Dear Valued Customer,

We realize you're a busy professional with deadlines to hit. Whether your goal is to learn a new technology or solve a critical problem, we want to be there to lend you a hand. Our primary objective is to provide you with the insight and knowledge you need to stay atop the highly competitive and ever-changing technology industry.

Wiley Publishing, Inc., offers books on a wide variety of technical categories, including security, data warehousing, software development tools, and networking — everything you need to reach your peak. Regardless of your level of expertise, the Wiley family of books has you covered.

- For Dummies® – The ***fun*** and ***easy*** way™ to learn
- The Weekend Crash Course® –The ***fastest*** way to learn a new tool or technology
- Visual – For those who prefer to learn a new topic ***visually***
- The Bible – The ***100% comprehensive*** tutorial and reference
- The Wiley Professional list – ***Practical*** and ***reliable*** resources for IT professionals

The book you hold now, *Windows Server 2003 Bible,* is your 100% comprehensive guide to working within this newly expanded platform. Whether you are new to this platform, or are an experienced Windows Server administrator, *Windows Server 2003 Bible* is everything you need to install, upgrade, convert, manage, and more. Beginning with an explanation of the Server architecture and the .NET Framework, the coverage expands into planning, installation, networking, Active Directory, and management issues and wraps up with an exploration of the critical services of Windows 2003 Server.

Our commitment to you does not end at the last page of this book. We'd want to open a dialog with you to see what other solutions we can provide. Please be sure to visit us at www.wiley.com/compbooks to review our complete title list and explore the other resources we offer. If you have a comment, suggestion, or any other inquiry, please locate the "contact us" link at www.wiley.com.

Thank you for your support and we look forward to hearing from you and serving your needs again in the future.

Sincerely,

Richard K Swadley

Richard K. Swadley
Vice President & Executive Group Publisher
Wiley Technology Publishing

Bible

FOR DUMMIES

Wiley Publishing, Inc.

Windows® Server 2003 Bible

Windows® Server 2003 Bible

Jeffrey R. Shapiro, Jim Boyce, Marcin Policht,
Brian Patterson, and Scott Leathers

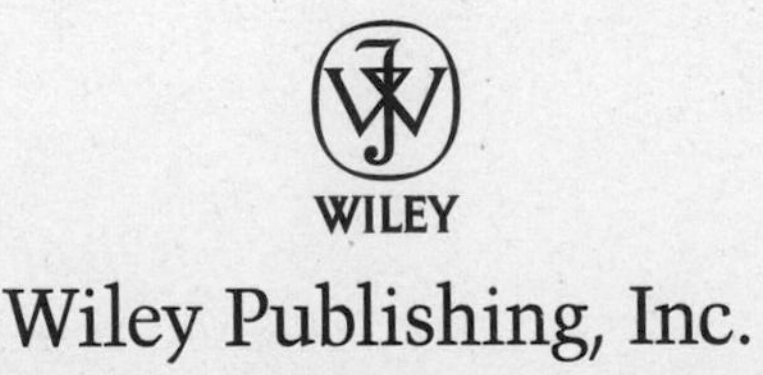

Wiley Publishing, Inc.

Windows® Server 2003 Bible

Published by
Wiley Publishing, Inc.
10475 Crosspoint Boulevard
Indianapolis, IN 46256
www.wiley.com

Published by Wiley Publishing, Inc., Indianapolis, Indiana

Published simultaneously in Canada

ISBN: 0-7645-4937-5

Manufactured in the United States of America

10 9 8 7 6 5 4 3 2 1

1O/QT/QU/QT/IN

LOC: 2002115041

About the Authors

Jeffrey R. Shapiro is the author of *Computer Telephony Strategies* (Wiley) and has authored more than ten books about Windows NT, Windows 2000, software engineering, networking, and so on. He has written numerous features for magazines such as *Call Center*, *Computer Telephony*, and *NetworkWorld*, and he is also the editor and publisher of the newsletter, *Systems Design Age*. A consulting engineer for more than 13 years, Jeffrey has worked with hundreds of companies such as Microsoft, Novell, and IBM, a number of public institutions, and several governments.

Jim Boyce is the author or co-author of nearly 50 books on computer software, hardware, programming (VB), and system administration. Jim is a former contributing editor and monthly columnist for *Windows Magazine*, has also written numerous features for print publications, and is a frequent contributor to online sites such as techrepublic.com. His Web site at `www.boyce.us` offers hundreds of Windows Server 2003 Professional tips, technology news, and more.

Marcin Policht has been involved in IT administration, engineering, development, and training for 10 years. Currently he works in one of the world's largest financial institutions managing Windows 2000/XP environment. He demonstrated his writing skills as the author of the first book covering scripting with Windows Management Instrumentation and as a contributor to `www.swynk.com`—one of the most popular Web sites dealing with Windows technologies. He has been also been very active in the certification area, not only as one of the first recipients of MCSE 2000 title, holder of MCSD, but also as a Microsoft Certified Trainer and a member of the team that established criteria for the Windows 2000 clustering certification exam.

Brian Patterson currently works as a software developer in central Illinois. Brian has been writing for various Visual Basic publications since 1994 and has co-authored several .NET related books, including *Migrating to Visual Basic .NET* and *C# Bible*. In his spare time Brian likes to program, write about programming, and read about programming. You can generally find him posting in the MSDN newsgroups or you can reach him by e-mail at `briandpatterson@msn.com`.

Scott Leathers spends his days as a Senior Software Architect primarily working with Visual C++. He has more than eight years of professional programming and networking experience. Scott has professional experience working with Windows NT, Windows 2000, and .NET Server 2003. He spends his spare time with his wife and kids.

Credits

Senior Acquisitions Editor
Sharon Cox

Project Editor
Chandani Thapa

Technical Editor
Todd Meister
Chris Thibodeaux

Copy Editors
William A. Barton
Nancy Rappoport
D&G Limited

Editorial Manager
Mary Beth Wakefield

Vice President & Executive Group Publisher
Richard Swadley

Vice President and Executive Publisher
Bob Ipsen

Vice President and Publisher
Joseph B. Wikert

Executive Editorial Director
Mary Bednarek

Project Coordinator
Ryan Steffen

Graphics and Production Specialists
Beth Brooks
Amanda Carter
Jennifer Click
Sean Decker
LeAndra Johnson
Heather Pope

Quality Control Technicians
Dave Faust
Andy Hollandbeck
Carl Pierce
Charles Spencer

Proofreading and Indexing
TECHBOOKS Production Services

To the late Dr. Michael Edwards for his contribution to the "science" of enterprise analysis and to Lesley Kalish for being there for me.

—Jeffrey

Preface

Windows Server 2003 is much more than an upgrade to Windows 2000. It offers many new and improved features that present you with both exciting and daunting challenges. This book is the culmination of thousands of hours spent testing, evaluating, and experimenting with just about everything that Windows Server 2003 can throw at you.

Gone are the days when the Windows server operating systems could be covered in a single book or a week's crash course at a training center. If we told you that this is the only book that you need about Windows Server 2003, we would be lying. Many of the features that we cover warrant advanced treatment under separate cover. We have attempted to build as complete a hands-on reference as possible while still providing a broad scope of coverage to give you a detailed look at the most important aspects and implications of the Windows Server 2003 platform, specifically for the Windows Server 2003 Enterprise Edition.

Although the conventional wisdom is usually to wait for the first service pack to begin moving to new software, Windows Server 2003 presents some compelling reasons to convert sooner rather than later. Windows 2003 offers expanded hardware support and support for Plug-and-Play. Windows Server 2003 incorporates numerous new technologies and improves on several existing ones, particularly for Windows Server 2003 Enterprise Edition, the focus of the *Windows Server 2003 Bible*.

One of the most pervasive changes in Windows 2000 was the Active Directory, and Windows Server 2003 expands on and improves the implementation of the Active Directory. The AD affects most aspects of Windows Server 2003, including the areas of security and user and group administration, network and domain topology, replication, DHCP and DNS, and more. Other important changes include changes to the Distributed File System (Dfs), which enables you to build a homogenous file-system structure from shares located on various servers across the network. These changes give you greater flexibility in deploying Dfs, including the capability to create multiple Dfs roots on a single server.

In a similar fashion, volume mount points, a feature of NTFS 5.0 (introduced in Windows 2000), enable you to mount a volume into an empty NTFS folder, making the volume appear as part of the structure of the volume in which the NTFS folder resides. Mounted volumes do much the same for a local file structure that Dfs provides for a network file structure. Changes in DNS and DHCP enable DHCP clients to dynamically request updates of their host records hosted by Windows Server 2003 DNS servers, enabling you to maintain up-to-date host records for all systems in the enterprise, even if they are assigned an IP address dynamically or their host or domain names change.

If you have been creating and managing Windows 2000 networks, you should find many features in Windows Server 2003 welcome improvements. A good example is Group Policy. You know from Windows 2000 that you cannot implement a Windows 2000 network without Group Policy. But Group Policy is difficult to master without supporting tools. Windows 2003 greatly improves Group Policy technology with increased functionality, such as resultant set of policy (RSoP) and the capability to more easily report on Group Policy application.

These changes are just a few of the many new features and modifications offered by the Windows Server 2003 operating platform.

Who Should Read This Book

Windows Server 2003 Bible is for anyone involved in network administration, server management, MIS, and so on. If the questions you have are along the line of "How do we handle this?", this book's for you.

Granted, Windows NT and 2000 administrators have a leg up on their Unix and NetWare comrades, but Windows Server 2003 makes waves in all IS infrastructures. The audience covers a wide spectrum . . . as broad as the number of services that the product offers. Not only do we cater to network or server administrators, but many chapters also are aimed at people tasked with certain responsibilities, such as security, user-account administration, service level, customer-relationship management, e-commerce, and so on.

Although we assume that you are familiar with the Windows environment (from Windows 9*x* through Windows XP), much of what we have written is of value to administrators working in heterogeneous environments — even midrange and mainframe facilities. We have also focused on issues of concern to managers and information offices. This is very much an integration book, so you find conversion tips aplenty, culled from an eagle eye cast on every process that may create problems for business systems and processes that are still in place.

Whether you're just trying to get a handle on what's new in Windows Server 2003 and the effect that it's sure to have, looking at installing new Windows Server 2003 systems, considering an upgrade from Windows 2000 Server, or are tasked with converting from Windows NT Server to Windows Server 2003, you find a wealth of information between the covers of this book that can help you meet your goals.

Everything that we discuss in these pages has been tested and deployed in a number of early adoptions, in one form or another. So step into our shoes and get a heads up on the road ahead. You will no doubt go on to learn a lot more about Windows Server 2003, as will we. If you would like to point out anything or add to what we've written, we value your contributions. You can write to us at `jeffrey.shapiro@mcity.org` or `boyce_jim@compuserve.com`.

How This Book Is Organized

The *Windows Server 2003 Bible* is divided into several logical parts, each focusing on a specific feature area or technology in Windows Server 2003. The following list summarizes the topics covered and how they are structured:

Part I: Windows Server 2003 Architecture

Part I provides extensive coverage of the Windows Server 2003 architecture in three key areas: system design, the Active Directory (AD), and security. Chapter 1 covers the system architecture to give you an understanding of how Windows Server 2003's components function and interact with one another. Chapter 1 also covers several higher-level components, such as Internet services, power management, plug-and-play, and so on. Chapter 2 focuses on Active Directory to give you an overview of the AD's purpose and design. Chapter 3 takes a broad look at security in Windows Server 2003, including Kerberos, certificates, encryption, and many other security-related topics. Chapter 4 rounds out the part with a look at .NET Framework Services, including architecture and installation issues.

Part II: Planning, Installation, and Configuration

Part II is where you turn if you're ready to start planning your Windows Server 2003 deployment, whether on a single system or a wider-scale deployment. Chapter 5 helps you decide whether you need to upgrade your hardware, plan deployment across the enterprise, and deal with several other pre-installation issues. Chapter 6 covers the actual installation of Windows Server 2003 and discusses machine or platform configuration, hardware selection, choosing services, and so on. Chapter 7 takes you to the next step after installation and explains how to configure services, the user interface, and other Windows Server 2003 options and properties.

Part III: Active Directory Services

Active Directory represents one of the most significant additions in Windows Server 2003 over Windows NT. Part III provides a complete look at AD, starting in Chapter 8 with a look at AD's logical structure and what it really represents. Chapter 9 examines the issues involved in developing a logical domain structure. Chapter 10 explores the physical structure of AD to explain it in the context of domains, sites, servers, and security. Chapter 11 covers AD planning, installation, and deployment. Chapter 12 explores AD management. Managing users and groups is covered in detail in Chapter 13, and Chapter 14 finishes the section with coverage of change management and how Group Policy facilitates change control over users, computers, security, and the workspace.

Part IV: Networking and Communication Services

Part IV explores in detail several key networking and communications services in Windows Server 2003. Chapter 15 lays the groundwork by covering the ubiquitous TCP/IP protocol, along with routing, troubleshooting, Network Address Translation (NAT), SNMP, and legacy protocols. You find detailed coverage in Chapter 16 to help you configure and deploy DHCP for automatic IP-address assignment and administration. DNS and WINS server configuration and client management are covered in Chapter 17, and the Routing and Remote Access Service is covered in detail in Chapter 18.

Part V: Availability Management

Windows Server 2003 builds on Windows NT and 2000 for fault tolerance, storage management, recovery, and other availability issues. Storage management is covered in detail in Chapter 19 to include removable storage, fault tolerance, RAID, general file-system management, and related topics. Chapter 20 helps you develop and implement a backup and recovery strategy and explores the new Windows Server 2003 Backup utility, configuring removable storage, and media pools. Chapter 21 teaches you to develop a disaster recovery plan. The Windows Server 2003 registry and registry management are explored in Chapter 22, with auditing explained in Chapter 23. Chapter 24 takes a detailed look at Windows Server 2003's service-level tools such as System Monitor, Performance Logs, and Alerts. Chapter 25 rounds out the section with an explanation of scalability and availability issues to help you deploy solutions that stay up and online day after day and still accommodate disasters if they occur.

Part VI: File, Print, Web, and Application Services

Part VI explores critical services in Windows Server 2003, with Chapter 26 detailing the various file systems available in Windows Server 2003. Chapter 27 explains how to configure and optimize file sharing and security and manage file sharing effectively. It also provides thorough coverage of the new support for file and folder encryption. Higher-end print topics such as Internet printing, printer management, and troubleshooting are covered in Chapter 28. Chapter 29 offers a detailed explanation of Web, SMTP, FTP services and intranet services to include such topics as service configuration and security, certificates, SSL, and so on. Chapter 30 is dedicated to Terminal Services, which are fully integrated into the operating system. This chapter kicks off with a reality check of client/server computing and explores the growing trend of thin-client deployment. The chapter also covers setting up Terminal Services, configuring application servers, and tips garnered from actual Terminal Services projects.

Conventions Used In This Book

Throughout this book, we've followed certain conventions to make the material clear and useful to you. New terms are presented in *italics*, followed by their definitions. File names, directories, URLs, and code are presented in `monospace` font, and any text that you should type at the keyboard is presented in **bold**.

The following margin icons are used to help you get the most out of this book:

Notes are used to highlight information that is useful and should be taken into consideration.

Tips provide an additional bit of advice that makes a particular feature quicker or easier to use.

Cautions are meant to warn you of a potential problem that could adversely affect your system or network.

Watch for this icon to learn where in another chapter you can go to find more information on a particular feature.

Acknowledgments

God knows how hard writing a book is . . . and then to get it published. So we are thankful for the team that has helped us bring this baby into the world.

We would first like to thank our agent, David Fugate, of Waterside Productions, for his effort in bringing us together with the team at Wiley Publishing. If an Olympic team for computer writers existed, David would be the head coach, for sure. Special honors also go to the Wiley Publishing editorial team. In particular, we would like to "flag" our production editor, Chandani Thapa, who did an outstanding job of bringing together the pieces of the puzzle.

The technical-editor "Oscar" goes to Todd Meister and Chris Thibodeaux not only for reading our lines, but for reading in between them as well. And we would no doubt have gotten no farther than this Acknowledgements page without the expert red pencils of our copy editors.

For every hour spent writing these words, at least ten were spent testing and toying with Windows Server 2003. So how do a bunch of authors get this far? Simple—you gather around you a team of dedicated professionals who help you build a killer lab and help you to test everything from the logon screen to the shutdown command.

Most of this book was written throughout 2002, a very difficult year for IT. But it would not have been survivable for me without two special souls that I worked with. Omar Martinez takes the gold for always being available for advice on just about any subject that involves a PC or a server . . . hardware or software. He is the best Microsoft engineer I have worked with and redefines the meaning of "operating system." Also on the team was Stephen Ryczek, a highly capable individual and one of the coolest project managers around.

The "home" team always gets the last mention, but without their support, input, and love, the soul in this work would not have taken flight. Special thanks to Kim and Kevin Shapiro and the ever-expanding Boyce clan.

Contents at a Glance

Contents

PART I

Windows Server 2003 Architecture

✦ ✦ ✦ ✦

In This Part

✦ ✦ ✦ ✦

CHAPTER

Introducing Windows Server 2003

✦ ✦ ✦ ✦

In This Chapter

Understanding the Windows Server 2003 architecture

Integrating Windows Server 2003

Understanding Windows Zero Administration Windows (ZAW) and total cost of ownership

Windows Server 2003 collateral services

✦ ✦ ✦ ✦

Windows Server 2003 is a complex operating system that is very different from Windows 2000 and earlier. In this book you will learn the fundamental differences between Windows Server 2003 and its predecessors. You will also gain valuable insight in the enhancements Microsoft has provided us which help with system stability, lower time needed for administration and help you understand why Windows Server 2003 has a massive performance gain over previous versions of Windows. This chapter introduces the product's architecture and provides guidelines to begin creating your strategy to adopt and support it.

Welcome to Windows Server 2003

After Windows NT 4.0 emerged in 1996, many organizations adopted the operating system, although Microsoft shipped service packs before the actual launch date for the software. This obviously begged the question—How stable can it be when service packs were created based on bugs detected by only Beta testers; surely the quantity and severity of bugs would increase now that it is gold? Many years later, people reluctantly made the leap to Windows 2000 Server so that they could reap the benefits of all the features that it contained, such as Active Directory. Unlike its predecessors, Windows Server 2003 enjoyed an extreme amount of production installations while still in Beta. This obvious support for a Beta operating system may seem rather odd considering the amount of service packs and security bulletins many have seen concerning the sibling operating systems such as Windows NT 4.0 and Windows 2000. That aside, the beta to this much-anticipated operating system has proven that it is very stable, provides a wealth of new features to aid the system administrator, and achieves an incredible performance gain over that of Windows 2000.

Windows Server 2003 doesn't give you one degree of separation from your customers right out of the box, but it does provide all the tools that you need to place yourself there such as the .NET Framework and IIS 6.0. Among these many tools are integration with the .NET Framework, improved Active Directory, improved DNS Server, and more configuration wizards than you can shake a stick at.

In the past few decades, only the big companies could afford big iron mainframes from the likes of IBM and Digital Equipment Corp. Now, however, that firepower is in the hands of everyone with enough money to register a dot-com. We, the System Administrators, are fighting a network war in which the competition can obtain weaponry and firepower never before thought possible in computer science.

Viral warfare is surging beyond belief, with thousands of computer viruses released every month. Hackers are penetrating corporate networks all around the world. Business people are hiring geeks to bombard their competition with datagram attacks and denial-of-service bombs. And fraud is just around the next router. You need an operating system that can protect you at home and away from home, at every portal, and at every location. Today, no operating system competes with the vastness of Windows Server 2003.

Before you look into the architecture that supports Windows Server 2003, you need to understand that the Operating System is not all peaches and cream. Windows Server 2003 still has a few shortcomings and we discuss these where appropriate. We should mention here, however that a huge hurdle to overcome — besides the long-winded name, of course — is the learning curve that you face with this product. No version of Windows NT (in fact, no other server operating system) is as extensive, as deep, and as complex in many places as Windows Server 2003.

Although Windows Server 2003 was created to cater to the demand for operating systems that cost less to manage and own, yet also provide performance that can compete with operating systems that cost several times more, realizing the benefit is a long and costly journey for many. Windows Server 2003 is not the only culprit; Unix, NetWare, and the midrange systems also have a long way to go before they can truly claim to reduce the total cost of ownership — not only in terms of operating systems and software, but also in terms of all technology ownership and management.

You can decide what you want to do about Windows Server 2003 in two ways. (For a start, know that all your competitors are in the same boat. Whoever takes the plunge and adopts first is sure to be better off down the road.) You can ignore Windows Server 2003 for the next six to 12 months on the premise or misguided advice that you should wait for the OS to ship at least two service packs, or you can take the plunge now and deploy it in labs and development environments and be ready whenever the inevitable "we need it now" memo arrives.

Throughout this book, we suggest the latter approach. Put the OS into controlled development and pilot projects and deploy selective components that provide better services than what is available under NT/2000. You cannot learn the OS overnight, so learning as much as you can makes sense.

With ongoing systems to support, Windows Server 2003 typically requires a skilled network engineer or systems analyst to invest about six to eight months into the OS. And even after eight months of intense study, you still can't consider yourself an expert. Perhaps the best way to tackle the learning curve — besides spending a lot of money on courses, where end-to-end training runs into five figures per administrator, and without the cost of absence from work during the training — is to divide up the key service areas of the OS.

To a large extent, we divide this book along the following key service lines:

- Windows 2003 Architecture
- Active Directory Services
- Security Services

✦ Network Services

✦ Availability Services

✦ File and Print Services

✦ Application Services

This chapter deals with Windows 2003 architecture and introduces you to key services that fall under the *Zero Administration Windows* (*ZAW*) initiative.

Understanding the Windows Server 2003 Architecture

Making the effort to understand the architecture of an operating system is a lot like making the effort to understand how your car runs. Without knowing the details, you can still drive, and the vehicle gets you from A to B. But if something goes wrong, you take your car to the shop and the mechanic deals with it. The mechanic can tell you that you should have changed your oil earlier, that your tires needed balancing, or that your spark plugs are fouled. Had you known how the car operates, you would have taken more care of it and prevented excessive wear and tear. You could possibly have serviced it yourself.

The same can be said about an operating system, although it is a lot more complex than a car's engine. If you understand the various components of the kernel (the OS), the file system, and how the OS uses processors, memory, hardware, and so on, you are better at administering the machine.

Operating system modes

Windows 2003, built on Windows 2000 Server, is a modular, component-based operating system. All objects in the operating system expose interfaces that other objects and processes interact with to obtain functionality and services. These components work together to perform specific operating-system tasks.

The Windows 2003 architecture contains two major layers: *user mode* and *kernel mode*. The modes and the various subsystems are as shown in Figure 1-1.

The system architecture is essentially the same across the Standard, Enterprise, Datacenter, and Web server editions.

User mode

The Windows 2003 user mode layer is typically an application-support layer for both Microsoft and third-party software, consisting of both environment and integral subsystems. It is the part of the operating system on which independent software vendors can make operating-system calls against published APIs and object-oriented components. All applications and services are installed into the user mode layer.

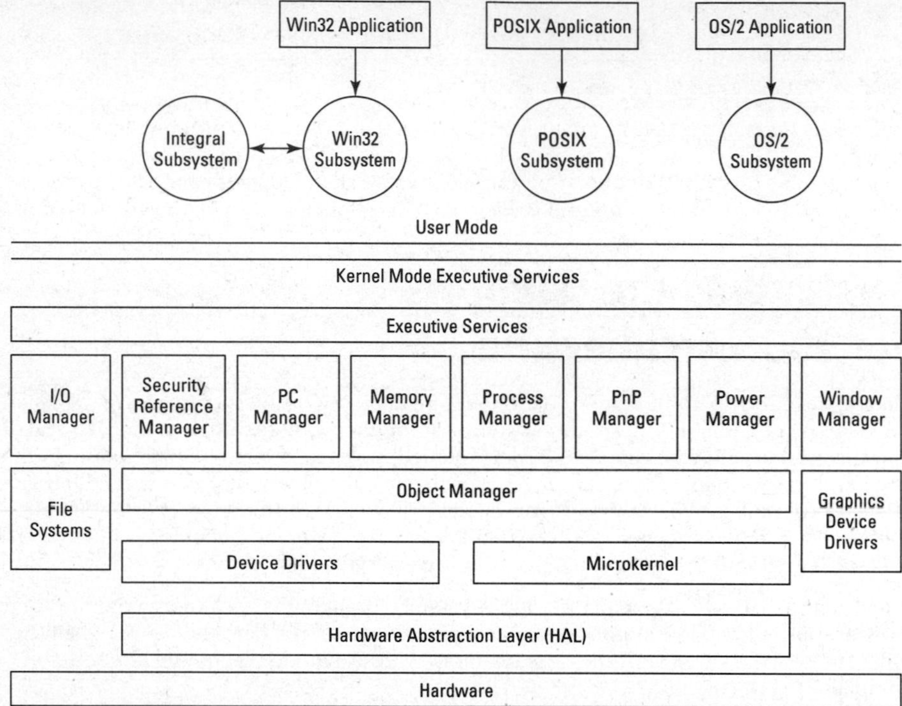

Figure 1-1: The Windows Server 2003 system architecture (simple).

Environment subsystems

The *environment subsystems* provide the capability to run applications that are written for various operating systems. The environment subsystems are designed to intercept the calls that applications make to a particular OS API and then to convert these calls into a format understood by Windows 2003. The converted API calls are then passed on to the operating-system components that need to deal with requests. The return codes or returned information that these applications depend on are then converted back to a format understood by the application.

These subsystems are not new in Windows 2003, and they have been greatly improved over the years compared to those of Windows NT. Reports in some cases indicate that the applications run better on Windows 2003 than they do on the operating systems they were intended for. Many applications are also more secure in Windows 2003. Windows 2003, for example, without affecting server stability, terminates DOS applications that would typically crash a machine just running DOS. Table 1-1 lists the Windows 2003 environment or application subsystems.

Table 1-1: Environment Subsystems

Environment Subsystem	*Purpose*
Windows 2003 Win32 (32-bit)	Supports Win32-based applications. This subsystem is also responsible for 16-bit Windows and DOS applications. All application I/O and GUI functionality is handled here. This subsystem has been greatly enhanced to support Terminal Services.
OS/2	Supports 16-bit OS/2 applications (mainly Microsoft OS/2).
POSIX	Supports POSIX-compliant applications (usually Unix).

The non-Win32 subsystems provide a basic support for non-Win32 legacy applications and no more. No real demand exists for either subsystem, and they have been maintained only to run the simplest of utilities that make very direct and POSIX- or OS/2-compliant function calls, usually in C. The POSIX subsystem, for example, caters to the likes of Unix utilities `vi` and `grep`.

The POSIX subsystem is not retained as a means, for example, of advanced integration of Unix and Windows 2003, such as for running a Unix shell on Windows 2003. For that level, you need to install Unix Services.

Several limitations and restrictions are imposed on non-Windows applications running on Windows 2003, by the underlying Operating System. This is demonstrated in the following list, which for the most part also includes user mode, Win32-based applications:

✦ **Software has no direct access to hardware.** In other words, if an application requests hard-disk space, it is barred from accessing hardware for such information. Instead, it accesses user mode objects that talk to kernel mode objects, which talk down the operating system stack to the Hardware Abstraction Layer. The information is then passed all the way up the stack into the interface. This processing is often known as *handoff processing*. The function in the Win32 code essentially gets a return value, and developers have no need to talk to the hardware. This is good for developers and the operating system. APIs that check the validity of the call protect the OS, and developers get exposed to a simple call-level interface, which typically requires only a single line of code and not 10,000 lines.

✦ **Software has no direct access to device drivers.** The philosophy outlined previously applies to device drivers as well. Hardware manufacturers build the drivers for Windows 2003 that access the hardware. The drivers, too, are prevented from going directly to the hardware, interfacing instead with abstraction objects provided by the device-driver APIs.

✦ **Software is restricted to an assigned address space in memory.** This constraint protects the operating system from rogue applications that would attempt to access whatever memory they can. This is impossible in Windows 2003, so an application can mess up only in the address space that it is assigned.

✦ **Windows 2003, as does Windows 2000, uses hard disk space as quasi-RAM.** Applications are oblivious to the source or type of memory; it is transparent to them. *Virtual memory* is a combination of all memory in the system and combines both physical memory in the machine and a swap file that is used to store information that cannot reside in hardware RAM.

✦ **Applications in the user mode subsystems run as a lower-priority process than any services or routines running in the kernel mode.** This also means that they do not get preference for access to the CPU over kernel mode processes.

Integral subsystems

The *integral subsystems* are used to perform certain critical operating system functions. Table 1-2 lists these services.

Table 1-2: Integral Subsystems

Integral Subsystem	*Purpose*
Security subsystem	Performs the services related to user rights and access control to all network and OS objects defined or abstracted in some way in the OS. It also handles the logon requests and begins the logon authentication process.
Server service	This service is what makes Windows 2003 a network operating system. All network services are rooted in this service.
Workstation service	The service is similar in purpose to the server service. It is oriented more to user access of the network. (You can operate and even work at a machine that has this service disabled.)

You need to manage very little with respect to these systems. These services are accessible in the Service Control Manager and can be started and stopped manually.

Kernel mode

The Windows 2003 *kernel mode* is the layer that has access to system data and hardware. It comprises several components (refer to Figure 1-1).

The Windows 2003 Executive

The *Executive* is the collective noun for all executive services. It houses much of the I/O routines in the OS and performs the key object-management functions, especially security. The Executive also contains the systems services components (which are accessible to both OS modes) and the internal kernel mode routines (which are not accessible to any code running in user mode). The kernel mode components are as follows:

✦ **I/O Manager:** This component manages the input to and from the devices on the machine. In particular, it includes the following services:

- **File System:** Translates file-system requests into device-specific calls.
- **Device Drivers:** Manages the device drivers that directly access hardware.
- **Cache Manager:** Buried in the I/O manager code, it manages I/O performance by caching disk reads. It also caches write and read requests and handles offline or background writes to the hardware.

- **Security Reference Monitor:** This component enforces security policies on the computer.
- **Interprocess Communication Manager (IPC):** This component makes its presence felt in many places in the OS. It is essentially responsible for communications between client and server processes. It comprises the Local Procedure Call (LPC) facility, which manages communications between clients and server processes that exist on the same computer, and the Remote Procedure Call (RPC) facility, which manages communications between clients and servers on separate machines.
- **Memory Manager** or **Virtual Memory Manager (VMM):** This component manages virtual memory. It provides a virtual address space for each process that manifests and protects that space to maintain system integrity. It also controls the demand for access to the hard disk for virtual RAM, which is known as paging. (See the section "Windows 2003 memory management," later in this chapter, for details.)
- **Process Manager:** This component creates and terminates processes and threads that are spawned by both systems services and applications.
- **Plug and Play Manager:** This component is new to Windows 2003. It provides the plug and play services and communicates with the various device drivers for configuration and services related to the hardware.
- **Power Manager:** This component controls the management of power in the system. It works with the various power-management APIs and manages events related to power-management requests.
- **Window Manager** and **Graphical Device Interface (GDI):** The driver, `Win32K.sys`, combines the services of both components and manages the display system, as follows:
  - **Window Manager:** This component manages screen output and window displays. It also handles I/O data from the mouse and keyboard.
  - **GDI:** This component, the hardest interface to code against and keep supplied with memory in the days of Win16, handles the drawing and manipulation of graphics on-screen and interfaces with components that hand off these objects to printer objects and other graphics rendering devices.
- **Object Manager:** This engine manages the system objects. It creates them, manages them, and deletes them after they are no longer needed, and it manages the resources, such as memory, that need to be allocated to them.

In addition to these services (and as indicated in Figure 1-1), three other central core components complete the makeup of the kernel mode: the *Device Drivers* component, the *Microkernel*, and the *Hardware Abstraction Layer* (*HAL*).

Device Drivers

This component simply translates driver calls into the actual routines that manipulate the hardware.

Microkernel

This component is the core of the operating system. (Some regard it as the operating system itself, with everything else just services.) It manages process threads that are spawned to the microprocessor, thread scheduling, multitasking, and so on. The Windows 2003 Microkernel is preemptive, which means, essentially, that threads can be interrupted or rescheduled.

Hardware Abstraction Layer

The *H*ardware *A*bstraction *L*ayer, or *HAL*, essentially hides the hardware interface details for the other services and components. In other words, it is an abstraction layer above the actual hardware, and all calls to the hardware are made through the HAL. The HAL contains the necessary hardware code that handles hardware-specific I/O interfaces, hardware interrupts, and so on. This layer is also responsible for both the Intel-specific and Alpha-specific support that enables a single executive to run on either processor.

Windows 2003 processing architecture

Windows Server 2003 is built around a *symmetric multiprocessing* (*SMP*) architecture. This means that, first, the operating system can operate on multiple CPUs, and, second, it can make the CPUs available to all processes as needed. In other words, if one CPU is completely occupied, additional threads spawned by the applications or services can be processed on other available CPUs.

Windows 2003 combines its multitasking and multithreading capabilities with its SMP capabilities. And if the threads waiting for execution are backed up, the OS schedules the processors to pick up the waiting threads. The thread execution load is evenly allocated to the available CPUs. Symmetric multiprocessing thus ensures that the operating system uses all available processor resources, which naturally speeds up processing time.

Windows Server 2003 Standard edition supports four-way (four CPUs) symmetric multiprocessing. The Enterprise server edition supports eight-way SMP, and Datacenter server supports up to 32-way SMP, while the Web edition limits you two a maximum of 2 CPUs. If you have the muscle, you can get the code from Microsoft, under hefty contract, to compile the OS to your SMP specifications.

Windows 2003 memory management

Windows 2003's handling of memory is almost identical to that of Windows 2000 Server in that it has been vastly improved over Windows NT 4.0. It consists of a memory model based on a flat, linear, albeit still 32-bit, address space. Two types of memory are used in the Windows 2003 operating system. First is *physical* memory, which includes the memory in the RAM chips installed on the system motherboards, typically in the form of SDRam, DDRam or RAMBus RAM. Second is *virtual* memory, which is a combination of all memory in the system and how it is made available to the OS.

The *Virtual Memory Manager* (*VMM*) is used to manage system memory. It manages and combines all physical memory in a system in such a way that applications and the operating system have more memory available to them than is provided in the actual RAM chips installed in the system.

The VMM also protects the memory resources by providing a barrier that prevents one process from violating the memory address space of another process, a key problem of the older operating systems such as DOS and earlier versions of Windows.

Every memory byte, whether physical or virtual, is represented by a unique address. Physical RAM has limitations because Windows 2003 can address the memory only according to the amount of physical RAM in the system. But virtual addressing is another story. Windows 2003 can support up to 2GB of RAM in the Web edition, 4GB with Windows Server 2003 standard edition, 64GB in the Enterprise edition and 512GB with Datacenter editon running with 64-bit processors.

The VMM manages the memory and has the following two major functions:

- ✦ The VMM maintains a memory-mapped table that can keep track of the list of virtual addresses assigned to each process. And it coordinates where the actual data mapped to the addresses resides. In other words, it acts as a translator service, mapping virtual memory to physical memory. This function is transparent to the applications, which continue to behave as if they have access to physical memory.
- ✦ If RAM is maxed out, the VMM moves the memory contents to the hard disk, as and when required. This process is known as *paging.*

Thus Windows 2003 basically has access to a 4GB address space, although the space is virtual and can be made up of both RAM and hard-disk space. Although you talk about a 4GB address space, this space is actually relative to how the system uses memory. In actual fact, the address space available to applications is only 2GB and is even less than that, because the 2GB assignment is shared by all processes running in user mode, and the other 2GB assignment is reserved for kernel mode threads.

You talk about an *upper* and a *lower portion* of the 4GB space, both containing 2GB addressing. The upper portion is reserved for kernel mode processes only, and the lower space is reserved for both user mode and kernel mode processes. The upper portion also reserves certain lower regions of its address space that are directly mapped to hardware.

The lower portion is also maintained in paging pools. It has a nonpaged pool and a paged pool. The paged pool can be swapped out to disk and is usually assigned to applications. The nonpaged pool must remain in physical RAM. The size of each page is 4K.

Paging in-depth

Paging is the process of moving data in and out of physical memory. If the physical memory pool becomes full and Windows needs more, the VMM reallocates data that is not needed in the physical memory out to the disk in a repository known as the *page file.*

Each process is assigned address space in pages that are either identified as *valid* or *invalid pages.* The valid pages are located in the physical memory and are available to the application. The invalid pages are not available to any application. The invalid pages are stored on disk.

Whenever applications need access to data that has since been moved to offline memory in an invalid page, the system acknowledges this need in what is known as a *page fault.* A page fault process is similar to a thread of execution that takes a different route in terms of routines after it encounters an error or exception. In this case, the fault is handled intentionally, and the VMM "traps" the fault, accesses the data in the page file that relates to it, and restores it to RAM. Other data that is now no longer needed is bumped out and sent offline to disk. This is one of the reasons why fast and reliable hard disks are recommended in data- and memory-intensive applications.

The VMM performs the following series of housekeeping chores as part of the paging routines:

- ✦ The VMM manages the data in the page file on disk on a first-in, first-out basis. In other words, data that has been on disk the longest is the first to make it back to physical memory after RAM frees up. The VMM continues to move the data back to RAM as long as RAM keeps freeing up and until no data is left in the page file. The data that the VMM keeps tabs on in this fashion is known as the *working set.*

✦ The VMM performs what is known as *fetching* as it brings back data from the page file. In addition, the VMM also performs what is known as *page file clustering*. Page file clustering means that, as the VMM fetches, it also brings back some of the surrounding data in the page file, on the premise that data immediately before and after the required data may be needed in the next instant as well. This process speeds up data I/O from the page file.

✦ The VMM is intelligent enough to work out that, if no space is present in RAM to place fetched data, it must first move out other recent data to the page file before attempting to place the fetched data back into faster RAM.

The parameters in which the VMM operates and the factors, such as the size of the page file, can be managed and controlled by you. We discuss this further in the performance management and troubleshooting techniques discussed in Chapter 24.

The Zero Administration Windows Initiative

The *Zero Administration Windows* (*ZAW*) initiative was a bold move to reduce the Total Cost of Ownership (TCO) and administration of Windows networks or environments. Though this was introduced in Windows 2000, take one look at the size of the Windows 2003 Resource Kit and decide whether your administrative burden has been reduced in any way. As we did, you were probably wondering just whether ZAW was a figment of Microsoft's imagination.

ZAW, however, is very much alive and apparent in Windows 2003. Consider the following to avoid having a heart attack: Understand and accept that you have a learning curve to climb in comprehending Windows 2003 in general and Windows Server 2003 in particular. The ZAW technologies, which have been added by the boatload to Windows 2003, do in fact reduce administration. We know what you are thinking: "How many nights must I stay up armed with pizzas and dozens of cans of soda before I figure out how this all works?" Here's the comforting statement from our team, which spent about 5,000 hours trying to make heads or tails of Windows Server 2003 for this book: ZAW is here and now in Windows 2003, but you must put it together now to achieve the long-term benefits.

After you put together all the pieces to your own satisfaction and understand how the new technologies come together, you begin to see ZAW emerge. Take it from us that Windows 2003 is the first operating system ever that is truly client/server. It can also be thin-client/server, fat-client/server (some call it rich-client/server), client/thin-server, and client/fat-server. Windows 2003 can also be client-client and server-server in many different variations.

When we say "truly client/server," we mean that the client operating-system processes, no matter whether they consist of a remote workstation running on Windows XP Professional or a server operating system, are very tightly integrated and meshed with the server operating processes and features. This is true regardless of the physical location of the server. This is not only apparent in the capability of a user to log on to any computer running Windows 2003 and find his desktop exactly as he left it and with access to all resources required and used previously, but also in the transparent availability of these resources. This is made possible by several key technologies that we discuss in the following sections, the first of which is Active Directory.

Active Directory

Active Directory is extensively discussed in Chapter 2 and in Part III in this book, so we do not go into too much detail other than to say that all the configuration and preferences relating to the services that we discuss in this section are stored in Active Directory. If you face a learning curve, Active Directory is where it starts. Unfortunately for larger businesses, Active Directory involves more than what is apparent to small businesses.

Active Directory is very much the hub of the network. Without Active Directory, you really do not have a Windows 2003 network. Though you will still run across quirks here and there, the number of tools that have been added since the Windows 2000 implementation is impressive. As time progresses, I'm sure it will grow ever more powerful with a whole new set of tools and utilities to help the Server Administrator.

Microsoft Management Console

The *Microsoft Management Console* (*MMC*) was deployed on Windows NT to support BackOffice applications such as Exchange, IIS, and SNA Server (now known as Host Integration Server). In Windows 2003, the MMC is used system-wide for managing just about everything on Windows Server 2003. A management module, known as a *snap-in*, exists or is created for each service. Each snap-in offers peculiar features and choices, depending on the service targeted for configuration.

We cover the MMC in Chapter 7.

Server and client in unison: IntelliMirror

Several technologies work to improve the integration between client and server. The *IntelliMirror* is a group of technologies that enables a user's settings, preferences, applications, and security to follow that user to other computers on the network. IntelliMirror also extends to laptops running Windows XP Professional and enables the user to maintain a disconnected state that is automatically restored seamlessly whenever the user reconnects to the network.

Group Policy, discussed in Chapter 14, is mostly responsible for the mirror, and of course, all configuration is stored in the directory. Clients access the data from the directory as needed. IntelliMirror is really an umbrella term that refers to the following technologies and features:

- **Offline folders:** Offline folder technology enables you to obtain a copy of a file that is usually stored on the server and to work with that file after you're disconnected from the network. If you disconnect from the server, the file that you were working on is managed as if it is still residing on the server. For all intents and purposes, your application thinks that it *is* still connected to the server. You save normally as if saving to the network, but instead, you are actually saving to an offline resource that is a mirror of the file and the folder on the server. After you reconnect to the network, the file is synchronized again, and the latest changes to the file are saved to the server's copy.

- **Folder redirection:** This is another IntelliMirror feature that makes a folder redundant. If the server disconnects from you but you are still connected to the network, the next time that you save your file, you are redirected to another copy of the folder residing on another server.

- **Roaming profiles:** These were inherited from Windows NT profile management philosophy, but they are much more sophisticated under Windows 2003. The idea is that your user profile follows you wherever you go.

- **Remote Installation Services (RIS):** These services are provided by several components and services that makes possible remotely installing Windows XP Professional and Windows XP Home to desktops and notebook computers.

✦ **Application publishing and software installation and maintenance:** By using Active Directory services, you can remove and install software remotely to users' workstations.

A lot of overlap does, of course, exist between the IntelliMirror-cum-Active Directory services and *System Management Server* (*SMS*). SMS manages the deployment of software over multiple sites as part of its complex change-control and change-management services. It is also an extensive scheduling and inventory management system. SMS is a BackOffice product worthy of description within its own book covers, which is why we do not cover SMS in this book.

Group Policy

Managing Windows Networks and Windows Server 2003 just got a lot easier with the new *Group Policy* technology. Group Policy is used to manage user settings, security, domain administration settings, desktop configurations, and more. In short, most of the workspace is managed through Group Policy.

Group Policy is applied at all levels of the enterprise in Active Directory, from domains down to organizational units and so on. The tool used for the job is the *Group Policy Editor* (*GPE*). GPE enables you to create objects that are associated or referenced to *organizational units* (*OUs*) in Active Directory. *Group Policy Objects* (*GPOs*) can be secured with NTFS permissions in the same fashion as files and folders.

Group Policy is discussed in detail in Chapter 14.

Availability services

Availability, as it relates to information systems, is the effort to keep systems and IS services available to users and processes all the time. We usually talk in terms of 24 × 7 availability, which, if possible, would be 100 percent availability. But 100 percent is possible only in a perfect world, so the target that we strive for is 99.9 percent. Few systems are capable of 99.9 percent availability. Trust us; we work in an environment of mainframes, Unix servers, NT clusters, AS/400s, and many other high-end servers, and no one can claim to have achieved perfect availability.

Availability is very important for companies that have service-level agreements with their customers. *Service Level Agreement* (SLA) is an IT/IS term used to refer to the availability of host systems that customers depend on for service from their suppliers. But SL is no longer applicable only to host systems or supplier-customer relationships. It is now important to all entities that depend on systems being available "all the time." Of particular importance are the Internet services because of the increased dependence that e-commerce companies place on Windows Server 2003. If your server goes offline, that situation can result in mounting losses that can easily be calculated and related in hard-dollar amounts. Taking a server down on an Internet site is like closing the physical doors to the store, which would send your customers to the competition. Cyberstores cannot afford that.

Every server administrator thus needs to zero in on this subject with the determination to maintain high availability of servers and services at all times. In fact, all services and components in Windows 2003 should be listed on an availability chart or a risk-assessment chart. The following list enumerates several areas that have been built by Microsoft with high availability criteria on the agenda:

✦ Bouncing server syndrome

✦ Clustering and server redundancy

- Storage redundancy
- Disaster recovery
- Security

Bouncing server syndrome

We are not sure who first used the word *bounce* to refer to the act of rebooting a server. But the term has caused many good laughs. In mid-1999, we were joined by a good-natured but overly serious VMS administrator who took over the management of a nationwide network of DEC VMX machines. One day, he came over to network administration and told us that he had just received the strangest call from one of the remote centers. "They say that they need me to bounce the Coral Gables VMX, but this is the first time I have heard such a term." And we replied: "Yes, you need to pick it up and drop it on the floor . . . do you need help?"

From that day on, our VMX administrator would often tease us about the number of times that you must "bounce" NT (a lot more than a VMX machine). Another term that is often used in IT circles is *IPL*, which stands for *I*nitial *P*rogram *L*oad (an operating-system restart) and which is rooted in legacy host systems and midrange talk. All systems require you to reboot, bounce, or IPL. Availability is rated on how often you must reboot.

Windows NT has a horrible availability rating. Just about any configuration change that you make demands a reboot. If you have administered NT for any number of years, you know that you just need to open the network configurations utilities and look at the settings and be told that you must reboot. Often, we would just ignore the warning and hit Cancel. Far too many changes, however, require you to reboot an NT server. At times, we wondered whether just breathing on the monitor would require a bounce.

Microsoft has improved the reboot record in the Windows 2003 kernel tremendously, both for new services and situations where applications and services crash. Improvement is especially noticeable in areas where you typically make a lot of changes, such as the network configuration and so on. Static IP address changes are, for example, immediate, as are reconfiguring network interface cards (NICs) and the like. A number of areas still need to be improved. Installing software (such as service packs) is a good example. Although a service pack reboot may be forgiven, reboots while installing new user applications on the server devoted to terminal users is not. A reboot after promoting a domain controller, however, is understandable. Still, we hope that later versions of Windows Server 2003 require even fewer reboots.

Clustering and server redundancy

Windows 2003 Enterprise Server now has clustering services built in, which is a big improvement over the Cluster Server product that was shipped as an add-on to Windows NT and Windows 2000. *Clustering* is a form of fault tolerance that enables users connected to one server to automatically connect to another server if the former server fails. This situation is technically known as a *failover* in clustering terms. (We have not dealt with clustering in this book because our scope of coverage is Windows Server 2003.)

Clustering, however, is not only applicable to redundancy, but also to *load balancing*, and particularly network load balancing, which clusters network resources. With technologies such as IntelliMirror and Group Policy, your users need never know which server in a farm of 50 machines is currently servicing their needs. The distributed files system, folder redirection, offline files and folders, and more all play their part in clustering and availability.

Storage redundancy

Storage services in Windows 2003 play a critical part in availability. Windows 2003 supports all available levels of disk arrays. The distributed file systems and NTFS 5.0 have several key features that support the high availability initiative.

Disaster recovery

Disaster recovery is managed by using Windows 2003 remote and removable storage services to maintain reliable backup sets. The *System Recovery Console* is also a new feature that enables you to boot to an NTFS-supported command line that enables you to access NTFS volumes. In addition, Windows 2003 also boots to a menu of "safe mode" choices in the event of serious system instability and gives you the opportunity to provide a description of why the system went down for logging purposes.

Security

Security services are critical to Windows 2003. In our opinion, you cannot have enough tools to protect the network. We discuss this topic further in the following section, in depth in Chapter 3, and in places in this book where security configuration is required. You would do well to take stock of the thousands of hacker sites on the Internet and join as many security groups as possible. The age of e-terrorism is upon us, and Windows Server 2003s are among the main targets.

Distributed Security

Microsoft has loaded Windows 2003 with security services unparalleled in any other operating system. Just about every port can be encrypted and protected in some way or form . . . all the way to 128-bit keys, which is now the world-wide encryption level in the wake of the e-business and e-commerce phenomenon. Windows 2003 also supports MIT's Kerberos version 5.0 protocol, now a de facto Internet standard that provides authentication of network logons by using symmetric key encryption and digital certificates, and the *Single Sign-On* initiative (SSO).

We devote a whole chapter to a discussion of Windows 2003 security (Chapter 3).

Interoperation and integration services

A homogenous network in a large company is a pipe dream in our opinion, and Microsoft probably concurs despite evangelizing to the contrary before the advent of the World Wide Web. All large companies deploy a hodge-podge of interconnected systems running on different platforms. The aim is to reduce the number of different systems as much as possible. At best, you can get down to supporting just Windows 2000, Windows Server 2003, Unix, AS/400, and possibly some legacy stuff. NetWare, once king of the LAN, still manages a foot in the door (especially with attorneys and high schools), and OS/2 died for most companies on December 31, 1999, a legend of the 20th century.

Microsoft has invested heavily in Unix integration, which is very strong. Microsoft has acquired new technology that, after it's deployed into Windows 2003, all but turns Windows 2003 into a Unix box. (Okay . . . we are exaggerating just a little.) These services existed with Windows 2000 but many of you may not have heard of them because they were very prone to bugs and used very infrequently. Not only does Windows Server 2003 communicate natively with Unix by using TCP/IP, but it also runs the Unix shell, giving administrators who work in both systems the best of both Windows and Unix worlds.

Hardware support and plug and play

Do not try to count the number of drivers that have been made available to Windows 2003; you'd be at it for hours. Remember the bad old days when critics berated the first version of NT for not having support for a lot of the hardware that was being shipped on Windows 95? Now the hardware teams for Windows 2003 and Windows 98 share the device-driver testing for all operating systems because they are the same drivers. More than 2,000 printer drivers, for example, already ship with Windows 2003, as well as many other drivers that are not even available to Windows 2000.

Did we just say that Windows 2003 and Windows 98 device drivers are the same? Thanks to the long-awaited *Windows Driver Model* (*WDM*) initiative, all device drivers created for Windows 98 and its successor that conform to the WDM can support hardware in both operating systems because they are the same drivers.

Hardware vendors can also bring their products to market a lot faster because, if they build device drivers to the WDM, they need to add only the final code to an extensive device-driver template that has already been written by Microsoft.

The WDM also caters to media streaming and image architecture, enabling support for a wide variety of scanners, plotters, digital cameras, image-capturing equipment, and more.

Storage and File System Services

Windows 2003 Storage and File Systems Services has been vastly improved over that of 2000. Many new features were added; some of them are mind-blowing, to say the least. The following list highlights the key services that you can expect to affect your administration routines and how you view both file and storage services in the future:

- Disk Administrator
- Removable Storage
- Remote Storage
- Microsoft Dfs
- NTFS 5.0

Disk Administrator

Windows Server 2003, like Windows 2000 supports dynamic disks, which enable you to merge volumes or extend them across multiple disks. Software RAID (Redundant Array of Independent Disks) support is built in to a much-improved disk-management utility that is now an MMC snap-in. You have full control over RAID volumes and can manage the volumes for the most part without needing to reboot the server. The MMC enables you to connect to any remote server and manage its hard disk resources as if they were local. This is hard-disk nirvana all the way.

Removable Storage

Removable Storage enables you to manage removable-storage media, such as tape drives and other removable media, to such an extent that doing so is almost an art form. Tape drives are now no longer managed as part of the backup and restore services. NTBackup (`ntbackup.exe`) is still there, but in a much-improved form (and labeled as Microsoft Backup which is a scaled down version of Veritas Backup Exec) . . . although it's still not quite as professional as we would have liked. Removable Storage enables you to create media pools that are assigned to various backup regimens and removable storage routines.

Remote Storage

Remote Storage is a service that takes files that are no longer accessed or used by the user or local process and moves them to removable storage media. An active file marker is placed in the place of the file with the data. This service thus frees up hard-disk space on demand by looking at which files can be relocated. If the user requires the files, they are returned from remote storage. The access may be slow at first, depending on the location or the technology used by the remote and removable storage service.

Microsoft Dfs

Microsoft Dfs (named *Dfs* so as not to be confused with the DFS standard) works a lot like the Unix NFS, in which folders and the directory tree are local to the network and not to any particular server. In other words, you can locate the files and folders that you need without needing to browse to any particular server or needing to map to a network drive from a workstation, as is the case with Windows NT.

NTFS 5.0

The Windows *NTFS 5.0* file system has been given extensive performance boost enhancements and supports mounted volumes, encryption, a folder hierarchy that extends multiple servers, and so on. Perhaps the most notable service that sits between the storage services and NTFS 5.0 is enforceable disk quotas which was introduced with Windows 2000. Disk quotas are set on a per-volume basis and enable you to warn and deny access to hard-disk space as or before the user reaches the quota level set.

Internet Services

Internet Information Server 6.0 is part of Windows Server 2003. You now have extended support for the SMTP and NNTP protocols besides FTP. In other words, whenever running the Internet services, the server also behaves as a mail or news host, enabling relay support and more.

The fully integrated support for IIS enables you to host multiple Web sites on one server with only one IP address. Each site can also have its own user-related databases, which thus supports multiple DNS domains.

Communication Services

What is a network without the capability to communicate? Windows 2003 is loaded with new and improved communications services. The Internet communications services have been highly optimized and advanced with e-mail, chat capability, and the wholesale support for the NNTP (Network News Transport Protocol) protocol, which is the pipeline to the newsgroups. For starters, Outlook Express, which is an Internet e-mail client with extensive support for security and attachments, is built into all versions of Windows 2003.

You also find new support for *Virtual Private Networking* (*VPN*) services, enabling connection to the enterprise network from remote networks such as the Internet. These services fully support both the *Point-to-Point Tunneling Protocol* (*PPTP*) and the *Layer Two Protocol* (*L2TP*).

Terminal Services

Windows NT enabled a single interactive session from the console, usually someone sitting directly in front of the monitor attached to the server. If you needed remote access to the server, you would usually need to use pcANYWHERE or CarbonCopy. This single interactive session is now completely obsolete with Windows Server 2003. *Terminal Services*, inherited from the Windows 2000 Terminal Server, is built into all versions of Windows Server 2003. You can, without license restrictions, connect remotely to the machine using the Remote Desktop feature.

Terminal Services enables a user to establish a session on the server from a dumb terminal or with terminal-emulation software running on just about any device that can connect to the network. The model, known as thin-client/server computing, works just the same as the mainframe model of a fat server to which many terminals can attach and obtain interactive sessions. The only difference here is that the "frame" sends back the Windows 2003 desktop to the user's terminal and not some arcane and bland collection of green characters, typical of midrange and mainframe systems.

The Windows 2003 kernel now includes a highly modified Win32 subsystem to support interactive sessions running in the server's allocated process space. Looking at it from dizzying heights, you would essentially take the Win32 subsystem and "clone" it for each user attaching to the server and running a workstation service. Have a look back at Figure 1-1. Now just make numerous copies of the Win32 subsystem, and you have Terminal Services in action.

For the most part, Terminal Services are not managed separately from the rest of the server. You have a few user-specific settings to manage related to sessions and session activity. Terminal Services are extremely important and are expected to garner wide adoption.

Summary

This chapter serves as an introduction to Windows 2003. First, you look at the Windows 2003 System architecture. It is the same architecture as Windows 2000 and the same foundation but with some dramatic changes.

Some major paradigm shifts are demonstrated in Windows 2003. The most significant is the shift back to terminal-mainframe environments. The mainframe, however, is Windows 2003, and the terminal gives you the Windows 2003 desktop and not a screen chock full of green characters and a blinking cursor.

We also introduce you to some of the key additions to the operating system. Almost all the topics that we introduce in this chapter are extensively covered in depth in the remaining 29 chapters.

We also warn that the learning curve you are about to face is steep. Experienced Windows 2000 administrators have less of a climb than newcomers, but much is new to Windows 2000 administrators as well, such as the .NET Framework, Active Directory changes, and so on.

You have no time to waste in getting down to learning Windows Server 2003 and starting on the road to deployment and rollout.

✦ ✦ ✦

CHAPTER

Windows 2003 and Active Directory

✦ ✦ ✦ ✦

In This Chapter

Understanding the origins of Active Directory

Understanding the elements of Active Directory

Comparing Windows NT and Windows Server 2003 domains

✦ ✦ ✦ ✦

Since the days of Windows 2000, Active Directory has become one of the hottest new technologies on corporate networks. If you are familiar with the Windows 2000 implementation of Active Directory then you are probably also familiar with its shortcomings. Understanding Active Directory is thus a prerequisite to any management or deployment of Windows Server 2003.

In the 1970s, all the computing resources you needed, or could use, were on the same computer or the terminal you logged on at. In the 1980s, with the advent of the PC LAN, many files were located on remote machines and there were definite paths to these machines. LAN users shared the files and printers, and exchanged e-mail on the LAN. Before the end of the 1990s, we witnessed the beginning of the paradigm shift where all information *and* functionality could be accessed on any server on any network anywhere . . . and the user did not need to know where the objects were physically located. Now it's 2003 and not only can you access any file on any server across a corporate network but you can access it with PDAs, cell phones and any number of wireless devices.

This is the ideal computing model, in which all network objects—servers, devices, functionality, information, authentication, and the transports—combine to become a single continuous information system and computing environment. This environment allows users, whether human or machine, to attach—or remain attached—to systems from a consistent user interface at any point of entry on the network. No matter what users require—be they functions of a device, communication, process, algorithms, or perhaps just information and knowledge—they must be able to access such an object without regard for its physical location.

The Active Directory is Microsoft's bold leap toward realizing the dream of a truly distributed environment and IS architecture. It has been talked about for many years. Headlines in the technical trades were always gloomy. And thus, many network administrators and systems engineers forgot about the directory and worked hard to refine or improve what was already in place, at considerable investment. But now the directory is here and with Windows 2003 comes many enhancements. And you probably have little idea what it is and how to use it. You should not feel ashamed, because not only are you not alone, but if you are unfamiliar with Windows 2000 then it is unlike anything you have ever used before.

In this chapter, we discuss the elements of Active Directory. We will kick off with a brief discussion of how and why we will use Active Directory, and where it came from. Then we break it down into its constituent components (its logical structure), and finally we discuss how the components work and interoperate with each other. You will notice that the subject of Windows domains and trusts will be left until after a full discussion of Active Directory.

This chapter also features the second appearance of Millennium City (MCITY), or `mcity.org`, which is the example Windows 2003 network infrastructure we use throughout the book (it was originally introduced in the Windows 2000 Server Bible). It's a network that runs the infrastructure of an entire city, and its Active Directory is what we used to test the limits of what Microsoft says it's capable of. MCITY is essentially one huge Active Directory laboratory.

You don't need to be in front of your monitor for this chapter. Just curl up with some snacks and postpone any appointments you might have.

The Omniscient Active Directory: Dawn of a New Era

The Windows NT client-server architecture was a great improvement over other server and network offerings, both from Microsoft and other companies. However, it had a shortcoming that, had it not been resolved in Windows 2000, would have suffocated the advancement of this highly sophisticated operating system. Now, Windows 2003 has taken it a step further with increased performance and many enhancements that make configuration and management much easier. On Windows NT — actually any network — resources are not easily distributed. The interoperation and scalability of numerous NT servers, printers, shares, devices, files, knowledge resources, functionality, and the sustained availability thereof, collapse when the ability for all network components and objects to share information is absent. As discussed briefly in Chapter 1, one of the most significant additions to Microsoft's technology is the Active Directory. There is perhaps no other aspect of Windows Server 2003 that will have the impact the directory service will, because just about every new feature or ability of this product depends on a directory service.

Before we haul out the dissecting tools, know this:

- ✦ The Active Directory service is critical to the deployment and management of Windows Server 2003 networks, the integration and interoperation of Windows Server 2003 networks and legacy NT networks, and the interoperation and unification of Windows Server 2003 networks with the Internet. Its arrival is a result of the evolutionary process of Microsoft's server and network technology. One way or another, the directory service is in your future.

- ✦ Active Directory is a powerful directory service, either as part of a Windows network or as a standalone service on the Internet. In the latter role, it is an apt contender as a directory service in the same fashion Internet Information Server (IIS) is an apt contender for a Web server. In other words, no querying client on the Internet needs to know the directory is Windows Server 2003 Active Directory. Active Directory is 100 percent LDAP-compliant and 100 percent IP-compliant.

Why do we need directories?

A directory provides information. At its most basic level, it is like a giant white pages that allows a user to query a name and get back a phone number . . . and then possibly be connected to the person by automatically dialing that number. But a directory in the IT world is a lot more than a telephone book. Before getting into the specifics of Active Directory, let's look at some reasons why we need directories. We kick off by placing Active Directory at the center of all services provided by Windows 2000.

Single Sign-On and distributed security

Active Directory makes it easier to log in to and roam cyberspace. Imagine if you had to log in at every mall, highway, turnpike, newsstand, public facility, sports amenity, shop, fast-food outlet, movie house, and so on, in the brick-and-mortar world we live in. Why then should we have to do this in cyberspace?

In every company today, it is almost impossible to get anywhere on the network without going through at least three logins. Everyday, we log into Web sites, Windows NT domains, voice mail, e-mail, and FTP, to name a few; we won't go into how many accounts and logins we have.

Not only do we have to log in dozens of times a day, and remember dozens of passwords and user or login IDs, but we also have to know exactly where information and resources are located on the network. The uniform resource locator (URL) on the World Wide Web has alleviated the resource location problem to some extent (it obviates having to know exactly where something lives on the Internet), but it is still not ideal and not very smooth. URLs are perishable, and for the most part unmanageable in large numbers, which means they often do not get updated. They are not managed in any sensible, cohesive system.

The ideal is to have some sort of badge that allows us to log in once and then flash it wherever we go, much like a proximity badge that allows your presence to be sensed and your identity verified. For starters, every application and service on our LANs, from e-mail to voice mail to data access to printer access, should be made available to us through one universal login, at home or at work. The type or level of access we have will depend on the attributes or "clearance level" of our badges. The access token provided by Windows NT security comes close to this, but it is not accepted by other technologies as a valid means of authentication. Figure 2-1 illustrates several systems that should be accessed and managed from a central login authority. In many cases, this is already possible with Active Directory-compliant applications such as SQL Server 2000 and Exchange 2000.

As you will learn in Chapter 3 and in the chapters in Part III, the single login dream is achieved by using the services of Active Directory and Windows Server 2003 support for MIT's Kerberos authentication. This service is known as *Single Sign-On* (SSO). SSO has become a quasi-standard among supporters of the Kerberos protocol, such as Microsoft, Apple, Sun, and Novell.

Once a trusted user is authenticated via the Kerberos protocol, all other services that support the Kerberos protocol can accept and allow access to the principal. This is made possible by the Kerberos use of tickets — the badge idea previously discussed — which are issued by the directory service.

In Chapter 1, we also told you that the Microsoft network domain architecture in Windows Server 2003 has been radically overhauled to seamlessly integrate with Active Directory and to extend out to the Internet. Imagine being able to log in to your domain from anywhere.

Customers: Orders
Customers: Help Desk
Customers: Catalogs
Customers: Websites
Suppliers
Manufacturers
Public Relations
Partners
Investors
Extranet Applications
Security

Extranet Cloud

Administrators
Technical Support People
Groups and Users
Printers, Computers, Equipment
Data and SQL Server Users
ERP, CRM, SFA, and Payroll Systems
Helpdesk Users
E-mail and Groupware Users
Voicemail and Fax Users
Internal Applications
Remote Users and Road Warriors
Vertical and Horizontal Application
Security
Host Access

Intranet Cloud

Active Directory

Internet Cloud

LDAP entry point and other LDAP compliant directories
Organization White Pages
(e-mail, phone, and fax addresses)
Catalog Searching
Interconnection with other directories
Internet Users
Internet Road Warriors
Extranet Access
Security

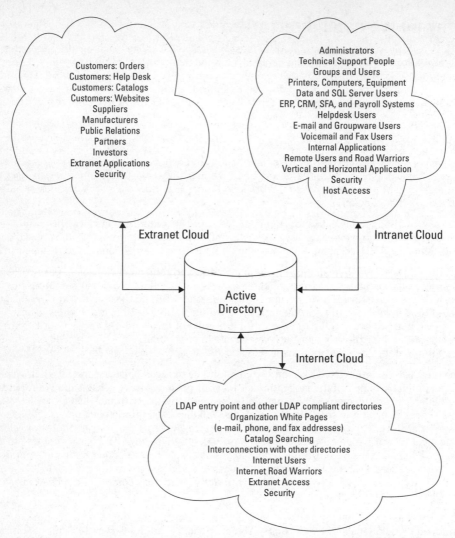

Figure 2-1: Active Directory is shown here in its rightful position as a central login authority.

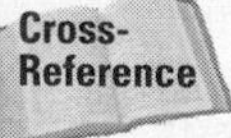

We will be discussing this in much more depth in Chapter 10.

Change management

Active Directory makes it easier to manage the roamers and users of cyberspace and corporate networks and the computers they use to attach to the network. We administrators want to be able to manage our users and computing resources in one central omnipresent repository. We don't want to repeatedly manage users in the voice mail directory, on the NetWare servers' directory, in the Host systems database, in our e-mail directory, on our Windows domains, and so on.

And we, as managers, need to be able to manage this information easier with change. Mergers, acquisitions, new products, and services need to be continually managed on a cohesive and consistent basis. Group Policy, the change control and change management service of Windows Server 2003, stores all user and computer information in Active Directory (as discussed in the section on ZAW in Chapter 1).

Distributed administration

Active Directory lets you delegate administrative function and responsibility and lets you parcel out chunks of the network or domain for controlled administration. A distributed directory service makes it possible to delegate the administration of network resources and users throughout the enterprise. On legacy Windows NT systems, you can create users and groups with administrative rights, but it is impossible to hide other network resources from these administrators.

Because Active Directory can be partitioned as a mirror of the structure or organization of the enterprise, it is also possible to partition the administration of the compartments. In other words, it makes more sense to appoint a member of a department to perform repetitive management of that department's resources.

You will see later how administration of the directory can be delegated to individuals who are given only selective access or right of passage to delegated areas of the directory.

Application management

Active Directory makes it easier to develop and distribute applications. Application developers need consistent, open, and interoperable interfaces and APIs against which they can code functionality that stores and manages information relating to applications, processes, and services in a distributed information store. We want to be able to create applications and store application and persistent data to an "invisible" repository through an open interface. This information should be available from anywhere and everywhere on the network, including from an intranet or even the Internet (thanks to the .NET Framework).

Developers want to be able to create methods that install an application into a directory on the network for initial configuration and manipulation over the lifetime or use of the application. We do not want to concern ourselves with the inner workings of the directory. We want to create our information or configuration object, initialize it, use it, and be done . . . no matter where the user installs or invokes our product. And wherever the object we created is moved to, it should always be accessible to the application.

With all of the above, the cost of access and management has in the past been high. We are looking for solutions that will, in the long- to medium-term, reduce the cost of both management and operation of cyberspace and the information technology systems running our companies and our lives.

What is Active Directory?

There are registries and databases that provide directory-type facility for applications and users. But not one is interconnected, share-centric, or distributed in any way. Active Directory is a universal distributed information storehouse through which all network objects, such as application configurations, services, computers, users, and processes, can be accessed, in a consistent manner, over the full expanse of a network or inter-network. This is made possible by the logical structure of the directory. And before you start scratching your head, you should understand that without Active Directory you cannot log in to a Windows Server 2003 domain, period.

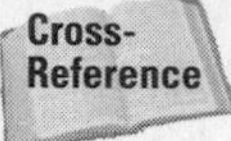

Chapter 10 discusses the Active Directory logical structure and illustrates the control you have over Active Directory's logical and physical structure.

We compare Active Directory to a database later on in this chapter.

The grandfather of the modern directory: The X.500 specification

The directory service as we know it began with an interconnection model proposed by the International Organization for Standardization (ISO) little more than 20 years ago. This model is popularly known as OSI, which stands for *open-systems interconnection.* In the late 1980s, OSI was given a huge boost by big business and government and quickly became the foundation for the information revolution we are experiencing today.

The OSI model and its seven layers lie at the root of modern information technology. Without a fundamental understanding of OSI, it is difficult to be an effective systems engineer, software developer, network administrator, CIO, or Webmaster. OSI is to IT what anatomy is to medicine. Although we assume that you are familiar with the OSI model, this brief discussion of X.500 serves to provide a common departure point for all systems engineers not familiar with a directory service.

The X.500 directory service can be found at the OSI application layer, where it sits as a group of protocols approved and governed by the International Telecommunications Union (ITU), formerly the CCITT. The objective of X.500 was to provide standards and interfaces to an open and interoperable global and distributed directory service.

X.500 is made up of many components (databases), all interoperating as a single continuous entity. Its backbone is the Directory Information Base (DIB). The entries in the DIB provide information about objects stored in the directory. Figure 2-2 represents the information contained in the DIB.

In order to access the information stored in the DIB, both users and computers needed a structure or model that would make it easier to understand where data could be located. The model proposed was an object-oriented, hierarchical structure that resembles an upside-down tree, as illustrated in Figure 2-3. The root of the tree is at the top, and the branches and leaves hang down, free to proliferate. This model assured that any object in the tree is always unique as long as it is inherently part of the tree and can trace its "roots" to the single node at the top. Active Directory trees (and DNS) work the same way, as discussed later. The tree is read from the bottom to the top.

The objects in the X.500 tree represented containers for information representing people, places, and things. These objects would also be organized or grouped into classes (for example, groups of countries, companies, localities, and so on).

The X.500 standard included the following container objects:

- Country
- Location
- Organizational unit (OU)

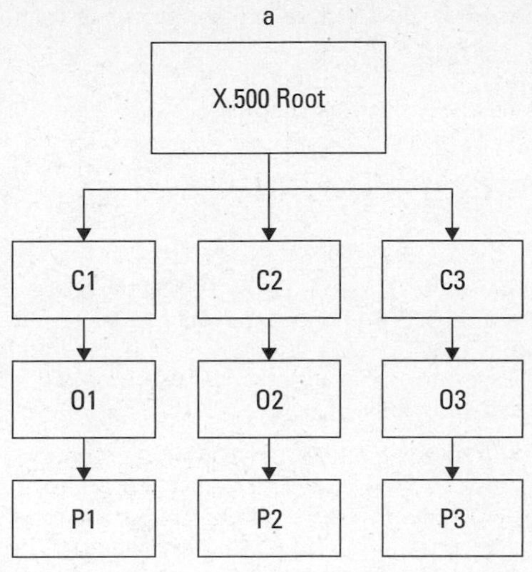

b

Entry Identifier	Classes	Attribute Values
P1	County Organization Person	US MCITY Jeffrey Shapiro

Figure 2-2: The X.500 hierarchy (a) and the DIB and the information it contains (b) are shown here.

Unfortunately, X.500 suffered from several limitations in its early days. It became bogged down under its own weight (the specification was exhaustive), and in many respects it was ahead of its time (especially with respect to its ties to OSI). It made its appearance in the late 1980s at a time when most innovators could not care less about managing information openly and globally, when we were all huddled in our garages inventing or writing code like crazy, and when we were all competing for market share at every turn.

X.500 was also born before the advent of the World Wide Web and the mass utilization of the Internet by both the public and businesses. And what really dragged it down was its ties to the OSI protocols (the datalink protocols — DLC — such as 802.2 and 802.3), which turned out to be its Achilles' heel, because the way of the Internet world was IP. Meanwhile, the Internet took off on the coattails of TCP/IP, leaving X.500 struggling in a protocol desert landscape.

Like so many innovations before it, X.500 provided nourishment for other inventions that followed. And much of the foundation for the modern directory service, especially Active Directory, can be directly attributed to the vision of X.500, as we will soon see.

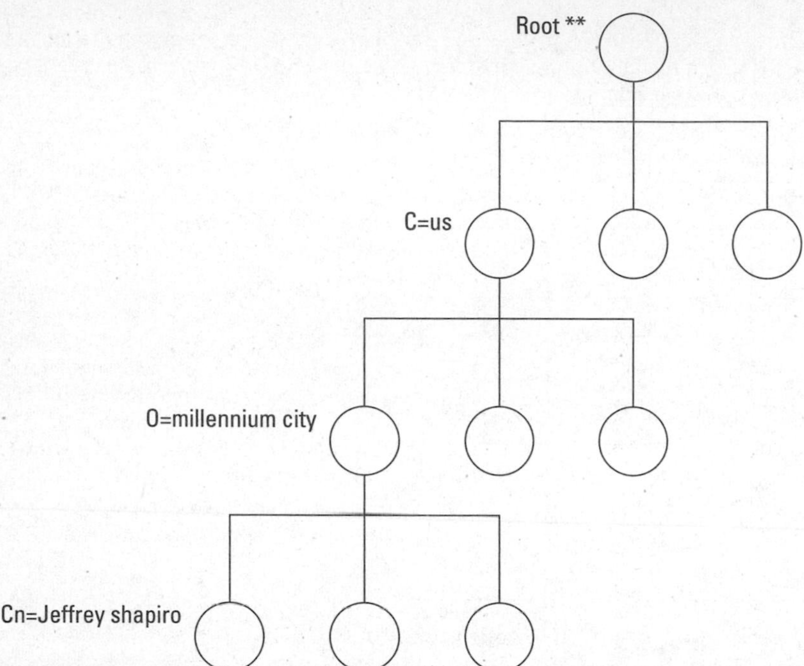

Figure 2-3: The X.500 tree structure illustrates the location of Active Directory domain information.

The father of the modern directory: LDAP

The X.500 specifications defined a protocol by which services would be able to access the information stored in X.500 databases. This protocol was known as the *Directory Access Protocol,* or DAP. It consisted of a comprehensive set of functions that would provide the capability for clients to add and modify or delete information in the X.500 directory.

DAP, however, was overkill and consisted of far more functionality than was required for the implementation of a directory service. Therefore, a simplified version of DAP was created, called the *lightweight directory access protocol* (LDAP). After several refinements, LDAP has begun to stand in its own right as a directory service. After adoption by the Internet Engineering Task Force (IETF), several important features of LDAP have garnered it widespread support:

✦ LDAP sits atop the TCP/IP stack rather than the OSI stack. This means that every client with an IP address, able to send and receive packets over IP, can access and exploit LDAP-compliant directory services. The client needs only to know how to "talk" to LDAP (IP). TCP, the transport, takes care of the rest.

✦ LDAP performs hyper-searching, which is the ability of a directory to refer to another for authoritative information. In other words, one LDAP directory can defer to another to chase information. An example of this is how Web-based search engines look to other search engines, via hyper-linking, for collateral information or information that does not exist in their own databases. Directory services on a worldwide Internet thus can become contiguous and distributed to form a transparent massive service, limited only by available servers and network resources.

✦ Early on its childhood, LDAP implemented a rich C-based API, making C the *de facto* programming language of the directory service. Using the most popular language of the day with which to call directory functionality ensured LDAP widespread support in the bustling developer community.

LDAP consists of the following components, which in some shape or form are the foundations of all modern directories, including Active Directory:

✦ **The data model:** This model represents how data is accessed in the directory. The data model is inherited directly from the data model of the X.500 specification. Objects are infused with information by way of assigning attributes to them. Each attribute is type-casted and contains one or more distinct values. The objects are classified into groups of classes, such as OUs or Companies.

✦ **The organization model:** This is the inverted tree paradigm we earlier discussed, which is also inherited directly from the X.500 specification. It is the structure adopted by all modern directory services. Of particular note is how the Domain Name System (DNS) of the Internet is arranged around inverted trees. The DNS consists of several trees, the root or topmost levels, that sprout downward and contain millions of leaves (or nodes). Figure 2-4 illustrates the DNS forest and the seven roots. It also illustrates the `.com` tree and how it has fired the Internet into the commercial juggernaut it is today.

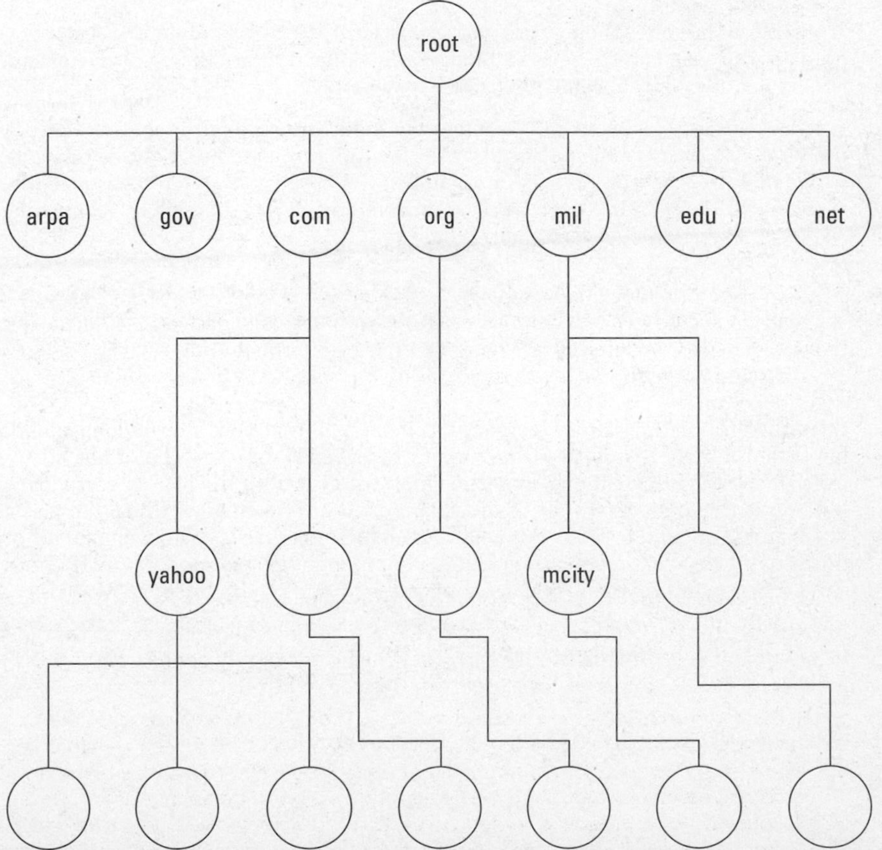

Figure 2-4: The organizational model revolves around the inverted tree, a hierarchical collection of objects.

✦ **The security model:** This model specifies how information is securely and safely accessed. LDAP adopted Kerberos password authentication and has since added additional authentication layers with the inclusion of the Simple Authentication Security Layer (SASL). This SASL provides a tiered architecture for a multitude of service providers. Version 3.0 of LDAP also supports the secure socket layer (SSL) of TCP/IP, which was developed independently by the Internet community. Windows Server 2003 supports SSL in its browser; Internet Explorer also supports SSL in its Web server, IIS.

✦ **The functional model:** This model specifies the methods for querying and modifying the directory objects. It includes operations to add entries and to edit, to populate the attribute fields, to delete, and to query objects in the directory.

✦ **The topological model:** This model specifies how directory services integrate or interoperate with other compliant directories. The ability of LDAP directories to refer or defer to other directories is inherent in this model.

LDAP's popularity flourished with the Internet. Today, many popular applications and server technologies support the protocol. It can be accessed from most e-mail applications, Web-based applications, and even embedded systems such as routers and gateway devices.

After X.500

A number of large technology companies are hard at work on directory services. The two of note who appear to have been at it longer than Microsoft are Banyan Systems and Novell. Others include Netscape and IBM (Lotus Notes).

Banyan perhaps has been at it the longest with its StreetTalk product that has been part of the Vines OS for more than a decade. Novell entered the market mid-way through the 1990s with a directory service aimed at its installed NetWare base, called the Novell Directory Service (NDS), and it has been working on versions of NDS that will be independent of the NetWare OS, including a version for Windows NT.

Despite its immaturity, Active Directory has been built on proven technology. One technology that it depends on heavily is replication, which comes from Microsoft Exchange. The Exchange site integration and replication technology has been proven on millions of installations around the world.

From the ground up, Active Directory has been built on open, international standards. It is important to note that Active Directory is not an X.500 directory, but it has borrowed heavily from the X.500 specifications. In particular, it uses LDAP as the access protocol, which opens it to everyone and everything. In short, Microsoft has taken everything that was great about X.500 and LDAP and combined it with proven technologies it has developed for other purposes over the years (such as Microsoft's Component Object Model [COM]). Active Directory can exchange information with any application or service that uses LDAP.

Active Directory also relies on DNS as its locator service, allowing clients to transparently locate domain controllers (Active Directory hosts) by merely connecting to a DNS server and looking up the IP addresses for the closest domain controller.

We will discuss the role of DNS in Active Directory in greater detail in Chapter 12.

The open Active Directory

Active Directory also provides a rich set of APIs to encourage the development of tools and applications. Active Directory will thus serve as a repository for application-specific information, particularly software that is group-driven. For example: We have developed a Customer Relationship Management (CRM) system for several medical and dental clients. Our users typically log in to the application and become apparent as a community of active users to the rest of the practice or hospital, once authenticated in Active Directory.

The application is able to obtain enterprise-wide information about the state of the application at any given time, and we are able to group users according to service and access levels, governed by objects in Active Directory. In particular, the application publishes information about who is logged in and using the system, the files (data) they have checked out of the database management system (such as SQL Server or Oracle), and what they are currently doing.

We do not need to provide users with a second login just to use the application. Instead, when they run the CRM, it checks to see if Active Directory has authenticated them, the machine they are accessing the system from, and what they are allowed to access. Based on this information, we populate the Graphical User Interface (GUI) that drives the CRM with information the user is allowed to see or use.

What about the registry?

Now that you can see why we need directory services and where they came from, where does the registry fit in? In the early days of Windows 95 and Windows NT, Microsoft improved the information repositories of applications running on the Windows platform with the creation of the registry. It was a great relief from the mess created by initialization and configuration files, insecure text files that anyone could access.

The registry, however, was more of a technology created to stabilize the OS, as a repository for managing information and the configuration of applications and computers. When users deleted their Windows 3.11 and earlier version `.ini` files in error, the application was, for better or worse, destroyed (if the `.ini` files were not backed up). The registry set out to change all that. Today, some of the largest software houses in the world still do not use it; I can't imagine why.

What's more, the registry also became the home for the so-called Security Account Manager (SAM). This database stores and manages all the security and access control authority of network resources.

There are some similarities between the registry and Active Directory. Specifically, the registry is all of the following:

- Also a database, somewhat cryptic and complex, but still a database.
- Open and accessible (except for the SAM part).
- Able to be programmed against.
- A replicating structure (single master), providing some vestige of a distributed system.
- A system of hierarchical structures, which contains records that hold configuration data.

For the most part, the similarities end there. Comparing the registry to Active Directory is like comparing a JetSki to the USS Kitty Hawk: Active Directory is a completely different animal. Yes, you can still use the registry to store configuration data, and you would still use the registry on a standalone workstation or server, even a domain controller. Specifically, the difference is that Active Director is also the following:

✦ A distributed multi-master database (peer directories update each other in real time, latency aside).

✦ Built on open, Internet-based standards.

✦ Object-oriented.

✦ Interoperable (almost coexistent) with DNS.

✦ Able to service any network client using TCP/IP.

✦ Able to grow to gargantuan proportions.

Unfortunately, many applications today still store configuration information in unguarded flat text files, ignoring the registry for the most part. Ignoring both the registry and Active Directory will likely render your application incompatible with Windows 2003, from both a functional perspective and as a Microsoft logo requirement.

Note

Active Directory does not set out to replace the registry. The registry still plays an important role in Windows Server 2003. In fact, even Active Directory uses the registry to store some configuration-related information. Microsoft began working on a directory or distributed information storage facility some time ago, possibly even at the same time it was developing the registry. I, for one, would one day like to see the registry based on an open standard such as XML.

From the outset, Microsoft believed it could only succeed with Active Directory by ensuring it was based on open standards and interoperable with the Internet, period. In other words, any IP-based (LDAP) client will be able to access the Active Directory, and like IIS, FTP, and other services, this access is transparent (in terms of what OS it is sitting on).

✦ Active Directory supports and coexists with both DNS and LDAP. Both are modeled on the X.500 standard, especially with respect to its structural and organizational model.

✦ Active Directory supports open and interoperable standards, especially with regard to the widespread naming conventions in use today.

✦ Active Directory is seamlessly integrated into the Internet by virtue of Microsoft's total adoption and commitment to TCP/IP. All other protocols that Microsoft supports essentially provide for backward compatibility with earlier versions of NT, other network operating systems, legacy transports such as SNA and the DLC protocols, and NetBEUI clients.

✦ Active Directory provides a rich set of C/C++, Java, VB, .NET Framework and scripting language interfaces, allowing it to be fully programmed against.

If you need to program complex code against Active Directory, I'd suggest using a language that is based on the .NET Framework, such as Visual Basic .NET or C++. These languages have a significant increase in speed compared to other languages.

✦ Active Directory is built into the Windows NT operating system (still at the core of Windows Server 2003 and Windows 2000), making it backward-compatible with earlier versions of Windows NT.

- Active Directory is a fully distributed architecture allowing administrators to write once and update everywhere from a single point of access, across any network.
- Active Directory is highly scalable and self-replicating. It can be implemented on one machine or the smallest network, and can scale to support the largest companies in the world. Resources and adoption permitting, once the kinks (and it has a few) are worked out, it will likely become a pervasive technology within a short time.
- Active Directory's structural model is extensible, allowing its schema to evolve almost without limits. In this regard, Active Directory has to comply with the X.500 specification that extending the schema requires you to register the new class with a X.500 governing body. This compliance is achieved by registering an Object Identifier (OID) with the authorities. In the United States, the authority is the American National Standards Institute (ANSI).

Active Directory has fully adopted the most popular namespace models in use today. It embraces the concept of an extendable namespace and marries this concept with the operating systems, networks, and applications. Companies deploying Active Directory are able to manage multiple *namespaces* that exist in their heterogeneous software and hardware.

The Elements of Active Directory

Active Directory is a highly complex product that will no doubt become more complex and more advanced in future versions. At the core of the product, we find a number of elements that are native to directory services in general and Active Directory in particular.

Namespaces and naming schemes

AD has adopted several naming schemes, which allows applications and users to access Active Directory using the formats they have most heavily invested in. These name formats are described in the following sections:

RFC822 names

RFC822 is the naming convention most of us are familiar with, by virtue of our using e-mail and surfing the World Wide Web. These names are also known as user principal names (UPN) in the form of `somename@somedomain`; for example, `thepresident@thewhitehouse.gov`. Active Directory provides the RFC822 namespace for all users. If you need to find a person's extension number at a company (if they publish it), you need only query the directory and look up `someone@somedomain.com` (your software will translate that into the correct LDAP query, as shown later). The UPN is also the login name or user ID to a Windows Server 2003 domain. Windows users can now log in to a Windows Server 2003 network by simply entering their user ID and password, like this:

```
User: jeffrey.shapiro@mcity.org
Password: *************
```

It is possible to assign any UPN to a domain for login. In other words, you might create a domain called MCITY but prefer users to log in as `someone@acmesales.com` so that they do not need to remember more than their e-mail addresses.

LDAP and X.500 names

The LDAP and X.500 naming conventions are known scientifically as *attributed naming,* which consists of the server name holding the directory (which we refer to as the *directory host*), username, OU, and so on. For example:

```
LDAP://anldapserver.bigbrother.com/cn=jsmithers,ou=trucksales,dc=bigbro
ther,dc=com
```

LDAP names are used to query the Active Directory.

Active Directory and the Internet

It is possible to locate Active Directory servers anywhere on the Internet or a private intranet. These Active Directory servers can be full-blown Windows Server 2003 domain controllers, or they can serve the single purpose of being LDAP directory servers. The information and access that users and clients enjoy from these servers is transparent.

The client needs only resolve the closest Active Directory server to it to get information. The closest server might be on the same site as the client, in which case the DNS server will resolve to an Active Directory server on the same subnet as the client. Or it may be located on a site far away. This means that Active Directory can and will be used as an Internet directory server without ever being accessed for domain authentication. Multiple Active Directory servers will link together to provide a global directory service that spans the continent.

Active Directory everywhere

Microsoft also set out to ensure that Active Directory was highly scalable and would become pervasive as quickly as resources permitted. Active Directory is easy to install and set up on a simple server. It is also easy to set up and install Active Directory as a single-user repository, and it carries virtually no noticeable overhead on the simplest configuration (we will discuss Active Directory configuration in Part III). In other words, when Active Directory needs to be small, it can be small, and when it needs to be big, it can grow at an astonishing rate.

This makes it ideal to use Active Directory for even the simplest of application information storage requirements. Although it is no substitute for database management systems that provide advanced information management services such as information analysis and data mining (or the management of corporate data), it may not be uncommon to find a single-user application deploying Active Directory in the hope that later scaling up will be as easy as merely further populating the directory. Active Directory even installs on a standalone 133-MHz desktop machine with 64MB of RAM, and is easily deployable as a domain controller supporting a small company (this configuration is not what Microsoft officially recommends, and such a configuration should support little else but a directory with a small helping of user and computer accounts).

On the other hand, it is possible to deploy Active Directory in such a way that it scales to astonishing levels. As a domain repository, Windows NT 4.0 maxes out at about 100,000 users, but Active Directory can scale to the millions — it can grow as large as the Internet. All the replicas of Active Directory are synchronized (which itself is quite an administration feat, as we will soon see). All copies of an organization's Active Directory system propagate changes to one another, similar to how DNS servers propagate domain records.

Note In practice, an NT domain becomes shaky at between 30,000 and 40,000 accounts, which is why many large companies create multiple resource and account domains. Since both Windows 2000 and Windows Server 2003 use Active Directory, you will find no significant difference between them when it comes to scalability.

The key to the scalability of Active Directory is the domain tree . . . a data hierarchy that can expand, theoretically, indefinitely. Active Directory provides a simple and intuitive bottom-up method for building a large tree. In Active Directory, a single domain is a complete partition of the directory. Domains are then subdivided or partitioned into organizational units, allowing administrators to model the domain after their physical organization structure or relevant business models. A single domain can start very small and grow to contain tens of millions of objects; thus, objects can be defined at the smallest corporate atomic structure without the fear of overpopulation, as was the case with Windows NT 4.0, and NetWare 3.*x* and 4.*x*.

Inside Active Directory

The core of Active Directory is largely accessible only to geeks who see heaven in a line of C++ and Assembly code (authors included). It does not ship with special viewer tools, like MS Access, that give you a feel for what exists in its structures or what these structures look like (a few Resource Kit tools provide some access). The following, however, describes the key components with the objective of providing an insight into the innards of this directory service.

If it walks like a duck

One area seriously lacking in administrator education is database knowledge. Database 101 should be in every engineering course. All too often, we see administrators "reinitializing" databases to free up space, only to discover that they wiped out valuable corporate data in the process. Later on in this chapter, we will study the anatomy of the directory from a very high level. To fully understand how the Active Directory engine works, the following is a mini-course on Active Directory, the database:

On the physical level, Active Directory is two things: It is a database and a database management system (DBMS) . . . pure and simple. The data it keeps can be viewed hierarchically. A *database* is a repository for data. It is a software structure in which data is stored, manipulated, and retrieved by any process seeking to gain access to and exploit the information it contains. If you are not sure this is a valid definition of Active Directory, then let's apply the definition of a database (the rules) to Active Directory.

A database is a database if the following are true:

✦ It contains functional layers — which include a schema — that define the structure of the database: how data is stored, retrieved, reviewed, and manipulated. Other functional layers include an "engine" that comprises I/O functions, maintenance routines, query routines, and an interface to a storehouse for the data. This is often known as a storage engine.

✦ The data, properties, and attributes of a thing are stored in containers, which comprise collections of records, known as tables (such as in a relational database) or some other cubby (such as in an object database).

The simplest definition of a DBMS is that it is a software application, on top of which sits a user interface, used to manage the data in a database and the database itself. A DBMS can be used to extract data (query), format it, present it to users, and print or transfer it into a comprehensible form. Modern DBMS systems, like SQL Server, provide users with the technology to interpret or analyze data, as opposed to simple quantification.

Users of databases and DBMS include both humans and machines. Software used by machines and computers saves and accesses data because it is a means by which a process can gain access to persistent information. Persistent data can and should be shared by multiple users, both human and man-made. For example, an engineer puts data into a database so that a robot can perform repetitive work based on the data.

Active Directory is all the above and more, but you would not use it to, say, extract records of a group of individuals who pose a credit risk to your company, because such support is beyond the purpose of a directory service. Whether Active Directory is a relational database or an object database brings us to debatable levels in our discussion, so we won't go there. Our analysis of Active Directory will help you to make that assumption on your own.

A relational database is made up of tables; it is made up of columns (collections) that represent things, such as a column or collection of first names. Information about each individual entry is stored chronologically (for example, the fifth *first name or fn* in the collection is David). Figure 2-5 represents a column of first names.

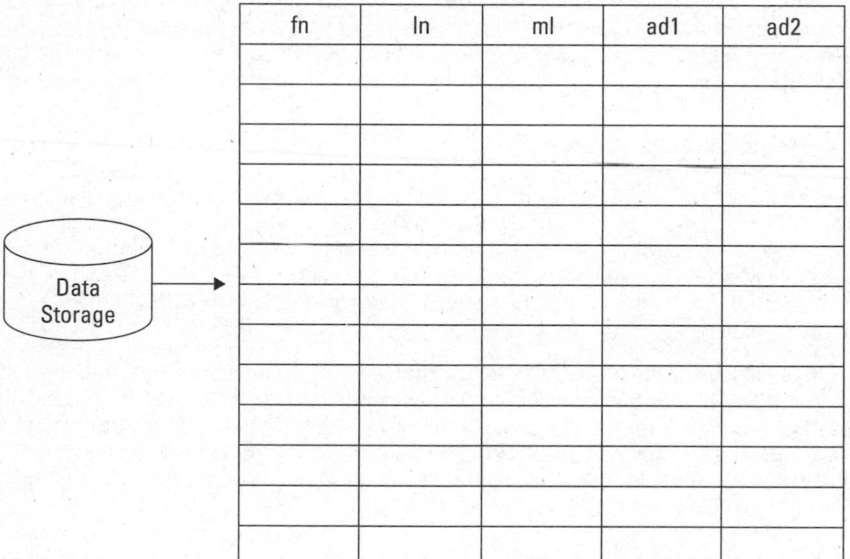

Figure 2-5: The column in a relational database contains records, which are members of collections or groups.

You can have multiple tables in a relational database. You can also have "things" in one table that relate to things in another table, not only by chance, but also by design and purpose. In relational tables, you access the properties of a thing, and the information that it represents, by referencing its place in the collection, as shown in Figure 2-6.

An object database is a little harder to define, mostly because many forms of object databases evolved from relational databases. An object model-compliant database might be more about how the information it contains is exposed to the users and how the underlying schema can be accessed than about the underlying makeup and technology or how it was created.

But an object database might also be best described as a database that conforms to the object model as opposed to the relational model. We do not know enough about how Active Directory works because at the very core, it is a proprietary technology. What we do know is that data is stored in Active Directory in a structure that resembles tables with columns and rows. In fact, Microsoft has used the very same database engine (Jet) it deployed in Exchange Server in Active Directory. It is thus a blood relative of Microsoft Access.

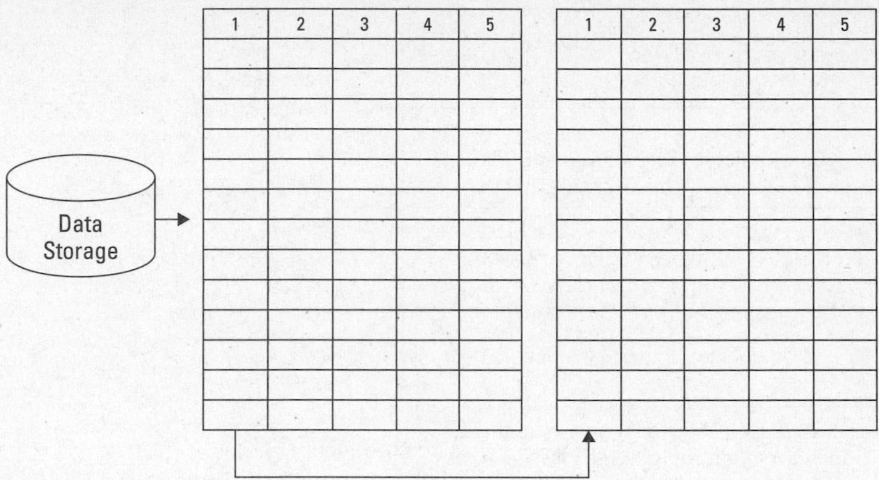

Figure 2-6: Two columns in a relational database contain records that are related to each other.

The Active Directory database structure

Active Directory has been implemented as a layered system comprising the Core Directory Service Agent (DSA), the Database Layer (DB), and the Extensible Storage Engine (ESE). Above these layers lie the interfaces that comprise the replication service, the Security Account Manager or SAM (as with the NT 4.0 SAM), the LDAP interface, and the API (ADSI). The LDAP interface, as you will see later, provides the interface or access to LDAP clients. LDAP is supported in all 32-bit desktop and workstation environments. LDAP is also built into Outlook. SAM provides the security interfaces to Active Directory and hooks in the access control technology. See Figure 2-7.

The time has come to dispense with the acronym SAM. The problem is that SAM stands for Security Account Manager, Security Accounts Manager, and Security Access Manager; Surface to Air Missile fits as well. If Microsoft would simplify this to SM for Security Manager, the industry and Microsoft's people might then agree on what the acronym stands for.

The ESE comprises two tables: a data table and a link table. The ESE database is used to maintain data on the structure of the directory and is not apparent to clients. The Active Directory database, `NTDS.DIT`, on the other hand, contains the following collection of database tables that users will relate to, either transparently, via some cognitive processing, or directly.

- ✦ **Schema Table:** The *schema* dictates the type of objects that can be created in Active Directory, how the objects relate to each other, and the optional and compulsory attributes applied to each object. It is important to note that the schema is extensible, and it can thus be expanded to contain custom objects that are created by third-party applications and services.
- ✦ **Link Table:** The link table contains the link information and how the objects relate to each other in the database.
- ✦ **Data Table:** The data table is the most important structure in the Active Directory database system because it stores all the information or attributes about the objects created. It contains all the compulsory and optional information that makes up the objects such as usernames, login names, passwords, groups, and application-specific data.

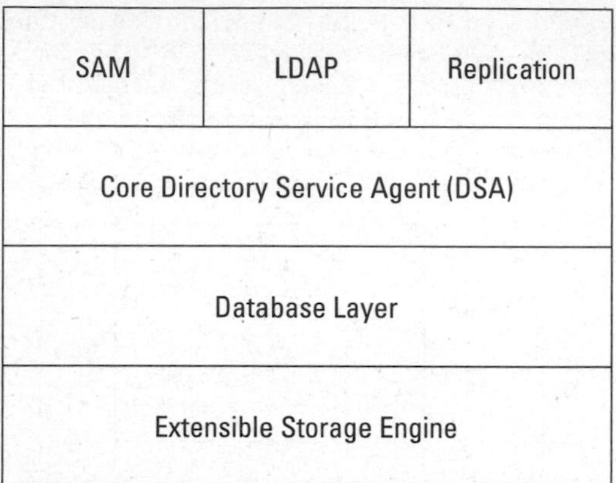

Figure 2-7: Active Directory consists of three functional layers, on top of which lie the access and replication layers and the Security Account Manager (SAM).

Active Directory objects

If Active Directory is a casserole, then the objects are its ingredients. Without objects, the directory is a meaningless, lifeless shell. When you first install Active Directory, the system installs a host of user objects you can begin accessing immediately. Some of these objects represent user accounts, such as Administrator, without which you would not be able to log in and obtain authentication from the directory.

Objects contain attributes or properties — they hold information about resources they represent. For example: The user object of a Windows Network contains information (the attributes) of the user pertaining to his or her First Name, Last Name, and Logon ID. Figure 2-8 is an object-oriented representation of a user object in the Active Directory. (The actual data structure is a table of columns or fields.)

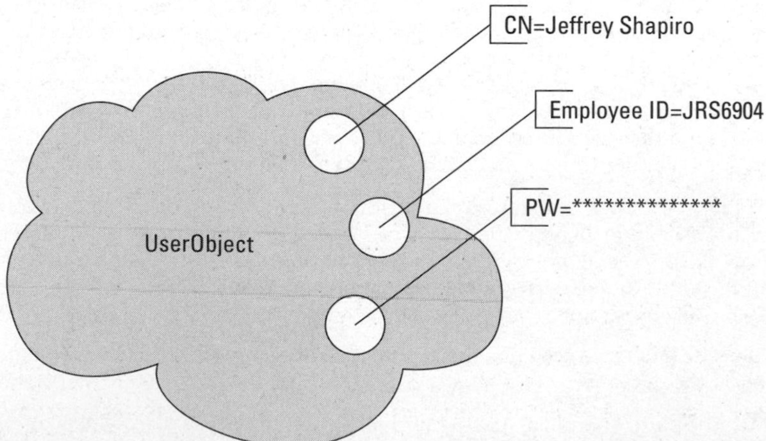

Figure 2-8: An Active Directory user object and three attributes or properties.

There can be many different objects in Active Directory. Some hold exploitable information, and some are merely containers for other objects. You might conclude that the entire Active Directory is one big object, inside of which are container objects, which contain other objects, and which in turn contain other objects, as illustrated in Figure 2-9. Here, we depict a *container object,* technically represented by a triangle, a popular storage symbol, which holds other container objects. This nesting can continue until the last object is a *leaf object,* which cannot be a container.

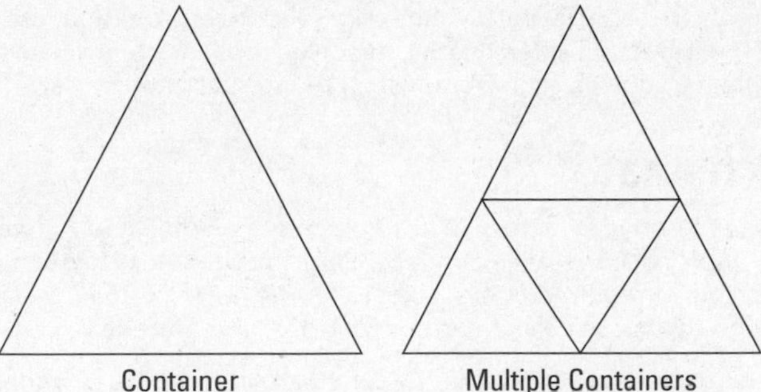

Figure 2-9: The container object contains other objects, which in turn may contain objects.

Objects that are not container objects, such as a user object, are known as leaf objects, or end node objects, as illustrated in Figure 2-10. When a leaf object is added to the container, the nesting ends there.

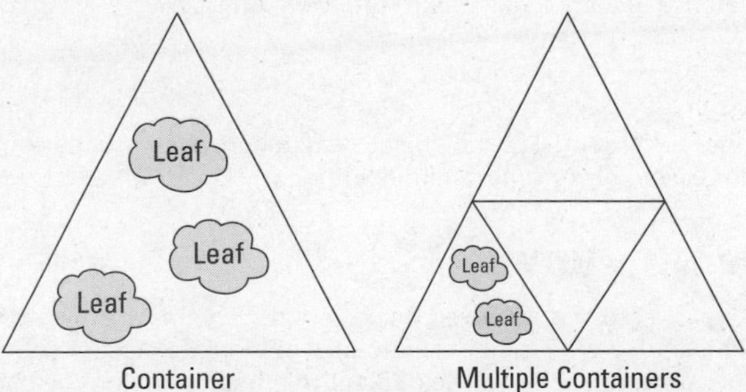

Figure 2-10: The leaf object or end node object does not contain other objects.

Active Directory is like one big babushka doll. Figure 2-11 provides a popular two-dimensional view of the container philosophy. However, the metaphor we are more familiar with in IT and Windows network administration is the object tree, which we will discuss shortly.

We also talk in terms of *object classes* when working with Active Directory. The object class is less a class in the object-oriented technology sense and is more a collective noun for the type and purpose of objects organized as groups. Object classes can be user accounts, computers, networks, and more; actually, they can be any of the objects that Active Directory currently supports.

Another way to look at the object class, or simply class, is that it is a definition of an object that can be created and managed by the directory. *Content rules* govern how an object can be attributed. Classes are also endowed with certain rules that dictate which classes of objects can be parents, which can be children, and which can be both.

We mentioned earlier that the Active Directory schema is extensible. This means that programmers can code against the API and create and manage their own objects (refer to the discussion on ADSI later in this chapter, in the "My active directory" section). This allows application developers to use Active Directory and save configuration and state information about applications. Of course, the registry is still a valid place to store information, especially for hardware settings, but Active Directory offers features such as replication, propagation, and a wider "gene pool" of objects, such as users, with which to interact and coexist.

Active Directory schema

The *schema* is the Magna Carta of Active Directory. When you create an object in Active Directory, you have to also comply with the rules of the schema. In other words, you have to supply all the compulsory attributes required by the objects, or the object cannot be created. The schema governs data types, syntax rules, naming conventions, and more.

As we just mentioned, the schema, which is stored in the schema table, can be extended dynamically. That is, a program can extend it with new custom classes and then provide the rules by which the schema can manage the classes. Once this has been accomplished, the application can begin using the schema immediately.

Extending or changing the schema requires conforming to programmatic and administration rules. That the schema is itself part of the directory means that it is an enterprise-wide service in Active Directory. And as such, a master schema has to be properly accessed before any peer schema receives propagated schema changes. We will not delve too far into this because it is a subject that belongs in a book devoted to programming Active Directory.

Object attributes

Objects contain *attributes.* Some are essential to the object's existence, such as a password for a user object. Some are not essential, such as a middle initial.

Walking the Active Directory

The route to an object in Active Directory is achieved by traversing a hierarchical path that resolves the object's name. This path includes all the container objects through which you can drill down to the end node. What might be a little difficult to grasp is that on the one hand, we talk about containership, while on the other, we talk about how you have to walk a long and winding road to discover the name of the leaf or end node object. The best way to try and understand this is by examining the diagram in Figure 2-11, which shows a system of boxes that contain smaller boxes, and so on. If we join all the left top corners of the boxes, we see the emergence of the hierarchical path about which we speak.

In Active Directory, this full path name (the names of all the dots joined together) is known as the *distinguished name,* or DN, of the object. The name of the final object itself, apart from the path, is known as the *relative distinguished name,* in this case "mis."

We say the full path to the object and the object name itself is *distinguished* because it is unique in Active Directory. No other object contains the identical object DN. In other words, the object itself is unique. The purpose of this naming and tracing mechanism is to allow an LDAP client to rapidly track down an object and retrieve its information as quickly as possible.

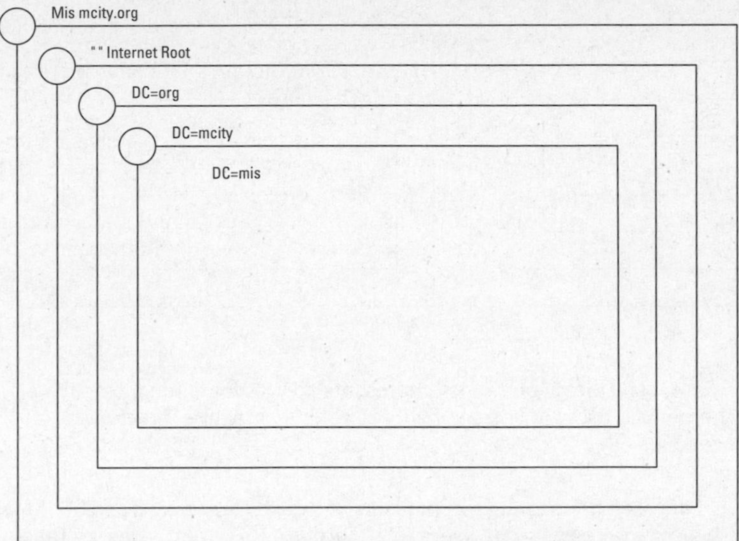

Figure 2-11: If we join all the dots representing the ID of each box, a systematic, hierarchical collection of boxes begins to emerge.

The relative distinguished name (RDN) of the object is the object name itself. The RDN is an attribute of the object. The RDN is not necessarily unique, although it is unique in its container in Active Directory, because such a name can exist at the end of another DN somewhere else in Active Directory, down some other path. Figure 2-12 illustrates how two objects can have the same RDN but somewhere up the chain the similarity will end, if finally at the root or the parent.

When we make a query to Active Directory, we naturally start at the root of the DN of an object and follow the path to the node. But in LDAP, we start at the RDN and trace the name parts to the root. In this fashion, the entire DN is constructed during such a query, such as:

```
cn=box1,root=,container5=,container6=,container7=,container8=..
```

It might help to clear things up for you at this point if you construct a DN on a scrap piece of paper. For the exercise, let's say that you need to construct a query to the user named jchang. To get to jchang, you need to start with the cn, which is jchang, then go up to office=232, floor=3, building=maotsetung, city=peking. LDAP works from the bottom up. Try not to think about an entry point into Active Directory, but to merely start at the object and parse your way up the path until a match is found when you hit the root object.

Naming convention

Each section of the DN is an attribute of an object expressed as `attribute_type=value`. When we talk about the object name itself or the RDN, we refer to the *canonical* or *common* name of the object, expressed in LDAP lingo as `cn=`. If we are talking about a user, the common name takes the format `cn=jchang`.

Conversely, each object's RDN is stored in Active Directory, and each reference contains a reference to its parents. As we follow the references up the chain, we can also construct the DN. This is how LDAP performs a directory query. This naming scheme is very similar to the mechanism of DNS, as illustrated in Figure 2-12.

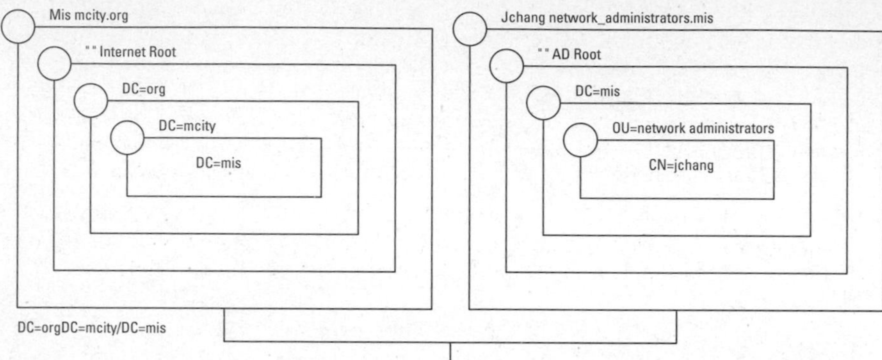

Figure 2-12: The domain hierarchy on the left represents a DNS domain namespace on the Internet. The domain hierarchy on the right represents an Active Directory domain namespace.

Now that we have discussed the naming mechanisms of Active Directory, you should know that Windows does not require everyday users to go through this exercise every time they access an object. The UI does all the work for you and hides this syntax. However, such attributes are required when you code directly to the Active Directory API (ADSI) or LDAP, or are using scripting languages or tools to query and work with Active Directory in a more advanced fashion than the standard tools allow.

Active Directory supports both LDAP v2 and LDAP v3 naming styles, which comply with the Internet's RFC 1779 and 2247 naming styles. This style takes the following form:

```
cn=common name
ou=organizational unit
o=organization
c=country
```

However, Active Directory drops the `c=country` and replaces `o=organization` with the `dc=domain` component. For example:

```
cn=jchang,ou=marketing,dc=mcity,dc=org
```

The use of commas in the DN is a separation or delimiter mechanism. LDAP functions parse the DN and go by the delimiters to break the DN into its relative parts.

In *dot notation,* this would read `jchang.marketing.mcity.org`. An LDAP algorithm translates LDAP names to DNS format and vice versa.

By complying with the LDAP naming convention, any LDAP client can query Active Directory via an LDAP Uniform Resource Locator (URL) as follows:

```
LDAP://ldapserver.mcity.org/cn=jchang,ou=marketing,dc=mcity,dc=org
```

Objects in Active Directory are stored and tracked according to an attribute consisting of the object's globally unique identifier or GUID (pronounced *gwid* by some and *gooeyID* or *gooID* by others). The attribute is called the *objectGUID.* The object can thus be moved around and changed, even renamed, but its identity will always remain the same. The GUID is the 128-bit number that is assigned to the object upon its creation. An object cannot exist in Active Directory without a GUID; it is one of the compulsory attributes that are automatically assigned when the object is created. The GUID is available for external process reference and programmatic function; in other words, you can reference the object in Active Directory from an external program by its GUID. This mechanism assures that the object will always be accessible as long as it exists. Ergo, wherever it is moved, it is still accessible.

Objects are protected in Active Directory via the SAM access control mechanisms and security through the functionality of access control lists (ACLs). In other words, you need to be able to prove ownership and rights over an object if you want to edit or delete it.

Domain objects

When you set up Active Directory for an enterprise, your first exercise will be to create your root domain or, in Active Directory terms, the root domain object. If this root domain will also be your Internet root domain, you should register it with an Internet domain administration authority (such as Network Solutions, Inc.) as soon as possible. If you already registered a root domain, you will be able to create an object that represents it in Active Directory and link it to the DNS server hosting or resolving that name. If you have not registered your domain, you might not be able to match it to your company name, because domain names are being claimed every second of the day. This root domain in fact becomes the first container object you create in your chain of objects that represent the "expanse" of your local network logon domain in Active Directory. Under this domain, you create more container objects that represent the organizational units (discussed next) within your enterprise. For example, you might create a domain called `mcity.org` and register it with the InterNIC. There are also security considerations we will address later.

For now, know that the domains you are creating here are full-blown security and administration entities of your network, in the same fashion that legacy NT 4.0 and earlier domains are. How they work will just confuse you now, so we have left this discussion for the chapters in Part III. Note, however, that we will not discuss integration and migration of legacy domains until Part III.

Figure 2-13 represents a path (from the bottom up) of a user all the way up to the domain root. As you now know, you can have only a single domain parent in Active Directory. It is entirely feasible, and good practice, to create sub-domains under the domain root that reflect the sub-division of resources, departments, politically and geographically diverse divisions of an enterprise, acquisitions, resource entities, and more.

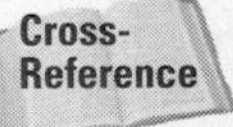

Chapter 10 presents some reasons you would or would not partition Active Directory into several domains.

For example, a root domain of ABC Company might be `abc.com`. You could then easily create a sub-domain of `abc.com` called `marketing.abc.com`. Note that the `.com` should not be your domain root, because the Internet authorities own that domain root. Keep in mind that we are still creating objects only from an Active Directory point of view. These domain objects are container objects, with name attributes for easy lookup and management (and GUIDs for internal tracking and identity). What we are actually asking Active Directory to do is to maintain the first domain as a root container object, which in turn contains subordinate domain objects.

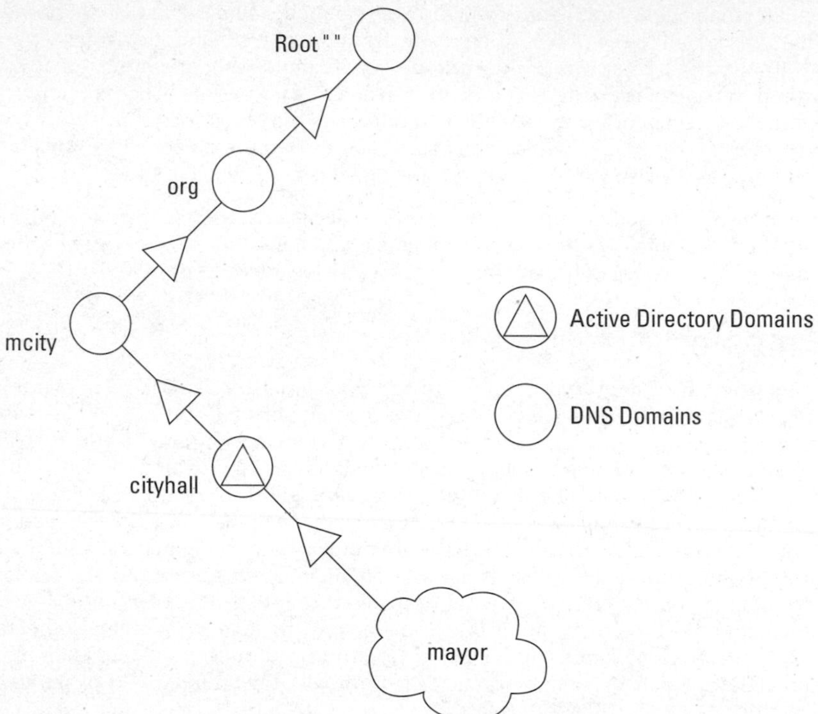

Figure 2-13: A user object (account) on an Active Directory local domain. There is a direct connection between the Active Directory domain and the DNS domain.

Organizational units

OUs are key container objects in which you can group classes of objects. OUs can, for example, contain objects such as user accounts, printers, computers, files, shares, and even other OUs. Figure 2-14 illustrates the "containerization" of a group of user accounts into an OU.

The OU is a welcome addition to network management in Windows Server 2003, as it was in Windows 2000. In Active Directory, you can create these containers to reflect your enterprise or organization. To illustrate, we re-created the organizational chart of a major U.S. city and merged it into the domain of a cyberspace city called Millennium City. This will become the sample enterprise we will return to during later discussions of Active Directory.

The organization chart on the left in Figure 2-15 shows the hierarchy of departments and divisions in Millennium City at the time a directory for this organization was being contemplated. We also see that the chart shows a diverse collection of departments, both local and geographically dispersed, and various sites and services. On the right in Figure 2-15, the same organization chart is represented with OU objects in Active Directory.

In any domain on the domain path, you can create organizational units, and inside these organizational units you can create group, user, and computer objects. You can also add custom objects to the domains and OUs. Active Directory lets you also create any end point or leaf object outside the OU.

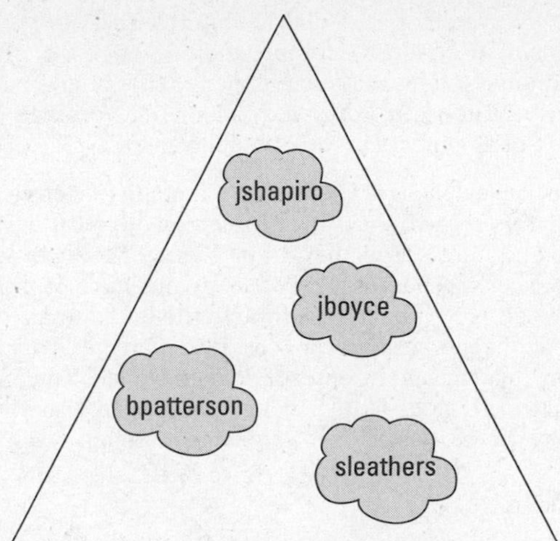

Figure 2-14: User accounts grouped in an OU container.

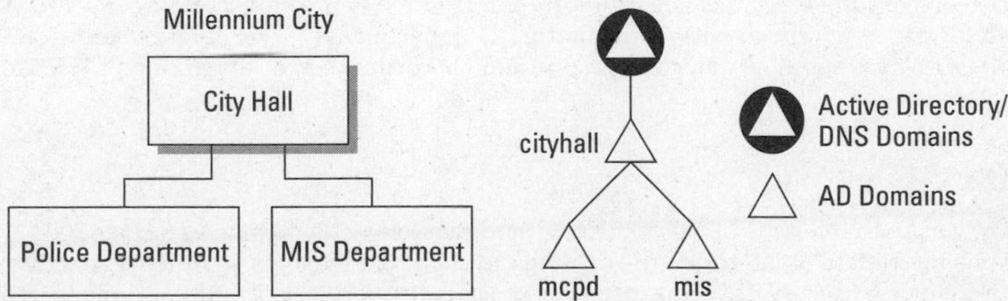

Figure 2-15: The left side of the figure represents an organizational chart. The right side represents the same organizational chart as an object hierarchy in Active Directory.

Trees

Active Directory refers to the domain structure we just studied as *domain trees.* Everything from the bottom of the object path is considered part of the domain tree—leading from the bottom up, all the way to the single domain parent at the top. The domain tree is unique in Active Directory, because no two parent domains can be the same. The schema does not allow it.

As demonstrated earlier, the domain tree is a systematic collection of Active Directory domain objects that belong to a contiguous namespace. Remember that in Active Directory, the root domain can be extended or partitioned into multiple subdomains that share a common parent. Sub-domain names must also be unique; however they all share a common directory schema, which is the formal definition of all objects in the domain tree.

Active Directory deploys the DNS naming conventions for hierarchical naming of Active Directory domains and domain devices. In this regard, the Active Directory domains and the devices therein are both identified in DNS and Active Directory. Don't worry, Windows Server 2003 takes full advantage of Dynamic DNS, so DDNS names, like WINS, do not have to be created in Active Directory and then manually entered into DNS. Although the two domain hierarchies have identical names, they still reflect separate namespaces. DNS manages your Internet namespace, while Active Directory manages your enterprise namespace. The enterprise namespace is, however, resolved via the services of DNS, which provides a directory to the servers that hold your Active Directory directories. This may seem confusing.

Forests

It is possible to create another parent domain in Active Directory and create objects under it that may appear identical to objects in adjacent domain trees. These collections of domain trees are called *forests.* Active Directory refers to a single domain tree as a forest of one tree. You can also set up trust relationships between these trees, and allow users of one tree in the forest to access the resources in another tree. You would find yourself adding trees to your forest, for example, when you acquire another IT department in a corporate takeover or merger, or when migrating objects from one domain to another, or integrating with legacy NT domains.

Trusts

Finally, we get to the issue of trusts. Like NT and Windows 2000, Windows Server 2003 domains interrelate or interoperate according to trust relationships. In other words, the security principals of one domain are trusted by the security services of another domain according to the trust relationship between the two domains. This is illustrated in Figure 2-16.

Figure 2-17 illustrates the three domains that are linked by transitive trust relationships. For those who are wondering about this new trait, *transitive* essentially means that if domain A trusts domain B and domain B trusts domain C, then A also trusts C. Another way to look at it is by stating that a friend of my friend is also my friend. Figure 2-17 illustrates the transitive trusts.

Transitive here really means that something is able to get from point A to point B by going via point *n.* Transitive can refer to the transient activity of other systems besides security. Replication is a good example.

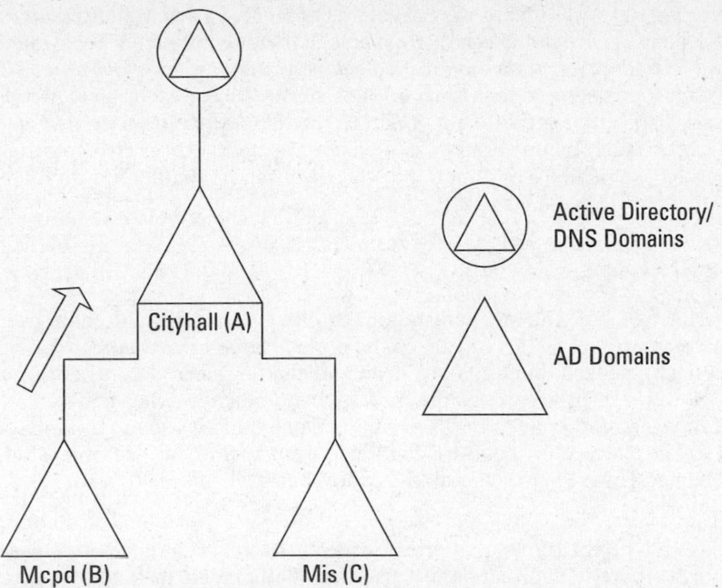

Figure 2-16: Domain A trusts domain B, and domain B trusts domain A . . . a two-way trust.

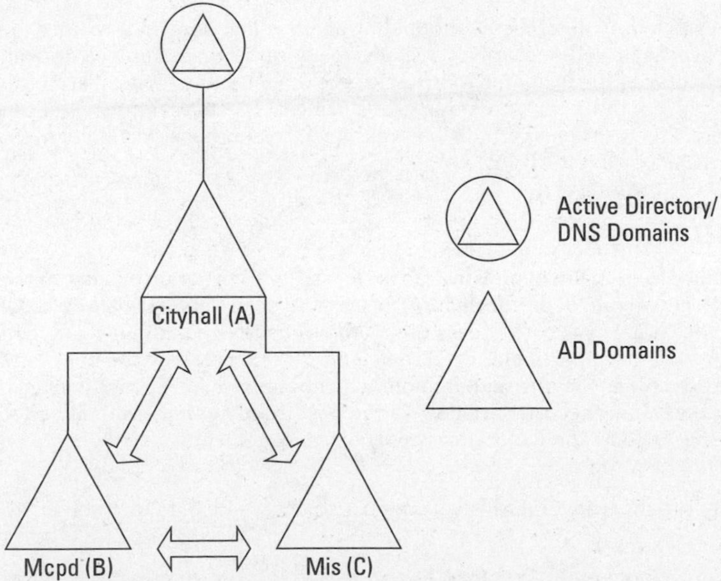

Figure 2-17: Transitive trusts: If domain A trusts domain B and domain B trusts domain C, then domain A trusts domain C.

You might be wondering why, then, Windows Server 2003 domains are automatically transitive while legacy NT domains are not. There is no magic in this, no nifty trick performed by Microsoft other than the adoption of an established security standard long overdue: Kerberos. The ticket-granting service that Kerberos and Active Directory bring to Windows Server 2003 creates a distributed security network. Like the Single Sign-on initiative discussed earlier, Kerberos tickets issued by one domain can be used as good currency in another domain. The Kerberos ticket is like a multinational visa or passport that allows the bearer to gain access to any territory that can accept the instrument.

The global catalog

As we discussed earlier, in LDAP, the mechanism for searching or parsing a domain tree is to start from the bottom and travel all the way up to the domain root. LDAP also works on a system of referrals in which a search that ends in a dead end can be referred to other domain trees in the forest. However, LDAP searches only work when you know what you are looking for; in other words, if you already have the DN or object name and all you are hoping for are the attributes you will be allowed to see. But what if you want to find, for example, all the printers in the OU named Town Planning or all the users that have access to a certain folder? Enter the global catalog (GC).

Active Directory supports directory deep queries by means of a GC that is created as soon as the first domain root is created. It contains the attributes of all objects in Active Directory that are, by their nature, searchable. Last or first names are a good example; organization names, computers, printers, and users can be searched by supplying certain attributes as keywords. Applications and users are thus able to query the GC by using a known, or assumed, attribute as a keyword to find possible matches.

The GC also allows you to find an object without knowing in which domain it resides, because the GC holds a subset of all the objects of all domains in a forest. For example, a domain member tells you that he or she is unable to log on to the domain. When you search the domain, you find no object that represents this user's name or logon attributes. You can then search the GC to find if the user has perhaps been assigned to another domain, if an account has not yet been created, or if it is disabled.

My active directory

Of extreme importance to domain administrators is the ability to program against Active Directory. Custom access to account information has always been a limitation in Windows NT 4.0. Microsoft provided no easy way to access the SAM for customized administrative functions. Every organization has a particular need that cannot be satisfied by the base functionality alone: A good example is the desire to find out which Windows NT accounts have dial-in access enabled, and who has used this privilege in the past three months. To build a tool to query this against the NT SAM and generate a report for management is like trying to add another face to Mount Rushmore.

But Active Directory provides several APIs you can use to access its data for such custom needs.

- ✦ **ADSI:** The most important API Microsoft has released is the *Active Directory Service Interfaces (ADSI)*. ADSI is a collection of Component Object Model (COM) objects that can be used to manipulate and access the directory. Since its release, Microsoft has added Java support (JADSI), which allows any Java tool to program against the ADSI interfaces; but given the litigious atmosphere around Java, you would be better off programming Active Directory from the LDAP API using Java, as described in a moment.

- **MAPI:** The Windows Open Services Architecture (WOSA) Messaging API. One of Microsoft's oldest APIs, Active Directory supports MAPI to allow mail-enabled directory applications to gain access to the MAPI address book provider.
- **LDAP API:** This is a C API, which is the *de facto* standard for programming against anything LDAP-compliant. The LDAP API can be programmed from C, C++, Java, and Delphi (essentially any programming language capable of calling C functions).

However, through ADSI, you can access any LDAP-compliant directory (Active Directory, LDAP repositories, and third-party directories such as NDS). This means that ADSI can be used by anyone looking to create applications that access any LDAP-compliant directory. In other words, write once to ADSI and support any directory (with Microsoft Windows, naturally).

ADSI provides an abstract layer above the capabilities of the directory (it wraps the LDAP API). In this fashion, it provides a single set of directory service interfaces for managing or accessing LDAP resources.

Developers and administrators will use ADSI to access LDAP directories in general and Active Directory in particular. This opens Active Directory and LDAP to a host of possible applications. Consider this: Under NT 4.0 and earlier, it was cumbersome to work with APIs to duplicate the functionality of User Manager for Domains and Server Manager. Administrators were pretty much saddled with these applications, no matter how creative they believed they could be in managing network resources through code or scripting.

ADSI will see both ISVs and corporate developers developing tools to make their administrative tasks easier and cheaper. Using traditional languages and scripting tools, a developer might create functionality that automatically sets up groups of users, applications, network resources, tools, devices, and more. These "applets" can also be targeted to the Microsoft Management Console (MMC), which makes their installation and deployment a cinch. And developers will be able to easily "directory enable" their applications.

ADSI has been designed to meet the needs of traditional C and C++ programmers, systems administrators, and sophisticated users. But it is as easily accessed with Visual Basic, making it the most comprehensively accessible LDAP product on the market. ADSI presents the services of the directory as a set of COM objects. For example, an application can use the ADSI PrintQueue object to retrieve data and to pause or purge the print queue, leading to applications that coexist with the underlying technology (as opposed to applications that just run on the platform).

Active Directory is also MAPI-compliant or, should I say, supports the MAPI-RPC address book provider. This support allows a MAPI-based application to look up the contact information of a user, such as an e-mail address or telephone number.

Bridging the Divide: Legacy NT and Windows Server 2003

One of Active Directory's primary features is its accommodation of earlier versions of Windows NT. Most companies will not switch their entire operations to Windows Server 2003 overnight, but will instead run Windows Server 2003 alongside Windows 2000 and Windows NT for some time.

Many companies will adopt the Active Directory domain controller or several controllers as the new "PDC" of legacy Windows NT domains. NT servers, workstations, and clients view Active Directory servers as PDCs in mixed-mode (Server 2003, NT, and 2000 mixed) environments. To users, applications, and services, the authentication by Active Directory is transparent, thus allowing NT domains to continue services oblivious that the PDC is in fact the proverbial disguised wolf, as Microsoft cunningly did with the File and Print services for NetWare, which made clients think the NT server was a NetWare server. (This requires a special upgrade to the NT registry and SAM to make it Active Directory-compliant, which starts with Service Pack 5.)

Active Directory achieves this magic by totally emulating Windows NT 3.51 and NT 4.0 domain controllers. In a mixed-mode environment, the Windows 2000 domain controller acts and behaves like a Windows NT 4.0 domain controller. Even applications and services (including the ISV and third-party products) that are written to the Win32 API will continue to work without modification in an Active Directory environment.

A term you will encounter in chapters ahead is *down-level compliance.* This down-level compliance allows many IT and LAN administrators to plan gradual and safe transitions to Windows Server 2003 domains in which Active Directory is the master logon authority. Thus, the transition in most cases will be evolutionary rather than revolutionary, while still guaranteeing that Active Directory gets deployed right at the very beginning. Transition by phased implementation is the route we will primarily advocate to you in the chapters to follow, and we will also discuss routes to Windows Server 2003-Windows NT integration that do not require Active Directory.

Note The routes to Windows Server 2003 and Windows 2000 Server are less of an issue since Windows 2003 is fully backwards compatible with Active Directory in Windows 2000 Server.

Active Directory provides or denies logon authority and access privileges to the network resources of a Windows domain. Before we proceed further with Active Directory, we deem it necessary to get certain information straight about Microsoft domains: Let's define "domains" in the Windows network sense (as opposed to what you have read about earlier in this chapter) so we all know what we are talking about. Not only should we try to clear up the confusion about domain generations or versions, but also you will almost certainly have to integrate or migrate legacy NT domains into Windows 2003 domains, and unless you understand the differences, you are likely to really foul things up. Philosophically, things are very different.

So now there are two types of Windows domains: the NT domain (now the legacy domain) and the Windows Server 2003 domain . . . a container object in Active Directory, a speck on the Internet, and conceptually the extent of your network. Both can be analyzed in terms of a logon "stack." And both share common traits.

Figure 2-18 represents the Windows NT and Windows Server 2003 local logon stack on the local machine, and the logical order (from the top down) of the process to authenticate access to the local services. At the top of the domain stack are client processes; these reside on local machines or on other client machines, workstations, and network devices. When the client process requires access to a service, the local Security Account Manager, using data stored in the local SAM, controls the access (this works the same for Windows NT and Windows Server 2003).

Figure 2-19 represents the Windows domain logon and authentication stack, which encompasses the Windows NT networking environment. The domain logon stack works in the same fashion, only the clients do not log on locally to a machine or network resource. Instead, the OS passes the access request to Active Directory, in Windows Server 2003, or the domain (PDC or BDC) registry (where an accessible copy of the SAM resides), on NT domain controllers.

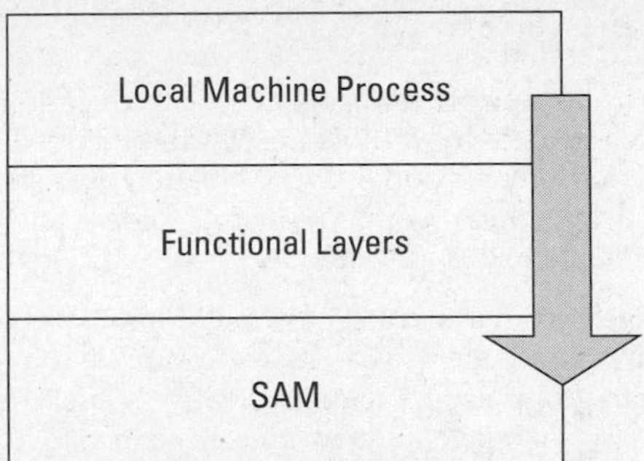

Figure 2-18: The Windows NT and Windows Server 2003 logon and authentication stacks.

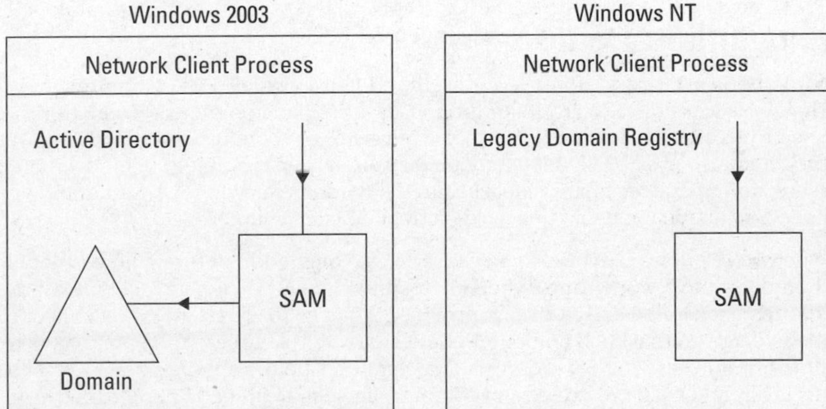

Figure 2-19: The Windows NT and Windows Server 2003 domain logon and authentication stacks.

The Windows Server 2003 domain is a single collective, albeit extendable, unit that comprises all the network objects considered to be members. In many respects, the domain structure is one huge distributed container that embraces all your company's networking and IT assets. You can view a domain as a "collective," much as a fleet of ships comprises a flotilla or a navy, or a group of marines comprise a brigade or a corps.

Before we discuss what's new about Windows Server 2003 domains, let's discuss some quick similarities, which for many will provide familiar turf. The NT domain begot the Windows Server 2003 domain, and that's probably the best way to compare them (even if the kid somehow came out very different).

Single point of access and administration

NT domains allow an administrator to log on to the network and gain access to the administration tools at a server or workstation (even via scaled-down tools on Windows 95 and Windows 98). The tools include User Manager for Domains and Server Manager. Users, groups, network devices such as printers and drives, and resources such as folders and sharepoints are accessible to administrators who have been assigned the necessary rights.

Windows Server 2003 domains provide the same single point of access and administration, but with a lot more flexibility to manage resources and users. The OU, for example, is a new entity in the Windows domain that allows you to group users in administrative structures, compartments, or diverse organization divisions or management entities. This means it is possible to create units and assign administrative functions to departments. For example: The materials management department is managed under the Mat-Mgt OU. And a user in this OU is assigned administrative rights to manage the contents of this OU and only this OU. This obviates the need to assign everything to a single administrator, or having an admin group with dozens of users gaining access to blanket administration authority on the domain.

Domains and more domains

The NT (or Windows network) domain represents a logical grouping of computers and devices that are accessible to a group, or groups, of users and computers, no matter their logon place or position. The domain provides a means of containing and controlling users on the network, and also provides a defined boundary and a security shield behind which computers, users, and operators function in a secured environment. Windows Server 2003 domains perform an identical function, as described in later chapters.

If you are new to Windows networking, here's a quick explanation of the Windows network domain: Compare it to a workgroup. When Microsoft launched Windows 3.11 and Windows for Workgroups back in the early 1990s, it provided a means for computers to connect to each other as peers so that each computer could share its resources. You would have to specifically permit access to the resources on a computer before anyone or anything could use it. This is already a pain to do at each computer in a small office of people, because each computer acts as a standalone server and has to be managed as such. Once your network begins to expand, it becomes impractical and well nigh impossible to manage.

The domain, on the other hand, was born of the ability to locate a central security, login, and access permissions authority on a master server, called the primary domain controller, or PDC. The SAM database, which lives inside the registry, provided a global access to the users in the central security database, to the resources on all the computers, and to devices attached to the network, such as printers, backup drives, and CD-Rs.

Intra-domain trust relationships

The ability of NT domains to trust each other (bi-directionally) is very apparent in Windows Server 2003 domains, but you will uncover big differences. The inter-operation of flat NT domains (4.0 and earlier) is tedious. It seemed to make no sense under NT 4.0 to create separate domains for a small to medium company, even across wide area networks. Any company of, say, 100 people that requires the establishment of more than 100,000 domain objects is doing something very wrong. Yet, small companies would often create multiple domains for no apparent reason other than to organize their thoughts.

Few follow the 100,000-object limit rule for a Windows NT domain because domains are in a constant state of change. It makes more sense to monitor the size of the SAM, which has a tendency to become unstable when it grows larger than 35 or 40MB.

The only time we have had to administer more than one domain in a company (70+ in one company is the record) was due to aggressive acquisitions, in which we inherited domains from the various takeovers. Daily, we would have problems trying to assign resources and absorb users. Nonetheless, many large companies ran out of registry space because they were so big, or they created separate resource domains where devices and other network services resided apart from "user" or "account" domains. These are typically companies with tens of thousands of users.

Windows Server 2003 domains are modeled on Internet domains, have depth and perspective, and can be partitioned almost infinitely. They inherently trust each other, in much the same way that a family trusts each other under the same roof, even though each member goes about his or her business in his or her own section of the house.

It makes sense to create multiple domains (actually domain extensions or partitions) on a Windows Server 2003 network, but for very different reasons, the most important, already mentioned, being devolution of power and delegation of management. As you will see later, you can create domains that encompass subnets, sites, departments, locations, and the like. And as long as your domains are attached to a common ancestor, the domain root, trusts between them are full-blown two-way. Although the term "transitive" relates to two-way trusts that exist between many domains, not only on the same tree, but also across trees in the forest, this naturally does not mean that two domain groups (the forests) can be somehow grafted into each other like you would two living plants. But it is a darn sight easier to migrate, move, and eventually eliminate orphan domains in a forest.

In short, Windows Server 2003 domains are modeled after Internet domains, have dimension, and can be partitioned. NT domains, on the other hand, are flat.

Access control lists and access tokens

When a user (human or service) logs into a domain, NT authentication and security management grants the user access to the network and resources it is permitted to use. This is done in the form of ACLs and access tokens. Seasoned or astute NT administrators will recall how it is possible to access and edit the ACL on a local machine. And if you do not know how, you will learn later. NT also provides the user (login) with an access token, which the user wears as it browses the network. The access token works like the security badge you wear to work. As you approach doors or devices, they either open for you or deny access. Windows NT domains and Windows 2003 domains both control access using ACLs. In Active Directory, the SAM ACLs (in the directory) control who has access to objects and the scope of that access.

All Windows Server 2003 services are referred to as objects. These objects are stored in either the local Security Account Manager (SAM), which is a registry tree, or else Active Directory is controlled by the ACLs. Each ACL contains permissions information, detailing which user can access the object and the type of access allowed (such as read only or read/write). ACLs are domain-object-bound; they are not transient entities.

Reality Check

It goes without saying that Microsoft, with Active Directory and Windows Server 2003, is taking us to a point from which we will be unable to return. Of course, we asked for this in our quest to be liberated from the old norms to the promises of e-commerce, DNA, and an information-ruled network society.

While the technology presented herein is impressive, there are several caveats to consider. Firstly, small companies will be able to install Windows Server 2003 far quicker than larger companies because the IT infrastructure of smaller companies is far less complex. A small Windows NT network is easier to convert than peeling a banana skin (provided you have supported hardware and current drivers). So, installing Active Directory for domain authentication and security in a small business is a relatively painless procedure.

Small companies typically do not currently drive their internal networks on pure IP and DNS. They still use NetBEUI and NETBIOS, and rely on IP and DNS only when it is time to take a trip on the Web or get e-mail. Larger companies, especially those that have long ago seen the sense of pure IP networks, already have DNS servers and IP infrastructures in place. This means that existing DNS support is likely to come into conflict with two factors, Unix-based DNS servers and Unix-based DNS administrators (asking a Unix administrator to adopt Windows-based DNS is like asking a cat to bark).

So, for some time to come, complex IT environments will likely run mixed networks (Windows NT, Windows 2000, NetWare, and Unix). And as long as NT domains (and Windows 9*x* clients) need to be supported, not all the wonders of Windows Server 2003 (such as SSO) can be accessible or appreciated. The entities that can most use the advanced features of Windows Server 2003 will mostly be the entities that take the longest to adopt the operating system or at least convert their domains to native Windows Server 2003. It all depends on the boldness of the people and the IT management at many firms.

And despite the enthusiasm for Active Directory, you need to be careful in your adoption strategy. The wish list for this directory-elect's next version already runs into dozens of pages at many organizations. The chapters in Part III are thus designed with these realities in mind.

Summary

In this chapter, we introduced Active Directory as one of the most exciting new additions to Windows networking: It is bound to be the technology that drives the transition from legacy NT domains, and probably from most other environments to Windows Server 2003 environments.

As applications developers, we need consistent, open, and interoperable interfaces and APIs against which we can store and manage information relating to applications, processes, and services. Many companies have risen to the challenge of providing directories. Directories and directory services will and must be free, open, accessible, and part of the network operating systems and technology we use. Active Directory is all this and then some.

Directories should not be seen as the next killer application; rather, they represent important evolutionary processes to support the existing and future revolutions in computing, communications, and information technology.

✦ ✦ ✦

CHAPTER

Windows 2003 Security

✦ ✦ ✦ ✦

In This Chapter

Understanding the ins and outs of encryption

Understanding Kerberos

Getting to know IPSec

Familiarizing yourself with Microsoft Certificate Services

Understanding logon and authentication

✦ ✦ ✦ ✦

This chapter starts you off with a discussion on the need for powerful distributed security before introducing you to the specifics of Windows 2003 distributed security services. It also reviews the new Windows 2003 security protocols, and protection of services and data.

An Overview of Windows 2003 Security

While the new era of computing and Windows 2003 will bring forth many benefits, it will also herald dastardly attempts to rob you, beat you up, and shut you down. There are many forces out there that have only one thing on their evil minds, and that is to find any way to break into your network to plunder and pillage.

Before you start building your new corporate infrastructure around Windows 2003, it will pay for you to become thoroughly versed in the security mechanisms the operating system offers and how to go about locking down your assets. Without a doubt, it is probably the most secure operating system available today. Not only has it inherited the Windows 2000 C2 security compliance, but also, if there were showbiz awards for security, Windows 2003 would clean up at the Oscars, the Golden Globes, the Grammies, and more.

But before we get into Windows 2003 security specifics, let's look at the problem holistically. You can then evaluate your current security status before devising a security plan.

You have probably heard the term "C2 security" everywhere, so what does it mean to you, the network, or server administrator? Absolutely nothing. C2 security is nothing more than a U.S. government sanction. The United States keeps a series of "books" that grade the security levels of operating systems. These specifications include object ownership, object protection, audit trail, memory protection, and user identification, all of which are discussed in various places in this book.

C2 is defined in the so-called "Orange Book," which is really titled the *Trusted System Evaluation Criteria.* C2 evaluation checks to see how secure a computer really is. However, C2 only applies to standalone computers. Microsoft is also testing to the specifications for network computers (Red Book and Blue Book). Microsoft has gone above and beyond C2 with Windows 2003. So, the term is really meaningless.

The operating system is not C2 out of the box. Everyone has access to everything. A vendor or security service provider has to set up a machine and the OS to be C2-compliant. This means locking down objects, setting up audit trails, creating user accounts with secure password philosophy, and so on. Only when a machine has been fully locked down can it be rated as C2-compliant . . . no matter if it's a washing machine or a file server.

Another reason that C2 is not important to you is that, as mentioned earlier, out of the box Windows 2003 is as locked down as the space above your head. You have to lock down every aspect of it; the network is only as secure as you make it. If Windows 2003 is not properly configured, claiming awards like C2 will not get you out of a jam when a hacker pulls your pants down on the Internet. We know we are being blunt, but security is part of the day-to-day life of a network administrator. If you don't have a security problem, you don't have a network.

The Need for Security

If you are new to network administration in general and Windows 2003 in particular, before you devise a security plan, you need to understand the risks to your network and yourself. Unless you plan to hire a security expert, you will probably have to come up with a plan yourself. Chances are your company will ask this of you . . . your superior will assume that you are well versed in the subject. If you are well versed in the security threat, you can skip this part and go directly to the section titled "Rising to the Security Challenge."

A company's data is its lifeblood, and it needs to be vigorously protected. As the network administrator, you will be required to ensure that data is kept confidential and that the data can be relied upon. There are numerous mechanisms in place to assist you with respect to data integrity and confidentiality, and they range from sensible access control policy to encryption, backup, and availability.

Data Input

Data is vulnerable to attack and capture from the moment a person types in a user ID and password. How often have you had to enter a password while someone was standing over your shoulder? You try to type as quickly as you can, but spies will watch you typing and pick up your passwords quicker than you think. Then, when you are not at your desk, they will get your user ID from the memo field at the sign-in screen and masquerade as you from any computer, anywhere.

With a smart card, the user is authenticated without the risk of being compromised because the thief needs the card to complete the hack. Smart card readers offer one of the most sophisticated domain authentication solutions available to Windows 2003.

Data Transport

The PC's or input device's operating system must transport the information down the network stack to the transport, all the way to the domain controller's (DC's) network interface and up the DC's respective stack. All along this route, the data is vulnerable to interception. If the data is not encrypted, or is encrypted very lightly, there is a risk that a person tapping the network will be able to pick up conversations between your input device and the domain controller, or any other partner for that matter.

To counter this, Windows 2003 employs extensive encryption technology both in data and network communications, and in file storage and protection.

Why the Threat Exists

There are many reasons people threaten your security. Let's look at a short list of threats that you are most likely to encounter during your life as a Windows Server 2003 administrator:

- **Espionage:** People need to break into your communications realm to learn company secrets, employee secrets, product plans, financial situation, strategy, and so forth. This level of threat is the most virulent. The attackers have strong motives to get the attack under way and to ensure they succeed. The attackers do not want to be discovered and will continue to hide in your environment as long as they need to. The damage is often irreparable if the attackers are undiscovered. This is the most difficult form of attack to counter because, for the most part, you do not know where they are hitting you or why.

  While bugging devices and spying are not usually the responsibility of the network or server administrator, espionage via the network is becoming more probable everyday because it is so easy and it is where all the jewels are located.

  Over the network, hackers will read files and e-mail, and try to log in to databases wherever they can to steal credit card numbers, bank account numbers, and so forth. An attacker can, for example, find out the password of your voice mail system and then listen to your messages.

- **Denial of Service (DoS):** These attackers are intent on destroying you. They can attack your physical premises or locations, which is becoming harder to do all the time, or they can target your network, which is becoming easier to do because you are connected to the Internet or because you provide users with remote access. This is fast becoming the favorable means of attack for stopping your work: firstly, because of the dependency your company has on the network, and secondly, because the attacker does not need to be physically present for the attack.

  DoS attacks are made by flooding your network portal (targeting your gateway to the Internet) with massive floods of e-mail, or with *syn* attacks, which are the low-level communication barrages that suck up all the server's resources, finally causing it to crash. Sometimes the objective is to crash the server just to trigger backdoor code that spawns a process. There could be a million places on a network to hide a sliver of code that gets executed when certain files are loaded. Good examples are the boot files and startup files like AUTOEXEC.BAT.

- **Hostile Applications:** Hostile applications are placed on the Internet for unwary surfers to download. Upon execution of the code on your internal network, the application can begin its dirty work, which for a while might be to do nothing that can cause it to be detected, but rather to find information that would be valuable to the attacker. Such applications are also called Trojan horses.

- **Virus Attacks:** By far, the most visible attack on the network comes in the form of viruses. Contrary to the claims that there are tens of thousands of viruses, only a handful of virus writers can actually claim to have invented one from start to finish. Most virus authors are not as brilliant as you may have been led to believe; they are just copycats. However, this information does not provide any relief.

  A lot of virus code is available on the Internet to be freely downloaded, manipulated, and enhanced or packed with a payload. This is the reason we see so many variations of viruses every month. Some can be detected by anti-virus software such as NetShield and cleaned up; others are more sinister, such as Backdoor-G, which can only be picked up by the anti-virus software after it has delivered its payload. Not only does it wreck your PC before it can be detected, but it also first attacks the anti-virus software.

Threats emanate from two locales: the external environment and the internal environment. A threat from the external environment is when the threat comes from people who have no contractual status with the enterprise. They are complete strangers. The attack comes from the outside. A threat from the internal environment is when the threat comes from people who have a relationship with the company, from employees to contractors to customers. This attack usually comes from the inside. In some cases, it comes from the outside, with inside information. Other times, the threat is not born out of revenge or criminal intent, but by ignorance.

The external environment

Not too long ago, the only way to threaten or attack an organization, its people, or its business was through some sort of physical act. This is no longer the case. It costs far less money and is much safer for a hacker to stay in a safe haven and attempt to break into a network through a RAS portal or connection to the Internet. For many, it means the possibility of financial reward; for others, it has to do with some form of demented feeling of achievement.

Now that many small companies can afford dedicated connections to the Internet, the pickings have become very attractive. While we have not yet realized the paperless office, almost all data is placed on the network in share-points and databases. The network and server storage silos are thus loaded with valuable information.

Attackers also no longer need to proactively choose their targets. They create hostile code that gets inadvertently downloaded from the Internet and gets executed by a number of mechanisms, from rebooting to the mere act of unzipping a file. The code then can gather intelligence and send it to its master. It is therefore essential that you establish policy to ensure that code downloaded from the Internet is authenticated and signed with the digital signature (a public key) of a trusted software publisher.

E-mail is now very much tangible property, and it can be used in court cases as evidence and as a source of information that can be used to plan an attack on a person or an organization. We all communicate more by e-mail than we do by snail mail, yet e-mail is treated like a postcard. We do not enclose our messages in an envelope and seal it. We just put it in the mail for anyone to look at.

E-mail needs to be secured on two levels. We need to be sure that the people with whom we communicate are really who they say they are. And we need to be sure that our e-mail is not being read or changed as it traverses the net. It is very easy to trace the route a message takes over the Internet and penetrate e-mail systems. Securing e-mail is becoming essential and falls under the auspices of public key encryption, which are discussed shortly.

The internal environment

The internal environment threat comprises employees who are either malicious, stupid, or who make honest mistakes. Threats come in the form of outright misuse of privileges to total ignorance or stupidity. For example, the perpetrator of outright misuse of privileges has administrative rights on the network and provides him or herself access to sensitive data.

The ignorance factor often involves users failing to keep anti-virus software current, or downloading all forms of rubbish from the Internet, thereby introducing malicious content to the network from the external environment.

Outright stupidity and honest mistakes that often cause headaches for administrators are usually deleted files, corrupted databases, deleted mailbox folders, and so on. Deleted data can usually be recovered from backups, as long as the backup regimen is well practiced in your company. Most of the time, recovering deleted files is just a waste of time spent doing administrative work to have to keep recovering files. Often, the problems are not user-related issues at all, but just bad management on the part of a lazy network or server administrator.

Rising to the Security Challenge

Over the years, there has been a lot of discussion about the security capabilities of Windows. Microsoft has often been criticized for not delivering a more secure operating system when, in fact, the opposite is the case. But it has not been all Microsoft's fault. For starters, the U.S. government has for years not allowed the export of 128K-bit encryption algorithms . . . although that did not deter many organizations from smuggling out the software.

And as for the comparison with Unix, Unix systems are more at risk today than Windows 2003. Because the Unix source code is open for all to see, many hackers can read the code to look for weak points and plot their attacks. Server for server, there are still more Unix machines on the Internet than Window NT or Windows 2003 machines. On Windows NT, hackers resort to scanning network communications to look for information with which to replay attacks. Data interception was and still is a common form of attack against an NT network.

For Windows 2003 to compete and even excel over the competition in the risky and exposed world of e-commerce, it needed to be *the* most secure operating system. The following sections explore the standard Windows 2003 security mechanisms Microsoft has implemented in Windows 2003:

✦ Kerberos

✦ IPSec

✦ PKI

✦ NT LAN Manager (NTLM)

All the fancy encryption algorithms you use will be useless if your server stands in the middle of an open-plan office for anyone to plunder or sneak out. Unless a server or key systems and data storage are locked up behind secured barriers, you might as well forget the rest of this chapter.

Before you tackle the protocols, you need to get up to speed on the cloak-and-dagger stuff.

Understanding Encryption Basics

This is a true story. A man walked into a diner one morning and ordered fried eggs. When the eggs were delivered, he changed his mind and advised the waitress that he had ordered scrambled eggs. The waitress, peeved at the cheek of the client, picked up a fork and with a quick whipping movement rendered the eggs into an unrecognizable heap. "There, now they are scrambled," she said, and stormed off.

The action of rendering the eggs into an unintelligible mess is known as scrambling. Data is scrambled in similar fashion; we call it encryption. At first, the data is in whole recognizable form, often called *plain text,* like the fried eggs. The motion to scramble them is known as the *algorithm* . . . and the result is often termed *cipher text.* In the anecdote, the algorithm is the technique, style, or "recipe" by which the waitress used her wrist and fork to turn a perfect pair of sunny-side-ups into a mound of yolk and white. If she only took a few stabs at the eggs, the patron might be able to claim he still had fried eggs (not a strong encryption algorithm).

Knowing the key that reverses the process is vital to the recovery of the data, but that is the only difference between egg scrambling and data scrambling. If we knew how to unscramble eggs, Humpty Dumpty might still be alive, and our world would be very different.

In computer science, the standard that governs the techniques and recipes for encryption of data is known as the Data Encryption Standard (DES). DES data encryption algorithms (DEAs) specify how to encrypt data and how to decrypt that data. A number of important bodies, such as the American National Standards Institute (ANSI) and the National Institute of Standards and Technology (NIST), govern the specifications for DES. Each algorithm is rated according to the strength of its encryption ability (and resistance to duplication, attack of the encryption/decryption key).

DES, actually the DEAs, needs to be continuously improved because the codes are often cracked by encryption experts (for science and crime). New standards are on the horizon, and soon the Advanced Encryption Standard (EAS) will replace DES. Other standards governed by these bodies include the Digital Signature Standard (DSS) and the Digital Signature Algorithm (DSA). Incidentally, the U.S. government does not regulate encryption.

For more information on encryption standards, see the RSA Laboratories Web site at `www.rsasecurity.com`.

Getting to Know Cryptography

Cryptography dates back more than 4,000 years. Over the past millennia, it has protected many a culture's communications and has brought them through wars, treaties with neighbors, and more.

In recent years, electronic data communications have escalated to such volume and importance in our lives that without electronic or digital cryptography we would not be able to continue on our logical course.

In fact, we owe our computerized environment to cryptography. If you have time during the locking down of your networks, you should read the biography of Alan Turing, who directed the British to build the first digital computers to break the German's Enigma code.

Pretty Good Privacy (PGP) is a software program written originally and distributed illegally for no financial gain by Phil Zimmerman, who believed that the cryptography algorithms that were being protected by patents should be made public property . . . worldwide. He created PGP back in 1991, and over the years, it was disseminated around the world on the "undernet." Even though its export was expressly forbidden by the U.S. government's International Traffic in Arms Regulations, which classified his software as a munition, it became available everywhere on bulletin board systems and the first pioneer sites of the World Wide Web. In the last decade, PGP was pretty much the only means of securing data and communications on the Internet and corporate networks of the world.

But encrypting data always required a user to make an effort to secure communications. Lethargy and a lack of knowledge have always left room for error and holes. Only with the incorporation of the encryption algorithms in the very core of the operating systems and standards-based network protocols would encryption become as pervasive and as transparent as air.

We have come a long way since Phil Zimmerman risked detention to make the slogan *encryption for everyone* a reality. Today, Windows 2003 incorporates it extensively. Only you, the administrator, need to ensure that it is configured correctly, through security policy, and everyone on the network will be able to use it, without even knowing it exists. Before we look at this native support for cryptography in Windows 2003 and how it is used, here is some cryptography 101.

Keys

Cryptography is a lock, a means of securing information by rendering it undecipherable without a key. The key, or cryptographic key, is held closely by people sending and receiving the communication. The following is the simplest example of cryptography:

The communication: Package color baby burger

The Key:

Package = meet

color = same

baby = grand central station

burger = 14:00 hours

Deciphered: meet me at the same place at Grand Central station at 2 p.m.

Obviously, if you have the key, you can unlock the code and decipher the message.

Private Keys

Private key encryption is also known as *Symmetric Key Encryption* or just *conventional cryptography.* This encryption uses the same key to decrypt and encrypt the data. In other words, the key you use to lock the door is the same key you use to unlock the door. In the previous example, both the sender of the message and the receiver share a common codebook or key. The sender encodes the message with the key, and the receiver decodes the message with the same key. This form of encryption is not the most secure in the public domain, because for widespread communications, numerous parties must hold the key. As soon as the key falls into wrong hands, then all bets are off. But it can be used in network authentication where the compromising of a key is highly unlikely.

Public Keys

Public key encryption uses two keys. One key is public, and the other is private. Both keys can encrypt data, but only the private key can decrypt the data. To be pervasive, the technology depends on a public key infrastructure (PKI), which Windows 2003 now supports (more about PKI later in this chapter).

A mathematical process is used to generate the two keys, and the keys are related to each other by the product of that mathematical process. Therefore, the message encrypted with one key can be decrypted only with the other. This is how it works:

You want to send an encrypted message. The receiver has a public key, which he or she makes publicly available for encrypting messages. You encrypt the message using the public key and send it. When the receiver gets your message, he or she can decrypt it using the private key, which is mathematically related to the public key. No one, including you, can decrypt the message with the public key.

It goes without saying that the private key must be closely held or your messages will be compromised.

Session Keys

The chief problem in making public keys widely available is that the encryption algorithms used to generate public keys are too slow for the majority of just-in-time communications (there are numerous algorithms used to create the keys, but the technology is beyond the scope of this book). For this reason, a simpler session key is generated, and it in turn holds the "key" to the encrypted data.

1. A session key is randomly generated for every communication that requires encryption. A *key distribution authority* (or the originator of the communication, or a vouchsafe process) creates the session key for the communication or message.

2. The data is encrypted with the session key.

3. The session key is then encrypted with the recipient's public key. The encryption of the data by the session key is a thousand times faster than the encryption of the data by the public key.

4. The encrypted data and the encrypted session key are then sent to the receiver, who can decrypt both by first decrypting the session key with the secret key and then decrypting the data with the session key.

Key Certificates

Key certificates are containers for public keys. Key certificates usually contain the public key of the recipient, the identity of the creator of the public key, the date the key was created, and a list of digital signatures.

Digital Signatures

We add our written signature to most things we do in the material world, so why not in the digital world? Most of us spend our working lives in cyberspace. Our customers deal with us on the net, they buy from us on the net, and they expect that when they send us confidential communications, they are sending it to the right people. We also want to know that when someone sends us a message, hits our Web site, or connects to our computers that they are who they say they are. We also need to use digital signatures to prevent repudiation. In other words, if someone places an order with you over the World Wide Web or via e-mail, or enters into some form of contract with you, they should sign the document so that they cannot turn around later and repudiate the transaction.

It is also not always necessary to encrypt a message, which taxes computer resources. Sometimes, the message or data content or information is not sensitive. Sending someone a publicly available encrypted price list would be an absurd idea. But what if someone intercepted that message and changed the content, which would affect the relationship? What if someone sent you a message saying, "Mary just had a little lamb," and a jokester intercepted the message and changed the content to read, "Mary just ate her little lamb?" The effects could be devastating.

Digital signatures are thus used to authenticate the sender, to legally bind parties in digital transactions, to authenticate content, and to be sure that content has not been changed or tampered with in any way.

Windows 2003 makes wide use of the encryption mechanics described previously. One of the most important implementations is in the use of the Kerberos protocol, which is now the most important means of authentication and protection of data in not only Windows 2003, but also all major operating systems.

Understanding Kerberos

What if we told you that every time you come to work, you have to go to a certain security officer who signs you in and issues you a clip-on tag that enables you to enter the building and go to your desk, but do nothing else? And that you had to check in with the officer every hour to renew your tag?

What if you then needed to go to this person for a new tag every time you needed to access a resource in the company, such as the file room or the copier machine? And then what would you think if we told you that you have to present this tag to guards that protect each resource so that they can verify that you are legitimate?

You'd say, "Wow, this is overkill. Why is security so tight here?" It would probably be hard to work in such an environment. But what if several companies, or a whole city, adopted such stringent security practices? Life in the city would be so secure that companies would be able to trust each other enough to share resources. But for all intents and purposes, it would still be hard to work in such an environment.

Yet, this is precisely how Kerberos works. The only difference is that the security check-ins and tag issues are handled transparently by the underlying protocols, and everything takes place in network transmissions. The user is oblivious to what is going on under the network hood.

Kerberos is based on a system of *tickets,* which are packets of encrypted data that are issued by a *Key Distribution Center (KDC)*—the security officer we just mentioned. This ticket is your "passport" and carries with it a myriad of security information. Each KDC is responsible for a *realm,* and in Windows 2003 every domain is also a Kerberos realm. Also, every Active Directory domain controller (DC) is a KDC.

When you log on to Windows, WinLogon and LSA kick in to first authenticate you to the KDC (see Chapter 2), which provides you an initial ticket called the *Ticket Granting Ticket (TGT),* which is akin to a right-of-way coupon at the fairground or a passport. Then, when you need to access resources on the network, you present the TGT to the DC and request a ticket for a resource. This resource ticket is known as a *Service Ticket (ST).* When you need access to a resource, your processing environment presents the ST to the resource. You are then granted access in accordance with the ACL protecting the resource.

The implementation of Kerberos in Windows 2003 is fully compliant with the Internet Engineering Task Force's (IETF) Kerberos v5, which was originally developed by MIT. This specification is supported by many, which means that tickets issued in a Windows 2003 domain (now also known as a Kerberos realm) can be passed to other realms, such as networks running Mac OS, Novell NetWare, Unix, AIX, IRIX, and so forth.

Trusts can therefore be established between the Kerberos Domain Controllers (KDCs) in the respective realms. The KDC trusts, for all intents and purposes, work just like trusts for Windows NT systems, which are set up between the primary domain controller (PDC) in each domain. And because Windows 2003 still speaks NT LAN Manager (NTLM), trusts are maintained to legacy Windows domains.

Kerberos, however, does require more tweaking and administration than you may be used to on Windows NT domains using NTLM. That's because users have to check in with the KDC several times a day. For example, if you are logged on for 12 hours straight, you will probably have to check in with the KDC about 12 to 15 times in that period. If the domain supports 1,200 users, that will result in about 18,000 hits to the KDC.

Also, trusts between heterogeneous networks are not as transparent as the trusts between Active Directory domains, in which the domain controllers can explicitly vouch for the users. Trusts between Windows 2003 forests, Windows 2003 and Windows NT, and Windows 2003 and other realms involve a manual setup between each domain's or realm's respective administrator. The process that takes place in the Unix or IRIX realm may be very different to the setup that takes place between Windows 2003 realms.

When planning the physical layout of the network, if you have multiple domains that communicate across a WAN, you will need to establish shortcuts or the best possible routes that ticket transmission can use to move from realm to realm. Shortcuts may be required so that authentication does not become bogged down in network traffic over a small pipe.

If authentication is slow due to slow links between networks, you may have a good reason to establish the site as a new domain. For more information on deciding when to create a new domain, check out Chapter 7.

Kerberos is, however, a very fast protocol and is an ideal environment for implementing the Single Sign-On paradigm in network authentication.

Kerberos and the Single Sign-On Initiative

Single Sign-On is long overdue. From a security angle, it provides tremendous benefits. If a user has six or seven passwords, it means he or she has six or seven more opportunities to compromise security. Many people are so sick of the different passwords they have to deal with that they would rather not have a password. This is a problem in systems where the password creation and application is in the hands of the user. A good example is a voice-mail system. Many, such as CallXpress for Windows NT, ask the user not to enter 1234 or to leave the password blank. But a review of the password history on the system usually shows that many passwords are left blank or are simply 1234.

Other users go to the opposite extreme and type their passwords into a password database or a spreadsheet, or worse, a simple text file. An intruder will go to town on a document loaded with keys. Password databases are the mother lode; it takes a few seconds to crack the password that locks the file.

With Single Sign-On, the user authenticates once, and that authentication is respected by other network applications and services. Made possible by Kerberos and Active Directory, Single Sign-On is supported in SQL Server .NET and Exchange .NET, and is supported by trusts set up between realms implemented by other operating systems and Windows 2003. It is the very reason that Windows 2003 trusts — between domains that share a common root or forest — are transitive.

Psst . . . This Is How Kerberos Works

Kerberos is built around the idea of "shared secrets." In other words, if only two people know a secret, then either person can verify the identity of the other by confirming that the other person knows the secret. The shared secret in Kerberos is between Kerberos and the *security principal* (the human user or a device).

Here's an analogy: Two people send each other e-mail regularly and need to be sure that each e-mail cannot be repudiated by the other, or that someone else is not masquerading as the sender. So to be sure that the sender or receiver is who they say they are, both agree offline that something in the messages between them will confirm that each one is "the one."

However, if someone is analyzing e-mail and spotting word arrangements, it will not take them long to discover the hidden confirmation message. On a network authentication mechanism, this can be quite a problem because it would not take long to intercept a message and fool an authentication service into thinking the user is genuine.

So how do the two correspondents devise a plan to be certain of their identities? The answer is symmetric-key cryptography. The shared key must be kept secret, however, or anyone will be able to decode the message. As discussed earlier, a symmetric key is a single key that is capable of both encryption and decryption. In other words, as long as the two correspondents share the same key, they can encrypt their messages and be sure that the partner is able to decrypt it.

The terms *secret key* and *symmetric key* are often interchanged when discussing the use of a single key to encrypt and decrypt text. However, it is entirely possible for a secret key to fall into the wrong hands.

The practice of secret key cryptography is not new and goes back to before the Cold War days when insurgents perfected secret key techniques and cipher science. In the Kerberos implementation, however, authentication is a done deal as long as the information is decrypted, or as long as one party can prove they are the real thing by being in possession of the decrypting key in the first place. But what if someone on the network steals the key, or manages to copy previous authentication sessions? Kerberos then makes use of an unalterable factor that goes back to the Big Bang . . . time.

Time Authentication

Kerberos authentication begins, literally, from the time a user tries to log on to the domain. When Kerberos receives an authentication request, it follows this series of steps:

1. Kerberos looks the user up and loads the key it shares with the user to decrypt the authentication message.
2. It then looks at the information in the message. The first item it checks is the time field, which is the time on the clock of the user's workstation or machine from where the user requested logon authentication. If the time on the sender's clock is out of synch by five minutes, Kerberos will reject the message without further ado (Kerberos will compensate for the different time zones and daylight savings time). However, if the time is within the allowable offset of five minutes, Kerberos accepts the message pending one more item.
3. Kerberos checks to see if the time is identical or older than previous authenticators received from the sender. If the time stamp is not later than and not the same as previous authenticators, Kerberos allows the user to authenticate to the domain.

However, it is also important to know that the authentication is *mutual.* Kerberos will send back a message demonstrating that it was able to decrypt the user's message. Kerberos sends back only select information, the most important being the time stamp that it obtained from the original authentication from the client. If that time stamp matches the client's information, then the client is sure that Kerberos, and not an imposter, decrypted the message.

Key Distribution

Authenticating to Kerberos works well for authentication to the domain, but what about accessing resources once the client has logged in? In that Kerberos is used for authenticating to domain resources, how does the client authenticate to other network resources?

Well, Kerberos is able to distribute keys. In other words, it acts as a broker. This, in fact, is where the name Kerberos comes from. In Greek mythology, you may recall that Kerberos was a three-headed dog that stood guard over the gates of Hades. Kerberos, the protocol, also has three heads: the client, the server, and a mediator or proxy. The proxy is known as the Key Distribution Center . . . it dishes out keys. In Windows 2003, the Key Distribution Center is installed on the Active Directory Domain Controller.

Okay, so now you are beginning to think one step ahead here, and you say, "Cool, that whole rigmarole of decrypting the message and checking the time stamps just has to be repeated between clients and servers." And you would be further correct if you assumed that the job of giving the network resources copies of every user's key would be that of the Key Distribution Center. However, you are correct in theory only, because so much key distribution would be a tremendous drain on resources. Every server would have to store keys from potentially thousands of users in memory. What, in fact, is implemented is quite ingenious in its simplicity.

Session Tickets

Instead of following the logical plan and sending the session key to the client and the server at the same time, the KDC in fact sends both copies of the key to the client and then gets out of the way. The client holds the server's copy of the key until it is ready to contact the server, usually within a few milliseconds. The illustration in Figure 3-1 may help you "decrypt" what is going on here.

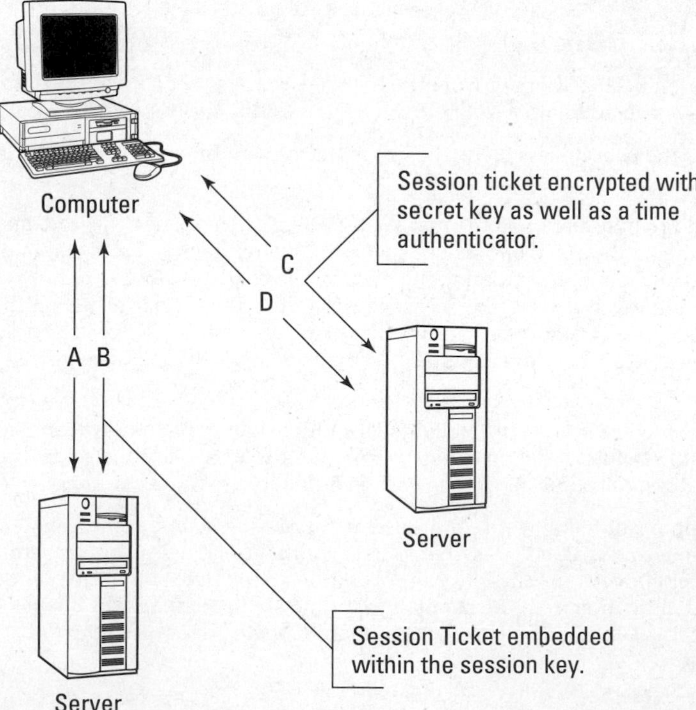

Figure 3-1: Key distribution and mutual authentication.

The KDC invents a session key whenever the client contacts it to access a resource (A). The server sends the session key to the client, and embedded in the session key is the session ticket (B). Embedded in the session ticket, which really belongs to the server, is the server's session key for the client. All that really happens here is that the KDC acts as a domain broker or proxy for secret key negotiations that take place between a client and the resource to which it requires access.

When the client receives the communication from the KDC, it extracts the ticket and its copy of the session key. It stores both items in secure volatile memory. Then, when the client contacts the server (C), it sends the server a message that contains the ticket that is still encrypted with the server's secret key and a time authenticator that is encrypted with the session key. The ticket and the authenticator make up the client's credentials in the same fashion as the logon authentication process.

If everything checks out, the server grants access to the client (D) because the server knows that a trusted authority, the KDC, issued the credentials. As soon as the client is done using the server, the server can get rid of the session key that the client was using to communicate with the server. The client will instead hold the session key and re-present it to the server each time it needs to access it.

Session tickets can also be reused, and as a safeguard against ticket theft, the tickets come with expiration times. The time to live for a ticket is specified in the domain security policy, which is discussed later in this chapter. Typically, ticket life usually lasts about eight hours, the average logon time. When the user logs off, the ticket cache is flushed and all session tickets and keys are discarded.

Kerberos and Trusts

Kerberos trusts are made possible by extending the concepts we just discussed beyond domain boundaries. When a trust is established between two domains, which happens automatically between domains that are part of a contiguous namespace (an Active Directory tree), the two domains share an *inter-domain key,* and one KDC becomes the proxy for the other and vice versa.

After this inter-domain key has been established, the ticket granting service in each domain is registered as a security principal with the other domain's KDC, allowing it to issue ticket referrals. Clients in their home or native domains still contact their local KDCs for access to the foreign resource. The local KDC checks to see that the resource needed by the client resides in another domain. It then sends the client a referral ticket for the resource in the other domain. The client then contacts the other domain's KDC and sends it the referral ticket. The remote KDC authenticates the user or begins a session ticket exchange to allow the client to connect to resources in the remote domain.

Locating KDCs

DNS is the locator service for Kerberos. The governing Request For Comment (RFC) 1510 specifies how DNS should resolve KDC hosts to IP addresses. Client computers need to send their messages to the IP address. If the IP address of the KDC cannot be resolved, it generates an error message to the client indicating that the domain cannot be located.

In a Windows 2003 domain, the KDC is usually installed on the Active Directory server. They are not connected in terms of application process space and run as separate services. However, because the KDC is always installed on the DC, it is possible to resolve a KDC by looking up the host address of a domain controller.

It is also possible to install Windows 2003 servers in non-Windows 2003 domains, and they can still participate in Kerberos authentication. You will need to ensure that they resolve to the correct host addresses, which will not be to Active Directory domain controllers. The utility called `ksetup.exe` is used to configure clients and servers to participate in Kerberos realms that are not Windows 2003 domains.

There is obviously a lot more to Kerberos than what we discussed here, but it exceeds the scope of this book. Numerous books have been written that deal exclusively with the subject. However, Kerberos security is the de facto pervasive security mechanism that protects Windows 2003 domains. Kerberos is a good reason to move to native domains as soon as possible. As ugly as it may sound, the three-headed hound guarding your network is a welcome addition to Windows 2003 domains.

Getting to Know IPSec

IPSec, which is a contraction of IP and Security, is an Internet Protocol (IP) security mechanism employed in Windows 2003 for the maximum protection of network traffic. IPSec is mainly used for communication over an insecure IP network. One such network springs to mind — it's called the Internet.

The protection, encryption, is applied at the IP layer and takes place between two computers. The encrypted packets are not filtered in any way by firewalls or routers and simply pass through. It is also thus transparent to the users and applications deployed on either side of the correspondence.

IPSec operates on four levels: encryption and encapsulation, authentication and replay tolerance, key management, and digital signing and digital certificates.

The encryption is also known as *end-to-end,* which means that it remains encrypted en route to the other computer, and it can only be decrypted by the other computer. IPSec also uses public key encryption; however, the shared key is generated at both ends of the encryption, and it is not transmitted over the network.

The IP Encapsulated Security Protocol uses 40/56-bit DES or 112/168-bit DES to encrypt the IP address of the sender along with the datagram. This thwarts attempts to grab the packets in transit between hops and prevents the attacker from learning the source or destination address, which would be required in order to mount an attack. The original packet is also encapsulated in a new packet, along with the contents of the packet and the header information. The packet is still transmitted to the destination IP address, but that is not apparent during transmission.

To guarantee data integrity, the secure data encryption algorithm (SHA-1 or MD-5 of RSA) ensures that the data cannot be tampered with en route. This is called IPSec anti-replay. Each datagram is tagged with a sequence number. When the datagram reaches its destination, its sequence number is checked to verify if it falls within the predetermined range. If it does not, the datagram is discarded.

The key management component is supported by the ISAKMP (Internet Security Association Key Management Protocol)/Oakley key management protocol v8 used to enable the use of a single architecture to secure transactions with different vendor products that are IPSec-compliant. The Digital Signature Standard (DSS) and RSA provide the proof of authorship for signatures on digital certificates.

IPSec also supports the ability to import your company's unique x.509 v.3 digital certificate into IPSec-compliant hardware and software. This means that you are essentially integrating

IPSec into your Public Key Infrastructure (PKI), which is discussed later in this chapter. The integration between IPSec and PKI provides even stronger network security.

This is how IPSec works:

1. Computer A sends data to computer B across an insecure IP network. Before the transmission begins, an algorithm on computer A checks to see if the data should be secured according to the security policy established on computer A. The security policy contains several rules that determine the sensitivity of the communication.

2. If the filter finds a match, computer A first begins a security-based negotiation with computer B via a protocol called *Internet Key Exchange (IKE).* The two computers then exchange credentials according to an authentication method specified in the security rule. The authentication methods can be Kerberos, public key certificates, or a predefined key value.

3. After the negotiations are underway, there are two types of negotiation agreements called *security associations* that are set up between the two computers. The first type is called *Phase I IKE SA,* and it specifies how the two computers are going to trust each other. The second type is an agreement on how the two computers are going to protect an application communication. This is known as *Phase II IPSec Sec Sas,* and it specifies the security methods and keys for each direction of the communication. IKE automatically creates and refreshes a shared secret key for each SA. And the secret key is created independently at both ends without being transmitted across the network.

4. Computer A signs the outbound packets for integrity and also encrypts (or not) the packets according to the methods agreed upon in the earlier negotiation. The packets are then transmitted to computer B.

5. Computer B checks the packets for integrity and decrypts them if necessary. The data is then transferred up the IP stack to the application in the usual fashion.

Although IPSec was designed to protect data on insecure networks, it can also be deployed on an intranet, especially in light of the widespread implementation of TCP/IP in a Windows 2003 intranet. It has obvious application to protect against many of the threats discussed earlier in this chapter.

However, all encryption carries with it the burden of the actual encryption overhead on CPUs. So you need to test IPSec in various situations before you deploy it.

Note Network Interface Card (NIC) vendors are supporting IPSec, and using a Windows 2003 IPSec driver may go a long way in reducing CPU usage. The idea is much like a hardware-based RAID controller that employs a CPU on the interface card to perform striping, as opposed to giving that burden to the main system CPU.

Similar to Kerberos, IPSec is managed under group policy, which is discussed extensively in Chapter 11. You define it per site, per domain, or per organizational unit (OU). And it can also be defined for computers that are not affected by domain or OU security policy. Specifically, IPSec can be configured to provide variations of the following services:

✦ You can specify the extent of authentication and confidentiality that will be negotiated between the communicating parties. For example, you can specify the minimum acceptable level of security allowed between clients, which is sending clear text over the network but hiding both sender and receiver information.

✦ You can set policy that communication over certain insecure networks takes place using IPSec, or not at all.

IPSec is discussed later in this chapter in "Security Planning," and in Chapter 11 under Group Policy.

SSL/TLS

Secure Sockets Layer/Transport Layer Security (SSL/TLS) has been around in several Windows NT or BackOffice products for a while. It is a widely supported protocol both on corporate networks and on the Internet. SSL/TLS has been supported in IIS and Exchange.

Windows 2003 uses SSL/TLS and X.509 certificates (discussed next) to authenticate smart card users for network and data protection. SSL/TLS is used to secure a wide range of communications such as network traffic, IIS traffic (Web and FTP), e-mail, and client transactions created in browsers.

Understanding Microsoft Certificate Services

There are two levels of public key cryptography at work inside Windows 2003. One level is implicit and expressly built into the operating system. It is at work in Kerberos, IPSec, and the Encrypting File System (EFS), and does not require attention from you, other than some minor configuration management. The second level is explicit. It requires you to build a public key infrastructure to accommodate a pervasive use of public key cryptography throughout the enterprise.

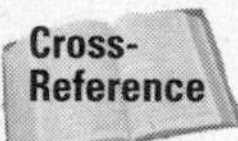

See Chapter 21 for a detailed discussion of EFS.

Public Key Infrastructure

A *Public Key Infrastructure* or PKI is a collection of services and components that work together to a common end. It is used to build a secure environment that will allow you to secure e-mail communications both on the intranet and over the Internet, to secure your Web sites and your company's Web-based transactions, to enhance or further protect your Encrypting File System, to deploy smart cards, and more.

A PKI gives you the ability to support the following public key services:

- **Key Management:** The PKI issues new keys, reviews or revokes existing keys, and manages the trust levels between other vendors' key issuers.
- **Key Publishing:** The PKI provides a systematic means of publishing both valid and invalid keys. Keys can also be revoked if their security is compromised. PKI handles the revocation lists so that applications can determine if a key is no longer to be trusted (akin to the revoked and stolen credit card lists published by the banks for the benefit of merchants).
- **Key Usage:** The PKI provides an easy mechanism for applications and users to use keys. Key usage is key (no pun intended) to providing the best possible security for the enterprise.

Digital Certificates

As discussed earlier in this chapter, public keys are packaged in digital certificates. A good example of a digital certificate is the visa you are given by a foreign country permitting access. The visa number is the key; it is what enables you to get into a country and move around. The visa, issued by the country's consulate, and which is usually laminated or expertly printed so that it cannot be tampered with, is the digital certificate, an object of trust that proves that you received the visa or "key" from a trusted authority, in this case the consular general, and that the number is authentic. Although visas can be forged and the authorities are constantly working to come up with better certificates, passport control officers use verification equipment to check the authenticity of the visa. If a visa is forged, the immigration authority at the port of entry will be able to detect the forgery and deny access. Digital certificates, however, rely on certificate authorities for verification.

But how do you verify a digital certificate? The answer is that a certificate authority (CA), the issuer of your key, or the equivalent of the consular authority in the previous analogy, signs the certificate with its digital signature. You can verify the digital signature with the issuer's public key. But who vouches for the issuer? The answer lies in a *certificate hierarchy,* a system of vouchsafes that extends all the way up to a group of root certificate authorities that have formed an association of vouchsafes. You can obtain the public keys for the CA from Microsoft, but it is all transparently taken care of in Microsoft Certificate Services.

Creating the PKI with Microsoft Certificate Services

A PKI is based on many different services and components all deployed in concert. For example, a Microsoft PKI depends on Active Directory for the publishing of information of issued keys. Also, certificates, revocation lists, and policy information are all stored in the directory. Knowing your directory service thus brings you closer to realizing the reality of the ultimate secured enterprise.

Managing a Microsoft PKI is not difficult and is even less time-consuming than managing users, printers, or the network. Actually, many tasks you perform in your day-to-day activities already encompass management of the PKI. Chapters 11 and 21 will thus offer pointers and guidelines specific to the management of your PKI on Windows 2003.

Support for Legacy NTLM

The NT LAN Manager (NTLM) is a legacy protocol that Microsoft has included in Windows 2003 to support legacy Windows clients and servers. We will not be covering NTLM in detail here because our predecessors have published much information on it over the years. Also, NTLM support is not configurable to the degree that Kerberos is, and it does not support transitive trusts and the Single Sign-On initiative.

In Windows 2003, the default authentication and security protocol between Windows 2003 machines is Kerberos. By continuing to support down-level or legacy Windows technology, you obviously leave room for infiltrators to maneuver; however, that does not mean NTLM is a weak protocol. After all, it has kept Windows NT networks together for many years and was key to the C2 award earned by the operating system back at version 3.51.

NTLM is omnipresent; it only stops working when the last process that needs it signs off. NTLM will be invoked under the following circumstances:

- ✦ You have legacy clients and servers that need to log on to the network or locally.
- ✦ You have Unix clients that need to continue talking to NT servers.
- ✦ You have Unix clients that are using the server message block (SMB) daemon that authenticates to NTLM.

Consider the following strategy for phasing out NTLM:

1. Move your legacy Windows NT and 9*x* clients to Windows 2003. Servers can be upgraded or replaced; clients can also be upgraded to support Kerberos or moved to terminal services (so the clients do not actually log on to the domain from a remote operating system).
2. Configure your Unix services to authenticate to Windows 2003 domains using Kerberos. Phase out SMB usage.
3. Deploy Microsoft's services for Unix packages.

Smart Cards

A smart card is really dumb looking. It is no bigger than a credit card and is carried around like one. Smart cards work just like ATM cards; you slide the card into a slot, and then you will be prompted for a personal identification number (PIN).

The smart card contains a smart chip that is wafer-thin and embedded in the card. The chip holds a digital certificate, the user's private key, and a load of other information that can be used for Single Sign-On, e-commerce, access control, and data protection and privacy, such as securing e-mail and Web access.

To install smart card technology, you must have a public key infrastructure established. You must also install smart card readers, which can be a little expensive, but capitalized over many users, it will pay for itself in TCO and security.

For further information on smart cards and Windows 2003, see the Smart Card White Paper "Smart Cards" at `www.microsoft.com/technet/win.NET/smtcard.asp`. RSA Laboratories at `www.rsasecurity.com` is also a good starting point for smart card research.

Domains

Let's look at the basics. *Domains,* or network domains, are the logical containers of a network, which controls access to all the resources placed in the custody of a domain. The domain does not exist in the physical sense, yet it is accessible from anywhere in the world if it maintains a portal to the Internet or a remote access service; all you need is a computer and connection to a network or a modem.

A domain means different things to different technology vendors. The term *domain* is not exclusively used by Microsoft. It is used on the Internet and by technologies such as SNA (mainframe protocols and services still believed by many to be superior to the TCP/IP domain).

A domain is a loosely defined term, and it represents a collection of computer and data processing devices and resources collected together under one "roof" or security boundary. For the benefit of new administrators to both Windows NT and Windows 2003, let's look at some basic facts about domains. Undoubtedly, what makes a domain a domain is that it is held together by a security policy that dictates the protection of the resources within the domain.

You gain access to a domain at the application level of the OSI stack. Interactive software to let you manually present credentials to the domain is available on the computer or via a device into which you insert a token for your credentials, such as a smart card or magnetic card.

Domains are held together by *domain controllers*. These controllers are keepers of databases that can authenticate a user by asking him or her or it to verify identity by confirming a password. This is known as *authentication.* The databases in question are the SAM in Windows NT and the Active Directory in Windows 2003.

Logon and Authentication

When you log on to a network, you do not have access to network resources. You simply land in a holding area (for a few milliseconds) before being further authenticated to the network's resources. Logon is much like using the international airport in a country after you've landed from abroad. You get rights of passage around the airport. Heck, you can even spend money on duty-free items, set up a home, get married, and pass out; but that's about all. If you want access to the city, you have to go through passport control and customs.

Windows 2003 Logon

When a user or machine logs onto a domain, he or she or it interacts with a collection of functions that make up the Windows Logon service, better known in development circles as WinLogon. WinLogon is now fully integrated with Kerberos, which provides the initial Single Sign-On architecture now part of Windows 2003. After the login, the user continues to be attached to the security protocol its client software best understands, which could be Kerberos, NTLM, or Secure Sockets Layer/Transport Layer Security. These protocols transparently move the user's identity around the network.

The authentication model of Windows 2003 is the same as Windows NT and almost every computer system in the world. (Refer to Chapter 10 for a discussion on the Local Security Authority.) However, it is not so much the model that causes problems in network security, but rather the other missing or weak links in the chain.

Bi-factorial and Mono-factorial Authentication

Network login is a *bi-factorial* exercise, meaning that it requires the user or device to present two factors to the authentication mechanisms of the network: a User ID (also known as an account name or ID), and Password (or what is also known in the secret service as the "cipher").

Every user ID must have a password. In order for the authentication system to validate the user, it asks for a password, and that is the only way it authenticates. However, the authentication is really weak. The authenticator cannot guarantee that the user is in fact the correct user; it could easily be a masquerader pretending to be the user.

Besides the network login (user ID and password), other examples of bi-factorial authentication are ATM cards, smart cards, and the like. The user presents the card and either types in a user ID or a password. Two components have to match to unlock the door. However, it is still not 100 percent secure. ATM cards get stolen, passwords can be discovered, and so forth.

Mono-factorial identification is a far more secure and convenient form of authentication for two reasons. It is more secure; there can be only one form, and it is more convenient for both the user and the authenticator.

The bottom line is that the user has to do less work to authenticate; he or she need not remember a password and does not have to type in a user ID. Examples of mono-factorial authentication include fingerprints, retinal scans, and voiceprints. These factors seldom require another factor of identification. A user has only one retinal pattern, voiceprint, and fingerprint in existence. In many cases, the password is not needed because the pattern itself is the cipher, and because it is attached to the user, there is no need to verify the user.

Trusts

For many reasons, it becomes necessary to create new domains. With Windows NT, big companies spawn domains like frogs' eggs because they are physically restricted by the technology (the SAM becomes unstable at more than 40MB in size). In Windows 2003, we create domains to compartmentalize or partition the directory, to represent distributed resources, corporate structure, ease of management (delegation), security, and much more.

It often becomes necessary for resources in one domain, such as users, to access resources in another domain. In order for this to happen, the domains, if "genetically" different, have to set up trust relationships. While domains that share a domain tree trust each other by default, domains on other trees in other forests, non-Windows 2003 domains, and realms from other environments do not, and you have to explicitly set up the trust. A domain that is trusted by another domain is known as a *trusted domain.* The domain that trusts the other domain is known as the *trusting domain.* This policy is the same in Windows NT as it is for Windows 2003.

If the trust is only one-way, we call it a uni-directional or one-way trust. In other words, Domain A trusts Domain B, but Domain B does not trust Domain A. This is illustrated in Figure 3-2.

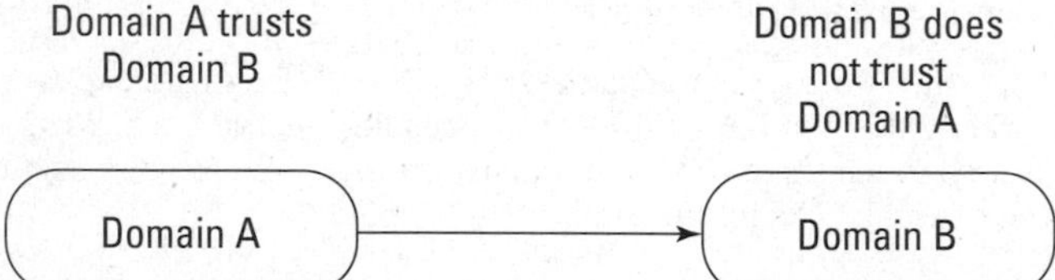

Figure 3-2: Uni-directional trust relationship between two domains.

When the feelings of trust are mutual, the trust relationship becomes bi-directional or two-way. Bi-directional trust enables the users or devices in each domain to access resources in each other's domains (see Figure 3-3).

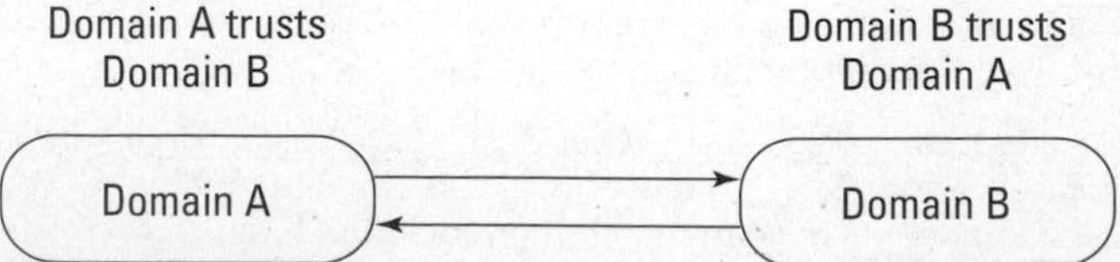

Figure 3-3: Bi-directional trust relationship between two domains.

Windows NT trusts are limited by the underlying database and security technology, which endows the operating system with a less than suitable "cognitive" ability. In other words, Windows NT domains are always mistrusting, and as such, whenever two domains need to interoperate, explicit trusts must first be set up between them.

What's more, Windows NT trusts are not transitive, which means that just because Domain A trusts Domain B, and Domain B trusts Domain C, Domain C does not necessarily trust Domain A, or the other way around. This is illustrated in Figure 3-4.

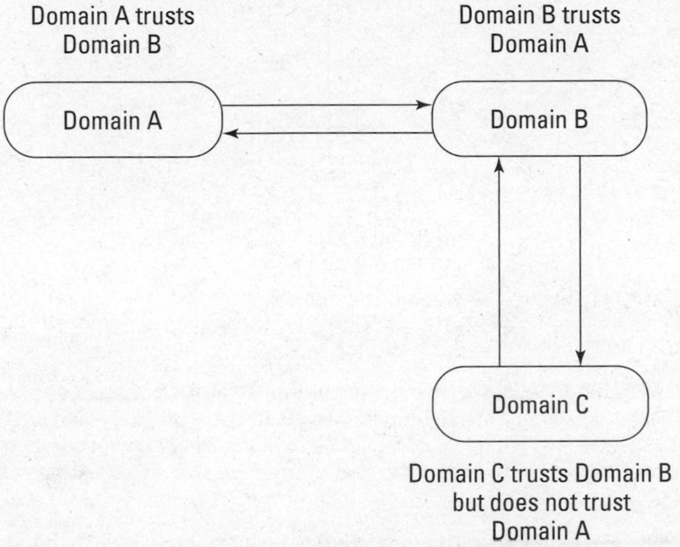

Figure 3-4: Non-transitive trust relationships between three domains.

The domain container and security technology of Windows 2003 is very different. Enabled by a robust directory service, a hot security technology, such as the Kerberos v5 protocol, and a powerful policing ability, Windows 2003 domains that are part of the same namespace, or family, and even of the same tree in a forest, implicitly trust each other. Not only are the trusts already implied, but they are also transitive, as illustrated in Figure 3-5.

However, domains from one forest do not automatically trust domains from another forest. Let's take this a bit further. There are several domains in Sherwood Forest. All these domains fall under the auspices of Robin Hood (the root domain in Active Directory). This means that as long as you live in Sherwood Forest, you pledge allegiance to Robin Hood and can visit any domain (access control, however, still applies).

But a domain that is part of another forest in the British countryside is not automatically trusted by Robin Hood's realm, Sherwood Forest. The administrators of both root domains need to get together and formalize a treaty before the two forests and domains will be able to trust each other.

Windows NT does not have a treaty with Windows 2003, partly because it speaks the wrong security language; that is, NTLM. In order for Windows 2003 and Windows NT users to exchange vows, you have to set up a bilateral trust. Windows 2003 will talk to NT using NTLM.

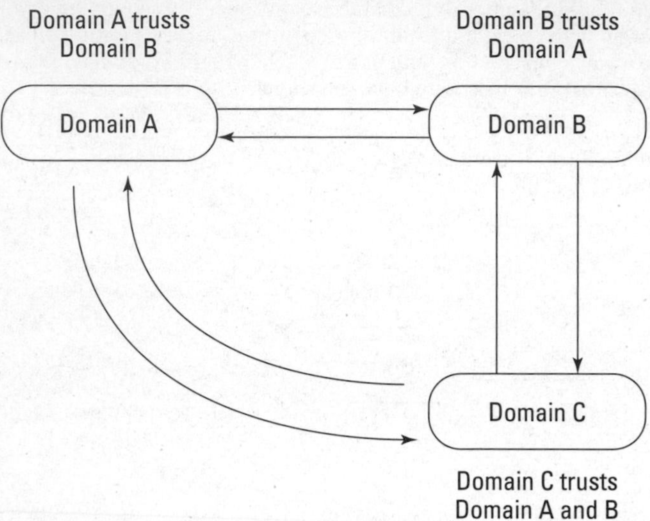

Figure 3-5: Transitive trust relationships between three domains in the same forest.

Setting up trusts is awkward, and whenever mistrusting administrators from two domains try and set up trusts, it usually takes an assertive individual to lead the way. But you have to know how to set up trusts between NT and Windows 2003; it is the only way for the two operating systems to coexist, and it is key to any conversion effort. The steps to creating trusts are explained in Chapter 8.

After authentication is successful, the user or application gains certain default rights to the network and its resources. The next level of protection steps in. It is called Access control.

Access Control

After a user or device account is authenticated to the domain, it is given permission, through certain default privileges, to network objects. The objects represent files, devices (such as printers and computers), and the file system's structure. In Windows 2003, these objects are stored in the Active Directory and "point" to the actual network location (in Windows NT, they are stored in the SAM portion of the registry).

To gain access to an object, the object has an Access Control List (ACL) associated with it. This access control list is also stored in the directory. An analogy might be to think of your ACL as a bouncer standing at the door to a club. When someone tries to gain entry to the club, the bouncer makes a check on his or her ACL. If the dude is not on the list, then entry is denied. The items on the ACL are known as Access Control Entries. You can view the ACL by opening the Security tab on an object's property sheet.

The property sheet lists the users and groups that have access to the object and the level of access they have, such as Read or Write or Execute. ACLs apply only to Security Principals — that is, user accounts, computer accounts, and security groups (as opposed to distribution groups). Security principals and ACLs are further discussed in Chapter 10.

Auditing

The word *auditing* strikes fear into the hearts of everyone. Even if you have nothing to fear, auditing is an ominous idea, a prying into your every move. But auditing is not only a practice defined within a security context, it is also an essential practice in troubleshooting and problem solving. An audit trail, a requirement for C2 security compliance, can lead you not only to the wolf's den, it can also lead you to a solution to a problem that was impacting network resources or causing users grief.

Auditing leaves a trail that you can follow to see what was done or attempted by network objects. If the network object has a username attached to it, your audit trail will then be a history of what was attempted by whom.

A good example of an audit trail is on the RAS. When a user calls to say he or she cannot logon to the network remotely, you can check the audit logs and trace his or her attempts by searching for information related to his or her user ID. The audit trail will then tell you why the person was rejected and give you a possible remedy.

Auditing of objects is not enabled by default. It has to be enabled and applied to the object. Auditing is discussed in depth in Chapter 19.

Security Planning

Before you go jumping up and down shouting, "Whoop, whoop, IPSec, PKI, SSL, way to go!" you should know that unless you are running a native Windows 2003 network, you will not realize the full potential many of these protocols have to offer.

Windows 2003 security is also so extensive that it is possible to get bamboozled in your efforts to provide the *ultimate* security. As you learn more about the capabilities of Windows 2003, you'll discover that the adage "less is more" applies to many Windows Server 2003 components in general and Windows 2003 security in particular. The subject of security planning is therefore coupled to the subject of planning for Windows 2003 in general and is discussed in the next chapter.

Firewalls

Firewalls are devices that protect your network and computers from malicious computer hackers. The Windows Server 2003 comes with what is known as the Internet Connection Firewall (ICF). This firewall is fairly simplistic but provides some very necessary firewall services to the machine it resides on, as well as any machine that may share its Internet connection.

Firewalls come in all shapes and sizes and can be a PC running Windows, or perhaps, an embedded device. Embedded devices have a definite advantage over computers running firewall software in that they typically can be used a lot faster and can inspect packets at a very high rate. Computers, on the other hand, have many other tasks to perform as well as packet inspection, and therefore can lose performance. In any event, a well-equipped machine running Windows Server 2003 and Routing services can be a very efficient firewall for your corporate network.

Active Directory Security Policy

Windows 2000/Windows XP implements the Key Distribution Center (KDC) as a domain service. It uses the Active Directory as its account database and the Global Catalog for directing referrals to KDCs in other domains.

As in other implementations of the Kerberos protocol, the KDC is a single process that provides two services:

- **Authentication Service (AS):** This service issues Ticket-Granting Tickets (TGTs) for connection to the ticket-granting service in its own domain or in any trusted domain. Before a client can ask for a ticket to another computer, it must request a TGT from the authentication service in the client's account domain. The authentication service returns a TGT for the ticket-granting service in the target computer's domain. The TGT can be reused until it expires, but the first access to any domain's ticket-granting service always requires a trip to the authentication service in the client's account domain.
- **Ticket-Granting Service (TGS):** This service issues tickets for connection to computers in its own domain. When clients want access to a computer, they contact the ticket-granting service in the target computer's domain, present a TGT, and ask for a ticket to the computer. The ticket can be reused until it expires, but the first access to any computer always requires a trip to the ticket-granting service in the target computer's account domain.

The KDC for a domain is located on a domain controller, as is the Active Directory for the domain. Both services are started automatically by the domain controller's Local Security Authority (LSA) and run as part of the LSA's process. Neither service can be stopped. If the KDC is unavailable to network clients, then the Active Directory is also unavailable — and the domain controller is no longer controlling the domain. Windows 2000/Windows XP ensures availability of these and other domain services by allowing each domain to have several domain controllers, all peers. Any domain controller can accept authentication requests and ticket-granting requests addressed to the domain's KDC.

The security principal name used by the KDC in any Windows 2003 domain is `krbtgt`, as specified by RFC 1510. An account for this security principal is created automatically when a new Windows 2003 domain is created. This account cannot be deleted, nor can its name be changed. A password is assigned to the account automatically and is changed on a regular schedule, as are the passwords assigned to the domain trust accounts. The password for the KDC's account is used to derive a cryptographic key for encrypting and decrypting the TGTs that it issues. The password for a domain trust account is used to derive an inter-realm key for encrypting referral tickets.

All instances of the KDC within a domain use the domain account for the security principal krbtgt. Clients can address messages to a domain's KDC by including both the service's principal name, krbtgt, and the name of the domain. Both items of information are also used in tickets to identify the issuing authority. For information on name forms and addressing conventions, see RFC 1510.

Secure Sockets

Secure Sockets is often referred to as the Secure Sockets Layer (SSL). SSL allows for a secure encrypted connection to a Web server. You will typically find SSL-enabled Web sites when you purchase goods online or perform other transactions that need to have a high degree of security so outside forces cannot intercept information.

SSL has changed a bit with Windows Server 2003, which has incorporated a new Windows Service application, W3SSL, to handle secure communications to and from the Web server. SSL uses encryption on all data sent and received to prevent people from intercepting information, such as credit card numbers.

Dealing with W3SSL directly is almost impossible with the lack of documentation provided, but if you wish to use it with an IIS application/Web site, this can be accomplished very easily by simply pointing and clicking.

Firewalls, Proxies, and Bastions

As we have discussed, firewalls keep people out of your network and away from all sensitive data that it may contain. Proxies, on the other hand, are another way of maintaining security on a network. Proxies allow computers on a network to maintain a degree of anonymity while users surf the Web. All requests from client computers to the Internet are sent to a proxy server. The proxy server requests information from the Internet, and then transmits this information back to the client PC that wanted the information in the first place.

Typically, Proxy servers also cache information so if people on your network, for example, typically go to the same Web sites, it can retrieve the Web pages much faster from its cache than it could from the Internet connection. Policies can be set on how long to cache Web pages and the maximum amount of space to use when it does so.

Because proxy servers are capable of caching data from the Internet and returning that data to a client request, it can greatly reduce the amount of traffic over your Internet connection. If you have a large number of people that need to be on the Internet and would like to conserve bandwidth, a proxy server may be the way to go. Aside from helping with the speed of the connection, a proxy server can almost always be set up to filter data as well. Setting up a proxy in a corporate environment would enable you to block Web sites that allow people to search for jobs. Setting one up at your home on a broadband connection would enable you to ensure that your children aren't looking at Web sites they should not really see. Even if you trust your Internet users to stick to sites where they belong, with the extreme amount of popup ads today, your users may be viewing other Web information whether they like it or not.

Introduction to the Public Key Infrastructure

Windows Server 2003 contains a very robust Public Key Infrastructure (PKI) that provides an integrate set of services and tools for deploying and managing Public Key applications. This allows application developers to take advantage of the shared-secret key mechanism and to provide the best security possible. The tools provided with the Windows Server 2003 enable administrators to manage these keys from a central location for an entire enterprise.

Setting up and Configuring a Windows PKI

A key element in the PKI is Microsoft Certificate Services that enables you to deploy one or more enterprise CAs. These CAs support certificate issuance and revocation. They are integrated with Active Directory, which provides CA location information and CA policy, and allows certificates and revocation information to be published.

The PKI does not replace the existing Windows domain trust-and-authorization mechanisms based on the domain controller (DC) and Kerberos Key Distribution Center (KDC). Rather, the PKI works with these services and provides enhancements that allow applications to readily scale to address extranet and Internet requirements. In particular, PKI addresses the need for scalable and distributed identification and authentication, integrity, and confidentiality.

Support for creating, deploying, and managing PK-based applications is provided uniformly on workstations and servers running Windows Server 2003s, Windows XP, Windows 2000 or Windows NT(r), as well as workstations running Windows 95 and Windows 98 operating systems. Microsoft CryptoAPI is the cornerstone for these services. It provides a standard interface to cryptographic functionality supplied by installable cryptographic service providers (CSPs). These CSPs may be software-based or take advantage of cryptographic hardware devices and can support a variety of algorithms and key strengths. Some CSPs, which ship with the Windows Server 2003, take advantage of the Microsoft PC/SC-compliant smart card infrastructure.

Layered on the cryptographic services is a set of certificate management services. These support X.509 version 3 standard certificates, providing persistent storage, enumeration services, and decoding support. Finally, there are services for dealing with industry-standard message formats. Primarily, these support the PKCS standards and evolving Internet Engineering Task Force (IETF) Public Key Infrastructure, X.509 (PKIX) draft standards.

For more information on the Internet Engineering Task Force (IETF) or X.509, please visit their Web site at `http://www.ietf.org`.

Other services take advantage of CryptoAPI to provide additional functionality for application developers. Secure Channel (schannel) supports network authentication and encryption using the industry standard TLS and SSL protocols. These may be accessed using the Microsoft WinInet interface for use with the HTTP protocol (HTTPS) and with other protocols through the SSPI interface. Authenticode supports object signing and verification. This is used principally for determining the origin and integrity of components downloaded over the Internet, though it may be used in other environments. Finally, general-purpose smart-card interfaces also are supported. These are used to integrate cryptographic smart cards in an application-independent manner and are the basis for the smart-card logon support that is integrated with Windows Server 2003.

Understanding Certificate Services

Microsoft Certificate Services, included with Windows Server 2003, provides a means for an enterprise to easily establish CAs to support its business requirements. Certificate Services includes a default policy module that is suitable for issuing certificates to enterprise entities (users, computers, or services). This also includes the identification of the requesting entity and validation that the certificate requested is allowed under the domain PK security policy. This may be easily modified or enhanced to address other policy considerations or to extend CA support for various extranet or Internet scenarios. Because Certificate Services is standards-based, it provides broad support for PK-enabled applications in heterogeneous environments.

Within the PKI, you can easily support both enterprise CAs and external CAs, such as those associated with other organizations or commercial service providers. This allows an enterprise to tailor its environment in response to business requirements.

Setting up and Configuring a Certificate Authority

Deploying Microsoft Certificate Services is a fairly straightforward operation. It is recommended that you establish the domain prior to creating a CA. You can then establish an enterprise root CA, or CAs. The Certificate Services installation process walks the administrator through this process. Key elements in this process include:

- **Selecting the host server.** The root CA can run on any Windows 2000 Server platform, including a domain controller. Factors such as physical security requirements, expected loading, connectivity requirements, and so on, should be considered in making this decision.
- **Naming.** CA names are bound into their certificates and hence cannot change. You should consider factors such as organizational naming conventions and future requirements to distinguish among issuing CAs.
- **Key generation.** The CA's public-key pair is generated during the installation process and is unique to this CA.
- **CA certificate.** For a root CA, the installation process automatically generates a self-signed CA certificate, using the CA's public/private-key pair. For a child CA, a certificate request can be generated that may be submitted to an intermediate or root CA.
- **Active Directory integration.** Information concerning the CA is written into a CA object in the Active Directory during installation. This provides information to domain clients about available CAs and the types of certificates that they issue.
- **Issuing policy.** The enterprise CA setup automatically installs and configures the Microsoft-supplied Enterprise Policy Module for the CA. An authorized administrator can modify the policy, although in most cases this is not necessary.

After a root CA has been established, it is possible to install intermediate or issuing CAs subordinate to this root CA. The only significant difference in the installation policy is that the certificate request is generated for submission to a root or intermediate CA. This request may be routed automatically to online CAs located through the Active Directory, or routed manually in an offline scenario. In either case, the resultant certificate must be installed at the CA before it can begin operation.

There is an obvious relationship between the enterprise CAs and the Windows Server 2003 domain trust model, but this does not imply a direct mapping between CA trust relationships and domain trust relationships. Nothing prevents a single CA from servicing entities in multiple domains, or even entities outside the domain boundary. Similarly, a domain may have multiple enterprise CAs.

CAs are high-value resources, and it is often desirable to provide them with a high degree of protection, as previously discussed. Specific actions that should be considered include:

- **Physical protection.** Because CAs represent highly trusted entities within an enterprise, they must be protected from tampering. This requirement is dependent upon the inherent value of the certification made by the CA. Physical isolation of the CA server, in a facility accessible only to security administrators, can dramatically reduce the possibility of such attacks.
- **Key management.** The CA keys are its most valuable asset because the private key provides the basis for trust in the certification process. Cryptographic hardware modules (accessible to Certificate Services through a CryptoAPI CSP can provide tamper-resistant key storage and isolate the cryptographic operations from other software that is running on the server. This significantly reduces the likelihood that a CA key will be compromised.

✦ **Restoration.** Loss of a CA due to hardware failure, for example, can create a number of administrative and operational problems, as well as prevent the revocation of existing certificates. Certificate Services supports backup of a CA instance so that it can be restored at a later time. This is an important part of the overall CA management process.

Summary

This chapter provided an overview of the key security protocols and mechanisms available in Windows 2003. Perhaps no other subject related to networking is as important as security. You can offer your users all manner of features and performance, integrate to perfection (almost), and maintain a server room that hums like a Rolls Royce engine. But, even the tiniest security breach can scuttle the entire boat.

The external environment of an enterprise is like an ocean of pressure, pushing and pushing until the rivets of your ship pop. Before you can plan your security strategy, you should first try to understand the technology that is at work in the Windows 2003 security subsystems.

In particular, this chapter covered security threats and risks, cryptography, the new authentication protocols, and the Microsoft Certificate Services, which are used to build a public key infrastructure to serve your enterprise.

✦ ✦ ✦

.NET Framework Services

✦ ✦ ✦ ✦

In This Chapter

Get to know the Common Language Runtime

Learn what the .NET initiative is.

Learn to configure .NET security

Understanding Garbage Collection in the .NET Framework

✦ ✦ ✦ ✦

The much anticipated .NET Framework is now included with Windows Server 2003. This framework for application developers allows your system to run very sophisticated programs that are extremely fast and extremely portable. Along with this power also comes security concerns. Presumably since the framework is integrated, applications that run under it can have a great deal of control over the server. To some degree this may be true, but this is where security comes into focus.

In this chapter you will learn about the many components that make up the .NET Framework. We will take a glimpse at the proper way to configure security as well as view how the garbage collection facility works and ways to monitor it.

Introduction to the .NET Framework

The average Windows Server 2003 administrator may not have a lot of interest in the .NET Framework. The .NET Framework is, in a nutshell, a library of "routines" that programmers can use in creating applications. This framework gives the programmer an extraordinary amount of control over the machine that it runs on, as well as over network operations as a whole. This may all seem a bit scary at first, but it also comes with a very sophisticated toolset for configuring security within the framework and applications that utilize it. The job of the Server 2003 administrator is to configure this security and deploy it across the network to protect network resources from rogue code.

Understanding the .NET Initiative

Defining exactly what the .NET Initiative is has been somewhat of a mystery. The .NET Framework is obviously a framework for application development, but what about Server 2003? It doesn't mean that Windows Server 2003 is meant for .NET Development, but one distinct characteristic of the Windows Server 2003 operating system is that it comes with the .NET Framework already integrated into the operating system, and you have no need to install it. Before we move on with a discussion of the .NET Framework, however, we first need to discuss what brought it about and what Microsoft hopes to accomplish with it.

The .NET Framework is a set of libraries that enable programmers to build applications. The difference between the .NET Framework and, for example, MFC is that the .NET Framework enables an extremely rapid development of applications that can be integrated very tightly with the operating system. Building a Windows Service application that monitors remote Windows Services — or processes, for that matter — would literally take a few minutes if you use the .NET Framework. This Framework also provides for Web Services and remoting, which can distribute an application throughout a network of servers. This can obviously be a nightmare for network and/or server administrators who need to maintain the security of their systems. Fortunately for administrators, the .NET Framework has extensive security built into it as well as a MMC snap-in that enables you to adjust these security settings. The snap-in is shown here in Figure 4-1.

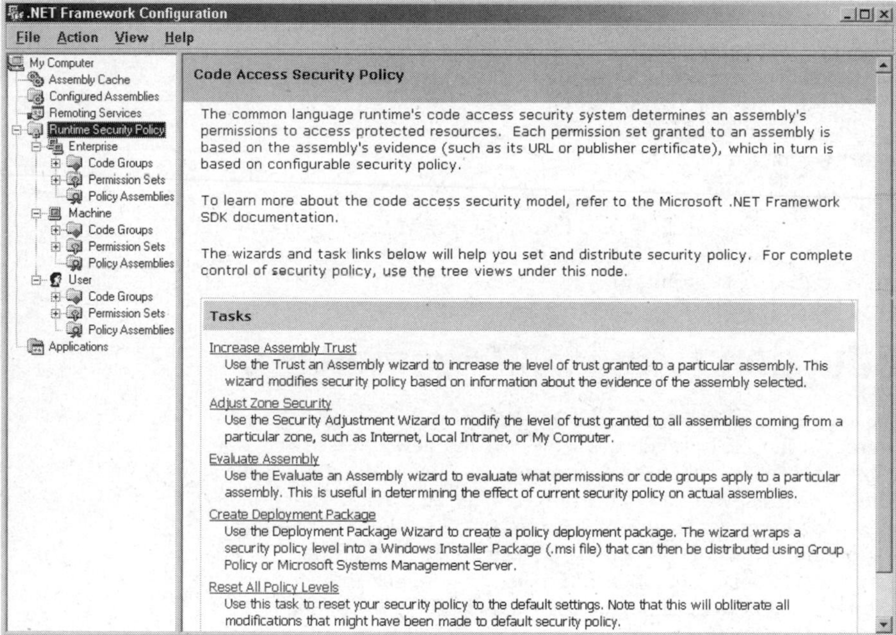

Figure 4-1: The .NET Framework Configuration MMC allows you to control all aspects of the frameworks settings.

The Common Language Runtime

The *Common Language Runtime* (*CLR*) is an environment that enables .NET languages to run while providing each application the same functionality set. The CLR also manages memory during program execution, as well as managing thread and other system services. The CLR also verifies that applications are permitted to run given the current set of security configurations.

The CLR can grant or deny security to items such as disk access, network access, memory, and peripherals such as printers. The CLR also implements strict type and code verification by use of the *Common Type System* (*CTS*), which is discussed in the following section.

Unlike interpreted languages, the CLR uses *Just-in-Time* compilation so that all applications are compiled into native machine language for the system that the applications are running on. This has severe performance gains over interpreted languages and also ensures less of a strain on the OS and limits the chance of memory leaks and the like.

Another definite benefit of the CLR is that it enables applications developed in separate languages to communicate with each other and maintain a high degree of integration. The benefit to Windows Server 2003 administrators is that they can write code in VB.NET or C# that performs in exactly the same way and uses the exact same function calls which means that one language doesn't have advantages over another. A benefit for writing scripts with a .NET Framework language (such as VB .NET, C#, etc.) would be, for example, importing a list of users and automatically creating logins for them within Active Directory.

Common Type System

We briefly touch on the Common Type System (CTS) in the preceding section, and now we're going to fill in a few of the details of CTS from a server administrator's point of view.

CTS ensures that all code within an application is *self-describing*, which means that the value of an integer type, for example, can be consumed by a long data type. Not a very thrilling concept for server administration perhaps, but CTS helps ensure that a programmer cannot insert bogus code within an application to intentionally cause an error. Why would someone do that, you ask? Well, say, for example, that you hire a programmer to write a few backend components for your Web site running on IIS 6.0. This programmer inserts a few lines of code that, if correctly accessed, cause an error that drops the user into the system allowing them complete access or maybe — even worse — crashes your server.

Keep in mind that the .NET Framework and all its components are very security-centric. The actual security details and operation of the framework are a bit beyond the scope of this book, but rest assured that any applications on your server that are written with a .NET Framework language can be configured for the utmost security conscious.

.NET Security

.NET Security can be configured in three different ways: at the enterprise level, the machine level, and the user level. This separation of security levels ensure that your enterprise not only can have a security policy in executing .NET applications, but it also ensures that, should your company hire contractors, a security policy can be applied to them as well so that they can't take advantage of your servers and the information that they contain (Figure 4-2).

To drill down even further, each level of security (enterprise, machine, user) can also contain custom code groups. You could make a code group for enterprise applications that need Internet access as well as a code group that needs access to corporate print servers (Figure 4-3).

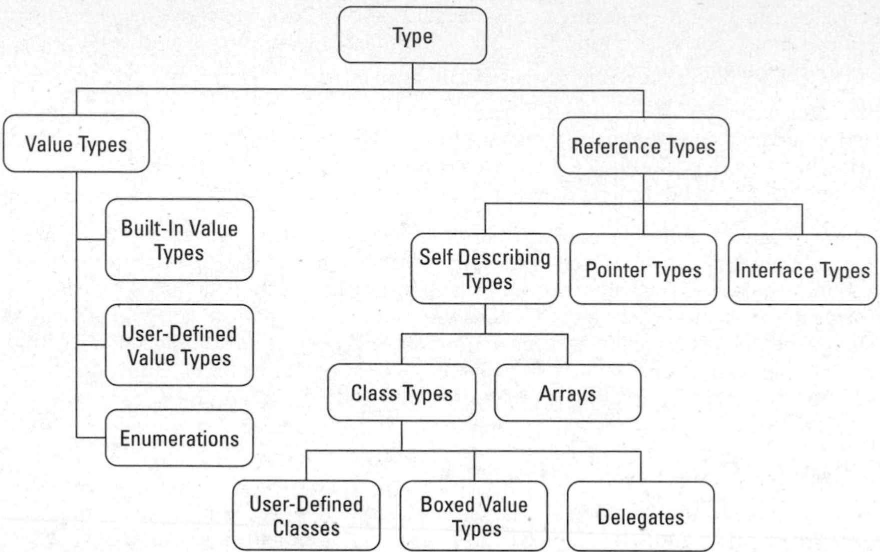

Figure 4-2: The three default security zones provide for a very robust security policy.

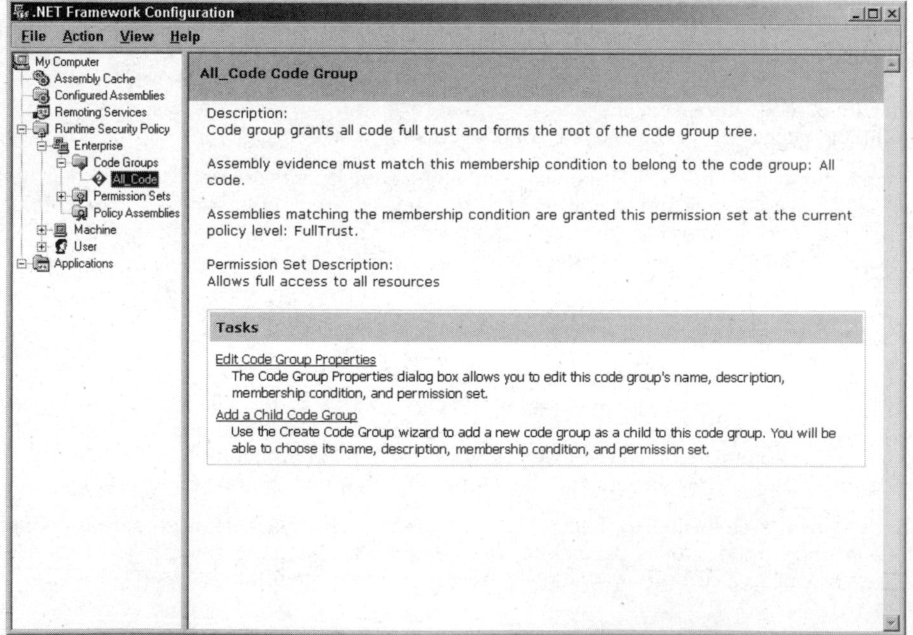

Figure 4-3: Code groups enable you to define different types of applications within each security "zone."

Setting restrictions on these code groups is as simple as pointing and clicking. If you navigate to the Administrative tools and open up the Microsoft .NET Framework Configuration console, you can examine the default access limitations on existing code groups.

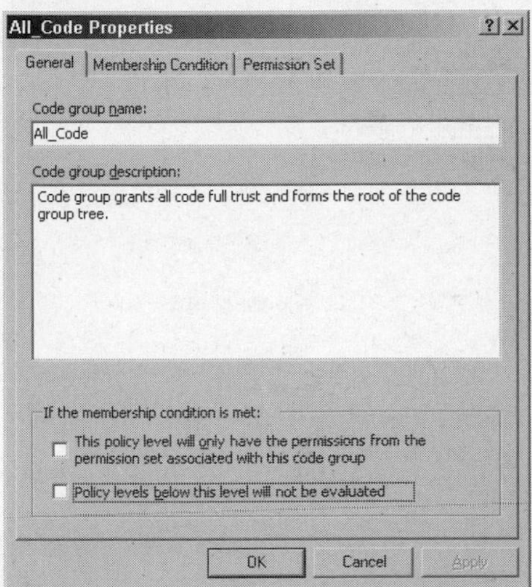

Figure 4-4: The All Code code group is granted full access.

As you can see in Figure 4-4, all code within the Enterprise security zone is permitted full access to the system and network — that is, of course, assuming that the other two security zones permit this behavior. After the .NET Framework determines security access, it essentially overlaps the three security zones and examines the privileges. If a privilege has been removed in any level, the specific action isn't permitted. This ensures, for example, that a user security policy doesn't override an enterprise policy.

To create a new code group — for a consultant, for example — you simply right-click the Security Zone where you want the rule added and then choose New. You can then type the name of this new code group and begin to add rules.

After you have created a new code group, you can change any number of details and even access to environment variables. To do this, expand the **Enterprise** security zone, expand the **Permission Sets** tab and then select **Everything**. **Environment Variables** is now shown in the right hand "Permission" window pane (Figures 4-5 and 4-6).

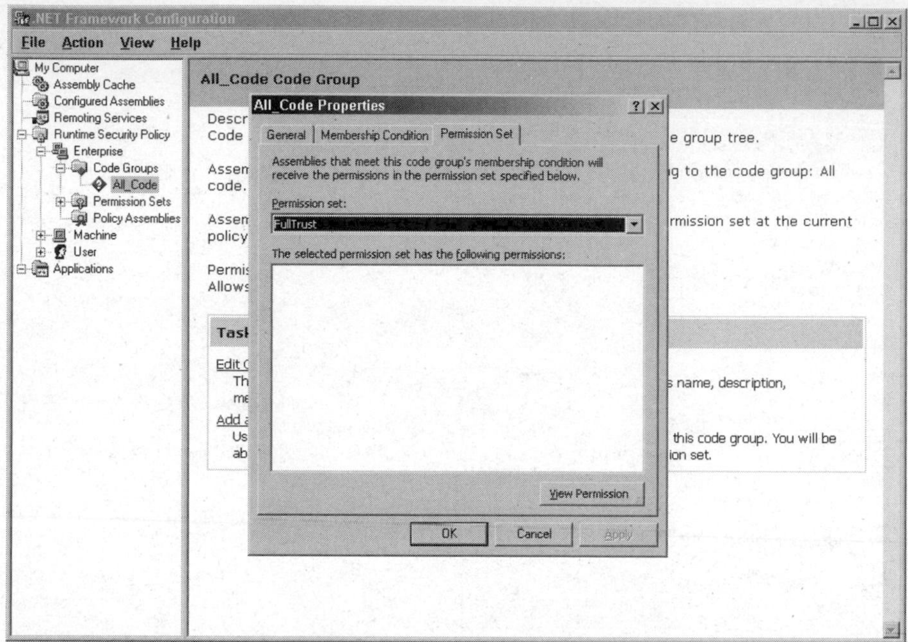

Figure 4-5: Creating a new code group for untrusted users is simple by using the Configuration Wizard.

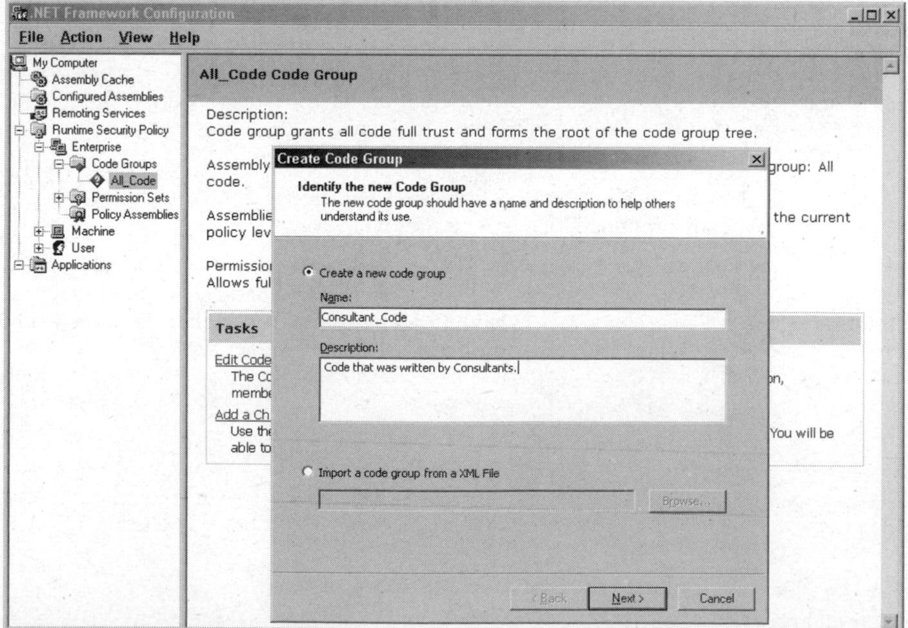

Figure 4-6: Controlling access to items such as environment variables is possible by using the .NET Framework Configuration console.

This kind of granular control is exactly what is needed for such a powerful programming framework.

Application domains

To better explain Application Domains, I'm going to start with an example that many of us have been through. The corporate mail server has been in desperate need of a way to process automated help desk tickets. To achieve this, the IT department has created a COM object that watches the mail go through the mail server and routes the help desk ticket to the correct person for the job. Several weeks after this COM object was installed, the Microsoft Exchange Server mysteriously crashes; this hasn't happened to Exchange since it was installed.

This particular example may not be familiar to all of you but the circumstances may be. So what happened to the Microsoft Exchange Server? The key to the mystery was that the COM object was an in-process object. The term *in-process* means that the COM object shared process space with Microsoft Exchange Server. Sharing process space allows the object (in this example it is the COM object) to share memory with the host application (Microsoft Exchange Server). This allows for an incredible amount of integration since both application and COM object can share all sorts of information. Unfortunately, this also means that if the COM object dies, the application and all other objects in the process space die as well.

This type of incident is pretty typical on Windows 2003 since not all applications are perfect and quite often applications crash. On Windows 98 and ME, you could expect different behavior however. These operating systems didn't have protected memory segments, which meant if one application crashed, it could quite possibly kill all running applications including Windows! Since Windows 2000 we have been shielded from this because an application dying within its process space couldn't harm other applications, nor could it harm Windows.

Application Domains has solved this problem with multiple objects in the same process space threatening the lives of the other objects. Application Domains involves a greater level of granularity. It allows multiple objects (or applications) to run within the same process space with isolation. This isolation means that even though multiple objects are executing, one of them can error and halt execution and not affect the others.

As a Windows Server 2003 Administrator, this means that the pesky programmers can't bring your servers to their knees. Application Domains are by no means foolproof, but they are a vast improvement over simple process space and a definite step in the right direction.

Garbage Collection

The *Garbage Collection* (*GC*) facility within the .NET Framework is in charge of releasing memory as objects run out of scope and are no longer used within an application. The fact that programmers have almost always needed to specifically free resources is the number-one cause of memory leaks within an application. Thanks to the .NET Framework, this is all handled behind the scenes.

This all sounds almost too good to be true, and the truth is that it may be. Although GC does free up memory, it does so at an undefined interval. Function calls available to the programmer enable a manual invocation of Garbage Collection but don't guarantee when Garbage Collection occurs.

On a positive note, included with the .NET Framework are performance counters that enable you to monitor Garbage Collection — when it runs, how long it runs, and the amount of memory it frees up, just to name a few.

.NET vs. the JVM

The *Java Virtual Machine* (*JVM*) has been around a lot longer than the .NET Framework, so most people think that it is probably a bit less buggy. We think that statement has yet to be determined, but the fact that the JVM is currently running more production applications around the globe than the .NET Framework is true.

That Microsoft took a long hard look at the JVM during the design phases of the .NET Framework is really no secret. So most of the useful features that you see in the JVM are also present within the .NET Framework. To avoid a war and lots of hate e-mail, we don't pick one over the other here, but we do tell you the two benefits to using the .NET Framework over the JVM:

The .NET Framework has a great deal of support for graphical user interfaces (GUI). Those who have ever tried to create a Windows-based application by using a text editor and the .NET Framework probably don't agree with us on this statement, but take our word for it. Not only can you design Windows applications by using the .NET Framework, but you also can design applications for the Web to be displayed in a browser, as well as applications for PDAs, cell phones, and many other Wireless Application Protocol (WAP)-enabled devices. Java simply doesn't offer this luxury; a third-party package is needed for GUI creation within Java.

The next obvious benefit of .NET over the JVM is performance gain. .NET simply beats the JVM in running almost any type of application, whether it is simply a GUI application with one screen or an n-Tier application accessing a database backend.

Configuring the Global Assembly Cache

Configuration of the *Global Assembly Cache* (GAC) should be done by a developer 99 percent of the time because developers are the most familiar with what their applications do and do not need. We touch on the GAC briefly here so that you, as a server administrator, have an idea of what its configuration actually entails.

The .NET Framework is capable of side-by-side DLL execution. So you can have two DLLs with the same name on the same machine and in the same directory. This enables applications to use the DLL that fits their needs. Application A may need version 1.0 of a certain DLL while a newer Application B may require version 2.0 of the same DLL. The .NET Framework Configuration MMC snap-in enables one to configure applications to use particular components. In the example just stated, Application A can be set to use only the `brian.dll` file, versions 1.0 through 1.76. This ensures that, if multiple `brian.dll` files are on the server, it uses the correct one, preventing the application from crashing.

To configure an assembly, right-click Configured Assemblies within the .NET Framework Configuration console and then choose New from the pop-up menu. You have the opportunity to choose an existing assembly (also known as a DLL) on the system or a new one that has not been registered in the GAC, as shown in Figure 4-7.

Because your server probably hasn't had the opportunity to be overrun by programmers and thus has no custom assemblies in place, you want to choose an existing assembly, as shown in Figure 4-8.

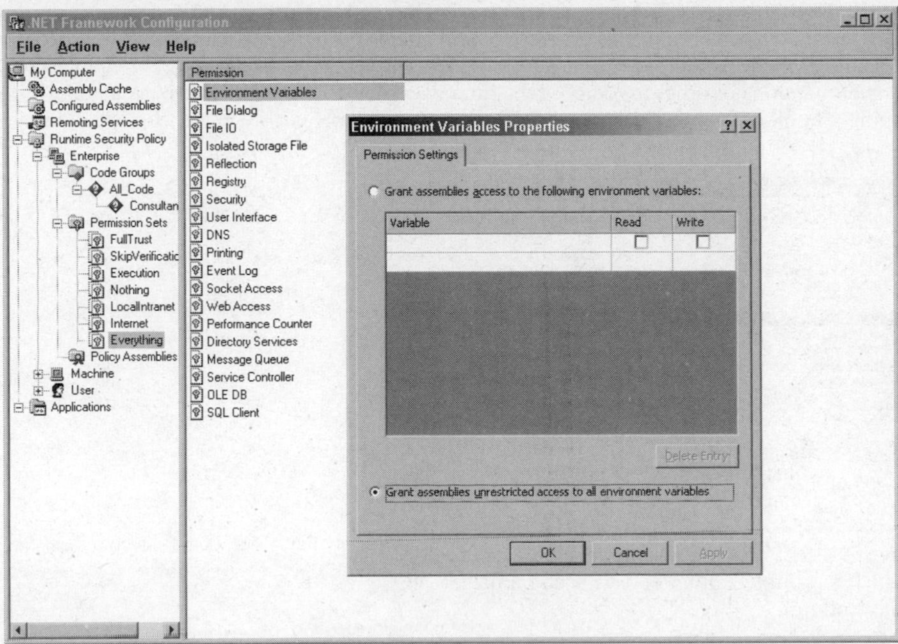

Figure 4-7: Configure assemblies by using the .NET Framework Configuration console.

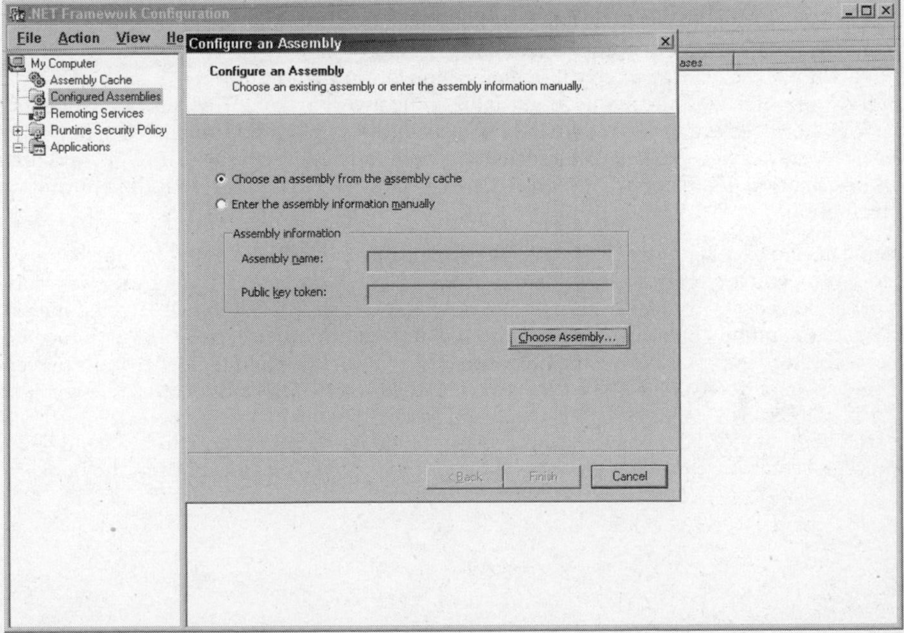

Figure 4-8: The .NET Framework Configuration console enables the user to choose an existing assembly.

The assembly name is shown along with its version and hash. These three items are how the .NET Framework distinguishes assemblies and enables them to operate side by side. Choose any one of these assemblies and click Open. You can instruct the assembly to operate with only certain versions of other assemblies that it may rely on, as well as a much richer set of settings. Binding applications to a particular version of an assembly is shown here in Figure 4-9.

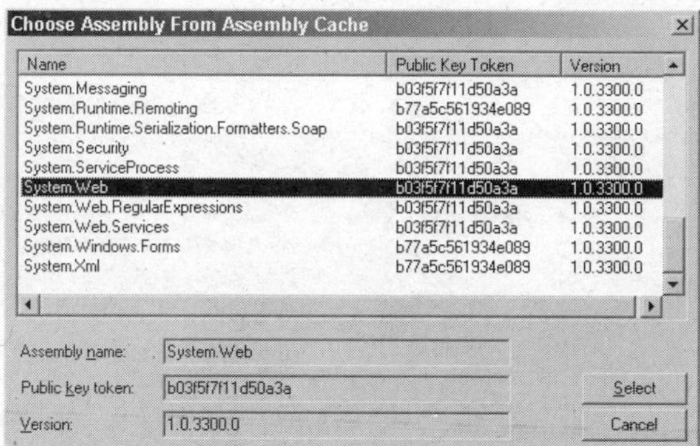

Figure 4-9: The codebase table allows you to define which assemblies operate with each particular .NET application.

Administering Web Services

Web Services are a means by which information can be transmitted and shared among systems using standardized protocols and data formats — namely HTTP, SOAP and XML. You can think of a Web Service as a typical Dynamic Link Library (DLL). Rather than this DLL residing on the computer with the application that is using it, it lives on a Web server. Requests from the Web Services are formatted in XML, packaged with SOAP and transmitted via HTTP to the service. The service extracts the information from the SOAP message and XML and processes the information. If a response it required, the Web Service responds with the appropriate information.

Seems like an excellent way to increase network traffic and add an undue burden to servers, right? Well, you are only partially correct. Think of it in these terms — you own a very large Internet bookstore. Your Web store has an obvious Web page front end where customers can navigate to and buy books. You've optimized your Web site to be compatible with the latest and greatest Internet Explorer. You, the CEO, come up with the brilliant idea of giving a percentage of sales profits to anyone who can sell items from your site. This means Stuart Laughlin in Peoria, Illinois creates his own homepage and wants to provide the functionality for people to search your site for books as well as purchase the books they find. Forcing Stuart to link to your site seems unreasonable since he may want to hide the real locations of the books.

I guess you could simply supply Stuart a file every night of all available books and their inventory levels, prices, and so on. However, you run into problems since you are performing batch transactions, and inventory levels will change so things just won't work correctly. To correct this problem you have your IT staff develop Web Services that allow queries to be passed in thus allowing book searches. Subsequently this Web Service should take the ISBN of a book and return the author names, abstract, Table of Contents, cover art, and all the information anyone could ever want. Now Stuart simply needs to program his Web site to call your Web Methods.

Note Much like DLLS that contain Functions and Methods—Web Services contain these and are generally referred to as Web Methods. This term denotes that the method in question isn't actually located on the current machine but out on a remote server.

The beauty to all this is that not only can users on the other side of the world make queries against your database, but other systems you have internally can as well. This may include Microsoft BizTalk Server 2002, Microsoft Portal Server, or Microsoft Commerce Server, which are all Web Service enabled.

Enough dreaming about making millions from book sales and on to what these Web Services mean to the server, how they are configured, and how they are monitored.

Web Service administration is handled exactly the same way as any Web site—with the Internet Information Services MMC. To begin, open this management console by navigating to your administrative tools or simply typing **inetmgr** from a console window. If you have the Web Administration utilities installed, you will see them listed with an icon shaped like a gear as seen here in Figure 4-10.

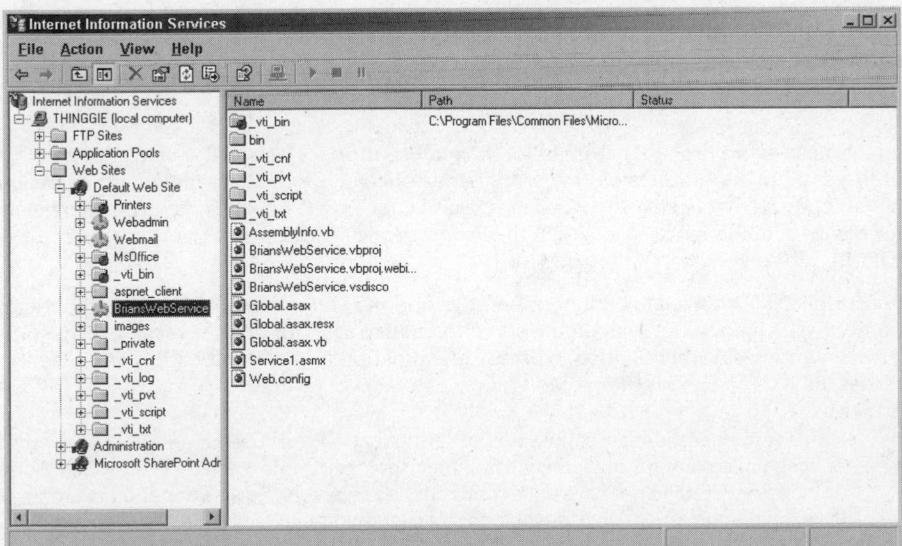

Figure 4-10: The Internet Information Services MMC is used to administer Web sites as well as Web Services.

As you can see from the figure, there are three Web services on the server: Webadmin, webmail and BriansWebService. Keep in mind that even though all of these have an icon that looks similar to a gear, they may not all be Web Services. IIS cannot differentiate between a Web Service and a typical Web application. The common link among all these is that they are all defined as Web applications, which changes the icon appropriately and are treated differently by IIS. As with any application, you can configure who may or may not use it as seen here in Figure 4-11.

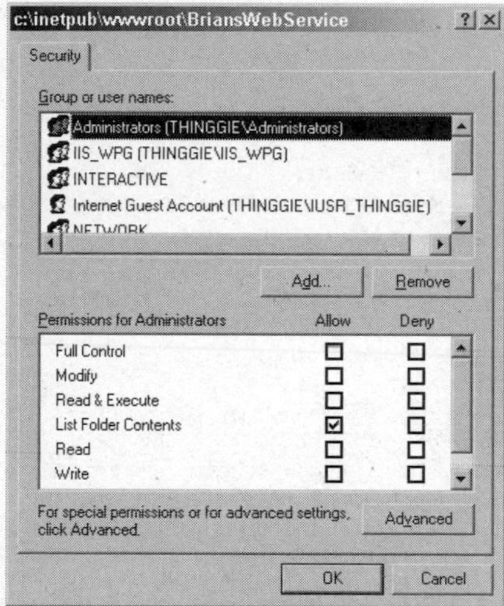

Figure 4-11: Directory security can be adjusted as with any application or file on Windows Server 2003.

Sometimes — and probably more often than not — directory security just isn't enough and imposes too many burdens on the Administrator because each user must have rights on that machine. By right- clicking the Web Service and choosing Properties, you can change security options with much more ease. When the Properties window opens, select the Directory Security tab as seen here in Figure 4-12.

IIS and the .NET allow many different security options and more specifically authentication methods that lighten the load on the server administrator. Among these are anonymous access, Windows Authentication, Forms Authentication and authentication provided by third parties such as Microsoft Passport.

Note

Forms Authentication is a simple way of saying that a list of usernames and passwords are provided in a Web site configuration file. The user logging into a secure portion of a Web site or Web Service need not have an account on the server where it resides and need only have their login information located within this configuration file.

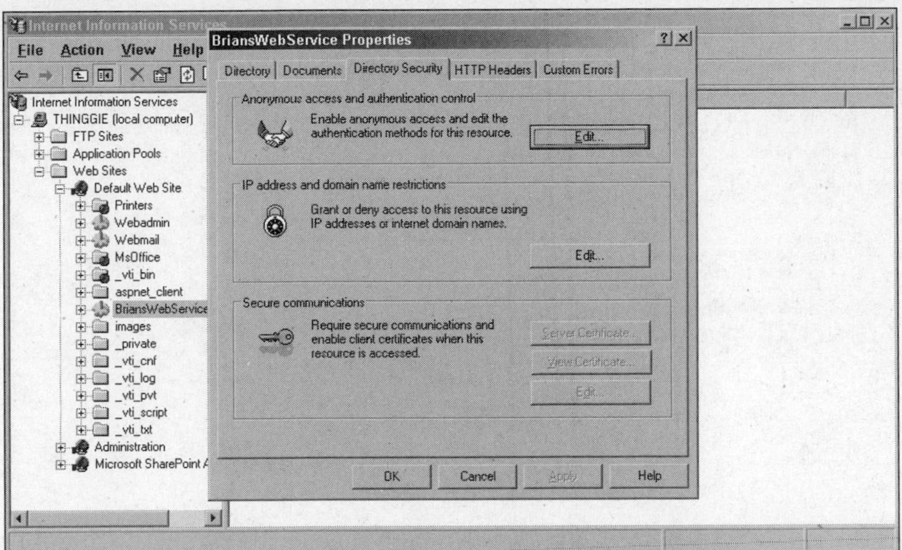

Figure 4-12: Many security options can be configured from the Directory Security tab with the Internet Information Service MMC.

The fact that this amount of authentication is provided means that user setup can be handled by a member of the development team or the administrator — or perhaps both. This also means that by using Windows Authentication, a user can browse to your Web site and be automatically logged in if they are a member of the domain and are currently logged into that domain — all authentication information is automatically passed from the client's browser to the Web server. This ensures that a visitor to your site cannot hack in by guessing name/password pairs since everything is handled in the background. That may seem a bit much if you haven't dealt with Web site administration — the fact that outsiders can log into a secure site and query a secure Web Service from anywhere on the Internet. Rest assured that you can also limit access by IP address as shown here in Figure 4-13.

As we have seen, the .NET Framework and IIS 6.0 take a lot of headache out of configuring a Web site or Web Service for not only security but ease of use. Administration of Web components can be a very large topic so you may want to invest in an IIS 6.0 book that covers administration topics in greater detail. Nine times out of ten, the developer of the Web server or a member of the IT staff will be directly involved with the configuration to ensure it works properly with the application it was built for.

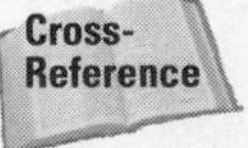

For more information on the framework, try picking up a book such as the *C# Bible* by Wiley Publishing.

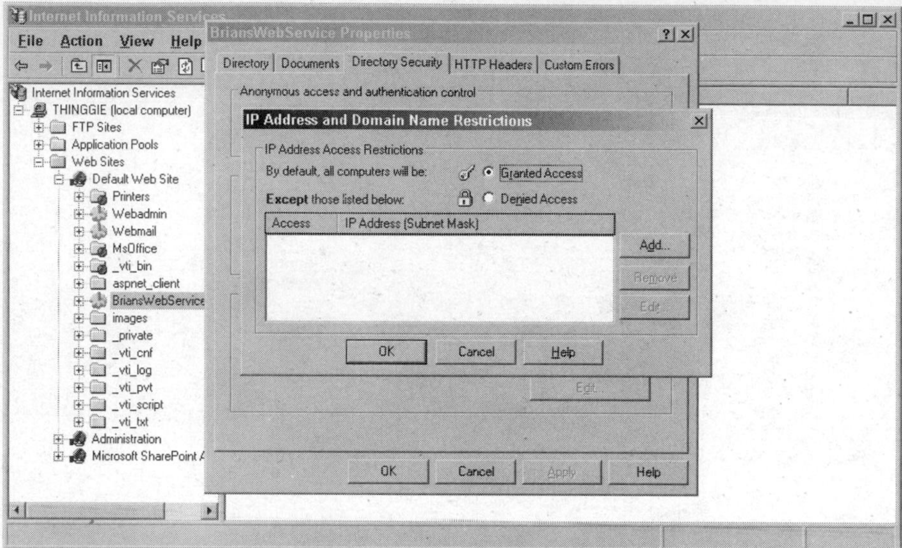

Figure 4-13: Login restrictions can be limited by IP address as well as network credentials.

Summary

The .NET Framework is a very powerful tool for application developers as well as server administrators. It allows you to create very powerful scripts to ease server administration—such as importing large lists of users and adding them to your network or simply to monitor system conditions. The framework also allows for side-by-side execution of same-name DLLs which quite often leads to application crashes. Using the .NET Framework, one can also build components that can communicate across the Internet and through firewalls using open standards and common protocols to help propel your business.

The .NET Framework is merely just that—a framework. It contains many tools and applications that let specialized applications run with its existence.

✦ ✦ ✦

P A R T

II

Planning, Installation, and Configuration

✦ ✦ ✦ ✦

In This Part

✦ ✦ ✦ ✦

Planning for Windows Server 2003

✦ ✦ ✦ ✦

In This Chapter

Understanding the steps to implementation

Implementing a Windows 2003 Server project

✦ ✦ ✦ ✦

No matter how small your network or your needs, you always need to plan your system installation, starting from user requirements and ending in installation and operational qualification at production time. This chapter covers project planning for Windows Server 2003 and takes you through the steps required to formulate and execute a sound project and deployment plan.

Steps to Implementation

Many of you are probably following the usual advice of some of your peers: Microsoft should release the first service pack or two of an operating system before you touch it. Here's our advice: You need to install .NET Server *now,* in your lab. Not after one or two service packs. Now. Are we paid Microsoft supporters? No. (Still no offers from Redmond.) But you cannot formulate a sound implementation plan for either yourself or a client without getting to know the product. And this means that you need to install the product in a lab, which becomes the proving and staging ground for all your projects.

You need to start testing now, understanding now, and learning now. You must plan for Windows Server 2003, and this advice is aimed not only at the multi-national company with 432,981 employees in 65 countries, but also at the single-person company that you find around the next corner. And you cannot successfully plan a .NET Server deployment project unless you know everything that you need to know about the product.

This advice is also as true for Windows Server 2003 as it was for Windows 2000 — perhaps more so. Windows Server 2003 provides such a huge competitive advantage, if wisely adopted, that the early implementers could end up well ahead of you and their competition — on the Web, in office productivity, in security, in lowering total cost of ownership (TCO), in administration, and more.

Got the message? So if you are wondering, "Where do I begin?" this is the chapter that takes you down the Yellow Brick Road. Put your worries and neuroses behind you and get cracking.

Formulating a plan

The first step that you need to take is to formulate a plan of attack. You can be very scientific about your planning for Windows Server 2003, and you can also overdo it. We urge you to keep the planning simple. The cliché that works for Windows Server 2003 is to make sure that you can see all the trees *and* all the forests. If you already have a well-organized Windows 2003 domain, you have lots of time; Windows Server 2003 is going to be around for a while.

You must come up with a formal document for management, proposing a project to evaluate and plan an upgrade or conversion to Windows Server 2003. If you take the CEO or CTO a 1,200-page tome, he is likely to freak out. Managers want to know how Windows Server 2003 is going to save them money, make them more competitive, and keep them secure. Most executives need nothing more than an executive summary with which to begin.

In this book, we talk about both *migrating* and *conversion*. *Migration* is a misnomer in referring to moving to Windows Server 2003 from Windows NT. Migrating implies that you can go back to where you came from. Migrating is not possible with Windows Server 2003 if you are coming from Windows NT. If you're trying to go back, you're in disaster-recovery mode. Your domains can coexist, which most of you are going to be doing for a while, and you *do* convert. But if you follow the advice in this book and in the next few chapters in particular, you do not need to climb down from Windows Server 2003 and reinstall Windows NT.

Migration, however, is possible from Windows 2000 to Windows Server 2003, because the two platforms are very closely related, especially if you're talking about Active Directory. As you progress through this book, you notice that much of Windows 2000 still exists in .NET Server (see Chapter 6).

Many ways to approach a project and a plan are possible. And we do not intend to teach project science here, so whatever works for you or is required by your organization is fine with us. We are not going to offer you the best way to approach the conversion. We do give you some pointers culled from many years of doing needs analyses and syntheses, as well as systems design, development, and deployment.

In the early days of the planning and testing phase, choose only a handful of energetic people to evaluate Windows Server 2003. You don't want too many people doing their own thing and becoming unproductive and uncoordinated. In the beginning, there will be little time for managing all the egos and eager beavers. If too many people join the project or you have subsidiaries and divisions setting up their own projects, the company on the whole loses out because you end up with disjointed installations everywhere, and the project drowns under the weight of everyone's two ounces of input.

In the Windows 2000 edition of the book, we suggested a plan of attack. It was a plan that we followed in testing Windows Server 2003, and it is the plan that we used to evaluate Windows 2003 for our own customers, clients, and companies, from our six-person insurance company to our huge multinational distributors. In this edition, however, we are going to introduce a more formal design methodology that we suggest you follow. You can either choose to make full use of this design methodology or steal bits from the information to formulate your own attack plan.

Implementing in phases

Phased implementation is a big phrase that represents a logical course to completing a difficult transition from one state to another. In this section, our objectives are to move from state zero (no Windows Server 2003) to a design phase, tests in the lab, pilot project, conversion, deployment and validation. This is often called the *System Development Life Cycle* (or *SDLC*). Depending on the nature of the implementation and your objectives, your project phases may vary or even be very different from ours. Each phase may itself become highly nested, with subphases, milestones, and sanity checks.

A well-planned design methodology and phased implementation enables you to stop at checkpoints along the way, assess results, and make changes as required. A Windows Server 2003 project consists of several phases, as shown in Figure 5-1. Some phases overlap and others are ongoing.

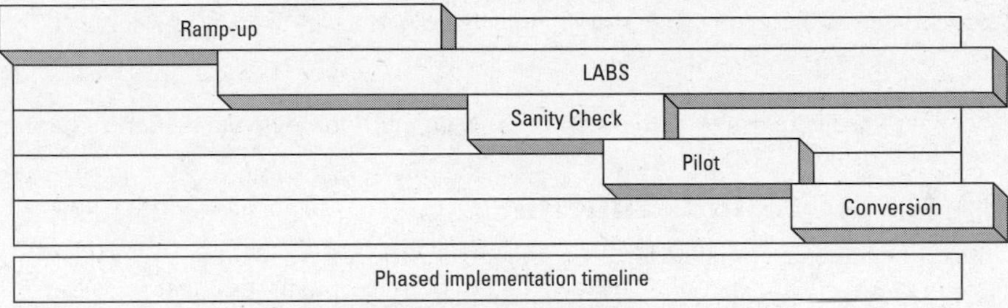

Figure 5-1: Drawing of a phased implementation plan.

You also have several steps within each phase. The conversion step is in itself a phased-implementation effort. Take care, however, not to overnest your project with too many phases. Our suggested phase-implementation structure is as follows:

- **Phase 1:** Analysis and Ramp-up
- **Phase 2:** Labs
- **Phase 3:** Test, Sanity Checks, and Proof of Concept
- **Phase 4:** Design
- **Phase 5:** Pilot
- **Phase 6:** Conversion and Deployment

The suggested steps that span all five phases are outlined in Table 5-1.

Table 5-1: Planning Steps

Phase	*Step*
Phase 1	Step 1: Establish a Timeline for Your Project
Phase 1	Step 2: Understand the Technology
Phase 1	Step 3: Understand How Your Enterprise is Currently Positioned
Phase 1	Step 4: Establish Budget
Phase 2	Step 5: Create and Secure the Lab
Phase 2	Step 6: Systems Architecture and Design

Continued

Table 5-1: (continued)

Phase	*Step*
Phase 3	Step 7: Test, Sanity Checks, and Proof of Concept
Phase 4	Step 8: Position the Enterprise on Windows 2003 (Gap Analysis)
Phase 4	Step 9: Evaluate
Phase 5	Step 10: Create Pilot Projects
Phase 6	Step 11: Begin Conversions, Migrations and Deployment

The design phase is revisited in the section, "Design methodology," later in this chapter.

Step 1: Establishing timelines

You need to establish a timeline for your project. For the record, plan on at least six months for a team of about three people. The ideal length of time from assessment to rollout is about 40 weeks. And that should cover everything that you need to do to integrate or infiltrate Windows 2003 into the core functions of your IT and telecom structures. If you are only one person, you need more time or you can bring in outside consultants for help.

You may get away with a shorter timeline for a small company. By *small*, we are referring to one employing not more than 20 people. Just because a company is small does not mean that it is not performing mission-critical work comparable to a unit in a Fortune 500 company. Remember that, if a unit in a large company goes offline for a few days, that state may hardly be noticed. Take a small company offline for a few days, however, and it could go insolvent.

A large company takes about two years to completely convert to a Windows Server 2003 (and this amount of time is a Microsoft recommendation). Smaller companies require less time, but no less than 24 weeks. You can possibly rush it, but to do so, you must study new material every day, seven days a week. You can also take classes and do a Microsoft certification in the middle, but that would not get you anywhere faster. An MCSE is a good idea in parallel with this project, but take classes so that you can interact with your instructors and clarify sticking points.

Step 2: Understanding the technology

If you have Windows 2000 experience, you can draw on that, because Windows Server 2003 is much like one huge Windows 2000 service pack. Windows 2000, of course, was a big leap from Windows NT, so system developers had a much harder time using Windows NT know-how for deploying Windows 2000.

If you are making the leap from Windows NT 4.0 (and, we hope, not anything earlier) or from some stagnant operating system such as NetWare, where you have the old NT domain architecture or Netware Directory Service (NDS) to contend with, you have a much tougher time. You can draw on any general IT/IS experience that you have, but for the most part, you're learning a lot of new stuff. Saying that you now know all that anyone can know about Windows 2003 after six months of shining a flashlight under the covers is also not sufficient; in fact, that's impossible. But understanding the technology — what Windows 2003 is and how it achieves its objectives — is vital.

Prerequisites

Windows 2003 architecture is highly complex. Key to understanding the technology is having a good grounding in general computer science and network engineering, but you must be willing to specialize. You are going to need expertise on your team, and the members of the team should be prepared to show proficiency in several IT areas.

Team members need a complete understanding and experience in all the following: network protocols and services; server hardware platforms; storage; Windows 2000 and Windows NT server administration and deployment experience; Windows 2000, Windows NT, and Windows *9x* workstation experience; Internet practices; and much more.

After you establish the timelines and pick a team of experts, you need to spend no less than two months — and possibly four — learning everything about the technology and the architecture, plus Active Directory (which adds six to eight weeks over and above everything else). Trust us. We work with engineers all day long, and they are very good at what they do, but on some Windows 2003 subjects, such as Active Directory, they still can only scratch their heads.

Where do you start?

Besides this book to break ground, the best place to start is the Microsoft Web site. Tons of white papers are there, as well as documents that can get you started on both the easy and difficult stuff. The Deployment Planning Guide in the Windows 2003 Resource Kit is also a worthwhile document to read.

Avoid books that are nothing but a rehash of the Windows 2003 Help files. They may have worked in the past but aren't necessary today. Not only are the current Help files very thorough, but they are also vast, covering many different functions and features of the server. And you can take them almost anywhere that you can take this book. . . on your Windows Pocket PC or CE handheld, for example, which connects you directly to the server by using a terminal session.

Also avoid books that attempt to teach you about subjects not really germane to Windows Server 2003 or that have been covered more times than the Oscars. You don't find instructions on how to format a hard disk in this book, for example, or how to use Windows Explorer. If you don't already know this stuff, you're not qualified to be involved in planning for and installing Windows Server 2003.

You also need new equipment. For the first few weeks, you need to read, read, read. You're going to experience payoffs. You find, for example, that people caught off guard start turning to you in desperate need of help to understand a complex Windows 2003 issue. Your peers who scoffed as you plastered your office walls with thousands of Windows 2003 white papers aren't going to be laughing now.

Step 3: Understanding how your enterprise is positioned to exploit Windows Server 2003

We know that positioning is difficult to do in the early stages of the project, but preparing yourself to take your early findings to management is very important. Although many projects are sanctioned or sponsored by people high up in the management channels, unless you come up with specific reasons to make changes to or enhance the existing IT infrastructure, your project may come to an abrupt end.

No matter how big or small the organization, change is always difficult, and you face the risk of business or work stoppages from unanticipated events that result directly from your conversion attempts. Believe it or not, many companies are still doing just fine on Windows NT . . . although don't expect to see them lighting up Wall Street.

Management, especially the CIO/CTO or MIS, is focused on keeping the business systems running. Without the systems, the business fails. Nine times out of ten, most senior executives cite the "wait until service pack 1" rule. Your job is to convince them to start testing now and then to get the initial sponsorship and budget for the project. And the only way to do that is to become an informed evangelist in less than two full moons.

Step 4: Establishing a budget

You need several stages of financing for your project, so think like an entrepreneur. The early stages can probably be catered to out of existing equipment, unused servers, hard disks, and so on. If you don't have surplus hardware, you need to get a few servers. And we don't need to tell you that the best means of providing servers for a project such as this is to buy the pieces and assemble the hardware in your lab. You not only learn about Windows 2003 hardware compatibility, but you end up saving a lot of money in the early stages.

Tip

Older brand servers, such as Pentium I Compaqs (sorry, we mean HPs) or Dells, are as risky for Windows 2003 (if not more so) than flea-market finds. eBay, however, abounds in good bargains that work wonders in the lab. One of the best lab servers for the price is the Compaq Proliant 1850R. The dual processor 400 MHz is a workhorse.

Step 5: Creating a lab

With your initial budget, you need to set up a lab. This should be a secure area where you can set up a number of servers, workstations, printers, and a slew of network components, such as routers and hubs. Depending on the size of your organization and the project, you want your lab to emulate an enterprise-wide domain structure, both physical and logical. In that case, you need to set up several domain controllers, role servers such as DNS and DHCP, and so on.

Tip

Strive to set up a lab that closely resembles your production network as far as possible.

Obtain a space in which you can comfortably fit about 12 rack servers and all collateral network equipment and printers and, naturally, a bunch of workstations. You may get away with a lot less, and you may need a lot more. One company that we know built a test domain complete with domain controllers for 24 large remote centers — that's *24 domain controllers*.

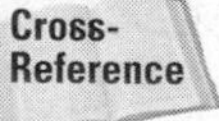

Cross-Reference

Follow Chapter 6 for specifics on installing the servers for different roles.

Step 6: Designing the logical and physical structures

After you have a budget and you are ramped up on the technology, you can begin designing your logical and physical domain structures in the lab. You need to set up key role servers such as domain controllers, certificate servers, license servers, DNS, and so on. In Chapter 6, we discuss issues directly related to the domain controllers and role servers. The logical and physical designs are discussed in Part III.

Step 7: Securing the lab

Pay particular attention to security during all phases of the test project. In other words, experiment with various levels of encryption and security practice (such as using smart cards). You are also setting up initial user accounts for your administrators and a selection of mock users for your organizational units (OUs) and groups in Active Directory.

Lab isolation is also very important. You need to make sure that the lab network at no time broadcasts out to the production network. Making sure that the production network does not inadvertently route packets to the lab network is also critical. The last thing that you need is for the lab DHCP server to reach out into production network and declare war on the production DHCP server.

Although hermetically sealing off the lab from the production network is the safest, doing so is not always practical. Often you need data and binary resources on the production network that cannot be transported on CDs, and the only way to move the data from the production network to the lab is over a router. You incur no risk to either network if you are handy with a router, a firewall, and networking.

A Windows 2000 or Windows Server 2003 can act as a suitable router between production and lab networks, and you can still use the machine for testing. The safest way to transport data between the two networks is to block packets from moving between the two NICs, a filtering technique explained in Chapter 15. But if you are filtering or blocking packet transport, how does the data get from one network to the other? Just upload data to the router's hard disk and then move it from there to the lab server. In other words, you set up the router's machines to appear as a member server on either network, which means that you are really sharing the hard disk between the two networks.

Step 8: Testing

After you design and create a logical and physical structure and apply security, you can begin to test. You are testing authentication, policies, DNS, WINS, DHCP, storage, files and folder access, and so on. During your tests, you should also pay attention to the position that your enterprise is currently in. Moving directly from Step 8 to Step 9 enables you to perform insightful gap analysis. (*Gap analysis* is used to determine the technology gap between the company of the present and the company of the future.)

Step 9: Positioning the enterprise on Windows Server 2003

During your test project and lab work, you need to assess the position that your organization now finds itself in and the position that it can be in during and after conversion. List, too, all the situations that the company would not want to be in during and after the conversion and phased implementation. The first situation that comes to mind that we would not want to be in, for example, is offline; another is being up but finding that users have lost access to their resources.

You should also consider the skills that are available to you or that you may need post deployment. One of the big problems facing IT operations and maintenance departments (O&M) is finding available skills. Although deploying a public key infrastructure for smart card authentication or encrypted e-mail may seem cool, such a service does not run itself or keep itself from falling apart. Although Windows 2003 ups the ante on self-healing technology, the day that the network no longer needs skilled administrators is the day that you see three moons on the horizon.

Step 10: Evaluating the project

You need to stop at predetermined intervals or milestones along the way for sanity checks and to evaluate how far you have come, how far you need to go, deadlines that may have been missed, and other problems. Toward the end of the project, you need to make the decision with your sponsors and management to move forward with a test or pilot project in which you are deploying servers in production environments.

Step 11: Creating pilot projects

The pilot projects can take on many forms. They can be limited to the installation of a role server, many role servers, the beginnings of Active Directory in the organization, and more.

Step 12: Beginning conversions

On the basis of successful pilot projects, you can, with the blessings of management or your own confidence, move forward with rollout and conversion.

A lot of material about planning is available on the Microsoft Web site. The material in the Windows 2003 Deployment Planning Guide is extensive. We found it too detailed in parts, however, and too verbose for the majority of installations. Many sections call for teams of experts that most companies could not afford. Indeed, a team of such experts, even for a month, would be beyond the budgets of all but a few companies.

The preceding steps are a starting point — something on which you can build. The following planning guide worked for us, suited our environment, and is based on many projects that came before Windows 2003 and during its beta cycles. Each step along the way was fully documented and evaluated. Indeed, you are holding much of the research and lab work that we did between these covers. Now to kick your implementation into high gear.

Analysis and Ramp-up

A huge difference exists between learning about Windows Server 2003 and understanding what the technology means for the enterprise. As components of Phase 1 which we describe in the section "Implementing in phases," earlier in this chapter, analysis and ramp-up set out to achieve both in logical order. We also touched on this in Chapter 1, where we placed Windows Server 2003 in the middle of Microsoft's architectural feast. Your planning efforts should thus be based on the following objectives:

- ✦ Understanding how to use the technology.
- ✦ Installing and deploying Windows Server 2003 with that knowledge.

Understanding the technology

Only after you have a thorough understanding of the technology and the architecture are you in a position to determine the benefits of the technology for the enterprise. Granted, you may have heard how wonderful Active Directory is. But you have probably heard rumors that it is "overkill for a small company." How do you know whether that statement is invalid until you fully understand how Active Directory works and what it can do for your company, no matter what the size? Just because Active Directory can hold a billion objects does not mean that it should not hold only a hundred. Understanding the various services that play domain roles is also important. Official documentation, for example, refers to three roles a server can play. The server can be any of the following, and *understanding* the differences between them is important:

✦ A Windows 2003 server can be a *standalone* server, which means that it is not joined to any domain and stands alone in its own workspace. Understanding how this server interacts or participates on the network provides you with the information that you need to assess needs and cater to them with the establishment of standalone servers. A standalone server, for example, is an ideal bastion. And it can be used as a firewall or proxy server without needing to be part of a domain. A certificate server, established for a public key infrastructure (PKI), is a good example of a standalone server.

Millions of Windows NT, Windows 2000 and Windows 2003 servers are on the Internet, and they are not part of any Windows domains. The machine is thus more secure as a standalone server than as a member server, because standalone servers are not given domain accounts nor are they authenticated on the domain. They can also be print servers and so on, but their resources cannot be published in Active Directory, short of mapping them to IP addresses (see Chapter 28).

Tip

If you are in a hurry to install Windows Server 2003, do not try to join it to any domain or promote it to a domain controller. Make it a standalone server that logs into its own workgroup. This type of setup enables you to configure it, because any domain influence or control is extended from Active Directory.

✦ Windows 2003 can be a *member* server, which means that it has an account in the domain. That account can be in a Windows NT domain, a Windows 2000 domain, or a Windows 2003 domain. As long as it is a member server, you can access its resources via the authentication mechanisms of Windows NT and the NTLM authentication service (see Chapter 3) or via Kerberos on a Windows 2000/.NET network. The Windows 2003 member server can therefore play certain worthwhile roles in an NT domain.

✦ A *domain controller* loads the Active Directory support infrastructure. You can install a Windows 2003 domain controller whenever you are ready to begin learning about Active Directory or if you are building your test domains in the lab. You can also install a Windows 2003 domain controller server into a Windows NT domain or a Windows 2000 domain.

Good examples of understanding the technology are coming to the conclusion that Windows Server 2003-DNS, Windows Server 2003-WINS, and Windows Server 2003-DHCP are ideal role servers to install in the existing environment, whether it's Windows NT or something else . . . and then figuring out how to integrate them. In fact, this is the design technique that forms the basis of our evangelism in this book in general and in Parts II and III in particular.

We call this technique *conversion by subversion*. The process is straightforward, as the following steps indicate:

1. Target the service that can be overthrown.
2. Move the role server into a position where it can perform the role of the target.
3. Take over the role.
4. Shut down the subverted server.

Now to look at this concept more closely. Take Windows Internet Naming Service (WINS). On NT, it's a stinker, causing more headaches for every new segment that you need to roll out. Face it: It is a Band-Aid for a service that was not meant to be used the way that it is being used, and we are talking about NetBIOS.

After years of complaints from thousands of IT managers, Microsoft has rolled out a new WINS. Managed behind the Microsoft Management Console (MMC), it's a new wave for a service that is not expected to last more than a few more years.

We have zoomed in on all the WINS servers at one of our clients — 19 servers to be precise. That's 19 targets to take over. After tests proved that the Windows 2003 WINS servers would work well in their new environments, we began a conversion project to take the legacy servers out one by one. Why could we deploy in this fashion? Because WINS .NET is not for pure Windows 2003 . . . it's for Windows NT and Windows 9*x* clients that need to resolve NetBIOS names to IP addresses (see Part IV).

Never install WINS on a domain controller if you have more than 20 or 30 users. It has a tendency to eat up precious processor cycles needed by Active Directory. This problem is further discussed in Chapter 17.

Focusing on capabilities and not features

We take this philosophy of understanding Windows Server 2003 further and implore you to focus on *capabilities* as opposed to features. If you focus on features, you lose sight of your enterprise needs and become a royal pain to everyone on your team. Rather than coming up with "Did you know . . .?" lines day in and day out, focus on, for example, why WINS .NET should be implemented *now*. (Because it supports persistent connections.)

If you support a large WAN with multiple sites and you still happen to be using Windows NT WINS, you're going to be glad to know that your days of endless forced replicating between "sterile" WINS servers is over. Does this mean much for the enterprise? It does if your sites are interconnected across low bandwidth WAN (56K circuits). Fixing broken WINS server services using the old WINS does not take much. But if users call because they cannot find their network shares and automatic file transfers fail, WINS .NET may be one of the first new services that you try to get into production and deployment.

Needs analyses-needs syntheses

A *needs analysis* or *needs synthesis* is a study of the needs of an enterprise for certain technology or solutions. This analysis can and should be done during the planning phase and before testing efforts and pilot projects are complete. This is your opportunity to "sell" Windows Server 2003 to your enterprise, based on user needs and user requirements. Here is a good example of a needs synthesis: One of our clients is a large multinational that is about to embark on the complex process of merging the IT departments of two recent acquisitions into its own IT infrastructure. Mergers and acquisitions can collapse if IT cannot get it right, and merging the network infrastructures and domains of once-competing companies can cause one's cholesterol levels to skyrocket.

For the foreseeable future — at least two years — the companies must operate as separate entities while IT converts key services and infrastructure into the acquiring (now parent) corporation.

The three companies have a total of 9,000 employees. Each company has a collection of Windows NT domains. The domains among the three companies number about 45, many still from earlier acquisitions and acquisitions of acquisitions, and all 45 need to be managed holistically. Many of the domains are NT account domains, collectively containing some 13,622 accounts. This is a daunting task. For starters, under Windows NT, all the domains interconnect across a large WAN, and thus all need to be related to each other with complex Windows NT domain bi- and unidirectional trusts.

Investigating the processes shows that several thousand folders also need to be shared among the entities. One of the biggest problems anticipated by all is the translocation of key employees, many of them moving from their old company to the new HQ. The translocated employees need to be given new user IDs and to the capability to log on to the new `HQDOMAIN`. They still need access to their old folders, however, and to shares back at the old offices where they logged in (for example, `EXDOMAIN`).

This situation means that administrators from both domains must cooperate, long distance, to make the resources available to the users. The effort is made much more difficult because the administrators from the acquired domains do not trust their peers. So administrators in HQDOMAIN must create user groups for the translocated souls, and the administrators from the old domains must implicitly add the new groups to the resources — for example, groups that need access to share-points.

The needs synthesis shows how Active Directory should be used to consolidate the file and folder resources to make them easier to access in a Windows 2003 domain hierarchy. Folders are published in Active Directory and made available to the users no matter where they log on.

The project, as you can imagine, is extensive. So between now and Part III in this book, take some time to ponder how you would go about such a project and where you would start.

Do not overlook your present needs

While doing your planning, you always need to make sure that you do not lose focus of what brings in the bread and butter today. Many companies are so busy with current projects that they cannot spare anyone to work on a Windows Server 2003 planning project.

A lack of project resources can be either a minus or a plus, depending on your circumstances. The example in the needs synthesis in the preceding section indicates how Windows 2003 can cater to present needs. On the other hand, you should not suggest or deploy Windows 2003 without first ensuring that you are not risking present systems. (Your lab work and pilot projects ensure that.)

Assessing your future needs

Looking to the future helps you and the team — and especially the managers who need to come up with the money — understand where Windows 2003 technology comes in. If you can show, as we did in the needs synthesis in preceding sections, that investing in Active Directory can cut six to eight months off the merger process, you make a lot of people sit up and take notice. If you can show how much you can save and how you intend to pave the way for the next big acquisition, which is expected to add another thousand accounts to the absorption process, you are likely to get double the funding that you need to take your project to the next level.

Assessing your strengths and weaknesses

We cannot stress how important assessing your strengths and weaknesses (translated to *risks*) is before you take your planning project to the second phase. This assessment must be done on several levels, specifically, the following:

- ✦ Support from management
- ✦ Available funds
- ✦ Available time
- ✦ Material resources
- ✦ Human resources
- ✦ Technical expertise
- ✦ Network infrastructure
- ✦ Technology or systems already in place
- ✦ Direction of the company
- ✦ What the competition is doing
- ✦ Administrative burden
- ✦ Risks posed to the company

The following sections explain these assessments in detail.

Support from management

Without champions for the project among your management team, you're dead. In one company, we know that the project was blocked from higher up because of the company's existing investment in Novell Directory Services (NDS). Don't take that the wrong way. NDS has been out there a lot longer than Active Directory and is a fine product, but the company was not willing to change to Active Directory in the middle of an NDS rollout. In such a case, it would be prudent not to focus on competing technology but to get support for other services, such as printing support, IIS, DNS, telephony, media, and so on.

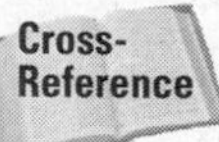

See Chapters 2 and 8 for information on the coexistence of NDS with Active Directory in particular and about meta-directories in general.

Available funds

Microsoft has made Windows 2003 available for 180-day trials. We do not believe that this period is sufficient time for a comprehensive project, however, and you face the added hassle of activation (now a part of everyday life for administrators). Many companies that we know have unused Windows NT 3.5 and 4.0 licenses lying around. If you need more time, a cost-effective option is to buy the Windows Server 2003 upgrade. Installing the upgrade, even on a virgin machine, is a painless process, as we explain in Chapter 6, as long as you have the original CDs.

You still must invest in servers, hardware, and time. Make a list of everything that you need and then estimate costs. Then ask management for twice that amount of money and work backward from there. Having money left over or demonstrating that the project was completed under budget is far better than needing to go back to management for another shot in the arm.

Of course, this last bit of advice sounds like project management gone nuts. Even in formal capital expenditure program (CEP) exercises, however, managers need to build in sufficient contingency, which almost always ends up getting used.

You may think that this is "seat-of-the-pants" budgeting, and it is, but given that IT people can be terrible at estimating costs and that you need to cater to unknowns, you must take care not to underestimate, even if you think that everything is going to go smoothly. If you are unskilled at preparing CEP documents for your projects, find someone in the company who can assist you or take on a consultant to write the contingency part.

If you are struggling with budget and need to buy a few months, consider making the leap to Terminal Services as opposed to buying Windows 2003 Professional. Microsoft gives you three months to deploy an application server before enforcing its licensing restrictions (see Chapter 30).

Available time

Make sure that you have the time to be involved in such a project. If you are planning a comprehensive technology assessment, test lab, pilot project — the whole thing — nothing short of a full-time commitment and a team of several souls is sufficient. Work out how much time you need to complete the job and then allot more time. If you are unsure of the amount of time, double that and work backward from there. We understand that "thumb-sucking" may not be realistic for many companies and individuals who often wish that they could multithread all the work processes that they have.

Project management expertise is not essential but is highly recommended for all IT projects, no matter how small. Many administrators are great engineers but are not good at managing their time. Understanding the differences between things such as labor and effort is a good idea.

Material resources

You need space, a test lab, hub space, rack space, monitors, storage, work benches, tape backup units, cartridges, CD burners (for cutting auto-installation CDs), and so on. Many companies have a lot of stuff lying around, so before you put pencil to paper to get a budget, first see how much can be requisitioned from the other departments or divisions.

You may still need to invest in new hardware, however, because Windows 2003 exploits new hardware services that the major manufacturers are bringing out on their new platforms. These include plug and play, Advanced Configuration and Power Interface (ACPI), and the Boot Information Negotiation Layer (BINL), which is the service that enables remote booting.

Human resources

You cannot hope to complete a full-scale Windows Server 2003 test or planning project single-handedly or with only a few hands. The conversion or upgrading process is tough on smaller companies that do not have many employees to spare, and — trust us — the MSCE on Windows 2003 does not prepare you sufficiently to convert a considerable infrastructure. Do not make the mistake of understaffing your project.

If you find yourself with insufficient technical resources you will need to contract with a technical recruiting firm that can hire the necessary temps for you, starting with a project manager. Or you might consider requesting a proposal from an independent contractor (outsourcing) to come in and do the entire job. The pros and cons of each approach are, however, beyond the scope of this book.

Technical expertise

This category is not quite the same as just having sufficient human resources. You need people with sufficient technical expertise for the project. Our own projects would have traveled a lot faster had several peer technicians been available. The mainframe and mid-range integration efforts, for example, needed to be pushed back because people were tied up in their validation efforts.

Network infrastructure

Having a sufficient network infrastructure to incorporate Windows Server 2003 can be a tough one. Collateral operating systems, protocols, topology, legacy applications, and legacy Windows (many copies of Windows NT are still in use) all have an effect on the design process. Your enterprise and gap analyses need to discover all the components. A so-called barrier to entry, for example, is the steep learning curve of DNS for many administrators who have never needed to touch it before.

If you support a highly complex network infrastructure, you should use products such as Microsoft System Management Server (SMS) to help you discover what you have. If you have not worked with discovery tools, you need to factor in ramp-up time and a learning curve to learn how to use such productivity or administration tools.

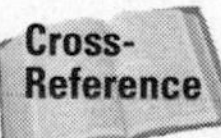

See Chapter 6 for a discussion on using Systems Management Server (SMS) to deploy Windows Server 2003.

And now for some words on Windows domains: Windows NT domains are not easily merged into Active Directory domains. Because of the limitations of the earlier technology, many companies were forced to create several domains to avoid blowing up the Service Accounts Manager (SAM) database. You may be tempted to upgrade the Windows NT domain to an Active Directory domain, but doing so is not an easy process and is risky because the NT domain controller is actually converted to an Active Directory domain controller and just not simply copied.

We have mixed sentiments about the conversion of Windows NT domain controllers (primary domain controllers [PDCs] and backup domain controllers [BDCs]) to Windows 2000 Server or Windows Server 2003, and we believe that Microsoft should have provided more tools to import accounts to the Active Directory, as opposed to converting the whole primary domain controller. We go into this topic in some depth in Chapters 6 and 10, where you benefit from a first-hand account of a disastrous PDC conversion.

If you have large and complex domains, you should explore using ADSI (Active Directory Services Interface) to programmatically copy user accounts to Active Directory. Your user accounts can be exported from the SAM database and then imported to Active Directory. You can also build a simple tool by using Microsoft's database technologies, such as the Active Data Objects (ADO or ADO.NET) and the Active Directory connectors service provider to perform your import. This process is much harder than it seems, especially if your network administrators do not write software — and most don't.

Regardless of how you plan to transfer user accounts to Active Directory from NT 4.0 domains, you can't get away from the amount of work that it involves. So you should plan now with Active Directory in mind, even if your conversion project is to begin a year down the road.

If you have investigated Active Directory really well, you should notice that many attributes or properties of the user-account objects are very different from the attributes of user accounts in NT (meaning all versions of NT). NT user accounts, for example, do not contain attributes for new services such as Terminal Services sessions or new fields for properties such as User Principal Names (UPNs); and home directories, policies, profiles, and passwords are all radically different in Active Directory. You thus need to consider whether your NT domain should be phased over rather than converted by the promotion of the domain controller. Although conversion may appear to be more desirable, certain caveats are involved with that process.

Many NT domains are a mess. They have thousands of accounts in them that are dormant, dead, or disabled and that should have been deleted and purged from the SAM in the last millennium. At one client, for example, generations of administrators failed to stick to procedure and policy. And the domain had accounts created according to combinations of *firstname, lastname* or *lastname, firstname* or contractions, middle initials, and so on. We deemed putting the domain "down" better than losing sleep trying to fix it.

Starting from scratch in creating user accounts in Active Directory may, therefore, pay because, otherwise, you may just end up with a huge list of user accounts that still require individual attention or that may give you further headaches. Of course, you need to adequately plan the installation of a parallel domain structure.

We, in fact, have declared several large clients that we surveyed for Windows 2003 and Active Directory as nonconvertible. And we would rather walk away from the business than attempt the impossible (as we discuss further in Chapter 6).

If a small client does not have a backup domain controller—and many do not—do not under any circumstances attempt to promote or convert the domain controller unless you are sure that you can quickly restore a failed conversion. If you find yourself faced with such a scenario, you have three choices: bring in a new machine and establish a BDC; bring in a new machine to be the Windows 2003 domain controller; or do nothing. As discussed in Chapter 5, we rate creating a domain controller from scratch to be the most logical choice in many situations.

Chapter 10, which deals with the installation and deployment of Active Directory, also provides guidelines for the domain conversion process. We have been to the "Promised Land," and we have returned empty-handed. The only way that some of Windows NT domains are going to be converted is to infiltrate the Active Directory domain controller into the user environment and, gradually, organizational unit by organizational unit, convert the users.

Technology or systems in place

This factor is closely related to the one that we describe in the preceding section, but existing systems may not be flexible. At one client, for example, we couldn't move a certain application because it depended on Pathworks, the long vanished Digital Equipment's protocol suite for VMS networks (now part of HP via its merger with Compaq), to connect to the NT sharepoint, and the replacement that worked on TCP/IP was not ready. We had to wait 10 months for the replacement.

At another client—this one more recent—authentication to an Oracle database on a Unix system depended on the eight-character user ID of the former network's Windows NT user account name. The User Principal Name (UPN) of the Active Directory account name (`someone@somecompany.com`) was not compatible with the legacy application. We thus needed to provide two accounts and authenticate to legacy database by using a proxy interface with the alternative account name. What a drag.

Direction of the company

You need to do things such as enterprise analysis to determine corporate requirements (covered in Chapter 8), gap analysis, and needs syntheses (establishing user requirements).

Chapter 7 delves into company types and philosophy and what drives management. If you work for a progressive company or one that is driven by change, you encounter a lot of support for the new era. If your company is stagnant or wavering, you may need to live with the status quo.

What the competition is doing

This factor is difficult to assess for obvious reasons. Larger companies often like to boast about their projects, however, and finding out that your competition is rolling out Windows Server 2003 *en masse* may prompt you or your management to get moving.

Administrative burden

User requirements that drive acquisition and design of systems should be considered against the administrative burden and skill sets required to support any systems in the future. You may, for example, think twice about deploying a certain system if you learn that the nearest qualified individual capable of maintaining the system lives 500 miles away. Wherever possible, your projects should strive to manage complexity and aim to prevent the overtaxation of your existing support staff.

You often need to train additional staff and to consider outsourcing certain support or hiring additional support staff. The design specifications of your systems should thus identify what support skills are required beyond what is currently available during the design phase, in terms of the skills of the permanent IT staff.

A guide to consider administrative burden should be provided to evaluate a technology in terms of what not having the technology may cost your company or customer vs. what supporting it costs.

Support costs are often not adequately factored into return on investment (ROI), but some systems are critically important to commission even if they do not seem to provide an apparent or visible benefit. In some cases, the cost of support and administration can be high. Supporting a Web server, for example, costs tons more than anti-virus support, which practically costs zero. Yet many companies spend no time on anti-virus support. Supporting a proxy service is not expensive either; not having a proxy service, however, may lead to an Internet security breach that could potentially close the company down.

Assessing the risks

You need to document and fully understand the risks involved in conversion or you risk missing key risk indicators and a chance to mitigate against them. Risk analysis is more a factor in the pilot phase and the conversion or roll-out phase than in the lab or formal test phase. Before components of the project are ready to come out of the sandbox, make sure that you have done your homework and that a disaster is not about to happen. Make a list of all the possible things that can go wrong; from systems being denied access to critical shares to users not able to log in. Always have a counterattack ready. Have your logistics ready. Understand and identify the risks and then decide whether you are ready for anything.

Perhaps the most valuable advice that we have to offer you in the limited space that we have is to introduce a formal risk-management process. This is something that we have learned to do for all our projects, whether systems or software products. The following section introduces the concept of a risk-management process.

Risk-management process

Every IT project needs a risk-management process, which is maintained for the life of the project and the System Development Life Cycle (SDLC) of each of your systems or solutions that you're providing.

A popular risk-management process to follow corresponds to Microsoft's Risk Management Process (RMP), which is derived from the risk-management process formulated by the Software Engineering Institute (SEI) at Carnegie Mellon University (at `www.seicmu.edu/programs/sepm/risk/index.html`). Your RMP should include the following phases:

✦ **Phase 1:** Risk Identification

✦ **Phase 2:** Risk Analysis

✦ **Phase 3:** Risk Action Plan

✦ **Phase 4:** Risk Tracking and Control

This RMP is the standard process used by the Microsoft Solutions Framework and is as shown in Figure 5-2.

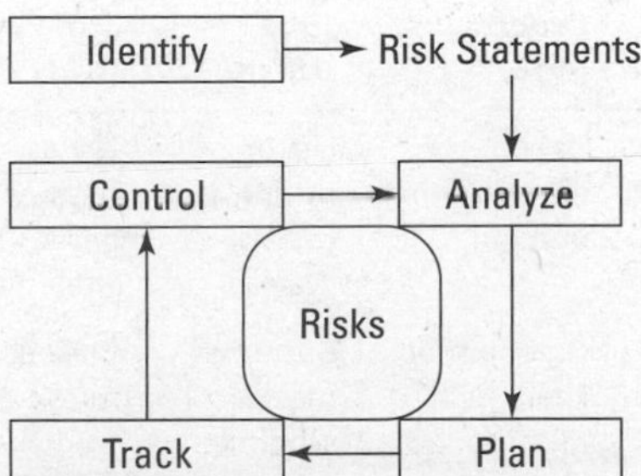

Figure 5-2: The Microsoft (MSF) Risk Management Process.

What is a risk? According to Webster's dictionary, a *risk* is simply the possibility of suffering a loss. You may experience a small loss, such as missing deadlines by a few days, which does not have any real effect, or the risk may be more severe. Not having a license key to install a critical piece of software can be considered a technical snafu that can quickly break the back of the project. What may not appear too important to the customer or stakeholder may be significant to an engineer, the systems architect, or the project manager.

Be prepared to qualify and quantify, as simply as possible, the effect and consequences of any risk. To one person, a risk may simply be a problem waiting to happen; to another, it may be a disaster waiting to happen.

Architectural models and frameworks

As a basis for planning the design phases or simply understanding the different levels of design, expressing systems architecture and high-level design according to a particular architectural framework is useful for organizing a structured approach to the analysis, design, and construction of computer systems.

Systems architects follow a number of architecture models. The three most popular are the *Index Model*, the *Gartner Group Model*, and the *Zachman Framework*. We particularly like the Zachman Framework because it is simple, easily understood by all the project participants (design engineers and testers alike), and clearly indicates the various levels of system design and abstraction, starting from the user at the top and ranging to the deployment engineer at the bottom.

Table 5-2 indicates the abstraction levels of the Zachman Framework. The first two rows are typically directed at the formulation of project management plans (PMP), user requirements specification (URS), and capital expenditure documents (CEP).

Much of what we discuss in this chapter and in the rest of the section is typically expressed according to an architect's view. This view is where overall architecture is expressed in the initial or defining (functional design) specifications. The designer and builder views are expressed in more detailed versions of specific design specifications and separate deployment and testing documents, respectively.

Table 5-2: The Zachman Framework Matrix

View	*Data (what)*	*Function (how)*	*Network (where)*	*People (who)*	*Time (when)*	*Motivation (why)*
Planner	List of items important to the enterprise	List of processes the enterprise performs	List of locations where the enterprise operates	List of organizational units	List of business events/ cycles	List of business goals/ strategies
Owner	Entity relationship diagram	Business process model (data-flow diagram)	Logistics network	Organization chart, with roles; security issues	Business master schedule	Business rules
Architect	Data model	Essential Data-flow diagram; application architecture	Distributed system architecture	Human interaction architecture (roles, data access); security requirements	Dependency diagram, timelines	Business rule model
Designer	Data architecture (tables and columns); map to legacy data	System design: structure chart	System architecture (hardware, software types)	User interface; security design	"Control flow" diagram (control structure)	Business rule design
Builder	Data design, physical storage design	Detailed Program Design	Network architecture	Screens, security architecture	Timing definitions	Rule specification in program logic

If you are unfamiliar with the architectural frameworks in general and the Zachman Framework in particular, the following paragraphs describe the views listed in Table 5-2 and tell how the views expressed in the far-left column (the so-called Zachman levels) drive the architecture and design of the systems:

✦ **Planner's view:** The planner's view, simply stated, is the view that tells or confirms to management what business the business is in. Strange as it may sound to us techies, who always know what operating system we support, management often needs to be told, by enterprise analysts, what the business is doing right and what it should not be doing. Remember how AT&T decided to go into computers? That was a mess. For the most part we do not really care what the planner's view advises or how it directs the company because it is up to the owner to translate the whims of management and shareholders into IT and user requirements.

✦ **Owner's view:** This level provides the specific user requirements based on the "thoughts" documented in the user requirements specification, or URS. The thoughts are often transferred to the IT manager or MIS from the users. For example, marketers ask for better mouse traps because the ones they have are operating poorly against the competition. So management take the "thoughts" to MIS or IT to translate the owner's view into specific requirements. This view is ignorant of specific systems or technology but expresses specific needs.

✦ **Architect's view:** This is the level that provides the overall architecture, integration, and interrelationships of the systems and services, traced back to the visions of planners and owners and the URS. At this level, the architect identifies the technology required to meet the needs expressed in the preceding levels and may even provide a certain level of detail. By the time that you are ready to write a design plan, you should have already chosen technologies for review, testing, proof-of-concept, and proof-of-design.

  Based on a design plan, the respective system designers develop design specifications with the level of detail warranted for the systems being reviewed. So this level provides the design plans that identify what specific items are modeled or designed, implemented, integrated, and deployed on Windows 2000 or Windows Server 2003. The design items must be traceable back to user requirements as identified in a formal URS.

✦ **Designer's view:** This level provides the actual design specifications of the systems, functional requirements, functional design, interfaces, system pseudocode, and specifics of how systems are built, tested, validated, and accepted. It is expressed in specific design documents that also contain specifications for hardware and software.

✦ **Builder's view:** This level provides deployment and migration details and describes the necessary steps to implement the design and deploy in the product environment after validation or acceptance. The builder's view is expressed in deployment documents, operational manuals, and failover and fallback procedures, backup and restore plans, and installation, operational, and performance metrics.

Design methodology

The *design methodology* or process begins at the architectural level — the architect's view — and extends down to the design level, or the designer's view. The higher the level, the more abstract are the specifications, and the lower the level, the more detailed are the specifications. Architects define specifications by providing proposed solutions to the customer or to satisfy the user requirements, taking into account all constraints. This level is known as the *defining design*, *initial design*, or *conceptual design* in the design document.

The initial design specifications should be kept as simple and abstract as possible. The user requirement, for example, may be "provide database system," but the architect provides an initial design in which Microsoft SQL Server is chosen for the implementation.

Further elaboration in the design document is achieved through lab testing for proof of concept, testing of systems for functionality, and capability to meet specific user requirements, such as "We want replication between SQL Server systems."

Through elaboration and iteration, a *detailed design* emerges that is eventually taken to the customer for acceptance. Some initial testing and acceptance by the customer may take place until a design specification at the level of *detailed design* is signed off on. Software and hardware vendors need to provide trial or development software long enough for designers to develop a detailed design. After the acceptance of a detailed design or obtaining design approval, designers and builders get the "all systems go" to begin rolling out their creations.

After the acceptance and acquisition of software and hardware, the detailed design document can be handed to an engineer (the builder) who builds the system in the lab. This level is known as the *build and test* level, or the *implement and test* level. The design document should be detailed enough for a fresh engineer to successfully implement the system in a lab environment and ready it for testing and acceptance and then rollout, deployment, and validation, as required.

As a result of testing and formal design qualification (DQ), further design work may prove necessary, especially if a limitation or risk arises that needs urgent addressing at the design level. The designer should also be able to easily enough return to the more abstract levels to explore certain alternatives and paths. (The build and test level must also provide the necessary metrics for validation at the deployment level.)

After testing is signed off on, deployment is scheduled and must follow validation procedures. Figure 5-3 demonstrates this design methodology.

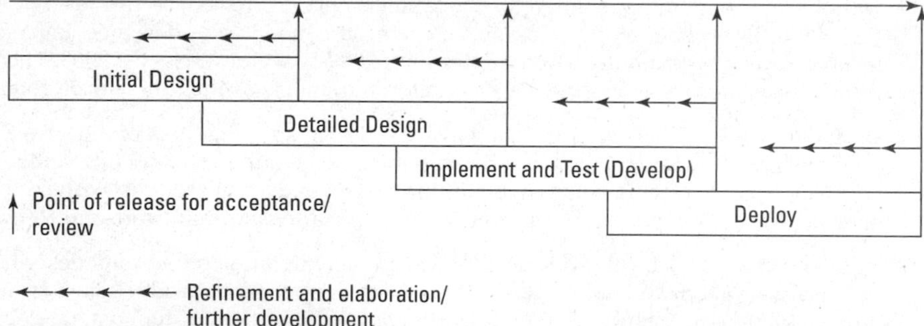

Figure 5-3: Design methodology.

The *detailed design* phase includes many tasks, which are typically listed in a project management schedule by using an application such as Microsoft Project. You need to prove concept on a number of items before a system or service can be said to meet a user requirement or the needs of the stakeholders. This "proof and discovery" stage takes place in your lab.

We use this stage to inspect third-party software that we may invest in, for example, test ways and means to migrate from NT or Windows 2000 to .NET Server, reaffirm assumptions and hardware and software choices, and consider the best options for deployment, disaster recovery, and so on. We especially take into consideration the factors that lurk in the People, Time, and Motivation columns of the Zachman matrix.

Design content or specifications for the systems and services that you develop include the following:

✦ Data, function, network, time, and interface design

✦ Motivation criteria

✦ Proof of design summaries

✦ Identification of system failure points and recovery criteria

✦ Risk-management issues

The design phase begins on acceptance by the client of the URS.

Design plan

If you sit down to design and develop more that a simple system, such as a whole network stuffed with services such as Systems Management Server, Exchange 2000, and .NET Server, a design roadmap helps. Such a roadmap typically exists in the form of a governing document known simply as a *design plan*.

Design plans normally also list the various approaches that you intend to take in your architecture and design methodology. Following is a short list of items that we put into our own design plans:

✦ Choice of architectural framework or approach, such as the Zachman Framework.

✦ Design methodology, such as the System Development Life Cycle model, Rational Unified Process (RUP), and so on.

✦ Risk-management approach.

✦ Documentation lists and various documentation styles.

Validation

Validation is a very complex subject, and we only touch on it in this book. If you work for IT departments that belong to government or federally regulated companies, you have your hands full with the formal validation process.

Validation is the process of ensuring that the production systems meet user requirements and qualify, under audit, to be deployed. Auditing usually consists of performing the formal Installation Qualification, Operational Qualification, and Performance Qualification (IQ, OQ, and PQ, respectively).

Tinkering in the labs

The following sections describe the components of Phase 2, which, in a sense, are launched in Phase 1. You no doubt managed to secure some space at the office or perhaps the company penthouse and then began tinkering around with Windows Server 2003 on some old beat-up Pentiums. If you have not touched the CD that comes with it yet, you are not ready to begin lab work. You should read the other chapters in the part and the Windows 2003 documentation before you start any lab work, but please read on for reference only.

Chapter 6, where you learn about installing Windows Server 2003, also caters to the ramp-up phase, the lab phase, and the pilot phase.

You cannot consider yourself ready to begin designing and testing until you have logged a hundred or more hours of study. And even then, not until you have installed role servers at least ten times, installed and trashed Active Directory at least eight times, screamed at the project manager, created boot disks, cut unattended install CDs, restored ghosted images, and so on . . . all dozens of times.

The how-to material and extensive Help files on Windows 2003 have a point of diminishing return. You can't read all the information, but you must start somewhere. The number of document pages at Microsoft covering Windows 2003 and collateral technologies, such as Windows XP and Windows 2000, runs into the millions and would take you much more than a year to read. Baptism by fire, as the saying goes, makes a good network and Windows Server 2003 administrator.

Creating the network infrastructure plan

Before you begin laying out the lab, bring in a huge white board and begin sketching up the topology and network infrastructure that you plan to create in the lab. The infrastructure may contain elements similar to the plan that we created in our labs. You can use our plan as a guideline. It contains the following elements:

- A domain and network representing our Active Directory root domain or namespace placeholder. In this case, we called this domain `Latinaccents` (see Chapters 8, 9, and 10).
- The `Latinaccents` domain and segment representing HQ, where most of our executive accounts and support staff live.
- The various hubs on the world-wide Active Directory forest. The hubs are connected with a 256-Kbps frame-relay network, provided by AT&T.

You may notice that our forest, `Latinaccents.biz`, currently goes down two levels. In other words, the forest currently comprises two domains, the root and a child. To recap: We have a root domain, or namespace placeholder, which we finally called `Latinaccents`, and a child domain called HQ.LATINACCENTS.BIZ (see Chapter 10).

Latinaccents.biz

In the examples given throughout this book, Latin Accents (the forest) contains four hubs. In the `Latinaccents.biz` domain, we have DNS servers in the various hubs, WINS servers, DHCP servers, and application servers running Terminal Services in application mode. We also installed RAS servers, VPN servers, and Exchange servers. Print servers were installed on file servers (a typical practice). Printers were connected to the network by using Lantronix and HP JetDirect printer servers that are deployed out at each printers location in the office.

Clients include Windows 2000 Professional and Windows XP Professional. We also have Windows NT 4.0 Servers in the domain to test connecting the NT 4.0 server to the Windows Server 2003 and to test the capability of the Windows NT 4.0 server to obtain WINS information, name services, and account privileges from the Windows 2003 network.

HQ-Latinaccents.biz

The HQ.Latinaccents.biz network contains the domain controller for Latin Accents and a DNS server. It also contains WINS, DHCP, and a RAS server for the low-bandwidth links. The RAS server is also multihomed to provide a second test site for network address translation. We also installed several Windows XP Professional clients to test access to network resources and group policy. The domain is a native-mode domain.

Setting up the lab

Your first task, if you are starting a lab from scratch, is to secure your lab and make sure that you can keep intruders out. If you cannot secure it behind closed doors and you must set it up in the corner of an open-plan office, put up a sign warning unauthorized personnel to stay out.

Creating the network

Before you bring servers into the lab, you first need to install the network. Lay down your hubs, routers, switches, network analyses, and network emulation and simulation tools according to the topological and network infrastructure plan that you develop. The mini network infrastructure that you create should represent, or clone, as far as possible the intranet in which you are eventually going to deploy.

To install Active Directory, you need to plug your domain controller machine into a hub even if no one else is on the network yet. Windows 2003 refuses to install Active Directory and promote the machine if the NIC is deactivated and you have no network. If you encounter the error, do not cancel the setup; just click back and install the hub and plug in the NIC cable. Windows 2003 sees the network automatically and switches on the NIC. If you don't have a NIC installed, Chapter 6 describes the installation process in more detail.

List the number of servers that you plan to install in the lab and then count the number of clients that you plan to test in the lab. If you are going to install about 24 machines, you need hubs with more than 48-port capacity. Depending on the servers that you are testing on, you may need at least three network drops per server. The three drops would typically cater to two network cards and a remote diagnostic component, such as HP's *Remote Insight Board*, otherwise known as a *RIB*.

If you are testing or interconnecting multiple domains, you need more than one hub for each new subnet. These hubs then cater to network equipment such as routers and gateways and give you enough room to expand. Remember that you may need to multi-home machines and make them network routers to obtain the desired network simulation. In your lab, you could dedicate Windows 2000 to do the job for you.

One good idea is to invest in network simulation tools to mirror your WAN and the interconnection topology between sites. If you need to test replication between domain controllers, DNS servers, and WINS, but you cannot afford a network simulator (which typically run about $30,000) and do not have access to a multisite network, consider setting up two networks and then connecting them by using RRAS-based routers.

If you use two 56-Kbps modems (which should be the same brand), such as two 3COM-US Robotics V.90 modems, you can simulate a 56-Kbps DDS frame-relay circuit, which is sufficient to test replication between the domain controllers (because it really gives you only about 36 Kbps). The great feature of modems is that you can force them down to 19 Kbps to simulate a busy network.

You have a number of ways to set up a test WAN. You can create another lab at a remote office and use your existing network infrastructure. Or, if you cannot afford to intrude on business or production traffic, you can connect the two sites directly or via a Virtual Private Network (VPN) across the Internet. The latter requires you to test VPN solutions, however, so that is a consideration. But splitting the lab over two or more locations is not ideal, because you lose some control of your test environment. You need to be present on two or more networks at the same time so that you can monitor what is going on and document your observations.

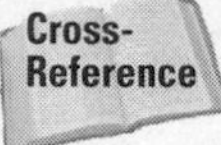

See Chapter 18 for information on VPNs.

An inexpensive solution is to invest in T1 or analog telephone-circuit simulators. We used equipment made by Teltone Corporation (at `www.teltone.com`), a company based in Bothell, Washington. By using this equipment, we could get one RAS server to dial the other RAS server and set up a link of 36 Kbps between the two networks (two 56-Kbps modems).

Using identical modems on each network (one dials, the other answers) is important to obtain the maximum bandwidth. Later, you can throttle the bandwidth by forcing either of the two modems to V34 or lower. The network diagram is as shown in Figure 5-4.

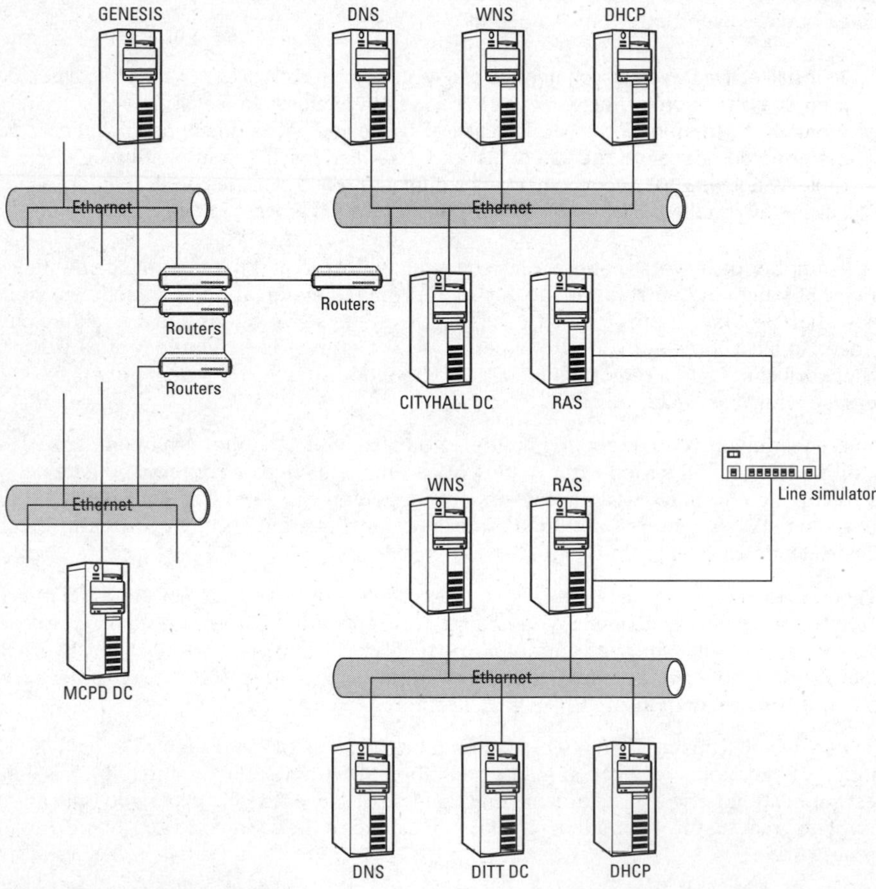

Figure 5-4: Network diagram for the lab.

Setting up two RAS servers in this fashion serves several purposes, as the following list describes:

✦ You get experience in setting up RAS and routing services.

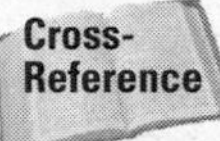

See Chapters 15 and 18 for a full description of setting up demand-dial routers by using Windows 2000 or Windows Server 2003s.)

✦ You get experience in setting up Network Address Translation (NAT), which is covered in Chapter 15.

✦ You get experience in multi-homing Windows 2003 servers and routing IP between the networks.

✦ You can test replication between your domain controller, DNS, and WINS partners.

✦ You can test user logons to domains in remote networks.

✦ You get to do some nifty TCP/IP exercises (subnetting, routing, addressing, and translation).

To set up a RAS and routing server, you need to install Windows Server 2003 on two machines and enable the Routing and Remote Access Service on both (RRAS). Servers need to be multi-homed, and you need to configure them to route IP between the NICs in each server. This setup is as shown in Figure 5-5.

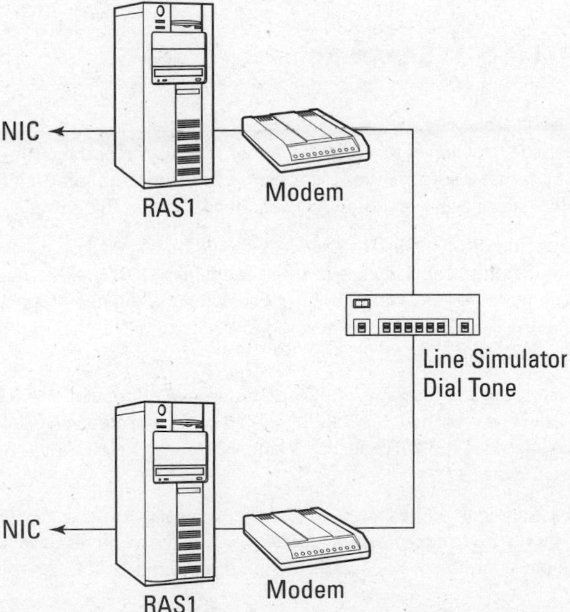

Figure 5-5: Configuring RAS servers to simulate a WAN.

If you have *Token Ring* (*TR*) environments, you need to test that in the lab as well, so if you are adding TR interface cards to the RAS servers as well saves time. (You need to put a TR card in only one machine really — the RAS-Router.) The object of putting a TR card in the machine is to test the TR segment (access to the domain controller) and to investigate transitioning the TR network to Ethernet.

To cheaply and effectively simulate a 500-Kbps T1 WAN, you can set up RRAS routers connected by a fast parallel cable. Chapter 18, which covers remote access, takes you through the ropes of setting up demand-dial routing by using modems and how to simulate a wide area network by using RRAS and a parallel cable.

Installing servers and services

Assuming that you have ramped up on theory, Table 5-3 lists the servers and services that you are advised to install in the lab. (Chapter 6 discusses the steps to installing some of these servers.) You can install many services on one server, but if you can afford to do so, you should install them on separate servers in the lab for several reasons. First, the more times that you install a server, the better you become at the process. Second, you may screw up a server big time, only to lose a good domain controller in the process. And third, at some point, you must install the service on a dedicated role server.

Another point about domain controllers: To experience Active Directory in full throttle, you should try to install as many domain controllers as you can, across root and child domains and between simulated hub and child sites. This process gets you experience not only in installing peer domain controllers across the WAN, but also in additional domains.

Table 5-3: Server Roles

Role	*Description*
DC	The domain controller, the host server for Active Directory. We recommend that this server be dedicated to directory services (flexible for small domains) and mirrored with replication partners for redundancy (see Chapter 10 for health tips for this server).
DNS	The *Domain Name System* (DNS) server. DNS services should be installed on a dedicated server (although this is also flexible in small companies). DNS servers should be partnered with secondary servers in large or busy deployments. You need to install only one DNS server in the lab. Chapter 17 is devoted to DNS and WINS. DNS can be installed on your DC.
WINS	The WINS server, which is used to resolve NetBIOS names into IP addresses. WINS can be installed on the DNS server for the lab work but should be a dedicated server on busy or large intranets, because the WINS service channels processor cycles away from directory services (see Chapter 17).
DHCP	The DHCP server for assigning IP address leases. You can also install this service to the DNS/WINS server. It should be installed on a separate machine, however, especially on a busy network. Please pay attention to the specific health tips offered for this server in Chapter 6.
IIS	The Internet Information Server, or IIS 6.0, that ships part-and-parcel with Windows Server 2003 (see Chapter 29). This server provides both Web and FTP services to the intranet and is an extremely powerful Internet server. IIS should most definitely be set up on a dedicated server, even in the lab, where it can be used as a public relations tool for the project.

Role	Description
Print	This server is configured specifically to provide logical printers to the network and to cater to queues and print spools. See Chapter 29, which is dedicated to print services.
File	This server is configured for advanced file services and storage (and it can also be the storage server); you can set it up for hierarchical storage management (HSM), however, and as a general file server for the enterprise. This server is usually configured for RAID-0 or RAID-5 arrays, failover and cluster arrangements, to provide high availability of file services to all users. In busy environments, this server should be dedicated, mirrored, or clustered, running on the Windows 2003 Advanced Server operating system.
Media	This server provides media streaming services to the network. It should be a dedicated server.
Telephony	This server is dedicated to telephony services – in other words, services that make full use of the Telephony API (TAPI). You typically dedicate this server to messaging, faxing, voice-over-IP (in tandem with media streaming services), and telephony services (such as switching, dial-tone access, and so on).
Cluster	Cluster servers can be built only on Windows 2003 Enterprise Server or the Data Center server. Setting up and running clusters in the lab is also essential, as is experimenting with network load balancing. Many of the services discussed in this book find their way into high-availability requirement situations, which require clustering or other methods of failover and load balancing, especially application servers. See Chapter 25, which covers high-availability solutions.
Database	This server can be set up to cater to database environments such as SQL Server .NET and others. You do not need to install anything special, but we suggest architecture and configuration for base requirements of database servers in Chapter 6.
MAIL	The server can be set up to route and forward e-mail. See Chapter 29 for information on setting up SMTP services.
.NET Server	Windows Server 2003 is the base or host operating system for all Microsoft .NET Server products, such as Exchange, SQL Server, SMS, SNA, and so on.
RIS	RIS is the service that performs remote installation of WindowsXP. It should be set up as a dedicated member server. We discuss options for RIS server installation in Chapter 6.
Backup	A backup server is dedicated to backing up other servers and storage units over the network and HSM or Dfs systems (see Chapters 19 through 21, respectively).
Application	The application servers are usually installed as dedicated member servers. They include component servers, Terminal Services, application servers, indexing, and message queuing services. Terminal Services installation is discussed in Chapters 6 and 30.
Certificate	Certificate services supply X.509 digital certificates for authentication. This is how you identify users on a nonsecure connection, such as the Internet. It is also used to secure communications.
License	The license server was created to ensure compliance with Microsoft licensing requirements. It is used for services such as Terminal Services.
Web server	The Web server is used for standalone Web services.

The number of services that are available from Microsoft and third parties is exhaustive. Depending on the application and the environment (number of users, networking, e-commerce, and so on), you can perhaps get away with installing multiple services on one server. Deploying Terminal Services to a small office of, say, five people, for example, and also using the same server for Active Directory is feasible. Other services, no matter the size of the company, require dedicated servers. A sophisticated firewall package is a good example. This topic is further discussed in Chapter 7.

The first server to install in the lab is the root domain controller. Begin installing Active Directory on this server only after you install everything that you need on this machine and the machine is stable. You do not touch the root host system again other than to install networking services, such as DNS, and to manage senior administrator accounts. (See Chapters 10 and 11 for detailed information on installing the domain controllers.)

After the domain controller is installed and you promote it to host Active Directory, you can begin setting up your administrator group and machine accounts. Consult Chapter 13 for information on setting up users and groups and Chapter 10 for specifics regarding installation of Active Directory.

The next server to install is the DNS server and then DHCP, WINS, and so on. The flow charts in Figure 5-6 suggest the logical progression of installing these services or servers. Remember that, as long as you are setting up a Windows 2003 domain, you first need a domain controller before you do anything else. However, Active Directory cannot function without DNS and if you do not already have a DNS server installed on the network the process of promoting a domain controller installs a DNS server on the DC. WINS, RAS and PKI are options and are not required for creation of a domain.

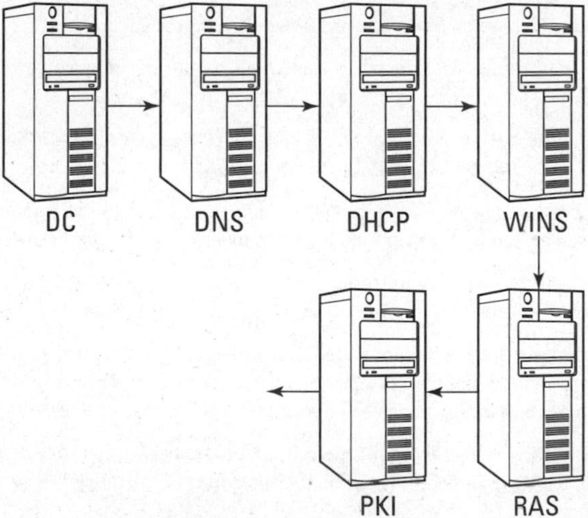

Figure 5-6: Setting up servers in the lab.

Lab-management pointers

The reason that you set up a lab in the first place is so that you can test Windows 2003 without risking production systems. It is also a place to test design and proof of concept on a number of items. The lab in every way simulates the real thing, however, and should easily be convertible to a production environment. Our Latinaccents lab, for example, contained more equipment than most small businesses ever need. And just because it is a lab does not mean that you should not treat it as if it *is* a production network in full throttle. Consider the guidelines in the following sections.

Lab isolation and security

The lab must be a sandbox. In other words, keep it off the corporate network and completely isolated. By isolating the lab, you are not only protecting production systems from anything unforeseen, but you are also protecting the lab from network intruders.

A good example of why isolation is important: Back in July 1999, while we were still testing the Windows 2000 betas, eager beavers in the IT department installed Professional on the network and adopted it as their new desktops. (It is very hard to resist.) Next day, the help-desk database crashed, and for two days, we sat with the vendors trying to figure out what was chewing up our Btrieve database files. After a lengthy process of elimination, the culprit turned out to be Windows 2000. We reported the problem to Microsoft, and new support was added by the next beta. After that, we made sure that no test systems were connected to the production networks. The fiasco cost us a lot of time and affected more people than we cared to know about in more than 25 U.S. cities, because it almost shut down the call center.

Keeping people who are not part of the lab team out of the lab and off the test network is also very important. This may prove very difficult to do in an open-plan office where you have taken over a cube that anyone can walk into. In such a case, run screen savers that lock access to the computers if they are left alone for a few minutes.

Why is security for the lab so important? Your lab should be treated in the same way that you treat a medical test laboratory. If someone does something unauthorized and it causes a problem, how are you going to work out what caused the problem? If a server crashes, you could spend days trying to replicate the problem and determining the cause.

Documentation and change control

Documenting everything that gets done in the lab is also highly important. Make all members keep journals and have them write down everything that they do. Deploy change-control management (see Chapter 14) and documentation software in the lab so that information is sensibly recorded. One or two people should be charged with keeping the documentation up to date. If members of your team do not update their documentation or forget to write down the steps taken to execute their test and the results, make them redo it.

Change control is a very important IT discipline to extend to the lab. For starters, make all the tests that you intend to run separate projects. If you are testing group policy, create a project and call it Group Policy Test (or Group Policy Security Test). List all the items that you plan to test, determine how you are going to test, document the results, and manage the whole project in project-management software, such as Microsoft Project.

As the team determines each project, list it in change control and have everyone sign off the change-control documentation. Change control keeps everyone on the same page. It is also key in determining the cause of problems and working back to restore a previously working condition. (The subject is discussed with Group Policy in Chapter 14.)

Deciding what to test

You cannot test everything that Windows 2003 offers, so you must decide what is important to test for the environment that you are planning to convert or integrate. Testing things that Microsoft and thousands of other beta testers have already tested does not make sense, unless you are on the beta program or learning about something specific.

One of the prime objectives of the corporate lab is to test how well Windows Server 2003 behaves in a production NT environment or how Windows 2000 behaves on a Windows 2003 domain.

You have two key segments to evaluate: *applications and processes* and *domain-wide integration*. Applications testing is usually focused on the server; you need to test how a particular application functions in the Windows Server 2003 environment. One of the things that we tested, for example, was an AS400-based process that needs to open an FTP session to the server and copy and retrieve files from it several times a day. We also test-ran batch files by using the `AT` command-line utility to run a process that performs unattended transfers of data to another network.

We also used our lab to test automated and unattended installations, especially on test Windows NT servers, to see how they would fare after upgrading them.

Domain-wide integration testing concerns how the new server, or *domain controller*, behaves on the network. We tested how NT and other legacy systems fared resolving to the new DNS, for example, or whether any problems arise in resolving NetBIOS names with the new WINS and whether the DHCP clients could obtain IP address leases.

We also tested Windows 9*x* clients logging into network shares and how NTFS 4.0 systems and NTFS 5.0 systems co-exist.

Whenever we tested various flavors of Unix with Windows 2003, we got mixed results. If we removed permissions from a file, for example, Corel Linux reported that a file it was trying access was "corrupted." Another version of Unix reported that the file no longer existed. These are not ideal messages to send to sensitive users. Unix is like a box of chocolates . . .

Table 5-4 provides a collection of test projects to get you started.

Table 5-4: Typical Test Projects

Aspect	***Components***
Active Directory	Logical domain structure, OU design, trusts, groups, publishing, Single Sign-On (SSO) (see Chapters 2, 8).
Active Directory	Physical domain structure, sites, replication (see Chapters 2, 9).
DNS	DNS namespace, zone replication, WINS integration, DHCP integration, standard replication, domain-controller replication (see Chapters 7, 17).
DHCP	DNS integration, client access (see Chapters 15, 16, and 17).
WINS	WINS replication, client access, DNS integration (see Chapters 15, 16, and 17).
Security	SSO, one-way trusts, Kerberos, NTLM, file systems, user access, Active Directory, RAS, IPSec, Encryption, Registry, Auditing (see Chapters 3, 9).
File Systems and Storage	Mount points, Dfs, HSM, Encryption, RSS (see Chapters 26, 27).
Workspace Management	Policies and change control (see Chapter 14).
Upgrading/ Converting NT	Converting PDC, BDC, cloning (see Chapters 5, 7, and 9).

Establishing Sanity Checks

You must always establish milestones and checkpoints along the way to take sanity checks, establish proof-of-concept and to obtain approval from reviewers. Although we have made sanity checks a component of Phase 3, which we described in the section "Implementing in phases," earlier in this chapter, sanity checks should start at the beginning of the project. After you have listed all the tests that you plan to perform, you can establish checkpoints after each step or after each project or group of projects. The sanity checks enable you and the team time to check in and determine progress made, areas that need to be revised, tests that need to be redone, new directions to take, and other directions to cancel.

Divide the entire lab phase into major checkpoints, enabling everyone to report in, discuss and determine the next steps, and then to take R&R for a few days. The chart in Figure 5-7 is an example of how the Latinaccents lab phase was divided up.

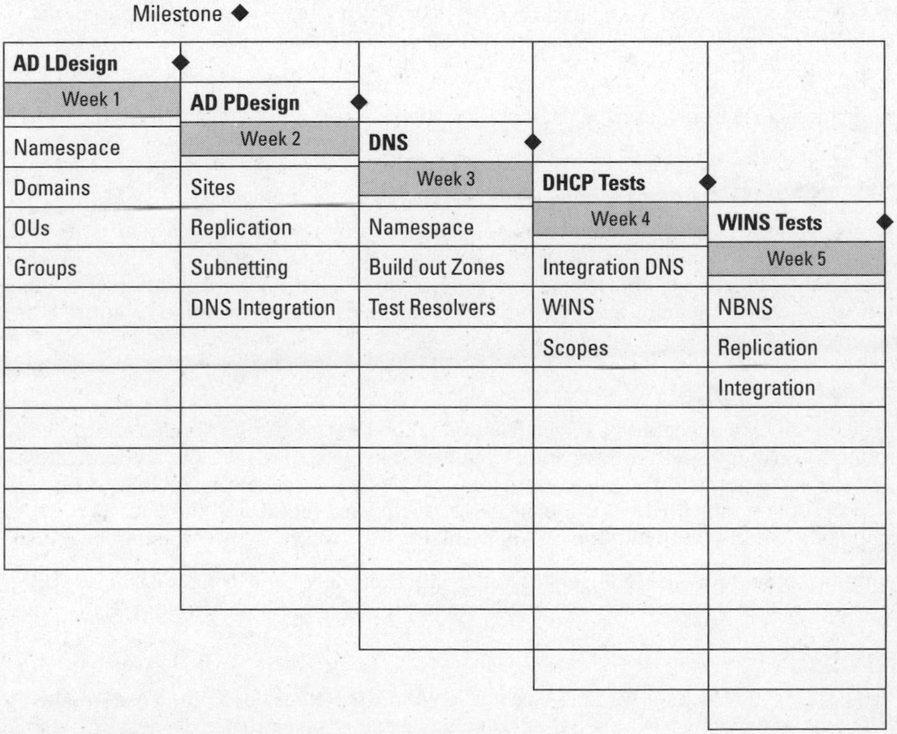

Milestone ◆

AD LDesign ◆	**AD PDesign** ◆	**DNS** ◆	**DHCP Tests** ◆	**WINS Tests** ◆
Week 1	Week 2	Week 3	Week 4	Week 5
Namespace	Sites	Namespace	Integration DNS	NBNS
Domains	Replication	Build out Zones	WINS	Replication
OUs	Subnetting	Test Resolvers	Scopes	Integration
Groups	DNS Integration			

Figure 5-7: Lab chart for Project Latinaccents.

Running Pilot Projects

The whole idea of the lab phase is to provide you with a controlled, isolated environment in which to test systems and applications that need to be deployed into production environments, and to assess risks.

The lab projects need to be completed and operating with all the parameters that would be expected in the production environment. Only after the lab phase project is considered complete can you promote it out of the lab or hand it over to the pilot-project team, which handles Phase 4. If you have any doubts about the success of a lab-phase project, you cannot hand it over to the pilot-project team.

The pilot phase enables you to place new or changed systems into a controlled and monitored production environment. Starting the pilot phase with only one pilot project is probably a good idea. Naturally, you have many different projects evaluating different things, but in the beginning, you should try and focus on one important or pivotal pilot.

Following are several items that need to be considered in a pilot project:

- Pilot scope
- Pilot objectives and timelines
- Participants or users
- Disaster recovery
- Communication

The following sections describe each of these items.

Pilot scope

The *scope* of the pilot determines how much and what you intend to place into the production environment. For now, examine two pilots: Latinaccents pilot and HQ. Both involved testing with the objective of deploying Windows Server 2003 into live production environments. In the case of HQ, the pilot was key to the company's existence, because its entire IT infrastructure had reached the end of its life.

Latinaccents pilot

The scope of Latinaccents was the installation of the `Latinaccents` domain controller into a production Windows NT network and to enable a select group of users to authenticate to the `Latinaccents` domain. The pilot tested the `Latinaccents` domain's capability to establish a one-way (out) trust with the NT domain. It also tested and monitored the `Latinaccents` users, paying particular attention to the capability of the users to access their resources as usual.

In addition, the pilot enabled users to log in with their new User Principal Names (UPNs) from anywhere and to access resources published in the `Latinaccents` directory.

HQ pilot

The scope of the HQ pilot was to place a role Windows Server 2003 into a NetWare environment, which, by using NetWare Services, masqueraded as a NetWare file server. Users in the HQ pilot continued to use legacy MS-DOS Database clients to access an insurance application that resided on the NetWare server. The users logged in to the NetWare server and thus gained access to executables, the databases, and the NetWare print-server services.

The databases currently installed on the NetWare volumes is backed up and moved to the Windows Server 2003. Phase 1 of this pilot enables the users to access the databases on the Windows Server 2003.

Pilot objectives

The *objectives* should be clear and stated in the pilot documentation. The pilot group members also need to fully understand the reason for the pilot and what is required of them during the pilot phase. Determining how long the pilot is to remain in force and the progression of one phase of the pilot to another is also necessary.

Latinaccents pilot objectives

The objectives of the Latinaccents pilot are as follows:

- ✦ To ensure that the domain controller works correctly in the NT domain environment.
- ✦ That users can consistently log on to the `Latinaccents` domain.
- ✦ That users can gain access to resources in the NT domain.
- ✦ That the trust relationship between the Windows 2003 domain and the NT domain works as expected.
- ✦ That using the UPN to log in does not cause any unexpected events to take place either on the `Latinaccents` domain or on the NT domain.

Additional objectives for Latinaccents could also be monitoring how users adapt to using the UPN, assisting them with peculiarities of Windows 2003, and learning how to support them in the process. We also used the pilot to test Remote Installation Services.

HQ pilot objectives

The objectives of the HQ pilot are as follows:

- ✦ That the Windows Server 2003 behaves in a NetWare environment, using IPX as the only protocol.
- ✦ That accessing the databases on a Windows Server 2003 is possible, even though the server is disguised as a NetWare server to the application in the client workspace.
- ✦ To reduce dependency on the NetWare-based volume for storage needs and to eventually begin a conversion of the applications to the Windows Server 2003.

Notice that the objectives of the HQ pilot and the nature of the pilot suggest that much of what was taking place in the Pilot phase should have been signed off on in the lab phase. It was, to some extent. The pilot phase enabled us to test continually in a controlled live environment with users. The databases were not moved to the Windows Server 2003 in the production environment until the move was tested in the lab with a backup of the databases.

Pilot users

You should use experienced users as far as possible in the pilot phase. With Latinaccents, we decided to test by using members of our own IT team. These people appreciated the scope and objectives of our pilot and were more-than-willing participants. We asked them to note problems, and we received a lot of help. Sometimes, however, they caused a few problems for us by being overly inquisitive.

In the HQ pilot, the users were at first oblivious to the fact that the databases were no longer on the original server. Although the users were presented with the scope and objectives of the pilot, they were not in the same camp as our willing Latinaccents users who were trained network administrators and support personnel. HQ users had a job to do and were concerned about finishing on time and were loath to be interrupted with network issues and training. In later phases, the HQ users were introduced to Terminal Services, which was a very delicate phase because they were being converted from DOS to Windows 2003 (a leapfrog over technology that spanned more than a decade).

Disaster recovery

You need a *disaster-recovery plan* with every pilot project. The disaster-recovery plan should explicitly detail the steps to take in the event that a problem occurs that requires rollback. In the case of Latinaccents, the disaster-recovery procedures involved the clients logging on to the NT domain with their old accounts. In HQ, it was a little more complex. In fact, we encountered a disaster shortly after the database move.

By using backups that we were taking of the new databases on the Windows 2003 server (employing the Backup utility on the Windows 2003 server), we could restore the database tables to the NetWare volume (on the NetWare server). The application kicked in, and the users could continue working after a two-hour break. We then proceeded to compare the two volumes and found a file that, for some reason, had not been copied along with the rest of the databases. (It may have been locked at the time.) We performed the move again, and the pilot continued forward.

Communication

Keep users and all pilot participants constantly informed of the progress of the pilot, the progression along the timeline given, and the expectations of all parties. Also provide feedback on how problems were resolved and the current status of the pilot.

Operating System Conversion

You are almost home. The conversion phase (Phase 5) is where rollout of your solutions begins. Conversion can start only after all problems encountered in the pilot project are ironed out.

By using documentation culled from the pilot phase, you can inform the new users, via e-mail, live conference, or conference calls, of the conversion and what is expected of them.

The conversion phase should contain the following elements:

✦ **Introduction to the conversion project:** Get all your users together and introduce them to the conversion project. You are telling them why they were chosen for conversion and so on.

✦ **Training:** Users need to be grouped into teams and trained on the new systems. For our HQ users, the learning curve was extremely steep. Users had never clicked a mouse before and were now expected to use e-mail and applications such as Microsoft Word.

✦ **Support:** The help-desk or support staff should be one of the first (if not the first) to be converted to any new systems or applications. After their training, you rely on them to assist newly converted users with problems. Support staff should have access to documentation and the steps taken to resolve problems all the way back to the lab phase.

✦ **Feedback and communication:** Users should be encouraged to report problems encountered and to make suggestions to the conversion team.

✦ **Disaster recovery and change control:** Ensure that change-control protocols are strictly adhered to, especially if your conversion project is to extend to users in far-off remote sites. Continually review disaster recovery (which you should be doing anyway) and keep support staff, and conversion, pilot, and lab people on their toes. You never know when a very tricky problem must be sent all the way back to the lab phase for a resolution.

You have no conclusion to implementation. New projects, lab work, pilots, and so on, need to be conducted all the time. Get ready for the next service pack.

Coming to Grips with Windows Server 2003

You may not be ready for Windows Server 2003 for any number of reasons. You also may not be in a position to set up a lab to test variations in deployment and conversion. Does this mean that you must sit around and do nothing? No. You can still do a lot, especially if you have an existing investment in Windows NT, to prepare you for the future — be it in two months, ten months, or over the next two years.

Consider the following steps to migration:

✦ Clean up your NT domains.

✦ Standardize on TCP/IP.

✦ Deploy DHCP.

✦ Deploy WINS .NET.

✦ Deploy DNS.

The following sections provide details on each option.

Clean up your old NT domains

The smaller the company, the smaller is the domain — and the easier it is to upgrade. The tools are available in the Windows Server 2003 Resource Kit, and they are discussed in Chapter 6 and Chapter 10.

If you are managing domains in a large company, however, the amount of domains that you have and the complexity of the structure of these domains, as well as the size of them, determine how risky the conversion is . . . after it finally must come. We have found that converting a domain of a thousand or more accounts (and we did this several times in the lab) is easily handled by Windows 2003. The problem arises in the restructuring that must take place after all the accounts are imported. In many cases, you may be better off starting from scratch. We deal with more of this in Chapters 7 and 10.

Clean up account domains

You can start cleaning up account domains now, even before you have a final decision on testing and investing in Windows 2003. Get rid of disabled or decommissioned accounts. You don't need to import them into Active Directory. By the way, Active Directory accounts contain much more information and thus can become untidy much more quickly than Windows NT directories can. If your housekeeping (or housekeeper) left a lot to be desired in the NT domain, start thinking replacement now.

Consolidate domains

Clean up your resource domains. If you have many resource domains, investigate consolidating them into one domain. And investigate not converting your resource domains and devising a plan to decommission them before the conversion to Windows 2003. Perhaps you are going to replace a lot of equipment and trying to convert these old domains would make no sense.

Trusts

Reduce the amount of manually configured trusts. Such trusts in Windows 2003 are for domains that are in other forests, which usually belong to other companies, partners, and associates. In Windows NT, trusts needed to be created between siblings, usually between resource and account domains. This is not the case with Windows 2003, and converting domains with trust relationships requires care.

User IDs

Start analyzing your user IDs. Windows 2003 user IDs can also be e-mail addresses. `Jshapiro` on the Latinaccents domain is also `jshapiro@latinaccents.biz`, which anyone who sends e-mail on the Internet is familiar with. But `js4po12` at Latinaccents `MCITY` does not make a good e-mail address . . . `js4po12@latinaccents.biz` is hard to remember. Keeping to one User Principal Name (UPN) as the universal sign-on makes life easier for everyone. UPN-type IDs are also easier to convert in an upgrade effort.

Stay ahead in the service-pack game

Windows NT gets a little antsy if it has only Service Pack 3 or lower and Windows 2003 arrives on the network. The best thing that you can do to cater to NT's inferiority complex is to upgrade to the latest stable service pack as soon as possible. For the record, Windows NT needs to be upgraded to Service Pack 5 at a minimum before it can be considered "educated" enough to talk to Windows 2003.

Keep track of the new features that are coming out in the service packs for Windows 2000, too; they are not only fixes for past infractions, but they may also contain important Windows 2003 compatibility features.

Standardize on TCP/IP

No matter the size of your network, you need to plan a wholesale conversion to TCP/IP in everything that you do. Windows 2003 without TCP/IP is like an eagle in a cage. As long as you maintain a hodge-podge of network protocols, such as IPX/SPX, NetBEUI, NWLink, AppleTalk, and the like, you cannot convert to a native-mode domain.

Besides the features of the native domain, maintaining several protocols makes for more network management, slower applications (the overhead of supporting more multiple protocols on the network), more opportunities to breach security, and the introduction of viruses, bugs, and so on.

Not only should TCP/IP be the network protocol of choice, but your applications should also be supporting it from one end of its stack to another. Begin binding the TCP/IP protocol to all network interfaces and start planning the logical design of a TCP/IP network if you have not already started doing so.

Take inventory of software and hardware that does not function on a TCP/IP network and devise the necessary plans to begin phasing them out. Work toward an end of systems' or applications' life dates for everything that does not support TCP/IP, just as you did with your Y2K systems and applications. In other words, standardize on TCP/IP and make it policy.

If you still need legacy applications that require support of the NetBIOS API, SNA, IPX, and so on, you obviously still need to support protocols, at least at the network topological level — that is, on routers, interface cards, and so on. That does not, however, mean that you are required to support these protocols on the Windows network infrastructure unless you still have a huge investment in legacy Windows operating systems and applications or in operating systems such as NetWare (prior to version 5.0).

We have small clients (four PCs) to large clients (1,000+ computers) beginning wholesale conversion to TCP/IP. The smaller the clients, the easier their conversions are to Windows 2003 on TCP/IP.

As for NetBIOS support, you just must use common sense. As soon as all NetBIOS-dependant applications and operating systems are shut down, you can end your reliance on the API and begin to plot the end of life for your WINS services. The writing is on the wall for NetBIOS, so if you are planning development that perpetuates the API on your systems, you are placing your bets on the wrong horse.

Deploy DHCP

The larger the network, the more important it is to deploy dynamic IP address assignment. So if you have not yet deployed DHCP, now is the time to start. Rather than invest in Windows NT DHCP, consider a Windows 2003 role DHCP server. Not only is it easier to manage than Windows NT DHCP, but it also gets you started in using the Microsoft Management Console, which is pervasive in Windows 2003. You really get to use MMC in Windows NT only with BackOffice products such as SNA Server and IIS.

Deploy WINS .NET

If you are dropping NetBEUI, you need to deploy WINS so that NetBIOS clients can resolve IP addresses to NetBIOS host names. If you already have a WINS presence, consider deploying a role Windows 2003 WINS server. It is not only easier to manage than the older versions, but it also has a lot of new features that make management a lot less troublesome.

Deploy DNS

Many companies do not use DNS, but they must do so whenever they start thinking about Windows 2003. If you are in such a position, deploy Windows 2003 Dynamic DNS (DDNS) on a role server (discussed in Chapter 15). If you support intranet-based Web and FTP servers, that is all the more reason to begin converting these servers to Windows 2003 role servers.

Summary

This chapter provides an overview of the key planning steps to deploying Windows Server 2003 as soon as possible.

We first discuss the steps involved in putting together a phased implementation plan. Our plan consists of several phases — essentially labs, pilot projects, and conversion. We also advise you to study as much documentation on the technology as possible before testing and deployment. A good example of understanding the technology is understanding that Windows Server 2003-DNS, Windows Server 2003-WINS, and Windows Server 2003-DHCP are ideal role servers to install in the existing environment, whether it's Windows NT or something else . . . and how to integrate them. Only after you know what you are dealing with can you move forward and test key solutions.

One of the prime objectives of the corporate lab, for example, is to test how well Windows Server 2003 behaves in a production NT environment or how NT behaves on a Windows 2003 domain. But just installing the server and watching it sit on the network serves little purpose. You need to devise specific experiments that test the new technology that you have learned about with applications and technology that you currently have in place.

After the lab phase, you need to roll out a pilot project, which gives you the capability to test your solutions in a controlled production environment. And if you are not ready yet to test or deploy Windows 2003, now is the time to get your Windows NT infrastructure in shape so that your conversion is a lot easier whenever it must come.

Installing Windows Server 2003

In This Chapter

Going through the hardware checklist

Understanding role server configuration

Installing from boot disks

Installing from the command line

Installing over the network

Understanding the boot file

This chapter reviews the installation of Windows Server 2003. It discusses a number of hardware configurations and setup options and reviews potential obstacles. Several recipes are discussed in this chapter; and most of them are using minimum hardware requirements; keep that in mind when ordering your server. We also prepare you for a fresh install or upgrade with many different server configurations. This chapter also helps you prepare for any troubleshooting issues that you may need to deal with for a successful installation. Several other topics such as SQL Server, ASP, IIS, and Exchange are covered to help you understand how they are incorporated into Windows Server 2003.

Installation and Configuration Strategy

If you have read Chapter 5 and have done your homework, you are now ready to begin installing Windows Server 2003 in your lab. You may be tempted (or you may have an urgent need) to go directly to a working or production system in a production environment. Perhaps your DHCP server died or a new DNS server is needed urgently and so on. Resist — or stick with what you know. If you have a Windows Server 2003 network and need to raise a new service to fill an urgent need, stick with Windows Server 2003.

On the other hand, if you are a seasoned administrator and you know what you're doing, you probably have items such as a hardware checklist, remote or unattended installation, hot standby, and so on well taken care of. So go directly to a production system only if you know what you are doing and the production system is part of a conversion and rollout project.

For the most part, you should always raise servers in a lab. Then you should *burn them in* (run them continually) for about a week; hit them with work for at least another week. After that, and if all test items check off, ship or go live. But no two environments are the same. The following sections look at the various installation and configuration situations, and then we go from there.

A lot of people ask how you burn in a server that is standing idle and has no users connected to it. One simple way is to set up NTBackup to run continually. Running backup is great physical therapy for a server. It works the hard disks, memory, system buses, access control, permissions and the NTFS, remote and removable storage functions, and more. You can also configure NTBackup (or any other backup utility, for that matter) to perform both pre- and post-backup routines, such as sending alerts and moving files around the house. Depending on your stress test, you may need to write a backup script to automatically overwrite media and so on. And if you want to test disk I/O and other routines, you may need to write some custom software for the job.

Getting psyched up about installing

This chapter takes you through the basic install routines and then to rollout and sophisticated deployment strategy. We are going to help you cook up a variety of server meals. Microsoft has spent many millions on the installation and configuration process. So, for the most part, Windows Server 2003 rises well for the power that it wields. It is certainly a lot smoother and friendlier to install than any other server operating system in existence (other than the machine you receive pre-installed from the factory).

We have installed the operating system more times than you care to know and on about ten different platforms with a variety of hardware from scrap piles to brand names. We have also deliberately sabotaged our systems (like taking away drives, drivers, memory, and certain system files) and tried a variety of recovery techniques. What we have to report to you is as follows: If you experience any difficulty installing Windows Server 2003, you must be using very unconventional methods, thrift store hardware, or not paying attention to details and recommended strategy.

Now sit back, close your eyes, and imagine that you are in a class going through installation training. You can feel good thinking that you spent no more than the cost of a nice dinner on this book and did not need to mortgage your house for a five-day course.

Server recipes

In evaluating the various needs in the enterprise, we classify our installation into various recipes of server installation, which are discussed in the following sections.

Low-road or bare-bones system recipe

This option consists of using minimum hardware requirements as recommended by Microsoft and some testing. All servers require a 133 MHz for x86-based computers except Datacenter server, which requires 400 MHz for *x*86-based computers. I would suggest a bare-bones minimum of 128MB of RAM for all servers except Datacenter Edition, which requires a bare-bones minimum of 256MB of RAM. You also want a CD-ROM, a 1.4MB floppy disk drive, a standard network card, and a mouse, keyboard, and monitor.

We have raised servers (Standard Server, Enterprise Server, and Web Server Edltion) on CPUs ranging from old Pentium 133s, 166s, 200s, Pro 200s, and 266s to Pentium II and III 300s, 450s, 500s, 700s, duals (two CPUs), quads, and so on. You can raise the mentioned server on 133-MHz and 166-MHz Pentiums, but we don't recommend it for anything more than the smallest test server, which we discuss in the section "An Overview of Hardware," later in this chapter. On the other hand, an old Pentium Pro with a lot of RAM serves many of your needs. You can usually pick these servers up on the Internet for a song, and if they are good brands, they do well for many years.

Small file and print server recipe

IT organization needs the capability to efficiently utilize file and print resources and keep them available and secure for users. Networks tend to expand, with greater numbers of users located onsite, in remote locations, or even in partner companies, and IT administrators face an increasingly heavier burden. Windows Server 2003 now provides many enhancements to the file and print infrastructure to help solve the never-ending administrators' burden.

You should still use the bare-bones components but add a second large IDE hard disk drive for file and print services, the usual peripherals, and so on. The amount of RAM that you need depends on the number of connections and users. Printing services require a lot more RAM than file services.

Your hard-disk demands are higher, and you should now consider adding a second drive. You can stick to a cheap IDE disk (even the cheap IDE or EIDE drives are good disks) or begin thinking about SCSI. But hold the thought about hard disks for the section "An Overview Of Hardware," later in this chapter.

You may have read information elsewhere calling for more firepower in Windows Server 2003. We would preempt that question with the answer that our assessment is based on various experiments, projects, pilot systems, and deployment. Every situation is different, and the only way to really know what you need to throw at a situation is to test.

Application-server installation recipe

The Windows Server 2003 application environment builds on the solid enterprise capabilities of Windows 2000 Server security, availability, reliability, scalability, and manageability. The application development seems to be more dependable because the environment can be managed by fewer people, and it delivers lower TCO with better performance. Developers are one of the most highly leveraged resources in IT. By integrating .NET Framework into the Windows Server 2003application-server development environment, developers are now freed from writing "plumbing" code and can instead focus their efforts on delivering business solutions.

You may want to install applications on servers for users who load them into local memory at their workstations. The application is thus loaded across the network, but the "footprint" and ensuing resource consumption is local to the user's hardware.

You may also have applications that are server-based or server-oriented. These may include database front-ends, communications software, processing-oriented software, and network-management applications. Hundreds of applications may be suited to server-side execution and need no user interaction, such as process-control applications and data processing.

You could use the recipe for file and print servers that we give in the preceding section; raising the ideal configuration for your purpose takes some testing. Depending on the availability requirements, you may need to add RAID, hot-swap drive-bays, and so on, which are discussed in the section "Hard Disk Drives," later in this chapter.

Terminal Services installation recipe

A terminal service application server is a whole new ball game. The WinFrame licensing arrangement between Citrix Systems, Inc., and Microsoft was the origin of Terminal Services. Terminal server, under the Hydra project name, first made its debut in Windows NT 4.0 in late 1997. It was then launched as a separate NT 4.0 operating system called Windows NT 4.0 Terminal Server Edition (TSE). Terminal Server in Windows Server 2003 is now called Remote Desktop Connection (RDC). RDC provides substantial improvements over previous releases.

RDC provides administrators and users with a simplified user interface that still connects to previous versions of Terminal Services (Windows NT 4–Terminal Server Edition and Windows 2000). Check chapter 30 for more detail on Remote Desktop Connection (RDC).

Windows Server 2003 Terminal Server supports more users on each high-end server than Windows 2000, and Session Directory in Windows Server 2003, Enterprise Edition, provides load-balancing support. Session Directory maintains a list of indexed sessions by username, therefore allowing the user to reconnect to the terminal server and resume working in that session. It also provides unsurpassed remote manageability by taking advantage of technologies such as Group Policy, and Windows Management Instrumentation (WMI), which provides management complete remote capabilities through a comprehensive read/write system.

With Windows Server 2003 acting as a Terminal Services application server, all your users run all their applications on the server. No such thing as a local Terminal Services client even exists. The client can be a browser, a fat client running a Terminal Services terminal application (such as a TN3270 character-based terminal running on Windows and accessing a DB2 database on the mainframe), a dumb terminal (known as *Windows-based terminals*), or terminals running on the Windows CE or Pocket PC platforms. Your users' terminals can also be installed on any non-Windows platform, such as Macintosh, DOS, and Unix, but these require the MetaFrame product suite from Citrix, which uses the ICA protocol.

Terminal servers can be raised with any of the recipes discussed so far. What matters, however, is not what you start up with but what the terminal users do after they are attached to the server. We have tested these services and deployed them in vigorous real-life situations since 1997, and the following configuration pointers, which apply to a different configuration recipe that we discuss shortly, are key:

✦ Restrict your users from having more than four applications open at a time. Make sure, for example, that they can comfortably open and run a database application, a word-processing application, e-mail, and a Web browser.

✦ Configure the applications to run without fancy splash screens, animations, or any resource-intensive software.

✦ Assign and enforce hard-disk quotas. This is important to do for all users but is especially useful if you are dealing with terminal users.

A server hosting no more than five terminal users should be running on a CPU of no less than 300 MHz. Each user (depending on the applications and the type of processing) should be assigned no less than 32MB of RAM. You should also install fast SCSI drives and support them in hardware RAID configurations on fast controller cards. In short, no bare-bones situation is possible for Terminal Services and application hosting. After all, if you were deploying to standard clients, they would likely each have more than 266 MHz with 32MB or more of RAM.

At 32MB each, the recipe thus calls for the following total server RAM:

✦ Operating system = 128MB

✦ Five users at 32MB each = 160MB

✦ Total RAM needed = 288MB

You're likely to have a hard time adding 32MB modules into a modern motherboard. Your configuration would thus be two 128MB modules and one 64MB module or a single 320MB or larger RAM module.

We have actually succeeded with less RAM, and you could count on a 300-MHz system with 128MB RAM and a couple fast IDE drives to service three to five users. But you should know that this setup works only if you can guarantee that the users keep no more than two applications open (say their e-mail and one work application, such as a database front-end). This latter "easier" configuration should be your bare-bones recipe for Terminal Services (to give users a reasonable work environment).

Role-server installation recipe

Role servers are servers running services such as DHCP, WINS, DNS, and Active Directory. Your application and needs may vary widely, depending on the service and how many subscribers it has. A small company may get away with a lightweight configuration, such as the small file- and print-server recipe offered in the section of that name, earlier in this chapter. In other cases, you may require much more firepower, especially on medium to large intranets. For the record, we've been running DHCP, WINS, and DNS on Windows Server 2003 on Pentium 200s with 128MB of RAM in each, servicing several thousand users across a nationwide WAN for several years. But you have a lot more replication and dynamic configuration overhead with Windows Server 2003, and you may need to shell out for a Pentium III or IV machine.

BackOffice, high-road, or mission-critical recipe

Mission-critical servers should have no less than 300 MHz in CPU capability. For the most part, and especially if you have more than a handful of users, your CPU should be more than 400 MHz. You may consider equipment running two-CPU configurations or possibly deploy quad systems.

Hard disk needs may vary, but you need to configure a second drive letter running at RAID 5 under hardware control. (In case you're wondering, these are SCSI devices, which we discuss in the section "Hard Disk Drives," later in this chapter.)

Redundant or standby system recipe

Any of the server recipes mentioned in the preceding sections can be cloned to provide an offline or hot spare. These are obviously not clustered or automatic failover machines. If the primary server goes down, you could pull dynamic volumes out of the primary arrays and install them into the hot spares. But a better solution, if you can afford it and have the budget, is to install Enterprise Server and run cluster services and network load balancing.

Large systems, clusters, and Datacenter Server installations

Advanced clustering (high availability) and Datacenter Server solutions are beyond the scope of this book, although most of the configuration information in this book applies to the high-end operating systems. Any large system calls for an external SCSI-based storage silo under hardware RAID-5.

The various recipes that we've discussed so far are summarized in Table 6-1.

Table 6-1: Hardware Guide for Server Recipes

Recipe	*CPU/MHz*	*RAM/MB*	*HDD*
Bare-bones	200	128+	IDE
Small File and Print	200-300	128+	IDE
App server	300+	128+	IDE/SCSI
Terminal Services	300+	300+	SCSI-RAID
Role server	266+	128+	SCSI-RAID
BackOffice	300+	128+	SCSI-RAID
Standby	300+	128+	SCSI/IDE
Large	450+	300+	SCSI-RAID

An Overview of Hardware

Choosing hardware is not a difficult exercise at all for Windows Server 2003. You really don't put a lot into your system. The list of hardware that we discuss in the following sections is as follows:

- ✦ Motherboards
- ✦ CPU
- ✦ Memory
- ✦ Hard-disk drives
- ✦ HDD controllers
- ✦ Network interface cards (NICs)

The Hardware Compatibility List (HCL)

Before you go buying parts, review the *Hardware Compatibility List (HCL)* at `www.microsoft.com/hwdq/hcl/`. The Designed for Windows logo identifies software and hardware products that have been designed for and work well with Microsoft products. Software and hardware products displaying the logo must pass rigorous testing to ensure that they provide ease of use and stability and that they take advantage of the new features in Windows products. Software is tested by an independent testing lab named VeriTest. All PCs and peripheral hardware must be tested by Windows Hardware Quality Labs (WHQL).

Businesses that use products meeting the Designed for Windows logo criteria stand to gain the following benefits:

- ✦ Lower support costs
- ✦ Support for mixed Windows environments
- ✦ Correct use of the operating system
- ✦ Compliance with the Americans with Disabilities Act and other equal-rights legislation

According to Microsoft policy, Microsoft does not support you if the item is not on the HCL, but not many items are on the HCL yet. And if you offer to spend $195 with Microsoft to figure out whether hardware is the reason a server does not start, do they refuse to take your money? They never have to date. Microsoft's paid support team is very responsive and helps you determine whether hardware is your problem. At least if they tell you that you have a hardware-compatibility problem, that's probably all the advice that you need.

The HCL aside, you should heed the following advice: Most large companies buy brands from the likes of IBM, Compaq, Dell, or HP, and so on. And if the budget is there, a small company looking for one business server should go this route as well. The servers are burned in and tested, and the manufacturer stands behind the compliance of its product running Windows Server 2003, logo-compliant or not. The servers also come with warranties and various levels of support.

If, however, you plan to build your own server, or if you need to upgrade a machine down the road, by all means, buy your own parts and knock together your own server. For best motherboard results, however, try to stick to made-in-America components or well-known and popular foreign imports. For RAM, only a handful of factories are left, but you're okay buying products from the likes of NEC, Compaq, IBM, TI, and others. For hard disks, IBM, Quantum, Western Digital, Maxtor, and Seagate are the leaders now and may soon be the only players. For CPUs, you have Intel, AMD, and Cyrix. If you are thinking PowerPC and other marginal CPUs, you need to talk to the likes of IBM or Motorola. The other peripherals do not interfere with your server.

Motherboards

The motherboard is, in many ways, the most important component in your computer (and not the processor, although the processor gets much more attention). If the processor is the brain of the computer, the motherboard and its major components (the chipset, BIOS, cache, and so on) are the major systems that this brain uses to control the rest of the computer. Having a good understanding of how the motherboard works is probably the most critical part of understanding the PC. The motherboard plays an important role in following vital aspects of your computer system (and notice how many are here):

✦ **Organization:** Everything is eventually connected to the motherboard. The way that the motherboard is designed and laid out dictates how the entire computer is going to be organized.

✦ **Control:** The motherboard contains the BIOS program and chipset, which, between the two, control most of the data flow.

✦ **Communication:** Almost all communication between the PC and its peripherals, other PCs, and you, the user, goes through the motherboard.

✦ **Processor Support:** The motherboard dictates directly your choice of processor for use in the system.

✦ **Peripheral Support:** The motherboard determines, in large part, what types of peripherals you can use in your PC. The type of video card your system can use (AGP, PCI), for example, depends on what system buses your motherboard uses.

✦ **Performance:** The motherboard is a major determining factor in your system's performance, for two main reasons. First, the motherboard determines what types of processors, memory, system buses, and hard-disk interface speed your system can have, and these components dictate directly your system's performance. Second, the quality of the motherboard circuitry and chipset themselves have an effect on performance.

✦ **Upgradability:** The capabilities of your motherboard dictate to what extent you can upgrade your machine. Some motherboards, for example, accept regular Pentiums of up to 133 MHz speed only, while others go to 200 MHz. Obviously, the second one gives you more room to upgrade if you are starting with a P133. I would not recommend anything less than a P4.

Motherboards come in a variety of sizes and shapes. The essential components of a motherboard are as follows:

✦ **Motherboard form factor:** Motherboards come in several sizes, as follows:

- **Full-AT:** This form factor is no longer produced because it cannot be placed into the popular Baby-AT chassis.
- **Baby-AT:** This size is almost the same as that of the original IBM XT motherboard, with modifications in the screw-hole position to fit into an AT-style case and with connections built onto the motherboard to fit the holes in the case.
- **LPX:** This size was developed by Western Digital when it was making motherboards and was duplicated by many other manufacturers. It is no longer made by Western Digital.
- **Full-ATX/Mini-ATX:** The ATX form factor is an advancement over previous AT-style motherboards. This style of motherboard rotates the orientation of the board 90 degrees, allowing for a more efficient design. Disk drive cable connectors are closer to the drive bays and the CPU is located closer to the power supply and cooling fan.
- **NLX:** This size was implemented in 1998 by Intel and is similar to the LPX form factor except for the improvements of support for the PII, AGP slots, USB, and DIMM slots.

We would stay with the ATX form factor. It seems to be the most preferred case style to date.

✦ **Slots:** Slots come in three standards: *ISA* (the older and slower slots), *PCI* (which caters to faster data transfer rates), and *AGP* (*A*dvanced *G*raphics *P*ort), which is more suited to graphics components (and not becoming of a server). Most motherboards include at least two of the three slot types. Because AGP is for a graphics interface card, usually only one AGP slot is present. Choose a motherboard that gives you at least one AGP slot and at least four PCI slots.

✦ **RAM slots:** The RAM slots include SIMMs and DIMMs. SIMM slots are the older 72-pin slots, and the modules must be mounted in pairs. DIMM memory is much faster. DIMM modules come in 168-pin slots, and the memory can be mounted as single modules. You can put more DIMM RAM in a server than SIMM, which is important for future expansion.

✦ **CPU sockets:** The CPU sockets include *Socket 7*, *Slot 1*, and *370/PPGA*. Socket 7 is the older Pentium Pro-type socket, which is inserted like a pancake into the motherboard sockets. Slot 1 CPUs are for the Pentium II and III CPUs, which go into a single slot and protrude away from the motherboard. Slot 370 CPUs are cheaper than Slot 1 CPUs and are for the Intel Celeron PPGA CPUs.

One of the top motherboards in the United States is SuperMicro, which supplies many leading brands. You can buy SuperMicro boards at `www.Motherboards.com`, which sells several other leading brands, including SOYO, ABIT, and INTEL. Another motherboard maker that has become popular is ASUS.

Central processing units (CPUs)

The leading CPU maker is still Intel. AMD and Cyrix, however, are making their own noises in the *x*86 market. Contact all three manufacturers for Windows Server 2003 compatibility, or check out the HCL (at `www.microsoft.com/hwdq/hcl/`), under CPUs.

Memory

DIMM is short for *dual in-line memory module*, a small circuit board that holds memory chips. DIMM slots are found in all new computers. A *single in-line memory module* (SIMM) has a 32-bit path to the memory chips, where a DIMM has a 64-bit path. Because the Pentium processor requires a 64-bit path to memory, you need to install SIMMs two at a time. With DIMMs, you can install memory one DIMM at a time. SIMM slots are almost obsolete; SIMMs hold up to eight or nine (on PCs) RAM chips. On PCs, the ninth chip is often used for parity error checking. Unlike memory chips, SIMMs are measured in bytes rather than bits. SIMMs are easier to install than individual memory chips. The bus from a SIMM to the actual memory chips is 32 bits wide. The DIMM provides a 64-bit bus. For modern Pentium microprocessors that have a 8-bit bus, you must use DIMMs.

The various slots that we have discussed so far are summarized in Table 6-2.

Table 6-2: Processor Minimum Memory Specifications

Processor	*Data Bus*	*30-pin SIMMs*	*72-pin SIMMs*	*168-pin DIMMs*
Pentium and MMX, K6, K6-2, K6-3	64-bit	N/A	2	1
Athlon, Duron, Pentium II, III, Celeron	64-bit	N/A	N/A	1
Pentium IV	8-bit	N/A	N/A	1

As shown in the preceding table, the RIMM eight-bit data bus is actually less than older Pentium II and III boards that use the DDR 64-bit data bus. The RIMM operates much faster than DDR, but the eight-bit data bus slows it closer to the speed of the DDR memory. Both are competing to become the standard.

Hard-disk drives

The biggest names in hard-disk drives (HDDs) are Seagate, IBM, Fujitsu, Quantum, Western Digital, Maxtor, and Hewlett-Packard, in no particular order. For small or bare-bone servers, you can escape with IDE or even Enhanced IDE (EIDE) drives. The IDE interface is closely related to the ISA interface — one of the general-purpose interfaces that can be found on the PC's motherboard.

ATA was the standard bus interface on the original IBM AT computer and is also called IDE, for Integrated Drive Electronics, and Ultra DMA, for Direct Memory Access. ATA is the official ANSI (American National Standards Institute) standard term. Most motherboards include two ATA 40-pin connectors each capable of supporting two devices (one master and one slave).

As the least expensive hard-drive interface ATA is, in general, slower than SCSI interface and is used for single-user PCs and low-end RAID systems.

SCSI is a high-performance peripheral interface that can independently distribute data among peripherals attached to the PC. Unlike ATA, SCSI incorporates those instructions needed for communication with the host PC. Freeing the host computer from this job makes it more efficient in performing its user-oriented activities. SCSI is a specification for a peripheral bus and command set defined in an ANSI standard X3.131-1986. SCSI drives are usually more suitable for high-end computer systems that require maximum possible performance. SCSI provides for higher data transfer rates and less CPU load than ATA but has higher cost and complexity in the setup. SCSI also supports more devices than ATA. Another important advantage of SCSI is that most SCSI products are backward-compatible. A faster, newer drive can still work with the older and slower controller, but does, of course, lose in performance.

Different flavors of SCSI are different in width (8-bit vs. 16-bit). Fast SCSI doubles the data transfer rate across the same 50-pin cable by using synchronous (vs. asynchronous) data transfer. Wide SCSI uses "wider" 68-pin cable to enable 16-bit data stream vs. 8-bit for 50-pin connector. A combination of both wide and fast technologies provides for the greater then 80MB data transfer rates.

The advantage of SCSI over IDE or EIDE lies in the following factors:

- **Speed:** SCSI drives are much faster in access time and transfer rate than IDE drives; however, new IDE drives are being introduced every month that outperform recent additions to the SCSI lineup.
- **Capacity:** SCSI drives are currently available from 9.5GB to 180GB (although this amount is sure to be out of date by the time that you reach the end of the chapter.)
- **Addressing:** Many drives or devices can be chained on a single cable. You can currently address up to 15 SCSI devices by using the Ultra SCSI standard.
- **Support:** More supporting technology is available for SCSI that is targeted to server solutions. These include high-end RAID controllers, hot-swap hardware, storage silos, and drive-array enclosures.

(Hot-swap is also an important consideration for server-class machines. Your servers should be configured with hot-swap drive hardware that enables you to remove a dead drive while a system is hot and online. This enables you to replace drives without bringing mission-critical servers down.

We can define hot-swap standards in four levels, as shown in Table 6-3.

Table 6-3: Removal and Insertion of SCSI Devices

Level	*Capability*
Level 1	Cold swap. System is offline; no power is applied to the drive.
Level 2	Hot swap reset. System is held in reset state; power is applied.
Level 3	Hot swap on an idle bus. Power is applied.
Level 4	Hot swap on an active bus. Power is applied to the drive.

Mission-critical or maximum-availability servers should be configured with Level 4 hot-swap capability.

HDD controllers

The standard HDD controllers that are built onto most motherboards suffice for most server and data-processing needs. Small business systems configured with IDE or EIDE cards work well with onboard controllers (that is, on the motherboard) or your vanilla controller that sells for less than $50.

SCSI drives need SCSI controllers. These can range from your standard SCSI controllers to faster cards and cards that support mirroring, disk duplexing, disk arrays, and so on. One of the best-known names is Adaptec. Most branded computers that are configured for SCSI usually make their own SCSI controllers or use Adaptec.

A good SCSI controller is of paramount importance, because it makes no sense to install a fast SCSI drive or drive array and then go cheap on controller cards.

Network interface cards

Any seasoned network administrator can tell you that you can buy a $10 network interface card (NIC) and spend hundreds of dollars trying to get it to work, or you can spend $75 to $100 and have it installed and bound in less than five minutes.

Stick with the brand name cards such as 3Com and Madge. Most of 3Com's products have been tested compatible with Windows Server 2003. You face zero setup effort with any of the latest 3Com NICs, and as long as you install any of 3Com's 900 series (such as the 3C905), you don't have any hassle.

Plug and play

This technology makes installing devices far less painful than was the case on Windows NT, which did not support PnP. For the most part, the operating system can detect your new components and automatically configure them for operation. You may need to provide only addressing or name configuration. We look at PnP and the Device Manager in the section "Post Installation," later in this chapter.

Getting Ready to Install

Before installation, you should prepare a checklist detailing what you are going to install and the items you need to have handy. The following checklists cover several types of installation.

Standalone servers

Standalone servers do not connect to any domain but rather to a workgroup. You can create a workgroup from one standalone server or join the server to another workgroup, Windows for Workgroups-style. Standalone servers can share resources with other computers on the network, but they do not receive any of the benefits provided by Active Directory.

For a standalone server, you need the following items:

- ✦ Workgroup name
- ✦ An administrator's password
- ✦ Network protocols
- ✦ IP address

- DNS IP addresses and host names
- NetBIOS name of host

Member servers

Member servers are members of domains. A member server is running Windows Server 2003, a member of a domain, and not a domain controller. Because it is not a domain controller, a member server does not handle the account logon process, does not participate in Active Directory replication, and does not store domain security-policy information.

Member servers typically function as the following types of servers:

- File servers
- Application servers
- Database servers
- Web servers
- Certificate servers
- Firewalls
- Remote-access servers

Member servers also have a common set of security-related features, as follows:

- Member servers adhere to Group Policy settings that are defined for the site, domain, or organizational unit.
- Resources that are available on a member server are configured for access control.
- Member server users have user rights assigned to them.
- Member servers contain a local security-account database, the Security Account Manager (SAM).

To install a member server into a domain, you need to add the following items to your checklist:

- Domain name
- Network Protocols
- IP address
- NetBIOS name of host

Role servers

A server within a domain can function in one of two roles: either as a domain controller or a member server.

As the needs of your computing environment change, you may want to change the role of a server. By using the Active Directory Installation wizard, you can promote a member server to a domain controller, or you can demote a domain controller to a member server.

To promote a role server into a domain controller, you need to add the following items to your checklist:

- ✦ Domain name
- ✦ An administrator's password
- ✦ Network protocols
- ✦ IP address
- ✦ DNS IP addresses and host names
- ✦ NetBIOS name of host
- ✦ Role service information

According to our definition, a member server can be a role server only if you install specific role services onto the server during installation, such as WINS, DNS, DHCP, and so on.

Domain controller

Two approaches to installing a domain controller are possible. First, you can raise the machine as a member server and promote it post-installation — and even post-burn-in. Or you can promote it to domain controller status during an automated installation.

We recommend against the latter option unless you are really confident about your machines and their configuration. If you are an Original Equipment Manufacturer (OEM), you would not need to be concerned about domain controllers and Active Directory because the domain specifics, such as creating a new tree or forest or joining existing trees and forests, is something that gets done on the customer's network. On the other hand, if you, as a consultant or network engineer, have created an extensive unattended or remote installation regimen that automatically raises the machine as a domain controller, you know what you are doing.

For now, you have several reasons for not promoting during or just after initial installation. First, promoting a domain controller is a time-intensive operation. (Active Directory goes through extensive self-configuration before the installation completes.) Second, if you experience a problem with the machine, you must demote the domain controller, which can be a complicated process. And third, after you have installed and raised a domain controller, you do not want to demote it because of a hardware problem or risk trashing your domain controller.

If Active Directory is demoted, it tears down everything that it created and restores the machine to the control of the registry and the local SAM. In fact, it is like watching a movie going backwards. Active Directory asks you for a new administrator account name and password for the rollback. All configuration changes made to the machine, such as desktop settings, are restored to the default, newly created settings. After you reboot the machine, you are back to where you started. You do not even get earlier changes that you made to the registry because the registry is essentially reinstalled after Active Directory comes down (because it is wiped out if you promote the server).

A good reason lies behind this. Everything configured on a domain controller is stored in the directory databases, and after the registry is restored, you can repromote it from scratch. Promoting a domain controller is dealt with in Chapter 11.

Burn in a domain controller machine for several weeks, if possible, before you promote and deploy it. A domain controller running Active Directory for several weeks has already accumulated an extensive configuration—not a good idea for a machine that must be replaced.

The checklist for a domain controller is as follows:

✦ Domain name

If you are creating a new domain, you need the name of the parent domain that you are installing under or the existing tree name (or the forest name if you are installing a new domain tree). If you are adding a domain controller to an existing domain, you need to have that name handy as well.

✦ An administrator's password

✦ Network protocols

✦ IP address

✦ NetBIOS name of host

✦ DNS IP addresses and host names

Installing Windows Server 2003

We have found, after dozens of installations, that the best practices for installing Windows Server 2003 is to follow the specific checklist of events that follows:

✦ Check system requirements—visit Microsoft's site and review the System Requirements for Windows Server 2003.

✦ Read the setup Instructions and release notes included with the Windows Server 2003 Installation CDs.

✦ Determine whether to upgrade or install.

✦ Determine what licensing schema to use: per server or per seat.

✦ Determine whether you want to the capability choose between different operating systems each time that you start the computer.

✦ Determine whether you need an NTFS or FAT32 file system.

✦ Partition information. (Is a special partition necessary for this installation?)

✦ Choose the correct components to install—determine the server's purpose.

✦ Determine how to handle networking, IP, TCP/IP, and name resolution.

✦ Determine whether you want workgroups or domains.

✦ Disconnect any UPS devices. The setup process tries to detect devices connected to serial ports; therefore, UPS equipment can cause problems with the detection process.

Start setup after you have considered each of the events in the following sections and prepared a checklist that is right for your installation.

Partitioning hard-disk drives

Give Windows Server 2003 a hand, and it takes an arm . . . or at least another drive. Installation assesses all the hard-drive resources in the system, and if you have two drives (or partitions), the OS attempts to use both. The first active partition gets snagged for the system files . . . the minimum required to raise the system to a point where you can run recovery tools or the Recovery Console. Windows Server 2003 calls this volume—you guessed it—the *system* volume.

Windows Server 2003 then snags a second drive or partition and uses it for the boot files . . . the files needed to boot the rest of the operating system all the way to the desktop where you can log in. Windows Server 2003 calls this volume the *boot* volume. (This is a reversal of the old naming convention for boot and system partitions.)

Two reasons exist for the dual disk consumption. First, Windows Server 2003 is optimized to use more than one hard-disk drive. Second, a minimum boot disk can be configured to hold just the boot files and be formatted as FAT or FAT32 instead of NTFS. The theory is that, if you lose the base operating system—that is, if you cannot boot to the desktop—you can at least boot to a DOS diskette and then, from DOS, copy new base files over the corrupt ones (or replace a defective drive). Many NT and NetWare systems have been configured this way. But a well-designed and managed system need not retain a FAT boot disk, which, because of its poor security, is a risk to the entire system because it does not support file-level security.

Windows Server 2003, however, enables you to boot to the Boot Options console (whenever it detects a disaster). Here you have several options, such as Safe Mode with Networking, and from there, you can attempt to boot without certain services and debug the problem after you have the OS up and running. You can also boot the Recovery Mode Console, which takes you to a command line that you can use to access NTFS partitions and the boot disks. So the idea of leaving boot or system files on FAT volumes is old-fashioned—the result of bad memories from Windows NT days. We recommend the partition arrangement options that we describe in the following sections.

Option 1: One HDD

This arrangement uses one hard-disk drive, which forces Windows Server 2003 to put both boot files and system files onto the same drive and partition. To use this option, follow these steps:

1. Configure the system with one hard-disk drive of about 2GB in size. (Microsoft's official recommendation is to supply at least a 1GB partition, but with service packs and new features coming down the road, you need to leave room for expansion.)
2. Format the partition during the install as NTFS.
3. Have Windows Server 2003 choose the default partition name

The pros of this partitioning option are as follows: First, you save on hard-disk drives. The system files take up no more than 20MB. Second, you can mirror this disk for fault tolerance. (Unfortunately, you can mirror the disk only under hardware disk mirroring because Windows Server 2003 does not enable you to mirror a disk that was installed as a basic partition . . . even if you make the disk a dynamic disk.)

The negatives of this partitioning option are that, if you must format the system or boot volumes as FAT, you end up with a disk consisting of numerous partitions. This is not necessary on a server and can later lead to problems, such as no capability to mirror or diminishing hard-disk space and the advanced features of dynamic disks. You may also have trouble providing dual-boot capability, but dual boot is not recommended, and besides, you have no need to provide dual boot on a production server.

You can dual boot a server to Windows 2000, Windows NT 3.51, Windows NT 4.0, Windows 95, Windows XP, Windows 98, Windows 3.1, Windows for Workgroups 3.11, MS-DOS, or OS/2. Some stipulations do exist with the NT operating system. It must be upgraded to Service Pack 5 or later. Service Pack 5 and later upgrade the NT NTFS to read Windows Server 2003 volumes. NT 4.0 with SP 4 and less cannot run on the new NTFS volume, and if you install Windows Server 2003 before adding at least SP 5 to the Windows NT side, you lose NT, period. Dual booting to any other operating system (non-NTFS) is not possible on an NTFS-formatted disk.

Option 2: Two HDDs

This arrangement uses two hard disk drives: Windows Server 2003 puts boot files on one disk and system files on the second disk. To use this option, follow these steps:

1. Configure the system with two hard-disk drives of about 2GB each in size.
2. Format the drives as NTFS during the install.
3. Have Windows Server 2003 choose the partition names and the default and put the files where it needs to.

The positive aspect of this partitioning option, as far as we can tell, is that you have the option of leaving the Boot volume formatted as FAT (or FAT32) and formatting the rest of the partitions and drives as NTFS.

The negatives of this partitioning option are that you use up a second drive for a small amount of hard disk space. But if you are bent on dual or multi-boots, the second drive can hold the additional OS.

Although you have a performance incentive to use a second hard disk, the increased performance is not worth the effort and the second drive, considering the speed and response of modern hard disks. We are also talking about the base operating system here and not Active Directory, SQL Server, or Exchange, which are built to take advantage of additional drives. You would be better off using a second drive as a mirror of the first to gain a fault-tolerance feature.

Performing a basic install

The CD install consists of several stages, prompting you for information, copying files, and restarting. Setup concludes with the Installation Server Wizard, which guides you through the server configuration.

Initial Setup: Using the boot disks

To use the boot disks for initial setup, follow these steps:

1. Insert Disk 1 into your A drive and then reboot your machine. Alternatively, you can run Setup from the DOS command line by typing **A:\winnt**.

   Executing Setup from the command line or from reboot loads a minimal footprint of Windows Server 2003 into memory. The code in memory contains the functions that start the Setup program. The machine is rebooted, and the text-based version of Setup starts.

2. The usual licensing information appears on-screen, and you are required to agree to the terms and conditions. The next step is disk partition.
3. Setup asks you to choose the partition on which to install the operating system. You can select existing partitions or choose to create a new partition.

4. Your next choice is the file system (FAT16, FAT32, or NTFS). After you select the file system, Setup formats the chosen partition. After the format, Setup immediately begins installing files to the partition. If you have more than one disk in the system and want to install to one disk, do not format or partition any other media at this time.

   Setup then saves the initial configuration and restarts the machine.

On boot up, the first screen that you see is the Windows Server 2003 Setup Wizard. The Windows Server 2003 operating system files are installed in the `C:\Winnt` folder.

If you do not have a local CD, you can run Windows 95, 98, or DOS boot disks with SmartDrive and network drivers installed. These boot disks put you on the network and enable you to connect to remote CD share-points. From the share, you can execute `winnt32.exe` (non-DOS mode) and launch the GUI-based initial setup screens.

Initial Setup: Installing from the CD

You can either make your CD bootable (if it is not so already) or execute the `winnt.exe` file from the local CD drive or from across the network. If you are already in Windows NT or Windows Server 2003 (a release candidate or beta), you can run `winnt32.exe` from the `I386` directory on the CD, or just simply run setup from the root directory on the CD. This method of install brings you to the graphical Windows-based installation dialog box, which prompts you to upgrade an existing installation or install a parallel operating system. Click the first option to install Windows Server 2003, as shown in Figure 6-1.

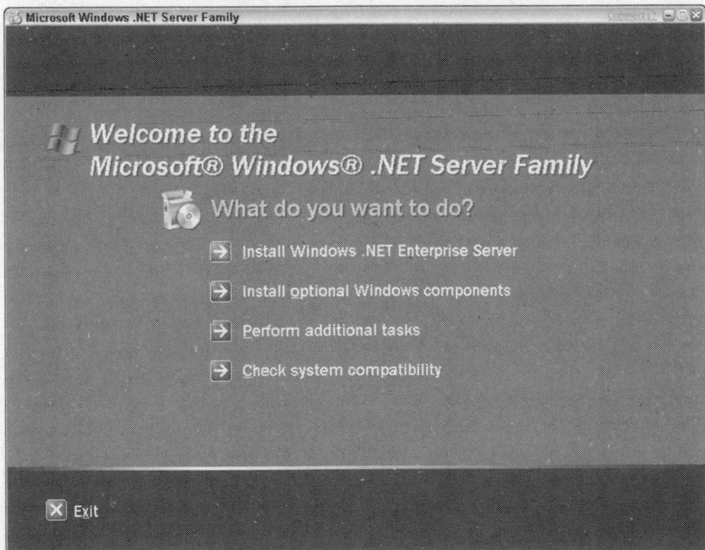

Figure 6-1: The Windows Server 2003 welcome and installation dialog box.

Running the Setup Wizard

The wizard now takes you through the second stage of the installation process. You are asked for information about yourself, the organization or company licensing the software, and the computer.

Windows Server 2003 takes this information and begins a noninteractive installation in which it copies software to support machine configuration, installed devices, and so on. After this phase, Windows Server 2003 prompts you for the following information:

✦ **Language Options:** You are asked to customize language, locale, and keyboard settings. If you are installing in the United States, you can, for the most part, leave these at the default settings. You can also configure the server to use multiple languages and regional settings. Choosing multiple languages forces Windows to install the character sets from multiple languages.

✦ **Name and Organization:** Here, you provide the name of the person responsible for the software and the name of the organization that owns the license.

✦ **Licensing Mode:** Here, you can choose to select licensing on a per-server or per-seat or per device basis. If you choose to license per seat, you must enter the number of client access licenses (CALs) purchased. If you are going to provide application services by using the Terminal Services in Application Mode, choose the CAL option.

✦ **Computer Name:** This is where you get to add the NetBIOS name. Windows Server 2003 chooses a default name for you, which you should change because it doesn't make very much sense. Coming up with a convenient naming convention that your users recognize is far better. In the examples given throughout this book, we use LA for `LATINACCENTS`, followed by the abbreviation for the role that the server plays and the role number. If the machine is destined to become a domain controller, for example, we name it MCDC, followed by the server number: LADC00 or LADC06. An example of a DNS server would be LADNS01.

Windows pretty much leaves you to your own devices in naming your computers. The best rule to follow is to name the machine according to any convention you dream up that works for your situation . . . just be consistent. Resist cute names for several reasons: The names may be hard for your users to relate to, and some may find them annoying. (Not everyone loves Disney.) Server names are also the prefixes for the new Dynamic DNS names assigned to the server. A simple machine name for the `genesis.mcity.org` domain name would be `LADNS06.LATINACCENTS.MCITY.ORG`, which is far better than `BULLWINKLE.LATINACCENTS.MCITY.ORG`. Be careful, too, however, in using names that attract security problems. We once used the name *Checkpointcharlie,* which was subsequently hacked the following week.

✦ **Password for the Administrator Account:** This account is installed into the local domain's Administrator account except for domain controllers.

✦ **Windows Server 2003 Components:** The next step is to add the optional components and services. Ignore most of these services in trial installations and go directly to the Networking Options. Here, you must provide DHCP information, the DNS server address, and others. Some of the services are selected for you by default, such as Transaction Server and IIS. If you are not going to use a service such as transaction server, deselect it. The Windows Server 2003 Components wizard is shown in Figure 6-2.

✦ **Terminal Services:** You are also asked to choose the operating mode of Terminal Services. Choose Administration mode. No point in choosing Application Server mode until you are ready, and the mode can be changed at any time.

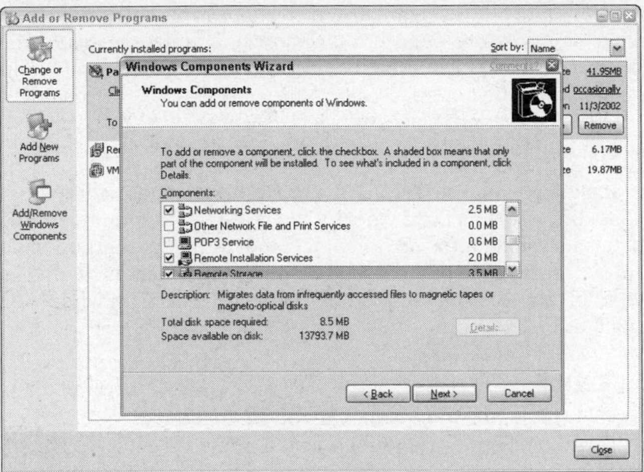

Figure 6-2: The Windows Components Wizard.

✦ **Display Settings:** These settings enable you to configure the screen resolution, number of display colors, and video-related information such as refresh rate. You can leave many of these settings to the default. Change your screen resolution, however, to at least 800 × 600. Many Windows Server 2003 folders and menus are jam-packed with icons and information. And 640 × 480 just does not work. In many cases, you should go with 1,024 × 768 resolution.

✦ **Time and Date:** These settings enable you to set time zones and daylight savings information and to adjust the current date and time. After this information is applied, Windows Server 2003 starts phase three of the installation process: the network install.

Windows network install

This phase installs the networking components. Windows Server 2003 attempts to detect the network interface cards (NICs). If you use standard well-known brands such as 3Com, you have no problems getting through the installation. The following list describes the steps, both automatic and interactive:

✦ **Network card detection:** After detecting and installing the drivers for the NICs, Windows Server 2003 attempts to locate a DHCP server on the network. It does this by broadcasting on DHCP Port 75 and then listening for a response from a DHCP server. If Windows Server 2003 cannot obtain an IP address, it uses the auto-configuration protocol and assigns itself an IP address. You can then continue with the installation, installing to a new workgroup, and make the necessary network connections later.

✦ **Networking components:** Next, you are asked to choose the networking components. The basic options to choose are the client for Microsoft Networks, File and Print Sharing for Microsoft Networks, and TCP/IP. You can install other services and components at any time after installation. If you are installing into an existing NT domain, which does not have DNS or WINS servers in place, install NetBIOS as well. You can also install IPX/SPX if you are going to integrate with Gateway Services for NetWare (GSNW).

✦ **Workgroup or domain:** If you are installing into a domain, you need the name of the account and password that has the authority to create new accounts in the domain. If you have problems installing into the domain, install into a workgroup. If you do not have a workgroup, create any workgroup name on the fly, such as *awshucks,* because you can always change it after installation or change to a domain whenever you are ready, post installation.

Final installation setup

This is the fourth phase of the installation, which involves final file copy, configuration, and removal of temporary files. The Setup program copies all remaining files to the hard disk. These include bitmap files, accessories, and services or component files that are either installed into service or left dormant until activated. Setup then applies configuration settings specified during earlier interactions.

The new configuration is saved in the registry databases and on disk to be used for the configuration after the computer starts anew. At this time, all temporary files are removed from the computer. After this activity, the machine is rebooted.

Installing from the network

You can also install servers from network share-points, which are called *distribution drives* or *servers*. Network installs should obviously be limited to local area network installation because anything less than the standard 10-Mbit/sec network speed makes installation an excruciatingly slow experience.

If you have not created a distribution share, simply copy the `I386`, `I386`, or `ia64` (for Itanium-based systems) folder on the Windows Server 2003 CD to a drive and share it. Apply the necessary access control to prevent unauthorized users from accessing the distribution files. The process, after you have a distribution point in place, is as follows:

1. Create a FAT partition on the target machine. This partition should be within the earlier recommended parameters. You can use the old faithful DOS `FDISK` command to create the partition, but if you are using a very large disk (more than 2GB), only Windows 98's `FDISK` for FAT32 enables you to configure all the space as one huge drive.
2. Boot to a network client. You can use Windows 95/98 boot disks, but a simple DOS may be all that you need. Your DOS client contains the following software:
   - TCP/IP protocol files
   - DOS operating system files for minimum machine life
   - Network interface card drivers (another reason to use good cards that require no configuration)
3. You also need to create configuration files that log the target machine onto the network and enable it to use the source distribution share-point.

After you have connected to the network share-point, you start the installation by executing `winnt.exe` from the distribution server. The following now takes place:

1. `Winnt.exe` creates the four Windows Server 2003 Setup boot disks using your local A drive as the target. Have four formatted disks available.
2. `Winnt.exe` creates the `$Win_nt$` temporary folder on your target machine.
3. `Winnt.exe` copies certain installation files to the temporary folder on the target server.

The process that now takes place is identical to installing from the boot disks, as described in the section "Initial Setup : Using the boot disks," earlier in this chapter.

Streamlining Setup from the command line by using winnt and winnt32

`winnt.exe` and `winnt32.exe` can take a number of parameters that help you streamline the install process. Use the network client to get the target server to the distribution folder. Then run `winnt` with the optional parameters. The syntax is as follows:

```
[pathtowinnt]\winnt.exe [parameter]
```

winnt

`winnt` starts the install process from a command line, while `winnt32` starts the installation from within another Win32 operating system. Table 6-4 provides the parameters for the `winnt.exe` command.

Table 6-4: winnt.exe Optional Parameters

Parameter	*Purpose*
`/a`	Turns on the Accessibility feature during the Setup process.
`/e:[command]`	Executes the command specified in `[command]` just before the final setup phase.
`/I:[inf file]`	Specifies the file name of the information file (`.inf`). This file is used for Setup and replaces the default `DOSNET.INF`. You do not need to include the path to this file.
`/r:[folder]`	Name of an additional folder to be created in the folder in which you install Windows Server 2003. This folder remains after Setup and can be used for custom installations or additional software. This is often used in OEM installations. You can create multiple folders by using this parameter.
`/rx:[folder]`	This parameter provides the same function as `/r:[folder]`, but the folder is deleted after installation is completed.
`/s:[sourcepath]`	This parameter specifies the location of the Windows Server 2003 Setup files. You need to provide a full path to the Setup files, either specifying a driver letter or by using universal naming convention (UNC) paths. You can also use multiple `/s` parameters.

Continued

Table 6-4 *(continued)*

Parameter	Purpose
/t:[*drive letter*]	This parameter specifies the drive to which you want Setup to copy its temporary files. Setup looks for a partition that has the most free space.
/u:[*answer file*]	The answer file is used in unattended mode. You also need to specify the location of the answer file by using the /s: switch.
/udf:[*id, UDF File*]	The udf parameter specifies a UDF file, which is a file that contains variable parameters to be used in unattended Setup. In other words, parameters specified in the answer file get replaced with parameters specified in the UDF file. *Example:* /udf: DomainName,NewDomain.udf. Be aware that, if you do not specify a UDF file, the unattended Setup suddenly requires human intervention to insert a disk containing the $Unique.udb file.

winnt32

To run winnt32 from within a Win32 application, simply open to the command line and execute the winnt32.exe file. To execute winnt32.exe with parameters, simply tack the parameter onto the end of the command as follows:

```
[pathtowinnt32]\winnt32.exe [parameter]
```

The winnt32 parameters are listed in Table 6-5.

Table 6-5: winnt32.EXE Optional Parameters

Parameter	Purpose
/checkupgradeonly	This parameter runs the compatibility test on the existing operating system to determine upgrade potential.
/cmd:[*command*]	Runs the command [*command*] that follows /cmd: before the Setup Wizard completes.
/cmdcons	This is the option that runs the Recovery Mode Console at boot for a failed installation. This can be run after the installation has failed and terminated.
/copydir:[*folder*]	This option enables you to copy an additional folder into the winnt installation folder. The folder remains after the setup is completed. You can reuse the parameter.
/copysource:[*folder*]	Same as the preceding option, but the folder is deleted after the installation.
/debug[*level:filename*]	This option creates a debug log file name with the specified level.
/m:[*folder name*]	This parameter specifies the location of the folder and its name containing the system file replacements. Setup first checks this folder for files to copy and then checks the installation folder.

Parameter	*Purpose*
/makelocalsource	This parameter tells Setup to copy all installation files to the local hard disk so that, if the CD or network drive becomes inaccessible, a local source exists.
/noreboot	This parameter tells Setup not to reboot after the first phase. This enables you to run additional commands before commencing with the reboot.
/s:[*sourcepath*]	This parameter specifies the location of the Windows Server 2003 Setup files. This must be a full path using the drive map letter or the UNC format. You can use multiple /s parameters.
/syspart:[*drive letter*]	This option specifies a hard disk to which to copy Setup's startup files. This is a disk, and the partition is then made active, and you can use the disk in another machine. After the new machine boots, the second phase of Setup starts automatically.
/tempdrive:[*drive letter*]	This option enables you to specify a drive for the Windows Server 2003 temporary files. The drive becomes the Windows Server 2003 installation drive. Setup uses the partition on this drive that has the most space.
/unattend	This switch enables you to perform upgrades in unattended mode. Run on an older operating system, Setup attempts to retain all the older settings. You cannot use this switch if you are an OEM, because the acceptance of the end-user license agreement (EULA) is implicit.
/unattend:[*num*:*answer file*]	This switch loads Setup in unattended mode and uses an answer file that you provide. The *num* value is a specification for the number of seconds Setup waits after copying the files and restarting the computer. This also is valid only if you are running Setup from Windows Server 2003. You also need to specify the /s switch to specify the location of the answer file.
/udf:[*id, UDF File*]	The UDF parameter specifies a UDF file, which is a file that contains variable parameters to be used in unattended Setup. In other words, parameters specified in the answer file get replaced with parameters specified in the UDF file. *Example:* /udf:DomainName,NewDomain.udf.
/dudisable	Prevents Dynamic Update from running. Without Dynamic Update, Setup runs only with the original Setup files. This option disables Dynamic Update even if you use an answer file and specify Dynamic Update options in that file.
/duprepare	Carries out preparations on an installation share so that it can be used with Dynamic Update files that you download from the Windows Update Web site.
/dushare	Specifies a share on which you previously downloaded Dynamic Update files.

The parameters in these tables are extensive, and many of them have long and difficult strings. Put all the parameters into a single DOS batch file and execute the batch file from a command line.

Troubleshooting the Installation

Although Windows Server 2003 installs smoothly most of the time, we do not live in a perfect world, and at times, an installation fails. This section provides some pointers to determine why an installation failed and what to do about it.

Tip

As Windows Server 2003 performs an upgrade, it first gathers information relating to installed hardware and software and reports this to you before installation begins. If some components preclude Windows Server 2003 from installing, you are given an option to remove those components or circumvent attempts by the installation process to support them in the new environment. After you have removed or dealt with the offending components, Windows Server 2003 enables the installation to proceed.

Setup occasionally may suddenly stop midway through the installation process. If this happens, you either get no information (the screen freezes up) or you get a stop error message. You can look up this error message if you have other functioning Windows Server 2003 systems, or you can look it up on the Microsoft Web site.

After dozens of flawless installations on a myriad of hardware and software platforms, we had become complacent. One large server, however, a Windows NT Primary Domain Controller (PDC) running on a Compaq 6000 with a full house of hardware (array controllers and RAID-5 configuration), failed. Only after several blue screens and after we had debugged all stop error messages and attempted various boot options could we get the machine up. Unfortunately, we never could promote it to a domain controller. The entire SAM had been corrupted in the upgrading process.

If you have a nonresponding system on hand and the three-fingered salute (Ctrl+Alt+Del) does not work, either hit the Reset button or switch the machine off. Wait for about 10 seconds and then restart the machine.

Several things may now happen. The worst case is that nothing happens and the machine hangs at a flashing cursor or something. If this happens, start the Setup process again and attempt to watch for what may be responsible for the problem. If the system freezes again, you need to look at the hardware you have installed in the machine and consider replacing parts until you get past the lockup. Specifically, look into the CPU, the system cache (which can be disabled), RAM (stick with the same brand of RAM if at all possible), the system BIOS, network and hard-disk controllers, and, especially, the video card. In fact, try replacing your video card before taking out any other device.

We know that this sounds a little longwinded, but a process of elimination may be your only solution. If the installation still freezes after you remove and replace several items, you may have a problem on the installation CD. This is, however, a rare situation and can obviously be confirmed if the same CD fails on another machine.

On the other hand, Setup may recover and return to a point that enables it to continue installation. In the event that you must reinstall, Setup detects the earlier attempt and prompts you to repair that attempt. At this point, you can either have faith that Windows Server 2003 can repair the damage or you can go with your gut and Windows NT experience and reinstall from scratch, whacking the partition and all.

A word of caution: If at any time you suspect that you may have a hardware problem, do not try to force the install by inching forward with repetitive installation attempts. If the server is going into production, it should pass a QC install first, which means flawless installation the first time around.

Post Installation

After you install the operating system and log in for the first time as an administrator, Windows Server 2003 automatically presents you with the Configure Your Server tool. This tool enables you to configure services such as Active Directory, DHCP, DNS, IIS, and so on. You do not need to use the tool, because all the shortcuts to the various consoles can be accessed from the menu items in Administrative Tools, from the Control Panel, and from the command line. So if you want to close it as soon as you log on, Windows Server 2003 does not stop you. The OS, however, presents this tool to anyone who logs onto a server interactively in the capacity of an administrator.

Introducing the Boot File

The *boot file* (`BOOT.INI`) is not a complicated element, but it is very important for many reasons. The file loads a menu onto the screen at startup and enables you to select preboot options. It also contains certain parameters that affect startup.

Table 6-6 looks at the variables of the `boot.ini` file and how they affect the startup of your server.

Table 6-6: Boot File Variables

Variable	*Usage*
`Timeout`	The number of seconds to display the loader. It is usually set to 25 seconds.
`Default`	The location of the default operating system that gets loaded on timeout.
`Multi`	Specifies the hard-disk controller number and the type used. You use the `SCSI` parameter for drives that are connected to a `SCSI` parameter.
`Disk`	The disk number on which the operating system resides. This value is `0` for IDE drives. For SCSI drives, you can specify the SCSI ID number.
`rdisk`	Also the disk number on which the operating system resides.
`Partition`	Represents the partition number of the disk on which the OS resides.
`\WINDOWS=`	Name of the OS between quotes. This value can be anything.

The following code represents a sample `boot.ini` file:

```
 Boot Loader Settings
--------------------
timeout: 30
default: multi(0)disk(0)rdisk(0)partition(1)\WINDOWS
```

If your OS loses its boot.ini file, you can create one and make sure that it points to the correct hard disk and partition. You notice that partition numbers are not zero-based as are the hard-drive numbers. The first and primary partition on each disk is labeled partition 1.

The boot variable switches in Table 6-7 are also worth knowing in the event that you have problems loading. These switches are used in the operating system section of the boot.ini file.

Table 6-7: Boot File Variables

Switch	*Usage*
/addsw	Adds operating system load options for a specified operating system entry.
/copy	Creates another operating system instance copy, for which switches can be added.
//dbg1394	Configures 1394 port for debugging.
/debug	Adds or changes the debug settings for a specified operating system entry.
/default	Designates the default operating system.
/delete	Deletes an operating system entry.
/ems	Enables the user to add or change the settings for redirection of the EMS console to a remote computer.
/query	Queries and displays the boot loader and operating systems sections.
/raw	Adds the capability to add strings to operating system sections of the boot.ini file.
/rmsw	Removes operating system load options for a specified operating system entry.
Timeout	Changes the operating system timeout.

Windows Server 2003 as a Communications Server and Microsoft Exchange

Microsoft Exchange Server unites users with knowledge anytime, anywhere. Exchange is designed to meet the messaging and collaboration needs of small organizations, large distributed enterprises, and everything in between. Microsoft Exchange seamlessly integrates with Windows Server 2003. We list a few of the Exchange Server main services in the following sections.

Internet Information Services integration

Exchange is also integrated with IIS to provide for high-performance mail protocols, SMTP protocols, and POP protocols. Exchange also provides a browser interface to access Microsoft Outlook Web Access client.

Active Directory integration

Active Directory which is covered in more detail in Chapter 6 is an enterprise directory service that is highly scalable and fully integrated with Exchange at the system level. Exchange takes full advantage of the Windows Server 2003 Active Directory; with but a single point of administration, it enables users to control all messaging services seamlessly. All directory information, including users, mailboxes, servers, sites, and recipients, is stored in Active Directory. Administrators benefit from the unified administration, experience no user-interface changes, and require no retraining after switching to Active Directory. Integration features of Exchange Server and Active Directory include the following:

- Unified administration of Exchange Server and Windows Server 2003 enables an administrator to manage all user data in one place by using one set of tools.
- Security groups in Windows Server 2003 can be automatically used as Exchange distribution lists, removing the need to create a parallel set of distribution lists for each department or group.
- Active Directory's schema extensibility enables the management of distributed information and easily configurable Exchange user and server information.
- Lightweight Directory Access Protocol (LDAP) is a native access protocol for directory information.

Distributed services

Distributed services enable subsystems to use storage, protocol, and directories on different computers, providing for scalability for millions of users. This system is extremely configurable, providing for growth and flexibility for system architecture.

Storage groups with datastores and clustering

The Datastores provide multiple groups of storage groups, and databases. You can simply define a storage group by using the Exchange Systems Manager snap-in. The storage group can be backed up, enabling the administrator to restore each table individually without server interruption.

Security

Exchange Server offers you the only messaging system that is fully integrated with the Windows Server 2003 security model. Administrators use the Windows Server 2003 security model to define the permissions for all messaging and collaboration services, including public folders. This means that administrators can learn a single permissions model for managing both Windows Server 2003 and Exchange and can create a single set of security groups to apply to either Windows Server 2003 resources or Microsoft Exchange objects. This helps simplify your workgroup administration. And Exchange Server enables permissions to be set at the item or document level. Security descriptors can be set for messages and components. These features provide for new levels of security.

Single-seat and policy-based administration

Microsoft Exchange uses a graphic administration and monitoring system that integrates with Windows Server 2003's Microsoft Management Console (MMC) (covered in Chapter 7) to provide single-seat administration. The MMC does not provide you with management capabilities, but instead provides you with a common interface that enables you to manage all your needs. The Microsoft Exchange System Manager, Microsoft Active Directory, and Internet Services Manager are snap-ins that provide the management for .NET Server 2003. Policy-based management provides the administrator with the capability to perform single operations made up of hundreds of objects. Policies are a set of objects defined by the administrator. Administrator can also define recipient policies that could potentially affect hundreds of thousands of users, groups, and contacts in active directory by using LDAP.

SMTP message routing

Exchange Server supports SMTP, POP, LDAP, IMAP, HTTP, NNTP, S/MIME, and X.509 version 3. This versatility enables Exchange Server to act as an organization's gateway to the Internet. Providing high-performance routing of e-mail services, SMTP is, by default, the transport protocol for routing all message traffic between servers, within an Exchange site and between sites. Your organization's use of SMTP results in increased performance and new opportunities for integration with the Internet. Exchange Server's message algorithms have been enhanced to provide fault-tolerant message delivery and to eliminate messages that bounce, even if multiple servers or network links are down. This provides for increased message bandwidth and performance. SMTP routing provides customers with considerable flexibility in designing a reliable, high-performance messaging backbone by using Exchange Server.

Internet mail content

Exchange Server can significantly increase performance of e-mail, because you use e-mail clients to store and retrieve Multipurpose Internet Mail Extensions (MIME) content directly from the base, without any form of content conversion. Client software such as Outlook enables you to stream data in and out of the database. This process helps performance immensely.

All the features discussed in the preceding sections provide low cost-of-ownership, which makes Microsoft Exchange Server a valuable asset to every organization.

System Monitoring by Using Windows Management Instrumentation

Windows Management Instrumentation (*WMI*) helps simplify the instrumentation of computer software and hardware. It provides you with a means of monitoring and controlling system components, both locally and remotely. The sole purpose of the WMI is to define a set of environment-independent specifications, thus helping you share management information that works with existing enterprise-management standards, such as Desktop Management Interface and the Simple Network Management Protocol (SNMP). The WMI provides a uniform model that complements these standards.

WMI is fully integrated with Windows Server 2003 to provide a simplified approach to management. Such tools as Microsoft Management Console help simplify the task of developing well-integrated management applications, therefore enabling vendors to provide Windows Server 2003 customers with enterprise-scalable management solutions. Combining local and remote events and the WMI query language provides you with the tools that you need to create complex management solutions.

The WMI also provides you with the Windows Driver Model (WDM), which is a kernel-level instrumentation technology. This technology provides you with consistent, open access to management data. WMI extensions are available for the following WDM capabilities:

- ✦ Publishing kernel instrumentation
- ✦ Configuring device settings
- ✦ Providing kernel-side event notification
- ✦ Publishing custom data
- ✦ Enabling administrators to set data security
- ✦ Accessing instrumentation by way of WMI

You can run WMI console from the command line in *interactive mode* or *noninteractive mode*. Interactive mode is used for entering commands at the computer, while noninteractive mode is useful for processing batch procedures.

The console installs the first time that you run it. If a change is introduced to the managed object format (MOF) files, the console automatically compiles the alias. To start the WMI console from a command prompt, type **wmic**. The prompt now should look as follows: `wmic:root\cli>`. The WMI console enables you to enter aliases, commands, and global switches, or you can enter /? for Help.

You can also run WMI console in noninteractive mode, where the command prompt returns to you after executing the command. An example is given as follows:

```
<PROMPT>wmic os get /format:hform>OperatingSystem.html
```

The output from the command is redirected to an HTML file; you can review the results in Figure 6-3. From here, the command line returns you to the command prompt where you started. Then you may proceed to enter other commands.

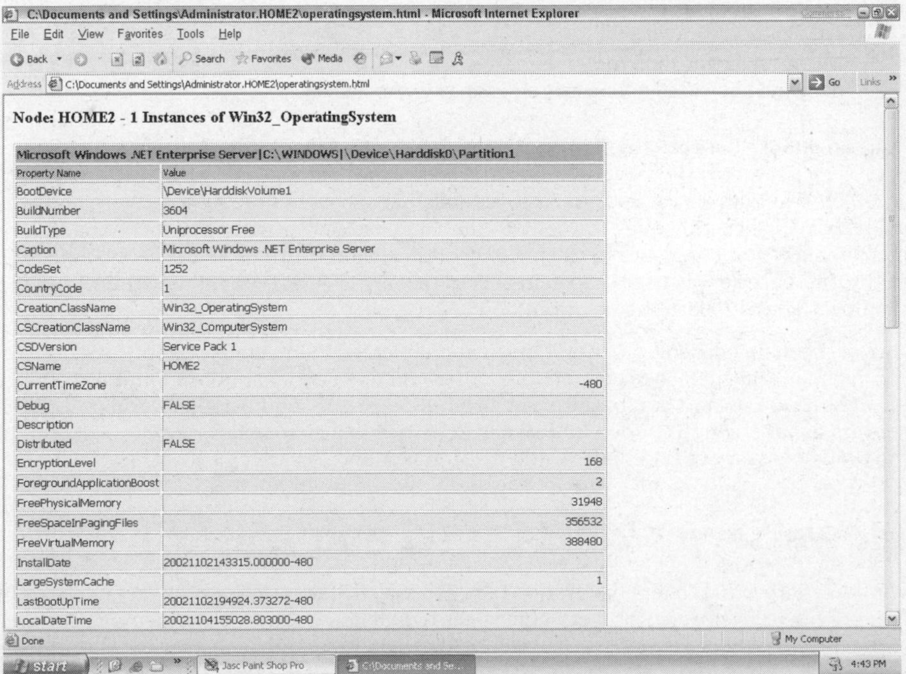

Figure 6-3: Results from the WMI console.

Windows Server 2003 for Database Services with SQL Server

If you have a modest understanding of database connectivity, you should find SQL Server's command syntax uncomplicated and easy to use. If you are an experienced developer, you are sure to appreciate the scalable, high-performance access that SQL Server provides.

If you are concerned about backward compatibility, we suggested connecting by using ODBC.

We want to avoid any security issues, as mentioned in the preceding Tip, so we are going to go through the steps to create an account for SQL Server to access data on a remote computer. Start by opening Enterprise Manager; then, in the console tree, double-click Microsoft SQL Server; then click SQL Server Group, followed by SQLComputerName. Double-click Databases and then double-click your database; proceed by right-clicking Users and then click the New Database User menu. The login name should be *domain\username*, and the Public check box should be selected for all the following items:

✦ db_owner

✦ db_accessadmin

✦ db_securityadmin

✦ db_ddladmin

✦ db_datareader

✦ db_datawriter

✦ db_backupoperator

Do not select db_denydatareader or db_denydatawriter. These options, if selected, deny members read and write permissions to the database.

You can choose between the TCP/IP Sockets and Named Pipes connection methods for accessing a remote SQL Server database. Named Pipes database clients must be authenticated by Windows Server 2003 prior to establishing a connection. Alternatively, connections using TCP/IP Sockets connect directly to the database server without connecting through an intermediary computer. And because connections made with TCP/IP Sockets connect directly to the database server, users can gain access through SQL Server authentication rather than Windows Server 2003 authentication.

One of the main challenges of designing a sophisticated Web database application seems to involve managing database connections. After you open and maintain a database connection, it can severely strain a database server's resources and result in stability issues. Database servers experiencing a sudden increase in activity can become backlogged, greatly increasing the time necessary to establish a database connection.

Windows Server 2003 for IIS and ASP.NET

Windows Server 2003 offers integration between Visual Studio.NET and IIS. This tight integration provides developers with very high levels of functionality. Now that the request-processing architecture is integrated with IIS 6.0, it should provide an improved experience for those of you using ASP.NET and the Microsoft .NET Framework.. The new Windows Server 2003 Web

Edition delivers a single-purpose solution for Internet Service Providers, application developers, and others wanting to use only the specific Web functionality.

Windows Server 2003 for Application Services

Windows Server 2003 builds on the core strengths of the Windows family, providing security, manageability, reliability, availability, and scalability across the board. Many advancements were made in Windows Server 2003 that provide benefits for application development, resulting in lower total cost-of-ownership and better performance. The following list describes a few of these benefits:

- Simplified integration and interoperability
- Improved developer productivity
- Increased enterprise efficiency
- Improved scalability and reliability
- End-to-end security
- Efficient deployment and management
- Simplified integration and interoperability

Windows Server 2003 delivers a revolutionary application environment to build, deploy, and run XML Web services. Microsoft has provided integrated support for XML Web services, which enables applications to take advantage of the loosely coupled principles of Internet computing. The Windows Server 2003 application environment improves the productivity of developers by providing integrated application services and industry-leading tool support. The following feature set helps increase productivity of developers:

- **ASP.NET:** By using the ASP.NET XML Web services features, developers can write their business logic, and the ASP.NET infrastructure is responsible for delivering that service via SOAP and other public protocols.
- **Automatic Memory Management:** .NET Framework runs in the common-language runtime, which is a garbage-collected environment. Garbage collection frees applications that are using .NET Framework objects from the need to explicitly destroy those objects, reducing common programming errors dramatically.
- **Industry-leading Tools:** Visual Studio.NET provides an integrated, multilanguage tool for building Web applications.
- **Microsoft .NET Framework:** By integrating the .NET Framework into the Windows Server 2003 application-development environment, developers are freed from writing the day-in, day-out code and can instead focus their efforts on delivering real business value.
- **Reusable Code:** Visual Studio .NET provides an architecture that is easy to learn and that enables improved code reuse.
- **Separate Code from Content:** Enables developers and content creators to work in parallel by keeping content separate from application code.
- **Server-Side Web Controls:** Visual Studio .NET Web controls are compiled and run on the server for maximum performance, and can be inherited and extended for even more functionality.

Applications that are developed by using Windows Server 2003 tend to be more responsive and available because Windows Server 2003 can be managed by so few people. This helps lower the total cost of ownership and provides better performance. Microsoft has also made many programming-model enhancements, providing component aliases, public and private components, process initialization, and services without components. *Component aliasing* enables you to configure the same physical implementation of a component as many times as you want. This provides component re-use at the binary level. The public and private components enable you to individually mark components as *public* for use in other applications or *private* if the component can be seen and activated only by other components in that same application. Process initialization provides the developer with the capability to execute code as the hosting process starts and finishes. This helps your component take the opportunity to take any action, such as initializing connections, files, caches, and so on. Services without components enable you to programmatically enter and leave a service domain. This enables you to build components that use transactions without needing to inherit from `ServicedComponent`.

Building and deploying your application on Windows Server 2003 gives you better performance and more options for the design and architecture of your system.

Windows Server 2003 Catalogs and Indexes

Microsoft offers the Windows Catalog as a comprehensive list of compatible products for Windows Server 2003. To access the catalog from Windows Server 2003, choose the Start menu then select the All Programs menu option, then select the Windows Catalog menu option. This redirects you to the Microsoft Windows Catalog Web page.

If you are interested in submitting products for listing in the Windows Catalog, follow this list of rules:

- ✦ Verify that the product corresponds with the Windows Catalog criteria.
- ✦ Obtain a VeriSign Code Signing ID (a Class 3 Organizational Certificate), which you use to digitally sign and upload your software, hardware drivers, and so on whenever submitting your products to the Windows Logo Program Qualification Service.
- ✦ Obtain an account for the Windows Logo Program Qualification Service for both hardware and software.
- ✦ Submit the hardware or software products to the Windows Logo Program Qualification program.
- ✦ Submit a description of the products that you are submitting. Refer to the How to Describe Products in the Windows Catalog sections of `www.microsoft.com`.

By following the preceding rules to be Windows Logo compliant, you are essentially helping your products gain recognition and prove that they work well with the Windows family of products.

Windows Server 2003 Domain Controllers

Member Servers or just standalone servers can be promoted to domain controller. The Active Directory wizard can help you install and configure components and enables you to provide directory service to network computers and users. Before installing or even considering a domain controller, however, review the following checklist:

- ✦ Review the Active Directory topic "Introduction to Active Directory" in your Windows Server 2003 Help guide.
- ✦ Make sure that you review the role of a domain controller.
- ✦ Review concepts about security.
- ✦ Review concepts about Domain Name Service (DNS) namespace planning and integration with DNS.
- ✦ Verify that the server has an NTFS partition.
- ✦ Verify that DNS is correctly configured.

Promoting member servers to domain controllers either creates new domains or adds additional domain controllers to existing domains. In creating the first domain, you must have already created one domain controller in that domain. The act of creating the domain controller also creates the domain.

If your organization needs additional domains, you must create one domain controller for each additional domain. New domains in a forest must be either a new child domain or the root of a new domain tree. If you decide to create a child domain, the name of the new domain must contain the full name of the parent. To hierarchically organize domains within your organization, make sure that you use the domain tree structure. If you would rather create the root of a new domain tree, make sure that its name is not related to the other domains in the forest.

To improve the availability and reliability of network services, add additional domains to a single domain. You can create new domain controllers across the network or from backup media.

Windows Server 2003 Active Directory

Windows .NET Standard Server 2003, Windows .NET Enterprise Server 2003, and Windows .NET Datacenter Server 2003 all support Active Directory. It uses a structured datastore for logical, hierarchical organization of directory information. The *datastore* is also known as the *directory*, and it contains information about Active Directory objects. Active Directory objects include shared resources such as servers, volumes, printers, and the network user and accounts. Refer to Chapter 8 for more detail.

Active Directory is tightly integrated with security through logon authentication and access control to objects. This makes managing directory data and organization throughout the network easy for an administrator. Schemas also help administrators with daily tasks by setting constraints and limits on instances of objects. *Schemas* consist of classes of objects and attributes contained in the directory. Global catalogs consist of the information about each and every object in a directory; therefore, Global catalog provides easy access to directory information regardless of which domain of the directory actually contains the data.

The following list summarizes the Active Directory features that are enabled by default on any domain controller running Windows Server 2003:

- ✦ The selection of multiple user objects and the capability to modify common attributes of multiple user objects at one time.

- The capability to drag and drop Active Directory objects from container to container or to a desired location in the domain hierarchy. You also have the capability to drag objects to group membership lists.
- Enhanced search functionality is object-oriented and provides an efficient search that minimizes network traffic associated with browsing objects.
- The capability of saving queries, enabling you to save commonly used search parameters for reuse in Active Directory Users and Computers.
- Active Directory command-line tools, which give you the capability to run directory-service commands for administration scenarios.
- You can now create instances of specified classes in the base schema of a forest and instances of several common classes, including country or region, person, `organizationalPerson`, `groupOfNames`, device, and `certificationAuthority`.
- The `inetOrgPerson` class is added to the base schema and can be used in the same manner as the user class.
- You can configure replication scope for application-specific data among domain controllers running Windows Server 2003.
- The capability to create additional domain controllers to existing domains by using backup media, thus reducing the time necessary for an administrator to create additional domain controllers.
- Universal group membership caching to help prevent the need to locate a global catalog across a WAN.

Active Directory can provide a company-wide network solution with one domain, reduced sign-on capabilities, and one single point of management. Active directory helps eliminate existing domains and reduces server hardware and maintenance costs.

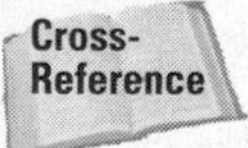

Please refer to Chapter 8 for a more in-depth view of Active Directory.

Windows Server 2003 for Resolutions Services

The following sections describe what is necessary for you to create a plan to help you prepare and configure your server by using DNS, WINS, and DHCP. These sections focus on decisions that you must make for a complete Windows Server 2003 installation.

DNS

Before you begin using DNS on your network, decide on a plan for your DNS domain namespace. Coming up with a namespace plan involves making some decisions about how you intend to use DNS naming and what goals you are trying to accomplish in using DNS. Some questions that you may have at this stage include the following:

- Have you previously chosen and registered a DNS domain name for use on the Internet?
- Are you going to set up DNS servers on a private network or the Internet?
- What naming requirements do you need to follow in choosing DNS domain names for computers?

Choosing your first DNS domain name

In setting up DNS servers, you should first choose and register a unique parent DNS domain name that can be used for hosting your organization on the Internet. Before you decide on a parent DNS domain name for your organization to use on the Internet, search to see whether the domain name is already registered to another organization.

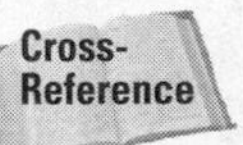

DNS is covered in more detail in Chapter 17.

DNS namespace planning for Active Directory

Before a DNS domain namespace can be correctly implemented, the Active Directory structure needs to be available. So you must begin with the Active Directory design and support it with the appropriate DNS namespace.

Active Directory domains are named by using DNS names. In choosing DNS names to use for your Active Directory domains, start with the registered DNS domain-name suffix that your organization has reserved for use on the Internet and combine this name with something significant in your organization to form full names for your Active Directory domains.

In planning your DNS and Active Directory namespace, we recommend that you use a differing set of distinguished names that do not overlap as the basis for your internal and external DNS use.

We suggest that you use only characters in your names that are part of the Internet standard character set permitted for use in DNS host naming. Permitted characters are defined as all letters (a-z), numbers (0-9), and the hyphen (-).

DHCP

If you are still in the decision-making process as you are deciding how many servers your organization needs, consider the locations of the routers on the network and whether you want a DHCP server in each subnet. If you are planning on extending the use of a DHCP server across more than one network, you may need to configure additional DHCP relay agents and use superscopes as well. If DHCP service is provided between segments, transmission speeds may also be a factor. If your WAN links or dial-up links are slower, you may need a DHCP server on both sides of these links to service clients locally. Currently, the only limit that a DHCP server can serve is determined by the number of available IP addresses.

Following are some Windows Server 2003 factors that could enhance DHCP server performance:

- The primary contributing factor to improving DHCP server performance is the amount of random access memory (RAM) and the speed of the server disk drives installed.
- You should carefully evaluate disk-access times and average times for disk read/write operations in sizing and planning for your DHCP-server hardware specifications. You should also try to increase RAM to the point where server performance is maximized.

For the best possible DHCP server design in most networks, we recommend that you have, at most, 10,000 clients per server.

Most networks need one primary online DHCP server and one other DHCP server acting as a secondary or backup server. If you choose not to implement two DHCP servers, using the 80/20 rule for balancing scopes, but want to continue to provide a measure of potential fault tolerance, you may consider implementing a backup or hot standby DHCP server as an alternative.

WINS

The first decision that you need to make is how many WINS servers your organization needs. A single WINS server can handle NetBIOS name-resolution requests for a large number of computers, but you must also consider the location of your routers on your network and the distribution of clients in each subnet as you decide how many WINS servers are actually required.

You now need to determine whether you want to configure WINS servers as pull or push partners, and you must also set partner preferences for each server. WINS servers are designed to help reduce broadcast traffic between local subnets; WINS creates some traffic between servers and clients. This can be particularly important if you use WINS on routed TCP/IP networks. You may want to consider the effects of slower speed links on both replication traffic between WINS servers and NetBIOS registration and renewal traffic required for WINS clients. Consider how temporarily shutting down a WINS server can affect your network. Use additional WINS servers for failure recovery, backup, and redundancy.

The following two factors can enhance WINS server performance:

- ✦ Installing dual processors on the computer running WINS. This can help increase performance by almost 25 percent.
- ✦ Installing a dedicated disk drive, separate from the system drive, for the WINS database.

After you establish a WINS server on your intranet, adjusting the renew interval, which is the time between a WINS client-name registration and name renewal, can help you trim server-response times.

You can also sometimes estimate WINS client traffic based on the behavior of the WINS clients. In estimating WINS client traffic, however, you also need to consider the network topology and the design or configuration of the network routers. In some cases, predicting the traffic load on a specific network router is not possible because the routers are configured to autonomously route traffic based on factors other than traffic load. By testing the performance of your network installation of WINS, you can better identify potential problems before they occur. Use WINS server performance counters, which are available through the use of System Monitor.

Summary

This chapter takes you through the Windows Server 2003 basic install procedure. We recommend that you install only what you need to get the system up and running. Later, you can begin adding advanced components to the server and establish its role on the network or promote it to an Active Directory domain controller.

We also take you through an exhaustive discussion of hardware. Unless you plan to install complex adapter or interface cards for specialized purposes, such as modems, telephony cards, sound cards, and so on, you do not have problems as long as you stick to tried-and-tested components.

The next chapter provides the information that you now need to configure and deploy your running server.

✦ ✦ ✦

CHAPTER 7

Configuring Windows Server 2003

✦ ✦ ✦ ✦

In This Chapter

Understanding the Microsoft Management Console (MMC)

Using Configuration Wizards

Working with MMC Tools

Configuring Data Sources (ODBC)

Exploring the Control Panel Applets

✦ ✦ ✦ ✦

This chapter explores the many tools for configuring and managing the system, managing users, and controlling other aspects of Windows Server 2003.

Using the Microsoft Management Console

One of the many changes in Windows 2000 from Windows NT that is expanded in the Windows 2003 interface and administrative structure is the switch to a more homogenous approach to administrative utilities. Although many system and operating properties still are controlled through the Control Panel, most administrative functions have moved to the Microsoft Management Console (MMC). The MMC runs under Windows 2003 Server, Windows 2000, Windows NT, and Windows 9*x*. This section of the chapter examines the MMC and its component tools.

You'll find additional information about the MMC as well as additional snap-ins at `http://www.microsoft.com/management/mmc`.

Understanding the function of the MMC

The MMC itself serves as a framework. Within that framework are various administrative tools called *consoles*. In particular, the MMC provides a unified interface for administrative tools. This means that after you learn the structure of one tool, you will be able to apply that knowledge to the rest, which are going to follow suit (within limitations imposed by the differences in the function of the various tools). Figure 7-1 shows the MMC with the Computer Management snap-in loaded (more on snap-ins shortly). As you'll learn later in this chapter, you use the Computer Management snap-in to configure most aspects of a system's hardware and software configuration.

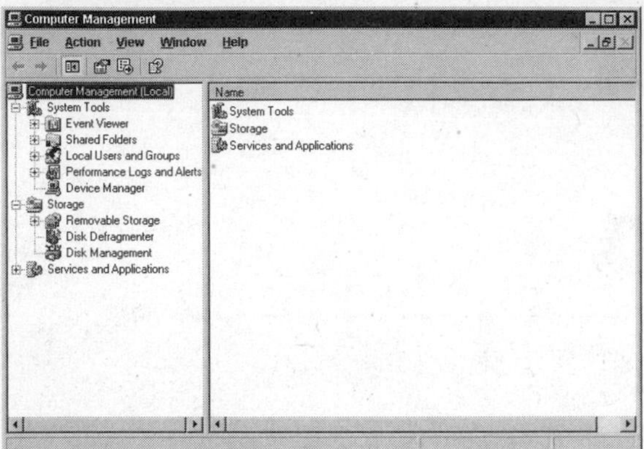

Figure 7-1: The MMC serves as a framework for a wide variety of administrative tools.

Perhaps more important than a unified interface is the fact that the MMC lets you combine administrative tools to build your own console configuration, which you can store by name on disk. The next time you need to work with it, you run the MMC console from the Start menu or double-click its icon or shortcut. For example, let's say that you want to put together a custom console for managing a Windows 2003 Internet server. You can integrate the tools for managing DNS, DHCP, Application Server, and IIS all under one interface. This custom console gives you quick access to most of the settings you need to configure on a regular basis for the server.

The MMC window consists of two panes. The left pane typically contains the Tree tab. The Tree tab generally shows a hierarchical structure for the object(s) being managed. When you use the Active Directory Users and Computers console, for example, the tree shows the containers in the Active Directory (AD) that pertain to users, groups, and computers.

The right pane is the details pane. The details pane changes depending on the item you select in the tree. When you select Services in the tree, for example, the details pane shows the list of installed services. The details pane typically offers two views: Standard and Extended. Standard view shows the columns or other items that you use to perform the management tasks; Extended view adds an additional area that typically shows instructions or additional information about a selected item.

MMC provides two different modes: *user mode* and *author mode*. In user mode, you work with existing consoles. Author mode lets you create new consoles or modify existing ones. Figure 7-2 shows the Services console opened in user mode. Figure 7-3 shows the Services console opened in author mode. As indicated in the figures, author mode offers access to commands and functions not available in user mode.

User mode actually offers three different options: full access, limited access with multiple windows, and limited access with a single window. With full access, an MMC user can access all the window management commands in MMC but can't add or remove snap-ins or change console properties. The limited access options limit changes to the window configuration of the console and use either a single window or multiple windows depending on the mode. A console's mode is stored in the console and applies when you open the console. Console modes can be changed via the Options property sheet (click File ➪ Options). Setting console options is discussed later in the chapter.

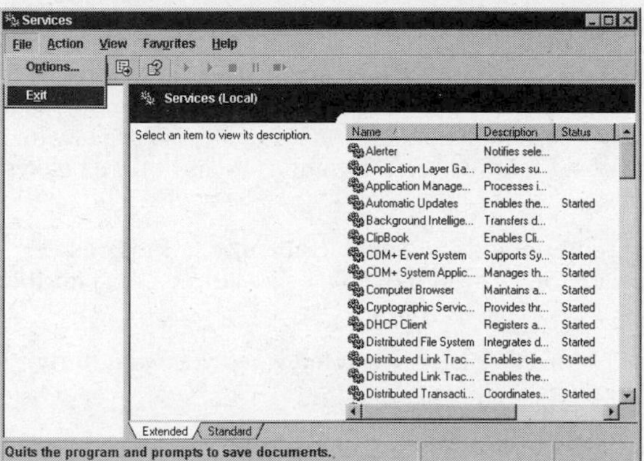

Figure 7-2: User mode restricts the actions that a user can perform within a console.

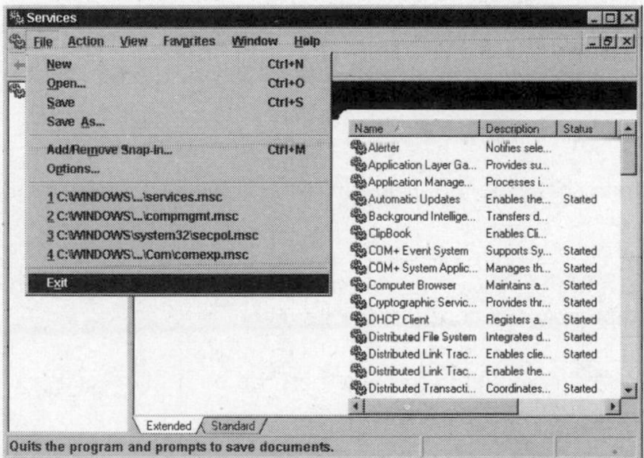

Figure 7-3: Author mode provides the ability to change console options and add new snap-ins.

The default mode in Windows 2003 is user mode — limited access, single window.

As mentioned earlier, you use author mode to author new consoles or modify existing ones. In author mode, you can add and remove snap-ins, change window options, and set options for the console.

Opening the MMC

You can open MMC consoles by selecting them from the Administrative Tools folder in the Start menu or by double-clicking their icons in Explorer. You also can start consoles using a command prompt. The format of the MMC command is:

```
MMC path\file.msc /a /s
```

The following list explains the options for MMC:

- `Path\file.msc`: Replace `path` with the path to the console file specified by `file.msc`. You can use an absolute path or use the `%systemroot%` variable to reference the local computer's path to the Windows 2003 folder. Using `%systemroot%` is useful when you're creating shortcuts to consoles for use on different systems (where the system root folder might be different).
- `/a`: Use the `/a` switch to enter author mode and enable changes to the console. Opening an existing console with the `/a` switch overrides its stored mode for the current session.
- `/32`: Start the 32-bit version of MMC. This is only needed when you want to run the 32-bit version on a 64-bit Windows version.
- /64: Start the 64-bit version of MMC. This option works only on a 64-bit version of Windows.
- `/s`: Use this switch to prevent display of the splash screen that normally appears when the MMC starts on Windows NT or Windows 9*x* systems. This switch isn't needed when running the MMC under Windows 2003.

For example, let's say that you want to open the DNS console in author mode to add the DHCP snap-in to it. Use this command to open the DNS console in author mode:

```
MMC %systemroot%\System32\dnsmgmt.msc /a
```

Tip You can right-click an `.msc` file and choose Author from the context menu to open the file in author mode.

After opening the DNS console, you add the DHCP console using the Add or Remove Snap-In command in the Console menu. Snap-ins are covered in the next section.

Tip If you prefer, you can open the MMC in author mode and then add both snap-ins using the Add or Remove Snap-In command in the Console menu.

Windows 2003 Server provides several preconfigured consoles for performing various administrative tasks. Most of these console files are stored in `\systemroot\System32` and have `.msc` file extensions (for Microsoft Console). Windows 2003 Server places several of these consoles in the Administrative Tools folder, which you access by clicking Start ➪ All Programs ➪ Administrative Tools. In essence, each of the preconfigured consoles contains one or more snap-ins geared toward a specific administrative task.

In an apparent effort to simplify the Start menu, Microsoft includes only some of these consoles in the Administrative Tools folder. However, you can open any console by double-clicking its file. When you do so, the MMC loads first and then opens the console. You also can open the MMC and add snap-ins to your own consoles. This gives you the ability to create a custom console containing whichever group(s) of snap-ins you use most often or that are targeted for specific administrative tasks.

Using snap-ins

Although the MMC forms the framework for integrated administrative tools in Windows 2003, the tools themselves are called *snap-ins.* Each MMC snap-in enables you to perform a specific administrative function or group of functions. For example, you use the DHCP snap-in to administer DHCP servers and scopes. The various MMC snap-ins serve the same function as individual administrative tools did in Windows NT. For example, the Event Viewer snap-in takes the place of the standalone Event Viewer tool (Figure 7-4). The Disk Management branch of the Computer Management snap-in replaces Disk Administrator. The Active Directory Users and Computers snap-in takes the place of User Manager for Domains, and so on.

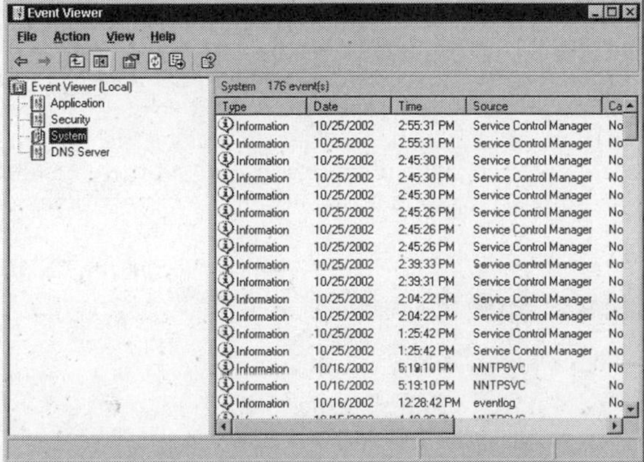

Figure 7-4: Snap-ins perform specific administrative functions and replace standalone tools such as Event Viewer.

Snap-ins come in two flavors: *standalone* and *extension.* Standalone snap-ins usually are called simply *snap-ins.* Extension snap-ins usually are called *extensions.* Snap-ins function by themselves and can be added individually to a console. Extensions are associated with a snap-in and are added to a standalone snap-in or other extension on the console tree. Extensions function within the framework of the standalone snap-in and operate on the objects targeted by the snap-in. For example, the Services snap-in incorporates four extensions: Extended View, Send Console Message, Service Dependencies, and SNMP Snapin Extension.

You can add snap-ins and extensions when you open a console in author mode. By default, all extensions associated with a snap-in are added when you add the snap-in, but you can disable extensions selectively for a snap-in.

To add a snap-in, open the MMC in author mode and choose File ⇨ Add/Remove Snap-In. The Standalone page of the Add/Remove Snap-In property sheet shows the snap-ins currently loaded. The Extensions tab lists extensions for the currently selected snap-in and allows you to add all extensions or selectively enable/disable specific extensions.

In the Standalone page, click Add to add a new snap-in. The Add Standalone Snap-In dialog box lists the available snap-ins. Click the snap-in you want to add and click Add. Depending on the snap-in, you might be prompted to select the focus for the snap-in. For example, when you add the Device Manager snap-in, you can select between managing the local computer or managing another computer on the network. Adding the IP Security Policy Management snap-in lets you choose between the local computer, domain policy for the computer's domain, domain policy for another domain, or another computer.

After you configure snap-ins and extensions the way you want them, save the console so that you can quickly open the same configuration later. To do so, choose File ➪ Save, or Save As, and specify a name for the console. Windows 2003 by default will place the new console in the Administrative Tools folder, which appears on the Start menu under Programs, but you can specify a different location if desired.

Getting to know taskpads

A taskpad is a page on which you can add views of the details pane and shortcuts to various functions inside and outside of a console. These shortcuts can run commands, open folders, open a Web page, execute menu commands, and so on. In essence, taskpads let you create a page of organized tasks to help you perform tasks quickly rather than using the existing menu provided by the snap-in. You can create multiple taskpads in a console, but the console must contain at least one snap-in. Figure 7-5 shows a taskpad for performing a variety of tasks in the DNS snap-in.

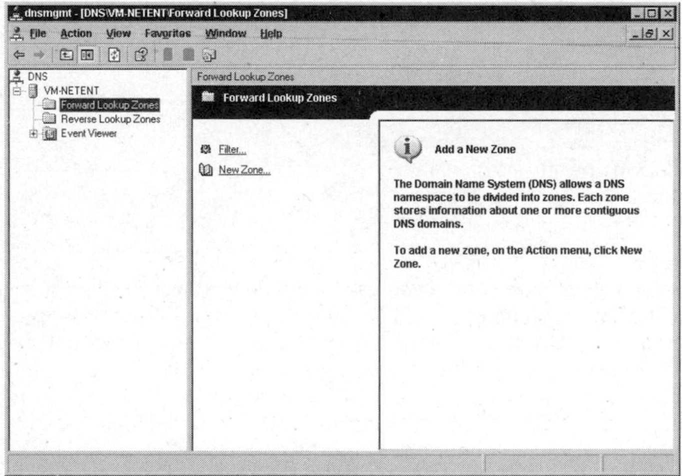

Figure 7-5: Taskpads let you create tasks for performing specific actions, such as these DNS-related tasks.

Tip You must open a console in author mode to create taskpads.

A taskpad can contain a list from the details pane in horizontal or vertical format. Horizontal works well for multiple-column lists (many fields per item), and vertical works well for long lists (few fields per item). You also can configure a taskpad to show no lists. In addition to the list, the taskpad includes an icon for each task with either a pop-up description or text description of the task. You click a task's icon to execute the task.

Creating a taskpad

To create a taskpad, right-click the object in the tree that you want to be the focus of the taskpad and then choose New Taskpad View. MMC starts a wizard to help you create the taskpad. In the second page of the wizard right after the introduction screen (Figure 7-6), you define the appearance of the taskpad. As you make selections, the wizard shows the results to help you determine the effect of your choices.

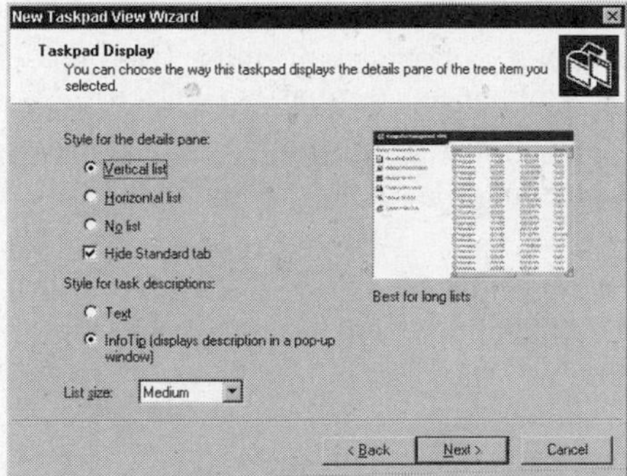

Figure 7-6: This wizard page helps you configure the way the taskpad appears.

In the next page of the wizard, you specify the items to which the taskpad applies. The following list summarizes the options:

✦ **Selected tree item:** This option applies the taskpad to only the selected item in the tree. Using the DNS snap-in as an example, creating a taskpad for Forward Lookup Zones and using this option will cause the taskpad to appear only when you click Forward Lookup Zones. It will not appear if you click Reverse Lookup Zones.

✦ **All tree items that are the same type as the selected tree item:** This option applies the taskpad to all objects in the tree that are the same type as the selected object. In the previous DNS example, choosing this option would cause the taskpad to display when you click either Forward Lookup Zones or Reverse Lookup Zones.

✦ **Change default display to this taskpad view for these tree items:** Select this option to have the MMC automatically switch to taskpad view when the user clicks the object in the tree associated with the taskpad. Deselect the option to have the MMC default to the normal view instead.

The next page of the wizard prompts you for a taskpad view name and description. The name appears at the top of the taskpad and on the tab at the bottom of the taskpad. The description appears at the top of the taskpad under the taskpad name.

On the final page of the wizard, you can click Finish to create the taskpad. The Start New Task wizard option, if selected, causes the Start New Task wizard to execute when you click Finish. This wizard, described in the next section, helps you create tasks for the taskpad.

Creating tasks

After you create a taskpad, you'll naturally want to create tasks to go on it. Select the Start New Task wizard option if you are in the process of creating the taskpad. Or, right-click the node in the tree that is associated with the taskpad, choose Edit Taskpad View, click the Tasks tab, and then click New.

The first functional page of the wizard prompts you to select the type of task to add. These prompts include the following:

✦ **Menu command:** Choose this option to execute a menu command. In the subsequent wizard page, you specify the source for the command and the command itself. The available commands fall within the context of the selected source. Select an object and then select the desired command.

✦ **Shell command:** Choose this option to start a program, execute a script, open a Web object, execute a shortcut, or perform any other task you can execute from a command line. The wizard prompts you for the command, optional command-line parameters or switches, startup folder, and window state (minimized, normal, maximized).

✦ **Navigation:** Choose this option to add an icon for an existing item listed in Favorites. See the section, "Favorites," later in this chapter to learn how to add to the Favorites list.

The wizard also prompts you for a task name, description, and icon to associate with each task and gives you the option at completion of running the wizard again to create another task.

Modifying a taskpad

You can modify an existing taskpad to add or remove tasks or change taskpad view options. Right-click (in the tree) the object associated with the taskpad and then choose Edit Taskpad View. MMC displays a property sheet for the taskpad. The General page shows the same properties you specified when you created the taskpad, such as list type, list size, and so on. Change options as desired.

The Tasks page (Figure 7-7) lists existing tasks and lets you create new ones. New starts the New Task wizard. Remove deletes the selected task. Modify lets you change the task name, description, and icon for the task but not modify the task itself. To modify the task, remove the task and recreate it. You also can use the up and down arrows to change the order of tasks in the list, which changes their order of appearance on the taskpad.

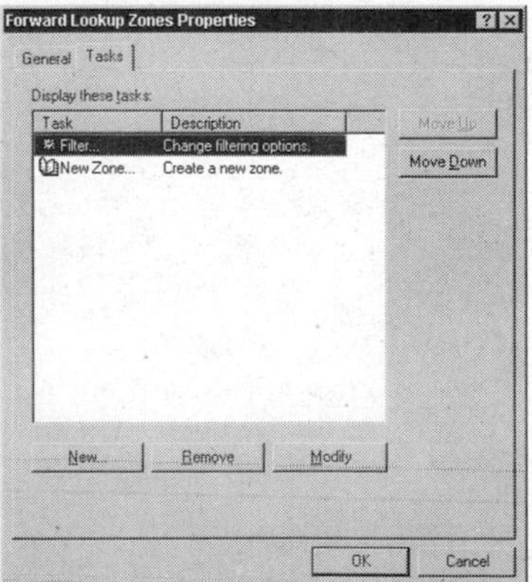

Figure 7-7: Use the Tasks page to add, remove, and modify tasks.

Other add-in tools

Snap-ins are just one of the objects you can add to an MMC console. Other objects include ActiveX controls, links to Web pages, folders, taskpad views, and tasks. The previous section explained taskpad views and tasks. The following list summarizes the additional items:

✦ **ActiveX controls:** You can add ActiveX controls to a console as the details/results view (right pane) for the selected node of the tree. The System Monitor Control that displays system performance status in Performance Monitor is an example of an ActiveX control. Choose Console ⇨ Add or Remove Snap-In, select ActiveX Control from the list, and then click Add. The MMC provides a wizard to help you embed ActiveX controls, prompting you for additional information when necessary.

✦ **Links to Web pages:** You can add links to URLs in a console, which can be any URL viewable within a browser (Web site, ftp site, and so on).

✦ **Folders:** Insert folders as containers in the console to contain other objects. You can use folders as a means of organizing tools in a console.

Would you like to add a local or network folder to a console? Just use the Link to Web page object and point it to the folder instead of an Internet URL.

Customizing MMC to suit your needs

Like most applications, you can customize the MMC to suit your needs or preferences. First, you can configure the settings for a console when you author it to determine the way it displays in subsequent sessions. For example, you might want to configure a console for user mode — limited access, single window, to limit the actions the users can perform with the console. To configure a console, first open the console in author mode. Choose File ⇨ Options to open the Options dialog box for the console (Figure 7-8). Specify settings and then save the console. The changes will take effect the next time the console is opened.

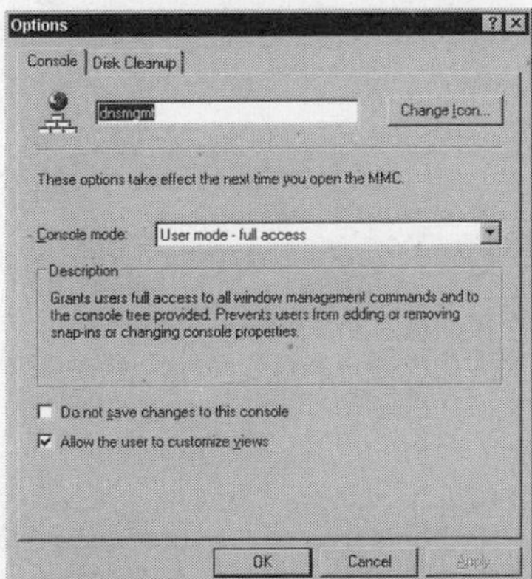

Figure 7-8: Use the Options dialog box to configure the console for future sessions.

The following list explains the available options:

✦ **Change Icon:** Click to change the icon associated with the .msc file. You'll find several icons in *systemroot*\system32\Shell32.dll.

✦ **Console mode:** Choose the mode in which you want the console to open for the next session. Choose between author mode and one of the three user modes discussed previously.

✦ **Do not save changes to this console:** Select this option to prevent the user from saving changes to the console — in effect, write-protecting it.

✦ **Allow the user to customize views:** Select this option to allow users to add windows focused on items in the console. Deselect to prevent users from adding windows.

You also can control view options within the MMC. To do so, choose View ➪ Customize to access the Customize View dialog box (Figure 7-9). The options in the Customize View dialog box are self-explanatory.

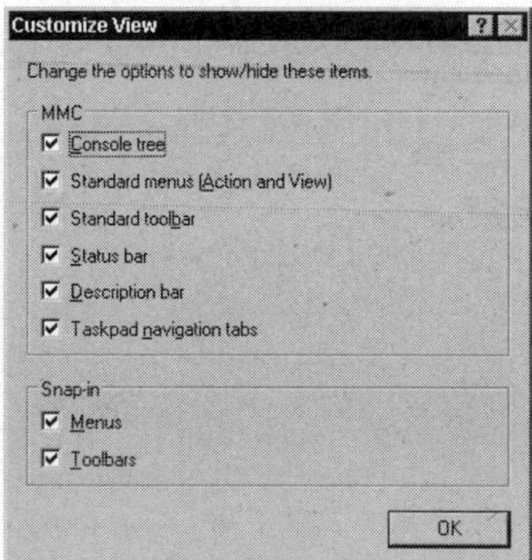

Figure 7-9: Use Customize View to set view properties in the MMC.

Control Panel versus MMC

Even though the MMC now serves as the focal point for many of the administration tasks you'll perform on a regular basis, the Control Panel hasn't gone away. The Control Panel is alive and well and contains several objects for configuring the system's hardware and operating configuration. The tools provided for the MMC do not take the place of the Control Panel objects or vice-versa. However, you will find some of the MMC tools in the Administrative Tools folder in the Control Panel.

The Control Panel in Windows 2003 works much like the Control Panels in Windows 2000 and earlier Windows platforms. In fact, many of the objects are the same or similar. Later sections of this chapter explore the Control Panel objects. The following section examines the core set of MMC tools for managing a Windows 2003 system.

Getting to Know the MMC Tools

As explained previously, Windows 2003 contains several predefined consoles for managing a variety of tasks both on local computers and across the network. The following sections provide an overview of these tools.

Certification Authority

The Certification Authority console appears in the Administrative Tools folder but is installed only if you configure the server as a Certification Authority (CA). Certificate services enables the server to create certificates for itself and for other servers, workstations, and users on the network, either locally or across the Internet. For example, if you need to configure your Web server to require SSL for authoring, you need to install a certificate for that purpose on the server (Certificate Services are not required on the Web server itself to support SSL, only the certificate). A Windows Server CA can generate the certificate, eliminating the need for you to purchase one from a commercial CA, such as Thawte or Verisign. However, unless the people viewing your site add your CA to their list of trusted sources, they'll receive certificate warnings when they view the site.

You use the Certification Authority console to manage certificate services on the local server or on a remote server. You can configure certificate policy settings, view pending and failed certificate requests, and view issued and revoked certificates. You also use the console to manage general CA properties such as the ability to publish certificates to the Active Directory, configure how the server responds to certificate request, control CA security, and other options.

Several sections in Chapter 3, including "Understanding Certificate Services," explain certificate services in detail and how to manage them with the Certification Authority console.

Cluster Administrator

The Cluster Administrator Console is available with Windows Server 2003 Enterprise Server and is the primary means by which you configure clustering. Clustering allows a group (cluster) of servers to function as a single logical unit for failover capability.

The Standard Server and Web Server platforms do not include clustering.

You can use the Cluster Administrator console to create and configure a cluster and for performing common tasks such as adding cluster nodes, configuring node and cluster properties, pausing the cluster service, and so on.

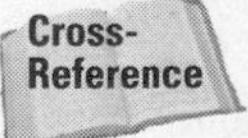

See Chapter 25 for a detailed discussion of clustering and cluster configuration.

Component Services

The primary function of the Component Services console (Figure 7-10) is to provide management tools for COM+ applications. COM+ provides a structure for developing distributed applications (client/server applications). The Component Services console lets you configure a system for Component Services, configure initial service settings, install and configure COM+ applications, and monitor and tune components.

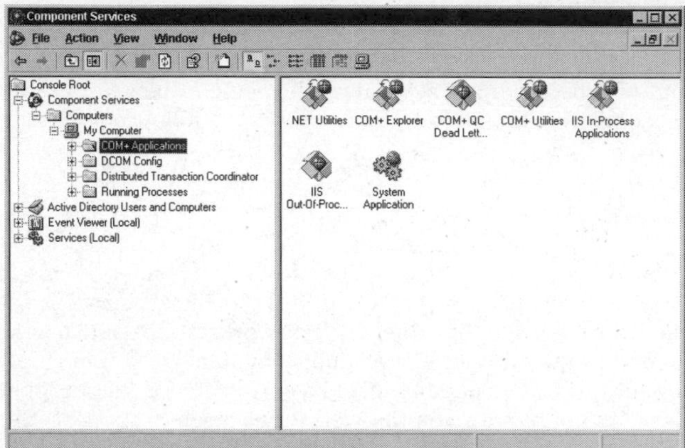

Figure 7-10: Use Component Services to configure COM+ applications as well as general Windows 2003 services.

Configuring COM+ applications goes hand-in-hand with COM+ application development. For that reason, this book doesn't provide detailed coverage of COM+ configuration.

The primary branches of the Component Services node under each computer are as follows:

- ✦ **COM+ Applications:** Use this branch to configure Component and Role properties and settings for COM+ components.
- ✦ **DCOM Config:** Use this branch to configure Distributed COM (DCOM) components, including setting security for them.
- ✦ **Distributed Transaction Coordinator:** Use this branch to view the DTC transaction list and monitor transaction statistics.
- ✦ **Running Processes:** Use this branch to monitor and debug running processes. Right-click an application and choose Dump to dump the application state to a file for debugging and analysis.

You'll notice that the Component Services console that is provided with Windows 2003 includes nodes for Event Viewer, Active Directory Users and Computers, and Services. These are also available as separate consoles. See the sections, "Event Viewer" and "Services," later in this chapter, for more details. See Chapter 2 for a discussion of Active Directory.

Computer Management

The Computer Management console (Figure 7-11) provides tools for managing several aspects of a system. Right-click My Computer and choose Manage or click Start ⇨ All Programs ⇨ Administrative Tools ⇨ Computer Management to open the Computer Management console. Computer Management is composed of three primary branches: System Tools, Storage, and Services and Applications. System Tools provides extensions for viewing information about the system, configuring devices, viewing event logs, and so on. Storage provides tools for managing physical and logical drives and removable storage. Services and Applications lets you configure telephony, Windows Management Instrumentation (WMI), services, the Indexing Service, and IIS. Other applications can appear under this branch as well, depending on the system's configuration.

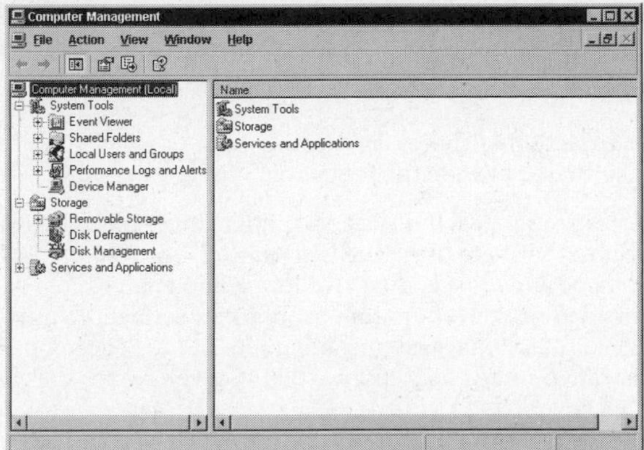

Figure 7-11: Computer Management integrates several snap-ins to help you manage a system, its storage devices, and services.

You can use Computer Management to manage either the local computer or a remote computer. Right-click the Computer Management node and choose Connect to another computer to manage a remote system. The tasks you can perform are usually the same whether locally or remotely, but some tasks can be performed within only the context of the local system. This chapter assumes that you're using Computer Management to manage the local system.

This section covers the snap-in extensions provided in the Computer Management console. However, many of these extensions can be used individually within their own consoles. For example, you can open `Services.msc` to configure services rather than using the Services node in Computer Management. Look in *`systemroot`*`\System32` for available snap-ins (`.msc` file extension).

Event Viewer

The Event Viewer snap-in takes the place of the standalone Event Viewer application in Windows NT. Use Event Viewer to view events in the Application, Security, and System logs, as well as to configure log behavior (size, rollover, and so on). See the section, "Using the Event Viewer," later in this chapter for more information.

Performance Logs and Alerts

The Performance Logs and Alerts branch of the Computer Management snap-in provides a tool for setting up performance monitoring. You can configure counter logs, trace logs, and alerts. This branch is useful only for viewing or modifying settings — it doesn't enable you to actually execute any performance monitoring. Instead, you need to use the Performance MMC snap-in. See Chapter 24 for detailed information on configuring performance logs and alerts and monitoring system performance.

Shared Folders

The Shared Folders branch of the Computer Management snap-in lets you view and manage shared folders, connections, and open files. It takes the place of features formerly found in the Windows NT Server Manager. The Shares node lets you view shares on the selected computer. In addition, you can double-click a share to view and modify its properties and share permissions. See Chapter 27 for information on publishing folders in the Active Directory.

Tip

You can create and manage shared folders through the Explorer interface. The advantage to using the Shared Folders console instead is that you can see all shares on the system at a glance.

You'll notice that a system includes a handful of shares by default, most of which are hidden shares (suffixed with a `$` sign). These shares include the following:

✦ *`drive`*`$`: Windows 2003 shares the root of each drive as a hidden share for administrative purposes. You can connect to the share using the UNC path `\\`*`server`*`\`*`drive`*`$`, where *server* is the computer name and *drive* is the drive letter, such as `\\appsrv\d$`. Members of the Administrators and Backup Operators groups can connect to administrative shares on Windows 2003 Professional systems. Members of the Server Operators group can connect to administrative shares on Windows 2003 Server systems, as well as Administrators and Backup Operators.

✦ `ADMIN$`: This administrative share points to the `systemroot` folder on the system (typically, \Windows or `\WINNT`) and is used by the system during remote administration.

✦ `IPC$`: The `IPC$` share is used to share named pipes and is used during remote administration and when viewing a computer's shares.

✦ `PRINT$`: This share enables remote printer administration and points by default to *`systemroot`*`\System32\spool\drivers`.

✦ `NETLOGON`: This share is used to support user logon, typically for storing user logon scripts and profiles. In Windows Server 2003 and 2000 Server domains, the `NETLOGON` share points to *`sysvol`*`\`*`domain`*`\Scripts` on the domain controller(s).

Cross-Reference

For a complete discussion of sharing and security, offline folder access, and related topics, see Chapter 27.

The Sessions node lets you view a list of users currently connected to the system. You can disconnect a user by right-clicking the user and choosing Close Session. Disconnecting a user could result in lost data for the user, so you might want to broadcast a console message to the user first. To do so, right-click The Shares or Shared Folders branch and choose All Tasks, Send Console Message.

Tip

When you are viewing sessions for a remote computer, your connection appears as an open-named pipe and can't be closed.

The Open Files branch lets you view files opened by remote users. Right-click an individual file and choose Close Open File to close the file. Or, right-click the Open Files node and choose Disconnect All Open Files to close all files. As when disconnecting users, closing files could result in a loss of data, so try to broadcast a console message to the user first.

Device Manager

Device Manager provides a unified interface for viewing and managing devices and their resources (DMA, memory, IRQ, and so on). Device Manager displays devices using a branch structure. Expand a device branch to view the devices in the branch. No special icon beside a device indicates the device is functioning properly. A yellow exclamation icon indicates a potential problem with the device, such as a resource conflict. A red X indicates the device is disconnected, disabled, or not in use in the current hardware profile.

Device Manager is the primary tool you use for configuring a system's hardware. To view or manage a device, locate it in the details pane and double-click the device (or right-click and choose Properties) to display the device's property sheet. The contents of the property vary according to the device type. Figure 7-12 shows a typical property sheet for a network adapter.

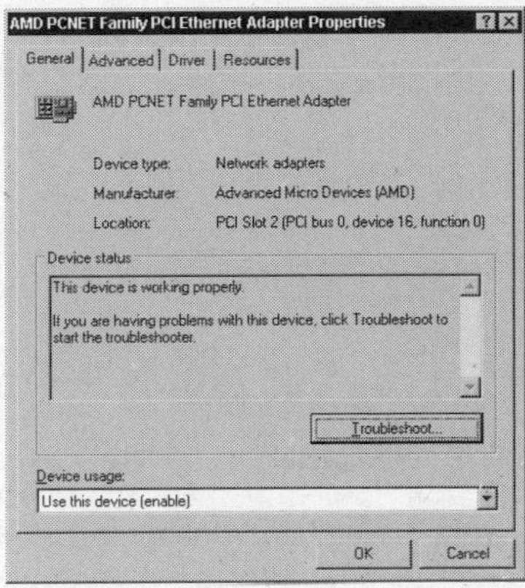

Figure 7-12: Use a device's property sheet to view and configure settings such as resource usage.

The General tab, shown in Figure 7-12, provides general information about a device, such as device type, manufacturer, and so on. Use the Device usage drop-down list to enable or disable the device. Click Troubleshooter if you're having problems with the device and want to use a wizard to help troubleshoot the connection.

It isn't practical to cover all the settings for all possible types of devices in this chapter. The following sections explain tasks common to most devices: changing drivers and modifying resource assignments.

Driver changes

The Driver property page lets you view details about, uninstall, and update a device's driver. Click Driver Details to view a list of the files that comprise the device's driver. This list is useful for checking the file or driver version to make sure that you're using a specific version of the driver. Use Uninstall if you want to remove the selected device's driver.

The Update Driver button opens the Upgrade Device Driver wizard. Use the wizard to install an updated driver for the device. The wizard gives you the option of searching your system's floppy and CD-ROM drives, other specific location (local or remote share), or the Microsoft Windows Update Web site. Just follow the prompts to complete the update. In some cases, changing drivers requires a system restart.

Resource assignment

Because it supports plug and play (PnP), Windows 2003 can assign device resources such as DMA, IRQ, I/O base address, and UMA memory allocation automatically. In some cases, particularly with legacy devices (those not supporting PnP), you'll have to configure resource allocation manually. To do so, open a device's property sheet and click the Resources tab. If the Resources page doesn't provide any resources to change, click Set Configuration Manually to switch the page to manual property configuration (Figure 7-13).

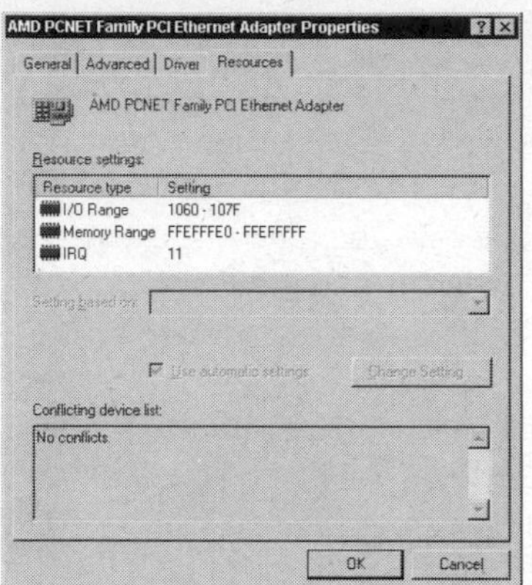

Figure 7-13: Set a device's resource utilization through its Resources property page.

In most cases, Windows 2003 provides multiple, pre-defined configurations for devices, such as a combination of a specific IRQ and I/O range. Deselect the Use automatic settings option and then select a different configuration set from the Setting based on the drop-down list. To modify individual settings, first click in the Resource settings list the resource you want to change and then click Change Setting. Specify the desired setting in the resulting dialog box and click OK.

Local Users and Groups

The Local Users and Groups branch of the Computer Management snap-in lets you create and manage local user accounts and groups on Windows 2003 standalone and member servers. This branch is disabled on a domain controller, because you use the Active Directory Users and Computers snap-in to create user accounts and groups in the Active Directory.

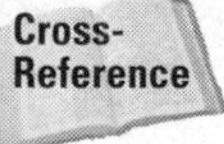

Users and groups are covered in detail in Chapter 13.

If you're familiar with creating user accounts and groups under Windows NT or Windows 2000, you'll have no problem using Local Users and Groups to create accounts. If not, see Chapter 13 for a detailed description of how to create accounts and groups. The primary difference between creating local accounts and groups and the same objects in the Active Directory is that the Active Directory provides for additional account and group properties. In addition, creating accounts and groups requires an understanding of permissions, rights, group policy, and user profiles, all of which are explained in Chapter 13.

Disk Management

The Disk Management node is the place to go to manage physical disks and volumes. Disk Management takes the place of the Windows NT Disk Administrator, and an important distinction is that unlike the Disk Administrator, Disk Management performs most tasks immediately. In Disk Administrator, you must commit changes for most tasks (such as creating or deleting a partition). If you're an experienced Windows NT administrator, keep this important point in mind when making storage changes with Disk Management.

Some of the tasks you can perform with Disk Management include managing partitions, converting basic disks to dynamic disks, creating volumes (basic, spanned, striped, mirrored, RAID-5), creating and deleting physical volumes, formatting disks, and so on.

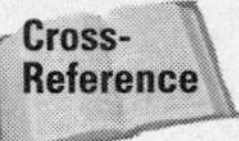

For a complete discussion of storage devices and management (including the Disk Management node), see Chapter 19.

Disk Defragmenter

As a disk is used over time, the data on the disk is scattered into noncontiguous clusters, becoming *fragmented.* Disk performance is greatest when data is not fragmented, as it takes less time to read the data (because the drive heads don't have to move as much to reassemble the data). The Disk Defragmenter node in Computer Management lets you analyze a disk for fragmentation and defragment the disk.

See Chapter 26 for a discussion of Disk Defragmenter and other options for improving disk performance.

Removable Storage

The Removable Storage node provides a tool for configuring and managing removable storage devices and media. You use Removable Storage to track media such as tapes and optical disks and their hardware devices (jukeboxes, tape changers, and so on). Removable storage is a technology subset of Hierarchical Storage Management (HSM) and Remote Storage Services (RSS). These new technologies provide a means for automatic data archival and retrieval of archived data.

The Removable Storage node lets you create and manage media pools, insert and eject media, mount and dismount media, view media and library status, inventory libraries, and assign permissions for security on media and libraries.

Telephony

The Telephony node provides a centralized tool for managing telephony properties for the selected computer, including configuring telephony providers and assigning user permission for various providers.

WMI Control

The WMI Control node in Computer Management provides tools for configuring and managing Windows Management Instrumentation (WMI) on a computer. WMI works in conjunction with the Web-Based Enterprise Management initiative to provide a means of collecting data about computers and their component devices both locally and remotely. WMI functions at the device-driver level, providing event notification from drivers and enabling WMI to collect data for analysis and management purposes. WMI is a key component in enterprise management. The WMI Control node provides a means for configuring general settings, logging, backing up and restoring the WMI repository, and security to control WMI access.

Services

In Windows 2003, *services* are applications that perform specific functions such as networking, logon, print spooling, remote access, and so on within the operating system. You can think of services as operating system-oriented applications that function by themselves or in concert with other services or user applications to perform specific tasks or provide certain features within the OS. Device drivers, for example, function as services. Windows 2003 Server includes several standard services by default, and many third-party applications function as or include their own services. A background virus scrubber is a good example of a possible third-party service.

Windows NT administrators will remember the Services object in the Control Panel that enables you to configure, start, stop, and pause services. In Windows 2003, the Services node in the Computer Management snap-in (and by itself as the Services.msc console) takes over that function (Figure 7-14). Services lists the installed services on the target system, and when Detail view is selected, displays description, status, startup type, and account the service uses to log on.

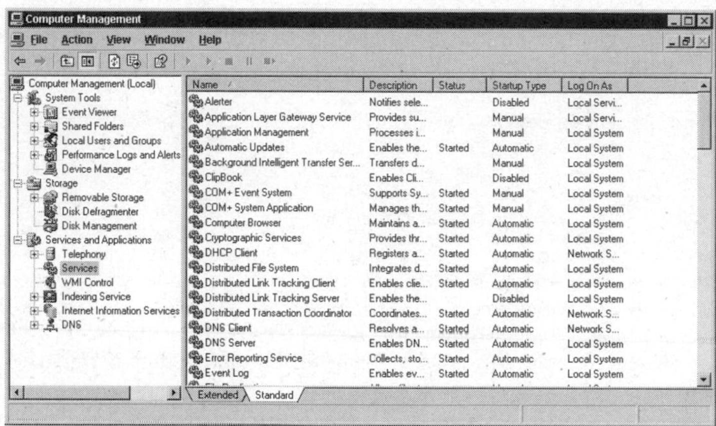

Figure 7-14: Use Services to configure, start, stop, and pause services, as well as view service dependencies.

Starting and stopping services

A running service processes requests and generally performs the task it was designed to accomplish. Stopping a service terminates the service and removes it from memory. Starting a service initializes and activates the service so that it can perform its task or function. For example, the DNS Client functions as a DNS resolver, processing requests for name to address mapping in the DNS namespace. If you stop the DNS Client service, it is no longer available to process DNS queries.

Windows 2003 supports three startup modes for services:

✦ **Automatic:** The service starts automatically at system startup.

✦ **Manual:** The service can be started by a user or a dependent service. The service does not start automatically at system startup unless a dependent service is set for automatic startup (therefore causing the service to start).

✦ **Disabled:** The service cannot be started by the system, a user, or dependent service.

You set a service's startup mode through the General page of the service's properties. Open the Services node in the Computer Management MMC snap-in (or open the Services.msc console in `systemroot\System32`) and double-click the service. Figure 7-15 shows the General property page for a typical service. From the Startup type drop-down list, choose the desired startup mode and click Apply or OK.

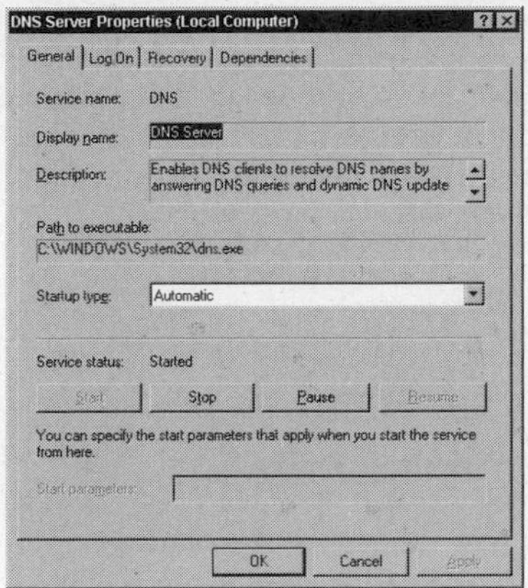

Figure 7-15: Use the General page to configure service startup, control the service (start/stop), and set general properties.

The General tab also lets you start, stop, pause, or resume a service. Starting and stopping were explained previously. Pausing a service causes it to suspend operation but doesn't remove the service from memory. Resume a paused service to have it continue functioning. Open a service's General property page and then click Start, Stop, Pause, or Resume, as appropriate.

You also can start and stop services from a console prompt using the NET START and NET STOP commands along with the service's name, which you'll find on its General property page in the Service name field. For example, use the command NET START ALERTER to start the Alerter service. Use NET STOP ALERTER to stop it.

NET START and NET STOP are very useful for controlling services remotely. If the telnet service is running on the remote computer, you can telnet to the computer and use NET START and NET STOP to start and stop services on the remote system.

Setting General service properties

Other settings on a service's General property page control how the service is listed in the details pane and how the service starts up. Use the Display name field to specify the name that will appear under the Name field for the service in the details pane. Specify the service's description in the Description field. Use the Start parameters field to specify optional switches or parameters to determine how the service starts. These are just like command-line switches for a console command.

Configuring service logon

The Log On property page for a service controls how the service logs on and the hardware profiles in which the service is used. Most services log on using the System account, although in some cases, you'll want to specify a different account for a service to use. Some types of administrative services often use their own accounts because they require administrative privileges. So, you would create an account specifically for the service and make it a member of the Administrators group or give it the equivalent permissions, subject to its specific needs.

Tip Avoid using the Administrator account itself for a service to log on. When you change the Administrator password, which you should do often if you use this account, you will also have to reconfigure each service that used the Administrator account to change the password in the service's properties. Using a special account for those services instead lets you change the Administrator account password without affecting any services. Check out Chapter 3 for a discussion of how to protect the Administrator account and discontinue its use.

The Log On property page contains the following controls:

- **Local System account:** Select to have the service log on using the local System account.
- **Allow service to interact with desktop:** Select to allow the service to provide a UI for the currently logged-on user to interact with the service. This setting has no effect if the service isn't designed to provide a UI.
- **This account:** Select and specify an account in the associated text box (or browse through the account list) to have the service log on with an account other than the local System account.
- **Password/Confirm password:** Enter and confirm the password for the account specified in This account.
- **Enable/Disable:** Select a hardware profile from the list of profiles and click Enable to enable the service in that profile or Disable to disable the service in the profile.

Configuring service recovery

Another behavior you can configure for services is what happens when the service fails. You can configure the service to restart, execute a file, or reboot the computer. In addition, you can configure a fail counter to track how many times the service has failed. You set a service's recover options through its Recovery property page (Figure 7-16).

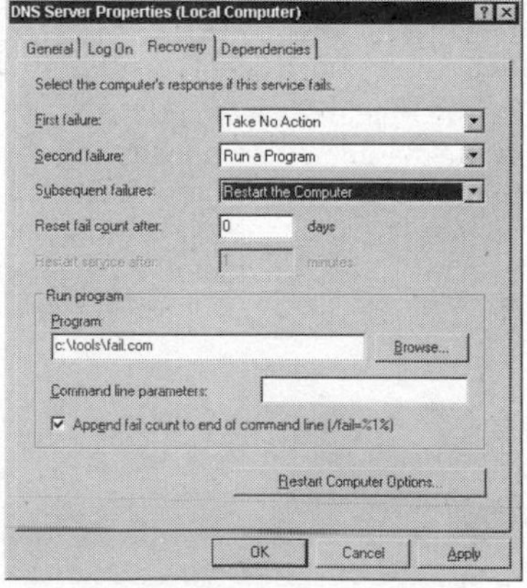

Figure 7-16: Configure service recovery option to specify what actions the service should take when it fails.

The Recovery page contains the following options:

- **First failure/Second failure/Subsequent failures:** With these three drop-down lists, select the action (or no action) to take on the specified failure. You can choose to take no action, restart the service, execute a file, or reboot the computer.

- **Reset fail count after:** Specify the number of days after which to reset the fail counter to zero.
- **Restart service after:** Specify the number of minutes that will pass between service failure and restart. Increase from the default of one minute if the system needs more time to stabilize after the service fails.
- **Run Program:** Use this group of commands to identify a program or script that will execute when the service fails. For example, you might create a script that broadcasts a message with the fail count and other information to the Administrators group. Use the Append fail count option to append the current fail count to the end of the command line (passing the fail count to the command for internal processing).
- **Restart Computer Options:** Click this button to specify the number of minutes to wait before restarting the computer and an optional message to broadcast on the network prior to restart (such as a reboot warning to your users).

Viewing dependencies

You can use the Dependencies page to view other services on which the selected service depends as well as services that are dependent on the selected service. This property page displays information only and doesn't allow you to configure or modify dependencies. The page is self-explanatory.

Indexing Service

The Indexing Service uses *document filters* to read and create a catalog of documents on a system and enables a quick text-based search through the catalog for documents that meet the search criteria. The document filter extracts information from the document and passes that information to the Indexing Service for inclusion in the catalog. You can search using the Search command in the Start menu, the Query the Catalog node of Indexing Service in Computer Management, or a Web page. You can search based on a variety of criteria including document name, author, contents, and so on. You might, for example, use the Indexing Service to build a catalog of internal documents or catalog your organization's Web site(s). The Indexing Service will index the following document types:

- HTML
- Text
- Microsoft Office 95 or later
- Internet Mail and News
- Other documents supported by an appropriate document filter (such as a third-party filter)

Tip

Indexing Service is useful even on a workstation to index user documents and to speed up searching for specific documents or groups of documents.

Use the Indexing Service branch of the Computer Management console to configure the Indexing Service and query the index for a list of documents matching your query criteria. The Indexing Service branch appears in Computer Management, even if the Indexing Service is not yet installed. To install the Indexing Service, open the Control Panel and run Add or Remove Programs. Click Add or Remove Windows Components in the left toolbar, select Indexing Service in the Components list, and then click Next and follow the prompts to install the service.

Planning for the Indexing Service

When planning for the Indexing Service, understand that the system configuration determines the service's performance. Indexing Service has the same minimum hardware requirements as Windows 2003 Server, but increasing the number of documents to be indexed increases the memory requirements. See the Help file for Indexing Service (press F1 with Indexing Service selected in Computer Management) for specific recommendations.

You also need to plan the file system to accommodate Indexing Service. Placing the catalog on a FAT volume will enable users to see the catalog even if they have no permission to view individual documents in the catalog. Placing the catalog on an NTFS volume offers the best security as Indexing Service maintains all NTFS security ACLs (Access Control Lists). Users will not see documents in the results list of a query if they don't have the permissions necessary to view the documents. In addition, the Indexing Service uses the System account to log on. If you deny the System account access to a given folder or file, Indexing Service will not be able to access the folder or file and won't index it. Also, encrypted documents are never indexed.

Where you store the index catalog(s) is also important. You should not store catalogs within a Web site (in the Web site's folder), because Internet Information Services (IIS) can lock the catalog and prevent it from being updated. Also, avoid running antivirus or backup software that locks the catalog files, which would cause Indexing Service to time out while attempting to update the catalogs. The best practice is to create a folder on an NTFS volume specifically for your catalog files and place each catalog in its own subfolder of that primary folder.

Tip You can change the location of the default System catalog created automatically when you install Indexing Service. First, create the folder to contain the catalog. Then right-click Indexing Service and choose Stop to stop the service. Open the Registry Editor and modify the value of HKEY_LOCAL_MACHINE\CurrentControlSet\Control\ContentIndex\Catalogs\System\Locatio n to point to the desired location. Close the Registry Editor and restart the Indexing Service.

Creating and configuring a catalog

You can create multiple index catalogs to suit your needs. To create a new catalog, open the Computer Management snap-in and right-click the Indexing Service branch. Choose New ➪ Catalog. Specify a name for the catalog and its location and then click OK. The catalog remains offline until you restart the Indexing Service.

Next, expand the newly created catalog in the Indexing Service branch in Computer Management. Right-click Directories under the catalog's branch and choose New ➪ Directory to display the Add Directory dialog box (Figure 7-17). Specify options according to the following list:

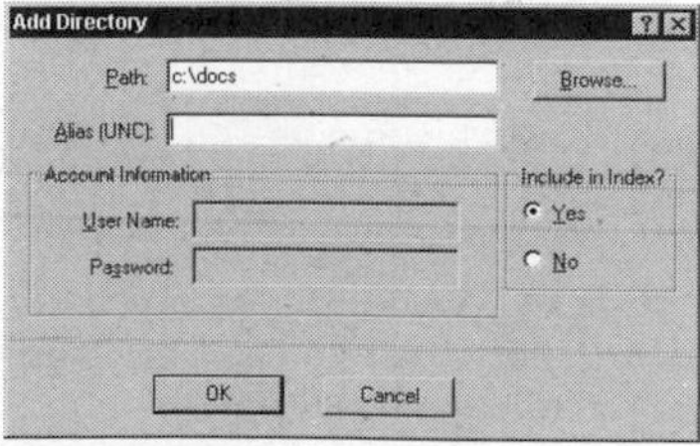

Figure 7-17: Add directories to a catalog to include their contents in the index.

✦ **Path:** Specify the path to the folder you want to add in the catalog or click Browse to the folder.

✦ **Alias (UNC):** If you're specifying a folder on a nonlocal computer, type the UNC path to the share in the form `\\computer\share`, where *computer* is the remote computer's name and *share* is the share where the folder is located.

✦ **Account Information:** For a directory on a remote computer, specify the domain\account and password to be used to access the computer.

✦ **Include in Index:** Select Yes to include the folder or No to exclude it from the catalog. This option enables you to exclude a subfolder of a folder that is included in the catalog. Add the parent folder and set it to Yes and then add the subfolder separately and set it to No to exclude it.

After you define the directories for the catalog, stop and restart the Indexing Service to populate the catalog. The Properties branch will be empty until you stop and restart the service.

Querying the catalog

As mentioned previously, you can query a catalog through a computer's Search command in the Start menu, a Web page, or the Computer Management snap-in. To perform a query using the snap-in, open the Indexing Service branch and click Query the Catalog under the desired catalog entry. Windows 2003 provides a query form in which you can specify the query criteria and options and view the results of the query.

Tuning performance

On a system with a large number of documents, you might want to fine-tune Indexing Service for best performance. Right-click Indexing Service in the Computer Management snap-in and choose Stop to stop the service. Right-click Indexing Service again and choose Tune Performance to display the Indexing Service Usage dialog box (Figure 7-18). The options on the dialog box let you specify how often Indexing Service is used on the computer, and Windows 2003 automatically configures the service based on your selection. Choose the Customize option and then click the Customize button to specify custom settings for indexing and querying. For indexing, you can set a slider control between Lazy and Instant. Lazy causes indexing to function more as a background task, and Instant grants it maximum system resources, which takes resources from other running tasks. For querying, you can set a slider between low load and high load, depending on how many queries the computer receives. Make sure to restart the service after you finish configuring it.

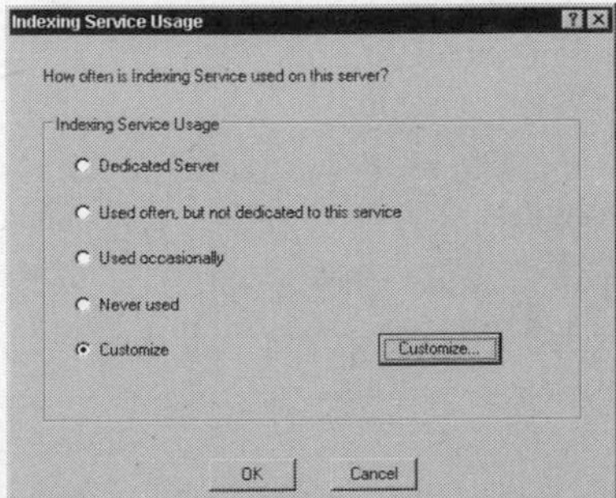

Figure 7-18: Use the Indexing Service Usage dialog box to optimize Indexing Service's performance.

Event Viewer

Microsoft defines an *event* in Windows 2003 as any significant occurrence in the operating system or an application that requires users (particularly administrators) to be notified. Events are recorded in *event logs*. Events and the event log are important administrative tools because they're indispensable for identifying and troubleshooting problems, tracking security access (logon, logoff, resource auditing, and so on), and tracking status of the system and its applications.

Some features are not available if you use the Event Viewer console within the Computer Management console. This section assumes that you are opening the Event Viewer console directly from the Administrative Tools folder.

Events fall into three general categories:

✦ **System:** These include system-related events such as service startup and shutdown, driver initialization, system-wide warning messages, network events, and other events that apply to the system in general.

✦ **Security:** These include events related to security such as logon/logoff and resource access (auditing).

✦ **Application:** These events are associated with specific applications. For example, a virus scrubber might log events related to a virus scan, cleaning operation, and so on, to the application log.

In addition to the three default event logs, other Windows 2003 services create their own logs. The Directory Service, DNS Service, and File Replication Service are some examples of services that create their own event logs. You view these logs with the Event Viewer, just as you do the three standard logs.

Events range in severity from informational messages to serious events such as service or application failures. The primary event categories include informational, warning, error, success audit, and failure audit. The severity of an event is identified by an icon beside the event in the log. For example, warnings use an exclamation icon and errors use an X in a red circle. Each event has common properties associated with it:

✦ **Date and Time:** This is the date and time the event occurred.

✦ **Source:** This identifies the source of the event, such as a service, device driver, application, resource, and so on. The source property is useful for determining what caused the event (cause and event source are not synonymous).

✦ **Category:** The source determines the category for an event. For example, security categories include logon, logoff, policy change, and object access, among others.

✦ **Event:** Each event includes an event ID, an integer generated by the source to identify the event uniquely.

✦ **User:** This property identifies the user that caused the event to be generated (if applicable).

✦ **Computer:** This property identifies the computer that caused the event to be generated (if applicable).

The Event Viewer MMC snap-in is the tool you use to view and manage the event logs. The Event Viewer presents the logs in the tree pane as individual branches. When you click a log, its events appear in the contents pane (Figure 7-19).

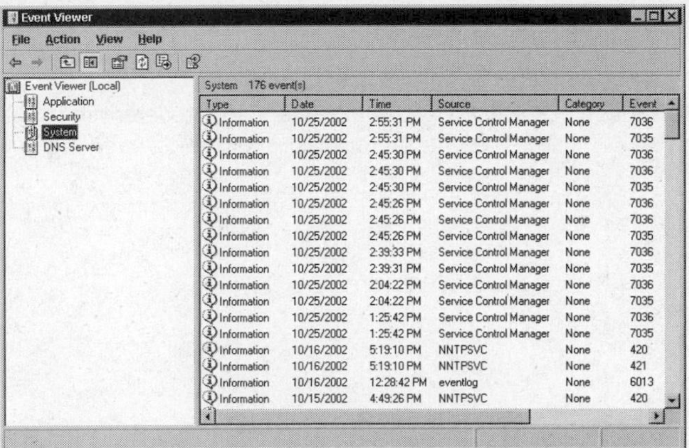

Figure 7-19: Use the Event Viewer to browse the event logs and configure log operation.

Viewing and filtering events

Viewing an event is easy — just open Event Viewer, locate the event, and double-click it (or select it and press Enter). Event Viewer opens a dialog box showing the event's properties (Figure 7-20). The top of the dialog box includes general information about the event such as time and date, event ID, and so on. The Description field provides a detailed description of the event, which most of the time (but not always) offers a decipherable explanation of the event. The bottom portion of the dialog box displays additional data included with the event, if any. You can choose between viewing the data in byte (hexadecimal) or DWORD format. In most cases, it takes a software engineer to interpret the data because doing so requires an understanding of the code generating the data.

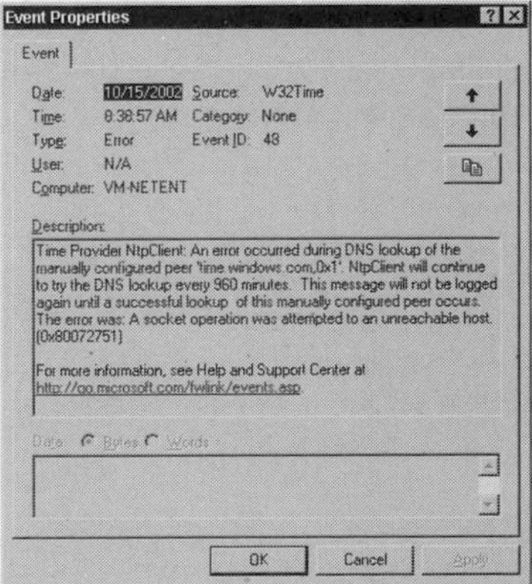

Figure 7-20: An event's property sheet provides detailed information about the event.

Use the up and down arrows in the upper half of the dialog box to view previous and following events, respectively. Click the document button to copy the selected event to the Clipboard.

By default, the Event Viewer shows all events for a selected log. In many cases, it is helpful to be able to filter the view so that Event Viewer shows only events that meet specific criteria.

To apply a filter, click a log and choose View ➪ Filter to access the Filter property sheet for the log (Figure 7-21).

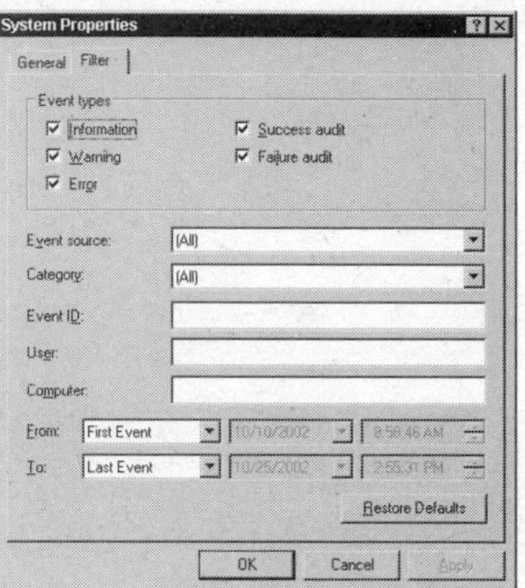

Figure 7-21: Use the Filter page to determine which events are displayed for the selected log in the Event Viewer.

You can choose to view events based on their type, source, category, ID, user, computer, or date range. For example, you might want to filter based on source if you're trying to troubleshoot a problem with a specific application, service, or driver. To create the filter, select your criteria in the dialog box and click OK. Choose View ➪ All Records to remove the filter and view all events in the log.

Setting log properties

Each log includes general properties that define the way the log appears in Event Viewer, the size of the log, how it reacts when the maximum size is reached, and so on. Select a log and choose Action ➪ Properties or right-click a log and choose Properties to display its General property page (Figure 7-22).

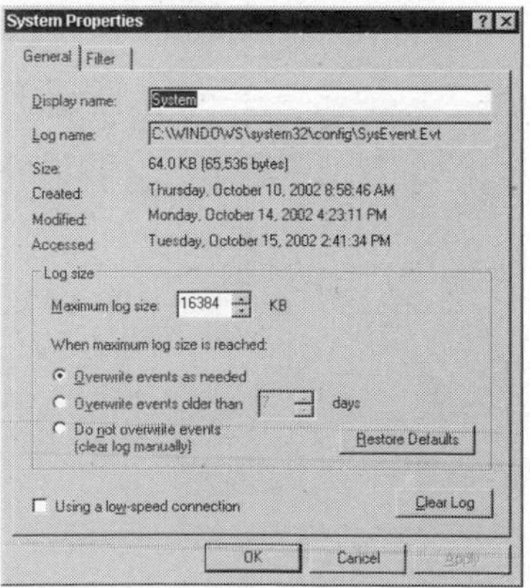

Figure 7-22: Configure a log's appearance and size through its General property page.

Some of the information displayed in the General page is read-only, such as the location of the log file. You can change the Display name property to change the name by which the log is listed in the tree pane in the Event Viewer.

The Log size group of controls specifies the maximum log size and the action Windows 2003 takes when the maximum size is reached. The options are generally self-explanatory. Keep in mind, however, that if you select "Do not overwrite events", Windows 2003 will stop logging events to the log when it fills up. Although Windows 2003 will notify you when the log is full, you'll need to monitor the event log and clear it periodically to make sure that you don't lose events.

Tip

Using a low-speed connection prevents Event Viewer from downloading all of the event data before you specifically request it and is useful when the logs are located on another computer, which is accessible through a slow network connection (such as dial-up).

Saving and clearing logs

Occasionally you'll want to save an event log and/or clear the log. Saving a log copies it to another event file of a name you specify. Clearing a log removes all the events in the log. You might want to create a benchmark, for example, prior to troubleshooting a problem. Or, you might want to periodically archive your event logs. In any case, you save the log and then clear it.

To save a log, select the log and choose Action ➪ Save Log File As or right-click the log and choose Save Log File As. Specify a name and location for the log file and click OK. After you save a log file, you can open the log again in Event Viewer to view its contents. Keep in mind that a saved log is static and doesn't gather additional events.

When it's time to clear a log, open the log's General property page and click Clear Log. Windows 2003 will prompt you to confirm the action.

Viewing logs on another computer

You can use Event Viewer to view the log file of other computers in your network (or across the Internet via a VPN connection). To open another computer's event logs, open Event Viewer, right-click the Event Viewer branch, and choose Connect to another computer. Specify the computer's name or browse the network for the computer and then click OK. Select the Local computer option to reconnect to the local computer's event logs.

Arranging the log view

You can arrange the Event Viewer results pane to specify which columns appear and their display order. If you seldom need to see the User or Computer columns, for example, you can turn them off.

To control column display, click any node in the Event Viewer and choose View ➪ Choose Columns to open the Modify Columns dialog. Add and remove columns as desired and use Move Up and Move Down to change the display order. Click OK to apply the changes.

Tip

You can drag columns in Event Viewer to change their display order.

Monitoring Performance

Monitoring and tuning system performance is an important administrative function in almost all situations. The Performance MMC snap-in lets you monitor a wide variety of system parameters regarding memory, processor, disk, I/O, and many other objects. The Performance snap-in takes the place of the Windows NT Performance Monitor.

Monitoring a system for optimum performance and fine-tuning the system is a fairly complex task requiring an understanding of the types of objects you can monitor and their relationships to one another. You'll find a discussion of performance tuning and the Performance snap-in in Chapter 24.

Server extensions

In addition to the MMC snap-ins described in previous sections, Windows 2003 Server incorporates several other snap-ins for managing specific services. For example, the DNS, DHCP, and IIS services all have their own snap-ins. Because these snap-ins are the primary means by which you control these services, they are best discussed in the context of the service. You'll find these snap-ins discussed throughout this book where appropriate.

Configuring Your Server Wizard

Windows 2003, like Windows 2000 Server before it, provides a Configure Your Server wizard to help you configure the server for specific uses. For example, you might want to configure a server as a file or print server. The wizard helps simplify the process. Where the wizard is most useful, however, is for setting up a server to perform more advanced functions, such as act as a domain controller.

You'll find the Configure Your Server wizard in the Administrative Tools folder. Within the wizard, you can choose a specific server function, as shown in Figure 7-23, and also view the server options currently enabled on the server.

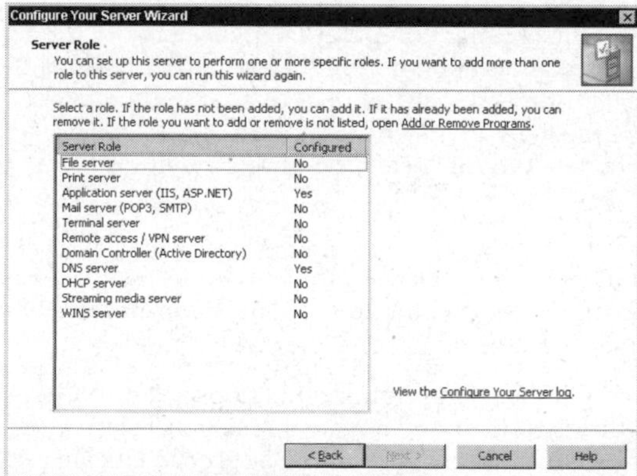

Figure 7-23: View and configure server options with the Configure Your Server wizard.

When you click on a server function in the wizard, the wizard displays a description of that feature and provides links to additional information about the service in question.

You should have no trouble enabling basic server roles with the wizard. Each of these functions is covered in depth in other chapters where applicable.

Managing Your Server Console

The Manage Your Server console provides a handy way to access configuration tools for specific server roles, such as Application Server, IIS, file server, and so on. Manage Your Server works in conjunction with the Configure Your Server wizard. For example, when you click Add or Remove a Role, 2003 launches the Configure Your Server wizard to accomplish the change.

As Figure 7-24 shows, Manage Your Server lists the currently enabled roles and provides quick access to the management consoles or Web interfaces for each role. More than that, however, Manage Your Server offers quick access to additional local and remote information about each role and how to configure it, as well as access to the Administrative Tools folder, server properties, Microsoft TechNet, and several other useful resources. Although Manage Your Server doesn't really offer anything in itself that isn't available elsewhere in 2003 or on the Web, it does bring together several of these resources into one location.

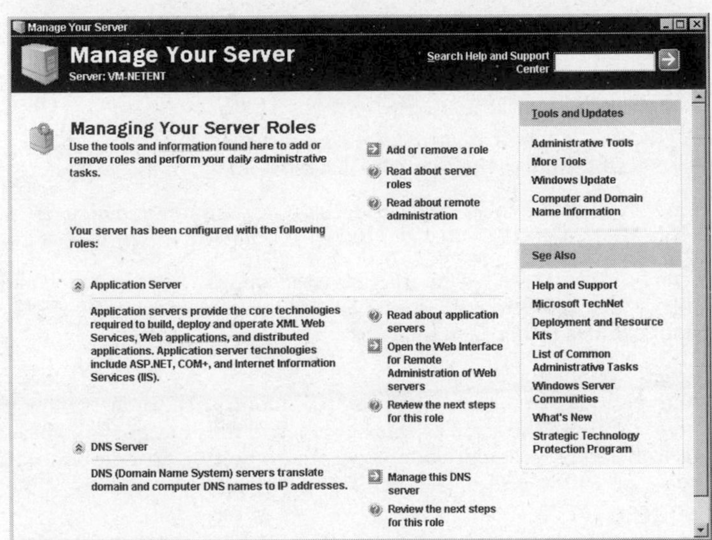

Figure 7-24: View and configure server options with the Configure Your Server wizard.

Because Manage Your Server doesn't offer features specific to its interface but rather relies on the other management tools included with 2003, we focus on those service-specific consoles throughout this book where applicable.

Working with Data Sources (ODBC)

ODBC, which stands for Open Database Connectivity, provides a framework for database engines to communicate with client applications. An example of such a client-server tool is WebBase, a tool from Expertelligence (`http://www.expertelligence.com`) that lets you integrate database queries in Web pages. WebBase makes SQL (Structured Query Language) queries through ODBC drivers to create a Web page based on the results of the query. So,

ODBC drivers serve as a middleman between a database and a client application, coordinating transactions and translating between the client and the database. In some cases, they can take the place of the database engine. For example, a server doesn't need Microsoft Access installed to enable clients to query an Access database file stored on the server, which is a typical practice of report engines such as Seagate Crystal Reports.

In order for client applications to communicate with a data source stored on a computer, you must configure the appropriate ODBC driver and connection on the target server. For example, if the client application needs to access an Access database, you need to first configure the Access ODBC driver on the computer where the database is located. The Data Sources administrative tool lets you configure and manage ODBC drivers and their associated data sources. This section of the chapter explains how to configure ODBC drivers.

The Data Sources tool is one of the few administrative tools that functions as a standalone utility rather than as an MMC snap-in.

Defining DSNs

You make data sources available to clients by creating a Data Source Name (DSN). Three types of DSNs exist:

✦ **User:** A user DSN is visible only to the user who is logged on when the DSN is created.

✦ **System:** A system DSN is visible to all local services on a computer and all users who log on locally to the computer.

✦ **File:** A file DSN can be shared by all users who have the same drivers installed and who have the necessary permissions to access the DSN. Unlike user and system DSNs, file DSNs are stored in text files rather than the registry.

The DSN identifies the data source, the driver associated with a data source, and other properties that define the interaction between the client and the data source, such as timeout, read-only mode, and so on. You use the same process to create a DSN for most database types. The exception is SQL Server, which provides a wizard for setting up a data source.

Defining a data source

To create a data source, you first open the ODBC Data Source Administrator. To do so, click Start ⇨ All Programs ⇨ Administrative Tools ⇨ Data Sources (ODBC). In the ODBC Data Source Administrator, click the tab for the DSN type you want to create and then click Add. Select the desired data source type and click Finish. Except in the case of the SQL Server driver, ODBC prompts you for information, which varies according to the driver selected. Define settings as desired and click OK to create the DSN.

Setting up an SQL Server data source

The Microsoft SQL Server ODBC driver provides a wizard to configure an SQL data source. This section explains the options you find when setting up an SQL Server ODBC driver. The first wizard page contains the following options:

✦ **Name:** This name appears in the Data Sources list on the DSN page for the data source.

✦ **Description:** This optional description appears with the DSN name on the DSN page for the data source.

✦ **Server:** Here, you specify the IP address or host name of the SQL server computer.

The second page of the wizard (Figure 7-25) prompts for connection and authentication options for the data source. The following list summarizes the options:

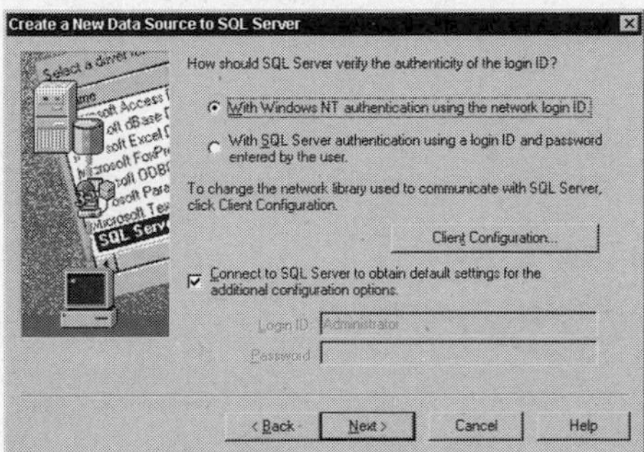

Figure 7-25: Specify connection and authentication options.

- **With Windows NT authentication using the network login ID:** Select this option to have the SQL Server ODBC driver request a trusted connection to the server. The driver uses the current client logon user name and password to authenticate the request on the server. In the case of a service or Web server, the credentials are assigned to the service or specified in the code that makes the query. The specified user name and password must have an association to a SQL Server login ID on the SQL Server computer.
- **With SQL Server authentication using a login ID and password entered by the user:** Select this option to require the user to specify a SQL Server login ID and password for all connection requests.
- **Connect to SQL Server to obtain default settings for the additional configuration options:** Select this option to have the SQL Server ODBC driver connect to the SQL Server identified on the first page of the wizard to obtain the correct settings for options in remaining configuration wizard pages. When you click Next with this option selected, the driver connects to the SQL Server and obtains the data. Deselect this option to use default settings rather than connect to the SQL server to obtain the information.
- **Login ID:** Specify the user name to connect to the specified SQL Server to retrieve the settings for subsequent wizard pages (see preceding bullet). This username and the associated Password field are not used for actual data connections after the data source is created, but are used only to retrieve information from the SQL Server for the remaining configuration pages.
- **Password:** Specify the password to use with the username specified in the Login ID field.
- **Client Configuration:** Click to use the Network Library Configuration dialog box. Usually you do not have to configure the network client configuration for the data source. Occasionally, however, you might need to specify the network connection mechanism and other options that define how the client connects to the data source. The options in Connection parameters are specific to the network connection type you select from the Network Libraries list of options.

In the next page of the wizard, you specify the database name and other options for the data source. Figure 7-26 shows the page. The following list describes its options:

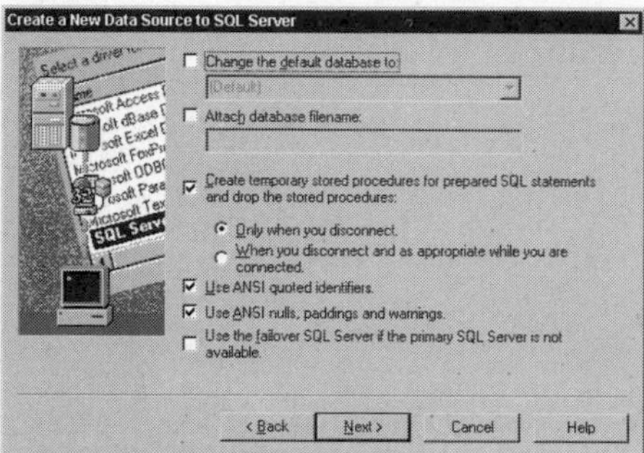

Figure 7-26: Specify the database name and other database options.

✦ **Change the default database to:** Choose a database from the drop-down list to define the default database for the data source, overriding the default database for the specified login ID. Deselect this option to use the default database defined for the login ID on the server.

✦ **Attach database filename:** Specify the full name and path of the primary file for an attachable database. The specified database is used as the default database for the data source.

✦ **Create temporary stored procedures for prepared SQL statements and drop the stored procedures:** Select this option to have the driver create temporary stored procedures to support the SQLPrepare ODBC function and then choose one of the associated options (see the following bullets). Deselect if you don't want the driver to store these procedures.

- **Only when you disconnect:** Have the stored procedures created for the SQLPrepare function dropped only when the SQLDisconnect function is called. This improves performance by reducing the overhead involved in dropping the stored procedures while the application is running, but it can lead to a buildup of temporary stored procedures. This particularly applies to applications that issue numerous SQLPrepare calls or that run for a long time without disconnecting.

- **When you disconnect and as appropriate while you are connected:** Have the stored procedures dropped when SQLDisconnect is called, SQLFreeHandle is called for the statement handle, SQLPrepare or SQLExecDirect is called to process a new SQL statement on the same handle, or when a catalog function is called. Using this option entails more overhead while the application is running, but it helps prevent a build-up of temporarily stored procedures.

✦ **Use ANSI quoted identifiers:** Enforce ANSI rules for quote marks so that they can only be used for identifiers such as table and column names. Character strings must be enclosed in single quotes.

✦ **Use ANSI nulls, paddings and warnings:** Specify that the ANSI_NULLS, ANSI_WARNINGS, and ANSI_PADDINGS options are set to on when the driver connects to the data source.

✦ **Use the failover SQL Server if the primary SQL Server is not available:** Have the connection attempt to use the failover server if supported by the primary SQL Server. When a connection is lost, the driver cleans up the current transaction and attempts to reconnect to the primary SQL Server. The driver attempts to connect to the failover server if the driver determines that the primary server is unavailable.

The final page of the wizard (Figure 7-27) prompts for miscellaneous options as described in the following list:

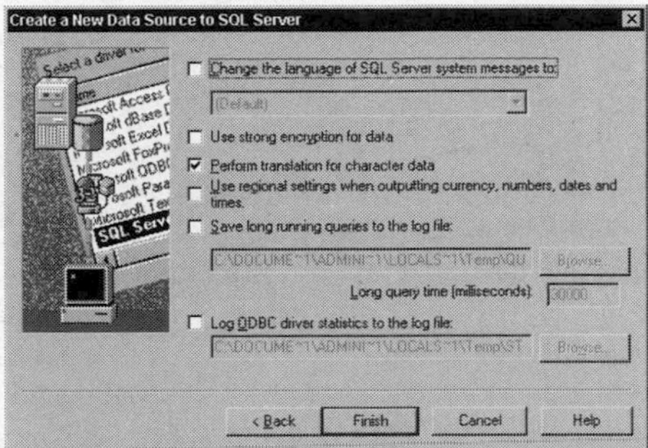

Figure 7-27: Specify miscellaneous database options.

✦ **Change the language of SQL Server system messages to:** Specify the language used to generate SQL Server system messages. The server can contain multiple sets of system messages, each in a different language. This option is dimmed if the server has only one language installed.

✦ **Use Strong Encryption for Data:** Encrypt data using strong encryption.

✦ **Perform translation for character data:** Select this option to convert ANSI strings using Unicode. Deselect the option to disable translation of extended ANSI codes.

✦ **Use regional settings when outputting currency, numbers, dates and times:** Select this option to have the regional settings of the client computer used to display currency, numbers, dates, and other region-specific elements.

✦ **Save long running queries to the log file:** Log any query that takes longer than the time specified in the Long query time field.

✦ **Long query time (milliseconds):** Specifies the maximum threshold value for logging long-running queries.

✦ **Log ODBC driver statistics to the log file:** Log driver statistics to a tab-delimited log file.

ODBC Component Checker

A non-homogenous set of ODBC components can lead to all sorts of strange and difficult-to-trace problems. For example, a Web application that queries an ODBC connection might receive a nonspecific server error when it attempts the connection if the ODBC component versions do not match one another. Keeping the components synchronized is therefore very important.

Microsoft offers a tool called the Component Checker to help you scan the system and determine if the Microsoft Data Access Components (MDAC) are synchronized. You'll find the Component Checker at `http://www.microsoft.com/data`. You'll also find the latest version of MDAC at the site, along with additional technical information on MDAC and ODBC.

Viewing Driver Information

The Drivers page of the ODBC Data Sources Administrator lets you view information about installed ODBC drivers. The Drivers page is useful for verifying driver version but doesn't provide any options you can change.

Tracing

Use the Tracing page of the ODBC Data Sources Administrator to configure tracing options to help you troubleshoot problems with a client connection. With tracing turned on, ODBC actions are logged to the specified file. You can view the log using any text editor.

Connection Pooling

Use the Connection Pooling page to specify whether or not ODBC drivers can reuse open connection handles to the database server. You can improve performance by eliminating the need for applications to establish new connections to a server, because the time and overhead involved in establishing the connection is reduced. Oracle and SQL connections are pooled by default, but others are not.

Understanding Control Panel Applets

As in other Windows platforms, the Windows 2003 Control Panel serves as a control center for configuring hardware and operating system settings. Some Control Panel applets control fairly simple sets of options, while others are relatively complex. The following sections explain the more complex Control Panel applets and their functions. Applets that require no explanation (such as configuring the mouse, game controllers, and so on) are not included. Also, note that not all applets appear in the Control Panel by default. The Wireless Link applet, for example, only appears on systems with infrared ports or similar wireless hardware.

You can configure the Start menu to display the Control Panel applets in the menu. This means you can access individual Control Panel applets through the Start menu without having to open the Control Panel folder. To display the Control Panel applets on the Start menu, right-click the taskbar and choose Properties. Click the Advanced tab, select Expand Control Panel in the Start Menu Settings group, and then click OK.

To open the Control Panel, click Start ⇨ Control Panel. If you've configured the Start menu to expand the Control Panel and want to open the Control Panel folder, click Start, then right-click Control Panel and click Open. You also can open the Control Panel from My Computer.

Accessibility options

This applet lets you configure interface and input/output functions designed to assist users with various physical challenges, such as reduced vision. You can configure a variety of settings and features for the display, keyboard, mouse, and sound.

Add or Remove Hardware applet

The Add or Remove Hardware applet, when selected, runs the Add or Remove Hardware wizard, which helps you add new hardware, remove hardware, unplug a device, and troubleshoot problems with devices. The wizard scans the system for changes and helps automate the process of installing drivers to support new devices.

If you choose to add or troubleshoot a device, Windows 2003 automatically performs a search for plug and play (PnP) hardware. If it finds and recognizes a new device, it takes you step-by-step through the process of installing support for the device. If it finds but can't recognize the device, the wizard prompts you to select the device from a list and manually specify the device's driver(s).

To troubleshoot a device, allow Windows 2003 to perform the hardware detection and then locate the device in the Choose a Hardware Device list and click Next. The wizard will help you perform steps to troubleshoot the device. To add a new device, choose Add a new device from the list and then click Next. Follow the prompts to insert the Windows 2003 CD or provide a path to the appropriate driver files when prompted.

If you choose to uninstall a device, Windows 2003 presents a list of all devices. Select the device you want to remove, click Next, and follow the prompts to complete the process. If you're unplugging a device, Windows 2003 presents a list of devices that can be unplugged. Select the device, click Next, and follow the prompts (if any) to complete the process.

Add or Remove Programs applet

The Add or Remove Programs applet (Figure 7-28) serves three functions. It enables you to change the installation of or remove existing programs, install new programs, or Add or Remove Windows 2003 components. The first two options are geared typically toward user-oriented applications. You use the latter to add or remove components such as Indexing Service, Certificate Services, IIS, additional tools, and so on, to or from Windows 2003. You also can use Add or Remove Programs to add and remove common Windows 2003 components such as the accessory applications (Notepad, wallpaper, games, and so on).

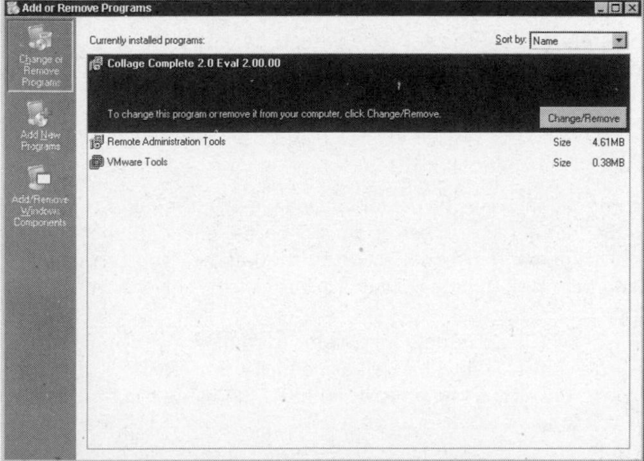

Figure 7-28: Use Add or Remove Programs to install, reconfigure, and remove applications and Windows 2003 components.

The left toolbar in Add or Remove Programs contains three buttons. The Change or Remove Programs button presents a list of installed applications. Select the application you want to modify or remove. Each application will include two buttons, Change and Remove, which will launch the application's Setup program to change the configuration or remove the application, respectively.

Add New Programs offers two functions: seeking the floppy drive or CD for a Setup program, or performing an update from the Windows Update Web site for new Windows 2003 components, device drivers, and system updates. In most cases, an application on CD will autoplay its Setup file, so all you have to do is insert the CD to start installation. Or, you can open the floppy or CD and execute `Setup.exe` (in rare cases, `Install.exe`) to install the application. So, although the Add or Remove Programs applet isn't all that useful for an experienced administrator in terms of installing new programs, it does give you a portal through which to access the Windows Update Web site (`http://windowsupdate.microsoft.com`). However, you could add a link to the site in your Favorites folder.

The Add or Remove Windows Components applet is your primary method for adding and removing Windows 2003 components. When you click Add or Remove Windows Components, Windows scans the system for installed components and displays a component list. Items with a check on white background are installed with all options (such as all accessory programs, for example). A check on a gray background indicates that some of the options for the selected component are installed. No check indicates that no options are installed for the selected component. To install a component, place a check beside it, click Next, and follow the remaining prompts to install the component. Select a component and click Details to view or select individual components.

Administrative Tools applet

The Administrative Tools applet in the Control Panel serves as a container for various administrative tools, including the Computer Management MMC snap-in, the Services snap-in, and others. Each of these tools is covered where appropriate in this chapter or in other chapters.

Date and Time applet

This applet is the same one that appears if you double-click the clock on the system tray. The resulting three-tab dialog box lets you set the server's date, time, and time zone, all of which are self-explanatory. The Internet Time tab, shown in Figure 7-29, lets you configure the server to automatically and periodically synchronize its local time with a remote time server such as `time.windows.com` or `time.nist.gov`. You can also use the tab to force a time synchronization immediately.

The Internet time synchronization occurs by default once a week but requires that the computer be connected to the Internet. If your server doesn't have a direct Internet connection but does have a dial-up or demand-dial connection to the Internet, you can connect the server to the Internet and then click Update Now to synchronize the server's time.

Having an accurate time on a server is extremely important for authentication purposes but is also important for error and event tracking, as well as security. For example, if you receive a denial-of-service attack from a particular dynamic IP address, knowing the time the attack occurred will enable you to track down the user of that IP at the specified time. Accurate timestamps are also important for reliable backup and restore operations.

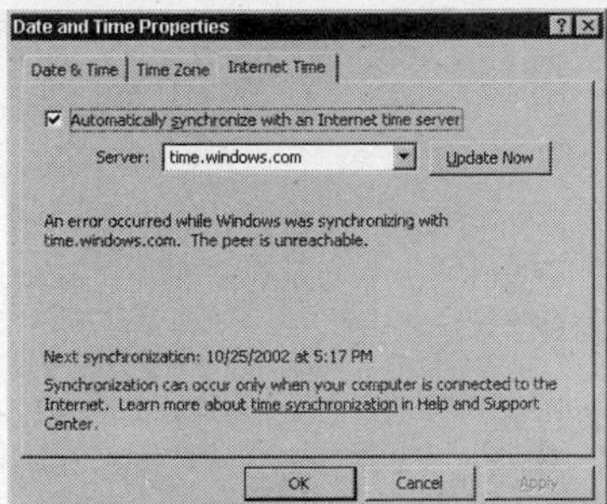

Figure 7-29: Use the Internet Time tab to configure time synchronization.

It's important to understand that computers in a domain perform their own synchronization. Workstations and member servers automatically synchronize with the domain controller serving as the operations master in the domain. This DC should be checked and adjusted periodically for the accurate time, but a better option is to configure it to take its time from an Internet time source such as `time.nist.gov`. Domain members will then receive an accurate time when they synchronize with the DC.

The Windows Time service is the component responsible for time synchronization. This service is set for Automatic startup by default.

You can configure time synchronization settings through group policy. You'll find the policies in the \Computer Configuration\Administrative Templates\System\Windows Time Service group policy branch. Use the Global Configuration Settings policy to enable and configure a wide variety of properties that determine the way the server handles the time samples it receives from time providers.

The policies in the Time Providers sub-branch control time synchronization from both a client and server standpoint:

- **Enable Windows NTP Client:** Enabling this policy allows the server to synchronize its time with the server specified in the Configure Windows NTP Client policy. Disable this policy if you don't want the server to synchronize its time.
- **Configure Windows NTP Client:** Enable this policy if you want the server to synchronize its time with a remote time server. When you enable the policy you gain access to several properties that specify the time server, update frequency, server type, and other time synchronization aspects.
- **Enable Windows NTP Server:** Enable this policy if you want the server to act as a time server, enabling it to service NTP requests from other computers on the network.

You don't need Windows 2003 to host your own time server. Windows 2000 and Windows XP also offer the ability to act as a time server.

Display object

The Display applet in the Control Panel lets you configure desktop settings such as wallpaper, background, color scheme, color depth, and desktop size (resolution). You also can configure a screen saver, enable and configure Web effects, and set general desktop effects and settings.

If the system contains multiple display adapters, you can configure settings for each as well as configure how each adapter fits into the desktop.

Folder Options applet

The Folder Options applet in the Control Panel lets you configure how Explorer folder windows appear and function. You can use it to enable/disable the active desktop, specify the type of window used for displaying folders (Web content or classic), specify whether new folders open in the same window or in a new window, and so on. You also can configure other options such as file associations and offline files.

Internet Options applet

The Internet Options applet offers several property pages that let you configure settings for Internet Explorer and related programs such as Outlook Express and NetMeeting:

- **General:** Set the default home page, delete cached files, clear the URL history, and set general properties such as fonts, colors, languages, and accessibility features.
- **Security:** Use the Security page to configure security level for various *zones.* A zone is a group of Web sites that share a common security level. Click one of the predefined zones and click Sites to add or remove Web sites from the zone. Then use the slider on the Security page to set the security level for the zone or click Custom Level to specify individual settings for the way Internet Explorer handles cookies, ActiveX controls and plug-ins, scripts, file downloads, and so on.
- **Privacy:** Use the Privacy page to change the way Internet Explorer handles cookies, both globally and for individual Web sites.
- **Content:** The Content page lets you enable and configure Content Advisor, which helps guard against access to restricted sites (such as sites with adult content). You also use the Content page to configure certificates for use on secure Web sites and for e-mail. Use the Personal Information group on the Content page to create a profile with your name, address, phone, and other information. Bear in mind that this information is visible to Web sites you visit unless you configure the security zones to prevent it.
- **Connections:** Use the Connections page to configure your Internet connection(s) and specify how and when Internet Explorer uses auto-connect to connect to the Internet. Click Setup to run the Internet Connection Wizard to create a new Internet connection. Click LAN Settings to configure proxy server settings.
- **Programs:** This page lets you associate specific programs with tasks such as e-mail, newsgroups, and so on.
- **Advanced:** This page contains several individual options that determine how Internet Explorer handles HTTP versions, multimedia, printing, security, and a variety of other properties.

Licensing object

Use the Licensing applet (Figure 7-30) to add licenses for Windows 2003 and applications. The two types of licenses are server and client access. A server license gives you the right to run the product on a particular computer but doesn't give you the right to connect clients to the server — for that you need client access licenses, or CALs. If you have 300 concurrent connections to a server, you need to have 300 CALs to be legal.

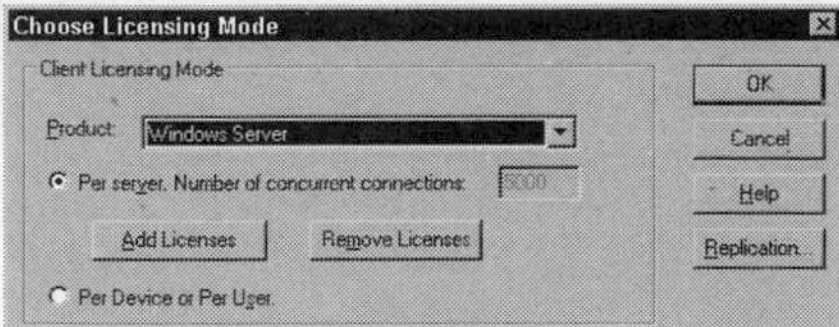

Figure 7-30: Choose between per server and per seat licensing for servers and applications.

You can choose between two licensing modes: per user or device, or per server. With the *per server* option, you specify the number of concurrent connections for the server or application. When that number of concurrent connections is reached, additional connections are refused. You then can use the Licensing applet to add licenses for the product (assuming that you've purchased the licenses in question).

You can also choose *per user or device* mode (also called *per-seat* mode), which does not track concurrent connections. Instead, per seat mode assumes that you've purchased a CAL for each computer that will access the server or application.

Network Connections applet

The Network Connections applet in the Control Panel opens the Network Connections folder. This folder contains icons for each of your network connections including LAN and dial-up connections. Right-click a connection and choose Properties to configure the connection's protocols, bindings, clients, services, sharing, and other properties.

For more in-depth coverage of network configuration, refer to Chapter 15.

You can take a shortcut to Network Connections by right-clicking My Network Places on the Desktop and selecting Properties.

Power Options applet

The Power Options applet in the Control Panel controls power-saving features on the computer, such as turning off system peripherals after a specified idle time and setting up hibernation (suspend to disk). You can configure power settings and save the configuration as a power scheme, making it easy to switch between different groups of settings.

The UPS page of the Power Options property sheet controls the UPS service. If a UPS is connected to the computer via one of the computer's ports, the UPS page shows UPS status such as estimated runtime and battery condition. You can configure the UPS through the UPS page or select a different UPS.

Printers Control Panel applet

The Printers Control Panel applet opens the Printers folder, which contains an icon for each installed printer, as well as a wizard for adding local or remote printers.

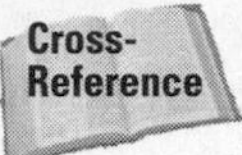

For detailed information on the Printers folder and printing services, see Chapter 23.

Scheduled Tasks folder

This applet opens the Scheduled Tasks folder, which contains tasks that are scheduled for execution on the system along with a wizard for creating a new scheduled task. The wizard helps you select the application to run, the frequency at which the task runs, username and password under which the task runs, and other properties. You can use scheduled tasks to automate a variety of tasks including file backup, executing scripts, and so on.

System applet

The System applet provides access to general system properties. You also can open the System applet by right-clicking My Computer and choosing Properties. The General page of the System property sheet provides basic information about your system, including OS version, installed memory, CPU type, and registration information.

Computer Name tab

The Computer Name tab is the place to go to change the workgroup or domain to which the computer is assigned, as well as to change its computer name. You also can change the primary DNS suffix for the computer, as well as its NetBIOS name.

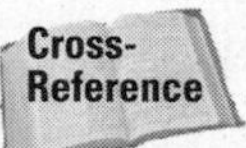

For more information on network settings and configuration, refer to Chapter 15.

Hardware page

The Hardware page offers a handful of features for controlling the system's hardware and resource settings (Figure 7-31). The Hardware Wizard was covered earlier in this chapter in the section, "Add or Remove Hardware." The Device Manager was covered earlier in the section, "Device Manager."

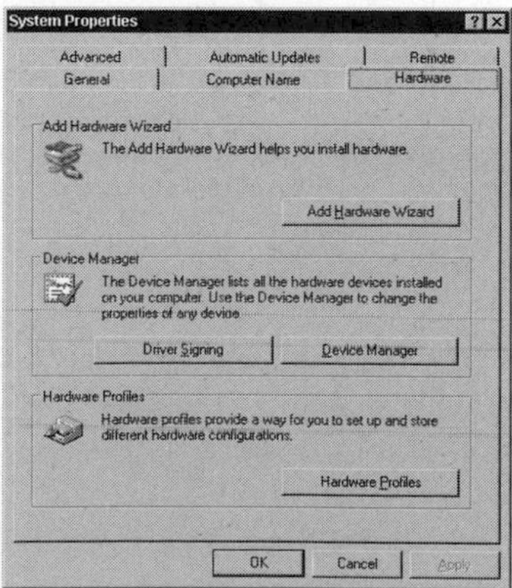

Figure 7-31: Use the Hardware page to add, remove, and configure hardware and hardware profiles.

In Windows 2003, drivers can be signed digitally by Microsoft to certify that the driver has been tested and meets certain compatibility criteria defined by Microsoft. Clicking Driver Signing opens a dialog box you can use to configure driver file signature verification. You can choose between the following:

✦ **Ignore:** Windows 2003 installs all driver files whether they have a valid driver signature or not.

✦ **Warn:** Windows 2003 displays a warning when you attempt to install a driver that isn't signed.

✦ **Block:** Windows 2003 prevents unsigned drivers from being installed.

Tip

You can configure driver signing behavior through group policy.

A *hardware profile* stores information about a specific hardware configuration, including which devices are enabled for a given profile and which ones are disabled. Each hardware profile has a name. When the system boots, it can automatically select a hardware profile based on the hardware it detects at startup. If the system can't determine the correct hardware profile, it prompts you to specify the hardware profile to use.

Hardware profiles are handy for working with different hardware configurations on the same computer. They are most applicable to portable computers, where in a docked configuration you might have a different network adapter, CD-ROM drive, monitor, or other peripherals that are not present when the computer is undocked, and vice versa. By disabling devices when they aren't in use, you can avoid hardware conflicts and make resources (IRQ, I/O base address, and so on) available that would otherwise be allocated to the disabled devices. For this reason, hardware profiles can be useful in a desktop system as well. You might have a piece of hardware you use infrequently that conflicts with another device. When you need to use the device, you can boot the hardware profile in which the device is enabled and then reboot with the other profile when you're through.

Windows 2003 creates a hardware profile automatically named Docked Profile on a portable and named Profile 1 on a nonportable system. You can work with this single profile, disabling devices as needed, or you can create a new profile. To work with hardware profiles, right-click My Computer, choose Properties, click the Hardware tab, and then click Hardware Profiles to display the Hardware Profiles dialog box (Figure 7-32). You create a new hardware profile by copying an existing one. So, select a profile and click Copy. Windows 2003 prompts you for a name for the new profile.

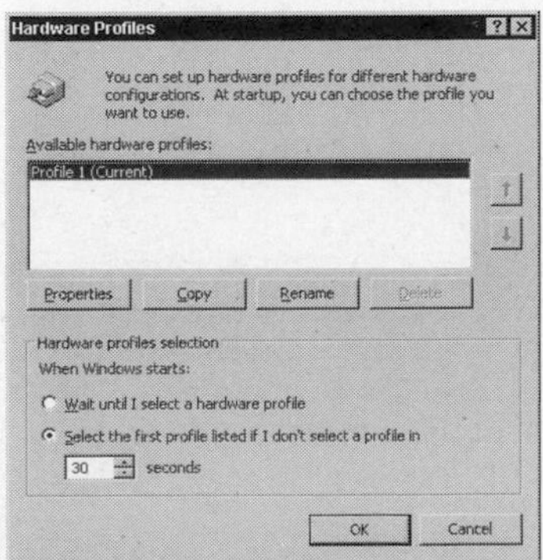

Figure 7-32: Use the Hardware Profiles dialog box to create, remove, and manage hardware profiles.

You can set general hardware profile properties in the dialog box, including specifying how Windows 2003 handles profile selection at boot. Click on a profile and click Properties to set properties for the profile. Within the profile's properties, you can specify whether the computer is a portable and direct Windows 2003 to always include the profile as an option when starting the system.

The Hardware Profiles dialog box gives you a means for managing hardware profiles globally. You use the Device Manager to enable/disable devices in a given hardware profile. On the Hardware page, click Device Manager and then open the property sheet for the device you want to manage. On the device's General page, select an option from the Device Usage drop-down list to specify if you want the device enabled, disabled in the current profile, or disabled in all profiles.

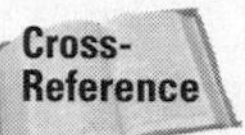

See the section, "Device Manager," earlier in this chapter for more information about the Device Manager.

Advanced

You can use the Advanced page of the System properties applet in the Control Panel to configure performance options for the computer, view and set environment variables, and configure system startup and recovery options.

User Profiles

User Profiles store a given working environment, including desktop configuration, mapped drives and printers, and other properties. When a user logs on, the user profile applies the desktop configuration and other properties. User profiles are most useful for providing a consistent user interface for each user even when other users share the same computer. They're also useful for providing a consistent UI for users who log in from a variety of computers (roaming users).

You access user profiles through the Settings button in the User Profiles group of the Advanced tab in the System property sheet.

User profiles are a Windows NT structure that is carried over into Windows 2000 and 2003. Group policy settings can override settings in a user profile, so user profiles are not necessary *per se* on Windows 2003 systems. However, they are still useful in mixed environments where Windows NT systems exist and provide an easy means of configuring the user interface even in homogenous Windows 2003 environments.

A user profile comprises a registry file and a set of folders. The registry file applies settings to the UI such as mapped drives, restrictions, desktop contents, screen colors and fonts, and so on and is a cached copy of the HKEY_CURRENT_USER portion of the registry. The folders include the user's My Documents, My Pictures, and other folders stored under the Documents and Settings folder for the user.

The three types of profiles are *personal*, *mandatory*, and *default*. Personal profiles allow users to modify their working environments and retain those changes from one logon session to the next. Mandatory profiles allow certain configuration changes (subject to restrictions in the profile itself), but those changes are not saved for future logon sessions. The only difference between a personal profile and a mandatory profile is the profile's file extension. Personal profiles use a `.dat` extension for the registry file portion of the profile, and mandatory profiles use a `.man` extension.

A default profile is preconfigured by Windows 2003 and is applied for new users that log on with no pre-existing profile. The profile then is stored as the user's profile for later logon sessions.

You specify a user's profile through the user's account properties when you create or modify the account. You use the Local Users and Groups MMC console to create and modify local accounts and use the Active Directory Users and Computers console to create and modify domain accounts in the Active Directory. The Profile page of the user's account properties (Figure 7-33) defines the path to the user's profile, logon script, and other properties. When the user logs on, Windows 2003 applies the profile located on the specified path.

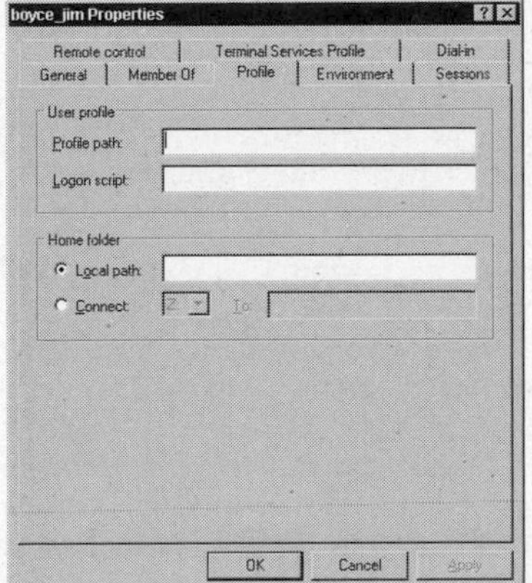

Figure 7-33: The Profile page defines the path to the user's profile.

Chapter 14 has more information about Group Policy objects and how they're integrated with Active Directory.

Creating a profile

Windows 2003 provides no utility specifically for creating user profiles. Instead, you first log on as the target user to a system with similar video hardware as the user's target workstation (because video settings are stored in the profile and you need to ensure compatibility). You configure the working environment as needed, mapping drives and printers, setting desktop schemes, and so on. When you log off, the profile is stored locally along with the user's folder structure.

Copying profiles

In order to copy a user profile from one location to another, you use the User Profiles page of the System object in the Control Panel. Open the User Profiles page on the system from which you're copying the profile. Select the profile from the list of profiles stored on the computer and click Copy To. Select the local folder or network share where you want the profile copied and click OK.

Supporting roaming users

A roaming profile is the same as a local personal profile except that the profile is stored on a network share accessible to the user at logon. You specify the UNC path to the user's profile in his account properties so that when the user logs on, the profile can be applied regardless of his logon location. If a profile exists on the specified path, Windows 2003 applies that profile at logon. If no profile exists on the specified path, Windows 2003 creates a new profile automatically, stores it on that path, and uses the profile for future logon sessions.

Creating a mandatory profile

You create a mandatory profile in the same way you create a personal profile, but with one additional step. After you create the profile and copy it to the target location (such as the user's local computer or a network share for a roaming profile), change the name of the profile's registry file from `Ntuser.dat` to `Ntuser.man`.

Performance options

Click Settings under the Performance group on the Advanced page to display the Performance Options dialog. The Visual Effects tab lets you configure a variety of interface options that can have an impact on overall system performance. In the default configuration, 2003 disables all visual effects except visual styles on windows and buttons. Essentially all of the visual effects are eye candy and have no significant administrative benefit, so you should leave them turned off.

You can select options on the Advanced tab to optimize the system for applications or background services. In most cases, you'll select Applications for a Windows 2003 workstation or Background services for a server.

The Performance Options dialog box also lets you change the system's virtual memory allocation (size of the system's swap file) and space allocated to the registry files. Why change swap file size or location? The swap file is used to emulate memory (thus the term *virtual memory*), making the system appear as if it has more physical memory than it really does. As memory fills up, Windows 2003 moves memory pages to the swap file to create space in physical memory for new pages, or it swaps pages between physical and virtual memory when an existing page stored in the swap file is needed. Windows 2003 automatically selects a swap file size based on physical memory size, but in some cases, you might want to increase the swap file size to improve performance. You also might want to move the swap file from the default location to a different disk with greater capacity or better performance (such as moving from an IDE drive to a SCSI drive).

Click Change on the Advanced tab of the Performance Options dialog box to access the Virtual Memory dialog box, shown in Figure 7-34. Select a drive for the swap file, specify the initial and maximum sizes (Windows 2003 will resize as needed within the range), and click Set. Specify the maximum registry size in the field provided and click OK to apply the changes.

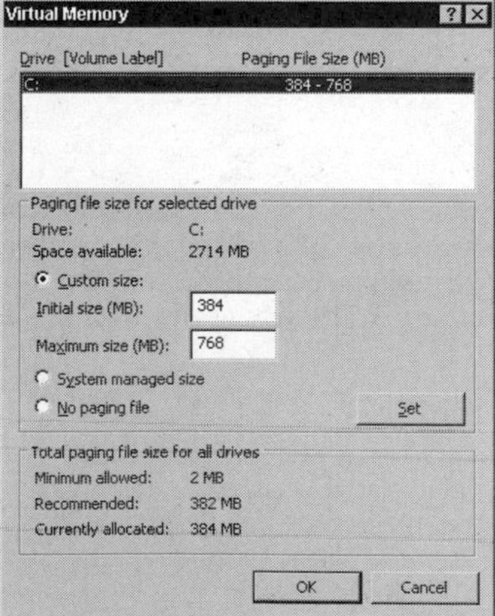

Figure 7-34: Use the Virtual Memory dialog box to control swap file size and registry size.

Tip

Changing the maximum registry size doesn't change the size of the registry. It imposes a maximum size that when reached, causes Windows 2003 to generate a warning message that the maximum registry size has been reached.

Environment Variables

Click Environment Variables on the Advanced tab to open the Environment Variables dialog box, which you can use to view, delete, and add environment variables. The variables you define in the upper half of the page apply to the user who currently is logged on. Variables defined in the bottom half apply to all users.

Startup/Shutdown options

The Startup and Recovery page (Figure 7-35) lets you configure boot options, how the system handles a system failure, and how debugging information is handled. The options in the System startup group let you specify which boot option is selected by default and how long the boot menu is displayed. These settings are stored in the `Boot.ini` file, located in the root folder of the drive where the boot loader is located. You can edit the file manually with a text editor to change values, if you prefer.

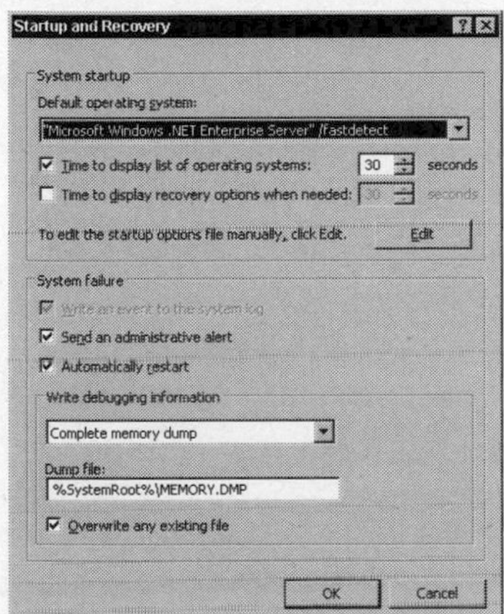

Figure 7-35: Configure startup, recovery, and debugging options.

Click Settings in the Startup and Recovery group on the Advanced tab to display the Startup and Recovery dialog box.

The System Failure group of controls determines how Windows 2003 reacts when a system failure occurs. The system always attempts to write an event to the system log, if possible. If you need to see the blue screen of death after a system failure to gather information for troubleshooting, deselect Automatically reboot.

Use the Write Debugging Information group of controls to specify the action Windows 2003 takes in creating a memory dump file when a system failure occurs. Microsoft support engineers can use the debugging information to determine the cause of the failure and recommend or develop a fix for the problem.

Automatic Updates

The Automatic Updates tab of the System Properties sheet (Figure 7-36) is the one that will probably give most administrators the most concern. This tab controls Windows 2003's dynamic update feature, which enables it to automatically download and install patches and updates. Microsoft thinks it's a great idea; most administrators would rather have complete control over the what and when of all upgrades and fixes.

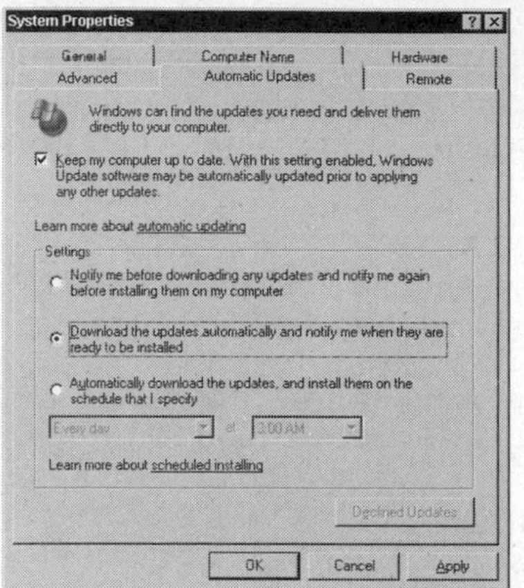

Figure 7-36: Control dynamic updates with the Automatic Updates tab.

If you prefer to manually initiate and control all updates, clear the option Keep my computer up to date. This will prevent Windows 2003 from scanning for and downloading updates. You can use the Windows Update Web site or other Microsoft Web site resources to obtain updates, patches, and service packs manually.

If you choose to enable automatic updates, you can choose between three options that determine the how updates occur and whether you are notified when they occur. At the very least, we recommend that you configure the server to notify you before installing updates. The worst thing you can do is configure the server to update silently, which will give you absolutely no version control over the server.

Remote tab

The Remote tab (Figure 7-37) controls Remote Desktop/Terminal Services access to the server, as well as Remote Assistance.

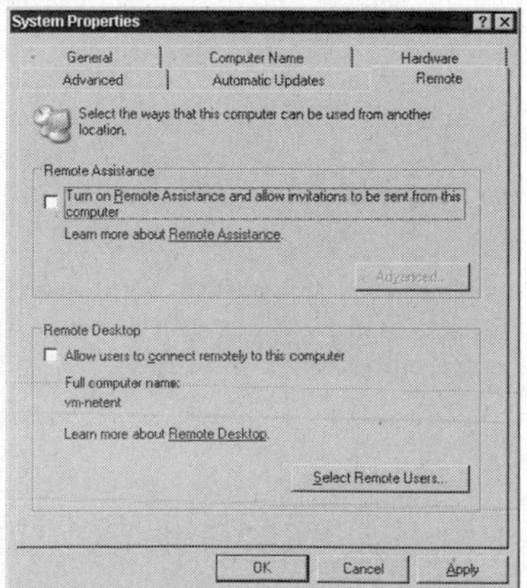

Figure 7-37: Use the Remote tab to configure remote control features.

The Remote Assistance group lets you allow remote users to connect to the server through the Remote Assistance feature. If you click Advanced, you can enable or disable the option Allow this computer to be controlled remotely. When this option is enabled, a remote user is allowed remote control over the server; disabling the option allows the user to view the server but not control it. You can also set the period of time a Remote Assistance invitation can remain open.

Tip

You can send Remote Assistance requests with MSN Messenger or by e-mail.

Remote Desktop is, essentially, a stripped-down version of Terminal Services. Enabling the Allow option in the Remote Desktop group allows remote users to initiate a Remote Desktop or Terminal Services connection to the server. Click Select Remote Users to specify the users that can log in through this service.

Windows XP includes a built-in Remote Desktop client that you can use to connect to Windows 2003. The Windows XP Professional CD includes Remote Desktop client software for other Windows platforms. In addition, users can employ a Terminal Services client to connect to the server through Remote Desktop. The Remote Desktop Web Connection ActiveX component allows Internet Explorer users to access a computer hosting Remote Desktop connections through their Web browser. Remote Desktop Web Connection is included with Windows XP and available by download from Microsoft's Web site.

As handy as it is for remote control and management, Remote Desktop certainly has security implications. You should read through Chapter 30 to make sure that you understand these security implications before enabling Remote Desktop on a server.

Tip

If you're having problems getting Terminal Services clients to connect to Windows 2003 running Terminal Services, make sure to enable the option Allow users to connect remotely to this computer option on the Remote tab of the System Properties sheet. Disabling this option prevents Terminal Services clients from connecting, even if you've enabled access through group policy.

Summary

Windows 2003 provides several tools for administering system hardware, operating environment properties, users, and other objects. Although most of the administrative functions are incorporated into Microsoft Management Console (MMC) snap-ins or extensions, a few — like the ODBC Data Source Administrator — still exist as standalone utilities. The Control Panel, as in Windows NT, still serves as a control center for configuring hardware and OS settings and properties.

Understanding the administrative tools available to you is an important step in configuring and monitoring a system. This chapter examined the majority of the administrative tools you'll work with on a regular basis. Other chapters cover additional administrative tools or cover in more detail some of the tools mentioned here.

✦ ✦ ✦

P A R T

Active Directory

✦ ✦ ✦ ✦

In This Part

✦ ✦ ✦ ✦

Planning for Active Directory

✦ ✦ ✦ ✦

In This Chapter

Understanding basic design principles

Domain planning

Forest planning

Administration planning

Migration planning

Backup and restore planning

✦ ✦ ✦ ✦

This chapter analyzes numerous models in planning for Active Directory and defines potential obstacles that may interrupt your planning process. Planning an Active Directory requires a methodology with a focus on your political and business needs. You also want to take into consideration the big picture and how it evolves as you integrate new applications with Windows Server 2003. This is a constant battle in the ever-changing technical world. This chapter can help network managers, systems integrators, and consultants prepare for the required tasks and decisions to plan an Active Directory.

Active Directory Overview

If you are an administrator or just a user of Windows Server 2003, gaining a good understanding of Active Directory is critical before you start your planning. Directory services are nothing more than orderly ways of classifying and managing resources on a network, whether users, printers, servers, or security parameters. Directories become the points of reference for user services and applications. They help find a printer in a field office, locate a user and direct an e-mail, or verify that a user has access rights to a particular file. They also provide Single Sign-On (SSO), which gives a user access to the whole network from a single log-on. Directories are becoming increasingly important as business networks expand to include connections with business partners and customers.

Four basic components make up an Active Directory structure: *domain plan*, *site topology plan*, *forest plan*, and *organizational unit plan*. We intend to help you create a planning document for each component, discussing the important decisions throughout this chapter. These documents then serve as a starting point for the Active Directory migration.

Basic Design Principles

As you prepare your plan for Active Directory, you should follow a few basic principles to help you through the decision-making process. One of the main principles is to keep it simple. Simple structures are easier to maintain, debug, and explain. You do realize some value in adding complexity, although you must make sure that you weigh the added value derived against the potential maintenance costs.

Certain costs are associated with everything that you create. If you create a structure without a well-defined plan or reason, it could cost you in the long run; you must, therefore, try to justify everything in your structure.

Another main principle is to plan for changes in your organization. Normal changes occur in every organization, from enterprise reorganization or acquisitions to employees moving though the organization. These changes affect your Active Directory structure. You need to plan for these changes and analyze the effects that such changes impose on your structure. Again, try to keep the design simple and general to fluctuate enough to handle significant changes.

Planning for the ideal structure, even if it does not currently reflect your domain or directory infrastructure, is important. Understanding what the ideal is, in the context of your organization, is useful, even if it is not actually in reach. Most designs require more than one attempt. You can compare multiple designs to devise the best design for your organization.

Active Directory Structure

Windows Server 2003 Standard Server, Enterprise Server, and Datacenter Server provide a directory service called *Active Directory*. Active Directory stores info about objects and enables administrators or users to easily access information. This information is stored in a *datastore* (also known as a *directory*) that provides a logical and hierarchical organization of information. The following plans help you model your Active Directory structure.

A domain plan

You need to consider several characteristics of a domain before attempting to create your domain plan. We discuss each characteristic in more detail in this section, providing you with a better understanding of the planning life cycle.

A *forest* consists of a database, where the database partitions are defined by the domains. This database is made up of many small databases spread across computers. Placing the individual databases where the data is most relevant enables a large database to be distributed efficiently. Each of these databases contains *security principal objects*, such as computers, users, and groups. These objects can grant or deny access to resources in your structure, and must be authenticated by the domain controller for the particular domain in which the object resides. Objects are thus authenticated before they are eligible to access the resource.

Domain administrators control every object in the domain structure; group policy is associated with that domain and does not automatically propagate to other domains in the forest. For the domains and the group policy to be associated, they must be explicitly linked, so security policy for a domain user account must be set on a per-domain basis.

A *domain* is identified by a *DNS name*, which provides a method for you to locate the domain controller for the given domain. This name indicates the domain's position within the forest hierarchy. The following list provides a step-by-step checklist for creating a domain plan for a single forest.

1. Determine the number of domains needed in each forest.
2. Determine the forest root domain.
3. Create a DNS name for each domain.
4. Create a DNS deployment plan.

5. Determine shortcut trust relationships.

6. Plan for changes in the domain and understand the effect of the changes.

7. Create teams to manage the network.

In determining the number of domains for the forest, consider a single domain model, even if your existing structure has more than one domain. Several reasons dictate that you create more than one domain, such as preserving the existing domain structure, administrative partitioning, and physical partitioning. But a good idea is to try to keep the plan simple, if at all possible. If you can justify more than one domain, you need to detail this justification for administration purposes. Remember that adding additional domains has a small cost associated with it, probably in the form of additional management.

If, by chance, you have NT domains in place, you may prefer to keep them as they are instead of consolidating them into Active Directory. If you decide to keep the NT domains, you should weigh the cost of maintaining more domains against the cost of migrating to Active Directory.

After you determine the number of domains that you need in your new forest, you need to determine the *forest root domain*. The *root domain* is the first domain created in the forest. Forest-wide groups, enterprise administrators, and schema administrators are placed in this domain. If your plan calls for only one domain, that domain must be the forest root. Consider the following possibilities in selecting the root domain:

✦ **Selecting an existing domain:** Usually, this domain is a critical part of your operation, and your organization cannot afford to lose this domain.

✦ **Selecting a dedicated domain:** This type of root domain serves solely as the root. It is an additional domain created for this purpose only.

After determining your root domain, you need to determine your *DNS naming structure* for your domains. DNS is globally recognized and can be easily registered. These DNS names are used by clients requesting access to the network to locate domain controllers. In creating your DNS hierarchy, you can break your domains up into trees, because a tree is a set of one or more contiguous named domains. (The names are contiguous because the names are different by only one label.)

Shortcut trusts are two-way transitive trusts that enable you to shorten the path in a complex forest. You explicitly create shortcut trusts between Windows 2000 domains in the same forest. A shortcut trust is a performance optimization that shortens the trust path for Windows 2000 security to take for authentication purposes. The most effective use of shortcut trusts is between two domain trees in a forest.

Shortcut trusts create performance optimizations that shorten the trust path for security; consider the following: If a user requests access to a network resource, the user's domain controller must communicate with the resource's controller. Considering that, you need to understand that the two domains must be related in a parent-child relationship; otherwise, the user's domain controller cannot communicate efficiently with the resource's domain controller. Depending on the network location of the controllers for that domain, the authentication hop between the two domains can potentially increase the chance of a failure. To reduce the chances of this happening, you can create a shortcut trust between the two domains, enabling them to communicate.

If you must change the domain plan after deployment, this is not a task to determine overnight. Domain hierarchies are not easily restructured after creation. Try to plan for such change so that you don't end up creating only a short-lived domain structure. Put a lot of thought into your domain design, and it will pay off in the long run.

A site topology plan

The *site topology* is layered on top of the physical network that reflects the underlying network topology. The domain structure sits above the site topology but below the network layer. Making a clear distinction between the domain structure and site topology plans is important. Domains contain objects, whereas sites reflect user groups. The domain is mapped to the site by placing a replica of the domain in the site, so the site contains the entire domain.

The site topology routes query and replication traffic efficiently and helps you determine where to place domain controllers within your structure. The site is known as a set of IP subnets; these subnets usually have LAN speed or better. Site links are used in the plan to model the available bandwidth between the sites. These links are usually slower than LAN speed. The following four parameters make up a site link:

- **Transport:** Used for replication.
- **Cost:** Determines the paths of replication.
- **Replication schedule:** Helps indicate when the link is available for replication traffic.
- **Replication interval:** Polls the domain controllers at the opposite end of the site link for replication changes.

After the user starts his computer, the computer communicates with the domain controller of the user's member domain. The user's site is then determined by the domain controller, based on the computer's IP address, and returns the name of the site to the user's computer. This information is cached and used for future queries. *Replication* uses the site topology to generate replication connections. A built-in process known as the *Knowledge Consistency Checker* (*KCC*) creates and maintains replication connections between domain controllers. The site topology is used to guide creation of the connections, and intrasite replication tunes the replication, while intersite communication minimizes bandwidth usage. Table 8-1 displays the differences in the site replication patterns.

Table 8-1: Differences between Intersite Replication and Intrasite Replication

Intersite replication	*Intrasite replication*
Bridgehead servers maintain replication connections.	Connections are made between two domain controllers located in the same site.
No compression is used to save processor time.	Compression is used to save bandwidth.
Partners notify one another if changes need to replicated.	Partners do not notify one another.
Replication uses the remote procedure call transport.	Replication uses the SMTP or TCP/IP transport.

You need to consider a few processes before starting your plan. You need to make sure that you define sites and site links by using your network's physical topology as the beginning point. You may also consult the team manager for your TCP/IP and forest planning group. These managers should be involved in this process. In creating the topology for your forest, again use the physical topology of your network for reference. Keep this plan as simple as possible, based on your current bandwidth. You also need to refer to the following section before you commit to creating your plan.

A forest plan

The *forest* is one of the main components of the Active Directory. It provides a collection of Active Directory domains. Forests serve two main purposes: simplifying user management within the directory and simplifying user interaction within the directory.

A few main characteristics also apply to the Active Directory: the *single configuration container*, the *schema*, *trusts*, and *global catalogs*. The *configuration container* supplies replication to all domain controllers in a forest. This container holds information about directory-aware applications that pertain to a forest, while the *schema* defines object classes and attributes of the object. These *classes* define types of objects that are created in a directory. The schema is then replicated to every domain controller. A *trust* automatically creates a two-way, transitive relationship between the forest and the domain and can be seen by any other group or user in all the domains in the trust. The *global catalog* contains every object in all domains in the forest, although it can see only a select set of object attributes, enabling fast, efficient full-forest searches. The global catalog also provides a seamless presentation to the end users.

We suggest planning to start with a single-forest scenario. This plan is sufficient in most situations. Remember to keep the structure simple unless you can justify the creation of additional forests. If you create a single forest, all users can see a single directory in the global catalog; they are, therefore, oblivious to the structure of the forest. The trust is automatically created for you, and configuration changes need to be applied only once. They flow through all forests.

If your design requires administration across divisions within your organization, you may be required to create multiple forests. Remember that, for each additional forest, you face an additional cost. Figure 8-1 represents a multiple forest configuration.

Additional forests must contain at least one domain, thereby causing additional costs. This is why we stress keeping the plan simple.

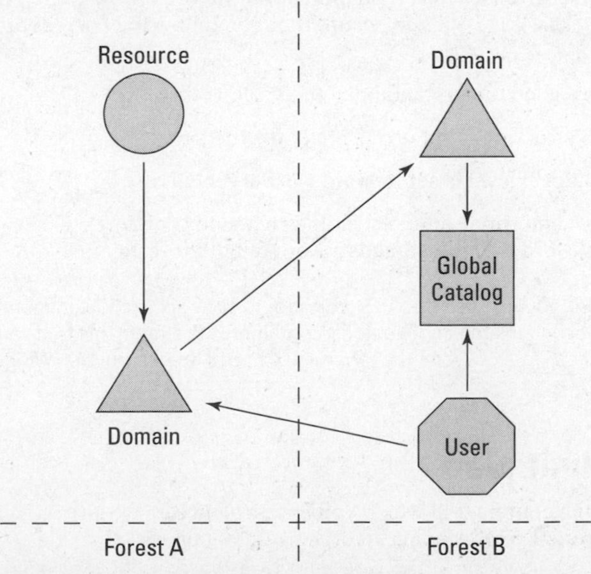

Figure 8-1: A multiple forest configuration.

The user who searches the global catalog in Forest B for a resource in Forest A can locate the requested resources and obtain direct access to the resource because of a one-way trust.

As you are determining how many forests are required, you need to keep the users' needs in mind and not those of the administrators. Do not create multiple forests to solve administrative problems because this setup could possibly distort the users' view of the forests. In certain cases, however, where having a consistent view is not important for the users, this type of setup is tolerable.

Each forest that you create should have an associated *forest change control policy* as part of your forest-plan document. You use this policy to guide changes that have forest-wide effects. You do not need to determine the individual processes before continuing, but understanding their ownership is important. The policy should include information about each of the shared elements in a forest.

Monitoring or setting up a schema change policy is also important. This policy would include the team names that control the schema administration, the total number of members of the group, and the guidelines for schema changes. You should also devise a configuration change policy that consists of the same policies as the schema policy, adding guidelines for creating or changing domains for the forest and modifying the topology.

A trust plan

The first step in creating a *trust plan* is to determine when you need to create a *trust* for your forest. If you create a forest trust between two forests, Windows Server 2003 by default creates a transitive relationship between every domain residing in the forest. Trusts are created only between the forest root in one directory and the forest root of another directory.

Before creating a forest trust, you need to make sure that all your domain controllers are running Windows Server 2003. The functional level must be set to Windows Server 2003, and you should verify that you have the correct DNS structure in place. The DNS structure must be authoritative for both forest DNS servers in which you want to create your trust, or you can create a DNS forwarder on both servers. (Refer to Chapter 17 for more information on DNS forwarding.) The following checklist can help you ensure that you follow the correct procedure in planning for a trust:

- ✦ Make sure that you have a good understanding of the various trust types.
- ✦ Make sure that your DNS structure is set up correctly for the trust.
- ✦ Make sure that your functional level is set to Windows Server 2003.

To create a trust, you must have enterprise administrator's rights on both forests. The new trusts each have their own password that the administrators of both forests must know.

Note

To determine the forest root, you can use the ADSI edit tool to connect to the configuration container. The domain that contains the configuration container is the root. This tool can be installed by running `suptools.exe` from the `support/tools` folder on the Windows Server 2003 CD.

An organizational unit plan

An *organizational unit* (*OU*) is the container in which you create structure within a domain. Consider the following characteristics in planning an organizational unit.

The organizational unit can be *nested*, enabling you to create a hierarchical tree structure inside the domain. OUs are also used to delegate administration and control access to directory objects, thus enabling you to delegate the administration of objects in the directory in a very granular manner. Remember that organizational units are not security principals, so you cannot make the organizational unit a member of a security group.

You can associate organizational units with Group Policy, enabling you to define desktop configurations such as users and computers. You can also associate Group Policy with domains, sites, and organizational units, enabling you to use different policies in the same domain.

In defining your plan, you do not need to consider the end users. An end user can navigate through resources in an organizational-unit structure but is not likely to do so because of the availability of the global catalog.

Planning for the Active Directory Enterprise

You need to have a good understanding of forests and trees, before you can start planning for the naming conventions in your organization. You must consider organizational growth in doing such planning. A good convention using meaningful names propagates down through all levels of your Active Directory.

Naming strategy plan

The organizational naming structure that you choose can reflect your company's organizational chart. Figure 8-2 shows a typical organizational naming structure of this type.

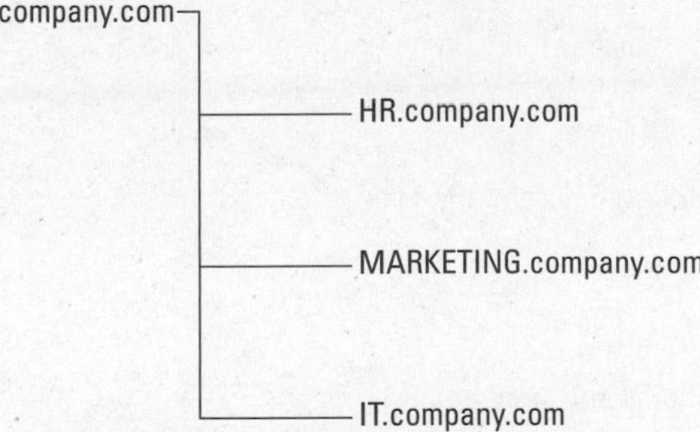

Figure 8-2: An organizational naming structure.

The naming structure shown in Figure 8-2 allows for growth but also has some disadvantages. What if your company decides to rewrite the organizational chart frequently? If this is the case in your organization, you can expect to reconstruct your network frequently. If the thought of such frequent restructuring scares you, this plan is not for you.

A *geographical naming structure* may be new to you. Depending on the size of your organization, the plan shown in the following figure may not fit your needs. This plan separates your organization by location into manageable units. Figure 8-3 shows a simple geographical model.

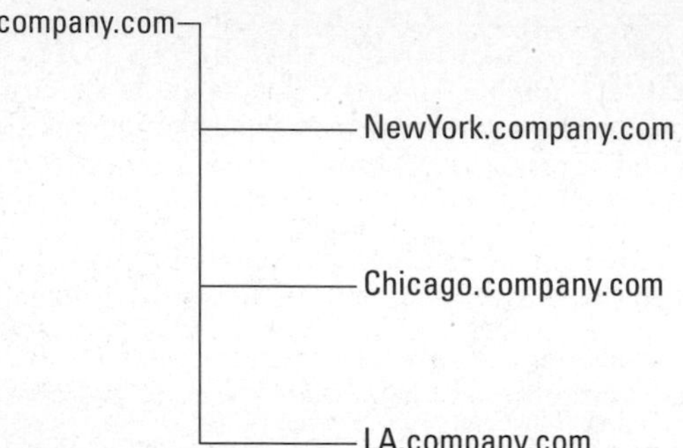

Figure 8-3: A geographical naming structure.

The geographical model tends to be consistent. After all, the names of the cities used in Figure 8-3 are not going to change anytime soon. This model tends to be more flexible compared to the organizational model. The major disadvantage is that geographic naming doesn't represent your company's true structure.

Another possibility is a mixture of the preceding two models. Because both models have some advantages and disadvantages, using the mixture approach may prove a benefit to your company. Figure 8-4 displays a simple mixed model. (The size and diversity of your organization greatly affects your naming schema.)

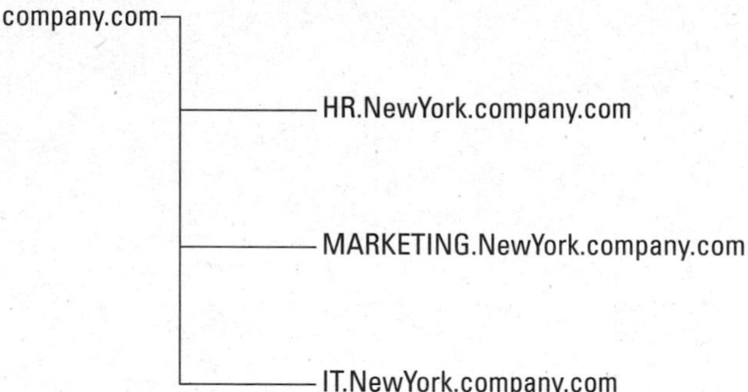

Figure 8-4: A mixture of the organizational and geographical naming models.

Generally in the mixed model, the first domain is assigned a DNS name; then, for every child of the existing domain, you use `x.dnsname.com`. Make sure that you use only the Internet standard characters, defined in the Request for Comments (RFC) 1123 as A-Z, a-z, 0-9, and the hyphen. Doing so ensures that your Active Directory complies with standard software. Using the preceding models as guides, you should have sufficient information to create your own plan for a naming schema.

Domain and organizational units plan

In planning your organizational units, you must first examine your company's organizational structure and administrative requirements so that you can form your company's OU structure.

This examination helps you determine when creating an OU is appropriate. The following list shows a few different reasons for creating OUs:

✦ **Helps simplify resource administration:** OUs are essentially container objects that store printers, file shares, users, groups, and other OUs. By assigning permissions at the container level, you are essentially assigning the permission to each of the OU's stored objects.

✦ **Helps in delegation of administrative tasks:** Grouping objects such as users, computers, and groups into an OU helps you define a distinct area of administration for delegation.

✦ **Helps divide users with policy requirements:** OUs help keep objects with identical security requirements together.

You must always create your first-level OUs unique to a domain. Doing so provides consistency throughout your structure. You have no limit to the number of OUs that you can put in a hierarchy, but the shallower that you can make your OU hierarchy, the better your administrators can understand it. Whenever you create an OU, make sure that it is meaningful, keeping in mind who is going to administer and view the OU.

Your organizational needs drive the OU hierarchy. We discuss in this section several common models that may help you determine your OU hierarchy. Remember that you may need to combine several of these models to complete your hierarchy.

The first model that we discuss is the geographic model. This model organizes your resources by location. Figure 8-5 shows North America, Europe, and Asia as examples of OUs. In using location as the factor for placing your OUs, you are laying the foundation for the OU organizational tree.

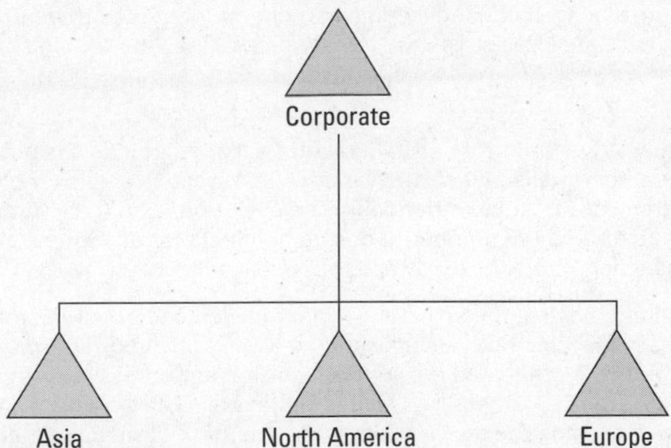

Figure 8-5: An OU organizational tree.

Geographic boundaries remain stable, helping administrators easily identify where resources are located. This model may not exactly mirror your business practices, however. But you may still want to use this model, making minor modifications to the design as necessary for your organization.

The *organizational model* divides OUs by department. This model looks similar to the geographic model, except that you are using your organization's structure to build your model. Because this model is based on your company's organizational structure, it is easily understandable by administrators, making the task of delegating administration easy. Departments can change, but that is not a problem, because the OUs are easily reorganized.

The *object-based model* is divided by object classes. Generally, these divisions would include your users, computers, groups, printers, and shares. This model helps make resource administration easier because OUs are designed by object types. Using this model may produce potentially larger numbers of OUs.

Remember that OUs are the smallest scope or unit that you can assign Group Policy or delegate administration to, enabling you, therefore, to manage resources based on your organizational model and to give administrators the capability to delegate administration on all OUs or a single OU.

Branch office plan

A *branch office plan* consists of numerous branch offices, with links to a corporate hub. It can be deployed in both large and small corporate environments. This plan covers only the branch office plan's basics; for corporate branch environments, you need to spend additional time planning, configuring, and monitoring for a smooth transition to branch offices.

Structural planning

Domain and forest partitions make up the two main pieces of the structural planning process. The two main reasons that most partition their Active Directory structure are to accommodate political organizational legal restrictions and to keep objects organized. If your organization does not agree on resource management and a common schema, you need to deploy multiple forests. In deploying multiple forests, you are greatly increasing your administration requirements. Your organization seems to have two options if separate security boundaries exist.

If the business units can acknowledge that no security isolation between domains is necessary and can agree on common operations and security guidelines, create a single forest; if your organization has a requirement for isolated domains, however, you need to create multiple domains. You are unlikely to exceed the number of possible objects for one forest. You can support many forests, assuming that your hardware supports such a need.

Domain partitioning is the second piece of the structural-planning element. You find several advantages and disadvantages in creating both a single and multiple domain directory. You can reduce the amount of data that is replicated during DomainNamingContext replication, thereby increasing the amount of global-catalog data that is replicated. The general amount of network traffic is reduced if you're using the multiple-domain structure. We suggest that you keep your plan to a single domain if your WAN can carry the load. Remember to keep the plan simple, if at all possible.

Replication planning

Active Directory replication and SYSVOL replication represent the two major components of domain- and forest-wide replication. These two components use the same replication topology but are run independently from one another. FRS SYSVOL replication starts as soon as a replication window is opened, while Active Directory randomly starts within the first 15 minutes of a replication window opening. Active Directory replication with multiple partners, therefore, starts at different times within that 15-minute interval, while the FRS SYSVOL starts at the same time for all partners.

Active Directory uses serialized inbound replication, where inbound replication is incoming data transferred from a replication partner to a domain controller. Because the data is serialized, the hub domain controller can handle inbound replication with one branch domain controller. This plays a big part in determining the number of bridgehead servers that your organization needs. A bridgehead server should not have more than 50 simultaneous active replication connections at any given time; try to keep the number lower than 50 which provides a significant effect on CPU utilization, network throughput, and I/O throughput. Data transfer form a domain controller to the replication partner is considered to be outbound replication. Outbound replication is not serialized, but it is multithreaded, thus causing the branch controller to pull changes from the hub domain controller.

The *file replication system* (*FRS*) is used by system policies and logon scripts stored in SYSVOL, causing domain controllers to keep SYSVOL for network clients to access. The FRS is a multithreaded, multimaster replication engine, meaning that changes to the SYSVOL can be made on any controller, and the controller then replicates the changes. FRS SYSVOL uses the timestamps on a file to determine the latest version of that file to distribute.

In determining your choice of bridgehead servers, you must first understand which servers should be bridgeheads. You also must understand the different load implications placed on a server depending on the replication type. Inbound bridgehead servers in a hub site travel through the list of replication partners one by one after the replication window opens. If the connection is slow and the window closes before the controller has finished replicating, it continues replicating until it is finished, potentially causing problems with the inbound sequences. Outbound replication is performed parallel; the only limiting factors, therefore, are the performance of the bridgehead servers, CPU load, and disk I/O. In determining how many bridgehead servers are needed, use inbound and outbound connections as the basis for the determination.

Hub site planning

Building the data center is the first step in the planning process, which includes configuration of DNS, root domain controllers, and bridgehead servers. Branch offices are usually connected through slow links to the hub, so setup of the domain controller first would mean replicating the whole directory. We don't think that you want to wait for that to occur. In many cases, no operations staff is located at the branches, so no one is willing to install and configure the domain controller. You have the option of using terminal services, but you still may need to be onsite to perform some configuration.

Administrators can install domain controllers in a central location, enabling them to create the domain controllers very quickly and then ship them out to the branch offices. This location where the domain controllers are installed and configured can be a data center but usually is a staging site. You must consider the differences between the sites — for example, their TCP/IP and link speeds. If hundreds of computers are to be set up, doing this in one location (staging site), where the process has been proven and tools and experienced personnel are on hand, is your best course. The setup process can cause increases in traffic for initial setup, so the staging site must have fast links for the replication process.

In building the root domain, make sure that the forest root domain controller is the first domain controller installed. Then the global catalog server must be installed; at least one domain controller in the forest domain must be the global catalog. The first domain controller that we installed was the global catalog server. We therefore installed global catalog on the domain controllers in the root domain. The global catalog role should be left on this computer. Additional domain controllers in the root domain should be only domain controllers. The forest root domain is special; it is the root of the Active Directory namespace. DNS configuration for the forest root domain controller is slightly different from all other domain controllers. DNS servers in the forest root domain (as long as they are domain controllers) hold a master copy of the _msdcs, which is used to store the CNAME records for replication. (The CNAME record is an entry in your DNS table that specifies another domain to which the user would be redirected.) You want to avoid isolation of a forest root domain controller after a configuration change; these DNS servers need to be configured to use another DNS server as the primary DNS server. You need at least two forest root domain controllers in the hub site, pointing to each other as primary DNS servers.

Five operation master roles exist in the root domain: the schema master, the domain naming master, the primary domain controller (PDC) emulator, the infrastructure master, and the relative ID (RID) master. The schema-master domain controller controls all updates to the schema. For you to update the schema of the forest, you must have access to the schema master. Only one schema master exists in the entire forest. The domain-naming master controls the addition or removal of the domains in the forest. The infrastructure master is responsible for updating references from objects in its domain to objects in other domains. The RID master processes all pool requests for the domain controllers of a particular domain. The PDC advertises itself as the primary domain controller to workstations, member servers, and domain controllers that are running earlier versions of Windows.

The root domain is usually a small domain, keeping the load to a minimum. Try to keep all roles on one server so that, whenever you take the server down, transferring the roles to a different domain is easy.

You need to plan for recovery, because the root domain is a crucial part in the Active Directory forest. It maintains the schema and the configuration information. If the root domain is lost, operations requiring the root domain do not operate correctly. Securing at least one domain controller of the root domain is of utmost importance. (Refer to Chapter 21 for more information on disaster recovery.)

Site staging planning

Your staging site can either be a separate site in your data center that helps you in preparing new domain controllers or possibly be contracted out to a third-party company for staging. If you have hundreds of computers to be manufactured, the best practice is to do all staging in one location. Your tools are then in one location for easy access, debugging, and configuration. This also helps your replication traffic, as branch offices generally have slower links that can cost you valuable time.

A staging site has a set of requirements that must be adhered to for successful staging. You must have at least one permanent domain controller in the staging site for replication of the new domain controllers. You also must have a permanent network connection between the staging site and the hub. Finally, this site must be large enough to capacitate all the new domain controllers. By providing a domain controller in the staging site, you can use it to replicate the existing directory while the installation wizard is running. The network connection provides the server configuration to the new domain controllers. A good idea is to keep domain controllers online for a while before they are shipped so that the RID pool is delivered, replication has sufficient time to complete, file-replication service replication succeeds, SYSVOL is shared, and the domain controller can advertise itself. You need a staging site that enables you to have sufficient time to complete the preceding processes and also provide enough physical space for all your needs.

Domain controller planning

Building a domain controller and then shipping it to the final destination can cause many problems. Many things can be done wrong if the domain controllers are built in a location that is different from the destination location. Risks are involved in even the most thought-out plans. Consider the following prestaging steps.

You need to install the correct operating system with the correct service packs, all troubleshooting tools, and monitoring tools. You may also have some in-house products that may need installation depending on your organization. You need to verify that the preceding step was successful, as well as to promote the server to a domain controller. You also need to verify that the promotion was successful, as well as to leave the computer online in the staging site. You then need to prepare your computer for transportation to its final destination.

In a perfect world, your new servers and domain controllers would be installed from a new image. This process is fast and less error prone. You should also document the software releases that were installed. You also need to perform configuration, and should prepare a checklist. Make sure that you verify that the computer name, DNS configuration, and IP configuration are all correct. Whenever the server is ready to be promoted to a domain controller, run the Active Directory installation wizard to promote the server. You need to specify the domain controller that is to be used to provide initial replication. As you install the domain controller into the staging site, it is automatically configured. Verifying that the new domain controller is replicating correctly with the rest of the domain controllers is crucial.

Before you prepare to pack and ship your server to its destination, you also need to verify that each domain controller is correctly configured.

Administration Planning

Administration planning provides you with an understanding of your server administration needs. This section covers topics from delegating administration to building an administration hierarchy. We hope that this section provides you with the information that you need to build your total administration plan. The point is to make administration as easy to manage as possible by preparing an administration plan.

Delegating administration

The main capability of Active Directory in Windows Server 2003 is the delegation of administration. Through this process, you can design a directory infrastructure to span multiple organizations that require unique management requirements. This helps your organization meet specific requirements for operational and structural independence. Administrators can delegate service management and data management to achieve isolation between organizations.

Many reasons exist to delegate administration, and you must realize why organizations may want to delegate administration. Table 8-2 shows several reasons to delegate administration.

Table 8-2: Reasons to Delegate Administration

Reason	*Description*
Organizational structure	Provide the capability to operate independently from the organization.
Legal requirements	Provide the capability to restrict access to sensitive information.
Operational requirements	Provide the capability to place unique constraints on configuration, availability, and security.

The administrative responsibilities that are delegated can be separated into two main categories, *service management* and *data management*. Service management generates responsibility for delivery of the directory service, and data management provides responsibility for the content stored in the directory service. The service administrator is responsible for administering service management, and the data administrator is responsible for the data management.

Delegating forests, trees, and organizational units

Three structures are used to delegate administration in forests, trees, and organizational units. You need to know when selecting a structure based on the delegation requirements is appropriate. You should fully understand the preceding section "Delegating administration," to continue.

The forest administrator is a member of a Domain Admins group and has control over the Enterprise Admins and the Schema Admins groups. This, by default, gives the forest administrator total control over the forest-wide configuration settings. The forest owner, therefore, controls the domain controllers, giving the forest owner the service administrator title. Domain Admins have control over domain controllers, giving them by default the title of service administrator. The OU object is controlled by the Access Control List; users and groups that have control over objects in the organizational unit, therefore, are data administrators.

Implementing object security

Active Directory objects, such as files and registry entries, have security identifiers associated with each object. This association creates a security-identifier presence, indicating that the resources in the directory can be secured in the same manner that files can be secured. By assigning a security identifier to each of the objects, you are essentially granting Read and Write rights to the object, to a grouping of properties, or to individual properties of that object. You therefore give administrators a granular-type control over the updating procedures of these objects and the users who can maintain and update the objects.

Simple and multilevel inheritance

Active Directory object permissions are automatically inherited, thereby causing objects in one container to inherit the permissions of that container or parent container. This form of inheritance is enabled by default to help minimize object administration.

This design of permission inheritance flows downward in the hierarchy to the object's child objects, if they exist. If you create an organizational unit named *marketing*, for example, and you permit the Marketing Admin group to have Full Control rights to the marketing organizational unit, after the child units are created they inherit the same permission settings, and the group administrator has Full Control permissions to the objects as well.

The domain and enterprise administrators have full reign in the following situation: They can enable or deny permissions for every object in the Active Directory, as can any other owners of the objects.

You can prevent this type of inheritance if you want to set a different level of security access to the child container than that of the parent container.

Defining object visibility in Active Directory

Object visibility is determined by the group scope that also determines what type of objects can be contained within a group. Three group scopes can essentially determine an object's visibility. These scopes are *universal*, *global*, and *domain local*. Members of universal groups can include other accounts and groups from any domain in the tree or forest; security groups cannot be created if using this type of scope when in native-mode. They can, therefore, grant permissions in any of the domains that belong to that tree or forest. Global groups could contain other accounts or groups from the domain in which the group is defined; they also have the capability to grant permissions to any domain in the forest. The domain local group incorporates groups and accounts from Windows Server 2003, Windows 2000, or NT. These groups can be granted permissions only within their respected domains.

Administrative roles

The administration team manages and maintains requirements as the system grows to meet your organization's needs. Depending on the size of your organization, the team may consist of one to two individuals or a series of interdependent groups. You need to identify who is going to perform administrative tasks such as account management and daily operations.

Efficient enterprise-wide group nesting

Organizational units can be nested to create a hierarchy in a domain structure. This structure is independent of the domain structure, enabling each domain to create its own hierarchy. Organizational units don't seem to affect performance. Group Policy can be applied to these organizational units to give administrators granularity in their administration of security.

Building the administrative hierarchy

Active Directory administration increases in complexity and difficulty with each administration level. The goal is to minimize the cost of administration, while providing a high level of service. Table 8-3 describes each tier of the administration model.

Table 8-3: The Three-Tier Administration Model

Administration Tier	*Description*
First-tier	Provides day-to-day administrative tasks such as creating users, help-desk support, and working with end users.
Second-tier	Provides in-depth knowledge of the organization's network and server apps. Administrators at this level are experts at problem solving and are required to use monitoring and troubleshooting tools.
Third-tier	Handles critical or cross-application problems that may be escalated to this level from the first or second tiers. Evaluates and rolls new server applications.

System administration may not always be clearly defined, as shown in Table 8-3; you usually find a hierarchy of administration based on the skills and experience of the administrator.

Migration Planning

During the migration planning stage, you make several important choices. These choices determine the functionality of certain features. We hope to help you make your migration choices much easier by covering the two main concepts of migration, which are *upgrades* and *restructuring*. Depending on your organization, you may need to upgrade first and then restructure or restructure first and then upgrade. This section should help you in making the preceding choices and help you complete your migration plan while identifying some areas of risk.

Upgrade plan

If you are planning on upgrading from Windows 2000 to Windows Server 2003, doing so enables you to take full advantage of the new features without restructuring your network configuration. Your existing directory service remains intact and provides you with improved group replication, application directory partitions, forest trust relationships, group caching, and an improved intersite replication-topology generator.

The three main tasks that you need to document in preparing your upgrade plan to Windows Server 2003 are *pre-upgrading*, *upgrading*, and *post-upgrading*. The pre-upgrading task takes you through all the necessary precautions that occur with a Windows Server 2003 upgrade. The pre-upgrade task's main focus points are securing all domain data and preparing your infrastructure.

The first task in pre-upgrading requires you to secure your domain data. This task may vary depending on the operations and procedures in your organization. You should at least allow for successful replication between two domain controllers in each domain, perform a full backup of all the domain controllers, and then successfully test all backups to make sure that they are not corrupt.

The second task in pre-upgrading requires you to prepare your infrastructure for the upgrade. The first step to completing this task is to successfully use the Active Directory preparation tool (`ADPrep.exe`) on the schema master to prepare the forest, and then once on the infrastructure master in each domain. You must make sure this program successfully executes, or Windows Server 2003 setup fails.

Use the following list to serve a checklist for the pre-upgrading plan:

- ✦ Back up all domain data and verify its validity.
- ✦ Use the ADPrep tool to prepare your forest and check for successful completion.
- ✦ Use the ADPrep tool to prepare your domain and check for successful completion.

The next step in planning your upgrade consists of the upgrade itself; this task involves installing Active Directory, upgrading the first domain, and upgrading the remaining domains. You can plan to upgrade your Active Directory installation by using the Active Directory Installation Wizard. The wizard enables you to create an additional domain controller and join it to existing domains, to configure the local server, to create directory partitions, or to install and configure DNS. By completing this task, you have a domain controller.

After installing Active Directory, allow sufficient time for replication to take place and for all member servers to synchronize with the new member server.

After you have allowed time for the replication to synchronize with the other domain controllers, you should upgrade your first domain controller. Then follow that by upgrading the remaining controllers.

As a checklist for the upgrading plan, make sure that you install Active Directory, upgrade your first domain, and follow that first upgrade by upgrading the remaining domains. You now need to follow up all the upgrading steps with your post-upgrade task. If you completed the preceding upgrade task successfully, you are now ready to raise the forest and domain functional levels. By default, the forest automatically functions at the Windows 2000 native functional level. If all your domains in the forest are in Windows 2000 native mode, raising the functional level of your forest to Windows Server 2003 automatically raises the domains' functional level.

As a checklist for the upgrading plan, make sure that you raise domain functional levels to Windows Server 2003 and also raise forest functional levels to Windows Server 2003.

Restructuring plan

Determining when to restructure is an important part of this plan. You need to restructure if your existing NT or Windows 2000 structure does not fit your target structure. You may also want to migrate gradually, maintaining your backwards compatibility. Before you make your decision, consider the following questions: Are you currently unhappy with your structure and believe that you could carry out a two-phase migration: upgrade to Windows Server 2003 and then restructure to fix any problems? Do you feel that you can't maintain a production environment while migrating to a new environment?

If either of the preceding questions apply to you, you should seriously consider restructuring. The main reason for restructuring is to maintain a network design in an ever-changing organization. What if you have department A and department B, each of which has its own individual domains, but then the departments decide to merge? In NT, you could create a trust between the two servers, but the two servers can never truly merge without recreating all the users in one of the domains. Windows 2000 and Windows Server 2003 provide a much easier interface for restructuring Active Directory to match the changing organization. Combining can still be a lot of work, but with Windows Server 2003, you never need to resort to reformatting the server.

As is the case with most types of network restructurings, you can't just sit down and revamp the entire network. You must plan your changes and determine how the changes may affect the network. You need to familiarize yourself with the tools used for restructuring Active Directory.

Migration tools

In the section "Upgrade plan," a little earlier in this chapter, we discuss the `ADPrep.exe` tool. This tool is essential in preparing Active Directory for Windows Server 2003. It prepares the forest and domain for an Active Directory upgrade by performing a collection of operations before the first domain controller is installed. This tool is located on the Windows Server 2003 CD, and it copies the files `409.csv` and `dcpromo.csv` from the `I386` directory or from a network installation to the local computer.

Current and old schema merge, preserving the previous schema modifications in your environment. You can run ADPrep `/forestprep` in a forest to accomplish the necessary forest preparation and ADPrep `/domainprep` to prepare a domain. To prepare the schema operations master, run ADPrep `/forestprep`.

The ADPrep program creates a log file each time that it executes. This log file helps you troubleshoot errors that may occur and also documents each step of the preparation process.

Test-lab plan

The test-lab plan is designed to help you prepare your testing strategy, basing it on a realistic scenario. In a test environment, you definitely need a realistic scenario that simulates your production environment. By preparing this scenario, you can verify your assumptions and uncover problems while optimizing the design. In doing so, you are verifying your plan and reducing your risk of errors and downtime.

Depending on your environment, you may even spread your test environments across numerous physical or even geographical locations. Several elements influence the type of lab that you choose, such as physical space or environmental limitations, budget, time and staff available for building the lab, existing labs, corporate culture, and the project's or corporate goals. Based on the previous elements, you have two types of labs to choose from — an *Ad Hoc lab* and a *Change Management lab*. The Ad Hoc lab provides specific project testing. After the project ends, the equipment can be redeployed, used for a production environment, or returned to the vendor. The total cost of ownership (TCO) for an Ad Hoc lab can vary, depending on the number of projects that you need it for, but the equipment can be redeployed, essentially keeping the TCO low. The Change Management lab presents a permanent environment. At first glance, you may think that the TCO for a permanent lab would be greater than for the Ad Hoc lab. But you view it across projects, the cost of a permanent lab is likely to be more reasonable. Ad Hoc labs are hard to track, and financial accountability is diluted. Change Management labs can be used in the following test environments:

✦ Network upgrades

✦ Service packs and software patches

✦ Business application compatibility

✦ Desktop configurations

✦ New hardware platforms

✦ Administrative and support processes

✦ Client computer management tools

In determining what model fits your goals, if circumstances (such as your budget) seem to dictate another approach to the one that you consider the best, try to come up with creative ways to support your solution.

After you make the decision for the correct lab model for your environment, you want to make sure that your lab simulates the full environment. You need to prepare a list of information about your environment that helps you design the lab. This list can include your current or new logical and physical network design, features that you want to explore and evaluate, administrative tools to explore or evaluate, and service packs, server drivers, and server bios that you need to configure and test.

This list needs to grow, depending on your own test-lab needs. After you compile your list and determine your test-lab design you need to focus on documentation. We know that this is hard to do, but it can prove essential and helps keep lab users up to date on design changes. Testers can use lab descriptions and diagrams whenever they design test-case scenarios to ensure completeness in the testing plan.

Backup and recovery plan

Backing up your Active Directory on a regular basis is critical. The Backup tool provides several features that keep this process simple. You should integrate your Active Directory backup routine into your regular server backup procedures without causing interruption to the network.

The Backup tool enables you to back up the domain controller while it is still online, causing no user interruption. The backup should consist of Active Directory, along with old system files and data files. The Backup tool provides methods for backing up the data that are supported for a normal backup. The normal backup marks each file as having been backed up and truncates the log files of database applications.

Before you attempt to make a backup, you should document the existing structure, including the resource registry keys that map to resources. We also suggest that you catalog your backups and create a repair disk for each node that you can use for restoring that node, if necessary. You should use the Backup tool to create emergency repair disks in case the system files become corrupt or damaged.

The Backup tool should back up all the system components and all distributed services on which Active Directory depends. This data is known as the *dependent data*, which is collectively known as the *system state data*. This data encompasses the system startup files, the system registry, the class registration database, file replication, the certificate database, the domain name system, and Active Directory. So whenever you use the Backup tool, you cannot back up Active Directory alone; all the system state data must be backed up. We recommend that you schedule regular backups and keep them well documented.

You have two basic plans for restoring Active Directory. The first plan involves reinstalling Windows Server 2003 as a domain controller and then enabling the other domain controllers to populate Active Directory through replication. This plan keeps Active Directory in current state.

The second plan is to restore the directory from the backup location. This automatically restores Active Directory to its last backed-up state. You have three options in restoring from backup: authoritative, primary, and normal restore.

The *primary restore* option is used for restoring servers of a replicated data set (`SYSVOL` and FRS). This should be used only if you are restoring the first replica set to the network. You should never use primary restore if you have already restored one or more of the replica sets; this restore should be your first replica restore. Primary restore is typically used if all domain controllers in the domain are lost.

The *normal restore* option is used in a nonauthoritative state. This restore keeps all original update sequence numbers intact, enabling replication to use this number to detect and propagate in the servers. If newer data is available from other servers, the newer data replicates to the server.

To use the *authoritative restore* option, you need to run the `Ntdsutil` utility after you restore the system state data but before you restart the server. This utility enables you to mark objects for authoritative restore and automatically updates the sequence number so that the data is new. You are, therefore, replicating through the server, thus making sure that you replace the data with restored data.

Caution If you decide to restore your system state data but you forget to designate a different location for the data, the backup erases the data and restores the system state data from backup. You therefore lose any data that was not on the backup.

Deploying the plan

After creating the appropriate plan for your Active Directory scenario, you need to organize your deployment team, based on their skill sets, and assign specific roles to the team members. The team should now be able to make projections on deploying the plan for your organization and on the final rollout. You then need to prepare a schedule and budget to meet the needs of your plan. If your plan requires additional resources, those issues need to be addressed and dealt with.

Summary

This chapter takes you through the basic planning process of Active Directory and the pieces that make up the Directory. Depending on your organization, you may need to build your own scenario. Several planning steps and stages are discussed in this chapter and we try to summarize all these plans into a basic plan that you can use for your own organization. We mention many times that you should try to keep your plan simple and consider alternative measures if needed, although doing so is not always possible.

The next chapter provides the information that you need to build your logical domain structure.

✦ ✦ ✦

CHAPTER 9

Organizing a Logical Domain Structure

✦ ✦ ✦ ✦

In This Chapter

Planning the Logical Domain Structure

Partitioning the domain

Using organizational units to create domain structure

Creating the design blueprint

✦ ✦ ✦ ✦

If you've read Chapter 8, you are probably pretty psyched about Active Directory. And you probably thought that we were nuts in the opening chapters of this book, where we urged you not to install Active Directory and to deploy standalone servers until you are at home with the new operating system. In this chapter, we are going to go overboard. We are going to tell you *not* to build your new domain until you have read this chapter, done a psychoanalysis of your company, and designed your domain on a whiteboard or a math pad and come up with a blueprint. Windows Server 2003 now provides a way for you to rename your current domains by using the new Active Directory domain-rename tools. We still feel that documenting your domain structure before creating the physical structure is very important. So before you start, know that, if you delete from the server either the root domain or the last domain on a domain tree (a process known as *demotion*), you uninstall the namespace. If you screw up the namespace and decide, after many hours of hard work, that you started wrong, you could end up losing all those hours that you spent creating user and computer accounts and configuring domain controllers. And if you go into production, you also take down several colleagues. We thus offer you a miniguide to enterprise analysis in this chapter in the hope that, as you get ready to break ground, you don't slice your toes off in the process.

Keepers of the New Order

As a Windows Server 2003 administrator, you now find yourself at the center of a paradigm shift. You are also a pivotal component in the change that is underway on the planet in all forms of enterprise and institutional management.

Windows Server 2003 is a great facilitator in that paradigm shift. Companies are changing; a new order is emerging. The way that businesses communicate with their customers is changing. Very little is currently regarded from a flat or unidimensional perspective. Today, corporate workers, owners, and administrators need a multifaceted view of their environment. Managers and executives need to look at everything from a 360-degree panorama of the business — its external environment and its internal environment.

You, the network administrator — specifically, the Windows Server 2003 network administrator — now have a lot more on your shoulders. Everyone is looking at you — what you're worth, what you know, how you conduct yourself — from the boardroom to the mailroom. You are the person to take the company beyond the perimeter of the old order.

The tools to facilitate the shift can be found, for one reason or another, in Microsoft Windows Server 2003. You learn a lot about the Windows Server 2003 architecture in Chapter 1, so we don't repeat it here, except to say that Windows Server 2003's Directory, Security, Availability, Networking, and Application services are in your hands and those of your peer server administrators. The tools that you use to manage all the information pertaining to these services and objects are the Active Directory and the Windows Server 2003 network.

As mentioned in earlier chapters, Windows Server 2003 domains are very different from legacy Windows domains. They are also very different from the network-management philosophies of other operating systems such as Unix, NetWare, OS/2, and the mid-range platforms such as AS/400, VMS, and so on.

Before you begin to design your enterprise's *Logical Domain Structure* (*LDS*), you have a number of important preparations to make. Besides items such as meditating, education, lots of exercise, and a good diet, you also have some network administration specifics to consider. We discuss these items in the following sections.

Active Directory Infrastructure Planning

Active Directory planning is a critical part of your Server 2003 deployment. The design of your Active Directory defines the success or failure of your organization's Windows Server 2003 implementation. A great deal of planning goes into an Active Directory infrastructure, such as that for creating a forest plan, a domain plan for the forests, planning the organizational units, and developing the site topology. These topics are all covered in more detail in Chapter 8, so if you study that chapter, you should have a good understanding of how to plan your Active Directory.

Planning for the Logical Domain Structure

In Chapter 5, we discuss the steps to installation and conversion. One of those steps is designing the Logical Domain Structure (LDS). If your task is the installation of or conversion to Windows Server 2003, the first item on your list should be to understand the steps to achieving the LDS and then implementing it. Unless you can create an LDS blueprint, the myriad other management functions, such as creating and managing user accounts, groups, policies, shares and more, are difficult to implement and cost you a lot in time and material. The following list represents the steps that you must take in this chapter to arrive at the point where you can begin the conversion process or even install in a clean or new environment:

1. Prepare yourself mentally for the task.
2. Assemble an LDS team.
3. Survey the enterprise.
4. Design the LDS.
5. Produce the blueprint.

Preparing Yourself Mentally

Long gone are the days when installing a Windows-based network could be handled with a sprinkling of administration experience gleaned from a few books or an education based on crammed MCSE courses.

Running a successful Windows Server 2003 domain (no matter what the size) is going to require more than a magazine education in networking, telecommunications, security, and administration. If you have been managing or working with Windows NT server, you have a head start on the new administrators and administrators from the other technologies who have chosen to defect. Nevertheless, the conversion and installation process is arduous and mentally taxing. And how much time you spend on fixing problems in the future depends on how well you lay your foundations now. The following sections offer some advice that can help stem the migraine tide from the get-go.

Forget about Windows 2000

Trying to create the LDS of Windows Server 2003 while thinking about Windows 2000 (and even managing Windows 2000) is like trying to meditate at a heavy-metal concert. In other words, it is very distracting. We would say that if you are involved in the day-to-day management of Windows 2000 domains, you should take a break from being an 2000 administrator while you're involved in the Windows Server 2003 LDS planning efforts, at least in the initial phases. You're almost certain to find working in both environments at the same time frustrating.

This is sobering advice if you must manage a 2000 domain while you plan a Windows Server 2003 domain. You need to make a special effort to separate the old from the new, the legacy from the up-and-coming.

Forget about conversion

Trying to think about retrofitting, upgrading, or converting your legacy Windows domains — and even your NetWare or Unix environments — only gets you into trouble. Forget about what everyone, including Microsoft, says about this, at least until you have the new domain structure in place and are fully versed in the techniques described in this chapter and the others described in this book. Only after you fully understand the possibilities and the limitations of Windows Server 2003 domains should you begin to plan your conversion process.

If you try to convert before the Windows Server 2003 LDS is in place, as discussed in more detail in Chapter 5, you risk an IT disaster and also risk losing money and opportunity in many respects. Set up a lab, as we discuss in Chapter 5. We can't tell you everything that you need to know or be aware of in this book, nor can Microsoft. Only you can discover how Windows Server 2003 accommodates your needs and how you accommodate its needs. No two organizations are alike.

Stay out of Active Directory

Before you break out into a cold sweat, this advice applies only to this chapter. The Windows Server 2003 LDS is just that — logical. Until you have your blueprint in place, your plans approved, and the budget in the bank, you don't need to do a thing in Active Directory.

Yes, Active Directory is the technology that makes the new LDS a reality, and yes, we would not be discussing the LDS in such direct terms as we do here if Active Directory were not a reality, but trying to design an LDS while tinkering around in Active Directory is counter-productive. Don't think that you can stumble your way to a design or blueprint.

We're not saying you shouldn't try to learn about Active Directory hands-on. Learn as much about it as you can. If you know nothing about Active Directory, you should not be in this chapter just yet, because you should have an understanding with Directory service terms and concepts.

If you are not yet up to speed with Active Directory, study Chapter 2, read the wealth of information in the Help system, download as much information as you can from Microsoft, and get stuck into books about Active Directory and LDAP. Chapter 2 is where you can test examples and concepts in Active Directory. In this chapter, you should be working with design tools and a whiteboard — a very large one.

For information on LDAP, you can download RFC 2254, 2255, 2307 from the Internet. These can usually be located at the Internet Engineering Task Force Web site (at `www.ietf.org`), but you can find these and many other LDAP references at any main search engine.

Assembling the Team

Before you begin, assembling a design team is vital. No matter whether you are a consultant or administrator for a small company and are attacking this single-handedly or a leader or part of a team working in a mega-enterprise, designing the domain requires the input of a number of people. In small companies that are adopting Windows Server 2003, the team may consist only of you and the owner or CEO.

The domain planning committee

Your domain planning committee should include a number of people, especially if the task is huge, who can assist you in the enterprise analysis that you need to undertake. Your team may be made up of the following members:

- **Assistant analysts and consultants:** People to help you quickly survey a large enterprise. The Millennium City example in this book, which is an Active Directory domain structure that spans an entire city, replete with departments and divisions, may need to employ about a hundred analysts to get the survey job done as quickly as possible. How many such members you need depends on how quickly you need or want to move. If you plan to use your IT department as a test case (going from development to production), you could probably get away with one or two analysts.
- **Documentation experts:** People to assist you in getting information down and in an accessible form as soon as possible. These people should, as far as possible, be trained in desktop publishing and documentation software, illustration and chart-making software, groupware, and so on. The documents should be stored in a network share-point.
- **Administrators:** People to be involved in preparing the installation and conversion process. These may include technicians and engineers currently involved in the day-to-day administration of domains, technical support, special projects, and so on.

Domain management

As the LDS plan progresses from enterprise analysis to approval and then to implementation and conversion, you need to appoint people who initially are involved in the day–to-day administration and management of the new domains.

If you have the resources at your disposal, appointing newly trained staff or hiring and training administrators from the legacy pool makes sense. These people can help you to build the new Windows Server 2003 domain and need to communicate with the administrators of the old domains and so on. If you are doing everything yourself, you have your work cut out for you.

Change control management

To provide your users with a higher level of reliability and a more managed infrastructure, you need to appoint a person responsible for change management. After the development domain is ready to be rolled to production, the teams need to communicate to assess the effect of the domain and to prepare for it. As projects become more complex in the computing environment, collaborating on complex projects becomes even more important.

Users need consistent, reliable experience, including a well-configured operating system, up-to-date applications, and data that is always available. The IT department must meet a variety of needs on a network. For this to succeed, IT must respond to the various changes that occur in the computing environment. The following list describes a few of the factors that require change management:

- New operating system and applications
- Updates to operating systems and applications
- Hardware updates
- Configuration changes
- New users and business requirements
- Security requirements

The change-control manager helps provide a lower total cost of ownership (TCO) by providing reduced downtime, reduced disaster-recovery costs, and reduced data loss because of hardware failure.

Domain security

Domain security is a serious issue; you therefore need to appoint at least one person to manage all aspects of domain security. That person's role is to test security in the development domain and to apply the appropriate security mechanisms in the production domains. In addition, such a manager can help you to determine domain policy, Group Policy, delegation, workspace management, and so on.

See Chapter 3 for information on Windows Server 2003 security and for information on security policies.

Intradomain communication

An important component is intradomain communication, or the communication between Windows Server 2003 domain users and legacy domain users. Depending on your environment, different levels of domain functionality are available. If all your domain servers are Windows Server 2003 servers, the functional level is set to Windows Server 2003 providing all the Active Directory domains and forest features to you. If you still maintain NT 4.0 or Windows 2000 domain servers, your features are limited.

In Windows 2000 Server, both native and mixed modes existed. If the domain was set to mixed mode, it supported NT 4.0 backup domain controllers but not the use of universal security groups, group nesting, and security identifier capabilities. If the server was set to native mode, it supported all capabilities. Controllers running Windows 2000 Server are probably not aware of forest and domain capabilities. Now, with Windows Server 2003, you have three domain functionalities. These functional levels are listed in Table 9-1.

Table 9-1: Domain Functional Levels

Functional Level	*Support*
Windows 2000 mixed	NT 4.0, Windows 2000, and Windows Server 2003
Windows 2000 native	Windows 2000, Windows Server 2003
Windows Server 2003	Windows Server 2003

Use caution in raising the domain functionality; after it's raised, the domain no longer supports legacy domains. A domain that is set to Windows Server 2003 for a domain functional level cannot add domains that are running Windows 2000 server.

You also need to appoint an Exchange administrator if you plan on integrating Exchange — or Lotus Notes administrators, Send Mail people, and so on.

A vital component of the LDS is that information can flow freely through the enterprise's information network and between the operational environments in which the company finds itself after a Windows Server 2003 domain greets the world.

Education and information

You need to generate information to keep management abreast of the development with respect to the conversion process and the emergence of the LDS. After a plan is approved, this information needs to be extended to educate people throughout the enterprise.

Surveying the Enterprise

Before you can begin to plan the LDS, you need to survey your enterprise. Consider the job of the land surveyor. A surveyor sets up the theodolite — an instrument that measures horizontal and vertical angles — and charts the hills and valleys, the lay of the land, the contours, and more. These scientists and engineers determine where it is safe to build a house or skyscraper, where to bring in a new road or a bridge, or where to place a town or a city. You need to do the same — not to determine where the company is going (which is what enterprise analysts do) but how to plan an LDS with what is already in place and what may be around the corner.

In surveying the corporate structure, you are not going to take on the role of offering management advice about its business, nor do you suggest that new departments or units should be added, moved, or removed to suit the new domain structure. Not only would that be impossible, but it also would likely get you fired or promoted out of networking.

On the other hand, the Windows Server 2003 LDS needs to be filtered up to the highest levels of management. In fact, the LDS blueprint is what the CIO or CTO is going to drop on the boardroom table, and the IT department is expected to implement the changes desired by management to affect the DNA, e-commerce, the paradigm shift, and more. The Windows Server 2003 LDS, because of what it may expose, may indeed result in enterprise or organizational change; just don't say it too loud.

Windows Server 2003 domains reflect the enterprise structure more than any other technology, and the domain structure is representative of the layout and the landscape of your company, from an administrative and a functional point of view.

Windows NT domain administrators, network administrators, and IT/IS managers have never before contemplated that their careers would take them into enterprise analysis. Large organizations are no doubt going to hire expensive enterprise analysts, but for the most part, that's an unnecessary expense unless some serious first aid is needed before a conversion to Windows Server 2003 can be considered.

In many cases, you already have the resources at hand. They exist in you and in your peers. You do not need to go overboard studying enterprise analysis, enterprise resource planning (ERP), and customer relationship management (CRM). Of course, having that knowledge helps and may even get you the job that you're after. This chapter serves as a guide if you are not sure where to start. The following sections discuss the key concepts of enterprise analysis.

Enterprise analysis

Enterprise analysis is enterprise land surveying and enterprise engineering come together for the future and good of the company. Enterprise analysts examine where the company is today, what business it is in (many don't know), and where it wants to go (or where the board or shareholders want it to go) and then make suggestions on how the company should go about achieving its objectives. Enterprise analysts help suggest changes at all levels of the enterprise — in particular, in information systems and technology. They provide management with critical, actionable information . . . blueprints that start the wheels of change turning.

Without technology, very few of the desires of the corporation can become a reality. You do not need to look far to see how misguided efforts in IT/IS have wrecked some companies, while making others more competitive and profitable. In your new role as enterprise analyst, you are surveying the corporate landscape to best determine how to implement a new Windows Server 2003-based logical domain structure.

You have two responsibilities. You must study the enterprise with the objective of implementing the new LDS as quickly and painlessly as possible. You may have a lot of money to work with, or you may not have much of a budget. In either case, you are going to need facts fast.

You also need to study the enterprise and forecast or project where it may be heading. Is the business getting ready for IPO, to merge, to file Chapter 11, or to be acquired? Is it changing focus? All these items and more affect not only the LDS of a company, but also the LDS of a city, a hospital, a school, or a government.

You may consider that you are doing the enterprise analysis for the good of the company, but you are doing it for your own good. You are expected to cater to any change that may happen between sunrise and sunset. And not having the wherewithal to implement or accommodate the sudden business direction that management may throw at you is not good IT administration.

So where do you start? As mentioned earlier in this section in "Planning for the LDS," you can't plan the LDS by just looking up all the groups that you created in Windows NT and figuring that just importing them all does the trick. That would be the worst place to start and the worst advice that anyone can take. Microsoft, we believe, makes too much noise about upgrading Windows NT; we believe that countermands *strategic* LDS planning.

The new Group Policy technology is so sophisticated that it makes upgrading an NT domain and inheriting its groups and user accounts a tricky business. Make sure that you fully understand Group Policy before you upgrade an NT domain. It is discussed in detail in Chapter 14.

Here is a short list of starting points. The following items may be better in another order for you, and you may add to the list as you deem fit:

✦ **Get management on your side:** This may not be difficult if you are the CIO or if the LDS directives come from the CIO or CTO. But to do the job well, you need access to more than would be expected of network or domain administrators. Management and HR, therefore, are going to need to trust you with sensitive information. We would like to add to this point: Get the CEO on board. You are going to need to set up appointments with the most senior staff in the enterprise. They need to know that your research is sanctioned at the very top. You are likely to encounter resistance at the departmental head level, where change may be deemed a threat. Advise department heads in writing that, if you do not get cooperation, their departments must be left out of the domain conversion or "new order." People tend to go crazy if their e-mail gets cut off, so you can use this as a foot in the door.

✦ **Get hold of organizational charts:** Most enterprises and organizations have these. If you're fortunate, they are up to date. If they are not or they do not exist, you are going to need to invest in a software tool that can make organizational charts.

✦ **Tell people what you are doing:** Being frank and open about the process, without exposing the team to security risks, is important.

Enterprise environments

Before you begin an exhaustive enterprise analysis project, take some time to understand the environments in which the enterprise or organization operates. Enterprise analysts often refer to these environments as *operational environments*. We have been teaching companies about their respective operational environments for several years, long before the advent of Windows Server 2003. The elements in these environments feature heavily on both the LDS and Physical Domain Structure (PDS).

Years ago, an enterprise operated in only two environments: *external* and *internal*. The advent of the Internet and wide area networks have resulted in a third environment: the *extra* environment, or the environment "in-between." An analysis of these environments is essential in the formulation of both the LDS and PDS.

To fully investigate the environments, you need to build lists of items to look for; otherwise, you do not know where to start and when to finish.

The external environment

The *external environment* is made up of several components: customers, suppliers, distributors, cleaning staff, and so on. At the physical level, the corporation or enterprise must deal with the elements of the external environment directly. Examples include providing access to cleaning staff, dealing with customers, delivery pick up, and more.

The most important technological factor in the external environment is the Internet. As do all enterprises and organizations, the Internet provides resources with which to deal with the elements in the external environment electronically and also offers a means of interconnecting partitions of the internal environment. Any modern company is as present in cyberspace as it is in the physical realm.

Today, the neural network in the external environment also is the Internet. The telephone system still plays an important and indispensable part, but it is becoming less pervasive as people find the Internet more convenient in many respects.

The enterprise depends on several components on the Internet that are vital to its existence in general. These include DNS, the locator service for the entity on the Internet, and the Internet registration authorities that provide the entity the right (for a fee) to participate in a global Internet infrastructure. These rights include the registration of your domain names and the assignment of IP addresses, without which you are unreachable.

The following is a short list of items that you should pay attention to as you examine the external environment:

- How is the company connected to the Internet?
- How does the company use the Internet's DNS system?
- What are the public domains used by the enterprise?
- Who keeps the domains and makes sure that the fees are paid on time?
- Are the domains that you need to register available?

The internal environment

The *internal environment* comprises all the departments, divisions, organizational units, and Key Management Entities (KMEs) that work together for the benefit of the enterprise. This environment includes employees, contractors, executives and management, subsidiaries, divisions, acquisitions, equipment, intelligence, information, data, and more.

The internal environment's neural network is the private intranet and its relative KMEs and administrative functions. The intranet is a private network, which is the medium for the Internet protocols TCP/IP. The local area network (LAN) is fast becoming a passé term, associated with outmoded and confining protocols such as NetBEUI, IPX, and more. Windows Server 2003 *is,* for all intents and purposes, an intranet operating system that still knows how to function on a LAN for backward compatibility.

Very important to consider in the internal environment are all the legacy systems and midrange systems that are going to need facilities in the new realm.

The following is a short list of items that you should pay attention to as you examine the internal environment:

- How many employees work for the company?
- How many remote divisions or branches does the company have?
- What functions do the remote divisions perform?
- How are the sites interconnected?
- Who is responsible for the management of the network that connects each of the sites?
- What is the bandwidth of the links between the sites?
- How is the company prepared for disaster recovery?

The extra environment

The *extra environment* is the interface—and the environment in the immediate vicinity of the interface—between the external environment and the internal environment. In some cases, the division may be obvious and thus easy to manage (such as a computer terminal in the public library or a voice-mail system). In other cases, the interface is harder to encapsulate or define and thus more difficult to manage (such as how people hear about your product).

Examples in the extra environment are e-mail; communications between the internal and external environments that may need to be monitored, controlled, and rerouted; corporate Web sites that enable customers to access portions of the internal environment; and so on.

The network environment supporting this environment and its technology is known as an *extranet*. A good example of such an extranet is FedEx, which enables customers to tap into the tracking databases to monitor their shipments.

The following is a short list of items that you should pay attention to as you examine the extra environment:

- What Web sites does the company use? Who manages them? Where are they located?
- What call center or help-desk functions are in place?
- How do contractors and consultants gain access to the enterprise to perform their work without risking exposure to sensitive data?

Working with organizational charts

With the organizational chart in hand, you can zero in on the *logical* units of the enterprise and begin enterprise analysis in a "logical" fashion. Figure 9-1 represents a portion of the organizational chart of Millennium City. (The entire chart is on the CD, in the Millennium City Domain Structure Blueprint PDF.) The chart has been adopted from the organizational chart of a major U.S. city, and we use it throughout the book to see examples of both Logical Domain Structure and Physical Domain Structure.

The full chart in Figure 9-1 is huge (more than 50 divisions and hundreds of boards and councils), but you must realize that the LDS that you are going to create may need to accommodate such an environment. Obviously, fully converting such an organization is going to take many years, and you're likely to be working with Windows 2005 before achieving 100 percent penetration with an organization of this size.

In fact, in organizations of this size, you're likely never to achieve a 100-percent pure Windows Server 2003 domain structure, and you wouldn't want to. Just a cursory glance at such a chart tells you that you are going to be up to your neck in integration with legacy and mid-range systems, Unix and Mac platforms, and more.

You need to start somewhere, however. You need to start conversion and installation with select departments, starting perhaps with your own department, where you can learn a lot about the conversion process, the fabric of Windows Server 2003, and the place to set up the labs and development environments that we discuss in Chapter 5.

We have selected three entities out of the chart to use as examples. We are going to convert the Mayor's office (City Hall), the Department of Information Technology and Telecommunications (DITT), and the Police Department (MCPD).

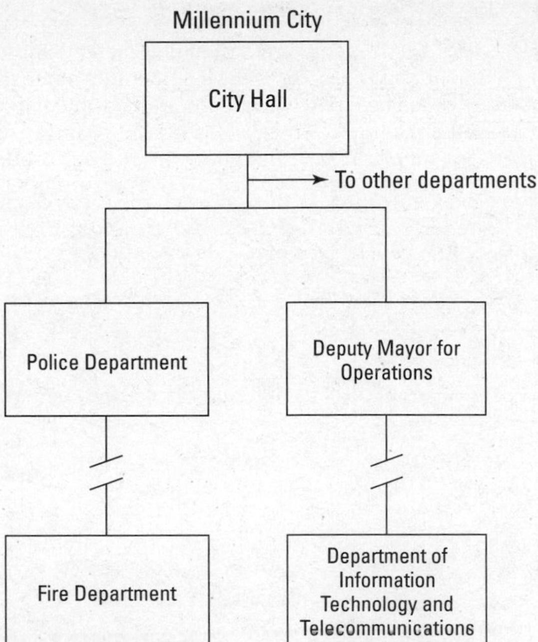

Figure 9-1: Abridged organizational chart of Millennium City.

Identifying the Key Management Entities

Key Management Entities (KMEs) are the management, administrative, or service components of a business or organization that, taken as a whole, describe what the entity does. These KMEs are not on the organizational chart and often span multiple departments. Payroll processing, for example, is a KME that spans the enterprise. Although the KME for payroll is concentrated in the Office of Payroll Administration, the KME spans Millennium City because it requires the participation of more than one logical or organizational unit. Every department processes its payroll by processing time sheets, data input (time/entry databases), sick leave, raises, check issues, check printing, bank reconciliation, direct deposits, and so on. The KMEs need not be physical groups; they can be logically dispersed between several departments and across several domain boundaries, remote sites, and so on.

All KMEs, after they're identified, are best represented on a matrix of the enterprise. Each KME represents an area of responsibility that must be measured and evaluated. After you have identified the KMEs, you can learn about the IT/IS systems and technologies that have been implemented to assist them and ultimately how both LDS and PDS can emerge to accommodate them. Figure 9-2 shows the KME matrix for MIS.

MIS people seldom research KMEs or even update previous reports and plans. An important benefit or payoff of such research is that MIS learns how it can improve efficiency in the KME.

Breaking the KMEs down further and extracting the components that require the services of IT/IS is also important. You need this information later as you identify where to delegate administration and control in various organizational units and domains.

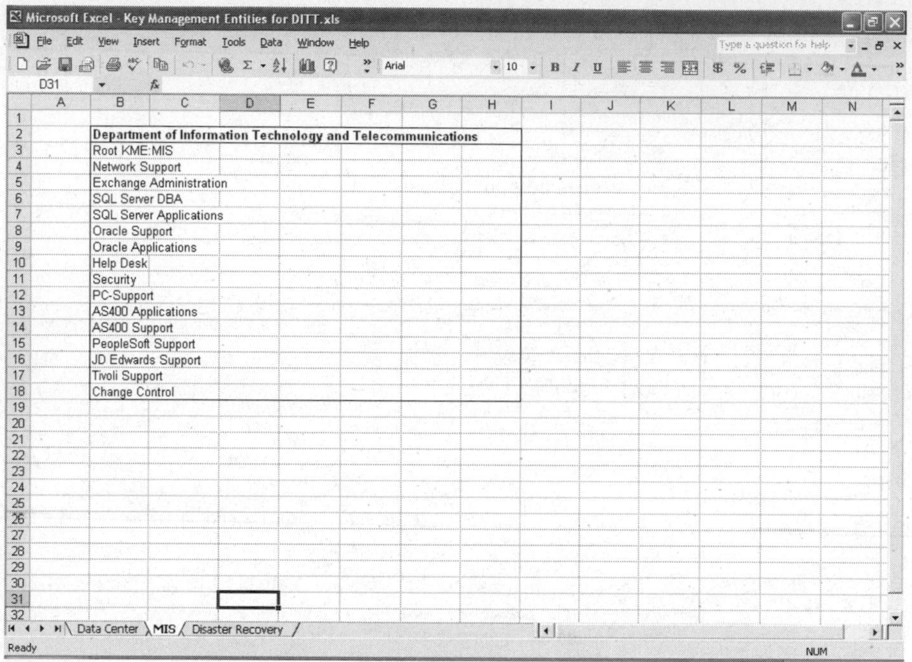

Figure 9-2: KME matrix spreadsheets prepared in Microsoft Excel.

Strategic drivers

In the movie *Wall Street,* Michael Douglas' character identifies greed as the *strategic driver* in his effort to raid companies and make huge profits. Greed certainly is a strategic driver in many companies and organizations, but many others exist, and you could argue that they are subordinate to greed and profit. The Internet is a strategic driver; the ambitions of the CEO and major shareholders are strategic drivers; mergers and takeovers are others, as are investment in new technology and more.

Strategic drivers are also new laws, new discoveries, new technology, lawsuits, labor disputes, and so on. Knowing what makes the company work and what can keep it working is important in domain planning and structure. You need to have as much information as you can about the enterprise and where it is headed so that you can give 100 percent where and whenever needed.

We contend that, if you know the strategic drivers of the organization you work for, you can be in a position to cater to any IT/IS demands placed on you. More important and in relation to the task at hand, you can implement a domain structure to cater to the drivers that influence the future of the enterprise.

Use your sixth sense, common sense, and logic in determining strategic drivers. Remember that with the new domain comes new threats, denial of service attacks, viruses, information and intellectual property theft, data loss, loss of service level, and more. A good example: In the weeks prior to New Year's Eve, Y2K, we anticipated that heightened security concerns would come from the CEO of the large distributor that we support. So we preempted the request and investigated how best to lock down the company's RAS and still provide access to key support staff that may be required to dial in during the night. We effectively locked down all access and created a secure zone on the RAS machine, which authenticated users locally before providing access to the domain. Being a good system administrator means going beyond the theories that you learn at MCSE school or computer science class. Windows Server 2003 is the wake-up call for stodgy sysadmins.

Identifying the logical units

Look at the organizational chart of Millennium City in Figure 9-1, and the *logical units* jump out at you. Every department or organizational unit within each department affects the LDS in some form or another.

The Mayor's office looks simple enough. It includes the mayor and the people who work for him, such as public relations people, advisors, and administrative staff. The Mayor's office is probably one of the simplest of the logical units to represent or quantify in the LDS plan. For all intents and purposes, it can be represented as a single organizational unit on the LDS.

In corporations, the offices of the CEO and executive staff can range from extremely complex to very simple. But the Department of Information Technology and Telecommunications is very different. What are the logical units within this department? We identify some of them in the following list (although we cannot deal with every OU within this department because the list would run into too many pages):

✦ **Operations:** This unit is responsible for disaster recovery and maintenance of critical systems. The people in this unit make sure that systems are online; they watch systems and applications for failures; they monitor production; they print reports; and so on.

  If Operations detects errors or problems, its members try to fix them within certain guidelines or parameters. They may be required to restore servers in the middle of the night or call the on-call staff as needed. Operations staff members are trusted employees with heavy responsibilities. They probably need high levels of access to certain systems; they may need to have authority to shut down servers, reboot machines, perform backup, and so on.

✦ **Help Desk:** This unit may be part of Operations or a separate unit. Help Desk is responsible for getting staff members out of jams with technology, teaching them how to use new applications, and more. Help Desk members also need special access to systems. Help Desk often needs to troubleshoot applications and systems in the context or stead of the users that its members need to help. They may need to log in to mailboxes, for example, troubleshoot print queues, and escalate calls to second- and third-level support.

✦ **PC Support:** PC Support is a separate organizational or logical unit within the Department of Information Technology. The people who work in this unit troubleshoot desktop PCs and upgrade, maintain, and ensure that all employees within the entire company — often across physical organizational divides — have the resources that they need to do their work.

✦ **Security:** Security staff members are responsible for catering to requests for user and machine accounts, changing passwords, access to resources, and more. The Security staff works closely with network support in determining group memberships, rights and permissions, access to shares and files, and so on.

✦ **Network Support:** That's where you (and we) come in. Network Support deals with the upkeep of the intranet, servers, and WAN resources, as well as dealing with network providers, routers, circuits and more. You also deal with the location of domain controllers and are responsible for upgrading servers; interconnecting protocols; establishing services; providing storage, backup and disaster recovery; and more.

Identifying the physical units

Between the various departments in an organization are numerous physical units to consider. Departments may be located in separate buildings and in other cities. In Millennium City, for example, the Mayor's office, or City Hall, is remote from the Department of Information Technology and Telecommunications. The Police Department is spread over numerous buildings all across town.

We have intranets to deal with, as well as WANs and dedicated connections between departments that cooperate closely. The Police Department of a city of this size employs its own technical team that manages network resources and systems at both the office of the Police Commissioner and at the individual precincts. The Police Department is also hooked into the systems at the Department of Transportation, the District Attorney's Office, the Department of Corrections, and so on.

Documentation

After you have thoroughly surveyed the enterprise and are familiar with its layout and organization, you need to document your findings. Be aware that, at this point in the LDS design process, the documentation is far from complete, but it nevertheless forms the basis or departure point from which the conversion or management team can begin planning and creating a blueprint. Remember, too, that the initial conversion project should be open-ended enough to permit you to slide into continuous domain administration and that the documentation should continue to evolve. It becomes the "bible" for the present and future administrative teams. The following short list is a suggestion of steps to take to complete documentation and move forward with your LDS and conversion plan:

1. Update the organizational chart and then circulate it to department heads for additions, accuracy, and comment.
2. List the KMEs throughout the enterprise and describe the extent of the administrative function in each KME. You are noting the size of the KME and complexity. Make a note of where the KME extends beyond departmental or divisional boundaries of the enterprise. The documentation of KMEs may take many formats. We suggest that you create a matrix on a spreadsheet, listing departments and divisions in the column headers and the KMEs that you have discovered as rows, similar to the one started in Figure 9-2.
3. Forward the KME matrix to department heads and invite feedback. The KME list is likely to grow, and you're probably going to be informed of more KMEs that you did not uncover.
4. Divide the organizational chart into sections or make a listing of the divisions or departments you believe or have decided are the best prospects with which to begin conversion. Note the reasons and mark them for debate at the next conversion team meeting.

The next phase of the LDS plan is the investigation of the administrative models in place over IT throughout the enterprise. What we present here isn't going to get you through Harvard, but it should be enough to give you something to think about.

Administrative modeling

Administrative modeling deals with management and administrative styles and practices. The following list illustrates several core management styles that may be in place in a company for one reason or another:

✦ The box-oriented company

✦ The human assets-oriented company

✦ The change-oriented company

✦ The expertise-oriented company

✦ The culture-oriented company

Understanding the definition of the term *box* is worthwhile because it influences the ultimate layout of your LDS. *Box* refers to the way that management controls a company. Enterprise analysts and corporate executives talk about soft-box companies and hard-box companies.

The *soft-box*-driven company management team does not rule with an iron fist and trusts its managers to act in the best interests of the enterprise. It goes without saying that these companies have a lot of faith in their people and have achieved a system that is comfortable for everyone. The soft-box company is likely to have a small, employee handbook and provides little direct control at certain levels, giving regional managers a wide berth.

The *hard-box*-driven company is very rigid. The employee handbook at this company is likely to be about two bricks thick and probably lists rules for everything from dress code to eating in your office.

Good and bad companies are in both models. The best exist somewhere between both extremes; a hard-box company, however, is more likely to employ a rigid, centralized administrative approach at all levels in general and with respect to IT in particular. "Softer" companies are likely to be more decentralized.

Centralized administration and decentralized administration models do not apply only to general administration, but also to IT, MIS, or network administration.

Centralized administration

The *centralized* approach dictates that all management takes place from a single or central department. In a small company, you really have no alternative. The smallest of companies that cannot afford nor need dedicated IT/IS administration usually outsources all their technical and IT/IS support, and the core executive team and the owners make all decisions.

Bigger companies that operate from a single location — or a clinic or a school — may employ the services of small technical teams and still outsource. The really big companies that still operate from single locations use a centralized administration model, supported by their own teams.

Decentralized administration

The *decentralized* approach dictates that management or administration is dispersed to geographically remote locations. This is usually a practice among the largest of enterprises. Departments, locations, and divisions, some of them on opposite sides of the world, are large enough to warrant their own MIS or IT departments.

Most multinationals today employ varying degrees of both approaches, and their operations dictate to what extent administration is both centralized and decentralized. This is probably the most sensible of the management models and varies from corporation to corporation.

Companies determine how much and what makes sense to delegate to the remote locations or seemingly autonomous divisions. They may, for example, dictate that remote administrators take care of responsibilities such as backup and printer management out at remote centers or depots.

Other systems, even ones located at the remote sites, may make more sense managed from a central location. If you have ten sites and need to install an e-mail server at each site, for example, hiring or training people at the remote sites does not make sense if a single e-mail administrator and possibly an assistant can manage all e-mail servers from a single location. Windows Server 2003 and a dedicated reliable network make managing a highly sophisticated IT infrastructure from a remote location, with no technical staffing on-site whatsoever, entirely possible. And investing in products such as Exchange or Lotus Notes, which are designed to function in clusters and are managed from a single location, regardless of where the physical equipment is actually located, would make sense and go a long way toward reducing TCO. The advent of such admin-centralized technologies is making the decentralized approach more feasible to adopt. From 1998 to the present, we have managed servers in more than 20 cities throughout the United States, and we have never physically been onsite.

The good, the bad, and the unwise

Each model has its pros and cons. The centralized model is often the most used from an IT point of view, and part of the reason is that legacy systems — both mid-range and Windows NT — do not lend themselves to any meaningful decentralized administration or controlled delegated responsibility. The Windows Server 2003 Security Accounts Manager SAM, for example, can be written to only at the primary domain controllers (PDC). Copies of the SAM on the backup domain controllers (BDC) can be read for service requests but not written to. If, at any time, the PDC became unavailable to remote locations (because of a loss of link, maintenance, and so on), delegated administration at remote locations becomes impossible.

On the other hand, many companies go overboard and delegate willy-nilly to all departments and divisions. Some companies have carried the decentralized model to the extreme, forcing the remote or otherwise separated units to request their own budgets and acquire and support their own systems. These companies are often impossible to deal with because they have no central buying authority and integration of systems is a nightmare.

Often, newly acquired companies in mergers and takeovers end up looking after themselves as management absorbs them at an agonizingly slow pace. What you end up with is a hodgepodge of systems that are incompatible and impossible to integrate. One side may support Compaq, for example, and the other IBM. Amicable mergers or acquisitions often turn sour because IT and MIS cannot get the two or more technology departments to speak the same language.

Windows Server 2003 enables you to delegate to various levels of granularity, all the way down to the organizational unit, in tandem with a highly distributed and redundant Directory service. As such, Windows Server 2003 provides the pluses of the centralized model, such as buying like systems and technology, with the undeniable benefits of decentralized administration, permitting a controlled delegation of administrative function and partial or substantial relief of the administrative burden at HQ.

At Millennium City, you have a strong decentralized administration in place. All budget and organization-wide IT planning, however, is done at the Department of Information Technology and Telecommunication. All technical hiring, firing, and requests from Human Resources for staff takes place at the DITT. New systems, maintenance, technical support, help desk, and more is also done here.

The Police Department (MCPD), however, is autonomous and distinct from the main offices of the City. MCPD is a separate administrative authority that relies on the DITT for investment decisions, choice of technology, and more, but local administrators keep it going and keep it secure.

DITT thus remains as the command center, ensuring that systems at MCPD can talk to systems at the DA's office or that crime units have familiar access to the Department of Transportation without needing to physically go and sit at the department's computers. DITT also ensures that an administrator at the DA's office can apply for an opening at MCPD without needing to be retrained on systems at MCPD that are different from systems at the DA. In short, one of the chief functions of the DITT is to strive for homogenous systems as far as possible throughout the city and that the heterogeneous systems are interoperable and can be integrated.

Logical Domain Structure: The Blueprint

The logical container for domains in Windows Server 2003 is a forest. Forests contain trees, which have roots, and domain trees make up a Windows Server 2003 network. Understanding forests is not necessary to design a namespace, and forests are discussed in various contexts in Chapters 2 and 8.

As stressed in the introduction to this chapter, after a domain root is created, you are, for the most part, stuck with it in Windows 2000, but this is no longer the case in Windows Server 2003, with the new directory-renaming tool. In the same breath, you must remember that the deeper the namespace, the more flexible it is, and objects can be moved around domains and between domain trees if you later get stuck. You don't, however, want to be tearing down domains that are already heavily populated. So use the information culled in the enterprise analysis wisely and plan appropriately. As we emphasize in Chapter 8, test everything.

The top-level domain

You cannot start or create a Windows Server 2003 network without first creating a root, or top-level, domain. What the root should be named and what role it should play perplexes a lot of people. If you are confused, you are not alone, because no clear-cut rules work for every company.

In referring to the role played by the root, we mean whether the domain should be populated with objects or should just serve as a directory entry point, in a similar fashion to the root domains on the Internet.

Naming the root

One of the first things that you must decide is what to name the top-level or root domain of your Windows Server 2003 domain. This name involves more than just identity. It is the foundation for your corporate Active Directory namespace. Your enterprise most likely already has a domain name registered with an Internet authority, in which case you already have a namespace in existence, even if you never thought much about it as a *namespace* . . . probably more as a parking space. You're probably thinking, "What the heck does the domain that we registered have to do with our corporate network?"

In our example, Millennium City is registered with the InterNIC (Network Solutions, Inc.) as `mcity.org`. But how *your* two namespaces coexist on your intranet and the Internet is not the issue. How you *integrate* the two namespaces is.

You have two options: You can leave your public domain name applicable only in the external environment, resolved by an ISP's DNS server, or you can use your public domain name also as the root domain in the directory and on your intranet.

If your domain name is listed in the .com or .org levels of the DNS, it becomes published on the public Internet and is available as a point from which to resolve your public Internet resources, such as Web servers and mail servers. A query to the root (.org) for mcity.org, for example, refers the client to the DNS server addresses that can resolve MCITY host names authoritatively to servers on the public Internet. DNS servers around the world that regularly service "hits" for the mcity.org can draw on cached records to resolve IP addresses for their clients.

In your case, would you then want to use the public domain name as the domain root in your LDS? In the MCITY example, we saw no reason not to. The results of your enterprise analysis may indicate otherwise, for a number of reasons. We discuss some of them here, as pros and cons.

Reasons to have identical external and internal DNS namespaces are as follows:

- The domain suffix is identical in both environments and is less confusing for users.
- You have only one namespace to protect on the Internet.
- You have only one namespace to administer.

Reasons not to have identical external and internal DNS namespaces are as follows:

- Domains remain separate, and a clear distinction exists between resources on the outside and resources on the inside. The corporate intranet is more protected, therefore, but you still need a good firewall.
- The company may change direction and also may change the name.
- Proxy configurations for separate namespaces are easier to manage. Exception lists can be created to filter the internal names from the external names.
- TCP/IP-based applications such as Web browsers and FTP clients are easier to configure. You would not need to make sure that clients that are connected to both the intranet and the Internet at the same time resolve the correct resources.

Several items in the preceding lists demand more discussion.

First, we have a way around the domain suffix problem — a late-feature addition. Windows Server 2003 clients can store more than one UPN name to an account, as shown in Figure 9-3. This is achieved by allocating additional domain suffixes to the domain, which must be carefully managed so as not to create conflicts with users in other domains. Down-level clients are stuck with the NetBIOS name assigned to the domain. To add more domain suffixes, you can open the Active Directory, open Users and Computers, open the account of the user, and select the Account tab. The drop-down list to the right of the User logon name is where you find the additional suffixes. By the way, any suffix suffices to log the user on.

We do not believe that the intranet is any more exposed if you have a single namespace, because whatever name you choose as an Active Directory root domain, the domain controller is hidden behind a firewall. It is assigned an IP address that belongs to your private network and is not locatable from the public Internet — hidden by the magic of network address translation and so on (see Chapter 15). Nor are any of your other resources locatable.

You're probably going to implement firewalls and network address translation to protect your resources. And you're likely to come under attack and face various threats regardless of whether your external DNS domain name is identical to your internal DNS domain name. Most companies already deploy mirrored sites on both sides of a firewall.

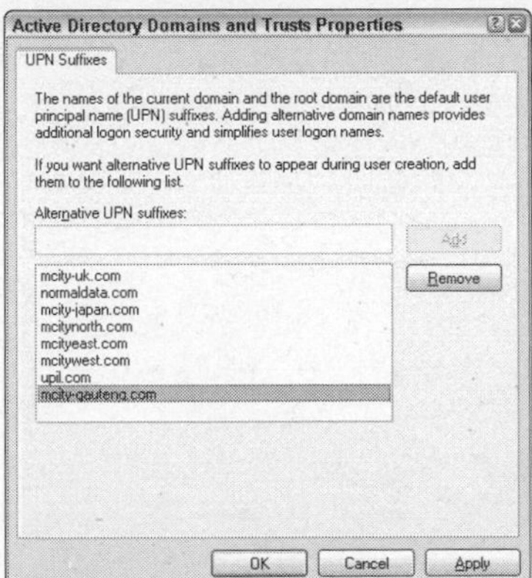

Figure 9-3: Changing the default domain suffix.

The second reason not to use your public domain name is that the identity of the company may change. You could get acquired or broken up, and changing the existing root domain to reflect the name of the new company would be almost impossible. This may, in fact, be a problem if you anticipate a merger or a name change soon (not usually something that server admins are privy to). This is why we devote such a lot of time and space to enterprise analysis.

You probably got excited about the advantages of the User Principal Name (UPN) that we discuss in Chapter 13. You should be aware that the UPN suffix is not locked into the root domain name by any means — or any other domain name, for that matter. You can change the UPN suffix at any time for your users if the name of the company changes or the public domain name changes. The underlying GUIDs never change, even if you relocate the objects to other regions of the domain tree or try to clone them with various resource kit tools.

If you need to plan for a merger or acquisition down the road or if you must deal with the outright sale of a certain division, you may be better off not naming your root domain after your public domain name at all.

Another discovery that you make in the external environment is that the public domain name and the enterprise name are different. Registering a domain name that is identical to the enterprise name is hard these days. Such a corresponding name would be nice, but obtaining it is not always possible. Take the company name Rainbow, for example. An infinite number of companies in the world must be called Rainbow something or another. But only one can be lucky enough to score the name `rainbow.com`. In such a case, you have no choice but to name the root domain whatever is the next-best name.

For the sake of example and because the name was available on the Internet, we went with `mcity.org` (and then, a week later, someone wanted to buy it from us). But a city is unlikely to change its name or be acquired, so if you are setting up a public institution, name changes are not be a major concern.

Getting back to the subject of the supplementary UPN, however, this should definitely reflect your public domain name so that e-mail addresses are the same internally and externally. If the public domain name changes and thus e-mail address suffixes change, you can apply the new domain suffix to the UPNs of all user accounts, as shown in Figure 9-4.

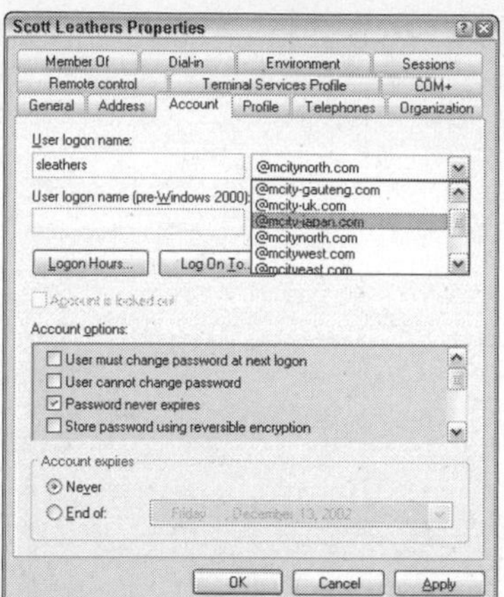

Figure 9-4: Adding multiple UPN suffixes to the domain.

The function of the root

The root domain of the first domain tree is the entry point to a forest. Forests are not part of any namespace and are located by attaching or connecting to the root domain in each forest. You can leave the domain root practically empty, with built-in accounts, or you can choose to populate it with OUs, security principals, and other objects. Most small companies never need a deep domain hierarchy, and even the root domain suffices in a company of several hundred employees. You should, however, seriously consider the following issues about the root domain:

✦ If the root domain is sparse, it replicates faster and provides an additional measure of fault tolerance. By ensuring that you always replicate the root, you serve to protect your domain "brainstem" in the event that a disaster takes out the lower levels. You can always create a domain and attach it to the root.

✦ The administrator in the root domain can reign supreme over the fiefdom like a shogun. A small group of forest-wide "samurai" administrators, serving the shogun, can be located in the root domain, which gives you tighter control over domain administrators in the lower-level domains.

The only drawback to this approach is the additional hardware for domain controllers that you need, but the root, being more ceremonial than functional, need not sit on an expensive server. Our first Active Directory was on a Compaq Pentium 133 Mhz, with 64MB of RAM.

Again, enterprise analysis points the way to justifying the reasons to add additional levels to the domain hierarchy, additional domain trees, and separate forests. Figure 9-5, however, shows the hierarchy that works for the `mcity` namespace. This is called an *extended* namespace, because it goes beyond what was envisioned by the DNS pioneers.

Here, we have chosen to stick to one namespace on the Internet, `mcity.org`. This enables the name servers, Web sites, FTP servers, mail servers, and more to be correctly resolved by the Internet DNS. The first domain controller in the city (`MCDC01`), however, becomes the second-level domain that serves as the domain root in the Active Directory forest. As Figure 9-5 shows, this server is located behind the firewall and is further protected by network address translation (see Chapter 13).

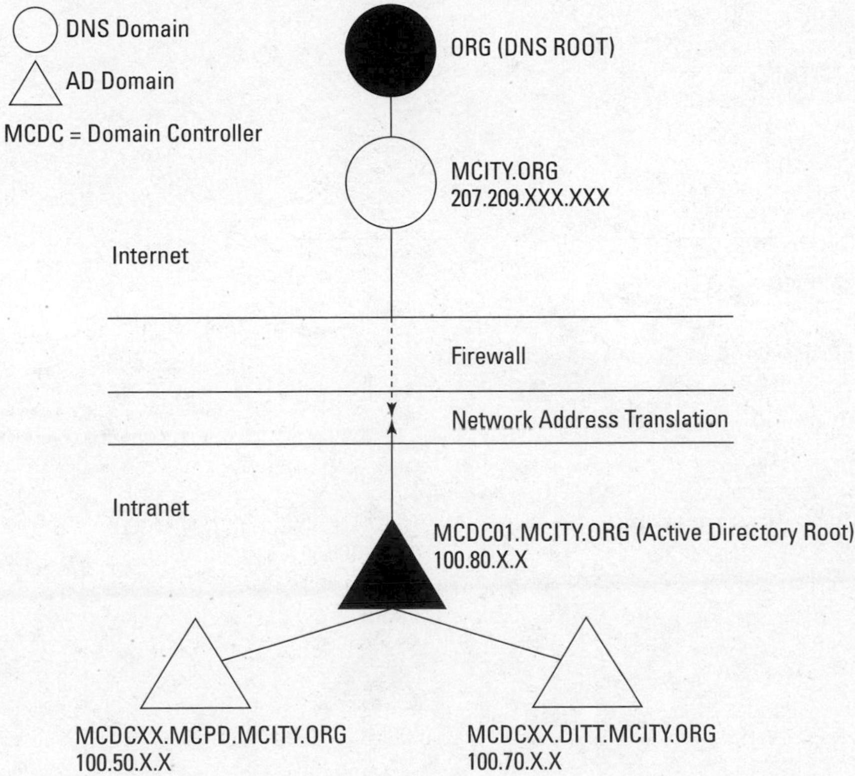

Figure 9-5: The `MCITY` DNS-Active Directory hierarchy in an extended namespace.

We can thus expose the directory to the Internet as `LDAP.mcity.org`, and it can serve as an LDAP directory global-catalog server in the so-called extranet, enabling users to look up e-mail addresses, phone numbers, locations, and more.

Under this root domain, we created second-level domains, such as `cityhall.mcdc10.mcity.org`, `mcpd.mcdc10.mcity.org`, and `ditt.mcdc15.mcity.org`. These second-level domains (third level from the Internet roots) are as safe as houses on the intranet, because they cannot be resolved, and they exist on private subnets behind a firewall. The intruders would need to break into the network through other backdoors, such as an unguarded modem, the PBX, the RAS servers, or stolen passwords.

This root structure also enables subsidiaries operating under the same Internet root to similarly extend the hierarchy. `mcnippon.mcity.org`, for example: is a perfectly legitimate scenario for a domain controller in Japan. So an enterprise-wide namespace/domain controller policy may be to make all first-layer domains under the root represent geographical, geopolitical, or departmental divisions. The second and third layers would then extend down into the division. This is shown in Figure 9-6.

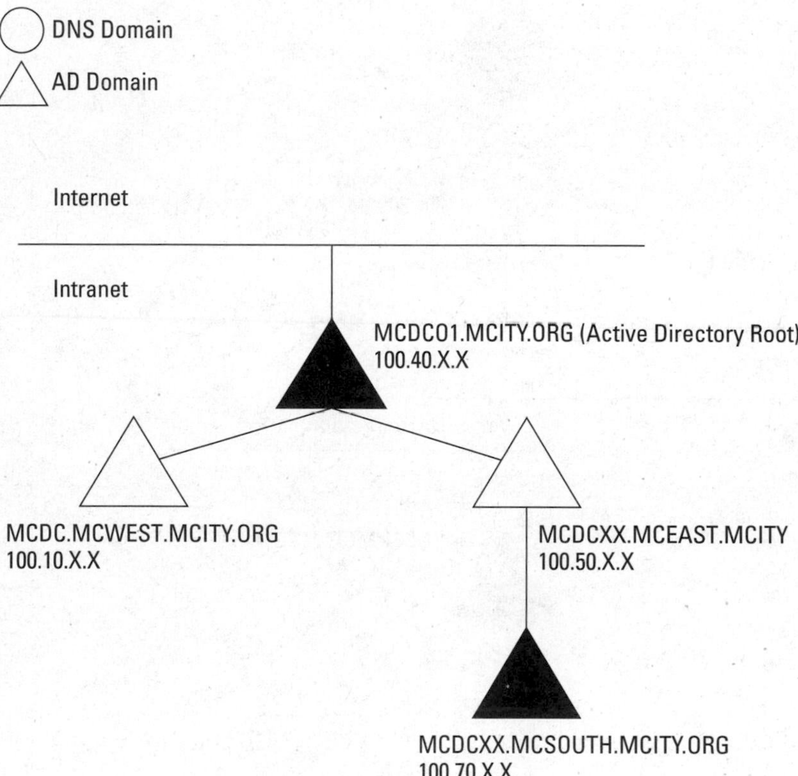

Figure 9-6: Enterprise-wide domain structure.

This approach involves only one caveat: Our shogun in the root domain may come under attack. But if anyone can take him out behind our secure server room, firewalls, NAT, Kerberos security, a highly sophisticated encrypted password scheme on a smart card, and myriad other protection schemes that we don't need to mention, we can all pack our bags and go home.

Your solution, however, may be different. Following are the alternatives:

- ✦ **Split namespace:** This namespace, as shown in Figure 9-7, is not connected. The root Active Directory domain cannot be resolved from the Internet by any means, yet it *is* a logical extension of the public DNS namespace. In other words, the Active Directory root appears to be an extension of the DNS root, yet it is in its own right an implicit namespace. The Active Directory side of the split namespace can become an extension of the DNS root at any time. Internet servers, such as DNS, mail, and FTP, can be installed on the Internet, on the intranet (protected behind firewalls and NAT), or in both places.

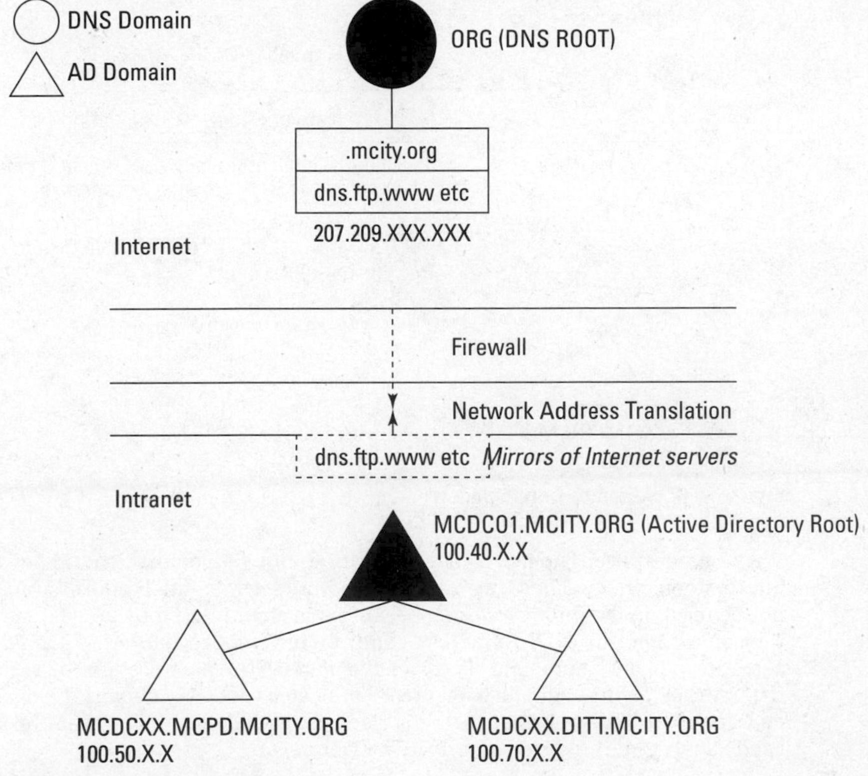

Figure 9-7: Split namespace.

- ✦ **Separate namespaces:** Both namespaces, as shown in Figure 9-8, are registered. They cannot be joined and both represent DNS roots. And one is an Active Directory root as well.

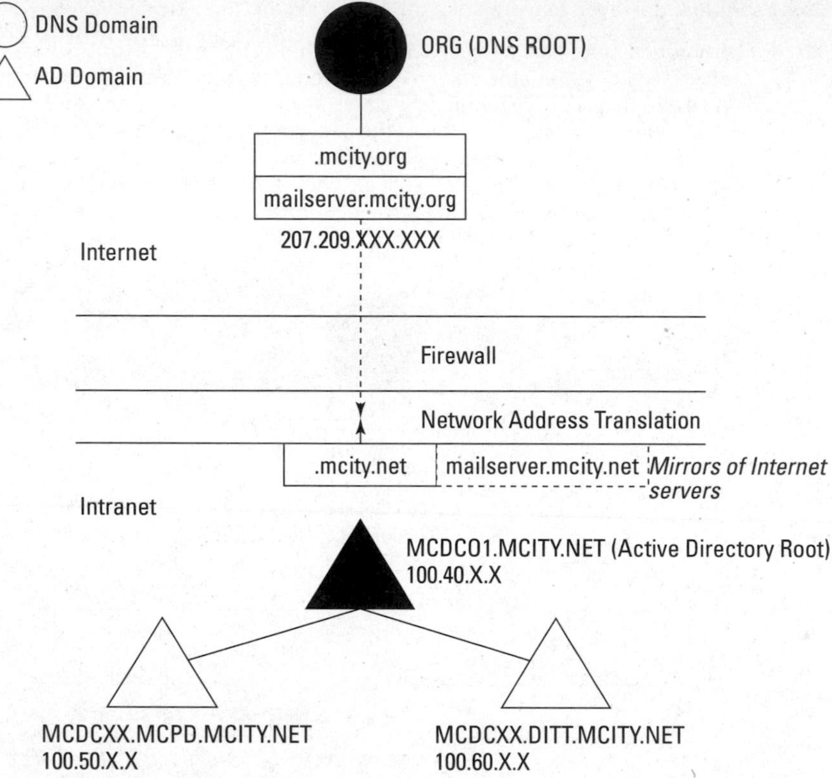

Figure 9-8: Separate namespaces.

✦ **Illegal namespace:** The illegal namespace does not get you brought up on charges of Internet conspiracy. (*Illegal network* is a network term for an IP address range that cannot be used on the public Internet, because it is already used by a registered owner.) If the name conforms to DNS standards and you have not registered it, it is *illegal* in a sense, especially if someone else owns the name. If the name cannot be registered on the Internet, as the example in Figure 9-9 indicates (possibly because nonstandard characters or DNS root domains), it is also considered illegal. Illegal addresses are used all the time, however, on private networks.

DNS naming practice

As mentioned in the section "Naming the root," earlier in this chapter, assigning names wisely and protecting them as you would a trademark or a copyright is good practice. Make sure, too, that they are registered with the Internet authorities. You should also start getting used to using good DNS language in the blueprint and LDS plan.

Use Internet DNS names

Use internationally recognized standard-approved DNS names for your Active Directory domains. See RFC 1123, which specifies that you can use A-Z, a-z, 0-9, and the hyphen (-). You notice that Windows Server 2003 supports nonstandard naming, and you can put almost any Unicode character in the name. Resist the temptation, however, even if you do not *yet* have a persistent connection to the Internet.

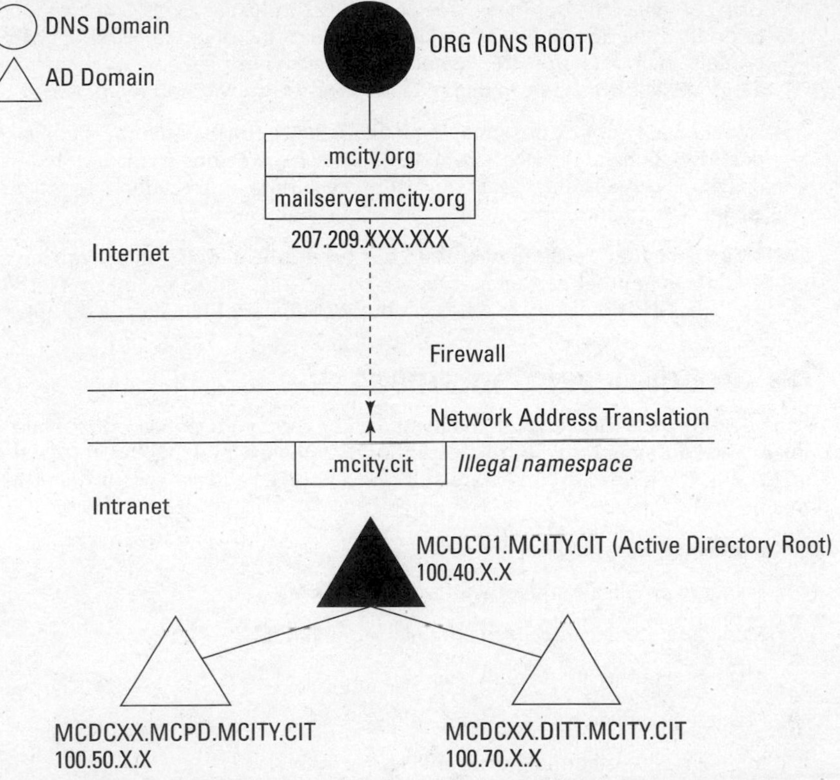

Figure 9-9: Illegal namespace.

Make sure that namespaces are unique

You cannot throw an exception on a whiteboard or a legal pad, so duplicate names go unnoticed and "cloned" namespaces may make their way to networks in the enterprise that are not yet connected. If your Active Directory conversion or rollout team is divided between offices and regions, for example, you may unwittingly be creating two or more domain trees in your forest that are identical but serving different divisions. After you connect them and go live, the whole kaboodle explodes like an egg in a microwave.

Keep legacy clients in mind

The deepest level in the DNS name for a newly created domain becomes the NetBIOS name for NetBIOS clients. This name need not bear any resemblance to the DNS name and can be changed. You get the opportunity to change this name only once — as you install the domain.

Pay particular attention to this name and keep in mind the following suggestions:

- **Make the NetBIOS name "palatable" to legacy clients:** Remember that they can see the NetBIOS name of the domain in the domain list in looking for a resource or trying to log on. Although Windows Server 2003 clients can log on as `someone@mcity.org`, NetBIOS clients, using the previous example, can log on only to the default NetBIOS name — such as `genesis` or `cityhall`. This is not too bad, but what if their domain is `eggonyourface.landofoz.mcity.org`. The example seems extreme, but then you never know.

Using an alias, the NetBIOS name can easily be changed to OZ. But you must remember to do it as the domain is created, because you cannot change it short of trashing the domain controller after the installation. Check your plan and make sure that the assigned NetBIOS name is marked in red for the conversion team.

Doing so may not be possible, but making the NetBIOS name the same as the last partition name in the DNS (from the top down or reading from right to left in English) provides a consistency that your users are sure to appreciate. If `genesis.mcity.org` is your DNS name, for example, `genesis` is your NetBIOS name.

- **Make sure that NetBIOS names do not get duplicated:** If you are raising a second domain in another region, make sure that the plan indicates unique NetBIOS names. The two DNS domains are different, but identical NetBIOS names do not work.

The second-level domains

To add second- and third-level domains under the root, you need good reasons. Each new domain adds administrative burden, additional expenses, and increased total cost of ownership (TCO). The following list, however, provides some valid reasons for creating additional domains levels:

- Managing separated departments.
- Managing replication overhead and network latency.
- Managing the decentralized administration models.
- Managing autonomous divisions.
- Managing a diversity of domain policy.
- Managing international partitions.
- Managing NT domains.
- Managing security requirements.
- Managing information hiding and resource publishing (a divergent view of the directory).
- Constructive partitioning of the directory.

Managing separated departments

If you examine the organizational chart of Millennium City, you can easily see how some divisions or departments are remote from the Mayor's office, or City Hall, and from the other departments. In fact, `MCITY` is so large that few departments share buildings and physical locations. The chasm between the departments is so vast that extending the root domain out to each site may prove impractical for many reasons.

This may also be the case in your enterprise. Perhaps you have several departments spread around the city. Often a company grows out of its present building and leases additional space across the road. And you must span the network backbone or collapse it between the two locations.

Key to your decision to create second-level domains is that users and network resources need to locate a domain controller nearest to them to authenticate. If you decide to extend the domain across several city blocks or between the suburbs and downtown, users in the remote department are likely to require a partner domain controller on their segment or suffer bottlenecks in trying to locate the domain controller and other network resources in the main building. Be aware that replication and authentication traffic is also hitting the pipe, along with the general network traffic. The domain controller for a new domain does not need to deal with the replication traffic generated between partner controllers in the same domain. You have two factors to consider: the size of the separate location and its distance from the existing domain.

The number of people in the separate location should be your guide, and this information should be in your enterprise analysis documentation. If the separate location is staffed by only a handful of people, the small amount of network traffic that they generate and the additional administrative burden that they cause cancel out any perceived benefits of creating a separate domain and locating a domain controller in their offices. (Think equipment costs, installation, and administration.)

The distance from the parent domain is also an important consideration. If the site is across the road, extending the backbone is easily handled with the appropriate permissions from the city planning department. If the parent domain is in the suburbs and the department is located uptown, however, extending the backbone even several blocks is likely to prove difficult — if not very expensive and impractical. You are likely to need to span a full or fractional T1 circuit or frame relay circuit to connect the two locations. Still, if the department is small and does not generate a lot of network traffic, you could get away without creating a child domain.

As the population of the separate location increases, you can first locate a collateral domain controller from the parent domain on its network segment, which enables the users and resources to authenticate faster without needing to touch the link. Just remember that you must watch replication bandwidth and the size of your pipe.

Later, other reasons besides being across the road or downtown determine the creation of a new domain. Following are a few alternatives to creating a child domain for a separately located department that does not have valid reasons to act as its own domain:

✦ **Consider Terminal Services.** Location of domain controllers and issues such as replication do not apply in a Terminal Services implementation. Even a dedicated Internet connection may be enough, depending on the type of work that your users are doing. Plus myriad other factors make Terminal Services feasible.

✦ **Upgrade the link** (your intranet connection) and increase bandwidth between the locations to relieve bottlenecks.

✦ **Install a partner domain controller.** First, however, compare the costs and TCO of installing additional bandwidth with the costs of installing a partner domain controller. This is further reviewed in Chapter 5, in covering the Physical Domain Structure.

✦ **A replication partner** gives you the added benefit of fault tolerance, and if you don't have one in the main location, installing one in the separate location provides this payoff.

Managing replication overhead and network latency

Replication overhead and bandwidth are causes for concern in extending the domain to remote locations that are farther away than the uptown-downtown example described in the preceding section. Again, you have many factors to consider before you create separate domains. Following are four important ones:

✦ Size and nature of the remote location.

✦ Distance from the existing domain.

✦ Number of remote locations.

✦ Resources required by the remote locations.

Bandwidth is your primary area of focus. The larger the pipe, the less latency it has in connecting to a remote domain controller. But dedicated networks are expensive to maintain; costs recur. A domain controller is a one-time purchase, virtually management-free if it is a partner. On the other hand, creating a separate domain substantially reduces replication traffic because only a small percentage of domain data is exchanged at the global catalog (GC) level (that is, in comparison to full-blown domain objects). If you must outfit many remote locations in any event, and they are large, the cost of a dozen or more T1 or bigger circuits outweighs the cost of creating new domains, one for each remote location.

Another factor, related to the next section, is the resources required by the remote locations. They may need local DHCP services, local WINS services, and local e-mail services. If the remote location is small enough and not too critical an operation, you may get away with installing all these services on one powerful server. So the cost of the domain controller is spread over the needs of the location.

Managing the decentralized administration models

These models dictate that you must transfer administrative authority — some call it power — to local or remote facilities. Such administration need not be in IT areas; it may be pervasive throughout the child entity. In this situation, you are not dealing with technological limitations as a reason to create child domains; rather, management has given you a valid reason to create child domains . . . *autonomy*.

The decision to create the child domain depends on the extent of the transference and the autonomy of the division. If delegation of administrative authority is minimal, you can achieve the decentralization or delegation initiative without needing to create a separate domain. Just delegate administrative power wisely, at the OU level or along well-defined KME-OU lines. (You find more information about KMEs and OUs in the section "Organizational Units," later in this chapter.)

Managing autonomous divisions

A good example of an autonomous division is the Millennium City Police Department (MCPD). This type of situation is also a good reason to create a separate domain. Although MCPD functions under the administration and control of the city and reports directly to the mayor — its CEO, the Commissioner, is a publicly elected official — its internal affairs and operations are very different from those of other departments. In fact, the city pays the bills and salaries of MCPD, but just about all other management decisions and administrative functions are handled by the department.

From the point of view of IT administration, MCPD has its own administrators — people who not only know IT but criminal science as well. They know how to leverage technology from the crime-fighting perspective, and their ideas of fault-tolerance, availability, and technological advantage are very different from those of the administrators in, for example, the Taxi and Limousine Commission.

A separate domain gives the MCPD the security and independence of its own domain, while still providing the benefit of being attached to the extensive systems at the Department of Information Technology and Telecommunications and City Hall. You may argue, and in your case you may be right, that an autonomous body such as a police department requires its own domain, in its own forest, and appropriate trust relationships between the forests. In our example, however, we believe that one forest suffices.

Managing a diversity of domain policy

As you create a domain, you need to apply domain policy to the domain. Domain policy governs many domain-wide properties, such as password expiration, account lockout, UPN style, and so on. Policy and the attributes of domain objects are generally restricted to domains. (Domains and their contents can also inherit policy from higher-level domains and from the site in which they are placed.)

So if your situation calls for such diversity, it can be achieved by creating separate domains. You need to be really sure that the reasons are valid and that the diversity cannot be simply achieved with OU and groups. Creating a domain with unusually stringent security policy just to house the accounts of the network administrators seems insane. Yet, we have seen this happening . . . incurring the cost of a new domain controller, Windows Server 2003 server license and all, just to hold the accounts of ten people. The bottom line is to analyze, evaluate, plan, and test before you come up with weak reasons to partition your directory into numerous domains.

Managing international partitions

International offices and locations provide many good reasons to partition to second- and third-level domains. The following list shows a few of these reasons, and you can probably come up with dozens of others:

- **Language barriers.**
- **Network limitations.** We may get away with extending the domain across the intercoastal waterway but not across the Atlantic.
- **Cultural barriers.**
- **Geographical and national remoteness.** We once needed to install an IBM OS/2 telephony system into one of Microsoft's foreign offices because the NT-based equivalent was not approved in that country (a true story). Redmond was a little upset about the "infiltration."
- **Political and security regulations.** In some countries, you may distrust the subsidiary enough to put it into a separate forest.
- **U.S. export regulations.**

Managing NT domains

We believe that upgrading or converting your Windows NT domains before you fully understand Windows Server 2003—and especially Active Directory and the new domain structure—is a bad idea. Don't convert until you have completed testing, development, evaluation, and your LDS plan. In fact, our plan calls for phased implementation as opposed to upgrading.

The conversion of a Windows NT domain must be controlled by a phased implementation plan that dictates having your NT domains around for a while. In some cases, we do not even recommend converting NT 4.0 domain controllers to Active Directory domain.

NT 4.0 domains cannot be attached to your domain tree, so you are just going to need to treat them as domains that belong in another forest, and this is going to mean setting up explicit trust relationships between the forests.

Managing security requirements

Windows Server 2003 is far and away the most secure network operating system in existence. You can lock down Windows Server 2003 so tight that not even helium can get in. Lockdown, however, is a relative thing; no system is flawless, and what matters is that it knows how to heal itself and that you pay attention to the necessary security details.

If your plan calls for more severe security restrictions in a segment of the namespace, restrictions that are likely to be intolerable for the majority of your users, you are left with no alternative but to create a new domain and possibly a new forest.

A domain is a security boundary for a collection of objects. And this security boundary cannot extend past the domain boundary to other domains without predefined trust protocol. Domain objects require the authentication of users and computers to access them. These so-called users requiring authentication are known as *security principals*. In other words, you can force all the users of one domain to log on with smart-cards — say in the MCPD domain — that have long, encrypted passwords, while requiring short, simple passwords in other domains. Domains thus provide this benefit, and varying levels of security can be established throughout the enterprise — specifically, as follows:

- ✦ Domain password policy, your ultimate security resource, dictates the password usage rules in each domain.
- ✦ Account lockout policy dictates the circumstances for intrusion detection and account closure.
- ✦ Kerberos ticket policy, per domain, dictates the life and renewal of a Kerberos ticket.

See Chapter 3 for more information on Kerberos tickets. Policy is discussed extensively in Chapter 14.

Managing information hiding and resource publishing

Separate domains partition the directory and can assist you in selectively publishing and hiding resources. You derive a lot of benefit from enabling users to see and know about only what they are permitted to see and know about. Active Directory enables you to publish resources and provide users with divergent views of the Directory service. This publishing and hiding of information is more critically achieved by using separate domains than by publishing in the domain itself. How objects are exposed is determined first at the domain level and then at the OU level.

Constructive partitioning of the directory

The beauty of Active Directory is that it lends itself to partitioning, and it is distributed. It can thus be scaled to support billions of objects (accounts, OUs, and custom objects). We don't suggest that you try to stuff a billion objects into a single domain. If you are analyzing an enterprise that supports tens of thousands of users, not partitioning into a deeper domain structure is counterproductive. The more objects that you need to create, the deeper or wider the structure is likely to be.

Partitioning the Domain

Several advantages and disadvantages result from partitioning the domain. The following list identifies several advantages in creating one or more domains:

- ✦ Defined security boundaries.
- ✦ Group Policies, security, and delegation need to be defined only once.

✦ Reduced File Replication System traffic.

✦ Reduced domain network traffic because of fewer changes that need to be replicated.

✦ Group Policies, security, and delegation need to be defined only once.

You also face several disadvantages in creating one or more domain partitions. You determine your needs as an organization and weight the disadvantages against the advantage to determine the correct partitioning. Following are several of the disadvantages of creating one or more domain partitions:

✦ Group Policies, security, and delegation need to be defined in each domain.

✦ Administrative overhead of managing a number of domains.

✦ Increased GC replication because of increased numbers of domains.

✦ Moving users from one domain to another is more administrative effort than moving them from one organizational unit (OU) to another.

✦ Increased global catalog size.

As discussed in Chapter 2, Windows Server 2003 domains are organized at two levels: the *organizational unit* (OU) and the *group*. Both are containers, but the difference between the two is that groups are *security principals* and OUs are not. Groups *contain* user and computer accounts and must be authenticated to enable their contents to access secured resources in a domain. OUs are not authenticated by the security subsystem and serve rather to structure and partition the domain and to apply Group Policy.

Many people have commented that OUs should have been endowed with security attributes and that Microsoft should have made them security principals. After all, Novell Directory Services (NDS) OUs are security principals, and NDS does not offer groups. But Active Directory OUs are not NDS OUs or even X.500 OUs.

Groups are also inherited from NT 4.0 and are not derived from any austere and otherwise bloated specification, such as the X.500 directory services. And some hardened NT administrators have ridiculed Microsoft for "porting" groups to Active Directory. But groups, for whatever is deemed good or bad about them, are built into the operating system and were around before the emergence of the Directory service. If Microsoft had removed groups from the NT security system, it would have been the operating system's undoing.

In this chapter, we have dispensed advice concerning the strategic analysis of the enterprise to build a Directory service and a domain structure. Our style and suggestions are derived from years of enterprise analysis of many companies, from the Thai fast-food place down the road to the likes of KLM Airlines and even Microsoft's own foreign subsidiaries. And we find that our own Key Management Entities (KMEs), discussed in the section "Identifying the Key Management Entities," earlier in this chapter, fit in well with the OU-group relationship and help clearly define the difference between groups and OUs.

Organizational units

Organizational units are, on Windows Server 2003 anyway, the *administrative principals* of the domain. They serve as an organization tool and as a keeper of Group Policy Objects (GPO), for administrative control, and as an object filing system. (See Chapter 2 for a more general discussion of OUs.)

Note The term *administrative principal* is not a Microsoft term (yet). The authors coined it, and you don't find it in the Windows Server 2003 documentation.

You learn from your enterprise analysis that how a company is run and how it is organized is not the same thing. At first glance, you would think that the OU would be used to reflect the departmental organization of the company. Companies, small and large, are split into divisions, and divisions are split into departments or business units. Thus structuring your domain by using the OU to reflect or mirror the organizational structure of the company may seem appropriate.

This approach may work in many situations, but enterprise organization (departments) should not be your exclusive guide. You usually find that you need to be flexible and creative in your approach and not create any shallow rules for creating OUs. Creating an OU to contain all the resources of a sales department in a small company, for example, may make sense. If the company employs ten people, you could easily create one OU for the sales department and then add groups to the OU that controls access to the resources in Sales. Delegate an administrator to the OU (if you have one), install policy to manage the workspace of the occupants of the OU, and be done.

But what if Sales employs several hundred people? One huge department would easily call for several OUs, many groups, and various levels of policy and administration. We thought about this and came up with the following suggestions for the creation of OUs, as shown in Figure 9-10:

- ✦ Create OUs not along departmental lines but, for the most part, along KME lines.
- ✦ Nest OUs only if the KMEs are large and contain child or already physically nested KMEs.
- ✦ Group KMEs that overlap into a single OU.
- ✦ Populate OUs with groups, as opposed to individual accounts.

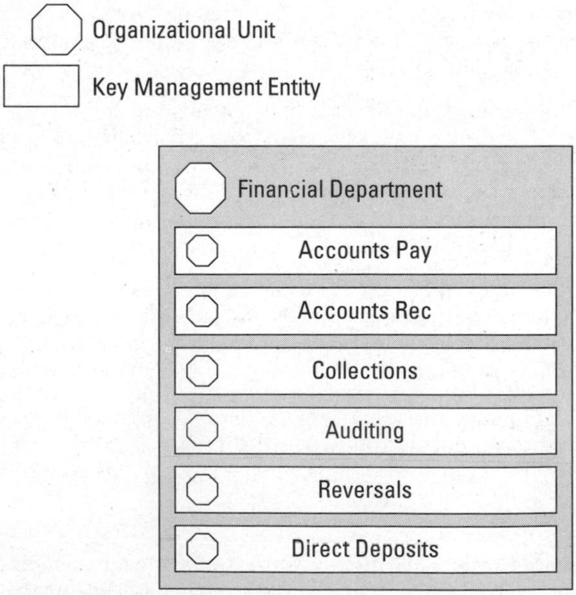

Figure 9-10: OU creation according to KMEs of the organization.

You then decide, with the OU leaders, the level of hardness desired in the Group Policy, access to applications, workspace control, security, and so on. From the OU level looking outward to the domain and inward to the groups, you begin to see a "social order" developing. This is not unlike the domain system that ruled Japan from the 1600s to the 1800s, where domains were also organized into units, trusted each other at the domain level, and all reported to the shogun. Management was decidedly decentralized.

Now you also see a structure taking shape — a box — and it may even influence business planners outside IT, where the shogun is the CEO sitting in HQ, and inside the forest, where the shogun is the administrator sitting in the root domain.

Look at your KME matrix and create OUs along the lines of the most significant entities. Creating an OU along the boundaries of the sales department would be a bad idea if the sales department were huge, divided up along product lines or regions. The matrix identifies several KMEs that make up the sales department, and creating OUs along those lines would make more sense, because you always find a gray area where you need to create an OU along something other than KME or administration lines or department lines — for example, a line of business.

We advise you to nest OUs only if the parent OU (which may turn out to be created along department lines) is large and contains child OUs. Within the financial department OU, for example, you can create OUs for accounts payable, accounts receivable, collections, and so on. If these KMEs are big or contain specialized KMEs within them, you can then create additional OUs and further nest the structure.

Avoid excessively deep OU nests, which are not only harder to manage but also require more computer resources. LDAP clients that do not understand the global catalog search long and deep and stretch the patience of your clients.

We advise you to collect all KMEs that overlap into a single OU. You could group niche KMEs in one parent OU, as long as you do not nest them just to create a hierarchy for "perspective." In some cases, you have a KME that has a wide embrace, such as accounts payable, and within that KME of, say, ten people, is one person who has a very different function or management mandate (such as a comptroller). In such a case, the smaller KME should not be defined by a nested OU but rather should be included in the parent OU along with its sibling.

So where do groups go?

After the OU is created along the KME lines, the administrators of the OU can decide, with the leaders or all members of the OU, what the OU requires in terms of resources (or, in other words, which objects the groups need to see or not see). We suggest populating your hierarchy of OUs with groups and not individual accounts.

Create groups and make the users who work in the KMEs members of the groups as needed. This practice, or policy, also serves to instill a discipline into the practice of assigning groups. NT 4.0 groups tend to show up everywhere at some lazy MIS departments. This way, unless a group is implicitly part of an OU, it should not be there.

What about users who work in KME *X,* are in OU *X,* but need access to the group in OU *Y?* Just "second" the user to the group in the other OU. You don't need to move the user account around. And for all intents and purposes, the user may be a resident in another domain.

User and computer accounts cannot be in more than one place in the directory. But, in fact, users often have more than one responsibility and, needing access to many things, appear in many groups. We may be working on applications during the week, for example, and be on call for the computer room over the weekends.

This approach—call it a philosophy—implies that all users be grouped into a single OU, possibly called HR. That concerned us, so we investigated the idea further. If you look at the attributes of user accounts, they are not variables that get managed often. Many are set once and then never changed. You can then locate your user accounts in your root OU, in one OU (such as HR), or in several root OUs, at least at the top level of your enterprise, reflecting organizational policy. In fact, as long as you ensure that your user or computer accounts are linked to required Group Policy Objects (see Chapter 14), you can put the accounts in any folder.

Figure 9-11 now provides a more complete logical domain structure framework from which to expand. It shows user accounts in root OUs along department lines and OUs within the root along KME lines. The child OUs contain groups needed to serve the KMEs. After you achieve an LDS, you are in a position to decide how and where and when to delegate administration of the OUs and apply policy.

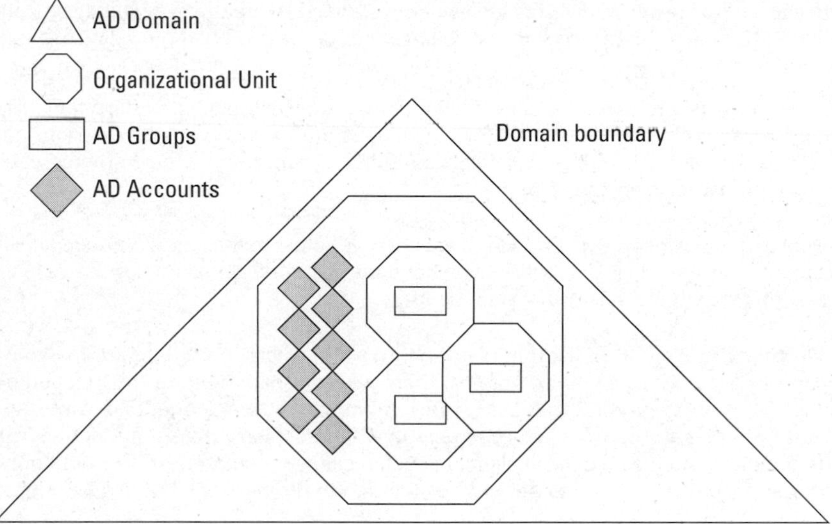

Figure 9-11: Logical domain structure.

Securing the partitions

Windows Server 2003 enables administrators to efficiently manage domain partitions in very large enterprises. The new Credential Manager helps by providing a secure store of user credentials and certificates. By selecting authentication services in the catalog you are automatically adding the credential manager to the system. When a users computer requests authentication through NTLM or Kerberos, the update default credentials or save password check box appears in the UI dialog box, enabling the credential manager to keep track of the user's name, password, and related information. The next visit caused the credential manager to automatically supply the stored credentials. Trusts also simplify cross-domain security issues.

If you have two Windows Server 2003 partitions or forests that are connected by a trust, authentication requests can be routed between partitions, thereby providing a seamless coexistence of resources. Authentication protocols can follow trust paths, so the service principal name of the resource computer must be resolved to a location in the partner partition. SPNs can be used to support authentication between a service and a client application. The SPN can be one of the following names:

- DNS domain name
- DNS host name

For users who access a resource from a computer that is located in another partition, Kerberos contacts the key distribution center on the domain controller within its domain for a session ticker to the SPN of the resource computer. Then the domain controller is responsible for finding the SPN.

Windows Server 2003 also introduced a new Group Policy management solution to unify all management of Group Policy. The Group Policy Management console integrates existing policy functionality into one simplified console. The following tools are all integrated into the Group Policy Management console:

- Active Directory Users and Computers snap-in
- Active Directory Sites and Services snap-in
- Resultant Set of Policy snap-in
- Access Control List (ACL) editor
- Delegation Wizard

These tools enable administrators to perform all necessary core Group Policy tasks from within the console. The following list shows a few benefits of the Group Policy Management console:

- Backup/restore of Group Policy Objects.
- Import/export and copy/paste of GPOs and Windows Management Instrumentation (WMI) filters.
- HTML reports for GPO settings and Resultant Set of Policy (RSoP) data. (These reports enable printing, saving, and read-only access to GPOs.)
- Scripting of Group Policy operations provided by this tool. (***Note:*** This does include scripting of settings within a GPO.)

The Group Policy Management console supports management to Windows 2000 server. Windows XP Pro must have Service Pack 1 and an additional post service pack 1 hotfix, along with the .Net Framework installed.

The Group Policy Management console also enables management across domain partitions, all within a simple user interface, by using drag-and-drop features. This management tool is available as a separate component that is downloadable from Microsoft's Web site at `www.microsoft.com/downloads`.

Summary

Creating a Windows Server 2003 domain, especially for large and complex entities, is a daunting task. You are strongly advised not to begin an upgrade or conversion from an NT domain until you have first performed a mission critical enterprise analysis of your organization and completed a blueprint of the Logical Domain Structure that is approved by the entire team and management. Additionally, you cannot start your rollout until you have done due diligence in the labs and have fully signed off on the Physical Domain Structure . . . and this is what we tackle in the next chapter.

✦ ✦ ✦

Active Directory Physical Structure

In This Chapter

Understanding past, present, and future

Understanding forests and trusts

Working with domain controllers and global catalogs

Understanding sites

Learning Active Directory replication

Using directory synchronization

Managing Active Directory site design and configuration

This chapter reviews the physical structures of Active Directory. This chapter also introduces you to the relationships between domain controllers (DCs) and the various roles of domain controllers, global catalogs (GCs), and sites.

Past, Present, and Future

Past operating systems had no awareness of the underlying physical network structure on which they were deployed. For small companies, or even reasonably large ones, the network layout, interconnection points and subnets, remote offices, and so on were either laid out long before Windows NT became pervasive or were installed independently of the network operating systems that depended on them.

We typically build networks for which the servers reside on 100-Mbps media, the backbone. There are 100-Mbps media between floors, and then this network is extended into a 10-Mbps network down to the users. Windows NT does not care if the network is 10 Mbps or 10,000 Mbps . . . it has no built-in means of catering to the available resources.

But this is no longer sufficient, because Windows Server 2003's physical structure and its multi-master replication technology, GC services, public key infrastructure, directory synchronization, Kerberos authentication, and more *do* need to be sensibly and carefully built according to the physical network resources. Fortunately, the OS also enables you to build a logical network and map it to a present or future physical network. With Active Directory services, you can tailor your Windows Server 2003 deployment to the available network and merge the two structures into a unified cooperative. The reason for this is Active Directory and its host domain controller server.

Windows NT and Windows Server 2003 network requirements are very different. Windows NT depends on a single primary domain controller (PDC), which holds the master database of the domain configuration, accounts, security, and so on. This PDC is a single master domain controller, meaning that only the database on the PDC machine can be written to. If this machine begins to shake or freak out, the network is frozen, in terms of its ability to make changes to the domain. Clearly, this is not a pleasant idea.

Backup domain controllers (BDCs) back up the PDC. The BDCs can service the domain, in terms of logon authentication, security, and the like. But their databases cannot be edited. To do that, you must promote a BDC to the role of PDC. Thus, the PDC and BDC exist in a single-master or master-slave arrangement. No matter where you are on a Windows NT network, changes you make to the domain are saved to the PDC, and the PDC replicates this information out to the BDCs wherever they are. The PDC does this automatically, or you can force the BDC and the PDC to synchronize their databases. Other than forcing it, there is little else you can do to manage or customize this synchronization.

In Windows NT, there is typically one BDC for every remote location and one or two on the local segment, and all reside on the same network. In other words, if the PDC is in Miami and the BDC is in Portland, Windows NT does not know that. The PDC functions independently of the BDC on the other side of the country. Naturally, if the BDC in Portland went down, the Portland users would have a hard time getting authenticated or using network resources, and if their segment lost connectivity to the office in Miami, they would be in trouble. This Windows NT single-master physical domain structure is illustrated in Figure 10-1.

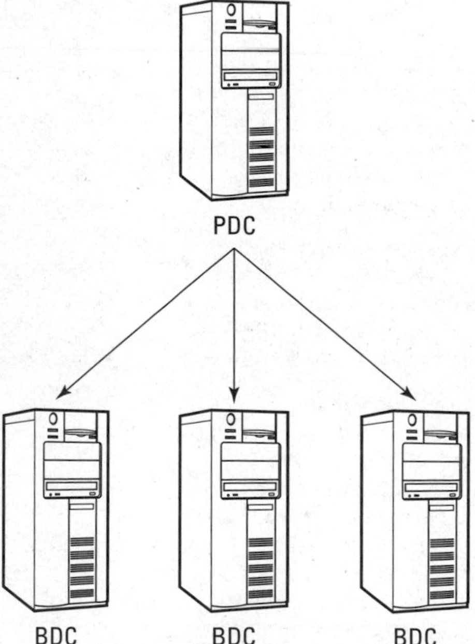

Figure 10-1: The network single-master domain structure of the Windows NT domain.

Windows 2003 Server is very different. Although the concept of DCs and BDCs remains the same, these services operate as masters, or in a multi-master peer arrangement. There is no PDC; all domain controllers can be edited and updated. Active Directory ensures that any changes or additions made to one DC directory are distributed to the other DCs. This is known as multi-master replication technology (and you could call it a philosophy as well). The multi-master arrangement is illustrated in Figure 10-2.

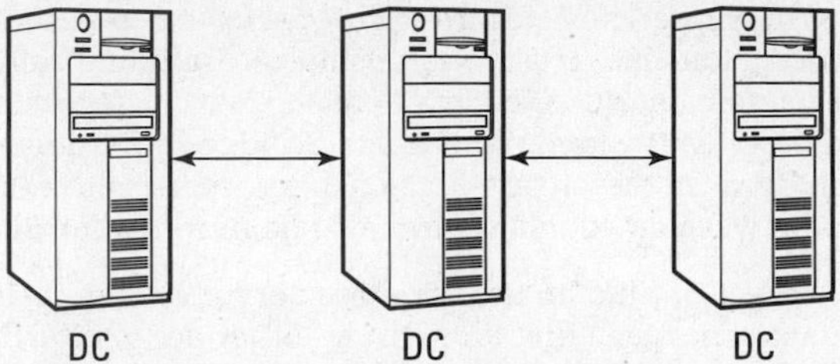

Figure 10-2: The network multimaster domain structure of the Windows Server 2003 domain.

To deploy an ongoing administrative approach in Windows Server 2003, you must first design the logical structures based on the enterprise's present and future needs, as discussed in Chapter 8. Then map that model to the physical network and ensure that you have the necessary structures to support it, in terms of bandwidth, subnet design, network routes, and so on. It is also possible, as you can see, to cater to areas of your network that do not ideally fit into any logical structures you have.

Windows Server 2003 and Active Directory enable you to map your logical network model to the physical network with DCs, GCs, and sites. And Windows 2003 Server ties everything together between the DCs, the GCs, and the sites with links, bridges, and connection objects to comprise a highly sophisticated directory, directory replication, and directory synchronization service. Before we get down to the railroad work, we should talk about DCs, GCs, and sites in less abstract terms than we have in previous chapters.

Forests and Trusts

Forests consist of one or more DCs that share common schemas and GCs. If multiple domains in a forest share the same DNS naming schema, they are referred to as a domain tree, as displayed in Figure 10-3.

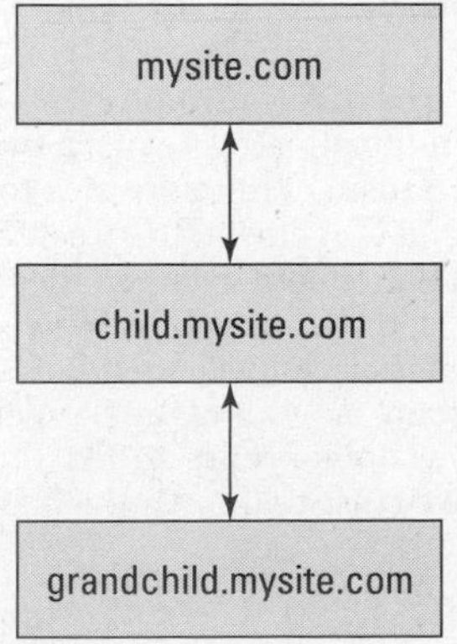

Figure 10-3: The Windows Server 2003 domain tree.

A forest can also be made up of one or more domain trees. The forest root domain is the first domain in the forest.

Windows Server 2003 computers use the Kerberos V5 security protocol over two-way transitive trusts to authenticate users between domains. Trust relationships are automatically created between adjacent domains when a domain is created in a domain tree. In a forest, a trust relationship is automatically created between the forest root domain and the root domain of each domain tree added to the forest. Because these trust relationships are transitive, users and computers can be authenticated between any domains in the domain tree or forest.

If you insist on upgrading a previous server product to the Windows Server 2003 domain, the existing trust relationships are maintained between that domain and other domains. Domain trusts enable users in one domain to access resources in another domain. Transitive trusts are two-way, meaning that both domains in the relationship trust each other. A transitive trust, therefore, is not bounded by the two domains in the relationship. Nontransitive trusts are bounded by the two domains in the relationship and don't flow to any other domains in the forest.

Table 10-1 can be used to assess the types of trusts available.

Table 10-1: Trust Types

Trust Type	*Direction*	*Transitivity*
External	Both	Nontransitive
Realm	Both	Nontransitive and Transitive
Forest	Both	Transitive
Shortcut	Both	Transitive
Parent	Two-way	Transitive
Tree-root	Two-way	Transitive

The Active Directory Wizard automatically creates tree-root, parent, and child trusts; therefore, external, realm, forest, and shortcut trusts must be created by the New Trust Wizard.

Windows Server 2003 forests are *transitive*, meaning that their trust relationships are not bound to any two domains. Each newly created child domain automatically creates a two-way transitive trust between the child and parent domain, causing transitive relationships to flow upward through the domain tree, causing relationships among all domains in the tree. Each newly created domain tree in a forest automatically creates a relationship between the forest root domain and the new domain. If no child domains are added, the trust path is between this new root domain and the forest root domain. If child domains are added, trust flows upward through the domain tree to the domain tree's root domain, extending the path created between the domain root and the forest root domain. If new domains are added, the forest is a single root domain or domain tree, causing the transitive trust to flow through all domains in the forest.

Figure 10-4 displays how transitive trusts flow through a forest.

In Figure 10-4, domain 1 has a transitive trust relationship with domain 2, therefore domain 2 has a transitive trust relationship with domain 3. Resources in domain 1 can be accessed by domain 3 users if they have the proper permissions. Domain A has a transitive trust relationship with domain 1, giving users in domain 3 access to resources in domain b, assuming they have the correct permissions.

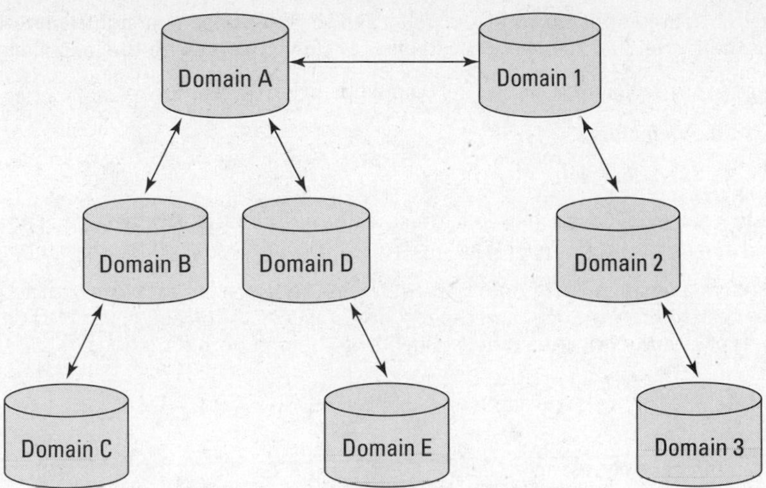

Figure 10-4: Transitive trusts for Windows Server 2003.

You also have ways to explicitly create transitive trusts between Windows Server 2003 domains in the same forest or domain tree. These shortcut trust relations can be used to shorten the trust path in large and complex forests.

Nontransitive trusts are bound by two domains in a trust relationship and do not flow to any other domains in the forest.

Windows Server 2003 domains are nontransitive relationships between Windows NT domains. If you upgrade from a Windows NT domain to a Windows Server 2003 domain, all trusts are preserved.

All nontransitive trusts are, by default, one-way. It is possible to create a two-way relationship by creating two one-way trusts. The following scenarios describe a nontransitive trust relationship:

- ✦ A Windows NT domain and a Windows Server 2003 domain.
- ✦ A Windows Server 2003 domain in one forest and a domain in another forest that are not joined by a forest trust.

Understanding that trusts refer to domains that are trusted to have access to resources is important. Figure 10-5 illustrates the flow of a one-way trust. *Trusting resources* means all resources, whereas *trusted accounts* refer to users that gain access to the trusted resources.

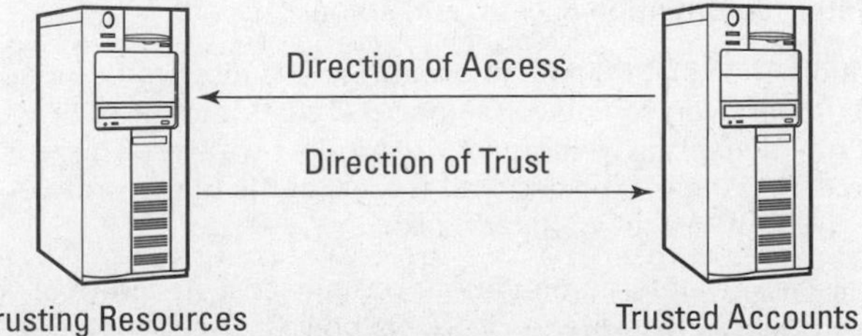

Figure 10-5: The one-way trust for Windows Server 2003.

A one-way single trust relationship, as displayed in Figure 10-5, consists of nontransitive trusts. A Windows Server 2003 domain can establish a one-way trust with the following:

- ✦ Windows Server 2003 and Windows 2000 domains in a different forest.
- ✦ MIT Kerberos V5 realms.
- ✦ Windows NT 4.0 domains.

Because Windows Server 2003 domains in a forest are linked by transitive trust, it is not possible to create one-way trusts between Windows Server 2003 domains in the same forest.

Figure 10-6 displays a two-way trust. Both of the domains shown trust each other, granting the accounts access to the resources and the resources access to the accounts. This enables both domains to pass authentication requests between them in both directions.

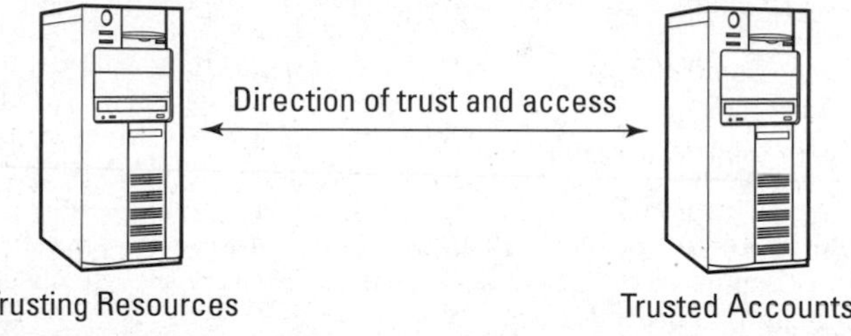

Figure 10-6: The two-way trust for Windows Server 2003.

Domain trusts in Windows Server 2003 forests are two-way transitive trusts. If you create a new child domain, a two-way transitive trust is created between the new child and the parent domains.

Domain Controllers and Global Catalogs

The three components of Windows Server 2003 and Active Directory networks are domain controllers (the directory hosts), global catalogs, and sites. They are all interrelated, so a discussion of each individually and then collectively is warranted. We kick off with the DCs that you have been reading so much about.

Domain controllers

A *domain controller* (DC) houses Active Directory (AD); it is the Active Directory's host. And as you have learned in the previous chapters, Active Directory is the brain or control center of the central nervous system that authenticates users and manages security and access control, communications, printing, information access, and so on.

Active Directory is also a lot more than just domain information. It is also a storehouse of enterprise information, a place where you can place "signposts" that point or redirect users to information and objects of functionality anywhere on the local or wide area network. It is also a place where you can go to find people, places, and things. In the future, Active Directory becomes the local "hangout" for all applications.

In addition, Active Directory also stores information about the physical structure of your network. To use the brain analogy again, Active Directory knows how your network is structured and what is required to keep it in good health and service it correctly.

But the one thing we cannot do with our brains is replicate the information in them. If we could, life would be very different. Also, imagine blowing out your brains and then just replacing them with a "hot" standby, *a la* plug and play. Fortunately for us, our brains, left alone, look after themselves pretty well for a period of 70 to 100 years. Active Directory brains are not as fortunate; they can be carried off, fused, trashed, and corrupted.

Imagine that the only DC running a Windows Server 2003 domain gets fried. Knowing what you do now, the network is frozen until the DC can be restored. This is not a fortunate position to be in. For starters, your backups (usually taken the night before) are only able to restore you to the state you were in 8 to 12 hours ago. Second, what now authenticates the restore service writing to the new machine? Although we explain how to restore a single Active Directory in Chapter 17, losing the DC is not a pleasant event, akin to a human going into a coma and not returning for a few weeks or years, if ever.

So having another "equal partner" DC is essential, even for a small office. It need not cost an arm and a leg, as we discuss in Chapter 9, but you should have one all the same.

The number-one rule about Active Directory availability on a Windows Server 2003 network is to place the DC as close as possible to users. In larger companies, it makes sense to place DCs on remote sites, segments, separated offices, or large offices, because the nearer your clients are to the DCs, the quicker they can authenticate and gain access to resources, printers, and communications. Having more than one DC also spreads the load around, a practice called *load balancing*. An office of more than a thousand people all hitting one lonely DC does not make sense.

All the DCs in an enterprise coexist as a "cluster" of sorts, each one backing up the others. They are all responsible for maintaining the identical information about a certain domain, as well as any information that that directory has concerning the other elements and domains in the forest. The DCs keep each other abreast of changes and additions through an extensive, complex, and complicated replication topology. It is certainly far too complicated to grasp at its DNA level. And it is both with tongue in cheek and in reference to a design style that we soon discuss that we refer to a Windows Server 2003 network as a *matrix*.

The matrix, however, becomes a growing consumer of network bandwidth the larger and more complex the enterprise becomes, or the more it begins to depend on directory services. So one of the first tasks that you or your administrators have in the management of the domains and directories is the replication provisioning that must take place. The GC service also uses bandwidth and Active Directory and DC resources, as we soon discuss.

As discussed earlier, this cooperation among all DCs on the matrix is what we call a multimaster arrangement. And if the packets are routed over limited bandwidth, you see that the router or gateway is a lot more vulnerable to bottlenecks than in the Windows NT domain arrangement of single-master operations.

Now to look at some core facts about DCs that cannot be ignored (and we summarize as we go):

- Each domain must have a DC (or one copy of Active Directory). As with the brain, if the last DC goes into a coma, the network comes to a dead stop.
- DCs provide users with the means to function in a workplace, to communicate, and to keep the enterprise alive. Take that away and you have a lot of unhappy people.
- You need more than one DC in a domain (or a very good backup/restore plan or even a RAID in a small office).
- The various parts of the DC that must get replicated to the other DCs in the same domain are *schema* changes, *configuration* changes, and the *naming contexts*. The naming contexts are essentially the tree namespaces, the names of the actual objects on the tree, and so on.

By now, you have probably realized that your DC can service only one domain. How much more sensible and easier would it be if a good machine with tons of resources could be used to host multiple domains? We hope to see this emerge in future generations of Active Directory.

Although Active Directory replicates everything to the other DCs, it has some built-in features that facilitate replication. Before we discuss them, look at the illustration in Figure 10-7. Imagine if you poured water in either side of the tube. Your knowledge of science tells you that gravity and other forces in the cosmos act to balance the two sides. It does not matter which side you pour the water into, nature still acts to create equilibrium. This is how Active Directory works; it has automatic built-in mechanisms that ensure that if more than one DC is on the matrix, it receives the share of information it needs or deserves.

If you limit the width of the U-piece, or the tunnel, however, creating the balance takes longer. And, naturally, if you block the U-piece, the balance cannot occur.

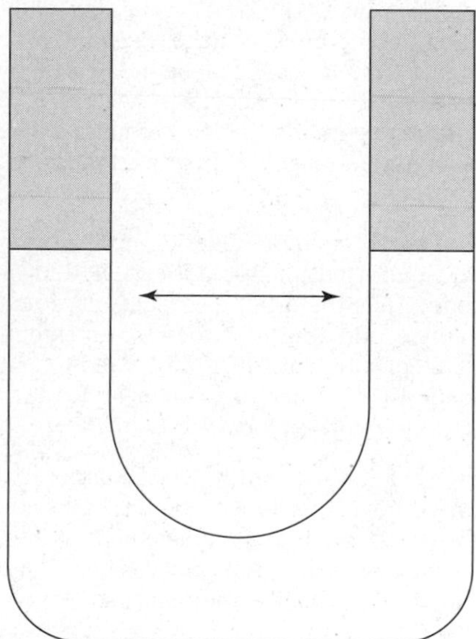

Figure 10-7: Active Directory replication is automatic and, for the most part, transparent.

Specifically, Active Directory acts in the following manner to make sure that the replication occurs and that it occurs as painlessly as possible: Only the changes to objects or new objects get replicated to the other DCs. Also, you can specify how the replication is handled. For example, you can schedule how often and when replication occurs.

By using these features, you can control the bandwidth usage between DCs. And if you have remote sites, sensible use of replication services and bandwidth may obviate the need for a separate domain, especially if you are catering to a small office and you do not have a lot of network traffic hitting that U-piece on your network.

Global catalogs

The main purposes of the *global catalog* (*GC*) are as follows:

- It provides the point of contact and interface for authentication of users into Active Directory domains, which means it holds a full replica of all user accounts in its custodian domain.
- It provides fast intra- and interdomain searches of Active Directory without actually iterating the trees, or performing what is known in directory service language as *deep searches*.

The GC is essentially a subset of the domain that, for search purposes, holds only the attributes or property information necessary to find an object belonging in a domain other than the one it directly serves. That may sound confusing because philosophically the GC sits above the domain hierarchy. In fact, the GC is not in a hierarchy at all and is not part of the Active Directory domain namespace.

When you search Active Directory, you know what you are looking for or you have at least a vague idea. (By *you,* we also mean any application that needs to look up an object for some reason.) As we discussed in Chapter 2, a user object is a leaf or end node on the Active Directory domain tree that is read from right to left (or bottom to top). The user object `scottleathers.genesis.mcity.org` tells you that if you start at the top of the namespace and from `org` you work your way down three domain levels, you find `scottleathers`. You of course also find other objects at the end of this namespace, but at least you have limited your search to a contiguous namespace.

But what if you do not have any information about the root domains? What if you or the application has no entry point (an LDAP shallow search needs at least a root from which to start a search) from which to begin? You would have to commit to a deep search of the forest to find the object. By *deep search,* we mean that you or your application would have to traverse every tree in the forest to find the object you are looking for, and this is done through a system of referrals.

A directory service with the potential of `MCITY` and all its departments would be very long and tiresome to search. That's where the GC comes in. We know this seems like a *deep* explanation, but many have found it confusing at first why there is a catalog when you can, theoretically, search the domain trees. The illustration in Figure 10-8 demonstrates how easy it is to search the GC.

The GC contains a partial replica of every domain in the forest and a copy of the schema and configuration-naming contexts used in each forest. In other words, the GC holds a copy of every object in the forest. However, it holds only the key attributes of each object that are useful for searching. You can thus easily find an object or a collection of objects just by specifying an attribute. Figure 10-8 shows the result after we provided a letter and the search returned several objects. In this manner, a user or application can locate an object without having to know in which domain the object resides.

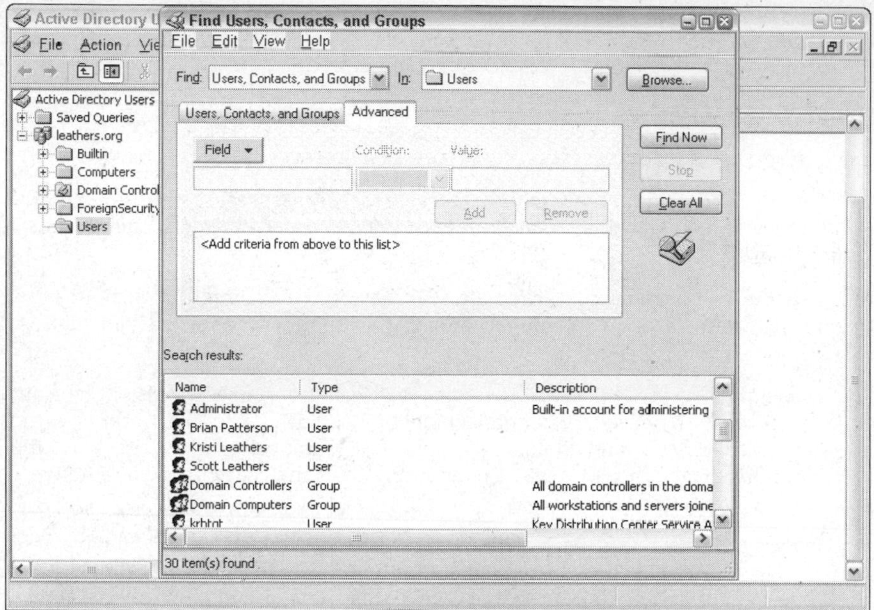

Figure 10-8: Searching for a user in Active Directory.

The GC is optimized for queries. The query mechanism is based on the LDAP system but uses basic queries that do not return referrals (LDAP referrals pass the search flow from tree to tree, but the GC is not hierarchical; it is a flat database). The following attributes are important considerations:

- ✦ A GC is located by using DNS.
- ✦ A GC is created in a domain tree; it is housed on a DC.
- ✦ You should install at least one GC per DC site.
- ✦ The members of universal groups are stored in the GC; although local and global groups are stored in the GC, their members are not. Universal groups are available only to native-mode domains. Mixed-mode domains do not need a GC for authentication.

By the way, the GC also holds the access control information of the objects so that security is not compromised in any way.

The GC network carries an overhead separate from the DC network. Remember that they are not integrated; they are separate resources. The GC, in fact, has no understanding of how a domain works, nor does it care. Here are some specifics to keep in mind:

- ✦ The GC generates replication and query traffic within a site and between sites. So, keep in mind that your network is now going to be hit with both DC and GC traffic. Also, a GC is required for logging onto a native-mode domain. If there is no GC on the local segment, a GC on a remote segment is used for authentication.
- ✦ Users may need to be shown how to query the GC, which is an administrative overhead. Or, you must make sure that your objects are populated with relevant information. if you

store only the e-mail address of a person in his respective object, for example, and someone looking up this person's e-mail address submits only what he knows, such as a last name or first name, the chance, albeit remote, exists that the search returns `NULL`.

✦ You need at least one GC in a domain, but if that domain is spread far and wide (which is possible), you can add the GC to other DCs (we discuss doing exactly that in Chapter 9). Get used to the idea of managing or working with more than one GC, because down the road many applications begin taking advantage of a permanent catalog service on the network, and we are not talking about only BackOffice stuff such as Exchange and SQL Server.

GCs are built by the Active Directory replication service, which we talk about shortly.

The DC and GC locator services

You may have been wondering, with all this superficial discussion of DCs and GCs, how a user locates the correct DC to log on to and how the user locates a GC to search. After all, you would imagine that you at least need an IP address or some means of locating the domain, because NetBEUI or other NetBIOS services are no longer a requirement on a Windows Server 2003 network. The answer is simple, but the architecture is a little arcane and thus may appear difficult to understand. On a very small network, you might be forgiven if you opt out, for now, of trying to understand the locator services; but on a reasonably large network that extends beyond more than a handful of offices and network segments, understanding this is very important.

Network clients deploy a special set of algorithms called a *locator service* that locates DCs and GCs. The latest version of the Windows locator service serves both Windows Server 2003 clients and legacy Windows clients. Thus, both clients are able to use DNS and NetBIOS APIs to locate the DC and GC servers. How do they do this?

If the client can resolve DCs in DNS, which is what all Windows Server 2003 clients are empowered to do, the client's locator service searches for the DC that is positioned closest to it. In other words, if the client is located on network segment 100.50.*xxx.xxx*, it checks a DNS server provided to it for a DC on the same network segment, regardless of whether the DC it gets is in its "home" domain.

If the domain the client is searching for is a Windows NT 4.0 domain, the client logs on to the first DC it finds, which is either a PDC or any of the BDCs. The upshot of all this locating is that the client first logs onto a site-specific DC and not a domain-specific DC. The next steps that the client takes are worth paying attention to.

If the DC closest to the client (on the same subnet) is the home DC of the client, then well and good, and no further referral or buck-passing is required. But what if the client is located in another network segment, far away from the home DC? A good example is a busy executive who spends every week in a different location, and therefore attaches to a different network each time. The notebook computer the executive is carrying around receives an IP address of a new network segment that could be many "hops" away from the last segment containing the executive's original domain.

As illustrated in Figure 10-9, the client contacts the nearest DC (A). The DC looks up the client's home site and then compares the client's current IP address with the IP address of the closest site containing a domain controller that hosts the client's domain. With that information, the client is then referred (B) to the DC in that nearest domain and obtains service.

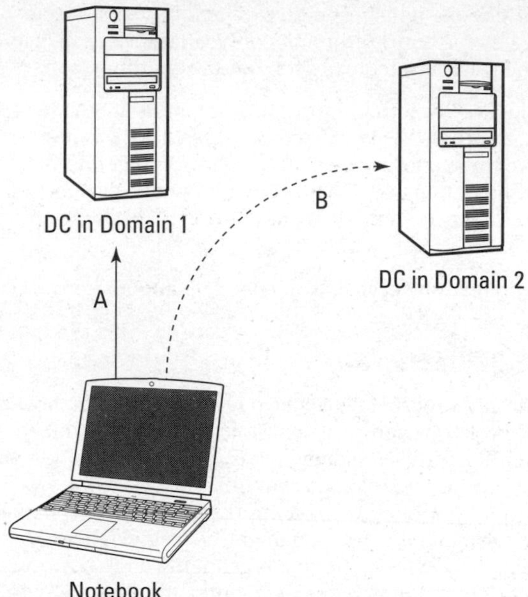

Figure 10-9: The locator service used by clients to look up their domain controllers.

This entire matrix of DCs and GCs, replication, and referral services for logon is accomplished by a sophisticated mechanism, built into Windows Server 2003, known as a *site*.

Sites

A *site* is a representation of a network location or a group of network locations abstracted as an Active Directory object above one or more TCP/IP network segments. It is managed as a logical unit within the Windows Server 2003 domain controller matrix.

A site is identified or addressed in Active Directory according to the TCP/IP subnet on which it resides, and it is resolved to that segment via DNS. A site is directly related to a domain as far as intra- and intersite replication is concerned. But a site is also indirectly related to the other elements in the forest, with respect to the other naming contexts such as the GC, the schema, and so on. A site is also a logical container that is totally independent of the domain namespace.

Active Directory requires that a site be *well connected.* That term may be relative and somewhat obscure in that a well-connected site, for example, in Swaziland, may be a disaster in the United States. Nevertheless, the definition, according to Microsoft, is that the site should also be accessible via a reliable connection, which would thus preclude the term *site* being used to refer to a machine hanging off the end of a 28.8-Kbps modem. You find that, in the real world, you may need to deal with sites of 56 Kbps and 64 Kbps, which is not a lot of bandwidth.

Windows Server 2003 also requires that the site be fast enough to obtain domain replication in a timely and reliable manner. By defining a site according to a TCP/IP subnet, you can quickly structure an Active Directory network and map it to the physical structure of the underlying network.

Most important, however, is that a site is used for determining replication requirements between networks that contain DCs, and for that matter all other replication services, such as WINS, DNS, Exchange, NDS, and more. All computers and networks that are connected and addressed to the same IP subnet are, in fact, part of this site.

A site is used to control several functions, as follows:

✦ **Authentication:** A site is used to assist clients in locating the DC and GC that are situated closest to them. As discussed earlier, the DC maintains a list of sites and determines which one is closest to the client, based on the IP address information it has on hand.

✦ **Replication:** Whenever changes occur in directories, the site configuration determines when the change is made to other DCs and GCs.

✦ **Collateral Active Directory Services and Applications:** Services such as Dfs can be made site-aware and can be configured according to the site information they obtain from Active Directory. In the future, applications may also look up specific site information.

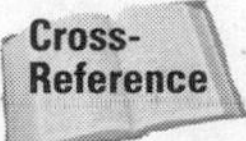

A site is also a conveyor of Group Policy, as discussed in Chapter 14.

Replication within sites

Windows Server 2003 supports a process known as the *Knowledge Consistency Checker (KCC)*. This technology has been adapted from Exchange Server, which uses it to replicate between Exchange servers. In this case, KCC is used for the replication services between DCs within a site.

The KCC essentially sets up replication paths between the DCs in a site in such a way that at least two replication paths exist from one DC to another and a DC is never more than three hops away from the origination of the replication. This topology ensures that even if one DC is down, the replication continues to flow to the other DCs.

The KCC also sets up additional paths to DCs, but in such a way that there are no more than three connections to any DC. The additional connections swing into action only when the number of DCs in a site reaches seven, thus ensuring that the replication three-hop rule is enforced. This is illustrated in Figure 10-10. The site on the left contains six domain controllers, and each DC supports two replication or KCC connections. The site on the right contains more than six DCs, and so the KCC makes additional direct connections to the DCs to ensure the three-hop rule.

Active Directory also enables you to define *connection objects*. These are essentially manually configured points of replication between domain controllers. The KCC sets up connection objects automatically; however, these objects have been made available for administrator access so that you can create a specialized replication topology of your own if you need to. For the most part, you can leave the KCC to its own devices and have it set up the connection and replication environment for you.

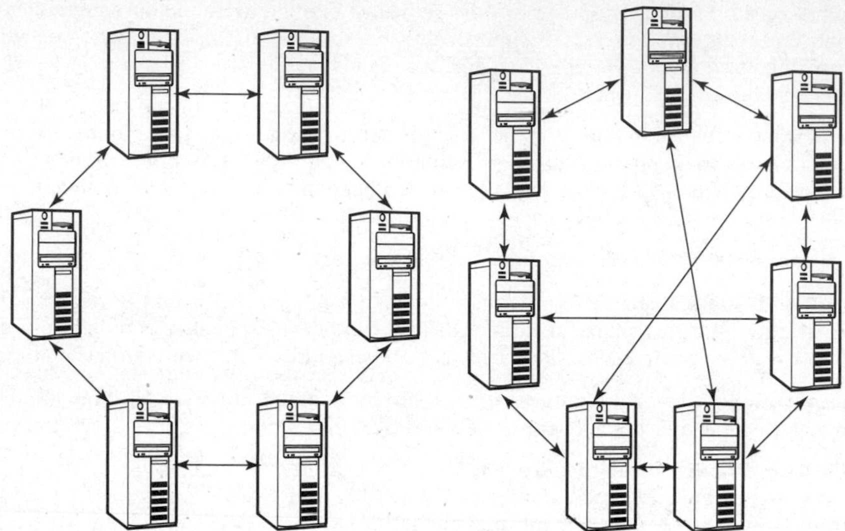

Figure 10-10: KCC connections enforcing the three-hop rule.

Site links

Site links connect two or more sites together. Site links are similar to Exchange connectors and are configured similarly. The links are unidirectional and, like Exchange and WINS, are used to set up the replication network topology.

You need to do very little work to create site links because Active Directory automatically creates them when you create sites and add DCs to them. You can, however, manually configure sites, and it may become necessary as you set up links to deal with special circumstances, redundancy, and the like.

Because site links are unidirectional, you need to establish them in two directions. There are a number of options you can set, because site links are managed according to the existing infrastructure of a wide area network. The configuration options are as follows:

✦ **Transport provisioning:** This option governs which technology you use to transfer the actual data between the DCs. Active Directory offers you the choice of RPC or SMTP. SMTP is a mail protocol and not a reliable logon authentication data transfer protocol, but it does not require very much CPU bandwidth. RPC, on the other hand, compresses data and is thus more efficient, especially over narrow pipes. You can, however, use SMTP for replication of the GC information, schema, and file replication services (FRS), because there is no support for compression in these technologies.

✦ **Cost routing:** You can set a cost value to a site to determine which route to the site is the cheapest. You do not want to route over links that cost per transmission as opposed to the total monthly or annual service. You should configure cost for site links wherever you can so that Active Directory can use the route of least cost.

✦ **Frequency:** The frequency value of the site link is used to determine in minutes how often the site link should be checked for replication.

✦ **Schedule:** The schedule governs when replication *can* occur on the link. If the site is very busy during the day, and the network requires all available resources for mission-critical applications, you should prevent replication during these busy periods.

The default settings for site links are 100 minutes for the frequency and every three hours (180 minutes) for the replication schedule. You learn more about links later, when we get into the actual configuration.

Site links are simple tools to ensure that replication flows from one domain to another and vice versa. However, for complex structures, they can get a bit tedious. Site links are not transitive. In other words, in a situation where Site A replicates to Site B, and Site B replicates to Site C, no replication between A and C takes place if B goes down.

The way around this is another feature in sites known as *site link bridges.*

Site link bridges

Breaking Active Directory into sites can reduce replication-related network traffic, but simply dividing Active Directory into sites is not enough. In order for sites to exchange Active Directory information, you must implement site links. These links provide information to Windows Server 2003, telling it which sites should be replicated and how often. When you link more than two sites using the same link transport you are essentially causing them to be bridged. Figure 10-11 shows three sites linked by IP site links; by forming a linked bridge these sites can communicate directly with each other.

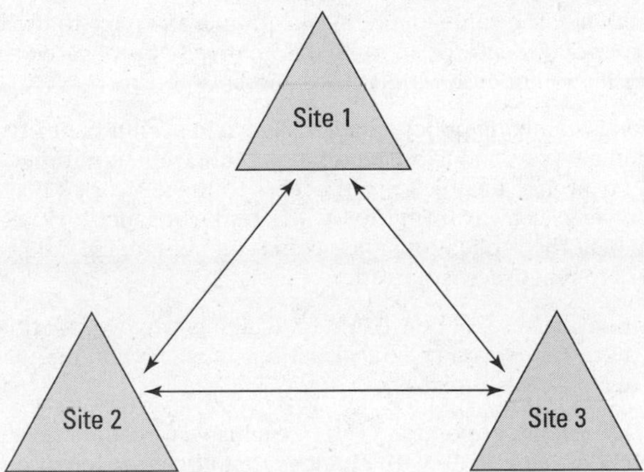

Figure 10-11: Sites can communicate directly with each other through a linked bridge.

When a site is bridged it is known as transitive, meaning that when you create a site link, any sites in the link are bridged automatically. You never even need to create a site as long as all your sites are on a routed IP network.

The site link bridge costs are the sum of all the links included in the bridge. Your service provider can reconcile link costs with you.

Connection objects between sites

As discussed earlier, connection objects can be manually created and managed for replication topology design. We discussed the connection objects in terms of tools used to manage replication topology between DCs on the same site. But you can also use them to manually configure replication between DCs in different sites.

In other words, the replication topology of Active Directory is flexible (which is why we recommend you explore other uses for it, such as DNS replication). You can manage your replication manually, which means you can create all the connection objects yourself. You can also let Active Directory fully automate replication and join all sites to the site link bridges. Alternatively, you can configure some links automatically and others manually.

If you have special needs or you have a special link that can only be configured manually, use the manual options. Otherwise, leave KCC and automatic configuration to its own devices.

Active Directory Replication

If you manage a wide area network or intranet of any particular size, from a connection between two small sites to a worldwide service, replication in the Active Directory infrastructure is something you would do well to understand.

What replication is

To recap, as soon as you have more than one DC controller on a network, you have network replication because of the multi-master replication activity that takes places between DCs of one domain and DCs and GCs of many domains. Replication takes place between DCs servicing the same domain or between DCs in the same forest. Replication is a service that enables changes made at any remote corner of the enterprise to be automatically propagated to other DCs servicing the enterprise. Replication occurs within a site and between sites.

A good example of this replication is changing policy related to certain accounts or organizational units in the Los Angeles domain (say, a lockout) and having those changes reflected in the London domain. A locked-out user may be able to gain access to the network if his or her account is disabled by logging on very far away from the DC where the account lockout was made. He is unlikely, however, to beat the replication, and, even if the remote DC did not receive the change in time, access to resources is barred.

All DCs can be updated, and their databases can be written to, which is why we call this a *multimaster* situation. However, there are certain special situations in which you do not want any DC to be able to make changes to Active Directory.

The first DC in the forest is also, by default, appointed certain exclusive forest management responsibilities. These responsibilities have to do with changes that affect the forest on the whole. In this role, the DC is known as the *single-master DC.* The roles of the "root" DC are as follows:

✦ **The Schema Master (SM):** This DC is the only one in the forest that is allowed to make changes to the schema. Any DC can actually be the schema master. However, you need to promote a DC to the position of schema master before it can play this role. This promotion leads the new SM to ask the old SM to transfer over the role of the SM.

✦ **Domain Naming Master:** This DC is the only one that can make changes to the domain namespace. This DC can, for example, add or delete domains or reference external directory services.

✦ **PDC Emulator:** Only one DC can be the PDC emulator. This role enables a DC to provide so-called *down-level* services to the Windows NT 4.0 clients and servers. It also fools the down-level Windows NT 4.0 BDCs. Also, as long as a PDC emulator or advertiser exists on a mixed-mode domain, it receives preferential replication of password changes.

- **RID Master:** This role DC manages the resource identifier (RID) pool. RIDs are used to create the security principals, groups, and accounts for users and computers (which are identified according to security identifiers or SIDs). RIDs form part of the SID and are allocated to each DC in blocks of 512 RIDs. Every time a DC uses up the 512 RIDs, it contacts the RID master for an additional allocation. The RID master is also used to move an object from one domain to another.

- **Infrastructure Master:** This role DC maintains references to objects in other domains.

If you deploy a small network, the preceding roles are likely to all be the responsibility of one DC. In larger, multi-domain environments, you may allocate these roles to several DCs in the domain. It is important to be aware of these roles in the event a server in charge of say, RIDs, falls over and leaves you RID-free. Each forest must contain the RID, PDC, and Infrastructure Master roles. These roles must be unique to each domain. The forest can contain only one instance of SM and Domain Naming Master roles. For the most part, these DC roles are self-healing between the different DCs, and you are unlikely to encounter any errors relating to the operations.

How replication works

Replication has been well designed because it is so important to Active Directory infrastructure, and Microsoft has gone to great lengths to ensure that the most up-to-date changes are distributed as efficiently and effectively as possible, without placing undue stress on already overloaded networks. In this regard, the following three crucial duties are performed by the replication algorithms:

- Identifying which changes must be replicated.

- Preventing unnecessary replication.

- Resolving conflicts.

The DC replication algorithms are self-learning and self-healing. DCs are able to keep track of the changes that have been made to their data and can also discover the changes that have been made to other DCs. If the DC deduces that it is missing crucial changes made at another DC, it is able to request that those changes be transferred so that it can update its databases accordingly.

How does this extensive replication network remain in sync? Remember the fairy tale of Snow White and the Seven Dwarfs? The wicked witch constantly strives to stay one step ahead of Snow White by looking in the mirror and requesting updates on who is better-looking. The Active Directory replication algorithms behave in a similar fashion, but they have fortunately not been endowed with ego or one-upmanship, lest a DC decide to send a poison apple to another DC.

Romantic tales aside, every DC uses a numerical sequence algorithm, or *USN,* to track the changes made to its databases. Active Directory does not use timestamps to compare changes, as similar replication services do. Active Directory, in fact, only uses timestamps to settle replication collision disputes and in the timestamp field of Kerberos tickets, which checks for replay attacks.

The USN is a 64-bit number held by each DC and is important only to that DC. Each object or attribute in Active Directory has two USNs assigned to it. Each object has a *USNcreated* value and a *USNchanged* value assigned to it.

Whenever an object or property is successfully changed, the `changeUSNs` are advanced and the new value is stored with the object. Each DC maintains a table known as the *high-watermark-vector* that states the highest `changeUSN` received from a DC's replication partners. Whenever a DC changes an object or a property, it sends the new USNs to the other DCs. In turn, the other DCs check their USN tables, and if the value of the `changeUSN` they have just received is higher than earlier ones received, or new, the DC requests a copy of the new information, which is saved to its databases. Each DC is constantly trying to stay current with the other DCs.

This replication strategy is also extremely fault-resistant. If replication fails for some reason (say, for example, that the DC receiving the update is restarted), the replication attempt starts again exactly from where it left off because the receiving DC has not incremented its USNs in its high-watermark vector table. If the change does not complete, the DC that was interrupted simply requests the information again.

Obviously, because we live in a world of friction and gravity, the DCs cannot always be totally in sync. And, in fact, the replication model used is termed *loose consistency* because at any given time that a change may be updated or propagated, another change may already be on its way.

The only time that a DC network is 100 percent current is when there is only one DC or when no changes are made to any of the DCs for a certain period of time. During quiet times or designated periods when changes are forbidden, DC states converge and become current. This is known in distributed systems lingo as *convergence*. It is thus recommended on large networks that a change "blackout" be enforced at certain times to facilitate convergence.

Active Directory also employs some nifty algorithms that prevent an endless cycle of updates from roaming around the network and DCs from endlessly firing off update requests and USNs. This technology is known as *propagation dampening*. Without it, a DC network simply grinds to a halt because DCs trying to update each other use up all the available bandwidth. The exact processes that are taking place in propagation dampening are fascinating, but beyond the scope of this book. If you need the torture, you can check the replication white papers at Microsoft for the excruciating details.

The same goes for collision detection. Using version numbers and the timestamp and other binary operations, Active Directory is able to resist the highly remote (but possible) chance that two administrators make a change to the same object in the Active Directory infrastructure at exactly the same time. In fact, only an application designed to do that can succeed, which is what Microsoft did to test collision resistance and assure us all that two DCs do not bump heads and blow up.

Directory Synchronization

No replication topology would be complete without synchronization traffic in the picture. At first glance, you may think that synchronization and replication are one and the same thing. They are not. Replication is information exchange between heterogeneous directories, while synchronization is information exchange between the same or homogeneous directories for the purpose of keeping each replica current.

For example: If you want to exchange information between Novell Directory Services and Active Directory, the technology to enable this is a *directory synchronization tool*. The following three strategies facilitate the interoperation of different directories:

- **Convert existing directories to Active Directory:** In case you decide to convert your existing directories to Active Directory, you need to obtain a directory conversion tool. One such tool for NetWare is the Microsoft Directory Migration snap-in. As a result of this course of action, the Novell directory meets the end of its life after the conversion. In this case, you replicate or transfer the information from one directory to the other. Yet other examples are in Microsoft's own backyard: All current BackOffice directories, such as MS Exchange and SQL Server, are converted to Active Directory.
- **Integrate directories:** If you choose rather to integrate directories, the tools you need to deploy are known as directory synchronization tools. These tools enable you to deploy two directories, each for its own good. Information is shared between them through the synchronization tool. A good example of such integration is an enterprise that is running both Exchange and Lotus Notes.

  Directories can be integrated with third-party tools, or you can make your own using the likes of ADSI or LDIFDE tools. (*LDIF* stands for *L*DAP *D*ata *I*nterchange *F*ormat, and *LDIFDE* stands for LDAP Directory Exchange.) It is worth noting that you can write code similar to SQL against the LDAP directory and move information between LDAP directories.
- **Deploy more than one directory:** This option is worth considering if you are a while away from deploying Active Directory, you have a huge investment in your current directory services, or your existing systems depend far too much on your current directory infrastructure. You may consider just deploying more than one directory, each one serving a special need, until you are ready to convert or synchronize.

Directory synchronization is no small matter. We recommend that you tread carefully here until the tools and techniques mature before you burn up time synchronizing or converting.

Whatever your decision, if you already deploy a directory service other than Active Directory or a BackOffice tool, you need to take into account the synchronization and replication traffic that is also added to your new Active Directory traffic.

Active Directory Site Design and Configuration

The first thing that you find out after you start Active Directory inter- and intrasite design is how well or how poorly your TCP/IP network has been designed. But before you start configuring anything in Active Directory, you first have to make sure the physical network is optimized, in terms of addressing, subnetting, and topology.

Check that the computers on the network that are attaching to Active Directory are obtaining the correct IP addresses. They should not be sitting on a different subnet from the one you are installing or getting the wrong dynamic IP addresses from a DHCP server. If the IP design is not sensible, location services are not going to resolve DCs as quickly as they should, and the logon experience becomes disappointingly slow for the user.

Topology

A good place to start when designing the physical structure is network topology. Begin by drawing a topology diagram of each site and then diagrams showing the links between each site.

After you have the site topology sketched out, you can create a network diagram showing the links between the different sites and how everything feeds back to corporate or enterprise HQ. Show the speed between the links and the different IP subnets that are in place. Also list the names of the routers on the links, the quality and transports being used, and so on. For example, in the WAN network in Figure 10-12, we indicate the IP addresses of the routers, the DHCP scope being used on that segment, the brand and model of the router, whether the site is Token Ring or Ethernet, and so on.

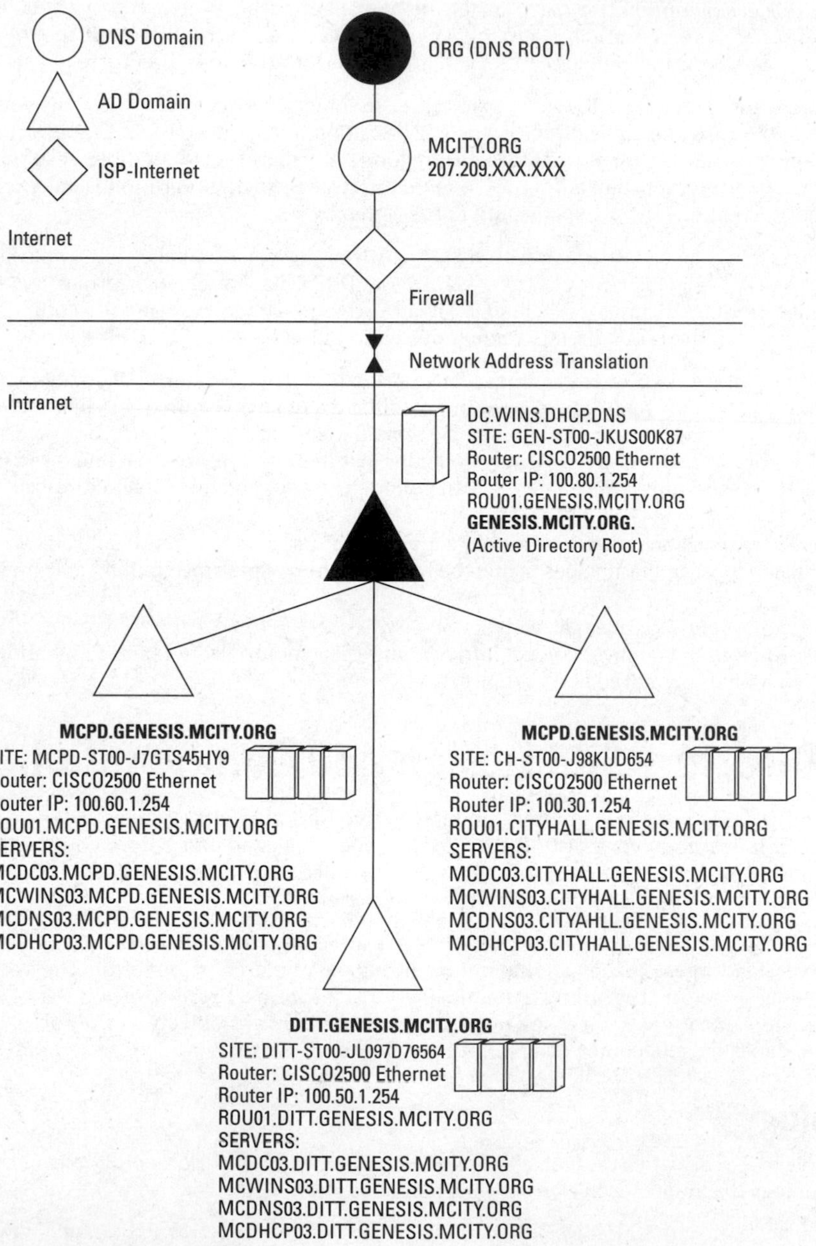

Figure 10-12: The network diagram of a portion of the Millennium City wide area network.

Also indicate on the diagram or in supporting documentation the following:

- ✦ Indicate the speed of the link and the traffic. Your service provider can give you a breakdown of the bandwidth you are using, spikes in traffic, and your busiest times.
- ✦ Describe the cost of each link in as much detail as possible. Especially important to note is if a link is pay-by-usage. This enables you to determine replication strategy to such a site.
- ✦ Describe the quality and reliability of the link.
- ✦ Define your site links by using the actual network topology that is already in place as a starting point. After all, if you have a network that is already down, no matter how bad it is, you have to start somewhere. If the links between the sites are reliable, you should map your Active Directory structure to this network as a foundation. Changes can be made later.

Creating DC sites

To begin creating DC sites, take your list of segments and locations and the topological plan and follow these steps:

1. Create a DC site for each network segment, location, or collections of locations that are part of your so-called reliable WAN or intranet, and assign each location a DC site name. In our case, our first DC site name is zero-based and called GEN00-R. Formulate a naming convention for your sites and for your servers and resources (see Chapter 5). The *R* in our name means reliable. You may notice that we have used only letters, numbers, and the hyphen. This is because the DC sites are going to be used in the DNS. It is a good idea to stick to the standard RFC DNS names and resist underscores and letters that make your DNS names not only incompatible with RFC DNS but also looking like alphabet soup as well. Another reason for keeping the names simple is that most seasoned administrators go directly to the command line when debugging DNS. If you ask an admin to type **nslookup somethingcrazy**, you are likely to get some nasty remarks sent your way.
2. Create a DC site for each segment that is accessible only via SMTP mail. An SMTP site name on our plan would be named something like GEN05-S, the *S* standing for SMTP. You can also add information that tells a network engineer more about the site than just protocols.
3. Take network segments that are not self-contained DC sites and merge them with other sites, as long as the bandwidth between the sites is fast and reliable enough for the two segments to operate as a single combined DC site. Remember that site configuration in Active Directory has to do with replicating, so although the site may actually be a physical site, it is not a DC site, so to speak.
4. Make a list or a database of the sites that are added to your topology chart and record all the subnet address schemes. It is worthwhile to record all the sites, not only the ones that have a DC in them. You can make the site in the database a DC site. This helps you identify the site as an Active Directory site.
5. Your next step is to mark on your topology diagrams where you are going to place DCs. In other words, mark the sites as being DC sites. Chapter 7 assists you in determining how to partition your forest and plan domains. Now is the time to put that planning and logical design into place.

Deploying domain controllers

Place your DCs in the sites selected in the following manner:

1. Place the root Active Directory DC in the so-called home site. In the example in this book, this site is `GENESIS`, and if you choose such a domain hierarchy, this site need only consist of a privately addressed subnet that uses network address translation to maintain the segment in such a way that it does not conflict with live networks. A root domain protected in this way is a worthwhile investment. Ignore the replication issue right now.

2. Place a DC in the "home" or head-office site. Your typical first-home DC is HQ. If you have followed a pilot project or you have performed lab work on Active Directory, you might also consider positioning the next site in the MIS Department. Depending on your network and topology, MIS might be on the same subnet as HQ. In the case of Millennium City, we placed the `CITYHALL` domain above `DITT` in the namespace hierarchy, but, in fact, it was the second DC that was raised.

3. Using the logical plan and the site or network topology link information, place your next DCs according to the following criteria:

   - Enough users are in the site to warrant a DC on their network segment.
   - The link is unreliable. If the link goes down a lot, users have a problem authenticating. If a DC is placed into that site, users can continue working. In the same spirit, if the link is an on-demand service, you want to drop a DC in there so that users have authentication round the clock.
   - The site can only receive e-mail or is open only to SMTP mail. In such a case, users must have a local DC because they cannot request logon authentication over SMTP.

While you are placing your DCs, keep in mind the need for GCs. Remember that GCs add to replication traffic, but they are also essential to log on. To refresh, GCs contain a complete copy of their parent domains and a partial replica of all other domains in the forest.

Try not to get confused between sites and domains. Site links, although configured in Active Directory, are not related to domains or domain hierarchy. A site can contain any number of domains (by virtue of the presence of DCs).

Securing domain controllers

As you have discovered in the preceding chapters, DCs are packed with highly sensitive information. In fact, if a DC in a large enterprise is stolen or accessed while online, anyone with malicious intent or thoughts of enrichment can do a lot of damage.

DCs need to be locked in secure rooms or cabinets with limited and controlled access. You may consider using the `Syskey` tool.

Deploying GC servers

As we warned earlier, it is imperative to place GC servers into your DC sites. We find it necessary to keep reminding ourselves that the GC handles the logon authority for its "custody" domain and is essential for native-mode domains — and the application of Universal groups.

It is also worth noting that you should place a backup GC in a sensitive or mission-critical domain, or have an online backup that can scream to the rescue. Losing the DC means losing the GC as well, and if that happens, your users must log on with their imaginations.

Understand that the GC holds the membership of the Universal Groups and, as such, when a logon request is made of a native-mode DC, the DC requests the GC to calculate the complete group membership access level of a particular user. With that level of security, if the GC has taken leave, your user is denied logon.

The only time that you can be lax on the GC availability scene is when you are dealing with a single domain. If this is the case, the GC is used mainly for search and seek.

Deploying DNS servers

Without DNS, you are in the dark. You can deploy a million DCs and GCs, but they run deep and silent without the locator service provided by DNS. Not only do the clients need to use DNS to locate network services and DCs, but DCs also need to use DNS to locate other DCs and other servers. We have dedicated an entire chapter to DNS (Chapter 17).

You should place at least one DNS on a DC site and designate secondary DNS servers on other segments and DC sites. The local DNS servers should be authoritative for the locator records of the domains in the DC site. This obviates the need of clients to query offsite servers for local resources.

You can also install a DNS server on the actual DC and have it integrated with Active Directory. The advantages are that the DNS and the DC are "co-located," which saves the cost of additional equipment; Active Directory automatically keeps DNS well fed, and the DC's replication service is ideal for DNS replication. DNS-Active Directory-specific configuration information is included in Chapter 17.

Before deploying your DNS server, make sure you have gone through the necessary planning. The following list helps you make sure that you are ready for deployment:

- Is your domain name standard for your organization?
- Do you have a plan for dividing up your DNS domain name and network address space into forward and reverse lookup zones as needed?
- Do you have a plan to determine how many servers you need to use and where to put them on your network?
- Use DNS performance tools for optimizing and monitoring to make sure that server performance is up to par.
- If you are upgrading from a prior server product make sure to review migration issues.
- Did you register your organization's domain name with the Internet domain name registrar?
- Do you need to consider the use of forwards for your network so that clients can resolve external DNS names?
- Create a plan on how to manage DNS client resolver configurations.
- Have you completed configuration for zones on your DNS server?
- Have you completed installation and configuration for additional DNS servers if they are to be used as secondary servers for your initial zones?

- Have you completed your DNS resource records, such as A, PTR, CNAME, and MX records?
- Consider enabling or disabling dynamic updates for zones as needed.
- Consider using the monitoring features of the DNS console to verify that DNS servers are operating correctly.

If you are planning on using a second-level, or parent, DNS domain name, it only needs to be registered if you plan to use this name on the Internet.

DNS server performance can also be very important. DNS server benchmarking helps you predict, estimate, and optimize your server's performance. Windows Server 2003 provides performance counters that you could use with System Monitor to measure DNS server activity. Performance counters help you measure and monitor server activity with the following metrics:

- Calculated statistics providing the number of queries and responses from your DNS server.
- Measurement of transport protocols such as Transmission Control, as well as Datagram protocols.
- Measurement of registration, as well as update activity by clients.
- Measurement of system memory usage and memory allocation patterns.
- Measurement of WINS lookups when WINS is integrated with DNS.
- Measurement of Zone transfers.

Deploying WINS and DHCP servers

Your organization may have a WINS infrastructure in place, or it may still rely on other methods of NetBIOS name resolution, such as `LMHOSTS`. If your organization does not currently use WINS, you need to consider deploying it based on your needs.

The strategy we use for meeting our deployment objectives considers functionality, availability, security and total cost of ownership. If you currently have a WINS server, make sure the server meets the hardware requirements described in Chapter 6. A dual-processor machine can increase performance 25 percent, and a dedicated disk drive can help increase replication response time.

In determining the number of WINS servers needed, use the following list to help:

- The number of WINS clients per server and network topology helps determine the number of WINS servers and their locations.
- Each server's usage patterns and storage capabilities determine the number of users it can support.
- You must be conservative when setting client counts for a WINS server to minimize client query response times.

Replication design of your WINS servers is essential to availability and performance; multiple servers distribute NetBIOS name resolution across WANs and LANs, confining traffic to local areas. WINS servers then replicate local entries to other servers. You now must determine whether you want your WINS server configured as a push or pull partner. Replication is usually set up using the Hub-and-Spoke or T Network Configuration strategies. You may want to look at Chapter 17 for more details.

DHCP is, of course, critical to all clients: down-level, up-level, and penthouse. The only places on a DC site that take static IP addresses are the servers.

In deploying DHCP, you should have already given the following issues some thought:

- Determine how many DHCP servers to use.
- Determine how to support DHCP clients on additional subnets.
- Determine how to handle routing for DHCP networks.

When determining how many DHCP servers you need, consider the location and whether you want a DHCP server in each subnet. If you are planning on using a DHCP server across several networks, you may need to configure relay agents or superscopes.

DHCP segment speed is another key factor. You want to consider a DHCP server on both sides of a slower WAN or dial-up link. This helps serve clients in a more efficient manner. There is no maximum number of clients that a DHCP server can serve, although your network has practical constraints due to the IP address class you have selected to use.

When addressing performance factors of your DHCP server, consider the following:

- One of the primary factors in improving performance is the disk drives and the amount of RAM installed. Make sure to evaluate disk-access time and read/write operations.
- You also want to limit the DHCP server to a maximum of 1,000 scopes. Adding additional scopes uses more space because of the server registry and server paging file.
- The recommended limit of clients per DHCP server is 10,000. This helps protect you from unusual traffic conditions.

DHCP servers are critical, and their performance must be monitored. When troubleshooting DHCP performance, Windows Server 2003 provides a set of tools. The tools can monitor all types of DHCP services, such as messages sent and received, processing time of message packages sent and received, and the number of packets dropped.

You may also want to consider the configuration of a standby server. You need at least one primary DHCP server, but you may want to keep a second DHCP server on standby or for backup purposes. If you planned to implement two DHCP servers for balancing scopes, you may want to consider a backup or hot standby as an alternative.

The chapter that follows takes you through actual deployment and installation of several different domains, their interconnection and replication matrix, and so on. Before you embark on this, consider the following:

- **Do a sanity check on the site concept:** It is one thing to hit a graph pad or Visio and knock out the Windows Server 2003 network of the millennium; it is another problem to try to map it to the physical reality. If there is already an installed network, you mostly need to work with what you already have, which may mean making the location a separate domain or taking care of replication as if you had the last network in the world.
- **Make network logon and access to resources your primary focus:** This should be your first consideration in the actual deployment plan. Get an idea of what slow logon or access to network resources entails and what your network feels like over low-bandwidth connections, and make that your point of departure. If it is impractical to have a new domain at the location, you must either open the pipe for better replication or be very creative with your replication scheduling.

✦ **Make network replication traffic your secondary focus:** As soon as you have laid the necessary foundations to ensure that your users have fast logon authentication and access to all the resources to which they are entitled, you should then work in your replication plans. You need to make sure that you can pick up propagation from the other domains and that you can get all your necessary updates from the root domain controllers and other domains in the forest, as well as the updates intended for the global catalog, the other naming contexts, and so on.

Summary

In this chapter, we introduce you to the physical structure of Active Directory. We look at the three concepts in this physical world that make up Active Directory's physical structures: domain controller (DC) servers, global catalog (GC) servers, and sites. We also discuss how essential it is, even for a small company, to either back up Active Directory regularly or maintain a redundant (hot) DC.

By maintaining a redundant DC, you ensure the domain has a hot failover should one of the DCs stop working; however, you learned that DCs and catalogs replicate information to one another to keep the network of controllers current. The degree of currency depends on the situation. For example, DCs supporting the same domain eventually become 100 percent replicas of each other, whereas DCs belonging to different domains only partially replicate to each other.

We discuss how replication is achieved by a complex collection of heuristic algorithms and how replication consumes bandwidth. On fast Ethernet networks, where there is a thick backbone, the replication traffic is tolerable. Between locations connected with slow links, however, replication traffic may be too slow to maintain a single domain. An additional domain may be needed to lessen the replication load.

You learn how you can calculate replication traffic by using information derived from the Active Directory technical specifications, such as the size of attributes. You discover that the attribute size remains fairly constant and that replication traffic is predictable and can easily be catered to.

Another management item on your checklist is directory synchronization. Directory synchronization differs from replication because it is an information exchange mechanism that takes place between unlike directories.

The next chapter takes the theory of the past several chapters and puts what you have learned into practice, starting with the installation of domain controllers and the deployment of Active Directory.

✦ ✦ ✦

Active Directory Installation and Deployment

In This Chapter

This chapter deploys an Active Directory infrastructure. Working from the deployment plan blueprint described in this chapter, you will be able to identify and modify the elements of the deployment plan that will suit your configuration. You can make the necessary changes, be it a solution for a small network or a WAN connecting multiple domain controllers and an extensive Active Directory tree.

Getting Ready to Deploy

This chapter takes you through the actual installation of the domain controllers for an Active Directory domain. We will be using our fictitious city, Millennium City (MCITY), as the demo. So far, we have put several structures into place according to the blueprint we will discuss next. You may take this blueprint and deployment plan and use it as a template for your own project, expanding or cutting and pasting to and from it as you need, or just use the examples to establish your own strategy. If the plan appears to be a real-life example, that's because it is. This Windows 2003 network and namespace have actually been deployed.

What we espouse here is not the gospel on Active Directory deployment by any means. It works for our environment, situation, and the diversity of our demo organization. Smaller companies may find it too expensive to implement some of our suggestions; others may garner some deep insight. Our purpose is to show a rich implementation.

Note While Millennium City is a fictitious city (modeled on the organizational chart of a real U.S. city), the following deployment plan was executed and actual domain controllers were set up across a simulated WAN in a test environment. We also upgraded a large Windows NT Primary Domain Controller (PDC) containing several hundred accounts from a live domain, and joined it to the MCITY namespace and the GENESIS forest as part of a live pilot project involving actual users.

Millennium City Active Directory Deployment Plan

The MCITY deployment plan consists of several phases. These phases are described in the plan according to the following contents:

A. Executive Summary

B. Deployment Phases

Phase I: Install and Test Root Active Directory Domain.

Phase II: Install and Test Child Active Directory Domains.

Phase III: Create Organizational Units.

Phase IV: Create Groups and Users (Chapter 13).

Phase V: Establish and Implement Security Policy (Chapter 14).

Executive Summary

The following summary describes the deployment specifics for the GENESIS forest on the MCITY.ORG and GENESIS.MCITY.ORG namespaces.

MCITY Network

The MCITY network (MCITYNET) is managed in the Department of Technology and Telecommunications (DITT). The backbone at DITT connects to a bank of Cisco 4000 series routers that connect MCITYNET to an ATM backbone. The routers and physical network are provided and managed by a major long-distance provider that offers managed network services (MNS). MCITYNET comprises both the Internet services required by the city and the private wide area network (WAN) and intranet, known as the GENESIS network.

DITT connects to the CITYHALL and MCPD over a dedicated IP network, and to smaller departments over an MNS T1 network. Several locations are connected on smaller pipes from 64 Kbps to 250 Kbps, and so on. The configuration of the GENESIS segment of MCITYNET is outlined in Table 11-1.

Table 11-1: Genesis Network Configuration

Location	*Genesis*	*Cityhall*	*DITT*	*MCPD*
Subnets	100.10.0.0	100.45.0.0	100.50.0.0	100.70.0.0
DHCP scope	100.10.2.1 to 100.10.2.254	100.45.2.1 to 100.45.5.254	100.50.2.1 to 100.50.5.254	100.70.2.1 to 100.70.254.254
Domain Controllers Reserved Names	MCDC00 to MCDC09	MCDC10 to MCDC49	MCDC50 to MCDC69	MCDC70 to MCDC129
Sites	GEN-ST00 – ST09 JKIJS09K87	CH-ST00 – ST09 J98KIJD654	DITT-ST00 – ST09 JKP09KLJ	MCPD-ST00 – ST40 JKDOP843D

The GENESIS Domain

The root Active Directory (AD) domain and the forest for Millennium City will be called GENESIS. The forest is also called GENESIS because Active Directory forces the forest to take its name from the root domain. After several months of extensive research and testing of Microsoft's Active Directory services on Windows Server 2003, the Millennium City Windows 2003 testing team has come to a decision on how to best deploy Active Directory services.

It has been decided that for an organization the size of Millennium City, the root domain of the organization's Active Directory namespace needs to be a secure domain accessible only by a small group of senior administrators. These administrators will have the organization's highest security clearance. There will be no user accounts in the domain outside of the core administrators, and no active workplace management — other than what is needed for security, domain controller (DC) lockdown, and to protect and administer in this domain — will be put into place. There are several reasons for the need to establish such a domain.

First, the root domain in any large organization is a target for e-terrorists. If the root domain contains many user and computer accounts and a lot of information, the organization could suffer extensive damages if this domain is destroyed either physically (removal or destruction of the DC servers) or by a concerted network attack, or if its data is accessed by unauthorized personnel. Naturally, a small concern might not need such a "bastion" root domain, but any large enterprise should seriously consider it.

Second, all MCITY first-, second-, and third-level domains are extensively populated by user and computer accounts (security principals) and many groups. There are also numerous organizational units (OUs) in these domains and thus many administrators at various levels of the domain's OU hierarchy. We thus deemed it necessary to establish a root domain with no more than a handful (preferably no more than five) administrators who by virtue of having accounts in the root domain would have the widest authority over the city's namespace, starting from GENESIS down.

Third, the root domain is critical to the city. It might be feasible — if Microsoft makes it possible — in the future to disconnect the root domain from the rest of the domain tree, and graft the tree to another root. However, at present it is not, and losing the domain root would result in the loss of the entire domain tree, taking with it all levels subordinate to the root, in fact everything on the tree. To thus protect the root domain, we will establish partner DCs of the root domain at several remote locations, primarily for redundancy and to locate the root domain over a wide area. These locations will initially be as follows:

✦ Location 1: DITT's Network Operations Center (NOC)

✦ Location 2: City Hall's Network Operations Center

✦ Location 3: MCPD (Police Department) Network Operations Center

The lightweight (user accounts) nature of the root domain, which in addition to the built-in accounts only contains a handful of users, makes it easier to replicate its databases around the enterprise.

Finally, the root domain controller is also our *Schema Operations Master* and *Domain Naming Operations Master* for the forest and holds the master schema and other naming contexts that affect the enterprise as a whole, such as the global catalog (GC), that can only be changed on the operations master.

The Schema Operations Master is where all schema updates will be performed, and the Domain Naming Operations Master is where we can make changes to the domain namespace on an enterprise-wide basis.

Physical location of GENESIS

The GENESIS domain's first and second DCs will be secured in the main server room of DITT's network operations center (NOC). These DCs will not be attended to by DITT's operators, but instead will be administered to by the GENESIS administrators. As stated earlier, GENESIS DCs will also be placed in MCPD and CITYHALL, supported by reliable, high-bandwidth pipes.

Although it is important to locate the GENESIS root DC in a secure location, it is also important to make the services of the GENESIS DCs and GC easily available in as many GENESIS locations as possible. This will enable users to obtain the following services without having to contact the DC over many hops on the WAN:

- Users should not have to look up the network address of any GENESIS DC, or any DC for that matter.
- High availability. The GENESIS DCs need to be in as many places as possible in the city so that the most up-to-date replicas of the GC and other information are nearby.
- Reliable query results. Strong and closely located GCs should facilitate rich queries, and users must be able to rely on the data's currency. They must be able to obtain information on users, groups, and other network services without any interruption in services or lack of data.

Network specifics of GENESIS

The GENESIS domain will be established on a segment of the physical network on which the Department of Technology and Telecommunications (DITT) currently runs. This network currently is supported on a 100 Mbps backbone on which the DITT supports its AS/400, Unix, and Windows NT systems. GENESIS will be established on the same network, but on its own IP subnet. This IP address space is a network supported by Windows 2003 routing services. It can also be supported behind network address translation services (NAT) running on a Windows 2003 role server.

GENESIS site object specifics

In order to support replication to and from other MCITY domains (inter-site) and between domain controllers belonging to the same domain (intra-site), an Active Directory site will support GENESIS. This site will be named GEN-ST00-JKIJS09K87, as illustrated in Table 11-1. The following DC names have been reserved for this site: MCDC00.GENESIS.MCITY.ORG to MCDC09.GENESIS.MCITY.ORG MCDC50. The NetBIOS name range of these DCs is MCDC00 to MCDC09.

GENESIS subnet object specifics

The subnet address 100.10.0.0 will be assigned to a subnet object. This subnet object will be associated with the GENESIS site object described previously.

Domain health and security

Two partner DCs will support the domain in the main DC site. The main DC site will also house a copy of the GC for the entire MCITY Active Directory namespace.

The administrators in the GENESIS domain will have administrative authority over the resources in the GENESIS domain. The GENESIS domain also has administrative and security authority over the subordinate domains.

The CITYHALL Domain

The CITYHALL domain is the first of the Windows 2003 populated domains. There will be several hundred user and computer accounts in this domain. This domain will support the accounts and network resources for the Mayor's office and the various departments that fall directly under the Mayor.

Physical location of CITYHALL

The CITYHALL domain controllers will be located at City Hall and will fall under the authority of the City Hall network administrators who work directly for the Mayor. We will supply at least two DCs to support the initial deployment of Windows 2003 into City Hall.

Network specifics of CITYHALL

The CITYHALL domain is to be established on the actual network segment assigned to CITYHALL by DITT. This segment is the 100.45.0.0 network. CITYHALL currently is supported on a 100 Mbps backbone between the ten floors, and the network is collapsed into a 10 Mbps network that services the workstations, printers, and other network devices.

City Hall's IT department also supports AS/400 systems, CICS on IBM S390, and several technologies supported on Unix systems, such as Oracle and Informix database management systems.

CITYHALL site object specifics

In order to support replication to and from other MCITY domains and several remote locations that will belong to the CITYHALL domain, an Active Directory site will support CITYHALL. The main site will be named CH-ST00-J98KIJD654. The following DC names have been reserved for this site: MCDC10.CITYHALL.GENESIS.MCITY.ORG to MCDC50.CITYHALL.GENESIS.MCITY.ORG. The NetBIOS name range of these DCs is MCDC10 to MCDC50.

CITYHALL subnet object specifics

The subnet address 100.45.0.0 will be assigned to a subnet object. This subnet object will be associated with the CITYHALL site (CH-ST00- J98KIJD654) object described previously.

Domain health and security

At least three partner or peer DCs will support the CITYHALL domain in the main DC site. We have decided to locate one DC in the secure server room of the floor on which the Mayor's office is located. The remaining two DCs will be located in the main server room in City Hall's network operations center (NOC). The DCs will also house copies of the GCs for the entire MCITY Active Directory namespace.

The administrators in the CITYHALL domain will have administrative authority over the resources only in the CITYHALL domain. Some administrators in CITYHALL are also administrators of the GENESIS domain.

The DITT Domain

The DITT domain contains the resources for the Department of Information Technology and Telecommunications. There will be several hundred user and computer accounts in this domain. This domain will support the accounts and network resources for the IT staff and consultants, and the various departments, that fall directly under DITT.

Network specifics of DITT

The DITT domain is to be established on the network segment 100.50.0.0. See Table 11-1 for the configuration specifics of DITT.

The MCPD Domain

The MCPD domain contains the resources for the Millennium City Police Department. According to the configuration, a large number of IP addresses are required for this network. The IP address range in the DHCP scope will support hundreds of workstations, terminals, and other network devices. This domain is the most complex of the four domains, because numerous domain controllers and sites will have to be configured to cover an extensive network connecting the precincts to the commissioner's offices, the DA's office, and various law enforcement agencies.

Network specifics of DITT

The MCPD domain is to be established on the network segment 100.70.0.0. See Table 11-1 for the configuration specifics of the MCPD.

Installing and Testing the Active Directory Domain Controllers

There are several deployment phases outlined in this plan. Phase I covers the installation and deployment of the GENESIS, CITYHALL, MCPD, and DITT domains.

Instead of repeating the full installation and deployment of each domain, we will first briefly install the root domain. We will then fully demonstrate the promotion of the CITYHALL domain controller and how it joins the GENESIS domain tree and forest. The other domains will join GENESIS in the same fashion. Each domain will then be administered as a separate entity, while still being covered by any policy that might derive from the root. The root administrators have the highest power of administration over all the domains in the forest.

The following sequence of events describes the creation of all the domain controllers. These activities will take you through machine preparation to final deployment:

1. Install the DC machine.
2. Promote the server to domain controller.
3. Make the server the root DC or join forest and trees.
4. Establish the DC in DNS/WINS.
5. Establish the DC in the Active Directory site.
6. Build the initial OUs.
7. Delegate OU administration.
8. Secure the DC further and follow disaster recovery protocol.

Installing the DC Machine

Follow the procedures described in Chapter 20 for installing Windows Server 2003. Ensure that the machine is stable. The best way to do this is to keep it running for about two weeks. You can use Backup/Restore as discussed in Chapter 20 to "burn in" the machine. After several DCs are all built or acquired on the same hardware configuration, you might consider reducing the burn-in period to several days instead of two weeks. If your machine is still running under load after several weeks, consecutive machines configured on identical hardware will likely run without problems. However, a few days of tests are required to be certain.

You do not need to go to the additional expense of using Advanced Server for a domain controller. All Windows Server 2003s can be promoted to a domain controller. Providing a failover service or a cluster for Active Directory is also a waste of resources and money. A fully redundant server will not only be cheaper, it will make for a more secure Active Directory deployment.

Server name

Pick a name for your machine from the list provided in the deployment plan. This is the NetBIOS name you will use to construct your DNS name. This name is going to be used again when you promote your server to a domain controller. We used the name MCDC00 for the standalone machine that became the root DC for GENESIS. When we promoted this machine, we reassigned this name and DNS resolved this machine as MCDC00.GENESIS.MCITY.ORG. In the case of CITYHALL, the server name reserved for the first DC in this domain is MCDC10. Its DNS name will thus be MCDC10.CITYHALL.GENESIS.MCITY.ORG. Remember, in the case of CITYHALL, it is the first level down from the root GENESIS domain, and also two levels down from MCITY and ORG, which are both Internet domain names. To check this information, open the Active Directory Domains and Trusts and select the domain in the tree, on the left-hand pane. Then, right-click the domain name and select Properties.

Server IP address

Give your machine a static IP address. You do not need to concern yourself about the subnet address you use now because you will change it later in the next phase of the deployment. However, make sure the IP address you choose is not used on any other machine on the network or as part of any DHCP scope listed in Table 11-1. Create a pool of static IP addresses, or reserve a segment of your scope, that you can use in the lab specifically for the purpose of installation and testing.

Choosing a workgroup

During the installation of the server, you will be asked to join it to a domain or a workgroup. You are also given the option of skipping the name and returning to it later. We prefer that you put it in a workgroup and that you name the workgroup after the server's name. This name cannot be the same name as the server — the installation will not allow that — so just add "wg" after the server name to keep it simple. For example, MCDC00 is the name we gave the server that was destined to become the first DC for GENESIS. The workgroup name is thus MCDCWG00. Joining a domain is not a good idea because that will force you to create a computer account for the server in the domain, which you have to remove later anyway when you install the server into its new domain. Not only is this inconvenient, but you also have to then ensure that you can "see" the network and that the server will be able to find the DC of the domain it wants to join.

Services

Leave as many services out of the installation as possible. It is worth repeating here that it is better to first get a bare-bones machine running before adding additional services. However, there is one exception, as described next.

Choosing a Terminal Services mode

There is one service that we deem to be the most important, and that is Terminal Services (TS). You will have to select TS from the Windows Components dialog box. You do *not* have to select licensing as well; that is only for application server servers. While choosing services, you will also be asked to choose the mode for TS, so select Remote Administration mode. This will allow you to attach to the machine remotely when it is installed in the new location. The machine can be promoted from the remote location or in the lab, but you should also provide a means to administer it remotely. This is demonstrated shortly. Remote Administration mode, as discussed in Chapter 30, allows up to two concurrent sessions to be used for remote administration without licensing.

Promoting to Domain Controller

The steps we take you through in this section demonstrate installing a root domain and a child domain into an existing domain tree. You would perform these same steps to install Active Directory for any new domain controller. The only difference is that you need to choose to create a domain controller according to the choices outlined in Table 11-2. If you are not sure what you need to be installing, you need to do some more preparation and planning. Read the fine print on the dialog boxes until you are sure about your actions, but do not overly concern yourself until the last step because you can always go backwards and forwards in these dialog boxes until you are sure.

Table 11-2: Domain Controller Promotion Choices

Action	*GENESIS*	*CITYHALL*	*DITT*	*MCPD*
DC for a new domain	Yes	Yes	Yes	Yes
Additional DC for an existing domain	Yes, at any time you need more DCs	Yes, at any time you need more DCs	Yes, at any time you need more DCs	Yes, at any time you need more DCs
Create a new tree	Yes	No	No	No
Create a new domain in an existing tree	No	Yes	Yes	Yes
Create a new forest	Yes	No	No	No
Place domain tree in an existing forest	No	N/A	N/A	N/A

The creation of the root DC is the easiest. You just need to follow the instructions to create a new domain and a new domain tree in a new forest. This will essentially be the first Active Directory domain you will create for your enterprise, and it is known as the root domain. We recommend a root domain structure similar to the one created here. Your own "Genesis" domain need not be on an expensive server. In fact, our first GENESIS server was a Pentium 133 MHz with 64MB RAM. The replica we show in this chapter is a Pentium PRO 200 MHz. We plan to add a super-server DC for GENESIS capable of holding a huge database and taking many thousands of concurrent queries and logon requests.

Before you begin promotion, make sure your server can talk to the network. The server does not necessarily have to send packets out to other machines. Unlike Windows NT 4.0 Backup Domain Controllers, there is no need to immediately begin synchronization with the primary domain controller (PDC). However, Windows 2003 will not let you promote the server and install Active Directory if it cannot detect that it is attached to a network. Connecting the server to a hub is good enough, even if it is the only server in the hub.

If the server cannot be contacted from the network, you will obviously not be able to promote it remotely, nor will it be able to join the domain tree. We will now begin the promotion of the DCs and the creation of child domains. You will need to take the following steps to complete the promotion:

1. Promote the server using the command DCPROMO or using the Configure Your Server utility. You can use the DCPROMO command from the command prompt, which is quicker and easier if you plan to promote many servers. The Configure utility is illustrated in Figure 11-1. To open the utility, click Start ➪ Programs ➪ Administrative Tools ➪ Configure Your Server.

Figure 11-1: The Configure Your Server utility.

2. In the Configure Your Server utility, select the *Domain Controller (Active Directory)* item in the menu on the left of the dialog box as seen here in Figure 11-2.

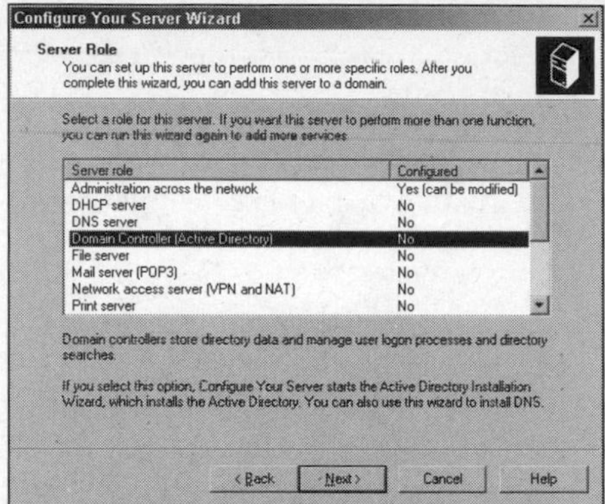

Figure 11-2: Adding Active Directory to a server is as simple as point and click.

At the bottom of this dialog box click Next. When the *Active Directory Installation Wizard* loads, as seen below in Figure 11-3, you may continue by clicking the Next button.

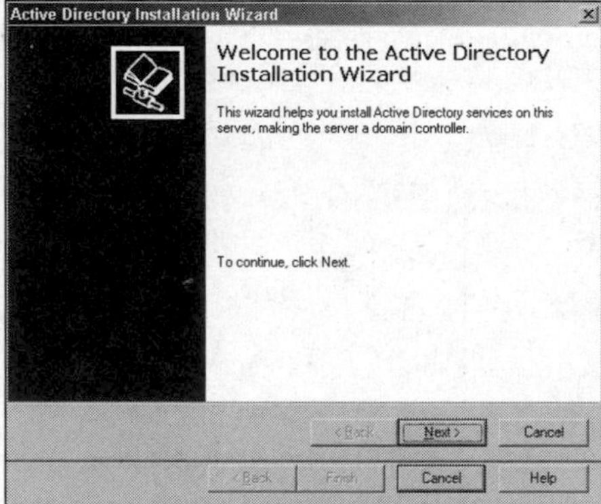

Figure 11-3: The Active Directory Installation Wizard guides you through the domain creation process.

3. The Domain Controller Type dialog box loads, as shown in Figure 11-4. Make sure to check the option "Domain controller for a new domain." This is the first DC for the domain GENESIS or CITYHALL or any other new domain. The creation of the root domain from here on is a no-brainer. Without an existing forest or domain tree, you cannot install anything else. We will now proceed to install a child domain . . . CITYHALL. Click Next.

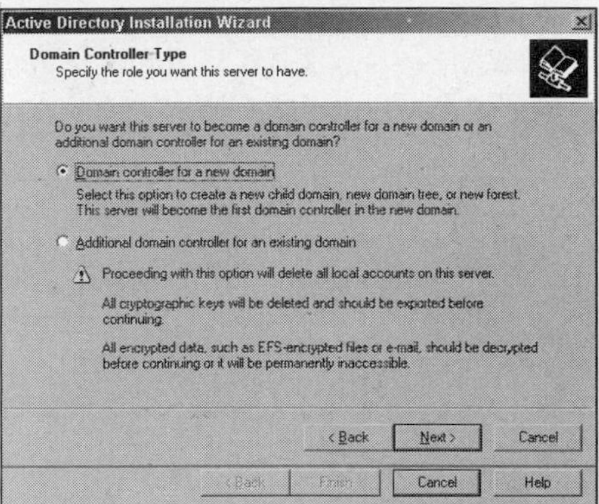

Figure 11-4: Use the Domain Controller Type page to pick one of two controller configurations.

4. The Create Tree or Child Domain dialog box loads. Select the option "Create a new child domain in an existing domain tree." Your screen should resemble that of Figure 11-5. After you have selected the appropriate domain type, click Next.

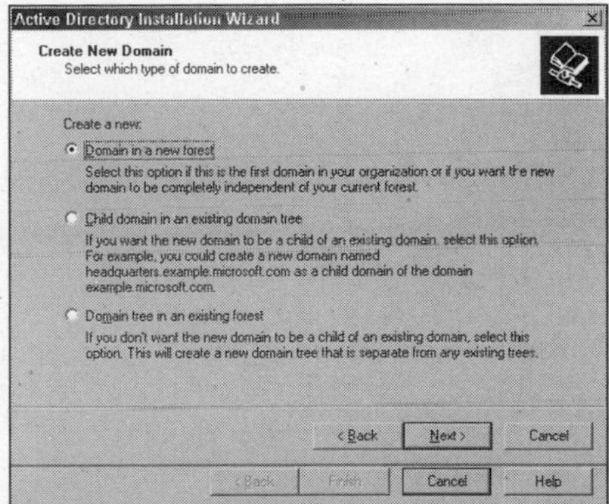

Figure 11-5: The Create New Domain page allows you to create a domain in a new tree or position into an existing tree.

5. The Network Credentials dialog box now loads. Here, you are asked to enter the name of a user account in a domain in the existing forest that has the authority to create the domain and join it to the domain tree. Enter the name and password and click Next. In our case, we entered the name of an administrator with such authority in the GENESIS domain.

6. The Child Domain Installation dialog box now loads. Here, you are asked to enter the parent domain. In the example for MCITY, we will add GENESIS for the parent and CITY-HALL for the child domain. The DNS name is automatically constructed, as illustrated in Figure 11-6. You can also browse for the correct domain if more than one already exists. Upon browsing, we find that only one other domain exists: the root GENESIS.MCITY.ORG (so far, so good). Only enter the name of the domain itself and not the entire DNS name, which will be automatically built for you. As illustrated in the example, this can be used as the NetBIOS name for a domain as well. Click Next when you are sure you have entered the right information. If you are unsure, go back and check the deployment plan, which is why you create such things.

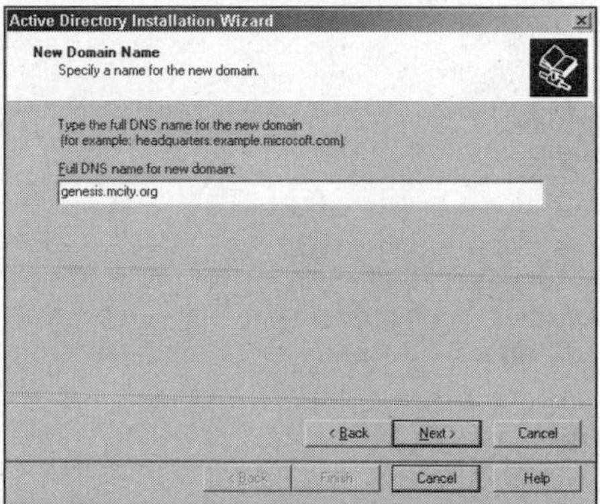

Figure 11-6: Specifying a DNS allows the Wizard to dynamically generate DNS entries for you.

7. The next dialog box to load is the NetBIOS name we just touched on, and the title of the dialog box is "NetBIOS Domain Name." Choose the default. Check back over previous chapters concerning the choice of names. Domain names should be simple. They need to be accessible to humans, not computers. In this example, we chose the NetBIOS name CITYHALL. Be sure you choose the right name, because you cannot change it after you promote the server. This dialog box is shown here in Figure 11-7. To continue click Next.

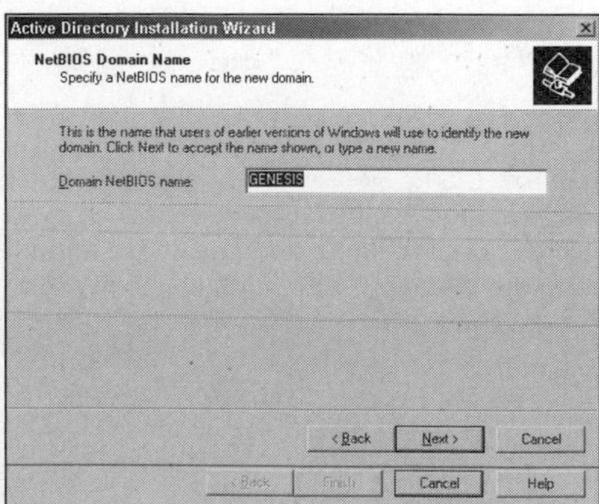

Figure 11-7: A NETBIOS domain name is needed for backwards compatibility.

8. The Database and Log Locations dialog box now loads. If you have separate disks, then choose a separate drive letter for the logs, as illustrated in Figure 11-8. This technique is inherited from Microsoft Exchange, which is the foundation for the Active Directory database and replication engines. You will get better performance if you choose two disks. If you are using RAID and only have one drive letter, then configure both locations to point to the same drive letter. Click Next.

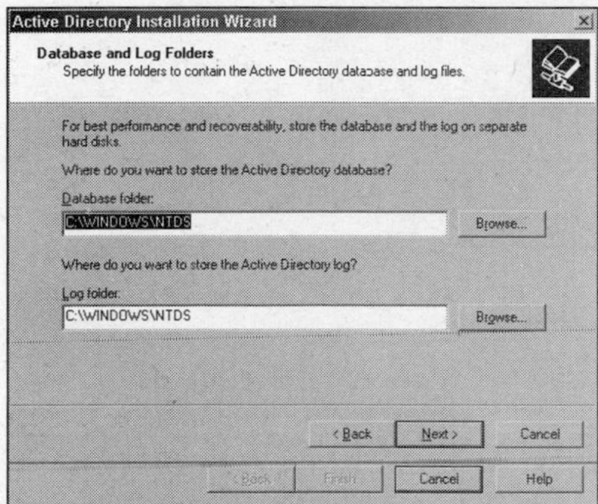

Figure 11-8: Locate the database and log files on an NTFS drive for increased security.

9. The Shared System Volume dialog box loads. You can usually leave this to the default chosen by the server. The Shared System Volume dialog box is shown here in Figure 11-9. To continue click Next.

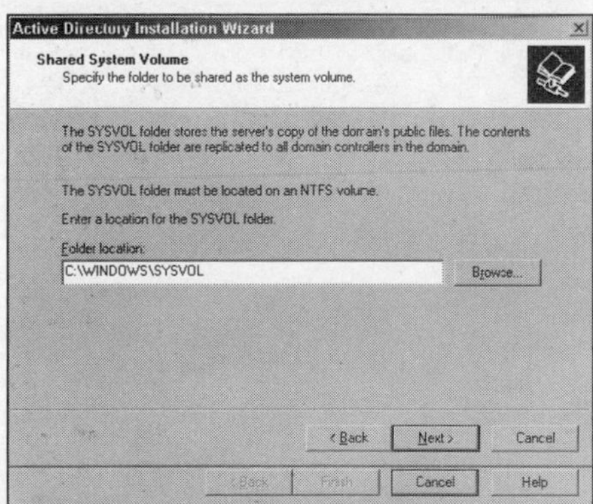

Figure 11-9: The SYSVOL folder contains a copy of information that is replicated to other servers.

10. The Permissions dialog box loads, as illustrated in Figure 11-10. If you have Windows NT servers that need to access information on this server, then choose the first option. For security reasons, we have chosen to upgrade all our NT servers in CITYHALL and deploy only Windows 2003 (we have ways and means of spending our taxpayer's money). CITYHALL will then be a native mode domain. Click Next.

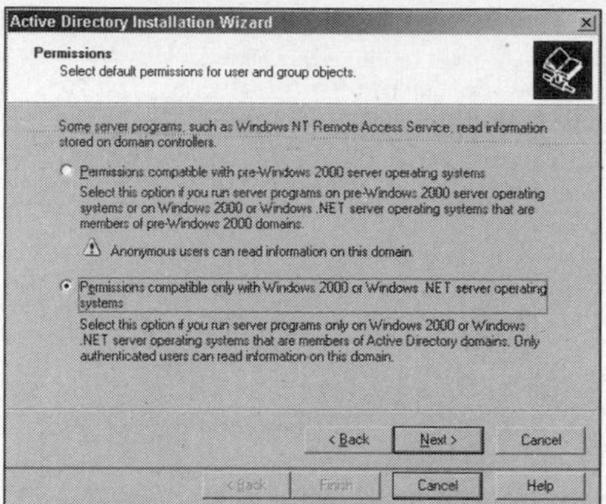

Figure 11-10: The Permissions page determines if pre-Windows 2000 systems will have access to this domain.

11. The Directory Services Restore Mode Administrator Password dialog box loads as seen below in Figure 11-11. This parameter is the password of the user account that is authorized to start a domain controller in Restore mode for the purpose of restoring system state. Enter the password twice and click Next.

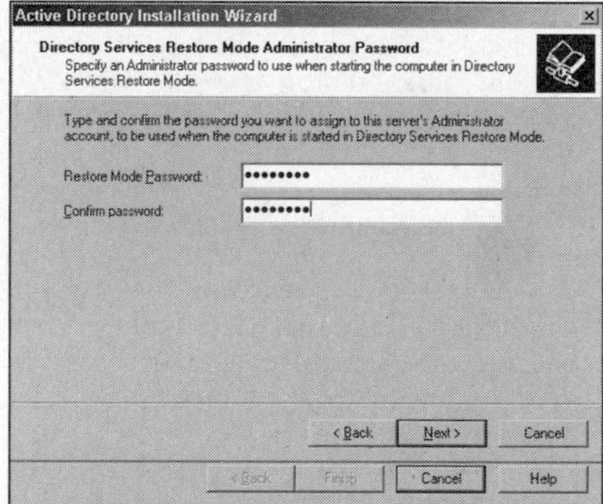

Figure 11-11: The Restore Mode Password is used to log in as administrator should you need to perform maintenance on Active Directory.

12. The Summary dialog box loads. This means that you are almost done. Check over the details carefully to ensure that you have made the right choices. At this point, you can always go back and change a value or parameter. Once you click Next, however, there is no undoing any mistakes. You can only demote the server and start the whole process all over again. Click Next to begin the promotion, the installation of Active Directory, and the joining of the domain to the tree. If you see the dialog box illustrated in Figure 11-12, you are doing fine.

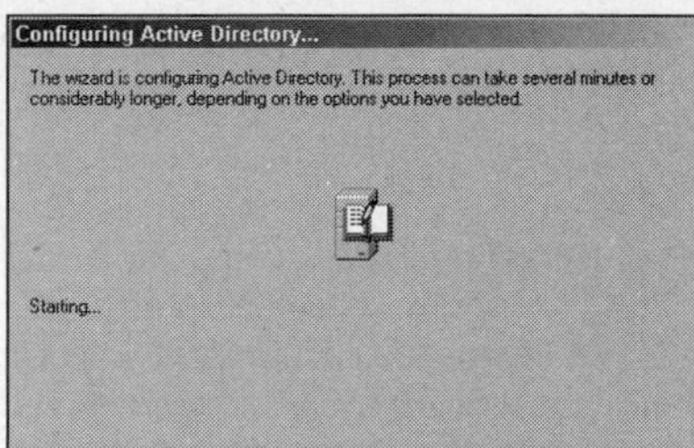

Figure 11-12: The process of installing Active Directory is under way.

The wizard then starts the installation of Active Directory on the local server. This process can take several minutes. At this point, you can leave the DC to finish; no further human intervention is necessary.

Figure 11-6 illustrates that the new DC has been able to contact the parent DC on the network. In this case, CITYHALL has been able to contact GENESIS. Replication is then started between the two domains. You will notice processor activity related to the replication on the parent domain.

Next, the wizard sets up a trust relationship between the new domain CITYHALL and its parent GENESIS. Because the domains are part of the same domain tree in the same forest, they can exchange security credentials, which allows trusts between the domains to be transitive and bi-directional.

If all went well, and if the installation took place on the same network segment as the parent, you will notice that the new child domain was placed into the same site as the parent domain. We can leave this as is for now and move it to another site later. Also notice that the Back button has been disabled. There is no going back; the server has now been promoted to a domain controller running Active Directory services. You will now have to restart the server.

The entire promotion and installation process should take no longer than an hour on a well burned-in machine and on the local area network. On a very powerful machine with very fast hard disks, it can take as little as five minutes. If the process takes longer, or if Windows 2003 seems to be taking hours or even the whole day to write information to the disks, then you have a problem and need to terminate the effort (just be sure the bottleneck is not due to replication that is taking place over a slow link to a remote site). Powering down the machine is the only way to terminate the effort. This, by the way, happened to us only once in more than 30 promotions. After restarting the machine, we started the effort again, and it ran all the way in about an hour.

Towards the end of the promotion period and before restarting, there is usually no way of accessing any former shares or resources on the new DC.

Establishing in DNS/WINS

Several important items needed to be taken care of when we first created the root domain GENESIS, or more correctly, GENESIS.MCITY.ORG. You will encounter the same problem when you install your root domain controller, the first domain in your forest. During the installation, you will be asked for the address of a Domain Name System server, or DNS, or you can choose to install DNS on the server if this was not done before you began the DNS promotion. The Active Directory installation procedure will look for a DNS server into which it must install a new zone and new domain information.

It is a good idea to choose to install and integrate DNS and WINS on the root domain controller. It will make installation a lot smoother. For example, if the new Active Directory cannot locate a DNS server, it will be unable to register any domain, host, or site-specific information into the DNS databases.

During the installation of child domains, however, you will not be prompted for DNS information, even if you installed DNS on the server when you originally set it up as a standalone server. This may change with subsequent releases and service packs. Unless you manually install the new domain into DNS, there will be no way of authenticating to the child domain or managing it from another domain controller. You will get the error message that Active Directory Domains and Trusts is unable to find the domain, or that the server was not started. If your new DC is, in fact, started, then the problem is DNS.

So, let's manually install the new domain into DNS.

1. Open the primary DNS snap-in by clicking Start ⇨ Administrative Tools ⇨ DNS, or run the snap-in from the command line as described in Chapter 6. The DNS snap-in will load. In this example, the DNS server is hosted on our root DC, MCDC00.

2. Drill down to your root Active Directory domain. Notice that we have the higher-level Internet domains of MCITY and ORG on this DNS as well. Select the root Active Directory domain and right-click. The menu options load, as illustrated in Figure 11-7.

3. Go down to the menu option New Domain and select it. The New Domain dialog box will load. In this example, we are going to add the new domain MCPD to GENESIS namespace, so we type **MCPD** in the dialog box.

4. If the domain exists, DNS will immediately pull all the records it needs into its databases. This is illustrated in Figure 11-8, which shows CITYHALL expanded down to the point where we can resolve both the Kerberos and LDAP services on the CITYHALL domain.

5. Close the DNS snap-in.

Testing DNS and WINS

If your domain controllers have been established in DNS and WINS correctly, you will be able to resolve them. The following tests provide the proof.

1. Check your DNS records: Open the command console and type **NSLOOKUP** and the domain name, as illustrated in Figure 11-9. If the domains have been correctly installed in DNS, you will be able to resolve them. In the illustration, we can correctly resolve CITYHALL and GENESIS to their respective domain controllers. Notice that you cannot yet resolve MCPD to its domain controller. There is a very good reason for this: The domain does not yet exist. Consult Chapter 17 for a more in-depth discussion of DNS.

2. Check your WINS records: Open the command console and ping the host of the domains from any workstation, as illustrated in Figure 11-10. If you just ping the NetBIOS name, you will be able to resolve it to an IP address as illustrated. You should also be able to ping the entire DNS name, which gets resolved in DNS, not WINS. Remember that clients will need DHCP-assigned IP addresses, which automatically give them DNS and WINS IP addresses. DHCP thus needs to be up and running before clients will be able to resolve anything on the network.

If DNS and WINS check out, you are on your way to happy administration. Check that you can open the child domain from its parent DC. This is demonstrated in the next section.

Testing Active Directory domains and trusts

If your domain controllers have been established in DNS and WINS correctly, you should be able to log on to the remote domain and administer it. Open Active Directory Domains and Trusts by clicking Start ⇨ Administrative Tools ⇨ Active Directory Domains and Trusts. The snap-in will load, as illustrated in Figure 11-11. Notice that a domain tree is now apparent. Right-click the child domain and select Manage. If trusts and authentication are all working, you will be able to enter the domain for management, as illustrated in Figure 11-11.

One last exercise before we look at sites and subnets again: Check the trust relationships between the newly created domains. To do this, go to the Domains and Trusts snap-in as illustrated earlier. Select a domain and right-click. Choose Properties and click the Trusts tab. You will see the child domain information in this dialog box. The Trusts tab also tells you that the trust is transitive and working. Notice that we have a nontransitive trust between GENESIS and an NT network. If your trusts are working right, you will be able to drill down into the directory and access a domain.

Creating Sites

When you promote the first domain controller, Active Directory creates a default site named *Default-First-Site-Name* and places the domain controller server into that site. You can change the name of the default site to reflect the conventions in your deployment plan, or you can create a new site after the promotion and move the server into that domain. We chose the latter for demonstration purposes. The moved server object is illustrated in Figure 11-12. This is further demonstrated when we create the CITYHALL domain.

Note It is not necessary to create subnet objects for replication between servers. In the GENESIS setup, Active Directory would be able to replicate to each server in the site.

Active Directory sees the root DC server in the site we created in Chapter 11 and puts the root DC of the child domain in that site. Remember that an Active Directory site is associated with an IP subnet. The Active Directory replication topology is built via the site and subnet topology, between the domain controllers, or both. This technology is derived from the Exchange replication mechanisms, and it works on the principal of joining an Exchange server to a site.

When you have two domain controllers on the same site, which is what we have done in the earlier example for expediency, the replication that takes place between the controllers happens very quickly, or at the speed of your local area network to be more precise. This could be anything from 10 to 100 Mbps.

With subnets, Active Directory gets the information it needs to build the replication topology. In the previous example, it automatically added the second domain controller to the site we created for GENESIS because they shared an IP subnet. But we are going to take the CITYHALL DC and ship it to its new location, which is the 100.45.0.0 subnet, and this means that we have to manually move the DC object from the site in which it was initially installed to the correct site. Before we do that, we need to make a new site for the DC. This is done as follows:

1. Load the MMC snap-in Active Directory Site and Services. To find the snap-in, go to Start ⇨ Administrative Tools ⇨ Active Directory Sites and Services, or load it from the command line. The snap-in loads.

2. Select the site item in the tree and right-click it. Choose New Site from the Context Menu. The New Site dialog box appears and allows you to create the new site. Enter the appropriate site information and choose the transport (IP or SMTP). Click OK to add the site.

Let's now look at the site object more closely.

The site object

You will notice that each site has a *servers* container. This container holds the DCs that have been placed into this site. There is also an attribute named *Licensing Site Settings* and an attribute named *NTDS Settings*.

The Licensing Site Settings property is used to specify the computer and domain that licenses the site. In the NTDS Settings object, you can disable the Knowledge Consistency Checker (KCC) settings that determine the automatic generation of the replication topology within the site or between this site and other sites. These settings allow you to create additional settings to augment the replication topology of the KCC, but this depends on your situation.

Creating server objects

There is no difference between the server objects you create manually or the server objects created automatically by the AD, save that you have to remove manually what you create manually. The KCC does not know about these objects nor does it care about what happens to them. To create such objects, you need to perform the following steps:

1. Select the server's NTDS Settings property in the console tree and right-click it. Choose the menu option New Active Directory Connection from the context menu. The Find Domain Controllers dialog box loads.

2. Select the DC to create a connection and click OK. This will then open the New Object - Connection dialog box.

3. Supply a name for the new connection object and click OK.

You change the configuration of your connection object easily after creating it by simply opening the connection object's Properties dialog box. Note that you can also set the security levels and access control on the object. But most interesting is the Change Schedule button on the first tab. This allows you to change the replication schedule to suit your environment.

You can, for example, schedule replication to run at night when there is no traffic on the network. But remember that the schedule for a connection object is only one way. To schedule the full replication load, you have to configure the connection object on the other domain controllers as well.

Creating the subnet objects

The Subnets folder holds the IP subnets that are associated with specific site objects. To create a subnet object, you need to perform the following steps:

1. Drill down to the Subnets container in the console tree in the Sites and Services MMC snap-in. Right-click the container and choose New Subnet from the shortcut menu. The New Object - Subnet dialog box loads.

2. Type the new subnet's network address and mask. This is automatically translated into a properly bit-masked subnet.

3. Now select the site in the list to which the subnet is to be associated and click OK.

Now, all servers that reside on this subnet that become DCs will automatically be added to the site associated with this subnet.

Creating the site link objects

Create the site link objects according to the criteria mentioned previously. To create the object, you will need to perform the following steps:

1. Drill down to the IP or SMTP transport listed in the console tree of the Site and Services snap-in and right-click the transport. Select New Site Link from the Context menu. The New Object - Site Link dialog box loads.
2. Specify a name for the new object and then choose the sites that the link connects.
3. Click OK, and the site link object is created.

Note When you choose site links, you need to know what you are choosing, and this should be in your deployment plan. For example, if you are going to connect sites to a T1 network, there will typically be only two sites to be linked, one at each end. Adding a third site to the link would be worthless. If you are working with a network cloud, you can also configure a site link bridge, which ensures that all sites get replication due to the transitive link structure that is created with site link bridges.

To configure the site link, right-click the new object and choose Properties from the context menu. The site links properties for the specific site load. Add a description for the site link and add the sites to the link by moving them from the pane on the left (Sites not in this Site link) to the pane on the right (Sites in this Site link).

You can then configure the cost of the site links and any special replication schedule.

Creating the site link bridge object

The process involved in creating the site link bridge object is identical to the process for creating site link objects. The only difference is that you select two or more site links instead of sites.

Now, let's create some facilities for our administrators in GENESIS.

Creating Organizational Units

To recap, OU stands for organizational unit. In the Active Directory, the OU represents a partitioning of the domain, yes; but it is more than that. An OU holds security policy, and it is the location for delegating administrative authority (also known as delegation of control).

Now and in the future, the Active Directory OU is going to be compared to the OUs of other directories, such as Novell Directory Services (NDS). Since the publishing of the Active Directory Services Interface (ADSI), the OU has already been slammed for not being a security principal. What is a spade in the hands of one gardener may be something else in the hands of another. Seasoned NT administrators may find it difficult to think in terms of another security principal to replace groups.

Note Had OUs replaced groups completely, it might have made upgrading very difficult.

OUs are different from groups; groups are security principals and can be given access or denied access to any network, computer, or domain resource — in fact, any object defined in the local registry or in the Active Directory. We like OUs because it is possible to model the OU to Key Management Entities (or KMEs); therefore, they play a role in enterprise administration as opposed to being gatekeepers.

To extend security policy over groups and users, you place them into OUs. OUs are themselves "locked down" with security policy and access control. The policy governs how the users and the groups are allowed to conduct themselves domain- and forest-wide. Most important for security, however, is that the OU is also your computer lockup. This is essentially how you should understand and plan the enterprise group policy. For now, we will take you through the steps of creating an OU.

To create an OU, you need to perform the following. Open the Active Directory Users and Computers MMC snap-in.

1. Drill down to the domain in the console tree and right-click it. Choose New and then choose Organization Unit from the ensuing menu.
2. Enter the name of the OU according to the naming conventions you are using and click OK.

Tip

Do not try to create an OU hierarchy for the benefit of your users. It's a waste of your resources. In fact, you should do your best as an administrator to hide the OU structure from your users and the network. The user base has a network folder hierarchy to navigate and folders that you may publish in the directory. The OU structure is there for the benefit of change control and management, security policy, and workplace administration.

You can nest an OU inside another OU hierarchy; but you should avoid deep OU nests because they are harder to manage.

Delegating OU Administration

At this point in the creation of your Active Directory DC, you may decide to create additional OUs, or you may come back to the task of OU creation later. One of your most important chores will be to delegate administrative control and management over the OU to an administrator or responsible party. And you might find it useful to assign the task of creating OUs to another individual, preferably a person trained in domain security.

There are two reasons to begin delegation at this point:

1. Delegation can help you manage a complex directory structure by delegating the work as early in the directory-building process as possible.
2. Delegation is an important security consideration. By delegating, you essentially block others from interfering with the workings of a particular OU. Delegation also obviates the need to create special OU security groups or OU administrators, which, if given power by group membership to administer an OU, essentially have the power to administer all OUs.

Start the Delegate Control Wizard to perform the delegation. This is done by first selecting the OU to which you wish to delegate control and then by right-clicking the selection. The OU context menu loads. Select Delegate Control, which is the first option in the menu. The Delegation of Control Wizard launches. Select Next and then click Add to load the list of domain security principals. Choose a user or group account from the list and then click the list of Active Directory users and groups. Click Add to add the user or group and then click Next.

The next screen allows you to select the task to delegate to the user or group. You can select from a predetermined list of tasks, or choose to build a custom list of tasks. If you choose the latter, you will be able to apply a finer control over the task to delegate. The customer list gives you two options: an extensive list of individual objects that can be manipulated by the intended administrator or group, or a shortcut that specifies the OU, all objects in the OU, and any new objects that are created.

If you do not want the delegated party to be able to create new objects, choose the list of objects and uncheck the specific objects that grant control.

When you are done, click Next and the summary page will appear. Check the delegation summary and then click Finish.

Securing the DC and Following Disaster Recovery Protocol

To properly secure a DC, you should ensure that all objects are properly protected by Access Control Lists or ACLs. ACLs on Active Directory objects contain Access Control Entries that apply to the object as a whole and to the individual properties of the object. This means that you can control not only the administrators or users that you want to see the object in its entirety, but also which properties should be exposed to certain groups or individuals.

Securing the directory is a complex task and time consuming, but it is essential. Each object, just like all other operating system objects, can display a Properties page. You launch the Properties page by right-clicking the object and selecting Properties. The object's Properties page loads.

Click the Security tab. You can now add or remove security accounts from any trusted domain and select the property pages (tabs) that can be read.

In addition to protecting the directory and its contents, it is also important to lock down the server . . . the domain controller. You should first ensure that the Administrator account or any other omnipotent security principal is not logged onto the console, and you should strive to ensure that such omnipotent accounts are not allowed to be disseminated. Meanwhile, lock down the server and only allow accounts to access regions of the directory to which they have been delegated.

By locking down the server, you are not only protecting the directory service but also other critical components of a vital server, such as the registry, storage facilities, and so on.

Be sure to schedule a backup of the directory as soon as the current tasks have been completed.

Summary

In this chapter, we successfully demonstrated the promotion of several servers to domain controllers, which hold the Active Directory namespace and all the functionality that goes with it from (A)ctive to (Z)one.

We also took you through the paces of creating and configuring your replication topology. Finally, we reviewed the creation of OUs. We did not dwell too much on the subject of OUs because they are discussed in detail in other places in the book, particularly Chapter 2.

Now that we have the Active Directory domain structure in place, it is time to learn a bit about managing it. Management tools here we come. . .

✦ ✦ ✦

CHAPTER 12

Active Directory Management

✦ ✦ ✦ ✦

In This Chapter

Learning to manage replication

Familiarizing yourself with catalog server installation

Learning to perform online and offline Active Directory backups

Learning how to move Active Directory among servers

✦ ✦ ✦ ✦

This chapter deploys an Active Directory infrastructure. Working from the deployment plan blueprint described in this chapter, you can identify and modify the elements of the deployment plan that suit your configuration. You can make changes as you need, whether you need a solution for a small network or a WAN connecting multiple domain controllers and an extensive Active Directory tree.

Installing New Directory Services into an Existing Infrastructure

You should take several things into consideration when installing directory services into an existing infrastructure. The first thing to take into account is uptime. If you are dealing with a network that can be down for several hours at a time, perhaps after normal business hours, things get a lot easier. However, if your company maintains 24 × 7 services, you can't very well down servers to upgrade them.

One of the most important things to remember when upgrading a network is to remove an existing Backup Domain Controller (BDC) to maintain network integrity. If something should go wrong during the upgrade process, you can fall back on the BDC.

If you are in a 24 × 7 environment, follow these steps to begin the upgrade of your domain controllers:

1. Choose a BDC on the network and ensure that it has a current copy of the User Account database. Back this server up and then unplug it from the network. If a power failure or other catastrophic event happens during the upgrade of the Primary Domain Controller (PDC), you can always promote the BDC to a Primary to resume normal network operations.
2. Begin the operating system (OS) upgrade phase on the PDCs. During this phase of the upgrade, network requests are handled by the BDCs.
3. After the operating system has been upgraded on the PDC, you should upgrade the OS on all the BDCs, except for the BDC that was unplugged from the network.
4. When all operating systems have been upgraded, run the Active Directory Installation Wizard on the PDC, followed by all the BDCs.

If server uptime isn't much of a concern, you can upgrade concurrently, but this isn't recommended.

Replication Management

Replication management is handled with the Active Directory Sites and Services Manager, which is implemented as a Microsoft Management Console (MMC) snap-in. This is where you see how replication happens between servers; however, you lack the capability to monitor replication or to force replication to happen.

The `repadmin.exe` utility enables you to check replication for consistency between partners, monitor the status of replication, view the metadata contained within the replication, and force replication events.

Installing New Domain Controllers

Before you install a domain controller, verify DNS; we touch on this topic again shortly.

After you install the OS on the server, ensure that it has an active network connection and that it can properly communicate with the DNS server. During the Active Directory installation phase, the OS needs to query DNS for domain names for the installation to complete successfully. If you will be installing Active Directory on a server that exists within an existing forest, the network connection of this server can be configured to use more than one DNS server. This is necessary because an existing forest may have many DNS servers for each "branch" of the forest, and the Active Directory Installation Wizard on this new server must be able to locate all servers in the forest.

Don't worry if you are installing Active Directory into a network without an existing forest. The Active Directory Installation Wizard actually installs and configures a DNS server on the local machine. Keep in mind that the DNS settings of this server are automatically changed to point to the local server. You are free to change this after the Installation Wizard has completed its task. If you do change this setting, you need to point it to a DNS server that is still capable of seeing all the servers on your network. Without this, Active Directory will fail to operate correctly.

If, by chance, you already have DNS installed, you need to verify all records before you attempt the Active Directory installation. Specifically, you must verify that the appropriate service (SRV) resource records and the corresponding address (A) resource records exist in the DNS server.

A DNS SRV record enables administrators to use several servers for one domain. These records designate where services are located. For example, ftp can be located on one server while another server can host a Web server or Active Directory. A DNS A record simply maps a server name to the IP address.

If these DNS records are missing or invalid, the installation will die a miserable death; so it's critical that you add or correct these records.

After you have verified that all DNS records are present and accounted for, you need to ensure that your DNS server allows for dynamic updates. You do this in the authoritative DNS zone. To locate the authoritative DNS zone within your network, simply find the primary DNS server hosting the zone. This zone will have the DNS name of the Active Directory domain or the name of a parent zone. For example, if the name of the Active Directory domain is authors.wiley.com, the authoritative DNS could be one of the following:

✦ Authors.wiley.com

✦ wiley.com

✦ com

If you aren't sure whether your DNS server allows for dynamic updates, see your software documentation.

At the time of this writing, the Microsoft DNS server included with Windows Server 2003 is fully compatible with dynamic updates. The current version of BIND (a very popular UNIX-based DNS Server) is also capable of dynamic updates.

If you'd prefer not to configure your DNS for dynamic updates, you need to add all records manually. A list of all resource records that should be registered by a domain controller is stored in the following location:

```
%systemroot%\system32\Config\netlogon.dns
```

Installing New Catalog Servers

Configuring a domain controller to server as a global catalog server is a fairly straightforward process. To begin, open the Active Directory Sites and Services management console. When it opens, expand Sites within the tree view. Below the Sites node, expand your site's name; then expand the Servers node where your server's name is listed. Expand this node and find the NTDS node. Right-click on it and choose Properties. On the General page of the Properties dialog box, select the Global Catalog check box.

To open Active Directory Sites and Services, click the Start menu, click on All Programs, point to Administrative Tools, and then click on Active Directory Sites and Services.

Each Windows Server 2003 site or Windows 2000 site containing Microsoft Message Queue 1.0 clients running on Windows NT 4.0, Windows 98, or Windows 95 computers must contain at least one Windows Server 2003 domain controller running the Message Queuing directory service (Downlevel Client Support) configured as a global catalog server. Alternatively, you can have at least one Windows 2000 domain controller running a Message Queuing server and configured as a global catalog server from the domain of each such client. This is required to enable such clients to send queries programmatically to Message Queuing servers.

If you currently use a Windows NT 4.0 primary enterprise controller (PEC), this box is automatically promoted to a domain controller configured as a global catalog server when it is migrated.

The first domain controller in a Windows Server 2003 forest is automatically configured as a global catalog server.

Protecting Active Directory from Corruption

To ensure that Active Directory operates in a smooth and consistent manner, it may be necessary to perform integrity checks, repair, move, recovery, and defragmentation of the Active Directory database.

Online and offline database defragmentation

By default, Active Directory automatically performs an online defragmentation every 12 hours as part of its Garbage Collection process. Online defragmentation is very effective, but it doesn't reduce the size of the database file (`Ntds.dit`). It does, however, optimize data storage in the database and reclaim space in the database file to create new objects. The defragmentation process does prevent data storage problems, but if your database file is getting large you won't get much help here–you will ultimately need to perform an offline defragmentation. The process of offline defragmentation creates a brand new compacted version of the database file. If you have a large network where objects are added and removed quite often, it is quite likely that the resulting defragmented file will be considerably smaller.

To perform an offline defragmentation of the Active Directory database, follow these steps:

1. Back up Active Directory! Regardless of the software you are using to back up your server, if you are choosing to back up everything on the server, the registry will be backed up by default. If you choose not to back up everything on the server, ensure that you are backing up the System State, which will include all Active Directory information.
2. Restart the domain controller; then press and hold down the F8 key before the operating system starts. You are greeted with the Windows Server 2003 Advanced Options Menu.
3. Choose Directory Services Restore Mode and press Enter. To start the boot process again, press Enter.
4. Log on to the server using the Administrator account with the local admin password defined in the offline SAM.
5. After Windows Server 2003 starts, click the Start menu and choose Programs ➪ Accessories ➪ Command Prompt.

Note You can get to a console window quickly by clicking the Start menu, selecting Run, and typing **cmd** followed by Enter.

6. At the command prompt, type **ntdsutil** and press Enter.
7. After the utility opens, type **files** and press Enter.
8. Type **info** and press Enter. Current information about the path and size of the Active Directory database and its log files is displayed. Be sure to pay special attention to the path. You might want to write down this path information as shown in Figure 12-1.
9. Locate a spot on your drive that has enough free space for the compacted version of the database to reside. Type **compact to <*drive*>:\<*directory*>** where <*drive*> and <*directory*> represent the path that you recorded in the previous step. The database file is then compacted, and a progress bar displays the compaction rate as shown in Figure 12-2.

Note As with any directory path, if the path contains spaces, you must surround the path with quotation marks.

When the compact function is finished, `ntdsutil` displays the location of the compacted database file as well as the location of the log file (see Figure 12-3).

```
C:\WINDOWS\System32\cmd.exe - ntdsutil
Microsoft Windows [Version 5.1.3604]
(C) Copyright 1985-2001 Microsoft Corp.

C:\Documents and Settings\Administrator>ntdsutil
ntdsutil: files
file maintenance: info

Drive Information:

        C:\ NTFS (Fixed Drive   ) free(6.3 Gb) total(7.9 Gb)

DS Path Information:

        Database    : C:\WINDOWS\NTDS\ntds.dit - 10.1 Mb
        Backup dir  : C:\WINDOWS\NTDS\dsadata.bak
        Working dir: C:\WINDOWS\NTDS
        Log dir     : C:\WINDOWS\NTDS - 30.0 Mb total
                        res2.log - 10.0 Mb
                        res1.log - 10.0 Mb
                        edb.log - 10.0 Mb
file maintenance:
```

Figure 12-1: The `info` command displays the location of all relevant database files.

```
C:\WINDOWS\System32\cmd.exe - ntdsutil
        C:\ NTFS (Fixed Drive   ) free(6.3 Gb) total(7.9 Gb)

DS Path Information:

        Database    : C:\WINDOWS\NTDS\ntds.dit - 10.1 Mb
        Backup dir  : C:\WINDOWS\NTDS\dsadata.bak
        Working dir: C:\WINDOWS\NTDS
        Log dir     : C:\WINDOWS\NTDS - 30.0 Mb total
                        res2.log - 10.0 Mb
                        res1.log - 10.0 Mb
                        edb.log - 10.0 Mb
file maintenance: compact to c:\
Opening database [Current].
Executing Command: C:\WINDOWS\system32\esentutl.exe /d"C:\WINDOWS\NTDS\ntds.dit"
 /t"c:\ntds.dit" /p /o

Initiating DEFRAGMENTATION mode...
            Database: C:\WINDOWS\NTDS\ntds.dit
      Temp. Database: c:\ntds.dit

                  Defragmentation Status (% complete)

          0    10   20   30   40   50   60   70   80   90  100
          |----|----|----|----|----|----|----|----|----|----|
          ...........................................
```

Figure 12-2: The compact process can be monitored with the progress bar.

```
C:\WINDOWS\System32\cmd.exe - ntdsutil
                  Defragmentation Status (% complete)

          0    10   20   30   40   50   60   70   80   90  100
          |----|----|----|----|----|----|----|----|----|----|
          ...................................................


Note:
  It is recommended that you immediately perform a full backup
  of this database. If you restore a backup made before the
  defragmentation, the database will be rolled back to the state
  it was in at the time of that backup.

Operation completed successfully in 6.238 seconds.


Spawned Process Exit code 0x0(0)

If compaction was successful you need to:
   copy "c:\ntds.dit" "C:\WINDOWS\NTDS\ntds.dit"
and delete the old log files:
   del C:\WINDOWS\NTDS\*.log

file maintenance: _
```

Figure 12-3: Upon completion, the compact process displays the location of the resulting file.

10. A new database named `Ntds.dit` is created in the path that you specified.

11. To exit, type **quit** and press Enter. To return to the command prompt, type **quit** again.

You can now copy the new `Ntds.dit` file over the old `Ntds.dit` file in the current Active Directory database path that was recorded earlier. Restart the computer normally.

Ensure database integrity

Active Directory is implemented on a transactional database system. Log files enable rollback segments, which ensure that transactions are committed to the database. In the event of a power failure, there's no chance of a partial commit of data.

The Active Directory database system is commonly referred to as the Jet database. The Jet database is the native database used by Microsoft Access. The Jet database engine has been around for quite a while and is quite well established. For large systems, you may consider moving your database to SQL Server to increase performance.

To check the integrity of the contents of the Active Directory database, you can use the `ntdutil.exe` tool. This tool contains a semantics checker that can be invoked by selecting the Semantic database analysis option. This tool is automatically invoked during Active Directory's Restore mode. During this time, any errors are written into `dsdit.dmp .xx` log files. A progress indicator indicates the status of the check.

The following is a list of the functions that can be performed with the `ntdutil.exe` tool:

✦ **Reference count check:** Counts all the references from the data table and the link table to ensure that they match the listed counts for the record.

✦ **Deleted object check:** Deleted objects are checked to ensure that the date and time stamp have been removed.

✦ **Ancestor check:** Determines whether the current Distinguished Name Tag (DNT) is equal to the ancestor list of the parent and the current DNT.

✦ **Security descriptor check:** Looks for a valid descriptor.

✦ **Replication check:** Ensures that every object has property metadata.

Moving Active Directory from Server to Server

To move an Active Directory database, you use the `ntdsutil.exe` command-line tool in Directory Services Restore mode. In the event that you experience a corruption of a drive or a drive failure, you would need to move the `Ntds.dit` or the logs files to another drive.

To move the Active Directory database to a different file system on the same server or to a different server, follow these steps:

1. First and foremost, back up the Active Directory database. Windows Server 2003 Backup will handle this for you if you choose to back up the entire system. If you don't want to back up the entire machine, at least back up the System State, which includes all the Active Directory database information.

2. Restart the domain controller; then press and hold F8 until the Windows Server 2003 Advanced Options menu appears.

3. Choose Directory Services Restore Mode as you did earlier when you defragmented the Active Directory database.

4. Log on via the Administrator account by using the password defined for the Local Administrator account in the offline SAM.

5. Click the Start menu; choose Programs ⇨ Accessories ⇨ Command Prompt.

6. At the command prompt, type **ntdsutil.exe** and press Enter.

7. Type the word **files** and press Enter.

8. Type **info** to display the path and size information of Active Directory and the log files. Write this path information down because you will need it later.

9. Find a location that has enough drive space to hold the Active Directory database and the log files.

10. Type **move DB to *<drive>*:*<directory>*** and press Enter; *<drive>* and *<directory>* represent the location of the database and log files you wrote down earlier.

11. The `Ntds.dit` database file is moved to the location you specified.

12. Type **quit** and press Enter. To return to the command prompt, type **quit** again and press Enter.

After you have completed these steps, you can restart the computer as you normally would.

You can also move log files from one location to another by using the `move logs to` command, which moves the files and updates the registry entries to point to the new location of the log files.

Integrating Active Directory with Other Services

Many Microsoft products integrate very tightly with Active Directory. Installing and configuring these products is quite a long process and would merit an entire book. In the following sections, however, we mention a few of the products and what you stand to gain by using them within an Active Directory domain.

Active Directory and SQL Server

Active Directory is quite capable of using SQL Server as its mechanism for data storage. The missing ingredient in this scenario, however, is access control. In the event that you need to provide both access control and the performance that only SQL Server can provide, it is recommended that you use both Active Directory and SQL Server. It is well beyond the scope of this book to describe the installation procedures involved in using both SQL Server and the Active Directory data store.

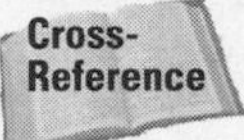

For more information on using Active Directory and SQL Server, grab a copy of *Microsoft SQL Server 2000 Bible* by Paul Nielsen (published by Wiley).

Active Directory and Microsoft Exchange

Similar to SQL Server, Microsoft Exchange can also be highly integrated with Active Directory. When Microsoft Exchange is installed on a server running Active Directory, it defaults to storing all user and account information in the Active Directory data store. By doing this, the software is ensuring that there is no duplication of data and that information could not be out of sync.

Trust and Replication Monitoring

The Active Directory Replication Monitor (`Replmon.exe`) is a graphical tool that you can use to view low-level status and performance of replication between Active Directory domain controllers. The Replication Monitor can monitor the following replication features:

- Automatically detects all directory partitions on the selected server, including global catalog servers. The Replication Monitor can display whether the server being monitored is a global catalog server. In graphical form, it also displays all the replication partners. When a partner's replication fails, the icon of the server changes to denote this condition.
- Displays servers with which the computer is replicating both directly and indirectly. It also allows administrators to display the properties for the monitored server. Some of the properties that can be viewed are the server name, the DNS host name of the computer, the location of the computer account in Active Directory, and the replication connections.
- Displays the number of failed attempts, reasons, and flags used for each partner for direct replication partners.
- Offers a server wizard that lists all servers so the administrator can choose the server from a list. As an option, you can create an INI file that contains a list of the servers to monitor. Keep your fingers crossed that in the future this will be replaced with an XML file.
- Automatically detects the domain of the client and displays the appropriate option.
- Displays a graphical view of the intrasite topology. By using the context menu for a specific domain controller in the view, it enables the administrator to quickly display the properties of the server and any intersite connections that exist.
- Gives administrators the capability to display how remote domain controllers are configured (for example, whether they have the PDC emulator role).
- In Automatic Update mode, polls the server at an administrator-defined interval to get current statistics and replication state. This is useful to generate a history of changes for each server that is monitored.
- Enables administrators to trigger replication on a server with a specific replication partner, with all other domain controllers in the site, or all other domain controllers within a site and between sites.
- Enables administrators to trigger the KCC to recalculate the replication topology.
- Enables the paranoid administrator to log all the tool's activities that it performs.

✦ Keeps a log file showing the history of all the replication states of the servers. This is very handy should you a have a server that intermittently misses replication. You can review this log file to keep tabs on the replication states of the server in question.

✦ Keeps track of failed replication attempts. You can set maximum fail levels so that if a server fails to replicate *n* times, it can write event log entries as well as send an e-mail.

✦ Enables administrators to show which objects have not yet replicated from a particular server computer. It also displays the metadata of an Active Directory object's attributes, which include the attribute name, the version number, and the time the attribute was last changed, to name a few.

✦ Generates very robust reports to help with technical issues. These reports can contain almost all the intricate details of Active Directory and the replication process so that a support technician can aid with replication issues. As well as generating a report that can be e-mailed or printed, this report information can be uploaded to a Jet database for historical purposes.

✦ Enables you to specify multiple logins in your domain. It can log in to and monitor servers across all forests if necessary.

Log On without the Global Catalog

If you have a WAN with many remote sites, it may be in the best interest of your network to place the global catalog remotely to improve the performance of log in times, searches, and other actions requiring the global catalog. This placement can dramatically reduce the traffic on your network. It not only provides better server response times but also provides better response with other applications that rely on the network to move data. For these reasons, and to reduce administrative tasks, you may choose to place a copy of the global catalog remotely. By doing so, you are essentially duplicating the functionality of the backup domain controller.

As you probably realize, there is still a problem. Even though a copy of the global catalog is placed remotely, the domain controller is still needed to authenticate users as they log in to the network. Therefore, if the remote site doesn't have a global catalog, and a global catalog server is unavailable, no one can log in. That means 100% down time for any remote offices that rely on a WAN connection to contact the PDC in the event the link goes down.

Before modifying the registry, which will be discussed in the following paragraph, we strongly suggest that you back up your system and registry settings.

To remove the need for a global catalog server at a site and avoid the potential denial of user log on requests, follow these steps to enable log ons when the global catalog is unavailable:

1. Start the Registry Editor (`regedit.exe`) and locate the following key in the registry editor: `HKEY_LOCAL_MACHINE\System\CurrentControlSet\Control\Lsa`.
2. Choose Edit ➪ Add Key and add a key name of **IgnoreGCFailures**. No value is required for this key.

You can now quit the Registry Editor and restart the domain controller for the changes to take effect.

This key needs to be set on the domain controller that performs the initial authentication of the user.

By bypassing the global catalog for authentication purposes, you could be introducing a major security hole. Examine all your options before making these changes to your server.

Active Directory and DNS

DNS is the primary means by which a Windows Server 2003 domain locates Active Directory services and servers. The clients and tools of Active Directory use DNS to locate domain controllers for administration and logon. You must have a DNS server installed within each forest of your domain to have Active Directory function correctly.

In earlier versions of Windows, NetBIOS name resolution is still required to resolve network resources on an Active Directory network. To achieve this, a WINS server, LMHosts file, or NetBIOS broadcast file is required. It's no secret that the WINS server is known for causing undue network traffic on a network.

Installing the DNS Server supplied with Windows Server 2003 is really just a matter of point and click for simple configurations. If you are an experienced administrator, you can also install BIND on a UNIX or Windows machine should you want to do so. Installing the DNS Server on Windows will quite possibly require WIndows Server 2003 to complete the installation.

We recommend that you stick with the Microsoft DNS server when installing DNS on an Active Directory network. If you choose not to install the Microsoft DNS server, ensure that the server you do install supports the dynamic update protocol.

Version 8.1.2 and later of BIND (a popular DNS server implementation) supports both the SRV RR and dynamic updates. (Version 8.1.1 does support dynamic updates, but it has flaws that were fixed in 8.1.2.) If you are using a version of BIND or any other DNS server that does not support dynamic updates, you need to manually add records to the DNS server.

Microsoft DNS, as included with Microsoft Windows NT 4.0 Server, does not support the SRV record. You can, on the other hand, use the DNS Server supplied with Windows Server 2003 or Windows 2000 Server, which both support dynamic updates.

When you add a DNS Server to a network that will eventually become an Active Directory network, you should install DNS on a standalone server. This server can then be promoted to a domain controller at a later time. Also ensure that this server has a static IP address No servers on a network should use DHCP because it can cause undue network traffic when clients attempt to connect to the server.

Summary

Management of Active Directory involves many tools and can only be effective with practice. This chapter covered the process needed to back up as well as move the Active Directory database. Using this technique, you can ensure that the database continues to provide peak performance and doesn't consume excessive disk space. You also learned how to correctly modify the registry so that a log in without the global catalog is possible. When editing the registry, it is very important that you maintain an up-to-date backup of the registry. Registry changes can render your server useless, and a backup of the registry enables you to get things going again. Employ these measures and practice, practice, practice.

✦ ✦ ✦

Managing Users and Groups

In This Chapter

Understanding groups

Creating user accounts

Creating groups

Managing users and groups

If you are passionate about being a network or domain administrator, managing users and groups can give you a lot of satisfaction . . . it can be a very powerful position in a company. On the other hand, unless you understand the fundamentals, manage the processes sensibly, and learn the tools and resources, the task can become an extremely frustrating responsibility. Our administration mantra is to use your common sense and learn to do it right before you take up the task. This chapter helps you get the best out of the Windows Server 2003 user and group-management philosophy and tools.

Despite Microsoft's Zero Administration Windows (ZAW) initiative, user and group management has become a lot more complex in Windows Server 2003. The complexity has a lot to do with the User and Group objects and their support in Active Directory, which was inherited from Windows 2000. Combined with the burden of integrating Windows NT 4.0 and earlier networks, the administrative task is not easy in the short term.

This situation may improve over the years, because many companies and, especially, administrators are certain to develop tools for the Active Directory that automate the repetitive stuff and enhance the experience of working with Active Directory (and we touch on that in this chapter). In that the directory is open and supports a widely available API (ADSI) and access protocol (LDAP), we must give credit where credit is due. You can, for example, extend the User and Group objects to suit your enterprise requirements or custom applications. What you learn in this chapter puts you on the road to such advanced administration.

In this chapter, we study User and Group objects and understand their function. We entertain user-management practice and policy with respect to users, groups, and computers. We also discuss the process of integrating legacy Windows NT and Windows 2000 accounts with Windows Server 2003 domains and how to sensibly manage users and groups on Windows Server 2003 mixed and native mode networks.

This chapter does not discuss management of the user workspace. Advanced items such as Group Policy, user profiles and logon scripts, workspace management, and so on are discussed in Chapter 14.

The Windows Server 2003 Account: A User's Resource

No one can work in a company, use any computer, or attach to any network without access to a user account. A user account is like the key to your car. Without the key, you cannot drive anywhere.

What is a user?

This question may seem patronizing at first, but in a Windows network domain (and also the local computer), the definition of *user* relates to autonomous processes, network objects (devices and computers), and humans. Human users exploit the networks or machines to get work done, meet deadlines, and get paid. But any process, machine, or technology that needs to exploit another object on the network or machine is treated as a user by the Windows operating systems. In a nutshell, the Windows Server 2003 security subsystem does not differentiate between a human and a device that is using its resources. All users are viewed as *security principals*, which at first are trusted.

After you install Windows Server 2003 (not do an upgrade) or create a new Active Directory domain, the operating system and many elements are exposed by default. This makes sense: Keep the doors open until the jewels have been delivered. As soon as you begin adding users to the system, and they begin adding resources that need protection, you should begin using the tools described in this chapter to lock down the elements and secure the network.

User objects are derived from a single user class in Active Directory, which in turn derives from several parents. Machine accounts are thus derived from the User object. To obtain access to the User object, you need to reference its *distinguished name* (*DN*) in program or script code. This is handled automatically by the various GUI objects, but if you plan to write scripts that access the object, you should be referencing the object's GUID.

What are contacts?

Contacts are objects that were introduced with Windows 2000 networks. They are derived from the same class hierarchy as the User object; the Contact object, however, does not inherit security attributes from its parent. A Contact is thus used only for communication purposes: for e-mail, faxing, phoning, and so on. Windows Server 2003 distribution lists are made up of contacts.

You can access Active Directory contacts from the likes of Outlook and Outlook Express and any other LDAP-compliant client software. The Contact object is almost identical to the object in the Windows Address Book (WAB).

Local users and "local users"

The term *local user* is often used to describe two types of users: users local to machines that log on locally to the workstation service and users who are local to a network or domain. Using the term interchangeably can cause confusion among your technical staff . . . and you have enough confusing things to deal with.

We believe that referring to local users as users who log on locally to a workstation or PC or a server makes sense. In other words, the local user can log on to the machine that the user is actually sitting at, where accounts have been created, or into a remote machine that has granted the user the "right" to log on locally, such as an application server that is accessed by a terminal session on a remote client.

In referring to generic users on the domain or users collectively, referring to these users as *domain users* or *domain members* makes more sense. A user can also be a member of a local domain, and such an account is also often referred to as a *local user*. On legacy NT domains, this was further confused by the capability to create a "local account," which was meant for users from nontrusted domains. This is no longer the case with Windows Server 2003 domains. Whether you agree or not, we suggest that you decide what the term *local user* means to your environment and then stick to that definition.

What is a group?

Groups are collections of users, contacts, computers, and other groups (a process known as *nesting*). Groups are supported in Active Directory (much to the horror of directory purists) and in the local computer's security subsystem. How Windows Server 2003 works with groups is discussed in the section "Groups versus organizational units," later in this chapter. Figure 13-1 shows the group-container philosophy.

Figure 13-1: Groups are collections or concentrations of users, computers, and other groups.

You would be right to wonder why Microsoft gives us both groups and organizational units (OUs) to manage. Groups, however, are a throwback to the Windows NT era. Remember that Windows Server 2003 is built on .NET, and groups were thus inherited from the earlier technology and enhanced for Windows Server 2003. Although groups may appear to be a redundant object next to OUs, they are a fact of Windows Server 2003 and are here to stay. They are also extremely powerful management objects.

Specifically, you create and use groups to contain the access rights of User objects and other groups within a security boundary. You also use groups to contain User objects that share the same access rights to network objects, such as shares, folders, files, printers, and so on. Groups thus provide a security filter against which users and other groups are given access to resources. This critical role of the groups is shown in Figure 13-2.

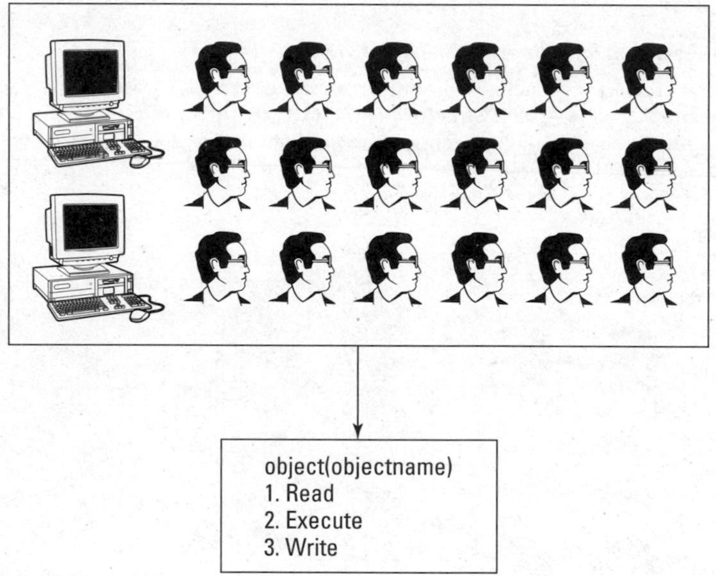

Figure 13-2: Groups provide a security "filter" against which users and other groups are given access to resources.

Sticking user accounts into every nook and cranny of a Windows domain is not good practice. If you start that practice, you soon have a domain that resembles a bowl of rice noodles at your local dim sum. It is a wonder that Microsoft engineers still enable us to stick a user account anywhere, because that practice is very rare on a well-run network. We believe that the only place that you should put a user is into a group . . . even if the group never sees more than one member. Make this your number-one user-management rule: "Users live in groups. Period."

We can also use groups to create distribution lists (a new type of group). We can, for example, create a group, and every user in the group receives any e-mail sent to it. This is a boon for e-mail administrators.

Groups versus organizational units

Many now feel that the Group object has been rendered redundant by the OU. That may be the case if OUs were recognized by the security subsystem and the access-control mechanisms — that is, if they were security principals. But the Group object is a sophisticated management container that can bestow all manner of control over the user accounts and other groups that it contains.

What we believe is good about the group is that it can be used to contain a membership across organizational and multiple-domain boundaries. An organizational unit, on the other hand, belongs to a domain. Complex mergers and acquisitions, along with companies that are so dispersed that their only "geographical" boundary is between the earth and the moon, are excellent candidates that could use groups to contain memberships from the organizational units of their acquisitions or member companies and departments. Figure 13-3 shows one group called *Accounting* that can contain the department heads and key people from several Accounting departments throughout the enterprise.

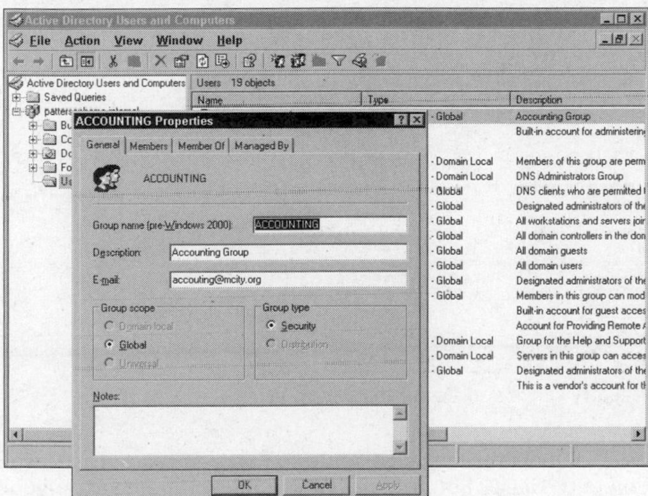

Figure 13-3: The Accounting group enables its members to access resources in the departments of several corporate domains in a forest.

What is a network from the viewpoint of users and groups?

A *network* has several definitions. From the perspective of users and containers of users, a network is a collection of resources (a collection of network objects as opposed to devices) that can be accessed for services. Users exploit network objects to assist them with their work. Network resources include messaging, printers, telecommunications, information retrieval, collaboration services, and more.

Administrators new to Windows Server 2003 should get familiar with the meaning of *Network object*, for it is used to reference or "obtain a handle" on any network component, both hard and soft.

Exploring the Users and Computers management tools

Windows Server 2003 ships with tools to manage local logon accounts and Active Directory accounts. These tools are *Users and Passwords* and *Local Users and Groups* on standalone machines (including workstations running Windows Server 2003 Professional) and member servers and *Active Directory Users and Computers* on domain controllers.

The *Active Directory Users and Computers* MMC snap-in is the primary tool used to create and manage users in network domains. It is launched by choosing Start ⇨ Administrative Tools ⇨ Active Directory Users and Computers. Figure 13-4 shows the Users and Computers snap-in. This snap-in is almost certain to become more sophisticated as the use of Active Directory increases.

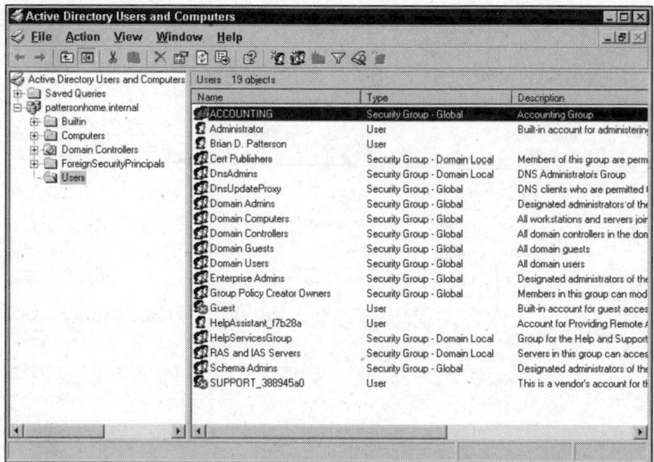

Figure 13-4: The Active Directory Users and Computers snap-in.

Run the snap-in. First, put the snap-in into advanced mode so that you can see all the menu options in the Users and Computers MMC library: Select any node in the tree and right-click it. Choose View ⇨ Advanced Features from the pop-up menu that appears. A check mark appears on this right-click context menu, meaning that the entire snap-in is in advanced mode, and you can access all menu options.

You may notice that you can also select the command above Advanced Features on the pop-up menu, the Users, Groups, and Computers as Containers menu command. But this may give you too much information to deal with in the learning phase. Select this feature after you know your way around this snap-in.

In the left pane, the snap-in loads the tree that represents the domain that you are managing. Notice that you can select a number of built-in folders, as the following list describes:

- ✦ The **Built-in** folder contains the built-in or default groups created as you installed Active Directory and promoted the server to a domain controller.
- ✦ The **Computer** folder contains any computers that are added to the domain that you are managing. It is empty if you have not added any computers to the domain at this stage.

- The **Domain Controllers** folder always contains at least one computer . . . the domain controller that you are currently working on.
- The **ForeignSecurityPrincipals** folder is the default container for *security identifiers* (*SIDs*) associated with objects from other trusted domains.
- The **Users** folder contains built-in user and group accounts. After you upgrade Windows 2000 Server to Windows Server 2003, all the user accounts from the old domain are placed into this folder. This folder is not an OU, and no OU group policy can be linked to it. For all intents and purposes, this folder should be blank or at least should not contain any accounts as you first do a clean install of Windows Server 2003 and promote it to Active Directory. Instead, the built-in accounts should have been placed in the Built-in folder, period. We guess that it is one of those things that the folks at Microsoft did without very much forethought. But they did provide the capability to move items from folder to folder, and moving all the built-in objects to the Built-in folder may make more sense to you . . . especially as you cannot delete them.
- The **LostAndFound** folder contains objects that have been orphaned.
- The **System** folder contains built-in system settings.

Now, before you proceed, know that understanding how user accounts work involves two levels. You can cover the basics of user accounts by poking around in the Active Directory User and Computers snap-in MMC panels, or you can make an effort to learn about the most important attributes of user accounts at a lower level. If you are a serious network and Windows administrator, we suggest the latter. Why?

First, as an administrator, knowing the stuff of which user accounts are made takes your management knowledge and skills to a higher level. You can contribute much more to the overall management of your enterprise network if you know how to perform advanced searches for users, scientifically manage passwords, better protect resources, troubleshoot, and so on. If you think administrators do not need to know how to program, think again; it could make a $20K difference, positively, on your salary package.

Second, senior administrators and corporate developers may need to circumvent the basic MMC panels and code directly to the Active Directory Service Interfaces (ADSI). On Windows 2000, senior administrators often created scripts that would block manipulate the accounts in the security accounts database. User Manager for Domains was often too dumb to be of use in major domain operations, such as changing the security privileges for a large number of users. Top Windows Server 2003 administrators need to know how to code to Active Directory and write scripts (which require basic programming knowledge) that make life easier and lessen the administrative burden. Knowing everything about User objects makes your services that much more in demand.

Windows Server 2003 user accounts

A Windows Server 2003 user account can be a *domain account* or a *local account.* As you first install any version of Windows Server 2003 or promote a server to a domain controller, a number of domain and local accounts are automatically created. If you install Active Directory on a server—that is, if you promote it to a domain controller—the local accounts are disabled.

Domain accounts

Domain accounts or network accounts are User account objects that are stored in Active Directory and that are exposed to the distributed Windows networking and security environment. Domain accounts are enterprise-wide. Humans, machines, and processes use domain accounts to log on to a network and gain access to its resources. Each logon attempt goes through a "security clearance," whereby the system compares the password provided by the user against the password stored in the Password Attribute field in the Active Directory. If the password matches the record, the user is cleared to proceed and use network resources, perform activities on computers, and communicate.

Remember that Active Directory is a "multimaster" directory service. This means that changes to users and groups are replicated to other member DCs (but not to a local account database). You can manage users on any DC on the network and not worry about locating a primary DC, as was the case in Windows NT 4.0 and earlier. User objects also contain certain attributes that are not replicated to other DCs. These attributes can be considered of interest only to the local domain controller. The attribute `LastLogon`, for example, is of interest only to the local network's domain controller; it is of no importance to the other domain controllers in the domain or the forest.

You can also create a user account in any part of the AD . . . as long as you have rights to create or manage that User object. Although container objects such as OUs and groups serve to assist in the management of collections of users, you have no mechanism other than admin rights to prevent a user account from being created anywhere in a forest.

Local accounts

Local accounts (users) are identical to network accounts in every way, but they are not stored in Active Directory. Local accounts are machine-specific objects. In other words, a local user account can be validated only against a local security database — the *SAM* or *Security Account Manager*. Second, local accounts provide access only to resources within the "boundaries" of the machine "domain" and no further. An analogy may be that the key to your house only enables you to enter your house. All other houses in your neighborhood are off-limits.

If you are new to Windows networking, you may be wondering why machines on a Windows Server 2003 network would have local accounts. As you know, you can create a network of machines and not manage it by using Active Directory at all, which would certainly send your cost of ownership soaring. But good reasons why these accounts are better off on the local machine rather than sitting in Active Directory also exist. Active Directory users can "connect" to local machines from remote services (such as to the local FTP account), which is achieved by virtue of having the "right" to log on locally at the target machine. Local user accounts can also exist on machines that are part of Active Directory domains and that are not the domain controllers. You can also make a domain controller an application server for a small business and enable a number of users to log on locally to the DC by way of terminal sessions.

Local user accounts are restricted to the Access Control List of the local computer. The local domain itself does not replicate this information off the local machine because it matters only to the local account system, which is not distributed.

The tools to manage the local machine's native domain can be accessed through the Users and Passwords and Administrative Tools applications in Control Panel.

Predefined accounts

After you install Windows Server 2003, as either a standalone or member server or as a domain controller supporting Active Directory, the operating system establishes default accounts. On a standalone machine (server or workstation), the default accounts are local to the machine native domain and established in the SAM. On a domain controller — in Active Directory — the default accounts are network accounts. Built-in accounts cannot be deleted, but they can be renamed or moved from one container to another.

The default accounts include administration accounts that enable you to log on and manage the network or the local machine. Windows Server 2003 also installs built-in machine or Guest accounts and anonymous Internet user accounts. You may notice that these so-called accounts are disabled by default and must be implicitly enabled.

A good idea, as soon as it's feasible, is to rename the Administrator account to hide its purpose and thus its access and security level. (Hiding was not possible on Windows NT but was added to Windows 2000.) If you have security fears, you can audit the activity of the Administrator to determine who or what is using the account and when.

If you demote a domain controller (DC) to a standalone server, and especially if it is the last DC on the network, the OS prompts you for the password to use for the local Administrator account. In the process of stripping away AD and its administrator accounts, the OS ensures that you can log on locally and gain access to the machine after the conversion. As AD departs from the server, it hands control of the machine back to the machine-specific domain and Security Account Manager (SAM).

Administrator account

The Administrator account is the first user account created after you install Windows Server 2003, regardless of which version of Windows Server 2003 you are installing. The Administrator account is created in both the local SAM and in Active Directory.

The Administrator is the CEO on Windows Server 2003 and all earlier versions. By logging on as the Administrator, you get total access to the entire system and network. Without the power of this built-in user, setting up the first objects would be impossible.

The Administrator account is dangerous, however. Over time, the password to this account gets handed around, and your network goes to hell. We have even seen situations where the Administrator's account password finds its way around the world in large corporations, even enabling users in foreign domains to mess things up without the key MIS people at HQ finding out. In one situation, it ended up in the hands of a subcontractor who managed to bring an office to a standstill for a week.

So how do you protect this account from abuse? For starters, you cannot delete or disable the account because then getting locked out of the system or falling victim to a denial-of-service (DoS) attack would be all too easy.

But you can rename this account, which presents an opportunity to conceal the Administrator's true identity and lock down access to it. Recording the Administrator password in a document and then locking it away in a secure place before new (flesh and blood) administrators are added to the domain then makes common sense. To do so, follow these steps:

1. Rename the Administrator account. Remember to provide a UPN and rename the down-level or NETBIOS name as well, because renaming merely changes the hidden attribute and label.
2. Create a new user as a decoy Administrator and endow it with administrator power by assigning the account to the Administrators group. Or leave the account with no powers of administration.
3. Appoint the Administrator (which can be under the new name) account as the manager of this account. This is done on the Organization tab of the User Manager, in the Manager field.
4. Cease using the real Administrator and lock away the password.

You would now be correct in saying, "But that still does not stop someone from getting hold of one of the other administrator accounts and abusing it." But now you have accounts that can be monitored, audited, disabled, and deleted if they become a security risk. And deleting and recreating administrators at certain intervals may pay off in certain circumstances.

To rename the Administrator account, you need to first give an Administrator account the "right to rename the Administrator account." This right is granted by Group Policy, which is discussed in Chapter 14. After you have renamed the real Administrator, you can create a decoy Administrator account.

Another wise move is to move the Administrator and administrator type accounts out of the Users folder. We give you this advice for several reasons, as the following list describes:

✦ Anyone looking for the Administrator is sure to go there first, and denying access to this folder may be impractical.

✦ The security policy governing the Users folder is inherited from the root domain. This means that, if for any reason the default or root domain policy changes, it may affect the account without you being aware of the event.

✦ The Administrator accounts are better grouped in the main IS OU, where access is controlled by specific OU policy, focused management, and delegated responsibility.

To move the Administrator account, follow these steps:

1. Open Active Directory Users and Computers. Double-click the Users folder.
2. Select the Administrator account in the right-hand pane and right-click it. Now choose Move from the pop-up menu. The list of folders and OUs appears.
3. Drill down to a different OU of your choice. Select that OU and click OK. The Administrator account is now moved to the new OU.

Another means of protecting the network and the Administrator account and a sophisticated means of management and troubleshooting is to use the *RunAs* service. Also known as the *secondary login*, it enables a user who is logged on with his regular user account to perform functions with the privileges of another account—typically, an administrator's. RunAs is demonstrated in the section "Getting familiar with RunAs," later in this chapter, where we discuss the configuration of user accounts.

Guest account

The Guest account is the second of the default accounts that are prebuilt as you install Windows Server 2003 the first time and after you create a domain controller and install Active Directory. The account is useful for guests and visitors who either do not have accounts on any domain in the forest or whose accounts may be disabled.

The Guest account does not require a password, and you can grant it certain access and rights to resources on the computer. (See the section "Rights and Permissions," later in this chapter, for details.) We believe that the Guest account on any domain should be relocated to an OU with a security and account policy that is appropriate for managing security risks. You can leave the Guest account in the Users folder (which is a domain folder and not an OU), but the security policy governing that account in the Users folder is inherited from the root domain. So if for any reason the default or root domain policy changes, it affects the Guest account without you being conscious of the event. The Guest account is also automatically placed into the Guest group, which you may want to also place in the Visitors OU. You can move the Guest account by using Active Directory Users and Computers. In our Millennium City network, we've moved the Guest account to the City Hall-Visitors OU.

In the User folder, the Guest account is granted the right to log on locally to a local computer or member server. In the City Hall-Visitors OU, you can grant specific access to the domain resources, such as e-mail, access to printers and devices, and so on. You can also create several Visitor accounts for accounting and auditing purposes and to keep track of the objects that each visitor accesses.

By using logon scripts and profiles, you can track activity between each logon and logoff period and use that to generate reports. From these reports, you can run invoices, statements, bills, and so on. If you run a service bureau, this is the direction that you should be considering.

Some organizations do not believe in Guest or Visitor accounts and keep these disabled from the get-go. If you disable the Guest account, you are denying anyone who does not have an account from logging on. In highly secure environments, this policy may be valid. And this was, and still is, the case in many Windows NT domains that do not provide for the additional protection of the OU security policy. But these accounts can be handy even in sensitive environments. Consider the following before taking the easy way out and disabling the account:

- ✦ By using a Guest account, a new user awaiting a user account can get some work done on a computer. Such users can, for example, begin reading company policy or the employee handbook, and they can fill in employee forms and so on.
- ✦ By using a Guest account, a user who has been locked out for whatever reason can at least log on to the domain and gain access to the company intranet and local resources. Say that you have an intranet Web site that enables the user to access the help desk and open a ticket; then a user who cannot log onto the domain can still generate a ticket for an account lockout problem. Lockouts can and do happen often.
- ✦ An employee suspected of a misdeed can be asked to log on to a Guest account while the reason for an account lockout is being investigated. This may help diffuse a situation that has the potential of becoming tense. The user's account can also be transferred out of his usual OU to the Visitors OU or a holding OU. This gives the user the impression that he can log on to the domain, but certain access rights have been removed.

The Internet user account

Windows Server 2003 also provides default or built-in accounts for anonymous access to IIS. Such accounts can be manipulated, but doing so is strongly discouraged because the default settings are generally sufficient for IIS.

Account policy

Before you go creating users, you must first take the time to fully understand how account policy on Windows Server 2003 affects account creation and management on an account-by-account basis.

The Windows *Group Policy* technology (which also includes account and security policy) governs how all accounts can be configured on both standalone servers and in the Active Directory. If you create users from the get-go, the accounts are set up with the default account policy attributes. They remain this way until Active Directory site, domain, or OU policies override this (which occurs whenever a domain controller and Active Directory is installed and sites, domains, and OUs are created).

What you should be aware of here, especially if you have been given certain responsibility to create an account and set up a computer, is the order of precedence for security and account policies. The order of precedence, from the highest to the lowest, is as follows:

- Site policy
- Domain policy
- OU policy
- Local policy

The local policy governs the local accounts that you set up on the computer itself, in its native or machine-specific domain. But the local policy is overridden by the policies of higher precedence, unless you take the steps to avert that behavior.

Security principals and the logon authentication process

The onus of "good behavior" rests on the shoulders of User and Group objects in Windows Server 2003. As mentioned earlier in this chapter, these objects have the total trust of the OS on first being installed. They are often referred to as *security principals* and *trustees.* Every other object that is not a security principal or that does not exist in AD within a security context is rejected by the security subsystem and thus cannot present for rights and access. The Contact object is a good example of an object that is not a security principal. You may create other nonsecurity objects and register them in Active Directory.

Several security principals are defined to the security subsystem by default. These include groups such as Domain Users, Domain Admins, and so on.

If a user attempts to log on to Windows Server 2003 by way of the AD or the Local Security Authority (LSA), the security system checks to determine whether the user exists and whether the password provided matches the password stored in the relevant database. If the user is authenticated, Windows Server 2003 creates an *access token* for the user.

If the domain controller does not receive the correct password or the user account is unknown, the user is gracefully returned to the logon dialog box. But after a user is authenticated, Windows then proceeds to activate whatever rights and permissions the user has on the network.

The process that Windows Server 2003 uses to "follow" the user through the domain is known as *access token assignment.* In other words, the access token is assigned to the user for the duration of the logon and acts as a security tag that a user wears in "roaming" from computer to computer and from resource to resource. User account information is replicated to all domain controllers in the enterprise, even across slow WAN links.

Security identifiers

The *security identifier* (*SID*) is a unique value of variable length that is used to identify an account (known as a *trustee* to the kernel) to the security subsystem. Windows refers to the SID rather than to the user or group name in referencing these objects for security purposes. The SID is not the same thing as the *object identifier*, or *OID*. SIDs guarantee that the account and all its associated rights and permissions are unique. If you delete an account and then recreate it under the same name, you find that all rights and permissions of the deceased account are gone. This is because the old SID was deleted with the original account.

As you create an account, the system also creates the SID and stores it in the security structures of AD or the SAM. The first part of the SID identifies the domain in which the SID was created. The second part is called the *relative ID* (*RID*), and that refers to the actual object created (which is thus relative to the domain).

Whenever a user logs onto the computer or domain, the SID is retrieved from the database and placed in the user's access token. From the moment of logon, the SID is used in the access token to identify the user in all security-related actions and interactions.

Windows NT, Windows 2000, and Windows Server 2003 use the SID for the following purposes:

- ✦ To identify the object's owner.
- ✦ To identify the object owner's group.
- ✦ To identify the account user in access related activity.

Special well-known SIDs are also created by the system during installation to identify the built-in users and groups. If a user logs on to the system as Guest, the access token for that user includes the well-known SID for the Guest group, which restricts the user from doing damage or accessing objects they are not entitled to.

SAM and LSA authentication

The Windows Server 2003 SAM is inherited from the Windows 2000 SAM and works the same. It no longer, however, plays a part in network domain management. Standalone and member servers use the Windows Server 2003 SAM to authenticate or validate users that have local accounts, including autonomous processes. The SAM is still buried in the registry and plays an important role in Windows Server 2003, and it is an integral part of the Local Security Authority (LSA). LSA authentication exists for the following several reasons:

- ✦ To process local logon requests.
- ✦ To enable ISVs and customers with special requirements to use the LSA to gain local authentication services. An access control application may use the LSA to validate holders of magnetic access control cards and so on.

- To provide special local access to devices. For a device to be installed and gain access to system resources, it may need to be authenticated by the LSA. Such an example is a tape-backup device driver, which may need to gain access to a local database management system or to machine-protected processes that require it to be logged on locally.
- To provide heterogeneous local authentication. Not everyone can take advantage of the Active Directory authentication and logon process, and not everyone wants to. The LSA thus provides these "users" (processes) with a local logon facility that they were accustomed to, or built for, on Windows NT 4.0 and earlier.

As you set up a standalone server, Windows creates default or *built-in* accounts. These are actually created in a local Windows 4.0-type domain stored in the local SAM. The two local domains created are `Account` and `Builtin`.

As you first install Windows Server 2003, these local domain systems are named after the NETBIOS-type name of the machine. If you change the machine's name, the domain name is changed to the new machine name the next time that you restart the server. In other words, if you set up a standalone server named LONELY1, a local domain named `LONELY1` is created in the local SAM. The OS then creates the built-in accounts for this domain. Later, you can create any local user in the local legacy domain. Services also use the local domain for system accounts.

Active Directory includes a SAM service provider that enables Windows Server 2003 domain controllers to interoperate with NT 4.0 domain controllers. Such service providers also exist for other directory services, such as Novell NDS.

User Accounts in Action

A user account is like a bank account. Without a bank account, you have no way to access the services of a bank, store money, pay bills, take out loans, and manage your financial affairs. If a user comes to work and cannot log on, the scene that ensues is like that for a bank account that has been closed unexpectedly.

Getting familiar with RunAs

Before you proceed with account creation and management, you should take some time to understand the *RunAs* application and service. It is invaluable to you in your administration endeavors, especially for troubleshooting account problems.

RunAs is also known as *secondary* or *alternate logon*.

RunAs enables you to execute applications, access resources, or load an environment or profile and so on by using the credentials of another user account, without needing to log off from the account that you initially logged onto your computer with. RunAs is a nongraphical executable that resides in the `%System%\System32` folder of your server or workstation. It is also a service that can be accessed from various locations in the operating system. You can link to it from the desktop or create scripts and applications that make use of its services. You can also create a shortcut to an application and enable it to be executed by using the credentials of any another user account (provided that you have the password to the other account).

RunAs essentially enables you to operate an environment or application in the security context of another user account, while remaining in your current security context or in your current logged-on state. The simplest, but very useful, feature of RunAs enables you to test a logon name and account password without needing to log off from your workstation. Perhaps the best way to describe RunAs usage is to provide a simple example.

Create a shortcut to the Command Console on the desktop and enable it to be used to test a User ID and password, as follows:

1. Create a shortcut to the command prompt on your desktop.
2. Right-click the shortcut and choose Properties from the pop-up menu. On the Shortcut tab of the Properties dialog box that appears, select the Run as Different User check box.
3. Click OK.

You now notice that, whenever you right-click the shortcut, the Run As line is added to the context menu in bold type. But you can just double-click the shortcut icon and the Run As Other User dialog box appears. You can then enter your user's account, domain, and password.

If you investigate RunAs further, you discover that you can test alternative logons and troubleshoot problems such as access to shares, printers, and so on. You can log on and switch to the environment provided by the alternative account, and you can enable users to run an application in the context of another account.

Naming user accounts

You can make your life as a user administrator more enjoyable if you follow the recommended convention for naming user accounts. You can and should plan your user namespace carefully, publish the rules and policy surrounding the chosen convention, and stick to it. Nothing is worse than inheriting a directory of accounts where no naming convention exists.

To set up your naming convention checklist, consider the following:

✦ User account names must be unique in the domain where the accounts are created. You cannot, for example, have two names set up as `mcity\john samuels` or `johns@mcity.org`. One must become `johns1@mcity.org`. You can, however, create an account with the same UPN prefix in another domain — for example, `johns@mcity.mcpd.org` or `mcpd\johns`.

✦ The user account prefix can contain a maximum of 20 characters in any case. The logon process is not sensitive to the case. The field, however, preserves the case, enabling you to assist in naming convention, such as `JohnS` as opposed to `johns`.

✦ The following characters are not permissible in the account name: " < > ? * / \ | ; : = , + [ ].

✦ You can use letters and dashes or underscores in the name to assist with convention, but remember that account names may be used as e-mail addresses. Follow the suggestions in the UPN naming conventions, described in the section "User Principal Name," later in this chapter.

Passwords

Accounts do not always need to have passwords, this is controlled by Group Policy. Many administrators use the method of combining initials and numbers for passwords and keep them consistent throughout the enterprise.

To set up your password convention checklist, consider the following:

- ✦ The passwords can be up to 128 characters in length. That does not mean that Microsoft expects you to saddle your users with a password that takes all day to input. But smart cards and noninteractive logon devices can use a field of that length.
- ✦ Do not create passwords that contain fewer than five characters; a minimum of eight is recommended.
- ✦ The following characters are not permissible in the password: " < > ? * / \ | ; : = , + [ ].

Password management is a nightmare for everyone. Most administrators we know keep lists of passwords in various database files and help desks because users often find themselves locked out of domains and resources for "no apparent reason." To troubleshoot and assist the user, we often need to log on to that user's account and "experience" what may be going wrong. Many administrators troubleshoot this way; being in the user's context helps in troubleshooting. The new RunAs service that we describe in the section "Getting familiar with RunAs," earlier in this chapter, is a useful tool for managing user accounts and troubleshooting passwords.

The password issuance and management-style questions are similar from platform to platform, especially from NetWare to Windows NT and Windows Server 2003. In giving users passwords, you have the following three choices that can be adapted and become policy:

- ✦ Assign the passwords.
- ✦ Enable the user to choose the password.
- ✦ Assign passwords to certain users; enable others to set their own.

All three choices have their pros and cons, and every company has a reason for going with one option or the other.

If you go with the first option, you must either adopt a password-naming scheme that lends itself to easy recollection by administrators (as secure as an open field) or enter the users' passwords in a secure database.

The former is not really secure because figuring out the scheme that the administrators are using would not take much effort. A popular password-forming approach is to join the users' initials and parts of their social security numbers, driver's licenses, or some other form of number that society issues—for example, *jrs0934*. This scheme has been in place at several companies where we worked. In that several thousand accounts were set up under the scheme, changing it has been a nightmare.

The second approach, enabling users to select their own passwords, is more secure but fraught with danger. First, users who have lots of sensitive stuff on their machines and in their folders often assign weak passwords that can easily be cracked. We have found users choosing *12345678* and giving us the excuse that they were going to change it later . . . three months later.

Second, enabling users to choose their own passwords can be nightmarish on corporate networks. In troubleshooting problems, administrators often need to ask for the passwords over the telephone (for all to hear) and in e-mail. And then come the occasions where you must reset the password anyway because the owner is either not present or Windows Server 2003 rejects the password.

We believe that the best policy is to go with the third choice: Assign a password for most corporate users and enable selected users (who demand the security and who can justify it) to set their own passwords. The latter users fall into groups that have access to company financial information, bank account numbers, credit card numbers, personnel records, and so on. Paranoid executives fall into the latter group as well.

Generate secure passwords (as opposed to obvious acronyms). Record the password in a secure place: either a database management system that is hard to crack, such as an encrypted Microsoft Access database file, or in an SQL server table. The one weakness of this option is giving new users their passwords. Often, the password ends up going through several hands before ending up at the user. You could create a temporary password assignment scheme.

You may also try your hand at adding a field to the Active Directory User object that displays the password in plain text. (The schema is there to be extended.) You can secure the objects in the AD so that only certain administrators have access to the field. You would also need to create a GUI to read the field, because the Account tab on the User Properties dialog box is off limits to such wild ideas.

Protecting passwords is more important under Windows Server 2003 than under Windows NT—or any other OS, for that matter. The reason is the Single Sign-On initiative (SSO) and the Kerberos ticket-granting service discussed in Chapter 3. On older OSs, you need new user IDs and passwords for just about any service, such as voice mail, fax mail, SQL Server, Internet access, and so on. As more applications support the SSO, one password eventually suffices for all. But this is a double-edged sword. If the password or access falls into mischievous hands, the culprit has access to everything authenticated in the SSO process.

Understanding logon

We have discussed the concept of local logon in various places, but this is a right and not an automatic privilege. For a user to connect to the machine standing next to him or to a remote machine across the network, he needs authority in the following two places:

- ✦ The domain that the user is a member of must enable the user to request logon permission from a machine. The default is to enable the user to request logon from any machine, which means the target machine's SAM gets to say yes or no and not the domain.
- ✦ The target machine must give the account the right to log on locally.

Unless the target machine has special software on it that requires local logon and authentication, providing access to resources on remote machines via domain groups makes more sense.

Granting remote access

Remote-access privileges are the most sought-after rights in any organization. By being given access to Remote Access Services (RAS), users may be permitted to telecommute, work from home, or access the network and servers from the road. Road warriors also give you the most headaches because remote policy is by its very nature governed by more stringent security requirements.

In setting up groups, creating remote user groups in specific OUs may also pay. You are certain to run into problems putting every remote user into an enterprise-wide remote-user group. Users who are restricted at certain levels as they work on the premises often find life more open and accessible in connecting from home. And users who have a wide berth in the office may find life claustrophobic on the outside.

Creating a user account

In the example in this section, we're creating user accounts for the Driver Compensation Program (DCP) in Millennium City. They exist in the DCP OU, which resides in the `CITYHALL` domain.

Select the domain, right-click the DCP OU that you created earlier in this chapter, and choose New ➪ User from the pop-up menu. The New Object - User dialog box opens, as shown in Figure 13-5. The most important information that you need here is the old SAM account name of the user who is connecting or a new NetBIOS name. This is the name that the user used or still uses to log on to the legacy NT domain. It is not the name of the machine that is connecting. Remember that this is a NetBIOS name; it must contain fewer than 20 characters, and you need to watch for the illegal characters discussed earlier in this chapter.

You can create a new user account anywhere in the domain and later move it as needed.

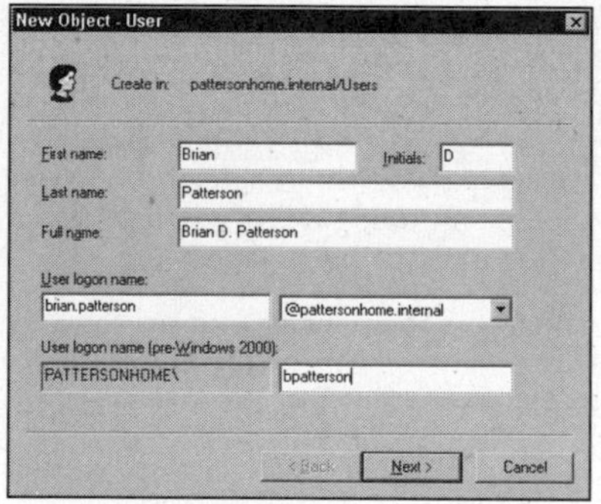

Figure 13-5: The New Object - User dialog box.

The User Principal Name

In the beginning, on legacy NT, you had little flexibility with logon names. You would typically use contractions of first and last names, such as *jshapiro* or *jeffreys*, or names typically assigned to people serving 25 years to life, such as *psjrs08676*.

Now, everything is different. The user's logon name and e-mail addresses are the same. Good reasons exist to do this. First, this change supports the SSO initiative, better known as Single Sign-On. As long as the resources that the user needs access to support TCP/IP, RFC 822 naming, and Kerberos authentication, the user ID or the resulting authentication certificates can be relayed to these technologies. Second, the UPN enables you to use an e-mail address to log on to the domain from anywhere on the Internet. As long as the domain controller is exposed to the Internet or the packets find the DC through a firewall, logging on and accessing resources is possible.

If you can resolve CITYHALL.GENESIS.MCITY.ORG on the Internet, you can log in. The prefix part of the UPN provides the so-called user ID, while the suffix identifies the domain.

So, given that life would be easier if your users' logon IDs and e-mail addresses were the same, you have some serious restructuring to do. Perhaps the best place to start is at your e-mail server. Here, all the accounts are set up with UPNs already. And if you have been running an Exchange server, all the better. Simply dump all the names into a comma-separated file (.csv) and use these as the basis for your UPNs.

Using first and last names as a UPN is a good idea. RFC 822 requires that you separate the elements of the UPN with acceptable characters. Obviously, the @ sign is not acceptable, nor is the & (ampersand). Simple dot notation works the best: user.name@adomain.com or jeffrey.shapiro@mcity.org.

Figure 13-5 shows you the two logon types that can be used, the UPN (brian.patterson) and the down-level NetBIOS name (bpatterson). In the first one, the user enters the prefix part of the UPN as the user ID and the suffix as the domain name. This may be less comfortable for people accustomed to logging on to Windows NT domains or NetWare.

If you are not yet ready to move users to Windows Server 2003 but plan to in the near future, now is the time to start preparing for UPNs. If your e-mail server accounts do not make attractive UPNs (such as zp-badboy5.shapiroj@wierdestofcorps.com), for example, now is the time to change them. You seldom if ever need to type your e-mail address every time that you send a message, but you do need to type at least the prefix every time that you log on to Windows Server 2003. Try keeping the UPNs as short as possible without turning everyone's name into an acronym. Using jshapiro, for example works better than jeffrey.shapiro, which is better than js. Anyone who ends up with a UPN of more than, say, eight letters may never want to log in again.

Before you add the name, you need to check that the UPN that you entered as you created the account conforms to the standards that you have set for your network. This double-checking exercise is worthwhile here because, many times, the UPN must be entered after the account is created. If you copy an account, the UPN field must be updated. Remember that the UPN conforms to the Internet standard e-mail address governed by RFC 822, such as jeffrey.shapiro@mcity.org or jeffreys@mcity.org.

Click Next to fill in the password in the next dialog box, as shown in Figure 13-6. Click Finish after you're done. That's all that creating a user involves. Next, you need to set the properties for the user.

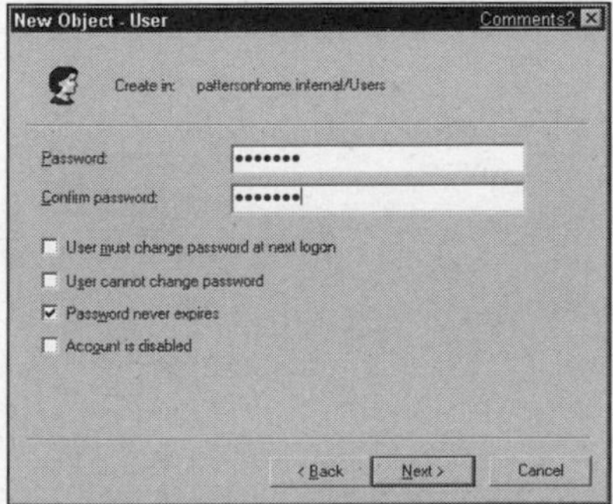

Figure 13-6: Adding the password to the New Object - User dialog box.

Setting properties

After the account is created, you need to set the properties to define the user's rights and privileges, access to resources, contact information, and so on. To access the property sheets of the user account object, simply double-click the account in Active Directory or right-click it and choose Properties from the context menu. In this example, you double-click Brian D. Patterson, and Brian's Properties dialog box loads, as shown in Figure 13-7.

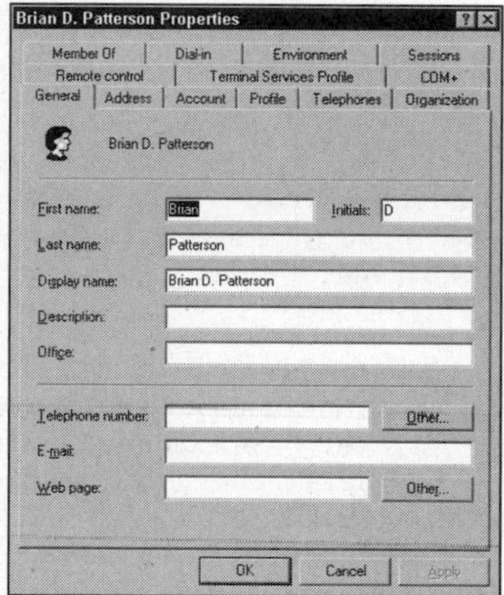

Figure 13-7: The user's Properties dialog box.

The Properties dialog box for the user has a lot of tabs that you can use to configure the User object and populate it with information. Many of the tabs are self-explanatory, so the following sections do not describe them all but only the ones that you need to set in creating a new user account.

Account tab properties

The options on the Account tab are security options, and they need to be managed carefully. If you've used the Windows 2000 User Manager application, you may recognize many of the following options:

✦ **Account Expires:** Set this option to Never to indicate that the account never expires. Set one of the other options, X and Y, if you want the account to exist for only a certain period of time. Locking a person out at some future date is valuable for applications services and for temps and subcontractors, who are classified a security risk at some future date.

✦ **Home Folder:** This should be a directory on a file server somewhere. After the user logs in, his home directory is immediately accessible. You can set this path to a folder on the user's local machine. In this case, you want to set the path to a share on the SQL Server 2003 machine so that the user has immediate access to data-entry tools on that server.

✦ **First, Last, and Initial:** After you enter the First, Last, and Initials, the display name is formed automatically. You can also change the display name to suit a company standard or policy. You want to leave the display name as is for the current example — that way, wherever users of `CITYHALL` are logged on, you can spot them immediately in open file lists, connection lists, owners, and so on.

- **Description:** This information can describe the purpose of the account, or it can be information that better identifies it. The bigger the network, the more important filling in this field is. In this case, you insert DCP Entry Team Leader to describe the purpose of the account.
- **Office:** Enter the user's physical office address.
- **Telephone Number:** Enter the user's telephone number and extension, if any.
- **E-mail:** Enter the user's e-mail address. For this field to default to the UPN may seem intuitive, but it doesn't. The field is also not e-mail format-sensitive, however, so if an SMTP format is out, you can enter a `cc:Mail` address, an X:400 address, or something else. Keeping the entries here consistent is important because access to this field is open via the ADSI, and the field is no doubt a key repository of information for many people-tracking tools, ERP apps, communications applications, and more. At the time of this writing, we don't know what e-mail applications may be using this field, but it is available to access.
- **Web Page:** Enter the user's home page, if applicable. The idea of this field may be foggy at first, because why would you have all your users worry about home pages? These fields can be used for other applications, however, such as an ISP with user accounts that "rent" homepages. If you are an ISP, you can set up user accounts in the directory to manage access and accounting from the directory. The field is a string data type, so an IP address is feasible here, too.
- **Address:** On the Address tab, enter the user's address.
- **Logon To:** This is the path of the workstation or server to which the users can log in. For an administrator, leave this at the default. If the employee is new or questionable, we would restrict him to the department's machine and lock the person out of the other MIS machines. For the sake of demonstration, Figure 13-8 shows this restriction in force. This restriction applies to all member machines and not just to workstations, as it may suggest. By not setting any values in this dialog box, you give the user access to all machines on the network.

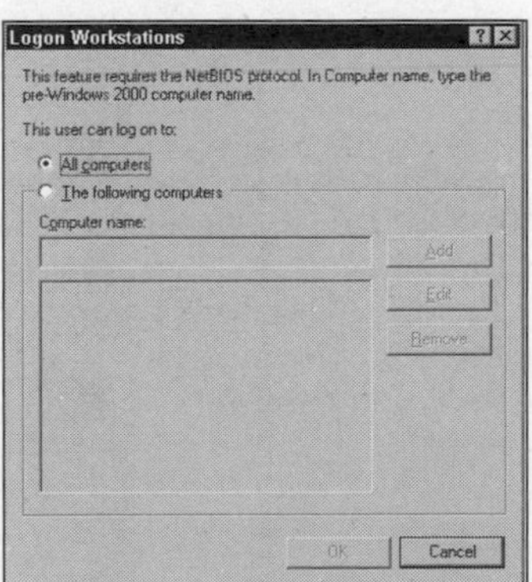

Figure 13-8: Logon restrictions.

By forcing the users to log on to their own workstations, you are by omission barring them from logging on locally to any other machines. Of course, you can restrict the local logon at the target machine.

✦ **Account Options:** This is where you set password policies. To comply with the Millennium City password policy, select the User Cannot Change Password and Password Never Expires check boxes. Choose a secure password for the user.

More account options

The Account Options section on the Account tab determines how users and computers are authenticated on the network. The following options are self-explanatory:

✦ **User Must Change Password at Next Logon.**

✦ **User Cannot Change Password.**

✦ **Password Never Expires.**

✦ **Store Password Using Reversible Encryption.** Use this option if the user is authenticating from an Apple computer.

✦ **Account is Disabled.** Select this option to prevent the user from authenticating.

✦ **Smart Card Is Required for Interactive Logon.** This option requires that the user have a card reader attached to his machine before he can log on.

✦ **Account Is Trusted for Delegation.** This option enables the user of this account to delegate administrative function in the domain tree to others.

✦ **Account Is Sensitive and Cannot Be Delegated.** This option negates the option of enabling the user to delegate.

✦ **Use DES Encryption Types for this Account.** DES supports multiple levels of encryption, including MPPE Standard (40-bit), MPPE Standard (56-bit), MPPE Strong (128-bit), IPSec DES (40-bit), IPSec 56-bit DES, and IPSec Triple DES (3DES). See Chapter 3 for further information on DES and security.

✦ **Do Not Require Kerberos Pre-Authentication.** Refer to Chapter 3 for more information on Kerberos.

Logon hours

The Logon Hours controls, as shown in Figure 13-9, are available from the Account tab. By default, logon time is set to always, meaning that users can log in whenever they want, but you may want to restrict this for several reasons. `MCITY` is set up to deny access to the domain controllers every Saturday night for about 12 hours. This is the time, once a week, when we power down the servers and perform maintenance. You may have a tighter security arrangement, for example, that only permits logon during working hours.

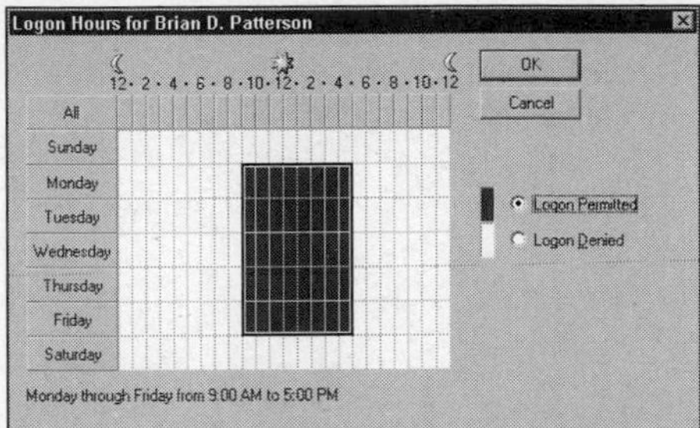

Figure 13-9: The Logon Hours controls.

To set logon hours, follow these steps:

1. On the Properties dialog box, select the Account tab and click the Logon Hours button. The Logon Hours dialog box opens.
2. To enable a user to log on at certain hours, click the rectangle on the days and hours for which you want to deny or permit a user logon time. The blue boxes denote logon times permitted, while the white boxes denote logon times that are denied. By default, the entire box is blue, indicating that logon is permitted all the time.
3. After you click OK and close the dialog box, the logon hours are saved.

Profile tab properties

The Profile tab contains a User Profile group box and a Home Folder group box. The User Profile fields enable you to enter information that determines the resources that a user connects to as soon as the user authenticates to the domain. You can also enter logon script information, if applicable. The Home Folder fields enable you to enter the path to the user's personal folder, which can be a folder used by a group as well. This folder can also be redirected according to Group Policy. The following list describes:

- **Profile Path:** Enter the user's profile path here. In the case of the current example, it's `\\mcdc01\profiles\amartinez`.
- **Logon Script:** If you're using logon scripts for your users, enter the appropriate file name here. For the current example, you enter `\\mcdc01\profiles\eredmond\eredmond.scr`.
- **Local Path:** Enter the path to the folder on a network server or workstation. It can be to a local folder as well, and you can just leave this field blank to default to the default local folder on the user's local hard disk. (Get used to entering information here, especially if you are going to set up resources for terminal users. Remember that terminal users' local paths are the servers that they sign onto by default, and if you redirect users to any of a number of servers, you need to define Home Folders.)
- **Connect:** This information enables you to map a drive letter to the Home Folder path.

Organization tab properties

The Organization tab enables you to provide information about the user's organization, title, and superiors. Remember that this account information is entered into a directory, which is used by people researching information related to users. The options available on this tab are as follows:

✦ **Title:** This is the user's title — for example, VP or CEO.

✦ **Department:** This is where the user works.

✦ **Company:** This is the name of the company.

✦ **Manager:** This is the user account of the individual who manages this user or account.

✦ **Direct Reports:** This is a list of users who directly report to this user account (information supplied in the Manager field in other accounts appear in this list).

Member Of tab properties

This tab enables you to add the user to a group on this domain or in groups in other domains in the forest. Enter the names of groups that the user is required to be a member of. This is done by clicking the Add button and selecting the groups from a domain that appears in the Select Groups list.

Dial-in tab properties

This tab enables you to give the user dial-in (RAS) privileges, authentication options, and IP addressing options.

Renaming user accounts

Windows Server 2003 enables you to rename user accounts because the SID remains the same. All you are doing is changing the values of certain attributes in the object. To rename a user account, you can either right-click the account in Active Directory Users and Computers and choose Rename from the pop-up menu or click the entry once. After you single-click it, the entry can be renamed in the same manner as you can rename any other object name in Windows Server 2003, such as a file or a folder name.

Whenever you rename an account, you are changing only the name property as you see it in the AD list. This is very different behavior from legacy NT account management, where the username and account name were the same thing. Changing the account name does not change the logon name (UPN) or the legacy NetBIOS name.

Deleting and disabling user accounts

Common sense tells you not to delete accounts willy-nilly. After the account is deleted, you can never get it back. The SID can be tracked, but it can never be resurrected. You have no undelete feature, and the account and SID are lost forever as active objects. If you want to render an account unusable, disable it. If you are an experienced administrator of Windows NT, this practice is not new to you, and disabling an account in Active Directory is easy. Just select the account in Active Directory Users and Computers and right-click. Choose Disable Account from the pop-up menu.

You can consider adopting a policy to delete any disabled account within a certain time frame — say, six months. Unless you have a very good reason to delete the account, however, leave it disabled indefinitely. Deleted accounts are like zombies. They return from their graves to haunt you. Often, temps leave the company, only to return six months later to perform similar duties, and needing to recreate the same account all over again, with the same access rights and permissions, group memberships, and so on, is an exercise in futility.

Copying accounts

Copying accounts is a no-brainer. Simply right-click the account that you want to copy and choose Copy from the pop-up menu. Copying accounts may not save you a lot of time if you have a lot of accounts to create. You may be better off using a script or special program, especially if many of the account attributes for each user are different.

Consider having new employees fill in a form in a database or on the intranet. Then parse the form and use the values to create the user account in a script.

Computer Accounts

A *computer account* is also a security principal, a direct descendant of the User object. For a computer to participate in a Windows network, whether Windows Server 2003 or NT 4.0, it must be capable of logging on securely to a domain in some manner. Windows 2003 adds additional security and control over the computer by requiring it to have an account — just as a user does.

Whenever you join a computer to a domain, you create an account for the computer, and Windows generates a SID. The procedure is identical to that of creating human user accounts.

The first computers that you add to a Windows Server 2003 domain are the domain controllers. These servers are the domain security outposts. You cannot create a Windows Server 2003 domain without first “raising” a domain controller. The act of promoting a machine to domain-controller service demotes any authority the local SAM had. Directory services are created, and full domain security is located in Active Directory.

After you add the first member server, standalone server, or Windows 2003 Professional workstation to the domain, Windows establishes two new groups to assist with machine management: the Domain Admins Group and the Domain Users Group.

Creating a computer account is simpler than creating the User account. You need only to select the OU in which you want to place the computer and choose New ➪ Computer from the snap-in’s menu bar. Obviously, you need authority to create the account. By placing the computer into an OU, you place it under the influence of Group Policy.

Group Accounts

Group management in Windows Server 2003 is a vast improvement over legacy NT group management. The group’s role as an administrator-appointed mustering or container tool has been replaced by the OU, which means that administrators can create and use groups more scientifically, now that its only purpose as a security principal is to provide and control access to computer and network resources.

A group is nothing more than a container for managing user accounts. The most important role of a group, however, is that you can assign permissions to it rather than needing to grant permissions to individual users. You rarely need to create a user who is so peculiar to an organization that he has rights and access to resources that no one else has. Even the Administrator account, of which you have only one, is placed into several groups to gain access to sensitive resources and information.

Windows 2003 groups come in two flavors, *security group* and *distribution group*, as the following list describes:

✦ **Security group:** This is the standard Windows Server 2003 security principal, stored as an entry in the ACL. Security groups, however, can now be mailed to. In other words, all the members in the security group who have an e-mail address stored in their User account objects can receive e-mail.

✦ **Distribution group:** This group is not a security principal and is used only as a distribution list. You can store contacts and user accounts in the distribution group. Because contacts do not contain the overhead of user accounts, including contacts only in large groups makes more sense. This group is also compatible with Microsoft Exchange and can play a large part in your telephony and messaging applications as well. After you upgrade Exchange to support Active Directory, you can eliminate the Exchange distribution lists and reduce the administrative burden on the e-mail administrators.

The scope of groups

Both group types have three scope types. Scopes determine the capability to contain members and nest groups from other domains and forests across the enterprise and even on an intra-enterprise relationship basis. The three scope types are *Universal*, *Global*, and *Domain Local*. Windows NT supported only Global and Local group types. The following list describes all three group types:

✦ **Universal groups:** These groups can include members from any Windows NT or Windows Server 2003 domain in a forest. The members can be groups of any of the three scope types, and they can come from any domain in the forest. This scope was created for users who need access to resources in other domains. A good example of a Universal group is a user who works mainly in USA-Domain but who frequently travels to London where the user logs onto UK-Domain. This user could log on to UK-Domain and still gain access to his USA-Domain resources. Members of Universal groups can be given access and permissions for any resource in any domain in the forest.

✦ **Global groups:** These groups can include members only from the originating domain. These members can be other Global groups and Contact groups. Global groups can be given access to resources in any domain in the forest, and the members can be members of any of the groups in the forest. You can nest Global, Local, and Universal groups in a global group.

✦ **Domain Local groups:** These groups can include members from any domain in the forest. Members of such a group can be any user or group from anywhere in the forest. You can, however, nest only other Domain Local groups from the same domain. The members of this group scope cannot be members of groups set with the Global and Universal group scope types.

Group scopes can be elevated only if they do not belong to other groups in the lower level and only on native-mode networks. In other words, you can move a Global group to a Universal group only if the global group does not belong to another global group. You may also notice that you cannot change the scope of a Universal group, because Universal scope objects are the weakest security principals of all the groups.

The following text recaps common group use and management on Windows NT, which helps you understand Windows Server 2003 groups. On legacy NT domains, you create and work with two types of groups, *Domain Local* and *Global* groups. Domain Local, or just Local, groups are restricted to the domains in which they are created; they cannot be given entry into other legacy NT domains. Global groups, on the other hand, can be given entry into other legacy domains — and even Windows Server 2003 domains, for that matter.

Local groups can contain Global groups from the local domain and any trusted domain, but a Local group cannot contain, or nest, any other local group.

Good management practice on legacy NT domains is to create Local groups as resource groups that access the domains as the primary security principals, almost as bastions, to borrow a Unix term. In other words, Local groups are the front-line containers holding the access and permissions control that users require to get to their resources. (This practice continues in Windows Server 2003 domains.)

If a collective of local users — or even one user — requires access to the resources in their "home" domain, you give them access or membership to the Local group. If a foreign group of users — that is, users from another domain — requires access, you give that Global group membership to the Local group. This enables you to restrict user access permissions to the local resource groups while retaining Global groups for intradomain access and organizational grouping.

The Global group is also a security principal, however, and is used to control access in the same way as the local group. This capability has led many companies, especially those that have only one local LAN, to abolish the use of the Local group (except in the case of built-in groups) and make every group *Global.* Why worry about Local groups if Global groups serve both as security principals and as organizational "departments" into which members who do similar work and need the same resources can be assembled? Table 13-1 provides a list of scopes and their limitations.

Table 13-1: Group Scopes and Their Limitations

Group Scope	*Members*	*Permissions*	*Nesting*
Universal group	Can come from any domain in the forest. The members can be other Universal groups, Global groups, and users and contacts from any domain in the forest. Cannot host Local groups.	Can be granted on any domain in the forest.	Can be a member of any Local and Universal group in the forest.

Continued

Table 13-1 *(continued)*

Group Scope	*Members*	*Permissions*	*Nesting*
Global group	Can come only from the owner domain. Can host other Global groups and users from the owner domain. Cannot host Universal groups.	Can be granted on any domain in the forest.	Can be a member of any group in the forest.
Local group	Can come from any domain in the forest. Can host Global groups and users and contacts from any domain in the forest. Can also host other Local groups from the owner domain.	Can be granted only by the domain owning the group.	Can be a member only of other local groups in the owner domain.

Finding Global groups such as *Accounts Payable, Shipping,* and *Logistics* is not uncommon in many NT domains. Although you cannot do much harm in such management practice, Microsoft did not intend groups to function as tools of business administration. Enter the organizational unit (OU). We have touched on OUs but we need to discuss them here briefly in the context of managing groups and users. Organizational units are created to provide hierarchical administrative delegation, organizational structuring, and for setting Group Policy. Groups are used for granting and denying users access to computer and network resources. Global groups also traverse domain boundaries. A group can contain users and global groups from other domains, both on a single domain tree and across a forest of domains. OUs are valid only on a contiguous domain space in the domain that they were created in.

So now that you have abolished the group role as an organizational tool, you need to be sure of its purpose in life. Instead of granting individuals access rights in every corner of the domain, you should instead grant them membership to certain access groups.

First creating a group with a predetermined purpose, such as "access to the very large label printer," is far easier. You would then assign security and management definitions to this group and assign any necessary permissions to the group. After the group is set up, you need to merely add a user to the group, and the group's restrictions and access permissions are cumulative to the permissions that the user may have already applied elsewhere in other groups or individually and would override any weaker values assigned elsewhere. The first trait of a group is the permissions that are assigned to it. Permissions enable the users of a group to gain access to resources and information to which the group as a unit has been given access. In other words, the group permissions define the mode or level of access that members of the group gain.

Think of this in terms of classes on a plane. Business people may join the First or Business Class to gain access to better meals, more room, and seating arrangements that can accommodate in-flight board meetings, room to work with files and documents, and so on. If a flyer does not have a First or Business Class ticket, he does not have access or privileges to any services paid for by the First and Business Class flyers.

The following list summarizes what you've learned in this section:

- Groups are mostly collections of user accounts.
- Users or members of groups inherit the blanket permissions assigned to a group.
- Users can be members of more than one group.
- Groups can be members of organizational units, which can be members of other OUs. Groups can also be members of other groups.

This flexibility offered by OUs and groups is somewhat dangerous, however, because it can result in an overnested organizational mess if taken to the extreme. You should plan this carefully, before you find that you can't see the forest for the trees.

The elements of groups

As do User objects, Group objects exist in two places in Windows Server 2003: in Active Directory and in the local registry. Groups are used for the following purposes:

- To manage user and computer access to network objects, local objects, shares, printer queues, devices, and so on.
- To create distribution lists.
- To filter Group Policy.

In Windows Server 2003, you specify the purpose of the group as you create it. If the group is meant to contain security principals, you set it up as a security group. Otherwise, you specify the group as a distribution list containing contacts.

Windows Server 2003 groups operate identically to Windows NT groups but with more functionality. In fact, the underlying group technology has merely been elevated to the Active Directory level. Instead of adding individual users to resources (such as shares and device access), the best management policy is to add them to a group that needs the necessary access. Even if you have only one user who needs access to a share-point, create a group for that user. Do not fall into the habit of adding individuals to shares, because before long, you have these lonesome access cases spread all over the place, which is a security risk.

Installing predefined groups

As does legacy NT, Windows Server 2003 installs predefined groups as you install certain components or features of the operating system. You do not automatically get all the groups installed at the same time just by installing every service that ships with the OS. You do not see *Domain Admins*, for example, listed in the Users and Computers Snap-in until you create the first computer account. The following list defines the base built-in groups installed when you install the first domain controller and create a computer account.

Take some time out to study this list and understand what each group bestows on its members. The groups are created for your convenience and serve broad purposes. But they represent a quick start to setting up a domain. Later, after your planning is underway (it is never complete), you can create new groups that serve security needs as tight as clams. These lists are not exhaustive, and you find many more groups listed in the Users and Computers snap-in. Many third-party applications also create additional groups that are specific to their applications. A good example is groupware applications such as helpdesk, CRM, and ERP applications. The following predefined groups are shown in Figure 13-10:

✦ **Administrators:** The only user account placed into this group at installation is the Administrator. You can add any user account to this group to immediately bestow wide access and power to the user.

  Administrators do not get access to everyone's files and folders by virtue of the wide power that they are given in this group. If a file or folder's permissions do not give access, Administrator is also locked out. This ensures protection and enables owners or managers of sensitive shares, files, and folders to lock down their resources securely.

✦ **Users:** The local Users group is the default group for any user account created in Windows Server 2003. Do not confuse this group with the Users folder into which the Anonymous and Guest accounts are placed.

✦ **Account Operators:** This group gives wide administrative power to its members. Operators can create users and groups and can edit and delete most users and groups from the domain (permissions permitting). Account operators can also log on to servers, shut down servers, and add computers to the domain.

  Account operators cannot delete Administrators, Domain Admins, Backup Operators, Print Operators, Server Operators, or any Global or Universal groups that belong to these Local groups. They also cannot modify the accounts of any members of the superior groups.

✦ **Backup Operators:** Members can back up and restore systems. But they can use a backup program only to back up files and folders. They can also log on to domain controllers and backup servers and shut them down.

✦ **Print Operators:** Members can create, delete, and manage the print share-points on print servers. They can also shut down print servers.

✦ **Server Operators:** Members can manage member servers.

✦ **Replicators:** This is not a group that contains human users. It contains only the user account used to log on to the Replicator service to perform replication functions.

✦ **Guests:** This is the built-in group that contains accounts for casual users or users who do not have accounts on the domain. Users in this group can usually log on without passwords and make very limited or controlled use of the system. It is an ideal group for service-based systems. Earlier in this chapter, we recommended moving the accounts from this group into a visitor's OU, which can be further secured with Group Policy.

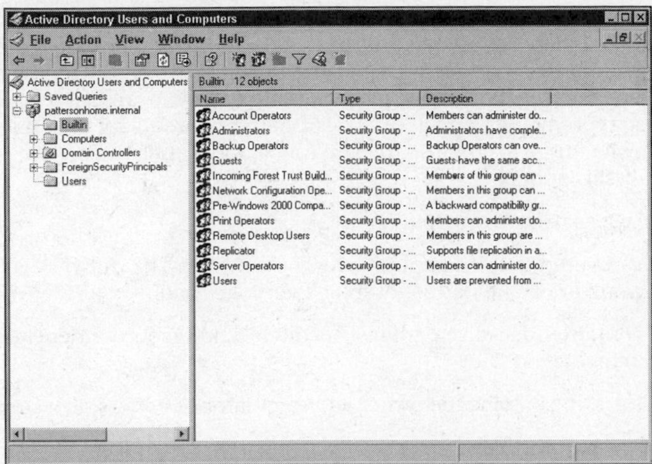

Figure 13-10: Windows Server 2003's default built-in groups are created automatically on installation.

The following list presents the important Global groups. These automatically have membership in Local groups.

- ✦ **Domain Admins:** Use this group to provide administrative powers to administer the domain, domain controllers, and member servers and workstations. You can prevent anyone from accessing a member server simply by removing this group from the member's Administrators group. This group, by virtue of being a Global group, can be added to the Local groups in other domains and can be added to Universal groups.
- ✦ **Domain Users:** The Domain Users group is a Global group, and so including every user in your domain in this group makes sense, regardless of the other groups they are in. You can then add this group to the Users Local group, and whenever you need to grant access to "all," simply admit the group to the object granting permission. We put "all" in quotes and did not use the term *everyone* for a good reason: The *Everyone* group that Windows admits to shares and folders by default means exactly that — everyone. If you create a user account from the command line by using the `net user` command and do not specify group destination or domain, the user is automatically sent to the Domain User group. The account is also physically located in the root of the domain, however, and not in any folder or OU. You can move it to a folder or OU after you create it.

The following list includes several "special" groups that are also created. These groups cannot be edited, disabled, or deleted, and do not have the capability to add members to these groups. They can be removed from shares, folders, and permission lists but are not apparent in the Active Directory Users and Computers snap-in. Windows Server 2003 stores objects into these groups that need to be presented to the security subsystem:

- **Everyone:** This "group" means everyone that uses the computer and the network. By admitting this object to a share, you implicitly open all doors to the object, even if the user is an account on an alien OS on a far-away planet. If they exist, they can access your object. We believe that removing the *Everyone* group from your resource and using the Users group (containing Domain Users) is a better course. Any time that you get a call to get someone out of an open share, you can simply knock the person out of the Domain Users or Users group.
- **Interactive:** All local users using the computer.
- **Network:** All users connected to the computer over the network. The Network group and the Interactive group are combined to form the Everyone group.
- **System:** This group contains specialized groups, accounts, and resources dependent on by the operating system.
- **Creator Owner:** This group contains the owner and/or creator of folders, files, and print jobs.

Groups on member servers

There is another good reason why the Domain Admins group is a Global group: It can be admitted to the Local group on a member server (and even a workstation for that matter). As discussed, the domains created in the local machine environment are, for all intents and purposes, full-blown "domains" used to manage these computers.

The users and groups in the local domains work the same way as in the network domains. After you attach a nondomain-controller machine to Windows Server 2003 domains, the Domain Admins group is automatically added to the member computer's Users group.

Another group worth mentioning on the local machine is the Power Users group. This group has a similar role to the domain's Domain Admins group, except that members of this group do not have total control. This setup enables the managers of these computers to keep tight control over the local users.

Nesting groups

Nesting groups is an efficient way of delegating the management of group membership. In native mode, you can create a Universal group and delegate the control over membership to an enterprise or senior administrator whose job it is to manage the membership of the Global groups. Global group administrators are the ones responsible for managing the membership of the Global groups . . . granting membership to users or Local groups.

Nesting is useful in enterprises that are dispersed across geographical boundaries or that have built multiple domains. At `MCITY`, we have created a universal group called GENESIS DCP that contains the senior users from `GENESIS.MCITY.ORG\DCP`. In the example in Figure 13-11, the universal group `DCP.GENESIS.MCITY.ORG` has been nested into the `CITYHALL` Local DCP group.

Domains must be in native mode to nest security groups. The Universal group is not available in mixed mode. See the section "Mixed mode versus native mode," later in this chapter.

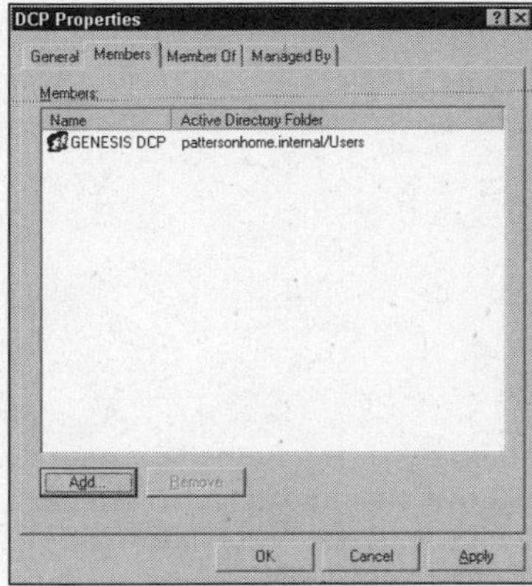

Figure 13-11: Nesting in action: The local group DCP contains the universal group GENESIS DCP from the `pattersonhome.internal` domain.

Group creation

This section describes an example of how to create a new group.

Run the MMC Users and Groups snap-in and double-click an organizational unit that you created earlier in this chapter. Navigate to the OU where you want to create the group. Choose Action ➪ New ➪ Group from the menu bar. This action opens the New Object (Group) dialog box, as shown in Figure 13-12. The options in this dialog box are as follows:

- **Group Name:** This is the unique name that you give the new group.
- **Group Name (Pre-Windows 2000):** This is added for you automatically and is based on the name that you provided the new group. (You may need to provide a down-level name that differs from the Windows Server 2003 name.)
- **Group Scope:** The options here are Domain Local, Global, and Universal.
- **Group Type:** The options here are Security and Distribution. Keep in mind that if you choose a group of type Security, the weak Universal group is not an option in a mixed-mode domain.

Enter the information into the fields shown in Figure 13-12 and click OK.

Setting up the group

After the group is created, navigate to the newly created group; right-click it and choose Properties from the pop-up menu. You can also just double-click its name in the list. By using the Properties dialog box for the group, as shown in Figure 13-13, you can specify the settings that you need to set up the group.

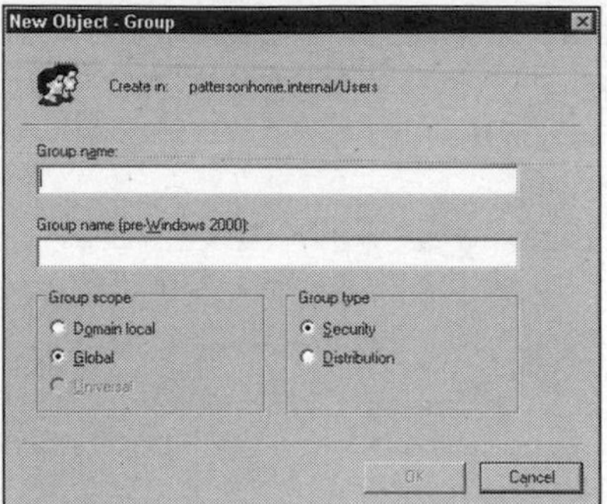

Figure 13-12: Creating a new group.

General tab

This tab of the Properties dialog box for the group contains fields for the general information that you need to add to the Group object. You can also change some of the information that you added as you created the group, as discussed in the following list:

✦ **Group Name (Pre-Windows 2000):** Enter the legacy Windows group name here. If the name that you provided as you set up the group later causes problems, you can edit it at any time.

✦ **Description:** Enter a brief description of the group. What you enter here appears in the Users and Computers snap-in Description column.

✦ **E-mail:** Enter an e-mail address for the group. Any e-mail sent to the group is distributed to its members.

✦ **Group Scope:** These radio buttons enable you to change the group scope. If the group is in a mixed-mode domain, the Universal scope option remains disabled. You also cannot change a group's scope from Global to Domain Local and vice versa.

✦ **Group Type:** These radio buttons enable you to change the group type.

✦ **Notes:** Enter text in this field to assist in the documentation of your domain objects.

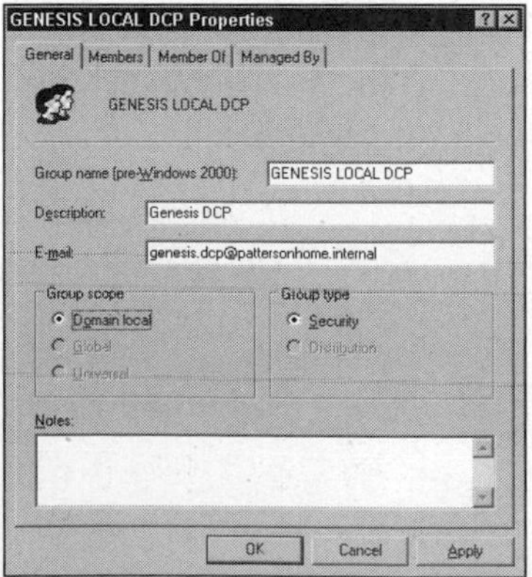

Figure 13-13: The General tab of the group's Properties dialog box enables you to enter or edit the base properties of the group.

Members tab

The Members tab enables you to add members to the group. You can add computers, users, groups, and contacts to the Members list, as follows:

✦ **Add:** Click Add. The complete list of all objects that can be given membership of this group appears. Double-click a user, and the user's name is added to the list. Click OK.

Member Of tab

The Member Of tab provides a view of membership from the membership lists of other groups. It also enables you to join other groups, as follows:

✦ **Add:** Click Add. The complete list of all container objects to which this object can be given membership appears. Double-click the Users group and click OK.

Managed By tab

The Managed By tab provides a host of fields that identify the name, address, and contact information of the person who manages the group but you change only one, as follows:

✦ **Change:** This is the only item that you can add or change on this tab. The other properties are inherited from the manager's User object. You can protect the object at the permissions level later.

More about adding users to groups

You can add many objects to a group. These objects, all called *group members,* can be users, other groups, contacts, or computers. Adding computers to groups has some interesting consequences for management. For now, however, we want to add only a single user account to a group of choice. To add members requires only a few steps. Simply select the group in Active Directory Management and right-click the selection. Then click Properties. The Properties dialog box appears and is labeled *YOUR DOMAIN'S GROUP* Properties. Select the Members tab and click the Add button at the bottom-left corner of the dialog box.

A second-level dialog box appears, named Select Users, Contacts, or Computers. Now select the user. (Notice that you can "look in" several places or domains for the user account, and you can search the entire directory.) After you have located and selected the user account, click Add. Your user is now added into the currently selected group, as indicated in the Members list. You can select more than one user in the top list by pressing and holding the Ctrl key as you select usernames. You can also press and hold the Shift key and drag the cursor over the list to select multiple users. In this case, however, you are interested in only one user. Notice, too, that after you click Add, the accounts are listed serially in the Name field for confirmation. (This option really should have been a drop-down list.) Clicking OK puts them into the Object list at the bottom of the dialog box.

Managing groups

In Windows Server 2003, an individual or group can be delegated the task of managing users, or members, of specific organizational units. In our case, we are likely to assign the management of the GENESIS DCP group to the DCP manager, who also maintains the GENESIS DCP organization unit. In addition, Group Policy is used to control the work environments of the users in these groups and OUs. The DCP group that we created may be refused access to the RAS, while another group that works remotely is granted access to RAS via the Group Policy.

You need to fully understand how Group Policy works, and what you learn here is insufficient to perform the task without making mistakes and needing to redo things. Only practice and a lot of experience, working with many, many users over a few years, can prepare you for the job.

Rights and permissions

The Windows Server 2003 security system controls access to network objects and protects network and machine-specific resources in two ways: through rights and through permissions. *Rights* are granted to users and groups. (And don't forget that includes processes, threads of execution, and so on that operate in the context of a security principal.) Many rights would not normally be exploited by a human user, such as the right to lock a file in memory, which prevents it from being paged out to disk. But a thread of execution, requiring the capability to do so, would.

Permissions belong to the objects that are the essence of the operating system. With that bit of information in hand, you may be pleased to know that objects are given rights to perform certain things, but as objects in Active Directory, you need permission to manage them. The difference between rights and permissions has confused administrators for years. Whenever Windows Server 2003 enables you to do something on a machine or on the network, that is a right, making rights something granted to users. Rights, for example, include the right to *log on locally*, the right to *log on as a service*, and the right to *act as part of the operating system*. But if you need to access an object in a defined way, you need to obtain permission. Permissions include permission to change objects, read them, execute them, delete them, and so on. A printer is a good example of an object that you need permission to use. Another way of looking at the difference is that rights involve the capability to function, while permissions control access.

Permissions are granted by both the file system (over its objects) and by the Active Directory over its respective objects.

Rights come in two flavors: *Privileges* and *Logon Rights*. They can be bestowed on individuals by enabling rights in a Group Policy object (User Rights Assignment and Logon Rights Assignment) and linking the object to the user account. Association does this . . . and it takes place whenever you place a user account into an OU. The user account can also inherit any privilege defined in the GPO of a domain or site.

Bestowing privileges and rights through group membership rather than on an individual basis, is the best course. Whenever you need to remove a privilege or logon right, you need only remove the user account from the group.

Privileges

The rights bestowed to users and groups to provide them with the capability to perform certain functions in the computing environment are known as *privileges*. Privileges often override permissions, where necessary. A good example is the Right to Backup Files and Directories, which overrides any permission that denies access to a user. The Backup Operators group needs the capability to read and change (reset the archive bit or overwrite during a restore) the files that it is backing up, no matter what permissions the owner of the objects has. Table 13-2 explains the privileges, their purpose, and to whom they are assigned by default.

Table 13-2: Privileges and Predefined Groups

Right	*What It Enables*	*Default Groups Assigned To*
Act as part of the operating system.	Enables a process to operate as in the context of a secure or trusted part of the OS.	Everyone, Authenticated Users, Power Users, Administrators.
Add workstations to domain.	Enables a user to add workstations (computer accounts) to a domain.	Not assigned to a default group.
Back up files and directories.	Enables users to back up files and folders.	Administrators, Backup Operators.
Bypass traverse checking.	Moves between folders to access files.	Everyone.
Change the system time.	Sets the internal clock of the computer.	Administrators, Power Users.
Create a pagefile.	Enables the user to create a pagefile.	Not assigned to a default group.
Create a token object.	Enables a process to create an access token via the LSA.	Not assigned to a default group.
Create permanent shared objects.	Enables a user to create permanent objects.	Not assigned to a default group.
Debug programs.	Debugs low-level processes and threads.	Administrators.
Enable computer and user accounts to be trusted for delegation.	Delegates responsibility.	Administrators.
Force shutdown from a remote system.	Shuts down a remote computer.	Administrators.
Generate security audits.	Generates security audit entries.	Administrators.
Increase quotas.	Enables a user to increase the disk quotas.	Administrators.
Increase scheduling priority.	Increases the execution priority of a process.	Administrators.
Load and unload device drivers.	Installs and removes device drivers.	Administrators.
Lock pages in memory.	Enables a user to prevent pages from being paged out to `pagefile.sys`.	Not assigned to a default group.

Continued

Table 13-2 *(continued)*

Right	*What It Enables*	*Default Groups Assigned To*
Manage auditing and security log.	Specifies which objects can be audited.	Administrators.
Modify firmware environment values.	Modifies system environment variables.	Administrators.
Profile single process.	Performs profiling on a process.	Administrators.
Profile system performance.	Performs profiling on a computer.	Administrators.
Remove computer from docking station.	Unlocks a computer from the docking station.	Administrators.
Replace a process-level token.	Enables a user to modify a security access token.	Not assigned to a default group.
Restore files and directories.	Enables users to restore files and folders.	Administrators, Backup Operators.
Shut down the system.	Shuts down Windows Server 2003.	Administrators, Backup Operators, Everyone, Power Users, and Users.
Synchronize directory service data.	Enables a user to synchronize directory service data.	Not assigned to a default group.
Take ownership of files or other objects.	Enables the user to take ownership of all objects attached to the computer. This right overrides permissions.	Administrators.

Logon rights

Logon rights dictate how a user can log on to a computer or a domain. Logon rights are also bestowed in Group Policy. They are defined in the GPO and specifically linked to groups and users (preferably via group membership) through association with a site, domain, or OU. Table 13-3 explains the logon rights.

Table 13-3: Logon Rights and Predefined Groups

Right	*What It Enables*	*Groups Assigned To*
Access this computer from the network.	Enables a user to connect to the computer over the network.	Everyone, Authenticated Users, Power Users, Administrators.
Deny access to this computer from the network.	Revokes this right.	Not assigned to a default group.

Right	*What It Enables*	*Groups Assigned To*
Deny logon as a batch job.	Revokes this right.	Not assigned to a default group.
Deny logon as a service.	Revokes this right.	Not assigned to a default group.
Deny logon locally.	Revokes this right.	Not assigned to a default group.
Log on as a batch job.	Enables a user to log on by using a batch-queue facility.	Administrators.
Log on as a service.	Enables a security principal to log on as a service, which enables the process to operate in a security context.	Not assigned to a default group.
Log on locally.	Enables a user to log on to a local machine at the keyboard.	Print Operators, Authenticated Users, Server Operators, Backup Operators, Administrators, Power Users, Account Operators.

Mixed mode versus native mode

Your domains must be in *native mode* to use the advanced group features in Windows Server 2003. Specifically, you cannot create a Universal security group in mixed mode. (You can create only a universal distribution list, which is not a security principal.) You also cannot nest security groups in mixed mode nor convert groups from one scope to another. This is a severe limitation, and you may want to consider promoting the scope as soon as doing so is feasible. Mixed-mode domains support Windows NT 4.0/ Windows 2000 domain controllers (the legacy Backup Domain Controllers or BDCs).

Before committing to new Windows Server 2003 applications, check with the ISV to determine what groups are required by the application and the features that it needs to use. Some applications may require you to promote the domain to native mode even if doing so is not practical for you.

The Zen of Managing Users and Groups

Managing users is demanding and requires an assertive personality in an administrator. Managing a small group of, say, 25 people may not be such a big deal (you think), but as the number of users grows, the task becomes more and more complex. Users depend on the network to get their jobs done. And thus the life of the administrator or user manager is a never-ending exercise in tolerance, assertiveness, concentration, and understanding. The less savvy are your administration skills, the more you have your work cut out for you.

A good idea for any serious administrator is to take a course in *enterprise resource planning* (*ERP*), human resources, *customer relationship management* (*CRM*), business management, and administration in general. Understanding how the various departments function autonomously and in concert with the rest of the company goes a long way to effective user management.

User management is not simply the task of enabling users to log on to a network. You need to provide access, protect resources, track utilization, audit activity, and much more. Setting up users and groups is often easier than managing them in the long term. Just moving a group from one domain to another can be a complex process. And if your company happens to absorb or acquire the IT department of another company, you could be saying goodbye to 40-hour weeks for a long time, especially if nobody knows who owns what shares, folders, files, and so on.

So where do you start? The preceding material in this chapter gives you a thorough understanding of Windows Server 2003 user and group architecture and how user and group accounts are created and deployed. With that information, you now need to plan the best way to use this information to manage the network. Every company is different, and thus you are the one who can best determine your own needs. You do, however, need to plan ahead and use common sense. We may suggest task lists as the best way to begin user and group management projects. Before you begin, establish the following protocols:

- Create an IT-HR/Windows Server 2003 physical workgroup to oversee new policy or changes in policy and change control with respect to user management and access to resources. The capability to create objects and delegate their management and control (down to the finest grain) to individuals, groups, teams, and project leaders can prove very beneficial but also very dangerous.
- Your team needs to consider new policy and the ramifications of delegated responsibility with respect to managing user accounts and the collateral services such as security, access to shares, devices, information, and other information-based resources.
- You need to set up new policy with respect to the delegation of control and management of objects. You need to decide at what level IT and MIS is prepared to give control to the department heads and group leaders and the people that they delegate.
- This team may be called the Directory Administrator's Team, with a leading figure such as the CIO or MIS in charge.
- Appoint a person (employee or consultant) to work with HR and analysts to establish or improve corporate structure. Many organizations do not get remodeled or restructured for some time because few really care. But now you can involve IT directly in the corporate structure, especially as the Active Directory enables several teammates to collaborate on setting the corporate structure and model in the directory, as opposed to doing it on paper or in flow charts and diagrams. The task ahead is to create organizational units based on the layout and scope of the entire organization.
- A term often used in business or corporate analysis is *Key Management Entity* (KME). Key Management Entities are all the key aspects of a business that need to be managed. Accounts Receivable, Accounts Payable, Materials Management, Shipping, QC, and QA are examples of KMEs. These KMEs can now also be modeled in AD, inheriting directly from the models and structures typically associated with corporate analysis software and ERP technology (such as the likes of products from SAP and Baan).
- Appoint teammates who are responsible for migrating users to the new OUs and groups on a per-OU basis. If you are relocating users from Windows NT, these members need to be members of the old Domain Admins group. The problem many companies face is that shares and permissions are just dished out with no record of what groups, shares, user policies, profiles, file permissions, and so on are in place. This would need to be thoroughly documented. Adequately extracting information that documents the NT domain is almost impossible.

✦ Invite the people responsible for customer relationship management (CRM) to join the directory administrator's forum with a view to incorporating help desk and the external environment into the directory. What if the group decided, for example, that setting up OUs for user groups (customers) may prove worthwhile?

Delegating responsibility

The best means of putting policy and change control under management is to involve the department heads and team leaders across the board. Several items in this regard need to be considered if you delegate, as the following list describes:

✦ Do the respective department heads want the new responsibility? Do they carry sufficient weight to shirk the idea of managing their own groups? And do they carry sufficient weight to manage their peers?

✦ If policy dictates that they must participate, are managers behind the new initiative to enforce the policy?

✦ After the department heads have agreed to participate in the management of their own groups, do they need to delegate the function to a member who requires some training in managing?

Change management for users and groups is even more important under Windows Server 2003, because with the devolution of administrative power comes decentralization, even in a central location. Setting up a permissions request or user access request committee, consisting of members of HR, MIS-Security, and the network administrators, is thus worthwhile.

The teams or individuals responsible for new users (employees) should receive user and group account requests from HR after new employees are cleared. An e-mail or form is sent to the MIS-Security person who is responsible for setting in motion the steps to set up the user with his basic needs, inside the organizational unit to which the user is assigned. Such a person is equipped with sensitive information about all various resources in operation at the company. This person is aware, for example, of what shares represent what on the Payroll server or how access is provided to the AS/400, the Remote Access Server, and so on.

Employees and team leaders can also motivate or request changes to the profiles and rights of the workers under them — for example, if a user gets promoted or assigned new administrative functions. The user may now need certain Read-only rights changed to Full Control or rights to delete, copy, and move files. The requestors do not need to know what groups they are in. The HR manager's job is to help the department requesting a new employee clear the employee to work for the company and set the new employee up with all the resources that the person needs to do his job as efficiently as possible.

The MIS-Security checklist or account request and setup form may contain the following information:

✦ **User ID (logon):** An ID such as `jeffrey.shapiro@mcity.org`.

✦ **Password:** Made up according to a system or policy.

✦ **Devices:** Printers, drives, scanner, modems, and so on.

✦ **Share-points:** Folder or directory shares.

✦ **Applications:** For the discussion of policies and profiles, see Chapter 14.

- **Facility:** Help, training, setting up workstations, and so on.
- **Logon hours:** Regular hours and overtime.
- **Messaging:** E-mail, voice mail, fax mail.
- **Organizational Unit:** Assigned by HR.
- **Description:** Gives the user's needs and any special circumstances.

After this list (which may be longer or shorter) is complete, it can be given to the network administrator or engineer responsible for user account creation in the respective organizational unit. This person does not question how or why the account is set up or what is assigned; he just creates the account.

Under the Windows Server 2003 domain, the preceding practice now takes place on a department or OU basis, as opposed to being enterprise-wide or centralized under the control of a handful of techies. Requests from users and organizational units or departments should be directed to the help desk. A good idea is to use e-mail forms or an HTML form on the company's intranet Web site.

Of course, you can still appoint a single administrator to manage user accounts. But on Windows Server 2003, encouraging decentralized management makes sense (to a point, of course).

User and Group Management Strategies

The objective behind this section is to discuss strategies that lessen the burden on the administrator. Starting with the management of groups and users, so much power is now in the hands of the Windows Server 2003 and domain administrators that, without care and forethought, becoming bogged down in a quagmire of administrative spaghetti is all too possible. As with many other management systems and technologies, you can abuse the power (such as that involving Group Policy, coming up in Chapter 14) and end up with a situation that is counter to the intention of order and sanity.

Keep your eye on TCO

What is *TCO*? It stands for *T*otal *C*ost of *O*wnership. In a nutshell, it means that the total cost of a computer, a network, an application, or an entire IT department, for that matter, greatly exceeds the cost of its acquisition. After the asset is acquired, it must be managed and kept up, and all the functions that keep the system going contribute toward TOC.

Many habits of administrators can send TCO to the doghouse. A seemingly simple oversight can cause hours of downtime and can cost the company thousands in consulting fees and technical support from Microsoft. At $195 a pop, getting Microsoft on the line to help identify your mistakes is a sure way of making certain that you are not around by the next service pack release.

Almost all the items that we discuss in the following sections affect TCO. The two basic considerations? Don't manage users, manage groups; and refuse new group requests.

Don't manage users, manage groups

Illogical user management contributes to the TCO bottom line, so where at all possible, you do not want to manage the access and security needs and privileges of users on an individual basis. We discussed this aspect of user management but at times, you may have no choice but to provide a user with "direct" access to a resource, without first putting that person into a group. If you do so, make sure that you keep that situation as temporary as possible. Then, as soon as you can, add the user to a group and get rid of the solitary assignment.

Refuse new group requests

The first rule that you need to learn is to be as stubborn and assertive as possible regarding new group requests. Every time that you create a new group, you add to TCO in the following several ways:

✦ You add traffic to your network and systems. New groups require permission to access resources, they need storage space in the Active Directory, and they need to be replicated to domain controllers, global catalogs, and so on.

✦ Creating groups for every little need is a waste of time. If two groups need access to the same resource, such as a printer, why admit two groups to the resource? Keep one group and either add all users that need the same level of access to the group or nest the groups.

✦ You give yourself more work in documenting and maintaining the groups.

To lessen your load, first do the following before creating new groups:

1. Check to determine whether a built-in group can satisfy the needs. Creating a group for every little device makes no sense. If a printer object admits everyone, for example, you don't need to create another group for it (unless you have specialized auditing or security needs).

2. Check to determine whether a group that you or someone else earlier created can suffice to meet the user's needs. Nine times out of ten, you can easily find several dozens of groups that have become redundant, because people create new ones without checking whether others exist that serve their purpose.

Determine the access and privileges needed

From the request form, you can generally determine the needs of the users or the group in determining what group-creation or management action you need to take. If you find that you need to keep going back to people for more information, the forms are not working correctly or people are not complying with the protocols. In determining these needs, you need information concerning the following:

✦ **Access to applications and libraries:** If the applications are on the servers or users are Terminal Services clients, they need access to the shares and folders containing the applications. They also need access to policy and script folders, home directory, specialized paths, attachments (such as to SQL Server), and so on.

✦ **Access to data:** Applications and users need access to data: database tables, freestanding data files, spreadsheets, FTP sites, storage, and so on. Determine what data is needed and how best to access it.

- **Access to devices:** Users and applications need access to printers; communications devices, such as fax servers and modem pools; scanners; CD changers; and so on. All network devices are considered objects, and their access is also governed by permissions.
- **Communications:** Users need accounts on mail servers, voice messages boxes, and in groupware applications.
- **Privileges and logon rights:** Users need certain rights and power to perform their duties efficiently and in the shortest possible time.

Most of the time, requests are easily fulfilled: User X requires an account and needs to be placed in the B group for access to the C share. X needs e-mail and must have the capability to dial in to the RAS at any time of day or night and so on. This is not a difficult request, but if you get complicated requests, you need as much information as possible.

Determine the security level

The request form should be clear on the security needed over the user and the resources that the user is accessing. If the data is extremely valuable or very sensitive, you may need to consider auditing objects, tracking file and folder access, and so on. The levels or lengths that you go to protect the resources depend on the needs of each organization. You may, for example, consider short-term passwords, restricting logon hours, restricting logon location, and so on.

Protect resources and lessen the load by using Local groups

The best practice in group management has been inherited from experience with Windows NT: First create *gatekeeper* groups, which are Local groups that control the access to resources and expose what needs to be exposed for broad and even tightly controlled purposes. Then nest Global and Universal (if in native mode) groups in the Local groups, providing a second level of access control and permissions.

The practice of creating gatekeeper groups also encourages a delegation of responsibility and a form of decentralized management that is still safe and not out of touch. Assign people, who need to admit Global or Universal groups only as requested, the responsibility of managing Local groups. Then assign the membership of the Global groups to the department or organizational unit administrators.

Delegate with care

In line with the item in the preceding section, delegating with care is important. Over time, we expect that administrative power will become decentralized, but you still need to maintain a watchful eye over the "higher level" administrators. You may need to create admin groups for each OU where you have delegated responsibility or create one OU admin group and manage the individuals via OU Group Policy and so on.

Keep changes to a minimum

If you do a good job managing users and groups, you don't need to keep changing things around. The fewer changes that you need to make, the better. Remember, too, that every time you change something in the domain, the change needs to be propagated around the network to all the domain controllers. If you have a wide area network and your domain traverses geographical divides, constant changes can cause latency and costly delays while remote domain controllers lag behind in updates and replication.

Summary

In this chapter, we discuss how the new User and Group objects in the Active Directory enable you to more cohesively manage users and groups on Windows Server 2003-based networks. We also discuss the creation of users and groups and how to best administer them.

Most important, we stress using common sense in creating and managing users and groups and delegating responsibility. We move on to a more complex subject in the following chapter . . . managing the workspace.

✦ ✦ ✦

Change Control, Group Policy, and Workspace Management

In This Chapter

Group Policy overview

Creating policy and change-management plans

Applying Group Policy

Managing Group Policy

This chapter discusses Group Policy, a collection of technologies that enable administrators to enjoy centralized workplace management and change control over workstations, servers and services. Group Policy governs many aspects of the computing environment on a Windows network, such as security, communications, application delivery and so on.

What Is Change Control?

Change control is simply the capability to control change. As you are aware, nothing remains in stasis; even stasis itself "constantly" changes. For network administrators, the capability to control change at the desktop and at all layers of the network is critical. Without the capability to control change, serious network and work interruptions are inevitable.

During the writing of this chapter, one of our clients almost lost a small fortune in business because of a lack of change control. Our client is a small insurance broker (only five people). One of the brokers, Dave, writes marine insurance, and on a fine, cool January day in Florida, he got the break that the company was waiting for — an order for a policy to insure a $10 million yacht . . . the premium would be a killer.

He returned from the marina shaking and shivering, realizing that he was about to write the policy of his career. The commission would be staggering, and from this, many more deals would flow. You get a name for writing big policies such as this. Nothing would stand in his way . . . nothing but his faithful workstation.

Dave likes to fiddle with his computer. Whenever he is not looking for insurance business, he likes playing around with his desktop settings, fonts, resolution, and more. Dave lives in the Control Panel more than in his apartment. We had maintained a "loose" change-management policy in this company. In other words, we maintained minimal desktop control because Dave was the only wild card and was considered an advanced user. The company had been our client for several years, and we had never had an issue with users changing anything that could cause a problem.

On the day that Dave needed to write up his policy, his desktop went berserk. He logged into his workstation as usual, but after he opened the insurance application, the application began to tremble and then the session froze. If you know insurance, you know that, if you cannot write the policy, the client makes another call. Dave was getting ready to jump off the jetty with an anchor around his neck.

We jumped in and disabled Dave's account. And because we were deploying the Windows Desktop and Agency software applications through Terminal Services, we could get Dave back to his policy writing in record time. He admitted that he had changed his font again, along with some other "things" that he could not remember.

The client learned a lesson and decided that no employee (all four of them) could tamper with the applications or desktop sessions. But we learned a bigger lesson. Change control is as important for our small clients as it is for the big ones. It cannot be ignored anywhere.

Change control on Windows NT and other server environments has been lacking since the invention of client/server. Policy and profile maintenance is possible on Windows NT and Windows 9*x* desktops, but it is not secure, and users can override settings with little effort. A Windows NT workstation/server environment is more secure. But change-control empowerment is still lacking.

Windows 2000 and Active Directory changed all this in late 1999 with the introduction of *Group Policy*. Group Policy governs change-control policy on many facets of the operating system. These include the following:

- Hardware configuration and administration
- Client administration and configuration (desktop settings, logons, connection, and more)
- Operating-system options and policy, such as IntelliMirror and remote OS installation
- Application options and policy (such as regional settings, language and accessibility, deployment, and more)
- Security options and policy
- Network access

We are not going to take you through every detail of creating and managing Group Policy objects, because the Windows Server 2003 Help system adequately handles that. But we do show you how to take control of the change-control issue, apply security policy, and more. Before we get to that, we discuss the science and philosophy of change control and management.

Understanding Change Management

In the highly complex worlds of information technology and information systems, the only constant is change. The more complex and integrated that IS systems become, the more important having change control becomes. Managing change has thus become one of the most important MIS functions in many organizations. If you do not manage change, the unexpected results of an unmanaged change could render you extinct.

Processes, routines, functions, algorithms, and the like do not exist in vacuums or some form of digital isolation from the rest of the universe. Just as in life, all processes depend on or are depended on by other routines or processes. If you change the way that a process behaves, you alter its event course. In other words, you alter its destiny. Altering the event course of a process is in itself not the problem. Problems arise if processes dependent on a particular course of events are no longer afforded what they were expecting.

Think about how you feel and are inconvenienced if a person that you were going to meet does not turn up or cancels the engagement unexpectedly. In software and computer systems, such events can have catastrophic results. They in turn fail, and their event courses are also altered. Whenever processes begin to crash, an unstoppable domino effect takes place, leading to systems failure and disaster from one end of the system to the other. This is why troubleshooting is such a difficult exercise: The best troubleshooters are the ones that look beyond the evidence of failure and seek to discover what caused the problem or what event led up to system failure.

In addition to the example in the preceding section, when Dave's job was almost toasted, following are other examples of change control short comings:

✦ The FTP service on a server is turned off. AS/400 connections expecting to find the connection up cannot transfer route information to a network share. A process that was expecting the information to be in the FTP folder cannot calculate the daily routes for orders that need to go out. The trucks do not arrive, and the orders do not get established. The orders are not shipped. Clients place more than $10 million in business elsewhere.

✦ Norton Antivirus causes a domain controller to hang because its update feature results in a memory leak that gradually starves the DC to death. The result is that authentication on the network comes to a halt and servers begin to drop like flies.

✦ A software engineer makes a change in source code that introduces a bug into the process pool. Programs begin to collapse because the receiving data function does not know how to deal with data.

✦ A user downloads new software from the Internet onto his company's notebook computer. The new software contains a backdoor virus that silently attacks the notebook's anti-virus suite. It inserts a replacement file into the anti-virus software and causes the software to reload the old inoculation data file, which is akin to taking an antibiotic that has expired. After the user connects back to the corporate network, the hostile code moves to the network servers and does the same thing. After it's on the servers, the virus shuts down the company systems, and the company almost goes insolvent as a result.

These examples sound far-fetched, but they are not. We have seen all three of them on our networks. Such is the need for change control. In fact, the unit of time in which no change takes place is too small to be studied by humans.

So you must control change; moreover, you must manage it in such a way that the effects of change are planned for and that all dependencies are informed and enabled to compensate whenever change comes. In a nutshell, no change can take place unless the proposed change is put to a board of change management for consideration; the consequences of the change are fully investigated; and the change is deemed necessary. Because change is always inevitable, another factor comes into change control — contingency planning, of which disaster recovery is a part.

In the past, problems caused by unmanaged change affected standalone systems. Because computers were previously islands and isolated, the effects of the change were local and confined. After people started to network, change-control problems began to affect the global corporate or organizational environment. But the effect was — and still is to a large extent — confined to the corporate or enterprise information network.

In the world of e-commerce, however, change control has become critical, because any change that causes an unplanned-for new course of events affects the external environment where systems crashes can have catastrophic results and cause untold damages and liability. In the world of Internet banking, for example, a change-control disaster can affect many people who have no relationship with the bank, in addition to its innocent account holders.

In Chapter 24, we also discuss service level and quality of support. As you know, more and more people are signing service-level agreements that guarantee availability of systems all the time. These agreements must be covered by effective change-control management.

The change-control or change-management board reviews all changes and, based on the board's research, consultation, and findings, a change request is either approved or denied. (In the companies that we consult for, all change-management approvals must be signed off by the officer in charge.)

But the problems arise if you have a fully functional board and compliant team leaders but no means of enforcing change-control policy at all levels of the enterprise. To figure out how this all comes together, you need to take a look at change-control conceptually. The respective parts of change-control or change-management systems resemble the justice system or at least the enforcement parts of it. They include the items listed in Table 14-1.

Table 14-1: Change Control

Description	*Purpose*
Change control board	A group of people in an organization responsible for reviewing change requests, determining validity, deciding change of course or procedure, and so on. This board also determines regulation and enforcement protocol and deploys change-management resources.
Change management	Functions to manage signed-off or approved change or contingency. Change management may include lab tests, pilot projects, phased implementation, incremental change, performance monitoring, disaster recovery, backup/restore, and so on.
Change control policy	Rules and the formulation thereof governing change control and management.
Change control rules and enforcement	The enforcement of policy and the methods or techniques of such enforcement.
Change control tools	On Windows 2000/Windows Server 2003 networks, these include local security policy to protect machines, Group Policy to enforce change policy throughout the forest, security policy throughout, auditing, change request applications and so on.
Change control stack	The change-control "stack" comprises the various layers that are covered by change control.

To better understand where in the information-systems environment change control needs to be enforced, consider the change-control stack shown in Figure 14-1.

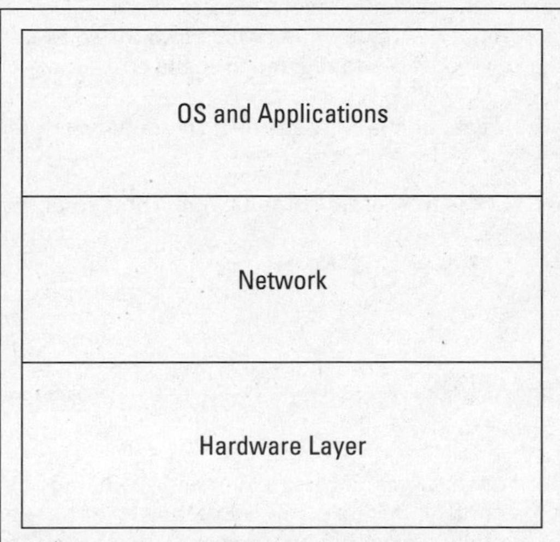

Figure 14-1: The change-control stack.

At the bottom of the change-control stack (CCS) shown in Figure 14-1 is the *hardware (physical) area*. Objects in this layer that you place under change-control enforcement are all hardware, computer components, and hardware requirements. The following list provides an idea of what is covered by change control at the hardware or physical layer:

- ✦ Hardware compliance with the existing infrastructure.
- ✦ Hardware acquisition and determination of hardware needs.
- ✦ Technology deemed necessary or not.
- ✦ Protection and security of storage and access to media (such as FDDs and CD-ROMs).
- ✦ Protection of network-interface cards.
- ✦ Access to memory and system components.
- ✦ Availability and stability of hardware device drivers.
- ✦ Hardware problem abandonment point. (When do you give up trying to fix a part or computer and buy a new one?)
- ✦ Parts replacement (such as procedure for replacing media and so on).
- ✦ Hardware availability (such as RAID, clustering, load balancing, and so on).

Next up is the *network layer*, which encompasses change control on the data link, network, transport, and session layers of the Open Systems Interconnect (OSI) model.

According to Newton's Telecom Dictionary, The Open Systems Interconnect (OSI) model of the International Standards Organization (at `www.iso.ch`) is the only accepted framework of standards for interconnection for communication between different systems made by different vendors. The OSI model organizes the communications process into a system of layers. OSI has become the foundation model for many frameworks in both software and computer hardware engineering. The OSI model is also referred to as the *OSI stack*.

The following list includes areas that are targets of change control at the network layer of the CCS:

✦ Security needs (encryption, IPSec, access to routers, circuits, hubs, and so on).

✦ Quality of service.

✦ Network bandwidth.

✦ Topology.

✦ Transport technology (Ethernet, SNA, Token Ring).

✦ Routing, bridging, switching.

As you get higher up the CCS, the number of variables begins to increase. (You have more opportunities for change and thus change control, because you are getting into the area where the user lives.) The following list includes areas that are targets of change control at the *operating systems and applications layer* of the CCS:

✦ Logon/user authentication.

✦ Network services.

✦ File systems and storage.

✦ Network protocols.

✦ Device driver installation and version control.

✦ Device operation.

✦ Application services.

✦ Disaster recovery services.

✦ Internet/intranet services.

✦ Media services and telephony.

✦ File transfer.

✦ Sharing and access control.

✦ Virus protection.

✦ Directory services.

✦ User levels/access to resources.

- Communications.
- Desktop configuration (menus, shortcuts, icons, access to folders, and so on).
- Access to information (such as access to the Internet).
- Cultural and regional options.
- Accessibility (the ease of access to computing resources, specifically to people with handicaps).
- Access to software/applications.
- Access to data.

Not only are more factors or "opportunities" for change control in this top layer, but it also is the most vulnerable of the layers. Although certain parts of the operating system and the lower layers provide a barrier to entry because of their complexity, change control should not be any more lax or less important. The more obscure the service is, regardless of the layer it resides in, the higher is the risk of a skilled attacker doing undetectable and lasting damage. The biggest threat to the stability or health of IT/IS systems, however, comes from users. Most of the time, the problem is just a case of "curiosity killed his computer." (Remember Dave?) But users also generate security threats, introduce viruses, download hostile applications (most of the time unwittingly), and so on.

The user

First, the term *user* rarely refers to a single biological unit. This is why you have security groups, as discussed in Chapter 13. As soon as you define or categorize the levels of user groups that you need to support in your organization, you can apply change-management procedures that can be enforced on those groups.

If you are involved in client management, you should make an effort to become a member of the change-control team. You should also get to know your users, the type of software and applications that they need, and how they work with their computers, treat their computers, and interact with their computers.

You have two main types of user or worker, as discussed in the following list:

- **Knowledge workers:** Your knowledge workers are usually the workers who are applying a particular skill set or knowledge base in their job. These people are your engineers, technical-support people, accountants, lawyers, designers, and so on. Knowledge workers usually have a permanent office. These people use their computers for most of the day. Their machines are constantly in use, and losing them would be costly for the company. They can be considered advanced users.

- **Task-oriented workers:** These workers are data-entry personnel, receptionists, office assistants (to varying degrees), order takers, and so on. Most of these users would not need more than a terminal and a terminal service account to perform their duties. These users can be considered your basic users.

The computer

The two main types of users are further broken down into the following categories (by computer resource used):

- **Stationary (office) workstation user:** This user (usually a knowledge worker) does not need a notebook computer because he needs the machine only at work. This machine is usually a small-footprint workstation running Windows NT Workstation, Windows 2000 Professional, or Windows XP Professional.
- **Remote workstation user:** This worker connects to the network from home or a remote office across a WAN connection or modem. The user still uses a fixed desktop computer because he does not move around.
- **Notebook/docking station user:** This user uses his computer at work *and* at home. The user is usually accommodated with a docking station at home and at the office, which makes connecting and disconnecting from the network easier.
- **Multi-user workstation:** This computer does not belong to any specific user. Users making use of this resource are usually guests, users who move around from location to location, temp staff, shift staff (such as call-center or customer-service representatives), and so on. This computer is also known as a *kiosk*.
- **Mobile computer:** This computer is usually a notebook or laptop computer, sans docking station, that spends most of its life in a carrying case stuffed inside the cubby of a jetliner. Mobile users can either connect to the office from the road (such as a hotel or conference center) or from branch locations where they can connect to the corporate network.

In each of these cases, you need to establish workstation and user-management policy for each type of user and computer. Further tagging your user as advanced or basic in the literacy level of computer usage often makes more sense than dumping them in one group. We have had knowledge workers who caused endless problems for the administrators and basic workers who should be writing software instead of using it. We get back to the subject of how much power to give your user in the section "Workstation lockdown," later in this chapter. First we need to deal with the issue of applications.

Create a list or database of these categories and, in each category, list a computer name and a username. Take, for example, the following list of mobile computers:

- Mobile Computer Accounts
  - MCPD98
  - MCPD99
  - MCPD100
  - MCPD101
- Mobile Computer Users
  - Henry R. James
  - Catherine H. Anderson
  - Jill J. Smith
  - Michael F. Wolf

Taking Control

You, the network administrator, have control over a number of critical areas. The three main areas are easily identified according to the following high-level network administration areas:

- **Applications:** This area is one of the most important to put under strict change control. Users must in no way, shape, or form install and manage their own software.
- **Security:** To maintain a secure network, you need the authority to set security policy or to enforce the policy required by the business owners at both the servers and the workstations.
- **Operating System Environment:** Our modern operating systems, such as Windows 2000 and Windows XP, are extremely complex. Management and control of these systems and their myriad configuration needs to be firmly in the hands of experienced network technicians, support personnel, and administrators.

These three areas merely encapsulate what amounts to thousands of possible management scenarios. We discuss each one in more detail in the following sections.

Applications

What's the big deal enabling users to obtain and install their own applications? Actually, it's a very big deal. First, users really do not understand (for the most part) software piracy laws and how easily they can fall foul of them. Many people borrow software from friends and family, often unaware that they are committing a felony that carries as much as 20 years in jail for the crime.

Falling victim to software piracy laws is very easy. All that's necessary is for one disgruntled employee to report that your company "steals" software, and the ensuing raid by the software piracy police makes an IRS "raid" seem like Sunday at the church fund raiser.

If application usage is managed by the IT department and only technical-support people can install software, the risk is greatly reduced. Software metering and strict adherence to licensing requirements can keep the CEO or the CIO out of jail.

Enabling users to install their own software can cause administrative burdens to go through the roof. Most users do not understand the changes that an operating system undergoes whenever software is installed on the operating system.

Software should also be distributed from a central location or server. This practice saves technicians from needing to make the trip to the users' desktops for the installation. Remote software deployment or electronic software distribution goes a long way toward keeping administrative burden to a minimum.

To protect your company from extensive application support and administrative burden users need to use only the applications that are approved or sanctioned by the company. The best way to manage this approach is to create groups or collections of users and assign to them various applications. These groups and collections can be named after the applications that the members use, such as OfficeXPUsers and AcrobatUsers.

You need to create another list for each user that determines what software and hardware each requires to perform his functions. You create two lists. The first is for basic users who need no more than the standard applications adopted by the enterprise. If your company has adopted Microsoft Exchange 2000, for example, Outlook 2000 and later is on that list, as is MS Word, Excel, and other applications . . . if, of course, the company has standardized on Microsoft Office components, which is very common.

A second list next to the first one is an advanced-user choice list. The user (if policy permits) can choose a specialized list of software for which he must justify deployment. This justification, by the way, is presented to change control or management for review. A good example is a software engineer who is hired to create a certain application. He then requests that a development tool or component be installed or made available to complete the task.

Managing software is a daunting task for anyone. In a small organization, one person can typically be saddled with the job of managing anywhere in the region of 10 to 20 applications. In large companies, the number of software components can run into the thousands. Defining and enforcing policy regarding installation and configuration of applications is thus critical. Why do you need to do this? Consider the following problems that may occur if you permit users to install their own applications:

- The application may be unstable and could damage existing systems. During the early beta testing of Windows 2000 Professional, for example, a technical-support engineer at one of our clients installed the Release Candidate 3 code on his workstation to check it out. The code corrupted the databases belonging to the help desk and shut down the call center for three days.
- Applications may not be legally obtained. If you do not enforce change-control policy, your enterprise may be risking lawsuits and criminal charges. You cannot claim ignorance of users using illegal or pirated software. Your boss goes away for 20 years or more if your users steal software.
- The act of installing the software can introduce viruses and security risks to the network. If the user installs from a source on the Internet, you face the risk that the download may bring with it hostile applications. We have seen backdoor viruses pop out of downloaded zip files and kill a machine in less than a minute.
- Users are likely to run into problems and come to you for help with an application that you likely know nothing about. (Amazing how the network or server administrator is expected to know everything about every application that has ever been invented.)

Another category in addition to applications is *application management and configuration*. This involves determining and managing the deployment process, local and remote installation, configuring the software, user education, user support, and so on. Windows Server 2003 provides some services to manage automatic deployment and configuration.

Security

As does application management, security must be managed centrally. In fact, whenever you join a workstation to a domain, any security settings that you apply or enforce at the local workstation level are overridden by domain security settings.

Security policy needs to govern and enforce issues such as password usage, lockouts, and attempts to crack passwords by using elimination processes. If users maintain short passwords that never change or that can be easily figured out (such as the names of their dogs), before long, an intruder can learn the password and do some damage.

Other security policies that you need to manage centrally include public keys, certificates, digital signatures, and so on. What a user can and cannot do on the workstation or at a server is also important. The capability to log on to a domain controller, for example, is a privilege that only a handful of administrators should have.

Operating-system environment

The operating system is a complex piece of machinery, and it is becoming more complex to manage as software and hardware become more sophisticated and powerful. Consider the Windows XP operating system: Tens of thousands of settings and preferences can be set on it.

For your own sanity, all workstations in the enterprise must be managed as a single unit—or at least in only a handful of variations.

You should strive, for example, to make sure that all workstations have the same screen-saver settings—usually the corporate logo—and that users do not have the capability to change the corporate screen saver. If you don't, before long (a few days at the most), you can count on having as many as 20 different screen savers in use. Not only can the custom screen savers be doing damage (especially if they are freebies found on the Internet), but some may also be downright offensive. A few years ago, some users in a company were downloading screen savers that involved a female portrayed in a derogatory light. A sexual-harassment lawsuit ensued after the requests to remove the screen saver were ignored.

You don't want users constantly changing display settings, fiddling with network devices, and installing hardware that can damage the computer systems.

Workstation lockdown

Of course, the capability to centrally control and manage your user's computing experience can also be too powerful for some situations. Certaln classes of users may need more administrative control over their work environment.

Remote users on notebook computers that connect to the network for no more than 30 minutes a day may need more privileges to manage their own computers than do the users who work from the office all the time.

Although roving notebook users should possibly be permitted to set their own printer drivers and configurations, because they typically move from one printer to another during their sojourns, this does not mean that they should have the capability to change their network-device settings. Remote notebook users rarely need to set static IP addresses, and the DHCP stuff that they receive at each site is sufficient for them.

You find many settings in the Control Panel, however, that users rarely need to play with. Leaving these locked down until the user comes into the office and the notebook is handed to the technical people for a tune up is usually sufficient.

Getting ready for change-control policy

You now have a lot of information with which to determine how best to lock down workstations. The following list recaps what you know, or should know, before you enter the world of the Group Policy creators:

✦ You should know what type of user you support (basic to advanced or technically inclined).

✦ You should know the category of workstation that the user needs (mobile, workstation, handheld, and so on).

- You should also know what applications are required and how they are used (usage level). Is, for example, the user advanced or basic? If the user is given Access XP, can he wreck Access 97 databases?

- You should know the list of applications that your classes of users need.

In addition to what is on the preceding list, understanding the following information before you can begin to determine how best to enforce policy is imperative:

- Have users logged onto their computers as the local administrator or as a member of the local *Administrators* group? (This is common practice on workstations where logging onto the domain is not always possible or desirable.) If users can access the local account and registry, they may circumvent change-management policy. Decide which users fall into this category and which may be candidates to obtain a Windows 2000 Professional or XP desktop or session. Then ensure that these workstations have a local policy that as far as possible shadows group policy.

- Do your users install their own unauthorized software on their computers? If you do not have a policy to control this malady in an enterprise, you need to formulate one as soon as possible.

- Do your users store data on their own workstations? If they do, you need to plan or devise a strategy to have them move the data to network share points or folder resources published in Active Directory folders. Understand that the data is at risk in such practice, because workstations do not typically get backed up, which means that data can be lost if a computer crashes or is stolen. A feature of Windows 2000 and Windows Sever 2003 called *folder redirection* is a way of making sure that a user's documents or data folders reside on the server where the data is backed up. You find more information about this in the section "Types of Group Policy," later in this chapter.

- How often do users call with "broken" workstations or desktop configurations? A broken configuration is usually the outcome of a user trying to install his software or hardware on the machine. Another form of broken configuration results from users tampering with the operating systems, fiddling with registry settings, Control Panel applets, and so on. The problem stems from users who have a false sense of security because they have a home computer that they have mastered. They then eschew policy that strips them of that power at work. Only your administrators — and only a few, at that — or power users who are testing software as part of change-management board activity, however, should have such rights over the enterprise or corporate computer property. The risk of a change causing damage to the workstation or network services is just too high to be up for discussion with users who consider themselves "kings of computers."

Users also need to use the Internet wisely and in a way that does not compromise the enterprise. Although you can trust some users to do just that, you also need power and tools to ensure that users use the Internet only according to the organization's business rules. You can and should control Internet Explorer use and enforce proxy-access rules, browsing preferences, and so on.

Windows 2000 and Windows Server 2003 security is extremely powerful, but unless you can extend the security to workstations and ensure that users follow corporate requirements and business rules with respect, your life as a network or workstation administrator can prove very frustrating.

Understanding Group Policy

The change-control tool on Windows Server 2003 is the *Group Policy Object Editor* (*GPOE or just GPE*). As shown in Figure 14-2, this application is an MMC snap-in from which policy can be applied to the security principals — computer, users, and groups — of a Windows 2000 and Windows Server 2003 network.

Group Policy, which gets its name from the idea of grouping policy, can be applied to items such as security management and hardware configuration as well.

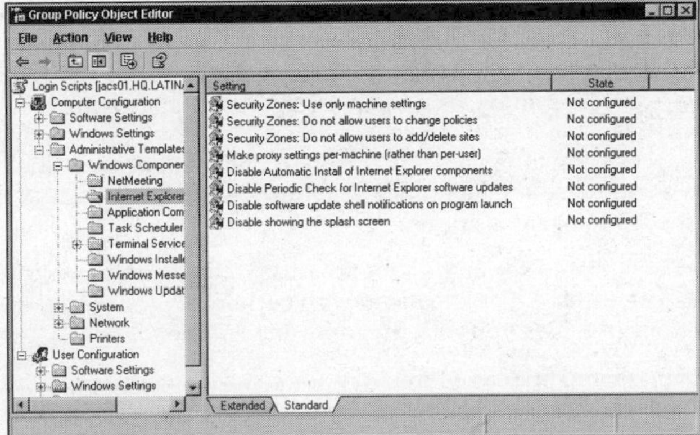

Figure 14-2: The Group Policy Object Editor snap-in.

Group Policy is applied by creating an object that contains the properties that extend control of the computer and the user's access to network and machine resources. This object is known as the *Group Policy Object*, or *GPO*. The policy is created from various templates stored on the workstation or server.

If an object is a member of a container that is associated (linked) to the GPO, that object falls under the influence of that GPO. If a container is linked to multiple GPOs, the result is that the effects of all GPOs on the linked container are merged. This is as shown in Figure 14-3.

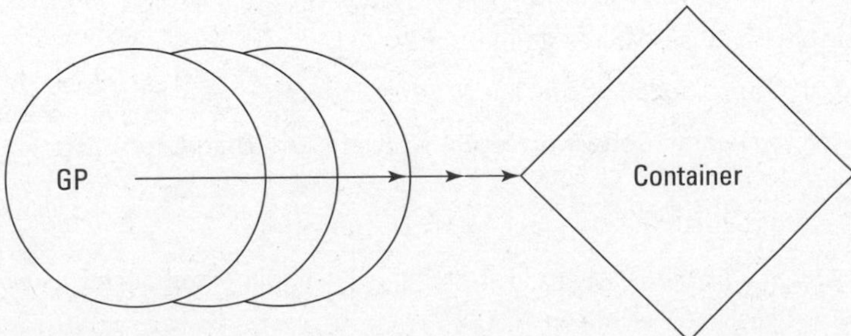

Figure 14-3: Multiple Group Policy Object policies merge to affect the container.

Sophisticated object-oriented engineering is at work in the GPO application process. The Group Policy architecture is complex, spans hundreds of pages, and is beyond the scope of this book. It is, however, well worth studying if you are an engineer at heart, because such advanced knowledge can only make you a better server or network administrator. You can search for the GPO architecture papers on the Microsoft Web site by searching Microsoft's white papers.

Group Policy is not applied directly to an individual security principal (although you can attain such granular control by creating specific OUs) but rather is applied to collections of security principals. Security principals gather under one roof on a Windows Server 2003 network in three places: the *site*, the *domain*, and the *organization unit*. As GP applies to all three types of containers, you can refer to this as a *GP hierarchy*.

Group Policy is vast and extremely powerful. It takes some getting used to, and you need to spend a lot of time trying different things. In large companies, the role of managing GP should be assigned to individuals, possibly members of the change-management board. Managing GP can easily become a full-time occupation for an administrator. GP becomes your main technology with which to manage change, user configuration and desktop settings, workstation lockdown security, software installation, and so on.

GPOs have more than 100 security-related settings and more than 700 registry-based settings, and the GP technology can also be extended or enhanced with certain APIs and custom templates. Specifically, GP technology provides you with the following functionality:

- The GPO is configured and stored in Active Directory. GP can also be defined at the local level — that is, at the workstation. Standalone computers are secured or locked down with local policy, but we provide more information about that in the section "How Group Policy Works," later in this chapter. GP, however, depends on Active Directory.
- You apply GPOs to users and computers in AD containers (sites, domains and OUs).
- The GPO is secure. (You can lock down a GPO just as you can any other object in the operating system.)
- The GPO can be filtered or controlled by membership in security groups. This, in fact, speeds up application of policy on the membership of the security group.
- The GPO is where the concentration of security power is located on Windows networks.
- The GPO is used to maintain Microsoft Internet Explorer.
- The GPO is used to apply logon, logoff, and startup scripts.
- The GPO is used to maintain software, restrict software, and enable software installation.
- The GPO is used to redirect folders (such as My Documents).
- The GPO does not expose the user profile to tampering if policy is changed, as was the case with Windows NT 4.0.
- GP settings on the computer are not permanent. In other words, unlike with older technologies for management or locking down workstations, the Registry is not permanently tattooed. The settings and configuration can be lifted at any time and easily changed.

Types of Group Policy

Group Policy has influence over just about every process, application, or service on a Windows network. Both servers and workstations are influenced by GP, and, therefore, unless you deploy Windows 2000 Professional or Windows XP, GP is *not* pervasive throughout the enterprise. Windows 9*x* and NT 4.0 Workstations are not influenced to the same extent as Windows 2000/XP clients, because client-side extensions that pull down and read policy are not present in these legacy desktop operating systems.

A network consisting of many different versions of Windows (in some cases, as many as five versions), therefore, is also going to be less secure or at least not as manageable. Obviously, a hard-to-manage or -control network is going to be a lot more expensive to maintain in the long run. The initial cost of upgrading to Windows Server 2003 throughout the enterprise pays off in the long run. In terms of security, such as the capability to stave off a hacker thanks to encryption or the capability to save critical data thanks to folder redirection — and we could give you many more examples — you can not only save a bundle by going "native," but you may even save the company as well. The more versions that you eliminate, the more secure and more manageable life is going to be for you.

You can have many different types of Group Policy "collections." (The term *policy collection* is not a Microsoft term as far as we know, but it is useful for describing the policy types.) The following list describes the "intent" of these collections:

- **Application deployment:** These policies are used to govern user access to applications. Application deployment or installation is controlled or managed in the following ways:
  - **Assignment:** GP installs or upgrades applications and software on the client computers. The assignment can also be used to publish an icon or shortcut to an application and to ensure that the user cannot delete the icon.
  - **Application publication:** Applications can be published in Active Directory. These applications are then advertised in the list of components that appears whenever a user clicks the Add/Remove icon in Control Panel.
- **File deployment:** These policies enable you to place files in certain folders on your user's computer. You can, for example, take aim at the user's My Documents folder and provide him with files that he needs to complete a project.
- **Scripting:** These policies enable you to select scripts to run at predetermined times. They are especially useful for ensuring that scripts get processed during startup and shutdown or whenever a user logs off a machine and a new user logs onto the same machine. Windows Server 2003 can process VB scripts, JScripts, and scripts written to the Windows scripting host.
- **Software:** These policies enable you to configure software on user workstations on a global or targeted scale. This is achieved by configuring settings in user profiles, such as the desktop settings, Start menu structure, and the other application menus.
- **Security:** Perhaps no other collection in Windows Server 2003 is as important as the security policies, given that, in current times, the next hacker who wipes out the assets could be the kid next door.

In addition to *eventually* reducing the total cost of ownership (through lowering the cost of administration), you should consider that Group Policy has other roles. It exists not to create problems for users and administrators, but to secure the environment and enhance the work and user environment. You thus need to make sure that you have the wherewithal to balance the two needs; if you don't, you could end up with cold pizza instead of glazed sirloin for dinner.

In your endeavors to secure the environment, you no doubt come across conflicts that violate the tenet to maintain a "user-friendly" environment. Going wild on password length is a good example. If you set password length too long to increase security, users not only get peeved, but they also start sticking the passwords on their monitors because they are so hard to remember. That is not security. If you must have tight security, your choice in such a matter may be to take the security need to management and suggest smart cards or biometrics. Remember that locking down an environment should not lock out the user at the same time.

The environment can be enhanced in many different ways. If users need access to new software, you need to determine which of the following three methods of delivery is more pleasing or enhancing to the user from the user's perspective:

- ✦ Waiting hours or days for the administrator to show up at your desk with the new software.
- ✦ Being asked to log on to a network distribution point and install the software yourself.
- ✦ Taking a break while the software mysteriously installs itself onto your machine with seemingly no human intervention.

Enhancing the users' environment also means helping them easily locate applications, intelligently redirecting folders or mapping their folders to resources, and automating processes during the twilight times of the workstation — namely, at logoff and logon.

Before you study how Group Policy works, you should at least take some time to get familiar with the technology.

The elements of Group Policy

A programmatic discussion of the elements is beyond the scope of this book. Understanding the various elements with which you interact, however, helps. Several components make up GP from the administrator's perspective. These components include the following:

- ✦ The Group Policy Object.
- ✦ Active Directory containers.
- ✦ Group Policy links.
- ✦ The policy of Group Policy (such as the Group Policy refresh intervals).
- ✦ *Explain* text, which elaborates on the objective of the policy.
- ✦ The Group Policy Editor.
- ✦ Computer Configuration and User Configuration nodes.
- ✦ GP Containers and GP Templates.
- ✦ The `gpt.ini` file.

The Group Policy Object

The *Group Policy Object*, or *GPO*, is the object that contains Group Policy properties. The GPO is really a container, at the highest level, into which properties or attributes are stored. Policy is conveyed by association with a GPO . . . that is, its properties "rub off" on a user or computer object contained inside a GP recipient. GPOs must be created and named before their policies can be used.

Active Directory containers

Active Directory containers are the default targets of the GPO. In other words, the contents of a container that a GPO is linked to receive the Group Policy settings by default. By establishing a link with a GPO, a container falls under the influence of the GPO and its policies. This happens automatically if you create a GP object. The containers that can be linked to GPOs are *sites*, *domains*, and *organization units*. But GP can also be associated with a standalone computer; and all computers can be linked to their local GPO.

Group Policy links

GP links are the means by which containers are associated with GPOs. You can research links for a particular domain, as discussed in the section "How Group Policy Works," later in this chapter. By "discovering" the links, you can establish which GPO is influencing a particular container and, therefore, its members. (See the section "How Group Policy Works," later in this chapter, for more information.)

The policy

The *policy* is the *property* of the GPO. The policy is the actual setting that is applied through the association as discussed in the section "Active Directory container," earlier in this chapter. All GPOs have the same policies. You do not add or remove a policy from a GPO. But policy is activated in several ways. The policy first must be *defined* and then possibly *enabled* or *disabled* or otherwise activated in the particular GPO or applied to a security group. After it is enabled or defined, you can then manipulate the settings that comprise the policy.

Figure 14-4 shows a policy that needs to be defined before it can be made useful. In the figure, we have chosen to define a policy for the DNS Server. After the policy is defined, you can set its startup criteria. In this case, we have defined the DNS Server and set its startup parameter to *Automatic.* Other policies require you to simply enable or disable the policy, while others require definition, enabling, and then further configuration or setup.

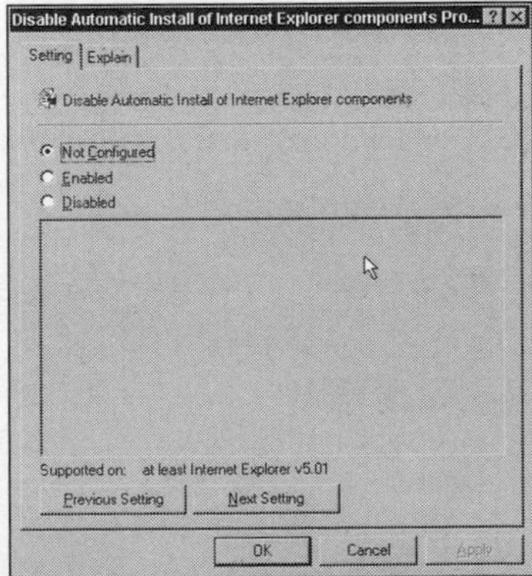

Figure 14-4: Defining a policy.

Explain text

The *explain text* is accessed on the Explain tab of a policy, as shown in Figure 14-4. Not all policies have an Explain text tab. Explain text essentially describes what the policy achieves and any instructions as to how to apply the policy and even circumstances where you *shouldn't* apply the policy.

The Group Policy Editor

The *Group Policy Object Editor* (*GPOE*) is the Microsoft Management Console (MMC) snap-in that provides access to the configuration of a GPO. To edit or create a GPO for a container, you first must load a used or new GPO into the GPE. The GPE is shown in Figure 14-5.

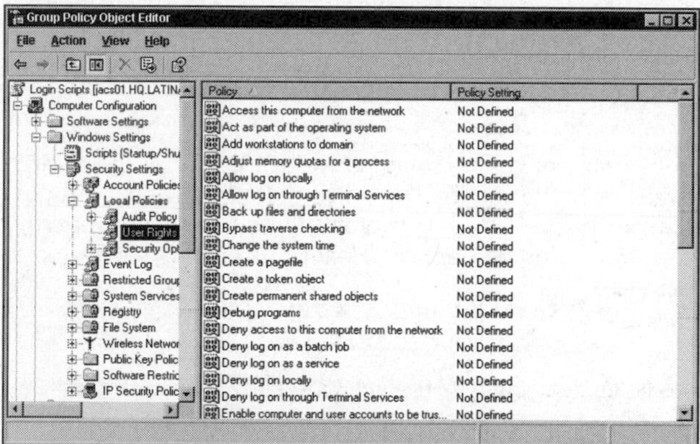

Figure 14-5: The Group Policy Object Editor showing User Rights Assignment expanded.

Computer Configuration and User Configuration

A GPO is divided into two nodes. These nodes are known as the *Computer Configuration* and *User Configuration*. Each node contains the policies for the respective security principal. You can apply policy to either of the nodes for any GPO.

Where GPOs live

All GPOs store their information in two locations: the *GP Container* (*GPC*) and a *GP Template* (*GPT*). These objects are identified by a globally unique identifier (GUID), which keeps the objects in the two locations synchronized. After a GPO is born, information associated with it is transferred to the two locations.

For the GPT, the OS creates a folder for its use in the `Sysvol` structure in the `systemroot`. The actual folder name of the GPT is its GUID. A typical GPT folder looks as follows:

```
%systemroot%\SYSVOL\sysvol\genesis.mcity.org\Policies\{31B2F340-016D-
11D2-945F-00C04FB984F9}
```

The GPC lives in the Active Directory. It builds itself a hierarchy of containers in the space that it is given in the directory in which to store computer and user configuration information.

The GPC deals with the version (used for synchronization), status (enabled/disabled), and settings (of extensions) and any policy settings defined by extensions. The SYSVOL side of the GPO holds a list of client-side extensions, User Configuration settings, Computer Configuration settings (`registry.pol`), and Registry settings that derive from administrative templates.

As a general rule, policy data that is small and seldom changes is stored in the GPC, while data that is large and changes often is stored in the GPT.

Group Policy Template structure

The default contents of the Group Policy Template structure are security related, but as you configure the user and machine environment, the GPT structure begins to fill up with folders and information related to a broad range of GP and change-management information.

Table 14-2 lists some of the folders and information that find their way into the GPT structure.

Table 14-2: The Group Policy Template Structure

Folder	*Purpose*
\ADM	This holds the ADM files that are associated with a GPT.
\MACHINE	This holds the `registry.pol` file that relates to machine registry settings.
\MACHINE\APPLICATIONS	This holds the AAS files used by the Microsoft Windows Installer.
\MACHINE\DOCUMENTS & SETTINGS	This holds files that are used to configure a user's desktop whenever the user logs on to this computer.
\MACHINE\MICROSOFT\ WINDOWSNT\SECEDIT	This holds the `gpttmpl.ini` Security Editor file.
\MACHINE\SCRIPTS	This contains the startup and shutdown folders.
\MACHINE\SCRIPTS\STARTUP	This holds scripts and other files related to startup scripting.
\MACHINE\SCRIPTS\SHUTDOWN	This holds scripts and other files related to shutdown scripting.
\USER	This holds the `registry.pol` file that relates to user registry settings.
\USER\APPLICATIONS	This holds the AAS files used by the Microsoft Windows Installer.
\USER\DOCUMENTS & SETTINGS	This holds files that are used to configure a user's desktop.
\USER\SCRIPTS	This holds logon and logoff scripts.
\USER\SCRIPTS\LOGON	This holds scripts and other files related to logon scripting.
\USER\SCRIPTS\LOGOFF	This holds scripts and other files related to logoff scripting.

The gpt.ini file

In the root folder of each GPT, you also find a file called the `gpt.ini`. Two important entries in this file are related to local GPOs, as follows:

- `Version=x`: This entry is the version number of the GPO, and *x* is the placeholder for a number placed by a version-counter function. Typically, the version number is zero-based, and each time that you modify the GPO, this counter is incremented by 1. However, this number is a decimal representation of an eight-digit hexadecimal number (a DWORD), which is the data type the group policy processes understand. The four least significant digits represent the Computer Settings version number, and the four most significant digits represent the User Settings version number. In other words, if you see Version=65539 the computer understands this as hexadecimal is 0X00010003, which tells it that the Computer Settings version is 3, and the User Settings version is 1.
- `Disabled=y`: This entry refers to the local GPO and tells the dependant functions whether the local GPO is disabled or not. If you disable the GPO, the value placed here is 0, and if you enable it, the value is changed to 1.

How Group Policy Works

The Windows Server 2003 Group Policy (GP) application hierarchy is typically site first, domain next, and then OU. In other words, if GP is set for a site, all objects in that site feel the effects of the GP, including the domain and all its members. If you then apply GP to a domain, the merged GP for all objects in the domain is inherited from the site and the domain. If you further apply GP to an OU, if GP is set for the domain and the site, the GP on any object in the OU is a combination of all three.

So the combined control in the OU may be derived from the domain policy and the site policy as well, unless the inherited policy is expressly blocked by a built-in override mechanism that can be enabled or disabled (discussed in the section "Group Policy application," later in this chapter) and the access-control mechanisms on groups and users, discussed in Chapter 13 and Chapter 27.

You can also force policy directly on an object by linking the GPO to the object and then setting the link to forbid overriding.

Local or nonlocal Group Policy Objects

Group Policy Objects also come in two flavors — *local GPOs* and *domain-bound GPOs* — and because the local GPO is applied to a computer before the domain GPO, the actual inheritance hierarchy for a computer is local GPO, non-local site, domain, and finally OU. Local GPO is first applied to the computer, and then any policy that is to be applied from the DC takes place after the user logs in.

What happens to the policy that is applied to the computer? Group policy application is successively applied. In other words, the last policy that is enabled for a setting is applied. So if a local policy is defined and a site policy undefines it, the site policy setting wins. If the domain setting then defines the setting again but the OU policy undefines it, the final result is that the setting is undefined and does not affect the objects that are affected by the GPO. In this example, the OU policy wins over all others.

For a local GP, if the setting is undefined from on high, the local policy wins. To keep your network secure while ensuring that users can continue to work, to some extent, with their computers, you should set up local policy as if no domain policy is forthcoming.

One part of GP, however, always wins over local policy, and that is the security policy from the domain. Security policy always overrides local security policy, even if the local security policy is stronger. If no security policy is defined at the domain level the security policy at the local level remains undefined. You can test this by running a report for a Resultant Set of Policy, which we show you how to do in the section "Taking control of Group Policy by using FAZAM 2000," later in this chapter. Each Windows computer has only one local GPO that governs it. You can open the local GPO by running `gpedit.msc` from the command line on any Windows Server 2003, Windows 2000 Server and Professional or Windows XP computer, or you can pull up the MMC snap-in from installed menu items. (To customize the MMC, refer to Chapter 7.) But remembering that a nonlocal GPO can override the local GPO is important. More about this is coming up in the following section.

Group Policy application

The architecture of Active Directory dictates that policy applied later to an object overrides policy that is applied earlier. In other words, if you remove the rights that enable a person to log on to a computer locally in the local GPO and then later restore that right in a site or domain GPO, the restored setting becomes the effective control because it was applied later—possibly even last. The exception is that anything not defined does not change the existing control, and any control specifically enabled or disabled earlier persists.

Any GPO control state that is disabled or enabled in an earlier container persists. But if something higher up is undefined, and then, at the local level, it is defined, the defined setting survives. This is useful for controlling access and certain security mechanisms on individual computers, where specifically disabling an option prevents an administrator from enabling it unintentionally or on purpose at the nonlocal (domain) level.

You also can create multiple GPOs for a container. The order of control application is that policy applied later overwrites policy applied earlier. In other words, if you have two GPOs to an OU, any settings that say "yea" in the first GPO in the list are then overwritten by GPOs that say "nay" later in the list. This is called *administrative order*, and the order can be rearranged by using the Up and Down buttons on the Group Policy tab of the OU's Properties dialog box, as shown in Figure 14-6. (This dialog box appears when you right-click an OU and select Properties from the context menu.)

If you set a No Override on a GPO by checking this option, GPOs that are linked at the lower levels cannot override the higher GPO's effective settings. The use of No Override also prevents GPOs that are linked at the same level from overriding. If you have several links at the same level in the AD that are set to No Override, you need to arrange them according to a priority that you determine. Links that are higher in the list have the priority.

Understanding priority in applying GP to a domain or even to a site is important. You want numerous settings to remain in force, and a local administrator may attempt to override you. As long as you set the No Override on the higher GPO, the setting that you enable is enforced at the lower levels of the directory.

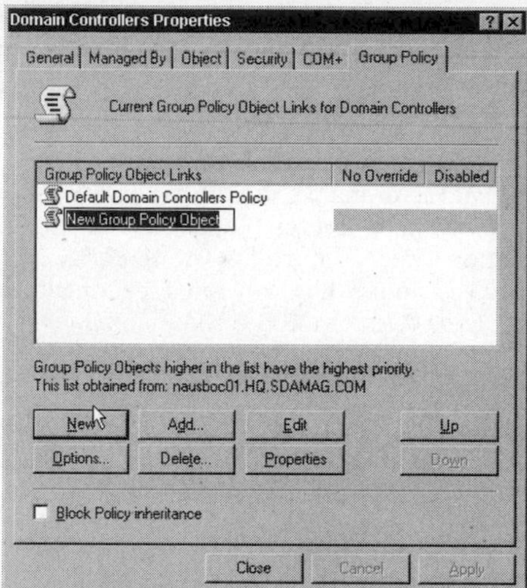

Figure 14-6: Applying the GPO link.

The No Override setting is applied to a link rather than to the actual GPO. The Block Policy inheritance setting is applied to the domain or OU, and it thus applies to all GPOs linked at that level or higher. Sites do not have a higher authority.

Conversely, you can also block inheritance of GP from higher GPOs. This is done by checking Block Policy inheritance on the GP tab of the Properties sheet of the domain or OU. This option does not apply to sites, because in terms of GP, they are the highest in the hierarchy. There is a catch (just when you thought you found a security flaw); the No Override option— if enabled—takes precedence.

To investigate the links maintained by a GPO, follow these steps:

1. Open the OU's Properties dialog box as just described and select the Group Policy tab.
2. Select the GPO and then click the Properties button. The dialog box shown in Figure 14-7 loads. Select the Links tab and then click the Find Now button.

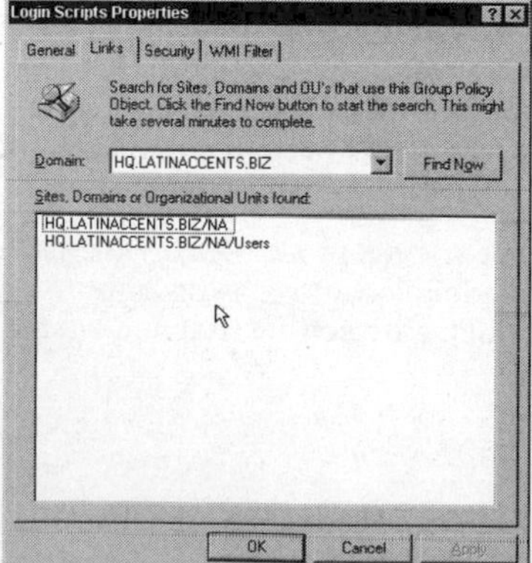

Figure 14-7: The Links tab in the GPO Properties dialog box.

Whenever you edit a GPO, any settings that you change are not immediately applied to the container's possessions, but the change in policy is immediate. The GPO settings are then applied to the object by default every 90 minutes. The refresh time can be changed, however, and we discuss how in the section "Group Policy refresh rate," later in this chapter.

Conflicts can possibly arise from the application of GP. An account lockout, for example, can occur if you set the number of attempts at a logon password too low. If a user gets the password wrong several times in succession, which can easily happen if the user has the Caps Lock key on, you need to reset the lockout posthaste.

An account lockout could be the result of several security policies doing what they were supposed to do but the results not being the original intention. To unlock an account in such a case, open the Active Directory Users and Computers snap-in and go down to the user account. Right-click the account and select Properties from the menu. On the Properties page that appears, select the Account tab. You see that the Account Lock Out check box is selected. The OS did this in compliance with GP. Deselect the box, and the user can now log in (as long as the Caps Lock key is off).

Although the GP of a parent container can override a child's GP, if the child's GP contradicts the parent, the child prevails. Rather than creating a tug of war between the override, inheritance, and access control associations, you should strive to keep things simple and fully document all GP, group memberships, and any peculiar associations.

Filtering policy

GP can also be filtered out of the range of security principals residing in security groups. In other words, you can narrowly define which security group of users or computers is influenced by GP, irrespective of the relationships the group has with an OU. This is achieved by setting the discretionary access control list (DACL) permissions on the group. Not only does the GPO take effect on the security principals much faster, but you can also restrict a specific security policy from creating AD links to GPOs.

The DACL is a list of permissions on an object (in this case, a GPO). You use the DACL to permit or deny access to the GPO according to the membership in the group. You can apply the filter in either of the following two ways:

✦ Right-click the root node of a Group Policy Object in the GPOE it is open in; then choose Properties from the pop-up menu. The Properties dialog box loads. Select the Security tab, which shows groups and users and their associated permissions.

✦ You can also open to the container in Active Directory (site, domain, or OU), right-click it, and choose Properties from the pop-up menu. Then click the Group Policy tab on the Properties page that appears and select the GPO in the GPO list on this tab. Right-click the GPO, choose Properties from the pop-up menu, and then select the Security tab on the dialog box on the dialog box that appears. (You can also simply click the Properties button to get to the same destination.)

Now you can specify which groups are influenced or not in the container by checking or unchecking the Apply Group Policy access control entry (ACE). You should also know that, by default, authenticated users have both the Apply Group Policy and Read permissions checked but not Write or Full Control. What this means is that the users cannot modify the GPO. And you can thus also apply more stringent access to the GPO.

These techniques also enable you to use the Security tab on the GPO to determine which administration group can modify GP. We use such techniques to tighten the security of our domain, as demonstrated in the section "Security at the local Group Policy Objects," later in this chapter.

Delegating control of GP

GP can be delegated as follows:

✦ Delegate GP link assignment for a site, domain, or OU.

✦ Delegate the creation of GPOs.

✦ Delegate the management of GPOs.

Delegation is performed through the delegation of rights to use MMC consoles and particular management snap-ins related to GP. These are themselves controlled through GPOs. To delegate access to GPO duties, you essentially control who has access to the Group Policy MMC snap-ins. The path to this is as follows: Expand the container in AD and right-click the item. Choose Properties ➪ Group Policy from the pop-up menu. Select a GPO or, if one is not yet created, make one. Click Edit and you load the Group Policy console. Expand the User Configuration node of the Group Policy Object to Administrative Templates, Windows Components, Microsoft Management Console, and, finally, Group Policy. Under the Group Policy node, you find a bunch of folders and policies related to Group Policy snap-ins.

Administrators can administer Group Policy by being a member of a domain administrator group or the built-in administrators group. Non administrators must be given *log on locally permission* before they can administer GP, and this is done by expanding Computer Configuration to Windows Settings, Security Settings, Local Policies, User Rights Assignment, and, finally, Allow Log On Locally. Enabling many people to log on to the DC is not very secure or wise; and thus you're best off assigning Active Directory tools, such as the Active Directory Users and Computers tool, which gives rise to the Group Policy Editor console, to network administrators or the help-desk consultant's workstations. Given the appropriate rights, these administrators need never enter the server room and camp out at the DC.

Security at the local Group Policy Objects

The local GPOs that exist on every Windows Server 2003 machine have only security settings configured (and most of them are disabled). The local GPO is stored in the `%SYSTEMROOT%\SYSTEM32\GROUPPOLICY` directory. The following permissions are set through the DACLs:

✦ Administrators (Full)

✦ System (Full)

✦ Authenticated Users (Read and Execute)

How Group Policy is processed

Group Policy is almost entirely processed from the client side. The only service using GP that processes entirely from the server is the Remote Installation Service, and that's because a client-side OS does not yet exist to process policy.

A group of DLLs called *client-side GP extensions* performs client-side processing after first making a call to a DC for a GPO list. The processing order is obtained from the GPO list. The rule of precedence in processing is that Computer Configuration gets preference over User Configuration. But what if a user is placed in one OU and his computer is placed in another OU? Which GPO becomes the effective GP conveyor? In Chapter 9, we suggest putting all your users into a small collection of OUs and then placing their computers into other OUs that can be associated with key management entities (KMEs).

The following GP behavior transpires to keep a sanity check on things. A feature known as the *Group Policy loopback* enables you to bestow GP based or dependent on the computer used. The loopback feature enables you to choose two modes by which you can govern the choice of User or Computer Configuration.

Merge mode

Whenever a user logs onto a computer and the loopback feature is in *merge mode*, the GP objects are read according to the User Configuration and then again according to the Computer Configuration. By reading in the Computer Configuration last, the Computer Configuration is given priority. So the computer-related GP has a higher precedence than the user's GP. If the user's specific GP is not affected by the computer's configuration, the User Configuration policy is applied.

Replace mode

The *replace mode* forces GP to ignore the user's GP configuration. In other words, only the GP in the Computer Configuration applies.

The Merge mode and Replace mode setting, as well as all GP processing options, can be toggled in a GPO under its Computer Configuration\Administrative Templates\System\Group Policy.

GP processing streams

GP processing can be performed asynchronously or synchronously. Asynchronous processing can occur on other threads, and thus the processing happens much quicker. Synchronous processing threads wait for one process to complete before they start. You can customize the processing behavior of GP processing, but you would consider this only for specialized applications in which you need to apply the GP as quickly as possible. The rule is that, for speed, use asynchronous processing and, for reliability, use synchronous processing.

Although the latter rule worked well for Windows 2000, the Windows XP operating system muddies the GP pool a bit. Windows XP is designed to start up fast if GP is applied asynchronously, and thus it can start up too fast. Users may therefore be on their desktops and working before all policy is applied. Have no fear, because that does not mean that, while your user is working, some policy, such as folder redirection, happens to come along ten minutes into a document edit and whips the word-processing file away from the user's fingertips. Some policies — and folder redirection is one of them — are not processed synchronously.

One annoying issue with Windows XP and asynchronous processing is how software distribution is affected. If you assign applications to workstations, you may need to force the user to log on and off numerous times before the software policy takes root and the software gets installed. This is not a cool scenario if your idea of software distribution is that the software gets installed "now" and not after the user logs on and off for the whole morning just to pick up another new application.

Group Policy refresh rate

The default refresh rate is every 90 minutes. Thus any changes made to the GP that apply to a particular user or computer become effective only in this default time. You can change the default by using the GP setting in Administrative Templates. A setting of zero forces the refresh to kick off every seven seconds. You would configure a narrower refresh interval for tighter security application or for a specialized processing situation. The default refresh rate seems long and can be shortened to at least 60 minutes.

Setting shorter refresh intervals causes increased network traffic, and very tight intervals on user computers can interfere with the work environment. Very long refresh intervals are easier on the network but make for a less secure environment. The longest time is 45 days, and if you need to make a security policy change, such a time would be useless.

To change the setting, you need to edit the Default Domain Controllers GPO. This is linked to the DC's OU. Open the GPO and expand to the Computer Configuration node of the GPO. Select Administrative Templates and expand it through System and Group Policy, until you arrive at the Group Policy Refresh Interval for Computers node.

On several domain controllers that we installed, the refresh policy was disabled. You may want to check that this is not the case on your DCs. The documented DC refresh rate is five minutes.

Administrative GP settings, such as Folder Redirection and Software Installation, take place only during or after the computer starts up or after the user logs on and not during the periodic refresh period described earlier in this section. The obvious reason for this is that you would not want software to start removing itself while your user was still using it.

Optional Group Policy processing

Every client-side extension has a policy parameter for controlling the processing of GP. By default, the client-side extension updates the GP only if it determines at the refresh interval that the GP has changed. This is done for performance optimization. But for security purposes, you can make sure that, at every refresh interval, GP is refreshed even if the policy has not changed.

You should be very selective in how you use this setting because you see increased network bandwidth and slower GP refresh as a result.

Group Policy processing over low bandwidth

Group Policy sets a flag on the client-side extension if low bandwidth networks are detected. If the flag is raised, the following GP processing takes place:

- Security policy is always processed.
- Policy in Administrative Templates is always processed.
- Software installation is skipped.
- Scripts are turned off.
- Folder redirection is skipped.
- Internet Explorer maintenance is turned off.

How does GP detect low bandwidth? The client-side extensions simply ping the DC and analyze the response data. But low bandwidth is relative. What's low to you and me in Miami could be as fast as blazes in the Land of Oz.

Using a built-in algorithm, GP works out the response rate based on data and time parameters and the connections being used. If the result of the calculation is equal to the 500-Kbps default, GP considers that a slow link and makes the necessary adjustments in GP processing. But you can change the default as you deem fit in the Group Policy options of the GPO. The exact policy is *Group Policy slow link detection*. Remember to set this for users as well in the User Configuration node. The target policy in User Configuration is identical.

User Profiles also have a timeout policy over slow links. This is located in the Computer Configuration node, and the target policy is the Logon node of the GPE. If the extension cannot ping the server, it defaults to measuring file-system performance, which is how NT measures performance. The policy can be configured for a connection speed threshold in Kbps and a threshold transit time in milliseconds.

We are currently administering a domain in which hundreds of Windows XP workstations have been scattered around the U.S. They have been configured to receive policy over a 32-Kbps connection once a day. So far, they are not complaining.

Specifying domain controllers for GP

In setting up your Active Directory infrastructure, you need to make sure that GP settings are correctly propagated and disseminated throughout the enterprise and that replication is not a course for corrupted GP information.

You have several considerations. If you support a small enterprise that usually contains one DC on the same network as everyone else, you should not need to concern yourself where GP is edited. But in a large enterprise, you may want to studiously control the target DCs for GP changes and who has the capability to make such changes.

We have discussed how you can delegate (or restrict) power to edit GP, and you can also determine which DC is the target to receive the changes. Problems can occur if you have more than one DC receiving GP edits and more than one administrator applying changes. Your GP edit may become overwritten during replication, and you could suffer GP editing collisions. And depending on the location of the DC, it may not always be accessible for GPO editing and creation.

You have two routes to setting domain controller options for GP. One way is via the GPO Editor snap-in. The other way is via GP settings that enable you to set DC options by editing policy in the Administrative Templates node.

To access the setting in the former option, you need to open the Default Domain Policy into the GPOE and then select the root. Choose View ➪ DC Options from the menu bar. The dialog box shown in Figure 14-8 appears.

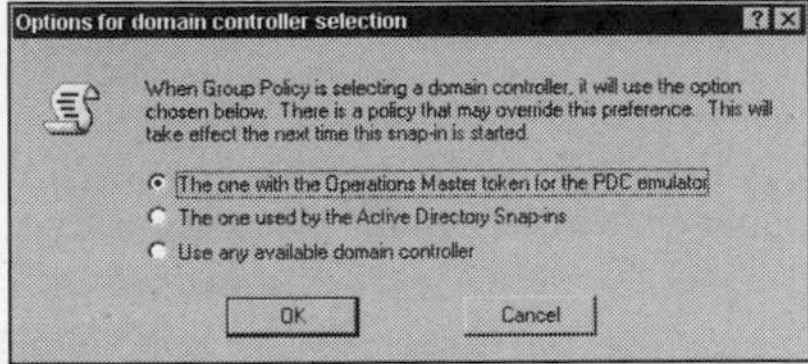

Figure 14-8: Choosing the domain controller to receive changes.

The dialog box contains three options. Choose the option that best applies to your network environment, as follows:

✦ **The one with the Operations Master token for the PDC emulator:** This is the default option according to Microsoft documentation, but we have found that not always to be the case, especially if you have more than one DC on the same network segment. This option ensures that only one DC is the target for GPO creation and editing, however, and that the other DCs receive GP updates from one source. This option forces the console to use the same DC every time that you or someone else uses it, which is why the option is part of the console and not the snap-in in the first place. In addition, you should limit the number of people that can apply GP in a certain domain, or you should schedule the GP tasks as part of change management. (The DC with the Operations Master token is usually the first DC created for a forest, but it can abdicate this honor if forced to.)

✦ **The one used by Active Directory Snap-ins:** Snap-ins include an option that enables you to change the DC that is the focus of the snap-in. (All MMC consoles enable you to choose a computer.) As long you are sure that you are "aimed" at the right DC, this option works. But if you don't pay attention to detail, this could become a problem down the road.

✦ **Use any available domain controller:** This option is the least desirable but would suffice, such as in a situation where you're working with a close-knit group or cluster of DCs on a fast network.

The option that we prefer overrides all the preceding ones . . . by setting the option in GP. The GPO makes sure that all snap-ins select the primary domain controller emulator for a domain in editing a GPO.

You can also use the policy to specify how GP chooses the domain controller. In other words, you can specify exactly which DC should be used by setting the option as policy.

To configure the correct settings, open the default domain GPO as just described and, in User Configuration, expand down through Administrative Templates and System to Group Policy. The options in the policy are the same as the ones demonstrated in the DC Options dialog box shown in Figure 14-8 and discussed earlier (although the various help texts describing these option varies). The exact policy is called *Group Policy domain controller selection*.

Putting Group Policy to Work

As discussed in the section "How Group Policy Works," earlier in this chapter, two key areas of GP and change management are *software change control* and *security*. These represent two key areas in change control and change management, which are serviced by the GP technology of Windows Server 2003.

The software policies

The software policies include policy to manage applications and Windows Server 2003 and its respective components. In the following examples, we demonstrate the modification and manipulation of the settings and environment by using the GPE snap-in.

To edit software GPOs, follow these steps:

1. Open the Active Directory Users and Computers snap-in and go to the site, domain, or OU in which you want to locate your GPO. (These are often referred to as the *SDOU containers*, which stands for *S*ite, *D*omain, or *O*rganization *U*nit container.)
2. Right-click the container, choose Properties from the pop-up menu, and then select the Group Policy tab from the dialog box that appears.
3. Select the GPO link to edit or create a new GPO. Click the Edit button.
4. Expand the User Configuration node from its root through Administrative Templates and Control Panel to Display. In this example, you are going to set a policy by disabling the Background tab so that the user cannot change the pattern and wallpaper on the desktop.
5. Right-click the policy to modify it and then choose Properties from the pop-up menu.
6. Check to determine whether the policy is implemented, defined, or enabled. If it is not enabled, define or enable the item by checking it. Then choose the setting for the policy. Click Apply and OK to get back to the console.

That's all that making a simple policy change involves. You may notice as you browse the software-related policies that some of these require you to add more details, such as the path name and similar information.

The security policies

These policies govern the extent of the security configuration of Windows Server 2003 networks. Security GP is available for deployment at every port that poses a security risk to the system as a whole, such as logon/logoff, communications, file systems, hardware and media, and so on.

Table 14-3 lists the GP related to security areas.

Table 14-3: Security Group Policy

GP	*Purpose*
Account Policy	These policies configure passwords, account lockout, authentication, Kerberos, and so on.
Local Policies	These policies configure auditing, user-rights definitions, and so on.
Restricted Group	These policies group membership for security sensitive groups. The built-in Administrator group is an example of a restricted group.
System Services	These policies configure security and the default startup behavior for services running on the computer. (Refer to Figure 14-4, which provides an example of applying policy on a service.)
Registry	These policies configure security on the registry keys.
File System	These polices configure security on the file system.

Continued

Table 14-3 *(continued)*

GP	*Purpose*
Active Directory	These polices configure security on directory objects in each domain.
Public Key	These policies configure the encrypted data-recovery agents, trusted certificate authorities, and other parameters related to your public-key infrastructure or PKI.
IP Security	These policies configure policies related to IPSec.

Group Policy and Change Management: Putting It All Together

The number-one rule of change-control policy engagement is this: *Change control policy is enforced over the user by way of the computer.* In other words, the target of change control is the user's computer.

If you can enforce change policy over the computer, you are effectively enforcing the policy over the user. If the user has no control over the computer, the user is no longer in a position or in power to circumvent policy. Although the GPO is divided into two configuration nodes, User and Computer, the Computer Configuration takes precedence.

Caution: With the power that GP yields, all the elements of Windows – access control, GP inheritance, GP override blocking, GP refreshing, GPO links, OU nesting, domain nesting, and more – you can potentially cook up a GP soup that no one can fathom, so take care in the planning stage.

But restricting a user to any particular computer becomes impractical. Terminal Services sessions are impossible to manage, and you have a hard time managing computers for roaming users and task-oriented staff. So the user's identification to the network, or logon ID, *and* the workstation's identification on the network are merged or combined to provide the change-control "blanket" that filters rights and privileges, and thus control, to the user *and* on the computers that he uses.

This power is not only a boon with security and change control, but it is also the main player in the functionality of IntelliMirror . . . having the user's desktop follow him to any PC, local or remote. After you have determined that you need change management and control, you also need enforcement. In other words, you create the change-control body, provide policy to carry out the whims of the change-control board, and enforce change control at all levels of the enterprise through GP (and other mechanisms that you find and customize to suit your environment).

Don't accept the default policy

In dealing with GP, an unsafe attitude is to assume that whatever Microsoft has installed as default Group Policy is adequate. Believing that the default settings are adequate is foolish for several reasons. First, every enterprise is different, so what you set in GP may work for you but not for the company around the corner. Second, the criteria that Microsoft has used to set the default GP is not widely known and is not appropriate for the majority of users (and we don't think that Microsoft intended that either). And third, what Microsoft documented as the default was, in many cases, found not to be the actual default after we installed and tested the services and components.

Where then do you start with GP? You can follow the cowboys who have stated that planning is for politicians and that the best way to tackle a Windows network is to just install it and to heck with all this ramp-up, pilot-project, testing, lab tripe. Or you can take the more conservative approach and perform testing and validation. You may find a place for yahoo-type antics. If you need to get a server up and running just to use a particular service as soon as possible, you can get away with the install-and-run approach.

What we recommend is that you go back to the lab and browse GP. This is probably the best method of getting to know GP, and at the same time, you find out how the server is configured from the time that you reboot it, after Active Directory promotion.

Without worrying about desirable change-management policy for now, open the GPE of your new domain controller and start at the top of the directory. Starting with the site, work your way down through each container in the SDOU hierarchy and investigate the GPO links that are in place. You do so as discussed in the section "How group policy is processed," earlier in this chapter — by opening up the Properties page of the container and selecting the Group Policy tab. Edit each link that you see in the container and then investigate the settings defined or enabled in each object, in both User and Computer Configurations.

At the birth of a new domain, any settings are unlikely to be blocked or overridden in any way. So you can safely assume that the policy that has been set up for the site into which you have placed your root DC filters down to the "bottom" of the directory. In other words, any OU that you now create inherits from higher up. The domain, of course, is in the middle of this hierarchy, so you need to then investigate the GP that is applied at the domain level to determine what effects that may have on your desired control at the OU level. Each domain created gets a default domain GPO. Study the information and document it on your help desk or change-management system. If you do not have a change-management system, even a database or word-processing document works — it may get unwieldy eventually, but for now, it serves the purpose.

Establishing a GP attack plan

We discussed OU strategy and groups and users extensively in the previous chapter of the book. But before you start, first sit down with the policy required by change management and security and separate out policy required from one end of the forest to another from policy that is required from one end of a domain to another. If only one domain is in the tree, this process should not take long. This research does not need to be exhaustive because the list is going to change and is going to get very much longer.

With that Global Policy wish list, you edit the GPO first for the site in which you have located your root DC — the one that sits at the very top of the namespace in the twilight world between the Active Directory domain and the Internet domain or namespace. In that site, establish the policies that you want to see defaulted throughout the enterprise. A good example is password length. If no GPO linked is to the site, create one and open it up for editing.

Whatever policies that you set at this level then filter down to the various domains and OUs that you create. Notice that, as you first went into the policy, the setting for password length was not even set. Then, if you open the domain GPO, you find that the default length is 0 characters. That level of security is about as secure as a ripe apple in a tree. That's like asking the burglar to mind the store while you go out for five minutes.

Go through all the policies in the site and define what satisfies your change-management and security plans for now. Your first objective no doubt is to lock down the network and install some form of security. Later, and before you deploy, you can batten down the hatches further as your needs dictate.

Dealing with computer accounts

Look at the logical plan that we discuss in Chapter 9. Concentrating your computer accounts into the OUs that represent your KMEs is feasible most of the time (and we say "most of the time" because every company has its own requirements). With that in mind, you can create OUs along key management entity (KME) lines or functions and collect your computers for the KME into the respective OU. You can also group all your computer accounts into a Computers or Workstations OU, which is done often, and all of your users into one large Users OU.

You can also — and doing so makes more sense — add a bunch of computers to a security group and then locate that security group in the respective OU. Wherever that computer group is added — and the group may be linked to other OUs through association — the computers are influenced in the order that they receive policy. For a group of computers, that order is, first, the OU in which they reside alone or in a group and then, later, any other structure that is affected by GP that the group is admitted to. Remember that the last GP applied overrides the previous GP unless you expressly forbid it or block inheritance.

Getting Started

To discuss all the possible ways and means of enabling change control and management would require more than the scope of this book permits. The best place to start, however, is to ensure that you fully understand the concepts. First, understand that the change control and management or configuration technologies deployed in Windows Server 2003 fall under an umbrella philosophy called *IntelliMirror*, which all started with the *Zero Administration Windows* (*ZAW*) initiative (see Chapter 1) some years ago.

You could literally start implementing the IntelliMirror technologies anywhere in your enterprise. You may start with installation and rollout of the operating system, with software installation and configuration, or with user settings and so on. Every segment of the change-management matrix is extremely complex.

The following suggestions provide a starting point for change configuration using GP- and IntelliMirror-related technologies. We prefer to start by configuring the logon/logoff scenario, locking down desktops, customizing and locking down the Start menu, redirecting folders, and various settings in the Administrative Templates These areas represent, for us, the most urgent needs for clients already in business for some years and who are well entrenched in their business processes and resources. We can't go over everything here because Group Policy alone has more than 700 settings to consider, so after you digest this short review, you need to review all related technologies and stack them up against the change management that you have begun to implement or are planning.

Customizing logon/logoff

A void time (where the user stares at the screen) exists between the computer starting up and the presentation of the login screen (where the user is asked to press Ctrl+Alt+Del). A void time is also present just after the user logs off.

In this void time, you can use policy to run various options. You can run an anti-virus checker, for example, or pull or push something to the network, synchronize offline files and folders, run diagnostics, or gather intelligence into a data file that represents the user's activities while logged on at the machine. Depending on the applications, you can have a million reasons to run something (via scripts of course) in void time during logon/logoff.

Locking down the desktop

Locking down the desktop is an important component in change control and takes you back to the first anecdote at the beginning of this chapter.

You can also create custom configurations for Internet Explorer to enforce download and browsing policy and so on. Other policies that are extremely useful can achieve the following:

- Prevent users from changing the path to their My Documents folders. This policy is often used if you need to ensure that users' documents and other work-related files are redirected to a server folder where they are certain to be backed up.
- Disable the Control Panel, which prevents users from fiddling with the settings that govern their displays, network connections, communications, and so on. You can also hide specific Control Panel programs if your users need access only to certain items.
- Hide access to the CD-ROM and the floppy disk drive. By taking away these ports, you prevent users from introducing viruses or rogue software to the network, and you ensure that the enterprise can control software piracy. (Remember that you need to lock down access to the Internet and e-mail as well to be 100 percent sure that no viruses are being introduced to the systems.) You can also hide the hard disk drives from the users.
- Disable the Command Console so that users cannot execute commands from the command line. For hackers, accessing the command line on a computer is like making it to the first floor.
- Disable access to the registry editing tools such as `Regedt32` or `Regedit`.

Controlling the Start menu

GP enables you to disable portions of the Start menu so that they are not visible to the user. You can also customize the Start menu to reflect the needs of change management. You can, for example, do any of the following:

- Remove the Run menu item from the Start menu. This option also locks down the keyboard shortcut that opens the Run menu.
- Add the Logoff item to the Start menu, which you want to do for terminal session users.
- You can also disable the drag-and-drop shortcut menus on the Start menu. This serves to prevent users from reordering or removing items and the sequence of items from the Start menus.

Folder redirection

Each user is given access to a number of personal folders on a domain and on a workstation. These include My Documents, My Pictures, and Application Data. To protect a user's files, the intellectual property of the enterprise, and application data, a valuable feature of Group Policy enables you to redirect every user's collection of personal folders and application data to a network server.

This practice bestows three important benefits on the enterprise. First, by forcing data to be stored on the network server, both personal and application data can be regularly backed up.

Second, the data and files can be regularly frisked for viruses. Data that is stored on local machines in an enterprise is usually never backed up, and forcing antiviral technology onto every workstation is not a 100 percent surefire solution to the virus malady. Despite installing virus checkers onto every workstation, you can never ensure that everyone has the latest data file on the thousands of new viruses that are being launched every month. Protecting one server is easier than setting up processes to make sure that every computer is adequately protected.

Third, you can ensure that, no matter where users log on, even as terminals on an application server, they always have access to their same folders, and their application data is always saved and remains accessible from the same place.

Redirecting folders is easy and can be done from any special folders that you place into service. You can also redirect everyone to a share point, and folder redirection can be enabled by group membership as well.

To enable folder redirection, expand the User Configuration node through Windows Settings to the Folder Redirection node in the SDOU of choice, as explained in the section "Putting Group Policy to Work," earlier in this chapter.

To redirect a folder, follow these steps:

1. Right-click the folder — for example, My Documents — and choose Properties from the pop-up menu. The dialog box for that folder loads. (In this example, it would be the My Documents Properties dialog box.)
2. Select the Basic - Redirect Everyone's Folder to the Same Location option from the Setting drop-down list. Or, to redirect according to group membership, you can choose the Advanced - Specify Locations for Various User Groups option.
3. Enter a target folder in the Target Folder Location field. You need to enter a UNC name here and use the `%username%` variable if you need to. You can also select the path via the Browse option. If you selected Advanced in Step 2, you need to select the group that this policy applies to by clicking the Add button in the dialog box.
4. Click the Settings tab on the dialog box to further configure the redirection criteria, such as rights, removal policy (which kicks in after policy is removed), and so on. Click Apply and then OK after you are done configuring the redirection criteria.

After all that work, you need to make sure that your backup and virus checkers "sweep" the new redirected resources.

Older versions of Windows

As mentioned in the section "Types of Group Policy," earlier in this chapter, a mixed environment is problematic. No user or computer logging into versions of Windows earlier than Windows 2000 can be influenced by Windows Server 2003 GP. To protect your environment, you need to continue to work with the older technologies, such as the System Policy Editor on Windows NT 4.0 (`poledit.exe`). Consider moving the older environments to Windows Server 2003 as soon as possible. Of course, this means upgrading to Windows 2000 Professional or Windows XP or adopting Terminal Services, as discussed in Chapter 30.

Change Control Management for Group Policy

The fact that the premier technology for managing change control in Windows Server 2003 could use some change management itself seems ironic. One of the biggest problems with the development, deployment and management of GP is that the technology is extremely difficult and complex to manage. Microsoft has been promising better tools to make management of GP easier, but they have been slow in coming.

Before we discuss this difficulty, further consider how technology is usually deployed under strict quality-management and validation procedures. First, systems are designed on paper and in Visio or Rational Rose before discovery and proof of concept in the lab. Then, on approval of the design and testing in the lab environment, the systems are migrated from the lab or torn down and built anew according to design specifications. After this process is complete — and following essential change control — a formal validation is carried out. This formal validation involves checks to make sure that systems are installed correctly, that they operate correctly, and that they meet performance metrics.

After the systems are deployed, they are maintained according to maintenance procedures, disaster recovery practices, and change control.

Group Policy implementation should follow the same practices in design and build-out, as described in Chapter 5. The technology has profound and far-reaching influence on the technical operations of an enterprise, yet it is neither practical nor possible to follow good design and management philosophy because of several shortcomings in the GP creation and application architecture itself.

For starters, you can design and test Group Policy in the lab and get it approved, but to copy and paste it into production is not possible, because GP must be created from scratch in a production environment. You have no way to migrate GP into production by using Windows Server 2003 tools. So you must document, usually in spreadsheets or databases, exactly what was tested in the lab, and then you must recreate everything in production.

Not only must the Group Policy be created from the ground up, but after the object is saved — which occurs as soon as you exit the editor — it is immediately in production and starts to work. So any validation or testing is meaningless. The GP is immediately linked to the container that it was created in. If the GPO is created in the main OU and turns out to have hostile tendencies toward all computers, you cannot always undo the damage easily or quickly.

From development to production with Group Policy

To ease the burden of deploying GP, you should thus create a staging OU in your domain where all GP is created. This OU must be at the lowest level in any OU tree—preferably, one that is not nested too deep. This enables you to create the GPO without it linking to any production OU that is populated with unsuspecting computers and users, or that affects any users or computers beneath it. After the GPO is created, it can be unlinked from the staging OU (deleting the link) and linked to any OU of your choosing, or it can be applied to a group somewhere in the domain.

This form of GP quarantine thus enables a measure of phased-implementation. After the GPO is created, you can gather a collection of test computers and users in a test OU and move the GP out of the staging area. If the GPO is doing what it is designed to do, you can then take it through change control and roll it out into production As you saw in the section "How Group Policy Works," earlier in this chapter, this is achieved by simply linking the GPO to another container or by applying it against a group of users or computers.

Change control for Group Policy

The next biggest headache that you face is maintenance and change control of Group Policy. You cannot extend or test or return the GPO to the lab for a tune up without affecting your live users. So you typically must create a new GPO for the new features, extend the old one, or partition it.

Wrecking and corrupting a GPO is certainly possible. Applying a setting that has less or more than the desired effect is also possible. Sure, you want to implement strict change control for GP, but for the most part, managing change in your GP architecture is extremely difficult.

Extending an existing GP has two downsides: First, the new definitions and settings of the GPO add to the complexity of the object. The more stuff that you implement in a GPO, the harder maintaining it or moving it around your domain becomes. Think about this concept for a second. A GPO with fancy login script settings is difficult to extend. If you add administrative settings for Access XP in the GPO, your users who are affected by the login script settings also feel the effect of the Access XP restrictions. You cannot, therefore, scale the GPO to all users of Access without interfering with login script settings.

Planning and Troubleshooting GP by using RSoP

If you have experience in Windows 2000 GP management, you know that you have no easy way to troubleshoot problem GPOs or to easily predict or test how a GPO will work in production. *Resultant Set of Policy—RSoP—*which was introduced in Windows XP, goes a long way to providing the means to both plan GP and troubleshoot problems that arise at workstations that have applied GP. It now comes built into Windows Server 2003.

RSoP enables you to obtain a report of all the GP settings that apply to a user and machine. It thus enables you to troubleshoot GP and also to determine how the RSoP changes the desktop and work environment of a user's computer.

The native Windows XP and Windows Server 2003 RSoP functionality enables you to extract RSoP from both the machine that you are sitting at or any machine on the domain. You can also use the command-line utility, `GPRESULT`, to discover the sum of GP settings affecting a user and his computer. RSoP and `GPRESULT` are discussed extensively under the topic of troubleshooting GP in Windows Server 2003's Help files.

To use RSoP to plan GP application open Active Directory Users and Computers and select any OU in the tree. Right-click the All Tasks menu option and then select Resultant Set of Policy (Planning) from the context menu. This action loads the Resultant Set of Policy Wizard as shown in Figure 14-9.

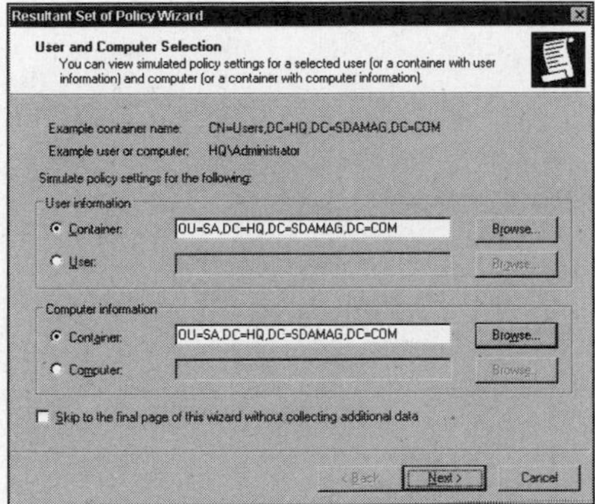

Figure 14-9: The Resultant Set of Policy Wizard.

Use this wizard to simulate GP application on a target OU, or users, computers and groups, with various settings such as loopback mode, slow network connection and Windows Management Instrumentation (WMI) filters.

The RSoP tool is, however, critical for troubleshooting. To build a report of RSoP on a target user and computer open the Resultant Set of Policy console (rsop.mmc) on the server. Before loading the console the RSoP gathers GP information targeting the current machine and logged on user. The RSoP console then launches with this information. You can then use the same console to target other machines (mainly workstations) and computers.

The RSoP console is, however, available on Windows XP and you can also target other workstations and users from a Windows XP support computer . . . provided you have permission, as the target machine's local administrator (which by default includes members of the Domain Admins group) to generate a RSoP report.

But generating reports for troubleshooting and simulating the resultant GP is about all that RSoP is good for. Making a mistake in the GPO — and even trashing it — is still very possible. It is not unheard of that a perfectly functional GPO gets ruined because some administrative templates overcooked the GP. Can you undo the changes, get a backup of the GP from the lab, or restore a backup? Not possible with the standard first-party tools that ship with the operating system. With these shortcomings in hand, you need to turn to a third-party software vendor for help.

Taking control of Group Policy by using FAZAM 2000

The one vendor to look at if you're experiencing problems with GP is the FullArmor Corporation, in Boston, Massachusetts. (This is not a marketing plug, by the way, and we have no relationship with FullArmor other than having tested and worked with its GP management tool, FAZAM 2000 — FAZAM being the acronym for FullArmor Zero Administration.)

No other tool on the market comes close to FAZAM 2000 for GP management, change control, and deployment. Before we discuss this tool a little further, you should also know that Microsoft includes a reduced-functionality version of FAZAM 2000 in the support folder on the Windows Server 2003 operating system's installation CD. And you no doubt can get a trial version of the software if you visit FullArmor's Web site at `www.fullarmor.com`.

FAZAM's RSoP also enables you to interactively point the tool to any machine in the domain and extract a marvelous HTML RSoP report of the GP affecting the machine and the user. The report, after it's created, can be printed. RSoP using FAZAM 2000 is driven from the FAZAM 2000 Administrator as shown in Figure 14-10.

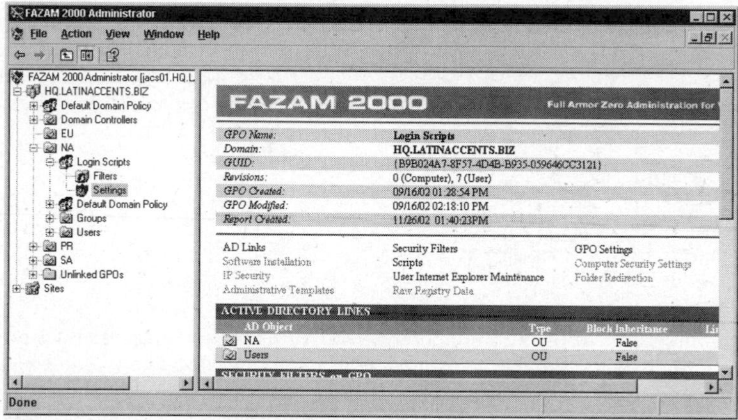

Figure 14-10: FAZAM 2000 Administrator.

Backing up and restoring Group Policy Objects

Currently, the only way to back up and restore a GPO is via full backup/restore procedure that involves also backing up and restoring the entire Active Directory. You have no way to selectively back up a single GPO and restore it to the Active Directory in the event that it becomes corrupted or accidentally gets deleted.

This functionality is provided by FAZAM 2000. Investment in GP design and construction is very costly. You can spend days on the process, if not weeks, and you can wipe out all that work simply by selecting the wrong radio button in the Delete dialog box.

If you corrupt, destroy, or somehow lose your Group Policy object (and many Windows 2000 administrators can tell you how the default domain policy or default domain-controller policy has been known to simply vanish), you have no choice but to restore the object from a backup tape — and part of the operating system with it.

You can, of course, use the `DCGPOFIX` command-line utility to restore the default GPOs, but that means that the settings in these GP are gone. Backing up and restoring a GPO by using FAZAM 2000, however, is very simple.

Implementing change management

The most useful feature of the FAZAM tool is its capability to create and test GPOs in a test domain and then save the policy definitions to a database repository. FAZAM 2000 enables you to create the object and store it in a local or desktop version of SQL Server or in a full-tilt production SQL Server 2000.

The repository architecture thus provides a full recovery system for GPOs, because you can load the GPO to the domain from its SQL Server storage location. The GPO is also fully recoverable. Corrupt or delete the object, and you are back in business with a simple connection to SQL Server — no more days or weeks (and tons of downtime) recreating the GPO that went with the wind.

This architecture is also ideal for implementing change control or change management of GP in Active Directory. FAZAM 2000 enables you to create and test GP in a lab domain, and then, whenever change control permits, the GPO can be migrated to the production domain (naturally after thoroughly testing it first).

Although Windows Server 2003 adds a host of new features that improve the management of GP, it is still a huge administrative burden and risky venture without the full coat of Titanium armor that is the likes of FAZAM 2000. A new GP management console is still under development at Microsoft as of Q1 2003; however, it is yet to be seen if it will offer the functionality of FAZAM.

Summary

This chapter discusses the importance of change control and change management and the capability to use Windows Server 2003 Group Policy to satisfy, as far as possible, the needs of the enterprise for change and security.

We look at how unmanaged change can lead to disaster. We also assess our user and security environment to better understand the elements that need to fall under change management in the enterprise.

Our study of Group Policy in this chapter is hardly a dent in this vast and critical component of Windows Server 2003. We look at the elements of Group Policy Objects, how they are created and applied, and how the policy that they embody is linked to objects that are deemed to require association with such policy.

We discuss how GP is inherited from sites to domains and then to organization units, and how GP can be filtered via security groups that are placed into various containers. We finally stress the importance of coming to grips with GP and understanding the effect that it has on the health of the enterprise.

This chapter caps our sojourn into Active Directory services that spans seven chapters. But plenty more is still there to tackle. The Windows Server 2003 Help files cover more specific elements of Active Directory and its management realm.

✦ ✦ ✦

PART

IV

Networking and Communications Services

✦ ✦ ✦ ✦

In This Part

✦ ✦ ✦ ✦

Windows Server 2003 Networking

✦ ✦ ✦ ✦

In This Chapter

Understanding TCP/IP on Windows 2003

Learning TCP/IP basics (IPv4)

Configuring TCP/IP

Understanding and using IPv6

Troubleshooting TCP/IP

Working with Legacy protocols

Understanding SNMP

✦ ✦ ✦ ✦

This chapter provides a detailed discussion of Windows 2003 networking, including an explanation of Transmission Control Protocol/Internet Protocol (TCP/IP), routing, network address translation (NAT), legacy protocols, and other topics related to Windows 2003 network configuration.

TCP/IP on Windows 2003

A little more than a decade ago, TCP/IP was used by a relatively small number of computers connected to the Internet. As the number of networks connected to the Internet grew explosively, and as companies expanded to include more and more networks within the enterprise, TCP/IP has come to be the protocol of choice for most organizations. The reasons are many but commonly include the organizations needs for standardization, the ability to route, and of course, Internet connectivity.

Windows 2003 offers strong support for TCP/IP. TCP/IP is the primary protocol for and the foundation of Active Directory (AD), which is the keystone of Windows 2003 networks. On the client side, the TCP/IP protocol enables full support for connecting to both peer and server computers running TCP/IP, the Internet, and TCP/IP-based services such as networked printers. On the server side, Windows 2003 offers the configuration and management tools you would expect, including support for dynamic address allocation through Dynamic Host Configuration Protocol (DHCP), name resolution through Domain Name System (DNS), Network Basic Input Output System (NetBIOS) name resolution through Windows Internet Name Service (WINS), and a full range of configuration and troubleshooting tools.

Windows 2003 builds on features introduced in Windows 2000 Server to support additional capabilities for TCP/IP clients. Windows 2000 and Windows XP DHCP clients, for example, can request updates for their host records with a Windows 2003 DNS server, enabling DHCP clients to have up-to-date host entries in their domains. Windows 2003 DHCP servers can also initiate updates on behalf of TCP/IP clients, including those that are not designed to support dynamic DNS. Windows 2003 DHCP servers can request an update of the client's pointer record in DNS as well.

Tip

Windows 2003 includes other features related to TCP/IP, such as the capability to bridge network connections; Internet Connection Sharing (ICS), which enables a single Internet connection to be shared by other users on the local network; and Internet Connection Firewall, a rudimentary firewall. For more information on ICS and other remote-access-related topics, see Chapter 18.

On both the client and server sides, Windows 2003 provides easy TCP/IP configuration. As with other Windows applications, you configure TCP/IP through various dialog boxes. But Windows 2003 also includes command-line utilities such as `ipconfig` to help you view and manage a system's TCP/IP configuration. A very useful feature is the ability to change IP addresses and other settings without requiring the system to reboot.

Before you begin configuring and using TCP/IP in Windows .NET, you need to understand the basics of how TCP/IP works, which are covered in the following section. If you're already familiar with TCP/IP and are ready to configure it in Windows .NET, turn to the section, "Configuring TCP/IP," later in this chapter.

Note

The following section explains IP version 4, generally referred to as IPv4. The latest version of the IP protocol, IPv6, is also included in Windows .NET. See the section, "Understanding and Using IPv6," later in this chapter, for a detailed explanation of IPv6 and its use.

TCP/IP Basics (IPv4)

The IP portion of TCP/IP provides the transport protocol. TCP provides the mechanism through which IP packets are received and recombined, ensuring that IP traffic arrives in a usable state. TCP/IP arose from the ARPANET, which was the precursor to today's Internet. TCP/IP is standards-based and supported by nearly every operating system, including all Microsoft operating systems, Unix, Linux, Macintosh, NetWare, OS/2, Open VMS, and others. This wide compatibility and the capability to interconnect dissimilar systems are the primary reasons TCP/IP has become so popular.

Although TCP/IP is most often used to provide wide-area networking (such as on the Internet), it is an excellent choice as a local network transport protocol, particularly where organizations want to serve network resources to local clients through an intranet. You can use TCP/IP as your only network protocol, or you can use it in conjunction with other protocols, such as NetBIOS Enhanced User Interface (NetBEUI). For example, you might use TCP/IP for Internet connectivity and use NetBEUI for sharing local resources. One main advantage to this option is that NetBEUI is non-routable and therefore relatively secure from unauthorized access from the Internet. As long as you don't bind the file and printer sharing client to your TCP/IP protocol, your local resources can be fairly safe from outside access.

Tip

Windows 2003 doesn't incorporate NetBEUI in the list of available protocols. Instead, it's located in the \VALUEADD\MSFT\NET\NETBEUI folder on the Windows Server 2003 CD.

IP addressing

Any device that uses TCP/IP to communicate is called a *host,* including a computer, a printer, and a router. As smart devices begin to pervade our daily existence, it's conceivable that even your washing machine or microwave oven will be a host, if not on the Internet, then at least on your home intranet. This will allow the device to notify the manufacturer (or you) when it needs service.

Each host must have a unique *IP address* that identifies it on the network so that IP data packets can be routed to and from it. IP data packets are simply data encapsulated in IP format for transmission using TCP. Each address must be unique; identical addresses on two or more hosts will conflict and prevent those computers from communicating properly. In fact, Windows 2003 shuts down the TCP/IP protocol on a computer if it detects an address conflict at TCP/IP initialization.

IP addresses are 32-bit values usually expressed in dotted decimal notation, with four octets separated by decimals, as in 192.168.0.221. Each IP address contains two separate pieces of information: the network address and the host address. How these two items of information are defined in the IP address depends on its *class*.

There are five classes of IP addresses, class A to class E, but there are only three classes you should concern yourself with for Windows 2003 networking: A, B, and C. Class A networks yield the highest number of host addresses, and class C networks yield the lowest number. Table 15-1 lists information about each class. The designation w.x.y.z indicates the portion of the IP address that defines network and host ID portions of the address.

Table 15-1: IP Address Classes

Class	*Network ID*	*Network Host ID*	*Number of Available Networks*	*Number of Hosts per Network*
A 1–126	w	x.y.z	126	16,777,214
B 128–191	w.x	y.z	16,384	65,534
C 192–223	w.x.y	z	2,097,151	254

As Table 15-1 indicates, the address range 127.x.y.z is missing. 127.x.y.z is reserved on the local computer for loopback testing and can't be used as a valid network address. Addresses 224 and higher are reserved for special protocols such as IP multicast and are not available as host addresses. In addition, host addresses 0 and 255 are used as broadcast addresses and can't be used as valid host addresses. For example, 192.168.120.0 and 192.168.120.255 are both broadcast addresses that are not available for use as host addresses.

The number of addresses in a given address class is fixed. Class A networks are quite large, with over 16 million hosts, and class C networks are relatively small, with just 254 hosts. The class you choose depends on how many hosts you need to accommodate, but most importantly whether you are using a public address range or a private one. The address ranges listed here are reserved by convention for private networks:

- 10.0.0.0, subnet mask 255.0.0.0
- 169.254.0.0, subnet mask 255.255.0.0
- 172.16.0.0, subnet mask 255.240.0.0
- 192.168.0.0, subnet mask 255.255.0.0

However, if you are not connecting your systems to the Internet, you can use any IP address class except the loopback addresses. For example, a Class A addressing scheme can provide a large number of host addresses for your enterprise. But if you're connecting the network to the Internet, at least some of the addresses need to be valid, public addresses that fall in the range described in Table 15-1 (excluding the private ranges mentioned previously).

If all your systems connect to the Internet directly rather than through a proxy server or other device that performs NAT, each host must have a unique, valid public IP address. If you use NAT, only those hosts on the public side of the Internet connection need valid, public addresses. Those hosts on the private side can use one of the private address ranges described previously, but only NAT and proxy services will allow the public addresses to translate to the private ones. This means you can accommodate a large class A network internally, if needed. Figure 15-1 illustrates a network that uses a private IP range but connects to the Internet through a proxy server and router with public addresses.

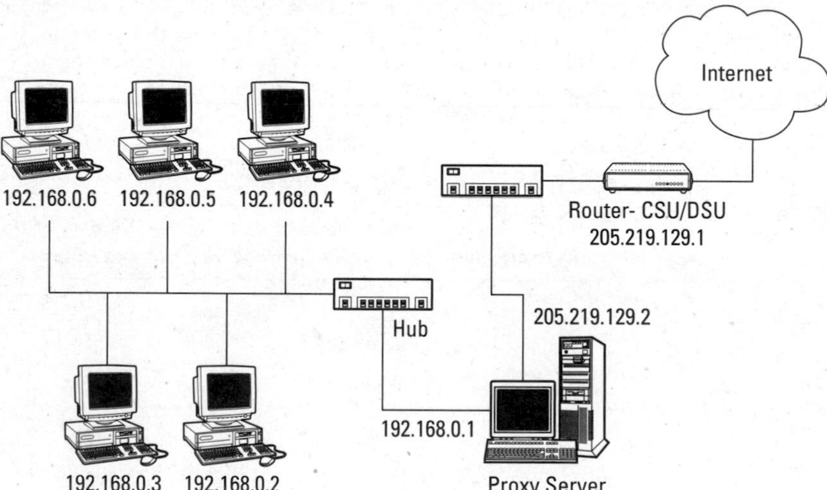

Figure 15-1: This network uses private IP addresses internally and a proxy server to connect to the Internet.

Subnetting

Each host, in addition to an IP address, needs a *subnet mask*. The subnet mask, like an IP address, is a 32-bit value typically expressed as four octets separated by periods. The subnet mask serves to strip the IP address into its two components, network ID and host ID, which enables traffic to be routed to the appropriate network and then to the destination host. Table 15-2 shows the subnet masks for the three standard network classes.

Table 15-2: Standard Subnet Masks

Class	*Binary Value*	*Subnet Mask*
A	11111111 00000000 00000000 00000000	255.0.0.0
B	11111111 11111111 00000000 00000000	255.255.0.0
C	11111111 11111111 11111111 00000000	255.255.255.0

In addition to masking the host ID from the network ID, a subnet mask also can serve to segment a single network into multiple logical networks. For example, assume that your small company obtains Internet access from a local ISP. The ISP uses a class C address space to accommodate a group of clients, of which your company is one. The ISP uses a subnet mask of 255.255.255.224 to divide the network into eight subnets with 30 hosts each. Table 15-3 lists the host ranges for each subnet.

Table 15-3: Sample Subnet

Subnet	*Host Range*
0	205.219.128.1 – 205.219.128.30
1	205.219.128.33 – 205.219.128.62
2	205.219.128.65 – 205.219.128.94
3	205.219.128.97 – 205.219.128.126
4	205.219.128.129 – 205.219.128.158
5	205.219.128.161 – 205.219.128.190
6	205.219.128.193 – 205.219.128.222
7	205.219.128.225 – 205.219.128.254

In this example, the ISP uses the first address range (subnet 0) for a routing *cloud* (a network subnet that functions solely for the purpose of routing) and the remaining seven subnets to accommodate the customers. You are the first customer and you get subnet 1, with addresses from 33 through 62. Figure 15-2 illustrates the network.

You can calculate subnet masks manually, but it's a real chore. Instead, download a copy of Net3 Group's IP Subnet Calculator from `http://www.wildpackets.com/products/ipsubnetcalculator`. Or, search your favorite shareware/freeware site, such as `www.tucows.com` for additional tools such as Advanced Subnet Calculator, also available at `www.solarwinds.net`.

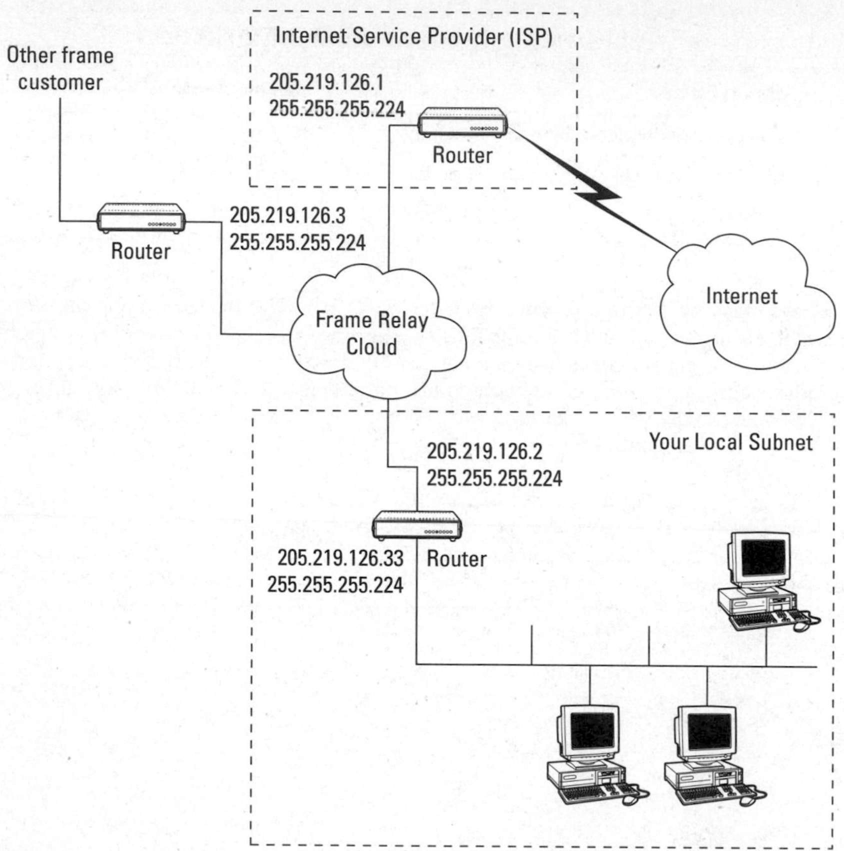

Figure 15-2: This ISP serves seven customers with a class C address space and a subnet mask of 255.255.255.224.

As you're designing your network and assigning IP addresses and subnet masks, keep in mind that all nodes on the same logical segment need to have the same subnet mask. This places them in the same logical network for routing purposes.

A full understanding of subnetting is essential for the deployment of Active Directory across multiple sites in an enterprise, or even the Internet. See Chapters 8 and 9 in Part III.

Classless interdomain routing notation

Given the length of a subnet mask, it isn't always efficient to specify an address using the address and subnet mask. Classless Interdomain Routing (CIDR) simplifies addressing notation by letting you specify the network ID using the number of bits that define the network ID. Table 15-4 illustrates the concept.

Table 15-4: Classless Interdomain Routing Notation

Class	Binary Value	Network Prefix
A	11111111 00000000 00000000 00000000	/8
B	11111111 11111111 00000000 00000000	/16
C	11111111 11111111 11111111 00000000	/24

For example, the class C address space 192.168.0.0/255.255.255.0 can be expressed using CIDR as 192.168.0.0/24.

Tip

CIDR is also known as *network prefix notation*.

CIDR is not limited to specifying these three network IDs. You can also use CIDR to identify the network ID for networks with different subnets. To determine the network prefix, simply add the number of subnet bits. For example, assume you create a subnet using the mask 255.255.255.224, or three additional subnet bits. The notation for the address range 192.168.0.*n* with this subnet mask would be 192.168.0.0/27. Table 15-5 shows the network prefixes for subnets of a class C network ID.

Table 15-5: CIDR Subnets of Class C Network ID

Number of Subnets	Subnet Bits	Subnet Mask/CIDR Notation	Number of Hosts per Network
1–2	1	255.255.255.128 or /25	126
3–4	2	255.255.255.192 or /26	62
5–8	3	255.255.255.224 or /27	30
9–16	4	255.255.255.240 or /28	14
17–32	5	255.255.255.248 or /29	6
33–64	6	255.255.255.252 or /30	2

Obtaining IP addresses

How you assign IP addresses depends on whether your systems are connected to the public Internet. Systems that are connected to the Internet directly, rather than through a proxy server or other device doing NAT, must have unique, valid IP addresses, often termed "legal" addresses. This means you can't arbitrarily choose an address range for these systems. Instead, you need to obtain an address range from your ISP to ensure that you are using unique addresses (and that proper routing takes place). The number of addresses you need to obtain depends on how many hosts you will have on the public side of your proxy server or other NAT device, if any. For example, assume you configure your network so that a proxy server sits between the router and all other hosts. You therefore need only three public addresses: one for each side of the router and one for the public side of the proxy server. The hosts on the private side of the proxy server can use private addresses.

If your network is not connected to the Internet, you could theoretically choose any network address range, including a public range in use by someone else, but you will not be able to connect your network to the Internet. You should, however, follow the convention of using one of the reserved address ranges for your private network (discussed previously in this chapter), because it will make life easier for you if you install NAT services, as discussed later in this chapter. You won't have to re-address all of your hosts later if you decide to connect the network to the Internet — you simply need to provide some means of NAT through a router (such as Routing and Remote Access Service (RRAS), discussed later) or a proxy server.

Gateways and routing

TCP/IP subnets use *gateways* to route data between networks. Usually, a gateway is a dedicated router, but it could be any device running routing services, such as a Windows 2003 server running RRAS. The router maintains IP address information about remote networks so it can route traffic accordingly. Traffic coming from the local network with a public address gets routed out through the appropriate port on the router. Figure 15-3 shows a simple network with two connections to the Internet. The second connection provides redundancy in the event the primary connection fails.

On the host, IP inserts the originating and destination addresses into each packet. The host then checks (using its subnet mask) the destination address to determine if the packet is destined for another host on the same local network or for a host on another network. If the packet is for a local host, it is sent directly to the local host on the same subnet. If the destination host is on a remote network, IP sends the packet to the local host's *default gateway*, which routes the traffic to the remote network. You can configure multiple gateways if more than one is present on the network, and the local host attempts to connect through them in turn. If the default gateway is down, the host attempts to reach the next gateway in the list. The packet then travels through (possibly) several other routers until it reaches its destination.

Standalone subnets do not require gateways because there is nowhere for the traffic to go — all traffic is local. Subnets connected to other subnets or to the Internet require at least one gateway.

Dynamic Host Configuration Protocol (DHCP)

Because every host must have a unique IP address, how you allocate and manage addresses is an important consideration when setting up an IP network. You can allocate addresses in one of two ways: *static addressing* or *dynamic addressing*. With static addressing, you simply assign a specific IP address to each host. The address doesn't change unless you manually reconfigure the host's TCP/IP properties (thus the term *static*). Static addressing is fine for small networks where you don't need to add or remove nodes or change addresses very often. As the number of nodes increases, however, static addressing can become an administrative nightmare. It's easy to accidentally assign conflicting IP addresses, and when subnet properties change (such as a default gateway address), you have to manually reconfigure those properties.

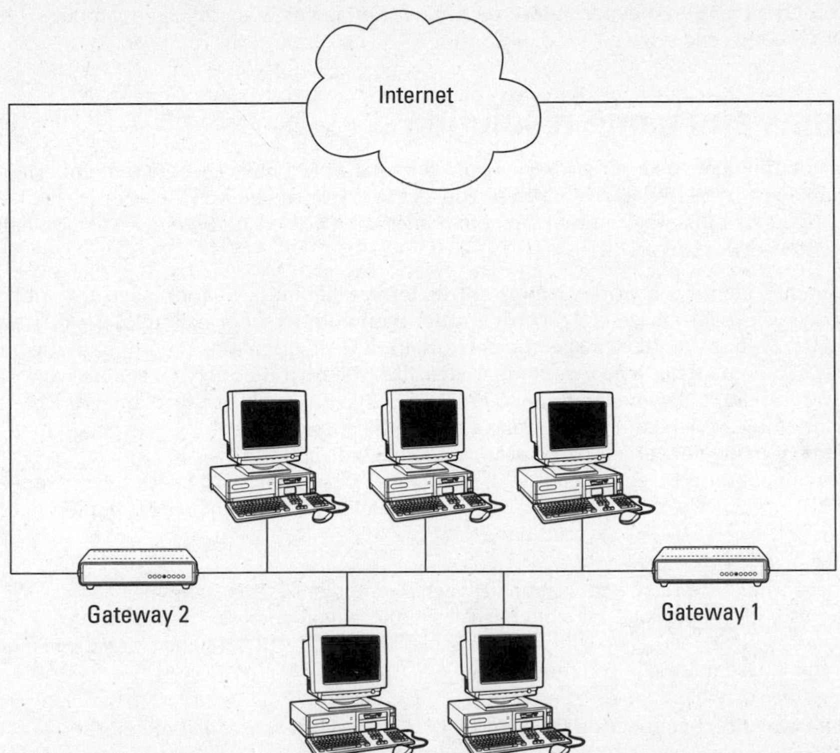

Figure 15-3: A simple network with two gateways to the Internet.

Dynamic addressing through DHCP is a much better solution than static addressing, particularly for large networks or dynamic networks in which IP properties change. DHCP enables a server to automatically allocate IP addresses and related properties (gateway, DNS servers, and so on) to clients as they boot. A dynamically assigned address and associated properties is called a *lease*. Depending on the configuration at the DHCP server, a lease can have an infinite duration or can expire after a certain period. If a lease expires, the client can *renew* the lease to obtain a new IP address (which could be the same as the one provided by the previous lease).

DHCP in Windows 2003 offers some additional benefits in its interaction with Windows 2003 and Windows 2000 Server-based DNS servers. A Windows 2000 or Windows XP DHCP client can request that the DNS server update its host address in the DNS namespace for its domain. This means that even if the client receives a new IP address each time it boots, its host record in DNS will remain accurate. Windows 2003 DHCP servers can also request host record updates on behalf of clients, including non-Windows 2000/XP clients that don't support dynamic DNS updates. It's important to remember, however, that the DNS records are updated locally. Servers that are hosting secondary records for the domain(s) will have to perform a zone transfer to retrieve the up-to-date records. Local clients that have DNS entries cached will obtain up-to-date queries when their caches expire.

See Chapter 16 for detailed information on DHCP and how to configure Windows 2003 DHCP clients and servers.

Domains and name resolution

IP hosts communicate using IP addresses, but humans would have trouble remembering more than a few IP addresses. How would you like to try to remember the addresses of all the Web sites you visit in a week's time? *Domain names, host names,* and *name resolution* help simplify internetworking for the user.

Domain names identify networks using a dotted format similar to IP addresses, except that domain names use letters (usually words) rather than numbers. For example, the domain `latinaccents.biz` identifies a specific network in the `.org` domain. Each host in the `latinaccents.biz` domain has a *host name* that identifies the host uniquely on the network. The host name and domain name combine to create a Fully Qualified Domain Name, or FQDN, that uniquely identifies the host. For example, a host in the `latinaccents.biz` domain might have the host name `server1`. The FQDN for the host would be `server1.latinaccents.biz`. If the domain contains delegated subnets, those figure into the FQDN, as well. For example, assume `latinaccents.biz` includes a subdomain called `support`. The host named `fred` in `support.latinaccents.biz` would have the FQDN `fred.support.latinaccents.biz`.

There is not necessarily a correlation between a computer's FQDN and e-mail address. While the user in the previous example might have the e-mail address `fred@support.latinaccents.biz`, there is no correlation with his computer's FQDN. The host name and e-mail account have nothing in common.

There isn't any direct connection between FQDNs or IP addresses, so some method is required to *map* host names to IP addresses. When you type `http://www.latinaccents.biz` in your Web browser, for example, some translation needs to occur to map `www.latinaccents.biz` to its IP address so your browser can connect to the site. That's where DNS comes in.

DNS

DNS provides a distributed database to enable host names to be mapped to their corresponding IP addresses. DNS name servers maintain records for domains they host and respond to queries for a given host name with the IP address stored in the DNS database for that host. For example, when you attempt to connect to `www.latinaccents.biz`, your computer submits a DNS request to the DNS server configured in your computer's TCP/IP properties to resolve the host name `www.latinaccents.biz` into an IP address. The DNS server looks up the data and passes the address back to your computer, which connects to the site using the IP address. The only interaction you provide in the process is to enter `http://www.latinaccents.biz` in your browser. Everything else happens behind the scenes.

The name resolution process described here is simplified for the purpose of this discussion. See Chapter 17 for a detailed explanation of how DNS works.

WINS

Another name resolution service provided by Windows 2003 is WINS. WINS provides much the same service for NetBIOS names that DNS provides for TCP/IP host names. NetBIOS is an application programming interface (API) that programs can use to perform basic network operations such as sending data to specific computers on the network. NetBIOS is used by earlier Microsoft operating systems such as Windows 95 and 98 and Windows NT to identify and locate computers on the network. Just as DNS provides a means for mapping host names to IP addresses, WINS provides a means of mapping NetBIOS names to IP addresses for systems running NetBIOS over TCP/IP.

NetBIOS is not required in Windows .NET, as Windows 2003 uses host names and DNS to locate hosts on the local network. See Chapter 17 for a complete discussion on how to configure WINS.

Unless you are using applications that use NetBIOS over TCP/IP, you don't need to configure WINS on your computer.

Obtaining a domain name

You should obtain a domain name if your network will be connected to the Internet and to protect a root Active Directory domain name (discussed in Chapters 2 and 9). The domain will identify your computers on the Internet. Until a few years ago, domain management was managed by a single organization, Network Solutions. Now, you can register a domain through any authorized domain registration organization or connect to `http://www.netsol.com` to register your domain. See Chapter 17 for additional information on domain names and domain registration.

Preparing for installation

You now have enough information to begin configuring TCP/IP. Before you jump in with both feet, however, do a little planning. Make sure that you have the following information:

- ✦ **Network address and domain:** Obtain valid public addresses from your ISP for computers connected directly to the Internet. Decide which private, reserved address space you'll use for computers on private network segments. Register your domain with Network Solutions or another domain registration authority. This step is required only if you intend to use DNS to enable users on the Internet to connect to your network and its resources.
- ✦ **Identify an IP address for the computer:** Obtain the IP address(es) you will be assigning to the computer if you are allocating them statically. If you're using DHCP, you don't need to obtain a specific IP, nor do you need the IP address of a DHCP server on your network. Windows 2003 TCP/IP locates the DHCP server automatically at startup.
- ✦ **Subnet mask:** Determine the subnet mask you'll need for the computer based on the way your network is configured.
- ✦ **Default gateway(s):** Determine the IP addresses of the router(s) that will function as the computer's gateway(s).
- ✦ **DNS servers:** Determine the IP addresses of the computers that will serve as the client's DNS servers.
- ✦ **WINS servers:** Determine the IP addresses of the computers that will serve as the client's WINS servers (if any).
- ✦ **Bindings:** Decide which clients and services you'll bind to TCP/IP. For example, you will probably not want to bind TCP/IP to the File and Printer Sharing service, in order to prevent users on the Internet from potentially gaining access to your computer's shared resources.

Setting Up TCP/IP

Windows 2003 installs TCP/IP by default unless you override the installation during setup. However, you can add the protocol later if it was not installed by Setup or was deleted after installation.

Setup installs TCP/IP by default when you install Windows .NET. In fact, you can't uninstall TCP/IP, although you can disable it for a particular interface.

Although you can't uninstall TCP/IP, there might be occasions when you would like to have that ability. For example, the registry settings for TCP/IP might have become so corrupted that you need to reset the protocol back to its initial post-Setup state. You can use the `netsh` command from a console to reset the protocol. The following example shows the syntax for the command:

```
netsh int ip reset c:\ResetIP.txt
```

The last parameter specifies the name of a log file in which `netsh` logs the results of the reset operation. When `netsh` completes, the TCP/IP registry keys and values will be reset to the just-installed configuration.

The following sections explain how to configure TCP/IP.

Configuring TCP/IP

Open the Network Connections folder from the Control Panel to configure TCP/IP. Right-click the network interface whose TCP/IP properties you want to change and then click Properties to open its property sheet. Double-click TCP/IP or select TCP/IP and click Properties to display the General property page (Figure 15-4).

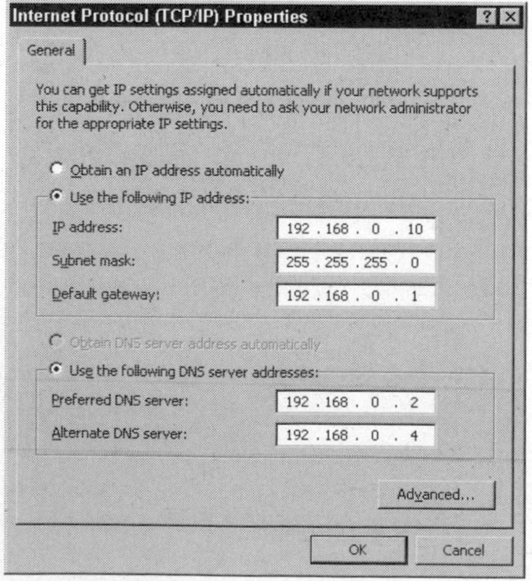

Figure 15-4: Use the General tab to set a static IP address or configure the server for DHCP.

Use the following list as a guide to configure options:

✦ **Obtain an IP address automatically:** Select this option to use DHCP to automatically obtain an IP address and other configuration properties.

✦ **Use the following IP address:** Select this option if you need to assign a static IP address.

✦ **IP address:** Specify a static IP address in dotted octet format.

✦ **Subnet mask:** Specify the subnet mask for the interface in dotted octet format.

✦ **Default gateway:** Specify the default gateway your computer should use to route nonlocal IP traffic.

✦ **Obtain DNS server addresses automatically:** Select this option to automatically retrieve the list of DNS servers from a DHCP server. This option is available only if you obtain the IP address automatically.

✦ **Use the following DNS server addresses:** Select this option to statically assign DNS server IP addresses.

✦ **Preferred DNS server:** Specify the IP address of the DNS server you want to use by default for resolving host names to IP addresses.

✦ **Alternate DNS server:** Specify the IP address of the DNS server you want to use for resolving host names if the preferred DNS server is unavailable.

These properties are sufficient for computers connected in a small private network, but in most cases, you'll need to configure additional properties. Click Advanced on the General tab to access the Advanced TCP/IP Settings property sheet. The following sections explain the options on each property page.

IP settings

Use the IP Settings tab (Figure 15-5) to configure additional IP addresses for the computer and additional gateways. The Add, Edit, and Remove buttons in the IP addresses section lets you add, modify, and remove IP addresses and associated subnet masks on the computer. You might add multiple IP addresses to a server to host multiple Web sites, for example, with each site at its own IP address. Click Add to display a simple dialog box in which you type the new IP address and subnet mask to add. Select an existing address and click Edit or Remove to modify or remove the address.

Use the Add, Edit, and Remove buttons in the Default Gateways section to add, modify, or remove gateways. In small networks, there is often only one gateway, but in larger networks, multiple gateways are used to provide fault tolerance and redundancy, enabling users to connect outside their local network should one gateway become unavailable. Click Add to specify the IP address of another gateway, or select an existing address and click Edit or Remove to respectively modify or remove the selected gateway. The metric value of a gateway specifies the relative cost of connecting through the selected gateway. When routing is possible through more than one gateway, the one with the lowest metric is used by default.

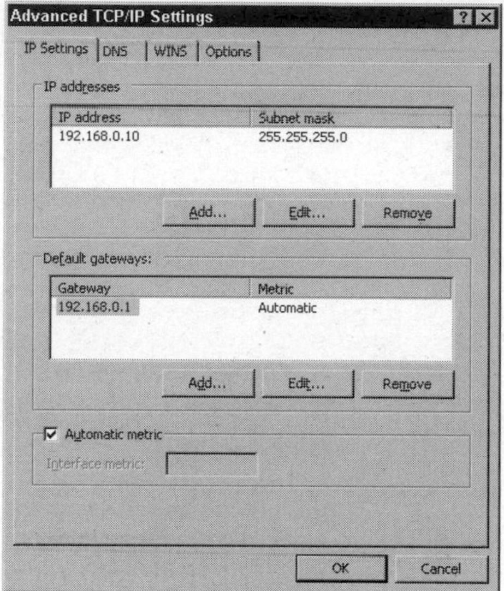

Figure 15-5: Use the IP Settings tab to configure additional addresses.

Here's an example of when the metric value comes into play. Assume your network has two connections to the Internet. Connection A is the one you want to use most because you pay a flat, monthly fee for it. Connection B is charged by bandwidth usage, and you only want to use B when A is unavailable. So, you'd assign a metric of 1 to A and a higher value to B to ensure that traffic always goes through A if it's available.

The Interface metric value on the IP Settings page specifies the relative cost of using the selected network interface. The default value is 1. This setting performs the same function for multi-homed systems (those with multiple network interfaces) as the metric value assigned to the default gateway(s). However, this value determines which interface is used to route traffic when multiple interfaces can be used to route the traffic. The interface with the lowest metric is used by default.

DNS

Use the DNS tab (see Figure 15-6) to configure DNS settings for the connection. In addition to specifying DNS servers, you can configure other options that control the way the client performs name resolution and enable dynamic DNS updates. The following list explains the available options:

✦ **Append Primary and Connection Specific DNS Suffixes:** Select this option to append the primary DNS suffix and connection-specific DNS suffix to unqualified host names for resolution. Define the primary DNS suffix for the computer through the computer's Network Identification property page (right-click My Computer, choose Properties, click Network Identification). The primary DNS suffix applies globally to the system unless overridden by the connection-specific DNS suffix, which you set in the property "DNS suffix for this connection" (described later). For example, assume your primary suffix is `latinaccents.biz` and your connection-specific DNS suffix is `support.latinaccents.biz`. You query for the unqualified host name `fred`. This option then causes

Windows 2003 to attempt to resolve `fred.latinaccents.biz` and `fred.support.latinaccents.biz`. If you have no connection-specific DNS suffix specified, Windows 2003 will attempt to resolve only `fred.latinaccents.biz`.

✦ **Append Parent Suffixes of the Primary DNS Suffix:** This option determines whether or not the resolver attempts resolution of unqualified names up to the parent-level domain for your computer. For example, assume your computer's primary DNS suffix is `support.latinaccents.biz` and you attempt to resolve the unqualified host name `jane`. The resolver would attempt to resolve `jane.support.latinaccents.biz` and `jane.latinaccents.biz` (attempting to resolve at the parent level as well as the computer's domain level).

✦ **Append These DNS Suffixes (In Order):** Use this option to only append the specified DNS suffixes for resolving unqualified names.

✦ **DNS Suffix for This Connection:** Use this option to specify a DNS suffix for the connection that is different from the primary DNS suffix defined in the computer's Network Identification property page.

✦ **Register This Connection's Addresses in DNS:** Select this option to have the client submit a request to the DNS server to update its host (A) record when its host name changes or its IP address changes. The client submits the full computer name specified in the Network Identification tab of the System Properties sheet along with its IP address to the DNS server. You can view the System properties through the System object in the Control Panel, or right-click My Computer and choose Properties.

✦ **Use this Connection's DNS Suffix in DNS Registration:** Select this option to have the client submit a request to the DNS server to update its host record when the host name changes or IP address changes. The difference from the previous option is that this option registers the client using the first part of the computer name specified in the System properties along with the DNS suffix specified by the option "DNS suffix for this connection" on the DNS page. You can use this option along with the previous option to register two different FQDNs for the host.

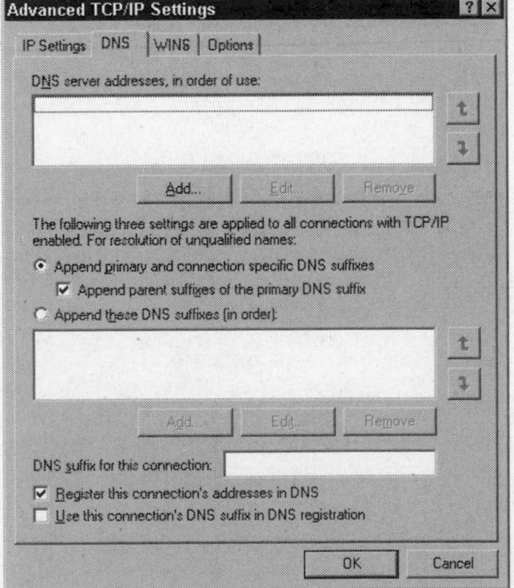

Figure 15-6: The DNS tab controls how the client interacts with DNS servers.

Use the DNS tab when you need to add more than two DNS servers.

WINS

Use the WINS tab (Figure 15-7) of the connection's TCP/IP properties to configure WINS services. You can use the Add, Edit, and Remove buttons in the WINS addresses group to add, modify, and remove WINS servers by IP address.

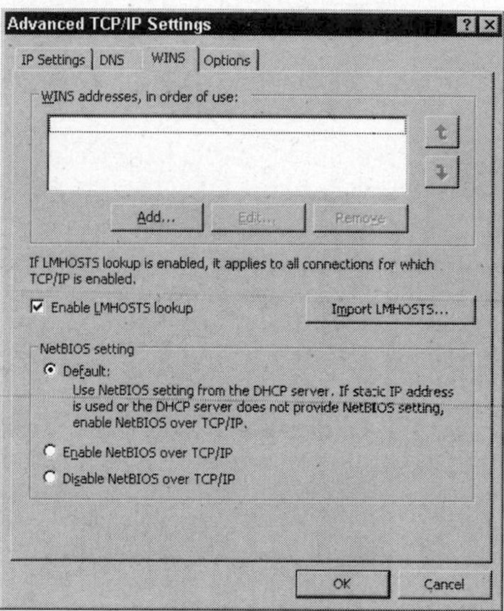

Figure 15-7: The WINS tab specifies Windows Internet Name Service properties for the interface.

The following list explains the other options on the page:

- ✦ **Enable LMHOSTS Lookup:** Select this option to enable the computer to use a local LMHOSTS file to resolve NetBIOS names to IP addresses. LMHOSTS provides a way to supplement or even replace the use of WINS servers to resolve NetBIOS names. See Chapter 14 for more information on using LMHOSTS.
- ✦ **Import LMHOSTS:** Click to import an LMHOSTS file into your local LMHOSTS file.
- ✦ **Default:** Use this option to have the DHCP server automatically assign WINS settings.
- ✦ **Enable NetBIOS Over TCP/IP:** Select this option to use NetBIOS over TCP/IP (NetBT) and WINS. This option is required if the computer communicates by name with other computers running earlier versions of Windows 9*x* or NT. NetBT is not required in a homogeneous Windows 2003 environment or when connecting to computers on the Internet through DNS.
- ✦ **Disable NetBIOS Over TCP/IP:** Select this option to disable NetBT in situations where it is not needed (see previous item).

Options

The Options tab (Figure 15-8) of the TCP/IP properties lets you configure IP Filtering options.

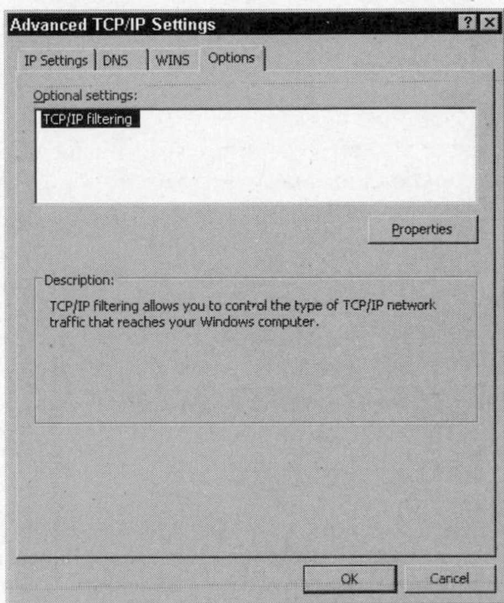

Figure 15-8: Use the Options tab to set IP filtering options.

TCP/IP filtering provides a less refined way than IPSec of controlling IP traffic to and from your computer, and is useful when you need to restrict traffic on a global scale and don't need the level of control offered by IPSec. Select TCP/IP Filtering and click Properties to configure filtering. Figure 15-9 shows the TCP/IP Filtering dialog box. As the illustration indicates, you can configure traffic for TCP ports, UDP ports, and IP protocols to permit all or permit only those ports or protocols specifically listed.

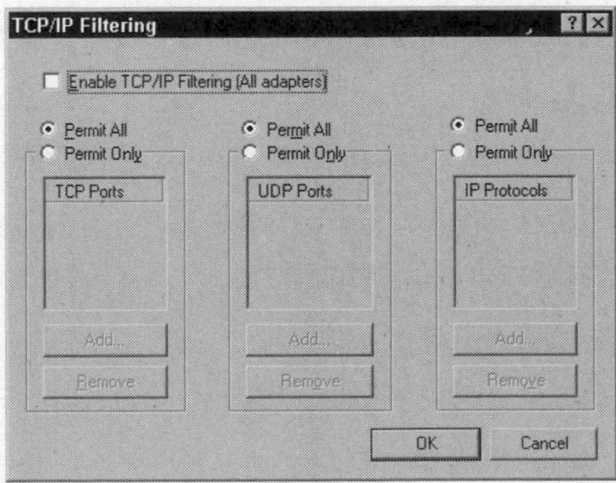

Figure 15-9: Use the TCP/IP Filtering dialog box to control traffic based on TCP ports, UDP ports, and IP protocols.

Understanding and Using IPv6

With the proliferation of IP-based devices, the pool of available IPv4 IP addresses will soon run dry. The lack of more addresses won't stop you from wanting that new integrated cell phone/PDA with wireless Internet connectivity, so something needs to be done about the dwindling pool of addresses. IPv6 is that something.

IPv6 is intended to be the eventual replacement for IPv4. The goals of IPv6 naturally include expanding the available address space, but also target routing performance improvements, Quality of Service (QoS) for low-latency applications, increased security, and other improvements.

IPv6 terms and concepts

As with IPv4, a *node* in IPv6 is any device that implements IPv6, and is either a router or host. The connection to a transmission medium through which packets are sent is called an *interface*. The medium used to transmit IPv6 is called a *link*, and can be loosely associated with an IPv4 subnet. *Neighbors* are nodes connected to the same link. Each link supports a specific maximum transmission unit (MTU) size, which is the maximum packet size that the link supports. The IPv6-capable portion of the Internet is called the *6bone*.

IPv4 supports both unicast and multicast routing; IPv6 supports these as well as anycast routing. Unicast traffic is directed at a particular interface. Multicast traffic is directed at a set of interfaces. Anycast addresses reference multiple interfaces, but anycast traffic is directed only to the closest interface to the sender rather than to all interfaces.

IPv6 addresses are also different from IPv4 addresses: Where IPv4 uses 32-bit dotted decimal values, IPv6 uses 128-bit hexadecimal values comprising eight 16-bit sections. Here's a typical IPv6 address:

```
ABCD:EF12:0000:7890:0000:3412:0006:A327
```

Fields that contain leading zeros can omit the leading zeros, so the previous example can be simplified as follows:

```
ABCD:EF12:0:7890:0:3412:6:A327
```

In addition, any fields that contain all zeros can be represented by a blank set (`::`), although a blank set can be used only once in an address. The following is an example:

- **Full address:** `ABCD:0:0:1234:0:0:0:5678`
- **Simplified address:** `ABCD:0:0:1234::5678`
- **Not acceptable:** `ABCD::1234::5678`

In addition, in mixed mode environments that support IPv4 and IPv6 nodes, the six leftmost fields use hexadecimal values but the remaining bits are entered as dotted decimal values, as in the following examples:

- `0:0:0:0:0:0:206.10.22.150`, or `::206.10.22.150` compressed
- `1234:FFFF:0:0:0:0:206.12.15.108`, or `1234:FFFF::206.12.15.108` compressed
- `::ACF5:0:206.142.68.11`

In an IPv6 address, a variable-length field of bits identifies the address type. This variable-length field is called the Format Prefix, or FP. The following sections discuss the various IPv6 address types and their corresponding FPs.

Unicast addresses

The FP value 11111111 or FF identifies an IPv6 address as a multicast address. So, any address with an FP value other than FF is a unicast address. As with IPv4, unicast addresses identify a single node on the link. There are several types of unicast IPv6 addresses.

You can assign a single unicast address to multiple interfaces on a single node as long as the interfaces are recognized by the upper layers of the protocol as a single logical entity.

There are two reserved IPv6 unicast addresses. The first, 0:0:0:0:0:0:0:0 or :: in compressed format, is called the *unspecified address*. This address is used during IPv6 initialization before a node has obtained its own address. You can't assign :: to a node, and it can't be used as the source address in a IPv6 packet or routing header.

The second reserved address is the loopback address and corresponds to the 127.0.0.1 loopback address in IPv4. The IPv6 loopback address is 0:0:0:0:0:0:1, or ::1 in compressed format. The loopback address lets the node send a packet to itself and is useful for testing proper function of the protocol stack.

Local-use unicast addresses support communication over a single link where no routing is required. They are also used for automatic configuration of addresses and neighbor discovery, which is the process used to discover neighboring nodes on the link. Table 15-6 shows the structure of a local-use unicast address.

Table 15-6: IPv6 Local-Use Unicast Addresses

10 bits	*54 bits*	*64 bits*
1111111010	0	Interface ID

Site-local unicast addresses provide connectivity within a single private network and are similar to reserved private addresses used in IPv4. Just as these private IPv4 addresses are not routed, IPv6 routers do not route traffic for site-local unicast addresses. Table 15-7 shows the structure of a site-local unicast address.

Table 15-7: IPv6 Site-Local Unicast Addresses

10 bits	*38 bits*	*16 bits*	*64 bits*
1111111010	0	Subnet ID	Interface ID

The third type of unicast address is an IPv6 address with embedded IPv4 address. This type of address is used for tunneling IPv6 packets over IPv4 networks and serves as a transitional mechanism to move from IPv4 to IPv6. There are two primary address types. In the first, only the 32 lower-order bits contain address data and the upper-order bits contain zeros. The second form is called an IPv4-mapped IPv6 address, and precedes the 32-bit IPv4 address with FFFF. Table 15-8 illustrates the structure of IPv6 addresses with embedded IPv4 addresses.

Table 15-8: IPv6 Addresses with Embedded IPv4 Addresses

80 bits	*16 bits*	*32 bits*
0000...0000	0000 or FFFF	IPv4 Address

Aggregatable global unicast addresses are used to allocate public address pools and are used primarily by ISPs to carve up the public address space on the 6bone. Table 15-9 illustrates the structure of aggregatable global unicast addresses.

Table 15-9: Aggregatable Global Unicast Addresses

Public Topology				*Site Topology*	*Interface*
FP	*TLA ID*	*RES*	*NLA ID*	*SLA ID*	*Interface ID*
001	13 bits	8 bits	24 bits	16 bits	64 bits

The Public Topology portion of the address hierarchy is managed by the large ISPs that maintain the structure of the 6bone and enable them to allocate address pools (aggregates) to smaller organizations, including individual companies and smaller ISPs. The Site Topology portion of the address hierarchy represents the internal routing information needed to route the packets internally. The interface ID provides the information needed to route to individual nodes. Table 15-10 defines the individual components.

Table 15-10: Aggregatable Address Components

Item	*Field*	*Bit Length*	*Description*
FP	Format Prefix	3	The value 001 identifies the address as an aggregatable global unicast address.
TLA ID	Top-Level Aggregation	13	Identifies the top-level authority for the routing hierarchy.
RES	Reserved	8	Reserved for future expansion of TLA and NLA fields, when needed.
NLA ID	Next-Level Aggregation ID	24	Used by top-level authorities to define and identify the routing hierarchy for the sites that they service.

Item	Field	Bit Length	Description
SLA ID	Site-Level Aggregation ID	16	Used by organizations to create the internal routing structure to support their networks.
Interface ID	Interface	64	Identifies the interfaces on a link.

Multicast addresses

IPv6 multicast addresses serve much the same purpose as multicast IPv4 addresses and replace broadcast addresses used in the IPv4 design. A multicast address is assigned to multiple nodes, and all nodes with the same multicast address receive the packets sent to that address. Table 15-11 shows the structure of a multicast address.

Table 15-11: IPv6 Multicast Addresses

8 bits	4 bits	4 bits	112 bits
11111111	Flags	Scope	Group ID

The Format Prefix of 11111111 identifies the address as a multicast address. The Flags field identifies the address type, and the first three bits of the Flags field are reserved as zero. A fourth bit of zero indicates a permanent multicast address assigned by IANA. A fourth bit of 1 indicates a dynamically assigned address not under the authority of IANA.

The Scope field defines the scope of the address, as identified in Table 15-12.

Table 15-12: Scope Field Values

Value	Scope
0	Reserved
F	Reserved
1	Node-local scope
2	Link-local scope
5	Site-local scope
8	Organization-local scope
E	Global scope
All others	Unassigned

The Group ID field identifies a particular group.

Anycast addresses

Anycast addresses use the same physical structure as unicast addresses. Unlike unicast addresses, however, anycast addresses are assigned to multiple nodes. Currently, only routers can use anycast addresses. A router that needs to send a packet to an anycast address uses a neighbor discovery mechanism to locate the nearest node that owns the specified address. The router then sends the packet to that node.

See the following section to learn how you can assign IPv6 addresses in Windows .NET.

Using IPv6 in Windows .NET

Windows 2003 includes support for the IPv6 protocol, so you can assign IPv6 addresses to Windows 2003 computers. Also, the RRAS in Windows 2003 supports IPv6 packet forwarding and route announcements. This section of the chapter explains how to install and configure the IPv6 protocol in Windows .NET.

Installing and configuring IPv6

Installing support for IPv6 in Windows 2003 is easy. Open the Network Connections folder from the Control Panel, right-click the interface on which you want to install IPv6, and choose Properties. On the General tab, click Install. Select Protocol and click Add. In the Select Network Protocol dialog box, select Microsoft TCP/IP version 6 and click OK. Then, click Close to close the interface's property sheet (Figure 15-10).

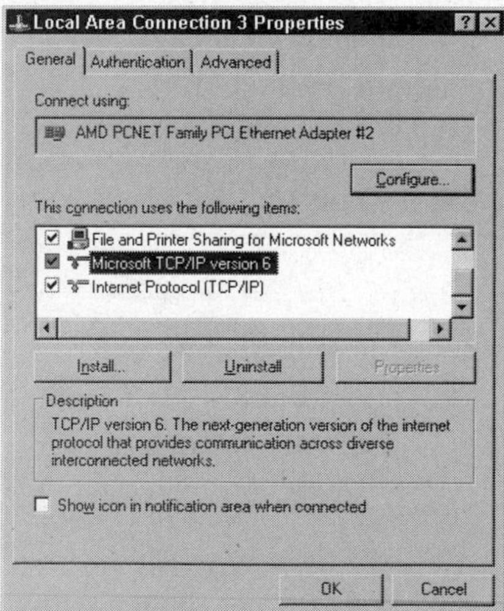

Figure 15-10: The IPV6 protocol appears in the interface's properties.

IPv6 address assignment

As with IPv4, IPv6 you can assign IPv6 addresses either statically or dynamically; however, the implications and implementation of automatic address assignment are very different from IPv4. Let's take a look at automatic address assignment first.

IPv6 address autoconfiguration

IPv6 doesn't require the use of a configuration protocol such as DHCP to assign addresses automatically, although IPv6 supports automatic assignment through DHCPv6 servers. Automatic configuration without a DHCPv6 server is called *stateless autoconfiguration*. With this method, the host configures its address using router advertisement messages received from the routers on its link. The end result is similar to IPv4 address assignment with APIPA (Automatic Private IP Addressing), which allows Windows platforms to derive a valid IP address from the private 169.254.x.x/16 address space (class B with subnet mask 255.255.0.0). Windows 2003 supports stateless autoconfiguration.

IPv6 also provides for *stateful autoconfiguration*, which relies on a DHCPv6 server to allocate the address. However, Windows 2003 does not at this point support stateful autoconfiguration, nor does the DHCP service included with Windows 2003 support DHCPv6 address allocation. So, you need to rely either on stateless autoconfiguration or configure the address and other properties manually.

Static IPv6 address configuration

Unfortunately, Windows 2003 doesn't provide a graphical means to configure IPv6. Instead, you must use the `netsh` command from a console to configure IPv6. Open a command console and issue the following commands to initiate a Netsh session to configure IPV6:

```
NETSH
INTERFACE IPV6
```

Next, add the interface and address using the following command:

```
ADD ADDRESS INTERFACE=string ADDRESS=address
```

Replace *string* with the string that identifies the IPv6 interface; *address* specifies the IPv6 address.

Generally, even if you assign the address statically in this way, the computer will determine the default router from router advertisements; however, you can assign the default router statically if need be. Still in the `netsh` IPv6 interface, execute the following command:

```
ADD ROUTE PREFIX=IPv6address/Integer INTERFACE=string
```

Replace *IPv6Address* with the valid IPv6 address and *Integer* with the prefix length. Replace *string* with the interface name on which to add the route. If you need to remove a route, use the following commands:

```
SHOW ROUTES
DELETE ROUTE PREFIX=IPv6Address/Integer INTERFACE=string
```

Use the results of the SHOW ROUTES command to determine the route prefix and interface index for the route to be deleted. Then replace the *IPv6Address*, *Integer*, and *string* values accordingly.

See Chapter 17 for a discussion of the implications of IPv6 for DNS. See Chapter 18 for a complete discussion of using Windows 2003 for routing and remote access.

Troubleshooting TCP/IP

When TCP/IP works well, life is good. Occasionally, however, TCP/IP connections will fail and you will need to determine the cause of the problem. Windows 2003 includes a handful of TCP/IP utilities you can use to test connectivity and troubleshoot connections. This section of the chapter examines TCP/IP troubleshooting in general and the tools included with Windows 2003 for that purpose.

Common troubleshooting concepts

As is the case when troubleshooting any problem, the first thing to consider when troubleshooting TCP/IP connections is whether anything has changed in the system's configuration. Problems with a newly installed computer typically point to an invalid IP address, wrong subnet mask, or incorrect default gateway. If TCP/IP has never worked on the system, open the TCP/IP properties for the connection and verify that they are correct.

For systems that have been working but have stopped, you need to more narrowly define the problem. For example, if you've been able to connect to a specific Web site but can't anymore, see if you can connect to other sites. If the problem lies with one site, it's almost surely a problem on the server side and not something you can correct on your end. However, if a range of Web sites work but others do not, you probably have a DNS or routing problem. The same holds true for FTP sites and for local resources such as other computers on your local segment.

A methodical, logical approach will help you identify the point of failure, if not the cause. While you could work from the problem backwards, we prefer to troubleshoot from the local computer outward until we find the point of failure, using Packet InterNet Groper (`ping`). For example, you should first ping the loopback address (type `ping 127.0.0.1` or `ping localhost` from a command prompt) to verify that TCP/IP is functioning on your computer. You can then begin moving farther out into the network and Internet until you find the point at which communication breaks down. Ping a computer on the local segment, and if successful, ping the internal side of the router. If that works, ping the external side of the router, then a system past the router. If the `ping` fails at any point, it typically indicates that the packets generated by the `ping` command are not being returned, either because the remote node is configured to discard `ping` traffic or a problem with the routing table is preventing the packets from being returned. If `ping localhost` fails, you probably have a problem with your network interface card or a corrupt TCP/IP protocol stack.

If you have problems pinging a particular host and know that the host does not discard ping traffic, verify that the host has a properly configured default gateway. If not, the ping traffic will not be properly routed back to you.

The following list describes common problems and potential solutions:

- ✦ **TCP/IP won't initialize on the host or a service fails to start:** These problems typically point to a configuration error. Open the properties for the interface and check the settings for TCP/IP closely to make sure they are correct, particularly that you haven't specified a conflicting static IP address. For multi-homed systems, check the priority order of the interfaces. To do so, open the Network Up Connections folder and choose Advanced ➪ Advanced Settings. On the Adapters and Bindings tab, use the Up and Down arrows for the Connections list to move the primary adapter to the top of the list. Also, verify in the same property page that TCP/IP is bound to the selected adapter.

✦ **Communication to other hosts fails, or other hosts don't respond:** This often results from an IP address conflict, network hardware failure, or possibly an incorrect DHCP lease. Use the `ipconfig /all` command to check your IP address, subnet mask, and default gateway settings.

✦ **Pinging localhost works but you can't communicate with local or remote hosts:** Verify that you have the correct subnet specified. The ability to ping local hosts but not remote hosts can be caused by incorrect default gateway setting or router problems.

✦ **You can ping the local computer by name, but you cannot ping remote computers by name:** You're having a problem with DNS. Verify that you are specifying valid DNS servers in the system's TCP/IP configuration and that those servers are available.

✦ **You can ping a non-Windows 2000/XP workstation but can't connect to it using a .NET console command:** You might be experiencing a problem with NetBIOS name resolution. Check WINS settings and verify that you haven't disabled NetBIOS over TCP/IP on the WINS page of the computer's TCP/IP settings. You might also have a problem with the workstation service on the local computer or the computer you are trying to connect to. This is not a TCP/IP problem, but you would not be alone thinking it is. If the workstation service is stopped, try restarting it. If you can restart it and still have the problem, then name-to-IP address resolving is the likely cause. If you cannot restart the workstation service, you will likely have to reboot the culprit machine. A dead workstation service points to an installation that went bad.

✦ **You can connect to a host or Web site by IP address but not by host name:** This is clearly a DNS issue. Verify that your system is configured for valid DNS servers and that the servers are available. (See Chapter 17 for troubleshooting DNS entries.)

Windows 2003 includes several utilities you can use to troubleshoot TCP/IP connectivity. The following sections explain these tools, starting with the most basic and sometimes most useful tool: the `ping` command.

ping

In its most basic use, `ping` works like a submarine's sonar: It bounces a packet off a remote host and listens for the return packet. If the packet comes back, you have basic TCP/IP connectivity between the two hosts. Lack of a response can indicate routing problems, a configuration problem with TCP/IP on the local host, unavailability of the remote host, or increasingly, that the remote host is configured to ignore `ping` traffic.

The `ping` command generates Internet Control Message Protocol (ICMP) packets and transmits them to the designated host, then waits for a response. The version of `ping` included with Windows 2003 sends four packets by default and waits for a period of one second for the response from each. You can specify the number of packets to transmit and the timeout period to override the defaults, if desired. For example, you might send a larger number of packets to test response time over a more realistic sample period. Following is a sample output from `ping`:

```
C:\>ping 192.168.0.6

Pinging 192.168.0.6 with 32 bytes of data:

Reply from 192.168.0.6: bytes=32 time=16ms TTL=128
Reply from 192.168.0.6: bytes=32 time<10ms TTL=128
Reply from 192.168.0.6: bytes=32 time=16ms TTL=128
Reply from 192.168.0.6: bytes=32 time<10ms TTL=128

Ping statistics for 192.168.0.6:
    Packets: Sent = 4, Received = 4, Lost = 0 (0% loss),
Approximate round trip times in milli-seconds:
    Minimum = 0ms, Maximum =  16ms, Average =  8ms
```

`Ping` is also useful in identifying name resolution problems. If you can ping a host by IP address but not by host name, one of the following could be the cause:

✦ There is no valid host record in the remote host's domain. Add an entry to the DNS zone or add an entry in your local Hosts file for the remote host.

✦ You have an incorrect entry in your local Hosts file for the host. Remove or correct the entry in the Hosts file. See Chapter 17 for a discussion of Hosts and Lmhosts files.

✦ Your DNS configuration is incorrect (pointed to wrong or unavailable DNS servers). Correct the configuration and try again.

Before you begin testing any connectivity problem, you should verify that you can ping your own workstation. Use `ping` to perform an internal loopback test that verifies whether or not TCP/IP is functioning on your computer. Use one of the following commands to ping your own computer:

```
ping 127.0.0.1
ping localhost
ping YourIPAddress
```

Following is the syntax for the `ping` command:

```
ping [-t] [-a] [-n count] [-l size] [-f] [-i ttl] [-v tos]
[-r count][-s count] [[-j HostList] | [-k HostList]]
[-w timeout] [-R] [-S srcaddr] [-4] [-6] target_name
```

Table 15-13 describes the switches you can use with `ping`.

Table 15-13: ping Command Switches

Switch	*Function*	*Use*
`-t`	Pings continuously until terminated by Ctrl+C. Press Ctrl+Break to view statistics.	Perform extended testing or check for intermittent problems.
`-a`	Resolves address to host name.	Test name resolution and troubleshoot Hosts file.
`-n` *count*	Specifies number of packets to send.	Perform extended testing.

Switch	Function	Use
`-l size`	Specifies packet size in bytes; the default is 64, the maximum is 8,192.	Check for packet fragmentation and response time.
`-f`	Sets Don't Fragment flag in packet.	Prevent routers from fragmenting packet.
`-i ttl`	Sets packet time-to-live.	Increase timeout on slow connections.
`-v tos`	Sets Type of Service field.	Specify type of action remote router should perform on the packet.
`-r count`	Records packet route; specify from 1 to 9.	Determine route of outgoing and incoming packets.
`-s count`	Sets time stamp for number of hops specified by *count.*	Set current hop count for the packet.
`-j HostList`	Routes packets using host list; specify maximum of 9 hosts.	Direct traffic through specific route; hosts can be separated by intermediate gateways (loose source route).
`-k HostList`	Routes packets using host list.	Similar to `-j` but hosts can't be separated by intermediate gateways (strict source route).
`-w timeout`	Sets packet timeout In milliseconds.	Increase timeout value to overcome timeout on slow connections.
`-R`	Trace a round-trip path.	Trace back to client; used on IPV6 only.
`-S srcaddr`	Source address to use.	Specify source address to ping from; used on IPV6 only.
`-4`	Force IPV4.	Force ping to use IPV4; not necessary if specifying IPV4 address.
`-6`	Force IPV6.	Force ping to use IPV6.
`target_name`	Specifies remote host(s) to ping.	Specify destination to ping.

ping and IPv6

You can use the `ping` command to test connectivity to systems that use IPv6. To test the function of the stack, ping the local interface using the following command:

```
ping ::1
```

If that works, try pinging the local computer using its IPv6 address rather than the localhost address. Use the following command to ping a link-local node:

```
ping address
```

Replace *address* with the link-local address of the other node. Next, try pinging a different host using the same format, replacing *address* with the IPv6 address of the remote node and optionally using `-s` to specify the source interface. See Table 15-13 for a list of additional command switches you can use with ping to test IPV6 connectivity.

ipconfig

Use the `ipconfig` command to display configured TCP/IP properties for all adapters, set certain properties, renew or release address leases, and update host records through dynamic DNS. The `ipconfig` command is useful for determining TCP/IP settings on any system, but is most helpful for determining settings on systems that obtain settings through DHCP. Knowing your address and related settings is the first step in troubleshooting any connectivity problem. In addition, you can use `ipconfig` to release and renew a lease, set a class ID, manage the DNS cache, and request an update of the host record in DNS.

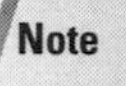

The equivalent tool for `ipconfig` in Windows 9*x* is WINIPCFG.EXE.

The following is the syntax for `ipconfig`:

```
Ipconfig [/all | /renew [adapter] | /release [adapter] | /flushdns |
/displadns | /registerdns /showclassid [adapter] | /setclassid adapter
[classid]
```

Table 15-14 lists the switches and their uses.

Table 15-14: ipconfig Command Switches

Switch	*Function*	*Use*
`/all`	Shows all TCP/IP properties, including MAC address.	Obtain complete information; omit to view only address, subnet mask, and gateway.
`/renew [adapter]`	Renews DHCP properties on *adapter*.	Omit *adapter* to renew DHCP properties on all adapters.
`/release [adapter]`	Releases current DHCP lease on *adapter*.	Release address, disabling TCP/IP for *adapter*; omit *adapter* to release all leases.
`/flushdns`	Purges local DNS resolver cache.	Overcome problems with bad cache entries.
`/registerdns`	Refreshes all leases and register host name with DNS.	Ensure up-to-date host records in DNS; dynamic updates require a Windows 2003 DNS server.
`/displaydns`	Displays contents of local resolver cache.	Check cache for potential bad entries.
`/showclassid`	Displays all class IDs allowed for *adapter*.	Class IDs allow DHCP to assign properties on a client-by-client basis, using the class ID as the client identifier.
`/setclassid`	Sets the current class ID for *adapter*.	See above.

netstat

The netstat command provides three primary functions: monitoring connections to remote hosts, viewing protocol statistics for a connection, and extracting the IP address of a host to which you've connected using domain names (or determining domain name if connected by address). The syntax for netstat is as follows:

```
netstat [-a] [-enos] [-p protocol] [-r] [interval]
```

Table 15-15 describes the options you can use with netstat.

Table 15-15: netstat Command Switches

Switch	*Function*	*Use*
-a	Displays all connections.	Show all connections, including server connections.
-e	Shows Ethernet statistics.	Use with -s.
-n	Shows addresses and port numbers in numerical format.	Use numerical rather than host.domain format.
-o	Displays owning process ID.	Show the ID of the process that owns each connection.
-s	Shows statistics on per-protocol basis.	netstat by default shows TCP, UDP, ICMP, and IP.
-p *protocol*	Shows connections for *protocol.*	View connections for a specific protocol.
-r	Shows contents of routing table.	Troubleshoot routing problems.
interval	Specifies interval for update; terminate with Ctrl+C.	Omit *interval* to display information a single time.

As mentioned earlier in this chapter, you can use netstat to determine the IP address of a remote host. To do so, issue the command netstat -n. The following examples first issue netstat with no parameters, then use -n to derive IP addresses:

```
C:\>netstat

Active Connections

  Proto  Local Address          Foreign Address        State
  TCP    bart:netbios-ssn       NOTE2KSRV:1117         ESTABLISHED
  TCP    bart:3454              ftp.BayNetworks.COM:ftp  ESTABLISHED

C:\>netstat -n

Active Connections

  Proto  Local Address          Foreign Address        State
  TCP    192.168.0.1:139        192.168.0.2:1117       ESTABLISHED
  TCP    209.105.38.181:3454    134.177.3.22:21        ESTABLISHED
```

This example shows two connections: a local connection to a server named NOTE2KSRV and another to ftp.baynetworks.com. Note that the second example displays the IP address rather than the host name.

hostname

Use the hostname command to derive the host name of the local computer. If no host name is set through the DNS properties for the computer, the computer name set in the Network Identification tab of the computer's properties is used as the host name. Using the hostname command is often easier than opening the properties for the connection to hunt for the host name. There are no options for the hostname command.

tracert

Being able to determine the route used to connect to a given host is extremely useful in troubleshooting routing problems. Use tracert to trace the route used to connect to another host and determine where, if at all, a connection is failing. For example, if you're having problems reaching sites on the Internet, you can use tracert to locate the problem and identify the router where the traffic is dying.

Like ping, tracert generates ICMP packets, but the tracert command sends a series of ICMP packets to the destination host using steadily incrementing time-to-live (TTL) values. Each gateway decrements the TTL value by one. The first packet has a TTL of 1, so it gets decremented to 0 by the first gateway, which then sends a ICMP Time Exceeded packet back to the originating host (your computer) along with the transit time in milliseconds. The local host then transmits the next packet with a TTL of 2. The first gateway decrements it to 1, and the second gateway decrements it to 0. The second gateway then sends back the ICMP Time Exceeded packet. Subsequent packets make it one gateway, or *hop,* further than the previous one before being expired. The result is a table showing the data for each packet. When the packets stop coming back, you've potentially identified the problem router.

The following is a sample output from tracert (text in bold is the typed command):

```
C:\>tracert ftp.happypuppy.com

Tracing route to ftp.happypuppy.com [199.105.102.130]
over a maximum of 30 hops:

  1   110 ms  109 ms   125 ms  USR1RRT-TS1.DialUp.rrt.net [209.105.38.198]
  2   109 ms   94 ms   125 ms  CISCO1RRTGW-TS.DialUp.rrt.net [209.105.38.50]
  3   281 ms  110 ms    94 ms  border1-h4-0.ply.mr.net [207.229.192.1]
  4   109 ms   94 ms   110 ms  core1-A0-0-0-722.PLY.MR.Net [137.192.7.141]
  5   125 ms  109 ms   109 ms  Serial5-1-0.GW2.MSP1.ALTER.NET [157.130.98.189]
  6   109 ms  109 ms   125 ms  152.ATM3-0.XR2.CHI4.ALTER.NET [146.188.209.134]
  7   141 ms  125 ms   125 ms  194.ATM3-0.TR2.CHI4.ALTER.NET [146.188.208.230]
  8   140 ms  141 ms   125 ms  106.ATM7-0.TR2.EWR1.ALTER.NET [146.188.136.126]
  9   141 ms  125 ms   140 ms  196.ATM6-0.XR2.EWR1.ALTER.NET [146.188.176.81]
 10   172 ms  141 ms   140 ms  192.ATM9-0-0.GW3.EWR1.ALTER.NET [146.188.177.169]
 11   907 ms  953 ms   891 ms  ftp.happypuppy.com [199.105.102.130]

Trace complete.
```

The following is the syntax for `tracert`:

```
Tracert [-d] [-h max_hops] [-j hostlist] [-w timeout] [-R] [-S srcaddr]
[-4] [-6] target_name
```

Table 15-16 describes the switches for `tracert`.

Table 15-16: tracert Command Switches

Switch	*Function*	*Use*
`-d`	Does not resolve names of interim systems.	Simplify output.
`-h` *`max_hops`*	Specifies maximum hops to trace.	Limit testing to specified number of hops.
`-w` *`timeout`*	Sets time in milliseconds to wait for reply.	Overcome slow connections.
`-j` *`hostlist`*	Specifies a loose-source route along *hostlist.*	Perform trace along specified route
`-R`	Traces round-trip path.	Use on IPV6 only to trace back to source.
`-S` *`srcaddr`*	Specifies the source address.	Use on IPV6 only to specify source IP address.
`-4`	Forces IPV4.	Force tracert to use IPV4; not necessary when specifying IPV4 address.
`-6`	Forces IPV6.	Force tracert to use IPV6; not necessary when specifying IPV6 address.
`target_name`	Returns FQDN or IP address of destination host.	Specify destination.

arp

The `arp` command, which stands for Address Resolution Protocol, lets you view the `arp` table on your local computer, which associates physical MAC addresses of other computers on the local network with their IP addresses. The `arp` table speeds up connections by eliminating the need to look up MAC addresses for subsequent connections. Viewing the contents of the `arp` table can be useful for troubleshooting connections to specific computers on the network.

The following are the syntaxes for the `arp` command:

```
arp -s inet_addr eth_addr [if_addr]
arp -d inet_addr [if_addr]
arp -a [inet_addr] [-N if_addr]
```

Table 15-17 describes the options for `arp`.

Table 15-17: arp Command Switches

Switch	*Function*	*Use*
`-a` or `-g`	Shows `arp` table data for all hosts.	Provide detailed view.
`-d` *`inet_address`*	Removes entry for *inet_address* from `arp` cache.	Clear up connection problem due to bad `arp` cache entry.
`-s` *`Inet_address eth_address`*	Adds new `arp` cache entry for *Inet_address* pointing to eth_address.	Add entry for specified host.
`-N` *`IfAddress`*	Displays ARP entries for interface specified by *IfAddress*.	Display ARP entries.

route

You can use the `route` command to view or modify entries in the local computer's static routing table. Static routes are used in place of implicit routes determined by the default gateway for the computer. For example, you can add a static route to direct traffic destined for a specific host through a gateway other than the default to improve response time, reduce costs, and so on. The `route` command is also useful for troubleshooting, either for identifying incorrect static routes or for adding temporary routes to bypass a problem gateway.

The syntax for `route` is as follows:

```
route [-f] [-p] [print|add|delete|change] [destination] [MASK netmask]
[gateway] [METRIC metric]
```

Table 15-18 explains the options for `route`.

Table 15-18: route Command Switches

Switch	*Function*	*Use*
`-f`	Clears all gateway entries from table.	
`-p`	Use with `add` to create persistent route.	Non-persistent routes are lost at each boot.
`print`	Prints a route.	
`add`	Adds a route to the table.	Use `-p` to make the route persistent for subsequent sessions.
`delete`	Deletes a route from the table.	
`change`	Modifies an existing route.	
`destination`	Specifies host address.	

Switch	Function	Use
MASK *netmask*	Uses subnet mask specified by *netmask*.	If MASK isn't used, defaults to 255.255.255.255.
gateway	Specifies address of gateway for route.	
METRIC *metric*	Specifies the metric, or cost, for the route using the value *metric*.	
IF *interface*	Specifies the interface for routing table to modify.	

You can use the wildcards * and ? with the print and delete switches. As with file names, a * matches any number of characters, and a ? matches one character.

nbtstat

Use the nbtstat command to display statistics for NetBIOS-over-TCP/IP (NetBT) connections. You also can use nbtstat to purge the name cache and reload the Hosts file, which offers the benefit of reloading the LMHOSTS file without rebooting.

The following is the syntax for nbtstat:

```
nbtstat [-a RemoteName] [-A RemoteAddress] [-c] [-n] [-R] [-RR] [-r]
[-S] [-s] interval
```

Table 15-19 describes the switches for nbtstat.

Table 15-19: nbtstat Command Switches

Switch	Function
-a *RemoteName*	Shows NetBIOS name table for computer *RemoteName*.
-A *RemoteAddress*	Shows NetBIOS name table for computer at the IP address *RemoteAddress*.
-c	Shows contents of the NetBIOS name cache.
-n	Shows NetBIOS names for the local computer.
-R	Purges the NetBIOS name cache and reloads LMHOSTS.
-RR	Submits Name Release packets to WINS, then refreshes.
-r	Shows NetBIOS name resolution statistics.
-S	Shows current NetBIOS workstation and server sessions by IP address.
-s	Shows current NetBIOS workstation and server sessions by name.
Interval	Returns number of seconds between subsequent display of protocol statistics.

Legacy Protocols

Although the previous sections of this chapter have been devoted to TCP/IP, Windows 2003 supports additional network protocols as well. The following sections explain these protocols and their properties, but do not provide a detailed explanation of how these protocols are structured or how they function.

NetBEUI

NetBEUI is one of two protocols that support NetBIOS, the name resolution method used by previous Microsoft operating systems, including DOS, Windows 3.*x*, Windows for Workgroups, Windows 9*x*, and Windows NT.

NetBEUI is useful on small networks because it is easy to install and configure. As the number of nodes on the network increases, however, NetBEUI becomes less practical because of the amount of network traffic it generates. Also, NetBEUI is not routable, which limits it to local segments only.

Tip

NetBEUI can be routed if encapsulated in PPTP or L2TP for a VPN connection. This enables you to use NetBEUI for accessing resources on remote networks, but it also requires a TCP/IP link between the two networks.

There are no configurable properties for NetBEUI. Simply install the NetBEUI protocol on the selected interface and ensure that all nodes using NetBEUI on the network have unique names.

IPX/SPX

Like TCP/IP, IPX/SPX is actually two protocols: Internetwork Packet eXchange and Sequenced Packet eXchange. IPX/SPX provides connectivity for Novell NetWare servers and clients, but it can also serve as a primary network protocol when no NetWare servers are present.

With IPX/SPX, two types of numbers are used to route traffic: the *external network number* and the *internal network number.* The external network number is associated with the physical network adapter and network. All nodes on the network that use the same frame type (explained shortly) must use the same external network number. You can specify an external network number manually or allow Windows 2003 to detect it automatically. The external network number is a hexadecimal value from one to eight digits.

The internal network number identifies a virtual network in the computer, and programs identify themselves as being located on this virtual network rather than the physical network identified by the external network number. Each virtual network appears as a separate network to the user. By default, Windows 2003 assigns the value 00000000 as the internal network number. The internal network number helps improve routing in multi-homed systems or in a system where more than one frame type is used on a single adapter.

The following are the configuration properties for the IPX/SPX protocol:

✦ **Internal network number:** This property defines the internal network number associated with the interface.

✦ **Auto frame type detection:** Select this option to allow Windows 2003 to automatically detect the frame type. If multiple frame types are detected in addition to 802.2, NWLink defaults to 802.2.

✦ **Manual frame type detection:** Select this option to manually configure frame type or configure multiple frame types. Specify the internal network number for each: Choose 802.2 for NetWare 3.3 or later on Ethernet; choose 802.3 for other Ethernet configurations; choose 802.5 for Token Ring adapters.

DLC

DLC stands for Data Link Control. All network adapters have a DLC address or DLC identifier (called a DLCI, or *del-see*). Some protocols, including Ethernet and Token Ring, use DLC exclusively to identify nodes on the network. Other protocols use logical addresses to identify nodes. TCP/IP, for example, uses the IP address to identify a node. However, at the lower layers of the network, some translation still needs to take place to convert the logical address to the DLC address. Address Resolution Protocol (ARP) performs this translation for TCP/IP.

DLC is required as a protocol only for those situations where DLC is used rather than a logical address. For example, DLC enables Windows 2003 computers to connect to IBM mainframe systems and use DLC-enabled network printers.

There are no user-configurable properties for DLC.

SNMP

Simple Network Management Protocol (SNMP) provides a standardized means for managing hosts on TCP/IP (and IPX) networks. SNMP enables hosts to communicate with one another and is commonly used for remote monitoring and configuration. For example, you might use an SNMP management tool to manage routers or other devices in your network, gather information about workstations on the network, detect unauthorized attempts to reconfigure certain network devices, and so on.

Understanding how SNMP works

SNMP functions through *SNMP management systems* and *SNMP agents.* A management system is an application that requests information from SNMP agents and directs agents to perform certain tasks, such as setting options on the remote device, returning configuration data, and so on. For example, you might have a non-Windows 2003 router on the network that contains firmware to enable it to function as an SNMP agent. You use a management system (SNMP-aware application) on your local workstation to manage the router, by viewing and changing the router's configuration and monitoring its status.

SNMP management systems send SNMP *messages* to agents, which respond to those messages. In most cases, the management system requests information from a *management information base,* or MIB, managed by the agent. The MIB is a set of objects that function as a database of information about the managed host. The only message an SNMP agent generates on its own is a *trap,* which is an alarm-triggered event on the agent host. A system reboot on the agent host is an example of a trap.

SNMP uses *communities* to provide a limited amount of security for SNMP and a means of grouping SNMP management systems with agents. Agents respond only to management systems in the list of communities to which they belong. The community name serves as a password for access by the management system to the agent. Agents can belong to multiple communities.

The SNMP service included with Windows 2003 enables a Windows 2003 computer to function as an SNMP agent to allow remote administration of the following:

- Windows 2000/.NET Server
- Windows 2000/XP Professional
- Windows .NET-based DHCP
- Windows .NET-based WINS
- Internet Information Services (IIS)
- LAN Manager
- Exchange 2000
- SQL Server 2000

Windows 2003 does not include any management system software, and the SNMP service functions only as an SNMP agent. However, there are third-party SNMP management tools for Windows 2003 and related services.

Installing and configuring SNMP

You add the SNMP service through the Add or Remove Programs object in the Control Panel. After you open Add or Remove Programs, click Add/Remove Windows Components. Open the Management and Monitoring Tools item and select Simple Network Management Protocol, then click OK. Click Next to install the software.

Also install the WMI SNMP Provider if you want to be able to manage the server through the Windows Management Interface.

The following sections explain how to configure the SNMP service (set community names and other tasks). You manage the SNMP service through the properties for the SNMP service. You can access the service through the Services console in the Administrative Tools folder or through the Services snap-in in the Computer Management console.

Configure agent properties

After installing the SNMP service, you need to configure agent properties, which includes general information such as who is responsible for managing the agent host and the types of services with which the agent will interact on the computer.

Right-click the SNMP service in the Services console and choose Properties to open the properties for the SNMP Service, or select the service and choose Action ⇨ Properties to display the service's property sheet. The General, Log On, Recovery, and Dependencies pages are the same as for other services. Click the Agent tab to configure the following agent properties:

- **Contact:** Specify the name of the person responsible for managing the host computer.
- **Location:** Specify the physical location of the computer or the contact's location or other information (phone number, extension, and so on).
- **Physical:** Select this option if the agent host manages physical hardware such as hard disk partitions.

- **Applications:** Select this option if the agent uses any applications that transmit data using the TCP/IP protocol.
- **Datalink and subnetwork:** Select this option if the agent host manages a bridge.
- **Internet:** Select this option if the agent host is an Internet gateway.
- **End-to-end:** Select this option if the host uses IP. This option should always be selected.

Configuring traps

Use the Traps tab of the SNMP service to configure computers to which the SNMP service sends traps. From the Community name drop-down list, select the community for which you want to assign a trap destination. If you have no communities set yet, type the community name in the combo box and click Add to List. Then, click Add to display a simple dialog box in which you specify the host name, IP address, or IPX address of the remote computer to receive the trap notification. Repeat the process to add other trap destinations as needed.

Configuring security

Use the Security tab of the SNMP Service's properties to configure the communities in which the agent participates and optionally a list of hosts from which the agent accepts SNMP packets. By default, the agent accepts packets from all hosts. This presents a security risk, however, so you should take care to configure security settings to allow SNMP traffic only from authorized hosts. The Security page contains the following options:

- **Send Authentication Trap:** Select this option to have the agent send a message to all trap destinations if the agent receives an SNMP request from a host or community not listed in the "Accepted community names" list or "Accept SNMP packets from these hosts" list. The message is sent to all hosts in the trap destination list on the Traps property page to indicate that a remote management system failed authentication (potentially indicating an unauthorized access attempt).
- **Accepted Community Names:** Use this list and the associated buttons to modify the list of communities in which the agent participates and the community rights for each. You can select from the following rights:
    - **None:** Prevent the agent host from processing any SNMP requests from the specified community. For example, you might configure None for the Public community for enhanced security.
    - **Notify:** Select this option to allow the agent host to send traps only to the selected community.
    - **Read Only:** Use this option to allow remote consoles to view data in the local MIB but not change it. This option prevents the agent from processing SNMP SET requests.
    - **Read Write:** Use this option to allow remote consoles to make changes on the managed system. This option allows the agent to process SNMP SET requests.
    - **Read Create:** Use this option to allow the agent to create new entries in the SNMP tables.
- **Accept SNMP Packets from Any Host:** Select this option to allow the agent to process requests from all hosts in the "Accepted community names" list.
- **Accept SNMP PACKETS from These Hosts:** Select this option to define a specific list of hosts from which the agent will process SNMP requests.

Translating events to traps

To trap events and enable the agent to transmit the traps to the management systems defined in its Traps properties, you need to first translate the event to an SNMP trap. For example, to trap a system shutdown, you need to convert the system event 513 to an SNMP trap.

Windows 2003 provides two utilities you can use to translate local events to SNMP traps. The first, `evntcmd.exe`, is a command-line utility you can integrate in batch files or use dynamically from a command console. For a description of command switches for `evntcmd`, issue the `evntcmd /?` command at a console prompt. The other tool, `evntwin.exe`, provides a graphical user interface for translating events to traps. Click Start ⇨ Run and enter `evntwin` to run the Event to Trap Translator.

To translate a trap, select the Custom option and click Edit to expand the dialog box to include the Event Sources and Events lists (Figure 15-11). Search through the Event Sources list to find the source of the event you want to trap (such as Security for system shutdown, startup, logon, and so on). In the Events list, locate and select the event you want to trap, then click Add. Windows 2003 displays the Properties dialog box, which lets you specify the following two options:

- **If Event Count Reaches:** Specify how many times the event can occur before a trap is generated.
- **Within the Time Interval:** Specify an optional time interval in which the number of events specified by the previous option must occur to generate a trap.

After you specify the properties for the trap, click OK to add it to the list. Repeat the process for any other events you need to trap.

Setting general properties

You can configure a handful of settings in the Event to Trap Translator to limit trap length and throttle the number of traps transmitted by the agent. With the Event to Trap Translator program open, click Settings to display the Settings dialog box. Configure the following options as needed:

- **Limit Trap Length:** Select this option to limit the length of data sent with the trap to the number of bytes specified by the following option.
- **Trap Length *n* Bytes:** Set the size in bytes for the trap. Any additional data is truncated if the trap exceeds the specified length.
- **Trim Insertion Strings First:** Trim insertion strings from the trap data before truncating the data when the trap exceeds the specified length.
- **Trim Formatted Message First:** Trim formatted message text from the trap data before truncating the data when the trap exceeds the specified length.
- **Apply Throttle:** Select to limit the number of traps that can be sent in a given period of time.
- **Don't Apply Throttle:** Select to allow an unlimited number of traps to be transmitted.
- **Number of Traps:** Set the maximum number of traps allowed in the given time frame when throttling is turned on.
- **Interval of Time (Seconds):** Set the interval in seconds that the specified number of traps can be transmitted before throttling takes effect.

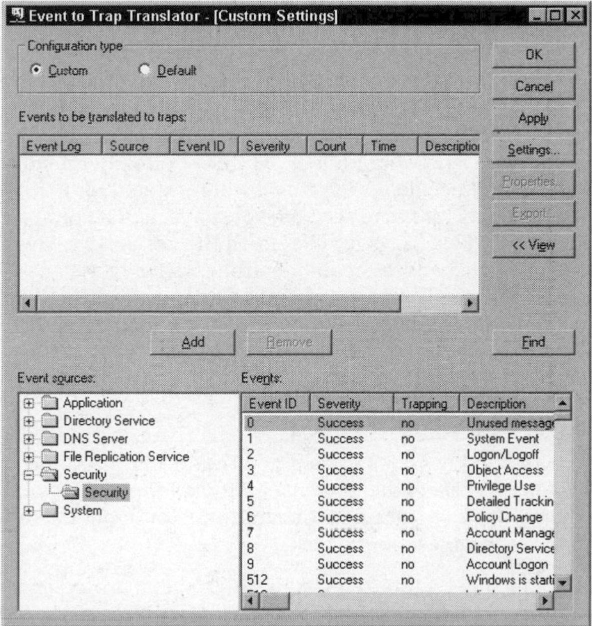

Figure 15-11: The Event to Trap Translator, expanded to show event sources.

Exporting the trap list

After you've taken the time to weed through the event list and create traps for a number of events, you probably will want to archive the data in case you experience a problem with the Event to Trap Translator or the system and need to reconfigure the traps. You might also want to configure the same traps on several other systems without having to reconfigure them manually. The solution in both situations is to export the trap list. After you have the traps configured as needed, click Export in the Event to Trap Translator. Windows 2003 prompts you for a file name. Save the file in an appropriate archive location or where you can access it from the other workstations. The file automatically receives a `.cnf` file extension.

Use the `evntcmd` command to load the event list into the system. For example, the following command will load the file `events.cnf` from a network share into the local computer:

```
Evntcmd \\srv2\config\events.cnf
```

Use the following command to load the file from a local file named `netevents.cnf` to a remote system named `work23`:

```
Evntcmd -s work23 c:\snmp-stuff\netevents.cnf
```

When configuring traps on a remote computer, the SNMP service need not be running on the local computer. You will, however, have to copy the `evntcmd.exe` application to the local computer, as it is not installed by default (it installs with the SNMP service).

Summary

The Transmission Control Protocol/Internet Protocol (TCP/IP) is rapidly becoming the protocol of choice for many networks, partly because of the proliferation of the Internet, but also for the flexibility the protocol offers. TCP/IP is a complex protocol, however, so there are several issues to address when you configure a network for TCP/IP. Once you understand addressing and subnet issues, you need to decide how systems will receive their IP addresses (statically or dynamically) and assignments for name servers, gateways, and so on. You can use DHCP to automatically configure TCP/IP settings for clients on the network, which simplifies administration and helps protect against address conflicts from statically assigned addresses. You can have local clients retrieve IP address leases from an external network through a DHCP relay agent. A Windows 2003 server running RRAS can function as a DHCP relay agent.

Although its use is currently rather limited, IPv6 will continue to build in use as development of the 6bone continues and companies come to realize the benefits offered by IPv6.

You'll find several tools included with Windows 2003 to help you troubleshoot TCP/IP connections. The `ping` command, for example, is one of the most useful tools for checking basic TCP/IP connectivity. Other tools enable you to trace network routes, view IP configurations, view routing tables, and perform other troubleshooting tasks.

In addition to TCP/IP, Windows 2003 includes support for additional legacy protocols including NetBEUI, IPX/SPX, and DLC. NetBEUI is a good choice for small networks and supports older Microsoft client platforms such as Windows 3.*x*, Windows 9*x*, and Windows NT. IPX/SPX provides connectivity to NetWare servers, but also can be used as the primary protocol when no NetWare servers are present on the network. DLC is used primarily for connecting to IBM mainframes and network-connected printers.

One final topic covered in this chapter is SNMP, or Simple Network Management Protocol. Windows 2003 includes an SNMP agent that enables the computer to respond to SNMP requests from local and remote management services. You can configure a Windows 2003 server to generate traps for specific events and have those traps transmitted to specific management services for monitoring and administration purposes.

✦ ✦ ✦

DHCP

This chapter covers configuring and managing a Windows Server-based Dynamic Host Configuration Protocol (DHCP) server and DHCP clients.

In This Chapter

Understanding DHCP

Understanding the Windows Server 2003 DHCP server

Installing and configuring the DHCP server

Defining and implementing user and vendor classes

Creating and using superscopes

Creating multicast scopes

Configuring global DHCP server properties

Managing the DHCP database

Configuring Windows DHCP clients

Overview of DHCP

The TCP/IP protocol, which is required for Internet connectivity and is rapidly becoming a protocol of choice for many intranets, requires that each node on the network have a unique IP address. This includes any individual network object, such as a server, workstation, printer, or router. You can assign IP addresses to network nodes either *statically* or *dynamically.* With a statically assigned address, you specify a fixed address for a given node, and that address never changes unless you manually change it. Static assignment is the option used when the network node must have the same IP address all the time. Web and FTP servers or devices such as printers that don't support anything other than static assignments are prime examples of devices with statically assigned addresses.

You also can assign IP addresses dynamically through the Dynamic Host Configuration Protocol. DHCP enables network nodes to take IP address assignments from a DHCP server automatically at startup. Although dynamic assignment means that IP addresses for network nodes can (and do) typically change each time the node is restarted, that poses a problem only if a computer needs the same IP address for every session. In all other situations, including for most workstations and many servers, dynamic assignment enables you to manage a pool of IP addresses more effectively to prevent address conflicts. DHCP also lets you allocate a smaller number of IP addresses than the number of computers using them, provided the maximum number of live nodes at any given time doesn't exceed the number of available addresses. An example of such a situation is when you're using a server to provide dial-up access for multiple users. You might allocate 20 IP addresses to accommodate 50 dial-in users. Each user would receive a unique IP address assignment from the DHCP server at connection time, to a maximum of 20 concurrent connections.

Perhaps the most important benefit to DHCP is in the area of administration. DHCP makes it much easier to manage the IP address configuration of clients because you can affect all changes from a central server, rather than requiring changes on individual clients. The more computers on the network, the greater the advantage DHCP brings to address management. Rather than manually reconfiguring network settings at several hundred (or more) workstations when a network change occurs, you can simply change the settings at the server and either push the changes transparently to the user or allow the changes to take place when the clients restart.

The Windows Server DHCP Service

Windows Server 2003 includes a built-in DHCP service that offers excellent functionality for allocating and managing addresses. The DHCP Server service is built on industry standards (Request for Comments or RFCs) defined by the Internet Engineering Task Force (IETF). This adherence to standards ensures that the DHCP service will accommodate not only Windows clients but other clients as well, including Unix, Macintosh, and so on.

As with other services, you manage DHCP on a Windows Server through the Microsoft Management Console (MMC). The DHCP service console snap-in enables you to create DHCP scopes (a range of addresses and corresponding properties), assign global properties, view current assignments, and perform all other DHCP administration tasks.

In addition to supporting the IETF standards, the Windows Server 2003 DHCP service extends the functionality of DHCP to include logging, monitoring, and other features that integrate DHCP with the Windows Server 2003 operating system. In addition, Microsoft added several new features in Windows 2000 to improve DHCP's usefulness, administration, and integration with other services such as DNS, and these features naturally carry over into Windows Server 2003 DHCP. These features are discussed in the following sections.

Support for dynamic DNS

DHCP provides for dynamic address assignment and can therefore make it difficult to maintain accurate name-to-address mapping in DNS servers. As soon as a node changes its address, records in the DNS database become invalid. Windows Server 2003 DHCP integrates with DNS by enabling the DHCP server and clients to request updates to the DNS database when address or host names change. This capability enables the DNS database to remain up-to-date even for clients with dynamically assigned IP addresses.

Dynamic DNS (DDNS) functions through a client-server mechanism. Windows 2000 and Windows XP DHCP clients support DDNS, and they can directly request that a Windows Server 2003 or Windows 2000 DNS server update their host resource records (also called A records) when the clients' IP addresses or host names change. Windows 2000 and 2003 DHCP servers can also submit requests on behalf of clients, although a DHCP server can request an update to both the clients' host and pointer (PTR) records. Host records are used for host-to-address mapping, and pointer records are used for reverse lookup.

A Windows Server 2003 DHCP server also can act as a proxy for non-Windows 2000/XP DHCP clients to perform dynamic DNS updates. For example, a Windows Server 2003 DHCP server can perform updates for Windows 95/98 and Windows NT clients, which do not natively support dynamic DNS and are unable to submit requests to either the DHCP server or DNS server to update their resource records. Figure 16-1 illustrates how DHCP and DNS interact.

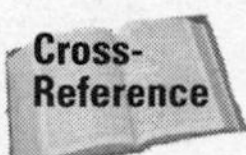

See the section, "Configuring Windows DHCP Clients," later in this chapter for an explanation of how to configure clients to use DDNS.

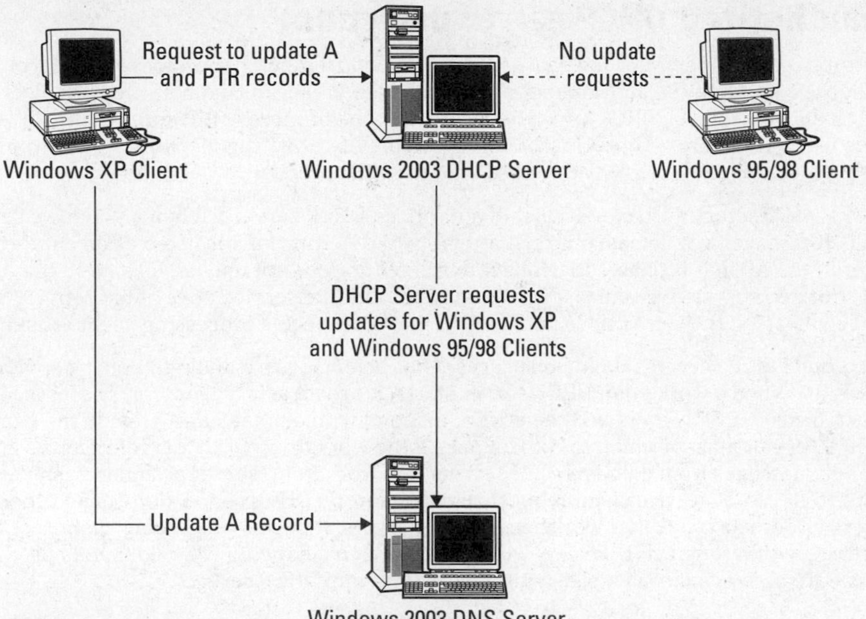

Figure 16-1: DHCP supports automatic updates to DNS when host name or IP address changes occur.

Vendor and user classes

Vendor classes enable you to define a set of DHCP settings for a specific equipment vendor and apply those settings to any node falling into that class. User classes enable you to do much the same thing, defining DHCP settings to apply to a specific group of nodes. Vendor and user classes offer enhanced flexibility in assigning custom settings to individual nodes or groups of nodes without affecting others on the same network. Through a vendor or user class, a node can request a custom set of DHCP settings to suit its configuration. For example, you might assign shorter lease durations to notebook PCs because they leave the network more frequently. You define a user class called Notebook and assign to it a shorter lease period; the client, which presents the user class to the server, receives the shorter lease based on that user class.

Multicast address allocation

Multicast addresses enable IP traffic to be broadcast to a group of nodes and are most commonly used in audio or video conferencing. A standard IP address is also known as a *unicast address* because traffic is broadcast to a single address. A multicast address, however, enables you to send a group of computers the same data packets with a single broadcast, rather than using multiple broadcasts to a group of unicast addresses. The use of multicasting enables a group of computers to receive the same data without duplicating the packets, thereby reducing packet traffic.

Unauthorized DHCP server detection

Unauthorized DHCP servers can cause real problems in a network by allocating incorrect or conflicting configuration information to clients. For example, an administrator or power user might install and start a DHCP server, unaware that one or more DHCP servers already exist on the network. There was previously nothing to prevent this "rogue" DHCP server from starting. Windows Server 2003 addresses that potential problem.

The Active Directory (AD) stores a list of authorized DHCP servers. When a Windows Server 2003 DHCP server in a domain starts, it attempts to determine if it is listed as an authorized server in the AD. If it is unable to connect to the AD or does not find itself listed in the AD as an authorized server, it assumes it is unauthorized and the service does not accept DHCP client requests. If the server does find itself in the AD, it begins processing client requests.

Workgroup DHCP servers (standalone servers not belonging to a domain) behave somewhat differently. When a workgroup DHCP server starts, it broadcasts a `dhcpinform` message. Any domain-based DHCP servers on the network respond with `dhcpack` and provide the name of the directory domain of which they are a part. If the workgroup DHCP server receives any `dhcpack` messages from domain DHCP servers, the workgroup server assumes it isn't authorized and does not service client requests. If a workgroup DHCP server detects no other servers or detects only other workgroup DHCP servers, it begins processing client requests. Therefore, workgroup DHCP servers will not operate on a network where domain-based DHCP servers are active, but can coexist with other workgroup DHCP servers.

Automatic client configuration

Windows 2000 and XP DHCP clients attempt to locate a DHCP server at startup and renew any unexpired leases (a lease is an IP address and the associated data allocated from a DHCP server). If no DHCP server is found, the client pings the default gateway defined by the lease. If the ping succeeds, the client continues to use the lease and automatically attempts to renew the lease when half the lease time expires.

If the client is unable to locate a DHCP server and pinging the default gateway fails, the client assumes that it is on a network without DHCP services, automatically assigns itself an IP address, and continues checking for a DHCP server every five minutes. The client assigns itself an address in the subnet 169.254.0.0/16 (Class B, subnet mask 255.255.0.0), but prior to assigning, the client tests to determine that the address is valid and doesn't conflict with other nodes.

Automatic address assignment is a useful feature, particularly for small peer networks, such as a home network, without a DHCP server. It enables users to move between networks with relative ease, and eliminating the need to reconfigure their systems. For example, a user can move his notebook from the office to home and have a valid address within the current network without having to reconfigure TCP/IP each time.

Improved monitoring and reporting

The DHCP service performs its own monitoring and logs events to the System log, which you can view with the Event Viewer console. DHCP in Windows Server 2003 also provides additional monitoring and statistical reporting. For example, you can configure DHCP to generate alerts when the percentage of available addresses in a given scope drops below a certain point.

Installing and Configuring the DHCP Server

The process of installing DHCP is relatively simple. Configuring a server and putting it into service is much more complex, however, particularly if you are new to DHCP. The following sections explain how to install the DHCP service and configure global and scope-specific settings.

Installing DHCP

As with other services, you add DHCP through the Add or Remove Programs object in the Control Panel. Open Add or Remove Programs, then click Add or Remove Windows Components. Open the Networking Services item and select Dynamic Host Configuration Protocol, click OK, then click Next. Follow the prompts to complete the software installation. After the software is installed, you can begin configuring and using DHCP without restarting the server.

You should configure a DHCP Server with a static IP address prior to adding the DHCP service.

Using the DHCP console

Windows Server 2003 provides an MMC console to enable you to manage DHCP servers both locally and on remote computers (Figure 16-2). You can perform all DHCP administrative functions through the DHCP console. To open the DHCP console, choose Start ➪ All Programs ➪ Administrative Tools ➪ DHCP.

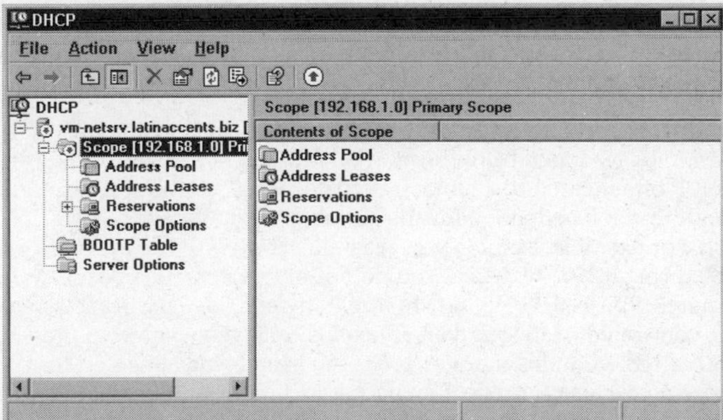

Figure 16-2: The DHCP console.

By default, the DHCP console connects to the local DHCP server, showing the server's IP address in the left pane. You can use the console to manage DHCP servers both locally and remotely. To connect to a different server, right-click the DHCP node (the top-most node) in the left pane, and choose Add Server. Type the name or IP address of the server you want to manage and then click OK. DHCP adds the server to the list.

Like most MMC consoles, DHCP functions as a two-pane console with the tree pane to the left and the contents pane to the right. The following sections explain how to configure DHCP using the console.

Creating scopes

A DHCP *scope* is a set of properties that define a range of IP addresses and related settings such as DNS servers, default gateway, and other information that the client needs to obtain from the DHCP server. Before you can begin using DHCP to assign addresses, you need to create at least one scope. Scopes can be active or inactive, so you also need to make the scope active before the server can allocate addresses from the scope to clients. This chapter assumes you are going to fully define the scope before activating it.

DHCP provides a New Scope wizard to take you through the process of creating a scope. To create a scope, right-click the server in the tree and choose New Scope. Or, select the server and choose Action ➪ New Scope. Click Next, and the wizard prompts for the following information:

- **Name:** This is the friendly name that appears in the DHCP console for the scope. An example might be "Miami Office scope."
- **Description:** This optional description appears on the scope's General property page (right-click the scope and choose Properties to view). Assign a description to help you recognize the purpose of the scope. For example, you might use the address range in the description.
- **Start IP address:** Specify the beginning address of the range of IP addresses you want to assign to the scope using dotted octet format.
- **End IP address:** Specify the ending address of the range of IP addresses you want to assign to the scope using dotted octet format.
- **Length** or **Subnet mask:** You can specify the subnet mask for the address range using either the address length or subnet mask in dotted octet format.
- **Exclusions, Start address and End address:** Use this page to specify one or more ranges of addresses to be excluded from the scope. Addresses in an excluded range are not used by DHCP or allocated to clients. If the addresses you want to exclude fall outside of the address range defined for the scope, you don't have to explicitly define an exclusion. For example, assume you create a scope with the included range 192.168.0.100 through 192.168.0.254. You do not have to create an exclusion for 192.168.0.1 through 192.168.0.99, which are implicitly excluded. Using this same example, however, you would need to create an exclusion if you wanted to prevent the address range 192.168.0.150 through 192.168.0.160 from being allocated to clients. If you choose an exclusion range, it must fall within the scope created on the previous page.
- **Lease duration:** This property defines the length of time an IP address assignment is valid and is applicable to all clients unless modified by a user or vendor class assignment (in effect, it is the default lease period). When the lease duration expires, the client must request a renewal of the address, and failing that (because the address might already have been reassigned while the client was offline, for example), request a new address lease. The default is eight days. See the section, "Defining and Implementing User and Vendor Classes," later in this chapter for additional information.

✦ **Configure other options:** The wizard gives you the option of configuring the default gateway and DNS server properties to assign to the scope. See the section, "Setting General Scope Options," later in this chapter for more information.

✦ **Activate the scope:** Although you can activate the scope immediately after creating it, you should make sure you've fully defined all required scope properties prior to activation in order to ensure that clients receive all necessary DHCP properties. You can activate the scope later after fully defining it.

After you create a scope, it shows up in the DHCP console as a branch under the server's node in the tree pane, as shown in Figure 16-2. You'll see multiple scope branches if the server hosts more than one scope. Each scope branch includes the following objects:

✦ **Address Pool:** This branch lists the included address pool for the scope along with any exclusion ranges. Each scope has only one inclusion range, but can contain multiple exclusion ranges.

✦ **Address Leases:** This branch lists current client address leases, including the IP address, name, and lease expiration.

✦ **Reservations:** This branch lists address reservations, which reserve specific IP addresses for specific users based on the user's MAC address (physical network adapter address). See the section, "Creating Reservations," later in this chapter for more information.

✦ **Scope Options:** This branch lists additional properties passed to clients when they receive address leases from this scope. Typical properties include default router, DNS server assignments, time server, and time offset. The following section explains how to configure these settings.

Setting general scope options

You can specify a wide range of scope properties in addition to those discussed so far. These properties are given to clients when they receive a lease from the server. For example, the scope's properties can assign the default gateway and DNS servers the client should use, a time server for synchronizing the client's internal clock with the network or server, and many other properties. In most situations, you will need to configure only the default gateway and DNS servers, although some situations might warrant configuring other properties as well.

To configure general scope options, open the DHCP console and then open the scope whose properties you want to modify. Right-click Scope Options and choose Configure Options to display the Scope Options property sheet, shown in Figure 16-3.

The General tab enables you to configure properties that apply to all clients receiving address leases through the scope. As Figure 16-3 shows, you select an item by clicking it, and then you specify the value(s) for the item in the lower half of the property sheet. Enable or disable properties by selecting or deselecting their check boxes in the list. Set the value for each one and then click OK.

The Advanced tab (Figure 16-4) enables you to configure global properties for specific vendor and user classes. The default vendor classes are as follows:

✦ **DHCP standard options:** These are the same options that appear on the General tab by default and apply to all client connections for which no vendor or user class is specified.

✦ **Microsoft options:** These options define Microsoft-specific DHCP properties for Microsoft clients.

✦ **Microsoft Windows 2000 options:** These options define Microsoft Windows 2000/XP-specific properties for Windows 2000 and Windows XP clients.

✦ **Microsoft Windows 98 options:** This selection can be used to define Windows 98-specific options, although by default none are defined.

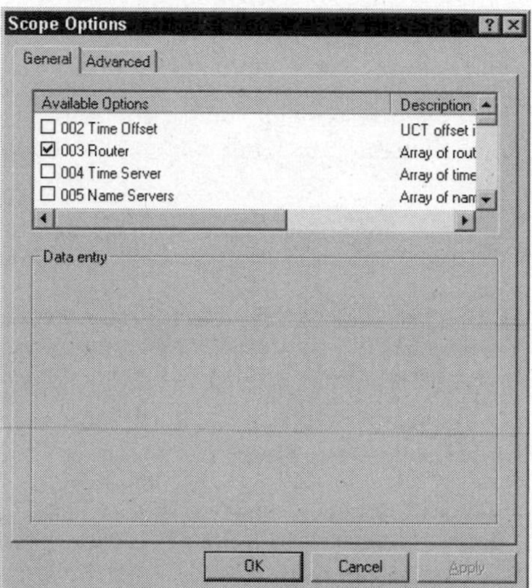

Figure 16-3: The Scope Options property sheet.

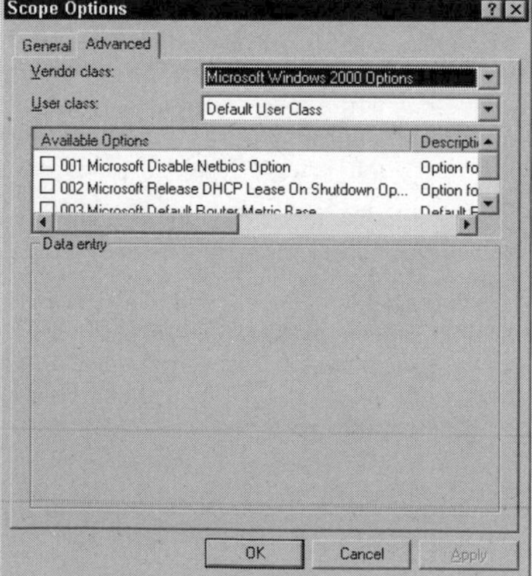

Figure 16-4: The Advanced tab.

By default, three user classes are defined:

✦ **Default BOOTP Class:** These properties apply to clients that receive a lease via `bootp`. The command `bootp` enables clients to retrieve a valid address along with a boot image that enables the computer to boot; it is typically used as a mechanism to boot diskless workstations.

✦ **Default Routing and Remote Access Class:** These properties apply to clients that receive a lease through RRAS connections.

✦ **Default User Class:** These properties apply to all clients not handled by a different user class.

See the section, "Defining and Implementing Vendor and User Classes," later in this chapter for detailed information on configuring and using vendor and user classes to customize lease properties for specific systems and users.

The following sections explain how to configure the most common DHCP properties.

Default gateway

The Router lease property defines the default gateway assigned to the DHCP client. You can specify an array of addresses, giving the client multiple gateways to use. If the client's primary gateway fails for some reason, traffic will route through the next available gateway, providing fail-over insurance against a loss of connectivity. To assign a gateway to the array, enter the IP address in the IP address box in dotted octet format, then click Add. You can enter a host name in the Server name box and click Resolve if you know the host name of the gateway but not its IP address. Clicking Resolve performs a DNS lookup and returns the IP address in the IP address field if successful. You can specify multiple IP addresses, clicking Add to add each one to the array. Use the Up and Down buttons to change the order of the list. The client then tries the routers in sequence, starting with the top router.

Domain name and DNS servers

In addition to assigning one or more gateways, you will probably also want to assign at least one DNS server. Select 006 DNS Servers in the list and then add the IP addresses of the DNS servers to the list, just as you would when adding a router to the router list. The order of servers in the list defines the order in which the client will attempt to resolve names to addresses. Use the Up and Down buttons to change the order.

Domain name

Another property you should consider setting is the domain name. This property defines the client's domain and is used to create the user's fully qualified domain name (FQDN). The client prepends its host name to the domain name to create the FQDN. You can specify the domain name within the client's DNS properties, but setting it through DHCP instead enables the domain name to be changed dynamically when the client is granted a lease. If all the systems on the network use DHCP, this enables you to change your entire organization's domain without changing any client settings — you simply change the domain name property in the DHCP server. Because of potential unseen pitfalls (clients with statically assigned domain names, for example), this isn't the recommended way of changing domain names.

Other scope properties

You can configure a wide range of other properties that are passed to the DHCP client when a lease is granted. Review the list of properties and configure those that apply to your network and client needs.

Configuring global DHCP options

Within each scope, you can configure properties such as domain name, gateway, and DNS servers, as explained in the previous section. These properties apply to all leases granted through the selected scope. You also can configure these properties to apply globally to all scopes defined on the server. These global options are used unless overridden by a scope-assigned property.

To configure global DHCP options, open the DHCP console, right-click the Server Options node, and choose Configure Options. The DHCP console displays the same property sheet you use to assign properties for a scope. Select and configure properties as needed.

Creating reservations

A *reservation* assigns a specific IP address to a specific MAC address. The MAC address is a unique hardware-based address that uniquely identifies a network adapter (Network Interface Card, or NIC) on the network. Reservations enable a specific adapter to receive the same IP address assignment from the DHCP server and prevent the address from being leased to any other adapter. In effect, reservations let you enjoy the flexibility offered by DHCP while still enabling you to assign a static IP address. Through reservations, you ensure that the NIC always has the same IP address, but enable other configuration changes to be applied dynamically (such as domain name, router, DNS servers, and so on).

Reservations do not assign the same IP address to a computer per se, because the reservation is associated with the NIC's MAC address, not the computer name. This is only a real distinction in multi-homed systems (those containing multiple NICs).

Before creating a reservation for an NIC, you need to know the NIC's MAC address. On Windows NT, Windows 2000, and Windows XP systems, you can use the `ipconfig` command at a console prompt to view MAC addresses for NICs in the computer. Open a console prompt on the system and issue the command `ipconfig /all`. The command lists network configuration data for each NIC, including the MAC address.

For Windows 9*x* and Me systems, use the WINIPCFG utility to determine the MAC address. WINIPCFG includes the adapter address in the information it displays, along with IP address, gateway, and other configuration information.

When you have the MAC address of the client's NIC, open the DHCP console and then open the scope where you want to create the reservation. Right-click the Reservations node and choose New Reservation to open the New Reservation dialog box (Figure 16-5). Use the following list as a guide to configure the reservation:

✦ **Reservation name:** This name appears in the DHCP console next to the reservation IP address (left pane). You can specify the computer's name, username, or other information to help you identify the NIC for which the address is reserved.

✦ **IP address:** Specify the IP address within the scope to reserve for the specified NIC.

✦ **MAC address:** Enter the MAC address of the NIC for which the address is reserved.

✦ **Description:** This optional description appears in the contents pane of the DHCP console.

✦ **Supported types:** You can designate the type of client (DHCP, BOOTP, or both) that can use the reservation.

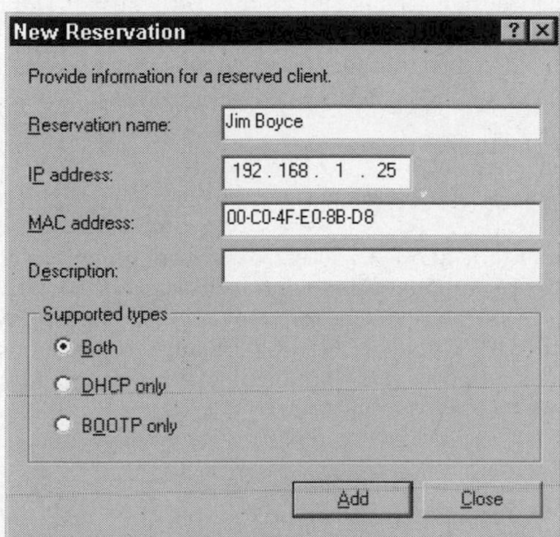

Figure 16-5: Reservations assign an IP address to a specific network adapter.

Setting global scope properties

Before you activate a scope and begin using it, there are a handful of properties you should configure that apply to the scope on a global basis. To set these properties, open the DHCP console, right-click the scope, and choose Properties to display the Scope Properties sheet. The General tab lets you modify the scope-friendly name, IP address range, lease period, and description. These options are self-explanatory.

The DNS tab determines how DHCP integrates with DNS. You'll find an explanation of how to configure DHCP clients to use DDNS in the section, "Configuring Windows DHCP Clients," later in this chapter. For now, you can use the following list as a guide to configuring settings on the DNS page:

✦ **Enable DNS dynamic updates according to the settings below:** Select this option to direct the DHCP server to attempt to update client DNS information in the DNS server. The server will, by default, attempt to update the client's host and pointer records to associate the client's host name with its IP address.

✦ **Dynamically update DNS A and PTR records only if requested by DHCP clients:** Select this option to have the server update the DNS records only if the client requests the update. Currently, only Windows 2000 and Windows XP clients can request the update.

✦ **Always dynamically update DNS A and PTR records:** Select this option to update the DNS records regardless of whether the client requests an update.

✦ **Discard A and PTR records when lease is deleted:** Select this option to have the DNS server discard the host record for a client when its lease expires and is deleted.

✦ **Dynamically update DNS A and PTR records for DHCP clients that do not request updates:** Select this option to enable the DHCP server to update host and pointer records with DNS for clients that don't support dynamic update (such as versions of Windows prior to Windows 2000).

The Advanced property tab lets you configure the types of clients the DHCP server will handle with the selected scope. You can support DHCP only, `bootp` only, or both. If you select `bootp` only or both, you can configure the lease duration for `bootp` clients using the lease duration group, specifying a lease duration or configuring the scope to provide unlimited leases to `bootp` clients.

Activating and deactivating a scope

At this point, you should have enough data in the scope to activate it, although you might want to further configure your DHCP server by implementing vendor or user classes, using superscopes or multicast scopes, and so on (both are discussed later in this chapter). When you're ready to activate the scope, open the DHCP console. Right-click the scope in question and choose Activate. To deactivate a scope and prevent it from being used to assign leases, right-click the scope and choose Deactivate.

Authorizing the server

An additional step for domain-based DHCP servers is to *authorize* the server. Authorizing a server lists it in the Active Directory as an authorized DHCP server. As explained earlier, Windows Server 2003 DHCP servers attempt to determine if they are authorized at startup and prior to processing client lease requests. Domain-based DHCP servers attempt to check the AD to determine if they are listed as an authorized server. If the server is unable to contact the AD or doesn't find itself listed, it does not begin servicing client requests. A workgroup-based DHCP server queries the network for other DHCP servers; if it identifies any domain-based DHCP servers, it assumes it is not authorized and does not service client requests. If no domain-based DHCP servers respond, however, the server starts servicing client requests. This means that multiple workgroup-based DHCP servers can operate on the network concurrently.

When you install the DHCP service on a domain-based server, the server is unauthorized by default. You must authorize the server before it can begin servicing client requests. Authorizing a server simply lists the server in the AD. To authorize a domain-based DHCP server, open the DHCP console, right-click the server in the left pane, and choose Authorize.

Defining and Implementing User and Vendor Classes

Vendor and user classes are new features incorporated into the Windows Server 2003 DHCP service. Vendor classes enable you to create new, predefined scope options without having to go through the lengthy process of submitting RFCs and getting approval for adding new options. You can use vendor classes to create options specific to a particular device or operating platform, and then assign those options based on user classes.

User classes enable you to assign unique scope options to individual clients. For example, you may apply a specific DHCP configuration to all notebook users that, among other things, sets the lease expiration at eight hours rather than the default of eight days. You can incorporate other special properties to suit that group's requirements as well.

Vendor classes

In many respects, a vendor class is really just a container object that groups together custom DHCP options. You name the vendor class and assign to it new scope options not otherwise defined by the standard options. To create a vendor class, you specify a display name for the vendor class, description, and ID. The display name and description are primarily for convenience and identification within the DHCP console. The ID uniquely identifies the vendor class.

Creating a vendor class

To create, modify, or remove a vendor class, open the DHCP console. Right-click the server on which you want to work with vendor classes and choose Define Vendor Classes. DHCP displays a DHCP Vendor Classes dialog box that lists all currently defined vendor classes. Click Add to display the New Class dialog box, shown in Figure 16-6.

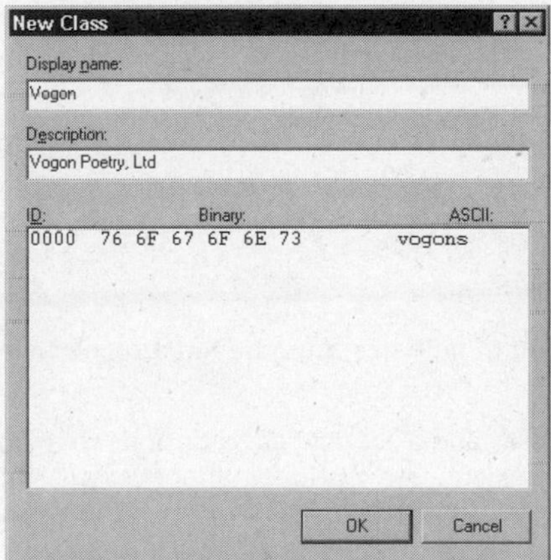

Figure 16-6: The New Class dialog box.

The Display name is the friendly name for the vendor class within the DHCP console. You can include an optional description to further identify the vendor class. The ID is the data that clients use to request a specific set of DHCP options based on their vendor class. Click in the ID box under the Binary column if you want to enter the data in hexadecimal, or click under the ASCII column to enter the ID in ASCII characters. Choose a string that uniquely identifies the vendor class but is also easy to remember (and perhaps easy to type). Bear in mind that this is an identifier string only and needs to have no real relationship with the actual vendor name or other product information. However, using the vendor name in the ID will help you recognize the purpose for the vendor class.

Configuring vendor class options

After you create a new vendor class, you need to specify the DHCP options that will be available to that vendor class. To do so, open the DHCP console, right-click the server on which you want to define vendor class options, and choose Set Predefined Options. DHCP displays the Predefined Options and Values dialog box. Select the option class you want to modify values for and then click Add. DHCP displays the Option Type dialog box, shown in Figure 16-7.

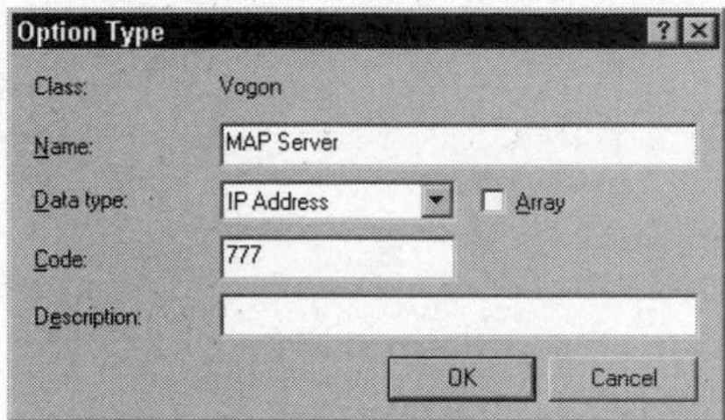

Figure 16-7: Use the Option Type dialog box to add vendor class options.

Provide information in the dialog box using the following list as a guide:

✦ **Name:** This is the name of the option as it appears in the Available Options list of the Scope Options property sheet. Specify a descriptive name such as Name Servers.

✦ **Data Type:** Select from this drop-down list the type of data represented by the class option (byte, word, long, IP address, and so on).

✦ **Array:** Select this option if you are creating an array, such as a DNS server list or gateway list.

✦ **Code:** Specify a unique numeric code for the option.

✦ **Description:** Specify an optional description to help describe the function of the option value.

You may have surmised that creating a vendor class and assigning class options to it can be a time-consuming task, particularly if you need to assign many options. Whenever possible, you should use standard DHCP options and override selected options with vendor class options only when needed.

Windows 2000 incorporates three predefined vendor classes: Microsoft Options, Microsoft Windows 2000 Options, and Microsoft Windows 98 Options. The Microsoft Options and Microsoft Windows 2000 Options currently define three options: Disable NetBIOS, Release DHCP Lease on Shutdown, and Default Router Metric Base. You can use these options to implement the associated features for Windows 2000 clients. There are no predefined scope options for Windows 98 clients.

User classes

Although vendor classes enable you to define new DHCP scope options, user classes enable you to allocate DHCP scopes (whether standard or vendor class-defined) on a client-by-client basis. Each client can be configured with one or more user class IDs that the client submits to the DHCP server. The server responds with an appropriate lease based on the settings defined for that user class ID. For example, you might create a user class ID called *notebook* and configure its DHCP options to decrease the lease period. Or you might have a group of computers that requires a different set of DNS servers or default gateway. You can use user class IDs in all of these cases to assign DHCP options on a selective basis.

User classes must be supported at the client level. Currently, only Windows 2000 and Windows XP clients support user classes. This capability is not included with Windows 98 or Windows NT clients.

When a client submits a class ID to a DHCP server, the server provides all the default options defined for the scope not otherwise defined by the class ID. You can allocate DHCP options using the default options for the scope and apply selective options with the user class. This means you do not have to duplicate the default settings for a user class; you need to configure only those settings that are unique to clients in that user class.

Creating a user class

You define a user class in much the same way that you define a vendor class. Open the DHCP console, right-click the server at which you want to define the user class, then choose Define User Classes. Click Add in the DHCP User Classes dialog box. As you do with a vendor class, specify a display name to appear in the DHCP console, an optional description, and the class ID. The class ID is the data you will configure at the client level to enable it to request a lease based on the class ID. You can enter the class ID in either hexadecimal or ASCII format.

Configuring user class options

After you create a user class, you need to assign to it the DHCP scope options that need to apply to each client having the specified class ID. To do so, open the DHCP console and expand the server in question. Right-click Scope Options, choose Configure Options, then click Advanced to display the Advanced tab, which is the same as shown in Figure 16-4. You can select options from the DHCP Standard Options vendor class or use any other defined vendor class. Select the desired user class from the User class drop-down list. The scope options that are predefined for the selected vendor class appear in the Available Options list. Browse through the list and configure scope options as you would the default options.

There is no need to configure options that will otherwise be assigned through the global options for the scope. Instead, you need to configure only those options that are unique to the user class. For example, if all you are doing with the user class is reducing the lease period, then you need to configure only the Lease value within the user class. All other settings can be assigned to the client through the global scope properties. When you have configured all necessary properties, click OK.

Configuring a client to use class IDs

You can assign multiple class IDs to Windows 2000 and Windows XP clients, although only the last one assigned is actually used to retrieve DHCP data. Each client, by default, assumes the class ID "Default BOOTP Class," which enables Windows 2000/XP clients that require `bootp` to retrieve settings from the DHCP server. If you assign any other class IDs, however, the class ID assigned last takes precedence and the client takes on all global scope options plus the scope options assigned to that last class ID. The scope options are not cumulative — the client will not take on all options for all class IDs assigned to the adapter in question.

Use the `ipconfig` command to assign a class ID to a Windows 2000/XP client. You can assign class IDs manually through a command console or startup script. The syntax for assigning a class ID is as follows:

```
ipconfig /setclassid [adapter] [ClassIDString]
```

To configure a client with the class ID "portable" on the default network connection (Local Area Connection), use the following command:

```
ipconfig /setclassid "Local Area Connection" portable
```

You might want to rename your network connections using simpler names, if only to make it easier to perform `ipconfig` commands. To rename a network connection, open the Network and Dial-Up Connections folder, right-click the connection, and choose Rename. For example, you might rename "Local Area Connection" simply, "LAN."

Creating and Using Superscopes

As Windows 2000 Server does, Windows Server 2003 supports a DHCP feature called *superscopes,* an administrative feature that enables you to create and manage multiple scopes as a single entity. You can use superscopes to allocate IP addresses to clients on a *multinet,* which is a physical network segment containing multiple logical IP networks (a logical IP network is a cohesive range of IP addresses). For example, you might support three different class C logical IP networks on a physical network segment. Each of the three class C address ranges is defined as one of three individual child scopes under a superscope.

In many cases, you won't plan or set out to use a multinet because using a single logical IP network is much simpler from an administration standpoint; however, you might need to use a multinet as an interim measure as your network size grows beyond the number of addresses available within the original scope. Or, you might need to migrate the network from one logical IP network to another, such as would be the case if you switched ISPs and therefore had to switch address assignments.

Superscopes are useful on high-speed wide area networks, especially when planning for and managing shallow Active Directory domain trees (trees with multiple Active Directory sites and few domains). This is discussed in Chapters 10 and 11.

You also can use superscopes to support remote DHCP clients located on the far side of a DHCP or `bootp` relay agent. This enables you to support multiple physical subnets with a single DHCP server. Figure 16-8 illustrates a single DHCP server supporting multiple logical IP networks on the local physical network, as well as logical IP networks on the far side of a relay agent.

Naturally, you will want to assign certain scope options, such as the default gateway within each scope, to place the option within the context of the scope. You can assign global options that apply to all scopes in a superscope at the server level. All scopes on the server, whether in a superscope or not, will use the global options when options are not specifically defined within the individual scopes. For example, all clients can probably use the same set of DNS servers, so you would define the DNS server array at the server level.

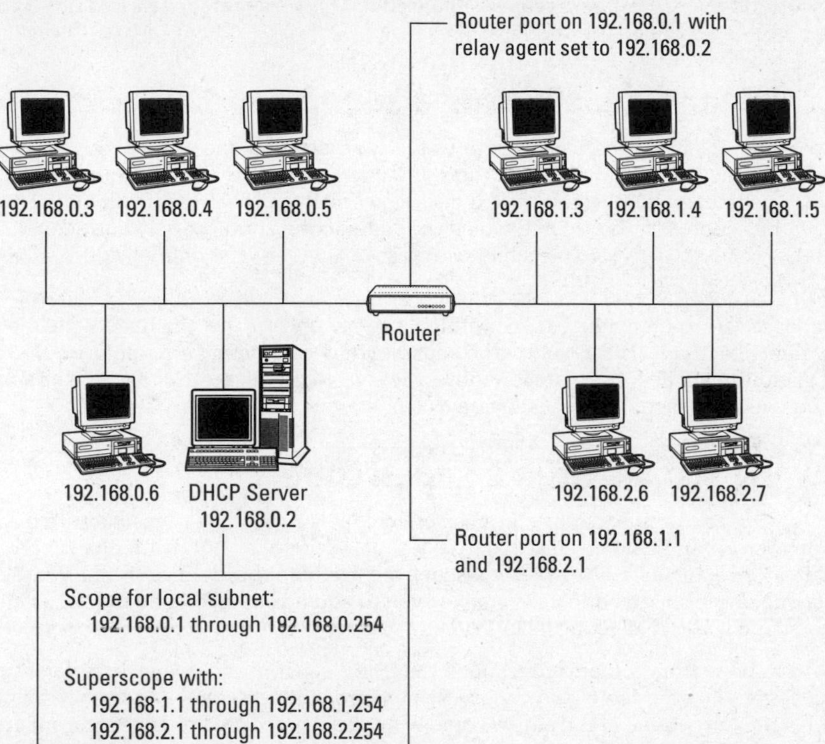

Figure 16-8: A single DHCP server can support multiple local IP networks and remote networks.

Keep in mind that superscopes are really just an administrative feature that provides a container for managing scopes as groups on the same server. A superscope does not actually allocate options of its own. DHCP options come either from the server (global) or from the properties of the individual scopes within the superscope.

Creating a superscope

You can create a superscope only after you define at least one scope on the server (this prevents you from creating an empty superscope). Windows Server 2003 lets you select which existing scopes will be moved to the superscope. You can create additional scopes within the superscope afterwards. You can create multiple superscopes and create scopes both inside and outside of a superscope. So, a given server might have two superscopes with four scopes each, along with three scopes defined at the server level that are not part of either superscope.

To create a superscope, open the DHCP console. Right-click the server you want to create the superscope in and choose New Superscope (the command is not available if no scopes exist on the server), then click Next. Windows Server 2003 prompts you to choose a friendly name for the scope and which existing scopes will be added to the superscope. Hold down the Shift key while selecting to choose multiple scopes.

Activating and deactivating a superscope

Windows Server 2003 automatically activates the superscope if one or more scopes in the superscope are active when you create the superscope. If not, you can activate individual scopes in the superscope, then activate the superscope itself. To activate individual scopes, right-click the scope and choose Activate. If the superscope contains only one scope, Windows Server 2003 activates the superscope as well. Otherwise, right-click the superscope and choose Activate.

You can deactivate an individual scope within a superscope, or you can deactivate the superscope, which deactivates all scopes in the superscope. Deactivating a scope prevents it from servicing additional client requests for address leases. Right-click either a scope or superscope and choose Deactivate to deactivate it.

Removing scopes from a superscope

You can remove one or more scopes from a superscope if necessary to restructure the scopes on the server. Removing a scope from a superscope does not delete the scope or deactivate it. Instead, it simply makes it a scope directly under the server branch rather than a child scope of the superscope. This enables you to add it to a different scope or eliminate the superscope without affecting its individual scopes.

To remove a scope from a superscope, open the DHCP console and open the superscope in question. Right-click the scope and choose Remove from Superscope. If the scope being removed is the only scope in the superscope, Windows Server 2003 removes the superscope because you can't have an empty superscope.

Deleting superscopes

Deleting a superscope removes the superscope and places its child scopes directly under the server branch of the DHCP server. The scopes are unaffected and continue to service client requests — they are simply no longer a member of a superscope. Open the DHCP console, right-click the superscope to be deleted, and choose Delete.

Creating Multicast Scopes

A *multicast scope,* as explained earlier, is used to broadcast IP traffic to a group of nodes using a single address, and is traditionally used in audio and video conferencing. Using multicast addresses simplifies administration and reduces network traffic because the data packets are sent once to the multicast address rather than individually to each recipient's unicast address.

A Windows Server 2003 DHCP server can allocate multicast addresses to a group of computers much as it allocates unicast addresses to individual computers. The protocol for multicast address allocation is Multicast Address Dynamic Client Allocation Protocol (MADCAP). Windows Server 2003 can function independently as both a DHCP server and MADCAP server. For example, one server may use the DHCP service to allocate unicast addresses through the

DHCP protocol, and another server may allocate multicast addresses through the MADCAP protocol. In addition, a client can use either or both. A DHCP client doesn't have to use MADCAP, and vice versa, but a client can use both if the situation requires it.

As the use of multicasting is somewhat specialized, this chapter assumes you have a working knowledge of multicast addressing, routing, and so on, and focuses on explaining how to configure a Windows Server 2003 DHCP server to act as a MADCAP server.

Tip

For additional information on using multicast scopes, open Help in the DHCP console and search for "multicast scope."

You can create multiple multicast scopes on a Windows Server 2003 DHCP server as long as the scope address ranges don't overlap. Multicast scopes exist directly under the server branch and cannot be assigned to superscopes, which are intended only to manage unicast address scopes. To create a multicast scope, open the DHCP console, right-click the server that you want to create the multicast scope in, and choose New Multicast Scope. Windows Server 2003 starts a wizard that prompts you for the following information:

- ✦ **Name:** This is the friendly name as it appears for the scope in the DHCP console.
- ✦ **Description:** Specify an optional description to identify the purpose of the multicast scope.
- ✦ **Address range:** You can specify an address range between 224.0.0.0 and 239.255.255.255, inclusive, which gives you a large range of addresses to use.
- ✦ **Time to Live (TTL):** Specify the number of routers the traffic must pass through on your local network.
- ✦ **Exclusion range:** You can define a range of multicast addresses to exclude from the scope, just as you can exclude unicast addresses from a DHCP scope.
- ✦ **Lease duration:** Specify the duration for the lease. The default is 30 days.

You can choose to activate the scope through the wizard or activate the scope later. Right-click a multicast scope and choose Activate to activate the scope.

Configuring Global DHCP Server Properties

After configuring scopes and other DHCP options, turn your attention to a handful of global DHCP server properties that you can configure to fine-tune your DHCP server. To configure these settings, open the DHCP console, right-click the server, and choose Properties. Some of the server override settings you configure at the scope level. For example, the settings on the DNS tab correspond to the settings covered earlier in this chapter in "Setting Global Scope Properties."

The General Tab (Figure 16-9) contains the following three settings:

- ✦ **Automatically update statistics every:** Use this option to have the DHCP server refresh statistics in the DHCP console at the specified interval. The statistics update when you open the console, and you can also refresh them manually by choosing Action ➪ Refresh. Use this option if you keep the console open for extended periods for monitoring.

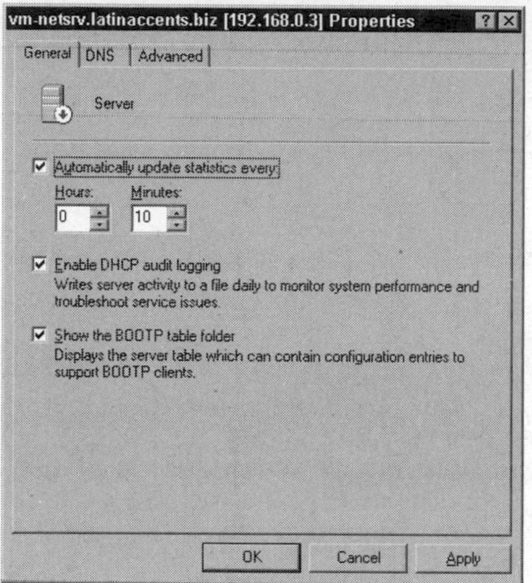

Figure 16-9: Configure global settings with the General tab.

- **Enable DHCP audit logging:** Enable this option (the default) to record DHCP server events to a log file. See the following information on the Advanced tab for more information.
- **Show the BOOTP table folder:** Enable this option to add a BOOTP Table branch to the DHCP console. You can then right-click the BOOTP Table branch and choose New Boot Image to display the Add BOOTP Entry dialog box (Figure 16-10). Use this dialog to specify the boot image file, path, and TFPT server for the boot image.

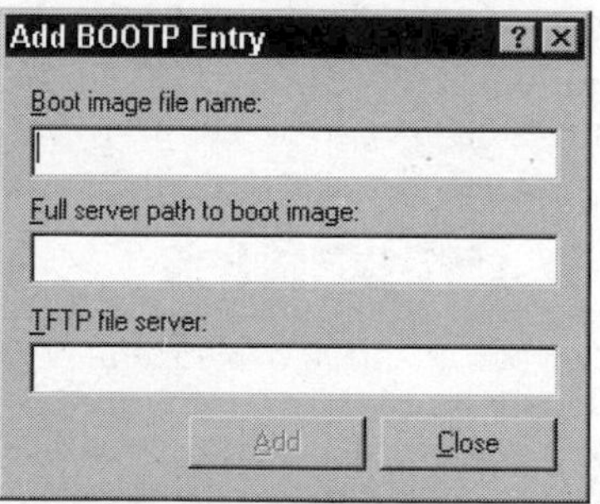

Figure 16-10: Add BOOTP images through the BOOTP Table branch.

The Advanced tab (Figure 16-11) provides several settings for logging, backup, network configuration, and authentication. These settings include the following:

- **Conflict detection attempts:** Specify the number of times the server should attempt to detect address conflicts before leasing an address to a client. Increase the value in situations where detection typically takes longer, such as in heavily saturated networks or where clients take longer to respond because they are operating in power-saving mode.
- **Audit log file path:** Specify where you want the DHCP server to place its audit log files. The default location is `%systemroot%\System32\dhcp`.

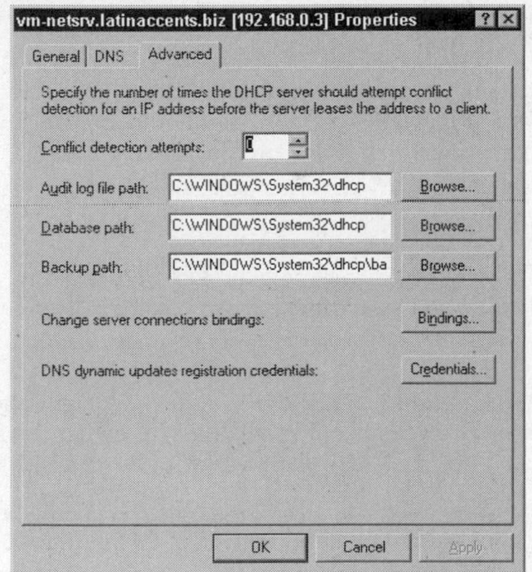

Figure 16-11: Configure a variety of settings with the Advanced tab.

- **Database path:** Specify the location where the DHCP server will place its database files. The default location is `%systemroot%\System32\dhcp`.
- **Backup path:** Specify the location where the DHCP server will back up its database. The default location is `%systemroot%\System32\dhcp\backup`. See the following section for information on backing up and restoring the DHCP database.
- **Bindings:** Click this button to open a dialog box in which you choose the network interfaces on which the DHCP server will respond to DHCP client requests. The list will be empty if the server has no static IP addresses.
- **Credentials:** Click this button to specify the account credentials, including domain, that the DHCP server will use when authenticating dynamic DNS requests to a Windows 2000 or .NET DNS server. You need to specify credentials only if the DNS server is configured to require secure updates.

Managing the DHCP Database

Windows Server 2003 makes it easy to back up and restore the DHCP database, which provides recoverability from server failures and an easy means to move DHCP data to a different server. The DHCP data you can back up includes all defined scopes, reservations, and leases, as well as all options at the server, scope, reservation, and class levels. The default location for the backup is `%systemroot%\System32\dhcp\backup`. You should consider moving the location of the backup folder to another server for improved recoverability in case the DHCP server fails and the backup folder is lost.

Backing up and restoring the DHCP database

The DHCP server provides three backup mechanisms. The DHCP server backs up its database automatically to the backup folder every hour, and Microsoft terms this a *synchronous backup*. You can also manually initiate a backup with the DHCP console, and

Microsoft terms this an *asynchronous backup*. The final method is to use the .NET Backup utility or third-party backup utility to perform scheduled or as-needed backups.

All of these methods back up the items mentioned previously, but do not back up authentication credentials, registry settings, or other global DHCP configuration information such as log settings and database location. Instead, you need to back up the registry key `HKEY_LOCAL_MACHINE\SYSTEM\CurrentControlSet\Services\DHCPServer\Parameters` to back up these additional items.

Tip

The easiest way to back up the DHCP registry key is to export the key from the Registry Editor. Open the Registry Editor, select the key, and export it to the same backup location as the other DHCP backup files.

To perform an asynchronous backup of the DHCP data, open the DHCP console, right-click the server, and choose Backup. In the resulting Browse for Folder dialog box, select the folder location where you want the data to be backed up. You can create a new folder through this dialog box, if needed.

To change the interval for synchronous backups from its default setting of 60 minutes, open the Registry Editor and open the key `HKEY_LOCAL_MACHINE\SYSTEM\CurrentControlSet\Services\DHCPServer\Parameters`. Modify the value BackupInterval as desired.

Tip

With the Edit DWORD Value dialog box open, switch to decimal view and specify a value in minutes for the backup interval.

If the DHCP server suffers a failure, you can quickly restore the DHCP service by restoring the DHCP database. Bring the server back online and install the DHCP service. If you backed up the DHCP registry key, stop the DHCP service, import the key, and restart the service; then, open the DHCP console. Right-click the server in the console, and choose Restore. Select the location to which you previously backed up the DHCP database and restore the data.

Caution

You can only restore a backup that you created manually with the DHCP console. Do not use the DHCP backup files created automatically by the DHCP service during a synchronous backup. This will cause the DHCP service to fail. The synchronous backups are used only by the DHCP service to automatically restore the database if the service detects that the DHCP database has become corrupted.

Moving the DHCP database to another server

Whether you are upgrading servers or simply migrating the DHCP service to another computer for performance reasons, moving the DHCP database is relatively easy. On the source server, open the DHCP console and back up the DHCP database to a location accessible by the target server. Stop the DHCP service on the source server and if needed, export the DHCP registry key to a file as explained in the previous section.

Tip

Stopping the DHCP service prevents the DHCP server from responding to client requests and potentially conflicting with the new server when it comes online.

Next, install the DHCP service on the target server. Stop the DHCP service and import the registry file. Copy the contents of the DHCP database backup folder from the source server to the appropriate location on the target server (the default is `%systemroot%\System32\dhcp`). Then, start the DHCP service.

Tip: Make sure you authorize the new DHCP server in the Active Directory.

Configuring Windows DHCP Clients

Configuring Windows 2000 and Windows XP clients to use DHCP is a relatively simple process. At the client, right-click My Network Places and choose Properties, or choose Start ➪ Settings ➪ Network and Up Connections to open the Network Connections folder. Right-click the connection you want to configure for DHCP and choose Properties. Double-click the TCP/IP protocol in the list of installed components or select it and click Properties to display its property sheet.

Note: On Windows 2000 systems, the Network Connections folder is named Network and Dial-Up Connections.

To configure a Windows 9*x* or Me client, right-click Network Neighborhood on the desktop or open the Network applet in the Control Panel. Locate and double-click the TCP/IP protocol in the list of installed network components.

You can configure the client to obtain its IP address from the DHCP server, obtain DNS server addresses through DHCP, or both. The controls on the General tab are self-explanatory.

Configuring DNS options for DHCP

You can configure a Windows 2000 or Windows XP client to use Dynamic DNS (DDNS) to automatically update its host record when its host name changes or its IP address changes (including through DHCP lease renewal). Click Advanced on the General property page for the TCP/IP protocol for the connection in order to display the Advanced TCP/IP Settings dialog box; then, click the DNS tab to display the DNS page, as shown in Figure 16-12.

Two settings on the DNS page control integration of DHCP and DDNS for the client, as follows:

- **Register this connection's addresses in DNS:** Select this option to have the client submit a request to the DNS server to update its host (A) record when its host name changes or IP address changes. The client submits the full computer name specified in the Network Identification tab of the System Properties sheet along with its IP address to the DNS server. You can view the System properties through the System object in the Control Panel, or right-click My Computer and choose Properties.
- **Use this connection's DNS suffix in DNS registration:** Select this option to have the client submit a request to the DNS server to update its host record when the host name changes or IP address changes. The difference from the previous option is that this option registers the client using the first part of the computer name specified in the System properties along with the DNS suffix specified by the option "DNS suffix for this connection" on the DNS tab.

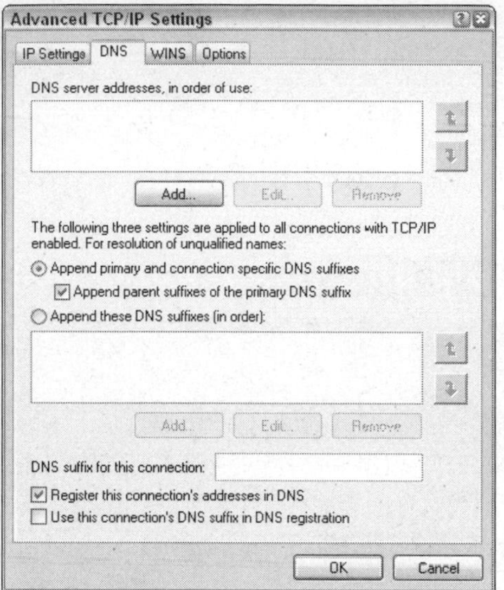

Figure 16-12: The DNS tab of the Advanced TCP/IP Settings dialog box.

Summary

DHCP provides a means through which you can allocate IP addresses to clients automatically when the clients boot, making it much easier to manage IP leases and corresponding properties in a network. Rather than modifying clients manually when a required change occurs (such as DNS server change, router change, and so on), you simply modify the properties of the scope on the DHCP server and allow the clients to retrieve the new data when they renew their leases. Through class IDs, you can allocate specific scope properties to clients to satisfy unique requirements of the client, such as gateways, DNS servers, lease duration, and so on.

The DHCP server service provided with Windows 2000 also enables a Windows Server to act as a multicast address provider, allocating multicast addresses to clients that require them. A server can function as a unicast scope server, multicast scope server, or both.

A new management feature provided with the DHCP server service is the ability to create superscopes, which essentially act as containers for scopes. You can use superscopes to manage a set of address scopes as if they were a single scope.

✦ ✦ ✦

DNS and WINS

CHAPTER 17

✦ ✦ ✦ ✦

In This Chapter

Getting an overview of the Domain Name Service (DNS)

Understanding Microsoft Domain Name Services

Configuring subdomains and delegation

Understanding DNS and Active Directory

Using Dynamic DNS

Using Windows Internet Name Service (WINS)

Configuring Windows Server 2003 clients for DNS and WINS

Using `Hosts` and `LMHOSTS` files for name resolution

✦ ✦ ✦ ✦

In Chapter 2 and the chapters in Part III, you learn that Active Directory domains are modeled on Internet domains. You also learn that Windows Server 2003/2000 networks rely on TCP/IP as the network protocol of choice. To resolve Windows Server 2003 domain controllers and many other hosts running Windows .NET services, you need to fully understand and know how to configure *Domain Name Service* (*DNS*). This chapter explains the services that you can use to create DNS. It also covers *Windows Internet Name Service* (*WINS*) name servers, and includes coverage of *Dynamic DNS* (*DDNS*), client configuration, and related topics.

Overview of the Domain Name Service

The Internet comprises many millions of devices, including computers, routers, printers, and other devices, and each device is called a *node*. Each node requires a unique IP address to differentiate it from others and enable traffic to be routed to and from the node. Intranets also can employ the TCP/IP protocol and require that each node have a unique address, although in the case of an intranet, these IP addresses can come from a nonpublic reserved address space such as 192.168.0.*x*. Nodes on the Internet must have a unique, public IP address. IP addresses are difficult for most people to remember, and their sheer number makes trying to do so impractical. The Domain Name Service (DNS) overcomes this problem by enabling users to work with names rather than addresses. In effect, DNS provides a means of *mapping* names to addresses. Rather than typing **207.25.71.9** to connect to CNN's Web site, for example, you connect your browser to `www.cnn.com`. DNS takes care of translating `www.cnn.com` into the appropriate IP address. Mapping a name to an IP address is called *name resolution*.

The Internet arose from a network called the *ARPANET*, which comprised a relatively small number of computers in the 1970s (mostly defense and educational systems). With few nodes, it was relatively simple to provide name resolution. The Stanford Research Institute (SRI) maintained a single text file named `Hosts.txt` that contained the host-to-address translations for all the ARPANET's hosts. The operating systems (predominantly Unix) used the `Hosts.txt` file to resolve names to addresses. System administrators copied the `Hosts.txt` file from SRI to their local systems periodically to provide an updated list.

As the number of hosts grew, the continued use of a Hosts.txt file to provide name resolution soon became impractical. In the mid-1980s, the DNS system was developed to provide a dynamic name resolution system that no longer relied on a static name-to-address map. Before you learn about the DNS system, however, you need to understand domain names.

Understanding domain names

As we mention in the preceding section, each device on an IP network is a node. Many nodes are also termed *hosts*. Generally, a host is a computer, router, or other "smart" device, but any device can be considered a host and have a host name associated with it. In Windows Server 2003, a computer's name as it appears on the LAN is typically its host name. Assume, for example, that your computer's name is tia and that your computer resides in the latinaccents.biz domain. The host name is tia, the domain name is latinaccents.biz, and the *Fully Qualified Domain Name* (*FQDN*) of your computer is tia.latinaccents.biz. The FQDN identifies the host's absolute location in the DNS namespace.

Domain names are not limited to a single level, as in the preceding example. Assume that the latinaccents.biz domain comprises several sites, each with its own subdomains. Assume, for example, that each domain is divided into three subdomains: east, midwest, and west. The domain names would be east.latinaccents.biz, midwest.latinaccents.biz, and west.latinaccents.biz. These domains could further be divided into subdomains, such as sales.west.latinaccents.biz, support.west.latinaccents.biz, and so on. Taking this example one step further, consider a host named tia in the support.west.latinaccents.biz domain. This host's FQDN would be tia.support.west.latinaccents.biz.

Table 17-1 lists the original top-level domains. Notice that the root of the domain namespace is a null, which is often represented by a dot (.). The dot is omitted from Table 17-1.

Table 17-1: Original Top-Level Domains

Suffix	Purpose	Example
com	Commercial organizations such as businesses.	microsoft.com
edu	Educational organizations such as colleges and universities.	berkeley.edu
gov	Governmental organizations such as the IRS, SSA, NASA, and so on.	nasa.gov
int	International organizations such as NATO.	nato.int
mil	Military organizations such as the Army, Navy, and so on.	army.mil
net	Networking organizations such as ISPs.	mci.net
org	Noncommercial organizations such as the IEEE standards body.	ieee.org

Table 17-2 lists new top-level domains.

Table 17-2: New, Additional Top-Level Domains

Suffix	*Purpose*	*Example*
`aero`	Restricted to air-transport industry.	`boeing.aero`
`biz`	Businesses.	`latinaccents.biz`
`coop`	Restricted to co-op organizations or those that serve co-ops.	`redriver.coop`
`info`	Informational sites.	`windows.info`
`museum`	Restricted to museums, museum associations, and museum professionals.	`smithsonian.museum`
`name`	Personal names.	`boyce.name`
`pro`	Restricted to credential-bearing accountants, lawyers, and doctors.	`shapiro.pro`
`us`	Individual, businesses, and organizations with a presence in the United States.	`ford.us`

Tip

See `www.icann.org` for information about the new domain namespaces.

Several other domain types exist in addition to the domain types specified in Tables 17-1 and 17-2. The `.us` domain, for example, is used by governmental, regional, and educational institutions in the United States. Other countries have their own domains, such as `.uk` for the United Kingdom, `.jp` for Japan, and so on.

NeuStar, based in Washington, D.C., has been assigned authority for the `.us` domain by the U.S. government. NeuStar's `.us` Web site provides links to enable you to research, register, and delegate within this domain. Point a Web browser to `www.nic.us` for more information on the `.us` domain or to request delegation for `.us` subdomains.

Until a few years ago, an organization called InterNIC was responsible for managing and allocating domain names within the top-level domains. InterNIC, however, became a for-profit business named Network Solutions and, therefore, had to give up its monopoly on the domain namespace. Network Solutions still can allocate domain names, however, as can a multitude of other companies on the Internet. To acquire a domain name for your organization, point your Web browser to `www.icann.org` to locate a domain registrar. You can use the Network Solutions site at `www.netsol.com` to look up domain names to determine whether the names are in use or are available, register new domains, modify domains, and so on. Other domain registrars provide similar services.

Today's DNS system

Today's DNS system functions as a distributed database through a client/server relationship between DNS servers and clients requiring name resolution. The entire namespace of all domains comprises the DNS namespace. By using a distributed database architecture, DNS provides for local control of each domain while still enabling all clients to access the entire database whenever needed.

The DNS namespace comprises a hierarchical structure of domains, with each domain representing a branch on the tree and subdomains residing underneath. At the topmost level are the *root servers* that maintain the *root domains,* such as `.com`, `.net`, `.org`, `.biz`, and so on. The root of the domain namespace is a null, often represented by a dot (`.`). Figure 17-1 illustrates the DNS namespace.

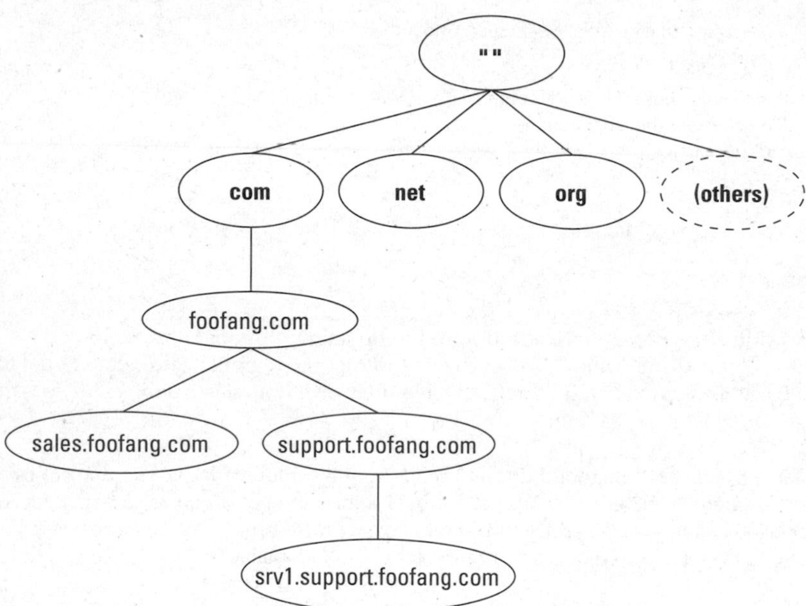

Figure 17-1: The DNS namespace is a hierarchical distributed database.

The root servers maintain only a limited amount of information about a given domain. Typically, the information includes only the name servers identified as *authoritative* for the zone (that is, those having authority over the domain's records). Records that map names to addresses within individual domains reside on the name server(s) for the domains in question. These name servers are typically managed by ISPs for the ISPs' clients or by companies that manage their own domains. Certain other domains are *delegated* to other organizations (ISPs, state agencies, educational institutions, and so on) that manage the domains for the respective domain holders. Distributing the DNS namespace in this way enables users to control their own domains while still remaining a part of the overall namespace.

Resolvers, name servers, and forward lookup

DNS clients called *resolvers* submit queries to DNS servers to be resolved into IP addresses. Assuming, for example, that you want to connect to `www.latinaccents.biz`, `www` is the host name (or could be an alias to a different host name), and `latinaccents.biz` is the domain name. The resolver on your client computer prepares a DNS query for `www.latinaccents.biz` and submits it to the DNS server identified in your client computer's TCP/IP settings, which in this case, we assume is a DNS server on your LAN. The DNS server checks its local cache (which stores results of previous queries) and database and finds that it has no records for `www.latinaccents.biz`. So the DNS server submits a query to the root server for the `.biz` domain. The root server looks up the `latinaccents.biz` domain and responds with the IP address(es) of the name servers for the domain. Your DNS server then submits a query to the specified DNS server for `latinaccents.biz`, which responds with the IP address of the host `www`. Your DNS server in turn provides this information to your resolver, which passes the data to your client application (in this case, a Web browser), and suddenly, the `www.latinaccents.biz` site pops up on your browser. Mapping a host name or alias to its address in this way is called *forward lookup.* Figure 17-2 illustrates a forward-lookup request.

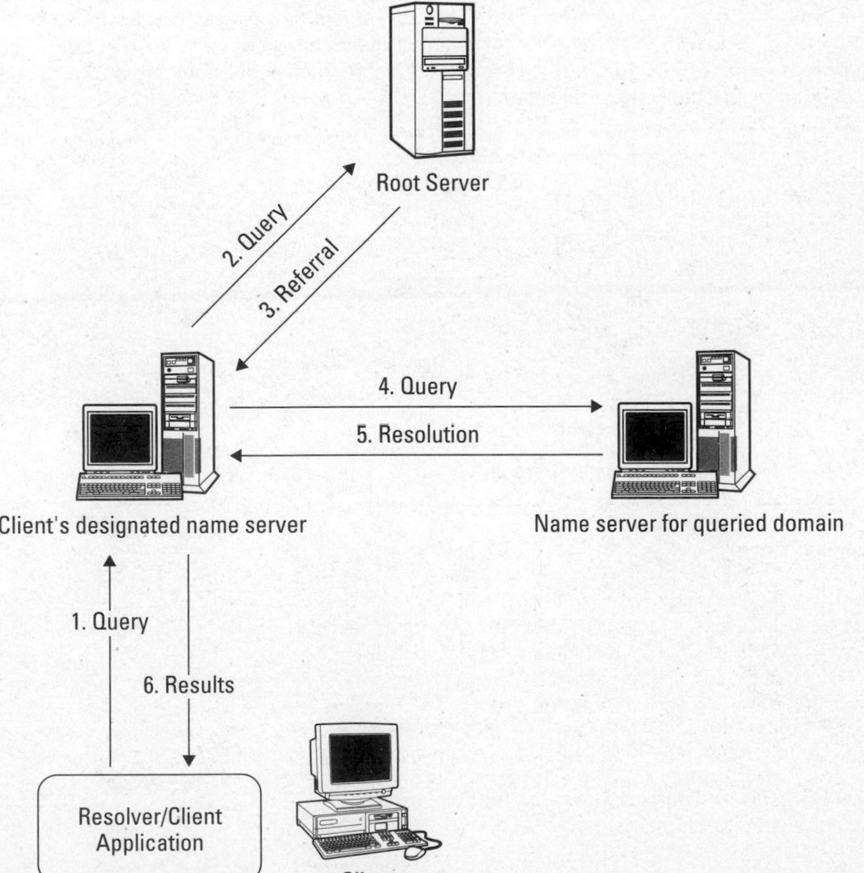

Figure 17-2: A forward-lookup query.

Tip

Keep in mind that domains and IP address ranges have no direct relationship. A single domain can use any number of different subnets, and host records in a domain can point to hosts outside your local network and even outside your domain. You might outsource e-mail for your organization, for example, which would mean that your domain contains mail-related records that point to a server outside your subnet and LAN.

Name servers range from the root servers all the way down to the name servers at your department or organizational level. In most cases, a given name server manages all the records for some portion of the DNS namespace called a *zone*. For the most part, the terms *zone* and *domain* are generally synonymous, but not always. A *zone* comprises all the data for a domain, with the exception of parts of the domain delegated to other name servers. (See the section "Configuring Subdomains and Delegation," later in this chapter, for details.) A zone is the *part* of the domain hosted on a particular name server. The *domain* comprises the whole of the domain, wherever its components reside. Whenever the entire domain resides on a single name server, *zone* and *domain* are synonymous.

A name server that has full information about a given zone is said to be *authoritative* or *has authority* for the zone. A given name server can be authoritative for any number of zones and can be both authoritative for some and nonauthoritative for others. In addition, a name server can be either a *primary master* or *secondary master*. A primary master maintains locally the records for those domains for which it is authoritative. The system administrator for a primary master can add new records, modify existing records, and so on, on the primary master. Figure 17-3 illustrates the relationship between zones and domains.

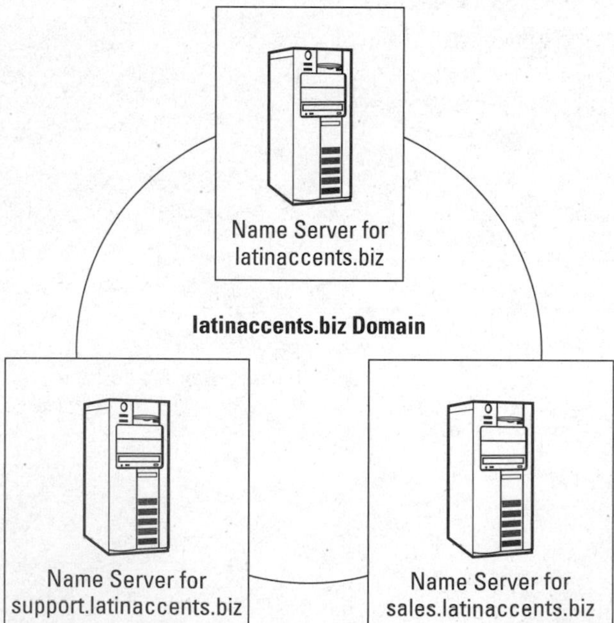

Figure 17-3: Portions of a domain can be delegated to name servers in subdomains.

A secondary master for a zone pulls its records for the zone from a primary master through a process called a *zone transfer.* The secondary master maintains the zone records as a read-only copy and periodically performs zone transfers to refresh the data from the primary master. You control the frequency of the zone transfers according to the requirements of the domain in question, the desired amount of network traffic (reducing network traffic by reducing zone transfers if needed), and any other issues pertinent to your domain(s). A secondary master is essentially a backup DNS server. A server can function as a primary master for some zones and a secondary master for others. The difference is in how the server handles the zones and not in the zones themselves.

Domain records and zone files

Each zone contains records that define hosts and other elements of the domain or a portion of the domain contained within the zone. These records are stored collectively in a *zone file* on the DNS server. A zone file is a text file that uses a special format to store DNS records. The default name for a zone file is `domain.dns`, where *domain* is the name of the domain hosted by the zone, such as `latinaccents.biz.dns`. Windows Server 2003 stores zone files in `%systemroot%\System32\Dns`. Windows Server 2003 provides an MMC console to enable you to manage the contents of the zone files with a graphical interface. (More on the console later in this chapter.)

Each zone contains a certain number of *resource records* that define the hosts and other data for the zones. Several different types of records exist, with each serving a specific purpose. Each record has certain properties associated with it that vary from one record type to the next. Table 17-3 lists the record types and their purposes.

Table 17-3: Windows Server 2003 DNS Resource Records

Record	*Purpose*
A	Maps host name to an address.
AAAA	Maps host name to Ipv6 address.
AFSDB	Location of Andrew File System (AFS) cell database server or Distributed Computing Environment (DCE) cell's authenticated server.
ATMA	Maps domain name to Asynchronous Transfer Mode (ATM) address.
CNAME	Creates alias (synonymous) name for specified host.
HINFO	Identifies host's hardware and operating system type.
ISDN	Maps host name to Integrated Services Digital Network (ISDN) address (phone number).
KEY	Public key related to a DNS domain name.
MB	Associates host with specified mailbox; experimental.
MG	Associates host name with mail group; experimental.
MINFO	Specifies mailbox name responsible for mail group; experimental.
MR	Specifies mailbox name that is correct rename of other mailbox; experimental.

Continued

Table 17-3 *(continued)*

Record	*Purpose*
MX	Mail exchange server for domain.
NS	Specifies address of domain's name server(s).
NXT	Defines literal names in the zone; implicitly indicates nonexistence of a name if not defined.
PTR	Maps address to a host name for reverse lookup.
RP	Identifies responsible person for domain or host.
RT	Specifies intermediate host that routes packets to destination host.
SIG	Cryptographic signature record.
SOA	Specifies authoritative server for the zone.
SRV	Defines servers for specific purpose such as `http`, `ftp`, and so on.
TXT	Associates textual information with item in the zone.
WINS	Enables lookup of host portion of domain name through WINS server.
WINS-R	Reverses lookup through WINS server.
WKS	Describes services provided by specific protocol on specific port.
X.25	Maps host name to X.121 address (X.25 networks); used in conjunction with RT records.

The primary record is the *SOA*, or *Start of Authority*. The SOA record indicates that the server is authoritative for the domain. Whenever you create a new zone, Windows Server 2003 automatically creates the SOA record for the zone. *NS* records identify *n*ame *s*ervers, and a zone should contain NS records for each name server in the domain.

Address, or *A* records, map host names to IP addresses. *Multi-homed hosts*—those that have multiple IP addresses—can be represented by multiple A records, each mapping the same host name to the different addresses of the host. A DNS lookup retrieves all matching records if multiple A records reference the same name. The name server sorts the address list so that the closest address is at the top of the list to improve performance if the resolver and name server are on the same network. Otherwise, addresses are rotated through subsequent queries to respond in round-robin fashion. One query responds with the address of the first address in the list, for example, and subsequent queries respond with the second and third, respectively.

CNAME (*Canonical Name*) records map an alias name to a Fully Qualified Domain Name (FQDN) and are, therefore, called *alias* records. So, A and CNAME records typically work hand-in-hand. You create a host (A) record for a host and then use CNAME records to create aliases. You may create a host record for `server.latinaccents.biz`, for example, and then use CNAME records to create aliases for `www` and `ftp` that point to that server.

Mail Exchanger, or *MX* records, are another common resource record type. MX records enable servers to route mail. The MX records in a zone determine how mail is routed for the domain hosted by the zone. An MX record includes the FQDN of the mail server and a preference number from `0` to `65535`. The preference number determines the priority of the mail server specified by the MX record. If multiple mail servers exist for a domain, the zone includes multiple MX records. Mail delivery is attempted based on the preference number, with the lowest-numbered server(s) tried first. If the MX records all have the same preference number, the remote mail server has the option of sending to any of the domain's mail servers with the given preference number.

Service Location (SRV) resource records offer the same flexibility for other services that MX records offer for mail routing. You create SRV records for specific services such as HTTP, FTP, LDAP, and so on. Resolvers that are designed to work with SRV records can use the preference number to connect to hosts offering the specified service. As with MX records, servers with lower preference numbers are attempted first.

The *Pointer* (*PTR*) record is another common record type. Pointers map addresses to names, the reverse of what host records do, in a process called *reverse lookup*. You learn more about reverse lookup in the following section. For now, simply understand that, whenever you create or modify resource records for forward lookup, the Windows 2003 DNS service can automatically create or modify the associated PTR record.

Each record has certain properties associated with it, and many properties are common to all records. Each record, for example, has a *time-to-live*, or *TTL* property. The TTL value, a 32-bit integer, specifies the number of seconds the resolver should cache the results of a query before it is discarded. After the specified TTL period is reached, the resolver purges the entry from the cache, and the subsequent query for the item is sent to the name server rather than pulled from the cache. Although the TTL value and caching can speed performance by caching often-used queries, the dynamism of the Internet requires that records can change. Mail servers, Web servers, FTP servers, and other hosts can and do change addresses, and those changes need to be reflected in the DNS namespace. The TTL value enables caching but also enable query results to grow stale and the resolver to query for fresh results. You need to adjust the TTL value for records to suit the type of record and how often you want the record updated across the intranet/Internet. If you're not sure what value to use initially, settle for the default value.

The TTL value is optional for most resource records. The minimum default value specified with the SOA record is used if no TTL is specified for a record. In addition, the Windows 2003 DNS GUI presents some data differently from the way it is stored. The TTL is a 32-bit integer in the data file, for example, but the GUI represents it in the format *DD:HH:MM:SS* (days:hours:minutes:seconds) for readability.

Reverse lookup

Forward lookup maps names to addresses, enabling a resolver to query a name server with a host name and receive an address in response. A *reverse query*, also called *reverse lookup*, does just the opposite — it maps an IP address to a name. The client knows the IP address but needs to know the host name associated with that IP address. Reverse lookup is most commonly used to apply security based on the connecting host name, but it is also useful if you're working with a range of IP addresses and gathering information about them.

Address-to-name mapping through the regular forward lookup mechanism is simply not practical, as it requires an exhaustive search of the entire DNS namespace to locate the appropriate information. Imagine scanning through the New York City phone book trying to match a phone number with a name; then multiply that task by the number of computers on the Internet, and you may understand that reverse lookup requires a special mechanism to make it practical.

The solution is to create a namespace of IP addresses or, in other words, a domain in the namespace that uses IP addresses rather than names. In the DNS namespace, the `in-addr.arpa` domain serves this purpose. The `in-addr.arpa` domain serves as the root for reverse lookup. To understand how the `in-addr.arpa` domain and reverse lookup work, you need to first examine IP addresses.

Each IP address is a *dotted octet*, or four sets of numbers ranging from `0` to `255`, separated by periods. An example of a valid IP address is `208.141.230.30`. The `in-addr.arpa` domain delegates each octet as a subdomain. At the first level is `n.addr.arpa`, where *n* represents a number from `0` to `255` that corresponds to the left-most octet of an IP address. Each of these domains contains 256 subdomains, each representing the second octet. At the third level are subdomains that represent the third octet. Using the IP address given in this example, the reverse-lookup zone is `230.141.208.in-addr.arpa`. Figure 17-4 illustrates the reverse lookup domain `in-addr.arpa`.

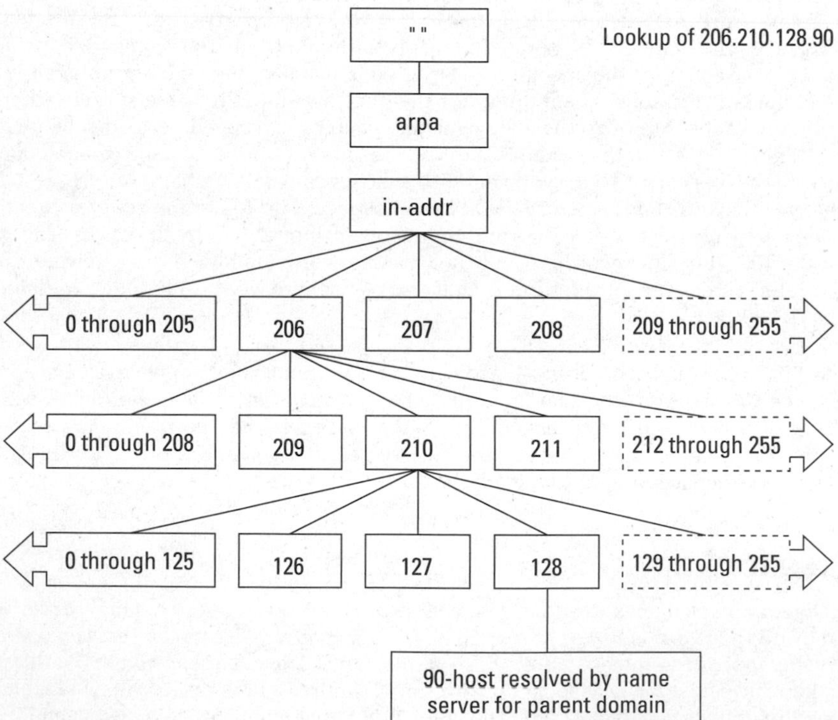

Figure 17-4: The domain `in-addr.arpa` provides the capability to perform reverse lookup, mapping addresses to host names.

As the example in Figure 17-4 illustrates, reverse-lookup zones are structured in reverse notation from the IP address ranges that they represent. Take a forward lookup as an example, assuming that you're querying for the host `bob.support.midwest.latinaccents.biz`. The lookup starts in the `.biz` domain, moves to `latinaccents`, to `midwest`, to `support`, and then finally locates the `bob` host record. Reverse lookups happen in the same way, moving from least significant to most significant, right to left. Using the address from the preceding example, the reverse lookup starts in `in-addr.arpa`, moves to the `208` subdomain, to `141`, and then to `230`, where it finds the PTR record for the `.30` address and maps it to a host name. Using reverse notation to create the reverse lookup zones enables the query to start with the first octet of the address, which in this example is `206`.

The upper-level reverse lookup domains are hosted primarily by large ISPs such as AT&T, which delegate the subdomains to individual customers (or handle reverse lookup for them). Your primary concern is probably creating reverse-lookup zones for your subnets. Creating a reverse-lookup zone is a relatively simple task and is much like creating a forward-lookup zone. The only real difference is that, instead of manually creating records in the reverse lookup zone, you rely on the DNS service to do it for you automatically as you create records in forward-lookup zones. (You find detailed steps for creating both forward and reverse lookup zones in the section "Microsoft Domain Name Services," later in this chapter.)

Delegation

Delegation is the primary mechanism that enables DNS to be a distributed namespace. Delegation enables a name server to delegate some or all of a domain to other name servers. The delegating server in effect becomes a "gateway" of sorts to the delegated domain, with individual domain records residing not on the delegating server but on those servers to which the subdomains are delegated. Figure 17-5 illustrates the process.

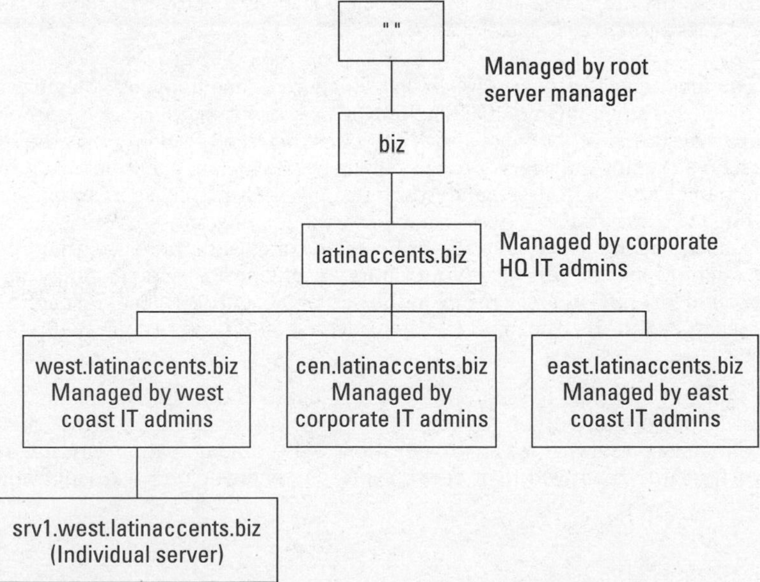

Figure 17-5: Delegation enables local control of subdomains where another organization has control and responsibility for the parent domain.

In the example of delegation shown in Figure 17-5, the root server for the `.biz` domain controls the `latinaccents.biz` domain. The `west.latinaccents.biz` domain is delegated to the West Coast IT staff, which hosts its own DNS servers and manages the DNS records for the subdomain. The subdomains for `cen.latinaccents.biz` and `east.latinaccents.biz` are managed by the corporate IT staff in Miami.

Delegation provides two primary benefits. It reduces the potential load on any given name server in the delegation chain. Imagine that all domains in the `.com` domain were hosted by one company. The company would need to host millions of domains, imposing an impossible load on their servers, but perhaps more important, this situation would place a significant load on the poor administrators who would administer the zones. This load reduction leads to the second benefit: Delegation enables a decentralized administration, further enabling other organizations, such as a subsidiary of the company, to administer their own domains and have control over their resource records. (See the section "Configuring Subdomains and Delegation," later in this chapter, for detailed steps on creating and delegating subdomains.)

Caching, forwarders, and slaves

The number of queries that could potentially hit an active and popular domain on the Internet could easily overwhelm a name server. *Caching* helps reduce that load and reduce network traffic. Each server caches successful and unsuccessful resolution queries for a period of time defined by the server's administrator. Whenever a resolver queries the server for an address, the server checks its cache first for the data and, if the data exists in the cache, submits the cached data to the client rather than looking up the data again.

Note Caching unsuccessful queries is called *negative caching.* Negative caching speeds response, reduces server load, and reduces network traffic by eliminating repeated queries for names that can't be resolved (such as nonexistent domains or hosts). As with positive caching, however, negative-cache results age and expire, enabling lookups to succeed if the domain or host record does become available.

Name servers can function as *caching-only servers*, which don't maintain any zone files and are not authoritative for any domain. A caching-only server receives queries from resolvers, performs the queries against other name servers, caches the results, and returns the results to the resolvers. So a caching-only server essentially acts as a lookup agent between the client and other name servers. At first glance, caching-only servers may seem to make little sense. They reduce network traffic, however, in two ways: Caching-only servers reduce zone transfers because the caching-only name server hosts no zones and, therefore, requires no zone transfers. Caching-only servers also reduce query traffic past the caching-only server as long as query results for a given query reside in the server's cache. Because the cache is cleared after the server restarts, the most effective caching-only server is one that remains up for extended periods.

A name server typically attempts to resolve queries against its own cache and zone files and, failing that, queries one or more other name servers for the information. In certain situations, you may not want all name servers for an organization to be communicating with the outside world for network security, bandwidth, or cost reasons. Instead, you'd forward all traffic through a given name server that would act as a sort of agent for the other name servers in the organization. Assume, for example, that you have a few relatively slow or expensive Internet connections to your site and one with higher bandwidth or that is less costly. Servers A, B, and C connect through the former, and server D connects through the latter. Rather than have all servers generating traffic through their respective links, you might want to funnel all traffic through server D. In this case, server D would act as a *forwarder*, which forwards offsite name queries for other name servers on the network. Servers A, B, and C would handle queries against their local caches and zone files and, failing those queries, would pass the query on to server D.

Name servers can interact with forwarders either exclusively or nonexclusively. If interacting nonexclusively, the server attempts to resolve queries against its cache and own zone files first. Failing that, the server forwards the request to the designated forwarder. If the forwarder fails the query, the server attempts to resolve the query on its own through other name servers. To prevent a server from doing this, you need to configure it as a *slave*, which makes it function in exclusive mode with the forwarder. If functioning as a slave, a name server first attempts to resolve a query against its cache and local zone files. Failing that, it forwards the query to the designated forwarder. If that fails, the forwarder responds with an unsuccessful query, and the local server fails the request to the client resolver without attempting any further resolution.

You also can configure a slave name server as a *caching-only slave*. In this configuration, the server hosts no zone files. It attempts to resolve queries against its local cache only and, failing that, forwards the query to the designated forwarder and takes no further action to resolve the query. It does not itself fail the request to the resolver.

Recursion, iteration, and referrals

Figure 17-6 illustrates a query for resolution of the host name `jane.west.latinaccents.biz`. As the figure shows, the name server directly queried by the client must perform several queries to find a definitive answer to the query. The other name servers do relatively little work, mostly responding with *referrals*, which simply point the originating server to a different name server farther down the namespace hierarchy. In effect, these other servers are s aying, "I don't have the answer, but so-and-so does," referring to the name server contained in the referral.

DNS uses two primary means to resolve queries: *recursion* and *iteration* (also referred to as *nonrecursive*). A recursive query is the method used by server A in Figure 17-6. In this example, the resolver sends a recursive query to server A, which starts the resolution process by querying the root server B. Server B responds with a referral to server C, which hosts the root of the `.biz` domain. Server C responds with a referral to server D, which hosts the `latinaccents.biz` domain. Server D responds with a referral to server E, which hosts the delegated `west.latinaccents.biz` subdomain. Server E contains the appropriate host record and returns the address for `jane.west.latinaccents.biz`. So, in a recursive query, the queried server (in this case A) continues to query other servers until it finds a definitive answer; then it returns that answer to the resolver. A recursive query places the most load on the client's name server.

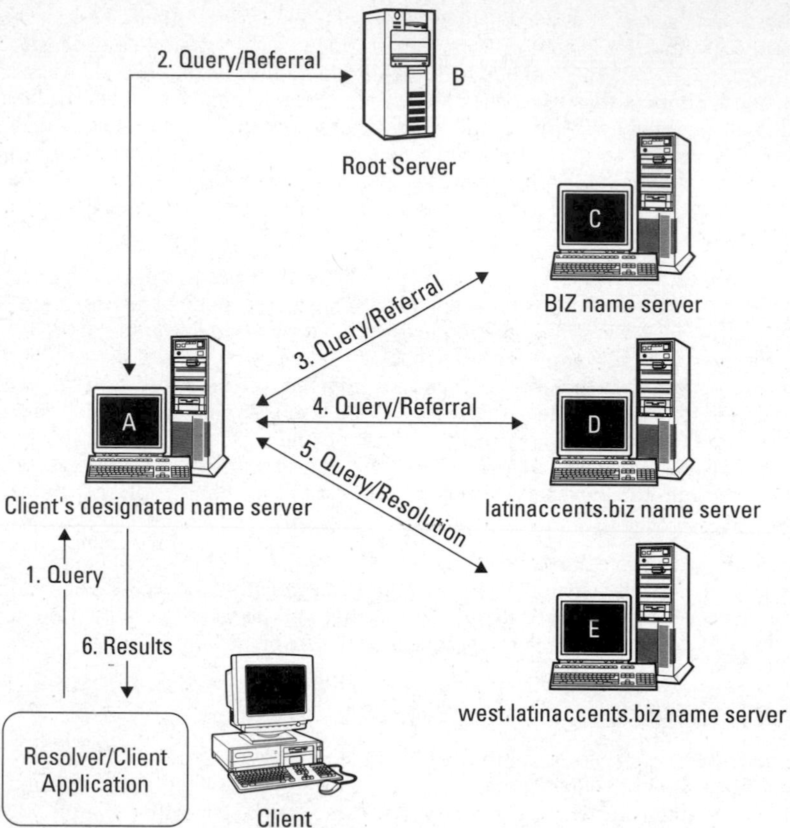

Figure 17-6: Resolution of the host name `jane.west.latinaccents.biz` shows recursion and referrals.

An iterative query places the majority of the load on the client. In the iterative query shown in Figure 17-7, the client resolver requests resolution of the same host, `jane.west.latinaccents.biz`. In this example, however, name server A simply responds with the best information that it already has for the query. If the resolved query resides in Server A's cache, it responds with that data. Otherwise, it gives the client a referral to a name server that can help the resolver continue the query on its own. In the case of Figure 17-7, Server A provides a referral to server B, which gives the client resolver a referral to C and so on, until server E finally provides the answer to the resolver.

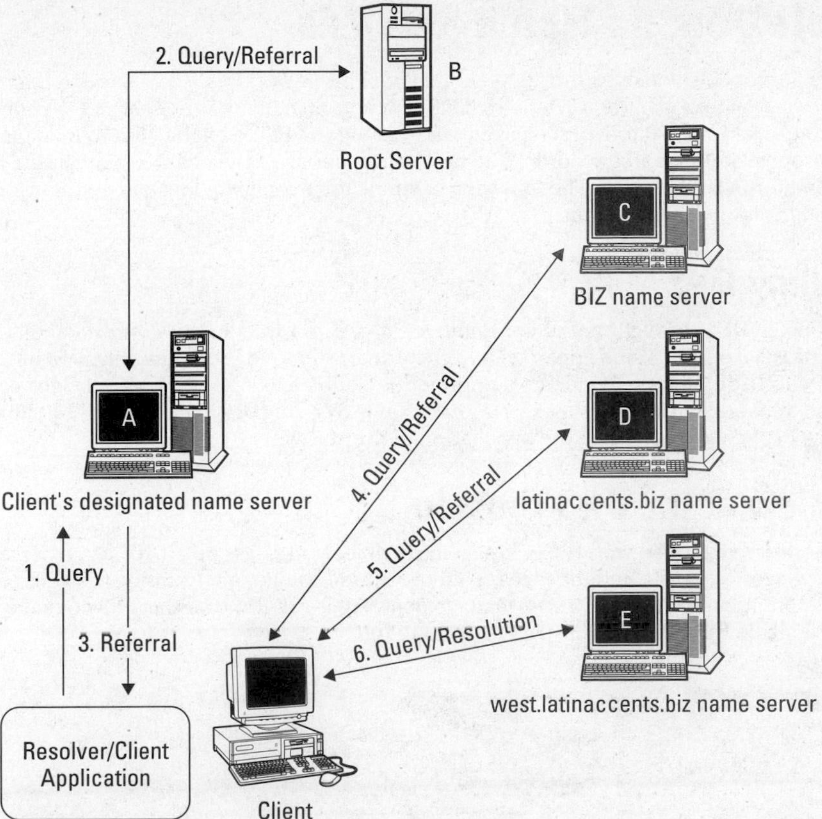

Figure 17-7: An iterative query of jane.west.latinaccents.biz.

One main difference between recursive and iterative queries is the fact that recursive queries place the majority of the responsibility for resolving the query on the name server, while the iterative query places the responsibility with the client resolver. To adequately process iterative queries, therefore, a client resolver must be more complex and "smarter" than one that relies only on recursive queries. Recursive queries also tax the client's designated name server(s) much more than iterative queries. Name servers in general and Windows Server 2003 in particular enable you to disable the server's support for recursive queries, forcing the clients to use iterative queries. You might choose this option in situations where you need to limit the load on the server. Another reason to disable recursion is if you're setting up a name server that services only the LAN or WAN and you don't want it to attempt to resolve queries for domains outside that general area.

Microsoft Domain Name Services

Windows Server 2003 includes the Microsoft *Domain Name Services* (*DNS*) service that you can use to set up and manage a Windows 2003 DNS server. As with other services, Windows Server 2003 provides a Microsoft Management Console (MMC) to enable you to manage DNS servers, zones, and resource records. The previous sections of the chapter explain the concepts behind the DNS service. The following sections focus on installing and configuring DNS and setting up zones and domains.

Installing DNS

You can install DNS through the Add or Remove Programs applet in the Control Panel. Open the Add or Remove Programs applet, and in the Add or Remove Programs window that appears, click Add/Remove Windows Components. Double-click Networking Services or select the item and click Details. Select Domain Name System (DNS) and click OK. Follow the remaining prompts to complete the installation of the software.

Overview of the DNS console

The *DNS console* included with the DNS service enables you to set up a DNS server, create and manage zones, create and manage resource records, and so on. In short, the DNS console is a single point of contact for all DNS management. Figure 17-8 shows the DNS console. Open the DNS console from the Administrative Tools folder.

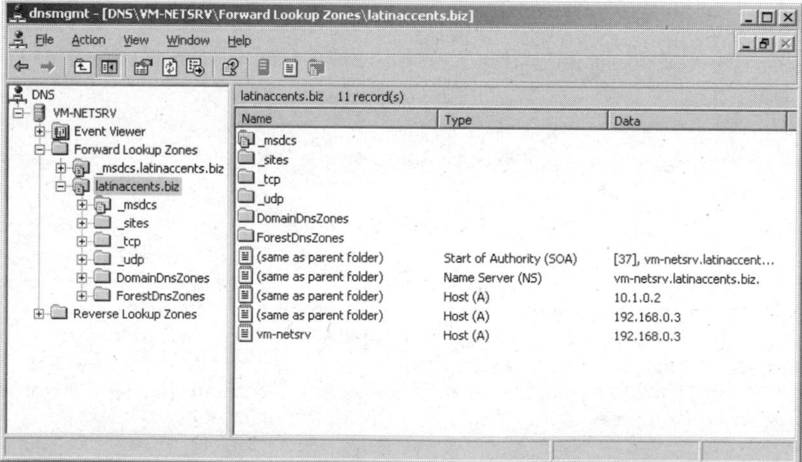

Figure 17-8: Use the DNS console to manage DNS servers locally and remotely.

By default, the DNS console shows the local server, but you can connect to any Windows Server 2003 or Windows 2000 DNS server through the console. To do so, right-click DNS in the left pane and choose Connect to Computer. Select The Following Computer radio button and then specify the computer's name or IP address in the corresponding text box. Click OK to connect.

After you connect to a server, you find two primary branches in the left pane: Forward Lookup Zones and Reverse Lookup Zones. Expanding the Forward Lookup Zones branch displays all forward-lookup zones, each under its own subbranch. Expanding the Reverse Lookup Zones branch displays all reverse-lookup zones in their own subbranches.

How the contents of a zone branch appear depends on whether the zone is for a Windows Server 2003 domain or simply a DNS domain. If it's for a Windows Server 2003 domain, you find additional branches for domain-related services and objects such as Kerberos, LDAP, sites, and so on.

The following sections explain how to use the DNS console to create and manage zones, resource records, and servers.

Creating forward-lookup zones

Each domain that you host for DNS requires a forward-lookup zone, zone file, and associated records. You create the zone in the DNS console by using one of the following three options:

- **Active Directory Integrated:** This option creates the zone in the Active Directory, or AD, which provides for replication, integrated storage, security, and the other advantages inherent in the AD. The zone file is stored within the AD. You can create an AD-integrated zone only on a domain controller . . . giving the DNS service direct access to the database mechanisms of AD. You can't create AD-integrated zones on member servers that function as DNS servers.
- **Standard Primary:** This option creates a standard primary zone using a `.dns` file in `%systemroot%\System32\Dns` (default location). You can add and modify resource records in a primary zone.
- **Standard Secondary:** This option creates a standard secondary zone using a `.dns` file in `%systemroot\System32\Dns`. This is a read-only copy of a zone on another server. You cannot create or modify resource records in a secondary zone.

Windows Server 2003 provides a wizard to help you create a zone. Right-click either the server name or on the Forward Lookup Zone branch and choose New Zone from the context menu to start the New Zone Wizard. In addition to prompting you for the type of zone (AD-integrated, primary, secondary), the wizard prompts for the following information:

- **Forward Lookup Zone/Reverse Lookup Zone:** Choose the type of zone that you want to create. In this case, choose Forward Lookup Zone.
- **Zone Name:** Specify the full name of the zone, such as `latinaccents.biz`, `west.latinaccents.biz`, and so on. If you are specifying a second-level zone such as `west.latinaccents.biz`, you should make sure that you first create the first-level zone for `latinaccents.biz` on its designated name server. You then delegate `west.latinaccents.biz` on that server to the current server.
- **DNS Zone File:** Specify a zone-file name under which to store the zone's records if you're creating a standard primary or standard secondary zone. Specifying an existing file enables you to migrate existing resource records to the new zone. AD-integrated zones are stored in the AD and don't require an external file.

After you create a forward-lookup zone, you can begin populating it with resource records. Before doing so, however, you should first create any required reverse-lookup zones. Creating the reverse-lookup zone(s) before creating the resource records enables DNS to automatically create the PTR records in the reverse-lookup zones for resource records that you create in the forward-lookup zones.

Creating reverse-lookup zones

You create a reverse-lookup zone in much the same way that you create a forward-lookup zone. The primary difference is that you specify the subnet for the zone and the DNS console converts that to the appropriate reverse zone name. Enter `208.141.230` after you're prompted, for example, and the DNS console creates the reverse lookup zone `230.141.208.in-addr.arpa`. You do not need to specify three octets unless you're creating a reverse-lookup zone for a domain that uses a class-C address space. Specify the appropriate number of octets to define your reverse lookup zone. In addition, you can choose to specify the DNS file name yourself, but remember to enter it in reverse notation.

Creating resource records

After you create a zone, you can populate it with resource records. As you create a zone, the Windows 2003 DNS service automatically creates the SOA record and NS record for you.

To create new records, right-click the zone in the left pane or right-click the right pane and choose New Host, New Alias, or New Mail Exchanger from the context menu to create A, CNAME, or MX records. Or choose Other New Records to create other types of resource records. The information that you provide varies slightly depending on the type of record that you're creating.

Host records (A)

Host, or A, records map a host name to an IP address and are the primary means by which names are resolved. Each host in your network that you want visible through DNS needs to have a host record in its corresponding zone.

In creating a host record, you specify the host name (such as `www`, `ftp`, `tia`, `server`, and so on) and the IP address to map to that host. You can't add a host name containing periods, as anything after the period is considered part of the domain name. Select the Create Associated Pointer (PTR) Record option after creating the record in the DNS console to have DNS automatically create a pointer record in the reverse-lookup zone for the domain. DNS chooses the appropriate reverse-lookup zone based on the IP address that you specify for the host.

If you need to create a host name that contains a period, first create a parent-level zone for the second half of the name. If you're attempting to create `joe.west` in the `latinaccents.biz` domain, for example, you first need to create a `west` zone as a subdomain of `latinaccents.biz`. Then create the host record for `joe` in the `west.latinaccents.biz` subdomain.

Alias records (CNAME)

Alias, or CNAME, records map an alias name to an existing FQDN. Assume, for example, that you're the administrator for `latinaccents.biz` and you have a server in your network named `srv1`, with a corresponding A record for `srv1` that points to the server's IP address. You want to use the server as a Web server. So you create an alias for `www` that points to `srv1.latinaccents.biz`. Users connect to `www.latinaccents.biz`, and DNS actually routes them transparently to `srv1.latinaccents.biz`.

In creating an alias record, you specify the alias name and the Fully Qualified Domain Name of the host to which the alias points. As with a host record, you can't include a period in the host name for the alias. The FQDN for the alias can and does have periods in it, as by definition, a FQDN contains the domain name in which the host resides.

Mail Exchanger records (MX)

Mail Exchanger, or MX, records enable mail to be routed through or to a domain. They specify *mail exchangers*, or servers that process mail for the domain. For MX records, specify the single-part name for the Mail Exchanger in the Host or Domain field. If you leave this field blank, the Mail-Exchanger name is the same as the parent domain name. In the Mail Server field, specify the FQDN of the server that acts as the mail exchanger. The FQDN that you specify here must resolve to a host (A) record in the zone, so make sure that you create the A record for the Mail Exchanger as well as the MX record. You can click Browse to browse the DNS namespace for the appropriate hostname if you're not sure what it is. Finally, specify the preference number for the Mail Exchanger in the Mail Server Priority field.

Service Location records (SRV)

Service Location, or SRV, records are another common resource record type that offers excellent flexibility if a domain contains multiple servers for specific services, such as multiple HTTP servers. SRV records enable you to easily move a service from one host to another and designate certain hosts as primary for a given service and others as secondary for that same service. You might designate a server as the primary Web (HTTP) server, for example, and two others as secondary servers to handle HTTP requests whenever the primary is heavily loaded or offline.

Resolvers that support SRV records submit a request to the DNS server for servers in the subject domain that provide a specific TCP/IP service (such as HTTP). The DNS server responds with a list of all servers in the domain that have a corresponding SRV record for the requested service type.

To create an SRV record, right-click the zone in the DNS console and choose Other New Records from the context menu. Select Service Location from the list and click Create Record to open the New Resource Record dialog box for SRV records (it opens to this tab), as shown in Figure 17-9.

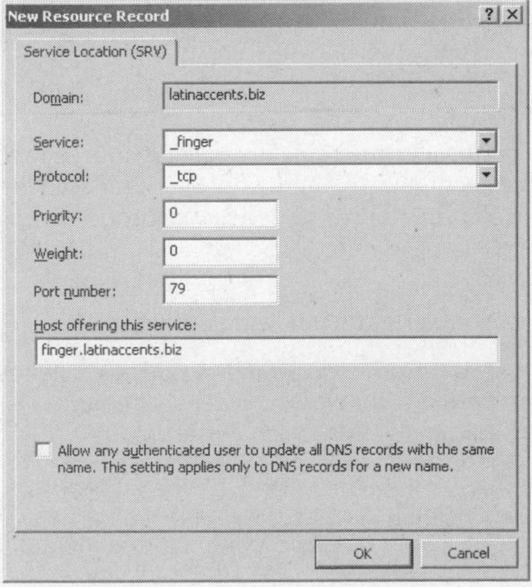

Figure 17-9: Use the Service Location (SRV) tab of the New Resource Record dialog box to create SRV records for specific services offered by specific servers.

Fill in the fields for the SRV record by using the following list as a guide:

- **Service:** Select the predefined service type offered by the target server (FTP, HTTP, and so on).
- **Protocol:** Select either `tcp` or `udp`, depending on the requirements of the service.
- **Priority:** Specify an integer between `0` and `65535`. This value specifies the preference order of the server, just as the preference number for an MX record identifies the priority of the target Mail Exchanger. A lower value places the server higher in the priority list (`0` is highest priority); a higher value gives the server a lower priority. The client tries the server with the highest priority first and, failing that, attempts connections to other servers in decreasing priority. Multiple servers can have the same priority value.
- **Weight:** Specify an integer between `0` and `65535` to allocate a weight to the target server for load-balancing purposes. If multiple servers have the same priority value, the weight value serves as a secondary priority indicator. Hosts with a higher weight value are returned first to the resolver client. Use a value of `0` to turn off weighting if you don't need load balancing. Using a value of `0` speeds up SRV queries and improves performance.
- **Port Number:** Specify an integer from `0` to `65535` to indicate the `tcp` or `udp` port number used by the target service.
- **Host Offering this Service:** Specify the FQDN of the target server offering the service. The FQDN must resolve to a valid name supported by a host record in the server's domain.

Other record types

You can create other types of resource records by right-clicking the zone in the DNS console and choosing Other New Records from the context menu. The DNS console displays the Resource Record Type dialog box. Select from this dialog box the type of record that you need to create and then click Create Record. DNS displays a New Resource Record dialog box that prompts for the required data, which varies from one record type to the next.

Configuring zone properties

A zone's properties determine how the zone performs zone transfers, ages resource records, and other behavior for the zone. The following sections explain the options available for a zone. To set these options, open the DNS console, right-click the zone, and choose Properties.

General zone properties

A zone's General property page enables you to configure the following options:

- **Status:** Click Pause to pause a zone and stop it from responding to queries. Click Start to start a paused zone. You might pause a zone while making extensive changes to the records in the zone or performing other administrative tasks on the zone.
- **Type:** You can change a zone's type on the General page to any of the three supported types (AD-integrated, standard primary, or standard secondary). If a server for a primary standard zone fails, for example, you can change its secondary zone on a different server to a primary zone.

✦ **Zone File Name:** Use this property to change the file where the zone records are stored. By default, the zone file name is `zone.dns`, where *zone* is the name of the zone. The resource records for `west.latinaccents.biz`, for example, would be stored by default in `west.latinaccents.biz.dns`.

✦ **Allow Dynamic Updates:** Use this option to enable/deny dynamic updates by Dynamic Host Configuration Protocol (DHCP) clients and servers to resource records in the zone and corresponding pointer records. See the section "Dynamic DNS," later in this chapter, for detailed information.

✦ **Aging:** Click to specify aging properties for records in the zone. See the section "Configuring scavenging," later in this chapter, for a detailed explanation.

Start of Authority properties

The *Start of Authority* (*SOA*) property page for a zone enables you to configure the zone's SOA record. This property page contains the following properties:

✦ **Serial Number:** DNS uses this value to determine when a zone transfer is required. The DNS service increments the value by 1 each time that the zone changes to indicate that the zone is a new version. Other servers performing zone transfers with the server use this value to determine whether a zone transfer is needed. If the value is higher than the remote server's records for the zone, the server initiates a zone transfer to update the remote server's zone records. Use the Increment button to increment the serial number and force a zone transfer.

✦ **Primary Server:** Specifies the host name of the primary master for the selected zone. If you need to change the value, type the host name of the primary master or click Browse to browse the network for the primary master. Make sure that you include a period at the end of the host name.

✦ **Responsible Person:** Specifies the e-mail address of the person responsible for managing the zone. The data takes the form of an FQDN. The address `administrator@latinaccents.biz`, for example, should be entered as `administrator.latinaccents.biz`, replacing the @ symbol with a period.

✦ **Refresh Interval:** This value specifies how often servers that host secondary copies of the zone should check the currency of their zone data against the primary zone data. The default is 15 minutes.

✦ **Retry Interval:** This value specifies the amount of time that must elapse before a server hosting a secondary copy of the zone retries a connection to the primary zone if a previous connection attempt failed. This value should usually be less than the Refresh interval and defaults to 10 minutes.

✦ **Expires After:** Specifies the period of time that a server hosting a secondary copy of the zone can wait before discarding its secondary data if its zone data hasn't been refreshed. This prevents the secondary servers from serving potentially stale data to client requests. The default is 24 hours.

✦ **Minimum (Default) TTL:** This value specifies the amount of time that querying servers can cache results returned from this zone. After this period expires, the remote server removes the record from its cache. The default is 1 hour.

✦ **TTL For This Record:** This value specifies the time-to-live for the SOA record itself. The default is 1 hour.

Name-server properties

The Name Servers page enables you to modify the NS records for the zone. The advantage to using this method rather than manually changing each record is that you can view all NS records in the zone in a single dialog box. To modify a record, select the record and click Edit. Windows 2003 DNS displays a dialog box that you can use to modify the host name, IP address, or time-to-live value for the NS record. If modifying the host name, make sure that the name contains a period at the end. You can click Add to add a new NS record.

WINS properties

The WINS page determines whether the DNS service attempts to resolve names through WINS that it can't resolve on its own. Use the following properties to configure WINS integration:

- **Use WINS Forward Lookup:** Select this option to enable the DNS service to query WINS for any names that it can't resolve on its own through DNS.
- **Do Not Replicate This Record:** Select this option to prevent the DNS server from replicating WINS-specific resource data to other DNS servers during zone transfers. You need to use this option if you are performing zone transfers to servers that don't support WINS (such as non-Microsoft DNS servers).
- **IP Address:** Specify the IP addresses of the WINS servers to query.
- **Advanced:** Click to set the cache timeout and lookup timeout periods. The cache timeout specifies the amount of time other servers can cache results returned through a WINS lookup. The lookup timeout specifies the amount of time that the DNS server can wait for a response from the WINS server(s) before generating a `Name not found` error.

Zone-transfer properties

The Zone Transfers page of a zone's properties specifies the servers that can request and receive a copy of the zone's data through a zone transfer. You can configure the zone to enable all servers to request a transfer, only servers listed on the zone's Name Servers property page or only servers included in a list of IP addresses that you define.

Click Notify to specify how other servers are notified of zone updates. You can configure the zone to automatically notify servers listed on the Name Servers property page for the zone or servers included in a list of IP addresses that you define. Deselect the Automatically Notify option if you don't want the DNS server to notify the other servers whenever the zone data changes.

Managing DNS Server Options and Behavior

You can use the DNS console to configure various options that determine how the DNS service functions. The following sections explain the different properties and behavior that you can configure, including how to set up a forwarder and perform monitoring and logging.

Configuring multiple addresses on a DNS server

By default, the DNS service responds on all IP addresses bound to the server. Why use multiple addresses for DNS on a single server? One good reason is that, whenever you register a domain, you must specify two name servers for the domain. But you may have only one DNS server because of the cost of the server or other considerations. You can assign two (or more) IP addresses to the server, assign two NS host names to the server, and use both host names and their corresponding IP addresses to register the domain.

Assume, for example, that `latinaccents.biz` has only one DNS server. You bind two IP addresses to the server, `192.168.0.2` and `192.168.0.3` (by using reserved IP addresses in this example). You then create two host records, `ns1` and `ns2`, that point to the `.2` and `.3` addresses, respectively. At the time that you register the domain, you specify `ns1.latinaccents.biz` on one public IP address and `ns2.latinaccents.biz` on a second public IP address. These two public IP addresses map in your firewall to the private `.2` and `.3` addresses, respectively. To the outside world, you appear to have two physical name servers, but you really have only one that responds on both IP addresses. The server runs only one instance of the DNS service, maintains only one zone file for `latinaccents.biz`, but appears to be two different servers.

You face no real performance penalty in enabling the DNS service to respond on all bound IP addresses, but in some situations, you may want to reduce the addresses to only those that you specifically want associated with the DNS service. You might allocate two addresses that are always used for DNS but, in effect, "reserve" the other IP addresses on the server for other uses. Assume, for example, that you have the addresses `192.168.0.2` through `.10` bound to the server. If you enable the DNS service to respond on all addresses, users may conceivably start using `192.168.0.10` for DNS if they know that it's there. A few months down the road, you remove `.10` from the server because you want to use it elsewhere. Suddenly, those users who have been using `.10` as a DNS server find themselves unable to resolve. If you start out limiting DNS to a specific set of addresses that is always used on the server for DNS, you can avoid the problem.

You configure the addresses on which the server responds through the Interfaces tab of the server's property sheet. Open the DNS console, right-click the server, and choose Properties from the context menu to open the property sheet for the server. On the Interfaces page, choose All IP Addresses if you want the server to respond to DNS queries on all IP addresses bound to the server. Choose the Only the Following IP Addresses option if you want to limit the server to responding on only the IP addresses listed in the associated box. Use Add and Remove to change the contents of the list.

Using a forwarder

The section "Caching, forwarders, and slaves," earlier in this chapter, discusses the use of forwarders and how they enable you to funnel DNS requests through specific servers for purposes of administration, access, or bandwidth control. You configure a Windows 2003 DNS server to use a forwarder through the Forwarders page of the server's property sheet. Open the DNS console, right-click the server, choose Properties to display the property sheet, and then click the Forwarders tab. Use the following controls to configure forwarding:

- **Enable Forwarders:** Select this option to direct the DNS server to forward initial requests from client resolvers to the DNS servers specified in the following box.
- **IP Address:** Specify the IP address of a server to which queries should be forwarded. You can specify multiple servers.
- **Forward Time-Out (Seconds):** Specify the time in seconds that the DNS server waits for a response from a listed forwarder. At the end of this timeout period, the local DNS server submits a query to the next server on the list until it receives a response or cycles through the list.

✦ **Do Not Use Recursion:** Select this option to configure the server as a forwarding-only slave, preventing the server from attempting to resolve queries on its own if the forwarder cannot resolve the query. Leave this option deselected (the default) to enable the local server to attempt resolution if the forwarders cannot respond to the query.

Configuring Advanced Settings

The Advanced page of a DNS server's property sheet enables you to set several advanced options that control the way the server functions. To configure the following settings, open the DNS console, right-click the server, choose Properties, and click the Advanced tab:

✦ **Disable Recursion:** Select this option to prevent the server from performing recursive queries. With this option selected, the server replies with referrals instead of recursively querying until a resolution is reached.

✦ **BIND Secondaries:** To optimize zone transfer speed, Windows 2003 DNS servers by default use compression and submit multiple resource records in a single TCP message whenever performing zone transfers. This method is compatible with servers running *BIND* (*B*erkeley *I*nternet *N*ame *D*omain) version 4.9.4 and later but is incompatible with earlier versions of BIND. To optimize performance, leave this option deselected if your server is not going to be performing zone transfers with these earlier systems. Select this option to have the Windows 2003 DNS server perform slower, uncompressed zone transfers for compatibility with these older systems.

✦ **Fail On Load If Bad Zone Data:** The Windows 2003 DNS service by default continues to load a zone even if it detects errors in the zone data, logging the errors but not failing. Select this option if you want the DNS service to stop loading the zone if the zone data contains errors.

✦ **Enable Round Robin:** The Windows 2003 DNS service by default rotates and reorders a list of host records if a given host name is associated with multiple IP addresses. This round-robin behavior enables an administrator to perform load balancing, directing traffic to multiple computers with the same host name but different IP addresses (such as multiple servers hosting `www.latinaccents.biz`). With this option selected, the server responds to queries with each address in turn. Deselect this option if you want to disable round robin and have the server return the first match in the zone.

✦ **Enable Netmask Ordering:** If a given zone contains multiple host records that map the same host name to multiple IP addresses, the Windows 2003 DNS service can order the response list according to the IP address of the client. Windows 2003 DNS checks the IP address of the client against the addresses of the host records, and if a record falls in the client's subnet, the DNS service places that host record first in the list. This directs the client to the requested host that is closest and typically fastest for the client to access, which is very important for Active Directory services. This option is selected by default. Deselect this option to prevent the DNS service from reordering responses based on subnet. Netmask ordering supercedes round-robin ordering, although round robin is used for secondary sorting if enabled and is also useful where subnets are in different geographical locations.

✦ **Secure Cache Against Pollution:** The Windows 2003 DNS service does not add unrelated resource records added in a referral from another DNS server to the Windows Server 2003 server's cache. It caches referrals that might not match the queried host name, however, such as caching a referral for `www.sillycity.com` if querying for `www.latinaccents.biz`. Selecting this option prevents the DNS service from caching nonrelated referrals.

- **Name Checking:** Internet host names were originally limited to alphanumeric characters and hyphens. Although this limitation was maintained after DNS was developed, it posed a problem in some situations, particularly for supporting international character sets. This option controls how the DNS service performs name checking. Windows Server 2003 by default uses the UTF8 (Unicode Transformation Format) character set, which provides the broadest and least restrictive character set support. Select Strict if you need to limit names to the standard format. Use Non-RFC to permit names that do not follow the RFC 1123 specification. Use Multibyte to recognize characters other than ASCII, including Unicode.
- **Load Zone Data on Startup:** The Windows 2003 DNS service by default loads zone data from the Active Directory (for AD-integrated zones) and from the registry. You can configure the server to load only from the registry or load from a BIND 4 boot file. This latter option enables you to essentially duplicate a BIND server under Windows Server 2003, importing all the zone data. Notice that the boot file—typically called `Named.boot`—must use the BIND 4 format rather than the newer BIND 8 format.
- **Enable Automatic Scavenging of Stale Records:** Stale records typically are those that point to hosts no longer on the network. Accumulation of stale records can lead to decreased storage space, degradation of server performance, incorrect name-to-address resolution, and no capability for a host to have the DNS service create its resource record (through Dynamic DNS). Scavenging, which is turned off by default, enables the DNS server to use time stamps and other properties to determine when a resource record is stale and automatically remove it from the zone. Records added automatically through DDNS are subject to scavenging, as is any record manually added with a timestamp that you have modified from its default of zero. Resource records with a timestamp of zero are not subject to scavenging. Select this option and configure the associated scavenging period. Notice that scavenging must be enabled for individual zones in their properties as well. For additional information on scavenging, see the section "Dynamic DNS," later in this chapter.
- **Reset to Default:** Select this option to reconfigure all advanced settings to their defaults.

Setting root hints

Root hints direct a name server to the root servers for domains at a higher level or in different subtrees of the DNS namespace and, in effect, provide a road map for a DNS server to resolve queries for domains outside of its area of authority. For DNS servers connected to the Internet, the root hints should point to the Internet root name servers. For DNS servers that provide services only to a private network, the root hints should point to the root server(s) for your domain or organization. Servers that function as forwarders for local clients requesting resolution of Internet names should have their root hints point to the Internet root servers, while the other name servers in the organization should point to the local root server for the organization's private network.

By default, the Windows 2003 DNS service uses a `cache.dns` file that contains the list of Internet root servers. You find `cache.dns` located in `\%systemroot%\System32\Dns`. Browsing the file in Notepad or WordPad shows you that the file contains entries for NS and A records for the Internet root servers. If you're connecting a name server to the Internet, use the `cache.dns` file to ensure that you have the appropriate root hints. If you're creating a name server for your internal network, however, you should instead use a `cache.dns` file that contains the NS and A records of the name servers higher in your local namespace rather than the root Internet servers.

You can edit the cache.dns directly by using Notepad or WordPad if you need to modify its entries. If you prefer, you also can use the interface provided by the DNS console to modify the cache.dns file. To do so, open the DNS console, right-click the server that you want to modify the cache.dns file of, and then choose Properties. Click the Root Hints tab to display the Root Hints page. Use Add, Edit, and Remove to add, modify, and remove entries from the cache.dns file, respectively.

Entries in the cache.dns file consist of an NS record and a corresponding A record for each name server, located on two separate lines. The first line specifies the NS record. This line begins with an @ symbol, followed by a tab, and then NS, another tab, and then the FQDN of the root server. On the next line, specify the FQDN of the server, a tab, and then A to indicate an A record, another tab, and finally the IP address of the server.

If you are running internal name servers that don't need root hints to servers higher in the local area, you should eliminate root hints altogether. The easiest way to do this is to rename or delete the cache.dns file and then stop and restart the DNS server.

Although the root name servers change infrequently, the root servers can change for a variety of reasons. You can acquire a new list of root server records via FTP from Network Solutions by downloading the file ftp.rs.internic.net/domain/named.root. You can use the file directly as your cache.dns file without modifications. You can also click Copy from Server on the Root Hints page to copy the root hints from another server. (You specify the IP address of the other server.)

Configuring logging

The DNS service by default does not perform extensive logging because the number of potential queries in a relatively small amount of time can be quite large, particularly for servers that serve a large portion of the namespace or a large number of clients. You can configure logging for reasons of troubleshooting, security, and so on through the properties for the DNS server. The service provides two types of logging: *event logging* and *debug logging*. The following sections explain these logging types.

Configuring basic logging

Basic logging is useful for identifying potential problems and basic troubleshooting. You configure basic logging through the Event Logging page of the DNS server's properties. Open the DNS console, right-click the server, choose Properties, and click the Event Logging tab. Select the items to be logged and click OK. The DNS service stores log entries in \%systemroot%\System32\Dns\Dns.log. If yours is a busy server, however, understand that logging even a few items can consume a lot of server time and create a potentially very large log file.

Using debug logging

If basic logging fails to help you identify the cause of a DNS server problem, you can enable *debug logging*, which records packets sent and received by the DNS server. Debug logging generates a very significant amount of log traffic and corresponding server overhead, so you should use debug logging only if basic logging does not provide the information that you need to address the problem at hand.

To configure debug logging, open the DNS console, right-click the server, and choose Properties. Click the Debug Logging tab to display the Debug Logging page of the server's property sheet (see Figure 17-10). Use the Packet Direction group of controls to log incoming packets, outgoing packets, or both. Use the Transport protocol to choose which protocol(s) to log.

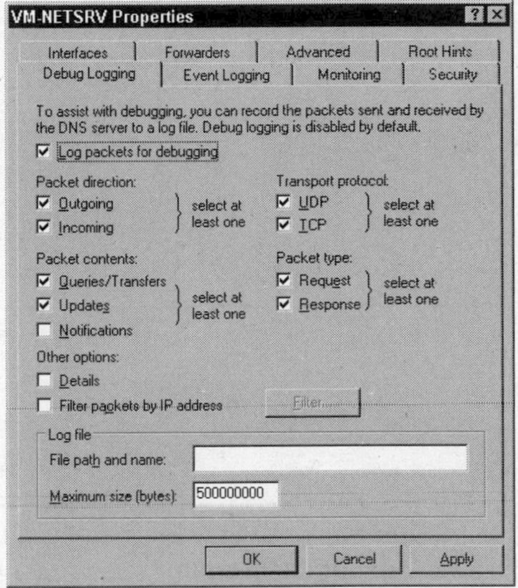

Figure 17-10: Configure extended logging on the Debug Logging page.

The Packet Contents and Packet Type groups of controls enable you to choose the types of packets that the DNS service logs. Enable the Details option if you want the entire contents of the packets logged rather than a subset of the contents.

If you're having problems with certain servers or clients, you can enable the Filter Packets by IP Address option, which causes the DNS service to log the IP addresses of the source and destination servers. You can then click Filter to specify a list of servers (by IP address) that are logged.

Finally, use the File Path and Name field to specify the path and file name for the log file and the Maximum Size field to specify the maximum log file size.

Monitoring and testing

The Monitoring property page for a DNS server enables you to issue test queries against the local server and recursive queries against other name servers. This helps you test the server and its capability to communicate successfully with other name servers. This is an extremely useful tool, as most other methods for this type of testing typically use a cumbersome command-line interface. To display the Monitoring page to perform testing, open the DNS console, right-click the server, choose Properties, and then click the Monitoring tab to display the Monitoring page, as shown in Figure 17-11.

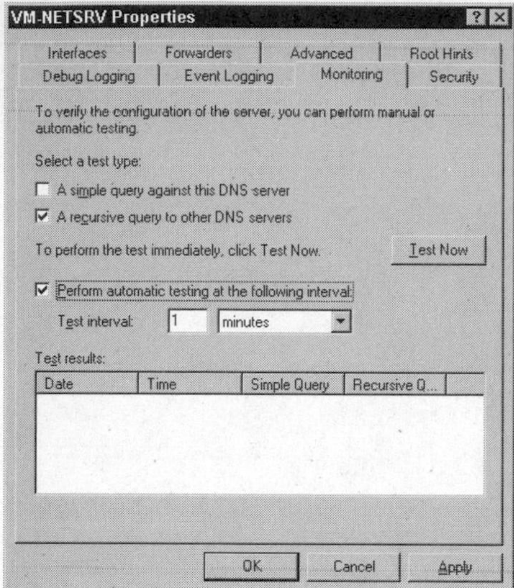

Figure 17-11: Use the Monitoring page to issue test queries.

The following list explains the options on the Monitoring page:

- ✦ **A Simple Query Against this DNS Server:** Choose this option to perform an iterative test against the local server.
- ✦ **A Recursive Query to Other DNS Servers:** Choose this option to perform a recursive query against other DNS servers (which start with the DNS servers defined in the local server's TCP/IP properties).
- ✦ **Perform Automatic Testing at the Following Interval:** Select this option to perform periodic, automatic testing by using the preceding two testing options.
- ✦ **Test Interval:** Specify the frequency of automatic tests.
- ✦ **Test Results:** This list shows the results of tests and includes the test date, time, and results.

Applying security

Windows Server 2003 provides the capability to restrict access to a DNS server and/or selected zones, enabling you to control who has the capability to modify the server, add records, remove records, and so on. You can configure security for a server overall only if the server is a domain controller participating in the Active Directory. You can't configure security on member servers that host the DNS service or on standalone DNS servers. In addition, you can configure security on individual zones only if the zones are stored in the AD (set up as AD-integrated zones).

To apply security to a server overall, open the DNS console and connect to the server. Right-click the server and choose Properties to display its property sheet. In addition to the property pages discussed in the preceding sections, you find a Security tab. Click the Security tab to display the Security page, which enables you to define the permissions that groups or users have within the DNS server. Security at the server level acts as the first line of defense in protecting the server in general and the zones housed on the server.

You also can configure security for individual zones as a second layer of security, enabling you to designate specific users or groups the capability to manage a given zone. Open the DNS console, right-click the zone in question, and choose Properties. Use the Security page in the zone's property sheet to configure security for the zone.

Managing the server and cache

You use the DNS console to manage the DNS server in addition to managing individual zones. The following lists common administrative tasks and explains how to accomplish them by using the DNS console:

✦ **Update data files:** The DNS service automatically stores changes to the data files at set intervals and whenever the service shuts down, writes changes in memory to disk. A good practice is to update the data files manually whenever you add a number of records or make other changes to ensure that those changes are written to disk in the event of a problem with the server that would otherwise prevent the updates from occurring. To update the data files within the DNS console, right-click the server and choose Update Server Data Files.

✦ **Stop, start, pause, resume, or restart the DNS service:** You can control the DNS service on the local computer through the Services branch of the Computer Management console (which you access by right-clicking My Computer and choosing Manage). You might find using the DNS console easier, however, particularly in managing a remote DNS server. In the DNS console, right-click the server, choose All Tasks from the context menu, and choose the desired action (Start, Stop, and so on).

✦ **Clear the cache:** If a server's cache becomes polluted with bad records or you're having problems correctly resolving queries, clearing the cache can fix the problem if the problem is related to the cached queries. In the DNS console, right-click the server and choose Clear Cache to clear the contents of the cache. Notice that this command does not affect the root hints defined by the `cache.dns` file.

Configuring Subdomains and Delegation

If yours is a small organization, you're likely to have only a single domain. Larger organizations, however, often segregate services and delegate responsibility and administration for different parts of the organization's namespace. Or you may simply be hosting the DNS records for another organization. You accomplish these tasks through *subdomains* and *delegation*.

A subdomain is a child of an existing domain. The domain `west.latinaccents.biz`, for example, is a subdomain of `latinaccents.biz`. The domain `west.west.latinaccents.biz` is a subdomain of `west.latinaccents.biz`. The `latinaccents.biz` domain serves as the primary domain for all of these. The `latinaccents.biz` name server could host the resource records for all its subdomains, providing centralized management of the organization's namespace. Queries for hosts in the subdomains would be handled by the `latinaccents.biz` name server(s). The `latinaccents.biz` domain, however, could also delegate the subdomains to other name servers, such as name servers hosted at the subdomain location. The domain `latinaccents.biz`—located in Florida—may, for example, delegate west.latinaccents.biz to the name servers for the support group located on the West coast. In this case, queries would come to the latinaccents.biz name server, which would refer the query to the west.latinaccents.biz subdomain. The only real difference is that, in the former example, all the zones and data reside on the latinaccents.biz server, and in the latter, they are parceled out to other servers as required by the domain structure.

Setting up subdomains

Whether or not you're hosting a subdomain on the primary name server for the organization or delegating it, the first step is to create the subdomain. You accomplish this task through the DNS console. In the console, open the server where you want to create the subdomain; then open the parent domain. To create the subdomain west.latinaccents.biz, for example, open the latinaccents.biz zone. Right-click the parent zone and choose New Domain. Windows Server 2003 prompts you for the subdomain name. Enter the single-part name (west in this example) and click OK. The subdomain appears as a subbranch under the parent domain. After you create the subdomain, you can begin adding records to it. Just right-click the subdomain and choose the type of record that you want to create. As in creating records for a parent domain, you can specify only the single-part name for the host. If you're creating a host record for jane.west.latinaccents.biz, for example, you would create a host record for jane in the west.latinaccents.biz subdomain.

Before creating resource records in a subdomain, verify that you have created the reverse-lookup zone for the subdomain. This enables the DNS service to automatically create pointer records for hosts that you define in the subdomain.

Delegating a subdomain

Rather than host a subdomain's records under the parent domain's name server, you may prefer to delegate the subdomain to another server. Assume, for example, that the Support group hosts its own DNS records on its own servers. In this case, you need to perform the following steps to delegate west.latinaccents.biz:

1. On the Support group's name server, create the zone west.latinaccents.biz and support reverse-lookup zone, as explained in the section, "Reverse lookup," earlier in this chapter; then populate the zone with the appropriate resource records for the hosts in west.latinaccents.biz.
2. On the parent name server hosting latinaccents.biz, open the DNS console and then open the latinaccents.biz zone. Right-click the zone and then choose New Delegation to start the New Delegation Wizard.
3. In the wizard, specify the delegated domain name (in this example, west). The wizard automatically assembles the FQDN for the delegated domain by using the parent domain as a postfix. Click Next.
4. On the Name Servers page, click Add to add the FQDN and IP address of the server(s) on which the subdomain's records are hosted. In this example, you'd specify the name and address of the server that hosts west.latinaccents.biz.
5. Repeat Step 4 to add other name servers that host the subdomain's records, click OK, and then click Finish to complete the process.

DNS and Active Directory

The Windows 2003 DNS service provides integration with the AD to provide to the DNS service the advantages inherent in the AD — security, ease-of-management, replication, and so on. In fact, DNS integration with the AD is required for domain controllers (DCs) because the Windows 2003 Netlogon service uses DNS for locating DCs. A DC can run the DNS service itself or rely on other servers in the domain to provide DNS services, but a name server that supports dynamic updates and that is authoritative for the domain must be present. (See the section "Dynamic DNS," later in this chapter, for more information on DDNS and dynamic updates.)

Integrating DNS in the AD provides a measure of fault tolerance for DNS. Because the DNS data for integrated zones is replicated throughout the DCs for the domain, any DC running the DNS service can handle client requests for resolution of names in the hosted domains. This means that you have no single point of failure for a given domain as long as it is hosted in an AD-integrated zone. One server can go offline, and others can continue to process requests for the domain. Changes to records in an AD-integrated zone also are automatically replicated to other DCs running the DNS service, simplifying administration. If you bring a new DC on line that is running the DNS service, the zone records are automatically replicated to the new DNS server. Synchronization of AD-integrated zones is also potentially more efficient than a standard zone transfer, as data is selectively transferred rather than transferring an entire zone.

Security, which was discussed in the section "Applying security," earlier in this chapter, is another important advantage to AD integration. You can apply access control lists (ACLs) to a server and to individual zones to define which users or groups have the capability to modify the server and records in the secured zones.

Only primary zones are supported for AD-integration. Secondary zones must be stored in standard zone files. By migrating all zones to the AD, however, you effectively eliminate the need for secondary zones, because the zones are replicated to other servers for redundancy and fault tolerance, the main purpose of secondary zones. If you maintain Windows NT-based DNS servers, however, you still need to rely on secondary zones.

Whenever you create a zone by using the DNS console, the wizard gives you the option of creating three types of zones: *AD-integrated*, *standard primary*, and *standard secondary*. Choose AD-integrated if you want to take advantage of the benefits offered by the AD for DNS.

The AD is a complex topic that requires quite a bit of explanation in its own right. Refer to Part III for a detailed explanation of the AD's structure, function, replication, and administration.

Dynamic DNS

Dynamic DNS (DDNS) enables a Windows 2003 DNS server to automatically update resource records for clients if their host names or IP addresses change. Host name changes can occur if the remote computer changes computer name or becomes a member of another domain (which implicitly changes its FQDN). The use of DHCP is another argument for DDNS. As DHCP leases expire, a client computer's address can and is likely to change. This makes maintaining accurate DNS records for hosts on the network that use DHCP for address allocation difficult. DDNS resolves the problem.

DDNS functions through a client-server mechanism. Windows 2000, 2003, and XP DHCP clients support DDNS and can directly request that a Windows 2003 DNS server update their host resource (A) records whenever the clients' IP addresses or host names change. Windows 2003 DHCP servers can also submit requests on behalf of clients, although a DHCP server can request an update to both the clients' host and pointer (PTR) records.

A Windows 2003 DHCP server also can act as a proxy for non-DDNS-capable DHCP clients to perform dynamic DNS updates. A Windows 2003 DHCP server can, for example, perform updates for Windows 9*x* and Windows NT clients, which do not natively support Dynamic DNS and, therefore, cannot submit requests to either the DHCP server or DNS server to update their resource records. Figure 17-12 shows how DHCP and DNS interact.

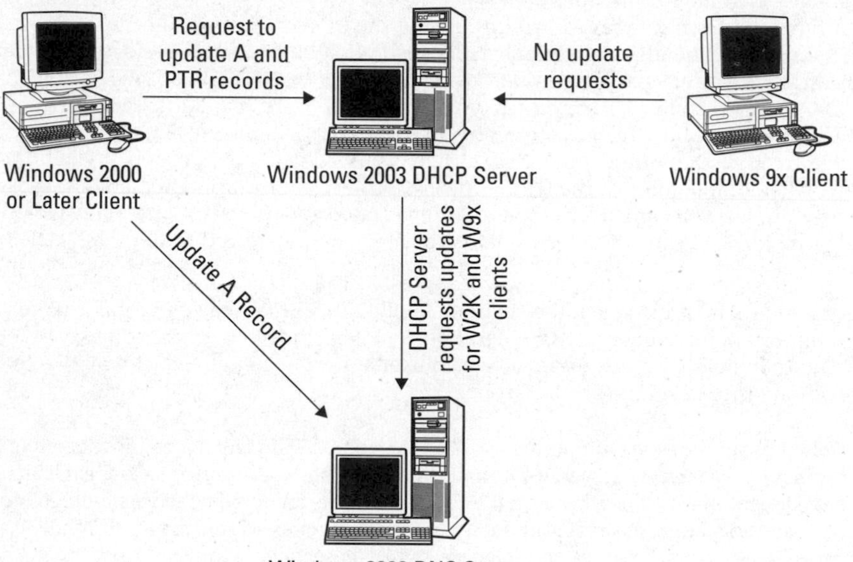

Figure 17-12: DHCP supports automatic updates to DNS if host name or IP address changes occur.

For a detailed discussion of configuring a Windows 2003 DHCP server to support DNS, see Chapter 16.

Configuring DDNS

Most of the configuration to support DDNS occurs on the client side. You do, however, have some configuration steps to take on the server side to implement DDNS. You enable dynamic updates on a zone-by-zone basis, and the types of updates permitted depend on whether the zone is stored in the AD. AD-integrated zones give you the additional option of permitting only secured updates, which use the ACL for the zone to determine who can perform an update. Standard zones not stored in the AD can be configured only for unsecured updates or no updates.

Windows Server 2003 clients by default attempt to perform an unsecured update and, failing that, attempt a secured update. If you're having problems getting client records to update from servers or clients outside of a domain, make sure that you have not configured the zone for secured updates only. For optimum security, you should avoid using a DC as a DHCP server, because updates from the DHCP server always succeed, even if the zone is configured for secure updates only.

You configure a zone's DDNS behavior through the zone's properties. Open the DNS console, right-click the zone, and choose Properties. The Allow Dynamic Updates option determines whether the server accepts dynamic updates for records in the zone. You can choose one of the following three options:

- **No:** Select this option to prevent DHCP clients or servers from updating resource records in the zone.
- **Yes:** Select this option to enable DHCP clients and servers, including those outside the domain, to perform unsecured updates to the zone's resource records. DHCP servers can also update pointer records for dynamically updated host records.
- **Only Secure Updates:** Select this option to require the DHCP client or server to authenticate in the domain to be capable of performing dynamic updates of host or pointer records.

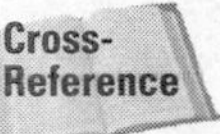

See Chapter 16 for information on how to configure a client for DDNS.

Configuring scavenging

As explained in the section "Domain records and zone files," earlier in this chapter, records can become stale in a zone. A notebook user's computer, for example, may update its host record in its zone, but then the user disconnects from the network without shutting down. The computer remains off the network for an extended period, but the computer's host record still remains in the zone. As a result, the record becomes stale and potentially points to the wrong IP address (or the user might change his computer's host name). You can configure Windows 2003 DNS to *scavenge* records, removing those that are stale.

Windows 2003 uses a timestamp to determine whether a record is stale. The server scans the data at an administrator-defined interval, checking the resource records' timestamps to determine whether they have exceeded the refresh interval. If so, the server scavenges the record (removes it from the zone). Scavenging by default applies only to dynamically created records and has no effect on records that you create manually. The DNS server, however, applies a timestamp to resource records that you create manually but sets the time stamp to zero to indicate that the record is not subject to scavenging. You can modify the value to enable the DNS service to scavenge these records as well.

You configure scavenging in two places: at the server level and at the zone level. At the server level, you enable scavenging globally for the server and set the scavenging frequency, or the frequency at which the server performs scavenging. The default value is seven days, and the minimum is one hour. To configure scavenging at the server level, open the DNS console, right-click the server, and choose Properties. Click the Advanced tab to display the Advanced property page. Select the Enable Automatic Scavenging of Stale Records option and then use the Scavenging Period control to specify how often the server should perform a scavenging operation. The more dynamic the network, the more frequently you should have the server perform scavenging. Choose a value that fits your network needs.

You also need to configure scavenging on a zone-by-zone basis. Scavenging can be applied only to primary zones. Open the DNS console, right-click the zone for which you want to configure scavenging, and choose Properties. On the zone's General property page, click Aging to open the Zone Aging/Scavenging Properties dialog box (see Figure 17-13).

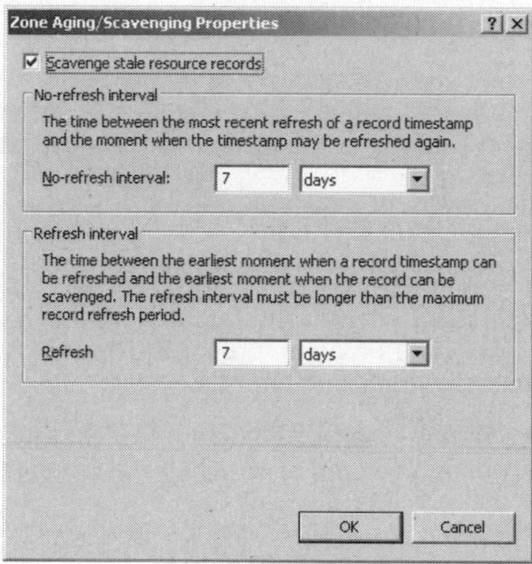

Figure 17-13: Configure the zone's scavenging properties in the Zone Aging/Scavenging Properties dialog box.

The dialog box contains the following two controls:

- **No-Refresh Interval:** This property essentially specifies the timestamp's time-to-live. Until this period expires, the record's time stamp can't be refreshed.
- **Refresh Interval:** This property defines the period of time that the timestamp can remain unrefreshed before the server scavenges the record.

Scavenging occurs automatically at the interval defined in the server's general scavenging properties. You can, however, manually initiate a scavenge. Open the DNS console, right-click the server, and choose Scavenge Stale Resource Records.

Windows Internet Name Service (WINS)

NetBIOS, which is described in Chapter 15, is a legacy API that has for many years served as the means by which you connect to file systems and network resources on corporate local area networks. But then along came TCP/IP and crashed the NetBIOS party, spiked the punch, and became the protocol of choice everywhere, not asking permission from authority higher up the OSI stack. As a result, many clients on a network cannot see the IP-flavored host names that map to IP addresses; instead, they can see only NetBIOS-flavored names. The solution? Map the NetBIOS names to IP addresses.

Windows Internet Name Service (WINS) was developed by Microsoft to provide a DNS-like NetBIOS Name Service (NBNS) to map NetBIOS names to IP addresses. The *Internet* in WINS is a little misleading, because a NetBIOS name on the Internet is like a goldfish trying to breathe in olive oil. But, in essence, it also signifies taking a NetBIOS name and turning it into a *neo-host* name that can be mapped to an IP address. And as long as IP rules supreme and you take the input/output out of NetBIOS, it is nothing more than a label, even at the functional or application levels of the network.

But WINS is more than just a name-IP address resolver. It enables centralized management of NetBIOS namespace data and eliminates the need to remotely manage multiple LMHOSTS files (which perform the same function for NetBIOS lookup that Hosts files perform for DNS lookup).

WINS also helps reduce NetBIOS broadcasts on the network to maximize bandwidth utilization, because clients can query the WINS server for a name-to-address mapping, enabling them to communicate directly with remote hosts rather than generating broadcast traffic on the network.

WINS is needed on old Windows networks because the only way that the down-level operating systems flag their presence is via NetBIOS, and in many respects, it has been convenient even since the days that TCP/IP first showed up. Imagine a Windows network where every server was listed under only its IP address.

WINS is also essential for getting those NetBIOS names resolved over TCP/IP subnets. NetBIOS is not routable, and it was never intended to be; nor are the primary protocols that carry NetBIOS names, such as NetBEUI (although they can be encapsulated in TCP/IP communication packets that can be routed, a practice often used to route SNA traffic over TCP/IP). The only way then for NetBIOS to coexist in the routable world of IP addresses and IP internetworks is via WINS.

Note WINS communications take place in datagrams over the UDP port 137, which is reserved for NBNS.

Microsoft's strategy, in line with all the other Internet builders, is to abolish reliance on NetBIOS and to support TCP/IP and its successors as the only routable protocol on all networks. This strategy enables network administrators to gradually abolish NetBIOS from their networks as they replace down-level or NetBIOS-named computers and devices and enables them to switch to native mode Windows Server 2003 deployment, which is more secure and rich.

But for many companies, expect WINS and NetBIOS to be around for many years. In fact, we predict that the last vestiges of NetBIOS, and thus WINS, are going to vanish no earlier than 2005. Change is not an overnight phenomenon in large corporate environments, where huge investments in corporate intranets are also underway. In fact, had it not been for Y2K, many companies would have kept Windows NT 3.51 around. The reasons to keep WINS around are patent if you consider the following two inescapable facts:

✦ **Investment in legacy systems.** NetBIOS has been the "driving" force on Windows networks since the advent of the networkable personal computer. In all those years, Windows has become the pervasive desktop operating system, and it is now poised to become the dominant server operating system.

  Our guess is that no one really knows how many copies of Windows are running in the world. And figures range from tens of millions to hundreds of millions. So a huge investment in legacy, or "so-called" *down-level*, Windows operating systems still exists, from simple clients to mega-servers, and is likely to remain so for many years to come. In so far as these systems, especially the servers, still use NetBIOS names, WINS is needed to resolve these names into IP addresses. In short . . . the best of both worlds — an entrenched namespace coexisting with an indispensable protocol.

✦ **Investment in legacy applications.** Many applications still use NetBIOS names in their code. So NetBIOS remains a fact on these networks until all applications are no longer dependent on NetBIOS or until they can be removed from your network and information systems.

How WINS Works

All Windows 9*x* and later operating systems can request services of WINS. To request a name-IP address resolution, the client queries any WINS server designated to it on the network. It tries to contact WINS servers in the order assigned in the WINS address list in its TCP/IP configuration. The client tries to connect to the WINS server three times before giving up and moving onto the next WINS server in the list.

After the client boots and authenticates on the network, it registers its name and IP address with the designated WINS server. If for some reason the client does not register automatically, the registration takes place whenever the client next makes a query or targets a folder on a remote server.

The process to connect to a NetBIOS name by using TCP/IP is as described in the following steps:

1. Computer MCSQL01 logs onto the network and makes a registration request with WINS. The NetBIOS name and IP address are thus recorded to the WINS database.
2. You come along and you need to connect workstation `SQLCLIENT` (at `10.5.4.132`) to `\\MCSQL01\SHARE1` (at `100.50.2.32`), which you see in the browse list. `SQLCLIENT` needs to make a request of the WINS server for the IP address of `MCSQL01` to effect a connection to the server via TCP/IP. In other words, the client needs to turn the target address `\\MCSQL01\MYSHARE` into `\\100.50.2.32\MYSHARE` because the only way to connect to the remote server, via several routers, is TCP/IP.
3. If the WINS server is unavailable, `SQLCLIENT` tries two more times before trying the next WINS server in its list. Assuming that `MCSQL01` happens to register with WINS and an IP address exists, the resolve is successful and the connection can be established.
4. Finally (and we do not mean to be cheeky because we have needed to do this on many occasions with the old WINS), if you cannot see or connect to the share, you can phone the owner or admin of the server and ask for the IP address. For network administrators to do this to troubleshoot connections is okay. For *users* to do this every time that they need a file or a printer, however, is not okay.

WINS registration

The WINS architecture is very different from that of DNS. WINS maintains a database of name-IP address mappings. It is not hierarchical. After a client registers a mapping, the WINS server issues a successful registration message to the client. Encapsulated in that message is a time-to-live (TTL) value, which is like a “lease” on the name, held in trust by WINS for a certain period of time.

But what if the name is already registered with WINS and the client makes a new registration attempt, or another client tries to register with the same NetBIOS name? WINS does not ignore the request; it sends out a verification request to the currently registered owner of the mapping. The request goes out three times at 500-millisecond intervals. If it has more than one IP address for the client, which is often the case on NT, 2000, or Windows Server 2003 servers, WINS tries each address that it has for the registered owner. This verification regimen continues until all IP addresses are “called” or the owner responds.

If the owner responds, the client requesting the registration gets a polite decline. If the owner does not respond, however, the client requesting registration gets free passage.

Mapping renewal

WINS mappings are not persistent, and the WINS database is in a constant state of change. Leases on mappings are assigned on a temporary basis to enable other computers to claim the mapping later. The short-term lease method also enables clients with DHCP-assigned IP addresses to register their new addresses with WINS.

If the WINS client remains online, it needs to renew its lease before expiration on the WINS server. The client achieves this task by renewing automatically after one-eighth of the TTL has elapsed. If the client does not receive a renewal notification from the server, it continues to attempt renewal every two minutes, until half the TTL has elapsed. After that, the client moves on to the next WINS in its list and begins the renewal attempt with that server. WINS is a multimaster replication architecture, and which of the WINS servers honors the WINS registration request doesn't matter as far as the client and the networking-resolving process are concerned. If the next WINS in the list fails to honor the request, however, the client "hits" the leading server again.

On a successful registration renewal, the client attempts to renegotiate the next lease renewal after 50 percent of the TTL has elapsed.

If WINS clients are powered down normally — that is, by issuing the shutdown command — they send a message to WINS requesting release of the mapping. The message includes the entire mapping NetBIOS-IP address. The WINS server honors the request as long as the records check out. In other words, the mapping must exist or the values for IP address and name must be the same as in the message. If the request checks out, the record is *tombstoned* (marked for deletion); otherwise, it remains in the database.

The New WINS

As important as WINS has been for many diverse Windows-based networks, the WINS service on NT 4.0 is not something that we look back on fondly, and for many with thousands of users spread over dozens of subnets, it has been more a case of WINS and "LOSSES."

Although WINS performed with a measure of fault-tolerance on small intranets, it often let us down on large networks, losing connections, missing replication with its peers, and collecting garbage that needed to be manually deleted from the database. Often, intra-domain communications between sites would break down because records were not updated and the clients could not succeed with connections to critical services in other domains. Many network managers pleaded with Microsoft to rebuild the WINS service, and Microsoft did so with Windows 2000 Server. So now, WINS is a very different animal under Windows 2000 and Windows Server 2003.

The new features do not mean much to new administrators working with WINS in Windows 2003, but they are welcome news for the old and the brave among you. Two important features are worthy of mention in this chapter: *persistent connections* and *manual tombstoning*.

Persistent connections

WINS should never be implemented as a single-server solution unless a very small collection of users depends on the service and the business can afford the downtime and collapse of service level. On networks serving a lot of users or small offices that need to maintain critical connections across the intranet, WINS should be implemented in groups of two or more servers. Not all servers need to be on the same subnet, however, because should a local WINS fail, the client can hit a secondary on another subnet because it already knows the static address (via DHCP) of the secondary WINS server.

WINS servers thus coexist as loose clusters. (They interoperate but do not really function as a single logical unit.) After a client registers with WINS or whenever WINS tombstones a record, the information is replicated out to WINS servers that are configured as replication partners. Often, replication on the old WINS on NT 4.0 would fail because requests to re-establish would not take place. This would result in widely dispersed WINS databases being inconsistent and out of touch with each other.

Users on the intranet depend on the maintenance of connections between clients and servers placed at opposite ends of the intranet. If WINS servers cannot comply with requests, the user usually gets the `Network Path not Found` error message, and the attempted connection fails. This message may seem as if the host is down, but often it is WINS that is at fault, so first try to `ping` the host by name to confirm a WINS problem before anything else.

Tip Always keep a database of your static IP addresses handy. If you can `ping` the host that is not being resolved by WINS and you can manually map to a known share on the host, for example, such as `\\192.168.4.8\shares`, you can be almost certain that WINS is in trouble.

Windows 2003 WINS can be configured to request a permanent connection across the intranet with any or all replication partners. Persistent replication offers two significant advantages.

Significant overhead associated with starting and stopping connections is reduced. Legacy WINS would need to re-establish connections with replication partners every time that it needed to replicate. A chance always exists on a very large intranet that a connection cannot be established automatically and requires human intervention.

The speed of replication has also been greatly increased, because the updates can be sent directly to the replication partner without needing to go through the motions of first establishing connections.

Manual tombstoning

You can now manually mark records for deletion by using the manual tombstoning feature in Windows 2003 WINS. This means that manual deletion requests get orderly and consistent propagation to replication partners. On Windows NT WINS, manual deletes on one server were problematic, because a chance existed that a replication partner could re-establish the previously deleted record.

If you manually tombstone a record, the information is propagated to all replication partners (which occurs quickly with the persistent connection option). Tombstoned records are deleted from all servers after the propagation and after all partners have received the tombstoned records.

WINS Installation and Configuration

WINS does not require a dedicated server or your most powerful CPU. The service can also be installed on a DNS, DHCP, or DC server — even on a Remote Access Service (RAS) server.

Installing WINS

To install WINS, the server needs a static IP address — preferably one dedicated to WINS traffic. So you can either *multi-home* the machine (that is, install more than one NIC) or assign another IP address to a single interface.

If you did not install WINS with the operating system, follow these steps:

1. Load the Add or Remove Programs applet from the Control Panel.
2. Click the Add/Remove Windows Components button. The Windows Components Wizard launches.
3. Go to the Components list box, select Networking Services, and then click the Details button. The Networking Services checklist box loads.
4. Scroll down and select the WINS option. (Do not uncheck anything; doing so only removes the other components.) Click OK and then click Next to begin the installation of WINS. After the installation, you need to configure the service.
5. Click Start ⇨ Control Panel ⇨ Network Connections. Right-click Local Area Network Connection and select Properties. The Local Area Connection Properties dialog box opens.

If the server is multi-homed, clicking Network Connections in the Start menu opens only a submenu. Right-click on the menu the network interface that you want to configure; then choose Properties.

6. Select TCP/IP from the Connections Protocols list on the first tab and then select Properties. In the Properties dialog box, that appears click the Advanced button. The Advanced TCP/IP Settings dialog box opens.
7. Select the WINS tab and then click the Add button. Enter the IP address installed on the local NIC that you are using. Repeat the process to add a secondary WINS IP address. Close the Advanced TCP/IP Settings dialog box and click OK all the way out. Installation is complete.

Configuring WINS

WINS, as does DNS and many other services in Windows Server 2003, now uses the Microsoft Management Console (MMC) for configuration and management. To launch the WINS snap-in, go to Administrative Tools and select the WINS option or (easier) open the Run dialog box and run the `winsmgmt.msc` shortcut. The WINS snap-in is as shown in Figure 17-14.

One of the perks of WINS is that clients register themselves with the service, and for the most part, you do not need to manually enter mappings. Exceptions do exist, however, one of them being non-WINS clients and static entries.

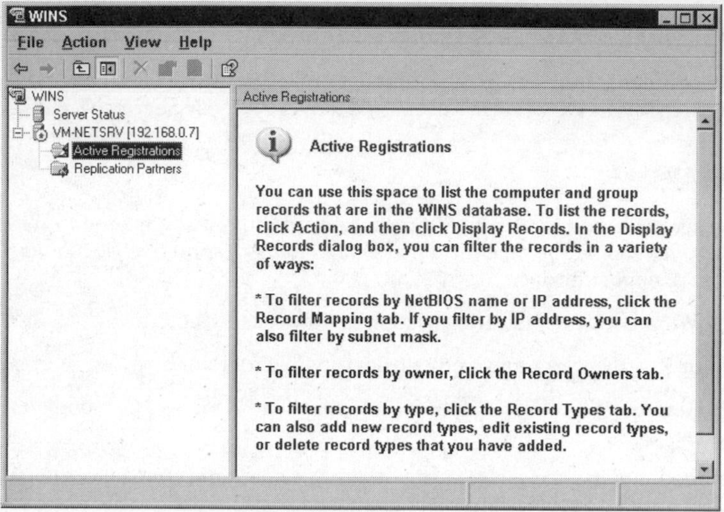

Figure 17-14: The WINS MMC snap-in.

Static entries

By entering static mappings, you ensure that WINS clients can resolve the IP addresses of non-WINS clients. Non-WINS clients include machines running under other operating systems, networks, network devices, domains, and so on. You can even insert a static IP address for another WINS server, if the connection to that WINS server is unreliable and you cannot afford to have the server lose a lease and not be capable of renewing it.

To create a static mapping, open the WINS console as explained in the previous section and follow these steps:

1. Right-click the Active Registrations node on the WINS tree. Choose New Static Mapping from the context menu.

2. In the New Static Mapping dialog box, type the name of the target to be resolved in the Computer Name field.

   Although you can add a scope name in the optional NetBIOS Scope field, this field should not be used because NetBIOS scopes are not recommended. The support is included for advanced NetBIOS solutions and applications.

3. From the Type drop-down list, select the type of name to be resolved. The following list explains the static entry types:

   - **Unique:** This is a unique name that can be mapped to a single IP address. Use this type if you need to add a static mapping for a server — usually another WINS server.

   - **Group:** Choose this type for a name that maps to a group. A group is a logical unit on the intranet. Group members, regardless of their nature, usually have their own IP addresses, but these do not need to be stored in WINS.

   - **Domain Name:** Choose this type to map an IP address to a domain name.

  - **Internet Group:** Choose this type to group resources, such as routers, hubs, and printers. You can store up to 25 members in an Internet group.
  - **Multihomed:** Choose this type for the name of a host that has more than one IP address. (*Multihomed* usually refers to a host with more than one network interface card, but Windows Server 2003 can assign multiple addresses to a single interface.)

4. In the IP Address field, enter the IP address of the client and click OK to store the entry.

The proxy agent

The *WINS proxy agent* extends the WINS services to non-WINS clients by listening for their name-registration requests and broadcast-resolution requests and then forwarding them to the WINS server. To set up this service, you need to tinker in the registry.

Open the Registry Editor and go to the following subkey:

```
HKEY_LOCAL_MACHINE\SYSTEM\CurrentControlSet\Services\NetBT\Parameters
```

Under the `Parameters` key, you find the entry for `EnableProxy`. Change this value to `1` (enabled). Unfortunately, you must then restart the server.

After it's enabled, the proxy agent forwards the non-WINS client's broadcasts requesting name registration to the WINS server. The name does not get registered; the intention of the proxy is to check that the name is not already registered.

Whenever the agent detects a name-resolution broadcast, it checks its NetBIOS name cache and attempts to resolve the name to an IP address. If the name is not cached, the agent forwards the broadcast as a resolve request to the WINS server. The WINS server responds to the agent, and the agent then responds to the non-WINS client.

Configuring Windows Clients for DNS and WINS

Configuring Windows clients to use DNS and WINS is a relatively simple task. It primarily means configuring the clients with the appropriate DNS and WINS server IP addresses. If you're using DHCP, you can configure the DHCP server to provide the DNS and WINS server data to the DHCP clients automatically.

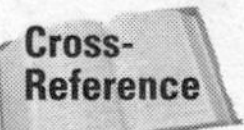

To learn more about DHCP and how to configure both DHCP servers and clients, see Chapter 16.

If you're not using DHCP or need to configure the DNS or WINS settings separately from the dynamically assigned IP address on the client, you can configure the client's DNS/WINS settings manually. To do so, log on to the client computer and open the properties for the client's TCP/IP connection. On the General page, locate the TCP/IP protocol in the list of installed components and choose Properties to display the TCP/IP property page shown in Figure 17-15.

If you select the Obtain an IP Address Automatically option, you can select the Obtain DNS Server Addresses Automatically option to receive the DNS server address list from the DHCP server. If you prefer, you can specify the addresses explicitly by choosing the Use the Following DNS Server Addresses option and then filling in the IP addresses of the preferred and alternate server. The client resolver attempts to resolve through the preferred server first, and if the preferred server fails to respond, the client tries the alternate server.

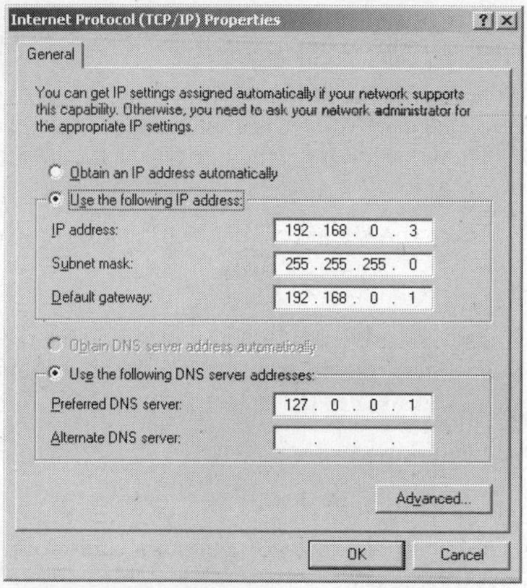

Figure 17-15: Configure DNS and WINS settings through the connection's property page.

To configure additional DNS properties, click Advanced and then click the DNS tab to display the DNS property page, as shown in Figure 17-16. As the figure shows, you can specify more than two DNS servers if you want and change the order of DNS servers in the list. The resolver tries the DNS servers in order from top to bottom.

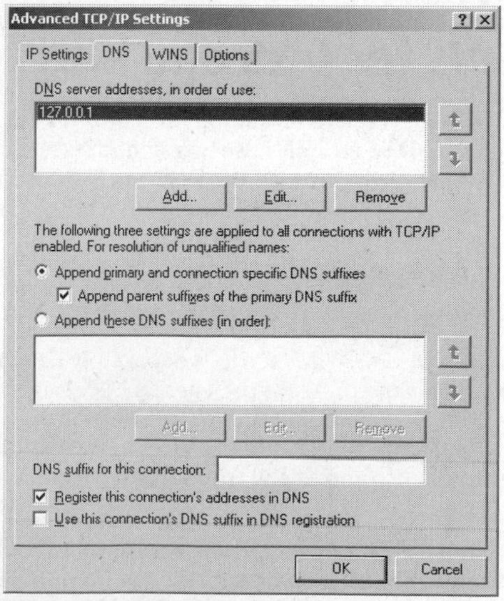

Figure 17-16: Use the DNS page to configure additional DNS options.

The following list explains the options on the DNS page:

✦ **Append Primary and Connection Specific DNS Suffixes:** Select this option to append the primary DNS suffix and connection-specific DNS suffix to unqualified host names for resolution. You define the primary DNS suffix for the computer through the computer's Network Identification property page (which you access by right-clicking My Computer, choosing Properties, and clicking Network Identification). The primary DNS suffix applies globally to the system unless overridden by the connection-specific DNS suffix, which you set in the property DNS Suffix for This Connection (see the following option). Assume, for example, that your primary suffix is `latinaccents.biz` and your connection-specific DNS suffix is `west.latinaccents.biz`. You query for the unqualified hostname `tia`. This option then causes Windows Server 2003 to attempt to resolve `tia.latinaccents.biz` and `tia.west.latinaccents.biz`. If you have no connection-specific DNS suffix specified, Windows Server 2003 attempts to resolve only `tia.latinaccents.biz`.

✦ **Append Parent Suffixes of the Primary DNS Suffix:** This option determines whether the resolver attempts resolution of unqualified names up to the parent level domain for your computer. Assume, for example, that your computer's primary DNS suffix is `west.latinaccents.biz` and you attempt to resolve the unqualified hostname `jane`. The resolver would attempt to resolve `jane.west.latinaccents.biz` and `jane.latinaccents.biz` (attempting to resolve at the parent level as well as the computer's domain level).

✦ **Append These DNS Suffixes in Order:** Use this option to append only the specified DNS suffixes for resolving unqualified names.

✦ **DNS Suffix for this Connection:** Use this option to specify a DNS suffix for the connection that is different from the primary DNS suffix defined in the computer's Network Identification property page.

✦ **Register this Connection's Addresses in DNS:** Select this option to have the client submit a request to the DNS server to update its host (A) record when its host name changes or IP address changes. The client submits the full computer name specified in the Network Identification tab of the System Properties sheet along with its IP address to the DNS server. You can view the System properties through the System object in the Control Panel, or you can right-click My Computer and choose Properties.

✦ **Use this Connection's DNS Suffix in DNS Registration:** Select this option to have the client submit a request to the DNS server to update its host record whenever the host name changes or IP address changes. The difference from the preceding option is that this option registers the client by using the first part of the computer name specified in the System properties, along with the DNS suffix specified by the DNS Suffix for this Connection option on the DNS page. You can use this option along with the preceding option to register two different FQDNs for the host.

Configuring Windows NT and Windows 9*x* clients for DNS is very similar to configuring Windows 2000/XP/Server 2003 clients. Right-click Network Neighborhood and choose Properties, or open the Network object in the Control Panel. Locate and double-click TCP/IP and then click DNS to set the DNS properties.

Using Hosts and LMHOSTS Files for Name Resolution

DNS servers resolve host names to IP addresses, and WINS servers primarily resolve NetBIOS names to IP addresses. In some cases, however, the capability to resolve host names to addresses without contacting a DNS or WINS server is helpful. You may, for example, have several hosts on the local network with host names and addresses that don't change, so you have no real need to put a load on the local name server for resolution if you can avoid it. Or you may not have a name server available for some reason but still need to enable an application to resolve host names.

Windows Server 2003 offers two methods for resolving host names to addresses that you can use in conjunction with or in place of name servers to provide name resolution. These two methods rely on ASCII files to store a database of host-to-address entries, just as the original ARPANET relied on the Hosts file for name resolution. You can use a local `Hosts` file in conjunction with or in place of DNS and a local `LMHOSTS` file in conjunction with or in place of WINS.

Using a Hosts file for name resolution

A *`Hosts` file* maintains a host table that maps host names to IP addresses. Windows can look up entries in the `Hosts` file to resolve names without needing to query a DNS server for resolution. Windows Server 2003 creates a file named `Hosts` in the `\%systemroot%\system32\drivers\etc` folder. `Hosts` is an ASCII file that you can edit in Notepad or any other word processor. The file uses the same format as the `Hosts` file on 4.3 BSD Unix (stored in `/etc/hosts`) and by default includes an entry that maps `localhost` to `127.0.0.1` (which is used for loopback testing and troubleshooting).

You should make a backup copy of the `Hosts` file before modifying it in case you experience any problems in modifying the file. Do not change or remove the entry for localhost.

Entries in the Hosts file take the format *`IP Address`* <tab> *`host name`*. You can specify more than one host name for a given IP address, but you must use multiple entries for hosts in different domains, each entry on its own line. Entries in `Hosts` are case-sensitive, so in the following example, the first two entries enable a correct resolution if the user specifies the host name in either uppercase or lowercase:

```
192.160.0.124     joe.latinaccents.biz
192.160.0.124     JOE.LATINACCENTS.BIZ
192.168.0.203     jane.west.latinaccents.biz
```

You can include a single host name for each entry or specify multiple host names for a single IP address if they fall in the same domain. The following, for example, are valid entries:

```
192.168.0.224     me     tarzan  jim.west.latinaccents.biz
192.168.0.198     you    jane    jane.east.latinaccents.biz
```

Each of the entries in this example specify three host names for each IP address.

Windows Server 2003 parses the entries in the `Hosts` file in sequential order until it finds a match. You can speed up lookup time by placing the most often-used host-name entries at the top of the file.

Using the LMHOSTS file for name resolution

Windows Server 2003 automatically resolves NetBIOS names for computers running TCP/IP on a local network. You can use an `LMHOSTS` file to resolve IP addresses of computers on other networks to which yours is connected by a gateway if a WINS server isn't available.

`LMHOSTS` is an ASCII file, with the entry format similar to entries in a `Hosts` file. In addition, `LMHOSTS` supports special keywords that are explained later in this section. Windows Server 2003 includes a sample `LMHOSTS` file in `\%systemroot%\system32\drivers\etc`. As with the `Hosts` file, you should make a backup copy of `LMHOSTS` before modifying it.

Windows Server 2003 parses each line in `LMHOSTS` sequentially at startup, which means that you should place often-accessed names at the top of the file for best performance. Following are a few rules for structuring an `LMHOSTS` file:

- Each entry must include the IP address in the first column, with the NetBIOS name in the second column. Additional keywords, if any, appear in subsequent columns. Columns are separated by at least one space or tab character. Some `LMHOSTS` keywords follow entries, while others appear on their own lines (discussed later in this section).
- Each entry must reside on a separate line.
- Comments begin with the pound (#) character, and special `LMHOSTS` keywords also begin with the # character. Reduce comments to a minimum to improve parsing performance. Place often-accessed entries near the top of the file for best performance.
- The `LMHOSTS` file is static. As with the `Hosts` file, you must manually update the file to create new entries or modify existing ones.

Windows Server 2003 TCP/IP reads the `LMHOSTS` file at system startup, and entries designated as preloaded by the `#PRE` keyword are read into the name cache at that time. Other entries are read only after broadcast name-resolution queries fail. The entire file is parsed at each query, so you should place often-used names near the top of the file and reduce comments to a minimum to improve performance.

You can include the following special keywords in an `LMHOSTS` file:

- **`#PRE`**: Preloads the entry into the name cache at startup. If you want names stored in a remote `LMHOSTS` file to be added to the name cache at startup, use the `#INCLUDE` and `#PRE` statements in combination, as in the following example:

```
#INCLUDE      \\srv1\public\lmhosts      #PRE
```

- **`#DOM:`*`<domain>`***: Designates remote domain controllers located across one or more routers. Entries that use the `#DOM` keyword are added to a special Internet workgroup name cache that causes Windows Server 2003 TCP/IP to forward requests for domain controllers to remote domain controllers as well as local domain controllers. The following example identifies a domain controller named *`server1`* in the domain `west.latinaccents.biz` and preloads the entry into the name cache at startup:

```
192.168.0.212   server1   #PRE   #DOM:west.latinaccents.biz
```

✦ #INCLUDE<*filename*>: Includes entries from separate LMHOSTS file. Use #INCLUDE to include entries from a common, shared LMHOSTS file or your own set of entries stored on your own computer. If you reference a remote LMHOSTS file on a server outside of your network in an #INCLUDE statement, you must also include an entry for the IP address of the remote server in the LMHOSTS file before the #INCLUDE statement that references it. Do not use #INCLUDE to reference an LMHOSTS file on a redirected network drive unless your drive mappings remain the same from one session to another. Otherwise, use the UNC path for the file. The following example includes an LMHOSTS file from a network server:

```
#INCLUDE   \\server1\public\Lmhosts     #Includes shared Lmhosts file
```

✦ #BEGIN_ALTERNATE: Signals the beginning of a *block inclusion,* which is a block of multiple #INCLUDE statements. The statements within the block designate primary and alternate locations for the included file, and the alternate locations are checked if the primary file is unavailable. Successful loading of any entry in the block causes the block to succeed, and subsequent entries in the block are skipped. You can include multiple block inclusions within an LMHOSTS file. Following is an example of a block inclusion:

```
#BEGIN_ALTERNATE
#INCLUDE     \\server1\public\lmhosts        #Primary source
#INCLUDE     \\server2\public\lmhosts        #Alternate source
#INCLUDE     \\netserv\shared\lmhosts        #Alternate source
#END_ALTERNATE
```

Tip

Addresses of servers specified in a block inclusion must be preloaded through entries earlier in the file. Entries not preloaded are ignored.

✦ #END_ALTERNATE: Signals the end of a block of multiple #INCLUDE statements.

✦ \0xnn: Use this keyword to specify nonprinting characters in NetBIOS names. Enclose the NetBIOS name in quotation marks and use the \0xnn keyword to specify the hexadecimal value of the nonprinting character. The hexadecimal notation applies to only one character in the name. The name must be padded to a total of 16 characters, with the hexadecimal notation as the 16th character. The following is an example:

```
192.168.0.89    "janetrs   \0x14"     #Uses special character
```

Summary

In this chapter, you learn that DNS provides the primary means through which Windows Server 2003 clients resolve host names to IP addresses. The client's computer uses a *resolver* to request resolution of a name from one or more DNS servers. The client can also use a Hosts file to statically map names to addresses and bypass the need to access a DNS server for name resolution.

DNS in Windows Server 2003 is dynamic and enables clients and DNS servers alike to request that a DNS server that is authoritative for the client's zone update the client's host and pointer records. A client can directly request an update of its host record, and a DNS server can request an update of both the host and associated pointer record on behalf of the client. Zones that are stored in Active Directory can be secured through ACLs to require authentication before dynamic updates are permitted.

WINS provides the same capabilities for resolving NetBIOS names to addresses that DNS provides for host names. Windows Server 2003 includes a WINS server service that enables a Windows Server 2003 server to function as a WINS server and also integrates DNS and WINS to provide additional capabilities. Although WINS is not always an optimum solution, it nevertheless offers several advantages for name resolution where NetBIOS names are still used.

✦ ✦ ✦

Routing and Remote Access

In This Chapter

Understanding Windows 2003 Remote Access Services (RAS)

Understanding RAS connection types and protocols

Configuring RAS

Configuring a router

Configuring a VPN server

Using Multilink and BAP

Using RADIUS

Applying a remote access policy

Examining security issues

Configuring dial-up networking connections

Using Internet Connection Sharing and Internet Connection Firewall

Troubleshooting RAS installations

Connecting to the Internet

This chapter covers the remote access services provided with Windows Server 2003 that enable dial-up access (client and server) for remote connectivity, including dial-up connections to the Internet. It also covers the many features in Routing and Remote Access Service (RRAS) that enable Windows 2003 to function as a router and limited firewall.

Windows 2003 RAS and Telephony Services

RAS stands for Remote Access Services. In Windows 2003, RAS enables Windows 2003 clients to dial other systems for access to remote networks, including the Internet, and enables Windows 2003 computers to act as dial-up servers for remote clients. The Routing and Remote Access Service (RRAS) enables Windows Server 2003 to function as a router. RAS and RRAS are integrated into a single service in Windows 2003. This chapter examines the dial-up networking features in RRAS that enable a Windows 2003 computer to function as both a dial-up server and dial-up client.

The following sections provide an overview of these RRAS features. Later sections explain protocol, security, and configuration issues.

Overview of Windows 2003 RRAS

Remote access enables a client computer to connect to a remote computer or network and access the resources of the remote computer or network as if they were local. For example, users who are frequently on the road can access the company file server(s), printers, mail system, and other resources from remote locations. Clients also can use remote access services to connect to public networks such as the Internet. Figure 18-1 illustrates one implementation of remote access.

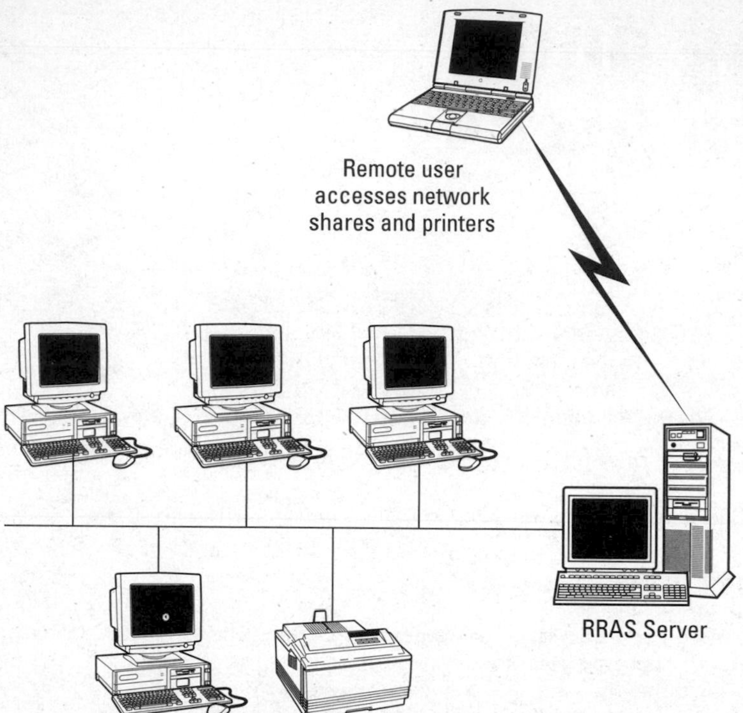

Figure 18-1: RRAS enables remote users to connect to the local computer or network and supports dial-out connections from Windows 2003 clients.

The Routing and Remote Access Service in Windows 2003 provides three primary functions:

✦ **Dial-up client:** You can use RRAS to create and establish dial-up connections to remote networks, including the Internet, through a variety of media such as a modem, ISDN, infrared, parallel ports, serial connection, X.25, and ATM. Windows 2003 dial-up clients support a wide range of authentication protocols and other connectivity options, which are discussed in depth later in this chapter. Support for tunneling protocols enables clients to establish secure connections to remote networks through public networks such as the Internet.

✦ **Dial-up server:** A Windows Server 2003 can function as a dial-up server, allowing remote clients to connect to the local server, and optionally to the local network, through the same types of media support for dial-out connections (see previous). You can also use RRAS to support terminal service client sessions because RRAS issues an IP address to the connecting clients and binds the necessary protocols to the RAS connection.

Windows 2003 supports several authentication protocols and can authenticate users against local or domain user accounts, or it can use Remote Authentication Dial In User Service (RADIUS), an industry standard authentication mechanism. Once connected, a remote user can browse, print, map drives, and perform essentially all other functions possible from either the local server or local area network.

✦ **Routing services:** The routing components of RRAS enable Windows Server 2003 to function as a unicast and multicast router. Windows 2003 provides for routing, packet filtering, connection sharing, demand-dial routing, and several other features that make it a good choice for LAN and WAN routing. Windows 2003 also adds limited firewall capability.

Although Windows 2003 RRAS integrates dial-up networking and routing into a single service, they are treated as separate issues in this book because of the different focus for each.

One of the key benefits of Windows 2003 RRAS is its integration with the Windows 2003 operating system. On the client side, integration means that once a remote connection is established, the client can access resources on the server transparently as if they were local resources. The client can map remote shares to local drive letters, map and print to remote printers, and so on. Except in very rare circumstances, applications can use remote resources seamlessly without modification to make them RAS- or network-aware.

On the server side, integration means that Windows 2003 can use a single authentication mechanism to authenticate users both locally and from remote locations. RRAS can authenticate against the local computer's user accounts or accounts in the domain, or it can use an external authentication mechanism such as RADIUS. Through its support for RADIUS, Windows 2003 RRAS enables a Windows Server 2003 to function as a gateway of sorts to the network while offloading authentication to another server, which could be any RADIUS platform including a UNIX server.

Remote Authentication Dial-In User Service (RADIUS) is a standard, cross-platform protocol for authentication commonly used for dial-in authentication.

Windows 2003 RRAS also provides close integration with Active Directory (AD). This AD integration provides users with the replication of remote access settings, including access permissions, callback options, and security policies, among others. AD integration also means simplified administration with other AD-related services and properties.

As you learn later in the section "RAS Connection Types and Protocols," Windows 2003 RRAS supports a wide range of connection protocols, including Point-to-Point Protocol PPP, Serial Line Internet Protocol (SLIP), and Microsoft RAS Protocol. Windows 2003 RRAS supports multiple authentication methods, including Microsoft Challenge Handshake Authentication Protocol (MS-CHAP), Extensible Authentication Protocol (EAP), Challenge Handshake Authentication Protocol (CHAP), Shiva Password Authentication Protocol (SPAP), and Password Authentication Protocol (PAP). Network protocols supported include TCP/IP, IPX/SPX, and AppleTalk to support Microsoft, Unix, NetWare, and Macintosh resources and clients.

New features of Windows 2003 RRAS

If you're familiar with RAS or RRAS in Windows NT or Windows 2000, you'll find all of those same features in Windows 2003 RRAS. You'll also find several enhancements to existing features along with many new features, including those discussed in the following sections.

AD integration

As mentioned previously, Windows 2003 RRAS integrates with the Active Directory (AD). AD integration enables client settings to be replicated throughout the organization to provide expanded access by clients and easier administration. Integration with the AD also can simplify administration by enabling you to browse and manage multiple RRAS servers through the AD-aware RRAS management console snap-in, providing a single point of management for RRAS services in an organization.

Bandwidth Allocation Protocol and Bandwidth Allocation Control Protocol

The Bandwidth Allocation Protocol (BAP) and Bandwidth Allocation Control Protocol (BACP) enable Windows 2003 RAS to dynamically add or remove links in a multilink PPP connection as bandwidth requirements for the connection change. When bandwidth utilization becomes heavy, RAS can add links to accommodate the increased load and enhance performance. When bandwidth utilization decreases, RAS can remove links to make the connection more cost efficient. You configure BAP policies through a remote access policy that you can apply to individual users, groups, or an entire organization.

MS-CHAP version 2

Previous versions of RAS supported Microsoft Challenge Handshake Authentication Protocol (MS-CHAP) to authenticate remote clients. MS-CHAP v2 provides stronger security and is designed specifically to support Virtual Private Network (VPN) connections, which enable remote clients to establish secure connections to a private network through a public network such as the Internet. MS-CHAP v2 provides several security enhancements:

✦ **LAN Manager coding of responses, formerly supported for backward compatibility with older remote access clients, is no longer supported.** This provides improved security. MS-CHAP v2 no longer supports LAN Manager encoding of password changes for the same reason.

✦ **Mutual authentication, which provides bidirectional authentication between the remote client and the RAS server is supported.** Previously, MS-CHAP only provided one-way authentication and did not provide a mechanism for the remote client to determine if the remote server actually had access to its authentication password for verification. Version 2 not only enables the server to authenticate the client's request, but also allows the client to verify the server's ability to authenticate its account.

✦ **Stronger encryption is provided in MS-CHAP v2.** The 40-bit encryption used in previous versions operated on the user's password and resulted in the same cryptographic key being generated for each session. Version 2 uses the remote client's password, along with an arbitrary challenge string, to create a unique cryptographic key for each session, even when the client password remains the same.

✦ **Better security for data transmission is provided by using separate cryptographic keys for data sent in each direction.**

Extensible Authentication Protocol

The Extensible Authentication Protocol (EAP) enables authentication methods to be added to RAS without redesigning the underlying RAS software base, much like new features in NTFS 5.0 enable new functionality to be added to the file system without redesigning the file system. EAP enables the client and server to negotiate the mechanism to be used to authenticate the client. Currently, EAP in Windows 2003 supports EAP-MD5 CHAP (Challenge Handshake Authentication Protocol), EAP-TLS (Transport Level Security), and redirection to a RADIUS server. Each of these topics is covered in more detail later in this chapter.

RADIUS support

Windows 2003 RRAS can function as a RADIUS client, funneling logon requests to a RADIUS server, which can include the Internet Authentication Service (also included with Windows 2003) running on the same or a different server. The RADIUS server doesn't have to be a Windows 2003 system, however, which enables RRAS to use Unix-based RADIUS servers or third-party RADIUS services you might already have in place. One of the advantages to using RADIUS is its capability for accounting, and several third-party utilities have been developed to provide integration with database backends such as SQL Server to track and control client access.

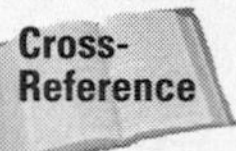

See the section "Using RADIUS" later in this chapter for detailed information on configuring and using RADIUS.

Remote access policies

Windows 2003 improves considerably on the flexibility you have as an administrator to control a user's remote access and dial-up settings. Windows NT RRAS gave you control only over callback options, and settings were assigned on a user-by-user basis. Although Windows 2003 still lets you assign remote access permissions through a user's account, as with Windows 2000 RRAS you also can use a remote access policy to define the remote access settings for one or several users. Remote access policies give you a fine degree of control over the users' settings, controlling options such as allowed access time, maximum session time, authentication, security, BAP policies, and more.

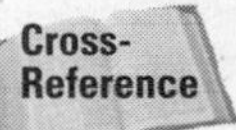

See the section titled "Remote Access Policy" later in this chapter for additional information on configuring and using RAS policies.

Support for Macintosh clients

Windows 2003 adds remote access support for Macintosh clients by supporting AppleTalk over PPP for Macintosh clients. This enables Macintosh clients to connect to a Windows 2003 RAS server using the standard PPP and AppleTalk protocols.

Account lockout

Windows 2003 RAS enhances security by supporting account lockout, which locks an RRAS account after a specified number of bad logon attempts. This feature helps guard against dictionary attacks in which a hacker attempts to gain remote access by repeatedly attempting to log on using a dictionary of passwords against a valid account. You can configure two settings that control lockout — the number of bad logon attempts before the account is locked out, and how long the account remains locked before the lockout counter is reset.

The Routing and Remote Access Management Console

Microsoft has integrated most administration and management functions into Microsoft Management Console (MMC) snap-ins, and RRAS is no exception. The Routing and Remote Access console snap-in enables you to configure and manage an RRAS server. Figure 18-2 shows the Routing and Remote Access console.

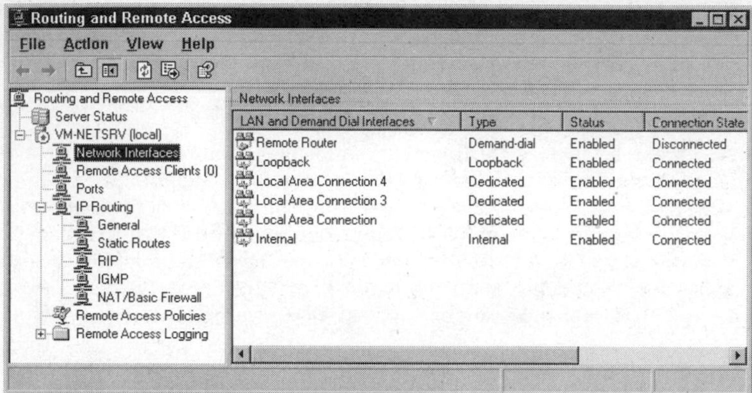

Figure 18-2: The Routing and Remote Access console.

The RRAS console serves as a central control center for managing most RRAS properties. In addition to configuring ports and interfaces, you can configure protocols, global options and properties, and RRAS policies through the RRAS console. Later sections of this chapter explain how to use the RRAS console to perform specific configuration and administration tasks. Open the console by choosing Start ➪ All Programs ➪ Administrative Tools ➪ Routing and Remote Access.

RAS Connection Types and Protocols

Windows 2003 supports several connection types and network protocols for remote access. The following sections explore these connection types and network protocols.

NetBEUI is not included with Windows Server 2003; therefore, Windows Server 2003 does not support NetBEUI for routing and remote access.

Serial Line Internet Protocol

The Serial Line Internet Protocol (SLIP) is a connection protocol that originated in the Unix realm. SLIP offers limited functionality in that it does not support error detection or correction. Windows 2003 clients can use SLIP to connect to Unix servers (or other servers requiring SLIP), but Windows Server 2003 does not support SLIP for dial-in connections.

Point-to-Point Protocol

The Point-to-Point Protocol (PPP) was developed as a standardized alternative to SLIP that offered better performance and reliability. Unlike SLIP, PPP is designed around industry-designed standards and enables essentially any PPP-compliant client to connect to a PPP server. Windows 2003 supports PPP for both dial-in and dial-out connections. On a Windows 2003 RAS server, PPP enables remote clients to use IPX, TCP/IP, AppleTalk, or a combination thereof. Windows-based clients including Windows 2003, Windows NT, Windows 9*x*, and

Windows 3.*x* can use any combination of IPX, or TCP/IP, but AppleTalk is not supported for these clients. Macintosh clients can use either TCP/IP or AppleTalk. PPP supports several authentication protocols, including MS-CHAP, EAP, CHAP, SPAP, and PAP.

Point-to-Point Multilink Protocol and BAP

The Point-to-Point Multilink Protocol (PPMP, or simply Multilink) enables multiple PPP lines to be combined to provide an aggregate bandwidth. For example, you might use Multilink to combine two analog 56Kbps modems to give you an aggregate bandwidth roughly equivalent to 112 Kbps. Or, you might combine both B channels of an ISDN Basic Rate Interface (BRI) connection to provide double the bandwidth you would otherwise get from a single channel.

The Bandwidth Allocation Protocol (BAP) works in conjunction with Multilink to provide adaptive bandwidth. As bandwidth utilization increases, BAP enables the client to aggregate additional connections to increase bandwidth and improve performance. As bandwidth utilization decreases, BAP enables the client to drop connections from the aggregate link to reduce connection costs (in cases where multiple connections incur their own charges).

See the section "Using Multilink and BAP" later in this chapter to configure and use multilink connections.

Point-to-Point Tunneling Protocol

The TCP/IP protocol suite by itself does not provide for encryption or data security, an obvious concern for users who need to transmit data securely across a public network such as the Internet. The Point-to-Point Tunneling Protocol (PPTP) provides a means for encapsulating and encrypting IP and IPX for secure transmission. PPTP is an extension of PPP that enables you to create a Virtual Private Network (VPN) connection between a client and server.

PPP frames in a PPTP session are encrypted using Microsoft Point-to-Point Encryption (MPPE) with the encryption keys generated using the MS-CHAP or EAP-TLS authentication process. PPTP by itself does not provide encryption, but rather encapsulates the already encrypted PPP frames. In order to provide a secure connection, the client must use either MS-CHAP or EAP-TLS authentication. Otherwise, the PPP frames are encapsulated unencrypted (plain text). Figure 18-3 illustrates how PPTP encapsulates data. PPTP is installed by default when you install Windows 2003 RRAS.

PPTP is a good choice for creating secure connections to a private network through a public network, such as the Internet, when the remote network isn't configured to support IPSec.

Layer Two Tunneling Protocol

Layer Two Tunneling Protocol (L2TP) is a protocol that combines the features of PPTP with support for IP Security (IPSec) to provide enhanced security. Unlike PPTP, which relies on MPPE for encryption, L2TP relies on IPSec to provide encryption. Therefore, the source and destination routers must support both L2TP and IPSec. Figure 18-3 illustrates how L2TP encapsulates data. L2TP is installed by default when you install Windows 2003 RRAS.

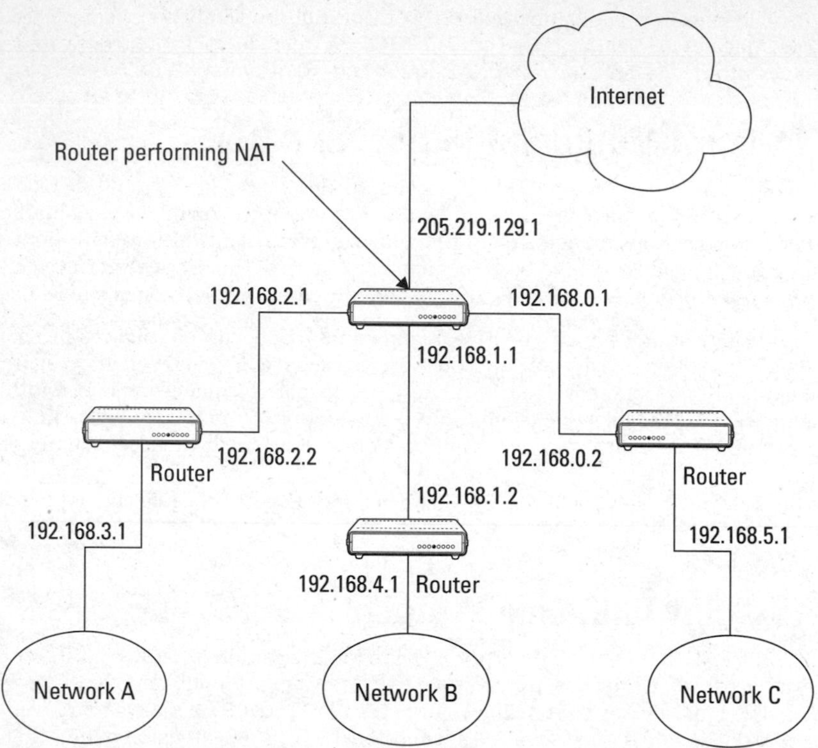

Figure 18-3: PPTP and L2TP use different methods for encapsulation and encryption.

Tip L2TP provides better security than PPTP by supporting IPSec. L2TP is a better choice for creating VPN connections than PPTP when the remote network is configured to support IPSec. See Chapter 3 for a discussion of Windows 2003 security and IPSec.

Transport protocols

As mentioned previously in this chapter, RRAS supports three network protocols: TCP/IP, IPX, and AppleTalk. A Windows 2003 RAS server supports all protocols for incoming connections. Windows 2003 RAS clients support all protocols except AppleTalk. When you install RRAS, Windows 2003 enables all currently installed protocols for incoming and outgoing RAS connections. As you learn later in the section "Configuring RAS for Inbound Connections," you can configure the supported protocols to enable clients to access only the RAS server or access the LAN. You configure access on a protocol-by-protocol basis.

TCP/IP

As a dial-out protocol, TCP/IP enables you to connect a Windows 2003 client to nearly any TCP/IP-based network, including the Internet. You can statically assign the IP address, subnet mask, default gateway, and other settings for the dial-out connection or allow the remote server to assign the connection properties. As a protocol for incoming connections, TCP/IP enables essentially any client that supports TCP/IP and PPP to connect to a Windows 2003 RAS server. As you learn later in the section "Configuring RAS for Inbound Connections," you can allocate addresses from a static pool or use DHCP to allocate addresses and other connection properties to remote clients. In addition, clients can request a predefined IP address (defined at the client side through the connection properties).

IPX

The IPX protocol is used primarily in environments where Novell NetWare clients or servers are used. Support for IPX enables a Windows 2003 RAS server to coexist with NetWare servers and enables clients to access NetWare resources through the RAS connection. A Windows 2003 RAS server hosting IPX also serves as an IPX router, handling RIP, SAP, and NetBIOS traffic between the local network and the remote client. In addition to using the IPX protocol, the remote client must run a NetWare redirector. The server must be running the IPX/SPX/NetBIOS-compatible protocol.

The Windows 2003 Professional NetWare redirector is Client Service for NetWare. In Windows Server 2003, the redirector is Gateway Service for NetWare.

A Windows 2003 RAS server allocates IPX network numbers and node numbers to connecting clients. The server can generate the IPX network number automatically or, as it can for TCP/IP, allocate numbers from a static pool assigned by an administrator. If assigning a number dynamically, the server first verifies that the number is not already in use on the network. The server then allocates that number to all remote access clients. Assigning the same network number to all clients reduces RIP announcements from the RAS server.

AppleTalk

The AppleTalk protocol is used by Macintosh network clients. Windows 2003 RAS supports AppleTalk to enable remote Macintosh clients to connect to the server and access resources shared by the server or other AppleTalk clients on the network. In order to use AppleTalk for RAS dial-in, you must install the AppleTalk protocol on the RAS server.

Enabling and Configuring RRAS

Although Setup installs RRAS by default when you install Windows Server 2003, you still need to enable the service to begin configuring and using it. To do so, choose Start ⇨ All Programs ⇨ Administrative Tools ⇨ Routing and Remote Access to open the RRAS console. Right-click the server in the left pane and choose Configure and Enable Routing and Remote Access to start the RRAS Setup Wizard. You can use the wizard to automatically configure RRAS for specific applications or configure the service manually.

If you enable RRAS and choose to configure it manually and then later decide you'd like to run the wizard, you can do so, but you will lose the current configuration settings. To reconfigure the service through the wizard, open the RRAS console, right-click the server, and choose Disable Routing and Remote Access. After the service stops, right-click the server again and choose Configuring and Enable Routing and Remote Access.

The wizard provides five basic options for configuring RRAS:

✦ **Remote access (dial-up or VPN).** Sets up the server to accept incoming remote access connections, whether dial-up or VPN.

✦ **Network address translation (NAT).** Sets up the server to provide NAT services to clients on the private network that need to access the Internet.

✦ **Virtual private network (VPN) access and NAT.** Sets up the server to support incoming VPN connections from the Internet and NAT-protected client connections from the local network out to the Internet.

✦ **Secure connection between two private networks.** Establish a demand-dial or persistent connection between networks with the server acting as a router.

✦ **Custom configuration.** Enables you to choose individual services you want RRAS to offer, such as NAT, LAN routing, and VPN access.

The following sections explain how to use the wizard and the custom configuration option to set up RRAS to perform specific functions.

IP Routing

Except in self-contained private networks, routing plays an important role in TCP/IP. Routing enables packets destined for external subnets to reach their destinations and for traffic from remote networks to be delivered to your network. Windows 2003 includes a service called Routing and Remote Access (RRAS) that enables a Windows Server 2003 to function as a dedicated or demand-dial router (establishing connections only as needed). This section of the chapter discusses IP routing and the routing elements of RRAS in particular.

IP routing overview

A *router* works in concert with other network hardware to direct network traffic to its intended destination. For example, when you open your Web browser at the office and connect to `www.foxnews.com` to check the current news, your network router directs the traffic out to the Internet. At that point, other routers take care of getting the traffic to the site and back again with the responses. Another example is when you dial into your ISP from home. The ISP's router(s) connects its network to the Internet and processes traffic going to and from your computer and to and from the computers of other connected customers.

A typical router essentially sits on the fence between two or more subnets. This fence is typically known as a *hop,* and each time a packet traverses a router, its *hop count* is incremented. The router exists on all subnets to which it is connected and therefore has connectivity to each subnet. When traffic comes into the router from a particular interface, the router directs the traffic to the appropriate interface. Figure 18-4 illustrates a typical routing situation. If the number of hops a packet takes to reach a destination is determined to be excessive by a router, the packet will be terminated and a message will be sent back to the sender indicating that the packet expired in transit. This is a safeguard that prevents data that cannot be routed to an interface from eternally moving around the Internet. The typical hop limit is 30 for most routers.

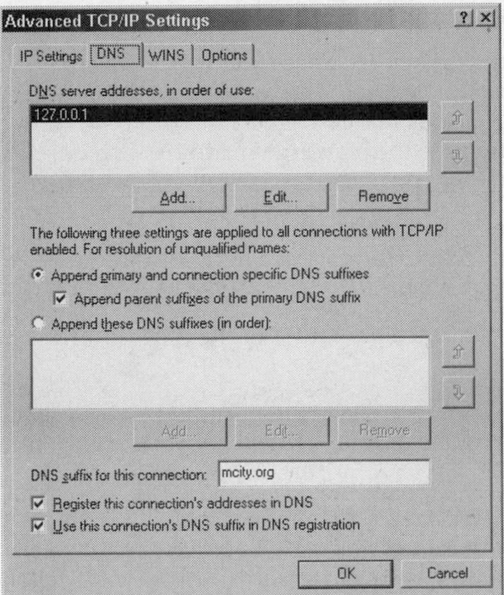

Figure 18-4: Several networks connected to the Internet through routers.

A router examines each packet that comes in to determine the destination network for the packet. It does this by examining the destination address stored in the packet's header. The router then decides which of its interfaces to use to route the traffic and sends it on its way. For example, assume that a router has three interfaces: one for the local network, one for another local network, and a third that connects to the Internet. Assume that the first local network (A) is on subnet 208.141.235.33 - 208.141.235.62 and the second local network (B) uses 208.141.235.129 - 208.141.235.158. A packet comes into the router from subnet A with the destination address 208.147.235.137. The router routes the packet out through the interface connected to subnet B. Another packet comes in with the destination address 205.135.201.130, so the router sends that packet out through the interface connected to the Internet because it doesn't belong in either of the local subnets.

Routers use *routing tables* containing *routes* to determine where to send packets. Routes help the router know where different networks are located relative to its interfaces so that it can send packets out on the appropriate interface and have them delivered to the proper destination. Each route in the routing table falls into one of the following types:

- ✦ **Network route:** These provide a route to a specific network ID, and therefore to all host addresses within that network.
- ✦ **Host route:** These provide a route to a specific host, defining not only the network but also the address of the host.
- ✦ **Default route:** The default route is used to route all traffic for which there is no specific network route or host route. For example, a router connecting a local network to the Internet would have a default route pointing all traffic to the Internet interface.

Each route in the routing table has certain general properties:

- ✦ **Network ID/host address/subnet mask:** These properties identify the destination network ID or host address and the destination subnet. The router checks the destination addresses in the packets against these entries to determine a match. If the packet address matches the criteria, the router uses the forwarding address and interface data associated with the route to process the packet.
- ✦ **Forwarding address:** The router forwards matching packets to this address. The address could be that of another router or the address of a network interface on the local router (directing the traffic out a specific port on the router).
- ✦ **Interface:** This is a port number or other logical identifier of the port through which the traffic is routed for the given route.
- ✦ **Metric:** The metric specifies the relative price of the route based on cost, available bandwidth, and so on. Where multiple routes exist to a given network or host, the route with the lowest metric is used.

When a packet comes in to the router, the router checks the destination address in the packet's header against the routing table to determine which route applies to the packet. If the router matches the destination address with a route, it forwards the packet using the forwarding address associated with the route. If the router finds no matching route, it forwards the packet using the default route (if one is configured on the router). The default route is used to handle any traffic for which there is not a specific route.

How do routers learn their routes? One method is for routers to learn routes dynamically from other routers and propagate them to other routers. Routers communicate with one another using routing protocols, with the two most common protocols for IP routing being Routing Information Protocol (RIP) and Open Shortest Path First (OSPF). Windows 2003 supports both (and can support additional protocols). RIP and OSPF are explained shortly.

A second method is for routers to use static routes. When you configure the router, you create the static route, which creates the static route entry in the routing table. A router can use static routes to handle all its traffic, a common situation for small to mid-sized organizations. For example, if you only connect a few local subnets to the Internet, you can use static routes to handle all traffic, with a default route handling traffic to the Internet. You can read more about static routes later in the section "Configuring Static Routes."

RIP

RIP for IP, one of the two routing protocols included with Windows 2003 for routing IP traffic, offers the advantage of being relatively easy to configure. RIP is appropriate mainly for small- to mid-sized businesses because it is limited to a maximum hop count of 15. RIP considers any address more than 15 hops away to be unreachable.

When a router using RIP first boots, its routing table contains only the routes for physically connected networks. RIP periodically broadcasts announcements with its routing table entries so that adjacent routers can configure their routes accordingly. After a router starts up, it uses RIP announcements from adjacent routers to rebuild its route table.

RIP also uses triggered updates to update routing tables. Triggered updates occur when the router detects a network change, such as an interface coming up or going down. The triggered updates are broadcast immediately. Routers that receive the update modify their route tables and propagate the changes to adjacent routers.

Windows 2003 supports RIP v1 and v2. RIP v2 adds additional features such as peer security and route filtering.

OSPF

OSPF offers an efficient means of handling routing for very large networks such as the Internet. OSPF uses an algorithm to calculate the shortest path between the router and adjacent networks. OSPF routers maintain a *link state database* that maps the inter-network. The link state database changes as each network topology change occurs. Adjacent OSPF routers synchronize their link state databases and recalculate their routing tables accordingly.

Because of its scalability, OSPF is geared toward large networks. It's also more complex to configure. If yours is a very large network, OSPF may be a good choice for your routing needs. For smaller networks, consider using RIP. In situations where you're only connecting a few networks together, static routes could be the best and easiest solution of all.

Routing with RRAS

In addition to providing remote access services to enable a Windows Server 2003 to act as both a dial-up server and client, RRAS enables a Windows Server 2003 to function as a router for persistent connections and as a demand-dial router, connecting only when requested by a client to do so. For example, you might have two divisions of a company that need to transfer data between networks only occasionally. Maintaining a leased line or a direct Internet connection between the two isn't feasible because of the cost involved, so you set up a demand-dial router that will call the other router (over a dial-up connection, for example) when any traffic needs to be routed to the other network.

All of the functions supported by Windows 2003 RRAS require routing. When you use the wizard to configure a RRAS server, the result is that routing is enabled on the server. In this section of the chapter, we limit RRAS specifically to functioning as a router to explain how to configure routes, protocols, and other components. Later sections explain how to configure a RRAS server to function in other ways (such as a VPN server).

Configuring a basic router

As mentioned previously, RRAS can use static routes, dynamic routes, or a combination thereof to provide routing services. This section of the chapter explains how to set up a simple router that uses static routes rather than dynamic routing. Most of the steps in this section also apply to a dynamic router. So even if you won't be using static routes, you should read this section before moving on to "Dynamic Routing," later in this chapter.

At this point, assume that you have yet to enable RRAS. To configure a LAN router, open the RRAS console by choosing Start ➪ All Programs ➪ Administrative Tools ➪ Routing and Remote Access. Choose Custom Configuration and click Next. Choose LAN routing, click Next, and click Finish. Click Yes when asked if you want to start the RRAS service.

Configuring the router address

By default, the router uses the first IP address bound to an interface to process routing tasks on that interface. An interface that has only one address assigned therefore doesn't require configuration of its address. You might, however, have multiple addresses assigned to each interface for other purposes. In such a case, you need to configure the address the router interface will use.

To do so, open the RRAS console, expand the IP Routing branch, and click General. In the right pane, right-click the interface you want to configure and choose Properties to display its property sheet. Set the IP address, subnet mask, and gateway (if required) for the interface on the Configuration page. Click Advanced if you need to specify a metric for the interface.

Configuring static routes

After you set up RRAS for routing, you need to either add static routes or configure the router to use RIP or OSPF. The exception is when you have only two networks connected by a router. In this situation, the router can route the traffic without a specific route.

To add a static route, open the RRAS console and expand the IP Routing branch. Click Static Routes, right-click the right pane (or Static Routes), and choose New Static Route to display the Static Route dialog box (see Figure 18-5).

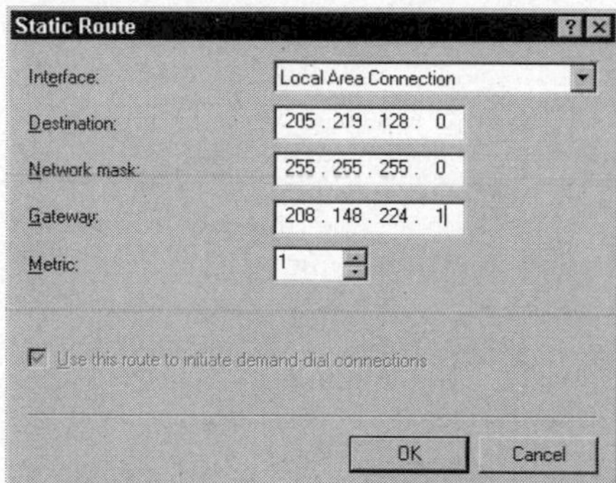

Figure 18-5: Use the Static Route dialog box to add a static route.

The following list explains the options in the Static Route dialog box:

✦ **Interface:** Select the network interface to be used to forward packets that fit the criteria for the route. For example, to route traffic destined for the Internet, select the network interface on the server that is connected to the Internet.

✦ **Destination:** Specify the address criteria for matching packets. RRAS will check the destination address in the packet header against this address to determine if the route applies to the packet. You can specify a network address, host address, or a default route of 0.0.0.0. For a network address, use the low broadcast address for the network. For example, for the class C network 205.219.128.*x*, use 205.219.128.0. For a host, specify the actual IP address of the host.

Creating a default route using 0.0.0.0 causes all traffic for which there is no other applicable route to be forwarded through the interface defined by the default route entry.

✦ **Network mask:** Specify the network mask for the destination network or host. For a default route, enter 0.0.0.0.

✦ **Gateway:** Specify the address to which the packets will be forwarded for this route and must be an address directly reachable on the router's external network segment (interface for the route). For example, you might specify the address of the router port on the same subnet for the next adjacent router.

✦ **Metric:** Specify a value to define the relative cost for the route. A lower metric indicates a lower cost. In many cases, administrators use the number of hops to the destination as the metric. When multiple routes apply to a given packet, the route with the lowest metric is used unless it is unavailable.

✦ **Use this route to initiate demand-dial connections:** Select this option to cause the router to initiate a demand-dial connection when it receives packets applicable for the selected route. This option is available only if at least one demand-dial interface is configured for the router.

Create static routes to accommodate each specific network segment in your network. Create a default route to handle all other traffic.

Adding and configuring a demand-dial interface

You need to add a demand-dial interface if you're installing RRAS to include the capability to function as a demand-dial router as well as a LAN router. A demand-dial router automatically dials a connection to a remote network when traffic from the local network needs to be routed to the remote network reachable through the demand-dial connection as defined by the route for that network.

To install a demand-dial interface, open the RRAS console and expand the server where you want to install the interface. Right-click Network Interfaces in the left pane and choose New Demand-Dial Interface to start the Demand-Dial Interface Wizard. The wizard prompts for the following information:

✦ **Interface name:** Specify a friendly name for the interface. RRAS by default suggests the name Remote Router. Keep in mind that if you configure the demand-dial interface to allow remote users (routers) to connect to this interface, the interface name is automatically used as the local account name. Using the suggested name Remote Router, for example, causes Windows 2003 to create a user account named Remote Router.

✦ **Connection type:** Select between physical devices such as modems, ISDN, network adapters, and so on, or specify that the connection will use a virtual private networking (VPN) connection. Selecting the VPN option will cause the wizard to prompt you for the tunneling protocol to use (PPTP or L2TP). You can also choose PPP over Ethernet (PPPoE).

✦ **Phone number or address/alternates:** For a dial-up device, specify the phone number of the remote interface. Specify the IP address of the remote interface if connecting through a non–dial-up device (such as a physical network connection).

✦ **Route IP packets on this interface:** Select this option to enable IP routing on this demand-dial connection. TCP/IP must already be installed on the server.

✦ **Route IPX packets on this interface:** Select this option to enable IPX routing on this demand-dial interface. IPX must already be installed on the server.

✦ **Add a user account so a remote router can dial in:** Select this option if you want to create a user account remote routers can use to dial in to this demand-dial connection. When the remote router receives a packet that needs to be forwarded to the local demand-dial interface, the remote router uses the account and password stored in its dial-out credentials to connect to the local router. The credentials at the remote router must match the account and password you create through the wizard. See "Dial-out credentials" at the end of this list to configure the local account and password that the local router will use when connecting to remote routers.

✦ **Send a plain-text password if that is the only way to connect:** Select this option to allow RRAS to transmit its credentials using plain text rather than encryption if the remote router doesn't support encryption or doesn't support the types of encryption supported by the local router.

✦ **Use scripting to complete the connection with the remote router:** Use this option to specify a script RRAS will use when connecting to the remote router. Scripts can be used to automate the logon process and other connection tasks. Scripts are most applicable to dial-up connections that require menu-based selections to authenticate and log on (such as SLIP servers). SLIP stands for Serial Line Interface Protocol and is a connection protocol typically found on older, Unix-based servers.

✦ **Dial-out credentials:** Specify the user name and password the local router will use to authenticate its access to the remote router. On a remote Windows 2003 router, you would use the option "Add a user account so a remote router can dial in" discussed previously to configure the associated account on the remote router.

Setting demand-dial filters

By default, RRAS allows all IP traffic through the demand-dial interface. However, you can create filters to restrict the type of traffic allowed. For example, you might want to restrict TCP port 80 to block Web browser traffic through the interface. You can create filters to restrict traffic going to or from specific networks, or you can create a filter that blocks specific packets to or from all addresses. The demand-dial interface will establish a connection to the remote router only if the packet is not blocked by the configured filters.

To configure filters, open the RRAS console and open the server on which you want to configure filters. Open the Network Interfaces branch. In the right pane, right-click the interface where you want to configure filters and choose Set IP Demand-dial Filters to display the Set Demand-dial Filters dialog box, shown in Figure 18-6.

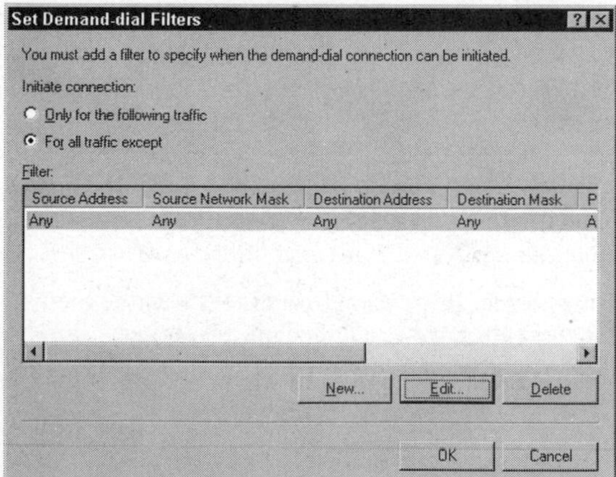

Figure 18-6: Use filters to restrict traffic through the demand-dial interface.

Configure the filter using the following list as a guide, then click OK and repeat the process to add any other required filters:

- **Source network:** Select this option to base the filter on the network from which the packet was sent. Specify an IP address and subnet mask to define the source network or host.
- **Destination network:** Select this option to base the filter on the destination address in the packet's header (where the packet is going). Specify the address and subnet mask of the destination network or host.
- **Protocol:** Specify the protocol type to filter. Select Any to filter all the traffic or select a given protocol type and specify the accompanying information, such as the source and destination ports.

Setting permitted dial-out hours

You might want to restrict a demand-dial connection to specific hours to limit the times at which the router will forward traffic on the interface. For example, you might want to disable the demand-dial interface during the weekend. To configure dial-out hours, open the RRAS console and then open the server you want to configure. Click the Network Interfaces branch, then right-click the demand-dial interface and choose Dial-out Hours. Use the Dial-out Hours dialog box to specify the hours at which the interface can be used. The options in the dialog box are self-explanatory.

Changing dial-out credentials

You can modify the credentials the router uses to connect to the remote router when it initiates a demand-dial connection. You might have entered it incorrectly when you set up the router, the remote administrator may have changed the account at the other end, or you might need to change the account and password for other reasons. Open the RRAS console and the server you want to modify. In the RRAS console, right-click the demand-dial interface you want to change and click Set Credentials. Specify the new user name, domain, and password as needed.

Setting dialing properties

In some situations, such as when you're using a modem connection, you'll want to configure dialing properties such as redial attempts, redial interval, idle time before disconnect, and so on. To configure dialing properties, open the RRAS console, open the Network Interfaces branch, right-click the demand-dial interface, and choose Properties. Use the controls on the General and Options property pages to configure the dialing properties. The options are self-explanatory.

Configuring security methods

RRAS gives you the ability to configure the security/authentication methods that RRAS uses for authenticating with the remote router for a demand-dial connection. To configure authentication methods, open the properties for the demand-dial connection and click the Security tab. The settings you can configure here for the authentication methods are the same as those you can configure for incoming RAS connections. For a detailed description of authentication methods, see, "Configuring RRAS for Inbound Connections," later in this chapter.

Modifying network settings

RRAS uses the protocols and other network properties configured for an interface when you add the interface. You might need to remove or add a protocol or make other network property changes for a routing interface. For example, you might want to add the ability to route IPX as well as IP, requiring that you install IPX on the interface. You can do so through the RRAS console. Open the property sheet for the routing interface, choose Properties, and click the Networking tab. You can configure dial-up server settings, network protocols and bindings, and other network properties.

Enabling or disabling routing

On occasion, you might need to enable or disable a router, such as taking the router down for maintenance. You can stop or pause the RRAS service to stop routing on all interfaces, or you can take down a specific interface. To stop, pause, or restart RRAS, open the RRAS console, right-click the server you want to manage, and choose the task you want to perform (stop, start, and so on) from the All Tasks menu.

To take down a specific interface, open the RRAS console and then open the IP Routing branch. Click General to display the routing interfaces, then right-click the interface to bring the menu down, and choose Properties. Deselect the option "Enable IP router manager" and click OK to take down the interface. Reselect the option and click OK to bring it back up.

Dynamic routing

If yours is a more complex network than the one described in this section, you might want to use a routing protocol such as RIP or OSPF to provide dynamic route table creation and management. The following sections explain how to add and configure RIP and OSPF. This section assumes that you have some knowledge of RIP or OSPF and primarily need to know where to go to add and configure routing protocols in Windows 2003 RRAS.

Adding and configuring RIP

Before you can configure RIP on an interface, you need to add RIP. In the RRAS console, open the server you want to manage, then expand the IP Routing branch. Right-click General and choose New Routing Protocol. Select RIP Version 2 for Internet Protocol from the list and choose OK. A new node labeled RIP appears under the IP Routing branch.

Next, you need to specify the interface on which RIP will run, as by default no interfaces are configured when you add RIP. Right-click RIP and choose New Interface. RRAS displays the available interfaces. Select the one on which you want to run RIP and click OK.

The next step is to configure RIP. RRAS presents a property sheet for RIP when you add the interface. You can also display the RIP properties by double-clicking the interface in the right pane with RIP selected in the left pane. The following sections describe the options you can configure for RIP.

General

Use the General page to configure how RIP handles updates, enable or disable authentication, and other general properties, as explained in the following list:

- **Operation mode:** Choose the method RIP uses to update routes. You can choose the auto-static update mode or periodic update mode. With auto-static mode, RRAS sends out RIP announcements only when other routers request updates. Any routes learned through RIP when in auto-static mode are treated as static routes and remain in the routing table until manually deleted, even if RRAS is restarted or you disable RIP. This is the default mode for demand-dial interfaces. The periodic update mode generates RIP announcements automatically at the interval defined by "Periodic announcement interval" on the Advanced property page. Routes learned through RIP with this mode are treated as RIP routes and are discarded if the router is restarted. This is the default mode for LAN interfaces.

- **Outgoing packet protocol:** Select the protocol RIP should use for outgoing RIP announcements. Select RIP version 1 broadcast if no other adjacent routers support RIP version 2. Select RIP v2 broadcast in a mixed environment with adjacent routers using RIP v1 and RIP v2. Select RIP v2 multicast to send RIP announcements as multicasts, but only when all adjacent routers are configured to use RIP v2 (RIP v1 doesn't support RIP v2 multicast announcements). Select Silent RIP to prevent the router from sending RIP announcements and to function in listen-only mode, listening for announcements from other routers and updating its routing table accordingly, but not announcing its own routes.
- **Incoming packet protocol:** Specify how you want the router to handle incoming RIP announcements. Select Ignore incoming packets to have the router function in the announce-only mode and not listen to announcements from other routers. Otherwise, select the required mode depending on the mix of adjacent routers and their support for RIP v1 and/or v2.
- **Added cost for routes:** This number is added to the hop count for a route to increase the relative cost. Increase the number to help limit the traffic on the route if you have other, less costly routes that can be used if they are available. The default is 1, and the maximum number of hops for IP and RIP can't exceed 15.
- **Tag for announced routes:** You can use this value to assign a tag number to be included with all RIP v2 announcements.
- **Activate authentication/Password:** Select this option to enable the inclusion of a plain text password for incoming and outgoing RIP v2 announcements, and then specify a corresponding password in the Password field. If this option is enabled, all routers connected to this interface must be configured for the same password. This option serves only as a means of identifying routers and doesn't provide security or encryption of RIP traffic.

Security

The Security tab lets you specify which routes to accept or reject that come in via RIP announcements from other routers. You can accept all routes, accept only routes that fall within a specified network range, or ignore all routes in a specified range. For outgoing RIP announcements, you can configure RRAS to announce all routes, announce only those routes that fit a specified network range, or exclude routes that fit a specified range.

Neighbors

The Neighbors tab lets you define how the router interacts with neighboring routers. The options are as follows:

- **Use broadcast or multicast only:** Select this option to issue RIP announcements only using the outgoing packet protocol specified on the interface's General property page.
- **Use neighbors in addition to broadcast or multicast:** Select this option to define specific routers to which RRAS sends unicast RIP announcements as well as to issue RIP announcements using the outgoing packet protocol specified on the General page.
- **Use neighbors instead of broadcast or multicast:** Select this option to define specific routers to which RRAS sends unicast RIP announcements and not issue RIP announcements through the broadcast or multicast protocol specified on the General page. Use this option in networks that don't support RIP broadcasts.

Advanced

You can use the Advanced tab to set several advanced options for RIP on the selected interface including the interval between RIP announcements, route expiration period, and other settings. The following list summarizes the settings:

- **Periodic announcement interval:** Specify the interval in seconds at which RIP announcements are issued from the local router. You can specify a value between 15 seconds and 24 hours (86,400 seconds), and this setting is only applicable if you've selected periodic update mode on the General tab.
- **Time before routes expire:** This value defines the time-to-live of routes learned through RIP. Routes that do not update in the specified time are marked as invalid. You can specify a value between 15 seconds and 72 hours (259,200 seconds). The setting only applies if the interface uses periodic update mode.
- **Time before route is removed:** Specify the number of seconds a route learned through RIP remains in the routing table before it expires and is removed. Valid values range from 15 seconds to 72 hours. This setting applies only if the interface uses periodic update mode.
- **Enable split-horizon processing:** Select this option to prevent routes learned on a network from being announced on the same network. Deselect the option to allow those routes to be announced.
- **Enable poison-reverse processing:** Select this option to assign a metric of 16 (marking them as unreachable) to those routes learned on a network that are announced on the same network.
- **Enable triggered updates:** Select this option to allow the router to generate triggered updates when the routing table changes. Set the maximum time between triggered updates through the option "Maximum Delay" on the General page of the global RIP property sheet. To view this property sheet, right-click the RIP node in the IP Routing branch of the RRAS console and choose Properties.
- **Send clean-up updates when stopping:** Select this option to have RIP announce all routes with a metric of 15 to adjacent routers when the local router is going down, indicating to the other routers that the routes are no longer available. When the router comes back up, RIP will announce the routes again with their appropriate metrics, making those routes available again.
- **Process host routes in received announcements:** Host routes in RIP announcements are ignored by default. Select this option to include them in received announcements.
- **Include host routes in sent announcements**: Host routes are not included by default in outgoing RIP announcements. Select this option to include host routes in outgoing announcements.
- **Process default routes in received announcements:** Default routes received in RIP announcements are ignored by default. Select this option to add them to the local routing table. Note that this could have the consequence of disabling routing if the default route is not applicable to the local router.

✦ **Include default routes in sent announcements:** Default routes are not included by default in outgoing RIP announcements. Select this option to include them. In most situations, you should not include default routes unless those default routes are applicable to all other networks on the selected interface.

✦ **Disable subnet summarization:** Select this option to have subnet routes summarized by class-based network ID for outgoing announcements on networks that are not part of the class-based network. Subnet summarization is disabled by default and requires RIP v2 broadcast of RIP v2 multicast support on all applicable routers.

General RIP properties

There are a handful of general properties you can set for RIP in addition to those discussed in the previous sections. To set these properties, open the IP Routing branch in the RRAS console, right-click RIP, and choose Properties. Use the General tab to configure logging and the Security tab to define the routers from which the local router will process RIP announcements.

Adding and configuring OSPF

You add and configure OSPF in much the same way as RIP, although the configuration properties are considerably different. To add OSPF, open the RRAS console and open the IP Routing branch for the server you want to manage. Right-click General and choose New Routing Protocol. Select "Open Shortest Path First (OSPF)" from the list and click OK. RRAS adds an OSPF branch to the IP Routing branch.

Next, specify the interface on which OSPF will operate. Right-click OSPF and choose New Interface. Select the network interface from the list and click OK. RRAS displays the property sheet shown in Figure 18-7. The following sections explain the properties for the connection. You can also modify these properties later by double-clicking the interface in the right pane with the OSPF branch opened.

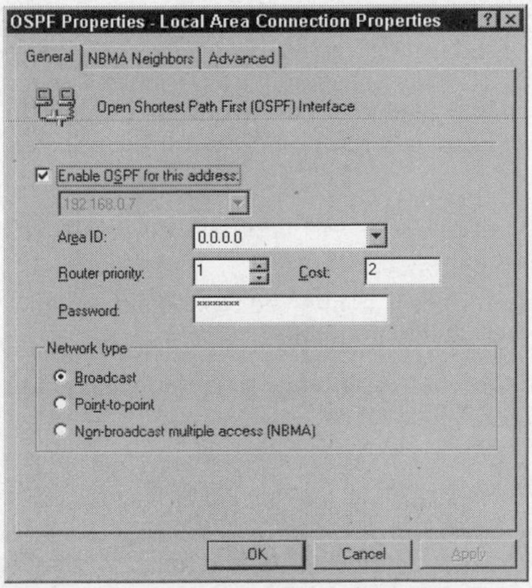

Figure 18-7: The OSPF Properties sheet.

Setting interface properties

The interface properties for OSPF define the way OSPF operates on the selected interface. If you have more than one router interface using OSPF, you need to configure each according to your network's needs and the neighboring routers. The following sections explain these interface properties. See the section titled "Setting global OSPF properties" later in this chapter to configure general OSPF properties.

General

Use the General tab shown in Figure 18-7 to specify the address on which the router interface responds, the area ID, and related properties. The following list explains the options:

- **Enable OSPF for this address:** Select this option to enable OSPF on the listed IP address for the selected interface. If you have more than one IP address bound to the selected interface, you must enable or disable and configure options for each IP address. The Area ID, Router priority, Cost, and Password apply to the IP address and can be configured differently for each address on the same interface if needed.
- **Area ID:** Select one area ID to associate with the previous address set. Each address can have a different area ID. By default, only the backbone area ID of 0.0.0.0 exists. Create other area IDs through the Areas tab of the general OSPF properties for the router. See the section titled "Setting Global OSPF Properties" later in this section for more information on creating area IDs.
- **Router priority:** The router with the highest priority number becomes the designated router when multiple routers exist on the network, and takes precedence. If the priority numbers are the same (causing a tie), the router with the highest router ID value takes precedence. Specify a value to set the router's priority as needed within the context of the other routers in the network.
- **Cost:** Use this option to set the interface's metric, or relative cost. When two or more interfaces can be used for a given route, the one with the lowest metric is used by default unless it is unavailable.
- **Password:** Specify the clear text string used for identification purposes to other routers in the area. The default password is 12345678, and all routers in the same area must use the same password. This option is dimmed if plain text passwords are disabled for the area. Open the global properties for OSPF and edit the properties for the selected area to enable the plain text password.
- **Broadcast:** Select this option if the interface is connected to a broadcast-type network such as Ethernet, Token Ring, or FDDI.
- **Point-to-point:** Select this option if the interface is connected to a point-to-point network such as T1/E1, T3/E3, ISDN, or other dial-up network.
- **Nonbroadcast multiple access (NBMA):** Select this option if the interface is connected to an NBMA network such as Frame Relay, X.25, or ATM.

NBMA Neighbors

The NBMA Neighbors tab of the interface's OSPF properties enables you to define the neighboring routers when you select NBMA as the network type on the General page. Select an IP address for the interface (if the interface has multiple addresses bound to it), then specify the IP address of neighboring routers.

Advanced

The Advanced tab lets you configure various intervals, transit delay, and MTU values for each address on the selected interface. These values are explained in the following list:

- **IP address:** Select the IP address for which you want to change the settings.
- **Transit delay:** Specify the estimated number of seconds required to transmit a link state update packet over the selected interface. The default is one second.
- **Retransmit interval:** Specify the number of seconds between the retransmission of link state advertisements for adjacencies. The value should be greater than the total expected round-trip time between any two routers on the attached network.
- **Hello interval:** Specify the interval at which the router broadcasts *hello packets.* Hello packet transmission is a means of discovering network structure (neighboring routers). Routing metrics are configured based on the length of time it takes a packet to make the trip between the source and the destination. The hello interval value must be the same for all routers on the common network. A shorter interval enables network topology changes to be detected more quickly but has the effect of generating more OSPF traffic in a given timeframe. The suggested value for X.25 is 30 seconds; for a LAN, the suggested value is 10 seconds.
- **Dead interval:** Specify the period after which adjacent routers will consider this router down. The other routers decide that the router is down if they haven't received a response to the hello packets within the specified amount of time. The value must be the same for all routers on the common network segment and should be set as a multiple of the hello interval. A common practice is to set the dead interval to four times the hello interval.
- **Poll interval:** Specify the period of time for network polls on NBMA interfaces. Network polls enable routers to determine if a dead neighbor has come back up or the connection has been restored. The poll interval should be at least twice as long as the dead interval.
- **Maximum transmission unit (MTU) size (bytes):** Specify the maximum size that IP datagrams can be transmitted without fragmentation. The default size for Ethernet networks is 1,500.

Setting global OSPF properties

RRAS provides several options that control OSPF globally. To configure these global properties, open the IP Routing branch in the RRAS console, then right-click OSPF and choose Properties. The following sections explain the global options in the OSPF property sheet.

General

The General tab configures the address identity of the OSPF router and logging options:

- **Router identification:** Specify the IP address on the server used to uniquely identify the OSPF router.
- **Enable autonomous system boundary router:** Select this option to configure the router to advertise routing information from other sources such as static addresses and RIP.
- **Event logging:** Select the desired logging level (self-explanatory).

Areas

You use the Areas tab to add and configure OSPF areas. Double-click an existing area or click Add to create a new entry. The following list summarizes the options for an area:

- **Area ID:** Specify a 32-bit number in dotted decimal format to identify the OSPF area. 0.0.0.0 is reserved for the backbone. While you can use the IP network number for a subnet, the number does not have to correlate to an IP address or IP network ID.
- **Enable plaintext password:** Select this option to require a plain text password for the area. All OSPF routers in the area on the same network segment must use the same password. Routers on different segments can use different passwords.
- **Stub area:** A stub area is an OSPF area that doesn't enumerate external routes but does accept external route data from other OSPF routers. Select this option to configure the area as a stub area.
- **Stub metric:** Specify the metric of the summary default route advertised into the stub area.
- **Import summary advertisements:** Select this option to import inter-area routes into this stub area. Deselect it to base all nonintra-area routes on a single default route.

Use the Ranges page to define ranges of IP addresses that belong to the selected area. The ranges are used to summarize the routes within the selected OSPF area.

Virtual Interfaces

Use the Virtual Interfaces tab to create virtual links between a backbone area router and an area border router that can't be physically connected to the backbone area. The virtual link is used to transmit routing data between the two. You can specify the transit delay, retransmit interval, hello interval, dead interval, and plain text password for each virtual link.

External Routing

If you select the option "Enable autonomous system boundary router" on the General tab of the global OSPF properties, you can use the External Routing page to define the route sources from which the router will accept routes. Select Accept or Ignore, then select the route sources from the list that you want to either accept or ignore. Click Route Filters to build a list of routes to be accepted or ignored, based on their destination addresses or network masks.

DHCP relay agent

A DHCP relay agent (BOOTP relay agent) functions as a sort of DHCP proxy, enabling DHCP clients on a given IP subnet to acquire IP leases from DHCP servers on other subnets. The DHCP relay agent relays messages between DHCP clients and DHCP servers. The DHCP relay agent component provided with Windows 2003 RRAS serves that function. Figure 18-8 illustrates a Windows Server 2003 functioning as a DHCP relay agent.

The DHCP relay agent can't run on a Windows Server 2003 that also is running the DHCP Server service or Network Address Translation (NAT) with automatic addressing enabled.

Setting up a DHCP relay agent is fairly simple. In the RRAS console, select the server you want to function as a DHCP relay agent. Open the IP Routing branch, right-click General, and choose New Routing Protocol. Select DHCP Relay Agent from the list and click OK to add it to the IP Routing branch.

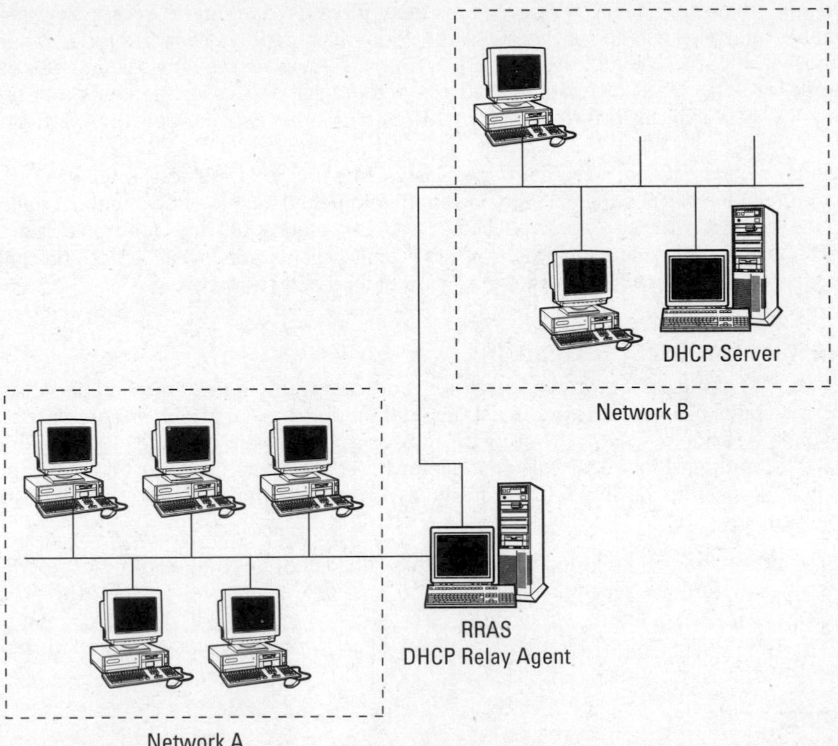

Figure 18-8: A Windows Server 2003 operating as a DHCP relay agent.

Next, add the interface(s) on which the DHCP relay agent will function. Right-click in the right pane or on DHCP Relay Agent and choose New Interface. Select the appropriate network interface and click OK. RRAS displays a property sheet for DHCP Relay that includes the following options:

✦ **Relay DHCP packets:** Select this option to enable DHCP relay or deselect it to disable DHCP relay.

✦ **Hop-count threshold:** Specify the maximum number of DHCP relay agents to handle DHCP relayed traffic. The default is 4; the maximum is 16.

✦ **Boot threshold:** Specify the interval the server waits before forwarding the DHCP messages. Use this option to enable a local DHCP server to have a chance to respond to requests before forwarding the message to a remote DHCP server.

The final step is to define the list of DHCP servers to which the local relay agent relays messages. In the RRAS console, right-click DHCP Relay Agent under the IP Routing branch and choose Properties. RRAS displays a dialog box you can use to specify the IP addresses of the remote DHCP servers.

IGMP – multicast forwarding

Most IP traffic is *unicast,* or directed to a single destination. A Windows Server 2003 running RRAS can function as a *multicast* router, broadcasting Internet Group Management Protocol

(IGMP) traffic to multiple hosts. Multicasting is most often used for audio or video conferencing to enable multiple hosts to receive the same data. Clients configured for multicast listen for the multicast traffic, and all others ignore it. Chapter 16 discusses how to configure multicast scopes for a DHCP server, enabling it to assign multicast addresses to clients that request them. This chapter explains how to configure RRAS to function as a multicast forwarder.

Note

Windows 2003 does not include any multicast routing protocols. Multicast routers exchange group membership information with one another to help determine how multicast traffic is routed. Windows 2003 only provides limited multicast routing, but does function as a multicast forwarder, forwarding multicast traffic to listening clients. Windows 2003 can be configured as a multicast router through the addition of third-party protocols.

Overview of multicast forwarding

A Windows 2003 multicast forwarder listens for multicast traffic on all attached networks and forwards the traffic (based on its multicast destination address) to attached networks where listening clients reside or to other routers for networks where participating clients reside. A Windows 2003 multicast forwarder also listens for IGMP Membership Report packets and updates its multicast forwarding table accordingly, enabling it to forward traffic to those destinations requesting it.

The IGMP routing protocol included with Windows 2003 is not an IGMP routing protocol per se, but enables a Windows Server 2003 to function as a forwarder. After you add the protocol to Windows 2003, you configure one or more interfaces to handle IGMP. You can configure the interface to function in either *IGMP router mode* or *IGMP proxy mode,* as explained in the following sections.

IGMP router mode

An IGMP interface running in router mode sets the network adapter for the interface in *multicast-promiscuous mode,* which passes all multicast packets received on the interface to the higher networking layers for processing.

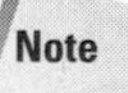

Note

Not all network adapters support multicast-promiscuous mode. If you're setting up a multicast forwarder, verify with the NIC manufacturer that the adapter supports this mode.

The interface also tracks multicast group membership, querying periodically for IGMP Membership Report messages and updating its forwarding table accordingly. Each entry in the table specifies the network ID where multicast clients are listening and the multicast address on which those clients are listening. The table does not reference individual hosts, but rather the interface forwards traffic to any networks where there is at least one client listening for multicast traffic.

Tip

When multiple routers in a network function as IGMP routers, one is automatically elected to be the querier and performs all membership queries.

IGMP proxy mode

IGMP proxy mode enables a local intranet router to pass IGMP traffic to and from multicast-capable clients and routers on the Internet (referred to as *multicast backbone,* or MBone).

An interface running in IGMP proxy mode functions as a proxy for IGMP Membership Report packets. RRAS listens on the selected interface for IGMP Membership Report packets and retransmits them on all other interfaces running in IGMP router mode. This enables IGMP multicast groups connected to the proxy mode router to have upstream routers update their multicast tables.

The interface running IGMP proxy mode also serves as a gateway of sorts for IGMP traffic coming to the local network from the upstream multicast router, forwarding that traffic to the appropriate clients. Traffic from local clients to the Internet also passes through the interface. For both incoming and outgoing traffic, TCP/IP itself handles the forwarding.

Setting up a multicast forwarder

The first step in configuring a multicast forwarder is to add the IGMP protocol to the router. In the RRAS console, open the IP Routing branch of the designated server, right-click General, and choose New Routing Protocol. Select IGMP from the list and click OK to add it to the IP Routing branch.

Next, add at least one interface for IGMP. Right-click IGMP in the left pane and choose New Interface. Or, select IGMP in the left pane and right-click anywhere in the right pane, then choose New Interface. Select the interface on which you want to run IGMP and click OK. RRAS displays the IGMP Properties sheet. The General tab lets you choose between router mode and proxy mode for the interface. Select the protocol version using the IGMP protocol version drop-down list if you select router mode.

The Router tab contains several options that control how IGMP functions on the interface:

- **Robustness variable:** This variable indicates the relative robustness of the subnet to which the interface is attached.
- **Query interval:** Specify the interval at which IGMP queries are broadcast on the interface.
- **Query response interval:** Specify the maximum amount of time the router should wait for response for General Query messages.
- **Last member query interval:** Specify the time, in milliseconds, the router waits for a response to a Group-Specific Query message, and the time between successive Group-Specific Query messages.
- **Startup query interval:** Specify the time, in seconds, between successive General Query messages sent by the router during startup. The default value is ¼ of the query interval.
- **Startup query count:** Specify the number of General Query messages to send at startup.
- **Last member query count:** Specify the number of Group-Specific Query messages sent with no response before the router assumes there are no more members of the host group on the interface being queried.
- **Automatically recalculate defaults:** Select this option to have RRAS automatically recalculate values for the Startup query interval, Startup query count, and Last member query count at startup. The default for the Startup query interval is ¼ the query interval. The default for Startup query count and Last member query count is the same as the Robustness variable.
- **Group membership interval:** This read-only property displays the calculated group membership interval, which is the period of time that must pass before the router decides that there are no more members of a multicast group on a given subnet. The value is calculated as (Robustness variable) × (Query interval) + (Query response interval).
- **Other querier present interval:** This read-only property displays the calculated querier present interval, which is the period of time that must pass before the router decides that there are no other multicast routers that should be the querier. The value is calculated as (Robustness variable) × (Query interval) + (Query response interval) ÷ 2.

Network Address Translation

Windows Server 2003's RRAS provides full-featured network address translation (NAT) services. Network Address Translation is not new, and was born out of the high demand for IP addresses. With the Internet growing the way it is, it is virtually impossible to obtain a large range of IP addresses, especially for a small company. The most an ISP will assign to a small company is less than one-sixteenth of a class C subnet, and you have to be spending a lot of money on dedicated Internet services to get that many addresses.

Most small businesses are deploying asymmetric digital subscriber lines (ADSLs), which are cheaper and often faster than dedicated Internet access connections, such as Frame Relay or dedicated ISDN. However, an ISP will usually only assign you a small range of addresses (sometimes just a single IP address). If you plan to install a number of hosts on your internal network, such as DNS, mail, Active Directory, Web, and FTP services, and need to route Internet traffic to these hosts, you will need a NAT.

Note

NAT services in Windows Server 2003 are typically aimed at small or home businesses. A larger company would most likely use a firewall, which has NAT built into its packet inspection technology. Most routers, even for small offices, now come with NAT support.

NAT alleviates the demand for a larger number of IP addresses by mapping externally assigned IP addresses to internally or privately assigned private addresses (translating from one IP address to another). This means that one IP address can typically be used to target a whole range of IP addresses on the concealed network.

Windows 2003 NAT and the RRAS service takes NAT further. NAT can inspect inbound packets to host names and query the internal IP address of the host from an Internal DNS. It will then route the packets that have arrived at the public address to the internal hosts, and route the packets to the correct service via the ports it has been configured to use.

Configuring NAT

As we discussed at the beginning of this chapter, you might typically assign the Class B network of 192.168.0.0 to an internal network in a small company. Armed with the IP addresses of your internal hosts and the IP addresses assigned to you by your ISP, run the RRAS Setup Wizard to configure the server for NAT (right-click the server in the RRAS console and Configure and Enable Routing and Remote Access). Select the option Network Address Translation, click Next, and provide the following information:

Note

You can also manually add NAT, as explained a little later in this section.

✦ **Use this public interface to connect to the Internet.** Select the network interface that is connected to the Internet. This might not actually be a public interface — a firewall or other private network segment might sit between the interface and a public presence on the Internet.

✦ **Create a new demand-dial interface to the Internet.** Select this option if you want to create a new demand-dial interface for the Internet connection.

✦ **Enable security on the selected interface by setting up a basic firewall.** Select this option to enable a firewall on the interface.

You can also manually add NAT if you have already enabled RRAS for another function. The following steps not only add NAT manually, but also take you through the configuration steps for NAT:

1. You need to first add NAT as a routing protocol, which you do by right-clicking the General node and selecting New Routing Protocol. Next, select the server in the console tree and expand its node down to NAT/Basic Firewall. The interfaces (NICs) appear in the details pane on the right.
2. Add the interface to the protocol. Right-click NAT/Basic Firewall and select New Interface. You will have the option to configure the interface for the internal network or the external network (Internet). Select an interface and click OK to display the Network Address Translation Properties dialog box. Specify whether the interface is connected to the Internet or private network, then click OK.
3. Select the interface to configure and right-click. Then select Properties. The Local Area Connection Properties dialog box will appear.
4. On the Address Pool tab, enter the IP address assignment provided by your ISP. In many cases with ADSL, you will be given a dynamically assigned address, which should remain persistent, which means the same IP address gets renewed every time the DHCP lease expires. But you can ask an ISP to reserve the number for you as well.
5. On the Services and Ports tab, place a check beside a service that you want translated. The Edit Service dialog box will load.
6. In the Private Address field, enter the IP address of the server hosting the specified service, then click OK.
7. If you need to add a service not listed, click Add to open the Add Service dialog box. Enter a name for the service in the Description of Service field.
8. In the incoming port field, type the Well-Known port number typically assigned to the IP service in question: for example, port 21 for FTP or port 25 for SMTP.
9. In the outgoing port field, type the private port you wish to assign to the same service. It could be a Well-Known port of the outgoing IP service or any port used by your internal resources. (Using high port numbers, such as 5000, provides additional security; this makes it more difficult for hackers to focus on unknown ports.)
10. In the Private address field, type the private address of the TCP/IP service (typically the host).
11. Enter the public IP address to be translated (as opposed to the interface) in the field on this address pool entry.

That's all there is to configuring NAT; however, you should plan the deployment carefully. To point clients to the Internet for browsing and other services, you would configure the private outgoing IP address on the NAT as your gateway to the Internet. NAT will translate this address to the correct public address.

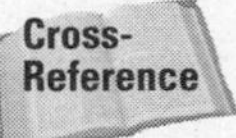

See the section on Internet Connection Sharing (ICS) later in this chapter for an easier alternative to using NAT. The following section explains how to configure the firewall.

You can also configure services and ICMP behavior for the interface. The Services tab lets you configure NAT translation to allow external requests coming from the Internet to be mapped to servers on the internal LAN. The ICMP tab contains settings that determine how the server reacts to ICMP messages it receives on the interface. You can configure these settings without enabling the firewall on the interface, but it's likely you'll do both.

Configuring Services and ICMP Messages

The next step in setting up NAT (or a firewall) on an interface is to specify the services that are allowed in. For example, if there is an FTP server on the internal network and you want external users to be able to access it, you need to enable FTP. In the RRAS console, click NAT/Basic Firewall and then open the properties for the network interface in question. Click the Services and Ports tab (see Figure 18-9).

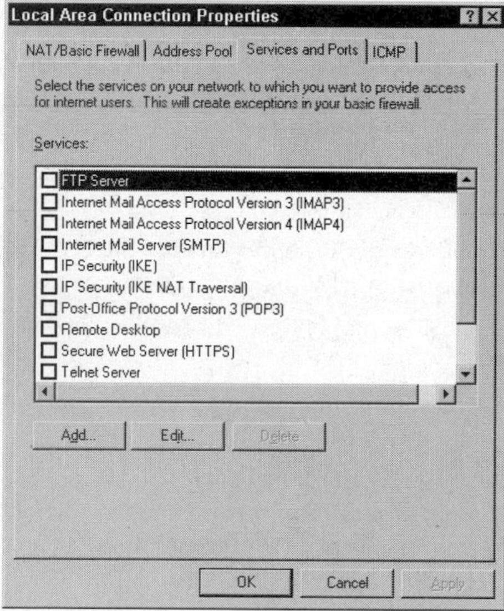

Figure 18-9: Use the Services and Ports tab to add or remove services allowed through the firewall.

Adding a standard service is as simple as selecting the check box beside the service. Windows 2003 displays the Edit Service dialog box (see Figure 18-10), which lets you configure the settings for the service such as the address of the server on the private network that provides the service. Using the FTP example, this would be the IP address of the internal FTP server.

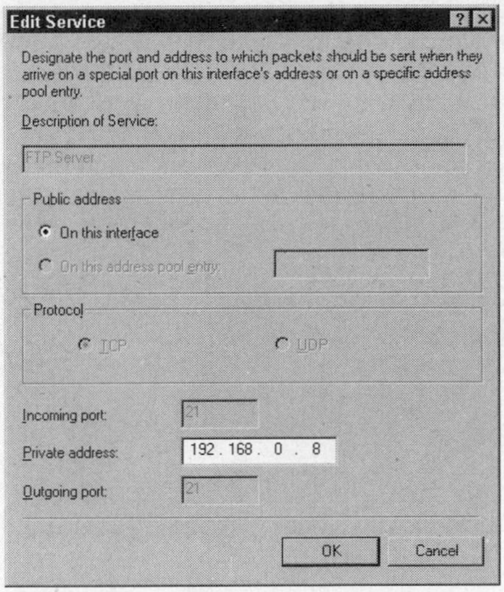

Figure 18-10: Configure the service settings on the Edit Service dialog box.

You can only specify the IP address of the server for all of the standard services listed in the Services and Ports tab. You can configure additional properties by creating a custom service. To do so, click Add to open the Add Service dialog box (see Figure 18-11).

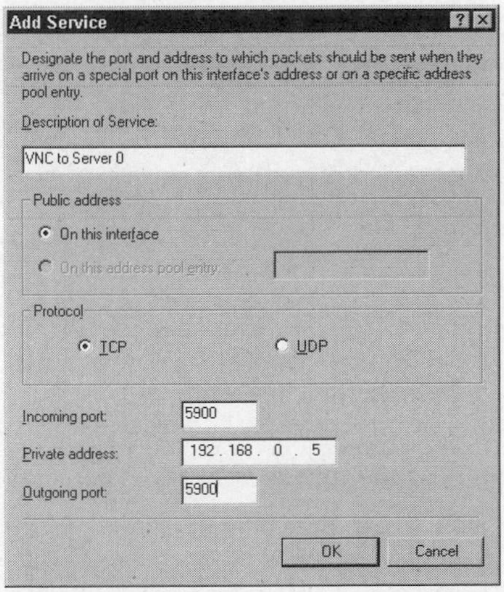

Figure 18-11: Define the settings for the custom service on the Add Service dialog box.

Enter a name for the service, and then select either TCP or UDP to specify the protocol for the service. In the Incoming Port field, type the port number to which the packets are targeted. For example, this would be port 80 for a Web server. In the Private Address field enter the IP address of the server on the internal LAN. In the Outgoing Port field, enter the port on the server to which the packets will be directed. In most cases, the Incoming Port and Outgoing Port values will be the same. However, you can use different port numbers to remap the traffic. For example, you might map incoming port 80 traffic to port 8080 on the server if the server uses that port for HTTP traffic.

You can use the ICMP tab (see Figure 18-12) to specify the ICMP traffic, if any, that the firewall will allow. Each item in the list includes a description — just click on an item to view its description. Items with a check are allowed; others are denied.

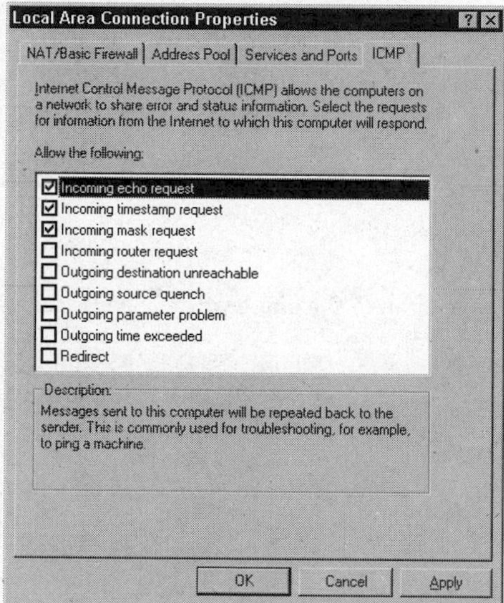

Figure 18-12: Use the ICMP tab to define how the server should handle ICMP traffic.

Configuring a Basic Firewall

The previous section explained that Windows 2003 includes a basic firewall with RRAS. While you probably won't use this basic firewall as your only protection for the network, Windows 2003's firewall can be useful for further restricting and controlling traffic through a server.

To configure a basic firewall, open the RRAS console, expand the IP Routing branch, and click the NAT/Basic Firewall node. In the right pane, right-click the network interface on which you want to establish the firewall and choose Properties. On the NAT/Basic Firewall tab (see Figure 18-13), select the option Enable a Basic Firewall on this Interface.

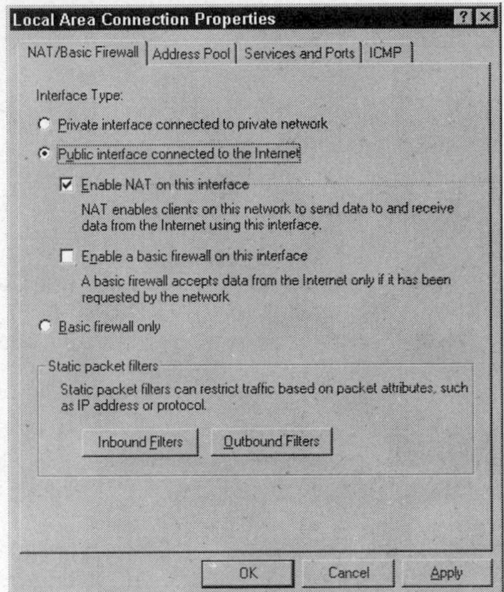

Figure 18-13: Use the NAT/Basic Firewall tab to enable or disable NAT and/or the firewall.

If you don't want to perform NAT on the selected interface but want to protect it with a firewall, choose the option Basic Firewall Only. This disables NAT for the interface and directs Windows 2003 to use Internet Connection Firewall (ICF) to control traffic through the interface.

Configuring RAS for Inbound Connections

RRAS in Windows 2003 really takes three distinct directions: routing, inbound connections (RAS server), and outbound connections (RAS client). This section explains how to configure a Windows Server 2003 as a RAS server. When you install Windows 2003, Setup by default installs RRAS, so you don't need to install it separately. You do, however, need to configure it. The following sections explain how to configure modems, ports, protocols, encryption, and other properties to set up and manage a RAS server.

Enabling RRAS

As explained earlier in this chapter, RRAS installs when you set up Windows 2003, but you need to enable and configure the service. The wizard offers a handful of options to help you automatically configure the service.

Remote access (dial-up or VPN)

Select this option to configure the RRAS server to enable remote access clients to connect through the server to access resources on the server or on the local network through a dial-up or VPN connection. You can choose either or both. The wizard prompts for the following:

✦ **Public interface:** For VPN connections, choose the public interface through which remote VPN clients connect to the RRAS server. You also have the option of enabling a basic firewall on the interface.

✦ **Network interface:** The wizard prompts for the network interface to which to assign remote clients, which determines where the addresses and other access properties come from. In a multi-homed server, select the network interface where the DHCP server is located, if allocating addresses through DHCP.

✦ **IP address assignment:** You can choose to assign addresses through DHCP (see the previous option) or from a static address pool. If you choose to use a static pool, the wizard prompts you for the range of addresses to use. See the section titled "Configuring protocols" later in this chapter for detailed information regarding address assignment.

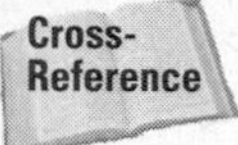

You can allow remote clients to request a preassigned IP address configured at the client side. See the section titled "Configuring protocols" later in this chapter for a detailed explanation.

✦ **RADIUS:** You can configure the RRAS server to use RADIUS for authentication and accounting. You specify the IP address or host name for the primary and alternate RADIUS servers, along with the RADIUS shared secret, which essentially is a password the RRAS server uses to authenticate its right to access the RADIUS servers. Windows 2003 includes a RADIUS server called Internet Authentication Service (IAS) that you can use for RRAS and other applications requiring RADIUS authentication, or you can use any RADIUS server. See the section titled "Using RADIUS" later in this chapter for more information.

Network address translation

This option helps you set up a Network address translation (NAT) server. Configuring NAT was covered earlier in this chapter.

Virtual Private Network access and NAT

Select this option to configure RRAS as a Virtual Private Network (VPN) server, enabling clients to use PPTP or L2TP to dial in from a public network such as the Internet (or direct dial-up) and to establish a secure connection to the local network. This option also sets up the server as an Internet gateway with NAT, enabling internal users to access the Internet through the server.

By default, RRAS configures 128 ports each for PPTP and L2TP, but you can add or remove ports as desired. The settings prompted by the wizard are the same as those settings explained previously in the section titled "Remote access (dial-up or VPN)," and the server also prompts for the network interface through which the RRAS server connects to the Internet. The VPN server must have a second network interface for the internal LAN.

Secure connection between two private networks

Select this option to configure the RRAS server to function as a router. The wizard prompts you to choose whether or not you want to use demand-dial connections to access remote networks. If you choose No, the wizard completes the configuration and terminates. If you answer Yes, the wizard asks if you want to assign IP addresses through DHCP or a static address pool (if IP is installed on the server). Choosing Yes does not cause the wizard to configure any demand-dial connections; you configure those through the RRAS console after the wizard finishes. The wizard adds NAT/Basic Firewall to the configuration automatically.

Custom configuration

Select this option if you want to choose which functions the RRAS server will perform. You can run the wizard again if desired to automatically configure the server, although you'll lose the current configuration settings. See the previous section, "Enabling RRAS," to learn how to restart the wizard.

The following sections assume you are configuring the server manually rather than using the wizard, or fine-tuning settings after running the wizard.

Configuring modems and ports

One of the first steps to take in setting up a Windows 2003 RAS server is to install and configure the hardware and ports that will handle the incoming calls. You configure a standard modem through the Control Panel. If the modem is not already installed, open the Control Panel and double-click the Phone and Modem Options object. Click the Modems tab, then click Add to start the Add/Remove Hardware wizard. You have the option of selecting the modem manually or letting Windows 2003 search for it. Repeat the process for any additional modems you are installing on the system.

Other types of dial-up equipment require different installation and configuration steps that vary from one item to the next. It isn't practical to cover all types in this chapter, so you might have to refer to the manufacturer's documentation to learn how to properly install the hardware. If you're setting up a server connected to the Internet to act as a VPN server for your local network, install the network hardware, connect the system to the Internet, and verify that the server has connectivity to both the LAN and Internet.

You configure ports for incoming access through the RRAS console. When you click on the Ports node, the console displays the installed RAS ports. Windows 2003 by default installs both the PPTP and L2TP protocols for VPN support and adds ports for each protocol (one incoming connection per port of each type.) You can view the status of a given port by double-clicking the port in the list or right-clicking the port and choosing Status. Windows 2003 displays a Port Status dialog box for the port that shows line speed, errors, and protocol-specific data such as IP address, IPX address, and so on.

To configure ports, right-click Ports in the right pane of the RRAS console and choose Properties. Windows 2003 displays a Ports Properties dialog box listing each of the port types. For example, all PPTP ports appear under a single item in the list, as do all L2TP ports and individual modems. Select the port type you want to configure and click Configure. Windows 2003 displays the Configure Device dialog box shown in Figure 18-14.

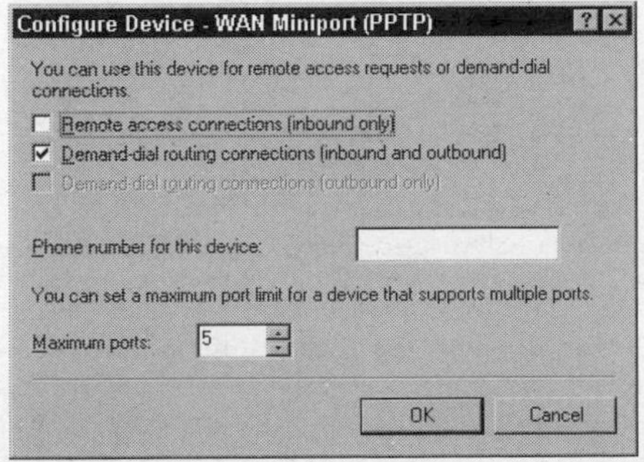

Figure 18-14: The Configure Device dialog box.

The following list explains the options in the Configure Device dialog box:

- **Remote access connections (inbound only):** Select this option to allow the selected port to handle incoming connections only and not function as a demand-dial router for outgoing connections.
- **Demand-dial routing connections (inbound and outbound):** Select this option to allow the port to handle incoming calls and function as a demand-dial router to service local clients for outgoing calls.
- **Phone number for this device:** This option is used for Called-Station-ID and BAP-enabled connections and to identify the IP address for PPTP and L2TP ports. Some devices support the automatic recognition of the device's phone number for Called-Station-ID, so you only need to add the number manually if the device doesn't support automatic recognition. The number must match the number defined in the Called-Station-ID attribute of the remote access policy that is in effect, or the call is rejected. For BAP, this property is passed to the client when it requests an additional connection so it knows what number to dial for the new connection. For PPTP and L2TP ports, enter the IP address in dotted decimal format you are assigning to the VPN interface of the server.
- **Maximum ports:** Use this control to specify the maximum number of ports enabled on a multiport device or protocol (such as PPTP or L2TP).

Configuring protocols

In addition to configuring the ports used by the RRAS server, you also need to configure the protocols to be used by remote access clients. You should verify that you have the necessary protocols installed prior to attempting to configure the protocols for RRAS. The following sections explain the options you have for each of the supported RRAS protocols.

TCP/IP

You can assign IP addresses to remote access clients using one of three methods: DHCP, a static address pool, or by allowing the client to request a preassigned IP address.

Assigning addresses through DHCP

When the RRAS service starts, it checks for the availability of a DHCP server (if configured to use DHCP for address assignment) and obtains 10 leases from the DHCP server. The RRAS server uses the first lease for itself and assigns the remaining addresses to RAS clients as they connect, recovering and reusing addresses as clients disconnect. When the pool of 10 addresses is exhausted, the RRAS server obtains 10 more, and the process repeats as needed. When the RRAS service stops, it releases all the addresses, making them available for other DHCP clients on the network.

The RRAS service will use Automatic Private IP Addressing (APIPA) if it is unable to locate a DHCP server at startup. APIPA enables Windows 2003 to assign addresses in the class B address range 169.254.0.1 through 169.254.0.254 (subnet mask of 255.255.0.0). APIPA is designed to allow automatic IP configuration when no DHCP server is available. Because APIPA is intended for use in internal, single-segment networks, it does not allocate settings for default gateway, DNS servers, or WINS servers.

RRAS by default selects a network interface at random from which to obtain the DHCP leases for RAS clients. You can, however, specify the interface to pull addresses from a specific network segment/server when the RRAS server is multi-homed (multiple network interfaces).

You do so through the IP page of the server's properties. In the RRAS console, right-click the server and choose Properties, then click the IP tab (see Figure 18-15). Use the Adapter drop-down list at the bottom of the property page to select the adapter, or choose "Allow RAS to select adapter" if you want to allow RRAS to automatically select an adapter.

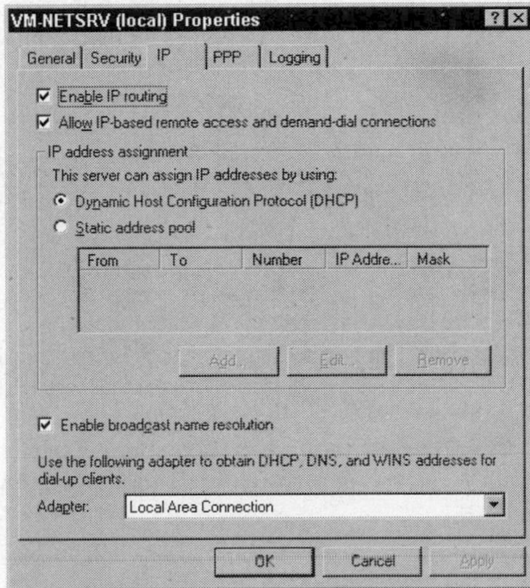

Figure 18-15: The IP tab.

The Adapter drop-down list only appears on multi-homed systems.

Using a static address pool

You can assign addresses to RAS clients from a static pool if you have no DHCP server on the network or simply prefer not to use DHCP for the RAS server. In previous versions of RRAS (Windows NT), you could configure included and excluded address ranges. In Windows 2003, however, you only create included ranges. You can achieve the same effect as an excluded range by simply creating multiple included ranges that don't include the address range you want to exclude.

You configure the static address pool through the IP property page for the server. In the RRAS console, right-click the server, choose Properties, and then click the IP tab. Select the option "Static address pool" and then click Add to display the New Address Range dialog box. You specify a starting address for the range, then either the ending address or the number of addresses to include in the pool. Windows 2003 determines the ending address for you if you specify the number of addresses, and it also determines the required subnet mask based on the selected address range. Click OK to add the range, then repeat the process if you need to add other ranges.

When defining static address pools for RRAS, make sure you don't use addresses already allocated to other systems or to DHCP servers on the network. If the static address pool is in a different subnet from the local network, you must either enable IP routing on the RRAS server (configured through the IP page of the server's global properties) or add static routes for the subnet.

Allowing clients to use preassigned IP addresses

In some situations, it's advantageous for clients to be able to use the same IP address for each remote session. For example, users might work with applications that expect remote users to be at specific IP addresses. Arbitrarily allowing clients to request preassigned IP addresses could lead to address havoc and potential routing problems, but Windows 2003 overcomes that problem by allocating the remote client's IP address through his or her account properties. Enabling a client to request a preassigned IP address requires two steps. First, you must configure the applicable remote access policy to allow the user to request a preassigned IP address. Second, you must specify the address in the user's account properties.

You configure the remote access policy through the RRAS console. See the section titled "Remote Access Policy" later in this section for detailed information on configuring and managing remote access policies.

Where you modify the user's account properties depends on the network configuration. On a standalone server (no domain), you modify the user's properties through the Local Users and Groups node of the Computer Management console. Open the account's properties and click the Dial-In tab. Select the option "Assign a Static IP Address" and specify the desired address in the associated text box. For information on other properties on the Dial-Up page, see the section titled "Remote Access Policy" later in this chapter. You'll find the same properties for users in a domain in the Active Directory Users and Computers console. Configure properties as you would on a standalone server.

Enabling/disabling IP for RRAS

Windows 2003 RRAS by default enables for RRAS all protocols installed on the server. You can selectively disable a protocol if you don't want to allow that protocol to be used for remote connections. To enable or disable IP for RAS, open the RRAS console, right-click the server, and choose Properties. On the IP property page, select or deselect the option "Allow IP-based remote access and demand-dial connections" to enable or disable IP for RAS, respectively.

IP routing and restricting access to the RAS server

By default, the RRAS server allows remote clients access not only to the local server, but also to the network (subject to permissions and policies applied to the remote client or local resources). As such, the RRAS server provides IP routing to the remote clients, routing traffic between the remote client and the LAN. You can prevent remote clients from accessing the LAN by disabling IP routing on the RRAS server. To do so, open the RRAS console, right-click the server, and choose Properties. On the IP page, deselect the option "Enable IP routing" to prevent remote clients from accessing the LAN and to restrict their access only to resources on the RRAS server.

IP routing must be enabled if you're using the RRAS server to provide LAN or demand-dial routing. See the section titled "IP Routing" earlier in this chapter for a detailed discussion of Windows 2003 routing through RRAS.

IPX

The first step in configuring IPX is to decide how IPX network and node numbers will be assigned to remote clients. You also can enable/disable IPX for RAS connections and control which resources the IPX clients can access. Open the RRAS console, right-click the server, choose Properties, and click the IPX tab to configure the following properties:

- **Allow IPX-based remote clients to dial into this server:** Select this option to enable IPX for RRAS; deselect to prevent remote clients from using IPX for remote connections.
- **Allow dial-in clients to access the entire network:** Select this option to allow remote IPX clients to access IPX-based resources (NetWare servers, for example) on the LAN to which the RRAS server is connected; deselect to allow remote IPX clients only access to resources on the RRAS server.
- **Automatically:** This option allows the RRAS server to automatically allocate IPX network numbers to remote access clients and demand-dial routers that request connections to the RRAS server.
- **In the following range:** Use this option to specify a range of IPX network numbers the RRAS server will use to allocate network numbers to remote clients and demand-dial routers.
- **Use the same network number for all IPX clients:** Use this option to have the RRAS server assign the same IPX network number to all clients, reducing RIP announcements and corresponding network traffic.
- **Allow remote clients to request IPX node number:** Select this option to allow remote access clients and demand-dial routers to request a specific IPX node number when the connection is established.

AppleTalk

There is essentially no configuration necessary for AppleTalk on a RRAS server. Use the AppleTalk page of the server's properties to enable or disable AppleTalk for remote connections.

Configuring authentication

After you have configured protocols on the RRAS server, you need to turn your attention to authentication and encryption, configuring the server to suit your needs.

Configuring PPP

Windows 2003 offers a few options you can configure that control PPP connections to the server. In the RRAS console, right-click the server, choose Properties, and click the PPP tab. The PPP page offers the following options:

- **Multilink connections:** Select this option to allow remote clients to request and use multilink connections. This option enables multilink connections but does not explicitly enable dynamic link management through BAP or BACP, which is controlled by the following option. See the section titled "Using Multilink and BAP" later in this chapter for additional information.
- **Dynamic bandwidth control using BAP or BACP:** This option enables the server and client to use Bandwidth Allocation Protocol and Bandwidth Allocation Control Protocol to dynamically multilink connections, adding links when bandwidth utilization increases and removing links when bandwidth utilization decreases.
- **Link control protocol (LCP) extensions:** LCP extensions enable LCP to send Time-Remaining and Identification packets, and to request callback during LCP negotiation. Deselect this option only if the remote clients don't support LCP extensions.
- **Software compression:** Select this option to have the RRAS server use Microsoft Point-to-Point Compression protocol (MPPC) to compress data transmitted to remote clients. Deselect this option if the remote clients don't support MPPC.

Configuring authentication

As mentioned earlier in this chapter, Windows 2003 RRAS supports several authentication standards. You can configure RRAS to accept multiple authentication methods, and the server will attempt authentication using the selected protocols in order of decreasing security. For example, RRAS attempts EAP first if EAP is enabled, then MS-CHAP version 2, then MS-CHAP, and so on.

You configure the authentication methods for RRAS through the Security page of the RRAS server's properties (accessed from the RRAS console). Click Authentication Methods on the Security page to access the Authentication Methods dialog box shown in Figure 18-16. Select the authentication methods you want to allow, then click OK. The following sections provide an overview of each method and where applicable, and how to configure and enable them.

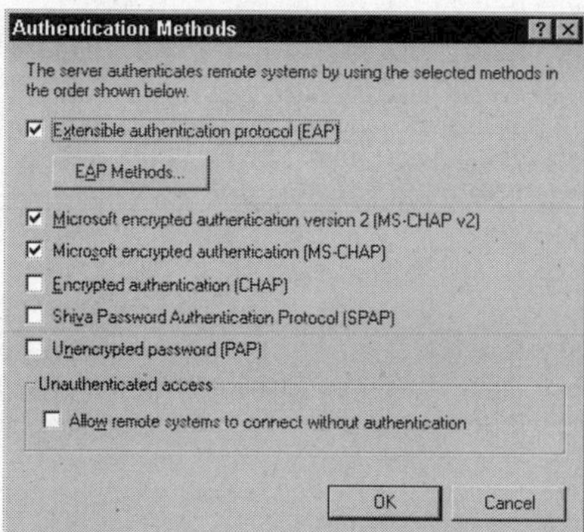

Figure 18-16: You can configure multiple authentication methods through the Authentication Methods dialog box, and RRAS attempts them in decreasing order of security provided.

You can require a specific authentication method for a client through a remote access policy. The following sections don't cover configuring authentication through a remote policy for each authentication protocol, but you will find coverage of that topic in the section titled "Remote Access Policy" later in this chapter.

EAP

Extensible Authentication Protocol (EAP) enables the client and server (or IAS, if used for RAS authentication) to negotiate an authentication method from a pool of methods supported by the server. Windows 2003 EAP provides support for two EAP types: EAP-MD5 CHAP and EAP-TLS. Both the client and authentication server must support the same EAP type for authentication through EAP, and you can install additional EAP types from third parties on a Windows Server 2003.

EAP-MD5 CHAP functions much the same as standard CHAP, but challenges and responses are sent as EAP messages. EAP-MD5 CHAP authenticates with user names and passwords. EAP-TLS, on the other hand, uses certificates to authenticate remote clients, using a secured private key exchange between client and server. EAP-TLS provides the most secure authentication of all the methods supported by Windows 2003.

Windows 2003 supports EAP-TLS only in domain environments (either mixed mode or native). RRAS on a standalone server does not support EAP-TLS.

Enabling RRAS to support EAP requires three steps. First, enable EAP as an authentication method in the Authentication Methods dialog box through the RRAS server's properties. Then, if necessary, configure the remote client's remote access policy to allow EAP, as explained later in the section "Remote Access Policy." Finally, configure the client to use the appropriate EAP type. See the section titled "Configuring Outgoing Dial-Up Networking Connections" in this chapter for a detailed explanation.

Configuring EAP-RADIUS

In addition to supporting the two EAP types described previously, Windows 2003 also enables authentication messages for any EAP type to be relayed to RADIUS servers (such as Windows 2003 systems running IAS). EAP-RADIUS encapsulates and formats the messages going from the RRAS server to the RADIUS server as RADIUS messages. The RADIUS server encapsulates the EAP response as a RADIUS message and passes it to the RRAS server, which relays it to the client. In this way, the RRAS server functions as a relay and doesn't actually perform the authentication, nor does it require the EAP type used to be installed on the RRAS server. Instead, the EAP type must be installed on the RADIUS server.

In addition to configuring the client to use EAP and the appropriate EAP type, you must enable EAP authentication on the RRAS server, configure it to point to the appropriate RADIUS server, and also install the required EAP type on the RADIUS server. You configure the RRAS server to accommodate EAP through the Authentication Methods dialog box for the server, as explained previously. To point the RRAS server to the RADIUS server, open the server's Security property page and select RADIUS Authentication from the Authentication Provider drop-down list. Click Configure ➪ Add to display the Add RADIUS Server dialog box shown in Figure 18-17.

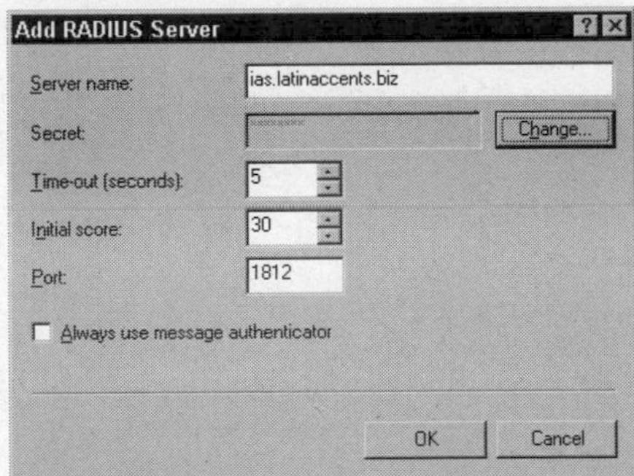

Figure 18-17: The Add RADIUS Server dialog box.

Use the following list as a guide to configure RADIUS server options:

- **Server name:** Specify the FQDN or IP address of the RADIUS server.
- **Secret:** Enter the secret string used by the RADIUS server to authenticate access to the RADIUS server. You can use any alphanumeric characters and special characters in the string, up to 255 characters. The shared secret is case-sensitive.

- **Time-out (seconds):** This is the period of time the RRAS server will wait for a response from the RADIUS server before timing out and failing the authentication.
- **Initial score:** This value indicates the overall responsiveness of the RADIUS server. This number changes dynamically as the responsiveness of the RADIUS server changes. RRAS queries the servers in order of highest to lowest score (the higher the score, the better the responsiveness). Use this option to specify an estimated initial score.
- **Port:** Specify the UDP port used by the RADIUS server for incoming authentication requests. The default is 1812 for newer RADIUS servers and 1645 for older RADIUS servers.
- **Always use message authenticator:** Select this option to force the RRAS server to send a digital signature with each RADIUS message. The signature is based on the shared secret. Ensure that the RADIUS server supports and is configured for receipt of digital signatures before enabling this option. If you're using IAS and the client for this server is configured to require the RRAS server to always send a digital signature, you must select this option.

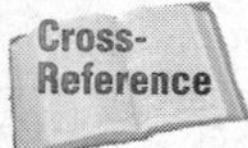

See the section titled "RRAS Logging and Accounting" later in this chapter to configure the RRAS server for RADIUS authentication.

Repeat the process described previously to add other RADIUS servers as required.

MS-CHAP version 2

Microsoft Challenge Handshake Authentication Protocol (MS-CHAP v2) is an improvement on the original MS-CHAP v1 that addresses a handful of security issues. With MS-CHAP v2, the authentication server sends a challenge to the client containing a session ID and arbitrary challenge string. The client returns the user name, an arbitrary peer challenge string, and a one-way encryption of the received challenge string, peer challenge string, session ID, and user password. The server checks the client response and returns a success/failure and an authenticated response that is based on the two challenge strings, the encrypted client response, and the user password. The client verifies the authentication and, if it's valid, accepts the connection. The RAS client terminates the connection if the authentication is not valid.

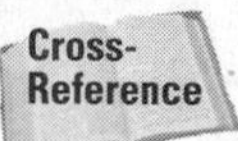

See the section titled "New Features of Windows 2003 RRAS" earlier in this chapter for a list of improvements MS-CHAP v2 offers over v1.

MS-CHAP v2 is enabled by default for authentication on Windows 2003 RRAS servers. There are no other configuration steps to take other than to configure the client to use MS-CHAP v2. See the section titled " Configuring Outgoing Dial-Up Networking Connections" later in this chapter for more information. To disable MS-CHAP v2 on the RRAS server, open the RRAS console and then open the property sheet for the server. On the Security tab, click Authentication Methods and then deselect the MS-CHAP v2 option.

MS-CHAP

MS-CHAP represents version 1 of the Microsoft Challenge Handshake Authentication Protocol. With MS-CHAP, the authentication server sends a challenge to the client containing a session ID and arbitrary challenge string. The remote client responds with the user name and encryption of the challenge string, session ID, and user's password. The server checks the supplied credentials and authenticates access if the credentials are valid.

MS-CHAP is enabled by default for Windows 2003 RRAS servers, and there are no other configuration steps except to verify that the client is configured to use MS-CHAP.

CHAP

This option enables the server to use Message Digest 5 Challenge Handshake Authentication Protocol (MD-5 CHAP, or simply CHAP). CHAP uses a standard mechanism for encrypting the authentication response and is supported by several nonMicrosoft remote access clients. As such, CHAP provides a means of supporting remote clients that do not support MS-CHAP or EAP (while still providing some level of encryption and security).

The first step to enable remote clients to authenticate on a Windows 2003 RRAS server with CHAP is to enable CHAP in the Authentication Methods dialog box. In the RRAS console, open the properties for the server and click the Security tab, then click Authentication Methods. Select "Encrypted authentication (CHAP)." Then, if you're using remote access policies to control allowed authentication methods, modify the policy as needed to allow the appropriate clients to use CHAP.

In order to support CHAP, user passwords must be stored using reversible encryption. While you can enable reversibly encrypted passwords for all users in the domain, you might wish to only enable reversible encryption for those clients requiring CHAP authentication. You can selectively enable reversible encryption if the accounts are stored in the Active Directory. To do so, open the Active Directory Users and Computers console, then open the user's property sheet. On the Account tab, select the option "Store password using reversible encryption" in the Account Options group, then click OK or Apply.

You need to modify the default domain policy if you want to apply reversible encryption for all users in the domain. On a domain controller, choose Start ➪ All Programs ➪ Administrative Tools ➪ Domain Security Policy. Open the branch Security Settings/Account Policies/Password Policy and enable the option "Store password using reversible encryption for all users in the domain." On a standalone server, choose Start ➪ All Programs ➪ Administrative Tools ➪ Local Security Policy to modify the password policy to enable reversible encryption.

Each user for which reversible encryption has been enabled needs to modify his or her password so that the new password will be stored with reversible encryption. Configuring the user's account or the domain or local policy for reversible encryption does not automatically change the way the passwords are stored. You can reset the users' passwords yourself or have the users change passwords during their next logon session. Because the users can't change passwords through CHAP authentication, they must either log on to the LAN to change their passwords or use MS-CHAP through the remote connection to change their passwords, and then switch to CHAP for future remote sessions. The alternative for those users who can't log on to the LAN or use MS-CHAP is for the administrator to reset the password.

The final step is to configure the remote client to use CHAP. See the section titled "Configuring Outgoing Dial-Up Networking Connections" to learn how to configure Windows 2003 remote access clients.

SPAP

SPAP stands for Shiva Password Authentication Protocol. Shiva is a corporation that develops and markets several remote access solutions, including the Shiva LAN Rover. Clients connecting to a Shiva LAN Rover use SPAP for authentication, as do Shiva clients connecting to a

Windows 2003 RRAS server. SPAP is disabled by default for a Windows 2003 RRAS server. SPAP offers a lower degree of security than the methods described previously, so you should enable SPAP only if you need to support Shiva clients. You can enable SPAP through the Authentication Methods dialog box in the RRAS server's properties.

PAP

Password Authentication Protocol (PAP) uses plain text to transmit passwords, making it susceptible to compromise. You should therefore only use PAP to support clients that do not support any of the other authentication methods, or in situations where security is not an issue. Enable PAP for the RRAS server through the Authentication Methods dialog box in the RRAS server's properties.

Unauthenticated access

You can configure a Windows 2003 RRAS server to allow unauthenticated remote access, enabling any user to log on whether he or she provides a valid user name and password or not. While unauthenticated access can pose a security risk, it nevertheless has some uses. Because unauthenticated access is applicable in few situations, it is not covered in detail here. To learn more about unauthenticated access, open the RRAS console, open Help, and open the topic Remote Access/Concepts/Remote Access Security/Unauthenticated Access.

Disabling routing (Remote Access Server only)

If you're using RRAS to only provide dial-in remote access and don't require routing, you can disable routing and allow the server to function as a remote access server only. This reduces some of the overhead in the RRAS server and can improve performance somewhat. You also might want to disable routing for security reasons that might be applicable to your network.

To disable routing, open the RRAS console and then open the properties for the server on which you want to disable routing. On the General page, deselect the Router option and leave the Remote access server option selected. Click OK and allow Windows 2003 to restart RRAS to make the change take effect.

RRAS logging and accounting

Windows 2003 RRAS, like many other services, logs events to the Windows 2003 System log, which you can view and manage with the Event Viewer console. You configure logging options on the Event Logging page of the RRAS server's property sheet. Open the RRAS console, open the property sheet for the server, and click the Logging tab. The Logging page offers a handful of options that control the amount of information logged to the System event log; the options are self-explanatory. You also can enable logging of PPP events for troubleshooting purposes–just enable the option Log Additional Routing and Remote Access Information.

By default, a Windows 2003 RRAS server uses Windows 2003 accounting, which means that certain aspects of remote sessions are logged to the log file designated by the entry in the Remote Access Logging branch of the RRAS console. Windows accounting is applicable when you are using IAS to provide authentication. If you're using a RADIUS server, however, you'll probably want to configure RADIUS to perform the accounting for you. The following sections explain both options.

Using Windows accounting

Windows 2003 RRAS by default does not log remote sessions, but you can enable logging for security and troubleshooting. To use Windows accounting, open the RRAS console, right-click the server, choose Properties, and click the Security tab. Select Windows Accounting from the Accounting Provider drop-down list, then click OK to close the property sheet.

Then in the RRAS console, open the Remote Access Logging branch. You'll find one item in the right pane labeled Local File. Double-click Local File, or right-click it and choose Properties, to display the Local File Properties sheet. The Settings page contains the following options:

- **Accounting requests:** Select this option to log accounting requests from the RRAS server to the accounting server to indicate that it is online and ready to accept connections or going offline, and to start and stop accounting for a user session.
- **Authentication requests:** Select this option to log authentication requests sent by the RRAS server to IAS on behalf of the client, along with responses from IAS to the RRAS server indicating the acceptance/rejection of the remote client's authentication request.
- **Periodic status:** This option enables you to log periodic status requests for a session sent by the RRAS server to IAS, although the option is generally not recommended because of the potentially large log file that usually results.

The Local File page of the Local File Properties sheet determines the format for the local log file as well as the log's location, file name, and how often a new log file is created. The options are generally self-explanatory.

Using RADIUS accounting

You configure RADIUS accounting through the Security tab of the RRAS server's properties. Open the RRAS console, right-click the server, choose Properties, and click the Security tab. Select RADIUS Accounting from the Accounting Provider drop-down list, then click Configure. In the RADIUS Accounting dialog box, click Add to add a RADIUS accounting server and configure its properties. The following list explains the options:

- **Server name:** Specify the FQDN or IP address of the RADIUS server.
- **Secret:** Enter the secret string used by the RADIUS server to authenticate access to the RADIUS server. You can use any alphanumeric characters and special characters in the string, up to 255 characters. The shared secret is case-sensitive.
- **Time-out:** This is the period of time the RRAS server will wait for a response from the RADIUS server before timing out and failing the accounting request.
- **Initial score:** This value indicates the overall responsiveness of the RADIUS server. This number changes dynamically as the responsiveness of the RADIUS server changes. RRAS queries the servers in order of highest to lowest score (the higher the score, the better the responsiveness). Use this option to specify an estimated initial score.
- **Port:** Specify the UDP port used by the RADIUS server for incoming authentication requests. The default is 1813 for newer RADIUS servers and 1646 for older RADIUS servers.
- **Send RADIUS accounting on and off messages:** Select this option to have the RRAS server send Accounting-On and Accounting-Off messages to the accounting server when the RRAS service starts and stops.

Configuring a VPN Server

A secure Virtual Private Network (VPN) connection enables remote access clients to establish secure connections to the RRAS server or to the local network to which the RRAS server is connected from a nonsecure network such as the Internet. Once connected by a VPN connection, the remote user has the same capabilities and security as he or she would have if connected locally to the network. A common use for VPN is to allow remote users to access files, printers, and other resources on the office LAN when they are on the road or working from other locations.

In a VPN connection, the data packets are encapsulated with additional header data that provides routing data to enable the packet to reach its destination. The segment of the connection in which the data is encapsulated is called a *tunnel.*

Data is encrypted before it is encapsulated to make the data secure as it travels through the public network. *Tunneling protocols* manage the traffic flow between the client and server. Windows 2003 by default supports two tunneling protocols: Point-to-Point Tunneling Protocol (PPTP) and Layer 2 Tunneling Protocol (L2TP). These protocols are described earlier in this chapter in the section titled "RAS Connection Types and Protocols." Windows NT, Windows 9.*x*, Windows Me, Windows 2000, and Windows XP clients support PPTP, and Windows 2003 clients support both PPTP and L2TP. NonMicrosoft clients that support PPTP or L2TP can also connect to a Windows 2003 VPN server.

When you set up a Windows 2003 RRAS server manually as a remote access server, Windows 2003 automatically installs both PPTP and L2TP and configures five ports for each protocol, meaning you can connect five remote VPN clients with each protocol. If you use the wizard to configure the server as a VPN server, the wizard creates 128 ports each for PPTP and L2TP. In either case, you can change the number of virtual ports available for connections through the Ports branch in the RRAS console (explained later).

The easiest way to configure a VPN server is to run the configuration wizard and select the desired VPN option. See the section titled "Configuring RRAS for Inbound Connections" earlier in this chapter for an explanation of the options offered by the wizard. The following sections explain changes you can make after installation or how to configure the server for VPN manually.

Tip

Don't forget to enable the remote clients' accounts for remote access either through the individual account properties or the remote access policy. This is required for VPN connections just as it is for standard RAS connections.

Configuring VPN ports

You use the RRAS console to make all changes to the VPN server's configuration. One of the changes you'll surely want to make at some point is the port configuration. Open the RRAS console, open the server to be changed, right-click the Ports branch, and choose Properties. The Ports Properties sheet shows the available ports, port type, and limited other information. Click a port type, then click Configure to display the Configure Device dialog box similar to the one shown in Figure 18-18.

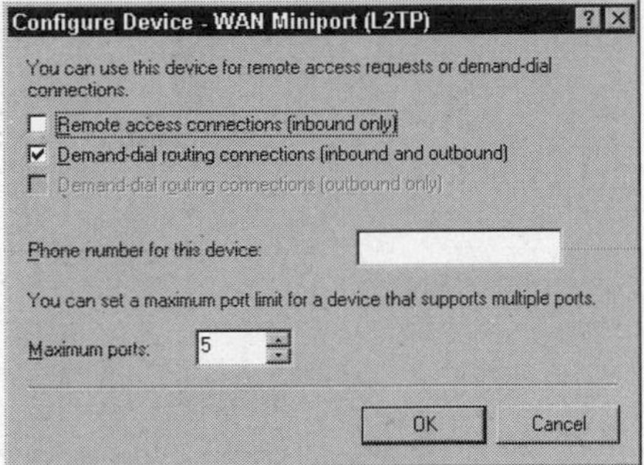

Figure 18-18: The Configure Device dialog box.

Use the Configure Device dialog box to configure port properties, which vary somewhat from one type to another.

Use the following list as a guide to configure port options:

- **Remote access connections (inbound only):** Select this option to enable the port type for incoming remote access connections. Deselect the option to prevent incoming connections on the selected port type.
- **Demand-dial routing connections (inbound and outbound):** Select this option to enable incoming and outgoing demand-dial routing on the port type. Deselect to disable routing for the selected port type.
- **Demand-dial routing connections (outbound only):** Select this option to allow only outbound demand-dial connections.
- **Phone number for this device:** For PPTP and L2TP ports, specify the IP address assigned to the VPN interface on the server through which the incoming connections arrive.
- **Maximum ports:** Change the number of ports of the selected type with this control.

Enabling L2TP for VPN

Windows 2003 by default configures five L2TP ports when you install RRAS for remote access and 128 ports if you install RRAS for VPN. There are some additional steps other than configuring ports that you need to take to ensure that L2TP provides a secure connection, as explained in the following sections.

Obtaining and installing a certificate

L2TP uses IPSec to provide encryption, which requires that you install a computer certificate on the RRAS server as well as the client to provide encryption/decryption capability for IPSec. You must have a Windows Server 2003 running Certificate Services on your network (or locally on the RRAS server) from which to obtain the certificate. This certificate server is called a Certificate Authority (CA). An enterprise root CA can be configured to allocate computer certificates automatically to computers in the domain. Or, you can use the

Certificates console to request a certificate from an enterprise CA. You also can connect to `http://server/cersrv`, where *server* is the address or name of the CA, to request a certificate. Use this last option if your RRAS server is not a member of a domain or if you need to request the certificate from a standalone CA.

Chapter 3 discusses IPSec, certificates, and Certificate Services.

Configuring L2TP over IPSec filters

Unlike PPTP, which uses Microsoft Point-to-Point Encryption (MPPE), L2TP relies on IP Security (IPSec) to provide encryption to secure the VPN connection. You therefore need to configure IPSec filters accordingly on the RRAS server's public interface to restrict all but L2TP traffic. This will ensure that only secure L2TP traffic moves through the RRAS server. To configure the filters, first note the IP address of the RRAS server's public interface (the one connected to the Internet). Then, open the RRAS console, open the IP Routing branch, and click General. Right-click the interface on which you want to set the filters and choose Properties.

On the General page of the interface's property sheet, click Inbound Filters to display the Inbound Filters dialog box. Click Add to display the Add IP Filter dialog box (see Figure 18-19). Select the option Destination Network, then in the IP Address field, specify the IP address of the server's Internet network interface. In the Subnet Mask field, enter **255.255.255.255**. Select UDP from the Protocol drop-down list, enter **500** in both the Source Port and Destination Port fields, and click OK.

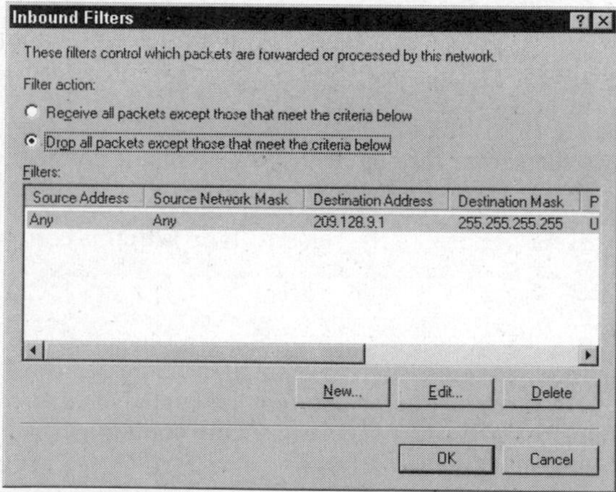

Figure 18-19: The Add IP Filter dialog box.

Back on the Input Filters dialog box, click Add again and add another Destination Network entry for the same IP address and subnet mask as the first entry, but add UDP port entries of 1701 for both Source Port and Destination Port fields. Click OK, then in the Input Filters dialog box, select the option "Drop all packets except those that meet the criteria below," and click OK.

Next, you need to add filters to restrict traffic for outgoing packets to the appropriate ports for L2TP. On the General page of the interface's property sheet, click Output Filters. Just as you did for the input filters, add two output filters for the server's public network interface IP address, subnet mask 255.255.255.255, with the first filter using UDP port 500 for Source Port and Destination Port and a second using UDP port 1701 for Source Port and Destination Port.

Using Multilink and BAP

As mentioned earlier in this chapter, Windows 2003 supports the use of multilink connections, which enables a client to connect to the RRAS server using multiple, aggregated links. Bandwidth Allocation Protocol (BAP) provides a means for the bandwidth utilization to be dynamic. As bandwidth usage increases, the client can request another connection to improve performance. As bandwidth usage decreases, connections can be dropped to make them available to other clients or reduce connection costs. Enabling multilink and BAP requires a few steps: enable multilink, configure remote access policies, configure the ports, and configure the clients.

First, open the RRAS console, right-click the server, and choose Properties. On the PPP page, select Multilink connections to allow clients to request multilink connections. Select "Dynamic bandwidth control using BAP or BACP" to enable clients to use BAP/BACP to dynamically manage aggregation. Click OK to close the property sheet.

The second step is to enable multilink in the appropriate remote access policy. The default policy allows all clients to use the settings defined globally for the RRAS server, so enabling multilink and BAP for the server enables it for all remote clients unless modified by a remote access policy. If you want to restrict the use of multilink and BAP to selected users, you need to modify the remote access policies accordingly. Apply one policy for those requiring multilink support and a different policy for those who do not.

In the RRAS console, open the server's branch and click Remote Access Policies. Double-click the policy you want to modify (or create a new one). Click Edit Profile and select the Multilink tab for the policy (see Figure 18-20). Configure the settings based on the following list:

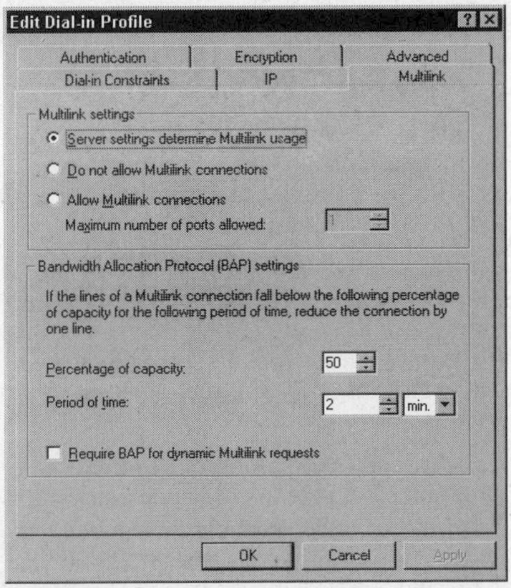

Figure 18-20: The Multilink tab.

- **Server settings determine Multilink usage:** Select this option to use the global settings defined by the RRAS server.
- **Do not allow Multilink connections:** Select this option to disable multilink for remote clients covered by the policy and limit them to a single connection.
- **Allow Multilink connections:** Select this option to allow remote clients covered by the policy to use multiple connections.
- **Percentage of capacity/Period of time:** Specify the utilization threshold value and duration the server uses to determine when to drop a link.
- **Require BAP for dynamic Multilink requests:** Select this option to require the client to use BAP to manage multiple links. If the client doesn't use BAP, multilink connections are refused and the client is limited to a single link.

Next, you need to specify the phone number for each port used for multilink connections to enable the server to pass that data to the client when the client requests another link. The client uses the link number to dial the next link. In the RRAS console, open the server, right-click the Ports branch, and choose Properties. Double-click the port for which you need to set the dial-in number, or select the port and click Configure. Specify the phone number in the field "Phone number for this device," then close the dialog box and the Ports property sheet.

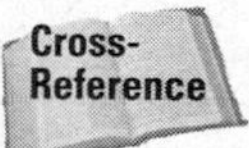

See the section titled "Configuring Outgoing Dial-Up Networking Connections" later in this chapter to learn how to configure Windows 2003 clients to use multilink and BAP.

Remote Access Policy

Although you can rely on global settings on the RRAS server to provide security and enable/disable access, you will find that you have much greater control over remote clients through the use of remote access policies. Like other group policies, remote access policies enable you to configure access on a user, group, or global basis. Windows 2003 RRAS by default creates a single remote access policy. You can modify this policy and/or create additional policies to suit your needs.

You manage remote access policies through the RRAS console. In the console, open the server to be managed and then open the Remote Access Policies branch. The right pane shows the configured remote access policies. The first default policy, "Connections to Microsoft Routing and Remote Access Server," prevents connections from RAS clients that use NetBEUI, because NetBEUI is no longer supported by Windows 2003.

The second default policy, "Connections to other access servers," is actually configured to deny access to all dial-up users. Double-click the policy and note that the option "Deny remote access permission" is selected. This setting applies unless overridden by per-user settings in each user's account, which effectively disables access for all users unless their accounts are configured to allow access. Selecting the option "Grant remote access permission" for this policy enables all users to gain remote access.

You can use the default remote access policies as-is, add other conditions to them, or create new policies to fit specific users, groups, or situations. For example, assume you want to grant remote access to a sales group but limit the group's members to one link (disable multilink). You want to also enable your Administrators group to gain access but allow them to use multilink. So, you need to create two policies. We'll use this example to illustrate how to create and configure policies. First, create the policy for the Sales group.

Configuring an RRAS server to use RADIUS authentication causes the Remote Access Policy branch to disappear from the RRAS console for the selected RRAS server. This is because the remote access policies on the RADIUS server take precedence. Also, configuring RRAS to use RADIUS accounting causes the Remote Access Logging branch to disappear from the console, as logging is handled by the RADIUS server.

Creating a new policy

In the RRAS console, open the server, then open the Remote Access Policy branch. Right-click the right pane and choose New Remote Access Policy to start the Remote Access Policy Wizard. You have two options in the wizard, create a typical policy for specific uses or create a custom policy. If you choose the former, Windows 2003 lets you choose from VPN, Dial-Up, Wireless, and Ethernet access methods, which sets the policy condition NAS-Port-Type matches *type*, where *type* specifies the appropriate connection type such as Ethernet. You can open the policy and view the NAS-Port-Type setting for the policy. All policies that you create in this way are set to deny access based on the specified condition(s).

For each of the four typical policy options you specify the policy name, which identifies the policy in the console. In addition to specifying the connection type, you must also specify the user or group to which the policy applies, as well as the authentication and encryption options.

If you choose the option to create a custom policy, the wizard prompts for the following information:

✦ **Policy name:** This is the policy name as it appears in the RRAS console. Specify a name that identifies the purpose of the policy or affected users. In this example, use Sales as the friendly name.

✦ **Policy Conditions:** Use the Select Attributes page of the wizard to specify the criteria by which the policy grants or denies access. In this example, click Add, select Windows-Groups, and click Add. Select the Sales group ⇨ OK ⇨ Next. (This example assumes a Sales group in the Active Directory, used by your Sales Department.)

✦ **Grant/Deny:** Click Next, then select which action is applied to the selected criteria. In this example, we want the Sales group granted access, so select "Grant remote access permission." If you wanted to explicitly prevent the Sales group from using remote access, you would instead select the "Deny remote access permission" option.

✦ **Edit Profile:** You can click Edit Profile to edit the other properties for the remote access policy or simply click Finish to complete the wizard. The properties you can change by clicking Edit Profile are the same as those made available by double-clicking the policy in the console (explained next).

If you click Edit Profile in the wizard or double-click a policy and then click Edit Profile in the policy's Settings page, RRAS displays the Edit Dial-In Profile property sheet shown in Figure 18-21. This sheet contains several tabs, which are described in the following sections. After you configure the Sales group's policy to deny multilink, you run the wizard again to create another policy for the Administrator's group, this time granting multilink permission.

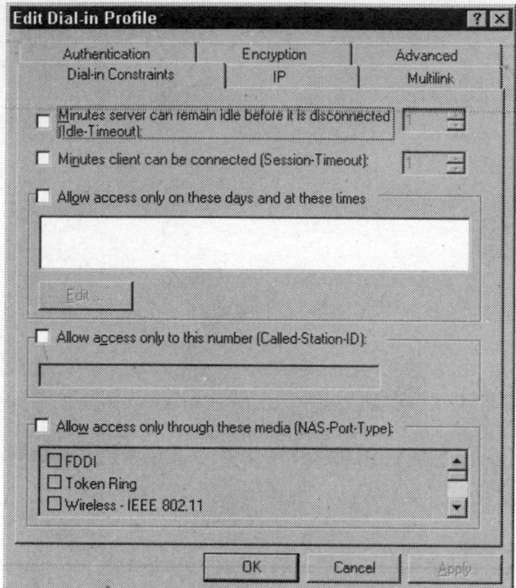

Figure 18-21: The Edit Dial-In Profile property sheet.

Dial-In Constraints

The Dial-In Constraints tab determines when the user can connect, for how long, and other properties that define the user's connection in general. The options in the bottom of the page let you specify which dial-in media types are available to users to whom the policy applies. For example, you might select Virtual Private Networking (VPN) to allow the remote users only to connect through a VPN connection. The options on the Dial-In Constraints tab are self-explanatory.

IP

The IP tab of the remote access policy's properties determines how the client IP address is assigned and which input/output filters, if any, apply to the connection. You can force the server to assign an IP, allow the client to request a specific IP, or let the global server settings define how the address is assigned (the default).

Click From Client if you want to apply a filter to incoming packets to limit them to specific protocols or ports. Click To Client to set up filters to control packets going to the remote client. See the section titled "Configuring L2TP over IPSec Filters" earlier in this chapter for more information on creating filters.

Multilink

The Multilink tab determines whether or not the remote client can use multilink, the maximum number of ports, and criteria that determine when BAP drops a link if bandwidth usage drops. These options are generally self-explanatory. See the section titled "Using Multilink and BAP" earlier in this chapter for additional information.

For our example, the Sales group needs to be denied the use of multilink. Select the option "Do not allow Multilink connections" to prevent anyone in the Sales group from using a multilink connection.

Authentication

The Authentication tab determines the authentication method(s) allowed for remote clients covered by the policy. Through this page, you can enable EAP or other authentication methods allowed for the remote clients. You can select multiple methods or select a single method if you need to ensure that the selected group always uses the same authentication method.

The option "Allow clients to connect without negotiating any authentication protocol" enables remote clients to establish a connection without authenticating. Although this capability is useful in a limited number of situations, it presents a security risk because you have no control over who can gain remote access. So, use this option sparingly.

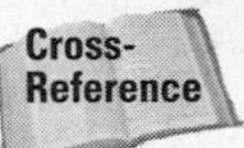

For more information on authentication methods, see the section titled "RAS Connection Types and Protocols" earlier in this chapter.

Encryption

The Encryption tab defines the levels of encryption that can be used by clients covered by the policy:

- ✦ **No Encryption:** Select this option to enable remote clients to connect without using encryption. If no other encryption options are selected, remote clients are prevented from using encryption.
- ✦ **Basic Encryption:** Select this option to enable remote clients to use IPSec 56-bit DES or MPPE 40-bit encryption.
- ✦ **Strong Encryption:** Select this option to enable remote clients to use 56-bit DES or MPPE 56-bit encryption.
- ✦ **Strongest Encryption:** Select this option to enable remote clients to use IPSec Triple DES (3DES) or MPPE 128-bit encryption.

Advanced

The Advanced tab enables you to configure additional RADIUS connection properties for remote clients covered by the remote access policy. Because there are so many, it isn't practical to cover all of them in this chapter. Click Add on the Advanced page and browse the list to determine which, if any, you require for the selection policy.

Prioritizing policies

Each remote access policy has a unique order number, and policies are evaluated and applied in the order of priority. You can change the order to define the way policies are applied, which determines the final applied result. To change the order, right-click a policy and choose either Move Up or Move Down to change its position and order number. You can also use the Up and Down arrows on the toolbar.

Using RADIUS

Windows Server 2003 includes a service called Internet Authentication Service (IAS) that enables a Windows Server 2003 to function as a RADIUS (Remote Authentication Dial-In User Server) server. In addition to providing authentication services, RADIUS also performs accounting and keeps track of user logon, session duration, logoff, and so on. You can use IAS to provide authentication for RRAS, IIS, or other services, including providing authentication for nonMicrosoft dial-up servers. Any dial-up modem pool that supports RADIUS, for example, can authenticate clients through a Windows Server 2003 running IAS.

Installing and managing IAS

You install IAS through the Add/Remove Programs object in the Control Panel. With the Add/Remove Programs object open, click Add/Remove Windows Components. Open the Networking Services item and select Internet Authentication Service, then click OK ➪ Next. Windows 2003 installs the IAS service without further prompting.

The IAS service does not have to be installed on the same server as RRAS. In fact, the IAS server could actually be located not only on a different server, but also in a different subnet. You specify the IP address or FQDN of the IAS server when you configure the RRAS server to enable RRAS to locate it.

Windows 2003 installs the Internet Authentication Service console to enable you to manage and configure IAS. Choose Start ➪ All Programs ➪ Administrative Tools ➪ Internet Authentication Service to start the IAS console. The following sections explain how to use the IAS console to configure and work with IAS.

Configuring IAS to accept connections

IAS uses certain security measures to restrict which services can connect to a RADIUS server for authentication. Services that use IAS to authenticate remote users are called *clients*. So, you need to configure IAS to allow specific clients — such as your RRAS server — to connect to a RADIUS server to authenticate users. To enable a client to connect, open the IAS console and then open the RADIUS Clients folder. Right-click RADIUS Clients, or right-click in the right pane and choose New RADIUS Client, to start the New RADIUS Client wizard. The wizard prompts for the following information:

✦ **Friendly name:** This is the client name as it appears in the IAS console. Select a name that identifies the client (such as RRAS Server 1).

✦ **Client address (IP or DNS):** Specify the client's IP address or FQDN. You can verify an FQDN by clicking Verify, which will attempt to resolve the name to an IP.

✦ **Client-Vendor:** Use this option to specify the client device manufacturer/type. This selection is optional unless you are using remote access policies to restrict access based on vendor type. Select the appropriate type from the list. Select Microsoft for a Windows 2003 RRAS server. Select RADIUS Standard if the client is a RADIUS proxy or if the client type doesn't appear in the list.

✦ **Request must contain the Message Authenticator attribute:** Select this option to require the client to send a digital signature attribute in access request packets for PAP, CHAP, or MS-CHAP authentication. IAS always requires the client to include the signature if you're using EAP. Authentication attempts that don't include a signature are discarded if this option is selected.

✦ **Shared secret/Confirm shared secret:** A shared secret is a string used as a password to enable the client to gain access to the IAS server. Like any password, the shared secret specified at both the client and server sides must match exactly. You can use any alphanumeric characters and special characters in the string, up to 255 characters. The shared secret is case-sensitive. Use a string containing a combination of letters, numbers, special characters, and different cases to help protect against dictionary attacks. You can use the same shared secret for each client or specify a different one for each (for better security).

Configuring IAS global options

There are a handful of global options you need to configure for IAS to control the way IAS functions. Open the IAS console, right-click the IAS server's main branch, and choose Properties.

Configuring service properties

The General page contains the following options:

✦ **Description:** Specify a friendly name to help differentiate this IAS service from others on the network.

✦ **Rejected authentication requests:** Select this option to write an event to the Windows 2003 Application event log each time the network access server (the client) sends a rejected or discarded authentication request. See the section titled "Configuring logging" later in this chapter for more information.

✦ **Successful authentication requests:** Select this option to write an event to the Windows 2003 Application event log each time a remote access client successfully authenticates. See the section titled "Configuring Logging" later in this chapter for more information.

Configuring ports

The Ports property page lets you configure the ports IAS uses for authentication and accounting. By default, IAS uses ports 1812 and 1645 for authentication and 1813 and 1656 for accounting.

Ports 1645 and 1646 are included to support older RADIUS clients, which by default do not use the new ports, 1812 and 1813. The RADIUS client must be configured to use the appropriate port. See the section titled "Configuring EAP-RADIUS" earlier in this chapter for more information on configuring RRAS for the appropriate RADIUS ports.

Configuring logging

Like RRAS, IAS can perform logging of accounting requests, authentication requests, and periodic status. You can configure IAS to use one of two file formats: IAS-compatible or database-compatible. Both options create a delimited text file. The latter is useful for importing the log file into a database such as Access or SQL Server. You can also configure IAS to log to a SQL Server directly (covered next).

You configure logging through the IAS console. In the console, click the Remote Access Logging branch, then double-click the Local File item in the right pane to display its properties. Use the Settings page to configure which events are logged. Use the Log File page to control the size of the log, how often the log is replaced, and its location.

Tip

See the branch "Remote Access Logging" in IAS Help for more information on interpreting IAS log files.

You can configure IAS to log to a SQL Server database. To enable SQL Server logging, double-click SQL Server in the right pane to open the SQL Server Properties dialog box. As with local file logging, you specify the types of events you want IAS to include in the log. Also specify the maximum number of concurrent client connections to the logging server, then click Configure to open the Data Link Properties dialog box, where you specify the target SQL Server, database name, authentication credentials, connection permissions, and initialization variables for the database.

Internet Connection Sharing and Internet Connection Firewall

In many small organizations or departments within larger organizations, users on the LAN need access to the Internet for e-mail or other Web access. Providing individual connections for each user is often impractical and expensive in terms of hardware, dial-up accounts, and administration. Through a feature in Windows 2003 called Internet Connection Sharing (ICS), however, multiple users can share a single Internet connection, thus overcoming the drawbacks to providing individual access.

A Windows 2003 computer sharing a connection through ICS in effect becomes a proxy server, name server, and router for the clients. More than that, however, the computer becomes a DHCP server, allocating addresses to the other computers on the network. ICS uses the class C address space 192.168.0.0 (mask 255.255.255.0) to allocate addresses. When you enable ICS for a dial-up connection, Windows 2003 automatically assigns the address 192.168.0.1 to the network interface through which other users access the shared connection. For example, a server with a single network card and a modem connection to the Internet would have its network card's IP address changed to 192.168.0.1 when the connection was shared. As other computers booted, they would be assigned addresses in the same address range, and 192.168.0.1 would be their default gateway (assuming they are configured for DHCP).

ICS is designed to enable small business networks to share an Internet connection and does not provide any flexibility of configuration. For example, you can't change the address range assigned by ICS to the LAN clients, disable the DHCP allocation, disable DNS proxy, or make other changes. For these small networks, however, ICS is almost a one-click configuration for setting up a shared Internet connection. If you need finer control over connection sharing, or if your network contains Windows 2003 domain controllers, DHCP servers, or DNS servers, you need to use Network Address Translation (NAT) instead, covered earlier in this chapter.

Configuring the server for ICS

You enable ICS through the properties of the Internet connection in the Network Connections folder. Once you've configured the Internet connection and tested it from the server to make sure it works, open the Network Connections folder, right-click the connection, and choose Properties. In the connection's property sheet, click the Advanced tab, shown in Figure 18-22.

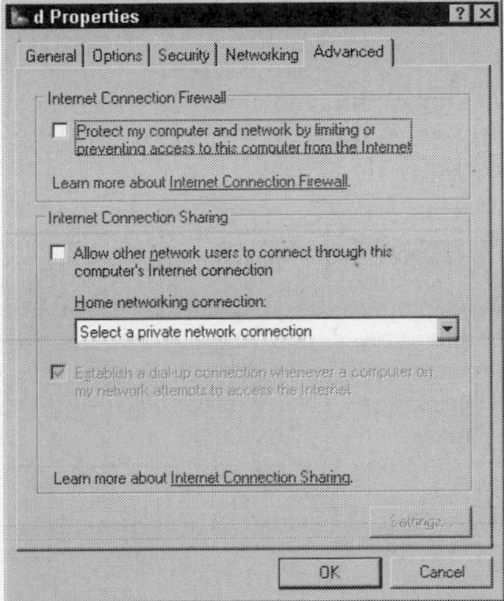

Figure 18-22: The Advanced tab.

A computer sharing a connection to the Internet through ICS must have two network connections. One is the connection to the local area network where the other clients reside, and the second is the connection to the Internet. This second connection can be a dial-up connection (modem, cable/DSL modem, ISDN, and so on) or a network adapter for a direct Internet connection.

The first step in sharing a connection is to create the connection and test it. Once the connection works as expected, you can configure it for sharing with other users on the LAN. Follow these steps to configure ICS:

1. Open the Network Connections folder; then open the properties of the interface you want to share. This is the connection that connects the ICS host computer to the Internet, not the local LAN connection.
2. Click the Advanced tab.
3. Select "Allow other network users to connect through this computer's Internet connection."

4. Select "Establish a Dial-Up Connection Whenever a Computer On My Network Attempts To Access the Internet," to allow other users to cause the connection to be dialed or to hang up the connection. This option is available only for a dial-up connection.
5. Click Settings if you want to configure applications and services, or click OK to allow all traffic.

Configuring Internet connection firewall

You can enable Internet Connection Firewall on the ICS interface to prevent certain types of traffic coming into your network from the Internet. Although ICF by no means gives you the type of firewall protection offered by products such as Microsoft's Internet Security and Acceleration (ISA) Server, CheckPoint, or other firewalls. However, it can be a reasonable solution for small businesses without the capital or staff to support more expensive or complex solutions.

To enable ICF, open the properties for the Internet connection and click the Advanced tab. Select the option Protect My Computer and Network by Limiting or Preventing Access to this Computer from the Internet.

Allowing Internet access to internal servers

When you enable ICS, the server performs NAT. If you need to allow access from the Internet to servers on the internal LAN, you need to create the service/port mappings to get the traffic to those servers. The process is essentially the same with ICS as it is when using RRAS. See the section titled "Configuring Services and ICMP Messages," earlier in this chapter for an explanation. To set up services, click the Settings button on the Advanced tab of the interface's properties.

Configuring the clients

The clients that connect through the ICS server don't need any special software or support for ICS, nor do you have to configure applications (such as Internet Explorer) to connect through a proxy server. All you have to do is to ensure that the clients reside on the same subnet as the ICS host and use it as their default gateway. The easiest way to accomplish this is to configure the clients to obtain their TCP/IP settings automatically (use DHCP).

If you prefer, you can configure the client computer settings manually, assigning each a static IP address in the Class C range 192.168.0.2 through 192.168.0.254, with a subnet mask of 255.255.255.0. Assign 192.168.0.1 as the default gateway for the client computers.

Configuring Outgoing Dial-Up Networking Connections

In addition to using RRAS to support dial-in users, you can also configure dial-out connections. For many users, this means creating a dial-up connection to the Internet, although with Windows Server 2003, it's more likely that you'll be creating demand-dial router or client connections to another server or to a router. Network Address Translation and routing are covered in detail earlier in this chapter. This section of the chapter assumes you need to configure Windows 2003 dial-up connections to a RAS server or the Internet.

Creating a connection

As with nearly every configuration issue, Windows 2003 provides a wizard to automate creation of dial-up connections. Click Start ⇨ Control Panel ⇨ Network Connections to open the Network Connections folder. Then double-click the Make New Connection icon to start the wizard. The wizard is generally self-explanatory. You specify the connection method (modem, broadband, and so forth.), authentication credentials, phone number, and other applicable information.

Configuring connection properties

After you create a connection, you can modify its properties. Most of the properties are self-explanatory, and you can configure such properties as the server's phone number or, in the case of a VPN server, the IP address, or FQDN. Other options configure such properties as redial attempts, idle time before hang-up, and so on. You should have no trouble configuring these settings. Simply right-click a connection in the Network Connections folder and choose Properties to access its property sheet.

The following sections explain a handful of configuration issues that are perhaps not as intuitive as the others.

Security and authentication

The Security property tab for a connection (see Figure 18-23) lets you specify the authentication method used for the connection. By default, Windows 2003 sets up the connection to allow unsecured passwords, which means the client can send the password in plain text, making it susceptible to interception.

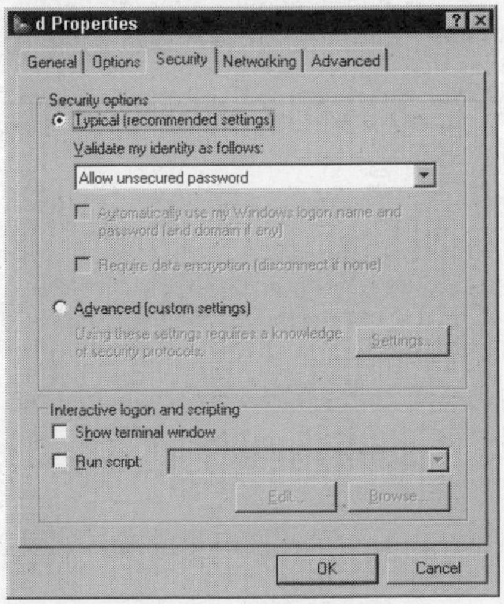

Figure 18-23: The Security tab.

You can select Require Secured Password from the "Validate my identity as follows" drop-down list to force the connection to require encryption for the password. The method used for encryption depends on the authentication method negotiated with the remote server. The following two options work in conjunction with the Require Secured Password option:

- **Automatically use my Windows logon name and password (and domain if any):** Select this option to have the connection automatically use your current logon name, password, and domain for logon to the remote server.
- **Require data encryption (disconnect if none):** Select this option to force data encryption for the connection and disconnect if the server doesn't offer a supported encryption method. You can prevent encryption through the Advanced properties (explained next).

You also can use a smart card for authentication. Select the option "Use smart card" from the Validate drop-down list to use a smart card for authentication. This option must be supported by the remote server for the connection to succeed.

Select Advanced on the Security page and click Settings if you want a finer degree of control over authentication settings (such as configuring EAP or other protocols). Use the Data Encryption drop-down list to specify if encryption can be used or is required for the connection. The options are self-explanatory.

If you choose any protocols other than EAP, you simply need to select which protocol(s) you want the connection to attempt. You can select multiple protocols. If dialing a Windows 2003 RAS server, the server will attempt authentication based on the security offered by each method, choosing the most secure whenever possible.

Configuring EAP

Configuring a client to use EAP takes a little more effort. Select the option "Use Extensible Authentication Protocol (EAP)," then select either MD5-Challenge or Smart Card or Other Certificate from the associated drop-down list. If you select Other Smart Card or Other Certificate, click Properties to display the Smart Card or Other Certificate dialog box. Select options using the following list as a guide:

- **Use my smart card:** Select this option if you have a smart card reader attached to your system and a smart card to use for authentication.
- **Use a certificate on this computer:** Select this option to use a certificate installed on your computer to provide authentication.
- **Validate server certificate:** Select this option to have your computer verify that the certificate provided by the server is still valid (not expired). Deselect the option to have the client accept the server's certificate without checking it.
- **Connect to these servers:** Use this option to limit connections to servers that reside in a specified domain. For example, enter `latinaccents.biz` if you only want to connect to servers in the `latinaccents.biz` domain (`server1.latinaccents.biz`, `ras.latinaccents.biz`, and so on).
- **Trusted root certificate authorities:** Select the trusted root certificate authorities for the server.
- **Use a different user name for the connection:** Select this option if the user name stored in the smart card or associated with the certificate you're using is not the same as the user name you need to use to log on in the remote domain.

Configuring protocols

Just as you can with a LAN connection, you can configure a dial-up connection for more than one protocol. Or, perhaps you have more than one protocol enabled for a connection and want to turn off the protocol for dial-up but leave it enabled for the LAN. To change your protocol settings, open the Network Connections folder, right-click the connection, and choose Properties. Click the Networking tab, then select/deselect protocols as desired. You can also remove a protocol, but keep in mind that removing it removes it from the computer altogether, and other connections won't be able to use it.

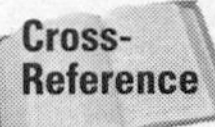

For more information on configuring network protocols, see Chapter 15.

Using Multilink and BAP

As explained earlier in this chapter, some dial-up servers support multilink connections that enable you to connect to the RAS server with multiple links (two or more modems, for example) to create an aggregate connection with a total bandwidth equal to the sum of all connected links. Windows 2003 dial-up networking supports multilink dial-out connections and can optionally use Bandwidth Allocation Protocol (BAP) to dynamically add and drop links as needed to accommodate changes in bandwidth usage. The remote server you connect to must support multilink and must also support BAP if you use BAP on the client side.

Most ISPs that support multilink also charge you for the ability to use multiple connections. Paying for multiple user accounts won't work for multilink, as Windows 2003 treats the individual connections as a single one and uses a single user name/password pair for establishing all links. Plus, the server needs to support multilink to enable bandwidth to be aggregated on the server side for your connections. Just dialing two separate accounts would give you two nonaggregated connections.

Before configuring multilink for a dial-up connection, you need to first install the multiple devices you'll be using to dial out. If you only have one device installed, the multilink options are not shown. If multiple devices are installed but only one is selected for the connection, the multilink options are dimmed.

After installing all connection devices, open the Network Connections folder, right-click the connection, and choose Properties. On the General page, select all of the devices you want to use to establish the multilink connection. If you need to configure different numbers for each one, make sure that the option "All devices call the same numbers" is deselected, then select each modem from the drop-down list and specify the number to dial through that modem. If the remote access server uses a single number with a hunt group to distribute calls, select the option "All devices call the same numbers."

Next, click the Options tab to display the Options property page. The drop-down list in the Multiple devices group provides three options:

✦ **Dial only first available device:** Select this option to only dial a single link (use one device only). This option enables you to dial a single link for the connection when other installed devices are busy. For example, you might use two modems to connect to two different remote networks. Selecting this option enables the second connection to automatically use the available device to dial.

✦ **Dial all devices:** Select this option to have Windows 2003 automatically dial all available devices to create a multilink connection to the remote server.

✦ **Dial devices only as needed:** Select this option to use BAP to manage bandwidth usage. Windows 2003 will dial other links for the connection depending on the settings you configure for BAP. Click Configure to display the dialog box shown in Figure 18-24. These four controls enable you to specify the criteria BAP uses to determine when to connect or disconnect links.

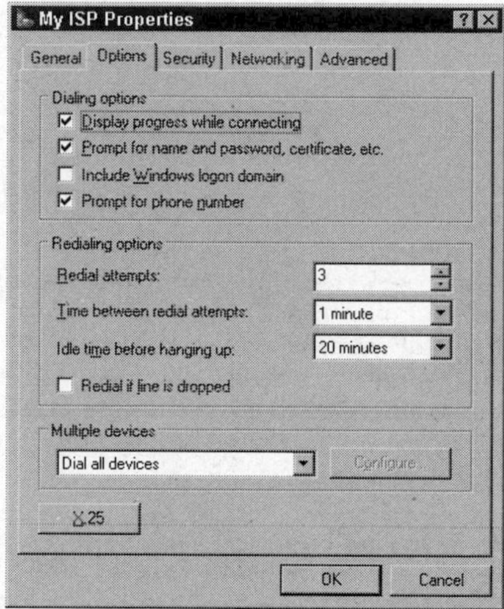

Figure 18-24: The Options tab.

Windows 2003 does not automatically reinitialize dropped multilink links unless you're using BAP. Selecting the option "Dial all devices" might get you an aggregate link, but there is nothing to prevent the connection from suffering attrition as links are dropped and not re-established. You can force links to reinitialize by setting relatively low usage conditions. Select "Dial devices only as needed" from the Options page of the connection's properties and then set automatic dialing to low values such as one percent for five seconds.

Configuring dial-up networking to connect to the Internet

In most cases, you can run the wizard to create a new dial-up connection to the Internet and use it as-is without problems. However, you might want or need to fine-tune some of your settings for cost or performance reasons. The following sections examine common properties you might want to modify.

Controlling disconnects

Most ISPs implement an idle-disconnect period, causing a connection to be dropped if there is no activity for a given amount of time. In most cases, the idle-disconnect works well, but some ISPs don't implement it and others that are configured for idle-disconnect seem to work sporadically. If you're paying for your connection by the hour, idle-disconnect can save you a lot of money if you forget to disconnect or want the system to disconnect after a long, unattended download.

You'll find the option "Idle time before hanging up" on the Options property page for the connection. If your ISP doesn't use idle-disconnect or you want to ensure your connection disconnects even if the ISP doesn't drop you, select the idle time that can occur before your system automatically hangs up the connection.

The other side of the disconnect issue is the fact that you might want your system to stay connected past the ISP's idle-disconnect period. For example, you might be performing a long, unattended download, but the remote server occasionally is idle for too long and the ISP drops your connection. In this situation, you can download and use one of the many connection utilities that keeps minimal traffic on your connection to ensure that it won't be dropped. You'll find several such utilities at `www.tucows.com`. Or, simply open your e-mail client and configure it to check your e-mail every few minutes. The traffic going to the mail server will be sufficient to keep your connection live.

Online security

Another potential problem is that in some cases, other users on the Internet can see your local folders and potentially gain access to your files. You can prevent that from occurring by disabling the File and Printer Sharing service from the dial-up connection. The default condition has this service disabled. Open the Network page of the connection's property sheet and deselect the File and Printer Sharing service. Also, deselect any protocols other than TCP/IP if they are enabled and you don't need them for a specific reason.

You should also consider enabling ICF on the interface. You'll find ICF on the Advanced tab of the connection's properties.

Summary

Windows 2003 RRAS integrates routing with remote access into a single service. Remote users can connect to a Windows 2003 RRAS server to gain access to resources on the server or to resources on the network. The users can authenticate against the server's local accounts, against domain accounts, or against a RADIUS server. Windows Server 2003 includes the Internet Authentication Service that you can use to configure a Windows 2003 computer as a RADIUS server, providing full authentication and accounting services. Windows 2003 supports several authentication methods offering varying degrees of security for both Windows authentication and RADIUS authentication.

Virtual Private Networking support in RRAS enables remote clients to establish a secure connection to a Windows Server 2003 or its network through a public network such as the Internet. In addition to supporting PPTP, Windows 2003 RRAS also adds support for L2TP, which provides additional security over PPTP. Demand-dial router connections can also use PPTP and L2TP, making Windows 2003 RRAS a good solution for establishing secure network-to-network connections over the Internet.

Dial-up networking in Windows 2003 enables all versions of the operating system to function as a remote access client. While RAS dial-out is more prevalent on workstations, the same capabilities are available in Windows Server 2003. You can create dial-up connections to private networks, the Internet, or individual computers. Support for Internet Connection Sharing enables a single dial-up connection to be shared by multiple users. Where flexibility of configuration is needed or when you need to support a large number of users, however, Network Address Translation should be used instead of ICS.

✦ ✦ ✦

P A R T

V

Availability Management

✦ ✦ ✦ ✦

In This Part

✦ ✦ ✦ ✦

Storage Management

✦ ✦ ✦ ✦

In This Chapter

Overview of Windows 2003 storage

Analyzing storage management

Learning Disk Management Service partition styles

Understanding removable storage

Understanding Remote storage and HSM

Working with The Disk Management snap-in

Understanding basic storage

Understanding dynamic volumes and fault tolerance

Using Hardware RAID

Understanding dynamic storage management

Managing storage with disk quotas

Troubleshooting

✦ ✦ ✦ ✦

This chapter introduces Windows 2003 storage. We will start by presenting the architecture of Disk Management Service (DMS), Remote Storage, Removable Storage Services (RSS), and Hierarchical Storage Management (HSM). (Removable storage and remote storage are covered in depth in Chapter 26.) We will also cover configuration and types of disks, partitions, and volumes (including a new partition style introduced in the 64-bit version of Windows 2003 Server); software-based fault-tolerant disk configurations (using a Redundant Array of Inexpensive Disks, or RAID); and disk quotas. We will conclude with an overview of troubleshooting common storage management problems.

Overview of Windows 2003 Storage

Although there are few certainties in life, in storage management you can be fairly sure that no matter how much disk space you plan for, sooner or later, you will run out of it. And you can expect a disk crash to happen at the worst possible time.

The failure of a storage device or even a shortage of disk space has, at the very least, negative impacts on running applications; more commonly, it leads to server downtime or data loss. This, in turn, translates into business losses measured in millions of dollars. You can help prevent these losses by taking the following proactive approaches:

- Evaluate your storage needs.
- Design and implement highly available storage solutions.
- Restrict and monitor storage use.
- Provide disaster recovery and backup/restore mechanisms.

Storage Management

Storage management can be analyzed functionally by dividing it into three areas: *performance and capacity*, *high availability*, and *recoverability*. Let's start by looking into access to storage.

Performance and capacity

Typically, a computer system requires local storage for system and boot files required by the operating systems (although Windows 2003 Server supports Storage Area Network (SAN) configurations where all disks are external). The boot partition (hosting the operating system) needs to be able to accommodate profiles of logged-on users, paging files, memory dumps, and installed programs. Make sure you set partitions large enough, especially because boot and system partitions, after being created, cannot be extended without third-party tools such as PowerQuest's Partition Magic.

> **Note** Throughout this chapter we will use the terms *boot partition* and *system partition*, a counterintuitive naming convention used by Microsoft for partitions containing boot files (system partition) and system files (boot partition). Contrary to what you might expect, a Windows-based computer boots from the system partition and stores its operating system files on a boot partition. These terms can refer to the same partition or two separate ones (separate boot and system partitions are mandatory on Itanium-based Windows 2003 installations, covered later in this chapter, and optional on Intel 32-bit computers).

On the other hand, ensure that your computer's BIOS supports Interrupt 13 Extensions, if you plan to make your boot or system partition larger than 8GB.

> **Note** One of the limitations of older versions of BIOS (Basic Input/Output System) was the way the hard disk access was handled, by using the BIOS internal code invoked through Interrupt 13. The addressing implemented in the code allowed access to partitions no larger than 8.4GB, which at the time of its inception (early 1980s) was more than anyone expected to ever need. Earlier versions of Windows (up to Windows NT 4.0) relied on this feature to read the system files necessary to boot before the operating system was fully loaded. This is why the size of boot and system partitions was limited in those systems to about 8GB. The problem surfaced if one of the files needed during the boot ended up (typically through fragmentation, especially after service pack updates, on systems with high disk space utilization) beyond the boundary reachable through BIOS. In the late 1990s, computer manufacturers developed extensions to the BIOS code handling Interrupt 13 that allowed it to work with much larger partitions (up to 9TB). The newer operating systems, starting with Windows 98 and Windows 2000, can take advantage of the Interrupt 13 BIOS extensions; however, you need to make sure that your computer's BIOS has this capability (you might be able to get updated BIOS from its manufacturer). Otherwise, make sure that your system and boot partitions are smaller than 8GB.

Do the disks storing boot and system volumes need to be particularly fast? Not necessarily, because access to boot files is needed only at startup and more frequently used operating system files are cached in the server's memory. However, you should ensure that the paging file resides on a fast volume (you might need to move it from its default location) because this will significantly improve the server's responsiveness.

To accommodate these varying requirements, you should separate the operating system from the data. This can be accomplished by first grouping disks into arrays based on their purpose and then attaching each group to dedicated channels or even disk controllers. Depending on your budget, you may be in a position to get faster disks, use striping volumes, or combine both by striping volumes on faster disks.

Collect information on applications to be installed, type of data, and number of users accessing the volumes. When dealing with extremely demanding applications such as busy commercial Web sites or On-Line Transaction Processing (OLTP) database management systems, take into consideration disk-related hardware parameters such as the following:

✦ **Access time:** This is the time it takes for a hard disk to register a request and prepare to scan the surface of a disk.

✦ **Seek time:** This is the time it takes for a hard disk to find and assemble all the parts of a file.

✦ **Transfer rate:** This is the time it takes for a hard disk to transfer data on and off the disk.

Closely observe the rate of disk consumption and plan accordingly. Leave a generous margin and ensure that your design allows for easy expansion. Make sure that you keep your space utilization below the 70 percent threshold. This will not only allow you to prevent sudden "Out of space" messages, but also help keep disks defragmented (for the built-in Disk Defragmenter to work efficiently, the disk should have at least 15 percent of total disk space available). Implement monitoring tools that will notify you when disk space utilization approaches the threshold defined by you.

If you find that the capacity of a single volume does not satisfy your disk space needs, you have the following options:

✦ Volumes can be spanned or extended (providing they are unformatted or formatted with NTFS and they are not system or boot volumes). Spanning refers to the process of chaining together areas of unallocated space residing on separate physical disks. Extending, on the other hand, involves adding extra unallocated space to an already existing volume. Extending is typically done when a volume runs out of free space and there is at least one unpartitioned area on the disk. This remaining area can be added on to extend the volume capacity. Dynamic volumes can be extended using any area from the same or different physical disk, but basic volumes are limited to contiguous areas on the same disk. We will explore this topic in more detail later in the chapter.

✦ If you want to increase the speed of I/O operations, you can create striped volumes (known also as RAID-0). Striped volumes, similar to spanned ones, are created using areas of unallocated space on multiple disks. What's different is the way data is written to the volume, which adds the requirement for striped areas to be of the same size. Another similarity between striped and spanned volumes is the lack of fault tolerance, meaning that the failure of any of the striped disks makes the entire volume inaccessible. If you want to add a level of fault tolerance (which is typically recommended), you can use striping with parity (RAID-5). This type of configuration provides redundancy by storing additional parity information as part of the volume. Another type of fault-tolerant volume, a mirror (RAID-1), creates an exact copy of the data, so it does not contribute in any way to increase available space (as a matter of fact, it wastes 50 percent of available space). Fault-tolerant solutions are discussed in the next section.

✦ You can enforce disk space quotas on per-user basis. As we will show later in the chapter, it is possible to specify a maximum amount of space that can be used by each user, for each server volume.

- ✦ You can mount a volume onto an empty folder on another volume. This way, from the user's perspective, the available storage is increased by the free space on the mounted volume. This topic is covered in Chapter 26.
- ✦ You can redirect shared folders on one server to a shared volume or folder on other servers. This functionality is available with Distributed File System (DFS), presented in Chapter 26.
- ✦ You can compress data on volumes. Compression is also covered in Chapter 26.
- ✦ You can take advantage of HSM. With the Windows 2000 Remote Storage snap-in and RSS, you can automatically move older files from a local volume to removable, locally attached media, such as tapes and portable disks. Refer to Chapter 26 for details.

The preceding options are frequently combined with each other (for example, disk quotas can be applied to a DFS residing on a RAID-5 volume).

Windows 2003 and SANs

A SAN (Storage Area Network or System Area Network), is essentially a collection of disks and storage controllers. What makes it different from the much more common Directly Attached Storage (local disks attached to a local disk controller) is the fact that a SAN is physically separate and independently managed. A single SAN can (and typically does) provide storage to multiple servers. It is linked to them through one or more dedicated interconnecting devices, which can be as simple as external SCSI buses or as complex as a multilevel, fully redundant network of fiber switches.

SAN is sometimes confused with Network Attached Storage (NAS), which, similar to SAN, is an external, separately managed collection of storage devices, but is connected through a regular TCP/IP network, most often shared with client computers. NAS offers the convenience of SAN at lower prices. Its performance, however, does not match that of SAN because available bandwidth between server and storage is more limited due to lower media speed and possibility, depending on design, of contention with client traffic. Windows 2003 introduces a number of improvements in the area of NAS, such as support for multipath I/O and Volume Shadow Copy Service. Interestingly, recent developments in iSCSI (Internet-SCSI) technology are changing traditional SAN design by allowing the use of IP protocol for server-to-storage communication. Unfortunately, Windows 2003 does not provide native support for iSCSI, due to lack of finalized iSCSI standards.

SANs, despite their high initial cost and increased complexity of management, are becoming a more popular choice for storage. Microsoft embraces this trend by introducing in Windows 2003 several new features geared toward SAN-based architecture, such as multipath I/O (the ability to simultaneously use several separate physical paths to storage devices), Winsock Direct (a protocol that bypasses networking layers and communicates directly with SAN hardware), support for SAN-based boot and system partitions, and the capability to turn off volume automounting (with the `MOUNTVOL.EXE` utility).

High availability

Besides providing a sufficient amount of fast storage, you also need to ensure its availability. You can use one of the following technologies to reach this goal:

✦ **RAID-1 (mirrored) fault-tolerant volumes.**

✦ **RAID-5 fault-tolerant volumes.**

✦ **Clustered servers:** This refers to two or more servers sharing (typically) common storage and capable of automatic failover. Server clustering, presented in the Chapter 25, is available only in Windows 2003 Enterprise and Datacenter Server.

✦ **Hot standby server:** This is a server synchronized with the original data source via a replication mechanism. You can use the File Replication Service built into Windows 2003 when dealing with regular file shares (there are also a number of third-party replication mechanisms available). Log shipping is one of the options for synchronizing replicas of Microsoft SQL Server.

Windows 2003's fault-tolerant dynamic volumes are given comprehensive coverage later in this chapter. You can also consider using DFS (described in Chapter 26) as another way of implementing high availability.

Recoverability

Recoverability features need to be able to secure your data against a number of threats, such as file corruption, theft, disasters, virus attacks, user-deleted files, or failed hard disks. The primary services that offer such support are:

✦ **Removable Storage Services (RSS):** This works with backup technology, media, and robotics to provide a comprehensive data protection media management system (you can find out more about it in Chapter 20).

✦ **The Backup/Restore Service:** This is fully discussed in Chapter 20 and as part of the HSM system in Chapter 26.

✦ **Remote Storage Services:** Also discussed in Chapter 26, Remote Storage is responsible for moving online data to offline backup. Remote Storage, RSS, and Backup/Restore work together as part of HSM system.

✦ **Volume Shadow Copy Service:** Introduced in Windows, this offers a revolutionary approach to backup and restore operations. It works by creating an instant copy (snapshot) of the original disk volume. As new files are created or existing ones modified, the service keeps track of only the changes to the state of the volume captured in the snapshot. This way, the volume can be backed up while the files are open and applications running (need for a backup window is eliminated) and a restore can bring back the volume to a specific point in time. The client portion of the service allows users to instantaneously restore previous versions of a modified file.

Issues with legacy systems

It is unlikely that you will run into issues relating to lack of support for Windows 2003 storage management features in previous versions of Windows. Older operating systems (other than Windows 2000, and XP Professional) are not capable of recognizing dynamic disks created by Windows 2003 Server unless these disks are local. The only scenarios in which this can happen occur when dual booting between .NET and legacy systems and when transferring disks between such systems.

The introduction of a 64-bit version of Windows 2003 on Itanium-based computers added another degree of incompatibility. Its new partition style, called GUID (Globally Unique Identifier) Partition Table (GPT), is not supported on any other operating system (including 32-bit versions of Windows 2003).

Note that the restrictions described in this section apply only to local disk access. Volumes residing on dynamic disk and GUID partitions can be accessed via network by any other operating system (providing proper permissions are granted).

Disk Management Service

The Windows 2003 DMS handles two types of storage: basic and dynamic. Basic disks are practically identical to (and compatible with) those used in previous versions of Microsoft operating systems. Dynamic disks, on the other hand, are more technologically advanced, scalable, and robust; they were introduced in Windows 2000 and are supported only in Windows 2000, XP Professional, and Windows 2003 Server.

Management of dynamic disks and their volumes is handled by Logical Disk Manager (LDM). One of its features is replicating data describing dynamic disk structure across all of local dynamic disks. This way, a corruption of such data on a single disk does not affect its accessibility. LDM is also the underlying component of DMS, which provides the following features:

- **Online Management:** This allows fault-tolerant RAID configurations and non-system or non-boot volumes to be created and rebuilt without rebooting the system (although your servers need to be hot-pluggable, if you want to replace a failed disk or extend an existing volume by adding a new disk).
- **Mounted Volumes:** This is the feature that maps an entire volume into an empty folder on an NTFS-formatted basic or dynamic volume. Mounted volumes provide a convenient and instantaneous way of adding disk space to a volume, by using an empty folder on the volume as an access point to another volume on one of local disks. If no local disks with free space are available, you can install another and use it for the mount. Removing a mounted volume is just as easy. Neither of these operations requires a reboot.

  Mounted volumes can use practically any type of storage, including removable media. This gives you plenty of flexibility in handling disk space shortages. For example, you can mount a new volume onto the d: drive using one of its empty folders and then extend that volume if you start running out of space on the d: drive again.

  Mounted volumes are available only if the volume where the mount point resides is formatted with NTFS, because reparse points (on which volume mounting is based) are not available in FAT or FAT32. However, the volume you mount can be formatted with any file system supported by Windows 2003, including FAT, FAT32, NTFS, CDFS, and UDF.
- **Disk Defragmentation:** This is the process of rearranging data on a disk to make it contiguous. This reduces seek time and effectively speeds up access to data. Disk defragmentation, introduced into Windows 2000, has been improved in Windows 2003 through the addition of a command-line interface (`defrag.exe`) and scheduling capabilities. We discuss it in depth in Chapter 21.
- **Disk Management Tools:** These are part of Windows 2003 Server and include Disk Management Console and several command-line utilities.

Disk Management is implemented as an MMC snap-in. It allows you to manage disks and volumes on local and remote systems. We will cover it in more detail later in this chapter.

The `diskpart.exe` command-line utility provides a shell from which you can launch multiple, disk-management-related commands. It is typically used to automate disk management tasks. It can be run in either interactive mode or in batch mode, using a text file containing multiple commands as an input.

The `fsutil.exe` command-line utility is used for the management of file systems and volumes. You can use it, for example, to find out volume characteristics (such as file system, volume name, and so on) or query how much free disk space a volume contains. Run the following code to display total and free bytes on the C: volume:

```
FSUTIL VOLUME DISKFREE C:
```

You can also run the following code to list additional information about the C: volume:

```
FSUTIL FSINFO VOLUMEINFO C:
```

Managing GPT disks involves a number of additional Itanium-specific tools, in addition to the preceding ones.

`MOUNTVOL.EXE` is a command-line tool used for volume mounting.

Partition Styles

Partition style describes the arrangement of partitions and volumes on a disk. All *x*86-based systems store information about disk layout using the structure called Master Boot Record (MBR). Itanium-based computers running the 64-bit version of Windows 2003 Server can also use the GPT partition style, with disk and volume information stored in the GPT. Because the partition style is set on a per-disk basis, MBR and GPT disks also exist.

Despite significant differences between MBR and GPT disks, most of their features are identical. Both can be configured as basic or dynamic disks. Both can also contain the same types of volumes, with the exception of logical volumes residing on extended partitions, since extended partitions are supported only on MBR disks.

MBR disks

Operating systems based on Intel *x*86 processors communicate with hardware via BIOS, which recognizes disks configured using the MBR partition style. MBR consists of a set of predefined fields storing disk configuration information, initial bootstrap code, and the partition table.

GPT disks

Itanium-based operating systems communicate with hardware using the Extensible Firmware Interface (EFI). EFI specifications also include definition of GPT partition style. GPT offers support for volume sizes of up to 18EB and up to 127 partitions on basic disks (compared to a practical limit of 2TB and 4 partitions with MBR partitions). It also includes performance and reliability improvements; for example, a GPT disk contains two copies of the partition table stored in a separate, hidden partition.

Itanium systems can use a mix of GPT and MBR disks, but they have to boot from a GPT disk. (In other words, the system partition on Itanium systems has to be created on a GPT disk. This partition, called the EFI system partition, has to be formatted using FAT and have a size between 100MB and 1GB.) System files must reside on another partition (called, as you probably recall, the boot partition) separate from the boot files stored on the system partition. Note that the files used during boot process of Itanium-based computers are different from the ones on *x*86-based systems.

GPT has its limitations. As we mentioned before, it is not backward-compatible. Only 64-bit operating systems running on Itanium computers (64-bit versions of XP Professional and Windows 2003 Servers) can access GPT-partitioned local disks. GPT partition style cannot be used for removable disks or for disks attached to shared storage devices on cluster servers in Windows 2003 Enterprise and Datacenter platforms. Also, the EFI system partition cannot be mirrored.

Conversion between MBR and GPT disks requires deleting all volumes and partitions. After all of them are removed, you can use the Convert to GPT Disk or Convert to MBR Disk options in the Disk Management Console or the Convert GPT and Convert MBR options of the `diskpart` utility.

Removable Storage

Removable storage includes any media that can (and is intended to) be easily swapped between multiple systems or relocated offsite for restore and disaster recovery purposes. Most commonly, removable storage consists of tapes, recordable and rewriteable CD and DVD disks, removable hard drives such as ZIP or JAZ disks, and optical drives.

Windows 2003 offers a uniform approach to removable storage management. It provides the same interface when dealing with single tape drive units similar to Quarter Inch Cartridge and highly sophisticated automated archive systems such as optical drive libraries or multi-drive tape silos. Removable media, regardless of their physical type, are organized into collections called *media pools*. The media pools are organized based on some common characteristics, typically related to their purpose. Tape devices and backup topics are discussed in Chapter 20.

Remote Storage and HSM

The Remote Storage snap-in for Windows 2003 bears many similarities to Unix. Its main component, HSM, was first made available in Unix and other mid-size operating systems.

HSM is more of a concept than a practical implementation and consists of numerous interrelated components and services. Its purpose is to control the transfer of data throughout a computing environment. This way, HSM not only provides data protection, but also takes care of space utilization by moving unused data off local storage. This can happen according to some arbitrarily chosen criteria, such as when the disks start getting full or at preconfigured intervals.

The hierarchical system of data storage has several levels. There is a *data retrieval level,* which starts out at the top of the hierarchy. Data at that level is online and immediately available. It resides on local fast hard disks, in fast-access network storage silos and SANs, or arrays of hard disks servicing clusters. The bottom of the hierarchy, known as the *storage level*, represents data that is offline (stored on tape cartridges, compact disc libraries, or tape libraries). Intermediate levels correspond to slower hard disk arrays.

How does the data get from the immediate-availability state to the other end of the hierarchy? This is the task of Remote Storage. A file that does not satisfy certain conditions, such as "time since last accessed" being shorter than the interval you defined, is moved off the fast disks down the hierarchy to slower media. In a well-designed system, the files that are not used at all end up eventually on library tapes. This file migration can be triggered when free disk space reaches dangerous limits.

Remote Storage replaces the moved file on the disk with a link pointing to its current location. From a user's perspective, the way of accessing the file does not change because the link emulates its presence (a user can tell whether a file has been archived, however; its icon is slightly modified and includes a tiny clock). At the first attempt to access it again, the file is checked out of the archive system and returned to its original location. The main drawback of this mechanism is the slower access time when opening such files, but this is a small price to pay in exchange for disk space savings.

When Remote Storage needs to move the data to a lower level of storage hierarchy, it interfaces with the removable storage system — via the previously described media pools — to copy the data to an available media library. You can deploy low-cost storage as a means of continually offloading stale data from the local disks that need space for applications and current data. You can use this strategy as long as you have available secondary, online storage media, such as tape or recordable DVDs or CDs.

It is important to remember that HSM is not a substitute for regular backups because only a single instance of the data exists. Make sure that you factor archived data into your backup strategy. Consider installing a system that makes regular, rotation-managed backups of the offline media.

The Disk Management Snap-in

The Disk Management MMC snap-in is automatically loaded into the Computer Management console, located in the Control Panel, under the Administrative Tools folder. You can also run it as a stand-alone snap-in by launching `diskmgmt.msc` or adding it to a custom console.

In the Computer Management tool, Disk Management Snap-in is a leaf or node on the Storage branch of Computer Management. The snap-in is illustrated in Figure 19-1.

The Disk Management snap-in is the main application for managing disks and volumes in a Windows 2003 system via graphical interface. You can use it to perform most operations on disks and volumes on both local and remote systems, as long as they are running Windows 2003 Server, XP Professional, or Windows 2000. We will describe use of Disk Management in the most common disk and volume tasks later in this chapter.

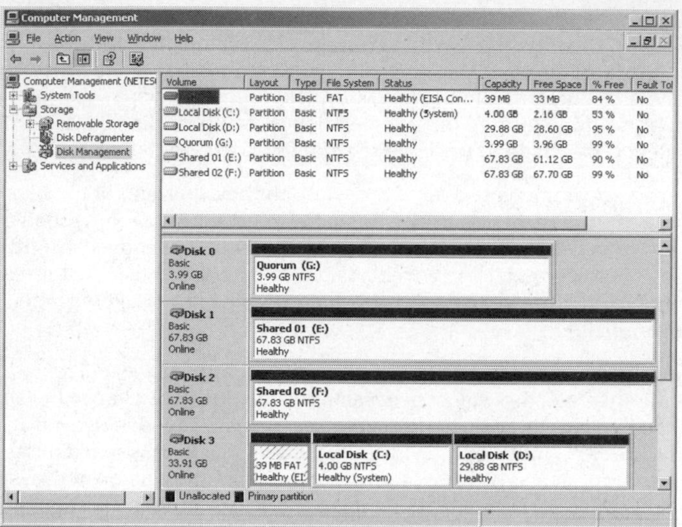

Figure 19-1: The Disk Management snap-in.

Basic Storage

All disks start as basic disks with structures that make the disk recognizable to the operating system. Specifics depend on whether the disk is MBR or GPT type (as previously described). Besides presenting the disk to the operating system, these structures store a disk signature, which uniquely identifies the disk. The signature is written to the disk through the process called initialization, which typically takes place when a disk is added to the system. Before a basic disk can be used to store any files, it has to be divided into partitions and volumes. Partitions are areas of a physical disk that can host one or more volumes, depending on whether the partition is primary or extended.

Primary partitions

Primary partitions can exist on both MBR and GPT disks. MBR disks are limited to four primary partitions, while GPT disks can contain up to 127 of them (plus Microsoft Reserved Partition). From a practical point of view, a primary partition is equivalent to a volume. One of its unique features is its capability to store a boot sector, which is used when launching an operating system. As explained previously in this chapter, such a partition is called a system partition. In order for a primary partition to become bootable, you have to designate it as active and install appropriate operating system boot files on it. In the pre-Windows 2000 operating systems, each primary partition was associated with the drive letter used to access it in Windows Explorer or via command prompt, but this is no longer the case. In Windows 2003 and 2000, you have the option of not assigning a drive letter to a partition (such a partition can be accessed, for example, by creating a mount point).

Extended partitions

Extended partitions are subject to several restrictions: They are supported only on MBR disks, only one such partition can exist per physical disk, and the operating system cannot boot from them. Their main benefit is the fact that they can contain multiple logical drives (volumes). You can use this feature if you want to work around the four-partition limit of MBR disks. Instead of creating four primary partitions, which translate into four volumes only, you can create three primary partitions and one extended partition. After the extended partition is created, you can divide it into any number of logical drives.

Basic volumes

Basic volumes are areas of the disk that can be independently formatted. The process of formatting assigns a specific file system to the volume (such as FAT, FAT32, or NTFS) and is required in order to store files on the disk. As mentioned previously, a basic volume can be located on a primary or extended partition. In the first case, a single volume occupies an entire partition; in the second case, one or more volumes can be created, with the portion of the partition unassigned to any volume left for later use.

When working with basic disks, you are limited to basic volumes only (which consist of a contiguous area of a single disk). To format any other type of volume (such as spanned, striped, mirrored, or RAID-5), you will first need to convert two or more disks to dynamic disks (at least three for RAID-5 and two or more for the other types).

Basic volumes can be extended, which essentially involves adding more space to an existing volume. This, however, is not possible in any of the following scenarios:

- The volume is formatted using FAT or FAT32 (only NTFS or unformatted volumes can be extended).
- The volume is used as a system or boot partition.
- Unallocated space is not adjacent to (immediately following) the volume to be extended.
- The volume was created as a basic partition on a Windows NT 4.0 or Windows 2000 installation that was subsequently upgraded to Windows 2003 Server.
- The simple volume has been modified using the `diskpart.exe` utility with the `retain` command (more about this later).

Note that you cannot extend a basic partition using Disk Management Utility, but have to use `diskpart.exe` instead.

Extending a volume does not affect data residing on a volume and it does not require a reboot.

Dynamic Volumes and Fault Tolerance

Dynamic storage was introduced in Windows 2000. Its main advantage is support for multi-disk configurations with additional performance or fault tolerance benefits. The basic units of dynamic storage are dynamic disks.

Dynamic disks

All dynamic disks start as basic disks. The conversion is manual and performed using either Disk Management Console or the `diskpart.exe` utility. The Conversion process creates a Logical Disk Management database containing the dynamic disk configuration for the entire system (shared with all other dynamic disks and updated for every disk configuration change). GPT disks store it in a separate, hidden partition, while MBR disks need roughly 1MB of free, unpartitioned space at the very end of the disk. The conversion fails if this space is not available. This will not happen if the MBR basic disk has been created in Windows 2000, XP, or .NET (as these operating systems always reserve sufficient space at the end of the disk when the basic disk is initialized) but it might happen if the system has been upgraded from Windows NT 4.0 and partitions fill out the entire disk. There is no workaround to this issue other than backing up the data, and deleting and recreating of all partitions.

Note

Storing disk information in multiple copies of the LDM database (one per disk) increases fault tolerance. This is a better approach than the one used for basic disks, where configuration information resides in the registry.

Conversion is a non-destructive operation, but to play it safe, make sure you have a solid backup before you start. When switching back from dynamic to basic disk, backup and restore is the only way to preserve the data because this operation requires deleting all of the disk volumes (along with their content).

Conversion of the disk from basic to dynamic typically does not require a reboot. The only exceptions to this involve conversion of basic disks containing system, boot, or paging files.

Dynamic disks are not supported on portable computers and removable disk drives. This is by design because laptop computers rarely use multiple disks and having a shared LDM database on a removable drive would require overwriting it every time the drive is transferred between computers. You also cannot use dynamic disks as shared storage devices for server clusters in Windows 2003 Enterprise and Datacenter servers.

You should not run the conversion for disks that contain other operating systems (on multi-boot computers) because this might prevent them from booting. This results from the fact that, during conversion, references to all partitions (except for system and boot) are removed from the MBR.

Volumes created on dynamic disks are called, as you might have already guessed, dynamic volumes. If the basic disk contained any primary partitions or extended partitions with logical drives, they are converted automatically into dynamic volumes. This does not apply to original equipment manufacturer (OEM) partitions (vendor-specific configuration partitions) and system partitions on GPT disks. Even though the maximum number of supported dynamic volumes per dynamic disk is 2,000, more than 32 are not recommended. There are five dynamic volume types, as follows:

✦ **Simple volumes:** A simple volume is limited to a single disk only. Simple volumes on their own do not provide any advantages over basic volumes, but they can serve as a starting point for extending storage space on the local system or building fault tolerance into it. You need to start with simple volumes if your goal is to extend or span volumes. If you have additional dynamic disks, you can also add levels of fault tolerance by mirroring them. Simple volumes can also be mounted to NTFS folders. Simple dynamic volumes can occupy contiguous or non-contiguous areas of the dynamic disk (after it is extended).

✦ **Spanned volumes:** If you have multiple dynamic disks with unallocated space, you can extend a simple volume beyond a single disk. At that point, your simple volume becomes spanned. Spanned volumes can occupy multiple, non-contiguous areas on up to 32 dynamic disks on the same system. To span a existing simple volume, it must be formatted using NTFS. You also have an option of creating a spanned volume starting with multiple, unallocated areas of free space on several dynamic disks.

Windows 2000 writes data to spanned volumes sequentially, filling all the available space on the first disk before starting with the next one. This means that spanned volumes do not provide any performance benefits — data is accessed in the same way as if it were written to a simple volume. There is also no improvement in terms of fault tolerance, since no data redundancy is provided. As a matter of fact, data stored on a spanned volume becomes even more vulnerable, because a failure of any disk renders the entire volume unusable.

✦ **Striped volumes:** On the surface, striping seems to be similar to spanning. In this case, you also combine areas of unallocated disk space from multiple disks into a single volume. The differences between them stem from the way the data on the resulting volume is written and read. Instead of the sequential approach used in a spanned volume, data is divided into 64KB pieces and written across all disks participating in the volume. This means that each disk is utilized to the same degree and the size of each stripe is the same (unlike in the case of spanned volumes, where you could arbitrarily choose the size of each area).

Due to their structure, striped volumes provide significant performance benefits. If dynamic disks can be accessed simultaneously (depending on the type of disk controller), I/O operations on each disk can be executed in parallel. Data vulnerability, however, is increased (just as with a spanned volume). This is the main reason that striped volumes are typically used for read-only data that can be easily restored.

A striped volume can consist of up to 32 dynamic disks.

Striped volume sets are also known as RAID-0 configuration.

✦ **RAID-1 volumes (mirrors):** This is one of two software-based fault-tolerant disk configurations available in Windows 2003. A mirrored volume set consists of two identical copies of a simple volume residing on two separate dynamic disks. If one of them fails, the system can still remain operational using the other copy until the failed hardware is replaced and the mirror is recreated. Mirrored volumes are part of standard fault-tolerant solutions.

✦ **RAID-5 volumes (fault-tolerant stripes):** This is the other type of software-based fault-tolerant disk configuration included in Windows 2003. As with striped volumes, data is written across all the drives in 64KB pieces. What is different is that for each of these pieces, the operating system adds parity information to one of the disks in the volume. The parity information is used to reconstruct the data if one of the disks fails. You need at least three dynamic disks to construct a RAID-5 volume. Fault tolerance and efficient use of disk space are two main advantages of RAID-5 volumes.

Simple and spanned dynamic volumes can be extended (just like the basic ones). They are subject to restrictions similar to those that apply when extending basic disks, except they do not require unallocated space to be adjacent; you can use free space on any dynamic disks. Essentially, it is possible to extend any non-system, non-boot, NTFS-formatted (or unformatted) dynamic volumes, as long as they have been created natively in Windows 2003. Note that it is not possible to extend striped, RAID-1, or RAID-5 volumes; if you are planning on using them, evaluate your space requirements ahead of time.

The fault-tolerant volume sets deserve more coverage.

RAID-1: Disk mirroring

Windows 2003 allows the creation of a mirror using any dynamic volume, including those containing system or boot files, as long as the unallocated space on the other disk is sufficient. When you create a mirror, you can start with a simple volume and an unallocated area on another dynamic disk or two unallocated areas on two dynamic disks. In the first case, the data from the existing simple volume will be copied to the other disk during the initial resynchronization process. In the second case, parts of the volume will be populated equally starting with the first write operation.

The main drawback of mirroring is its level of space utilization, which is always equal to 50 percent (e.g., when using two 18GB disks, your usable space is 18GB). However, RAID-1 is the only disk configuration that can provide software-based fault tolerance for boot and system partitions (this limitation does not apply to hardware-based fault tolerance, which we will discuss later in this chapter). With the costs of hard drives falling, configuring a server with a mirrored volume for system or boot files is a very cost-effective means of maintaining high availability.

Note that redundancy on the disk level does not prevent downtime if both dynamic disks participating in the mirror connect to the same disk controller. If availability of your system is critical, you might want to consider duplexing. Duplexing extends the concept of mirroring by using separate disk controllers, each connected to one of the mirrored disks.

RAID-5: Fault-tolerant striping with parity

RAID-5 is similar to a non-redundant stripe set. The main differences result from the fact that additional parity information is calculated and written across the disks to provide fault tolerance.

To set up a RAID-5 configuration, first evaluate your storage requirements; then determine how many disks will be needed to satisfy your needs. Remember the following three rules:

- ✦ Each of the striped areas across all disks has to be the same size.
- ✦ The redundant data will occupy up to $(1/n)$th of the total space, where n is the number of striped disks.
- ✦ A RAID-5 configuration can contain between 3 and 32 dynamic disks.

For example, if you have one dynamic disk with 9GB of unallocated space and two others with 13GB, the biggest RAID-5 configuration you can create will have 18GB of available space. This is because you are limited by the smallest of the areas that will be used for the volume (9GB in this case). Three disks with 9GB each will give you 27GB. One-third of it is used for parity; therefore, you are left with only 18GB.

The amount of wasted space (space used for parity information) is exactly equal to the size of the RAID-5 volume on a single disk. In other words, if you have 5 36GB drives, and each in its entirety is part of the RAID-5 volume, you will have 4 (36GB worth of usable disk space. This is much more efficient than mirroring, since the percentage of overhead in this case is 20 percent as opposed to 50 percent. With 32 disks in a RAID-5 volume (the maximum number of disk supported), you waste only 1/32 (100 percent or 3.125 percent. On the other hand, the more disks you have, the higher the probability that more than any two of them will fail.

RAID-5 is slower than other disk configurations because of the additional operations that need to take place to accommodate the calculation and writing of the parity information. Performance can be improved by using faster and more powerful hardware. Using drives of the same type and speed, as well as fast controllers with a large amount of battery-protected cache, will make a significant difference. Remember that within a RAID-5 configuration, the fastest and most expensive disk is only as good as the slowest and cheapest one.

Consider the type of data when determining the type of software-based fault-tolerant disk configuration. A mirror is the only type of volume that can be used for system and boot volumes; mirroring is also appropriate for storing data that is written sequentially (such as transaction logs). On the other hand, if you require large, fault-tolerant volumes that will be accessed randomly, use RAID-5. For example, for large application servers such as SQL Server or Exchange 2000, place their databases on a RAID-5 volume and mirror the transaction logs.

Table 19-1 presents a comprehensive comparison between the features of basic and dynamic disks.

Table 19-1: Feature Comparison between Basic and Dynamic Disks

Feature	***Basic***	***Dynamic***
Managing Legacy Volume Sets on Basic Disks	No[1]	N/A
Booting to Windows 2003 Server from a Volume	Yes	No[2]
Installing Windows 2003 Server to a Volume	Yes	Yes[2]
Creating/Managing BasicVolumes	Yes	No
Creating/Managing Spanned Volumes	No	Yes
Creating/Managing Striped Volumes	No	Yes
Creating/Managing Mirrored Volumes	No	Yes
Creating/Managing RAID-5 Volumes	No	Yes
Maximum Number of Volumes	4[3]	2000[4]
Creating/Managing Volume Mount Points	Yes	Yes
Extending Volumes	Yes[5]	Yes[5]

Continued

Table 19-1 *(continued)*

Feature	*Basic*	*Dynamic*
Support for FAT, FAT32, and NTFS	Yes	Yes
Support for Shared Storage on Server Clusters	Yes	No[6]
Support for Removable Drives (including USB and IEEE 1394)	Yes	No

[1]On Windows NT 4.0 and earlier, you could create mirrored sets, striped sets, spanned sets, and striped sets with parity on servers with basic disks (dynamic disks were introduced in Windows 2000). Support for these features was implemented by a driver, `ftdisk.exe`. For compatibility reasons, Windows 2000 continued support for these types of volumes on basic disks, but in limited capacity. After upgrading to Windows 2000, all fault-tolerant basic disk configurations were still accessible, but new ones could not be created. Windows .NET Server eliminates completely legacy fault-tolerant disk components implemented by `ftdisk.exe`. Keep this in mind if you migrate from Windows NT 4.0 servers using a multi-disk configuration. You have the following two options:

- You can back up data on the fault-tolerant volumes and restore it when Windows 2003 is installed.
- You can use `ftonline.exe` (part of Windows 2003 Support Tools, included on the Windows 2003 Server installation CD) to access the volumes after the migration and convert them to dynamic using Disk Management or `diskpart.exe` command-line utility. Keep in mind that `ftonline.exe` enables access to the legacy disk configurations only for the duration of the current session. After the machine is rebooted, access is lost and the tool needs to be run again to restore it.

[2]The capability to boot from a partition or a volume is strictly dependent on whether an entry for it appears in the partition table. This will happen if the dynamic disk has been converted from a basic disk that contained partitions created in earlier operating systems. It is also possible to use the `retain` command available in the `diskpart.exe` utility. This will force the simple volume entry to be retained in the partition table, even if the volume has been created in Windows 2003 Server.

[3]Basic disks using the MBR partition style support a maximum of four partitions; if one of them is extended, you can create unlimited numbers of logical drives to it. Basic disks using the GPT partition style support up to 128 primary partitions (including Microsoft Reserved Partition), but do not allow you to create extended partitions.

[4]Even though it is possible to create up to 2,000 dynamic volumes on a dynamic disk, the recommended maximum is 32.

[5]A volume can be extended if it is formatted with NTFS (or if it is unformatted) and is not used to store operating system or boot files. You cannot extend a basic volume that has been created in Windows NT 4.0 or 2000 and upgraded to Windows 2003 Server. Basic volumes can be extended using the area on the same disk only. In addition, this area has to be contiguous (immediately following) the one used by the basic volume. Similarly, you can extend a logical drive in an extended volume, as long as there is free contiguous space available. Basic volumes must be extended using `diskpart.exe` (this feature is not available through Disk Management).

[6]Dynamic disks can be used only for local storage on cluster nodes.

Hardware RAID

Our focus in this chapter has been on software-based RAID configurations available in Windows 2003. Although they can improve high availability or faster disk access, they are no match for equivalent hardware solutions. These range from relatively inexpensive internal RAID controllers to high-end, fiber-attached SANs containing hundreds of hot-pluggable drives, gigabytes of battery-backed cache memory, multiple, redundant, powerful, built-in storage controllers, and multi-channel I/O. They can also provide support for additional disk configurations such as RAID-1+0 (mirrored striped volumes) or RAID-0 + 1 (striped mirrors). This disparity is visible especially when dealing with RAID-5 configurations, where parity information needs to be calculated during data writes. Although software-based volumes use the local CPU, hardware solutions offload this task to dedicated processors on external RAID controllers.

Note that each of hardware-based RAID configurations is presented to the operating system as a single disk. Therefore, if you had five physical disks and you set up two of them via controller as RAID 1 and the remaining three as RAID 5, once you boot to Windows 2003, you would only see two disks in the Disk Management console.

Dynamic Storage Management

Your introduction to practical dynamic disk management will start with the conversion from basic to dynamic disk. Next, we will take a look at creating simple, spanned, striped, mirrored, and RAID-5 volumes.

Converting basic disks to dynamic

Upgrading a basic disk to dynamic takes only a few steps.

1. Start by backing up all data on any disks you intend to upgrade (even though the operation is non-destructive).

2. Launch Microsoft Management Console by typing **MMC.EXE** from the Command Prompt or Start ➪ Run text box. Select Add/Remove Snap-in from the File menu, click the Add button from Add/Remove Snap-in, and choose the Disk Management option from the list. You will be prompted for the target computer, so pick the local one or type in the name of a remote one. Close all dialog boxes and you will see the snap-in loaded in the tree pane (alternatively, you can use the Computer Management console, which contains the Disk Management node in the Storage tree. In all of the following sets of instructions, we will assume that this step has been taken.)

3. Make sure that either the top or bottom part of the details pane lists disks, not volumes. This is done by selecting View ➪ Top or View ➪ Bottom and then choosing either the Disk List or Graphical View option. Figure 19-2 shows the disk view in the top part of the pane and the graphical view at the bottom.

4. Right-click the basic disk you want to convert and select the option Convert to Dynamic Disk. The Convert to Dynamic Disk dialog box is displayed prompting you for confirmation (see Figure 19-3) and giving you an option to choose another disk or convert multiple disks at once. If the disk contains any partitions, you will be presented with another window, listing your selection and volumes to be converted for each disk. You will be reminded that after conversion other operating systems (other than Windows 2000, XP Professional, or .NET) will not be able to access the volumes on the disk. Finally, another message box will notify you that all volumes on the disk will be dismounted (so you should not keep any files on these volumes open during the conversion). If you are converting the disk containing the Windows directory, the reboot will be required.

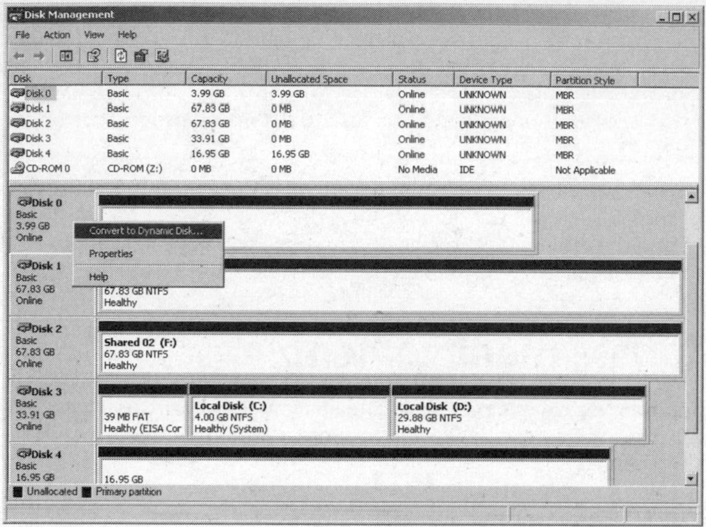

Figure 19-2: Selecting the option to convert a disk from basic to dynamic.

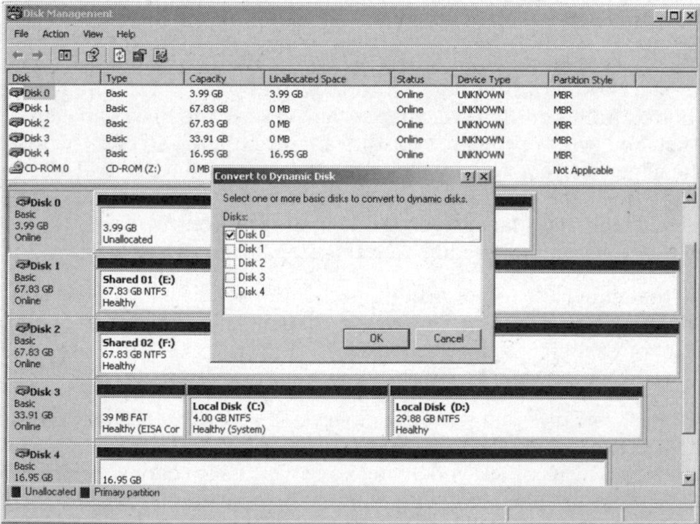

Figure 19-3: Confirming the action to convert to dynamic disk.

5. After you click on the Yes button on the final message box, the conversion takes place. The process is almost instantaneous.

If you want to convert a dynamic disk back to basic, you need to first delete all the volumes it contains. Obviously, this will destroy any data stored on them, so back it up first. After both steps are completed, select the Convert to Basic Disk option that appears in the context menu for each of the dynamic disks displayed in the Disk Management Console.

You can also use the `diskpart.exe` utility to perform both types of conversion by with the following steps:

1. At the Command Prompt on the target server, type **diskpart**. This will launch the tool and display the `diskpart>` prompt.
2. At the `diskpart>` prompt, type **SELECT DISK x**, where *x* is the number of the disk to be converted to dynamic (you can obtain a listing of disks by typing **LIST DISK** at the `diskpart>` prompt). This will make this disk a target of any subsequent operations.
3. Type in **CONVERT DYNAMIC**. This completes the conversion process.

To convert back to the basic disk, start by deleting all of its volumes. This is done by selecting each of them with the `select volume` command (after selecting the disk), then running the `delete volume` command for each. After this is done, execute `convert basic`. A quicker approach is using the `clean` command, which removes all disk configuration information from the disk. This command can also be used to convert the GPT disk to MBR. After running it, you will also need to re-initialize the disk.

Creating simple volumes

If a basic disk contains any partitions when it is upgraded, they all are automatically converted to simple volumes. You can also create them after the disk becomes dynamic. Simple volumes can exist only on dynamic disks.

Create a simple volume with the following steps:

1. In the Disk Management Console window, select the Graphical View from the View ➪ Top or View ➪ Bottom menu. This will display a listing of the disks with rectangles representing the layout of their volumes or partitions.
2. Bring up the context menu for the rectangle representing the disk layout of the dynamic disk where the simple volume will be created.
3. Select the New Volume option to launch the New Volume Wizard. Depending on the number of dynamic disks and their layout, you will have an option to create Simple, Spanned, Striped, Mirrored, or RAID-5 volumes. Select Simple and then click Next.
4. You will be presented with the Select Disks page of the wizard that lists Selected and Available disks that can contain the type of volume you chose. On this page, you can specify multiple simple volumes on multiple dynamic disks and provide the size individually for each of them. By default, the size of the simple volume is equal to the size of the remaining unallocated space on the disk (even if the areas of free disk space are not contiguous).
5. The next page of the wizard offers you three options: You can assign to the volume drive letter, mount it in an empty folder on an existing NTFS partition, or leave it the way it is, not mounted and without a drive letter assignment.

6. The next page gives you an option to format the volume. The only option available from Disk Management Console for volumes on dynamic disks is NTFS. You can, however, use FAT or FAT32, if you use `format.exe` from the command line. You can specify the allocation unit size and set the volume label. You can use quick format (if you are fairly confident that the disk does not contain bad sectors) and enable file and folder compression on the volume level.

7. The final page displays your choices. Click Finish to create the volume. If you decided to format the volume, without selecting the quick format option, the operation might take some time to complete (depending on a number of factors, such as volume size, system performance, disk speed, etc.). At any point, you can cancel formatting in progress and start the quick format by selecting the Format option from the Action ⇨ All Tasks menu.

Extending simple volumes and spanned volumes

As explained previously in this chapter, simple volumes, once created, can be extended, providing that they are formatted using the NTFS file system (or are unformatted), that they haven't been converted from basic volumes created in previous versions of Windows operating systems (other than Windows XP or .NET), and they do not function as system or boot volumes.

A simple volume can be extended by adding unallocated space residing on the same disk or by adding unallocated space from another disk on the same system. In the second case, your simple volume will become a spanned volume. Spanned volumes can also be created by combining multiple areas of unallocated disk space on multiple dynamic disks with the New Volume wizard (described in the previous section).

To extend a simple volume into a spanned volume, use the following procedure:

1. In the Disk Management Console, switch to the Graphical View in the lower part of the pane by selecting View ⇨ Bottom ⇨ Graphical View.

2. Right-click the existing simple volume and select the Extend Volume option from the context menu (the same option appears in the Action ⇨ All Tasks menu). This will start the Extend Volume Wizard.

3. You will be presented with a familiar Select Disk page. To convert a simple volume into a spanned volume, you need to pick another dynamic disk with unallocated space from the Available list and add it to the Selected box. You also need to decide how much space will be added to the existing volume. Because the existing volume is already formatted, the Format Volume page does not appear.

4. After clicking Finish, the volume will be extended and your simple volume will become spanned.

Create a new spanned volume with the following steps:

1. In the Disk Management Console, switch to Graphical View in the lower part of the pane by selecting View ⇨ Bottom ⇨ Graphical View.

2. Right-click the disk with unallocated space and select the New Volume option to launch the New Volume Wizard. The steps you go through are practically identical as before, although your selections will differ.

3. Start by selecting the Spanned option as the type of volume you want to create. Next, on the Select Disk page, all remaining dynamic disks with unallocated space will be listed in the Available box. Select the ones you want to include in the spanned volume and click Add. This will switch them to the list of Selected disks. For each disk, you can specify the amount of unallocated space you want to use for the spanned volume.
4. As with simple volume, you need to decide whether to assign a drive letter to the volume. You can also mount it using an empty folder on an NTFS partition.
5. Finally, specify the file system on the Format Volume page.

Spanned volume can be further extended by adding unallocated space from any of the local dynamic disks.

If you want to recover any of the space used by the spanned volume, you will have to delete the entire volume. Before you start, back up whatever data residing on the volume you want to preserve.

Delete a spanned volume with the following steps:

1. In the Disk Management Console, switch to Graphical View by selecting View ➪ Bottom ➪ Graphical View.
2. Right-click on any of the parts of the spanned volume. They will be displayed using the same color and will have the same label and drive letter (if assigned). Select the Delete Volume option, as illustrated in Figure 19-4. You will be reminded that all data on the volume will be lost.

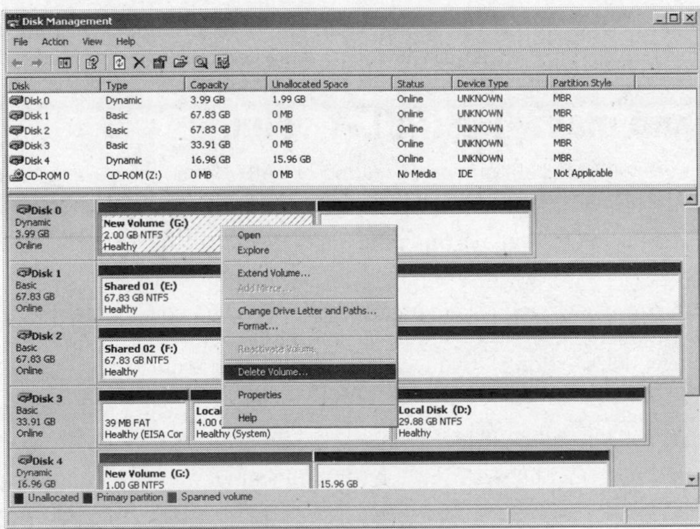

Figure 19-4: Deleting a spanned volume.

After the delete operation is completed, space used by the volume returns to the Unallocated state and can be used for any other type of disk configuration.

Creating and managing RAID-0 volumes (striping)

To create a striped volume, you need to have at least two dynamic disks with unallocated disk space. Each area from each of these disks used by the striped volume will have the same size. You do not need to be concerned about this when creating the striped volume because Disk Management will ensure that all pieces are equally large — it will simply allocate space on each disk using the size of the smallest unallocated space among all of them. But keep it in mind when designing the layout of your volumes. Remember that boot or system volumes cannot be parts of a stripe. Evaluate your storage needs carefully, since striped volumes cannot be extended.

Create a striped volume with the following steps:

1. In the Disk Management Console, switch to Graphical View by selecting View ➪ Bottom ➪ Graphical View.
2. Right-click the disk showing unallocated space and select the New Volume option. The New Volume Wizard launches and takes you through the previously described steps. Select the Striped option on the Select Volume Type page.
3. The remaining options are similar to the ones described in the previous section covering the creation of a Spanned Volume. The main difference is that once you decide which dynamic disks will be used for building the stripe, the amount of space allocated from each of them will be the same. This will be based on the disk with the smallest amount of unallocated space. If you manually type in a smaller number, the size of the areas to be created on each disk will automatically change. Total volume size is the result of multiplying the number of disks in the stripe times this amount.

To delete a striped volume, you would simply select the Delete option after right-clicking the volume. Obviously, this destroys all data stored on it, so back it up first.

Creating and managing RAID-1 volumes

RAID-1 volumes are fault-tolerant mirrors. Creation of RAID-1 volumes always involves two dynamic disks. You can create mirrored volumes in one of the following ways:

- ✦ Create a simple volume and mirror it afterwards using an unallocated area of the same or larger size on another dynamic disk.
- ✦ Create a mirror using two areas of unallocated space on two separate dynamic disks. As with striping, these areas do not have to be of the same size. Choose the smaller one and decide which portion of it you want to use. When the mirror gets created, an equally sized portion will be automatically allocated on the other disk.

Create a mirrored volume using the first method with the following steps:

1. In the Disk Management snap-in, switch to Graphical View by selecting View ➪ Bottom ➪ Graphical View.
2. Right-click the disk containing a dynamic volume you want to mirror and select the Add Mirror option.

3. You will be presented with the list of dynamic disks on your system with a sufficient amount of unallocated space to create the mirror. Select the one you want to use and click the Add Mirror button.

4. Right-click the disk containing a dynamic volume you want to mirror and select the Add Mirror option. This will start the process of synchronizing the content of the original simple volume with its replica. The length of time the process takes is dependent on the amount of data as well as your system's performance and utilization levels. After the synchronization is complete, your mirrored volume should display Healthy status.

Create a mirrored volume using the second method with the following steps:

1. In the Disk Management snap-in, switch to Graphical View by selecting View ➪ Bottom ➪ Graphical View.

2. Right-click one of the disks that will contain the mirrored volume and select the New Volume option. The New Volume Wizard will launch.

3. On the Select Volume Type page, select the Mirrored option.

4. On the Select Disk page, click the second dynamic disk listed in the Available box and click Add. The disk will appear in the Selected box. As with the striped volume, Disk Management will automatically adjust the size of space used for the mirror to match the smaller area of unallocated space between two disks (as illustrated in the Figure 19-5). You can make it smaller if you want.

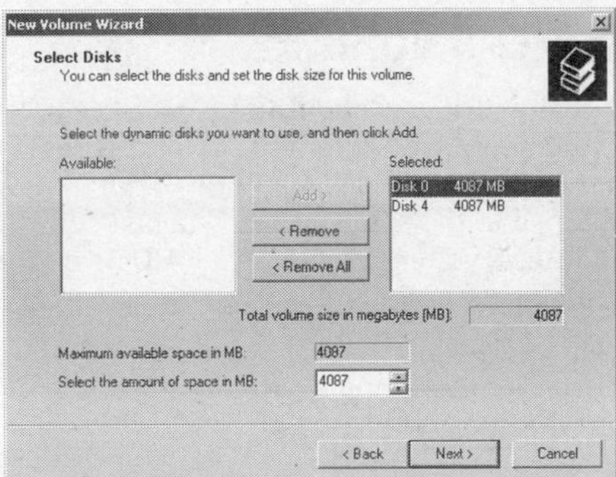

Figure 19-5: Selecting the disks used for a mirrored volume.

5. The two steps that follow—selecting a drive letter or mounting the volume and formatting—are the same as the ones used for other types of volumes. After you click Finish, the mirror will be created instantaneously because no resynchronization needs to take place.

Figure 19-6 shows the mirror set created and formatted (volume G:). It also illustrates that the mirror has been established on two areas of dynamic disk space equal to 3.99GB. Disk 4 still has close to 13GB worth of disk space left, which can be used for any other type of disk configuration.

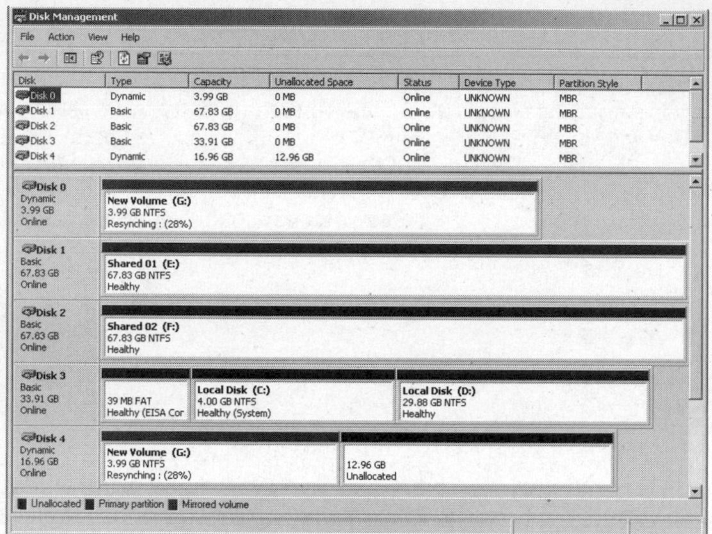

Figure 19-6: The mirror volume in the process of resynching, as displayed in Disk Management.

Creating and managing RAID-5 volumes

A RAID-5 volume is another type of fault-tolerant disk configuration available in Windows 2003 Server. In order to create a RAID-5 volume, you need to have at least three dynamic disks with unallocated space. As before, even though these areas might be of different sizes, Disk Management will ensure that only space equal to the smallest one will be used when creating the volume. It is not possible to extend a RAID-5 volume or create a RAID-5 volume using any existing volume.

To install RAID-5 volumes, do the following steps:

1. In the Disk Management snap-in, switch to Graphical View by selecting View ➪ Bottom ➪ Graphical View.
2. Right-click the dynamic disk showing unallocated space and select the New Volume option. The New Volume Wizard will launch and take you through the previously described steps. In the Select Volume Type box, select the RAID-5 option. For this option to be available, you need to have at least three dynamic disks with unallocated space.
3. As with striped and mirrored volumes, on the Select Disks screen you will select disks that will be part of the volume. The size will be automatically adjusted by Disk Management (you can also make it smaller).
4. After deciding on the drive letter assignment and formatting option, the wizard will display the final information page. Clicking the Finish button will instantly the create RAID-5 volume.

Importing disks

Typically, basic disks and dynamic disks containing simple volumes can be removed from one computer and installed into another Windows 2003 computer without any impact on the data stored on them. This is also possible when dealing with multi-disk volumes, as long as all the disks that the volume uses are moved together. The multi-disk volumes can be recognized on another system because information about their configuration is stored locally on each disk in the LDM database.

However, transferring dynamic disks between two systems requires an additional step called importing. This relates to the fact that all dynamic disks in a computer form a group, the name of which is computer-specific (derived from the computer name). In order for a dynamic disk to be imported into a new computer, its database information needs to be merged with the one existing on the new system and its computer group reference renamed.

Import foreign dynamic disks using the following steps:

1. Ensure that each disk is in a *healthy* state before removal.
2. After inserting the disks into the new host, open Disk Management Console. If the disk does not appear in the details pane, from the Action menu select Rescan Disks. You might also try launching Device Manager and selecting the Scan for Hardware Changes option from the Action menu.
3. Right-click the disk marked *Foreign* and then choose the Import Foreign Disks option.
4. The Foreign Disk Volumes dialog box will list all volumes detected on the disk to be imported. You can verify whether the list is complete. After you click OK, the disks will be imported into your system.

When the import process is completed, select the Rescan Disks option again to verify that the import worked.

Managing Storage with Disk Quotas

Disk quotas enable you to control space utilization of NTFS-formatted basic and dynamic volumes. In this section, we will take a closer look at the quota technology and the reasons for using it.

Why do you need disk quotas?

No matter how much hard disk space you think you need, it will never be enough. Insatiable appetite for space is common to users, applications, and operating systems. Just compare the current average size of a user's profile or home folder with the one a few years ago. Or take a look at the space requirements of Microsoft Office 97 and Windows XP.

Keeping track of available storage is an endless but essential effort. All computer functionality is affected by a lack of hard disk space. If your disk becomes full, services will stop, databases will crash, and backup jobs will fail.

Disk quotas provide a means of controlling and enforcing a user's ability to save data to a volume. It can be enforced at the user level and restricted on a per-volume basis. Typically, you set a user's quota and let Windows 2003 monitor the user's disk consumption. Then, as soon as the amount of a user's data on the volume exceeds the first threshold defined by your quota limits, the operating system will react with a warning. When the second threshold is reached, users can be prevented from saving any additional files until they free some of the disk space. This can be accomplished by either deleting files that are no longer needed, moving them to a different volume, changing file ownership (more about this last option next), or asking Administrator to change the quota limits. Quotas, thus, not only help you protect disk space, they also force your users to maintain their space utilization. Users can easily find out how much space they can use before reaching the second threshold by checking the volume properties. If the quota limits are enforced, volume properties will display only the amount of space left within their quota limits, rather than total amount of free space on the volume.

With disk quotas, you can set a limit on the hard disk space consumption for all your users. How do you do that? Let us now examine the quota system and learn how to apply and enforce quotas.

How the quota system works

The quota system is not difficult to set up and manage, but you should understand how it works and know its limitations.

Ownership

Quota calculations are based on ownership. Every time a file or folder is created on an NTFS volume or partition, the operating system adds an ownership attribute to it. Permissions have no bearing on the quota system.

Using ownership seems like a good idea, since the person who created a file should be held accountable for usage of the disk space occupied by it. Conveniently, ownership also gets properly transferred when a copy of an existing file is made, since copying actually involves the creation of a new file. Unfortunately, there are also some drawbacks to using ownership for controlling quotas, as follows:

✦ In many cases ownership of the file might unexpectedly change. The most common example is the restore scenario, where an administrator or a backup operator uses a staging area instead of restoring files directly to their original location. In this case, the next step after the restore would involve manually copying restored files to their final destination, where the user requesting the restore can access them. If this copy is done by someone other than the user, that person becomes the owner of the copied files, and they no longer count toward the user's quota limits. One solution to this problem is using a staging area on the same volume and moving files instead of copying, since moving files between folders on the same volume retains ownership.

✦ Fixing ownership problems might be difficult and time-consuming. Windows does not provide a method for granting ownership to another user (you can only take ownership if you have sufficient rights, which are controlled by Take Ownership of Files and Other Objects user rights and granted automatically to members of local Administrators groups).

There are several third-party products that can be used to grant ownership. Refer to `www.pedestalsoftware.com` and `www.mks.com` for details.

✦ Migration of data between servers needs to be done using methods that preserve file and folder ownership. The best approach is using Windows 2003 backup and restore (or third-party backup programs) that offer this feature. This, however, might create a problem if local groups (rather than domain local groups) are used to grant permissions to data.

✦ You need to pay special attention to services that are running in the context of a user account. Although typically such an account is a member of a local Administrators group, which is exempted from quotas, sometimes this might not be the case. In such situations, the service might suddenly stop running if an application using it exceeds disk space quota limits.

✦ Disk quotas can be assigned only on per-user basis since, with the exception of local Administrators, a group cannot be listed as an owner of a file or a folder. This introduces administrative overhead, unless you apply the same limit to all users.

Caveats of quota systems

Besides the ownership-related issues listed in the previous section, there are several other caveats of disk quotas in Windows. The quota system ignores compression, taking into account only the uncompressed size of a file when calculating space utilization. It uses the same rule with sparse files. Removing quota entries for individual users requires changing ownership for every single file owned by them on the volume (or deleting or moving these files).

As expected, quota limits do not apply to any accounts that are members of the local Administrators group. You can change this, though, by creating a separate quota entry for each of them. The only account that cannot be restricted this way is the built-in Administrator account.

When configuring quotas, you can instruct the quota service to write entries into the event log. You can build a custom solution that would use these entries to trigger a notification or even some type of cleanup activities.

Enabling quotas does not automatically enforce them, but enables you to collect the statistics about users' data. This, in turn, helps you make accurate estimates of disk space utilization and plan quota settings accordingly. Before you implement quotas, note that they impose a performance penalty. Its impact depends on the amount of data and overall system performance, so, just as with other solutions, you should test it properly first.

Remember that disk utilization statistics in the Quota Entries window are cached and might not reflect the actual values. You need to refresh the window by pressing the F5 key to update them.

Disk space/quota analysis

The quota service component, once enabled for a volume, gathers disk space usage information about all users who own files on it. This information is reported to the Quota Entries for Local Disk, as illustrated in Figure 19-7 (accessible from the Quota tab of the Volume Properties). This information is a convenient way of determining ownership of file objects in a volume, without having to analyze the entire file system by checking the security properties of each file and folder.

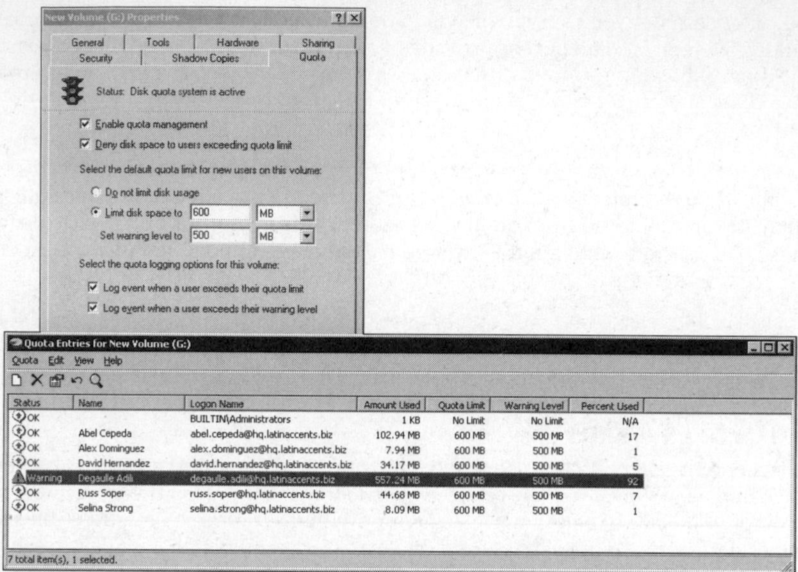

Figure 19-7: The quota entries for a local disk.

After collecting information utilization of the volume on per-user basis, you can start setting disk quotas.

Setting disk quotas

To set up quotas on individual volume, do the following:

1. Make sure you are logged on as a member of the local Administrators group on the server hosting the volume. This is required to set quotas. Ensure that the volume is formatted using NTFS. If not, you will need to run the `convert.exe` utility first, if you want to preserve the data residing on it. Otherwise, format it with NTFS using Disk Management Console, Windows Explorer, or the command line.

2. Launch Disk Management Console.

3. In the Disk Management snap-in, switch to Graphical View by selecting View ➪ Bottom ➪ Graphical View.

4. Right-click the volume for which you want to set the quotas and select the Properties option from the menu. This will display the Local Disk Properties dialog box. Click the Quota tab. This will display the content shown in Figure 19-8.

   If the volume has a drive letter assigned to it, you can also access it from the My Computer window by right-clicking that drive, selecting Properties from the context menu, and clicking the Quota tab. Both methods bring up the same dialog box, but the first one allows you to set up quotas on volumes (such as mounted volumes) without a corresponding drive letter.

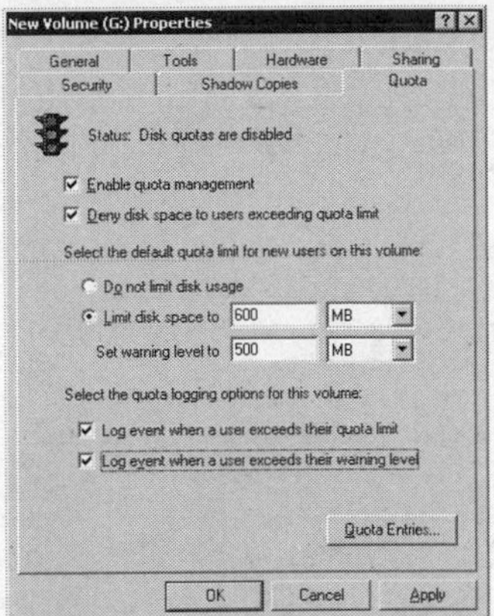

Figure 19-8: The Quota tab of Volume Properties.

5. Click the Enable Quota Management check box. This triggers the monitoring of user disk space consumption (the results can be viewed by clicking the Quota Entries button).

6. Click the Deny Disk Space to Users Exceeding Quota Limit check box. This option is required to enforce quota limits and send notification to users who exceed them. Checking this option is not sufficient, though, to enforce quotas. In addition, you will need to set appropriate limits for everyone, or for individual users through the Quota Entries for Local Disk window.

7. Leave the Do Not Limit Disk Usage option selected if you want to allow users to use as much hard disk space as they need; otherwise, check the Limit Disk Space to select box and specify the size limit. This value will apply to all users (with the exception of members of the local Administrators group).

8. Set the warning level to whatever amount you consider appropriate (but higher than the limit set in the previous step). This is the first threshold. After the warning has been issued, the users can continue using hard disk space until they reach the second threshold.

9. The last two check boxes on this tab control the logging of events of exceeding warning and quota limit thresholds in the Windows System Event Log. When searching for them, remember that they are listed as informational events.

Adding disk quota entries

In the previous section, we set the same quota thresholds for all users. If you want to be able to control disk space utilization in more granular fashion, you can create separate limits for individual users. To add quota entries, click the Quota Entries button in the Local Disk Properties dialog box for the volume. Insert quota entries using the following steps:

1. From the Quota menu, select the New Quota Entry option. This brings up the Select Users dialog box.

2. From the Select Users dialog box, enter the username to which the limit will apply and then click OK.

Common-sense disk quota management

Disk quotas can help you manage disk space utilization, but they can also make common, otherwise straightforward tasks more difficult. The following suggestions might help you with making your quota management more efficient:

- When assigning quotas, leave some extra disk space unassigned. This will be useful if you need to customize quotas on per users basis. This extra space will also be used by NTFS metadata (taking roughly 64KB per file) that is not counted towards a user's quota limits.
- Make users aware of the effects of disk quotas (without getting into details) and how to check the disk space available to them (all of them should be familiar with Windows Explorer). Most likely, enforcing quotas will bring them much closer to the space utilization limits than before. For example, let's say user JDoe owns 100MB worth of files on a quota-enabled volume with total disk space of 36GB. The same volume is used by 50 other users with very similar space requirements. Assuming (for simplicity's sake) that all of them currently occupy the same amount of space, JDoe will see 31GB of free disk space when checking the volume properties. Let's say that you set the quota threshold to 600MB, which you get by subtracting the 6GB "cushion" from the total of 36GB, and dividing it by the total number of users (obviously your users' requirements might, and probably will be, completely different). As soon as you check the Deny Disk Space to Users Exceeding Quota Limits check box in the Quota tab of Volume Properties, and set the quota limit, free disk space properties for JDoe will show the value of 500MB.
- Enable warning thresholds for all users and leave a sufficient buffer between the warning and hard disk limit. It makes no sense to warn users that they are about to run out of allocated space and then enforce a hard limit as soon as they try to save their files.
- Ensure that users will not be installing applications on the volume with the quota limits set. In rare cases when this happens, increase the quota limit to prevent application installations from failing or install it using an administrative account.
- Monitor hard disk usage on a continuous basis. Take corrective actions (for example, increase allocated space for power users) if you encounter problems.
- Avoid sharing user accounts. Such a solution is insecure and makes proper quota management difficult.
- Account for the size of a user's roaming profile in your estimates of space requirements if they happen to be stored on a volume with disk quotas turned on.
- If the spool directory resides on a volume with disk quotas, account for the sizes of print jobs. Their ownership is set to the users who created them, so they also count toward the quota limits. If possible, move a spool directory to a separate volume.
- Try using Group Policies, Windows Management Instrumentation scripts, or the `fsutil.exe` commandline utility to manage disk quotas. To simplify management, you can also export and import quota entries between the servers (as long as they are located in the same domain).
- Remove quotas for users who no longer need access to the volume. This requires, though, that you first delete, move, or take ownership (as Administrator) of users' files. The easiest way to handle this is from the Quota Entries dialog box. Attempting to delete an entry will trigger the display of the Disk Quota dialog box shown in the Figure 19-9. The dialog box contains the listing of all folders and files owned by the user. You have an option to delete, take ownership, or move individual files or select of multiple files. The only option available for folders is to take ownership.

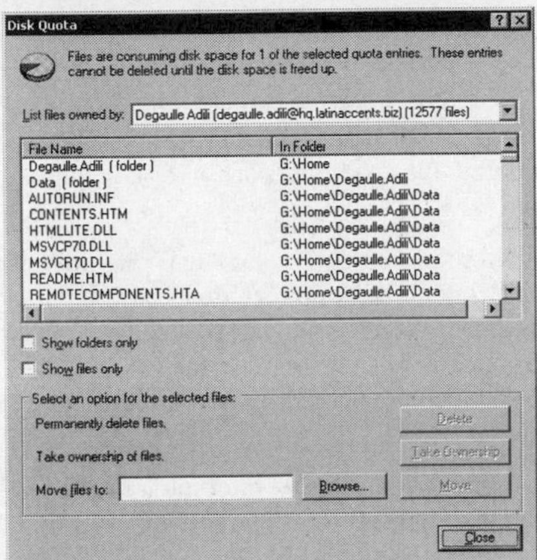

Figure 19-9: Disk Quota dialog box.

Troubleshooting

The last section of this chapter is dedicated to troubleshooting disk- and volume-related issues.

Disk and volume states

During the lifetime of a disk or a volume, its integrity may change. The disk management utility indicates the status of each disk and volume through its state. The status of disks and volumes can be also listed using `diskpart.exe` utility with the `list disk` and `list volumes` commands. Table 19-2 lists possible volume states and the meaning of each one.

Table 19-2: List of Common Types of Volume Status

State	*Description*
Healthy	The volume operates in the normal fashion and no known problems have been detected. This status is displayed for both basic and dynamic volumes. Healthy status can contain additional sub-status information. Two examples are listed next.
Healthy (At Risk)	The volume is available, but Windows 2000 has detected read and write (I/O) errors on the disk. This state is only reported for dynamic volumes.
Healthy (Unknown Partition)	The volume is not recognized. It might have been created using a different operating system or it might be non-recognizable OEM configuration partition. They can be deleted with both Disk Management and the `diskpart` tool (using the `delete partition` command with the `override` option).

Continued

Table 19-2 *(continued)*

State	*Description*
Unknown	The boot sector is corrupted. This might be result of disk corruption or a boot sector virus.
Resynching	This status applies to mirrored volumes. Resynching is the process of making both sets of data (one on each mirror) identical. The duration of the resynching process depends on the amount of data, and system performance and utilization. Try to limit access to the volume while resynching is in progress. When the resynching is complete, the disk status returns to healthy.
Formatting	The volume is being formatted. The percentage of the formatted volume is displayed to indicate the progress.
Regenerating	This status applies to RAID-5 volumes. It takes place after replacing a failed disk and involves writing missing information to a new member of the volume. Try to limit access to the volume while regeneration is in progress. When the regeneration is complete, the disk status returns to healthy.
Failed Redundancy	This status applies to mirrored and RAID-5 volumes. It indicates that one of the disks failed and the volume is no longer fault-tolerant. Even though the volume remains accessible, failure of another disk in the volume will cause loss of data. You should replace the disk as soon as possible and resynch or regenerate the volume.
Failed Redundancy (At Risk)	This status applies to RAID-5 or RAID-1 volumes. It means that the volume is no longer fault-tolerant and that I/O errors have been detected on the media. This status appears for each part of the volume on each disk. The Failed Redundancy state can also appear with other sub-states, such as System or Boot, for a failing non-mirrored system or boot volume.
Failed	This status applies to both basic and dynamic volumes. It indicates that the volume cannot be started and will require intervention. This status also might be displayed after importing incomplete multi-disk dynamic volume.

Table 19-3 lists possible hard disk states and the meaning of each one.

Table 19-3 List of Common Types of Disk Status

State	*Description*
Online	The disk is fully operational and no known errors have been detected.
Online (Errors)	The disk is operational but I/O errors have been detected. You might be able to return the disk to the Online state by running the `Reactivate Disk` command from the context menu of the disk. This status is available only for dynamic disks.

State	Description
Offline	The dynamic disk can not be accessed. This is typically caused by physical disk or connector failures. Try using the Reactivate Disk option from the Action menu of Disk Management Console. If this fails, you need to remove the physical disk from the computer and execute the Remove Disk option to remove references to the disk from the LDM database. This status is available only for dynamic disks.
Foreign	The disk has been moved from another computer. Import it using the Import Foreign Disks option from the disk's context menu.
Missing	The dynamic disk is damaged, corrupted, or disconnected. If the cause of the problem can be eliminated, you might be able to return the disk to Online status by selecting Reactivate Disk from the Action menu in Disk Management Console. Otherwise, use the Remove Disk option. This status is available only for dynamic disks.
Not Initialized	For MBR disks, a valid disk signature is missing from the Master Boot Record. For GPT disks, a valid GUID is missing from the GUID partition table. This typically happens if a new disk is installed in the computer. Initialization of the disk fixes the problem.
Initializing	This status is displayed when converting a disk from basic to dynamic. There is no need for intervention unless the system hangs and the status remains unchanged. Ordinarily, the status should return to Healthy.
Unreadable	The disk might be temporarily unavailable or corrupted. This status is available for both static and dynamic disks. Try rescanning the disk or rebooting the computer. If this does not change the status, replace the disk.

Fixing RAID redundancy failures

If the status of any volume reports "Failed Redundancy," "Failed Redundancy (At Risk)," or just "Failed," use one of the following procedures to fully recover it:

Procedure 1: To reactivate a volume in Failed Redundancy state, try the following:

1. In the Disk Management snap-in, switch to Graphical View by selecting View ➪ Bottom ➪ Graphical View.
2. If a disk hosting the volume is listed in Missing, Offline, or Online (Errors) state, right-click it and select Reactivate Disk. If the reactivation succeeds, the disk returns to Online and the volume to Healthy status.

Procedure 2: If a Failed Redundancy volume does not recover using the previous approach, try the following:

1. If the disk returned to the Online status, attempt to reactivate the volume manually. This is done using the Reactivate Volume option (although typically this should take place automatically after performing steps in Procedure 1).
2. If the disk is still listed as Offline or missing, the problem is most likely related to a non-functioning disk or loose or failed connectors. To replace a failed mirror, right-click any

of disk areas participating in the mirror, select the Remove Mirror option, and follow the wizard. Replace the bad disk and follow the instructions for creating mirrors using existing dynamic volume provided in the section, "Creating and Managing RAID-1 Volumes," earlier in this chapter. To repair a RAID-5 volume, first eliminate the cause of the problem. If the disk needs to be replaced, do so, initialize it, and convert it to dynamic. Then, use the `Repair Volume` command from the context menu of the RAID-5 volume.

Procedure 3: To attempt the reactivation of a volume in a Failed Redundancy (At Risk) state, try the following:

1. Try to reactivate the disk hosting the volume (typically listed with Online [Errors] status) in the same fashion as in Procedure 1. If necessary, attempt to reactivate the volume manually using Procedure 2.
2. Change of status to Failed Redundancy status (without At Risk part) after the first step is usually a good sign, and going again through the steps in Procedures 1 and 2 (if needed) should return the disk to Healthy status. The likely scenario is that the volume data is out of sync (for a mirror) or parity information needs to be regenerated (for RAID 5). Use the Reactivate or Resynchronize commands and then run `chkdsk` against the volume. If this fails, you may need to replace the hardware. You will need to have a valid backup.

Procedure 4: To replace disks, do the following:

1. If you have spare dynamic disks, import them using the Import Foreign Disk option. Otherwise, install the disks as basic and convert them to dynamic.
2. Using the methods described earlier in this chapter, return the volume to the original state.

Summary

This chapter provided a thorough review of Windows 2003 storage services. In particular, we covered the architecture of Disk Management Service, Remote Storage, and Hierarchical Storage Management, functionality and management of basic and dynamic disks and volumes, concepts and configuration of disk quotas, and troubleshooting disk and volume problems.

In the next chapter, we will cover other topics relating to storage, such as media pools, backup, restore, and disaster recovery.

✦ ✦ ✦

Backup and Restore

✦ ✦ ✦ ✦

In This Chapter

Understanding backup practice and procedure

Introducing removable storage and media pools

Using the backup tools that come with Windows Server 2003

Introducing Shadow Backup

✦ ✦ ✦ ✦

Every MIS or network administrator has a horror story to tell about backing up and restoring systems or data. One organization, where we now manage more than a dozen backup servers, has data processing centers spread all across the United States, and all are interconnected via a large, private wide-area network. Not long ago, a valuable remote Microsoft SQL Server machine just dropped dead. The IT doctor said it had died of exhaustion . . . five years of faithful service and never a day's vacation. After trying everything to revive it, we instructed the data center's staff to ship the server back to HQ for repairs.

The first thing we asked the IT people at the remote office was: "You've been doing your backups everyday right?" "Sure thing," they replied. "Every day for the past five years." They sounded so proud that we were overjoyed. "Good, we need to rebuild your server from those tapes, so send them all to us with the server." To cut a frustrating story short, the five years' worth of tapes had *nada* on them—not a bit nor a byte. Zilch. We spent two weeks trying to make sense of what was on that SQL Server computer and to rebuild it. We refuse to even guess the cost of that loss.

We have another horror story to relate later, but this example should make clear to you that backup administration, a function of disaster recovery, which we discuss in more depth in the next chapter, is one of the most important IT functions you can have the fortune to be charged with. Backup administrators need to be trained, responsible, and cool people. They need to be constantly revising and refining their practice and strategy; their companies depend on them.

This chapter serves as an introduction to backup-restore procedures on Windows Server networks, the Backup-Restore utility that ships with the operating system, and the Windows 2003 Server Removable Storage Manager. Before we get into this chapter, we should consider several angles on the backup/restore functions expected of administrators.

Why Back Up Data?

You back up for the following two reasons, and even Windows Server 2003, with its fancy tools, rarely highlights the differences:

- ✦ Record-keeping (such as annual backups performed every month)
- ✦ Disaster Recovery (DR) or System Recovery

You should make an effort to decide if a file is no longer valuable to the disaster-recovery period, and then it should be archived out for record-keeping. Depending on your company's needs, this period may vary from a week to a couple of weeks or from a month to a couple of months — and even years. No point buying media for annual backups for a site you know is due to close in six months.

What To Back Up

Often, administrators back up every file on a machine or network and dump the whole pile into a single backup strategy. Instead, they should be splitting up files into two distinct groups:

✦ *System files* comprise files that do not change between versions of the applications and operating systems.

✦ *Data files* comprise all the files that change every day, such as word-processing files, database files, spreadsheets files, media files, graphics files, and configuration files (such as the registry, and the DHCP, WINS, DNS, and Active Directory databases). Depending on your business, data files can change from 2 percent a day on the low side to 80 percent a day on the high side. The average in many of the businesses for which we have consulted is around 20 percent of the files changing every day. And you must also consider the new files that arrive.

Understanding the requirements makes your life in the admin seat easier, because this is one of the most critical of all IT or network admin jobs. One person's slip-up can cause millions of dollars in data loss. How often have you backed up an entire system that was lost for some reason, only to find that, to restore it, you needed to reinstall from scratch? "So why was I backing up the system," you may have asked yourself. And how often have you restored a file for a user who then complained that he or she lost five days' worth of work on the file because the restore was so outdated. It's happened to us on many occasions and is very disheartening if you are trying so hard to keep your people productive.

Nothing is worse than trying to recover lost data, knowing that all on Mahogany Row are sitting idle, with the IT director standing behind you in the server room, and discovering that you cannot recover. The thought of your employment record being pulled should make you realize how important is paying attention to this function.

We delve into these two subjects in more depth in this chapter and explore how Windows Server 2003 helps us better manage our recovery and record-keeping processes. We start by focusing on the data side of the backup equation and finally lead this discussion into system backup/restore.

Understanding Backup

Before you can get started using the Windows Server 2003 backup or any other backup program, you need to know how backing up works and have a basic backup strategy in mind.

Understanding archive bits

The *archive bit* is a *flag*, or a unit of data, indicating that the file has been modified. If we refer to the *setting* of the archive bit, we mean that we have turned it on or that we have set it to 1. Turning it off means that we set it to zero, or 0. If the archive bit is turned on since we last backed up the file, the file has been modified since it was last backed up.

Trusting the state of the archive bit, however, is not an exact science by any means, because it is not unusual for other applications (and developers) and processes to mess with the archive bit. This is the reason we recommend that a full backup be performed on all data at least once a week.

What is a backup?

A *backup* is an exact copy of a file (including documentation) that is stored on a storage media (usually in a compressed state) and kept in a safe place (usually at a remote location) for use in the event the working copy is destroyed. Notice that we placed emphasis on "including documentation," because with every media holding backups, you need to maintain a history or documentation of the files on the media. This is usually in the form of labels and identification data on the media itself, on the outside casing, and in spreadsheets, hard catalogs, or data ledgers in some form or another. Without history data, restore media cannot locate your files, and the backup is useless. This is why you can prepare a tape for overwriting by merely formatting the label so that the magnetic head thinks the media is blank.

Various types of backups are possible, depending on what you back up and how often you back it up, as the following list describes:

- **Archived backup:** A backup that documents (in header files, labels, and backup records) the state of the archive bit at the time of copy. The state (on-off) of the bit indicates to the backup software that the file has been changed since the last backup. When Windows Server 2003 Backup does an archived backup, it sets the archive bit accordingly.
- **Copy backup:** An ad-hoc "raw" copy that ignores the archive bit state. It also does not set the archive bit after the copy. A copy backup is useful for quick copies between DR processes and rotations or to pull an "annual" during the monthly rotation. (We discuss this in the section "Setting up schedules" later in this chapter.)
- **Daily backup:** This does not form part of any rotation scheme (in our book anyway). It is just a backup of files that have been changed on the day of the backup. We question the usefulness of the daily backup in Backup, because mission-critical DR practice dictates the deployment of a manual or automated rotation scheme (described later in the "Performing a Backup" section). Also, Backup does not offer a summary or history of the files that have changed during the day. If you were responsible for backing up a couple million files a day . . . well, this just would not fly.
- **Normal backup:** A complete backup of all files (that can be backed up), period. The term *normal* is more a Windows Server 2003 term, because this backup is more commonly called a *full* backup in DR circles. The *full backup* copies all files and then sets the archive bit to indicate (to Backup) that the files have been backed up. You would do a full backup at the start of any backup scheme. You would also need to do a full backup after making changes to any scheme. A full backup, and documentation or history drawn from it, is the only means of performing later incremental backups. Otherwise, the system would not know what has or has not changed since the last backup.
- **Incremental backup:** A backup of all files that have changed since the last full or incremental backup. The backup software sets the archive bit, which thereby denotes that the files have been backed up. Under a rotation scheme, a full restore would require you to have all the incremental media used in the media pool, all the way back to the first media, which contains the full backup. You would then have the media containing all the files that have changed (and versions thereof) at the time of the last backup.

✦ **Differential backup:** This works exactly as the incremental, except that it does not do anything to the archive bit. In other words, it does not mark the files as having been backed up. When the system comes around to do a differential backup, it relies on comparison of the files to be backed up with the original catalog. Differential backups are best done on a weekly basis, along with a full or normal backup, to keep differentials comparing against recently backed up files.

What is a restore?

A *restore* is the procedure you perform to replace a working copy of a file or collection of files to a computer's hard disks in the event they are lost or destroyed. You often perform a restore for no reason other than to return files to a former state (such as if a file gets mangled, truncated, corrupted, or infected with a virus).

Restore management is crucial in the DR process. If you lose a hard disk or the entire machine (for example, it gets trashed, stolen, lost, or fried in a fire), you need to rebuild the machine and have it running in almost the same state (if not exactly) as its predecessor was in at the time of the loss. How you manage your DR process determines how much downtime you experience or the missing generation of information between the last backup and the disaster — a period we call *void recovery time.*

Understanding how a backup works

A collection of media, such as tapes or disks, is known as a *backup set.* (This is different from a *media pool,* which we discuss in the following section.) The backup set is the backup media containing all the files that were backed up during the backup operation. Backup uses the name and date of the backup set as the default set name. Backup enables you to either append to a backup set in future operations or replace or overwrite the files in the media set. It enables you to name your backup set according to your scheme or regimen.

Backup also completes a summary or histories catalog of the backed-up files, which is called a *backup set catalog.* If your backup set contains several media, the catalog is stored on the last medium in the set, at the end of the file backup. The backup catalog is loaded whenever you begin a restore operation. You can select the files and folders you need to restore from the backup catalog.

Introducing Removable Storage and Media Pools

Removable Storage (RS) was introduced in Windows 2000. It takes away a lot of the complexity of managing backup systems. This service also brings network support to Windows for a wider range of backup and storage devices.

Microsoft took the responsibility of setting up backup devices and management of media away from the old Backup application and created a central authority for such tasks. This central authority is known as Removable Storage and is one of the largest and most sophisticated additions to the operating system, worth the price of the OS license alone, and a welcome member on any network. If you are not ready to convert to a Windows Server 2003 network, you may consider raising a Windows Server 2003 Backup server just to obtain the services of Removable Storage.

But Removable Storage is like an iceberg. In this chapter we can show you only the tip. Exposing the rest of this monster service and everything you can do with it is beyond the scope of this treatise, and a full treatment of the subject would run into several chapters. To fully appreciate this service — and if you need to get into some serious disaster recovery strategies, possibly even custom backup and media handling algorithms — you should refer to the Microsoft documentation covering both the Removable Storage Service and its API and the Tape/Disk API. A good starting place is the Windows Server 2003 Server Operations Guide, which is part of the Resource Kit. We do, however, provide you with an introduction to the service, coming up in the following section.

The Removable Storage Service

Removable Storage comprises several components. But the central nervous system of this technology is the Removable Storage Service and the Win32 Tape/Disk API. These two components, respectively, expose two application programming interfaces (APIs) that any third party can access to obtain removable storage functionality and gain access to removable storage media and devices. The Backup program that ships with the OS makes use of both APIs to provide a usable, but not too sophisticated, backup service.

By using the two services, applications do not need to concern themselves with the specifics of media management, such as identifying cartridges, changing them in backup devices, cataloging, numbering, and so on. This is all left to the Removable Storage Service. All the application requires is access to a media pool created and managed by Removable Storage. The backup application's responsibility is identifying what needs to be backed up or restored and the source and destination of data; Removable Storage's responsibility deals with where to store it, what to store it on, and how to retrieve it. Essentially, the marriage of backup-restore applications and Removable Storage has been consummated along client/server principles.

The Removable Storage Service can be accessed directly by programming against the API. You can also work with it interactively (albeit not as completely as programming against the API) in the Removable Storage node found in the Computer Management snap-in (`compmgmt.msc`) (Figure 20-1). The Removable Storage node is also present in the Remote Storage snap-in discussed in Chapter 19. Before we begin with any hard-core backup practice, we need to look at Removable Storage and how it relates to backup and disaster recovery.

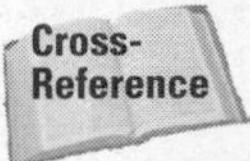

Removable Storage is also briefly discussed in Chapter 19.

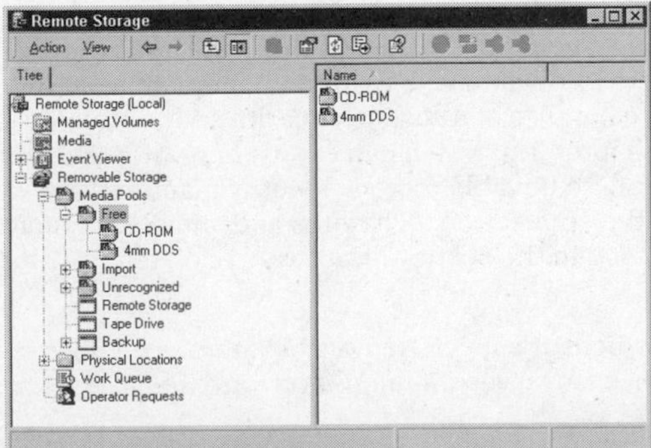

Figure 20-1: The Removable Storage snap-in.

The service provides the following functionality to backup applications, also known as backup or data moving and fetching clients:

✦ Management of hardware, such as drive operations, drive health and status, and drive head cleaning.

✦ Mounting and dismounting of cartridges and disks (media).

✦ Media inventory.

✦ Library inventory.

✦ Access to media and their properties.

Access to the actual hardware is hidden from client applications. But the central component exposed to all clients is the *media pool.* To better understand the media pool concept in Removable Storage, we first must discuss *media.*

Backup media ranges from traditional tape cartridges (discussed in the section "Hardware and Media formats," at the end of this chapter) to magnetic disk, optical disk CD-ROM, DVD, and so on. More types of media are becoming available, such as "sticks" and "cards" that you can pop into cameras and pocket-sized PCs, but these are not traditional backup media formats nor can they hold the amount of data you would want to store. DVD, a digital-video standard, however, is a good choice for backing up data, because so much can be stored on a single DVD disk.

As does the dynamic disk-management technology discussed in Chapter 19, Removable Storage hides the physical media from the clients. Instead, media is presented as a logical unit, which is assigned a logical identifier or ID. If a client needs to store or retrieve data from media, it does not deal with the physical media but rather with that media's logical ID. The logical ID can thus encapsulate any physical media, the format of which is of no concern to the client application.

Note Although the client need not be concerned about the actual media, you (the backup administrator) have the power to dictate onto which format or media type your backups should be placed by configuring media pools. If this concept is confusing to you, it becomes clearer after you understand media pools, which we discussed in more detail.

The benefit of the logical ID is patent, but a good example of its application is that the service can move data, represented by its *logical ID*, from one physical medium to another. This is desirable if media is approaching the end of its life and the data needs to be moved to new cartridges.

Media formats can be extremely complex. Some media enable you to write and read to both sides; others enable access to only one side. How media is written to and read from differs from format to format. Removable Storage handles all those peculiarities for you. Just as with the Print Spooler service (discussed in Chapter 28), which can expose the various features of thousands of different print devices, so can Removable Storage identify many storage devices and expose their capabilities to you and the application. (The pros and cons of each of the popular backup media formats are discussed in the section "Hardware and Media Formats," at the end of this chapter.)

Finally, and most important from the cost/benefit aspect, Removable Storage enables media to be shared by various applications. This ensures maximum use of your media asset.

The Removable Storage database

Removable Storage stores all the information it needs about the hardware, media pools, work lists, and more in its own database. This database is not accessible to clients and is not a catalog detailing which files are backed up and when they were backed up. Everything that Removable Storage is asked to do or does is automatically saved in this database.

Physical locations

Removable Storage also completely handles the burden of managing media location, a chore once shared between the client applications and the administrator. But the physical location service deals with more than knowing in which cupboard, shoebox, vault, or offsite dungeon you prefer your media stored in; it is also responsible for the physical attributes of the hardware devices used for backing up and restoring data. Understanding the information in this section is worthwhile, because you need such knowledge to perform high-end backup services that protect a company's data.

Removable Storage splits the location services into two tiers: libraries and offline locations. If a media is online, it is inside a tape device of some kind that can at any time be fired up to enable data to be accessed or backed up. If media is offline, you have taken it out of its drive or slot and sent it somewhere. As soon as you remove media from a device, Removable Storage makes a note in its database that the media is offline.

Libraries can be single tape drives or highly sophisticated and very expensive robotic storage silos comprising hundreds of drive bays. A CD-R/W tower, with 12 drives, is also an example of a library. Media in these devices or so-called libraries are always considered online and are marked as such in the database. Removable Storage also understands the physical components that make up these devices.

Library components comprise the following:

- ✦ **Drives:** All backup devices are equipped with drives. The drive machinery consists of the recording heads, drums, motors, and other electronics. To qualify as a library, a device requires at least one drive.
- ✦ **Slots:** Slots are pigeonholes, pits, or holding pens in which online media is placed in an online state. If media is needed for a backup, a restore, or a read, the cartridge or disk is pulled out of the slot and inserted into the drive. After the media is no longer needed, the cartridge is removed from the drive and returned to its slot. The average tape drive does not come equipped with a slot, but all high-end, multidrive robotic systems do. The basic slot-equipped machine typically comes equipped with two drives and 15 slots. Slots are typically grouped into collections called *magazines*. Each magazine holds about five cartridges, and one magazine maintains a cleaning cartridge in one of the slots. You typically have access to magazines so that you can populate them with the cartridges you fetched from offline locations.
- ✦ **Transports:** These are the robotic machines in high-end libraries that move cartridges and disks from slots to drives and back again.
- ✦ **Bar Code Readers:** *Bar coding* is discussed in the section "Labeling Media," later in this chapter. It is a means by which the cartridges can be identified in their slots. You do not require a bar-code reader-equipped system to use a multidrive or multislot system, because media identifiers can also be written to the media. But bar code reading

enables much faster access to the cartridges, because the system does not need to read information off the actual media, which requires every cartridge to be pulled from a slot and inserted into a drive—a process that could take as long as five minutes for every cartridge.

✦ **Doors:** *Doors* differ from device to device and from library system to library system. In some cases, the door looks like the door to a safe, which is released by Removable Storage whenever you need to gain access to slots or magazines. Many systems have doors that only authorized users can access. Some doors are built so strong that you would need a blowtorch to open them. On many cheaper devices, especially single-drive/no-slot hardware, the door is a small lever that Removable Storage releases so that you can extract the cartridge. Other devices have no doors at all, but after Removable Storage sends an "open sesame" command to the "door," the cartridge is ejected out of the drive bay.

✦ **Insert/Eject Ports:** IE ports are not supported on all devices. IE ports provide a high degree of controlled access to the unit in a multislot library system. In other words, you insert media into the port and the transport goes and finds a free slot for it. Another way to comprehend the IE port function is to compare it to a valet service. You hand your car keys to the valet, and he or she goes and finds a free parking space for you.

If the hardware you attach supports any or all of these sophisticated features, Removable Storage can "discover it" and use it appropriately.

You have dozens, if not hundreds, of devices from which to choose for backing up and storing data. Removable Storage, as we discussed in the preceding sections, can handle not only traditional tape backup systems, but also CD silos, changers, and huge multidisk readers. If you want to check whether Removable Storage supports a particular device, follow the steps to create a media pool discussed in the section "Performing a Backup," later in this chapter.

Media pools

A relatively new term in the Windows operating system is the *media pool.* If you are planning to do a lot of backing up or have been delegated the job of backup operator or administrator, you can expect to have a lot to do with media pools in your future backup-restore career.

A media pool in the general sense of the term is a collection of media organized as a logical unit. Conceptually speaking, the media pool contains media that belong to any defined storage or backup device, format, or technology assigned to your hardware, be it a server in the office or one located out on the WAN somewhere, 15,000 miles away. However, each media pool can only represent media of one type. You cannot have a media pool that combines DVD, DAT, and ZIP technology. But you can back up your data to multiple media pools of different types if the client application or function so requires it.

Thinking of the media pool in terms of the hardware devices that are available to your system (such as a CD-R/W or a DLT tape drive) may be easier for you. You should strive not to work with media pools from dissimilar devices, especially in backing up zillions of files. For example, you should stay away from creating media pools that consist of Zip drives, DLT tape drives, and a CDR-R/W changer. It would make managing your media, such as offsite storage, boxing, and labeling, very difficult, much like wearing a sneaker on one foot and a hiking boot on the other and then justifying walking with both at the same time because they both represent "pools" of walking attire.

Removable Storage separates media pools into two classes: *system pools* and *application pools.* The Removable Storage Service creates system pools as it is first installed. By default, the Removable Storage Service is enabled and starts up after you boot your system. If you disable it or remove it from installation, any devices installed in your servers — or attached on external busses — are ignored by Windows Server 2003 as if they did not exist. After Removable Storage is activated, it detects your equipment, and if compliant, they are used in media pools automatically created by the service or applications.

System pools

System pools hold the media that are not being used by any application. After you install new media into your system, the first action that Removable Storage takes is to place the media into a pool for unrecognized media. Then, after you have identified the media, you can make it available to applications by moving it to the free pools group. The system pools are built according to the following groups:

- **Free pools:** Free pools enable any application to access the media pools in this group. In other words, these media pools can be made available to any application requiring free media. Applications can draw on these media pools if they need to back up data. After media pools are no longer required, they can be returned to this group.

- **Unrecognized pools:** Media in these pools are not known to Removable Storage. If the service cannot read information on a cartridge, or if the cartridge is blank, the media pool supporting it is placed into this grouping.

- **Import pools:** This group is for media pools that were used in other Removable Storage systems, on other servers, or by applications that are compatible with Removable Storage or that can be read by Removable Storage. Media written to by the Microsoft Tape Format (MTF) can thus be imported into the local Removable Storage system.

Application pools

If an application is given access to a free media pool, either it creates a special pool into which the media can be placed or you can create pools manually for the application by using the Removable Storage snap-in, as shown in Figure 20-1.

A very useful and highly sought after feature of Windows Server 2003 media pools is that permissions can be assigned to pools to enable other applications to use the pools or to protect the pools in their own sets.

Multilevel media pools

You may be astonished to find out that media pools can be organized into hierarchies or nests. In other words, you can create media pools that hold several other media pools. An application can then use the root media pool and gain access to the different data storage formats in the nested media pools. Expect to see sophisticated document storage, backup, and management applications using such media pools.

An example of using such a hierarchy of media pools can be drawn from a near disaster that was averted during the writing of this chapter. One of our 15-tape DLT changers went nuts and began reporting that our tapes were not really DLT tapes but alien devices that it could not identify. The only way to continue backing up our server farm was to enlist every SCSI tape and disk device on the network into one large pool. After the DLT library recovered, we could go back to business as usual.

Work Queue and Operator Requests

You notice nodes for both Work Queue and Operator Requests in the Removable Storage tree. These services provide a communications and information-exchange function between the operator (the backup operator or administrator or the backup operator group) and Removable Storage, respectively.

Work queue

Working backup applications and the HRS/RSS (Remote Storage Service) service post their work requests to the Removable Storage service. To manage the multitude of requests that can come from applications and services, each request for work from the Removable Storage Service is placed into the work queue. The work queue is very similar in concept to a print queue discussed in Chapter 28.

The work queue provides information on queue states on a continual basis, and these are reported to the details pane in the Work Queue node. For example, if an application is busy backing up data, an In Process state is posted to the details pane identifying the work request and the state it is in. Table 20-1 describes the work queue states reported to the Work Queue details pane.

Table 20-1: Work Queue States

State	*Explanation*
Queued	The work item has been queued. It is waiting for the RS service to examine the request.
In Process	RS is working on the work item.
Waiting	The request is waiting for a resource, currently being used by another service, before work on the item can continue.
Completed	RS has handled the work item successfully. The request has been satisfied.
Failed	RS has failed to complete the work item. The request did not obtain the desired service.
Cancelled	The work item has been cancelled.

Operator requests

No matter how sophisticated Removable Storage is, it just does not do some things. These items are marked for the "human" work queue. For example, Removable Storage does not go and fetch cartridges from the cabinet or the storeroom. This is something you must do. The details pane in the Operator Requests node is where Removable Storage posts its request states for you, the operator. Removable Storage can also send you a message via the messenger service or the system tray, just in case you have the habit of pretending the Operator Requests node does not exist. Table 20-2 lists the possible Operator Request States.

Table 20-2: Operator Request States

State	*Explanation*
Submitted	The described request has been submitted, and the system is waiting for the operator's input.
Refused	The operator has refused to perform the described request.
Completed	The operator has complied and has completed the described request.

Labeling media

Removable Storage can read data written to the labels on the actual tape or magnetic disk as well as external information supplied in bar code format. The identification service is robust and highly sophisticated and ensures that your media does not get overwritten or modified by other applications.

You need to provide names for your media pools, and you should also, if you can afford a bar code reader, organize them according to serial numbers (represented as bar codes) for more accurate handling. If you are planning to install a library system, make sure that you get one that can read the bar codes from the physical labels on the cartridge casing. This information is critical in locating a few files that need restoring from five million files stored on 120 30GB tapes. (The bigger the enterprise, the more complex is the backup and restore regimen and management.)

Another reason we prefer a numbering or bar code scheme for identifying media, as opposed to labeling it according to the day of the week, is that a cartridge can often get inadvertently written to on the wrong day. If that happens, you may have a cart named Wednesday but with Tuesday data on it, which can get confusing and create unnecessary concern. With a bar code or serial number, you can simply make sure that the cart gets put back into the Wednesday box without needing to scratch out or change the label.

Practicing scratch and save

Although Windows Server 2003 does not cater to the concept of *scratch and save* sets, such sets are worth a mention because you should understand the terms for more advanced backup procedures. Simply put, a *save* set is a set of media in the media pool that cannot be overwritten for a certain period of time. A *scratch* set is a set of media that is safe to overwrite. A backup set should be stored and cataloged in a save set for any period of time during which the media should not be used for backup. You can create your own spreadsheet or table of media rotating in and out of scratch and save sets.

The principal behind scratch and save is to protect data from being overwritten for predetermined periods.

A monthly save set is saved for a month, for example, while a yearly is saved for a year. After a "safe" period of time has elapsed, you can move the save set to the scratch set. In other words, after a set is moved out of the save status into the scratch status, you are tacitly allowing the files on it to be destroyed. A save set becomes a scratch set if you are sure, through proper media pool management, that other media in the pool contain both full and modified and current and past files of your data and that destroying the data on the scratch media is safe.

Fully understanding the concept of save and scratch sets is important because it is the only way you can ensure that your media can be safely recycled. The alternative is to make every set a save set, which means that you never recycle the tapes . . . making your DR project a very costly and risky venture because tapes that are being constantly used stretch and wear out sooner.

Establishing Quality of Support Baselines for Data Backup/Restore

Windows Server 2003 provides the administrator with backup and recovery tools seen before only on midrange and mainframe technology (such as the capability to mark files for archiving). For the first time, Windows network administrators are in a much better position to commit to service level agreements and quality of service or support levels than before. Unfortunately, the new tools and technologies result in a higher and more critical administrative burden. (The service level shifts to the Windows administrator as opposed to being usually the domain of the midrange, Unix, or mainframe administrative team.) We need to consider some of the abstract issues related to backups before we get into procedures.

No matter how regularly you back up the data on your network, you can restore only up to the point of your last complete backup and then the subsequent incremental or differential backups. Unless you are backing up every second of the day, which is highly unlikely and impractical, you can never fully recover the latest OS data up to the point of meltdown (unless you had a crash immediately after you backed up) using standard backup software. Only advanced backup/restore systems that store data in specialized databases (like the SQL Server transaction log) can do that. You need to decide how critical it is that your business cannot afford to lose even one hour of data. For many companies, any loss could mean serious setback and costly recovery, often lasting long after the disaster occurs.

Considering the numerous alternatives for backup procedures and various strategies is, therefore, important if out-of-date data is considered inadequate recovery. You need to decide on a baseline for backup/restores: What is the least acceptable recovery situation? You also need to take into account the quality of support promised to staff and the departments and divisions that depend on your systems, plus the service level agreements (SLA) in place with the customers.

Note Service level and quality of support are discussed fully in Chapter 24.

First, before we consider other factors, we need to decide what we would consider adequate in terms of the currency of backed-up data. Then, after we have established our tolerance level, we need to work out how to cater to it and at what cost. Starting with dollars consider the following list:

- ✦ Data restored is one month or more old.
- ✦ Data restored is between one and four weeks old.
- ✦ Data restored is between four and seven days old.
- ✦ Data restored is between one and three days old.
- ✦ Data restored is between six and twelve hours old.
- ✦ Data restored is between two and five hours old.
- ✦ Data restored is between one and 60 minutes old.

Now, depending on how the backups were done and the nature of your backup technology, just starting up the recovery process could take anywhere up to ten minutes (such as reading the catalog), depending on the technology. So level 7 would be out of the picture for you as a tape backup proposition. In cases where backup media is off-site, you would need to take into consideration how long the media takes to arrive at the data center after you place a call to the backup bank. This could be anything from 30 minutes to six hours. And you may be charged for "rush" delivery.

Now look back at the preceding list and consider your options. How important (mission-critical) is it that data is restored, if not in real-time, almost in real-time? Many situations require immediate restoration of data. Many applications in banking, finance, business, science, engineering, medicine, and so on require real-time recovery of data in the event of a crash, corruption of data, deleted data, and so on.

You could and should be exploring or installing clustered systems, mirrors, replication sets, and RAID-5 level and higher storage arrays, as described in Chapter 19. But these so-called fault-tolerant and redundant systems typically share a common hard-disk array or a central storage facility. Loss of data is thus system-wide and mirrored across the entire array. A mirror is a reflection — no more, no less.

This brings us to another factor to consider: the flawed backup. You bring this factor into consideration if your data is continuously changing. The question to ask is, "How soon after the update of data should I make a backup?" You may decide, based on the previous list, that data even five minutes out of date is damaging to system integrity or the business objectives. A good example is online real-time order or delivery tracking. But backing up data with such narrow intervals between versions brings us to the subject of quality and integrity of backed-up data. (In the section "Establishing Quality of Capture)," later in this chapter, we discuss versioning and how technology in Windows Server 2003 facilitates it.) What if the file that just got hit by a killer virus is quarantined and you go to the backup only to find that it is also infected or corrupt? What if all the previous files are infected, and now, just opening the file renders it useless? It's something to think about.

Earlier this year, we rushed to the aid of our main SQL Server group, which had lost a valuable database on the customer ordering system (on our extranet). Every hour offline was costing the company six figures as customers went elsewhere to place their orders. Four-letter words were flying around the server room. We had to go back three days to find a clean backup of the database that showed no evidence of corrupt metadata.

Figure 20-2 illustrates data backed up on a daily basis, and in this case, bad data is backed up for three days in a row. You may consider some of the gray area as safe, where backup data is bound to have all the flaws of its source (corruption, viruses, lack of integrity, and so on), if you have other means of assuring quality or data integrity. Such assurances may be provided by means of highly sophisticated anti-virus software, quality of data routines and algorithms, versioning, and just making sure that people check their data themselves. Backing up bad data every ten minutes may be a futile exercise depending on the tools that you have to recover or rebuild the integrity of the data.

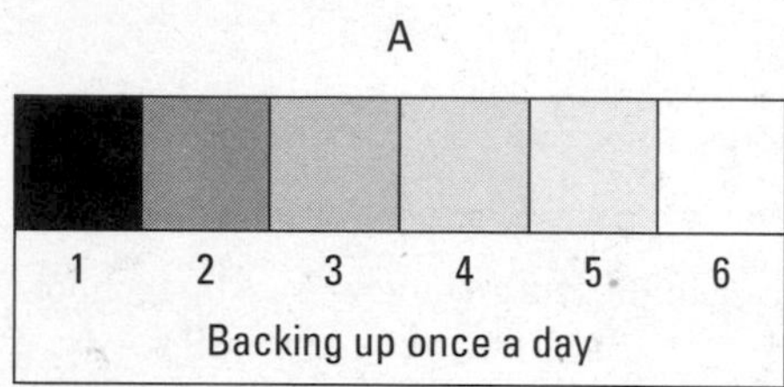

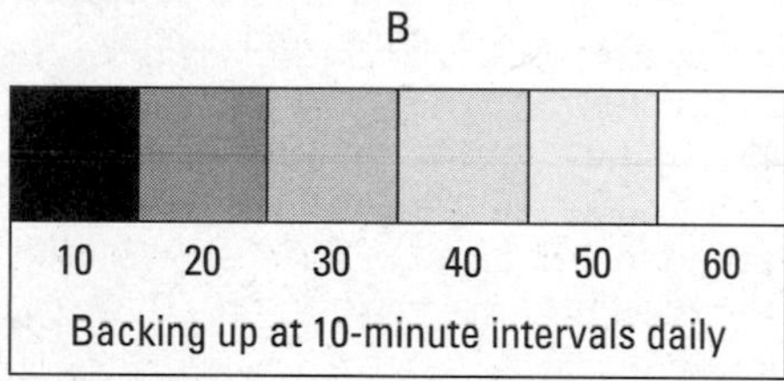

Figure 20-2: The narrower the interval between backups, the greater the chance that backed up data is also corrupted, infected, or lacks integrity.

Most companies back up data to a tape drive. (We discuss the formats later in this chapter.) The initial cost is really insignificant in relation to the benefit: the capability to back up and recover large amounts of data. A good tape drive can run anywhere from $500 for good Quarter-Inch Cartridge (QIC) systems to $3,000 to $4,000 for the high-speed, high-capacity Digital Linear Tape (DLT) systems, and a robotic library system can cost as much as $80,000. Now consider minimum restore levels, keeping the quality of backup factors described earlier in mind, as follows:

- Restore is required in real-time (now) or close to it. Data must be no longer than a few seconds old and immediately accessible by users and systems even in the event that the primary source is offline. In the case of industrial or medical systems, the secondary source of data must be up-to-date, and the latency may be measured in milliseconds and not seconds. Your SLAs may dictate that 24-7 customers can fine you if data is offline longer than *x* seconds or minutes. We call this the *critical restore* level.
- Restore is required within ten minutes of the primary source going offline. We call this *emergency restore.*
- Restore is required within one hour of the primary source going offline. We call this *urgent restore.*
- Restore is required within one to four hours of the primary source going offline. We call this *important restore.*
- All other restores that can occur later than the previous can be considered *casual restores.*

Figure 20-3 shows this in a visual hierarchy.

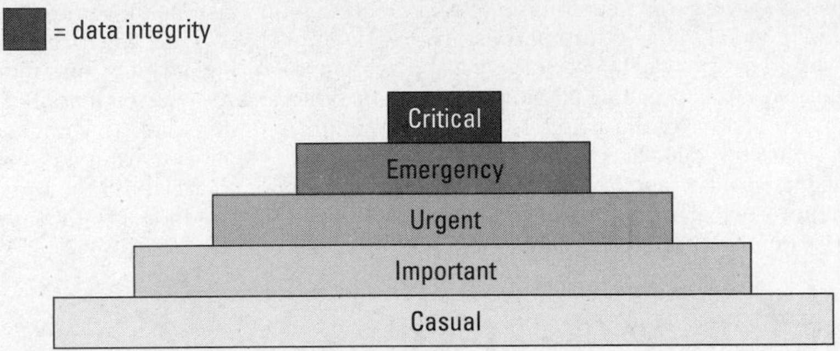

Figure 20-3: The data-restoration pyramid.

The pyramid in Figure 20-3 illustrates that the faster the response to a restore or recall of data request, the higher the chance of retrieving poor data. Each layer of the pyramid covers the critical level of the restore request. This does not mean that critical restores are always going to be a risk and that the restored data is flawed. It means that the data backed up closest to the point of failure is more likely to be at risk compared to data that was backed up hours or even days before the failure. If a hard disk crashes, the data on the backup tapes is probably sound, but if the crash is due to corrupt data or virus infection, the likelihood of recent data being infected is high.

Another factor to consider is that you often find that the "cleanest" backup data is the furthest away from the point of restoration or the most out-of-date.

If the level of restore you need is not as critical or the quality of the backup not too important, you could consider a tape drive system either to a backup server or local to the hosting machine. You could then set up a scheme of continuous or hourly backup routines. In the event data is lost (usually because someone deletes a file or folder), you could restore the file. The worst-case scenario is that the data restored is one hour out of date and at such a wide interval that a replacement of a corrupt file with another corrupt file is unlikely. Consider the following anecdote: We recently lost a very important Exchange-based e-mail system. Many accounts on the server could be considered extremely mission critical. Thousands of dollars were lost every minute the server was down. (The fallout from downed systems compounds damages at an incredible rate. The longer a system is down, the worse it becomes.)

The last full backup of the server was performed on the weekend. The system went down on Wednesday. Because we were backing up only the files that changed on Monday and Tuesday, we could restore the e-mail server to the state that it was in the night before. This was good news to the MIS director but not very good news to people who felt that losing six to eight hours of e-mail was unacceptable. (For many, that would mean losing an entire day of work and a lot of wasted time rewriting and resending e-mail.)

But the good news was short-lived after we discovered that the transaction logs covering the Monday and Tuesday backups were corrupt on the system and on the tapes. The result was that we could restore the entire system to the state it was in on Friday, essentially losing everything between Friday night and Wednesday afternoon. For backup administrators, this was an unacceptable event. In the section, "Backup Procedure," later in the chapter, we discuss how to prevent this from happening.

If you have several servers that need this level of protection, you must install some expensive backup equipment and advanced third-party software. Having a hot "clone" mirroring the entire system would be the way to go. Both disk and system mirroring, striping, and redundancy are discussed in Chapter 19. Full-blown redundant systems are required if applications need to continue, oblivious of the switch to alternative media and hardware. To summarize: Looking back at our checklists and matrices for a restore service level of five and up, you would be looking at regular tape backup systems. Anything more critical would require online libraries and a hierarchical storage management system — and yes, we look into this new service provided by Remote Storage Services (RSS) in Chapter 26.

Establishing Quality of Capture

In planning backup procedures and establishing quality of support levels for backups considering the quality of your backups before you begin designing rotation schedules and schemes and backup/restore procedures is vital. Every business is different. Even businesses in like industries do things differently, so what you work out may work for you but not for anyone else. What we suggest in the following sections are guidelines for establishing procedures. Before you get stuck in here, however, remember the following: Devise a plan, and if it works (after tests work under strict analysis), stick to it. If backup media gets out of sync or gets lost or damaged, you may have a disaster in trying to restore critical data.

Best backup time of day

Say that you decide to back up your data every night. One of the first items to consider is when you start your backups. If staff work late or your systems are accessed late into the night, you may wait until the early hours of the morning to begin backing up. In other words, the best time to start doing backups is whenever the files are least likely to be open and changing or whenever you feel that you are getting the last possible version change before people go home for the night and systems become idle again.

You may run into problems backing up earlier in the evening or even late at night if, for example, a process or department swings around at near midnight and updates 20 percent of the critical data you need to back up (such as night order processing). It can be especially tough to decide when to start backing up e-mail systems and database management systems, because they typically are in use around the clock, especially if your organization is a national or global entity.

Some organizations restrict access to systems at certain times to ensure that the best backups are achieved at that certain time. This would naturally need to be coordinated with other departments and change control, because making a system unavailable could crash other processes that may be running at the same time, or they may need access to the data. We believe that systems should never be taken offline even for backups. Also, in the age of the Internet, who would want to restrict access to systems? That's tantamount to closing shop in the middle of the day for international Web sites that view "after hours" as an obsolete term in the Information Age.

Length of backup

You should also work out how long your backups take. Starting your backups at one minute to midnight may be prudent, but if morning swings around and your backups are still churning away, you have hardly performed a backup, and the file may become locked or substantially changed after systems and people log in and seize control again.

If your backup devices are backing up multiple servers, you may not get to the last machines until the next day. Not much sense in a Thursday incremental backup that is part of a rotation scheme and that takes place only on Saturday.

You have a number of options to consider in striving to ensure that the best quality backups take place in as quick a time as possible, as the following list describes:

- **Files that do not change:** Repeatedly backing up system and application files is a waste of time. Many administrators, either from lack of time to plan their backups or ignorance, waste an incredible amount of time and resources backing up files that seldom change. System files are a good example, as are temp files and noncritical log files. You could consider dividing your backups into the categories described in the next paragraph.
- **Long-term system and system state files:** These files include program files and system state files that never change or change very seldom. As explained in the section "Rotation Schemes," later in this chapter, incremental and differential backup functions ignore these files after a full backup has occurred, but tying up time and media even on a weekly or monthly full routine that can often run into two or more days of continuous backup still makes no sense.
- **Short-term state files:** These files include system or application state files that do change often. Such files include configuration files, registry files, the Active Directory files, and so on. On servers, both registry and Active Directory files can change every day, whenever new users or resources are added or changed. So if short-term state files change daily on your servers, they need to be included in backups. Noncritical short-term state files, including `.pagesys` files, event log files, and temp files (`.tmp`), are not needed to restore downed systems, nor are they critical or useful to data.
- **Data and resource files:** These files include word-processing files, graphics-related files, database files, transaction logs, e-mails and other communications files, spreadsheets, voice and audio recordings, and so on. These files (and they can often be listed or categorized by their extensions) change often, are almost always critical, and should always be backed up or included in all backup routines.

If you intelligently include or exclude certain groups of files, you can control and keep backup times to a minimum. You also save on media (at $30 to $50 a pop for DLTs and not much less for small packs of DAT cartridges); you can save a lot of money and wear and tear on systems, media, and backup devices.

Redundant systems that use replication services in products such as Active Directory, SQL Server, Exchange, and so on are more effective, in many cases, than fancy backup technology for high-availability initiatives.

Backup of servers and workstations

If you have not by now separated your backup procedures into backup of systems and backup of data, now is the time to do it. Often, system administrators repeatedly back up Windows servers and workstations in their entirety for absolutely no reason. We cannot count how many full versions or backups of our systems we have in storage. This has a lot to do with the lack of thought that goes into backup practice and little to do with the inflexible backup technology of earlier versions of the Windows server platform.

In some cases, we have several years of system backups where the only files on the media that are different are the data files. From the get-go, you could probably recover 10 to 20 cartridges and put them back into the rotation without affecting your quality of service and backup integrity levels. (That could be worth a lot of money to you in media costs and time.)

How do you then deal with the backup of systems? If you have not already done so, you should consider taking an "image" of the system and saving it either on tape media, compact disk, DVD, or on a remote storage volume. We recommend against storing images on any remote storage volume or disk, because the hardware could fail or someone else may delete the file, even if you secure it (although Windows Server 2003 security provides more protection than Windows NT 4.0 and Windows 2000).

Instead, burn the system image onto a CD or use a product that specializes in so-called "bare metal" capture of all data. Several popular products specialize in bare metal recovery. The Stac Replica system, for example, boasts the capability to back up a server and then restore it to any another machine with zero reinstallation required.

Workstations are viable candidates for image storage because they usually never get backed up. Most system administrators tell their users to stick their data into server share-points where they are accessible to the groups that have interests in the files and the data gets backed up every day when the rotation sweeps around. Windows Server 2003 now offers such advanced control over the user's workspace that a policy dictating the storage of user's files on a server share is entirely enforceable. See Chapter 14 for information on how to redirect users' data folders to backup share-points.

Many users lose a considerable amount of computing time and inconvenience if they lose a workstation and no backup is there for it. Getting such a system back to what it was before a hard disk crash, fire, or theft can take more than a day. Many critical processes also take place from workstations.

To restore a system from an image is relatively simple, and in many cases, recovery can take place in a morning. Images can also be kept in a safe place at work for quick access.

The upshot of this method is that if a system is blown away, you need only to set up identical or very similar hardware and restore from the image to get back a machine that is at the same state as when the image was burned. You would then restore the data and any files that have changed since the image was burned.

Naturally, you need to ensure that you install the necessary service packs that were installed on the system from the time of the last image burning. Or you should reburn the image after a new service pack, application software, or new system libraries are applied.

The best candidates for the image burning and bare metal backup techniques are servers where the majority of files on the system are static system files. A print server is a good example, and the Windows Server 2003 Resource Kit includes such a utility (`printmig`) to back up logical printer shares. It may not be much of a savings to burn an image of a server where 89 percent of the storage space is dedicated to databases or e-mail files. On the other hand, a Remote Access Server, one of a group of WINS servers, and volumes that have no changing data on them are ideal candidates for image burns.

The open-files dilemma

Open files have always been the backup administrator's nightmare on Windows NT Server, and this is still very much the case on Windows 2000 volumes and Windows Server volumes. What are these open files? Any resource file on a system needs to be opened for exclusive or shared use by a user or device that is exploiting or updating its contents. Backup software, backup schemes and rotations, and backup administrators hate open files because of the following reasons:

- Open files cannot be backed up.
- Open files trash automated backup jobs.
- Open files cause the backup schedules to slow down and even grind to a halt.
- Forcing open files closed or shutting down services and systems causes headaches, inconveniences, missed deadlines, crashes and, worse, the Blue Screen of Death (although the latter is the least likely to occur).

Many relational database applications, for example, place "locks" on files while they are in use. The system also places locks on files. These files can range from simple configuration files, the registry and Active Directory files (their databases, for example), SQL servers, WINS servers, DHCP servers, and so on. E-mail applications are a good example of an open-files nightmare. These files are often huge and are almost always open and in use by the applications. Microsoft Exchange is a good case in point.

If a file is open or an exclusive lock is on the file, your backups are in trouble. On a mail server such as Exchange, the result of the open-files problem could be catastrophic for you. The information stores, the registry, the Exchange directory, the Active Directory, WINS, DNS, DHCP, and so on, are always open. If the backup fails because these huge files could not be backed up, you may be talking about hundreds if not thousands of users inconvenienced, at incredible cost.

Suppose that you face such a disaster: You do a full backup of Microsoft Exchange every weekend. Then, one day, your silent pager vibrates your hip joints with the message that the Exchange Server crashed. As you try to revive the system, guess what? It does not want to be revived. But that's okay because you have been diligently making full backups of Exchange every weekend. Only, after you do your backup, you find that the backup software was skipping exactly those files that you need to do the backup from. Career killer?

Database servers can cause even bigger headaches. Many, such as SQL Server, are self-contained domains of users and login mechanisms. From the outside world, you see only a huge database blob. In the case of SQL Server, it's the files with the `.mdf` extension, such as `hello.mdf`. In fact, any huge file that has a `.dat` or a `.?db` extension is likely to be a database.

Note Many high-end systems, such as SQL Server, now ship with their own built-in backup services.

You have several ways to deal with this bugbear, from the cheapest to the most expensive solution:

First, you can shut down the open application's services prior to backup or force closure of the files by requesting users to close applications and even log off. (Incidentally, any restore of SQL Server requires the database to be placed into single user mode so that the restore agent gets unrestricted access to the databases.) This is by far the cheapest method (software cost), and you can force closure of services and files prior to backup with several batch files and scripts. (We look at scripts shortly in the "Backup Batch file and Backup scripts" section. (If you have the budget then rather buy the backup agents for products like SQL Server and Exchange that allow you to back up open files or while these systems are still running.

The second solution is to install an open-files utility that provides the backup software with a "window" to the data in the open files. The plus in this solution is that your backup software gets access to open files across the board. One such product is the Open File Manager (OFM) from St. Bernard software (`www.stbernard.com`). You can install this tool on your systems and never need to worry about open files not getting backed up. So important to backup and recovery is this utility that it is worth a special mention here. But you should thoroughly test it on your systems before going live. As important as it is, the product tinkers with files deep into the abyss of the file system, as does anti-virus software. OFM and NetShield from Network Associates have been known to collide, so test your implementation before going into production.

The third and most expensive solution is an agent or API that works with the backup software you are using. Products such as Backup Exec and ARCserve provide their own technology that enable the Microsoft server products to be backed up while they are on line and in use.

Notice that, in this short list, we list the solutions in order of cheapest to most expensive solution. But that expense is only in terms of what buying the solution costs. In other words, if you think that you are saving money going for the option to shut down services, think again. This could be your most expensive solution. For example, just as you think you're being clever and shutting down services by using the nifty little batch files and scripts that we are about to create, the batch file breaks. For some reason, the service does not shut down, and the next day, your system crashes and you don't have a backup.

The open-files agents are also not airtight technology. We run nightly backups of several huge SQL Server databases, Oracle, Lotus Notes, and more. Often, we notice that the open-files agent stopped for some reason and the backup of critical data did not go through. You must watch the services like a cat sitting between a mouse and a hole in the wall.

The fact that Microsoft provides some limited open-file support for Exchange is worth mentioning here. Whenever you install Exchange, the installation updates the NT Backup utility to enable it to back up Exchange's directory and information store. No doubt, the new version of Exchange for Windows Server 2003 can similarly update Windows Server 2003 Backup.

Never, ever mix backup technologies on the same files. For starters, each backup job changes the state of the files to some degree, from changing the archive bit on one end to causing the applications to do housekeeping on the other end. Your restores may not work if a second backup application has altered the file system. Also, if a restore job fails, you can forget about getting support from a vendor if another product has interfered.

Shadow Copy technology on Windows Server 2003, however, presents a whole new ball game with respect to open-file issues. See the section "Working with Shadow Copy," later in this chapter, and in Chapter 26.

Backup Procedure

The Windows Server 2003 Server team can be credited for making the backup and restore process the lead member of its DR group, at least as far as classification goes. But consistency is not one of the team's credits: Why its members moved the menu item for Backup from Administrative Tools in Windows NT4 to Accessories ➪ System Tools on Windows Server 2003 is uncertain. An "accessory" is certainly not what a backup application should be to such a high-end operating system. Anyway, the aforementioned location is exactly where you'll find it. The path to Backup's door is Start ➪ All Programs ➪ Accessories ➪ System Tools ➪ Backup. Or just run the command line shortcut `ntbackup.exe`.

For most uses of your computer, the Backup utility is sufficient to archive and store data, and to recover it in the event of a disaster. However, that's as far as it goes. Microsoft has again chosen a custom-made version of Veritas Software, Inc.'s BackupExec product. You certainly want to stick with the third party products for enterprise-wide disaster recovery and data protection.

Before we get into the highs and lows of backup and restore, first we need to look at the limitations of the utility that ships with Windows Server 2003 Backup. For starters, it's a vast improvement over the Backup that was bundled with NT4, but it still has limitations. Naturally, Veritas wants you to come and pay extra for a pro version of this product, better known as Backup Exec. In our book, Microsoft should either have paid Veritas a higher royalty and put in features more in line with the advanced nature of the OS or left it out completely. We have several hundred servers in our server portfolio, and we don't use the NT4 version of NTBackup; we have just seen too many disasters with it. And after reviewing the new Backup, we are not likely to replace the third-party stuff we are using when we migrate to Windows Server 2003, although our small clients are using Backup just fine. Now to look at Backup's limitations.

Backup does not enable you to attach to other machines and perform backup and restores of state-related data, such as registries, directories, and system files. You can attach only to the drives and share on the remote computers. In short, it is not a network backup/restore solution. If you are trying to locate and back up domain controllers (especially pre-Server 2003 servers), don't even try. Windows Server 2003 Backup refuses to even give them a visitor's visa onto the source list.

Sure, you can attach with the appropriate permissions and pull over user files, but that's about it. This means that Backup is not really useful for managing a mission-critical DR project from a single server devoted to DR. If you manage a server farm, performing backups on each machine is a huge waste of time and resources and a drain on IT budget. The only advantage is better bandwidth, as we discuss in the section "Backup Bandwidth," later in this chapter. You would need to upgrade to a third-party suite if you want to devote to one server the job of backup system.

On the other hand, the Removable Storage Service is a great addition to Windows Server 2003. Earlier versions of Windows provided no professional means of managing complex and sophisticated storage media devices, such as DLT Libraries that automatically change out tape cartridges, read bar codes, and the like. We had to rely on third-party tools for these, which was a bit limiting. This is one area that belongs to the operating system. After we switched from one vendor to another, we would lose the entire storage setup. Now the storage device is managed and controlled at the OS level, just as a hard disk or CD-R or a printer is.

The most that Backup promises you is the capability to back up Exchange's system and data files, and the tape drive must be local to the Exchange Server. Many mail and groupware administrators want the capability to back up multiple Exchange Servers across the enterprise from a single DR location. If you use good equipment and sensibly manage an Exchange Server, you're unlikely ever to need to restore the machine and the databases in their entirety.

Any good Exchange administrator can confirm that 99 percent of all requests for restores to Exchange come from users who stand in your doorway drooping like basset-hound ears and saying, "I can't find my Inbox folder. I think it got deleted somehow."

The pro-backup utilities enable you to expand and collapse a mailbox tree in the backup software like an unfolding deck of cards. Trust us. If you have more than a handful of users (we manage about 3,000 on just one of our 67 domains), your Exchange DR is mostly about restoring a folder. Backing up and restoring folders piecemeal is often referred to as a *brick-level* or *object-level* backup and recovery.

Database servers are also an example of specialist applications where machines are almost entirely devoted to the database. Backing up a SQL server, such as Oracle or SQL Server, while it is in use is virtually impossible. The leading backup vendors have special agents that can attach to these servers as actual "users" (not domain accounts) created inside the database environment. If you have only a handful of users on a server or face no chance that anyone is using the server at certain times at night, you can probably get away with shutting down the database and all related services and backing up the closed files. In an enterprise-level DR project, this would be a practice unbecoming of the backup administrator, unless the entire domain was offline for maintenance.

Some advanced software suites come with "push" agents that send the files to the backup server. ARCServe, for example, provides backup agents that pump files to the server. The agents connect to the servers across IP or IPX, and any open files that cannot be pushed or that are in use are marked for later transmission after they are no longer being used.

And we have really discussed only backups. Restoring files on running systems can be even trickier because you are attempting to replace a file, not make a copy of it. High-end software suites enable you to restore by session, media, object in a tree, and so on.

As a rule of thumb, you need something a little more robust than Backup in a heterogeneous, mixed version, multivendor/OEM, chock-full-of-nuts environment. However, you always have a need to use Backup. We even know of one sad case where the Exchange administrator of a Fortune 500 company got so tired of waiting for the backup operator to get around to doing a brick-level system on her server that she went with Backup and "the heck with mailboxes." Next day, the CIO came over to whine about recovering his deleted mailbox, which he swore was more valuable than his 401K. It was the Backup administrator who was relocated to an oil rig in the North Sea, not the Exchange administrator.

Performing a Backup

In this section, we show you how to actually perform a backup by using the Backup utility. The whole thing starts with creating a media pool. Throughout this example, we assume that you're using a simple media pool composed of 4mm DAT cartridges.

You also use Backup to create an emergency repair disk (ERD).

Creating a media pool

Attach your DAT drive or whatever removable storage device you have to the computer. If you have not already done so, go to Add Hardware in the Control Panel and install the device. If the device was installed at the time you installed Windows Server 2003, the Backup media pool is probably using it already. If not, you must manually create the pool and allocate it to Backup or nest the new pool in the Backup media pool.

In Computer Management or Remote Storage, expand the Removable Storage option and select Media Pools. Right-click Media Pool and choose Create Media Pool from the pop-up list that appears. The Properties page for the media pool is presented, enabling you to select from dozens of supported media formats and technologies. This is illustrated in Figure 20-4.

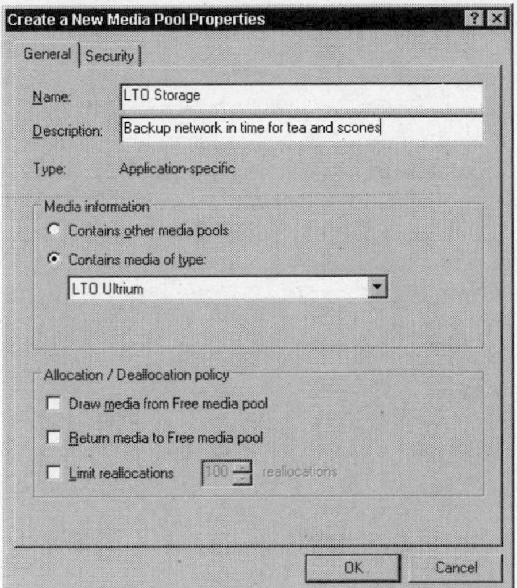

Figure 20-4: The Removable Storage media selection list.

Understanding rights and permissions

As with all Windows server platforms, you need certain rights and privileges to work with files. Windows Server 2003 does not permit you to back up or restore files for which you cannot claim rights to by virtue of your membership in a group, or *ownership*.

Here are the rules: If you are the owner of a file or folder, you can back up and restore the file on your domain or local computer, as long as you have logged on at the machine to restore to or have direct ownership. You must have access to the files in the form of one or more user permissions, such as read, write, or full access. You have no way to back up files if they are not yours.

Backup software services must use the account of a backup operator to access and back up files regardless of the rights associated with these files. If you are the administrator or you are a member of the Backup Operators group in a local group, you can sign on and perform backup and restores to the local machine.

To perform backup and restores from and to any machine on the network, you must be either the administrator (signed on as) or be a member of the domain's Backup Operator's group. As a domain Backup Operator, you can also do backups and restores in another domain if a trust exists between the domains.

Remember that you cannot back up the system-state of another computer even if you are the Angel of Administration. The advanced evolution of the Windows Server 2003 subsystem must have a lot to do with such a restriction. In the section "Performing a Backup" later in this chapter, we demonstrate a neat workaround that makes full use of Backup on every server and computer on the network while performing the backups from a single backup server, running any choice of backup software.

Understanding source and destination

We refer to sources and destinations when talking about backing up . . . on any system. So open Backup and click the Backup tab. (If this is the first time you have started Backup the Backup or Restore Wizard starts to provide the initial setup) In the left pane—your backup source—click the + box to expand your Desktop, as illustrated in Figure 20-5. You may also need to expand My Computer to expose the System State node of the source tree. In the Backup destination drop-down list box, select your tape drive. Notice that, if a tape drive is not installed, you can back up to a file. You can also back up to the media pool you created, but we save that for a command-line batch example in the section "Backup Batch files and Backup Scripts."

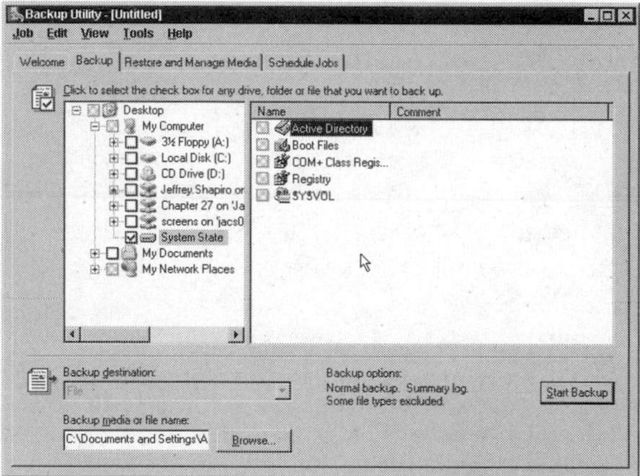

Figure 20-5: Selecting source and destination in Backup.

Now click the Start Backup button to open the Backup Job Information dialog box. In this dialog box, you can describe the backup. Windows Server 2003 inserts the time and date as the description. It also selects the time and date as the default label information.

The Advanced button enables you to select the backup type Normal, which you would do for any first full backup. You can also select Verify After Backup, which means that Backup compares the files backed up with the source data.

Verifying backups is not a bad idea, but you must understand that it adds a lot of time to the length of a backup; in many cases, it can take almost as long to verify a backup as the backup itself. If you have a lot of files and servers to back up, by the time you get to verify a file (compare the original against the backup), the original may have changed. This is a problem in many data centers where about 30 percent of the files backed up (usually during a 15-hour process) are changed before the verification starts. Many professional packages give you various levels of verification. You can on several, for example, check that the label and catalog information is intact or reliable and then make the assumption that the rest of the tape is okay.

We need to forgo all forms of verification (except for small jobs) because we back up so much data that not much interval time lies between backups. We have new backups starting back-to-back against old backups, and jobs collide and run into the following day's schedules.

If you have the time to verify your backups, by all means do it. But backup algorithms are so advanced today it is highly unlikely that a target file on the tape may not be the same as the source. Rather, set aside a day every so often (we do this once a month) to test restore the most critical data to a development server (even a special folder). You should also run disaster simulations, testing the restoration of the most valuable servers and their data.

Setting up schedules

Your next option is to start the backup now or schedule it to run at a later time. A later time may be whenever the computer is sure to be idle with no one logged on. On a Windows Server 2003 server, users can be logged on via terminals, shares, RAS, or via some network connection, such as FTP. You may consider shutting down certain services or denying access for the time the backup is running,

Notice that the Schedule Jobs option tab is a new addition to Backup. The old NT4 Backup could be scheduled to run at a later time only as part of a batch job triggered by the Task Scheduler; even that provided only the capability to repeat the process at various intervals. The Schedule Jobs tab on Backup provides a quasi-Backup wizard to achieve the manual task that we just performed. Some useful options are available in the Scheduler, so take some time to step through it and understand all the features.

To edit the job schedule, you can click the Schedule Jobs tab at any time and load the Schedule Jobs calendar. You can then double-click any day of the month to start the Backup wizard, or you can click a previously defined Job and load the Scheduler dialog boxes.

After you're in the Scheduled Job Options dialog box, click the Properties button to open the Schedule Job dialog box. The specifics of your task can now be edited or set in this dialog box.

That's really all that using Backup involves. Notice how everything we did here was very GUI-oriented. Next we look at how you can use media pools and command-line batch switches to run Backup as a covert scheduled backup operation. In the section "Restoring Data" later in this chapter, we look into advanced DR backup rotation schemes before getting to Restore operations.

Backup batch files and Backup scripts

Backup is accessible at the command line just as was its predecessors on Windows 2000 and Windows NT, and if running `backup` from the command line does not solicit a response from the server, try `NTbackup`. You still call the software by using `NTBackup`, so your Windows 2000 and NT 4.0 backup scripts can be easily ported; however not all commands are supported by NTBackup on Windows 2003 Server. You can type the command-line parameters and switches at the command line or prompt, and the OS loads and runs the backup routines (or you can just use the Run service).

Command line backups represent a complex and cryptic way of performing backups, but it has its uses. You can, for example, enter the commands into a batch file and have Windows run the batch file at a future date and time. Now to look at a few parameters and switches briefly; you can find details on all the parameters in the Windows Server 2003 online Help. You should recognize concepts and terms from our earlier discussions. Realize that the command parameters are the same ones set by the GUI, and that no different or alternative Backup application is at work under the hood.

You begin your command-line statement with the words `Ntbackup backup`. The first exercise at this point is to clone the job that we set up in Backup earlier, that of backing up the system-state. But as we promised in the previous section, we are going to use this backup in conjunction with a remote backup server. Open the command console (what we formerly called the MS-DOS prompt) and type the following:

```
ntbackup backup systemstate /f  "@c:\st\w2K001.bkf"
```

If you cannot find the command prompt option on your menus, follow these steps:

1. Click Start ➪ Run.
2. Add the run command path as follows: `cmd.exe`.
3. Click OK.

If you use the command console often, put the path into an icon and stick it on your desktop or in the menus. The `.bkf` file is the backup from the script file that was created in our earlier interactive example.

You do not need to enter zillions of parameters to see the backup launch from the command file. Open the Help File and search for NTBackup. From here, you can study the parameters and determine how they come together to perform a backup process from a batch file.

Notice that we have made a backup of the system-state in the preceding command-line example. And as we do not have a backup device defined or installed on the local machine, we have commanded NTBackup to back the system-state into a file named `w2K001.bkf`, which would identify this file as the system-state of Windows Server 2003 machine number 001. We can now back up this file to a remote system of choice.

Another NTBackup backup script

Although Backup is a greatly improved application over its predecessor, you still at times need to run a backup from a script. Remember that you can run the script only against a local tape or backup device.

Make sure that you meet all the previously discussed parameters to perform backups and gain access to shares and drives, such as a capable User ID and login password. You can use the Administrator account, although we don't recommend active use of this account, or you can use an account that is a member of the Administrator Group or Backup Operator group. Before you create your script, you should create a source list of the shares and devices (and all subfolders) that you intend to map to and back up. Each source operating system or environment requires peculiar login parameters. You may also need additional protocols and libraries to make the connection, such as Pathworks for a VAX share. To back up a Windows server, you need NTFS-level access, as follows:

```
Domain Name\Administrator (or Backup User ID)
```

The script that you create here enables you to connect to a local share. We use the command line `Net Use` option to map to the data or backup source. Then we use the NTBackup commands to perform the backup. After the backup and any post-processing is done, we again use the `Net Use` command to disconnect from the source. The NTBackup command reference is extensive and is available in Windows Server 2003 Help.

The following script enables you to back up a group of files to a Zip drive:

Wherever possible, use the environment variable `%windir%`, enclosed between percent symbols, as here, so that the script can be used on other machines.

The finished script should look as follows:

```
Rem: NET USE <new map>: \\<Server name>\<share name> <password> NET USE
K:\\MCDC01\MYBACKUPS\ *******
NTBACKUP BACKUP K: /D "MY WORD FILES" /HC:ON /M NORMAL /L:F
NET USE K: /DELETE /Y
```

The script can be thrown into a batch file and run from the Task Scheduler or the Command Scheduler. This script is very basic, and you should be able to expand it from here or concoct something for yourself . . . you could create quite an elaborate process. There are a number of parameters in the above script worth noting: /D lets you provide a description; /HC:ON is the switch for turning on hardware compression; the /M dictates the type of backup (such as normal, incremental, differential and so on; and /L:F specifies that you want full reporting to the log file. To check the full list of parameters, open a console and type `Ntbackup /?` .

Always disconnect a share that you no longer need so that another process can use it. *Delete* in a NET USE script prompts for a final Yes or No, so provide the `/Y` switch as needed.

You can now schedule this script to run at certain intervals. To check whether everything is in order with your scripts, open the dialog box illustrated in Figure 20-6.

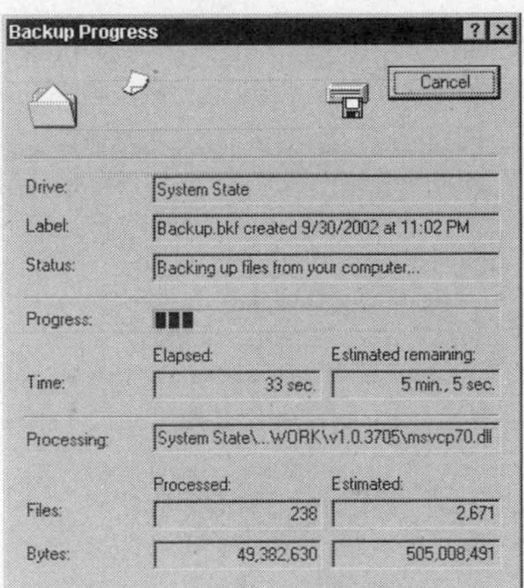

Figure 20-6: Backup progress.

Rotation Schemes

A *rotation scheme* is a plan or system by which you rotate the media that you use in your backup sets. At the most basic level, a rotation scheme may be a daily backup using one media. You would not have much of a DR scheme because you would be writing over the media every day; but this is a rotation scheme nonetheless. Another consideration in a rotation scheme is the dividing lines between what you consider archiving: data backup, version control, system-state, and recovery.

Figure 20-7 is one way to look at your data's value from a chronological point of view. The scale is a simple one, but it demonstrates the various stages of usefulness that backups go through, starting from the left. Data in the archival period need not be located on-site and is kept for record-keeping (annual backups), and data in the version control period is stored off- and on-site for access to full weekly generations of the data. Data in the recovery period is stored both on-site and off-site and (depending on the critical nature of the data) is either online or within "arm's length" of recovery.

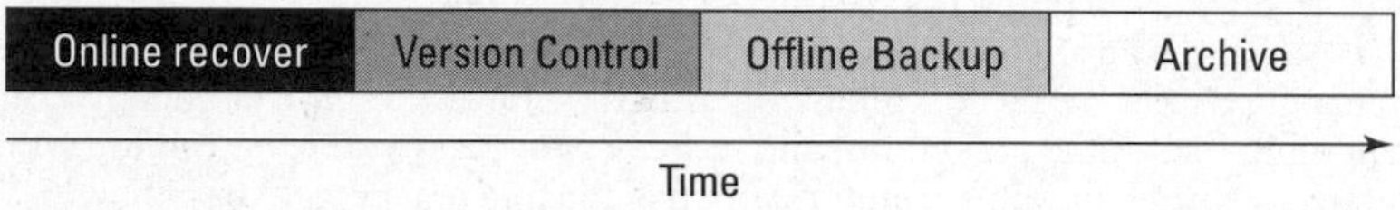

Online recover	Version Control	Offline Backup	Archive

Time →

Figure 20-7: The stages of a backup's life.

You can now expand our rotation scheme. The first option would be to rotate the media every other day so that you could be backing up to one tape while the alternate is in safekeeping somewhere. If the worst were to happen—a tape gets eaten by the device or something less common—you would still have a backup from the previous day. If the machine were stolen, you could restore it. But rotating every other day is useful only in terms of total data loss. So you have a full backup of all your files every day. What about wear and tear? A tape or a platter is a delicate device. Inserting it, removing it every other day, and writing to it over and over can put your data at risk. Tapes do stretch, and they do get stuck in tape drives. Tapes should be saved according to the scratch-and-save discussion in the section "Practicing Scratch and Save," earlier in this chapter.

And then what about version control? Rotating with multiple media—say, a week's worth—would ensure that you could roll back to previous states of a file. We could refer to such a concept of versioning as a *generation system* of rotation (not sufficient for critical restore, however). In fact, one such standard generation scheme is widely used by the most seasoned of backup administrators to achieve both these ideals—versioning and protecting media from wear and tear and loss. It is known as the *GFS system*, or *G*randfather, *F*ather, *S*on system.

You now want to create a GFS scheme to run under Backup. Most high-end backup software can create and manage a rotation scheme for you, but for now and always with Backup, you need a legal pad. So now put a label on one of your tapes or disks and call it Full, or First, Backup or Normal # 1—whatever designates a complete backup of the system and collection of files and folders.

The first backup of any system is always a full backup, and the reason is simple. Back up and you need a catalog or history of all the files in the backup list so that you can access every file for a restore and so that Backup can perform incremental or differential analysis on the media. Do your backup according to the procedures that we discussed in the section "Performing a Backup," earlier in this chapter. You should have enough practice by now. And you are ready to go from a development or trial backup to a production rotation scheme.

As soon as you make a full backup set, label the members as discussed and then perform a second full backup (or copy the first). On the first backup set, add the following information to the label:

- **Full_First:** January Server 2003
- **Retention:** G (for Grandfather) or one year — for example, dd-January-2003
- **Serial number:** Your choosing, or automatically generated

On the second set, add the following information to your labels:

- **Full_First:** Week1-January Server 2003
- **Retention:** F (for Father) or one month, Week1y-February-Server 2003
- **Serial number:** Your choosing, or automatically generated

The next day, choose a second set of media, but this time only the files that have been changed are backed up by using differential or incremental options. Say that you are doing incrementals here for example's sake.

On the incremental set, add the following information to the label:

- **I_First** (or a day of the week)**:** Monday, or First
- **Retention:** Seven days or every Monday
- **Serial number:** Your choosing, or automatically generated

The next day, put in a new backup set and perform the next day's incremental. This time, the label information is Tuesday or Second; retain these media in a seven-day save set and store them in a safe place. On Wednesday, perform the third incremental, and on Thursday, perform the fourth incremental. Now to look at what you are achieving.

You have created a Grandfather set that you store for a year. If you started this system in January Server 2003, you do not reuse these tapes until January 2003; the retention period is one year, the oldest saved data that you have.

The second copy set is the Father set of the scheme, and this set gets reused in four weeks' time. In other words, every four weeks, the set can be overwritten. This does not mean that you make a full backup only once a month. On the contrary: Notice that you made one full set and four incremental sets, so you are making a full backup once a week and four incremental backups Monday to Thursday. You retain the weekly set only for a month, meaning that, at the end of each month, you have five full backup sets, one set for each week, retained for a month, and one set for each month, retained for a year.

What about the incremental sets? These sets are the grandchildren of our rotation scheme. You save them for seven days and return them for scratching on the same day the following week. So what you back up on Monday gets written over next Monday, Tuesday gets written over on Tuesday, and so on. This also means that, at any given time, your people can access the previous day's data, the previous week's data, the previous month's data, and the previous year's data. What you have created here is a traditional rotation scheme for performing safe and accessible backups of data.

Variations on this theme are possible, and you need more than just seven of whatever media you are using. For example, for the full GFS rotation, you would need the following for a single server that used one DLT tape drive:

✦ **Daily backups** (incremental, rotated weekly): 4+

✦ **Weekly Full** (rotated monthly): 4+

✦ **Monthly Full** (rotated annually): 12+

✦ **Total tapes:** 20+

The best days for such a rotation scheme are Monday through Thursday for incremental and Friday for full. Even on big systems, you're unlikely to be doing an incremental into the following day. And on Friday, you have the whole day and the weekend to do the full backup, at a time when the system is most idle. You could start after the last person leaves on a Friday, and you would still have about 48 hours of backup time to play with.

Restoring Data

We left the subject of data restoring until now because it is usually the least time-intensive task to perform, and hopefully you are not asked to restore data too often. Backup has a restore option that enables you to select the files you need to restore from the source (the catalog or Backup history), as illustrated in Figure 20-8.

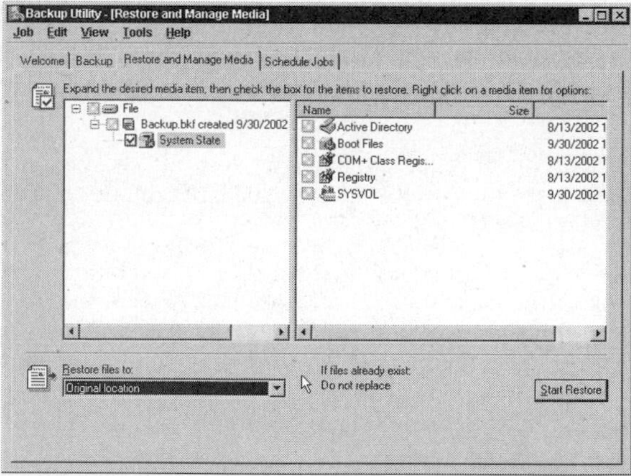

Figure 20-8: Selecting files to restore in Backup.

You also have the option of restoring some or all of the files to original location or an alternative. Backup, NTBackup, and all third-party software restores are handled in the same way. The following checklist thus applies to any restore that you are doing:

✦ Always make sure that restoring files to their original locations does not result in loss of data. Although making such a consideration seems illogical, restoring files often results in further damage. For example, if a file is corrupt but up to date and you restore a file that is not corrupt but out of date, how much better off are you?

Investigating saving the contents of the file that you want to replace or salvaging what you can before overwriting the file may be a better course. You could restore to an alternative location or rename the corrupt file. Better to check whether a "corrupt" file is recoverable before you blow it away with all chances of ever recovering your data.

✦ Consider, too, the consequences of restoring. Windows Server 2003 stores all manner of information about a file: the folder that it's in, the volume, EFS, DFS, RFS, quota information, share-points, archive information, and so on. Restoring a file restores not only the contents, but also any attributes and information known about the file at the time it was backed up. Anything new applied to the file and its relationship with the rest of the universe is not recorded in the restore. A good example is restoring a folder that several new groups and users were given access to after the last backup. The restore now blocks these new users, and a critical process may bring things crashing down if you turn your back. Again, restore to an alternative location if you are unsure of the results.

✦ Block user access while performing a restore to original locations. Nothing causes more problems than having users trying to open files that have not been completely restored. Blocking access results in calls to the help desk, so make sure that customer service or help-desk representatives know about the process. And don't waste your time calling people to tell them about the block. If it is a big share-point, you always have someone messing things up. On the other hand, if you are restoring a share that needs to be accessed by a critical process coming from another machine or software, let the owners of these processes know before their applications crash.

✦ Always check who is connected to the destination computer and what files they have open. If you restore to files that are open, you at the least get access errors, and at the worst, you could corrupt the files you are restoring. You can check who is connected to the server by opening the File Management Console (or Computer Management) and expand the Sessions node under the Shared Folders leaf. You can also see who is connected to what by running the `NET SESSIONS` and `NET FILE` commands at the Command Console. `NET SESSIONS` and `NET FILE` work for all versions of Windows Server.

One last item before we leave Restore. We spent a lot of time digging in the Remote Storage Manager looking for a place to erase, format, and catalog media. After all, RSM is where everything's supposed to happen for media. We guess Microsoft let this one slip by them, and we let them know. All is not lost. We discovered the missing erase and format utility in Backup. It is on the Restore tab, of all places. Just right-click the tape icon and format away your precious media.

Tape Location

Removing your valuable rotation sets from the premises as soon as the backup job is done, every day, and as long as online media are available is very important. You can find many reliable media pick-up companies in all cities in the United States. If you do not have access to a media pick-up firm, find a safe place (such as a safe deposit box at a bank) and move your media to this remote location every day. You could also buy a small fireproof safe and keep that on-site.

Following are two chief reasons for moving the media off-site: First, if a disaster were to take out your building, it would take out your backups as well. Here in Hurricane Land, Florida, USA, we move backups to a secure location every day.

Second, tapes and backup media grow legs and may walk out of your offices. Worse, someone may access your tapes and steal sensitive information without you knowing it.

We have a very secure computer room, and some time in the latter part of the last millennium, we removed a tape and then left the secure environment to fetch a new label. We were gone two minutes and returned to find the tape gone. We thought we had misplaced it and had to repeat a five-hour backup all over again. Later, we learned that, in those two minutes, another administrator had asked the computer-room staff for a spare tape and was given our unlabeled tape, thinking it was blank. Lesson learned: Never leave your backup media unattended, even for two minutes.

Backup Bandwidth

Bandwidth is an important item in your Hardware/Media/Support Level equation. From the get-go, you should forget about doing any significant backup over a WAN or Internet connection unless you have upward of a 1.5-Mbit pipe to the source (and even that is a stretch given the size of data files these days). Anything less (unless it is a very small collection of files) does not provide a suitable facility for backing up. The only time that you may try backing up over a low bandwidth connection (and for backup, low bandwidth could be considered anything under 10 Mbit) is if you need to grab a handful of important files. To back up a remote registry over a 64-Kbit pipe would take several hours.

On the other hand, we routinely back up thousands of server shares over a 10-Mbit Ethernet network; if you have a 100-Mbit backbone and have servers sitting directly on that, all the better. You need to remember, though, that even a 100-Mbit backbone is only as valuable as the speed of the server bus, network links, hard disk I/O, and the capabilities of the backup devices.

The minimum rate of backup you can expect over a 10-Mbit network is between 15MB and 45MB per minute, depending on the backup device. Local tape drives on fast computers using SCSI technology and high-end hardware can even achieve levels of around 200MB per minute and even higher on RAID systems and extremely high-speed disk arrays. However, as mentioned in Chapter 19, placing a high-end backup device on every server can be very expensive.

What you then need to do is work out how much data needs to be backed up and then figure out how long backing up all that data is going to take you. If the data is mission critical, you may want to back it up more often. Remember that data changes every minute of the day. Database applications can see as much as 20 percent of the data changing on the low end and as much as 80 percent changing on the high end. E-mail systems are changing just about every second of the day in busy organizations.

Here is a very simple formula to work out how long it will take to back up your data. Say that you want to back up *X* amount of data to a certain device in *Y* time. Starting with the desired unknown *Y*, you would want to first figure out how much data you are going to try to back up on the local machine or over the network. After you have calculated this, your equation resembles the following:

```
Y = S/T
```

Here, Y = time, S = amount of data in megabytes, and T = transfer time in minutes of hardware (locally or across the network). The data transfer or backup rate of the DLT 7000 is around 300MB per minute (hauling data off the local hard drives). Thus your equation would be Y = Server 2003/300, and 2GB would thus take just over six minutes to back up. Factor in another two minutes or more per 100MB for latency, cataloging, files in use, database updating, and so on. You would be safe to say that 2GB of data could get backed up in less than ten minutes. Across the local area network, you would be safe to divide the transfer rate by a factor of ten. The same 2GB over the network would take more than an hour to back up.

Hardware and Media Formats

Choosing hardware and media depends on the applications, size of the data pool or resources, size of the network (number of servers), number of users, critical nature of the data, and so on. In multiserver environments, you would be best off looking to invest in a tape library system. These sophisticated devices cost an arm and a leg (anywhere from $6,000 to $35,000), but what you save in time and frustration, as well as speed of restore, is worth it. Other choices of backup media include writeable compact discs, remote storage volumes, removable disks such as zip disks and flopticals, and DVD.

In the section "Establishing Quality of Capture" earlier in this chapter, we discussed Quality of Service and Service Level. Now comes the time to consider hardware purchase.

4mm Digital Audiotape

Still one of the most popular technologies, 4mm Digital Audiotape (DAT) is widely used in all business sizes. It now comes in three formats: DDS-1, DDS-2, and DDS-3—holding 2GB, 8GB, and 12GB, respectively. A single DDS-3 tape can thus hold as much as 24GB with high-end hardware compression.

The only major drawback of the DAT format is that the header is read every time the tape is used for backups or restores. This makes the format less hardy than its competitors (although a single tape is likely to live to 300 or more runs). Another problem with DAT is that the cartridge is not hardy and not much is necessary to damage it. We have seen several situations where a DAT was taken out of the drive and the media got caught up inside the system . . . unknown to the operator, who would then walk away leaving a trail of black tape streaming out behind him or her.

8mm Digital Audiotape

An improvement over its 4mm sibling, the 8mm format can hold up to 40GB of data with hardware compression running at 2:1. Another major advantage is the speed of 8mm DAT. It can typically back up 40GB of data in less than five hours. The Sony AME tapes are the most popular on the market and offer improved performance and reliability.

The 8mm cartridge is also dinky, however, and needs to be handled with care in busy server-room environments. Dropping one onto the floor or stepping on it can ruin the tape. The hardware, as can the 4mm hosts, can also be unkind to the media. We have had several situations where tapes got stuck inside the drives.

Digital Linear Tape

Digital Linear Tape (DLT) and now SuperDLT has become one of the most popular tape formats in high-end server operations for several reasons. It is fast, reliable, hardy, and you can store a lot of data on a single high-end version of the format. DLT is a Quantum format, which was introduced mostly to compete against DAT in the mainframe, midrange, and Unix platform arena. The adoption of DLT in the Windows and NetWare server environments has accelerated the success of the media.

DLT comes in several versions: DLT . DLT 4000, DLT5000, and DLT 7000. Capacity is 10GB on the low-end format to as much as 70GB compressed on the 7000 format. The SuperDLT format can pack as much as 200GB onto tape. Although DAT tends to be a faster technology, many manufacturers have introduced high-speed SCSI interface library systems capable of holding many drives and providing technology to deliver backup/restore on a continual basis.

The DLT cartridge is very sturdy, which makes it ideal in busy environments where tapes are moved around in robotic library systems all the time. Dropping a DLT cartridge or sending it flying across the server room floor (which often happens when the off-site delivery arrives and the backup admin has forgotten to remove the nightly backups from the system) does not make the slightest dent. You can also keep a DLT tape in service for a year or more, which makes it easy on the budget. DLT hardware is pretty sturdy; we have opened units in-house to reconnect slipped leader bands and to clean simple mechanical components that get clogged with dust and debris.

DAT and DLT technology differ in that DAT stores data in diagonal stripes across the media. The data is laid down by using helical scan technology. Helical scanning is achieved by rotating a drumhead across the media surface. DLT, on the other hand, lays down its data horizontally along the tape in tracks, by running the tape across the stationary head, much like the recording technology in four- and eight-track audiocassettes.

DLT also travels well, which is an important consideration if you manage a number of remote sites and they depend on you for supplies. We typically use retired DLT media, which may have another 50 runs of life left, to make a final annual backup of a system. This tape is then sent off-site into storage forever, called into service only on the remote chance that reference to old data is needed.

Advanced Intelligent Tape

For extremely large quantities of data and backup environments that never rest, the Advanced Intelligent Tape, or AIT, is another format from the Exabyte-Sony alliance. AIT tapes can typically stay in service for as many as 400 runs or backups per cartridge. Sony created a backup technology format for this media called Advanced Metal Evaporated (AME). The material is tough and comprises a carbon protective coating that keeps the tapes from "burning up" in the high-speed drives.

Tape libraries can support up to 8TB of data. So for speed and volume, this format is ideal for an online system for backup QoS levels 3 and lower. An advanced version of AME consists of a small EEPROM chip that is housed in the cartridge. This chip holds backup information, cataloging, and backup restore logs. The downside of AIT is that it is more expensive than the tape formats discussed in the preceding sections and holds less data (25-100GB) than formats like DLT and SuperDLT.

Quarter-Inch Cartridge (QIC)

QIC is the acronym for *Q*uarter-*I*nch *C*artridge and represents the most popular format for small business. The latest Travan cartridges (the T-series) can now back up as much as 8GB of data per cartridge. The casings are sturdy, making the format durable and easy to handle in situations where company servers are usually behind closets, in office corners, or on factory floors.

Unfortunately, QIC does not scale to large systems of magazine-loaded changers and robotic library systems. This also makes the format less than an ideal partner for RSS solutions. On the other hand, QIC hardware is also very affordable, costing $400 or less for top-of-the-line models.

Linear Tape-Open (LTO)

Linear Tape-Open (LTO), technology, which is used by systems such as the IBM Ultrium Scalable Tape Library, provides an ideal solution for cost-effectively handling a wide range of backup, archive, and disaster-recovery data-storage needs. The reliability, capacity and performance of LTO offers an excellent alternative to DLT, 8mm, 4mm, or 1/4-inch tape drives for streaming data applications such as backup. Consider the following specifications for an LTO system:

- Tape capacity, 100GB
- Two tape slots reserved for catalog backup
- One tape slot reserved for cleaning tape

With an Autoloader capacity, of say 18 tape slots, LTO solutions can be backing up a whopping 45TB of data. Here's some advice regarding investing in a backup hardware solution:

- Tape automation reduces errors and costs associated with manual operations.
- Consider cross-platform connectivity for networked storage environments.
- Open tape architectures provide seamless data interchange and true multivendor compatibility.

Working with Shadow Copies

In addition to the new design for backing up open files, the Shadow Copy function also goes a long way toward relieving the administrative burden on backup operators. How many times have you received a help-desk ticket or a call to retrieve a file that was mistakenly deleted or corrupted? If you raised your hand (and dropped the book), you're sure to be delighted with Shadow Copy's capability to restore previous copies of the documents directly from the shadow copy maintained in the file system.

Shadow Copy Backup/Restore enables you to create shadow-copy backups of entire volumes, which makes exact copies of files, including all open files (that open-file magic again). Even databases, which are almost always held open exclusively, are backed up. If you are also the SQL Server administrator, you know how frustrating it is needing to close down database connections so that maintenance on the database can be conducted and backups taken.

Any files under Shadow Copy management that are opened by an operator or the system are automatically backed up during a volume shadow-copy backup. Thus files that have changed during the backup process are copied correctly. This, of course, does not mean that you can obviate the need to backup "real" files to tape or some other media. But it ensures that backing up the shadowed files means that you have not lost data because of the open-files dilemma. If this is not a reason for you to rush out now and go buy Windows Server 2003, you've been suffering too many long nights restoring data.

Shadow copy backups have terrific utility in that they ensure the following:

✦ Applications can continue to write data to the volume during a backup.

✦ Open files are no longer skipped during a backup.

✦ Backups can be performed at any time, without locking out users.

Because we do not live in a perfect IT world, some applications and backup systems may not believe that everything about Shadow Copy is cool. Check with the manufacturer of your software or hardware if you have some doubts that shadow copies on third party products represent a reliable record of your data. Of course, you should always experiment with them in the lab before using them on your actual system.

To enable shadow copies, perform the following steps:

1. Open Computer Management (Local),. In the console tree, right-click Shared Folders and select Configure Shadow Copies. You can also right-click the volume in Explorer and select Properties, and then open the Shadow Copies tab. Whichever route you choose the dialog box tab shown in Figure 20-9 loads.

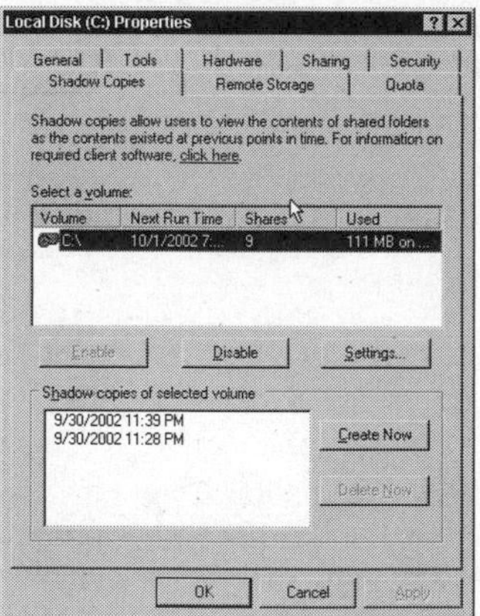

Figure 20-9: Selecting the volume for configuring Shadow Copies.

2. Select the volume in the list where you want to enable shadow copies and then click the Settings button. This will open the dialog box shown in Figure 20-10.

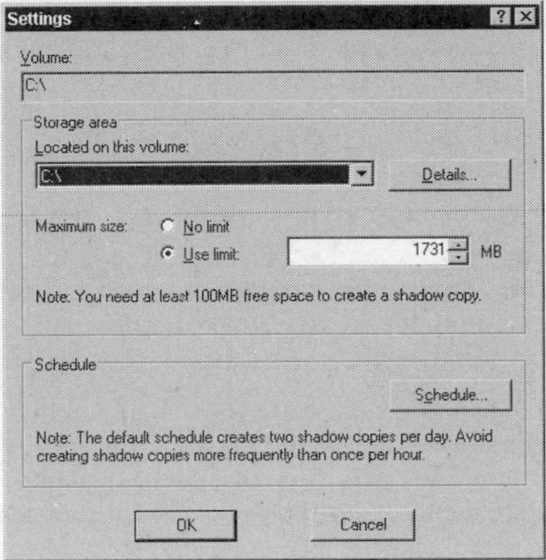

Figure 20-10: Selecting the volume for configuring Shadow Copies.

You can now configure Shadow Copy properties to suit your needs.

The Storage Volume option is for specifying where to store the shadow copies of the selected volume. The default is to use the same volume. Microsoft recommends that you use a separate volume on another disk because this approach provides better performance for heavily used file servers.

You can change the storage volume only if no shadow copies are present. If you need to change the storage volume for a volume that already is enabled, you must delete all the shadow copies on that volume before changing the storage volume.

Select the Details button to open a dialog box that lists the shadow copies that are currently stored. This dialog box also gives information about the total space and available storage space on the disk.

The Storage Limits option enables you to configure the size of the part on the volume that holds the source files being shadow copied. The default size is 10 percent of the size of the actual volume. If the shadow copies are stored on a separate volume from the source files, you should change this default to reflect the amount of the storage volume that you are willing to dedicate to shadow copies.

The storage limit must be at least 100MB, which permits only a single shadow copy to be retained. If you set a restrictive storage limit, you should test to ensure that the number of shadow copies that you have scheduled can fit within those restraints. If shadow copies are deleted prematurely because of storage limits, you may be defeating the purpose of enabling shadow copies of shared folders.

The Schedule button launches the Task Scheduler with the information that you need to create a task schedule for taking shadow copies of shared folders on a regular basis. Before creating the schedule, take a look at your current users' work patterns and design a strategy that schedules shadow copies at a time of day that works best for your users. The default schedule is Monday through Friday at 7 a.m. and 12 p.m. Following are some rules to consider in enabling Shadow Copy:

- Do not enable shadow copies on volumes that use mount points (see Chapter 26). Any drive mounted into the volume that is enabled for Shadow Copy is not included as the copies are taken.
- Shadow copies should not be used as a replacement for regular backups. Keep backing up as you usually do, but spend less time restoring from backup tapes.
- Do not schedule Shadow Copy to copy too often. The default schedule is set for 7 a.m. and 12 noon, but we went nuts on this feature and shadowed every hour. We ran out of disk space very quickly. If you decide that you need copies taken more often, make sure that you allot enough storage space and that you do not take copies so often that server performance degrades.
- Before deleting a volume that is being shadowed, delete the scheduled task for creating shadow copies. If the volume is deleted without deleting the shadow-copy task, the scheduled task fails and an `Event ID: 7001` error is written to the event log. Delete the task before deleting the volume to avoid filling the event log with these errors.
- In considering Shadow Copy, think about file permissions: If you're restoring a file, the file permissions are not changed. Permissions remain the same as before the restore. If you're undeleting a file, permissions are set to the default permissions for the directory.
- As storage area limits are reached, the oldest shadow copy is deleted and cannot be retrieved.
- Shadow copies are read-only. You cannot edit the contents of a shadow copy. You can work with the copy only after it is restored.
- Shadow copies are enabled on a per-volume basis. You cannot enable shadow copies on specific shares.

Summary

This chapter deals more with backup practice and protocol than actual software or technology. Most applications perform backups and restores in the same way. And the Microsoft tape and media APIs ensure that, at the file backup level, the data state resulting (integrity) from all backup technology is no better or worse from vendor to vendor.

Some third-party vendors, however, do have software that better manages the backup process. Backup is a useful utility, but in many respects, you are likely to use it for quick and dirty work or for recovery disks and ASR media. It is not a high-end utility for the application and data services that Windows Server 2003 is cut out to provide.

In addition, we stress how important it is to understand the difference between data backup and system backup. We also give you food for thought to enable you to manage backup procedures (QOST and SL) at a level becoming a professional administrator.

This chapter also touches on the new Shadow Copy facilities now built into the NTFS that comes with Server 2003.

✦ ✦ ✦

21 CHAPTER

Disaster Recovery

In This Chapter

Creating documentation

Setting up a response plan

Practicing recovery by using ASR

Recovering the operating system on a failed server

Dealing with a failed server is one of the most stressful parts of a system administrator's job. You face the pressures of reinstalling the operating system, recovering valuable data from the backup media, and then reinstalling all the key services needed for the correct operation of the server. Planning for disaster recovery involves a lot more than simply knowing how to operate your restoration software. In this chapter, we show you how to correctly use Automated System Recovery to recover a base operating system, as well as best practices for creating and documenting a Disaster Recovery Plan.

Disaster Recovery Planning

Disaster recovery is one of the single most important things that you can learn in system administration. Administering a server doesn't mean anything if you can't bring it back to life should something happen to it, such as a catastrophic disk failure or an Active Directory database corruption.

The fine art of disaster recovery not only includes restoring files from a backup device, but it also encompasses locating potential problems that could lead to a crashed server, restoring services after a reinstallation of the operating system, and a multitude of other duties.

Policy and protocol

The first step in disaster recovery is to define a policy and protocol. The policy should define what happens in what order to get things restored to their normal working condition. The protocol should define the conditions that must be met to perform certain actions. Under what circumstances, for example, should you reinstall the operating system and what determines whether you should merely attempt to repair the server operating system? These are the issues that need to be resolved.

Laying out a policy for disaster recovery doesn't make a lot of sense because it varies from company to company. You need to take several things into account: for example, does your business perform 24-7 operations? If so, your guidelines to disaster recovery should be much more strict than a company that operates only eight hours a day. You should define the response times to respond to an emergency as well as the estimated times that systems should take to be back up and running.

Documentation

Documentation is the cornerstone to any Disaster Recovery Plan. Without documentation, everyone involved in the disaster recovery plan must depend on memory. Considering the number of steps needed to bring a server back to life as well as to restore all data and ensure that all systems are functioning correctly, your memory alone probably isn't of much use.

In considering a Disaster Recovery Plan, you can take a clue from common household items. How many of you, for example, have a clock in your house that always flashes the ever-so-common *12:00*? More often than not, many people fail to read the documentation—whether about how to fix a clock or recover from a server crash—or just plain don't understand it. In writing a Disaster Recovery Plan, you need to ensure that your documentation is read and that it makes sense.

In developing your recovery plan, you need to plan for and expect budget overruns and time shortages. Typically, you find that if a Disaster Recovery Plan is running behind, time is taken from the documentation process to even things out. This obviously is a bad idea, but it is typically not a decision left up to the project leader in charge of the documentation process. You need to learn how to deal with a shortage of time and still develop usable documentation. Many technical writers and administrators suggest that a practical approach would be a layered document. The document outline would contain headings 1,2,3,4, and 5. Section 1 would be, for example, an overview of the Disaster Recovery Plan. The sections of the documents can be prioritized, which determines what is completed first. All sections that contain nonessential information (such as Section 1) could be held off until the end of the project in the event that time needs to be cut. Plan on prioritizing document sections according to the following information (low to high priority):

- ✦ Nonessential informational
- ✦ Important information
- ✦ Necessary information
- ✦ Essential information

By using this approach, you are sure to complete all the essential items before time is taken from the project.

Before you can develop a usable plan, you must know how the document will be used. In many organizations, the sales team considers the document valuable because it shows potential clients that your company is devoted to providing uninterrupted service. Managers may use the document to help with the budget increases for additional staff. Keeping all this in mind, you need to ensure that you don't try to squeeze everything into the document. Its purpose is as the company's recovery tool in the event of an emergency—not as a marketing tool. The portions of the document that marketing and managers find useful are most likely the portions that have a lower priority.

Equally important as being clear on the intent of the documentation is knowing who is likely to read the document. All companies have their own terms that are specific to their organizations. Using technical terms and phrases that your company doesn't typically use is pointless. If you happen to be a consultant in an unfamiliar company, you may want to learn the language and possibly read through other documentation that it may have.

Another important aspect of the creation of the documentation is to determine who has access to it. Quite often, these documents contain very sensitive information, such as the administrative password, firewall and router information, or user-account information. These documents, after they're developed, are usually stored on a network drive so that many other employees can proofread them, make corrections, and even add content. This location on a network drive must be accessible to only authorized users. You also need to determine who can access the documentation outside the directory. This directory is probably, for example, being backed up. You must know who has access to the backup media and can extract the information. If the backups are being performed across the network, you should consider that someone may be intercepting the packets. Extracting the sensitive information by using this method would prove fairly easy. You may also want to consider that, at some point, this document may be shown to people who shouldn't have access to the sensitive information. You should ensure that all the sensitive information is contained in a section that can be easily removed should the need arise—for example, in the appendix of the Disaster Recovery Plan. Should a salesperson need access to the document, you can then provide it to that person, with the exception of the section containing the sensitive information.

Most importantly, keep the document simple. You need to convey very complex information in an easy-to-read manner. If you can do this, readers of all types should have no problem following along.

Disaster recovery training and action planning

Before you begin the training process, setting objectives is a must. Without objectives, how can you know whether you have accomplished what you set out to accomplish? Take these suggestions to heart before you begin training so that you can create a list of the objectives that you want to accomplish.

In creating a Disaster Recovery Plan, you should use several layers for tasks and subtasks. Each one must have an objective and procedures to follow as you attempt to accomplish the objective. You can use Microsoft Word to generate a list of this sort because it is quite capable of numbering each item with the correct indentation for denoting levels. If you want a bit more control and the capability to set conditions on the items, subitems, and even predecessors, you may consider using Microsoft Project. Using this type of layout can serve as a road map for the plan that you are undertaking.

These plans are typically called *Use Cases*. A Use Case is actually a page (or pages) defining a typical scenario. For every possible scenario, you should have a Use Case.

Identifying Resources

As you are planning for disaster recovery, you need to identify several resources to make your job easier. If you have multiple people who manage servers, you need to initiate an *On-Call* schedule—a schedule of who comes in and performs the necessary steps should a server go down. If you have fewer than a dozen servers, having just one person respond may work. The more servers that you have, however, the more people you need to involve. Not only should you take administrators into account, but to effectively get things back up and going, you may also need a member of your network administration team on hand as well as those of any other team that your servers may affect.

After you have created this On-Call schedule, you should keep a list of hardware vendors that you can call on a moment's notice should you need additional hardware. Server administrators aren't always the best at actually installing hardware, so you may require a consultant or a vendor's support representative to get the necessary hardware installed and configured before you can restore the server to its normal operating condition.

Although planning for disaster recovery in a company that has one location is pretty tedious, imagine the additional steps necessary should a remote server go down. Not only do you need to ensure that someone local to the machine can respond, but you also must ensure that this person has intimate knowledge of the other servers on the WAN to make sure that everything is correctly set up. A handy tool in this case is a Keyboard, Video, Mouse (KVM) switch that accepts TCP/IP connections. A KVM switch enables you to remotely connect to a server, reboot it, and configure it and anything else—all from the comfort of your sofa.

Keeping a diagram of your servers handy may prove an excellent idea in helping you identify resources. This diagram should look something like a tree diagram that shows each server and what services and applications each server hosts. If a server goes down, you can see at a glance which systems it affected. By using this information, you can make a well-informed decision about who needs to be contacted for additional support or who should be informed that systems are currently down.

Developing Response Plans

Developing a response plan isn't something you can do overnight. You need complete knowledge of the servers as well as all the applications they are hosting. To get this kind of information, you more than likely need to interview several dozen people in your organization. After you have obtained a list of all the equipment and all the people you need to involve in the response plan, you can make a rough outline of the plan. Keep in mind that you could spend a full month writing this plan, but you can never make it completely foolproof. Some portions of it are sure to be lacking, and we're sorry to say that you usually must engage in a bit of trial and error to get the plan to work correctly.

Several software packages are available that enable you to inventory your systems, which is a first step in developing a response plan. These software packages provide an outline that you can use to begin your planning.

In developing your response plan, be generous on your allotment of response times. Assuming the worst and giving yourself ample time is better than taking 300 percent longer than the plan assumes to get all systems back up and running. After you have a response plan in place, the best way to determine whether it suits your needs is to test it.

Testing Response Plans

Disaster-recovery planning can often be thought of as similar to building a bridge with toothpicks. Just when you think you have the support beams in place, they float away. Disaster-recovery planning can be an enormous task—and proportionally so with a larger network.

You have probably heard the adage "If you fail to plan, you plan to fail." This really does represent the disaster-recovery process. You can develop a very robust plan, but if you never test it, how can you know how well it works? No matter what technique you choose in testing a response plan, keep the following points in mind:

✦ **Failures don't exist:** No matter what you do during a test, any results that you receive are worth something. The only failure would be not to test at all. All tests yield results, and these results help administrators gain a better knowledge of their system and the systems with which it interfaces.

✦ **Set objectives:** Because most Administrators have very limited time, a thorough plan with objectives can drastically reduce the time necessary to test a system. This plan and its objectives can usually be performed in steps. Completing all steps at once isn't necessary, but you can complete a few steps today and maybe a few more next week. You can also quite possibly test the steps out of order, which can help fit the schedule of the administrators. In testing a system, make sure that the objectives are well defined. Set time limits on the tests and compare those times to the actual results. This procedure ensures that the modifications you make to the test plan in the future accurately reflect the time that recovery takes for your particular system in its current environment.

✦ **Action items:** Every test should be timed and well documented, and all the steps and the final outcome also should be well documented. Doing so enables you to review all the steps and provide training material to other employees who may become responsible for portions of the system. Documenting a system, testing it, and then keeping all the results in your head doesn't do anyone any good. (If you should happen to, say, step in front of a bus, all progress is lost if you failed to document the test results.)

✦ **Frequency:** Test often! Creating a plan and testing it once is good until certain aspects of your system change enough to make your plan obsolete. Not only should you schedule regular tests on your system, but you should also ensure that you test it whenever anything major changes. If new routers or new servers are added or the network topology changes, you should automatically begin a new test of your plan. If enough changes in your system and its surroundings, the plan is quite likely to need updating.

✦ **Consultants:** Some consultants specialize in testing systems. Picking their brains and gaining some insight into the world of testing may prove helpful. Many software packages out there can also assist you in your testing. To be of any use, however, these software packages must be extremely configurable and may even contain a scripting language. Look into these products and try to locate a consultant who specializes in them.

Response plans and their testing is a very large subject that can consume not only a single book but literally volumes. For many of the sophisticated technologies out there today, you can pick up a book that can help you narrow your testing and get very specific with it.

Mock Disaster Programs

The best way to ensure that your disaster-recovery procedures are adequate is to put them to the test. Completely document several types of "disasters" and then play them out according to your disaster-recovery plan. Some of these events, especially a particularly catastrophic one, take a bit more time because they may involve going to a remote location, installing servers, and performing restores of data to get things going. Not only are test procedures for recovering servers and data necessary, but you also need to take into consideration communication lines and so on. To simulate simpler problems such as hard-drive failures, you can simply have a co-worker remove a SCSI cable from your drive array. Table 21-1 shows what you could expect from a number of disaster situations.

Table 21-1: Expectations During a Sudden Disaster

Disaster	*Expectation*
Operating-system drive failure	Typically a simple recovery, given a recent backup of the partition. Restore OS from backup with ASR and force replication.
Data-drive failure	Loss of the operating system can be dealt with, but a company works hard to build a large repository of data. This data could include orders, accounting records, client lists, and so on. With recent backups, you should still expect to lose some data.
Unknown hardware failure	An unknown hardware failure takes a fair amount of time to correct. Before you can check the validity of data or the OS, you must find the faulty hardware and fix it. This process can be very time consuming and may require consultants or vendors to be onsite.
Fire	Ouch! A fire means that your server may have suffered smoke, heat, fire, or even water damage. Expect long hours of setting up new equipment before you retrieve offsite backups to restore your servers.
Catastrophic event (tornado, hurricane, and so on)	Such an event would probably require an offsite restore to get your system back up and available so that the company can continue with its day-to-day operations.
Security breach	Your first concern here should be securing data. The hackers can destroy your OS if they want, but corrupting precious data could mean the death of your company. Secure the data and systematically shut the systems down to ensure your data's integrity.

Understanding Fault Tolerance

The idea of *fault tolerance* in a computer system revolves around the concept that the computer (or server, in this case) should have the capability to deal with a hardware or software failure. Probably the easiest failure to deal with is a power loss. To counter this type of failure, you can simply use an uninterrupted power supply (UPS). But would using a UPS actually constitute fault tolerance? A UPS doesn't have the capability to run forever, so you are actually merely postponing the inevitable. A better solution is to have two or more power supplies in the server that are both connected to uninterrupted power supplies. During a power outage, one UPS can supply power to the server, while the other one is charged offsite. Dual power supplies, however, brings up a topic all its own.

Having dual components is a must for any server that has to be extremely fault tolerant. To have a true fault-tolerant system, therefore, you would need two network interface cards, two power supplies, multiprocessors, and two drives. All these items seem to be good ideas, but what good would two hard drives do? Assuming that all the data from Drive 1 is copied to Drive 2, a failure would result in you needing to power down the machine and move Drive 2 into the Drive 1 position. That's why the use of a *Redundant Array of Independent Disks* (*RAID*) and hot-swappable drives is important.

You have several levels of RAID that you can use, but probably the most common is RAID Level 5. RAID 5 requires at least three drives and provides data-stripping and error-correction information. The drawback to RAID 5 is that it requires extremely complex hardware to function. A mid-level RAID 5 controller typically costs around $500. Having a RAID 5 controller with hot-swappable drives means that if one drive fails, you can remove it from the server while the system is still running and replace it with a new drive without the risk of losing any data.

If you who don't have tons of cash to throw around — or maybe you just need a RAID setup for an individual user and not particularly for a server — you can purchase a motherboard with a built-in RAID. One of these boards just happens to be our favorite: the SOYO KT333 Dragon Platinum.

Many boards contain the UDMA/ATA133 RAID controller functionality, and with most of these, you can expect the following:

- RAID 0,1,0+1 and Span
- Hot-swapping a failed hard disk in a mirror array
- Independent use of hard disks
- Hot spare-disk support
- Disk-error alarm

Although an IDE RAID configuration isn't as fast as a SCSI solution, it is very effective and can save you quite a bit of money.

Identifying the Weak Links

We're sure that most of you have heard that your system is only as strong as its weakest link. Failing to identify the weakest link in your system almost always leads to a catastrophe. Keeping the weakest links in mind is also very helpful should you experience problems; knowing the weakest links helps you identify where to start in the troubleshooting process.

In examining your system for possible points of failure, you should start with the most obvious:

- Hard-disk drives
- Power supply
- Network connection
- HDD controller card
- Processor

Ensuring that the preceding components don't fail is a fairly straightforward process — you double up on everything. Suppose that you have a dual-processor system, with a RAID-5 hot-swappable hard-disk system running with dual power supplies and dual network cards. All this is neatly bundled up and connected to a UPS or possibly a generator system. It almost sounds foolproof, right? So what do you do if your RAMBus RAM dies? What if the video card fails? A memory problem is easily fixed by ensuring that your system contains more than one stick of memory. You can even go so far as to use a board that supports hot-swappable memory modules. Having more than one stick of memory ensures that if one dies, the system doesn't crash to its knees. It's likely to suffer some errors, but at least you should have the opportunity to shut down the system and fix the problem without losing data.

Normally, you would have a serious problem if your video card died. How could you safely shut down the system to fix the problem? Fortunately for you, Windows Server 2003 supports a *headless configuration*. You can install the OS, configure all your applications, and then remove the video card, keyboard, and mouse, and the machine still operates. You can do all the configuration by using a remote desktop or even via Web administration.

After you have considered all possible points of failure in your system and have taken the appropriate steps to fix weak links, you should take a step back and look again. Your system may be the very definition of redundancy, but what if a router goes out that connects your system to the WAN? This isn't actually a point of failure in the server, but as a whole, it affects the system's operation. In planning your server configuration, you should also keep the network configuration in mind. The more that you look at and consider it, the better off you are when problems arise.

Recovery from Backup

Should the worst happen and a server goes down, one of the most important things that you must do is restore your system from a backup. Not only is this a time-consuming process, but you're probably under stress to get it done as quickly as possible. Without a computer system, most corporations are generally helpless. In this state, orders generally cannot be placed from vendors, nor can they be provided to customers. Time is money.

The restore process generally happens in two phases: the restoration of the base operating system and the restoration of configuration files such as Active Directory information.

Recovery of base operating systems

Restoration of the base operating system should be the second step that you take in the event that your server crashes. The first item obviously is the repair of the component that brought the system down in the first place — assuming, of course, that the reason for the crash was hardware related.

Restoring the operating system is really just a four-step process, as follows:

1. Boot to the Windows Server 2003 CD.
2. Press F2 during the CD boot process to initiate the Automated System Recovery (ASR) process.
3. Provide the Automated System Recovery floppy disk.
4. Choose the location of the full-system backup.

These steps assume that you have created a backup set by using the Microsoft-provided Backup application. Immediately after a full-system backup, you are prompted to insert a blank formatted floppy disk where three files will be placed: `asr.sif`, `asrpnp.sif`, and `setup.log`. A brief explanation of each file is given in Table 21-2.

Table 21-2: Files Created by a Full Backup for an Automatic System Recovery

File name	Description
`asr.sif`	This file contains the server name, Windows directory location, MBR information, partition information, and the location of recovery media.
`asrpnp.sif`	This file contains a list of plug-and-play items. It includes the monitor, hard-disk drives, BIOS, and so on.
`setup.log`	This file contains a list of all the files that were backed up during the backup process.

Now, take a closer look at this process. The more you understand about how the ASR functions, the more efficient you become at restoring a system, should such a procedure be required.

Note

Intentionally downing a server just to practice the art of restoration with ASR is a bit time consuming and may not be justifiable for your network. A smart approach should you want the practice is to use VMWare to install Windows Server 2003. You can then set up the OS, perform a backup, delete the OS from the drive, and perform an ASR for training purposes.

The first step on the road to recovery isn't actually attending AA—it's using the F2 key. After you boot to the Windows Server 2003 CD, you see a message for five seconds at the bottom of the screen that prompts you to press F2 to launch an Automated System Recovery, as shown in Figure 21-1.

An Automated System Recovery is the key to it all and enables the Windows installation to install a backup rather than a blank, new installation of Windows Server 2003. This type of installation is actually handled in 12 obvious steps. Rather than boring you with six pages of screen captures, we merely list the steps here. During restores, you can refer to the following list and anticipate what happens next:

1. F2 is pressed during the CD boot process to initiate ASR.
2. Partition information is gathered so that the drive can be partitioned and formatted.
3. The disks are examined.
4. A list of files to be copied is generated.
5. File copying takes place.
6. The configuration is initialized.
7. The system automatically reboots.
8. A graphical Windows Setup begins.
9. The ASR Wizard opens.
10. ASR enables you to select the backup set that must be restored.
11. Files are restored and the system is rebooted.
12. On reboot, the system is restored to its original state.

This list of events doesn't take into consideration any custom drives that may be needed for backup devices and is instead based on a backup set located on a secondary drive.

Figure 21-1: Pressing the F2 key begins the process of an Automatic System Recovery.

Recovery of configuration

Configuration information of the server — such as screen resolution, folder views, share information and so on — is all restored during an ASR. You're highly likely, however, to find that your Active Directory information is outdated. Backing up Active Directory information doesn't make a lot of sense if several servers are on your network. If additional servers are in place, all the information is updated after replication takes place. If you have only one server, first and foremost, shame on you! Second, you can rest assured that all Active Directory information is backed up during a full backup using the Microsoft Backup application.

Mirrored Services, Data, and Hardware

Mirroring data — that is, copying it to another drive in the same form — can be accomplished by using RAID, as we discuss in the section "Understanding Fault Tolerance," earlier in this chapter. To have a truly redundant system, you must mirror everything within your system — dual network cards, multiple processors, redundant power supplies, and so on. Without this type of hardware, your system is very prone to failure and down time.

Recovery of Key Services

Recovering key services can prove somewhat of a nightmare depending on the topology of your network. The following sections discuss some of the services that you may need to recover and what you should expect during the recovery process. All possible scenarios cannot be explained here because what you may face really depends on how your network is set up. We could assume that you are running all services on one server, in which case restoring a full backup to your server would fix everything. We doubt that this is the case, however, and expect that your services are spread across many machines.

Active Directory

A full backup of a server includes all Active Directory information. Whew! If your full backups are few and far between, make sure that you capture the System State on the incremental backups. The System State backup includes the Active Directory information. Without this information, you have a long road ahead in restoring the server to operating order.

If you happen to have more than one server in your forest, a full backup or System State isn't all that necessary. After you have reinstalled the server OS and the system is somewhat operational, all you have to do is add the server to the domain tree again and then kick back and wait for replication. If you can't just wait around for this to happen, you can use the tools provided to forcefully start the replication process.

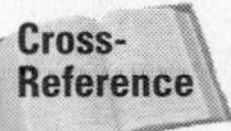

You can find more information on manually starting the replication process in Chapter 12.

Because the amount of data in Active Directory can be rather large, a full replication may seriously inhibit your network bandwidth. To make a good decision on what route to take, you need to weigh the amount of time required to restore a backup of this data against that of a full replication of your server.

DNS

By default, all DNS files are stored in `C:\windows\system32\dns`. Incremental backups should catch any changes made to these files. If you have enabled dynamic updates to DNS, you quite often see this file change. After you have restored the operating system on your server, you should ensure that the DNS server is indeed installed. If it wasn't installed during your last backup, you can perform a reinstall by using the Configure Your Server Wizard. Accept all defaults on this wizard, which are of little consequence anyway because you overwrite the configuration files with backups.

After you have verified that the DNS server is installed and running, you need only restore all `*.dns` files from your backup media. After you have restored these files, you need to shut down the DNS server and restart it to see the configuration changes.

Registry

The registry is probably one of the easiest things to restore after you have recovered from a server failure. A full backup of a server always includes registry information. Because incremental backups look at all changed files, the registry gets backed up then, too. If your registry does not appear to have changed since the last backup, something is definitely wrong — the registry is constantly changing, regardless of anything actually happening on the server.

Crash Analysis

After a crash has occurred, the single most-important thing you can do after you have restored the server and fixed all problems is to analyze the crash. If you don't fully understand what brought the system down in the first place, you cannot effectively prevent another crash from happening in the future.

Never take anything for granted in performing a crash analysis. Just because your RAID-5 array died doesn't actually mean that it was the root of the problem — it could be a defective cable or perhaps even the controller card. Put your CSI hat on for a few days and examine every inch of the system until you are 100 percent sure that you can explain the cause. After you have come up with a valid explanation, try to back it up. With this said, assuming, for example, that a cable was to blame, use the same cable in a new machine and try to get the system to crash. If it does crash, try to determine whether everything happened in the same order that it did on the other machine. If so, you have your culprit.

Summary

A Disaster Recovery Plan is like a smoke alarm in your house — you know that you need it, but you don't really appreciate it until disaster strikes. With the correct documentation and backups, as we describe in this chapter, you can quickly restore servers to operating condition and keep your business running — even after a major server failure. Not only is creating a Disaster Recovery Plan very important, but practicing it and keeping the documentation up to date as the need arises is also vital to the health of your system.

✦ ✦ ✦

The Registry

In This Chapter

The purpose of the registry

The registry structure

The registry editors

Securing the registry

The registry is the core repository of configuration information in Windows Server 2003, used for storing information about the operating system, applications, and user environment on standalone workstations and member servers (non-domain controllers).

The Purpose of the Registry

Early versions of the Windows operating system family, such as Windows 3.*x,* stored most of their configuration information in *initialization,* or `.ini` files. These files were text files containing various sections that stored settings for a variety of properties such as device drivers, application and document associations, user environment settings, and so on. Windows applications used `.ini` files as well to store their configuration settings. Even today in Windows Server 2003 and applications, `.ini` files are still sometimes used for storing user, application, and operating system settings. A quick search of your hard drive for `.ini` files will illustrate that fact.

Although they provide a simple means of storing and retrieving settings, `.ini` files offer some disadvantages, particularly for storing important OS settings such as device drivers, configuration data, user environment settings, and so on. First, Windows Server 2003 needs a fault-tolerant system for maintaining its settings to avoid the problem of an unbootable system due to a corrupt or missing `.ini` file. This information also needs to be secure, something `.ini` files can't really provide. Finally, managing all the settings needed to keep a Windows Server 2003 system up and running, plus applications and user-related settings, would be overwhelming if `.ini` files were the only solution. The registry comes to the rescue.

In Windows Server 2003, the registry stores configuration information about the system's hardware and software, both operating system- and application-related. The registry also stores information about users, including security settings and rights, working environment (desktop properties, folders, and so on), and much more. However, unlike Windows NT, it no longer stores domain user and computer accounts or information related to network objects; this job now belongs to the Active Directory, as explained in Chapter 2 and the chapters in Part III.

When you promote a member server to a domain controller, all registry settings that also apply to a domain controller server, such as the desktop settings, are absorbed into Active Directory. But when you demote the server, the original registry settings are not restored, and you are returned to a clean registry. (The demotion wizard even asks you for a new Administrator password because the original account is lost.) Keep this in mind when you demote a domain controller, because Active Directory can easily outgrow the host machine it was originally installed on.

The following list explains some of the ways certain components make use of the registry:

✦ **Setup:** When you install Windows Server 2003, Setup builds the registry based on your selections (or automated selections) during installation. Setup also modifies the registry when you add or remove hardware from the system.

✦ **Application setup:** The Setup program for an application typically will modify the registry to store the application's settings at installation. It also will typically read the registry to determine which components, if any, are already installed.

✦ **Applications:** Most applications that store their settings in the registry modify those settings during program startup, shutdown, or general operation to store changes made to application settings by the application or the user.

✦ **Ntdetect:** The `Ntdetect.com` program executes at system startup to detect hardware and attached peripherals, and it stores information in the registry about those items for use in subsequent boot steps to initialize device drivers for identified devices.

✦ **The kernel:** The Windows Server 2003 kernel reads the registry at startup to determine which device drivers to load and in which order, along with other driver initialization parameters.

✦ **Device drivers:** Most device drivers store their configuration and operating settings in the registry, reading the registry at initialization to determine how to load and function.

✦ **System:** The Windows Server 2003 operating system as a whole uses the registry to store information about services, installed applications, document and OLE (Object Linking and Embedding) associations, networking, user settings, and other properties.

✦ **Administrative tools:** One of the main functions of utilities such as the Control Panel, the various MMC consoles, and standalone administration utilities is typically to modify the registry. In this context, these utilities provide a user interface for registry modification.

✦ **The Registry Editor:** Windows Server 2003 provides one tool, `regedit.exe`, which lets you view and modify the registry directly. While you'll want to perform most modification tasks using other utilities, the Registry Editor makes possible tasks such as direct modification, selected registry backup, and others.

The registry is in many ways the "brain" of the Windows Server 2003 OS. Nearly everything the OS does is affected by or affects the registry. For that reason, it is important to not only understand the registry's function and how to modify it, but also how to protect it from catastrophe or unauthorized access. The following sections explain the structure of the registry and how to manage it.

The Registry Structure

The registry forms a hierarchical (tree) database with five primary branches called *subtrees*. A subtree can contain *keys*, which function as containers within the subtree for *subkeys* and *values*. Subkeys are sub-branches within a key. Values are the individual settings within a key or subkey. Perhaps the best way to understand the registry structure is to view it through the Registry Editor, as shown in Figure 22-1. (You'll find detailed information about the Registry Editor later in this chapter in the section, "The Registry Editor.")

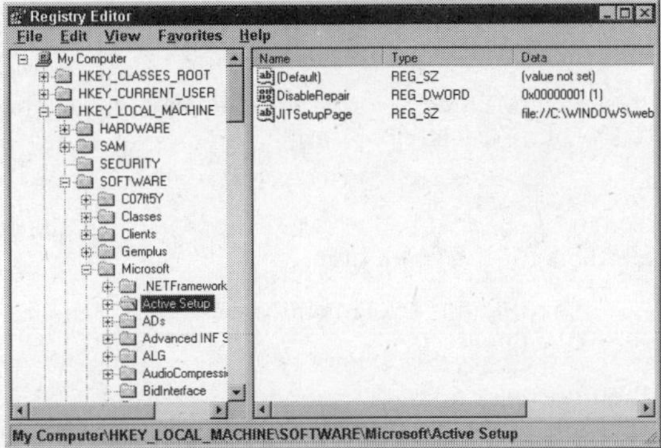

Figure 22-1: The Registry Editor shows the structure of the registry: a hierarchical tree, with each subtree serving as a primary branch.

There are two physical subtrees in the Windows Server 2003 registry: `HKEY_LOCAL_MACHINE` and `HKEY_USERS`, the former containing system- and hardware-related settings and the latter containing user-related settings. These two physical subtrees are divided into the five logical subtrees you see in the Registry Editor. Organizing the registry into five logical subtrees makes it easier to navigate and understand the logical structure of the registry. The five logical subtrees are as follows:

- **HKEY_LOCAL_MACHINE:** This subtree, often abbreviated as HKLM, stores settings that apply to the local machine, defining hardware and operating system settings that are the same regardless of which user is logged on. The settings in HKLM, for example, define device drivers, memory, installed hardware, and startup properties.

- **HKEY_CLASSES_ROOT:** Abbreviated HKCR, this subtree contains file association data, such as associating a document file type with its parent application and defining the actions taken on a given document type for various tasks (open, play, edit, and so on). This subtree is built from `HKLM\SOFTWARE\Classes` and `HKEY_CURRENT_USER\SOFTWARE\Classes`, with the value in HKCU taking precedence. HKCR provides user- and computer-specific class registration, providing different class registrations for each user. This per-user class registration is different from previous versions of Windows that provided the same registration data for all users.

- **HKEY_CURRENT_USER:** This subtree (HKCU) stores the user profile for the user who is currently logged on to the system locally. Settings include desktop configuration and folders, network and printer connections, environment variables, Start menu and applications, and other settings that define the user operating environment and UI. This subtree is actually an alias of `HKEY_USERS\`*`SID`*, where *SID* is the security ID of the current user.
- **HKEY_USERS:** This subtree (HKU) stores user profile data for users who log on to the computer locally, as well as the default user profile for the local computer.
- **HKEY_CURRENT_CONFIG:** This subtree (HKCC) stores hardware configuration data about the local computer identified at startup and includes settings relating to device assignments, device drivers, and so on. This subtree is an alias of `HKLM\SYSTEM\CurrentControlSet\Hardware Profiles\Current`.

Each of the subtrees listed previously represents a *hive*. Microsoft defines a hive as a body of keys, subkeys, and values rooted at the top of the registry hierarchy. An individual hive comprises two files:

- A registry file, in most cases stored in *`systemroot`*`\System32\Config`. This file contains the registry structure and settings for the given hive.
- A log file, stored in *`systemroot`*`\System32\Config`. This file serves as a transaction log for modifications to the hive registry file.

Table 22-1 lists the registry hives and their corresponding file names.

Table 22-1: Registry Hive Files

Hive	*Files*
`HKEY_LOCAL_MACHINE\SAM`	`Sam` **and** `Sam.log`
`HKEY_LOCAL_MACHINE\SECURITY`	`Security` **and** `Security.log`
`HKEY_LOCAL_MACHINE\SOFTWARE`	`Software` **and** `Software.log`
`HKEY_LOCAL_MACHINE\SYSTEM`	`System` **and** `System.alt`
`HKEY_CURRENT_CONFIG`	`System` **and** `System.log`
`HKEY_CURRENT_USER`	`Ntuser.dat` **and** `Ntuser.dat.log`
`HKEY_USERS\DEFAULT`	`Default` **and** `Default.log`

With the exception of `Ntuser.dat` and `Ntuser.data.log`, the hive files are stored in *`systemroot`*`\System32\Config`. The `Ntuser.dat` and `Ntuser.dat.log` files are stored in `\Documents` and `Settings\`*`user`* for systems with clean Windows Server 2003 installations or upgrades from Windows 9*x*. Systems upgraded from Windows NT store the `Ntuser.dat` and `Ntuser.dat.log` files in *`systemroot`*`\Profiles\`*`user`*.

Windows Server 2003 uses a process known as *flushing* to ensure a reliable, working copy of the registry at all times, guarding against attempted registry changes not being completed. Attempted changes to the registry, after a given number of seconds has passed or the modifying application explicitly requests it, are flushed or saved to disk. The following explains how flushing occurs for all but the `SYSTEM` hive (`HKLM\SYSTEM`):

1. Modified data is written to the hive log file so that the data can be reconstructed if the system halts or fails before the data is written to the registry file.

2. The log file is flushed upon completion of a successful update to the log file.
3. Windows Server 2003 marks the first sector of the registry file to indicate that it is in the process of being modified (dirty).
4. The changes are written to the registry file.
5. Upon successful completion of the write operation, the first sector is modified to indicate successful completion (clean).

When Windows Server 2003 reads the hive files to construct the registry, it checks the status of each file. If the system failed during a previous registry update operation, the registry file will still be marked as dirty. In that situation, Windows Server 2003 attempts to recover the registry file using the log file. The changes identified in the log file are applied to the registry file, and if successful, the file is marked as clean.

Having a backup of the registry is critical to being able to recover a failed system. Although Windows Server 2003 provides fault-tolerant management of the registry hive files, you should employ some additional procedures to ensure a valid, working copy of the registry. You'll find coverage of backup procedures in Chapter 21.

Registry hive files

As we mentioned earlier, the registry is divided into five logical hives. This section looks at each hive in a bit more detail.

HKEY_LOCAL_MACHINE

As explained earlier, the HKLM root key contains hardware and operating system settings for the local computer. HKLM contains the following subkeys:

- **HARDWARE:** This key stores the physical hardware configuration for the computer. Windows Server 2003 recreates this key each time the system boots successfully, ensuring up-to-date hardware detection/configuration.
- **SAM:** The Security Account Manager key contains security data for users and groups for the local machine.
- **SECURITY:** This key contains data that defines the local security policy.
- **SOFTWARE:** This key stores data about installed software.
- **SYSTEM:** This key stores data about startup parameters, device drivers, services, and other system-wide properties.

When corresponding settings are found in the HKCU key, those settings override settings in HKLM for the current user for certain data. If no corresponding settings exist, those in HKLM are used. For certain items such as device drivers, the data in HKLM is always used regardless of whether the data also resides in HKCU.

HKEY_USERS

The HKU key stores user profile data for users who log on to the computer locally, as well as the default user profile for the local computer. It contains a subkey for each user whose profile is stored on the computer, in addition to a key for the default user (`.DEFAULT`). It's virtually impossible to identify a given user from the SID, but you wouldn't want to try to modify settings in this key anyway except through the administrative tools that modify the registry. If you do need to modify settings directly, use the HKCU key instead.

HKEY_CURRENT_USER

As explained earlier in this chapter, the HKCU key is an alias for the KHC*SID* key, where *SID* is the SID for the current local user. In other words, HKCU points to the registry key in HKU where the currently logged-on user's registry data is stored. It contains the following subkeys:

- **AppEvents:** This key contains data about application and event associations such as sounds associated to specific events. Use the Sounds and Multimedia object in the Control Panel to modify settings in this key.
- **Console:** This key contains data that defines the appearance and behavior of the Windows Server 2003 command console (command prompt) and character-mode applications. Use the application or command console's Control menu to define settings in this key.
- **Control Panel:** This key contains data normally set through the Control Panel applets.
- **Environment:** This key contains environment variable assignments for the current user.
- **Identities:** This key contains user-specific identity information such as last user ID, last user name, and software-related identity settings for Outlook Express, the address book, and so on.
- **Keyboard Layout:** This key stores information about the user's keyboard layout and key mapping for international settings. Use the Regional Options object in the Control Panel to modify these settings.
- **Network:** This key stores data about the user's network connections.
- **Printers:** This key stores data about the user's printer connections.
- **RemoteAccess:** This key stores data about the user's Internet profile and dial-up connection settings.
- **Software:** This key stores data about the user's installed applications.
- **UNICODE Program Groups:** This key stores data about the user's UNICODE Program Groups and is usually empty.
- **Volatile Environment:** This key stores volatile operating environment data such as the user's application directory (usually `\Documents` and `Settings\`*`user`*`\Application Data`) and logon server.

Your system might include additional keys depending on the server's configuration.

HKEY_CLASSES_ROOT

The HKCR key stores data about file associations and is built from `HKLM\SOFTWARE\Classes` and `HKEY_CURRENT_USER\SOFTWARE\Classes`, with the value in HKCU taking precedence. It contains numerous keys, one for each file/document type. Use the File Types tab of the Folder Options object in the Control Panel to modify file associations.

HKEY_CURRENT_CONFIG

The HKCC key is an alias of `HKLM\SYSTEM\CurrentControlSet\Hardware Profiles\Current`, and it stores hardware configuration data about the local computer relating to device assignments, device drivers, and so on. It contains two keys: Software and System. The Software key stores settings for system fonts and a handful of application settings. The System key stores a partial copy of the `CurrentControlSet` key in `HKLM\SYSTEM\CurrentControlSet`.

Keys and values

As you've read up to this point, *keys* serve as containers in the registry. Keys can contain other keys (subkeys). Keys can also contain *value entries,* or simply, *values.* These are the "substance" of the registry. Values comprise three parts: the name, data type, and value. The name identifies the setting. The data type describes the item's data format. The value is the actual data. The following list summarizes data types currently defined and used by the system:

- ✦ **REG_BINARY:** This data type stores the data in raw binary format, one value per entry. The Registry Editors display this data type using hexadecimal format.
- ✦ **REG_DWORD:** This data type stores data as a four-byte number, one value per entry. The Registry Editors can display this data type in binary, hexadecimal, or decimal formats.
- ✦ **REG_EXPAND_SZ:** This is a variable-length string that includes variables that are expanded when the data is read by a program, service, and so on. The variables are represented by `%` signs, and an example is the use of the `%systemroot%` variable to identify the root location of the Windows Server 2003 folder, such as a path entry to a file stored in *`systemroot`*`\System32`. One value is allowed per entry.
- ✦ **REG_MULTI_SZ:** This data type stores multiple string values in a single entry. String values within an item are separated by spaces, commas, or other such delimiters.
- ✦ **REG_SZ:** This data type stores a single, fixed-length string, and is the most common data type used in the registry.
- ✦ **REG_FULL_RESOURCE_DESCRIPTOR:** This data type stores a series of nested arrays, such as a resource list for a device driver or hardware component.

The Registry Editor

Windows Server 2003 provides one Registry Editor, `regedit.exe`, for viewing and modifying the registry. Windows 2000 and previous versions of Windows NT included an additional Registry Editor, `regedt32.exe`, which provide a few features that Regedit lacked. These features have been merged (finally!) into a single editor.

Regedit lets you connect to, view, and modify a registry on a remote computer. Before you go tromping through the registry, however, keep two things in mind: you need to have a good backup copy of the registry, and you need to be careful with changes you make because you could introduce changes that might prevent the system from booting. That's why a backup copy is so important.

Also, before you start playing with the Registry Editor, keep in mind that most changes, whether for the system, user, service, application, or other object, should be made with the administration tools for that object. You should only use the Registry Editor to make changes not available through other administration tools.

Regedit.exe

Regedit displays the registry in a single, two-pane window. The registry tree appears in the left pane, and the results pane on the right shows the object currently selected in the tree. To view a particular key or setting, expand the tree and select the object you want to view.

Click Start ⇨ Run, type **regedit** in the Run dialog box, and click OK to start Regedit.

Modifying the registry

You can use Regedit to perform all registry browsing and modification tasks. You can even back up the registry by exporting it to a registry script; however, you should use Backup or a third-party backup utility that backs up other system data along with the registry. The following sections explain how to accomplish specific tasks in Regedit.

Creating and modifying values

You're most likely to modify the registry to change existing values rather than create new ones or modify keys. To change the value of a registry entry, locate the value in the editor and then double-click the value. Regedit displays a dialog box, shown in Figure 22-2, that varies according to the data type you're editing. Modify the data as needed, then click OK.

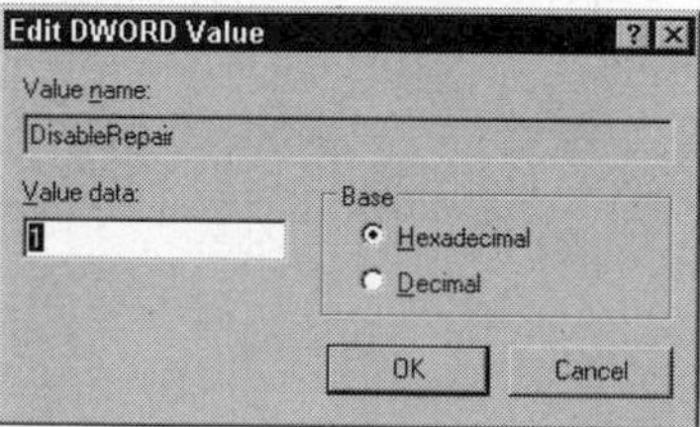

Figure 22-2: Regedit provides a dialog box tailored to the type of data value selected.

You can create a new value in an existing key. You might need to do this, for example, if a given application feature or property defaults to a hard-coded value in the absence of a registry value. Creating the value in the registry lets you control the application's behavior for that feature. To create a value, first locate and select the key in which you want to create the value. Click Edit ⇨ New ⇨ and select the type of value to create. Regedit creates a new value and names it New Value #*n*, but highlights the value name so you can type a new one to rename it. Then, double-click the newly created value to display a dialog box in which you set its data value.

Creating and deleting keys

Although you'll usually be creating and modifying values, you might come across a situation where you need to create a new key. As you do when creating a value item, first locate the key in which you want the new key created. Select Edit ⇨ New ⇨ Key. Regedit creates the key and highlights the name (New Key #*n* by default) so you can quickly change it. Type the desired key name and press Enter.

Deleting a key is even easier than creating one, which in a way is dangerous. When you delete a key, all of its contents are deleted as well. There is no undo feature, so make very sure you've selected the right key and really want to delete it before proceeding. Then, choose Edit ⇨ Delete. Click Yes to confirm the deletion or No to cancel it.

Importing and exporting keys

On occasion, you might find it useful or necessary to copy all or part of the registry to a file. For example, say you've gone through the trouble of installing an application that created its own registry section to store its settings. Now you want to move the application to a different computer but don't want to go through the whole installation process. Instead, you'd rather just copy the files over to the other computer. In this case, you can export the application's portion of the registry to a text-based registry file. After you copy the application's files to the other system, you can import the registry file into the other computer's registry. A similar example would be installing an application on several systems remotely. You copy the files to the computer and then edit each computer's registry remotely to add the application settings.

With Regedit, you can save a key and its contents to a binary file that you can later load into a registry. To do so, select the key and choose File ➪ Export, then specify a file name. From the Save as Type drop-down list, choose Registry Hive Files. Click Save to save the file.

You also can use Regedit to export a selected branch or export the entire registry to a registry script. There are other ways to back up the registry, so let's assume you want to export only a single branch (you use the same process either way). Locate and select the branch of the registry you want to export. Choose File ➪ Export. Regedit displays the Export Registry File dialog box shown in Figure 22-3. Specify a file name for the registry file and select either All or Selected branch, depending on how much of the registry you want to export. Then click Save to create the file, which will have a `.reg` extension by default.

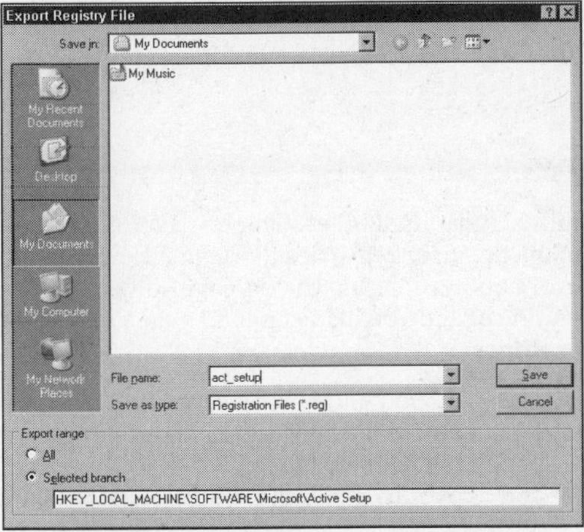

Figure 22-3: You can export a branch or the entire registry to a text file.

Tip

You can use any text editor to view and, if necessary, modify the exported registry file.

Importing a registry script adds the contents of the file to the registry, creating or replacing keys and values with the imported values. Using the application installation example described previously, you'd import the registry values for the application you want to add to the computer without running the application's Setup program.

In most cases, simply copying registry settings does not fully install an application, so importing and exporting application registry keys is seldom a replacement for running the application's Setup program. Using the registry copy method works only if the application doesn't create user-specific settings or perform other, non-registry modifications during installation.

You have two ways to import a registry file: import it in Regedit or simply double-click a registry script. To import a key in Regedit, choose File ⇨ Import and select a registry file. Locate and select the text file, then click Open. Regedit loads the registry file and applies its settings. Changes take effect immediately. In addition, double-clicking a registry script file causes Windows Server 2003 to incorporate into the registry the settings stored in the file (after prompting you to confirm).

You also can choose Start ⇨ Run and enter the name of the registry file to import the file's settings into the registry.

Editing a remote registry

You can edit the registry of a remote computer, subject to your permissions and rights on the remote computer, as well as how the remote system is configured. To open the registry from another computer in Regedit, click File ⇨ Connect Network Registry and specify the computer name or browse for it. The registry for the remote computer appears as a separate branch in the tree pane. You can view and modify settings just as you would for the local computer, although the tree includes only the HCLM and HKU keys for the remote computer; the others are not displayed. When you're finished, click File ⇨ Disconnect Network Registry, and the computer's registry disappears from the tree. You can connect to multiple remote systems concurrently, if needed.

Loading and unloading hives

Regedit provides the ability to load and unload individual hives, which is useful for managing individual hives from another system or managing user registries. For example, you might use Regedit to edit the hive of a system that won't boot, repairing the damage so you can replace the hive on the target system and get it running again. You also can load a user's copy of `Ntuser.dat` to modify the user's registry settings.

Loading a hive affects only the HKLM or HKU keys, so you must first select one of those keys before loading the hive. The hive comes in as a subkey of the selected hive rather than replacing the existing key of the same name (you specify the name for the new hive). You can modify the settings in the key, then unload the hive and copy it to the target system, if necessary.

To load a hive, open Regedit and choose File ⇨ Load Hive. Regedit prompts you for the location and name of the previously saved hive. Select the file and click Open. Specify a name for the key under which the hive will reside and click OK. To unload a hive, select File ⇨ Unload Hive.

Securing the Registry

As you've probably surmised at this point, the registry is a critical part of the Windows Server 2003 operating system. It also can present a security risk since virtually every setting for the OS and applications resides in the registry. For that reason, you might want to apply tighter security to certain keys in the registry to prevent unauthorized access that could potentially give a remote user or hacker the ability to change settings that would grant him or her access or cause damage. You also can prevent remote administration of a registry and protect the registry in other ways. This section of the chapter explains your options.

Preventing access to the registry

Perhaps the best way to protect the registry from unauthorized changes is to keep users out of it altogether. In the case of a server, keeping the server physically secure and granting only administrators the right to log on locally is the first step. For other systems, or where that isn't practical for a given server, you can secure the Registry Editor. Either remove the Registry Editor from the target system or configure the permissions on `Regedit.exe` to deny permission to execute for all except those who should have access. If you've removed the Registry Editor from a system and need to modify its registry, you can do so remotely from another computer that does contain a Registry Editor. See the section, "Securing Remote Registry Access," later in this chapter if you want to prevent remote editing of the registry.

Applying permissions to registry keys

Another way to protect the registry or portions thereof is to apply permissions on individual keys to restrict access to those keys. In this way, you can allow certain users or groups access to certain parts of the registry and deny access to others. However, you should use this capability sparingly. Changing the Access Control List (ACL) for a registry key incorrectly could prevent the system from booting. Either avoid configuring the ACL for pre-existing keys and change only those keys you create yourself, or be very careful with the changes you make.

In Regedit, select the key or subkey on which you want to set permissions. Choose Edit ➪ Permissions to access the Permissions dialog box (Figure 22-4). Add and remove users and groups as needed, then set permissions for each as needed. For more information about setting permissions, see Chapter 27.

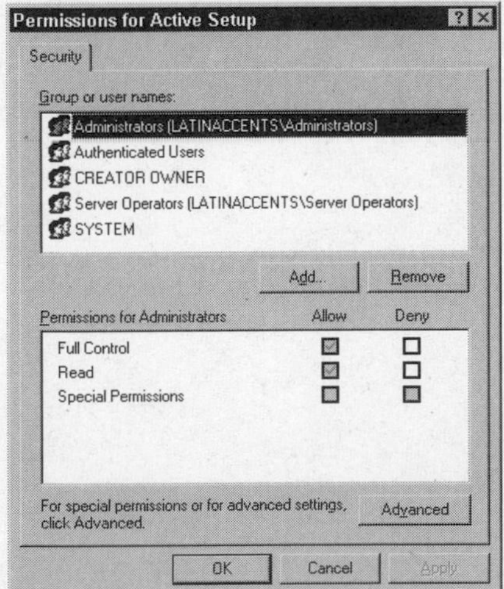

Figure 22-4: Use the Permissions dialog box to configure access permissions on registry keys.

Auditing registry access

If you do allow access to a system's registry, you might consider auditing registry access to track who is accessing the registry and what they're doing. Although you could audit all access to the registry, that would generate a potentially huge amount of load on the server. So, consider auditing only success or failure in modifying a key or value.

To enable auditing of the registry, you first have to enable auditing on the target system. You can do this either through the local security policy or through group policy. Open the branch `Computer Configuration\Windows Settings\Security Settings\Local Policies\Audit Policy`. Double-click the policy Audit object access and select Success and/or Failure, depending on which events you want to track.

Enabling auditing of object access doesn't configure auditing for a particular object, but instead simply makes it possible (that is, turns on the ability to audit object access). You then need to configure auditing for each object you want to audit. In the case of the registry, this means you need to configure auditing for each key you want to track. To do so, open Regedit. Locate and select the key you want to configure and choose Edit ➪ Permissions. Click Advanced, click the Auditing tab, click Add to select the user or group whose access you want to audit for the selected key, and click OK. Regedit displays the Auditing Entry dialog box shown in Figure 22-5. Select Successful/Failed as desired. Table 22-2 lists audit events you can configure for registry access.

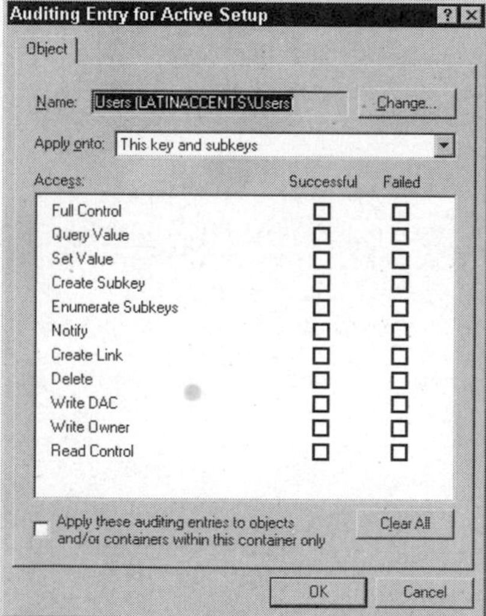

Figure 22-5: Use the Auditing Entry dialog box to configure auditing of the selected key.

Table 22-2: Registry Access Audit Events

Audit Event	*Explanation*
Query Value	Log attempts to view the key.
Set Value	Log attempts to set values.
Create Subkey	Log attempts to create subkeys.
Enumerate Subkeys	Log attempts to list subkeys.
Notify	Log attempts to open the key with Notify access.
Create Link	Log attempts to create links to the key.
Delete	Log attempts to delete a key.
Write DAC	Log attempts to determine who has access to a key.
Writer Owner	Log attempts to determine who owns a key.
Read Control	Log attempts to remotely access registry objects.

Securing remote registry access

A good security step to take to prevent hackers and others from making unauthorized changes to a system's registry is to prevent remote access to a system's registry. When a user attempts to connect to a registry remotely, Windows Server 2003 checks the ACL for the following registry key:

```
HKLM\System\CurrentControlSet\Control\SecurePipeServers\winreg
```

If this key is missing, all users can access the registry subject to the permissions assigned to individual keys. If the key exists, Windows Server 2003 checks the permissions on the key to determine whether or not the remote user can gain access to the registry (and levels of access). Individual keys then determine what these remote users can do with a given key. So, `winreg` is the first line of defense, and individual key ACLs are the second line of defense. If you want to prevent all remote access to the registry, make sure you set the permissions on the `winreg` key accordingly.

Summary

Despite the towering authority of Active Directory at the domain level, the registry still forms the repository of essentially all data that determines the Windows Server 2003 configuration for hardware, the operating system, and applications. Although you can modify the registry directly, most changes can and should be accomplished through the Control Panel or other administration tools for OS- and hardware-related settings, and through applications for each application's registry settings.

When you do need to modify the registry, you can use the Registry Editor (Regedit) to do so. You can use Regedit to view and modify the registry, as well as perform additional tasks such as loading an individual hive from another computer.

Security on the registry is also important. Restricting registry access is important to secure a system from local and remote viewing and modification of the registry. You can apply permissions on individual keys through Regedit and apply permissions to `HKLM\System\CurrentControlSet\Control\SecurePipeServers\winreg` to prevent unauthorized remote access to a system's registry. Auditing of registry access lets you track who is accessing the registry and the tasks they're performing on it.

✦ ✦ ✦

Auditing Windows Server 2003

✦ ✦ ✦ ✦

In This Chapter

Discovering how auditing works and why to use it

Configuring policies for auditing

Examining the audit reports

Enabling auditing — effective strategies for specific scenarios

✦ ✦ ✦ ✦

Auditing provides a means of tracking all events in Windows 2003 to monitor system access and ensure system security. It is a critical tool for ensuring security but can overwhelm a server if not configured and used correctly. In this chapter, we explain how and why you should implement auditing and provide some specific tips on how to configure and use auditing for different situations. As you read through the chapter, keep in mind that auditing is just one weapon in your security arsenal. Locking down the server, using firewalls, and other security-management tools are even more important.

Auditing Overview

In Windows 2003, *auditing* provides a means of tracking events and is an important facet of security for individual computers as well as the enterprise. Microsoft defines an *event* as any significant occurrence in the operating system or an application that requires users (particularly administrators) to be notified. Events are recorded in *event logs* that you can manage by using the Event Viewer console snap-in.

Auditing enables you to track specific events. More specifically, auditing enables you to track the *success* or *failure* of specific events. You may, for example, audit logon attempts, tracking who succeeds in logging on (and when) and who fails at logging on. Or you may audit object access on a given folder or file, tracking who uses it and the tasks that they perform on it. You can track an overwhelming variety of events in Windows 2003, as you learn in the section, "Configuring Auditing," later in this chapter.

Windows 2003 provides several categories of events that you can audit. The following list names these event categories and describes what they enable you to do:

✦ **Account Logon Events:** Track user logon and logoff via a user account.

✦ **Account Management:** Track when a user account or group is created, changed, or deleted; a user account is renamed, enabled, or disabled; or a password is set or changed.

✦ **Directory Service Access:** Track access to Active Directory.

✦ **Logon Events:** Track nonlocal authentication events such as network use of a resource or a remote service that is logging on by using the local System account.

✦ **Object Access:** Track when objects are accessed and the type of access performed — for example, track use of a folder, file, printer, and so on. Configure auditing of specific events through the object's properties (such as the Security tab for a folder or file).

✦ **Policy Change:** Track changes to user rights or audit policies.

✦ **Privilege Use:** Track when a user exercises a right other than those associated with logon and logoff.

✦ **Process Tracking:** Track events related to process execution, such as program execution.

✦ **System Events:** Track such system events as restart, startup, shutdown, or events that affect system security or the Security Log.

Within each category, you find several different types of events — some common and some specific to the objects or events being edited. If you audit registry access, for example, the events are very specific to the registry. So rather than cover every possible event that can be audited, this chapter explains how to enable and configure auditing and looks at specific cases and how auditing improves security and monitoring in those cases.

Configuring Auditing

Configuring auditing can be either a one- or two-step process, depending on the type of events for which you're configuring auditing. For all but object access, enabling auditing simply requires that you define the audit policy for the given audit category. You have an additional step for object-access auditing, however — configuring auditing for specific objects. Enabling auditing for the policy *Audit object access*, for example, doesn't actually cause any folders or files to be audited. Instead, you must configure each folder or file individually for auditing.

Enabling audit policies

Before you begin auditing specific events, you need to enable auditing for that event's category. You configure auditing through the computer's local security policy, group policy, or both. If domain audit policies are defined, they override local audit policies. This chapter assumes that you're configuring auditing through the domain security policy. If you need to configure auditing through local policies, use the Local Security Policy console to enable auditing. To configure auditing through the domain security policy, follow these steps:

1. Choose Start ➪ Administrative Tools ➪ Domain Security Policy.
2. Open the Local Policies/Audit Policy branch. As Figure 23-1 shows, each audit policy category appears with its effective setting.

If you want to configure auditing on the Domain Controllers OU for the local domain, open the Domain Controller Security Policy console from the Administrative Tools folder.

3. Double-click a policy in the right pane to display its settings in a dialog box (see Figure 23-2). You can enable the auditing of both Success and Failure of events in the selected category. You may, for example, audit successful logons to track who is using a given system and when. You may also track unsuccessful logons to track attempts at unauthorized use of a system.
4. Select Success, Failure, or both, as desired, and then click OK.

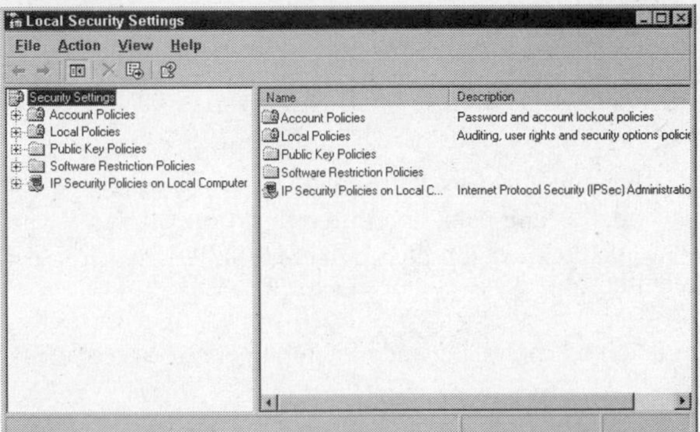

Figure 23-1: Use either the local security policy or domain policy to enable auditing.

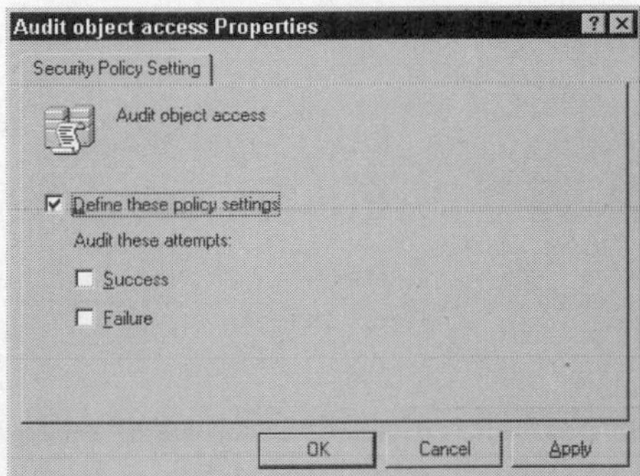

Figure 23-2: Select the types of events (Success or Failure) for which you want to enable auditing.

After you configure each category as you want, close the security policy console. See the following section if you're configuring the auditing of object access. Otherwise, audit events begin appearing in the Security Log. Make sure that you configure the Security Log's size and overflow behavior to accommodate the audit events. You can configure the log and view it in the Event Viewer, which is located in the Administrative Tools folder.

Auditing object access

The second step in configuring object-access auditing is to enable auditing on the individual objects that you want to monitor, such as folders, files, registry keys, and so on. You typically configure the objects where you find them in the user interface, such as in Explorer for folders and files, in the Printers folder for printers, and in `Regedit` for the registry keys. The types of events that you can audit for a given object depend on the object itself. Events for file access, for example, are different from events for registry-key access. To configure auditing for a folder or file, follow these steps:

1. Open Windows Explorer and then locate the folder or file. Right-click the object, and choose Properties from the context menu to view its property sheet.
2. Click the Security tab and then click Advanced to open the Advanced Security Settings dialog box.
3. Click the Auditing tab of the Advanced Security Settings dialog box to open the Auditing page and then click Add. Select a user, computer, or group that you want to audit, and click OK. Windows 2003 displays an object dialog box that lists the events that you can audit for the selected object (see Figure 23-3).

See Chapter 28 for more information on controlling and monitoring printer access.

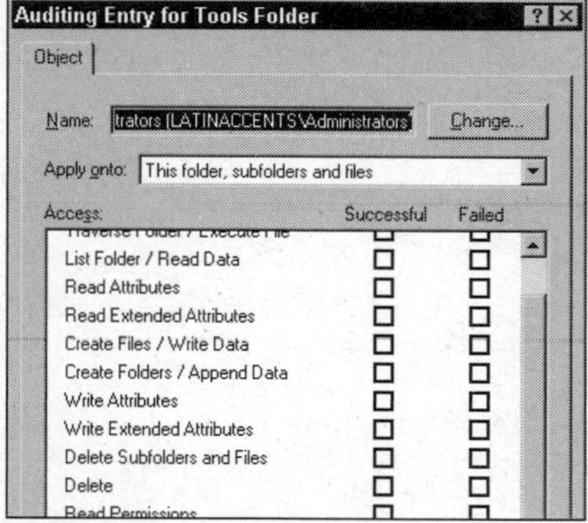

Figure 23-3: Select the Successful or Failed check box as needed to configure auditing for each event type for the selected object.

4. Select Successful for a given event if you want to record the successful completion of the event. Select Failed to monitor failed attempts. Selecting the Apply These Auditing Entries to Objects and/or Containers Within This Container Only check box applies auditing to only the contents of the selected container (such as the files in the selected folder). The contents of subfolders are audited unless this option is selected. After you're satisfied with the audit event selections, click OK.

As you're defining the audit policy for a selected object, keep in mind that you could potentially generate a huge number of events in the Security Log. Unless you have a specific reason to audit success on a given event, you should consider auditing only failure to reduce traffic to the log and load on the computer. Auditing failed access is typically most useful for tracking attempts at unauthorized access.

Repeat the preceding steps to add other users, groups, or computers to the list. In the Advanced Security Settings dialog box (see Figure 23-4), you find the following two options that control how auditing entries are affected by the parent object and how they affect child objects:

- ✦ **Allow Inheritable Auditing Entries from the Parent to Propagate to This Object and All Child Objects:** Select this option if you want auditing properties to be inherited by the current object from its parent object. Deselect this option to prevent audit properties from being inherited.

✦ **Replace Auditing Entries on All Child Objects with Entries Shown Here That Apply to Child Objects:** Select this option to clear and audit properties configured within child objects (such as subfolders) and to enable the audit properties for the current object to propagate to child objects.

Close the object's property sheets after you finish defining the audit policy for the object. Auditing begins immediately.

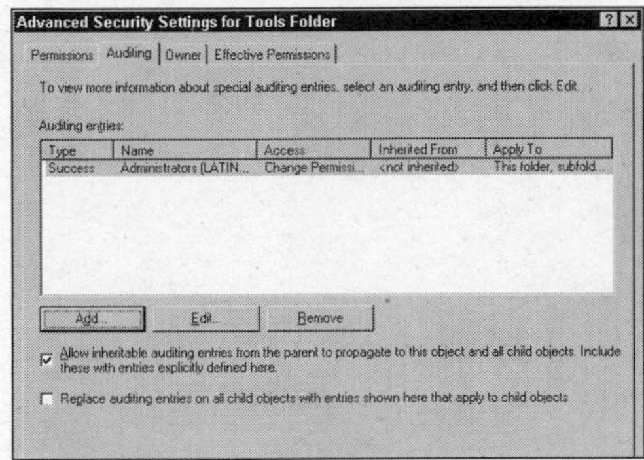

Figure 23-4: Use the Auditing tab of the Advanced Security Settings dialog box to configure auditing for a selected object.

Examining the Audit Reports

Windows 2003 records audited events to the Windows 2003 Security Log. You can use the Event Viewer console snap-in to view the event logs, save logs as log files for future viewing, and save the logs in either tab- or comma-delimited formats.

Using the Event Viewer

You can use the Event Viewer to view and manage the event logs. In addition to the Security Log, you can manage the Application and System Logs, as well as any additional logs created by Windows 2003 services or applications. By default, the Event Viewer displays the logs dynamically, meaning that new events are added to a log as you're viewing it. You also can save a log to disk to use as a benchmark or simply to archive a log before clearing it. Figure 23-5 shows the Security Log in the Event Viewer.

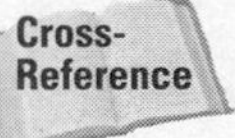

For detailed information on the Event Viewer console snap-in, including how to save logs and configure log behavior, see Chapter 7.

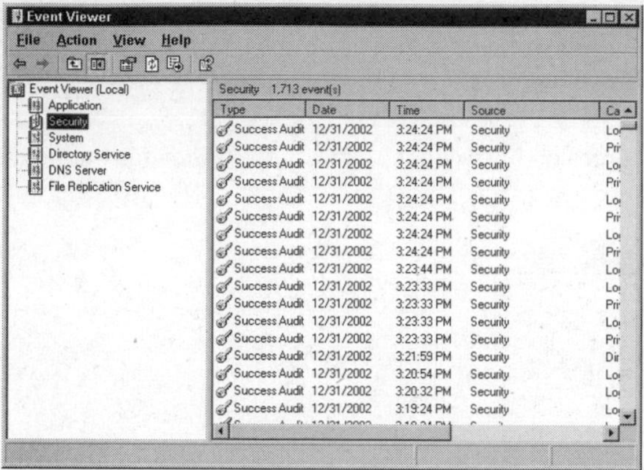

Figure 23-5: You can browse the Security log (and other logs) by using the Event Viewer.

Using other tools

The Event Viewer provides the means through which you configure event logs as well as view them. Because you can save a log to a text file, however, you can use other applications to view a log. You may save a log to a comma-delimited file, for example, so that you can import the file into Microsoft Access or another database application to create a database that you can easily organize by event ID, source, and so on. Or you may export the data to a text file and import it into a word processor to create a report. Just make sure that you pick an application that can import tab- or comma-delimited files and export the log files in the appropriate format.

A handful of other third-party tools exist for viewing a system's log files. One in particular worth considering is RippleTech's *LogCaster*. Providing a mechanism to manage the event logs is just a small part of what LogCaster does. It not only provides a unified interface for viewing the event logs, but it also serves as an excellent warning system for administrators. LogCaster provides real-time monitoring of the event logs, services, TCP/IP devices, performance counters, and ASCII logs. It provides automatic delivery of alerts through a variety of mechanisms, including paging, e-mail, ODBC, SNMP, and others. Whenever a given event occurs, you can have LogCaster automatically notify you regardless of where you are. Whether you're tracking system performance, want to be notified of audit events, or want to be warned of a possible system intrusion, you should find LogCaster an excellent resource. You can locate RippleTech on the Internet at `www.rippletech.com`.

You can also use several enterprise management tools to go beyond just managing event logs. Microsoft Operations Manager (MOM), for example, provides the capability to collect information across the enterprise from event logs, Unix syslog files, SNMP traps, and other sources to help you monitor availability and performance. MOM gives you an excellent set of tools for monitoring systems and Microsoft applications such as Exchange Server, SQL Server, and others. You find information on MOM at `www.microsoft.com/mom`.

Several other third-party enterprise-management tools are worth considering if you're looking for ways to improve data collection and monitoring. You should also consider CA Unicenter (at `www.ca.com`), HP OpenView (at `www.hp.com`), and the many tools from NetIQ (at `www.netiq.com`).

Microsoft Operations Manager is derived from NetIQ Operations Manager. Microsoft licensed the technology and integrated additional features to focus the product to Microsoft platforms and applications.

Strategies for Auditing

Although you could audit every event, doing so wouldn't be practical because you'd place an undue load on the system and either end up with an enormous log file or spend all your time worrying about archiving the logs. The following sections examine some specific situations and how you may employ auditing.

Leaving auditing off

The first option is to leave auditing off altogether, and this is not a bad option in some situations. If you're not concerned with security, you have no real reason to enable or perform auditing. Turning off auditing reduces system overhead and helps simplify log management; most organizations are or should be concerned with security at least to some degree, however, so this option may not fit your needs.

Turning all auditing on

At the other end of the auditing spectrum is complete auditing. If you're very concerned about security or shooting for C2 security certification, this may be an option; bear in mind, however, that your system is likely to generate a huge number of events requiring very active management of the Security Log. As an alternative to full logging, consider logging only failure events and not success events.

Auditing problem users

Certain users, for one reason or another, can become an administrator's worst nightmare. In some cases, it's through no fault of the user, but instead results from problems with the user's profile, account, and so on. In other cases, the user can be at fault, frequently using the wrong password, incorrectly typing the account name, trying to log on during periods when they are not allowed to, or even trying to access resources for which they have no permissions (or need). In these situations, you can monitor events associated with the given user and may even need to retain the information for counseling or termination purposes.

Which types of events you audit for a given user or group depends on the problem area. Audit account logon events, for example, if the user has trouble logging on or attempts to log on during unauthorized hours. Track object access to determine when a user or group is attempting to access a given resource such as a folder or file. Tailor other auditing to specific tasks and events generated by the user or group.

Auditing administrators

Auditing administrators is a good idea, not only to keep track of what administrators are doing, but also to detect unauthorized use of administrative privileges. Keep in mind, however, that auditing affects system performance. In particular, you should consider auditing account logon events, account management, policy change, and privilege use of an administrator only if you suspect an individual. Instead, control administrators by delegating through the wise use of groups and organizational units.

Auditing critical files and folders

One very common use for auditing is to track access to important folders and files. In addition to tracking simple access, you probably want to track when users make or attempt to make specific types of changes to the object, such as Change Permissions and Take Ownership. This helps you monitor changes to a folder or file that could affect security.

Summary

You learn in this chapter that auditing enables you to monitor events associated with specific users, groups, services, and so on. These events are recorded to the Security log. The capability to monitor these events is useful not only for troubleshooting, but also is an important tool for monitoring and managing security. You also learn how you can keep tabs on the actions of specific users or groups and monitor attempts at unauthorized access to the system or its resources.

As the chapter has explained, configuring auditing for most types of events is a one-step process. You configure the policy for Success, Failure, or both in the local or group security policy under Local Policies\Audit Policy. Configuring the auditing of object access, such as monitoring access to folders/files, printers, or the registry, requires the additional step of configuring auditing on each object to be monitored.

✦ ✦ ✦

Service Level

Preliminary benchmarks of Windows Server 2003 declare it a very capable operating system for running server-based applications. The speed increase in the operating system will appeal to many Windows NT and Windows 2000 users, and is noticeable from the moment the machine is booted and the OS starts. This will place tremendous burden and responsibility on Windows 2003 administrators to ensure the maximum availability of systems, and ensure that too much software clutter doesn't slow the system down. This chapter discusses service level and provides an introduction to Windows Server 2003 performance monitoring.

In This Chapter

Service Level Management

Understanding Windows Server 2003 Service Level Tools

Working with Task Manager

Working with the Performance Console

Performance Monitoring Guidelines

Understanding Service Level

If there is anything to be learned by this book, it is this: Windows 2003 is a major-league operating system. In our opinion, it is the most powerful operating system in existence . . . for the majority of needs of all enterprises. Only time and service packs will tell if Windows 2003 can go up against the big irons such as AS/400, Solaris, S/390, and the like.

Microsoft has aimed Windows Server 2003 squarely at all levels of business and industry and at all business sizes. You will no doubt feel the rush of diatribe in the industry: 99.9 this, 10,000 concurrent hits that, clustering and load balancing, and more. But every system, server or OS, has its meltdown point, weak links, single point of failure (SPOF), "tensile strength," and so on. Knowing, or at least predicting, the meltdown "event horizon" is more important than availability claims. Trust us, poor management will turn any system or service into a service level nightmare.

Note

One of the first things you need to ignore in the press from the get-go is the crazy comparisons of Windows 2003 to $75 operating systems, and so on. If your business is worth your life to you and your staff, you need to invest in performance and monitoring tools, disaster recovery, Quality of Service tools, service level tools, and more. Take a survey of what these tools can cost you. Windows Server 2003 out of the box has more built in to it than anything else, as this chapter will illustrate. On our calculators, Windows Server 2003 is the cheapest system going on performance-monitoring tools alone.

Windows 2003 is no doubt going to be adopted by many organizations; it will certainly replace Windows 2000 over the next few years and will probably become the leading server operating system on the Internet. With application service providing (ASP), thin-client, Quality of Service (QoS), e-commerce, distributed networking architecture (DNA), Web Services, and the like becoming implementations everywhere as opposed to being new buzzwords, you, the server, or network administrator are going to find yourself dealing with a new animal in your server room. This animal is known as the *service level agreement* (SLA).

Before we discuss the SLA further, we should define service level and how Windows 2003 addresses it.

Service Level (SL) is simply the ability of IT management to maintain a consistent, maximum level of system uptime and availability. Many companies may understand SL as quality assurance and quality control (QA/QC). Examples will better explain it, as follows.

Service Level: Example 1

Management comes to MIS with a business plan for application services providing (ASP). If certain customers can lease applications online, over reliable Internet connections, for *x* rate per month, they will forgo expensive in-house IT budgets and outsource instead. An ASP can, therefore, make its highly advanced network operations center and a farm of servers available to these businesses. If enough customers lease applications, the ASP will make a profit.

The business plan flies if ASP servers and applications are available to customers all the time from at least 7 a.m. to 9 p.m. The business plan will only tolerate a .09 percent downtime during the day. Any more and customers will lose respect for the business and rather bring resources back in house. This means that IT or MIS must support the business plan by ensuring that systems are never offline for more than .09 percent of the business day. Response, as opposed to availability, is also a critical factor. And QoS addresses this in SL. This will be discussed shortly in this chapter.

Service Level: Example 2

Management asks MIS to take its order-placing system, typically fax-based and processed by representatives in the field, to the extranet. Current practice involves a representative going to a customer, taking an order for stock, and then faxing the order to the company's fax system, where the orders are manually entered into the system. The new system proposes that customers be equipped with an inexpensive terminal or terminal software and place the orders directly against their accounts on a Web server.

MIS has to ensure that the Web servers and the backend systems, SQL Server 2000, Windows Server 2003, BizTalk 2002 Server, the WAN, and so on, are available all the time. If customers find the systems offline, they will swamp the phones and fax machines, or simply place their orders with the competition. The system must also be reliable, informative, and responsive to the customers' needs by fully automating the process with auto-response confirmation e-mails and all the frills that go along with online ordering.

The Service Level Agreement

The first example may require a formal service level agreement. In other words, the SLA will be a written contract signed between the client and the provider. The customer demands that the ASP provide written — signed — guarantees that the systems will be available 99.9 percent of the time. The customer demands such an SLA, because it cannot afford to be in the middle of an order-processing application, or sales letter, and then have the ASP suddenly disappear.

The customer may be able to tolerate a certain level of unavailability, but if SL drops beyond what's tolerable, the customer needs a way to obtain redress from the ASP. This redress could be the ability to cancel the contract, or the ability to hold the ASP accountable with penalties, such as fines, discount on service costs, waiver of monthly fees, and so on. Whatever the terms of the SLA, if the ASP cannot meet it, then MIS gets the blame.

In the second example, it is highly unlikely there will be a formal SLA between a customer and the supplier. Service level agreements will be in the form of memos between MIS and other areas of management. MIS will agree to provide a certain level of availability to the business model or plan. These SLAs are put in writing and usually favored by the MIS, who will take the SLA to budget and request money for systems and software to meet the SLA.

However, the SLA can work to the disadvantage of MIS, too. If SL is not met, the MIS staff or CTO (Chief Technology Officer) may get fired, demoted, or reassigned. The CEO may also decide to outsource or force MIS to bring in expensive consultants (which may help or hurt MIS).

In IT shops that now support SL for mission-critical applications, there are no margins for tolerating error. Engineers who cannot help MIS meet service levels, will not survive long. Education and experience are likely to be high on the list of employment requirements.

Service Level Management

Understanding Service Level Management (SLM) is an essential requirement for MIS in almost all companies today. This section examines critical SLM factors that have to be addressed.

Problem Detection

This factor requires IT to be constantly monitoring systems for advanced warnings of system failure. You use whatever tools you can obtain to monitor systems and focus on all the possible points of failure. For example, you will need to monitor storage, networks, memory, processors, power, and so on.

Problem detection is a lot like earthquake detection. You spend all of your time listening to the earth, and the quake comes when you least expect it and where you least expect it. Then, 100 percent of your effort is spent on disaster recovery (DR). Your DR systems then need to kick in to recover from preceding events. According to research from the likes of Forrester Research, close to 40 percent of IT management resources are spent on problem detection.

Performance Management

Performance Management accounts for about 20 percent of MIS resources. This factor is closely related to problem detection. You can hope that poor performance in areas such as networking, access times, transfer rates, restore or recover performance, and so on, will point to problems that can be fixed before they turn into disasters. However, most of the time a failure is usually caused by failures in another part of the system. For example, if you get a flood of continuous writes to a hard disk that does not let up until the hard disk crashes, is the hard disk at fault, the controller card, or should you be looking for better firewall software?

The right answer is a combination of all three. The fault is caused by the poor quality of firewall software that gives passage to a denial-of-service attack. But in the event this happens again, we need hard disks and SCSI controllers that can withstand the attack a lot longer.

Availability

Availability, for the most part, is a post-operative factor. In other words, availability management covers redundancy, mirrored or duplexed systems, *fail-overs,* and so on. Note that *fail-over* is emphasized because the term itself denotes taking over from a system that has failed.

The clustering of systems or load balancing, on the other hand, is also as much disaster prevention as it is a performance-level maintenance practice. Using performance management, you would take systems to a performance point that is nearing threshold or maximum level; then you switch additional requests for service to other resources. A fail-over, on the other hand, is a machine or process that picks up the users and processes that were on a system that has just failed, and it is supposed to enable the workload to continue uninterrupted on the fail-over systems. A good example of fail-over is a mirrored disk, or a RAID-5 storage set: The failure of one disk does not interrupt the processing, which carries on oblivious to the failure on the remaining disks, giving management time to replace the defective components.

There are several other SL-related areas that IT spends time on and which impact SLM. These include change management and control, software distribution, and systems management. See Chapter 11 for an extensive discussion of Change Management.

SLM by Design

SLM combines tools and metrics or analysis to meet the objectives of SL and Service Level Agreements. The SLM model is a three-legged stool, as illustrated in Figure 24-1.

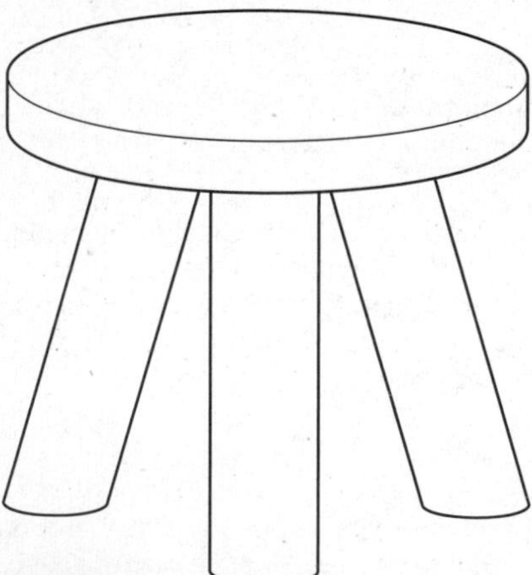

Figure 24-1: The SLM model is a three-legged stool.

The *availability* leg supports the model by guaranteeing the availability of critical systems. The *administration* leg ensures 24 × 7 operations and administrative housekeeping. The *performance* leg supports the model by ensuring that systems are able to service the business and keep the systems operating at threshold points considered safely below bottleneck and failure levels. If one of the legs fails or becomes weak, the stool may falter or collapse, which puts the business at risk.

When managing for availability, the enterprise will ensure that it has the resources to recover from disasters as soon as possible. This usually means hiring gurus or experts to be available on-site to fix problems as quickly as possible. Often, management will pay a guru who does nothing for 95 percent of his or her time, which seems to be a waste. But if they can fix a problem in record time, they will have earned their keep several times over.

Often, a guru will restore a system that, had it stayed offline a few days longer, would have cost the company much more than the salary of the guru. However, it goes without saying that the enterprise will save a lot of money and effort if it can obtain gurus who are also qualified to monitor for performance and problems, and who do not just excel at recovery. This should be worth 50 percent more salary to the guru.

Administration is the effort of technicians to keep systems backed up, keep power supplies online, monitor servers for error messages, ensure that server rooms remain at safe temperatures and air circulation, and so on. The administrative leg manages the SL budget, hires and fires, maintains and reports on service level achievement, and reports to management or the CEO.

The performance leg is usually carried out by analysts who know what to look for in a system. These analysts get paid the big bucks to help management decide how to support business initiatives and how to exploit opportunity. They need to know everything there is about the technology and its capabilities. For example, they need to know which databases should be used, how RAID works and the level required, and so on. They are able to collect data, interpret data, and forecast needs.

SLM and Windows Server 2003

Key to meeting the objective of SLM is the acquisition of SL tools and technology. This is where Windows Server 2003 comes in. While clustering and load balancing are included in Advanced Server and Datacenter Server, the performance and system monitoring tools and disaster recovery tools are available to all versions of the OS.

These tools are essential to SL. Acquired independently of the operating systems, they can cost an arm and a leg, and they might not integrate at the same level. These tools on Windows NT 4.0 were seriously lacking. On Windows 2003, however, they raise the bar for all operating systems. Many competitive products unfortunately just do not compete when it comes to SLM. The costs of third-party tools and integration for some operating systems are so prohibitive that they cannot be considered of any use to SLM whatsoever.

The Windows 2003 monitoring tools are complex, and continued ignorance of them will not be tolerated by management as more and more customers demand SL compliance and service level agreements. The monitoring and performance tools on Windows 2003 include the following:

- System Monitor
- Task Manager
- Event Viewer
- Quality of Service
- Windows Management Interface
- Simple Network Management Protocol (SNMP)

We are not going to provide an exhaustive investigation into the SLM tools that ship with Windows 2003, or how to use each and every one. Such an advanced level of analysis would take several hundred pages, and it is thus beyond the scope of this book. Performance monitoring is also one of the services and support infrastructures that ships with Windows 2003 but takes some effort to get to know and master. However, the information that follows will be sufficient to get you started.

Windows 2003 System Monitoring Architecture

Windows 2003 monitors or analyzes storage, memory, networks, and processing. This does not sound like a big deal, but the data analysis is not done on these areas per se. In other words, you do not monitor memory itself, or disk usage itself, but rather how software components and functionality use these resources. In short, it is not sufficient to just report that 56MB of RAM were used between time *x* and time *y*. Your investigations need to find out what used the RAM at a certain time and why so much was used.

If a system continues to run out of memory, there is a strong possibility, for example, that an application is stealing the RAM somewhere. In other words, the application or process has a bug and is leaking memory. When we refer to *memory leaks,* this means that software, which has used memory, has not released it after it is done. Software developers are able to watch their applications on servers to ensure they release all the memory they use.

What if you are losing memory and you do not know which application is responsible? Not too long ago, Windows NT servers used on the Internet and in high-end mail applications (no fewer than 100,000 e-mails per hour) would simply run out of RAM. After extensive system monitoring, we were able to determine that the leak was in the latest release of the Winsock libraries responsible for Internet communications on NT. Another company in Europe found the leak at about the same time. Microsoft later released a patch. It turned out that the Winsock functions responsible for releasing memory were not able to cope with the rapid demand on the sockets. They were simply being opened at a rate faster than the Winsock libraries could cope with.

The number of software components, services, and threads of functionality in Windows 2003 are so numerous that it is literally impossible to monitor tens of thousands of instances of storage, memory, network, or processor usage.

To achieve such detailed and varied analysis, Windows 2003 includes built-in software objects, associated with services and applications, which are able to collect data in these critical areas. So when you collect data, the *focus* of your data collection is on the software components, in various services of the operating system, that are associated with these areas. When you perform data collection, the system collects data from the targeted object managers in each monitoring area.

There are two methods of data collection supported in Windows 2003. The first one involves accessing registry pointers to functions in the performance counter DLLs in the operating system. The second supports collecting data through the Windows Management Instrumentation (WMI). WMI is an object-oriented framework that allows you to instantiate (create instances of) performance objects that wrap the performance functionality in the operating system.

The OS installs a new technology for recovering data through the WMI. These are known as managed object files (MOFs). These MOFs correspond to or are associated with resources in a system. The number of objects that are the subject of performance monitoring are too numerous to list here, but they can be looked up in the Windows 2003 Performance Counters Reference, which is on the Windows 2003 Resource Kit CD. However, they include the operating system's base services, such as the services that report on the RAM, Paging File functionality, and Physical Disk usage, and the operating system's advanced services, such as Active Directory, Active Server Pages, the FTP service, DNS, WINS, and so on.

To understand the scope and usage of the objects, it helps to first understand some performance data and analysis terms. There are three essential concepts to understanding performance monitoring. These are *throughput, queues,* and *response time.* From these terms, and once you fully understand them, you can broaden your scope of analysis and perform calculations to report transfer rate, access time, latency, tolerance, thresholds, bottlenecks, and so on.

Understanding Rate and Throughput

Throughput is the amount of work done in a unit of time. If your child is able to construct 100 pieces of Lego bricks per hour, you could say that his or her assemblage rate is 100 pieces per hour, assessed over a period of *x* hours, as long as the rate remains constant. However, if the rate of assemblage varies, through fatigue, hunger, thirst, and so on, we can calculate the throughput.

Throughput increases as the number of components increases, or the available time to complete a job is reduced. Throughput depends on resources, and time and space are examples of resources. The slowest point in the system sets the throughput for the system as a whole. Throughput is the true indicator of performance. Memory is a resource, the space in which to carry out instructions. It makes little sense to rate a system by millions of instructions per second, when insufficient memory is not available to hold the instruction information.

Understanding Queue

If you give your child too many Lego bricks to assemble, or reduce the available time in which he or she has to perform the calculation and assemblage, the number of pieces will begin to pile up. This happens too in software and IS terms, where the number of threads can begin to back up, one behind the other, in a queue. When a queue develops, we say that a *bottleneck* has occurred. Looking for bottlenecks in the system is key to monitoring for performance and troubleshooting or problem detection. If there are no bottlenecks, the system might be considered healthy, but a bottleneck might soon start to develop.

Queues can also form if requests for resources are not evenly spread over the unit of time. If your child assembles one piece per minute evenly every minute, he or she will get through 60 pieces in an hour. But if the child does nothing for 45 minutes and then suddenly gets inspired, a bottleneck will occur in the final 15 minutes because there are more pieces than the child can process in the remaining time. On computer systems when queues and bottlenecks develop, systems become unresponsive. Additional requests for processor or disk resources are stalled. When requesting services are not satisfied, the system begins to break down. In this respect, we reference the response time of a system.

Understanding Response Time

Response time is the measure of how much time elapses between the firing of a computer event, such as a read request, and the system's response to the request. Response time will increase as the load increases because the system is still responding to other events and does not have enough resources to handle new requests. A system that has insufficient memory and/or processing ability will process a huge database sort a lot slower than a better-endowed system with faster hard disks and CPUs. If response time is not satisfactory, you will either have to work with less data or increase the resources.

Response time is typically measured by dividing the queue length over the resource throughput. Response time, queues, and throughput are reported and calculated by the Windows 2003 reporting tools.

How Performance Objects Work

Windows 2003 performance monitoring objects contain functionality known as *performance counters.* These so-called counters perform the actual analysis. For example, a hard disk object is able to calculate transfer rate, while a processor-associated object is able to calculate processor time.

To gain access to the data or to start the data collection, you first have to create the object and gain access to its functionality. This is done by calling a `create` function from a user interface or other process. As soon as the object is created, and its data collection functionality invoked, it begins the data-collection process and stores the data in various properties. Data can be streamed out to disk, in files, RAM, or to other components that assess the data and present it in some meaningful way.

Depending on the object, your analysis software can create at least one copy of the performance object and analyze the counter information it generates. You need to consult Microsoft documentation to "expose" the objects to determine if the object can be created more than once concurrently. If it can be created more than once, you will have to associate your application with the data the object collects by referencing the object's instance counter. Windows 2003 allows you to instantiate an object for a local computer's services, or you can create an object that collects data from a remote computer.

There are two methods of data collection and reporting made possible using performance objects. The objects can *sample* data. This means that data is collected periodically rather than when a particular event occurs. All forms of data collection place a burden on resources, which means that monitoring in itself can be a burden to systems. Sampled data has the advantage of being a period-driven load, but the disadvantage is that values may be inaccurate when a certain activity falls outside the sampling period or between events.

The other method of data collection is *event tracing.* Event tracing, new to Windows 2003, is able to collect data as certain events occur. Because there is no sampling window, you can correlate resource usage against events. For example, you can watch an application consume memory when it executes a certain function and monitor how and if it releases that memory when the function completes.

The disadvantage of event tracing is that it consumes more resources than sampling, so you would only want to perform event tracing for short periods where the objective of the trace is to troubleshoot, and not to just monitor.

Counters are able to report their data in one of two ways: instantaneous counting, or average counting. An instantaneous counter displays the data as it happens; it is a snapshot. In other words, the counter does not compute the data it receives and just reports it. On the other hand, average counting computes the data for you. For example, it is able to compute bits per second, or pages per second, and so on.

Other counters are able to report percentages, difference, and so on.

System Monitoring Tools

Before you rush out and buy a software development environment to access the performance monitoring routines, you should know that Windows 2003 comes equipped with two primary, ready-to-go monitoring tools: the Performance Console and Task Manager. Task Manager provides an instant view of systems activity, such as memory usage, processor activity, process activity, and resource consumption. Task Manager is very helpful for an immediate detection of system problems. The Performance Console is used to provide performance analysis and information that can be used for troubleshooting and bottleneck analysis. It can also be used to establish regular monitoring regimens such as ongoing server health analysis.

Performance Console comes with two tools built in: System Monitor and Performance Logs and Alerts . . . but more about them later. The first tool, due to its immediacy and as a troubleshooting and information tool, is the Task Manager.

Task Manager

Task Manager provides quick information on applications and services currently running on your server. It provides information such as processor usage in percentage terms, memory usage, task priority, response, and some statistics about memory and processor performance.

Task Manager is very useful as a quick system sanity check, and it is usually evoked as a troubleshooting tool when a system indicates slow response times, lockups or errors, or messages pointing to lack of system resources, and so on.

Task Manager, illustrated in Figure 24-2, is started in several ways:

1. Right-click the taskbar (the bottom-right area where the time is usually displayed) and select Task Manager from the Context menu.
2. Select Ctrl+Shift and hit the Esc key.
3. Select Ctrl+Alt and hit the Del key. The Windows Security dialog box loads. Click Task Manager.

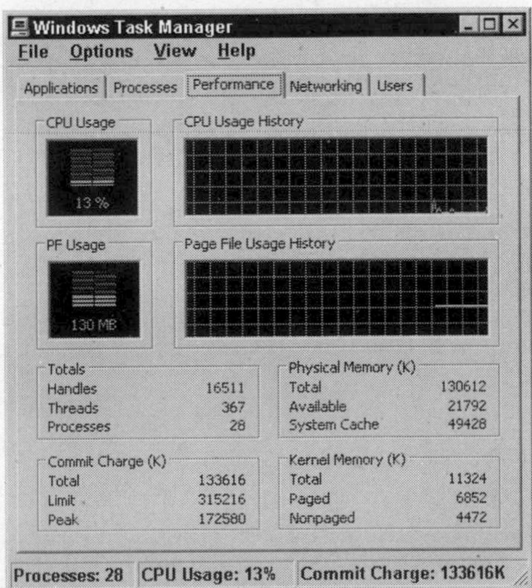

Figure 24-2: The Task Manager opened to the Performance tab.

When Task Manager loads, you will notice that the dialog box has three tabs: Applications, Processes, and Performance. There are a number of useful tricks with the Task Manager:

- ✦ The columns can be sorted in ascending or descending order by clicking the column heads. The columns can also be resized.
- ✦ When the Task Manager is running, a CPU gauge icon displaying accurate information is placed into the system tray on the bottom-right of the screen. If you drag your mouse cursor over this area, you will obtain a pop-up menu of the current CPU usage.
- ✦ It is also possible to keep the Task Manager button off the system tray if you use it a lot. This is done by selecting the Options menu and then checking the Hide When Minimized option. The CPU icon next to the system time remains, however.
- ✦ You can control the rate of Refresh or Update from the View ⇨ Update Speed menu. You can also pause the update to preserve resources and click Refresh Now to update the display at any time.

The *Process* tab is the most useful and provides a list of running processes on the system. It measures their performance in simple data. These include CPU percent used, the CPU time allocated to a resource, and memory usage.

There are a number of additional performance or process measures that can be added to or removed from the list on the Processes page. Select View ⇨ Select Columns. This will show the Select Columns dialog box that will allow you to add or subtract Process counters to the Processes list.

A description of each process counter is available in Windows 2003 Help.

It is also possible to terminate a process by selecting the process in the list and then clicking the End Process button. Some processes are protected, but you can terminate them using the kill or remote kill utilities that are included in the operating system (see Appendix B for more information on `kill` and `rkill`). You will need authority to kill processes, and before you do, you should fully understand the ramifications of terminating a process.

The *Performance* tab (shown in Figure 24-2) allows you to graph the percentage of processor time in kernel mode. To show this, select the View menu and check the Show Kernel Times option. The Kernel Times is the measure of time that applications are using operating system services. The remaining time, known as User mode, is spent in threads that are spawned by applications.

If your server supports multiple processes, you can click CPU History on the View menu and graph each processor in a single graph pane or in separate graph panes.

The *Application* tab lists running applications and allows you to terminate an application that has become unresponsive or that you determine is in trouble or is the cause of trouble on the server.

Performance Console

Performance Console includes the System Monitor, which is discussed first, and Performance Logs and Alerts, which is discussed next. System Monitor is really a new version of Performance Monitor (known as *perfmon* on Windows NT). It can be opened from Administrative Tools ⇨ Performance ⇨ System Monitor. Performance Console can be loaded like all Microsoft Management Console (MMC) snap-ins from the Run console, Task Manager, or command line as `perfmon.msc`.

When the Performance Console starts, it loads a blank System Monitor graph into the console tree.

System Monitor

System Monitor allows you to analyze system data and research performance and bottlenecks. The utility allows you to create graphs, histograms (bar charts), and textual reports of performance counter data. System Monitor is ideal for short-term viewing of data and for diagnostics.

System Monitor is illustrated in Figure 24-3 and includes the following features:

- ✦ System Monitor is hosted in MMC, which makes it portable. The snap-in can take aim at any computer and monitor remote processing on that computer.
- ✦ It provides a toolbar that can be used to copy and paste counters, purge or clear counters, add counters, and so on.
- ✦ You have extensive control over how counter values are displayed. For example, you can vary the line style and width and change the color of the lines. You can also change the color of the chart and then manipulate the chart window.
- ✦ Legends indicate selected counters and associated data such as the name of the computer, the objects, and object instances.
- ✦ System Monitor is an ActiveX control named `sysmon.ocx`. You can load the OCX into any OLE-compliant application, such as Microsoft Word or Visio, and even an HTML page on a Web site. The OCX is also useful in applications that can be specifically created for performance monitoring and analysis.

Note OCX is the file extension of certain ActiveX controls.

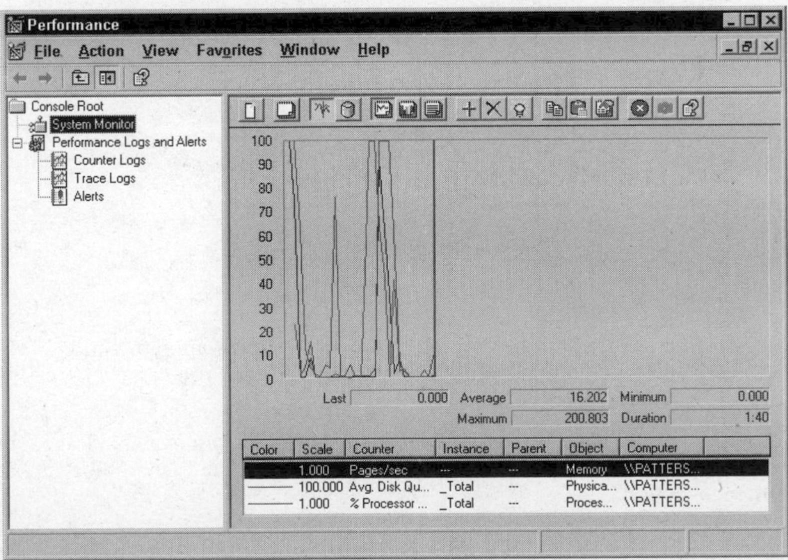

Figure 24-3: The Performance Console.

The monitor can be configured using the toolbar or the Shortcut menu. The Shortcut menu is loaded by right-clicking in the blank-graph area and selecting the appropriate option. The toolbar is available by default.

Using the toolbar, you can configure the type of display to view by clicking the View Chart, View Histogram, or View Report buttons. In other words, the same information can be viewed in chart, histogram, or report format.

The differences in the view formats should be noted. The histograms and charts can be used to view multiple counters; however, each counter only displays a single value. You use these to track current activity, and view the graphs as they change. The report is more suited to multiple values.

Your data source is obtained by clicking the View Current Activity button for real-time data. You can also select the View Log File Data button, which will allow you to obtain data from completed or running logs.

Of course, you first have to select counters. The counter buttons in the middle of the toolbar include Add, Delete, and the New Counter Set button. The latter resets the display and allows you to select new counters. When you click the Add Counters button, the dialog box, illustrated in Figure 24-4, is shown.

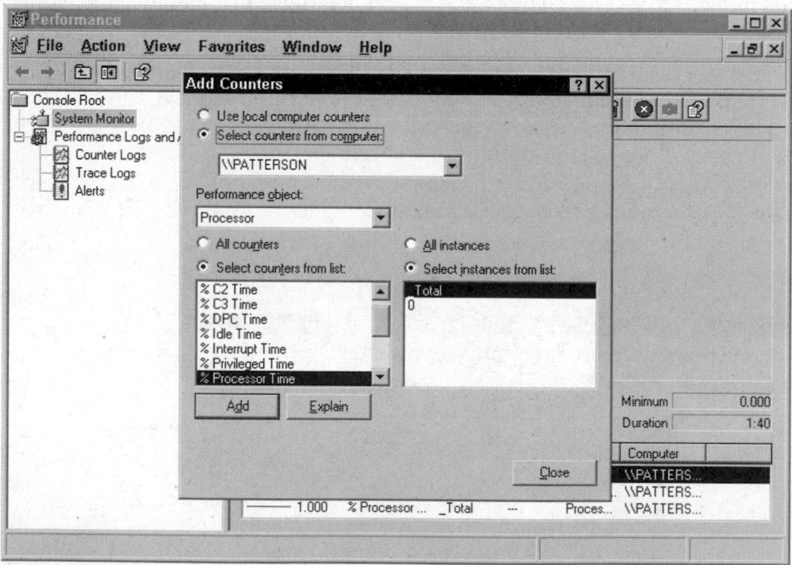

Figure 24-4: The Add Counters dialog box.

This dialog box allows you to select the computer you are aiming to monitor, and to select performance objects and counters. Also notice the Explain button. You can click this to learn more about the individual counters you select.

In addition, you update the display with the Clear Display option. You can also freeze the display with the Freeze Display button, which suspends data collection. Click the Update Data button to resume collection.

Clicking the Highlight button lets you highlight chart or histogram data. This serves the purpose of highlighting the line or bar for a selected counter with a white or black background.

The display can also be exported. You can, for example, save it to the Clipboard. Conversely, a saved display can be imported into the running display.

Finally, the Properties button allows you access to settings that control fonts, colors, and so on. When you click it, the System Monitor Properties dialog box loads, as shown in Figure 24-5.

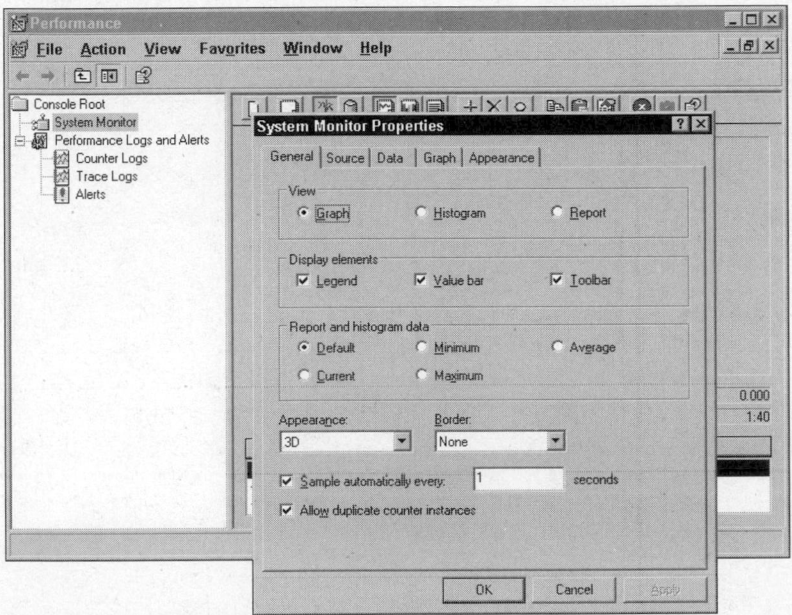

Figure 24-5: The System Monitor Properties dialog box.

There are several ways you can save data from the monitor. Besides the clipboard option described previously, you can add the control to a host application, as discussed earlier. But by far the easiest means of preserving the look and feel of the display is to save the control as an HTML file. Right-clicking the pane and saving the display as an HTML file does this, and it is the default Save As format.

Alternately, you can import the log file in comma-separated (CSV) or tab-separated (`.tsv`) format and then import the data in a spreadsheet, database, or report program such as Crystal Reports.

Working with the Add Counters dialog box, you can select all counters and instances or specific counters and instances to monitor from the list. Keep in mind that the more you monitor, the more system resources you will use. If you monitor a large amount of monitors and counters, consider redirecting the data to log files and then reading the log file data in the display. It makes more sense, however, to work with fewer counters and instances.

Note

It is possible to run two instances of System Monitor (in two performance consoles). This may make it easier to compare data from different sources.

In the instances list box, the first value, _Total, allows you to add all the instance values and report them in the display.

The lines in the display can also be matched with their respective counters by selecting the line in the display.

Performance Logs and Alerts

The Windows 2003 Performance utilities can produce two types of performance-related logs: counter logs and trace logs. These logs are useful for advanced performance analysis and record-keeping that can be done over a period of time. There is also an alerting mechanism. The Performance Logs and Alerts tree is shown in Figure 24-6. The tool is part of the Performance console snap-in and is thus started as described earlier in this chapter.

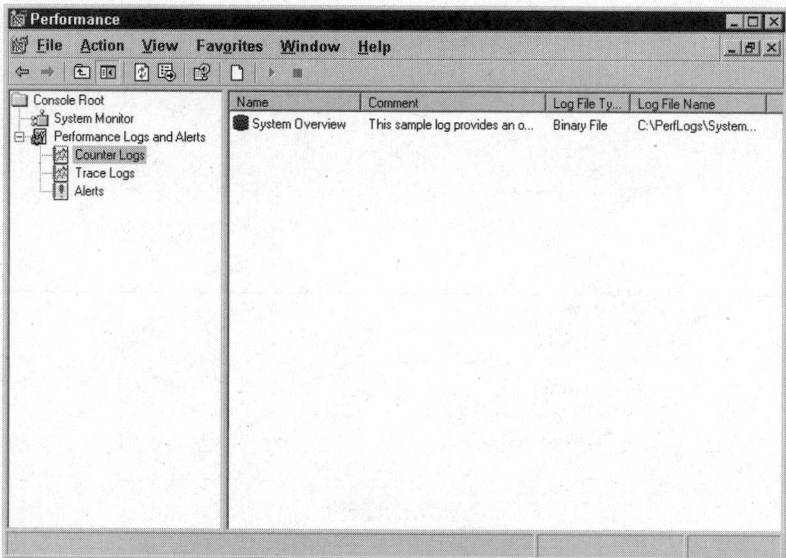

Figure 24-6: The Performance Logs and Alerts tree.

The Counter Logs record sampled data about hardware resources and system services based on the performance objects described earlier. It works with counters in the same manner as System Monitor. The Performance Logs and Alert Service obtains data from the operating system when the update interval has elapsed.

Trace logs collect event traces. With trace logs, you can measure performance associated with events related to memory, storage file I/O, and so on. As soon as the event occurs, the data is sent to the logs. The data is measured continuously from the start of the event to the end of the event, as opposed to the sampling that is performed by the System Monitor.

The Performance Logs data is obtained by the default Windows 2003 kernel trace provider. You can analyze the data using a data-parsing tool.

The alerting function is used to define a counter value that will trigger an alert that can send a network message, execute a program, or start a log. This is useful for maintaining a close watch on systems. You can, for example, monitor unusual activity that does not occur consistently and define an alert to let you know when the event has been triggered. Security-related events are good candidates for the alert service. When you are trying to catch a hacker, there is no better time than when he or she is in the act.

You can also configure the alert service to notify you when a particular resource drops below or exceeds certain values, thresholds, or baselines that you establish.

Counter Logs can also be viewed in System Monitor, and the Counter Log data can be saved to CSV and TSV files and viewed in a spreadsheet or report software. You can configure the logs to be circular, which means that when the log file reaches a predetermined size, it will be overwritten. Logs can be linear, and you can collect data for predefined lengths of time. Logs also can be stopped and restarted based on parameters you set.

Like the System Monitor, you can save files to various formats, such as HTML, or import the entire control OCX into an OLE container.

Using Logs and Alerts

To start using Logs and Alerts, right-click the details pane and select the New Log Settings option. You are first asked to name the log or alert before you can define its properties.

To use Logs and Alerts, you need to have Full Control access to the following registry subkey: `HKEY_CURRENT_MACHINE\SYSTEM\CurrentControlSet\Services\SysmonLog\Log_Queries`. This key is open to administrators by default, but access can also be given by way of the Security menu in Regedit32. Also, to run or configure the service, you will need the right to start or configure services on the system. Again, administrators have this right by default, but it can be conveyed through security group membership and Group Policy.

Upon choosing the Properties option, the Counter Log Properties or Trace Log Properties dialog box loads, as illustrated in Figures 24-7 and 24-8, respectively. The Log and Alert properties are configured, as demonstrated next.

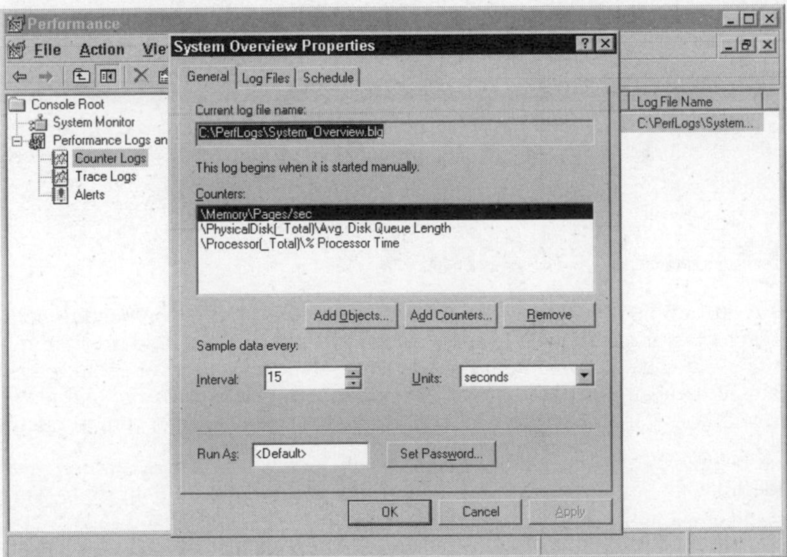

Figure 24-7: Counter Log properties.

To configure alerts, you first need to configure counters for the alerts, the sample interval, and the alert threshold. You then need to configure an action to take when an event occurs. These can include running a program, sending a message, triggering a counter log, or writing to the event log.

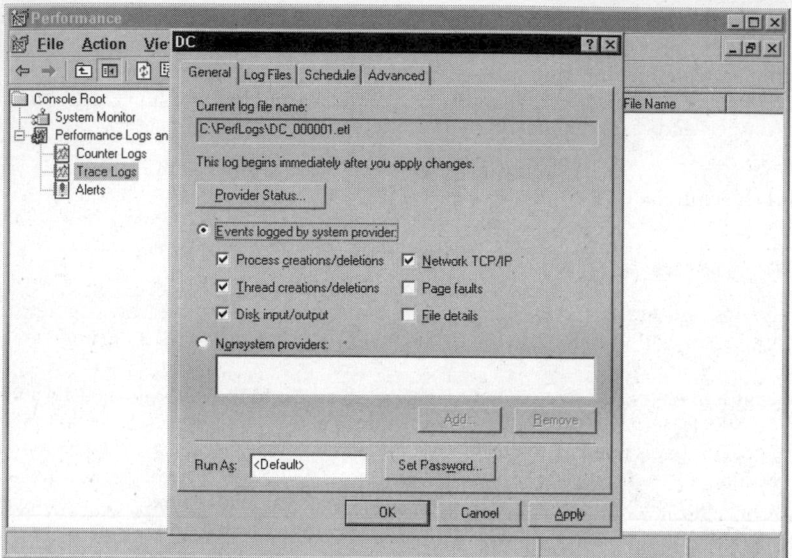

Figure 24-8: The Trace Log properties.

Alert startup can also be configured by providing Start and Stop parameters.

To configure Counter Logs, you need to set the Counter Log counters and provide a sample interval. To write to log files, you need to provide a file type, size, path, and any automatic naming parameters needed. The Counter Logs should be defined as SCV files or TSV files, text files, or binary linear or circular files.

Counter Logs can also be scheduled to start automatically, but you cannot configure the service to automatically restart if a log file is configured to stop manually. The same criteria apply to Trace Logs.

Getting to Know Your Servers

To maintain service level and keep servers and applications available, you need to become familiar with each of your machines, the applications running on them, and the resources they use. But it is insufficient to maintain a subjective feel for how a server is "supposed" to operate. Mission-critical applications, server attacks, and system failures can happen suddenly. System monitoring is thus a chore in which you should be engaged continuously.

When you first begin to monitor a system, you basically have nothing to compare it against. After a considerable amount of data has been collected, you will have a data set to work with. You will need to collect data over several weeks, possibly even months, and then based on the assessment of that data, you need to establish baselines against which to base future observation. Normal for some machines may be aggressive CPU usage, while other machines may sit idle for most of their lives.

If a system is unstable collecting data, setting alerts like crazy is only going to compound the problem. Your first option will be to determine the cause of the instability and then set up monitoring and alerts to determine the cause of the instability in the first place. In the event of an unresponsive system, your first option will be to run Task Manager and attempt to end the tasks, applications, and processes that are causing the problems.

With a baseline in hand, you will quickly be alerted to performance that is out of the ordinary. For example, if you notice that at night your mail server's responsiveness begins to diminish suddenly, you may find that the server is being hacked for its relay services, which can be compared to riding on a train without paying the fare. A memory counter would be the object that alerts you as to when this is taking place.

Your information should also reflect various points in system performance. You should note what constitutes normal on a server. For example, we noticed that a client's mail server was low on RAM and had begun to page out to disk excessively. When we queried this with the MIS, he advised it was "normal" for this time of the day due to replication services.

Therefore, it is important to note periods of low usage, average usage, and high or peak usage. Systems that provide real-time communications are good examples of servers that should be monitored continuously for this type of information.

Tip

Make baseline performance information available within an arm's reach of your server. This can be in the form of clipboards or journals into which you can paste data. This will allow other system operators to look up a server and determine what might be considered normal.

Do not expect to obtain any meaningful insight into system performance from the get-go, because the baselines you develop will establish typical values to expect when your system is not experiencing problems.

Monitoring for Bottlenecks

As described earlier in this chapter, when the system performance deviates from your established baselines, bottlenecks occur. It helps to have some guidelines, so Table 24-1 suggests thresholds for a minimum set of system counters.

Table 24-1: Suggested System Counter Thresholds

Item	*Resource*	*Object*	*Counter*	*Threshold*
1	Disk	LogicalDisk	%Free Space	15%
2	Disk	LogicalDisk	%Disk Time	80%
3	Disk	PhysicalDisk	Disk Reads/sec	
			Disk Writes/sec	Check the manufacturer's specifications
4	Disk	PhysicalDisk	Current Disk Queue Length	Number of spindles plus 2
5	Memory	Memory	Available Bytes	4MB, best not to go below 16MB
6	Memory	Memory	Pages/sec	20 per second
7	Network	Network Segment	% Net Utilization	30%
8	Paging File	Paging File	% Usage	Above 70%

Continued

Table 24-1 *(continued)*

Item	*Resource*	*Object*	*Counter*	*Threshold*
9	Processor	Processor	% Processor Time	85%
10	Processor	Processor	Interrupts/sec	1,500 per second
11	Server	Server	Bytes Total/sec	N/A
12	Server	Server	Work Item Shortages	3
13	Server	Server Work Queues	Queue Length	4
14	Multiple Processors	System	Processor Queue Length	2

These values are recommended for a minimum performance monitoring set. Some of these options may vary and still be satisfactory for your server. The following list of notes provides some additional guidance (the notes are numbered according to Table 24-1):

✦ Item 1: A threshold of 15 percent free space may be too low depending on the purpose of the machine. You can also ensure the threshold is never suddenly exceeded with disk quotas. Although not all processes can be blocked from using disk space, it is a good idea to configure alerts to signal you when the threshold is exceeded.

✦ Item 2: The value given for Disk Time is a usage period. We are saying that the disk should not be used more than 80 percent of the time. You need to check this value against the advice of the manufacturer. Disks that exceed this usage may not last long. We have seen disks easily overheat and crash when the threshold scaled to 100 percent.

✦ Item 3: The transfer rate information of your disk is usually printed on the disk. Program alerts you if the monitor reports that your rates are exceeding this rate. If the applications are hammering your disks, you should upgrade to faster technology, such as Ultra Wide SCSI.

✦ Item 4: The number of spindles is a snapshot; you should observe this value over several intervals. You can also use the Avg. Disk Queue Length counter.

✦ Item 5: If memory drops below 4MB, paging activity will begin to increase and the system response will begin to wane. If the condition continues, you will get an error message advising that system resources are getting low.

✦ Item 6: If memory use increases, watch that this threshold does not exceed your baselines.

✦ Item 7: This value depends on the type of network you are running. For an Ethernet network, your typical threshold will be around 30 percent.

✦ Item 8: You should fully understand how paging works before trying to make sense of this counter, because the threshold varies according to the nature of the hardware and the number of applications you have running (see Chapter 1 for some guidelines).

✦ Item 9: The Processor Time can be easily observed in the Task Manager, as described earlier in this chapter. Any processor usage at the 85 percent and higher mark is cause for concern. You can also use Task Manager to identify the process that is using up your CPU's bandwidth. If it is a critical function, such as Exchange or SQL Server, you might need to add another processor or upgrade to a faster CPU. On stable or inactive machines, you will notice that the System Idle Process uses the CPU most of the time.

- Item 10: This counter can be used to signal hardware problems. If the counter increases dramatically without a corresponding increase in server activity, a piece of hardware is responsible for the flood in interrupts. The hardware could be a disk controller, a network interface card, or something similar.
- Item 11: Using the server counter, you can sum the total Bytes Total/sec for all servers, and if the value is equal to the maximum transfer rate for the network, you may have some segmenting to do.
- Item 12: If the value exceeds three, you may have to change parameters in the registry. Look up information on WorkItems in the Microsoft knowledge base for a complete discussion of the Work Item Shortages counter.
- Item 13: Server work queues is another snapshot counter that may signify a processor bottleneck. You should observe this counter over several intervals.
- Item 14: The processor queue length is also a snapshot, and you should monitor the counter over several intervals. A value higher than two over several intervals requires investigation.

Understanding Server Workload

In addition to the starting points just described, you might find useful the following monitoring suggestions for workload monitoring on some standard server configurations. The following list provides a short description of objects to monitor by the server role:

- **Application Servers:** These include standard application servers and Terminal Services, or application, servers. Terminal Services are more demanding and require constant performance monitoring. The heaviest resource usage on these servers is memory and CPU. Objects to monitor include Cache, Memory, Processors, and System.
- **Backup Servers:** These servers can create bottlenecks on the network and suffer from extensive CPU usage. They may also place a burden on the remote computer to which they connect. Consider monitoring the System, Server, Processor, and Network Segment objects.
- **Database Server:** Disks and CPU are the most taxed resources on database servers. You would think that available memory is a taxed resource, but most advanced database server technologies, such as SQL Server 2000, only keep a small amount of "hot" data in memory (by caching records) for the majority of queries. You particularly need fast hard disks for database servers, like SQL 2000 or Oracle. Objects you should monitor include the PhysicalDisk, LogicalDisk, Processor, and System.
- **Domain Controllers:** Domain controllers can eat up a lot of different resources, including CPUs, disks, memory, and networks. You should monitor Memory, CPU, System, Network Segment, Network Interface, and the protocol counter objects, such as TCP, UDP, IP, NBT, connection, NetBEUI, NetBIOS, and so on. You can also monitor Active Directory's NTDS service objects and the Site Server LDAP service objects. WINS and DNS also have applicable objects that can be observed.
- **File and Print Servers:** These servers consume a lot of hard disk space and network resources. Intensive color and graphics rendering (see Chapter 23) can tax a CPU. Monitor here for CPU, Memory, Network Segment, Physical Disk, and Logical Disk. You can also monitor the PrintQueue object to troubleshoot spooling, and so on.
- **Mail Servers:** Mail servers, such as Exchange, use CPU, disks, and memory the heaviest. You can monitor the memory collection, Cache, Processor, System, PhysicalDisk, and LogicalDisk objects. Exchange also ships with specialized counters.

- **Web/Internet Information Server:** These servers consume extensive disk, cache, and network components. Consider monitoring the Cache, Network Segment, PhysicalDisk, and LogicalDisk objects.

Performance Monitoring Overhead

Monitoring performance requires resources, which can adversely affect the data you're trying to gather. Therefore, you need to decrease the impact of your performance monitoring activities. There are several techniques you can use to ensure that performance monitoring overhead is kept to a minimum on any server you are monitoring.

- The System Monitor application can be demanding on resources. You can use logs instead of displaying a graph, and then import the data into report programs and databases. Save the logs to storage that is not being monitored, or to a hard disk that is not the object of analysis. Also, ensure that the logs are not growing too big. You should set a quota and alert on the disk space, or make sure to keep your eye on the disks.
- Do not use many counters at the same time. Some counters are costly and can increase overhead, which will be counterproductive, and besides, it is hard to monitor too many things at once. What each counter consumes in overhead is available on the Windows 2003 Resource Kit.
- Tight collection intervals can also be costly. Microsoft recommends a ten-minute interval for data collection.
- While taking care not to impact available resources, you should continue monitoring during peak usage periods to obtain the best assessment of resource usage. It makes no sense to monitor a system that is idle.
- Consider monitoring remotely. Remote monitoring allows for a centralized data collection. You can also collect data from several servers and save the data to the local machine. You must be aware, though, that what you save on the swings, you might lose on the roundabout. Network bandwidth increases with the more data you are collecting and the more often you collect. Consider keeping the number of servers in a monitored group to no more than about 10 or 15. To increase network bandwidth, consider saving the remote data to log files on the remote servers and then either copy the data to the local computer or view it remotely.

Summary

This chapter introduced Service Level and Service Level Management. More and more companies and business plans are demanding that MIS maintain SL standards. To ensure that MIS or IT and IS managers adhere to the performance requirements of the business, the Service Level Agreement, or SLA, is going to be seen a lot more often in many enterprises.

As the e-commerce phenomenon continues to explode, so too will the number of applications and business processes that demand SL adherence. The customer will be more and more directly involved in the health of your systems. These include data interchange systems, Web servers, applications servers, ISP equipment, and so on.

SL and SLM have, for the past few years, been the domain mainly of mid-range and legacy systems. SL tools have been lacking on server operating systems for years. Now Windows 2003 rises to the challenge by providing an extensive performance monitoring and reporting architecture that will allow you to monitor systems' health in the ongoing effort to support SL, methodically troubleshoot problems, and maintain server and service health. These tools will also allow you to plan capacity and provide feedback to management to ensure that IT continues to support the business models and marketing plans being adopted.

We have discussed the Performance Console, System Monitor, Log and Alerts, and Task Manager in very loose terms. Our definitions have also been very broad. The number of monitoring objects is so extensive that you will need to fully understand what they collect and how they impact the available resources. The Windows 2003 Resource Kit includes a number of tools that can be added to your SLM arsenal.

✦ ✦ ✦

Windows 2003 High Availability Services

✦ ✦ ✦ ✦

In This Chapter

Windows 2003 and Server Clustering

Windows 2003 and Network Load Balancing

Windows 2003 and Application Center 2000 Component Load Balancing

Hybrid Clustering Solutions

✦ ✦ ✦ ✦

Analyzing Scalability and Availability Issues

Enterprises constantly place new demands on processing power and reliability of servers running business-critical applications. These demands force hardware and software vendors to produce economically and technologically sound solutions that are:

- ✦ **Scalable:** Accommodate drastically increasing network and processing loads
- ✦ **Highly available:** Gracefully handle failures of both individual system components as well as entire systems

This chapter presents several Microsoft technologies, described collectively as clustering solutions, which deal with both scalability and availability issues.

Scaling Out versus Scaling Up

In general, there are two ways of resolving scalability issues. The first one, known as "scaling up," describes a process of maximizing the computing power of a single system by upgrading its individual parts. This typically involves replacing existing hardware components with faster and more powerful ones. For example, the addition of one or more CPUs to a single processor system may produce a significant boost in its computational capabilities. Processing time can be shortened by increasing processor and storage controller caching or by installing large amounts of fast memory.

Unfortunately, this approach has several drawbacks. System upgrades might be expensive and inflexible. They also typically require system downtime, (although new technologies, such as Hot Add Memory supported in Windows 2003 Enterprise Server help prevent it). Replacing existing components might not be possible because of hardware or software incompatibility issues. Overcoming certain types of bottlenecks, such as the width or speed of a system bus or the number of supported processors, might require major system overhaul. In addition, taking full advantage of symmetric multiprocessing depends on the capabilities of application software, not just on an operating system. It might be also difficult to fully utilize old hardware elsewhere. Finally, maintaining a single system, no matter how powerful it is, introduces a single point of failure.

The second method, called "scaling out," takes a very different approach. It uses a number of systems, instead of one, to handle processing load. This provides scalability as well as availability. With this type of solution you can reuse existing systems, which constitutes an advantage from financial point of view. Among other benefits is the ability to perform routine maintenance procedures, such as software or hardware upgrades, without affecting overall resource availability. However, the complexity of typical administrative tasks, such as installation, configuration, monitoring, and troubleshooting increases substantially. Administrators of scaled out systems face several new challenges, such as ensuring the proper synchronization, replication, and mutual communication between its parts. These extra functions are necessary for a number of separate servers to operate as one. Unfortunately, they also create an additional set of processing tasks on each server. In spite of this overhead, the overall performance level improves, because the total number of servers increases.

Load Balancing versus Failover

Load balancing is an example of the "scale out" approach. In a load-balanced configuration, specially designed software or hardware distributes evenly requests for a shared application or service. All systems participating in this configuration are identical, equally capable of handling requests. Such a solution provides not only load balancing but also increases the availability of a shared resource. Unfortunately, its practical usage depends to a large extent on what constitutes a shared resource (for example, databases or writeable flat data files do not yield themselves easily for load balancing scenarios). In cases where load balancing is not possible, availability can still be substantially increased through a failover.

Failover configuration also uses a number of identical systems. Unlike before, though, some of them, known as hot standby, are idle during normal operations. They get activated only if a primary system fails through a process called failover.

Fault Tolerance versus High Availability

Scaled-out systems are able to handle failures of their individual members. Technologies providing this capability can be grouped into two categories: fault tolerant and high available. Level of availability is measured using percentage of uptime, expressed typically as a number of nines. For example, the term "six nines" designates 99.9999% availability, which translates into 32 seconds of downtime a year. Solutions satisfying this criterion qualify as fault tolerant.

As you can expect, building such systems tends to be very expensive. They are not only based on specialized software and hardware, but also on a very high degree of redundancy. In many situations (such as processing credit card and securities transactions), this extra expense is fully justified. The most popular fault tolerant products operating in a Windows environment come from HP (NonStop line) and Marathon Technologies (Endurance).

High availability configurations start below "five nines" (corresponding to 5.3 minutes of downtime a year) and typically occupy the area of "four nines" (no more than 52.6 minutes of downtime a year). This tends to satisfy typical needs of more demanding environments. At the same rate, purchase and support costs of high availability products are acceptable even by companies with very limited budgets.

Concept of a Cluster

A cluster is a group of servers, referred to as cluster nodes, that (even though physically distinct) can be viewed, accessed, and managed as one (or more) virtual entities. This is accomplished by using specialized software, hardware, or combination of both. Even though each node of a cluster is capable of operating independently of the others, under normal circumstances, all of them work closely together. In the case of a hardware failure of one or more nodes, the cluster still continues to function, as long as there is at least one operational node left. Clusters also support the addition or subtraction of components in a way that is transparent to the clients connected to it.

A cluster virtualizes the identity of its resources (that is, it hides its dependency on individual server hardware). This identity is typically based on either a unique name (NetBIOS or hostname) or address (IP or MAC). Such a name or address becomes part of a clustered resource rather than being assigned to one of the cluster nodes. As a result, requests from clients targeting this name or address are handled by clustering software. If multiple identical resources are available, a cluster redirects requests to a preferred node based on preconfigured settings (such as node preference or a hashing algorithm) and the current state (such as node availability and, in some cases, utilization).

Microsoft offers three clustering solutions differing in degree of high availability and load balancing capabilities. Each of them has a prominent position in .NET distributed architecture:

- **Server clusters:** Are geared towards high-availability (through failover) but also allowing some degree of load balancing. They are typically used for backend applications, such as database or messaging servers or file and print services.
- **Network load balancing clusters:** Offer excellent scalability and load balancing but limited failover. They are best suited for front-end services, such as Web, Terminal, or VPN servers. A group of servers working together in a single NLB cluster is often referred to as a cluster farm.
- **Component load balancing clusters:** Were developed specifically for the load-balanced handling of requests for middle-tier COM+ components. These requests are generated by front-end tier applications in order to process backend tier data.

A server cluster is built into the Windows 2003 Enterprise Server and Windows 2003 Datacenter Server. Network Load Balancing is available in all versions of the Windows 2003 Platform (Standard, Web, Enterprise, and Datacenter). A component load balancing cluster can be used only as part of Application Center 2000.

Server Clusters

Server clusters have been available as part of Microsoft operating systems since the Windows NT 4.0 Enterprise Edition. Initially known as Microsoft Cluster Service (or its Beta codename Wolfpack), the server cluster evolved into Cluster Service in Advanced and Datacenter Servers in Windows 2000 and Windows 2003 Enterprise Server and Windows 2003 Datacenter Server.

Server clusters provide high availability through failover with support for up to eight nodes, but not dynamic load balancing. Static load balancing, however, is possible by the manual distribution of resources among multiple cluster members.

Server Cluster Concepts

The primary goal of server clusters is providing high availability of its resources. This goal is accomplished through the virtualization of application and services. Because they are no longer associated with individual servers, but become parts of cluster, they can be owned and managed by any server. This way, if one or more cluster members fail, the remaining ones can still maintain clustered application and services online and keep responding to client requests. Server failure is transparent to clients, who, in the worst case scenario, experience only a short interruption of service.

Each clustered service or application consists of a set of resources. For example, network access to a shared folder on a clustered disk is provided by combining four resources: physical disk, IP address, network name, and file share. Because most of the resources do not allow simultaneous access, requests serviced by multiple cluster members need to be properly arbitrated. This issue is most apparent when dealing with physical disk I/O. Depending on how this arbitration is handled, clustering solutions are categorized as either "shared disk" or "shared nothing."

The "shared disk" clustering design was developed by engineers from Digital Corporation in the early 1980s and was implemented using their VAX computing platform. This solution used the distributed lock manager mechanism for the arbitration of disk access. Clusters based on this design were very reliable and offered virtually no downtime. However, they were also very expensive, relied on proprietary hardware, and did not scale easily.

When Microsoft engineers (among them Dave Cutler, who was part of the original Digital team) started working on their version of clustering, they decided to use a shared nothing approach. This design is based on the principle that any resource is, at any moment, controlled (or owned) by a single cluster node only. This exclusive ownership can, however, be quickly transferred to any other member of the same cluster. In order to maintain all cluster members working together as a single unit, cluster state information is kept in a dedicated resource called a quorum. Existence of this quorum is essential to the proper functioning of a cluster.

Microsoft's implementation of a quorum has to be stored on a disk (there are third-party solutions that support other types of quorum devices). Depending on the location of this disk, there are three categories of clusters supported on the .NET server platform:

- ✦ Single shared quorum: A multi-server configuration with a quorum stored on a disk attached to a storage bus (SCSI or Fibre) shared among all the nodes
- ✦ Single local quorum: A single server configuration with a quorum stored on the server's local disk
- ✦ Majority of Nodes quorum: A multi-server configuration with or without a shared storage bus and a quorum distributed across the entire server

An overwhelming majority of cluster implementations use a single-shared quorum. In this configuration, each cluster member maintains its own local replica of this database, residing in the `%systemroot%\cluster` folder. The database contains cluster configuration, which loads as a separate registry hive (named Cluster) under HKEY_LOCAL_MACHINE tree. To keep the copies of the database consistent across all nodes, its snapshot and transaction log are maintained on the quorum resource. A node that is a current owner of this resource is responsible for performing regular updates (which are replicated across the remaining nodes). The snapshot is stored in the file (called a checkpoint file) residing in MSCS folder and named CHKxxxx.TMP, where xxxx is a sequential number increased on every update. The same folder hosts a quorum log named quolog.log, which keeps track of the individual changes. Updates take place in regular time intervals, but can also be triggered by several types of cluster events. For verification purposes, a quorum log also records the checksum of a checkpoint file on each update.

A checkpoint file and a quorum log are needed when a cluster is formed. This takes place when the Cluster Service on the first server in a cluster starts (typically during the operating system's startup). The server checks whether the checkpoint file is valid by computing its checksum and comparing it to the value stored in the quorum log. Once verification completes successfully, the server compares the local database against a checkpoint file and updates it, if necessary. A quorum is also used by the nodes in order to establish whether the cluster is operational. When a server starts, it attempts to communicate with other members of the same cluster. If this attempt is successful, the server initiates the process of joining the cluster. In case a connection with the quorum owner cannot be established, it tries to form the cluster on its own. This, however, can happen only if the server can take ownership of the quorum resource. Using the quorum as the resource necessary to form a cluster prevents so called "split-brain syndrome." This refers to a situation where nodes lose communication with each other and attempt to independently form the same cluster.

The local quorum resource can be used for installations of single node clusters only. Obviously, such a cluster has no failover capabilities. It still, however, offers several benefits that will be discussed later in the chapter.

The Majority Node Set cluster, introduced in Windows 2003 Enterprise Server and Windows 2003 Datacenter Server, stores identical copy of cluster configuration data on the local disks of each node. By default, this cluster is running as long as the majority of servers participating in the cluster can communicate among each other. The majority is the smallest integer larger than a number representing 50 percent of total node count. For example, in a 6-node cluster, the majority would be 4, and in a 5-node cluster it would be 3. Quorum data, in this configuration, is stored locally on each node in the shared, hidden subfolder of `%systemroot%\cluster folder` (named after the globally unique identifier [GUID] of the Majority Node Set resource). The changes to the cluster configuration are automatically replicated among these subfolders for all cluster nodes. These nodes rely exclusively on network connections (because no shared shared storage device is available) to determine the cluster state. Majority Node Set clusters are likely to require an additional replication mechanism to maintain consistency between clustered resources.

Microsoft's approach to clustering, based on the "shared nothing" design, eliminates the complexity associated with the distributed lock manager implemented in the shared-disk approach. This increases scalability and lowers the cluster price because proprietary hardware is no longer necessary. Unfortunately, the "shared nothing" design is inferior to the "shared disk" alternative rival in the area of availability. If a server that controls a resource fails, that resource needs to be transferred to another member of a cluster. The resource remains unavailable until the transfer completes. The period of downtime varies, depending on several factors (such as a type and number of clustered resources or the level of cluster utilization), but it typically lasts several seconds.

Cluster nodes communicate periodically with each other via network connections, which link all cluster members together. These network connections, (preferably dedicated) are known as interconnects. The absence of subsequent heartbeat messages from a node indicates its failure. To limit the amount of interconnect traffic in clusters with three or mode nodes, multicast heartbeat signals are automatically used (providing that the network infrastructure supports multicasting).

A collection of related resources is called a group. When a server cluster is installed, a single group, called Cluster Group, is created. It contains the Cluster IP Address, Cluster Name, and Cluster Quorum resources. This group should not be modified. The ownership of resources is group based, which means that at any given time access to all resources within a group is controlled by a single server cluster only. This also means that the transfer of ownership, in case of a server failure, will take place for all resources within a group. This transfer is known as a failover. A failover cannot only result from a server failure, but can also (depending on configuration) be caused by a failure of an individual resource. The reverse process of bringing the group back to the original owner is called failback. Failback can be configured to take place as soon as the original group owner becomes available. However, because failback, just as failover, temporarily prevents the availability of cluster resources, it is possible to restrict it to a specific time window or to prevent it altogether. In the last case, the group can be moved between nodes manually using a cluster's administrative tools.

It is common for resources to depend on one another. For example a network name has little value without an existing IP address to which it resolves. This dependency has a direct impact on resource availability—if an IP address for some reason becomes unavailable, the network name ceases to function. Dependencies are restricted by group boundaries—a resource cannot depend on another resource outside its own group. Dependencies also affect the resource startup sequence—the ones that others depend on have to be activated first. Resources can be moved between groups, but if there is a dependency between them, they have to be moved together.

Each resource functions according to its restart policy. Depending on policy settings, the resource might attempt a restart multiple times. The number of the attempts is limited by a threshold value within a configurable time interval (this allows recovery in case of intermittent software or hardware failures). If all of the restart attempts fail, a resource can (again, depending on its policy) cause the failure of the entire group of which it is part. This failure, in turn, triggers a failover, which causes the group to move to another cluster node (this ensures recovery in the case of persistent software or hardware problems). The new owner will attempt to bring up each resource within the group in the order determined by their dependencies. The number of resource restart attempts is determined by the same resource policy that was used on the original node (because configuration, stored in quorum database, is the same on all nodes). If all attempts fail, the rest of the process repeats as well. A threshold and time interval values determine the maximum number of failovers allowed within a specified time period. If the threshold is reached within the time interval, the group fails. These two properties assigned to each group prevent so called "cluster trashing." This term describes a situation where a group continues failing over from one server cluster to another, wasting valuable cluster resources.

For a node to participate in the failover of a group, it has to be configured as a possible owner of each of its resources. By default, all cluster nodes are assumed to be possible owners. On the group level, you can also specify a list of preferred owners. The selection of a preferred owner is significant during failover and failback. If a group belongs to a nonpreferred owner and failback is allowed, the group will be moved back to a preferred one. In case of a group failover, if among the remaining cluster nodes there is a preferred owner, the group will be allocated to it.

From the client's point of view, resources are typically accessed as components of virtual servers. A virtual server contains at least four resources: an IP address, a corresponding network name, a physical disk, and a resource providing some type of service (such as file sharing, print spooling, or database storage). All resources that belong to a virtual server are part of the same group. However, there is a significant difference between a group and a virtual server. A group is a collection of resources that is visible only to cluster members. It sets boundaries for resource dependencies and processes of failover and failback. A virtual server, on the other hand, exists for the purpose of providing clients a view of the resources. A group can contain multiple virtual servers, although a one-to-one relationship between them is most common.

Virtual servers in Windows 2003 server clusters have the capability to become computer objects in Active Directory with the full support for Kerberos authentication (this feature is configurable). Replacing NTLM with Kerberos not only increases security, but also allows the use of features that are not possible with NTLM-based authentication, such as delegation and the authentication of connections initiated by the Local System account. Delegation is a common requirement in authenticating connections in multi-tier systems. The authentication of connections initiated by the Local System account takes place when Group Policies are used to deploy software to computers. In this case, software installation is launched at the computer startup, before any user logs on. Because source files for software to be installed are most commonly stored on a remote share, the connection needs to be first properly authenticated. The main problem with this is the fact that the installation of the software assigned or published to a computer is launched in the security context of the Local System account, which cannot be used across the network. This was not the case with NT 4.0 systems and Windows 2000 clusters, which were limited to NTLM authentication only. However, if both source and target computers are able to participate in a Kerberos ticket exchange, it is possible to authenticate using computer accounts rather than the Local System account. In Windows 2003, after the virtual name resource is registered in Active Directory, its account can be used to establish a Kerberos-authenticated connection with the client computers. The practical implication is that it is possible to use cluster-based file shares for storing source files for Group Policy-based software deployment.

Registering virtual servers in Active Directory simplifies the task of locating and referencing them using standard Active-Directory access methods (such as ADSI). In addition, Active Directory aware services (such as Message Queuing) are automatically published in the Active Directory as part of the virtual server of which they are part. Note, however, that Group Policies do not apply to virtual servers, but only to cluster nodes.

Clustering architecture consists of the following objects:

- **Cluster Service:** Is the main component of the architecture responsible for controlling cluster activity. Each node runs its own instance of the service but maintains regular communication with cluster services on other nodes.
- **Resource dynamic link libraries:** Implement and manage individual cluster resources and detect their failures.
- **Resource Monitors:** Handle communication requests between a cluster service and the resource-dynamic link libraries.
- **Cluster database:** Contains cluster configuration and helps maintain cluster integrity.
- **Cluster Automation Server:** Is the set of COM objects that can be used to automate cluster-related tasks using scripting languages.

Each of the resource dynamic link libraries implements one or more resource types. The following ones are implemented by default in the Windows 2003 server clusters:

- **Dynamic Host Configuration Protocol (DHCP) Service:** Is a networking service that provides dynamic IP configuration to network clients. Information about installing the DHCP Service resource can be found in the section titled "Clustering Network Services (WINS, DHCP)" in this chapter.
- **Distributed Transaction Coordinator:** Is a service operating as part of COM+ runtime environment. Its purpose is to provide transactional support for any activities that might require it, but for which such support is not natively available. For example, it can be used for operations involving distributed file systems or message queues. It can also be used when dealing with multiple databases (although databases typically support transactions, this is typically not the case when working across different databases). Component Services, Microsoft Message Queuing, and SQL Server 2000 rely on Distributed Transaction Coordinator for a number of their features. The procedure for creating a clustered DTC resource is provided in the section titled "Clustering Applications" in this chapter.

- **File Share:** Is a network file share or Dfs root. Information about setting up File Share resources is provided in the section titled "Clustering File Services and Dfs" in this chapter.
- **Generic Application:** Can be used for an application that has not been designed to operate in a clustering environment. Information about creating a Generic Application resource is provided in the section titled "Clustering Applications" in this chapter.
- **Generic Script:** Is a custom script written in a language supported by any of the scripting engines present in the .NET platform (such as VBScript or JScript). Script controls the execution of the application by detecting its failure. This failure, in turn, is communicated to a resource monitor, which triggers a failover. This is, essentially, the same way that other types of clustered resources maintain high availability. Specific ones are described in the section titled "Clustering Applications" in this chapter.
- **Generic Service:** Can be used for a service that has not been designed to operate in a clustering environment. Such services need to be installed on each cluster node designated as a possible owner. A cluster service is able to determine when a service is failing by checking its state with service manager. The ability to cluster a service depends on its ability to maintain its configuration data after a failover. COM+1.x server applications can be configured as services, which makes them suitable for clustering through the use of a generic service resource.
- **IP Address:** Is an IP address and its corresponding subnet mask. When creating this resource, you need to provide an address and subnet mask, and select an appropriate network adapter. You also can specify whether communication passing through it will support NetBIOS. The value of this setting is determined based on the requirements of clustered applications, the capabilities of operating systems on clients' workstations, and the name resolution methods in use.
- **Local Quorum:** Is a special type of quorum that enables the installation of cluster service when a system does not have a shared disk device. This option provides a very cost-effective way of testing or developing cluster-aware software. However, using a local quorum limits the cluster to a single node and eliminates failover capabilities.
- **Majority Node Set:** Is a special type of quorum designed for geographically distributed clusters. Using a Majority Node Set quorum eliminates the dependency on Fibre or SCSI bus distance limits. Microsoft does not recommend using this type of quorum for generic configurations but rather as part of custom solutions developed and offered by third-party vendors.
- **Message Queuing:** Is a service that provides a distributed mechanism for the asynchronous delivery of messages. It is part of the COM+ runtime environment and enables reliable communication between applications or systems that might not be running at the same time. The procedure for creating a clustered Message Queuing resource is provided in the section titled "Clustering Applications" in this chapter.
- **Network Name:** Is a name that resolves to its respective IP address (on which it depends) and to which clients connect in order to access the resources residing in the same group. A Windows 2003 server cluster has two new settings for this resource type:
    - *Domain Name Service (DNS) Registration Must Succeed:* Forces the registration of this name with the DNS server.
    - *Enable Kerberos Authentication:* Enables using the virtual server name for Kerberos authentication. For this feature to work properly, an object corresponding to this virtual server needs to be created in Active Directory. This process is

handled automatically by Cluster Service, providing that a Cluster Service account has the appropriate permissions. By default, this account has the Add Workstations to domain user right, which in Windows 2003 allows the creation of ten computer objects only. You can work around this limitation by granting to the Cluster service account the Create Computer Object permissions on the Computers container in Active Directory. You can view the NetBIOS, DNS, and Kerberos status of the network name resource on the Parameters tab.

- **Physical Disk:** Is a logical drive residing on a shared storage device. Typically, this resource would be created using a drive created with a hardware-based RAID configuration.
- **Print Spooler:** Is used to create a clustered print server. Information about creating Print Spooler resource is provided in the section titled "Clustering Print Services" found at the end of this chapter.
- **WINS Service:** Is a networking service that provides name registration and resolution in the Windows environment. Information about installing a WINS Service resource is provided in the section titled "Clustering Network Services (WINS, DHCP)" found at the end of this chapter.

Windows 2003 server clusters do not support IIS, NNTP, or SMTP Server Instance resources, which were available in server clusters in previous versions of Windows. It is, however, possible to install Internet Information Services (with SMTP and NNTP support on a server cluster) and support Web and FTP sites through a Generic Script resource. The process is described in the section "Web Server Clusters: at the end of this chapter.

Additional resource types become available during installation of cluster-aware applications (for example, Microsoft SQL or Exchange Servers). The maximum theoretical number of resources supported by a server cluster is 1674, with 62 resource monitors, each overseeing the operations of 27 resources.

Resources can exist in one of the following states:

- **Online:** Fully operational. Online resource can either be placed manually in an offline state (for example, in order to perform maintenance procedures) or in an automatically transition to failed state in case of its failure.
- **Offline:** Administratively down. Resources are also placed in the offline state when they are initially created. Offline resource can only be placed in an online state. Placing a resource in on offline state does not initiate a restart. If a group is moved or fails over to another node, offline resources are not brought online.
- **Failed:** Not operational. A failed resource can only be placed in online state.
- **Online pending:** A transitional state takes place when the state of a resource is changed from offline or failed to online. The maximum duration of the online pending state is controlled by the pending timeout period, which is configurable on a per resource basis. If a resource does not reach online state within this timeout period, its state is switched to failed.
- **Offline pending:** A transitional state takes place when the state of a resource is administratively changed to offline. The maximum duration of the offline pending state is controlled by the pending timeout period, which is configurable on a per resource basis. If a resource does not reach an offline state within the timeout period, its state is switched to failed.

The following states are permitted for groups:

- **Online:** Indicates that all resources are fully operational.
- **Partially Online:** Indicates that one or more (but not all) resources in a group have been placed in the offline state.
- **Offline:** Indicates that all resources in the group are administratively placed in an offline state. Placing a group in an offline state does not initiate a failover.
- **Failed:** Indicates that one or more resources in a group are in a failed state.
- **Pending:** Indicates that a group is waiting for its resource to switch to one of the non-transitional states.

2, 4, 8, and n-way clusters

With new and enhanced clustering solutions, Microsoft is venturing into areas occupied until recently only by high-end Unix-based servers and minicomputers. Windows 2003 Enterprise and Datacenter Servers support up to eight nodes per server cluster. 64-bit versions of both operating systems are available for servers operating with Intel's Itanium processors.

In addition, Microsoft develops High Performance Computing solutions. Windows-based superclusters have been proven fully operational in configurations with 64, 128, and 256 nodes. To learn more about Microsoft HPC initiative, visit the Microsoft Web site at `www.microsoft.com/windows2000/hpc`.

Server Cluster Requirements

Even though the process of installing a server cluster in the Windows 2003 Enterprise Server and Windows 2003 Datacenter Server is straightforward, there are a number of requirements that need to be satisfied first. Most of them are hardware related, but there are others, resulting from cluster dependencies on other factors, such as the configuration of the operating system and network components, or the domain and network infrastructure.

A server cluster requires the Windows 2003 Enterprise Server and Windows 2003 Datacenter Server. .NET clusters must be running the same version of the .NET Server, although in two-node clusters, it is possible to have a .NET and Windows 2000 Servers. All servers should have the same regional and country options.

Hardware compatibility must be verified against the Microsoft Hardware Compatibility List (HCL). Microsoft's regularly updated version is available on their Web site at `www.microsoft.com/hcl`. A copy of the HCL is also provided in the support folder found on the .NET Server Installation CDs. You must search for your configuration in the product, not component category, because this is the only way to guarantee that your system will be supported (this means that the compatibility of individual cluster node components does not ensure the compatibility of the cluster). Use identical hardware for each cluster node, including firmware revision (especially when selecting network adapters and storage controllers). In the case of Majority Node Set clusters, both hardware and software configuration needs to be certified by Microsoft.

Cluster shared storage is implemented as shared Storage Arrays or Storage Area Networks. In both configurations, each node should have a separate PCI storage adapter (SCSI or Fibre Channel) connecting to a shared storage device. As mentioned before, it is possible to install a cluster without it. If a system has multiple internal disks (such as one attached to EIDE and the other to a SCSI controller), a single node cluster can be built with one of the disks functioning as a quorum. As a matter of fact, you can build a single-node cluster even with only single drive by using a Local Quorum configuration. (It is also possible to set up a Majority Node Set quorum cluster with a single local disk, although, of course, use of such configuration would be limited to testing or development).

Fibre Channel controllers must be used instead of a SCSI controller when the number of nodes exceeds two. A Fibre Channel controller is also required if the nodes are running a 64-bit edition of Windows 2003 Server. Multi-channel shared storage controllers help limit I/O contention. Ideally, each of the clustered disk resources should reside on a separate channel. It is sufficient to have a quorum drive of about 500MB in size. This drive should be used exclusively for a cluster database and quorum log.

Typically, shared storage is configured first using firmware utilities created by the storage vendor, with the specifics varying with the implementation. For example, with shared SCSI devices on the Intel x86 platform shared storage is configured by running tools stored in the BIOS chip on the SCSI adapter. Equivalent functionality on Itanium computers is provided by an Extensible Firmware Interface.

If your nodes connect to shared storage via internal RAID controllers, make sure that you disable their write-back caching feature. Otherwise, a failover could easily cause a loss of data. This typically does not apply to external RAID controllers because the content of their cache is either shared or mirrored across all cluster nodes. In such situations, keeping write-back caching enabled improves the I/O performance.

When configuring shared SCSI devices using internal RAID controllers, proper SCSI ID numbering and termination is critical. Because each device on an SCSI bus must have a unique ID, you will need to change the ID of one of the SCSI adapters in the cluster nodes from the default (typically 7) to a different, unassigned value (for example, 6 — as long as this ID is not used by any other device on the bus). Also, in order to prevent the dynamic assignment of SCSI IDs upon startup, you will need to disable the SCSI ID reset feature (configurable usually through the BIOS utilities of an SCSI adapter). Ensure that the internal termination on the SCSI adapters is disabled and use a trilink or Y terminators at each end of the SCSI chain instead. This will allow you to shut down or disconnect a node from shared bus without affecting the other nodes. Note that using SCSI adapters limits a cluster to two nodes only.

Configure the disks on a shared storage bus as basic. Dynamic disks, software RAID, and volumes are not supported. Format logical drives on these disks with NTFS (clustered drives can take advantage of such NTFS features as Encrypted File System and mountpoints). For the 64-bit edition of Windows 2003 Enterprise Server and Windows 2003 Datacenter Server, shared cluster disks need to be partitioned as Master Boot Record (MBR) basic disks. GUID partition table (GPT) disks, which are available in the 64-bit edition of Windows 2003, cannot be used.

Boot and system partitions are typically local to each node. However, the Windows 2003 server cluster also supports configurations where boot, system, and paging files are located on the Fibre Channel-attached Storage Area Network (SAN) disks. If you decide to follow this design, in order to increase availability you should use redundant Host Bus Adapters for connections to the SAN. Among other SAN-related enhancements is the use of the targeted reset of storage devices instead of a full bus reset (providing sufficient hardware support).

Assign distinct and meaningful names to shared volumes and network connections. Naming network connections as public and private helps avoid confusion when configuring IP parameters or setting network priorities. Similarly, volume labels will help you identify them during the initial stage of configuration, when each of them must be assigned the same drive letter through the Disk Management utility.

All cluster nodes use synchronous IP-based traffic for both cluster-to-client and intra-cluster communication. The flow of this traffic varies, depending on the cluster type:

- Single-quorum clusters should have two separate physical network connections (single network connections configurations are not supported by Microsoft). One of them, known as interconnect, is intended for intra-cluster communication, which includes heartbeat signals and cluster configuration updates. Interconnects among all of the nodes form a so-called private network. The other types of connections forming a public network primarily carry traffic between cluster and clients. It is required (for Microsoft to accept the configuration as supportable) to provide redundancy for the private network. This is typically accomplished by configuring a public network as the backup. You should also consider increasing the level of availability of the public connections. Many vendors offer fault tolerant solutions (such as network adapter teaming) configurable via network adapter driver-based utilities. Unfortunately, teaming must not be used for private connections and is discouraged on public ones.
- Majority Node Set cluster nodes typically use an adapter listed first on the Adapters and Bindings tab in the Advance Settings of Network Connections window for both client communication and intra-cluster traffic.

Private interconnect can use any hub or switch, as long as the round trip latency is no longer than 1/2 of a second (this limitation becomes a more significant consideration when designing geographically dispersed clusters). In a two-node cluster, it is sufficient to use a crossover cable.

Ensure that the design does not introduce a single point of failure anywhere in the communication path. For example, use separate switches and separate network cards (instead of separate ports on a dual port card) for private and public networks. If you have a larger number of clusters in your environment, you can improve cost-efficiency by sharing switches among all private networks. In such a case, though, you should also provide additional redundancy on the switch level.

Switches or routers (to which public network cards are connected), need to be able to accept gratuitous ARP (the term ARP stands for Address Resolution Protocol and refers to the network protocol used to resolve IP address to corresponding hardware address) sent during a cluster startup or failover. This updates the IP to a MAC address translation when a virtual server or cluster group changes its owner (failover causes a clustered IP address to be assigned to a different physical network adapter).

You need to designate two subnets, one for a public network and one for a private network, with a sufficient number of IP addresses on each. The number of required IP addresses depends on the number of clustered resources and can be determined using the following guidelines:

- One IP address on a public network card per cluster node
- One IP address on a private network card per cluster node
- One cluster IP address on a public network per cluster (for cluster administration)
- One IP address on a public network per virtual server (for client access)

For example, for a two-node cluster with a virtual server providing the file access to users, six IP addresses are required. Four of them are located on a public network and the remaining two on a private network. This number increases with every new node or virtual server.

When designing geographically dispersed clusters (such as Majority Node Set clusters), the need for placing all network connections on the same subnet becomes an especially important consideration. If the underlying physical networks are distinct (as typically is the case), this condition is satisfied by creating VLANs and linking them together.

Although DHCP is supported for both private and public network adapters, it is recommended that you use the statically assigned IP addresses. If you are forced to use DHCP, create reservations and increase the lease time. Then, assign to the private network adapters IP addresses from one of three ranges reserved by Internet Assigned Numbers Authority (IANA) for private use:

- 10.0.0.0 through 10.255.255.255
- 172.16.0.0. through 172.31.255.255
- 192.168.0.0 through 192.168.255.255

Ensure that the range of addresses you select does not conflict with any of your existing subnets.

Verify the binding order for all network connections by checking the listing on the Adapters and Bindings tab in the Advanced Settings screen, which is accessible from the Advanced menu in the Network Connections window. A public connection should appear at the top of the list, followed by a private one. Disable File and Printer Sharing for Microsoft Networks and Client for Microsoft Networks on the private connection. Also, ensure that the private adapters do not have default gateway, WINS, and DNS server settings configured (they should be blank.) For private connections, also disable NetBIOS over TCP/IP (intra-cluster communication uses Remote Procedure Calls on IP Sockets over UDP, without any dependency on NetBIOS). It might be possible to disable NetBIOS on the public network connections, as long as none of the resources (or down-level clients) requires it. However, even though Cluster Service no longer depends on NetBIOS, some of the Cluster Administrator functionality will be lost (such as browsing for a cluster or connecting to it using its name).

Do not use auto settings on network adapters, but instead configure them with the same network speed, duplex mode, flow control, and media type values. Set the speed to match the one set on the ports of your interconnecting device (switch or hub) and the ones that network cards are capable of. When using crossover CAT5 cable for private connection in a cluster, you can configure network connections with 100 Mbps speed and full-duplex mode (although the more conservative 10 Mbps with half-duplex mode will suffice). Because clusters are easily impacted by problems with name resolution, ensure that your WINS and DNS infrastructures are functioning properly.

Network connection media sensing, which used to cause problems in Windows 2000, is by default disabled on the Windows 2003 clusters.

Using IPSec for securing access to clustered applications is generally discouraged because Internet Key Exchange Security Associations are not transferred between nodes during failover. This forcibly terminates all IPSec connections until the expiration of the previously created Security Associations (by default, five minutes) and the establishment of new ones.

Cluster servers have to be either member servers or domain controllers (although the latter is not recommended, due to the negative impact on performance) in the same domain. It is not possible to install a cluster on servers in a workgroup. One of the reasons is the fact that Cluster Service must run in the security context of a domain account. Its group membership, permissions, and user rights are set automatically during the cluster's setup. You should, however, ensure that its password is set not to expire. If this is unacceptable due to your strict security policies, you will be forced to change it periodically. Fortunately, this process works better than in previous versions of server cluster (it can be scripted and it does not require the interruption of Cluster Service). I present it in the section on server cluster installation and configuration.

You should ensure that the Advanced Power Management/Advanced Configuration and Power Interface (APM/ACPI) power options (configurable from Control Panel) are disabled. This applies especially to disabling the hard disks and standby/hibernate features.

Satisfying all requirements listed in this section will help limit the possibility of problems during the installation of clustering software. However, a trouble-free cluster operation depends also on the skills of software developers who create the clustered applications. In general, applications can be divided into the following categories, depending on their ability to function in a clustered environment:

- **Cluster management applications:** Are used for the administration and monitoring of server clusters. Microsoft provides two of them: Cluster Administrator and CLUSTER.EXE. There also are a number of third-party management applications on the market.
- **Custom resource types:** Implement new resource types, thus extending a number of applications and services that can run on the server clusters.
- **Nonmanagement applications that are cluster aware:** Are applications that can run in both a clustered and nonclustered configuration but they were developed using clustering APIs. They can take advantage of every clustering feature. They can also communicate with Cluster Service and receive cluster status and event notifications.
- **Nonmanagement applications that are not cluster-aware:** Are applications that are not based on clustering APIs (that is, they have not been designed with the ability to run in the clustered configuration). A number of them still can be configured for failover by using Generic Application or Generic Script resource. Configuration of Generic Application resource is presented in detail in the section titled "Generic Application Resource" found later in this chapter.

Server Cluster Design and Capacity Planning

While the primary goal of server clusters is to provide high availability, they can also increase the degree of scalability with static load balancing. The term static indicates that the load distribution is not adjusted according to changing performance characteristics of the individual nodes. Instead, each node owns an originally assigned set of groups. A group ownership can only change as a result of a manual administrative action (by using Cluster Administrator or CLUSTER.EXE to move group between nodes) or as a result of a failover or a subsequent failback.

Designing load-balanced clusters with multiple active nodes introduces a new factor that is not a consideration in clusters configured strictly for failover. If a node that is a recipient of a failover group is active, then it is important to ensure that the cumulative load after failover will not exceed its capacity. For example, in a four-node cluster where all the nodes are active and configured as possible owners of all resources, the average workload on each server should not exceed 25 percent. Providing that you satisfy this condition, the cluster would be able to handle the failure of three nodes and still remain operational (although the application's responsiveness will most likely be severely affected).

In a cluster with a larger number of nodes, you have more flexibility in setting up the various failover scenarios. For example, you can configure failover to happen only between node pairs. This will limit high availability, because a failure of two nodes in each pair would cause the failure of the groups they own. On the other hand, this would allow you to increase the utilization level on each up to 50 percent. Clearly, the design decision is an issue of trade-off between the level of utilization and high availability.

With a local quorum, a cluster can consist of a single node only. In such a case, design is trivial. A single node model does not offer high availability or load balancing. It also cannot be used with some, otherwise cluster-aware, applications (such as SQL Server 7.0). However, it still provides several benefits, such as:

- Resources on the server that can be arranged into cluster groups (including virtual servers) in order to match business or administrative preferences
- Applications that can take advantage of the automatic restart feature
- Developers that can test their cluster-aware applications against them
- Additional nodes that can be added at any point to form a multi-node cluster

With a single-shared or a majority node set quorum, you can choose from one of a variety of the following cluster models (depending on desired goals and available budget):

- **N-node failover pairs cluster:** Is a group of clusters that are configured to failover only between pairs of nodes in a cluster. As explained previously, this design limits the failover capabilities because a failure of two servers in a pair results in a failure of all the groups they own. On the other hand, it increases permitted utilization levels up to 50 percent. To configure N-node failover cluster, do the following:
    1. Divide all cluster nodes into pairs.
    2. Assign groups to each pair.
    3. Set the possible owners for each resource within each group to both nodes within a pair.
    4. The next step depends on whether a node pair is set up as active/active or active/passive. In active/passive, designate only one node as preferred for a group (or groups). In active/active, distribute groups between two nodes and set the current owner of each group as preferred.
- **Hot-standby server cluster:** Is a cluster where only a single node is designated as a hot standby failover for all the remaining nodes. You need to carefully evaluate and monitor the level of utilization of the active nodes. The hot standby server cluster should be able to handle the unlikely event in which all active nodes fail. Note, however, that this model limits high availability, because a failure of any of active nodes and a hot standby server cluster will result in a failure of that group. Depending on the results of your analysis and the level of high availability required, you might decide to switch to the N+I cluster model. To configure hot-standby cluster, do the following:
    1. Distribute groups among all the servers except for the one designated as the failover.
    2. Set the possible owners for each resource within each group to its current owner and the failover node.
    3. Set the preferred owner for each group to its current owner.
- **N+I server cluster:** Is a cluster where the N nodes are active and the I nodes function as a hot standby failover. This model might evolve from a hot-standby server cluster, if it turns out that the high availability requirements are not satisfied. Its main drawback is its increased cost without a return in processing power, because the larger number of

nodes remain idle most of the time. However, after a failover, the level of service remains approximately the same. To configure N+I cluster, do the following:

1. Distribute groups among N servers.
2. Set the possible owners for each resource within each group to its current owner and one of the I failover nodes.
3. Set the preferred owner for each group to its current owner.

✦ **Failover Ring cluster:** Is a cluster where each node is active. Its groups are configured to a failover in a specific sequence. This cluster offers a good utilization of resources and good failover capabilities. However, make sure that you evaluate a meaningful sequence of failover and do not allow overloading of the individual nodes if a failover takes place. To configure a failover ring cluster, do the following:

1. Distribute groups among all nodes.
2. Set the preferred owner for each group to its current owner.
3. Create a circular list of nodes that will be used to establish a failover sequence.
4. For each group, add all the remaining nodes as preferred owners according to their position on the list.

✦ **Random cluster:** Is a cluster where the order of a failover is random, because there are no possible or preferred owners set. During failover, ownership can be transferred to any node. This might be a preferred solution in clusters containing a large number of nodes and groups, where the other models are not suitable or too complex to implement. To configure a random cluster, simply ensure that the list of preferred owners is empty for each group.

For load balancing the different applications, follow the rules previously outlined. If you intend to load balance the same application across multiple nodes, you also need to decide whether such applications will be cloned or partitioned. Which one you choose depends to a large extent on the nature of data with which the application deals.

Cloned applications are identical, both in terms of the code they execute and the data they access. Running identical applications requires installing them on all cluster nodes and distributing the load by pointing different groups of clients to different application instances. Keeping data identical can be accomplished by treating it as read-only, pointing each instance of the application to the same data location, or, in case of read-write data, by ensuring some kind of replication mechanism. Obviously, not every application is a good candidate for cloning.

While cloned applications access the same data, each of the partitioned applications has its own data set with which to work. The best candidates for such applications are database management systems, where the content of a database can be easily separated, based on some criteria (such as periods of time, geographical location, alphabetical order, and so forth). For more details on such applications, refer to the section titled "Federated Server Setup and Deployment" later in this chapter. Just as with cloned applications, the determination of whether the application can be partitioned needs to be done on an individual basis, after analyzing the nature of the application code and data.

Your decision on which clustering model to use will depend on analyzing several factors: the price and high-availability requirements, the price and scalability requirements, the number and type of clustered applications, and the number and type of resources and groups. Focus first on the cost analysis. The main question is whether the decreased possibility of a system failure will justify a significant increase in price. Statistics show that downtime in certain sectors of the economy tends to be very expensive. The proper analysis, showing the current rate of server and application failures, in addition to estimated losses due to these failures, will help in making the right choice. Keep in mind that server clustering is considered to be a highly available (rather than fault tolerant) solution. Failover itself causes a temporary disconnection from the clustered data or application.

You must carefully design cluster groups, because they affect other cluster characteristics (such as failover and failback policies or the ability to load balance). In the group design, take into consideration the resource dependencies. As explained previously, it is not possible to create dependencies between resources residing in different groups. Another factor affecting group structure is a need to keep related resources together. These resources might have a common business or administrative purpose or need to be available at the same time.

To design group structure, Microsoft recommends creating a resource dependency tree. This is a diagram containing all resources, with arrows between them representing the direct dependencies. When building a dependency tree, the following dependency rules should be used:

- IP Address
  - No dependencies
- Network Name
  - Placed directly on the IP Address to which the name resolves
- Local Quorum
  - No dependencies
- DHCP Service
  - Placed directly on the physical disk containing the DHCP database
  - Placed directly on the IP Address of the DHCP virtual server
  - Placed directly on the network name resolving to the IP address of the DHCP virtual server
- Distributed Transaction Coordinator
  - Placed directly on the physical disk, which stores the transaction log
  - Placed indirectly on the IP address of the virtual server containing the DTC resource
  - Placed directly on the network name through which the DTC is accessed
- File Share (a nonDfs root): Even though no dependencies are required, the following are recommended:
  - Placed directly on the physical disk containing the shared folder
  - Placed indirectly on the IP address of the virtual server hosting the shared folder
  - Placed directly on the network name resolving to the IP address (and the dependent on it)
- File Share (a Dfs root)
  - Placed directly on the network name of the virtual server where the Dfs root folder is located
  - Placed indirectly on the IP address that resolves to this name

- Generic Application
  - No dependencies
- Generic Script
  - No dependencies
- Generic Service
  - No dependencies
- Majority Node Set
  - No dependencies
- Message Queuing
  - Placed directly on the physical disk
  - Placed indirectly on the IP address of the virtual server hosting the Message Queuing
  - Placed directly on the network name resolving to the IP address used for client connections
- Physical Disk
  - No dependencies
- Print Spooler
  - Placed on a physical disk storing spool directory
  - Placed indirectly on the IP address of the virtual server hosting the Print Spooler
  - Placed directly on the network name resolving to the IP address
- WINS Service
  - Placed directly on the physical disk storing the WINS database
  - Placed directly on the IP address of the virtual server hosting the WINS database
  - Placed directly on the network name resolving to the IP address

After the group structure and content is decided on, you will need to develop a strategy for failover and failback. Both failover and failback take place and are configurable on a per group basis. Because both are associated with the temporary loss of connectivity to resources within an affected group, you want to minimize their frequency. You can, for example, prevent failback from happening automatically after the preferred owner of the group comes back online or restrict it to specific hours only. You can also prevent excessive failovers by setting a threshold for the number of failovers during a specific time period. By default, this threshold is set to ten failovers over the period of six hours. If a resource in a group happens to be unstable and causes constant failovers, the group fails after reaching the configured threshold.

Similar settings can be configured on a per resource basis. You can set a threshold on the number of consecutive restarts within a specific period. The default sets the threshold to three restart attempts in a 900-second time period (configurable from the Advanced tab of resource Properties window in the Cluster Administrator interface). If the threshold is reached, the resource will, by default, initiate a failover of its group. This might not be a desired behavior in some cases. To prevent this behavior, you can change the default so that the resource failure will not the affect the group.

The cluster depends in several ways on the presence of a domain. Server clusters have to operate as either member servers or domain controllers in the same domain. Cluster Service has to be able to access a domain controller for a number of functions that it performs. Configuring cluster nodes as domain controllers ensures this access, even in the case of network problems. But in general, clustering domain controllers should be avoided for performance reasons. When configuring cluster nodes as member servers, ensure that you have fast, reliable (preferably redundant) connections to a domain controller. You should also provide redundancy on a domain authentication and name resolution level (by setting up at least two domain controllers, global catalogs, and DNS servers).

In addition to the high availability offered by the cluster on a server level, also consider increasing the high availability on a component level. For example:

- ✦ Use multiple-teamed public network adapters connected to separate hubs or switches. (Remember though, that adapter teaming is not supported for private network adapters.)
- ✦ Install redundant, hot swappable power supplies and UPS devices.
- ✦ Configure your disks as hardware RAID 1, 5, 1+0, or 0+1 (remember that software RAID is not supported on clustered storage devices).

Take advantage of the extra features included in the Storage Area Networks (SANs) products offered by all the major storage vendors (such as EMC, HP, IBM, or Hitachi), when setting up high-end clustered systems. Besides fast and reliable external storage, these SANs also offer other benefits:

- ✦ Replication technologies ideal for disaster recovery scenarios
- ✦ Ability to create, configure, and expand disk arrays with no downtime (Windows 2003 DiskPart utility allows dynamic, online expanding of the clustered drives once their underlying hardware array has been expanded)
- ✦ Clusters spanning large distances
- ✦ Hardware based on snapshot backups

If your design involves a geographically dispersed area, you should consider using a Majority Node Set clustering. The main advantage of this solution is removing the distance limits imposed by a shared storage bus. The main drawback is the fact that the failure of the majority of the nodes (or network connectivity between them) will cause cluster failure. This is different from a traditional single-shared quorum implementation, which can stay operational even if only one node remains running (although an increased load in such case needs to be seriously considered when evaluating the feasibility of such a configuration). You can, however, through registry modifications, force the creation of a Majority Node Set cluster with fewer nodes than normally allowed. This procedure is described in a troubleshooting section found later in the chapter. Unfortunately, the process requires manual intervention. As mentioned previously, this configuration type should be properly evaluated by the vendor of a clustered application and by clustering hardware.

Step-by-Step Server Cluster Installation and Configuration

After all the prerequisites are satisfied and your design is complete, you are ready to create a server cluster. Start by ensuring that only one of the servers connected to the shared storage device is active. Turn all the remaining servers on, but stop the startup process at the boot menu screen, thus preventing the operating system from loading. The active server should recognize all the disks attached to the shared storage device. As mentioned previously, you should configure the disks according to the manufacturer's instructions. Specifics are hardware dependent, but in general, you should create a number of fault tolerant disks arrays and initialize them (for example, in case of Storage Area Networks, disks can be grouped into so-called zones that, in turn, can be assigned to particular groups of servers. In such case, a server should be able to see only the disk devices within the zone to which it belongs. SAN zoning utilities are provided by the SAN vendors). The resulting logical drives should have the same letters when viewed from each node. Launch the Disk Management and verify that all of the shared disks are visible and set as basic. Then, partition the disks (when working on 64-bit version of Windows 2003 servers, keep in mind that MBR partitioning has to be used), create the logical drives, assign letters to each, label them in a meaningful way, and format with NTFS. Label the network connections according to their intended role (public or private).

After this is completed, shut down the first server and power up the next one that will be participating in the cluster. Use Disk Management to verify that each of the drives you configured previously is accessible. Make sure that the drive letters match (using the previously assigned labels as the guide). Repeat the same process for all of the remaining servers. Remember that at no point, prior to creation of a cluster, no more than one server should have access to shared storage devices at the same time. Violating this rule can result in the corruption of the file system on shared drives. Once this procedure is completed, leave one server running and connected to the shared storage device. This server will become the first cluster node. Log on either directly to the server (at the console or via a Remote Desktop Protocol connection) or another Windows XP or .NET Server system that has the Administrative Tools installed. For logon, use a domain account with local administrative privileges to the target server.

Before you continue, ensure that you have all the following information available:

✦ Name of the domain in which your cluster will reside (which is the same as the domain of all servers participating in the cluster)

✦ NetBIOS name of the cluster

✦ Name of each server that will become a cluster node

✦ Cluster IP address (on the same subnet as the IP addresses of the public network adapters)

✦ Cluster service account name and password. This can be a regular domain account. On member servers, New Server Cluster wizard will automatically grant it the appropriate privileges. However, when clustering domain controllers (which generally is discouraged) you need to also ensure that the account will have the right to log on locally to the domain controllers. This, by default, is granted only to a handful of predefined administrative groups (Administrators and Backup, Account, Print, and Server Operators). To modify this setting, launch Group Policy editor for Default Domain Controllers Policy and drill down to Computer Configuration ➪ Windows Settings ➪ Security Settings ➪ Local Policies ➪ User Rights Assignment node. Then click on the Allow log on local policy and allow the user account (or a designated group that the account is a member of) to the list. Remember that this account should also have write access to the root folder on all the cluster disks.

The process of creating a server cluster is different from the previous versions of Windows. Instead of running a separate setup process, a cluster is created using the cluster administrative tools. First we will take a look at accomplishing this task with Cluster Administrator, then with the CLUSTER.EXE command line utility.

Cluster Administrator is much easier to use, because of its intuitive graphical interface. However, CLUSTER.EXE has some advantages over its GUI-based counterpart. First of all, it can be easily incorporated into batch files or script. It is also faster, especially when dealing with clusters with large number of groups and resources over slow network links. Finally, it offers features not available otherwise (for example, resetting the password for a Cluster Service account). CLUSTER.EXE has standard `/?` and `/help` options, which display the full syntax of the command and is documented in online help.

In spite of the advantages of CLUSTER.EXE, Cluster Administrator still remains the primary administrative tool for managing Windows 2003 Server clusters. Unlike the majority of other Administrative Tools, it is a standalone program CLUADMIN.EXE, not a snap-in to Microsoft Management Console. A shortcut to it is located in the Administrative Tools menu. It is used to create new server clusters as well as manage existing ones. Although you can connect it simultaneously to multiple clusters, each one of them is managed independently (in a separate window).

Launch the Cluster Administrator console (initially empty). The Open Connection item of the File menu brings up the Open Connection to Cluster dialog box. This gives you the options to create new clusters, add nodes to the cluster, and open the connection to the cluster. Choosing the first option launches the Create New Cluster Wizard. Alternatively, you can select New ➪ Cluster from the File menu. The first page after Welcome window, the Cluster Name and Domain page shown in Figure 25-1, requires you to type in a cluster name and to select a domain name in which the cluster will be created.

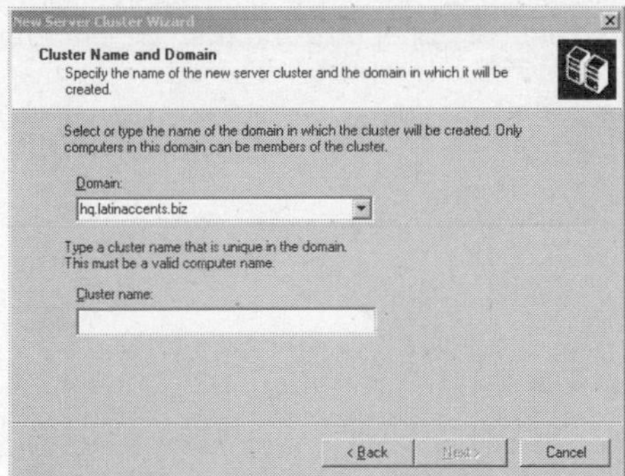

Figure 25-1: Cluster Name and Domain screen of New Server Cluster Wizard.

After you click on the Next button, the next page of the wizard prompts you for the name of computer where the new cluster will be set up. By default, the wizard will automatically locate all shared storage devices attached to the target computer and include them in the cluster. If, for some reason, you want to avoid this default behavior, click on the Advanced button and select the Advanced (minimum) configuration option. If you do so, you will need to add shared devices manually, after the wizard completes the last page.

The wizard uses information you provided to analyze all the factors necessary for cluster creation to succeed. This analysis, shown in Figure 25-2, consists of five main steps:

1. Checking for an existing cluster: Verifies that a cluster with the same name does not exist on the network.
2. Establishing node connection(s): Connects to the target server and initializes the cluster creation process.
3. Checking node feasibility: Establishes whether the target server satisfies all the prerequisites.
4. Finding common resources on nodes: Determines the availability of the shared resources. This involves enumerating the shared disk resources (in order to create a quorum) and network adapters (in order to set up cluster networks).
5. Checking cluster feasibility: Verifies that a cluster creation is possible and designates a resource for a quorum.

Each of the steps is marked with icons indicating success (check mark), failure (red cross), or warning (yellow triangle with an exclamation mark), as shown in Figure 25-2. If you encounter a problem, you have a chance to correct it and repeat the analysis by clicking on the Re-analyze button. Note that if you selected the Advanced configuration option, the Checking cluster feasibility step will be marked with a warning icon, because the detection of collisions between the local and clustered drive letters is skipped. This, however, is intended behavior, so you can safely ignore it (although this also means that you are responsible for verifying that the drive letters do not conflict). You might also see the same warning icon if you are using a crossover cable to connect to the other server, which will become part of the cluster (possible only in the two-node cluster), and that server is shut down when running the wizard (rather than being disconnected from the shared storage). This warning, which indicates that only one network adapter was found on the current node, can also be ignored (providing, of course, that you actually have at least two network adapters and they are both properly installed). If any of the steps in analysis results in a failure, you will need to eliminate its cause before the wizard allows you to continue.

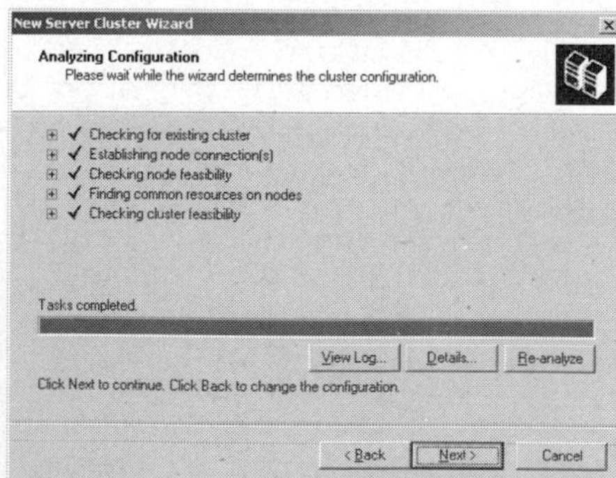

Figure 25-2: Analyzing Configuration page of the Server Cluster Wizard.

After a cluster's feasibility is verified, you will be asked for the cluster's IP address. This is a unique IP address that the cluster name will resolve to. In the next page of the wizard, type in the information about the cluster service account. The account will be placed in the local Administrators group and granted the appropriate privileges on the target server. The next page of the wizard will summarize all the information that you provided so far.

In case you need to perform any troubleshooting at this point, the following page contains the View Log button. Clicking it provides you with instant access to the ClCfgSrv.log file, containing information about all the steps performed so far. This button remains available throughout the installation process.

If you have multiple resources that can be used as the quorum, you will have an opportunity to select the most appropriate one using the Quorum button. You will be presented with the following choices (shown in Figure 25-3):

✦ Local Quorum

✦ Physical Disk (one for each physical disk on the disk controller other than the one used for the system drives)

✦ Majority Node Set

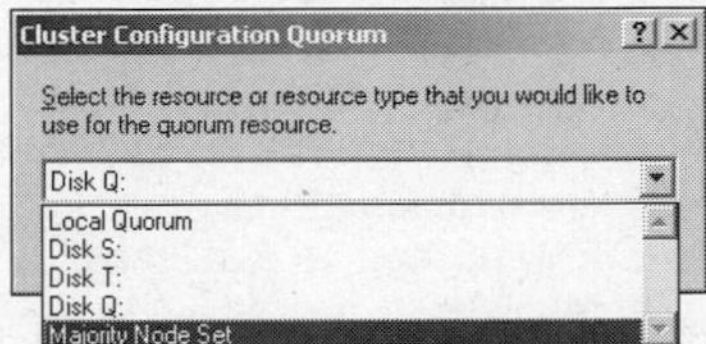

Figure 25-3: Selecting a quorum resource.

After selecting the appropriate quorum resource and clicking on the Next button, the creation of the cluster will start. This process is divided into five main steps:

1. Re-analyzing the cluster: Repeats the steps initially performed when checking cluster feasibility. Once this feasibility is verified, the cluster configuration is initialized.

2. Configuring the cluster services: Forms the cluster, configures a cluster service account by assigning it to the right groups and granting the appropriate user rights. Then, it creates and starts cluster-related helper services (such as Cluster Network Provider and ClusDisk), creates and configures the cluster database, and creates and starts the Cluster Service.

3. Configuring the resource types: Configures the "Generic Script" and "Majority Node Set" resource types.

4. Configuring the resources: Creates, configures, and starts the resources in the cluster group (including the quorum resource).

5. Deleting the local quorum resource: Uses a local quorum temporarily during the cluster creation process. Once a shared storage device becomes available, the local quorum is deleted. This step is skipped if you decided to use a local quorum.

Each of these actions is displayed with a visual indication of the outcome. As discussed previously, success is marked with a check mark, failure with a red cross, and a warning with an exclamation mark in a yellow triangle. If the failure of any of the steps prevented a cluster from being created, you can click on the Retry button after correcting the problem. This completes the cluster setup process. After you click the Finish button, you will be presented with a view of the newly created cluster in the Cluster Administrator console.

When using the typical (default) configuration options of the New Server Cluster Wizard, each of the shared disks becomes a resource in its own group (named Group 0, Group 1, and so on.). The quorum disk is allocated to the (previously described) Cluster Group that also contains two other resources — Cluster IP Address and Cluster Name (in which values are set according to the information provided when running the wizard).

On the other hand, the advanced (minimal) configuration option does not create any additional groups beside the Cluster Group (regardless of the number of shared disk devices). The type of quorum included in the Cluster Group will depend on the type of quorum you choose when running the wizard. If you leave the default, Local Quorum resource will be created. To change it, add a disk resource to the Cluster Group, bring it online, and select it from the Quorum Resource drop-down list on the Quorum tab of the cluster properties dialog box (you can remove Local Quorum resource afterwards).

After the cluster is running on the first node, additional ones can be added. At this point, you can connect them to the shared storage device and power them up. Adding nodes to a cluster can be done using either Cluster Administrator or the CLUSTER.EXE utility. Cluster Administrator simplifies the process with the Add Nodes Wizard, which can be launched from the context-sensitive menu of any of the nodes appearing in the left window pane. The same wizard launches after selecting the Add Nodes to Cluster option from the drop-down list of Open Connection to Cluster dialog box (it also can be accessed from the File ⇨ New menu option). After you type in the new server name (or select it after clicking the Browse . . . button), the Add Nodes wizard will lead you through the following sequence of steps:

1. Analyze the Configuration screen (identical to the one generated by the New Server Cluster Wizard).
2. Enter the Cluster Account password at the prompt (its name will be provided for you and you will not have a chance to change it).
3. Add the nodes to the cluster (identical to the one displayed by the New Server Cluster Wizard).

After the wizard completes successfully, Cluster Administrator will display additional node.

If you want to remove a node from an existing cluster, highlight it in the left window pane of Cluster Administrator and select the Evict option from the File (or context sensitive) menu. This will also remove the cluster configuration on that node. If you run this procedure on the last node of the cluster, the cluster will cease to exist. Adding or removing nodes to a cluster does not require a reboot.

You should remember that evicting a node from a cluster does not remove the Cluster Service account from the local Administrators group.

Cluster Administrator, shown in Figure 25-4 provides a friendly interface for configuring the cluster properties. The top-level node of the Cluster Administrator interface represents the cluster itself, under which the next level nodes — Groups, Resources, Cluster Configuration, and individual cluster nodes (up to eight) — can be found.

Using the top-level node, you can configure the quorum type and parameters (partition, root path and maximum quorum log size), the network priority assigned to all the networks used for internal network communication (ensuring that, in case of a single quorum cluster, the private network appears first on the list), and the security settings (for controlling access to the cluster's management).

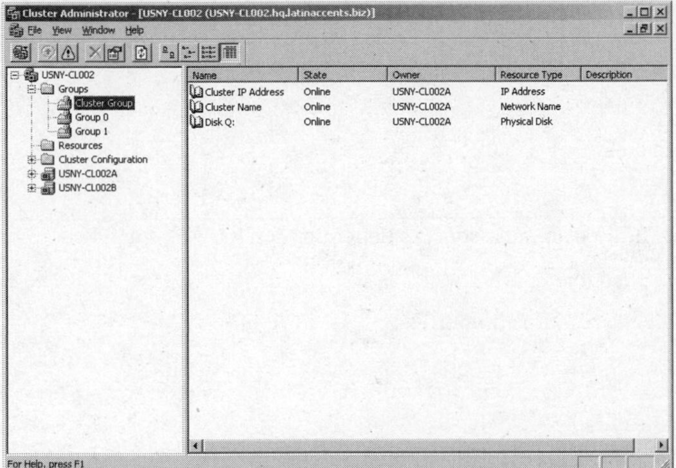

Figure 25-4: Cluster Administrator screen with two nodes.

The Groups node contains all of the groups for a currently managed cluster. From the context sensitive menu, you can create new groups, resources, and virtual servers (using the Configure Application menu item). When clicking on any of the group nodes, its resources are listed in the Details pane of the console. The context sensitive menu provides options for the cluster group operations such as:

- ✦ Taking a group offline
- ✦ Bringing a group online
- ✦ Moving a group to a different node
- ✦ Deleting or renaming a group (before a group can be deleted, all of its resources have to be either deleted or moved to another group)
- ✦ Configuring the following group properties:
    - Name
    - Description
    - Preferred owners: Designates a primary server for the group. If a failback policy is in effect, the group's membership will be transferred to this server. Also, if a current group's owner fails, the group is automatically transferred to a node that was selected based on a preferred owner list.
    - Failover threshold and period
    - Failback policy: Determines whether automatic failback should be prevented or allowed. If the allowed option is selected, then failback can be limited to a specific time window, or it can be configured to take place as soon as the primary server is back online.

Remember that you should not modify the Cluster Group. Resources should not be added to or removed from it. Because Cluster Service relies on its availability, its failure causes the entire cluster to fail.

The Resources node lists all the resources in a cluster, their states, owners, group membership, and resource types. Bringing a pop-up menu for each resource allows you to perform the following:

- ✦ Take the resource offline.
- ✦ Bring the resource online.
- ✦ Initiate a failure.
- ✦ Change the group (if there are no resources dependent on it).
- ✦ Delete or rename a resource.
- ✦ Configure the following resource properties:
  - Name
  - Description
  - Possible owners: Designates nodes that are permitted to own a resource.
  - Run in a separate Resource Monitor: Isolates a resource from the others (used when dealing with unstable resources that tend to crash frequently).
  - Resource dependencies: Lists the resources that a current resource depends on. Only direct dependencies should be listed.
  - Restart policy
  - Affecting group: Determines whether a failure of the resource will cause the failover of the group to another node.
  - Threshold and period: Contains the maximum number of restart attempts within a time interval before a resource fails.
  - Looks Alive and Is Alive intervals: Cluster service checks whether a resource is available by querying their respective resource monitors, according to the values of Looks Alive and Is Alive intervals. Looks alive is, by default, more frequent but less thorough (and therefore less resource intensive). Is Alive happens less frequently but at the expense of a higher resource utilization. Their default values depend on the resource types and are recommended in normal operating conditions. Change these values only for troubleshooting purposes.
  - Pending timeout: Is the maximum amount of time that a resource can remain in an Online Pending or Offline Pending state. If this limit is reached and the resource's state is still pending, its resource state changes to Failed.
  - Parameters: Are the resource-specific values (for example, the IP address and subnet mask for an IP address resource, the NetBIOS name for a Network Name resource, and so forth).

The Cluster configuration node has mostly informational value. The Resource Types node lists the resource types with the associated resource data description languages (DLLs). For each resource type, you can modify its default "Looks Alive" and "Is Alive" intervals.

The Networks node gives you the name, current state, role, and subnet mask information of the cluster networks. For each network, you can also specify its role in cluster traffic, which can be set to Public, Private, or Mixed (also referred to as Client Access Only, Internal Cluster communications, and All communications). By default, all networks are set up initially for "All communications". You should keep this default for the public network so it can function as a backup for the private one. Majority Node Set clusters, as mentioned before, cannot take advantage of such redundancy. Instead, they use the network connection that is listed first on the Adapters and Bindings tab in the Advanced Settings of Network Connections window (which typically is a public network). Network problems, in this case, might result in a failure of the entire cluster. The Procedure for recovery from these types of problems is described in the section titled "Troubleshooting Server Cluster" of this chapter.

The Network Interfaces node lists the network adapters for each member of the cluster, along with the network they participate in, their state, type of adapter, IP address, and description.

There is also a node for each cluster member. This type of node contains a listing of the active groups, active resources, and network interfaces in their respective containers. Its menu options allow you to pause, resume, and evict nodes, as well as start and stop the Cluster Service on each.

Creation of the groups and resources is straightforward and requires only specifying the values of the parameters described earlier in this section. You can create them by selecting New ➪ Group or New ➪ Resource from the File menu or the context sensitive menu of any node. When creating a group, the only parameters you need to specify are group name, description, and preferred owner(s). After the group is created, you can also customize the values determining the failover and failback policies. The number and type of parameters needed when creating resources are resource-type specific, but for each resource you will need to specify the name, resource type, group it belongs to, whether it should run in a separate resource monitor, its possible owners, and its resource dependencies. Cluster Application Wizard (invoked from the Configure Application menu option) simplifies the creation of virtual servers.

To delete a resource, you can just highlight it and press the Delete key, or select the Delete Resource option from the menu. Taking a resource offline is no longer necessary (as it used to be in earlier versions of Windows). If there are existing dependencies on the resource that you want to delete, you will need to either delete dependent resources (which can be done in the same step), remove the dependencies, or replace the dependency on the resource to be deleted with another, equivalent one. Remember that in order to modify the dependency for a resource, you will need to take it offline.

Creation of the server cluster and adding the remaining nodes to it can also be accomplished using the CLUSTER.EXE command line utility. `/create` switch accepts the parameters specified at the command line or stored in an answer file. The format and content of the answer file is documented in the UNATTEND.DOC file on Windows 2003 installation CDs. For example, the following command will create a new cluster named usny-cl002 with the cluster IP address 172.16.0.103 and subnet mask 255.255.255.0, assigned to a network adapter named "Public" on the server usny-cl002a, and using the cluster service account USNYCluSvc002 from the domain `hq.latinaccents.biz` with a password set to `Pa$$w0rd` (entire command needs to be typed in as a single line, either at the Command Prompt or in a batch file):

```
CLUSTER.EXE /cluster:usny-cl002 /create
/ipaddr:172.16.0.103,255.255.255.0,"Public" /password:Pa$$w0rd
/user:hq\USNYCluSvc002 /node:usny-cl002a
```

Adding one or more nodes to an existing cluster can be done by using the `/add` switch command. For example, the following command adds the node netsrv002b to usny-cl002 cluster:

```
CLUSTER.EXE /cluster:usny-cl002 /add:usny-cl002b /password:Pa$$w0rd
```

where the password option specifies the Cluster Service account password.

Removing a node from a cluster is accomplished with the node /evict parameters. Because the evicted node has to be offline, the Cluster Service on that node needs to be stopped first (this rule does not apply to the last node in the cluster). For example, the execution of these two commands results in evicting the node usny-cl002b from cluster usny-cl002:

```
CLUSTER.EXE /cluster:usny-cl002 node usny-cl002b /stop
CLUSTER.EXE /cluster:usny-cl002 node usny-cl002b /evict
```

Server Cluster Management

After the server cluster is configured and the appropriate groups and resources created, the main administrative tasks involve cluster monitoring, upgrades, backups, restores, and disaster recovery. We will start with the tasks that can be accomplished with Cluster Administrator or CLUSTER.EXE (Windows 2003 cluster operations are also supportable via Windows Management Instrumentation [WMI], which makes them suitable for scripting, but the details of this management technology are beyond the scope of this chapter).

To administer a cluster, you can connect to it using a Cluster name, a cluster IP address, the names or IP addresses of any of its nodes, or (if logged on directly to one of the nodes) a single dot (.) (designates a local node). The same options can be used with CLUSTER.EXE.

The following are examples of performing most common administrative tasks using Cluster Administrator and CLUSTER.EXE. They deal with the cluster called usny-cl002 with the two nodes usny-cl002a and usny-cl002b.

Viewing the node status:

- ✦ Cluster Administrator: Icons provide the graphical indication of the status
- ✦ CLUSTER.EXE: Run from the command prompt:
  CLUSTER /cluster:usny-cl002 node usny-cl002b /status

Starting the Cluster Service:

- ✦ Cluster Administrator: Highlight a node on which the service needs to be started. From the File or “right-click” menu, select Start Node.
- ✦ CLUSTER.EXE: Run from the command prompt:
  CLUSTER /cluster:usny-cl002 node usny-cl002b /start

Stopping the Cluster Service:

- ✦ Cluster Administrator: Highlight a node on which the service needs to be stopped. From the File or “right-click” menu, select Stop Node.
- ✦ CLUSTER.EXE: Run from the command prompt:
  CLUSTER /cluster:usny-cl002 node usny-cl002b /stop

Pausing a node (pausing a node keeps it operational, but prevents resources residing on other nodes from failing over to it):

- ✦ Cluster Administrator: Highlight a node on which the service needs to be paused. From the File or “right-click” menu, select Pause Node.
- ✦ CLUSTER.EXE: Run from the command prompt:
  CLUSTER /cluster:usny-cl002 node usny-cl002b /pause

Resuming a node:

- ✦ Cluster Administrator: Highlight a node on which the service needs to be resumed. From the File or "right-click" menu, select Resume Node.
- ✦ CLUSTER.EXE: Run from the command prompt:
  CLUSTER /cluster:usny-cl002 node usny-cl002b /resume

Changing a quorum disk (to S:\MSCS on a Disk S: physical disk resource)

- ✦ Cluster Administrator: Select the cluster icon (top level node). Bring up its properties, click the second tab, which is named Quorum, select another physical disk resource, and specify the partition, root path, and maximum size of a quorum log (if different from the defaults).
- ✦ CLUSTER.EXE: Run from the command prompt:
  CLUSTER /cluster:usny-cl002 /quorumresource:"Disk S:" /path:"S:\MSCS" /
  maxlogsize:4194304

  to set the new location and maximum size of the quorum resource.

Keep in mind that the cluster operations that involve changing the quorum parameters (especially its location) should be performed only when all nodes are active.

Changing the Cluster Service account password no longer requires stopping all the cluster nodes (this was the case in previous versions of Windows). Instead, CLUSTER.EXE provides the `/changepassword` switch. The following command changes the password from `OldPa$$w0rd` to `NuPa$$w0rd` on the cluster usny-cl002:

```
CLUSTER /cluster:usny-cl002 /changepassword:NuPa$$w0rd,OldPa$$w0rd
```

For this command to work, the "User cannot change the password" setting must to be unchecked for the Cluster Service account.

If you intend to change the Cluster Service account, you need to be familiar with its group membership and the privilege levels that it requires. The account has to be a domain account that belongs to a local Administrators group on each node. Its password expiration setting should be disabled. It also requires the following user rights:

- ✦ Act as part of the operating system
- ✦ Adjust the memory quotas for a process
- ✦ Back up the files and directories
- ✦ Increase the scheduling priority
- ✦ Log on as a service
- ✦ Restore the files and directories

Start by assigning these rights using a Local Security Policy Microsoft Management Console (MMC) snap-in on each cluster node (appropriate entries are located in the User Rights Assignments folder under Computer Configuration ⇨ Security Settings ⇨ Local Policies). You can assign the rights to the local Administrators group or directly to the cluster service account (the latter approach is more secure).

Next, you will have to stop the Cluster Service on all nodes (you can do this by using a Services MMC snap-in) because at any point, every node must use the same account and password. Once every instance of the Cluster Service is stopped, launch the Services MMC snap-in for each node, display the properties of the Cluster Service, and provide the new account name and password from the Log On tab. This process needs to be repeated on each node. Finally, restart the services.

The backup and restore procedures for the server clusters are more complex than for standard servers. This relates to the fact that the cluster relies on disk signatures and partition layouts to locate a quorum and other disk resources. In order to back them up, use Windows 2003 Automated System Recovery (ASR), which is part of the Backup and Recovery Tools. You should run it separately on each cluster node. Ensure that Cluster Service is running on the node being backed up in order to include a disk signature and partition layout information. ASR automatically includes System State, which contains, among other configuration data, a checkpoint file and a quorum log, which are necessary for maintaining cluster consistency. Ensure that you also back up each of the shared disks and each of clustered applications, according to their standard backup procedures. Note that the local backup on any of the cluster nodes can only access disks that are owned by this node.

Interestingly, Backup Operators do not have rights to run ASR on the cluster nodes. To fix this, you need to grant them permissions to manage the cluster (via the Security tab of the Cluster Properties dialog box of Cluster Administrator).

The restoration of a quorum will differ, depending on whether the restore should be applied to a single node only (backup is sometimes referred to as nonauthoritative) or an entire cluster (also known as authoritative) and whether it involves a quorum resource:

- ✦ If you need to restore only a single node (but the remaining nodes, and, hence the cluster, are still operational), run the ASR process on that node using its ASR floppy disk and media. This will restore the operating system and System State data on this node. After restore is complete, start the Cluster Service on the newly restore node. This will automatically update the local copy of the quorum to reflect the current cluster state. Verify that the node properly joined the cluster and redistribute the resource groups.
- ✦ If you need to restore an entire cluster but the quorum database on the quorum disk is still intact, restore a single node using Automated System Restore (which will include System State data). Once restore is completed, try starting the Cluster Service. Assuming that the quorum resource is functioning properly and the quorum disk signature has not changed, the first node should be able to form a cluster using the existing database on the quorum disk. Otherwise, you should use procedures outlined in the "Troubleshooting Server Cluster" section. Starting Cluster Service will also update the state of the local quorum using the shared copy. After the cluster is up and running, restore the remaining nodes using the ASR. After you start Cluster Service on each node, they should automatically join the cluster.
- ✦ If you need to restore the entire cluster, including the quorum database and log (included in the System State backup), then use the Advanced option during the ASR restore. The Restore Wizard will then allow you to select "Restore the Cluster Registry to the quorum disk and all other nodes". If the cluster is operational when the restore starts, during its first stage Cluster Service will be stopped only on the local node. After the reboot, Cluster Service will be also stopped on all remaining nodes (so the quorum database can be replaced with its newly restored version). After restore is completed, you will need to start the Cluster Services manually or restart all the cluster nodes. This procedure will also restore the quorum signature to the quorum disk, which comes in handy if the disk has been replaced due to its failure.

Expanding clustered drives can be performed online using the Windows 2003 DiskPart utility, as long as such an operation is supported by the shared storage device.

You can grant rights to manage a cluster using Cluster Administrator. First highlight the icon representing the cluster (found in the upper left corner). Using the Security tab of its Properties window, you will be able to grant Full Control over cluster administration to additional users or groups.

Troubleshooting Server Cluster

The most valuable cluster troubleshooting information is provided in the cluster logs. Configuration log ClCfgSrv.log, which contains entries describing the actions performed when running the New Server Cluster and Add Nodes wizards, is located in the `%Windir%\System32\LogFiles\Cluster` folder on the computer from which the wizards are run. A diagnostic log stores information about all other cluster activities. Its location is controlled by the value of the ClusterLog system environment variable, which is set by default to `%Windir%\Cluster\Cluster.log`. The `ClusterLogSize` system environment variable determines the maximum size of the log in megabytes (the default sets it to 8MB).

Although it takes some time to become familiar with the cryptic notation of the log entries, they contain a wealth of information about the cluster activities, and most of the time allow you to pinpoint the cause of cluster-related problems. Each entry in the log is time-stamped (in Greenwich Mean Time, so ensure that you account for the time difference when analyzing its content) and identifies a process and the thread that generated it. Most of the resource references use their GUIDs instead of names, but you can look up the corresponding names by checking the keys in the `HKEY_LOCAL_MACHINE\Cluster` portion of the registry. A detailed tutorial on the analysis of the cluster log can be found in the Microsoft Resource Kit.

More significant cluster events are also written to the Windows System Event Log. Using the CLUSDIAG Resource Kit Utility, you can compare cluster-related events from multiple nodes of the same cluster.

If problems are related to the lack of stability of a particular type of resource, you can assign to it a separate Resource Monitor. This will isolate failures to the resource only, without affecting the rest of the cluster. This option is available from the General tab of the resource properties window.

The most severe problems are caused by quorum-related failures. If a disk containing a quorum fails, or a file system, checkpoint file, or log become corrupted, then a cluster will not be able to function. You also will not be able to use the Cluster Administrator or CLUSTER.EXE utility as long as the Cluster Service is stopped. To start recovery, shut down all the cluster nodes, leaving only the one on which you will perform the restore and the shared storage device running.

Next, launch the Services console from the Administrative Tools menu on one of the cluster nodes, locate Cluster Service, open its Properties window, and type in the `-fixquorum` parameter (with the leading dash) in the Start parameters text box. After you click the Start button, the Cluster Service will start without a quorum resource. Even though all of the resources (including quorum) will remain offline, you will be able to take one of the following actions to fix the problem (which one you choose will depend on the cause of the failure):

- ✦ Change the quorum location (using the steps described in the section titled "Server Cluster Management"). A local quorum can be used if no other shared disk is available. In order to connect to the cluster using Cluster Administrator, you will have to use either an individual node name (or single dot, directly from the node's console). You will not be able to connect to the cluster via its IP address or name, because both resources are offline.

✦ Run Chkdsk with /f and /r switches to fix the file system corruption. Prior to running it, you will have to manually bring the quorum disk online (otherwise, you will not be able to access it). Running chkdsk against a clustered disk creates a log that can be reviewed in order to determine the level of corruption and final outcome.

✦ Replace the quorum disk and restore the original signature (and quorum database, if desired) with ASR described in the previous section. A mismatch in the disk signature for a quorum disk manifests itself in the form of event ID 1034 in the Windows System Event Log. You can also use ClusterRecovery from Resource Kit to reset the disk signature without running ASR.

After you manage to successfully complete one of the three actions described previously, verify whether you have a recent backup of a quorum disk. If so, restore it and restart Cluster Service in normal fashion, without any parameters. Otherwise, stop the cluster service and restart it using the resetquorumlog parameter. This will create new quorum files by copying the content of the local cluster database of the node from which recovery is run.

If a quorum is corrupted on one of the local nodes (this would be indicated by the System Event Log entries), you can either perform the System State restore, or copy the current checkpoint file from the shared quorum disk to the %WinDir%\Cluster folder and rename it to CLUSDB (by overwriting the corrupted one). You can also copy the CLUSDB from another node, however, this will require stopping the Cluster Service on that node and unloading the Cluster registry hive using REGEDIT.EXE.

When operating with a Majority Node Set server cluster, a quorum might fail if a majority of the servers becomes unavailable. Most commonly, this happens as a result of network problems (this is not an unlikely event, considering that the Majority Node Set cluster uses the same network for public and private network traffic). If this happens and there is no chance of quick recovery, it is possible to create a quorum with remaining nodes only. This is accomplished by creating a ForceQuorum REG_SZ entry in the registry at HKEY_LOCAL_MACHINE\SYSTEM\CurrentControlSet\Services\ClusSvc\Parameters. This entry needs to contain a comma-separated list of names of the servers that are supposed to form the quorum set. The same result can be accomplished by using the CLUSTER.EXE utility with the /forcequorum option.

Problems that occur during the transition of a group membership during failover or failback and the joining of a cluster are frequently related to failing network connectivity. Network problems might prevent authentication requests from reaching the domain controllers. Healthy WINS and DNS infrastructures are required for the proper name resolution and registration. You should also verify that the WINS and DNS parameters are properly set in the TCP/IP configuration of your cluster network adapters. If your servers point to different DNS servers for name resolution, DNS replication delay can cause problems when adding nodes to a cluster.

Remote Procedure Call (RPC) connectivity problems typically affect failover. A RPCPing utility (from the Exchange 2000 installation CD) or a network analyzer (such as Network Monitor that is available on the Windows 2003 Server) can be used to verify whether this is the case.

When troubleshooting network connectivity issues, keep in mind that the cluster nodes are capable of detecting network failures. The state of the network interfaces participating in cluster communication (both public and private) is displayed in the Network Interfaces node in the Cluster Administrator. Windows 2003 Servers check for hardware failures by employing the Network Driver Interface Specification (NDIS) network driver features. The server cluster also periodically pings external resources in order to determine whether connectivity with the rest of the public network has not been lost. The state of the public network connections is also taken into consideration when determining a quorum owner in the case of a private network failure.

Network Load Balancing Clusters

Network Load Balancing is a successor of a relatively unknown product from Valence Research called Convoy, which is available for the Windows NT 4.0 server platform. The product has been renamed to Windows Load Balancing Service after the company was acquired by Microsoft. Its name changed again to Network Load Balancing with the advent of Windows 2000.

Network Load Balancing is included in all Windows 2003 Server products.

NLB Cluster Concepts

Network Load Balancing (NLB) clusters combine load balancing and high availability for TCP/IP based services and application. Load balancing is accomplished by running separate, but identical copies of applications or services simultaneously on each cluster node. Note that this is different from server clusters, where only a single instance of an application is allowed to run at any given time. Running multiple applications capable of sharing a load provides an increased degree of scalability and is a perfect example of scale-out design. High availability in NLB clusters is based on the ability to detect a server failure. Typically, within 10 seconds, a failed server is excluded from participation in the cluster and, as result, new client connections are redirected to the remaining servers.

Load balancing software is implemented as an NDIS-packed filter driver named WLBS.SYS. As far as the protocol stack is concerned, NLB is located between the network adapter driver and network layer occupied by IP. NLB monitors the incoming traffic and checks their source and IP addresses, transport layer protocol, and destination port. Their values affect the NLB behavior. Load balancing does not, however, adjust dynamically to the changing utilization levels of cluster members (this feature is available in Component Load Balancing clusters, which are discussed later in this chapter). This fact makes proper design critical for optimal scalability and performance.

The NLB impact is limited only to a certain type of network and transport layer traffic, such as TCP, UDP, and Generic Routing Encapsulation (GRE protocol used by Point-to-Point Tunneling Protocol [PPTP]). Other protocols, such as ICMP, IGMP, or ARP are not affected by it in any way.

NLB can be used for clustering:

- Web and FTP servers
- Proxy and Internet Security and Acceleration servers
- VPN servers (with support for both PPTP and L2TP/IPSec)
- Windows Media servers
- Telnet servers
- LDAP Directory Services servers
- Terminal Services servers
- UDDI servers
- Message Queuing servers

NLB fits well in distributed environments, where the front-end servers load balance the client traffic and redirect it to backend servers. This is a common scenario in larger Exchange 2000 deployments, where the front-end consists of protocol servers, accepting HTTP, IMAP4, or POP3 requests and forwarding them to public folders and mailboxes located on backend servers. In the .NET environment, http-based SOAP communication is also a good candidate for network load balancing.

Cluster configuration is determined by a number of parameters. Some of them, known as shared, apply to an entire cluster. These parameters include the following:

- Cluster virtual primary IP address and subnet mask
- Cluster full Internet name
- Cluster MAC address
- Unicast or multicast mode
- IGMP support (in multicast mode only)
- Remote control and password

Host parameters, such as priority ID, initial state, and dedicated IP address and subnet mask, are set individually on each node. Incoming traffic is load balanced according to one or more rules. Known as port rules, they are composed of several parameters:

- Target IP address(es)
- Target port number(s)
- Transport layer protocol(s)
- Filtering mode
- Affinity
- Load weight (with the option of equal load distribution)

The cluster (or virtual) primary IP address is set to the same value across all cluster nodes. This IP address is bound to a network adapter named appropriately by the cluster network adapter. You can bind additional IP addresses (one per clustered application) to the same adapter. IP packets targeting any one of these IP addresses will be load balanced.

Load balancing parameters for each IP address (and its associated clustered applications) can be configured independently.

The load balancing mechanism works by delivering every IP packet simultaneously to all cluster nodes. Then, each node independently determines which one should be responsible for processing that packet. This determination is based on port rules, cluster parameters, and a statistical algorithm. Because the rules, parameters, and algorithm are shared across a cluster, all nodes end up with the same selection. Effectively, only one server processes a packet while all the others discard it.

Clients typically do not use an IP address to reach a clustered resource but refer to it using a name. You must ensure that the appropriate name resolution method is in place. DNS should contain the appropriate records for a cluster, fully qualified, domain name and the names of additional clustered resources. In absence of DNS, local HOSTS files can be used, although this is a less preferred alternative.

The NLB software creates a "virtual" cluster MAC address, which is shared among all nodes. This can be either a unicast MAC address (always starting with 0x02) or a multicast MAC address (always starting with 0x03). The address used depends on your selection of the mode in which cluster is running. The rest of the cluster MAC address is constructed using a cluster IP address, so it is guaranteed to be unique on the network.

In unicast mode, this "virtual" MAC address is used instead of the original one, and it is hard-wired into the cluster network adapter by its manufacturer. In multicast mode, both a multicast MAC address (which is assigned by NLB), as well as the original hard-wired unicast MAC address are used.

Sometimes, it might be necessary (such as for monitoring or content replication) to connect to a specific node of a cluster. Because clustered IP addresses are load balanced, they are not suitable for this purpose (because you would never know which node you end up connecting to). A dedicated IP address allows you to bypass this limitation. This IP address, assigned to the clustered network adapter, uniquely identifies each cluster node. In unicast mode, this IP address resolves to a "virtual" cluster MAC address. This means that packets directed to a dedicated IP address will still be delivered to every node. However, because such packets contain a dedicated IP address as their target, only one node (with its matching IP address) will process them.

Unfortunately, as long as a dedicated IP address is bound to the same network adapter as a cluster IP address, traffic sent to one will always affect the bandwidth available to an entire cluster. In order to overcome this limitation, you can use another network adapter or switch to multicast mode. With two network adapters, a cluster adapter is used strictly for load-balanced client traffic while the other one handles management, monitoring, and content replication. In multicast mode, the original MAC address is still used, which enables the dedicated IP address to get resolved properly to the MAC address of the target network card.

In multicasting mode, you can also enable Internet Group Management Protocol (IGMP) feature. This feature is used by network hosts to send information about their multicast addresses to switches that they directly connect to. This way, multicast packets can be sent only to the appropriate switch ports, rather than flooding all of them (as is the case in unicast mode). Cluster members send IGMP messages every 60 seconds.

Switch flooding can also be avoided in both a unicasting and multicasting configuration by creating a separate VLAN for ports connected to cluster nodes. This flooding, however, requires a VLAN-aware switch and available ports on a router, because cluster-bound network traffic needs to be routed between a cluster VLAN and the rest of the network.

The remote control feature allows the use of the NLB.EXE command line utility to manage cluster nodes from a remote computer. Enabling this feature introduces security risks, such as the possibilities of password or denial-of-service attacks. At the very least, you should set up a complex remote control password. If your NLB cluster serves Internet clients, you should also configure your firewalls to protect NLB clusters by blocking UDP ports 1717 and 2504.

In addition to a dedicated IP address, each node has a unique numeric value assigned during the configuration of NLB software. This value, ranging from 1 to 32 (where 32 is the maximum number of nodes in a cluster), is called a host priority ID. The host priority ID determines how to process incoming traffic that is not covered by any of the port rules defined for a cluster. The host with the highest priority (lowest numerical value of Priority ID) processes all such traffic.

The choice of the initial state of a cluster node typically depends on a clustered application. If such an application startup takes place considerably later than the startup of the NLB driver, then the initial host's state may need to be changed to inactive (rather than the "Started" default setting). Otherwise, a heavy client request load may create a large backlog of requests to be processed.

Port rules are collections of configurable settings that determine the load-balancing algorithm used by cluster nodes. Port rules have to adhere to the following guidelines:

- Each rule applies to a specific range of ports and is assigned to one or more clustered IP addresses.
- The range is a set of consecutive values between 0 and 65535. If there is a gap between ports used by traffic that you want to load balance, multiple rules have to be defined. For example, File Transfer Protocol (FTP) uses two port ranges: 20 to 21 and 1024 to 65535. This requires creating two separate port rules (unless you have a single rule covering all ports between 20 and 65535).
- You can create multiple rules covering the same port ranges as long as they apply to different IP addresses. However, it is not possible to create a different rule for UDP and TCP traffic for the same port and IP address pair.

If an incoming packet matches the IP address, port range, and protocol defined in a port rule, NLB software examines the filtering mode for that rule to determine how to proceed. The filtering mode can be set to disabled, single, or multiple.

The disabled mode prevents traffic that satisfies port rule conditions from being processed. This effectively blocks such traffic and makes NLB clusters behave similar to a basic firewall.

In the single filtering mode, traffic matching the port range and protocol is always handled by a single node. This node is the one with the highest Handling Priority value (the lowest numeric value) for this port range in a cluster. This value (ranging between 1 and 32) has to be unique on each cluster node. Note that this parameter is different from Host Priority ID (which takes care of all the traffic not covered by port rules). Instead, Handling Priority applies to a specific port rule only. This means that, for example, it is possible to have all FTP traffic handled by a different host than HTTP traffic.

The multiple filtering mode offers true network load balancing. In this mode, nodes balance the processing tasks based on the load weight parameters. Load weight is a numeric value between 1 and 100 that is assigned to each node. This value is used to calculate weighed average. Weighed average is the result of adding a load weight value for each node, dividing the outcome by the total number of nodes and finally expressing it as a percentage value. For example, if you have three nodes and you want the first one to process twice as much traffic as each of the other two, you can set their load weights to 40-20-20 (although 60-30-30 or 80-40-40 would work just as well). If each server has the same capacity, this parameter can also be set to equal, which causes even distribution.

When using multiple filtering mode, you might need to control how subsequent requests from the same client should be handled. This is accomplished by using an affinity parameter, which can take on none, single, or class C value. Choosing the right affinity setting is important, because some applications require session coherency. This term describes the ability to maintain a session state when exchanging information between a client and a server. With some protocols or applications (for example, FTP communication), this capability is provided by design. With others, ensuring session coherency might require additional configuration.

Most commonly, session coherency becomes an issue with Web applications. HTTP is connectionless and was not designed to support sessions. If communication relies on, for example, the ability to uniquely identify a client, then workarounds have to be used. One of them is provided by cookies, which are small text files sent to a client by a Web server during the initiation of communication. These files typically identify the Web site, but can also be used to establish a client's identity, allowing the linking of new requests to previous clients. However, including any type of confidential information in cookies is strongly discouraged, because cookies are regular test files. Instead, a client's identity that is contained in a cookie can be verified by a password or certificate, and it then can be used as a key for locating the client's data (including session information) stored either on the Web server or, preferably, in some kind of backend database. The session information can also be included (or munged, if some level of obfuscation is needed) in a URL string or stored in hidden HTTP fields and exchanged as part of the communication between the Web client and Web server. ASP.NET (built into Internet Information Server 6.0) offers ways of automating both URL munging and storing information into the backend database, as well as a state server that can manage state for all cluster nodes.

The previously described methods are sufficient to maintain a session state when communicating with an individual Web server. However, when dealing with a load-balanced cluster, due to the connectionless nature of HTTP protocol each new request for a Web page from the same client might be redirected to a different server every time. If session information is stored on a Web server that handled the original request, the session coherency will be broken. With Network Load Balancing, this can be prevented by setting affinity to either single or class C.

Single affinity forces all packets from the same source IP address to be always processed by the same node. The traffic from different clients is still distributed to multiple nodes, but it's unlikely that the distribution is balanced evenly. If one group of clients tends to generate more traffic than groups, you will see higher levels of utilization on servers that process their requests. Load balancing will also be negatively affected if the client requests are passing through a proxy server, because they all will be arriving to cluster nodes with the same source IP address.

Class C affinity works in a similar way, but instead of assigning the same node based on a single source IP address, it uses an entire class C network. This is used in situations where a session state is stored on NLB cluster nodes (rather than in the backend database) and clients access the cluster from behind multiple proxy servers. This type of configuration will provide session coherency as long as all proxy servers serving the same set of clients are located on the same class C network.

Because this is not always true (typically when dealing with large Internet Service Providers), another alternative is the use of Web request forwarding. Unfortunately, this feature is available only when using Application Center 2000 for managing NLB cluster nodes. Web request forwarding is based on the automatic creation of nonpersistent session cookies, which identify a cluster member that handled the original request from a client. This cookie is then included in every exchange of HTTP packets for the session's duration. Based on the cluster member identifier, Application Center 2000 forwards the incoming request to the appropriate server. The Web request forwarding feature should be used in combination with a single affinity of Network Load Balancing, otherwise, a large amount of packets could be forwarded among the cluster members. Using Web request forwarding tends to be expensive in terms of additional processing and the amount of additional network traffic generated, therefore, it should be used only when necessary.

The best solution to problems relating to session coherency is not storing session state information on cluster nodes. Instead, this information should be located in a backend database shared between servers, or (if confidentiality is not required) carried in client cookies. In the traditional ASP-based environment, this type of configuration required a rather complex design. ASP.NET, on the other hand, offers a natively process independent, Web-Farm compatible session state, which can easily be stored as part of a process space on a separate server or persisted in a database. After the session state information is no longer associated with individual cluster nodes, the affinity parameter should be set to None.

When using a single or class C affinity, mapping between the client's IP address and a server handling its requests remains constant. This mapping changes only if the affinity settings are administratively changed to none or as the result of convergence.

Convergence is a process in which node availability, cluster parameters, host parameters, and port rules are updated and synchronized across all cluster nodes. Convergence can be prompted by several types of events, such as a node joining or leaving a cluster. Administrative changes, such as adding, removing, or modifying port rules (changing load weight values, for example) also trigger convergence. Typically, convergence takes less than five seconds.

Change in several cluster members is dynamically detected by nodes, based on the unicast or multicast (depending on the mode) heartbeat messages that are exchanged in regular intervals. The absence of five consecutive responses from any node initiates convergence. Both the number of missed responses and the interval between them are configurable via a registry and are stored in the following location: `HKEY_LOCAL_MACHINE\SYSTEM\CurrentControlSet\Services\WLBS\Parameters\Interface\{Interface_GUID}` where the name of the lowest level key is the GUID of the cluster network adapter.

✦ `AliveMsgPeriod` entry of type REG_DWORD controls the length (in milliseconds) of the interval between heartbeat messages. Its default value is 1000 (decimal) and can range between 100 and 10000.

✦ `AliveMsgTolerance` entry of type REG_DWORD controls the number of a node's heartbeat messages that can be missed before this node is marked as unreachable and the convergence process begins. Its default value is 5 (decimal) and can range between 5 and 100.

Modifying these entries should be done only after evaluating their impact on the available network bandwidth and responsiveness to a node failure.

Hardware load balancing solutions provide a viable alternative to software load balancing. However, because filtering the packets (performed by NLB) is generally faster than rerouting them (typical approach of hardware-based load balancing solutions), NLB performs favorably in most situations.

NLB Cluster Requirements

NLB is available on all versions of the .NET Server platform (Standard, Web, Enterprise, and Datacenter). When configuring NLB as part of Application Center 2000, you will need to meet other requirements beyond the ones listed in this section. For example, in such a configuration, two network adapters on each cluster node are required. For details, refer to the product's documentation.

It is possible to run multiple version clusters. For example, you can use a mix of Windows 2003 Enterprise Server and Windows 2003 Datacenter Server and Windows 2000 Network Load Balancing, as well as the Windows Load Balancing Service operating on Windows NT 4.0 servers. However, running Network Load Balancing on a server cluster is not supported.

NLB places a number of requirements on the network infrastructure (such as routers and switches) as well as on the network adapters installed in the cluster nodes. NLB can run on servers connected to FDDI, Ethernet, or Gigabit Ethernet networks, but it does not operate on Token Ring networks.

As mentioned previously, when using unicast mode, the MAC address of a network adapter is substituted with one generated by NLB, which may not be supported by some network adapters. Such adapters need to be replaced prior to cluster setup. Alternatively, configuration can be changed to the multicast mode, which retains the original MAC address and eliminates the need for replacement.

Having the same unicast MAC address (when in unicast mode) used across multiple network adapters might create problems if adapters are connected directly to the same switch. To prevent these problems, NLB (by default, when operating in unicast mode) does not use the cluster-shared MAC address for the outgoing packets. Instead, it creates yet another one, which is a combination of the "shared" MAC address and cluster node priority. As a result, the switch never learns the cluster MAC address. When a client request arrives with the frame destination set to the cluster MAC address, the switch forwards it to all of its ports (because no port is associated with this MAC address). As a result, each cluster node receives the frame (as intended). This behavior is controlled by the value of the registry entry `MaskSourceMAC` (of REG_DWORD type). The entry resides, along with other NLB settings, in the following registry location: `HKEY_LOCAL_MACHINE\SYSTEM\CurrentControlSet\Services\WLBS\Parameters\Interface\{Interface_GUID}` where the {Interface_GUID} stands for GUID of the cluster network adapter. Setting this entry to 1 causes the behavior described previously. Setting it to 0 places the cluster MAC address back in the outgoing packets.

This process, known as "switch flooding," works well, providing that the switch is used exclusively for clustered servers. Otherwise, other nonclustered systems connected to the same switch will also receive cluster-bound traffic. Network congestion then becomes even more of an issue in situations where multiple clusters share the same switch. As a workaround, a network hub can be placed between a switch port and the clustered nodes. After you disable the `MaskSourceMAC` registry entry (by changing its value to 0), the cluster MAC address will become associated with the single switch port (the one connected to the hub), thus preventing the switch flooding. This solution, however, introduces individual points of failure (a hub, its connection to a switch, and single port on the switch) that negatively impacts the level of high availability (the very reason for using NLB clustering). A preferred approach is to use a dedicated switch for the cluster nodes, configure VLANs on the existing switch, or configuring NLB in multicast mode.

When operating in multicast mode, switch flooding can be prevented by enabling the Internet Group Management Protocol (IGMP) multicast feature. IGMP is used by network hosts to advertise their multicast addresses to switches in which they have direct contact. In order for this feature to work, monitoring of the IGMP packets needs to be configured on the switch. This way, a frame targeting a specific multicast MAC address can be forwarded to the appropriate ports, rather than flooding all of them. Once the IGMP setting is enabled on the cluster nodes, the switch updates take place every 60 seconds.

As explained previously, in both unicasting and multicasting configuration it is possible to avoid switch flooding by configuring a separate VLAN for switch ports connected to cluster nodes (assuming that the switch has VLAN capabilities and there are available unused router interfaces).

NLB uses Address Resolution Protocol packets to update the ARP cache on routers with IP Address and MAC address pairs of the cluster's network adapters. The MAC address can be either unicast or multicast, depending on the cluster mode. Some routers, however, have problems processing ARP updates that contain different MAC address information in the ARP portion of the frame and a different source MAC address in its Ethernet header. Others (most notably some of Cisco routers) do not accept ARP updates that map a unicast (cluster) IP address to a multicast MAC address (this happens when cluster operates in multicast mode). Either one of these problems can be solved by creating a static ARP entry, which can be created on a router.

TCP/IP should be the only network protocol bound to cluster's network adapters. Dedicated and cluster IP addresses should be statically assigned. Both also need to be entered in the NLB configuration and TCP/IP properties of the cluster network adapter (this is done automatically if you follow Microsoft recommendations and use NLB Manager for cluster management).

All dedicated and clustered IP addresses should belong to the same IP subnet and share the same subnet mask. In addition, the dedicated IP address should appear first in the list of IP addresses in the TCP/IP properties dialog box (on top of the cluster IP address). Otherwise, outbound connections from a cluster node would use a cluster "virtual" IP address as the source and the returning packet would be load balanced and could possibly be redirected to a different node. The only exception applies to configuring NLB for clustered Virtual Private Network connections. In such cases, no dedicated IP address should be used at all — only a virtual cluster IP address should appear in the TCP/IP properties dialog box for a cluster network adapter.

Just as with server clusters, NLB places special demands on the applications and services it supports. These applications have to be IP based and communicate using TCP connections or UDP streams. They cannot depend on server names for establishing remote connections. They also should not require exclusive locks (for write access) on resources located on cluster nodes that might be simultaneously used by other clients. In general, data used by clustered applications and services can be located on the backend servers (shared among the nodes) or directly on the server nodes. In the first case, shared backend servers should be able to handle simultaneous access from cluster nodes. In the second case, some type of content replication mechanism should be put in place (to make the content of the nodes identical). One such mechanism, which is almost completely automated, is provided by Application Center 2000. The Content Replication System available on the Site Server offers similar, although more limited functionality. With .NET Web applications, which no longer rely on a registry to store component configuration information, content deployment in many cases is as simple as file copy (hence the term "XCOPY deployment"). Very common is a hybrid approach, where the static content (such as HTML pages on a Web server) is synchronized across cluster nodes, while dynamic data is kept on a backend server.

NLB Cluster Design and Capacity Planning

NLB clusters offer benefits of load balancing and high availability. Scalability greatly exceeds that offered by server clusters — a NLB cluster can have up to 32 nodes. As described earlier in this chapter, NLB clusters offer various ways of handling client requests. Solutions can favor either scalability or fault tolerance. A load can be distributed based on a number of configurable settings, such as percentage of overall traffic, host priority, or source affinity. Failover is emulated by running a separate but identical instance of the same application on each cluster member. As long as the session state and application data are maintained outside of the cluster, connections broken due to a server failure can be redirected to another server and the original sessions can be restored.

Network Load Balancing, like other clustering mechanisms, require intra-cluster communication (such as heartbeat messages and convergence traffic) as well as nonclient external connections used for management and content replication. The negative impact of this overhead traffic on client connectivity can be eliminated by using an additional network adapter on each node. Implementing multicasting instead of unicasting further improves the efficient use of network bandwidth.

A number of network adapters and types of traffic used in intra-cluster communication are the basis for grouping NLB clusters into the following categories:

✦ Single network adapters in a unicast mode

✦ Single network adapters in a multicast mode

✦ Multiple network adapters in a unicast mode

✦ Multiple network adapters in a multicast mode

Configuration with single network adapters in unicast mode (shown in Figure 25-5) is the simplest and the least expensive. It is also one that is guaranteed to work with any router. It has, however, a number of drawbacks. In a switched environment, it causes "switch flooding" (unless VLANs are used). It also does not allow communication from one cluster node to another. Finally, the available bandwidth for client connections is affected by the management or content replication traffic, because both compete for access to the same network adapter. This design might be sufficient for servers with relatively static content and low volume of traffic.

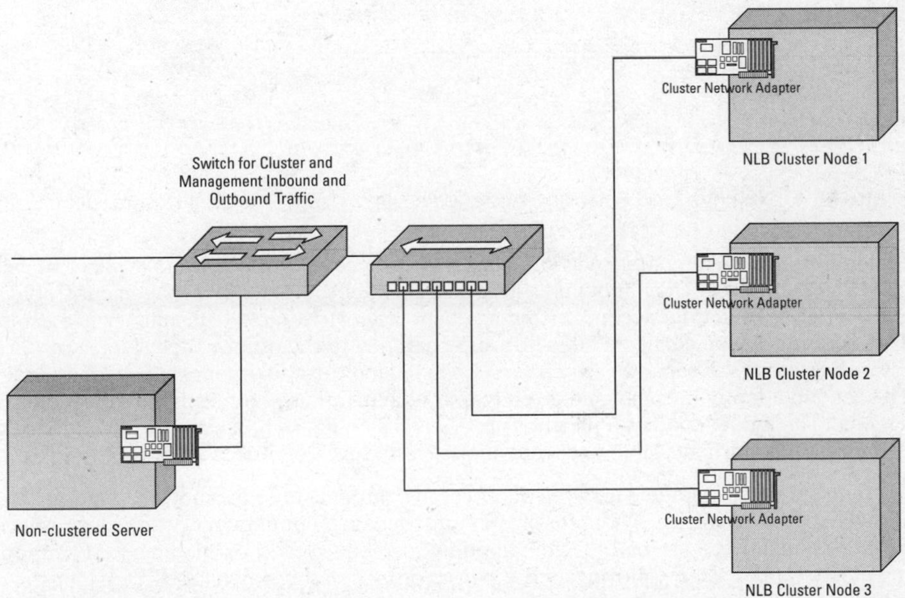

Figure 25-5: Network Load Balancing cluster with the single adapters in unicast mode.

Configuration with a single network adapter in multicast mode (shown in Figure 25-6) eliminates some of the drawbacks present in unicast mode (switch flooding can be eliminated through use of IGMP, as well as VLANs). Because dedicated IP addresses resolve to "hardwired" MAC addresses of network adapters on cluster nodes, intra-cluster communication is possible. However, if a local router does not support ARP updates containing a unicast IP address and a multicast MAC address, maintaining the manual entries in the router's ARP cache might be necessary. This configuration still suffers from the fact that client and management traffic compete for bandwidth on the same network adapter.

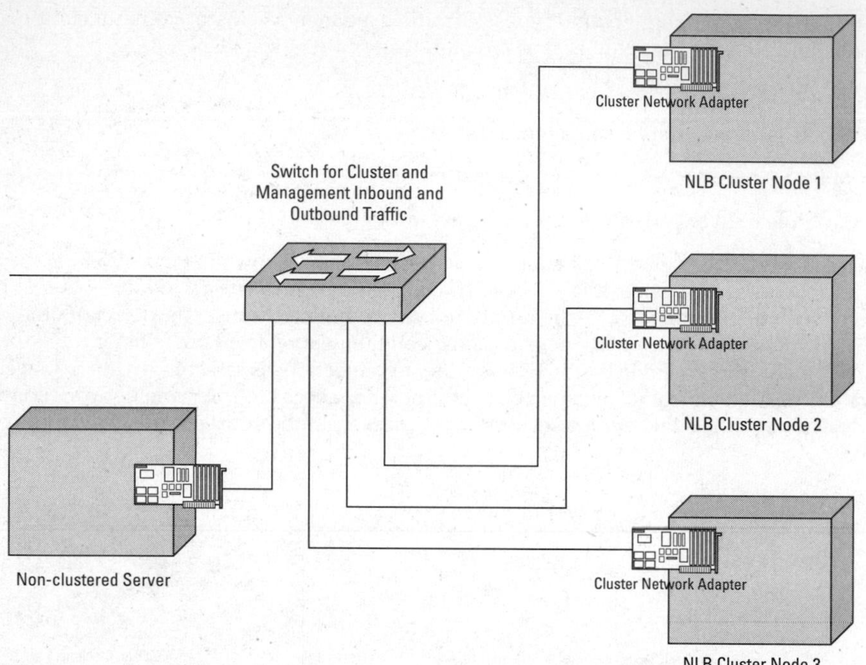

Figure 25-6: Network Load Balancing cluster with single adapters in multicast mode.

Configuration with a multiple network adapter in unicast mode (shown in Figure 25-7) allows for the separation of client inbound traffic and client outbound and management traffic. The cluster network adapter accepts incoming client requests targeted at a cluster IP address. This adapter can be connected to a hub and shared with the other nodes, in order to prevent "switch flooding". A separate switch (or VLAN) linking the cluster nodes is recommended. The second adapter is connected directly to a switch and used for both outgoing and management (including content replication) traffic. This configuration significantly increases the network bandwidth available to clients. In this case, ARP updates the work with any router.

Configuration with multiple network adapters in a multicast mode (shown in Figure 25-8) allows the use of a single switch for cluster and management network connections (as well as other, nonclustered systems). "Switch flooding" can be avoided by enabling IGMP support on the cluster and IGMP monitoring on the switch or by creating a dedicated VLAN for the cluster nodes.

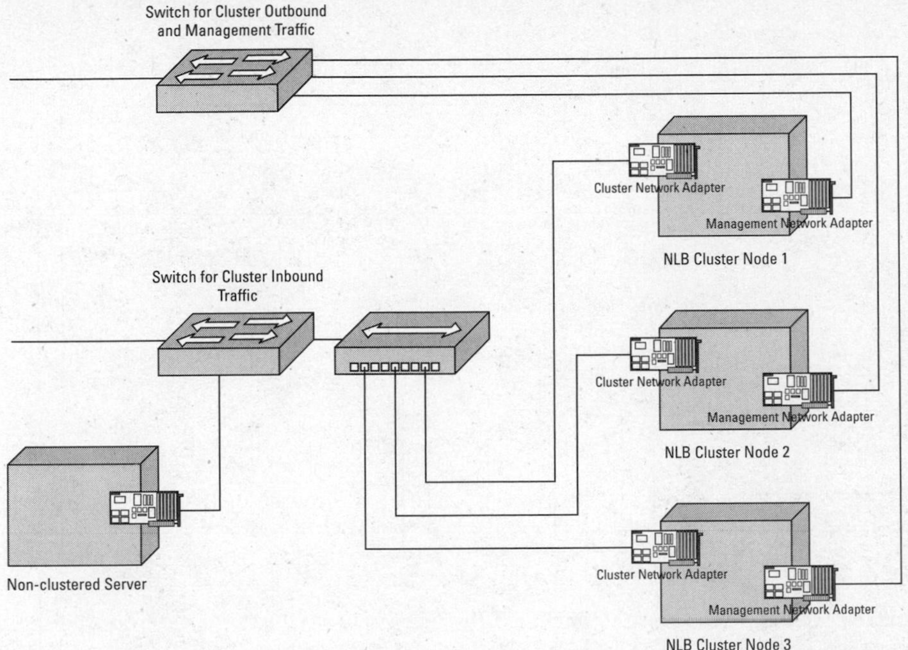

Figure 25-7: Network Load Balancing cluster with the multiple adapters in unicast mode.

Each cluster node can have only a single adapter that is bound to a particular NLB cluster. However, if a server has multiple adapters, then each of them can be associated with a different cluster.

In addition to deciding what configuration best suits your needs and budget, you also need to determine your optimum port rule settings. To obtain the best mix of load balancing and high availability, set the load weight to reflect the processing capacity of cluster nodes, and set the filtering to multiple host.

The choice of the affinity value will depend on whether communication will be session oriented and if so, whether the session information is maintained on cluster nodes or outside of them. The most even distribution is accomplished by using None affinity. None affinity is commonly used when directing client traffic to static Web pages residing on a Web farm. Reasons for using class C and single affinities ware explained in the previous section.

If your goal is high availability, but your application does not support load balancing, set the filtering mode to single host, and the preferred node should have its host priority set to the lowest numerical value.

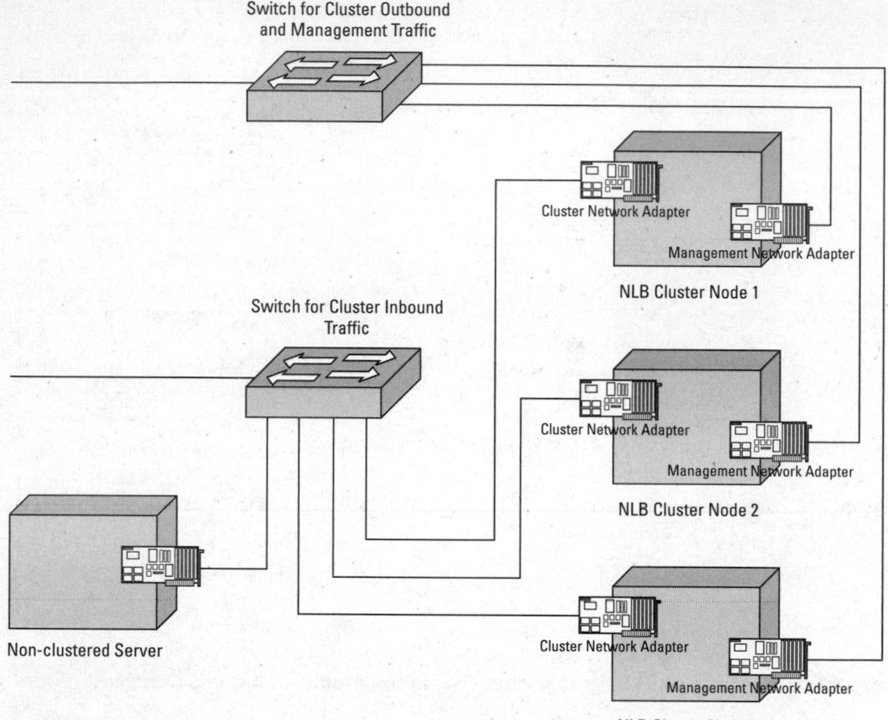

Figure 25-8: Network Load Balancing cluster with the multiple adapters in multicast mode.

Step-by-Step NLB Cluster Installation and Configuration

Network Load Balancing functions as a network component that is activated on a per network adapter basis. The software consists of a networking driver WLBS.SYS and control program NLB.EXE.

Before you start configuring NLB, you need to ensure that you have a number of available IP addresses. In a single network adapter configuration, you will need one for the "virtual" cluster, shared among all the nodes, and one dedicated per each node. They all should belong to the same subnet and share the same subnet mask parameter. In a dual network adapter configuration, you will need the "virtual" one for the entire cluster (shared among all the nodes), and two per node (dedicated and management). Cluster and dedicated IP addresses need to belong to the same subnet. All management IP addresses need to reside on a separate subnet. If a server has multiple network adapters, the default gateway parameter should be set only for the one that connects to the largest network. In the case of NLB clusters, this typically would be a cluster network adapter, connected to the public network and accepting load balanced client requests. Paths to other networks (such as the ones containing management workstations) need to be added manually to routing tables on each node.

Make sure that the network adapter that will be used for NLB is set with a static IP (not DHCP assigned). This static IP will be used as dedicated IP during the NLB configuration.

Also ensure that you perform all of the operations using an account that has administrative privileges to all servers that will become NLB cluster members.

An NLB cluster can be installed using the properties of a network connection in the Network Connections window, Network Load Balancing Manager, or with Application Center 2000. Using NLB Manager is the recommended method, but we will start with the first option for the sake of completeness (for information on configuring NLB with Application Center 2000, refer to its documentation). This will also help you appreciate the simplicity and robustness of the NLB Manager (which will be presented next).

Network Load Balancing appears as network component in Network Connection properties window. Enabling it involves checking a check box and modifying the parameters of the cluster, host, and port rules (this process needs to be performed on each node separately). To begin, bring up the dialog box displaying properties of the network connection that will be used as a cluster network adapter. The NLB option should appear in the list of installed components with a check box unchecked. If the option is not there, you will need to add it by clicking the Install button and selecting Network Load Balancing from the list of Services. After the option is selected and the check box checked on, the Properties button becomes enabled. Clicking it brings up the Network Load Balancing Properties dialog box from which most of the configuration settings are available.

The settings are grouped under three tabs:

✦ Cluster Parameters dialog box contains cluster-wide parameters shown in Figure 25-9.

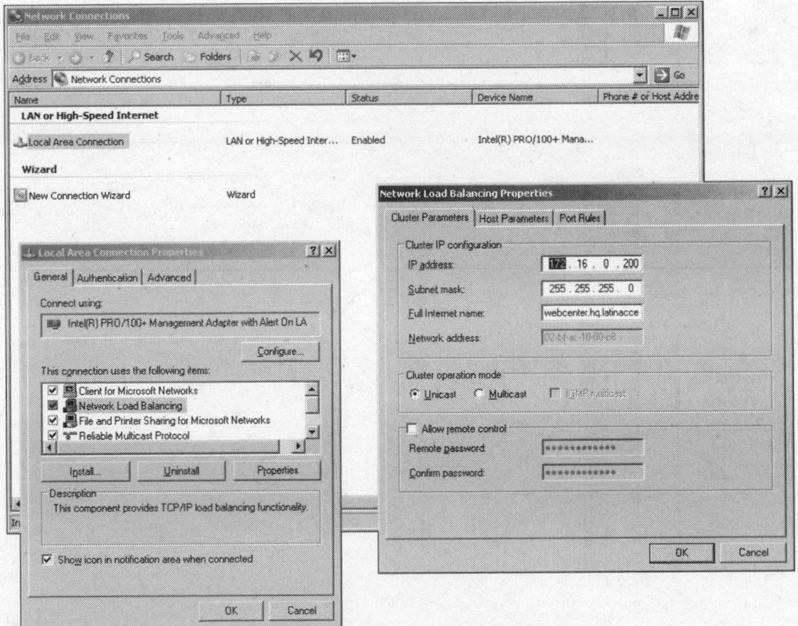

Figure 25-9: Network Load Balancing Cluster Parameters.

✦ Host Parameters dialog box contains settings specific to a node being currently configured, shown in Figure 25-10.

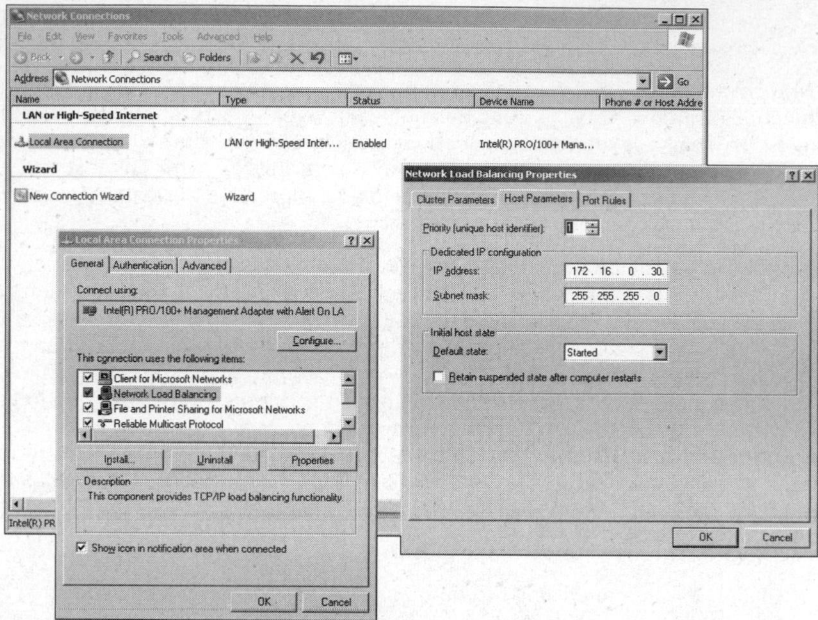

Figure 25-10: Network Load Balancing Host Parameters.

✦ Port Rules contains a list of port rules that consists of both cluster-wide and node-specific settings, shown in Figure 25-11.

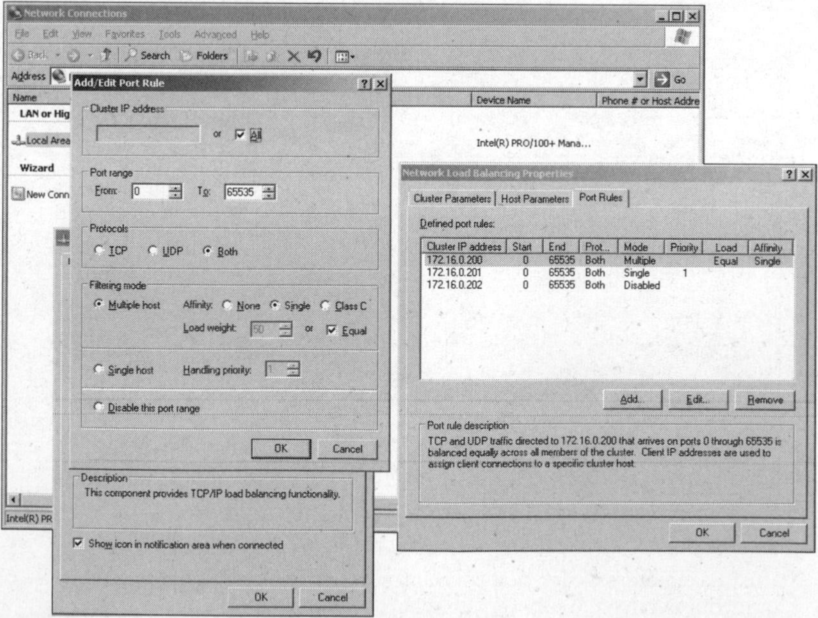

Figure 25-11: Network Load Balancing Port Rules.

After the cluster parameters, host parameters, and port rules are configured, you need to modify the TCP/IP properties for the same network adapter. Bring up its Internet Protocol (TCP/IP) properties dialog box, click the Advanced button, and add the cluster IP address with its subnet mask as the second to the list of IP addresses. The dedicated IP address should appear first in the list (this IP address should be already there because it has been statically assigned prior to enabling Network Load Balancing). In a dual network adapter configuration, you would also assign a management IP address to the other network adapter (using DHCP in this case is allowed). Once the cluster is installed, create entries on your DNS servers, resolving the Full Internet Name of the cluster into its IP address. The same applies to any other clustered applications that use unique DNS names.

To add another node to the existing NLB cluster, repeat the process described previously. When specifying the host parameters and handling priority, you need to ensure that you enter values different from those used on the existing cluster nodes. At the same rate, make sure that all of the remaining values are identical to those on the first node. Adjust the load weight to reflect the processing capacity of the new node.

When a node is removed from an NLB cluster (this is done simply by unchecking the NLB check box in the Network Connection properties window), the cluster IP address should be manually removed from the TCP/IP configuration properties of a cluster network adapter. Otherwise, an IP address conflict will result.

As you can see, using the Network Connection properties for configuring Network Load Balancing requires a number of repetitious steps and leaves plenty of room for error. This is the main reason behind recommending NLB Manager as the preferred tool for cluster management. NLB Manager helps to prevent issues resulting from misconfigured nodes and automates a number of tasks that would have to be performed manually otherwise (for example, the adding and ordering of clustered IP addresses to the TCP/IP properties of the cluster network adapter). It also simplifies the creation of a new cluster; adding or removing nodes; creating, deleting, or modifying port rules; and changing the host or cluster parameters. In addition, using this utility does not require access to the server (either via a console or an RDP connection). NLB Manager can run (like most administrative tools) from any workstation or server. The only exception applies to NLB clusters in unicast mode with single network adapters. In such a configuration, if NLB Manager is run directly on one of the cluster nodes, it cannot be used to manage the parameters of any other nodes. The reason for it is the fact that connection to cluster's virtual IP address originating from any of the cluster nodes would always be looped back to the same node (due to the matching destination IP and MAC address). You can still, though, use the Network Connection properties window to manage the cluster and host properties directly on each node. The practical implication is that you should not attempt to add more nodes to a single node NLB cluster by running NLB Manager from the first node, as long as the single adapter in unicast mode is used.

NLB Manager is part of the Windows 2003 Enterprise Server and Windows 2003 Datacenter Server Administrative Tools. Like Cluster Administrator, it is not implemented as a Microsoft Management Console snap-in but as an executable NLBMGR.EXE. Its main window (shown in Figure 25-12) is divided into three panes. The top left one contains a list of clusters and nodes. Once one of them is selected, its content (with properties) is shown in the top right window pane. The bottom portion of the window displays status messages generated by different actions invoked from the top or context-sensitive menus. You can connect to multiple NLB clusters from the same window.

To create a new NLB cluster, you need to select New from Cluster menu. This brings up the Cluster Parameters screen

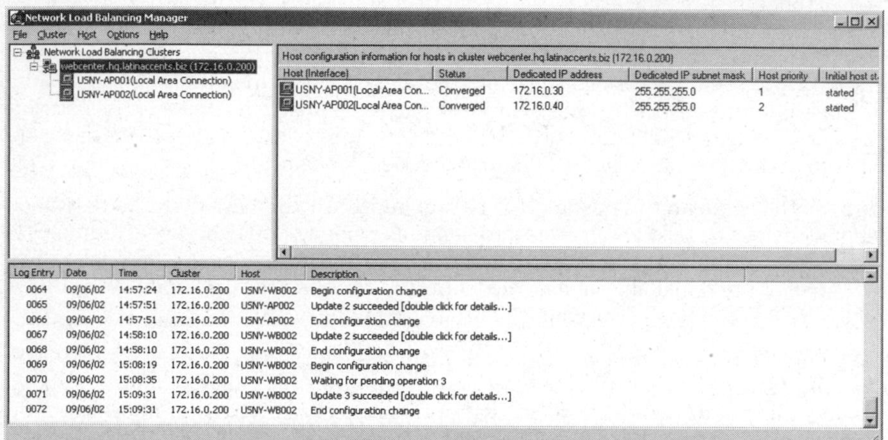

Figure 25-12: Main interface of Network Load Balancing Manager.

At this screen, enter the same parameters that you did in the Network Connection properties window. After typing them in and clicking the Next button, you have the option of adding more cluster IP addresses (besides the primary). The next dialog box allows you to define port rules, and is followed by the Connect screen (presented in Figure 25-13) where you can specify a host that will become the first member of the new cluster. After you type in its host-name or IP address and click Connect, you are presented with the list of interfaces available for configuration of a new cluster.

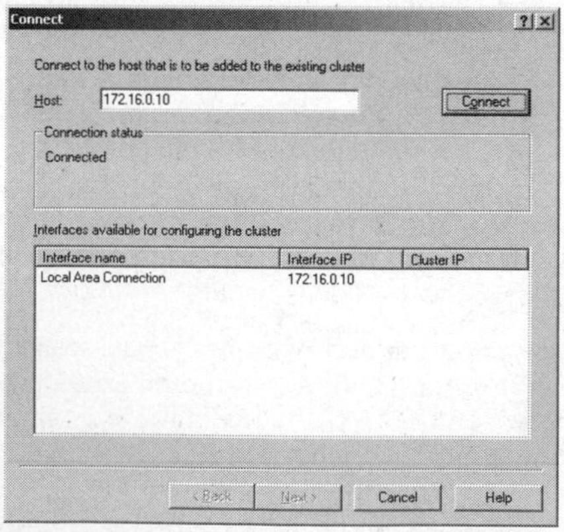

Figure 25-13: Designating the first host of an NLB Cluster using an NLB Manager.

Select the one that will be clustered and click Next again. You will be presented with the Host Parameters window, which is identical to the one provided by the Network Connection properties. From here, you can alter the default values, if you so choose. This step completes the setup of the first node of the NLB cluster.

To add another node, highlight the cluster in the upper-left window and select the Add Host to Cluster option from the Cluster menu. You will be prompted for the Host IP address with the same Connect dialog box that appeared when creating the cluster. After you click the Connect button (a target server has to be active), you will see a list of its IP interfaces (just as before). Select the one that the cluster IP address will bound to and click on Next. Then, specify the host parameters and click Finish. Repeat the same process for all remaining nodes.

Removal of the host is also straightforward — it can be performed by selecting the Delete Host menu option. This automatically removes IP cluster address from TCP/IP properties of a cluster network adapter on a target server.

To manage an existing node, use the Connect to Existing menu option (in the Cluster menu or right-click menu of NLB Clusters node). This will display the Connect dialog box, prompting you for the IP address or name of one of the cluster nodes. Be aware that you should not type in the clustered IP address here. Otherwise, you might have problems accessing some of the nodes' parameters.

The following list shows the port rule parameters for the most common types of services used with Network Load Balancing:

FTP: Because FTP uses two nonadjacent port ranges, two port rules need to be created.

Port Rule #1

Port range: 20 to 21

Protocols: TCP

Filtering mode: Multiple Hosts

Affinity: Single or Class C

Port Rule #2

Port range: 1024 to 65535

Protocols: TCP

Filtering mode: Multiple Hosts

Affinity: Single or Class C

Telnet:

Port Rule

Port range: 23 to 23

Protocols: TCP

Filtering mode: Multiple Hosts

Affinity: None (because only a single TCP connection is used)

HTTP:

Port Rule

Port range: 80 to 80

Protocols: TCP

Filtering mode: Multiple Hosts

Affinity: None (if session state is not stored on the cluster)

Single or Class C otherwise

HTTP over SSL:

Port Rule

Port range: 443 to 443

Protocols: TCP

Filtering mode: Multiple Hosts

Affinity: Single or Class C

VPN via PPTP/GRE or IPSEC/L2TP:

Port Rule for PPTP

Port range: 1723 to 1723

Protocols: TCP

Filtering mode: Multiple Hosts

Affinity: Single or Class C

Port Rule for IPSec

Port range: 500 to 500

Protocols: UDP

Filtering mode: Multiple Hosts

Affinity: Single or Class C

For VPN connection, NLB requires two separate network adapters. One of them is configured only with shared cluster IP address (no dedicated address should be assigned to it); the other uses a unique one. These addresses cannot belong to the same class C network. Default port rules can be used. Choose between a single and multiple hosts filtering mode, depending on whether you want to provide a failover or load balancing. This type of configuration is one of few exceptions, in which it is recommended to use unicast mode rather than multicasting.

On Windows 2003 Enterprise and Datacenter Servers, Network Load Balancing is capable of keeping track of IPSec sessions. This way, the existing connections are maintained even after such convergence-affecting events such as adding or removing a cluster node.

NLB Cluster Management

There are three separate utilities that can be used for management of an NLB cluster:

- ✦ Network Load Balancing properties dialog box in the Network Connection properties for cluster adapter for each cluster node.
- ✦ Network Load Balancing Manager, accessible from the Administrative Tools menu.
- ✦ NLB.EXE command line utility located in the `%SystemRoot%\System32` folder.

Configuration of the NLB properties available from the Network Connection Properties of a cluster adapter has been described in the previous section. We also have covered using an NLB Manager for creating a cluster, adding and removing nodes, and port rule changes. As previously mentioned, this is the recommended way of managing NLB clusters due to its robustness and ease of use (with the only exception being running NLB Manager directly from a cluster node configured in unicast mode with single network adapter). In addition, NLB Manager provides the ability to work with multiple clusters from the same interface (you can add them by selecting the Connect to Existing option from the Cluster menu). Unfortunately, the names of clusters and hosts you connect to are not retained between sessions, so every time you launch NLB Manager, the list of clusters in the upper-left window is empty. You can, however, save a list of hosts in a text file (each host name is separated by a line break) and load it next time you launch the tool. You can do this either by using Save/Load Host List options in File menu or by typing the following at the Command Prompt:

```
NLBMGR /hostlist HostList.txt
```

where HostList.txt is the file with line break-separated host list. This will launch NLB Manager with the connections to these hosts already open.

When using NLB Manager, remember that the interface is not automatically refreshed, so in order to see results of changes you applied, you might have to use the Refresh menu option or press the F5 key with the focus on the object with settings that you want to view (cluster or server).

Regardless of the tool you will be using for cluster management, you need to run it in the security context of an account with the administrative rights to each cluster node. This can be accomplished either by logging on with this account, running secondary logon (RunAs) utility, or, in the case of NLB Manager, setting default credentials (from the Options, Credentials menu option).

For the remainder of this section, we will concentrate on using NLB.EXE for cluster management. Even though more difficult to use, NLB.EXE has two main advantages. Probably the biggest one is its response time, which is much faster than that of the NLB Manager interface. Besides, NLB can be incorporated into batch files or scripts, allowing the automation of a cluster's administration.

NLB.EXE is the Windows 2003 replacement for WLBS.EXE, which is present in previous versions of Network Load Balancing. This name is derived from the Windows Load Balancing Suite, which was an implementation of the network load balancing developed for the Windows NT 4.0 platform. NLB.EXE and WLBS.EXE provide identical functionality. They can be used to configure and monitor an NLB cluster both locally and remotely, although some options are available only locally. In addition, in order to administer a cluster remotely, remote control has to be first enabled and a remote control password set. This password needs to be entered with `/PASSW` switch for every command executed remotely. The NLB.EXE utility has a standard help option (invoked by running NLB with `?` or help parameter or without any parameters).

There are several ways of referring to cluster nodes when running the NLB command remotely. You can reference an entire cluster by specifying a cluster IP address or full Internet name. If you want to refer to a specific node within a cluster, you can use a notation consisting of a pair of values. The first value needs to be the cluster's name or IP address followed by the node's hostname, IP address, or numerical value equal to host priority ID. A value of 0 designates a default host. In order to be able to use the Internet name of an NLB cluster, you need to create an appropriate host record on your DNS server.

For example, to stop the host USNY-AP001 with an IP address 172.16.0.30 and host priority ID 1, which is a member of a cluster webcenter with an IP address of 172.16.0.200, and a remote control password set to Pa$$w0rd, any of the following can be used:

```
NLB stop webcenter:usny-ap001 /PASSW Pa$$w0rd
NLB stop 172.16.0.200:172.16.0.30 /PASSW Pa$$w0rd
```

```
NLB stop webcenter:172.16.0.30 /PASSW Pa$$w0rd
NLB stop webcenter:1 /PASSW Pa$$w0rd
```

Here are some sample uses of NLB.EXE command:

```
NLB display
```

provides a variety of cluster- and local member-related information, such as the configuration parameters (including port rules), most recent event log messages, IP configuration of the local host, and cluster state. Unfortunately, the display option can only be used locally. The remaining options operate both locally and remotely, however, for the remote access you need to specify the IP address or the name of the target node and the remote control password.

```
NLB ip2mac 172.16.0.200
```

displays unicast and multicast MAC addresses generated for a given IP address. This command is useful when a router has problems processing ARP updates generated by NLB and a static entry needs to be added to a router's ARP cache.

```
NLB query 172.16.0.200 /PASSW Pa$$w0rd
```

returns the state of the remote cluster. This can be used to verify convergence status. For example, if a cluster node is in the converging state for an extended period of time (convergence should not take more than ten seconds), this might indicate that its configuration is inconsistent with the rest of nodes.

```
NLB start webcenter:usny-ap001 /PASSW Pa$$w0rd
```

starts the remote cluster node usny-ap001 on the cluster webcenter.

```
NLB start webcenter:usny-ap001 /PASSW Pa$$w0rd
```

starts the remote cluster stopped using the previous command.

```
NLB drainstop webcenter:usny-ap001 /PASSW Pa$$w0rd
```

prevents any new connections to the usny-ap001 node of the webcenter cluster. Once the last existing connection ends, the node is stopped. A draining process can be used in order to gracefully remove an NLB cluster member. This will prevent any new connections from being assigned to the selected server. You can accomplish the same result with the `Drainstop` option of the Control Host menu of an NLB Manager interface.

```
NLB drain 172.16.0.200:80 webcenter:usny-ap001 /PASSW Pa$$w0rd
```

prevents any new connections on the port 80 of the clustered IP address 172.16.0.200 to the usny-ap001 node of the webcenter cluster. A draining process can be used in order to gracefully stop traffic to a particular port or range of ports on an NLB cluster member. This will stop any new connections on all the ports controlled by the port rules that include a port specified by the command. You can accomplish the same result with the Drain option of the Control Host menu of the NLB Manager interface, which operates on a per-port rule basis.

```
NLB disable 80 webcenter:usny-ap001 /PASSW Pa$$w0rd
```

prevents new requests on port 80 from being accepted by usny-ap001 node of the webcenter cluster. This can be used to temporarily redirect traffic for a load-balanced Web site to other nodes (for example, if a current node needs to be reset). It is important to note that this command disables all the rules that include port 80 within their port range, so it might possibly affect other traffic as well (depending on how port rules are set up).

```
NLB enable 80 webcenter:usny-ap001 /PASSW Pa$$w0rd
```

allows new requests on port 80 of the same cluster node to be accepted (and, possibly, enabling traffic on other ports, depending on the ways port rules are set up) by enabling all the port rules that include port 80 in their port ranges.

Both enabling and disabling ports is also possible using the NLB Manager interface, although it is done on a per-rule basis. This truly reflects the way this command operates.

You should remember that changes to many configuration options (such as the modification of existing port rules, or addition and removal of a cluster node) trigger convergence. Convergence involves a number of actions, depending on cluster settings and the type of change detected. One of the effects is the re-evaluation of the role of default host. Change of the default host impacts, in turn, the distribution of traffic that is not covered by port rules. Other types of changes, such as modifying the host priority in a single filtering mode or changing the load weight values in multiple filtering mode also force the redirection of traffic. Because all these changes might break session coherency and, as the result, disrupt existing connections, they should be performed during off-hours.

Troubleshooting an NLB Cluster

Events related to the operations of an NLB cluster are recorded in the System Event Log. The most recent ones can also be retrieved by running the NLB command line utility with a display option (although this is limited to local cluster nodes only).

Common problems with NLB result from duplicate host priorities or other inconsistencies among cluster members, which prevent convergence from completing. This can be detected by running an NLB query command or checking the content of the System Event Log. To fix the problem, NLB on a host configured with duplicate priority or inconsistent port rules should be stopped. This can be done using the NLB command with a stop option. After the problem is corrected, the NLB start command would initiate the process of a node joining a cluster. In general, using NLB Manager for cluster configuration and management helps avoid such situations.

Component Load Balancing Clusters and Application Center 2000

Component Load Balancing (CLB) is the third type of clustering presented in this chapter. Its main purpose is the load-balancing activation of COM+ components residing in the middle-tiers of distributed Windows architecture. The Windows 2003 server platform does not offer native support for CLB. Instead, you need to use a separate Microsoft product called Application Center 2000. Application Center 2000, besides being required for setting up CLB clusters, also simplifies the configuration, management, and monitoring of NLB and CLB clusters, content synchronization, and COM+ application deployment.

CLB Cluster Concepts

To get familiar with the concept of Component Load Balancing, first we need to ensure that you have an understanding of technologies that led to its inception, such as COM, DCOM, and COM+.

Microsoft designed the Component Object Model (COM) as a software development framework. This framework included a set of rules that allow software components created by independent developers to interact with each other. This way, new applications could be written faster and without the duplication of effort, by taking advantage of already existing code. Using a feature implemented by an existing COM object is as simple as writing a couple lines of code to activate it. Once the object is activated, its methods and properties become available to a calling program.

Initially, a calling program and the COM objects had to reside on the same system in order to communicate. By introducing Distributed Component Object Model (DCOM), Microsoft extended reach of COM to remote systems. However, operating in a distributed environment introduced a new set of challenges. Using remote components made it difficult to provide the same level of reliability as when operating locally. Response time got longer, which frequently made synchronous communication methods (working perfectly for local components) not suitable. Another factor was the need for graceful handling of network or remote server failures.

To address these problems, Microsoft developed Microsoft Transaction Service (MTS). MTS applied a concept of database transactions to distributed operations in order to guarantee their consistency. Two phase commit (controlled by a software component called Distributed Transaction Coordinator) was used in order to check the status of a transaction throughout multiple stages of its processing. Only after all the systems involved confirmed a successful completion, the transaction was completed. Microsoft also addressed a problem of transactions, which required a reliable communication method with remote servers (that could be temporarily unavailable). The solution took the form of Microsoft Message Queue Server (MSMQ). MSMQ complemented MTS. It provided guaranteed asynchronous delivery by queuing requests for remote services until they could be processed.

COM, DCOM, MTS, and MSMQ were still, though, separate technologies. It required significant programming skills and experience to combine them together in order to take advantage of their benefits. The COM+ standard (first introduced in Windows 2000) integrated these technologies into the operating system. COM+ enhanced the functionality of the existing COM objects by creating an environment in which they can reliably execute. This environment functions like a wrapper, which disguises itself as a COM object to the outside world and intercepts all of its communication. This way, the COM+ object still acts like an original COM object, but also adds its own functionality. Extra features provided by COM+ include the following:

- ✦ Transaction support: Ability to ensure that each operation involving COM objects either completes successfully in its entirety, or rolls back, leaving the environment in its original state (feature offered originally by MTS)
- ✦ Component and application level security: Ability to control access to COM objects on the application and component level (also originally included in MTS)
- ✦ Concurrency support: Ability to support multiple threads executing the same code concurrently within COM object
- ✦ Just-in-time activation: Ability to activate and deactivate COM objects in response to client requests, which improves resource utilization
- ✦ Object pooling: Ability to maintain a number of COM objects once they are created, and to allocate them on as needed basis in response to COM object activation requests. Because COM object creation is typically an expensive (in terms of time and processing) operation, this improves the responsiveness to client requests.

.NET takes component sharing to the next level, by providing robust, flexible, and platform-independent infrastructure, with native memory management, garbage collection, and native support for versioning (in addition to all features supported by COM+). .NET is also fully compatible with COM+, both in the client and server role, hence all concepts presented in this section can be fully utilized on the Windows 2003 server platform.

COM objects have to be appropriately configured in order to be able to take advantage of the benefits provided by the COM+ runtime environment. With COM+, configuration can be done administratively without the need for code modifications. Administration is performed with the Component Services console located in the Administrative Tools menu. With Component Services, you can manage COM+ applications and their individual components. First, you need to create a COM+ application. Once an application exists, COM objects can be installed or imported into it from other computers. Installation registers the COM+ application and COM object in the COM+ Registration Database and creates the appropriate references in the Windows registry. Manual installation performed using the Component Services console is not suitable for large deployments. The process can be automated by a COMREPL tool, which is provided in Windows 2000 and Windows 2003 Servers (located in the `%SystemRoot%\System32\COM` folder). You can find out more about it from Component Services OnLine Help. If you have Application Center 2000 available, you can use its COM+ application deployment features.

There are three types of COM+ applications — library, server, and proxy. The main difference between them is the way they execute. A library application runs in the process space of a calling process. A server application, on the other hand, executes in a separate process space, which is provided in Windows 2003 by an executable DLLHOST.EXE, intended specifically for this purpose. Library applications execute faster because communication between the COM+ application and a calling process takes place within the same process space. Server applications execute slower because communication with the calling process needs to cross process space boundaries. On the other hand, using server applications provides more stability because their failure, or any type of performance problems affect only their own instance of DLLHOST.EXE, not a calling application. If one instance of DLLHOST.EXE fails, the next one is created on the next COM+ application invocation. Proxy application is a special case of a server application. Such an application forwards the request for execution to a remote system. Library and server COM+ applications can be installed on a single server. In this case, requests for the creation of COM objects are handled locally. Proxy applications need to be installed on two systems. One of them generates the COM object creation requests. These requests are forwarded to the other system, which is responsible for creating them.

Of all features of Application Center 2000, the most relevant one from our perspective is the ability to cluster COM+ applications. There are several ways of accomplishing this goal. New Cluster Wizard, included in Application Center 2000, offers three clustering options: General/Web cluster, COM+ application cluster, and COM+ routing cluster. The General/Web cluster uses Network Load Balancing. It provides high availability of COM+ applications, but without the true load balancing of COM object activation requests. It balances only network traffic arriving to a group of servers running NLB software. Each server is configured with the same set of locally installed and identically configured COM+ applications. Every new client request is handled according to the port rules and host parameters of an NLB cluster. Even though each server might handle approximately the same amount of network traffic, server utilization across the nodes might vary, depending on whether a client requests COM object activation. This type of cluster can be set up without Application Center 2000, because it requires features of Network Load Balancing only. Application Center 2000 can be used, however, to simplify deployment, management and monitoring tasks.

The remaining two cluster types — COM+ application and COM+ routing clusters — require Application Center 2000. This is due to the fact that both rely on one of its components, called Component Load Balancing, to load balance COM object activation requests.

COM+ application clusters (refer to Figure 25-14) typically belong to the second tier of load balanced COM+ architecture. Most commonly, the first tier consists of Web servers. All servers in the first two tiers have Application Center 2000 installed. In addition, all servers have the same set of COM+ applications deployed. Typically, the first tier servers are set up as an NLB cluster, which load balances incoming client traffic. These servers also run CLB software. CLB maintains an ordered list (called a routing list) of all servers in the second tier. The server names on the routing list are ordered based on the load, with the best performing server occupying the first position. CLB sends heartbeat signals to each server on the routing list every 200 milliseconds and keeps track of their responses. CLB calculates the delay in response, uses it as the indicator (in addition to arbitrarily chosen performance statistics collected through WMI) of the server load, and based on the outcome reorders the server names on the routing list. These dynamically updated values then are used to redirect COM object creation requests to the least utilized server in the COM+ application cluster. CLB accomplishes this by intercepting COM object activation requests before they leave the first tier servers and rerouting them based on the server order in the routing list. Component Load Balancing is applied only to COM+ components that are marked by selecting the check box "Component supports dynamic load balancing" on the Activation tab of the component's properties in the Component Services MMC snap-in (this check box is available only if Application Center 2000 has been installed). The same check box should be unchecked for the same components on all the second tier servers participating in the COM+ application cluster.

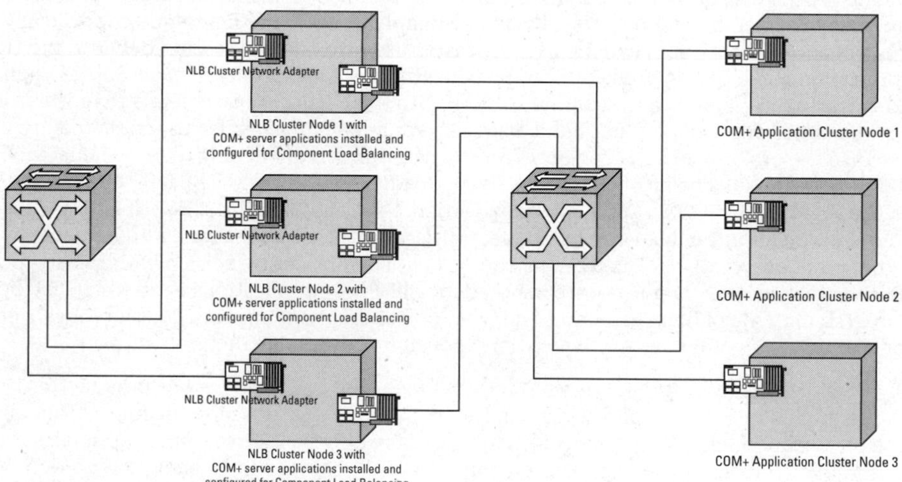

Figure 25-14: COM+ Application cluster configuration for balancing COM+ components.

The only limitation of this solution is the fact that the routing list can contain servers only from a single COM+ application cluster. If you want to be able to use multiple COM+ application clusters, each with a different set of COM+ applications, you need to use COM+ routing clusters. We will present its principles using an example.

COM+ routing clusters introduce an additional, intermediate tier into the COM+ load balancing architecture. All servers in all three tiers need to have Application Center 2000 installed. The servers found in the first tier are part of the NLB cluster that balances incoming traffic. We will consider a scenario with two COM+ application clusters in the third tier, COM+ Cluster1 and COM+ Cluster2. Each cluster has its own COM+ application, COM+ App1 and COM+ App2. The COM objects, which are part of the first COM+ application (COM+ App1), are configured as part of the COM+ application cluster (described previously). In our new design, this requires taking the following steps:

1. On the servers in the first tier, create a routing list of servers in the COM+ Cluster1.
2. Install COM+ App1 as the COM+ server application.
3. Check the "Component supports dynamic load balancing" check box on the Activation tab of COM+ App1.
4. Add servers in the COM+ Cluster1 to the routing list.
5. On the servers in the COM+ Cluster1 (last tier), install COM+ App1 as the COM+ server application.
6. Uncheck the "Component supports dynamic load balancing" check box on the Activation tab of COM+ App1.

To be able to load balance requests to the Cluster2 COM+ application cluster, we will implement COM+ routing clusters (refer to Figure 25-15) in the second tier (for COM+ App2 only). Each server in the second tier will have two network adapters. The first adapter, connecting to the first tier servers, will be used as a cluster adapter for NLB. The second adapter, connecting to the COM+ Cluster2 servers in the third tier, will carry COM object activation requests redirected by CLB. In addition, COM+ App2 will be installed on the servers in the first tier as a COM+ proxy application. The name used by the proxy application will match the virtual name of the NLB cluster in the second tier. This name is assigned by filling out the Remote Server Name box on the Activation tab of the application properties in the Component Services console. The setup can be summarized in the following steps:

1. On the servers in the first tier:
   - Install COM+ App2 as COM+ proxy applications and configure it with the name assigned to the NLB cluster in the second tier.
2. On the servers in the second tier (COM+ routing cluster):
   - Install the NLB and set the NLB cluster name to match the one used by the COM+ proxy application on servers in the first tier.
   - Install COM+ App2 as the COM+ server application.
   - Mark the "Component supports dynamic load balancing" check box on the Activation tab of COM+ App2.
   - Add servers in the COM+ Cluster2 to the routing list.
3. On the servers in the third tier (members of COM+ Cluster2):
   - Install COM+ App2 as the COM+ server application.
   - Unmark the "Component supports dynamic load balancing" check box on the Activation tab of COM+ App2.

When a server in the first tier requests the creation of a COM component of the COM+ App2 application, it uses the remote server name specified in the COM+ proxy application. Because this name matches the name of the NLB cluster in the second tier, such a request is forwarded to it and load balanced according to the NLB configuration settings. A server in the second tier, which is chosen by the NLB algorithm to handle this request, uses CLB to forward it to the least busy member of COM+ Cluster2. After the request reaches that server in the COM+ Cluster2, the component is created.

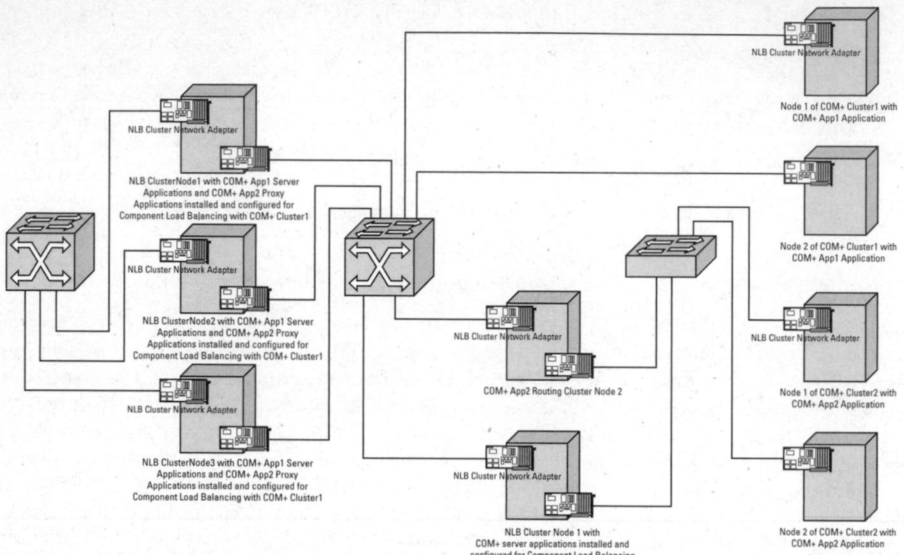

Figure 25-15: COM+ Routing cluster configuration for balancing COM+ components.

CLB Cluster Requirements

To operate on Windows 2003 Servers, Application Center 2000 needs to be upgraded to SP2 level. Windows 2003 servers also need to have Internet Information Services running. If NLB is to be used, each server also needs to have at least two network adapters. The CLB cluster supports up to 12 nodes with each version of Windows 2003 Server. For more detailed requirements of the Component Load Balancing Cluster, refer to the Application Center 2000 documentation.

CLB Cluster Design and Capacity Planning

When deciding whether to use CLB, you should not only consider its advantages but also keep in mind its drawbacks. For example, even though the COM+ clustering solutions benefit from load balancing and scalability, its performance is inferior to nonclustered solutions, because remote invocation of the COM+ objects is slower than a local one. The management and troubleshooting of clusters is much more difficult than individual servers, as is the level of complexity of multi-tiered COM+ configurations.

If you decide to use COM+ clustering, consider using a single-tier design with NLB, a two-tier design with NLB and CLB (and COM+ application cluster), or a three-tier design with NLB and CLB (and COM+ routing cluster).

These designs have been presented in the previous section, so we will now concentrate on discussing their strengths and weaknesses.

Single-tier design with NLB is the simplest and least expensive solution. It does not require Application Center to be installed. A single NLB cluster consists of servers with the same set of identically configured COM+ server applications. Incoming requests for COM object creation are distributed using NLB and handled locally, after a server is selected by the NLB algorithm. Some degree of load balancing is accomplished (although on network level only, without concern for server performance).

Benefits include the following: Local COM+ invocation is faster than the remote one; management, as well as content and COM+ application deployment, is simplified; and it has a lower cost (no need for Application Center 2000, less hardware required). Drawbacks include the following: The COM+ application cannot be shared between multiple Web clusters (because COM+ application resides directly on Web cluster nodes); it is difficult to separate the administration and development of the presentation tier and COM+ applications; COM+ applications can be easily affected by attacks directed as Web servers; and load balancing is based on network traffic, not server utilization. Two-tier design with NLB and CLB requires installation of Application Center 2000 on each server in both tiers. As before, client incoming requests for COM object creation are distributed using NLB on the first tier servers. If a request requires COM+ component activation, it is redirected to the second tier via CLB.

Benefits include the following: ability to separate administration and development of the presentation tier (Web servers) and COM+ applications, ability to place a firewall between the Web servers in first tier and COM+ application servers in the second tier, and load balancing based on network traffic and server performance. Drawbacks include the following: higher cost (two tiers of servers with Application Center 2000 installed on all of them), remote COM+ invocation, more complex management and troubleshooting, and no mechanism for distributing COM activation requests to multiple COM+ clusters.

Three-tier design with NLB and CLB requires Application Center 2000 on each server in all three tiers. NLB load balanced servers in the first tier have multiple COM+ proxy applications installed that point to the names of multiple NLB clusters in the second tier. If a client request requires component activation, it is forwarded to the appropriate NLB cluster in the second tier. CLB on the second tier server is selected based on the NLB algorithm that forwards these requests to the least utilized server in the COM+ application cluster in the third tier.

Benefits include the same as the two two-tier model plus the ability to distribute COM activation requests to multiple COM+ clusters. Drawbacks include the following: the highest cost of all three models, remote COM+ invocation (instead of the local one), and the most complex management and troubleshooting of all three models.

CLB Cluster Installation and Configuration

For details on the installation and configuration of the Component Load Balancing clusters, refer to the documentation included with Application Center 2000.

Hybrid Clustering Solutions

Any of the three clustering technologies presented in this chapter can function independently of the other two, providing high availability and scalability for applications and services. However, they can also work together and complement each other as parts of the distributed processing model. The model typically incorporates three tiers — front-end (also known as client or presentation), middle (referred to as application logic or business), and backend (or data). Each cluster type has its place in the model:

- Server clusters: Work well as backend systems, hosting databases or messaging applications.
- NLB clusters: Are intended primarily for front-end systems.
- CLB clusters: Are designed specifically for handling middle-tier COM+ components.

Clustering Network Services (WINS, DHCP)

Properly functioning network infrastructure is critical to the health of the Windows environment. DHCP and WINS services can be set up on a server cluster as clustered resources, although they are limited to a single instance per cluster only. NLB is not suitable for this purpose.

To set up high availability network infrastructure, start by installing DHCP or WINS service on one cluster node. This can be done from the Windows Components Wizard from Add or Remove Programs Control Panel applet or by selecting the Optional Networking Components item from the Advanced menu in the Network Connections window. This installs the appropriate files and configures DHCP or WINS with their default database locations. Next, create a virtual server by assigning an IP Address, Network name, and Physical Disk resources to it. Finally, set up the DHCP (or WINS) service resource by launching the New Resource Wizard. Besides specifying standard parameters, such as name, description, preferred owner, or dependencies (for both, you will need to provide IP address, network name, and physical disk for location of the databases and logs), you will also need to specify two (for WINS) or three (for DHCP) additional parameters: database path: For storage of the DHCP or WINS database, audit file path: (DHCP only) for storage of DHCP Service Activity Log (enabled by default), and backup path:

In case of DHCP, used by automatic backup that takes place by default every 60 minutes. The interval is configurable by modifying the BackupInterval registry entry located at `HKEY_LOCAL_MACHINE\SYSTEM\CurrentControlSet\Services\DHCPServer\Parameters`. The same backup path is used also by manual backup initiated from the DHCP console.

In case of WINS, backup takes place automatically every 24 hours once you specify the backup path. You can also set it to take place whenever WINS service is stopped (including server shutdown) or run it manually using the WINS management console.

These parameters need to start with the shared drive letter and end with a backslash (for example, `W:\dhcp\` or `W:\wins\`). As a result, local installation of the DHCP or WINS on the first node will be modified to reflect the new database, audit file, and backup path locations. After resources are configured and online on the first node, install services on remaining nodes (using Add/Remove Programs applet).

After installation of the DHCP resource, ensure that its bindings are set properly. Click the Bindings button located on the Advanced tab of the server properties in the DHCP console. This will bring up a window showing the bindings for all local network connections. Make sure that the check box corresponding to your private network connection is cleared and the one for public is checked. Repeat this procedure on each node.

Clustering File Services and Dfs

Access to the clustered file shares is available through the File Share resource on a cluster server. NLB is not suitable for clustering file share resources. The File Share resource can point to either a regular file share or a standalone Dfs root. Creating domain-based Dfs roots as cluster resources is not possible (you can still provide high availability for domain-based Dfs roots by setting up multiple root replicas). Limitation of a single Dfs root per server no longer exists in Windows 2003, so you can create multiple, independent Dfs namespaces using a single cluster (unless you are running a mixed version cluster).

The procedure for creating both file share and Dfs root are very similar. First, you need to ensure that the root Dfs or the file share with the same name does not exist on the same cluster. Then, create a folder on a shared drive that is part of the same group. Finally, launch the New Resource wizard and select File Share resource as resource type. The generic file share does not require any dependencies, but the Dfs root relies on a network name. On the last screen of the wizard, type in the full path to a folder on a shared disk and the name of a share (and, optionally, fill out the Comments field). Click the Advanced button and specify whether you want to create a normal share, Dfs root, or file share with shared subdirectories. This last option enables you to automatically share subdirectories (and optionally, make these shares hidden). It is typically used when creating user home directories under one common share. If you created a Dfs root resource, you can manage it and create a Dfs link using a Dfs console.

Do not assign NTFS or share permissions of file shares to local accounts from cluster nodes. Use domain accounts instead. Otherwise, permissions on a resource cannot be verified after failover. Set share permissions through the resource properties rather than through Windows Explorer. By default, the only permission set is Read granted to the Everyone group.

A new option in Windows 2003 allows you to set the Caching option on a shared clustered folder. The default — Manual Caching of documents — matches the one that has been in place in the previous versions of Windows.

Clustered drives support NTFS features such as the Encrypted File System and volume mountpoints (which maintain their information on failover). Support for the Encrypted File System, however, is possible only if several conditions are satisfied. First, virtual servers, where the encrypted files reside, need to have corresponding objects in Active Directory because Kerberos authentication is required. Second, all cluster nodes must be trusted for delegation. Finally, users whose files are encrypted need to be configured with roaming profiles, in order to make their private keys accessible from each node.

Clustering Print Services

Print Services can be clustered using Server Cluster (NLB does not offer any benefits in this case). Server Cluster provides the Print Spooler resource, which uses shared spool folder storing print jobs for clustered printers. Print Spooler depends on a Physical Disk resource, which hosts the Spool directory, IP address, and Network name resources. Clustered printers are accessed via the network name and can only reference network printing devices (that is, using printers attached to local ports of cluster nodes is not allowed). Each node needs to have the same set of printer monitors, ports, and drivers (print monitors need to be installed manually on each node, but ports and drivers are installed only once and automatically replicated among the cluster nodes). Because the Print Spooler resource maintains the Spool directory on a shared storage, in case of failover, all queued print jobs are transferred to another node and are subsequently printed.

After the Print Spooler resource is set up and online, you can start creating shared printers. First, make sure that appropriate print monitors are installed on every server participating in the cluster. A standard TCP/IP print monitor is installed by default, but LPR and proprietary print monitors need to be added manually if needed. Next, set up the printer ports. This is not done on individual nodes, but on the virtual server hosting the Print Spooler. To connect to it, type **\\VirtualServerName** from the Start⇨ Run dialog box. This will bring up a window with the list of shared resources on the server, including the Printers and Faxes folder. Once you double-click it, the Printers and Faxes on the VirtualServerName window will open. From the File menu, you can access the Server Properties dialog box. Add ports shared among all members of the cluster by clicking the Add Port button on Ports tab (note that only port types installed previously on individual nodes will be available). To install printer drivers on all servers, access the Drivers tab within the same window. Alternatively, double-click the Add Printer icon and follow the Add Printer Wizard prompts. Make sure that you set the printer as shared and provide a unique (per cluster) share name.

Clustering Applications

Both server and NLB clusters support a range of applications, although each one, as discussed, handles them differently. This section will concentrate on setting up clusters of the more popular types of applications.

First, we will take a look at the applications that are not cluster-aware. It is difficult to provide general rules for clustering such applications, because each needs to be analyzed separately and the decision needs to be based on a thorough review of its behavior and use of system resources. Typically, however, clustering can be accomplished by using Generic Application or Generic Script resources (assuming that clustering is possible at all).

A large number of applications depend on transactional and messaging features provided by the Windows operating systems. Microsoft developed clustered resources for two components offering these essential services: Distributed Transaction Coordinator and Message Queuing. They can serve both cluster nonaware and cluster-aware (such as SQL Server 2000) applications. Two subsections are dedicated to the description of the clustering procedures for these components.

High availability of client applications can be accomplished by installing them on a Terminal Server farm. This approach involves additional considerations, such as keeping track of the user sessions across the farm. The procedure for setting up such an environment and the way to maintain a session state is described in the next subsection.

Fortunately, the number of cluster-aware applications is growing. Microsoft SQL server, which is covered in the following subsection, serves as one of the best examples.

This section concludes with description of clustering procedure for a highly available Web farm.

Generic Applications Clusters

The Generic Application resource in a server cluster is used for providing high availability to cluster-unaware applications. Not every application, however, can be configured this way. To qualify for clustering, an application needs to use IP-based protocols, so any applications relying on NetBEUI, IPX, or AppleTalk do not qualify. The client portion of an application needs to be able to reconnect if the connection is temporarily lost. Any type of volatile data that an application relies on must be stored on shared storage drives. This, however, does not apply to registry settings, because Cluster Service can take care of their replication automatically. This is configurable using the Generic Application properties. If the destination of the installation is configurable, it is recommended to point it to one of the shared disks. Otherwise, an application should be installed to the same location on a local drive of every node. In both cases, the application's installation needs to be run separately for each node. If all conditions are satisfied, your application might be able to successfully failover, just like cluster-aware applications. However, even if this is not the case, you might still be able to take advantage of the clustering features. For example, if an application is unstable and tends to fail frequently, you can force its restart by setting the advanced properties of its application resource.

Generic Script Clusters

The Generic Script resource in a server cluster is a custom script written in a language supported by any of the scripting engines present in the Windows 2003 servers platform (such as VBScript or JScript). Even though such scripts would be application specific, they need to follow guidelines that are documented on Microsoft Development Network (available at `http://msdn.microsoft.com`). In short, the script has to implement at least the `LooksAlive`,and `IsAlive` functions, which return a Boolean value (`TRUE` or `FALSE`). These functions are periodically executed by a resource monitor, according to "Looks Alive" and "Is Alive" intervals. If the function returns `FALSE`, the resource monitor initiates a failover. The following script is the most trivial example of Generic Script resource:

```
Function Online()
End Function
Function LooksAlive()
   LooksAlive = TRUE
End Function
Function IsAlive()
   IsAlive = TRUE
End Function
```

Obviously, this is a sample of a self-serving resource that keeps itself alive that has no practical value, but it is used here to illustrate the most basic principles behind the Generic Script resource mechanism. For more meaningful examples, refer to the MSDN documentation. Interestingly, the Generic Script resource is used to create clustered IIS Web and FTP sites in a Windows 2003 server cluster. Information about installing IIS Web and FTP sites is provided in the section "Web Server Clusters" in this chapter.

Clustering Distributed Transaction Coordinator

Distributed Transaction Coordinator is a service that operates as part of the COM+ runtime environment. As mentioned previously, its purpose is to provide transactional support in environments where such support is natively not included. The features offered by DTC are used by Component Services, Microsoft Message Queuing, and the SQL Server.

Creating a clustered DTC is very straightforward (running COMCLUST.EXE on each node, as it used to be in previous versions of Windows, is no longer required. The only exception is setting up component-load balancing clusters, described later in this chapter). All you need to do is add the DTC resource to a group that is configured as virtual server (specifying all required dependencies in the process) and bring it online (there is no need to install DTC component, because, by default, it is included with the operating system). Keep in mind that if you do not specify a group, the DTC resource will be installed into the first group that contains the IP address, network name, and physical disk resources. The New Resource wizard creates the DTC log file MSTDC.LOG located in the MSDTC folder on the physical disk resource that is part of the virtual server. This log file is used by the DTC Transaction Manager to keep track of the active transactions. Its location can be changed using the Component Services Administrative Tool (by modifying the Location entry on the MSDTC tab of the My Computer Properties). The wizard also stores relevant DTC registry entries in the Cluster hive and configures the DTC service to run in the security context of a Network Service account. Only a single-clustered DTC resource can exist in a cluster. Adding a node to a cluster will automatically replicate the DTC configuration settings to it. Analogically, evicting a node will remove these settings. However, if you intend to run DTC locally on an evicted node, you will have to execute command `msdtc.exe` on it first.

Clustering Message Queuing

Message Queuing is a service that provides a distributed mechanism for the asynchronous delivery of messages. Its basic purpose is to ensure reliable communication between the applications or systems, even if they are temporarily unavailable.

In order to set up a clustered message queue, ensure that you have a group that contains physical disk, IP address, and network name resources, on which Message Queuing resource will build its dependencies. Then, on each node, install Message Queuing components (launch the Add/Remove Programs wizard, select the Add/Remove Windows Components, highlight the Web Application Server component, click the Details button, and choose Message Queuing from the list). Finally, create the Message Queuing resource using the New Resource wizard. Once brought online, it will run as a separate Active Directory-aware service (visible in the Services MMC snap-in). Its information is published in Active Directory and can be viewed using the Active Directory Users and Computers Administrative tool, providing that the "Users, Groups, and Computers as containers" option is selected from the View menu. This will reveal the msmq icon (representing Message Queuing resource) and its components under the Virtual Server icon that has Message Queuing resource installed on it. Keep in mind that in order for these entries to appear in Active Directory, a Cluster Service account needs to be granted permissions to create computer objects in the Computers container and write their properties. Note that the need for running the COMCLUST.EXE utility on each node and rebooting (required with previous versions of Windows) has been eliminated.

In the Windows 2003 Server cluster, Microsoft introduced support for Message Queuing triggers (which provide a way to detect arrival of a new message and use it to perform an arbitrary action). This allows the developers of clustered applications to take advantage of a more complete set of features than ever possible.

Maintaining Terminal Sessions across Clusters

Even though the Terminal Services installation is supported on Windows 2003 server cluster (which was not the case on Windows 2000 platform), Terminal Services in such configuration is neither load balanced nor highly available. Load balancing, however, can be accomplished by setting up Terminal Services as part of an NLB cluster (or by using other network load-balancing solutions).

One of the problems that must be solved in this case is the ability to gracefully handle disconnected sessions. Imagine a situation in which a user establishes a session to one of several load-balanced servers and for some reason (other than the server failure) temporarily loses the connection. Because the user never logged off, the session remains open on the server. Unfortunately, if the same user tries to reconnect, it is likely that the connection request will be redirected to another server (based on the load balancing algorithm).

To resolve this problem, Microsoft developed a service called Terminal Services Session Directory, which provides a database that stores information about user sessions for all cluster nodes. This database is automatically updated whenever a user connects to or disconnects from any server that registers with the same Session Directory server.

Whenever NLB directs the user connection request to one of the TS servers in a farm, this server checks first with the Directory server for an existing session. If the user already has established a session to some other server, the Directory server replies with that server's name. The first Terminal server returns to the user the name of the second server (that name was returned from Session Directory server) and request the user to reconnect. The initial session is terminated and the client reconnects directly to the second server.

The Session Directory service is installed (but disabled) by default on every Windows 2003 Enterprise or Datacenter server. To configure it, start by deciding which server will function as the Session Directory server. The server should be highly available (Session Directory is cluster aware, so it can be set up on a server cluster) and should not be running Terminal Services. Once you selected the target server, launch its Services MMC snap-in from the Administrative Tools menu, select the Terminal Services Session Directory Service entry, change its startup type to Automatic, and start it.

After the Session Directory is installed and activated (it runs as a service called Terminal Services Session Directory), it creates the local group "Session Directory Computers". You need to add to this group the computer accounts for all of the cluster members.

Configuration of Terminal Services Session Directory is handled most efficiently using Group Policies. To further simplify management, try placing all load-balanced terminal servers in the same Organizational Unit. Next, modify three entries in the OU's Group Policy Object under Computer Configuration ⇨ Administrative Templates ⇨ Windows Components ⇨ Terminal Services ⇨ Session Directory folder. The first one, Join Session Directory, needs to be simply enabled. The second one, Session Directory Server, needs to be enabled and set to the name of a server that will host Session Directory. Finally, Session Directory Cluster Name needs to be set to the name of the cluster formed by all of the servers reporting to the Session Directory.

Alternatively, you can configure the same settings on a per-server basis using the Terminal Services Configuration Tool (available from Administrative Tools). Click on Server settings, and double-click on Session Directory in the Details pane. Turn on the "Join session directory" check box in the upper-left corner and type in the Cluster and Session directory server names. The main advantage of this method is the ability to specify the IP address of the network adapter that clients can connect to using the virtual IP address of the Terminal Server cluster.

With both methods you can also configure the Terminal Server IP Address Redirection (additional setting), which determines whether the clients will attempt reconnecting to the actual address of a specific Terminal Server (if enabled) or to the virtual IP address of the cluster (if disabled). Typically, this setting should be enabled to allow clients to reconnect directly to a Terminal Server, which name was returned from Directory Services server. If the setting is disabled, clients will not be able to take advantage of the Directory Services unless the load balancing device supports routing token redirection.

When dealing with Terminal Services, you might want to also keep in mind the following general guidelines:

- User data should be stored on a backend server cluster. This way if one of the Terminal Servers becomes unavailable, sessions can be resumed on another one, with a minimal loss of data.
- Terminal Servers can be configured so that on a timed out or broken connection, a session will be disconnected but not terminated. This will allow the existing user processes to continue running.
- If, for some reason, you cannot implement a Session Directory, you can set NLB port rules to use single affinity, which will force users to always reconnect to the same server.

- Terminal Server connections are managed through the following port rule (used by RDP protocol):
  - o port range: 3389 to 3389
  - o protocols: TCP
  - o filtering mode: Multiple Hosts
- This rule does not apply if you are using Citrix Metaframe with ICA protocol (instead of RDP). Metaframe provides its own load balancing features.
- Affinity depends on the way a client application state is managed. Load weight settings depend on the performance characteristics of the cluster members.

MS SQL Server Clusters

Microsoft SQL Server 2000 is a high performance database management system and part of the Windows 2003 server platform. It is fully server-cluster aware but not suitable for NLB clusters. It can, however, be part of multitier design, where requests to front-end Web servers are load balanced using NLB and CLB, and redirected to a server-clustered SQL server on the backend. Windows 2003 Enterprise Server and Windows 2003 Datacenter Server clusters require the SQL Server 2000 Enterprise Edition.

SQL Server 2000 installation creates one or more (up to 16) instances of SQL Server. On a cluster, each instance needs to be set up as part of a virtual server (it is possible to have multiple instances per virtual server). These instances are distinguished by names that are arbitrarily chosen (with the exception of default instance, which uses the name of a virtual server to which it belongs). These names have to be unique across the entire cluster. Clients access an instance using a combination of the name of its virtual server name and the instance name, separated by backslash (this, again, does not apply to the default instance, which is accessed simply by using the virtual server name). Each instance requires at least one separate disk resource, although it is a common practice to split the database and transaction logs between two separate disks (with RAID 5 used for database and RAID 1 for transaction logs. RAID 1+0 is recommended for high-end systems).

The clustered SQL Server 2000 instance is installed as part of a virtual server that contains the following:

- SQL Network Name resource (one per virtual server)
- SQL IP Address resource (one per virtual server)
- Physical disk resource where the database and logs are stored (one or more per virtual server)
- SQL Server resource (one per instance)
- SQL Server Agent resource (one per instance)
- SQL Server Fulltext (Microsoft Search Service Instance) resource (one per instance)

The SQL Server resource depends on the SQL Network Name and physical disk resources. Each instance can function separately from others, although they have common dependencies on the following components:

- Microsoft Search Service (that SQL Fulltext resource relies on) is a standard service that needs to be running on each individual node.

- Microsoft Distributed Transaction Coordinator is limited to a single instance per server cluster. This component is required for distributed queries, two-phase commit transactions, and some replication features.
- Microsoft Message Queuing is also limited to a single instance per cluster.

Depending on the desired functionality (strictly failover or combination of failover and load balancing), different SQL Server cluster configuration can be created:

- Single-instance cluster: Offers strictly failover capabilities.
- Multiple-instance cluster: Although SQL Server supports up to 16 instances per system, it is recommended that you create only a single instance per node. Different models of load-balanced clusters have been discussed in the section titled "Server Cluster Design and Capacity Planning."

In load-balanced configurations, it is critical to properly evaluate the hardware requirements (especially memory for a cluster to remain functional after failover. You should also set a limit for the maximum amount of memory available to an SQL Server. The sum of "max server memory" values on each node should be less than the amount of memory on failover nodes. Otherwise, an SQL Server instance might fail to start after failover due to an insufficient amount of memory.

Keep the BUILTIN\Administrators account in the SQL Server System Administrators server role. This group is used by a Cluster Service account to communicate to SQL Server instances. Also make sure that the Cluster Service account has permissions on the Computers container in Active Directory sufficient to create a computer object for the virtual server and default SQL Server instance.

SQL Server 2000 is tightly integrated with the clustering software. For example, SQL Server service can be stopped by SQL Administrative tools (like Enterprise Manager or Service Manager), rather than by the Cluster Administrator. The best example of this integration though is the setup process. Prior to launching it, make sure that each cluster member is fully operational. SQL Server binaries are stored on the nonclustered drives, so make sure that there is sufficient amount of disk space on each server. To perform the setup, in addition to standard information (not cluster specific, such as authentication mode, components to install, or collation settings) you will also need the following:

- Domain account with sufficient permissions on cluster nodes (needs to be a member of local Administrators group on each node) and its password
- SQL Server (and SQL Server Agent, if not the same) service account name (needs to be a member of a local Administrators group on each node) and its password

and for each instance:

- Instance Name (with the exception of default instance, which uses the same name as the virtual server to which it belongs) of up to 16 characters in length
- IP Address (not used on the network)
- Port for TCP/IP sockets network library connections (default instance uses by default port 1433, while named instances have the port numbers dynamically assigned. This might need to be set manually if clients connect to the server via a firewall).

✦ Network Name of the virtual server (note that this name cannot be used on the network, which means that you cannot create a virtual server first and then install SQL Server on it. A clustered SQL Server setup will automatically create this virtual server with the associated IP address. The same applies to the IP address).

✦ At least one (preferably two or more) physical disk resource (ensure that this resource is owned by the node on which you are running the setup)

The setup process will detect that it is running on a cluster node and provide an option of installing an SQL Server instance on a virtual server, for which you will need to provide a name. As mentioned previously, this name cannot exist on the network. Next, you will be prompted for other information necessary to create this virtual server: IP address and network, cluster disk where data files will be placed, nodes that will participate in SQL Server clustering (on the Cluster Management screen), user account and password with administrative rights to both nodes, SQL server instance (default or named), and setup type (typical, minimum, or custom, for which you would specify a list of components to install). Note that while the destination folder for the data files will be on the shared drive you selected earlier, the destination folder for the program files will be on your local drive. However, running the setup separately on each node is not required. Instead, all nodes that were listed as Configured on the Cluster Management screen (mentioned earlier as part of the setup process) will automatically have SQL Server binaries installed on their local drives (removing the SQL server installation files from a node is also done from Cluster Management screen by excluding it from Cluster Definition). You will need to type in the name, domain, and password of the account to be used for SQL Server and SQL Server Agent services, choose between the Windows and Mixed authentication mode (if you choose mixed, you will also need to provide password for an SQL Server login), specify the collation settings and network libraries used for connecting to the server (Named Pipes and TCP/IP Sockets via port 1433 by default) and the licensing mode (per seat or per processor). After all this information is provided, the setup will install a Distributed Transaction Coordinator (unless it has not been already installed, because, as you might recall, there can be only one instance of DTC per cluster).

In order to perform configuration changes to an existing clustered SQL Server, you need to use the same setup program. In this case, though, when prompted for the computer name on the initial screen of the setup wizard, make sure that Virtual Server option is selected and type in the name of the existing Virtual SQL Server. This will allow you to upgrade, remove, or add components, modify IP address information, and add or remove nodes on which SQL Server is installed.

Federated server setup and deployment

SQL 2000 provides another (besides clustering), effective solution for scaling out. The solution is based on horizontal partitioning of the data. The term describes dividing data into groups based on some criteria and placing the resulting data sets in separate physical partitions. When applied to a relational database, this translates into separating rows of a single table into several distinct tables. Each one of them contains rows for which value in a key column belongs to a specific range of values. The ranges are chosen to reflect data access patterns. The goal is to load balance the distribution of queries by placing each table on a different server. If ranges are chosen properly, then for the majority of queries it should be sufficient to access a single partition only. For example, a table can contain sales data organized by the store location. The location code, stored in a key column, is used to assign each row to one of the tables (enforced with a CHECK constraint on the key column) distributed across separate servers. The collection of servers with partitioned data is known as a federation. Even though federated servers do not have to be clustered, ensuring high availability is recommended, because all partitions need to be reachable even if data you are looking for resides in only one of them.

Implementation of partitioned data and federated servers requires the proper data analysis and database design because the placement of data plays a critical role. Related data should be stored together. One way to accomplish this is to determine all the foreign keys referencing rows in a local partition and storing them on the same server. Another approach is based on observing data access patterns. Tables that do not qualify as good candidates for partitioning can be copied across federated servers and synchronized through use of triggers or replication.

There are three methods of accessing partitioned data: partitioned views, data-dependent routing, and a combination of partitioned views and data-dependent routing. For partitions to be transparent to users, distributed partitioned views are used. Such views combine all rows from all partitions and make them appear as a single table. Partitioned views can be read-only or read/write. The read/write type requires SQL Server 2000 Enterprise Edition or SQL Server 2000 Developer Edition. Data-dependent routing operates on the application level so it requires an application to be aware of the data location. For more detailed information, refer to the documentation of SQL Server 2000.

Web Server Clusters

Highly available Web sites can be built using server clusters, NLB clusters, or a combination of both (with or without CLB). However, while server clusters provide high availability only, NLB offers also load balancing. This results from the fundamental difference between them. A server cluster runs a single instance of an application, a NLB cluster runs multiple, identical instances in parallel.

Even though it is recommended that you set up your Web sites with NLB, there might be cases where you decide to use a server cluster instead. For example, your Web applications might not support load balancing or your network infrastructure might not be suitable for implementation of NLB. Note that the IIS Server Instance, SMTP Server Instance, and NNTP Server Instance resource types included in Windows 2000 clusters are no longer available on the Windows 2003 platform. Also remember that Front Page Extensions are not supported on clustered Web servers. In order to set up a Web or FTP site on a Windows 2003 server cluster, follow these steps:

1. First, make sure that Internet Information Services or/and FTP service with default Web or FTP sites are installed. If they are not present, install them using Add/Remove Programs applet from the Control Panel. For details on installing IIS and FTP, refer to Chapter 29.

2. Next, create a virtual server that will provide the IP address, network name, and physical disk used by the Web/FTP site. If your environment supports dynamic DNS, check the DNS Registration Must Succeed check box on the Network Name resource parameters. Otherwise, create the appropriate DNS records manually.

3. Within the same group, you need to create two Generic Script resources pointing to `%SystemRoot%\system32\inetsrv\clusweb.vbs` and `%SystemRoot%\system32\inetsrv\clusftp.vbs` to create the Web and FTP sites, respectively. It is recommended to make these resources dependent on the physical disk and network name resources of the virtual server.

4. Bring all of the resources online and make sure they stay operational.

5. Use the Internet Information Services console to create a Web or FTP site on the Virtual Server you created. Bind them to the IP address of the virtual server (do not use the All available setting). Create a home directory for the site on the physical disk resource. Set a home directory path parameter accordingly.

6. If a Web site requires a transaction support or uses applications relying on the Distributed Transaction Coordinator, create a DTC resource.

7. Use the `%SystemRoot%\System32\IISCNFG.VBS` script (included with IIS 6.0) to replicate portions of metabase across all the nodes. Refer to IIS On-Line Help for details about parameters used with `IISCNFG.VBS` or type at the Command Prompt:

   ```
   CSCRIPT IIsCnfg.vbs copy /?
   ```

If you prefer using graphical interface, you can accomplish the same goal with Internet Information Services MMC snap-in. Simply highlight the Web or FTP site you created on the shared disk on the first node and from the Action menu select All Tasks ⇨ Save Configuration to a File. This will create an .XML file containing site configuration. Copy the file to each of remaining nodes. Finally, on each one of them, highlight the Web Sites folder of IIS snap-in, and from the Action menu select New⇨Web Site (from file). You will be presented with the Import Configuration dialog box, prompting you for the name and location of the XML file you created previously. Once you provide its location and click OK, the metadata on the current node will be updated. If your Web site is using COM objects, synchronize registry and COM+ registration database settings with the Component Services console. You will not be able to use the IISSYNCH utility (available in Windows 2000) for this purpose, because it is no longer supported in Windows 2003 server.

When using NLB for clustering Web or FTP sites, assign their IP addresses to each clustered node. Include these addresses in the port rules for the cluster. You also need to replicate the content of the site across all the nodes. The replication process is identical to the one used for server cluster and depends on whether the Web application is utilizing COM+ or .NET architecture. In the case of COM+ applications, you can simplify your task by using the Content Replication from Microsoft Site Server or features of Application Center 2000. With the advent of .NET applications, the deployment is greatly simplified, because the Windows registry and COM+ registration databases are no longer used. Configuration files can be replicated among nodes with xcopy command.

Summary

This chapter covered high availability features built into the Windows 2003 server platform. Microsoft not only improved its server clustering technology in the areas of scalability and manageability, but also introduced support for new types of clustering resources and distributed clustering (through Majority Node Set). Similarly, Network Load Balancing ease of use and functionality have been significantly extended to allow load balancing of Terminal Services (through Session Directory) and VPN servers. We also presented Component Load Balancing, which allows COM+ activation requests to be evenly distributed across multitier Windows environments.

✦ ✦ ✦

File, Print, Web, and Application Services

PART

VI

✦ ✦ ✦ ✦

In This Part

✦ ✦ ✦ ✦

Windows Server 2003 File Systems

◆ ◆ ◆ ◆

In This Chapter

An overview of disk structure

Understanding FAT16 and FAT32

Understanding NTFS

Choosing a file system

Optimizing storage capacity

Managing the Distributed File System

Working with mounted volumes

Hierarchical storage management

File systems to support other platforms

◆ ◆ ◆ ◆

This chapter explores the many aspects of the Windows Server 2003 file system, including file system structure, the Distributed File System (Dfs), auditing, and system repair and recovery.

An Overview of Disk Structure

To understand the file system options in Windows Server 2003, you first need to understand some basic physical disk concepts and terms. This section covers concepts and terms that will help you understand file system structure in Windows Server 2003. This chapter does not cover basic hardware storage concepts such as heads and head gap in detail because these topics aren't germane to an understanding of file systems. This chapter focuses mainly on logical disk structure rather than physical disk structure.

The circular path a head traverses as it sits motionless over a disk platter is called a *track.* The tracks are magnetically encoded on the disk during formatting and define the physical structure of the disk's storage space. The tracks that reside in the same location on each platter form a *cylinder.* Each track is divided into a certain number of *sectors,* the number of which depends on the disk type and location of the track on the disk. Sectors are the smallest physical storage units on a disk, but they are grouped into *clusters*, which are the smallest *logical* storage units on the disk. Figure 26-1 illustrates basic disk structure.

Each cluster comprises a certain number of sectors. The number of sectors in each cluster depends on the drive type, partition size, and file system (explained in the following sections). When the operating system stores a file, the storage space is allocated not by sector, but by cluster. The cluster size has a significant impact on the amount of free space on a disk, as you'll learn later in the section titled "Optimizing Storage Capacity."

Basic disks in Windows Server 2003 contain one or more *partitions* that consist of a series of clusters. A partition has a beginning and an ending sector, and the number of sectors in between determines the partition capacity. Each partition uses a particular file system type (FAT16, FAT32, NTFS, and so on). Each basic disk can contain up to four partitions, all *primary partitions,* or three primary partitions and one *extended partition.* Each primary partition represents a single drive with a single drive ID, while an extended partition can contain multiple logical drives. Each logical drive can be represented by a drive ID, although drive IDs are not required per se. For the sake of simplicity and consistency, the term *volume* refers to a logical drive entity, such as a drive defined by a primary partition or a single logical drive in an extended partition.

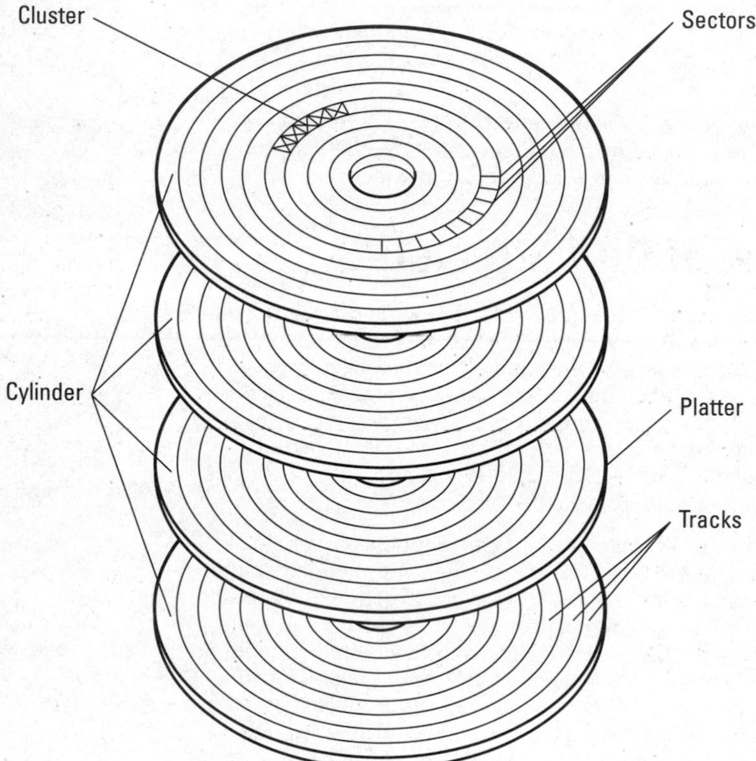

Figure 26-1: Physical disk structure.

Dynamic disks are new in Windows Server 2003 and overcome the four-partition limitation of basic disks. Dynamic disks don't contain partitions. Instead, they contain *dynamic volumes,* which are a lot like a logical drive within an extended partition in the sense that the disk can contain multiple volumes and each appears as a unique object. However, you can create an unlimited number of volumes in a dynamic disk, subject to disk capacity. As with partitions in a basic disk, each dynamic volume has its own file system (FAT16, FAT32, or NTFS).

Although you can manage existing fault-tolerant volumes on a basic disk with Windows Server 2003, you can't create or extend these volumes on basic disks. Full support (creation and modification) for fault-tolerant volumes now requires a dynamic disk.

The Enterprise Server and Datacenter Server versions of .NET also support a new disk partitioning style — first introduced in Windows XP — called GUID Partition Table, or GPT. Support for GPT volumes requires the 64-bit versions of these two Server platforms, which run on the Intel Itanium processor.

GPT offers several advantages over the Master Boot Record (MBR) partitioning scheme. First, GPT supports 2^{64} logical blocks. Assuming a typical block size of 512 bytes means a theoretical size for a single GPT volume of 8ZB (Zettabytes), although the practical size is limited to about 18 Exabytes. GPT also supports a theoretically unlimited number of unique partitions per disk. This means that a single disk can be considerably larger than with other partitioning schemes.

Windows Server 2003 systems with GPT disks can read and write to those disks, as well as to MBR-type disks. However, the 64-bit versions of .NET cannot boot from an MBR disk. The boot loader and boot partition must reside on a GPT disk. The GPT partition includes a structure called the Protective MBR, which starts at sector 0 and precedes the GPT partition on the disk. The Protective MBR exists for non-GPT-aware disk utilities, which would otherwise interpret the GPT partition as being unpartitioned space.

Note You will find more information about GPT at `www.microsoft.com/hwdev/tech/storage/GPT_FAQ.asp`.

Whether you choose to use basic disks with primary or extended partitions, or dynamic disks with dynamic volumes, each volume requires a file system. You can choose among three in Windows Server 2003: FAT16, FAT32, or NTFS. Each offers certain advantages and disadvantages. The following section explains the structure, advantages, and disadvantages of the FAT16 and FAT32 file systems.

FAT16 and FAT32

The FAT file system originated with DOS and is supported by DOS, all versions of Windows, Windows NT, Windows Server 2003, Unix, Linux, and OS/2. Because of that wide support, it is the most compatible between operating platforms (one of its advantages). FAT stands for File Allocation Table, which is the structure in a FAT volume that stores information about disk space allocation.

A disk formatted with the FAT file system contains five control areas. The first is the *reserve area,* which comprises one or more sectors depending on the disk type. The first sector in the reserve area is the *boot sector,* which contains the partition table and bootstrap program. The partition table stores information about the disk's partitions including type, starting and ending sectors, and which partition is active. The bootstrap program executes at startup and boots the operating system or boot loader in the active partition. The boot sector is always located at cylinder 0, head 0, track 1 (the first sector on the disk).

The *File Allocation Table (FAT)* is the second control area and serves as a reference table of the clusters in the volume. Each cluster's entry contains a value defined by those listed in Table 26-1. The value defines the cluster's status, indicating if the cluster is available, in use, bad, or reserved. A *backup copy* of the FAT makes up the third control area and can be used by utility applications to restore the file system when the primary FAT becomes corrupted.

Table 26-1: FAT Cluster Entries

Entry	*Meaning*
0	Cluster is available.
BAD	Cluster contains a bad sector and is unusable.
Reserved	Cluster is reserved for use by the operating system.
EOF	End of File; marks the last cluster of a file.
nnn	Number of the next cluster in the file.

The fourth control area is the *root directory table,* which works in conjunction with the FAT to define files in the root directory, subdirectories (which are really just files in the root directory), and the starting cluster of each file. The fifth control area is the area in which file data is actually stored in the volume. When applications request a file read operation, the OS reads the FAT to locate the beginning cluster for the file. It then uses the FAT as a sort of road map to locate the other clusters for the file, using the FAT as a lookup table to determine which clusters to read and in which order to put a file back together.

Windows Server 2003 automatically determines the number of sectors per cluster for a volume based on the volume size. Table 26-2 lists the default cluster size for FAT volumes. The sizes listed apply to disks consisting of a single partition and to logical drives in an extended partition. Floppy disks are not included. Cluster size is an important consideration when formatting a disk to optimize disk capacity.

Table 26-2: Default FAT Cluster Size

Volume Size	*Cluster Size*	*Sectors per Cluster*
Less than 32MB	512 bytes	1
33 to 64MB	1K	2
65 to 128MB	2K	4
129 to 255MB	4K	8
256 to 511MB	8K	16
512MB to 1GB	16K	32
1GB to 2GB	32K	64
2GB to 4GB	64K	128

The FAT file system originally used 12 bits to define the FAT entries. A 16-bit FAT, called FAT16, was introduced in DOS 4.0 to accommodate larger cluster values and therefore larger disks. FAT16 supports a maximum of 65,526 clusters, which limits FAT volumes to 4GB ($clustersize_{max} \times clusters_{max} = bytes$).

Windows 95 OSR2 introduced FAT32, which allocates 32 bits to the FAT, increasing the maximum number of clusters to 268,435,446. The maximum cluster size of 32,768 bytes means that FAT32 volumes can theoretically be up to 8TB (one terabyte equals 1,024 gigabytes), although the current hardware limitation of 512-byte sectors limits the actual size to 2TB. Windows Server 2003 limits the size of the FAT32 partition you can create within Windows Server 2003 to 32GB. However, it does support mounting any size FAT32 volume, including those larger than 32GB. The capability enables you to mount FAT32 volumes larger than 32GB created with another operating system or a third-party partitioning utility. Table 26-3 lists the default cluster sizes for FAT32 volumes of a given size.

Note Microsoft reserves the top four bits of each cluster in a FAT32 volume, so there are only 28 bits for the cluster number, not 32, and therefore the maximum number of clusters totals 268,435,446. In addition, BIOS limitations can limit volume size on any given system. Finally, the 512-byte sector size is also a limiting factor.

Table 26-3: Default FAT32 Cluster Size

Volume Size	*Cluster Size*	*Sectors per Cluster*
Less than 512MB	Not supported	N/A
512MB to 8GB	4K	8
8GB to 16GB	8K	16
16GB to 32GB	16K	32
More than 32GB	32K	64

NTFS

NTFS stands for NT File System, and NTFS is the third file system supported by Windows Server 2003. It offers several advantages over the FAT16 and FAT32 file systems, although NTFS is not the optimum choice in all situations, as you'll learn shortly.

One primary difference from FAT16 is that NTFS is a recoverable file system. If a failure occurs that affects an NTFS volume, Windows Server 2003 reconstructs the volume automatically when the system restarts. Another important distinction is security. FAT16 and FAT32 allow you to apply limited share permissions to control access to resources shared from a FAT16 folder. The share permissions apply to all subfolders and files within the share. NTFS, however, allows you to apply not only share permissions, but *object permissions,* as well. Object permissions provide a much more granular control over folder and file access, controlling access on a folder-by-folder and file-by-file basis. Object permissions apply not only to remote connections across the network, but also to local connections. NTFS, therefore, is the only Windows Server 2003 file system that provides adequate security for folders and files for users who log on locally. NTFS also allows object access auditing, something that is not supported for FAT16/FAT32 volumes.

Note See Chapter 23 for a detailed description of auditing.

Similar to FAT32, NTFS supports larger volumes than FAT volumes, with a maximum of 2TB per NTFS volume. Also, similar to FAT16 and FAT32, NTFS provides for a variable cluster size that adjusts automatically according to volume size. Table 26-4 lists the default NTFS cluster sizes for volumes of a given size.

Table 26-4: Default NTFS Cluster Size

Volume Size	*Cluster Size*	*Sectors per Cluster*
512MB or less	512 bytes	1
513MB to 1GB	1K	2
1GB to 2GB	2K	4
2GB to 4GB	4K	8
4GB to 8GB	8K	16
8GB to 16GB	16K	32
16GB to 32GB	32K	16
More than 32GB	64K	128

As with FAT16 and FAT32, you can change the cluster size for an NTFS volume when you format the volume to optimize storage capacity. The cluster sizes identified in Table 26-4 are the default sizes Windows Server 2003 uses unless you specify otherwise. See the section titled "Optimizing Storage Capacity" later in this chapter for an explanation of why you would choose a cluster size different from the default values.

NTFS Structure

The structure of an NTFS volume is considerably different from that of the FAT16 and FAT32 file systems. The boot sector, located at sector 0 in the volume, can be up to 16 sectors in size and comprises two structures: the BIOS Parameter Block (BPB) and the bootstrap program. The BPB stores information about the volume's layout. The bootstrap program loads the file `NTLDR`, which boots the system. NTFS stores a duplicate copy of the boot sector at the end of the volume for redundancy and fault tolerance.

How NTFS stores volume data also differs from FAT. NTFS uses a relational database called the *master file table* (MFT) to manage the contents of a volume. The MFT serves much the same purpose in the NTFS file system that the FAT serves in the FAT file systems. The MFT stores a record for each file and directory, including the MFT itself. Each entry includes the name, security descriptor, and other attributes. The MFT is an array of data with rows representing file records and columns representing attribute fields for each record, as shown in Figure 26-2. The size of each MFT record is constant and determined when the volume is formatted. MFT record size can be 1K, 2K, or 4K, depending on disk size.

The Data field for each record stores the file's data. With very small files, the data is contained completely within the Data field of one MFT record. When all of a file's attributes—including its data—reside in a single MFT record, the attributes are called *resident attributes*.

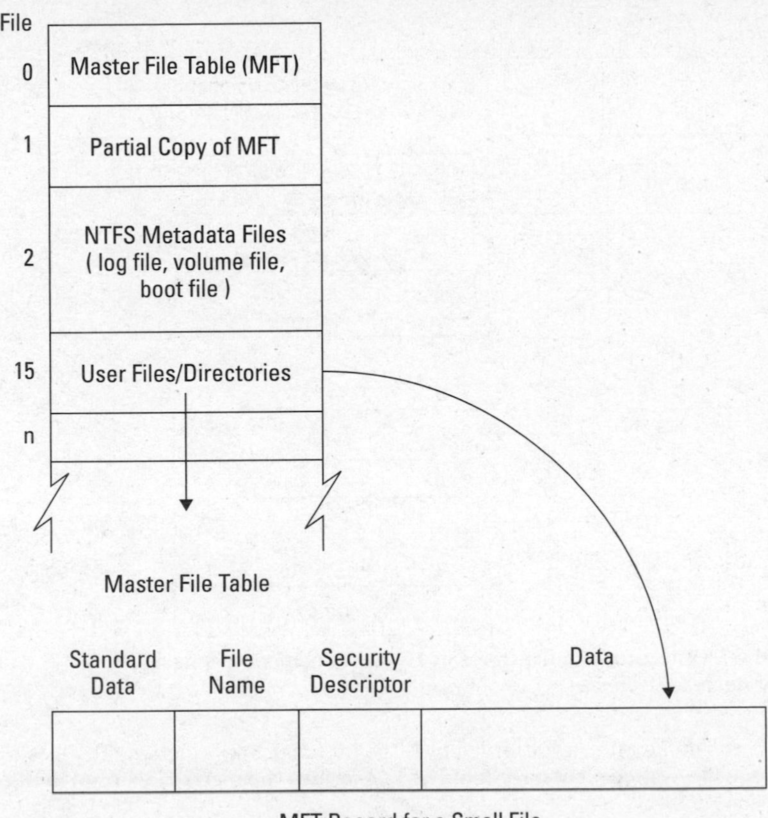

Figure 26-2: The MFT is a relational database that maintains the data on an NTFS volume.

As a file increases in size or becomes fragmented, however, it requires multiple records to store its data. The primary record in the MFT for a file that spans multiple records is called the *base file record.* The base file record serves as the starting point in the file's data chain. NTFS creates additional areas called *runs* on the disk to store the additional file data. With volumes that have a cluster size of 2K or smaller, the runs are 2K in size. Volumes with 4K or larger clusters use 4K-sized runs. Attributes that don't reside in the MFT but instead reside in runs are called *nonresident attributes.* NTFS adds additional runs as needed when the file size increases.

If you compare the way NTFS and FAT store information about data in the volume, you'll see that the MFT is similar to FAT. Windows Server 2003 uses the cluster entries in the FAT to locate the clusters in a file's data chain. Windows Server 2003 uses the records in the MFT to locate the data in a file's data chain. The clusters belonging to a file are referenced in the MFT using virtual cluster numbers (VCNs). Each file starts with VCN 0, and additional clusters are numbered sequentially up to the last cluster in the file. The Data attribute for the file contains information that maps the VCNs to the logical cluster numbers (LCN) on the disk. When there are too many VCN-to-LCN mappings to store in a single MFT record, NTFS adds additional records to store the additional mappings. Figure 26-3 illustrates VCN-to-LCN mapping in the MFT.

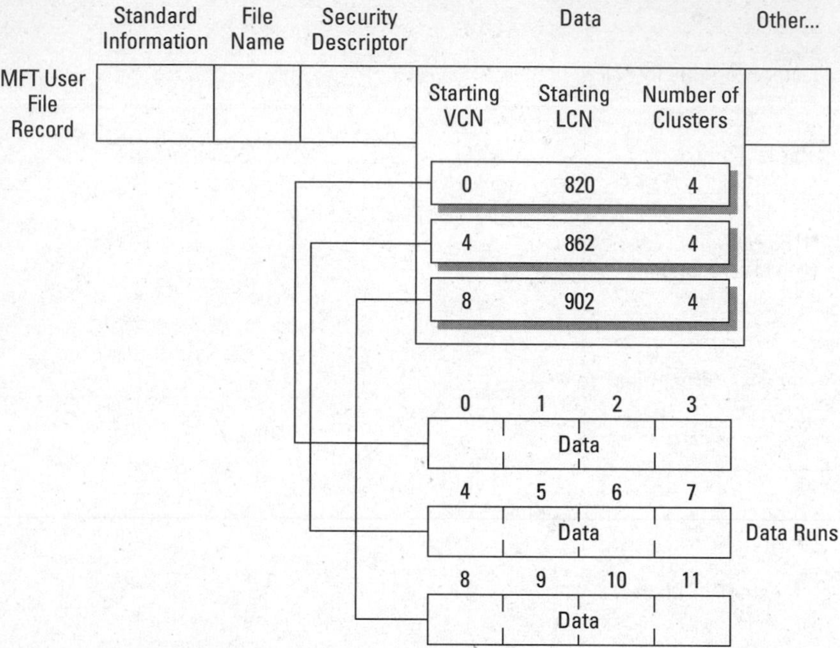

Figure 26-3: The MFT record for a file stores its LCN-to-VCN mapping, using multiple runs if necessary.

The first 16 records in the MFT are reserved by NTFS for *metadata,* which are the files NTFS uses to define the file system structure. Table 26-5 describes the metadata stored in the MFT.

Table 26-5: NTFS Metadata

MFT Record	*Description*	*File Name*	*Purpose*
0	Master file table (MFT)	`$Mft`	Stores base file record for each file and folder in the volume. Additional records are used when the number or size of files and folders exceeds the space available.
1	Master file table 2	`$MftMirr`	This duplicate MFT stores the first four records of the MFT to ensure access to the MFT in case of a failure. The boot sector stores the data segment locations for both `$Mft` and `$MftMirr` for recoverability.
2	Log file	`$LogFile`	Stores transaction history enabling NTFS to perform a recovery of the file system if an error occurs. The log can be up to 4MB in size.
3	Volume	`$Volume`	Stores volume data such as the volume version and volume label.

MFT Record	Description	File Name	Purpose
4	Attribute definitions	`$AttrDef`	Comprises a table of attribute names, numbers, and descriptions.
5	Root file name index	`$`	The volume's root directory.
6	Cluster bitmap	`$Bitmap`	Clusters-in-use table.
7	Partition boot sector	`$Boot`	Contains bootstrap program on bootable volume.
8	Bad cluster file	`$BadClus`	Bad cluster map.
9	Security file	`$Secure`	Stores unique security descriptors for all files in the volume.
10	Upcase table	`$Upcase`	Converts lowercase characters to uppercase Unicode characters.
11	NTFS extension file	`$Extend`	Enables file system extensions such as reparse points, quotas, and so on.
12–15			Reserved for future use.

While the MFT performs a similar function to the FAT, the similarities between the two file systems stop there. NTFS provides considerably more features than FAT because of the differences in structure. As mentioned previously, NTFS provides much better security and recoverability than FAT. NTFS also provides built-in compression capability, enabling you to compress files on a file-by-file basis. The NTFS driver handles decompression on the fly, making compression transparent to the user.

Note For detailed information on using compression on NTFS volumes, see the section titled "Using Disk Compression in NTFS" later in this chapter.

NTFS' structure also makes it an extensible file system, which means that new features can be added without completely redesigning the file system. Several new features were added to NTFS version 5 in Windows 2000, and these improvements carry forward into .NET. The following sections explain the most pertinent changes.

Disk Quotas

NTFS in Windows Server 2003 supports *disk quotas,* which enable you to restrict the amount of disk space a given account can use. Quotas enable you to more effectively manage storage space, because you can parcel out storage space on an as-needed basis. Quotas also force users to be conservative with their designated storage space, compelling them to delete files when no longer needed. You can configure how quotas are enforced when a given user's quota is reached, by either denying additional space to the user or simply displaying a warning message to the user (see Figure 26-4).

You assign quotas on a per-volume basis, which means that the entire volume shares the same quota properties. However, you can assign quota limits on a per-user basis, which means that each user can have a different quota limit, if necessary. You can also apply quotas on a per-group basis through the use of group policies. This flexibility enables you to tailor disk quotas to each user's or group's needs.

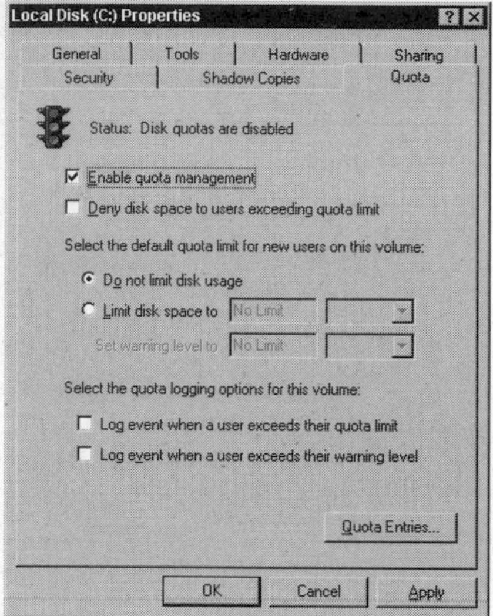

Figure 26-4: You configure quota settings on a per-volume basis through the volume's property sheet.

Although quotas apply to an entire volume rather than a single folder, there is a way around the per-volume nature of quotas. For example, assume you want to apply quotas only to `C:\Users` but not to the rest of drive C. *Mounted volumes,* also supported in Windows Server 2003, let you mount a physical volume to an NTFS folder. The mounted volume appears to both local and remote users as the contents of the host folder. In this situation, you can apply quotas to the mounted volume but not to the volume where it is hosted (drive C in this case). The net effect is that to the user, quotas only apply in the folder `C:\Users`.

For more information regarding quotas and quota assignment, see Chapter 19. See the section titled "Mounted Volumes" later in this chapter for a discussion of mounted volumes.

Reparse Points

Reparse points enable Windows Server 2003 to implement a handful of other features (described in the following sections). Reparse points are NTFS objects that carry special attribute tags. They are used to trigger additional functionality in the file system, working in conjunction with file system filters to extend the capability of the NTFS file system. The combination of reparse points and these additional file system filters enables features and functions to be added to the file system by both Microsoft and third parties without the need to redesign or restructure the file system.

In effect, reparse points are like red flags in the file system. When Windows Server 2003 encounters a reparse point during pathname parsing, it passes the reparse attribute tag (which uniquely defines the purpose of the reparse point) back up the I/O stack. Each installable file system filter in the I/O stack examines the reparse tag. When a match occurs, the driver executes the feature associated with the reparse point. So, this "red flag" tells

Windows Server 2003 that a driver other than the standard NTFS file system driver needs to process the file I/O to accommodate the added functionality made possible by that other driver.

Encrypting File System

The Encrypting File System (EFS) is one feature made possible by reparse points in Windows Server 2003 that enhances security for local files on NTFS volumes. EFS is useful for securing files on any system, but it is most useful on systems that can easily be stolen or physically compromised, such as notebook PCs. EFS is integrated within NTFS and therefore is applicable only to files on NTFS volumes. FAT16 and FAT32 volumes do not support EFS. Only files can be encrypted; folders cannot, even on NTFS volumes. However, folders are marked to indicate that they contain encrypted data. EFS is designed to protect files locally, and therefore doesn't support sharing of encrypted files. You can store your own encrypted files on a remote server and access those files yourself. The data is not encrypted during transmission across the network, however, unless you use Internet Protocol Security (IPSec) to encrypt IP traffic (and assuming you are using TCP/IP as the network protocol for transferring the file).

For a detailed discussion of EFS and how to implement it, see the section titled "Securing Files with the Encrypting File System" in Chapter 27.

Hierarchical Storage Management

Hierarchical Storage Management (HSM) is another feature in Windows Server 2003 made possible by reparse points. HSM allows some or all of a file to be stored remotely, and reparse points mark these files accordingly. The reparse point data stores the location of the remote data and allows NTFS to retrieve the data when needed. HSM works in conjunction with Remote Storage Services (RSS) and Removable Storage to enable files to be archived to tape or disk and automatically restored when requested by a user or process.

For more information on Removable Storage, see Chapters 19 and 20. Configuring the file system to support Remote Storage Services and HSM is discussed later in this chapter.

Directory Junctions

Directory junctions are another feature of NTFS. Directory junctions mark NTFS directories with a surrogate name. When the reparse point causes the path name to be reparsed, the surrogate name is grafted onto the original name. Directory junctions enable local volumes to be mapped to local NTFS folders, and also allow remote network shares to be mapped to local NTFS folders, thereby integrating these local and remote elements into a single local namespace. Directory junctions offer functions similar to the Distributed File System (Dfs), which is explained later in the section titled "Managing the Windows Server 2003 Distributed File System". Unlike Dfs, however, directory junctions work solely within the file system and don't require a client-side driver.

The primary purpose of directory junctions is to enable you to create a single local namespace using local folders, other local volumes, and network shares. All of these appear within the local namespace and appear to the local user as part of the local volume. Figure 26-5 illustrates the use of directory junctions to map local volumes and network shares into a local namespace.

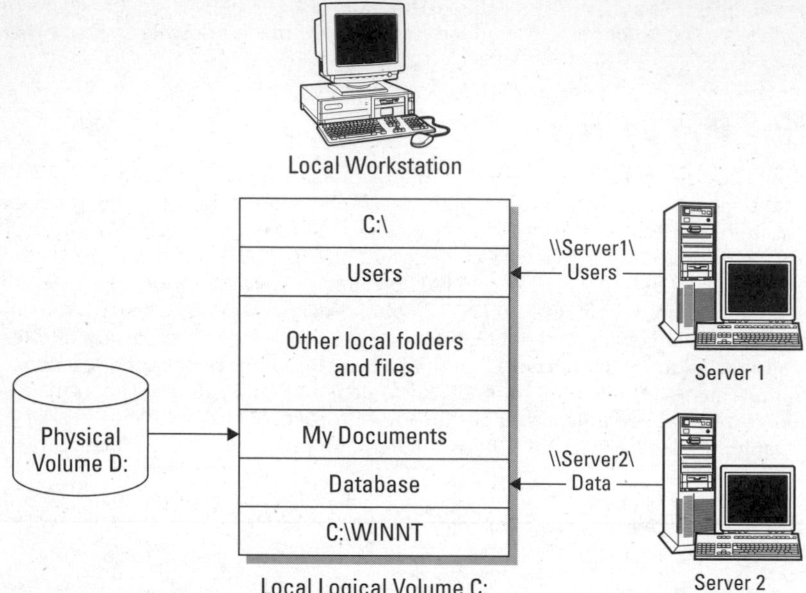

Figure 26-5: Directory junctions let you map local volumes and network shares into a single local namespace.

Mounted Volumes

Another reparse point feature, *volume mount points* (mounted volumes), brings to Windows Server 2003 the same advantages for local file systems that the Unix operating system offers through its distributed file system. In effect, this capability enables you to mount a volume to an NTFS folder on a different volume, making the mounted volume appear as if it were physically contained on the host volume. You can mount multiple volumes within a file system namespace, creating a homogenous file system from disparate physical volumes on the local computer. A single volume can be mounted to multiple NTFS folders if needed.

For a detailed discussion of mounted volumes, see the section titled "Working with Mounted Volumes" later in this chapter.

Choosing a File System

FAT offers a handful of advantages. First, it is compatible with nearly every PC operating system, which is useful for systems that must boot multiple operating systems and enable all (or multiple) operating systems to see a common FAT volume. FAT is also very recoverable because you can boot the system from a DOS diskette in the event of a failure and run one of many third-part FAT recovery utilities to repair and recover a volume. Finally, FAT offers better efficiency than NTFS for volumes smaller than 256MB (FAT32 does not support volumes smaller than 512M).

FAT also has some disadvantages. The fact that the boot sector is stored in a fixed location (first track on the disk) makes it more susceptible to failure. If that track goes, the drive goes. Also, the root directory structure in a FAT volume is limited by design to 512 entries, which limits the number of files in the root folder to 512, but more important, limits the number of folders under the root.

Another disadvantage of FAT16 is the 4GB limit it imposes on volume size, although in reality this isn't a true disadvantage as the overhead imposed by FAT16 on large volumes makes them undesirable. Also, the relatively large default cluster size in a FAT16 volume also makes FAT volumes less efficient in their use of storage space (see the section titled "Optimizing Storage Capacity" later in this chapter).

FAT32 offers its own advantages. The 32-bit FAT increases the storage capacity to 2TB, considerably higher than the 4GB supported by FAT16. The smaller default cluster size for a FAT32 volume means that FAT32 volumes store data more efficiently than similarly sized FAT16 volumes.

Aside from different default cluster sizes and maximum capacities, there are a few key differences between FAT32 and FAT16. First, FAT32 offers better performance than FAT16. In addition, FAT32 is more fault-tolerant than FAT16 because Windows Server 2003 can automatically use the backup copy of the FAT32 if the primary becomes corrupted. The boot record on a FAT32 volume also contains backup data necessary to recreate the volume in the event that the boot record becomes damaged.

NTFS offers several advantages over the FAT file systems. In terms of speed, NTFS is not always the fastest of the three. With many mitigating factors on either side (structure, cluster size, fragmentation, number of files) and the fact that today's hardware makes for quick file system performance regardless of the file system type, however, speed is not a factor in most situations. Choosing the right underlying disk subsystem is often more important (SCSI versus other interfaces, for example).

One of the primary advantages offered by NTFS is security. Neither FAT16 nor FAT32 provides any local security for files. The security you can apply to FAT volumes is very limited for shared network access. Only NTFS enables you to assign permissions on a file-by-file basis with a high degree of granularity. Support for compression is another advantage offered by NTFS that you won't find in FAT16 or FAT32 under Windows Server 2003.

Because you can control cluster size for FAT volumes under Windows Server 2003, as you can for NTFS, cluster size is not an advantage per se, but NTFS will always use a smaller default cluster size for a volume of a given size. Reducing cluster size improves storage efficiency by reducing sector slack (see the section titled "Optimizing Storage Capacity" later in this chapter), but it can also increase file fragmentation, which can reduce performance. Because of the difference in structure between FAT and NTFS, NTFS is more efficient at retrieving a fragmented file, which mitigates fragmentation as a factor in deciding on cluster size.

Thus, the primary advantages offered by NTFS are those that pertain to functionality and security rather than performance. Consider choosing NTFS for all new installations and converting existing FAT16 and FAT32 partitions to NTFS for upgrades. You'll not only gain the security advantages offered by NTFS' object permissions, but in addition you will be able to take advantage of Dfs, EFS, mounted volumes, disk quotas, and the other features discussed previously. The primary reason for retaining a FAT file system is to enable other operating systems on a dual-boot system to see the volume. While the additional overhead imposed by NTFS could be considered a disadvantage, most systems are so fast today that the overhead is transparent or negligible.

Optimizing Storage Capacity

Although quotas offer a means to help you manage storage capacity on NTFS volumes, there are also other issues to consider, including some that apply to FAT16 and FAT32 file systems. This section covers two topics that will help you optimize storage capacity: cluster size and compression.

Optimizing Cluster Size

As explained earlier in this chapter, a sector is the smallest unit of physical storage space on a disk. The smallest *allocation* unit, however, is the cluster. When Windows Server 2003 parcels out storage space, it does so by cluster. The significance of this is that cluster size has a direct impact on how efficiently the file system stores data. Take this example: Assume a volume uses a cluster size of 64K. You store several files, each 32K in size. Although two files could possibly fit in one cluster, that's not how Windows Server 2003 allocates the space. Instead, each file resides completely in its own cluster. That means that each file takes up just half of its allocated space, with the rest being unused. This is often called *sector slack.* Take it to the extreme in this example and assume that all your files are like this, and you'll waste half of the space on the volume. A 32GB volume would only hold 16GB of data.

In reality, most files are much larger than 32K, so the amount of wasted space is reduced. Overall, however, sector slack can have a significant impact on storage capacity, leaving as much as 25 percent or more of a disk unusable. You can reduce cluster size to reduce sector slack and make the most of the storage space you have. This has the net effect of increasing file fragmentation (see the next section), but a policy of frequently defragmenting the drive and the fact that NTFS efficiently retrieves even highly fragmented files can eliminate performance as an issue.

You can define the cluster size for a volume when you format the volume. To specify a nondefault cluster size for an NTFS volume, simply choose the desired cluster size from the Allocation unit size drop-down list on the Format dialog box (see Figure 26-6). There is no way to change the cluster size on an existing volume without reformatting the volume in Windows Server 2003, although you can use a third-party utility such as PowerQuest's PartitionMagic (`www.powerquest.com`) to dynamically modify cluster size without reformatting a disk.

The Format dialog box doesn't give you any options for using a nondefault cluster size for FAT16 and FAT32 volumes, however. You must format these volumes using the FORMAT command from a console prompt and specify the desired cluster size as a parameter of the FORMAT command. You can choose any of the cluster sizes defined in Tables 26-2, 26-3, and 26-4 for the respective file systems. In addition, FAT32 and NTFS support cluster sizes of 128K and 256K for volumes with a physical sector size greater than 512 bytes. For a description of the FORMAT command's syntax, open a command console and type `format /?`.

Defragmenting Volumes

Windows Server 2003 allocates storage space in contiguous clusters whenever possible. This improves file system I/O performance because the disk heads don't have to move much to read or write a file. As files are added and modified, however, the amount of available space changes and files become *fragmented,* or stored in noncontiguous sectors. The more fragmented a volume, the poorer the performance because the drive heads have to move more to piece together the file. Even drives that use an efficient cluster size for the size of volume and size of files on the volume can suffer from fragmentation that reduces performance.

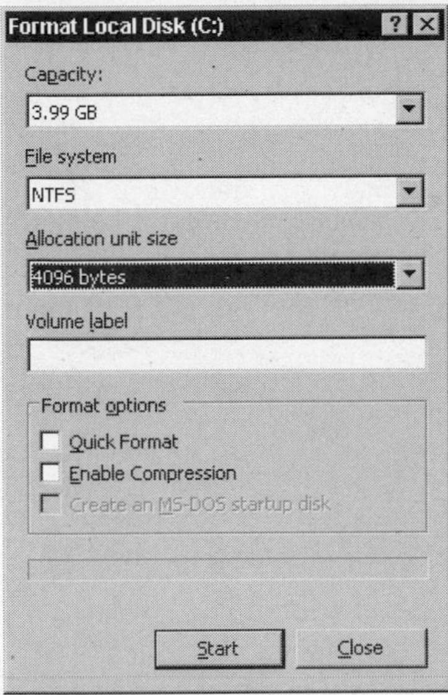

Figure 26-6: Use the Allocation unit size drop-down list to choose the cluster size when formatting a disk with NTFS.

Windows Server 2003 includes a defragmentation utility called Disk Defragmenter that you can use to defragment a volume. Disk Defragmenter analyzes disk fragmentation and provides a means to defragment drives that require it. It also provides a detailed fragmentation analysis report.

To defragment a volume, right-click the volume in My Computer and choose Properties. Click the Tools tab, and then click Defragment. Now open Disk Defragmenter (see Figure 26-7).

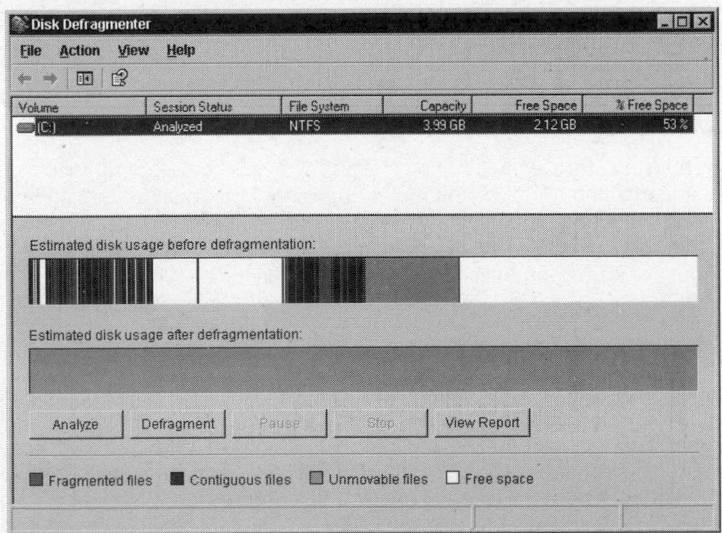

Figure 26-7: Use Disk Defragmenter to optimize storage space by defragmenting a drive.

You also can access Disk Defragmenter through the Disk Defragmenter node in the Computer Management console (right-click My Computer and choose Manage).

Disk Defragmenter requires no user-specified parameters or other input. Simply right-click a volume and choose Analyze to analyze fragmentation or Defragment to start the defragmentation process. The length of time required to complete an analysis or defragmentation depends on the size and fragmentation of the volume. To view a report from a previous analysis, right-click a volume and choose View Report (see Figure 26-8).

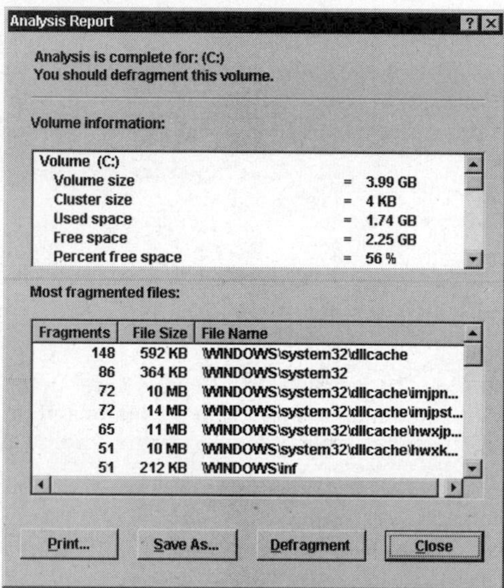

Figure 26-8: Disk Defragmenter provides a detailed analysis report on disk fragmentation.

Using Disk Compression in NTFS

Another means of optimizing storage capacity on NTFS volumes is to use compression. You can enable compression of an entire NTFS volume or configure individual folders and files for compression. Compression is not supported on volumes with a cluster size greater than 4K, however, because the tradeoff between storage capacity and performance degradation isn't worthwhile. The amount of storage increase achieved depends on the types of files being compressed.

Enabling and disabling compression

You can enable compression when you format a volume or turn on compression at any time for an entire volume, a folder, or an individual file. To enable compression for a volume when you format the volume, select the option Enable Compression on the Format dialog box. Use the `/C` switch if formatting a volume with the FORMAT command from the command prompt. In either case, folders and files added to the volume will be compressed by default.

You also can enable or disable compression for a previously formatted volume. Right-click the volume and choose Properties. On the General page, select the option Compress drive to save disk space, then click OK or Apply. Windows Server 2003 asks if you want to compress only the root folder or all folders and files. Select as desired and click OK. To turn off compression, deselect the option Compress drive to save disk space. Again, Windows Server 2003 asks if you want to apply the change to only the root folder or to subfolders and files.

To compress or decompress a single file, right-click the file and choose Properties. On the General property page, click Advanced to display the Advanced Attributed dialog box. Select or deselect the option Compress contents to save disk space, click OK, and then click OK or Apply.

You can use the COMPACT command to compress or decompress a folder or file from the command console. Issue the command `compact /?` to view the syntax and usage for the COMPACT command. Use COMPACT with no command line parameters to view the compression attribute of a folder or file.

Moving and copying files affects their compression attributes:

✦ **Moving an uncompressed file to any folder:** The file remains uncompressed, regardless of the compression attribute of the destination folder.

✦ **Moving a compressed file to any folder:** The file remains compressed, regardless of the compression attribute of the destination folder.

✦ **Copying a file:** The file takes on the compression attribute of the destination folder. A compressed file copied to an uncompressed folder, for example, is uncompressed at the destination.

✦ **Replacing a file:** If you copy a file to a folder that already contains a file by that name (and you replace the original), the file takes on the compression attribute of the file it replaced.

✦ **Copy or move from FAT16/FAT32 to NTFS:** The file assumes the compression attribute of the destination folder. Note that FAT16 and FAT32 do not support compression, so all files start out uncompressed and either remain that way if copied or moved to an uncompressed folder or are compressed if copied or moved to a compressed folder.

✦ **Copy or move from NTFS to FAT16/FAT32 or to floppy:** Files are uncompressed, as neither FAT16/FAT32 nor floppy drives support compression.

Performance considerations

Compression does affect performance, and the degree depends on a handful of factors. As files are moved or copied, even on the same volume, the file has to be uncompressed, then recompressed. Files are uncompressed for transfer across the LAN, so you don't get any benefit from compression in reducing network bandwidth use.

Windows Server 2003 can experience significant performance degradation when compression is used, depending on the server's function and load. In general, lightly loaded servers or those that are primarily read-only or read-mostly do not suffer from compression degradation as much as heavily loaded servers or those with a lot of write traffic. In addition, compressing certain types of files (jpg, zip, and so on) is counterproductive and can actually result in larger file sizes rather than smaller. The only real way to determine if compression will have an impact on a given system is to test it. If you find that you don't get the capacity savings you expected or if performance drops significantly, simply uncompress the volume or folders.

Managing the Distributed File System

Windows Server 2003 includes an extremely useful feature called the Distributed File System (Dfs) that enables you to simplify a user's view of the LAN and its resources. In essence, Dfs lets you bring local volumes, network shares, and entire multiple servers under a common file system namespace. Rather than require users to browse several different servers on the network for resources, those resources can all appear under the same namespace (such as a single drive letter). In other words, these distributed resources all appear to be located in the same place as far as the user is concerned, although they could actually be separated by continents.

Dfs provides other benefits in addition to providing a unified view of a distributed file system and simplifying access to the file system by users. First, Dfs uses link tracking to keep track of objects within the Dfs namespace, which makes it possible for folders and their contents to move without breaking the logical link and structure within Dfs. Because the users see the logical location for a given folder rather than the physical location, you can move a folder from one location to another, whether on the same server or to another server. The user sees no difference and can still access the folders from the same logical location even though they may have moved physically. In the case of a Web server, Dfs enables you to move portions of a given Web site without affecting availability of the site or breaking any links in the site. In the case of an enterprise, Dfs' link-tracking enables you to restructure storage as needs change without affecting users' access to the shared data or the way they access it.

Availability is another benefit to using Dfs when integrated with Active Directory (AD). Dfs publishes the Dfs topology to the AD, making it visible to all users in the domain. You also can replicate the Dfs namespace through AD-integrated replication, making the folders in a given Dfs namespace available even when a particular server is down or unavailable.

Load balancing is the third benefit offered by Dfs. You can bring multiple replicas of a share under a common share point, associating multiple identical shares with a single share name. While each user thinks he is accessing the folder or file from a specific location each time, it can actually be pulled from a different server based on load.

Dfs Structure and Terminology

Essentially, a Dfs namespace is a shared group of network shares residing under a *Dfs root,* which serves as a container for the namespace and performs much the same function for the distributed file system that a root folder serves for a physical volume. In other words, the Dfs root serves as the share point for the distributed file system. Rather than containing subfolders like a root directory does, the Dfs root contains links to the shares (local and remote) that form the distributed file system. Each link appears as a subfolder of the root share.

A server that hosts a Dfs root is called a *host server.* You can create *root targets* on other servers to replicate a Dfs namespace and provide redundancy in the event the host server becomes unavailable. A user can access the Dfs root using a UNC pathname in the form `\\host server\root name`, where `host server` is the network name for the server hosting the Dfs root and `root name` is the root's name. For example, if you created a root named `Shares` on a server name `FileServer`, users would access the Dfs namespace from their computers using the UNC pathname `\\FileServer\Shares`. What they see when they get there is a function of the Dfs itself and might include shares local to that server, shares on other servers, or even shares on the clients' own computers. Users can also specify more defined paths, such as `\\FileServer\Shares\George\Files\Somefile.doc`.

If you found yourself limited with Windows 2000 Server's Dfs implementation where a host server can host only one Dfs root (whether domain or standalone), you'll find more flexibility in Windows Server. Dfs in Windows Server now supports multiple standalone and domain roots, giving you greater flexibility for creating and managing roots.

Figure 26-9 illustrates a sample Dfs structure. The Dfs root is called `\\SRV1\root` and contains data in shares from SRV2 and SRV3, program files in a share from APPSRV1, and data from a Windows 98 workstation computer.

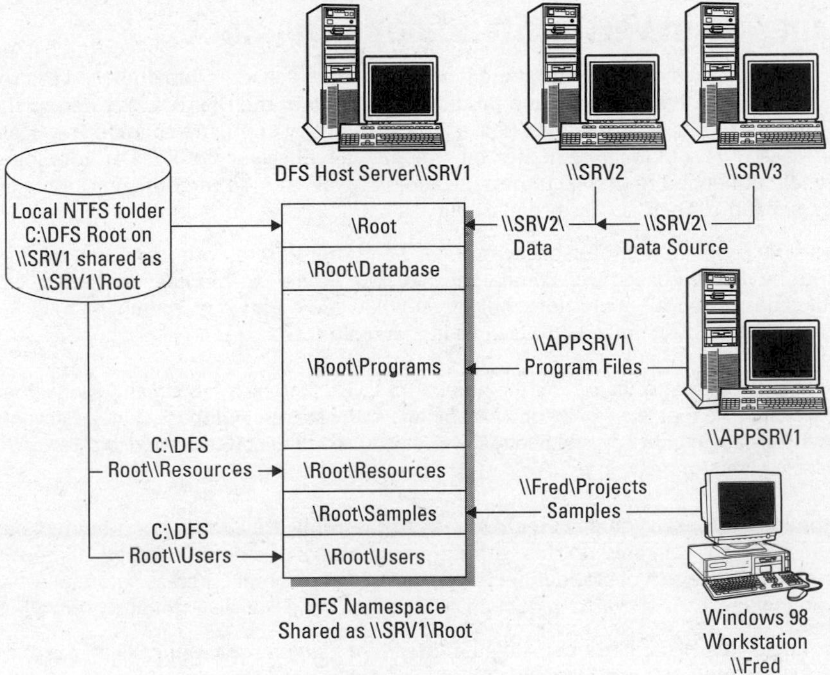

Figure 26-9: The Dfs structure (standalone Dfs root).

As illustrated in Figure 26-9, *Dfs links* connect a name in the root to one or more shared folders called *targets* (called *replicas* in Windows 2000), or simply *Dfs shared folders.* The links are essentially subcontainers within the root and serve much the same purpose as subdirectories in the root of a physical volume. Within the link object are one or more targets (pointers to shared folders) that define the share that a user sees when he or she opens the link. The ability to define multiple targets in a given link is what gives Dfs its failover capability. Dfs responds to a client request with the list of all targets in a requested link. The client then decides which one to use. If any particular target (share) referenced in a link is unavailable (the server sharing it is offline or times out, for example), the client can use a different one.

Although you may assume that each replica associated with a particular link will be a copy of the same folder, that assumption is wrong. Dfs does not provide any replication of data between replicas by default. There is nothing to prevent you from defining multiple replicas in a Dfs link, each pointing to completely different content. This presents interesting options for creating dynamic content on Web sites that use Dfs in their underlying structure. Provide a means of replication and synchronization if you need to ensure that the content in the multiple replicas is identical. See the section titled "Replication" later in this chapter for more information.

Domain-Based Versus Standalone Dfs Roots

Dfs supports two types of Dfs roots: standalone and domain-based. Domain-based Dfs roots integrate with the Active Directory and provide replication of the Dfs topology across the domain (but not replication of folders unless you specifically configure them for replication). A domain-based Dfs root must be hosted on a domain member server. The Dfs' topology is automatically published to the AD to provide access to all users in the domain (and in trusted domains), subject to their access permissions.

Standalone Dfs roots do not integrate with the AD and therefore do not provide the replication offered by domain-based Dfs. Standalone roots are limited to a single root target, while domain-based roots support multiple root targets. You can create a maximum of 10,000 Dfs links in a standalone root and 5,000 Dfs links in a domain root.

There is no explicit limitation on the number of levels that each target can have within its host share. The root really only contains pointers to the shares, and those shares can contain essentially any number of subfolders. However, you are subject to the Windows Server 260-character limit for pathnames.

As mentioned previously, you can create *root targets* to replicate a Dfs root from one computer to another. You can only do this within the framework of a domain-based Dfs root. You cannot create root targets of standalone Dfs roots. However, you can create a domain-based Dfs root on any member server in a domain. The server need not be a domain controller.

As with replicas in a Dfs link, there is no guarantee that a given root replica is an exact copy of another. Creating a root replica does not provide any means of folder replication or synchronization — it simply creates a logical relationship between roots on two or more servers that are referenced by the same name in the Dfs namespace. You must configure that replication and synchronization separately to ensure that users see the same content regardless of the server to which they connect.

Client Support

Dfs provides full support for clients to access shared resources through a Dfs root share point, as long as those clients support the underlying network structure and protocol and are Dfs-aware. These clients can browse both standalone and domain-based Dfs roots on the network. Windows 98 and Windows NT 4.0 with Service Pack 4 both include built-in support for browsing standalone and domain-based roots, as do Windows 2000, Windows XP, and Windows Server 2003. Windows 95 does not include any built-in Dfs support, so you need to install the Dfs service to enable Windows 95 clients to browse Dfs roots. You'll find the Dfs client for Windows 95 at `www.microsoft.com/ntserver/nts/downloads/winfeatures/NTSDistrFile/default.asp`. With this client installed, Windows 95 clients can browse both standalone and domain-based roots.

Windows 95, Windows 98, Windows NT, Windows 2000, and Windows XP clients all can host a replica (even Windows 95 clients without the Dfs service installed) because at that level Dfs simply represents a share-redirection mechanism. As long as the folder is shared on the client computer, any Dfs-aware client can be redirected to that share. In addition, the clients don't even have to be in the same domain (or in a domain at all) to host a shared folder, even with a domain-based Dfs root.

Replication

As mentioned briefly earlier in this chapter, Dfs can provide a level of redundancy to ensure that shares within a given Dfs namespace are available even if a server or share becomes unavailable for some reason. Dfs does this through replication, which copies the root or link (and underlying data) to one or more other servers. Because Dfs returns the complete list of root replicas or share replicas in response to a query, a client can try each one in the list to find one that functions if a particular server or share is offline.

See the section titled "Understanding and Configuring Site Costing/Affinity in Dfs" later in this chapter for information on how to control the targets a given client will attempt to use by default.

While Dfs by default does not provide replication of a Dfs root or any replicas associated with a given Dfs link, you can configure Dfs to replicate entire Dfs roots or individual shared folders (Dfs links). Dfs relies on the File Replication Service (FRS) included with Windows Server 2003 to perform automatic replication. After you create a root replica or a share replica, you can configure the *replication policy* for that object, which defines how the object is replicated. Automatic replication is only available for domain-based Dfs roots and can only replicate data stored on NTFS volumes. By default, FRS replicates the data every 15 minutes.

Automatic replication is not available for data stored on FAT volumes or for standalone Dfs roots or replicas. In these situations, you need to use manual replication. Manual replication is just what its name implies. You have to replicate the data manually by copying the data periodically through drag-and-drop or a similar method as you would manually copy any file from one place to another. Although you could automate the manual replication through the use of `AT` commands and batch files, that solution is something of an awkward solution. Automatic replication through the use of domain-based Dfs is by far the best method for sheer simplicity and low administration. Although you could configure a mix of automated and manual replication within a domain-based Dfs root, it's best to use one or the other to ensure that the copies remain synchronized.

You can configure your replication scheme such that one copy serves as a master and the other copies serve as read-only copies. To do so, first create the folder and share on the servers that will host the read-only copies. Set NTFS permissions on the main share folder to grant users read-only access but still allow FRS the control necessary to write changes to the share's child folders. Then set the replication policy for the root replica or folder replica to initiate the replication, specifying the dynamic source root or folder as the initial master.

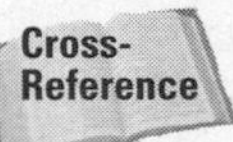

See the section titled "Configuring Replication" later in this chapter for more detailed information on configuring Dfs replication. See Chapter 12 for detailed information on managing replication within Active Directory.

Client-Side Caching

Dfs provides for client-side caching of requests to improve performance and reduce network traffic. When a client issues a query to a Dfs host server, the host returns the requested information along with a cache value. The client caches the returned results for the specified period of time. If the client makes another request for the same information within the cache period, the data comes from the client's cache rather than the host. If the cache period has lapsed, the cached data is purged and the host server provides the data, which again is stored in the cache during the next cache period. Data writes are not cached.

You can configure cache values for an entire root or for individual folder replicas. You configure the cache value when you create the root or link. Figure 26-10 shows the dialog box for creating a link, which includes a cache setting. You can also modify the cache value at any time through the object's properties. Right-click a root or link and choose Properties to view its property sheet, then change the cache value on the General page and click Apply or OK.

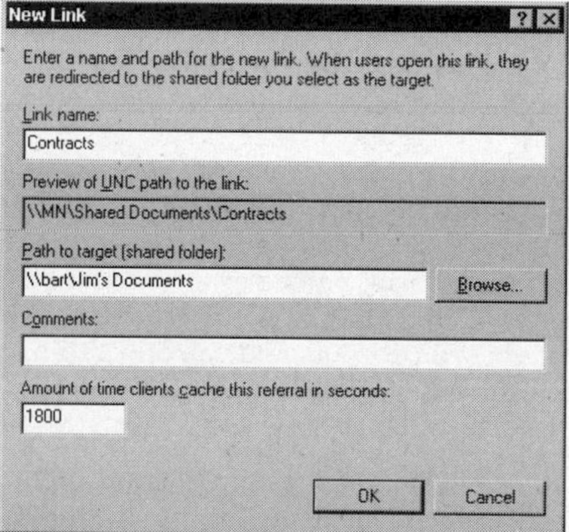

Figure 26-10: You can specify cache time when you create the root or link.

Working with the Distributed File System Console

As with most other administrative functions, Windows Server 2003 provides an MMC console for managing Dfs. To open the Distributed File System console, choose Start ➪ All Programs ➪ Administrative Tools ➪ Distributed File System, or execute the console file `Dfsgui.msc`. Figure 26-11 shows the Dfs console.

The Dfs console lets you manage multiple Dfs roots across the network, thereby providing a single point of management for all Dfs roots in your enterprise, subject to your access permissions within the enterprise. To view a Dfs root not listed in the console, right-click Distributed File System and choose Show Root. Specify the Dfs root name or server hosting according to the three naming formats described on the resulting dialog box. To remove a Dfs root from the console display but not delete the root, right-click the root and choose Hide Root.

The following sections explain how to use the Dfs console for specific tasks. See Chapter 6 to learn more about general MMC console operations.

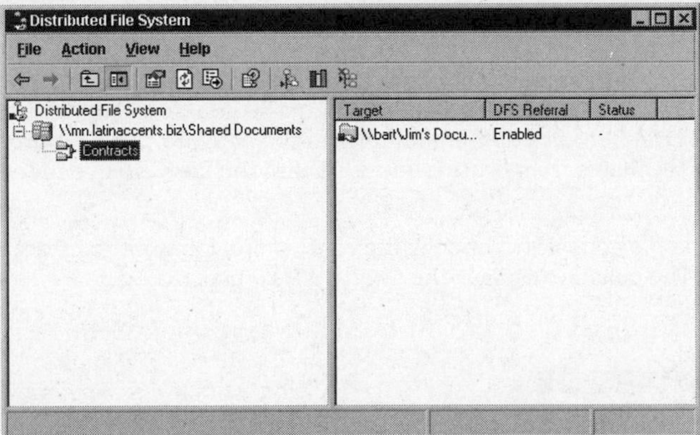

Figure 26-11: Use the Distributed File System console to manage Dfs roots and replicas.

Creating and Deleting Dfs Roots

You can create a standalone or domain-based root using the Dfs console. You can create either type on a member server or domain controller. You are not restricted to creating domain-based Dfs roots only on domain controllers. In addition, you can use the Dfs console to create a Dfs root on any appropriate target server in the network; you are not restricted to creating a Dfs root only on the local computer. You can create multiple Dfs roots on a server.

To create a Dfs root, open the Dfs console, right-click the Distributed File System node, and choose New Root to start the New DfsRoot Wizard. The wizard prompts you for the following information throughout the process:

✦ **Root Type:** Select the type of Dfs root you want to create. As explained previously, you can create either type of Dfs root on a workgroup or domain member server or domain controller.

✦ **Domain name:** Specify the domain name if you are creating a domain-based root.

✦ **Host Server:** The wizard prompts you for the name of the server on which the Dfs root will be hosted. Specify the server's UNC name (such as `\\someserver`) or the fully qualified domain name (such as `someserver.somedomain.com`).

✦ **Root name:** Specify the name of the share point on the host server where the Dfs root will be anchored.

✦ **Comments:** You can include an optional comment for the root that identifies its function or provides other information about the root. This information appears when you view the root's properties (right-click the root and choose Properties).

✦ **Folder to share**: Enter or select the folder that you want to serve as the root of the share.

To delete a Dfs root, right-click the root and choose Delete Root. Windows Server 2003 will prompt you to verify the deletion. Note that deleting a Dfs root prevents clients from accessing that root, although it does not delete the underlying folders or their contents.

Creating Dfs Links

The share you specify as a Dfs root's share point can contain subfolders and files, which users see when they connect to the Dfs root. The Dfs root can also contain Dfs links that point to shares on the local computer or other computers on the network. Dfs links are the mechanism that lets you bring shares from other computers into the file system defined by the Dfs root.

To create a Dfs link, open the Dfs console, right-click the root where you want to create the link, and choose New Link. The console displays the Create a New Link dialog box, shown in Figure 26-12.

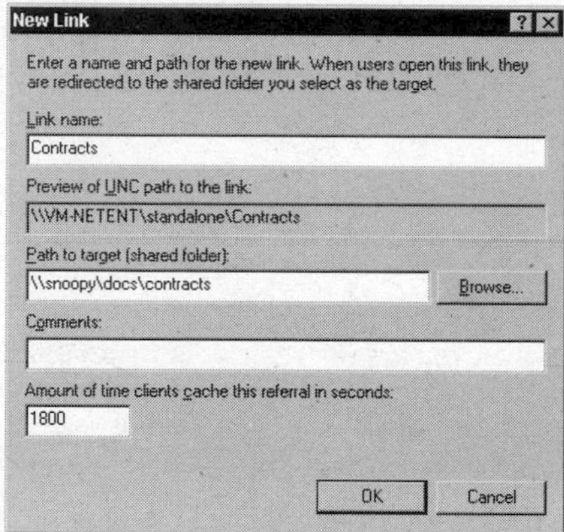

Figure 26-12: Dfs links serve as redirection pointers that associate a share point in the root with a physical share on the network.

The following list summarizes the options on the New Link dialog box:

- ✦ **Link name:** This is the virtual folder name the client sees within the Dfs structure.
- ✦ **Preview of UNC Path to the link:** This read-only value shows the UNC path that will result from the combination of server, share, and link names.
- ✦ **Path to target (shared folder):** Specify the UNC pathname for the local or network share to which the client should be redirected when accessing the folder defined by Link name. You can also click Browse to select a folder.
- ✦ **Comments:** This option appears when you display the link's properties.
- ✦ **Amount of time clients cache this referral in seconds:** Specify the cache-aging period for the link. Clients will cache the referral for the specified time, retrieving the data from their cache until the cache period expires.

Working with Targets

The previous section explained how to create a single target associated with a Dfs link. However, you can associate multiple targets (copies of a share) with a given link. This provides failover so that if the server hosting a particular target is offline or the share is unavailable, users can still access the data in the share. This failover process happens transparently to the user, who sees a single share under a given Dfs link, even though there might be several.

Windows Server 2003 uses the term *target* synonymously with *replica*. Windows 2000 refers to them as replicas.

To create a new target of a share (create multiple targets in a link, defining a *target set*), right-click the link and then choose New Target. Windows Server 2003 displays the New Target dialog box, shown in Figure 26-13. The following list summarizes the options:

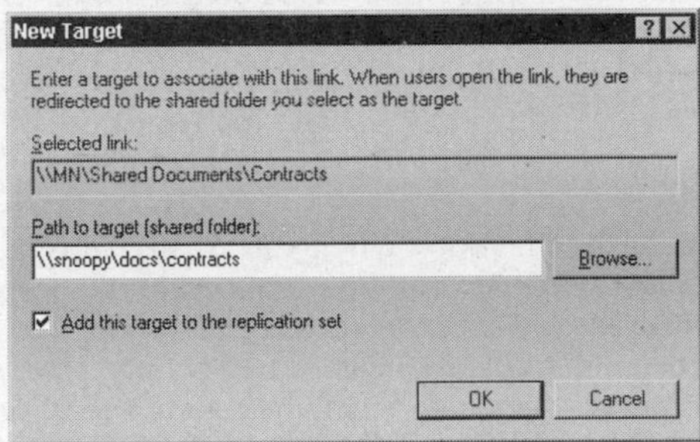

Figure 26-13: Specify the share name and replication type when creating a new replica.

- **Selected link:** Read-only; specifies the Dfs link name under which the replica is being created.
- **Path to target (shared folder):** Specify the UNC pathname for the local or network share to which the client should be redirected when accessing the folder defined by Link name.
- **Add this target to the replication set:** Replicate the folder using FRS if selected; do not replicate if not selected.

You can only specify a replication method when creating replicas within a domain-based Dfs root. The replication option is dimmed when creating replicas in a standalone root. After you create the replica, you can modify its properties to define its replication policy. See the section titled "Configuring Replication" later in this chapter for more information on configuring a replica's replication policy.

Creating Root Targets

A root replica, or *root target*, is a copy of a domain-based Dfs root's structure hosted on another server. When you create a root target, you copy the Dfs structure to the other server, but you do not copy any physical folders associated with links in the structure. You can create a root target from any server in the network on any other server on the network (or the local server), subject to your access permissions. After you create a root target, you can set its replication policy to define how it replicates (explained in the next section).

You can't create another root target of a standalone Dfs root. You can create multiple targets only of domain-based Dfs roots.

To create a root target, start by creating the target share on the new server. The share name must match the share name specified for the existing Dfs root. Then, open the Dfs console, right-click the root you want to make a replica of, and choose New Root Target. The New Root Wizard prompts you for the following information:

Tip

You can view the current share name in the root's properties. Right-click the root, choose Properties, and note the read-only share name on the General tab.

- **Server name:** Specify the name of the server or browse the network for the server that will host the root replica. You must choose a server that does not already host a root or root replica, as each server can host only one.
- **Folder to share:** This read-only value shows the share to be used on the target server for the new root. If you have not yet created the listed share, do so, set permissions as needed on the share, and then complete the wizard.

Configuring Replication

You can replicate roots and shares in domain-based Dfs roots. When you create a root target, you don't have the option of specifying a replication policy, but you can modify the properties after the root target is created. When you create a share target, you can specify that it participate in automatic replication. You can configure the replication policy only if there are at least two root targets. To modify the replication policy, right-click the root in the Dfs console and choose Configure Replication to display the Configure Replication Wizard, and then click Next.

The Configure Replication Wizard lists all replicas in the selected object (root or share). The list includes the name of the share and the location of the staging folder, which is used to store temporary files during replication. Click Staging and select the staging folder based on performance and disk capacity considerations.

You also must specify the replica that will serve as the initial master from which replication starts. Click the replica in the list to select it as the master and click Next to choose a replication topology (see Figure 26-14).

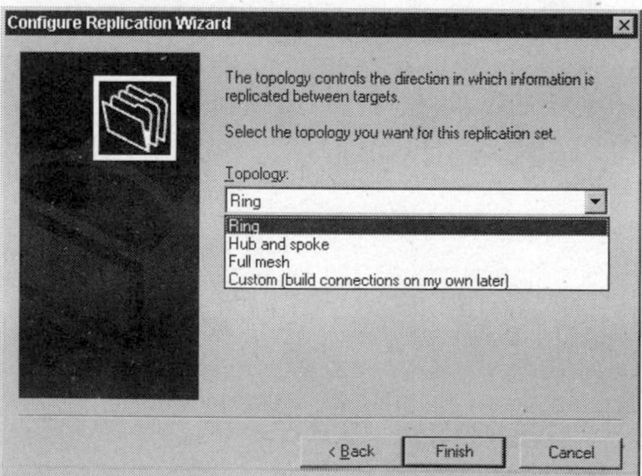

Figure 26-14: You must choose a replication topology for the replica.

For the next step, you need to understand the available replication topologies. These topologies, illustrated in Figure 26-15, include the following:

- **Ring.** The participating computers form a logical ring and each computer replicates with the computers on either side of it in the ring.

✦ **Hub and spoke.** One computer serves as the hub and replicates with each of the other computers in the topology.

✦ **Full mesh.** Each participating computer replicates with every other computer.

✦ **Custom.** You can manually define replication between participating computers.

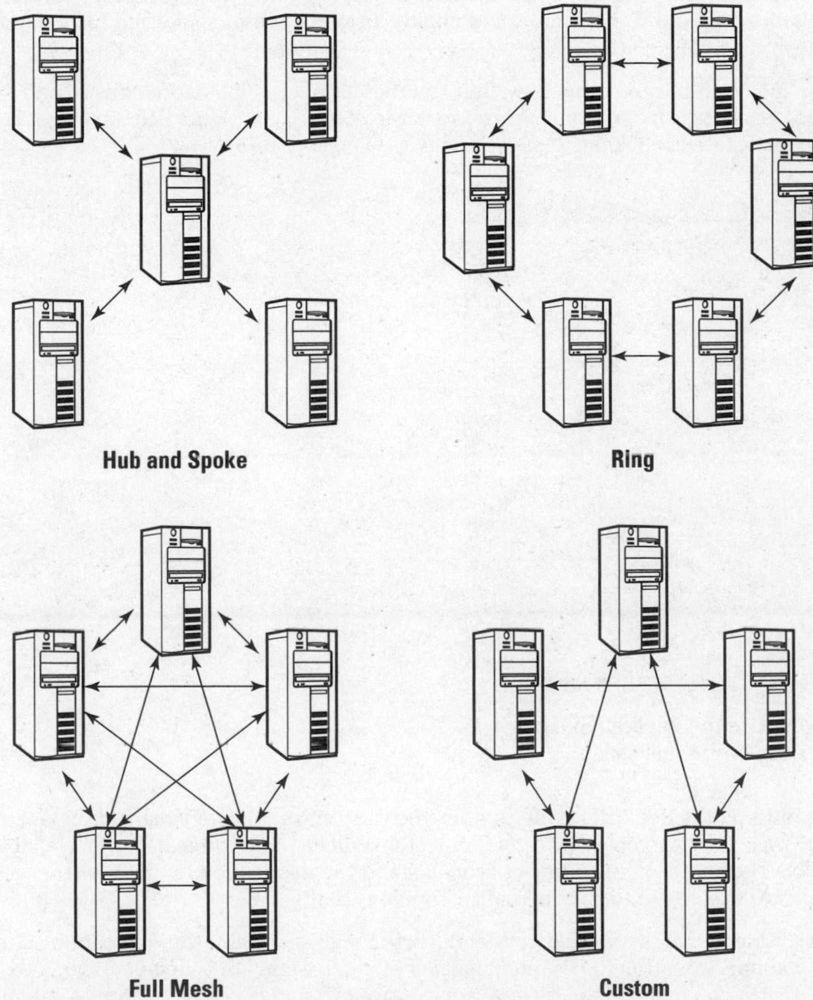

Figure 26-15: You can choose one of four replication topologies.

If you choose the hub and spoke topology, you must also select the computer that will serve as the hub. The wizard provides a drop-down list containing the FQDNs of all participating computers. Select the hub computer and click Finish. If you choose a different topology, you only need to click Finish — there are no other options to choose.

See Chapters 10 and 12 for more information on FRS and replication within domains.

Creating a Custom Replication Topology

If the default ring, hub and spoke, or full mesh topologies don't suit your needs, you can create a custom topology. For example, you might use a mix of hub/spoke and full mesh to achieve the results you need.

To create a custom replication topology, first run the Configure Replication Wizard and choose Custom as the topology type. After the wizard completes, right-click the target and choose Properties, then click the Replication tab (see Figure 26-16).

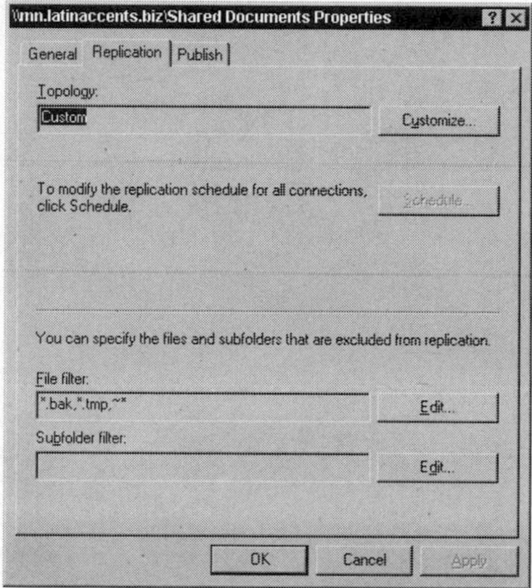

Figure 26-16: Use the Replication tab to fine-tune or customize replication.

Click Customize on the Replication tab to open the Customize Topology dialog box (see Figure 26-17). Click New to open the New Connections dialog box, which lists the available targets. Select the source in the Connect From list and the destination in the Connect To list, and then click OK to return to the Customize Topology dialog box.

After you've added all of the desired connections, you can customize the replication schedule. Select a connection from the list and click Schedule to open the Schedule dialog box (see Figure 26-18). Select a range of times (or a single time slot) and click Replication Not Available to prevent replication from occurring at the selected time. Click OK after you configure all the necessary "unavailable" time slots. Repeat the process for the other connections and click OK to close the Customize Topology dialog box, then OK again to close the properties for the target.

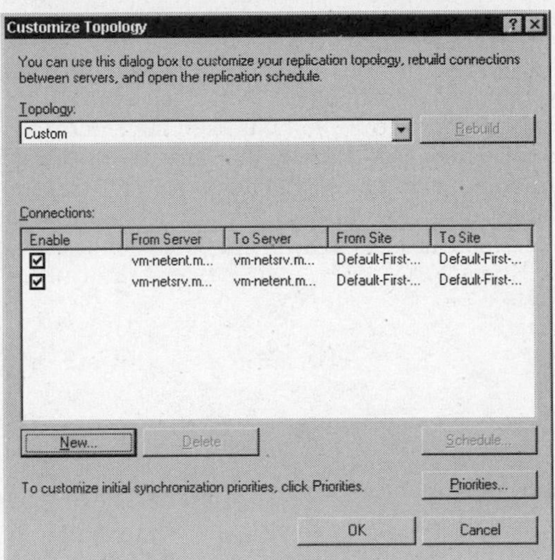

Figure 26-17: Create connections with the Customize Topology dialog box.

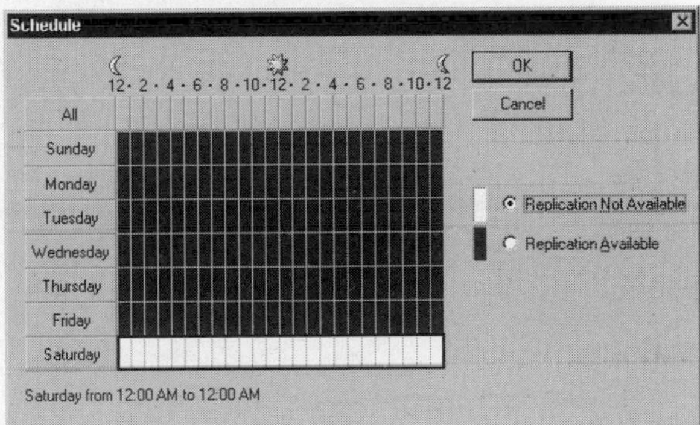

Figure 26-18: Set replication schedule through the Schedule dialog box.

Excluding Files and Folders from Replication

One additional step you'll probably want to take when configuring replication is to exclude certain folders and file types from replication. For example, if temporary files are created by applications in the target folders, you will probably want to exclude those files from replication. They're going to be deleted anyway, so why take up bandwidth replicating them?

To exclude files or folders, right-click a target and choose Properties, then click the Replication tab. Two controls on the Replication tab — File Filter and Subfolder Filter — enable you to specify a set of files or folders, respectively, that Windows Server 2003 will ignore during replication. Click Edit beside the appropriate list to open a dialog box you can use to add or remove items from the list.

Working with Mounted Volumes

The previous section discussed the Distributed File System (Dfs), which enables you to create a file system namespace using shares from multiple computers in the enterprise. Windows Server 2003 includes a feature called *mounted volumes* that does for the local file system what Dfs does for the enterprise. Mounted volumes, which rely on NTFS' reparse points, provide a means for you to mount local volumes under NTFS folders on the local computer. This enables you to create a homogenous file system from multiple volumes so that, for example, volumes D:, E:, and F: can all show up as folders under volume C:. Figure 26-19 illustrates how mounted volumes work.

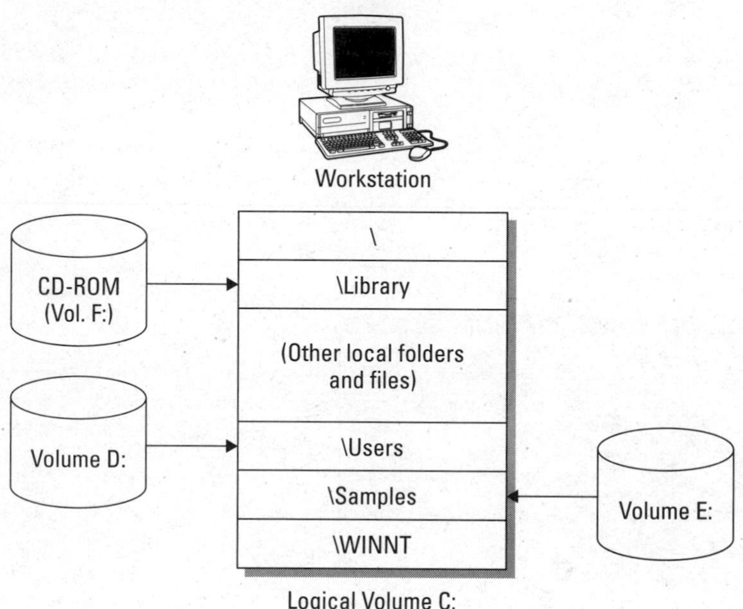

Figure 26-19: Mounted volumes let you create a homogenous file system namespace from multiple local volumes.

The primary benefit to mounted volumes is that they enable you to create a single file system namespace on the local computer that integrates multiple physical or logical volumes. This simplifies the user's view of disk resources and offers the following key advantages:

✦ **Selectively apply disk quotas:** As discussed in a previous section, you can apply quotas to a mounted volume to effectively apply quotas to a single folder within the logical namespace. This capability enables you to apply different quotas to different folders within a single logical volume. For example, you might apply different quotas to `C:\Users\Documents` and `C:\Users\Programs` to grant users different quota levels within each folder. (This example assumes that two different local volumes are mounted, one under each folder.) Because quotas apply to an entire physical volume, the only way to achieve different quota values is to mount separate physical volumes with different quota values to each folder.

- **Increase apparent volume size without hardware changes:** You'll probably find that in many situations, user storage-space requirements will surpass physical storage capacity over time, even when you apply quotas. Mounted volumes enable you to accommodate increasing storage requirements without replacing existing hardware. Instead, you add additional storage space locally and mount the new space to the existing volume. With servers that support the hot-swapping of drives and the ability to add new drives without taking down the system, the volume capacity increase can be accomplished without taking down the host server or affecting the services it provides.
- **Create a homogenous file system namespace from disparate volumes:** One of the chief benefits of mounted volumes is the ability they give you to create a single, homogenous file system namespace from various physical volumes.
- **Overcome the 26-letter drive ID limitation:** Mounted volumes do not require a drive ID, which overcomes the 26-volume limitation imposed by using letters for drive IDs. Rather than map local volumes to individual drive IDs, you can simply mount each one under its own NTFS folder on a host volume.

Although using a mounted volume can give you much the same effect as extending a volume, mounted volumes offer the advantages of selective quotas and can be used on basic disks. Extending a volume is supported only on dynamic disks.

Mounting a Volume

You use the Disk Management MMC console to mount volumes to NTFS folders. You can only mount a volume to an empty, local NTFS folder. The volume being mounted must also be local. To create a mounted volume, open the Computer Management MMC console and open the Disk Management node. Right-click the volume you want to mount and choose Change Drive Letter and Path from the context menu. Click Add to display the Add New Drive Letter or Path dialog box, as shown in Figure 26-20. Specify the path to the local NTFS folder in which you want to mount the volume and click OK.

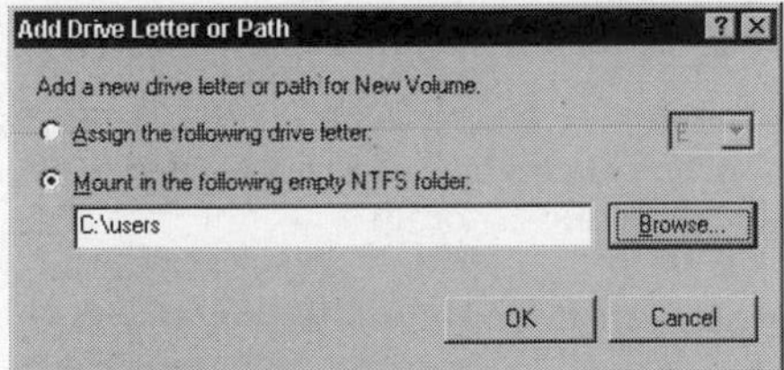

Figure 26-20: Specify the local NTFS folder to which you want to mount the volume.

The way a mounted volume appears in Explorer depends on the volume type. Hard disk volumes appear as drive icons instead of folder icons. CD-ROM volumes appear with a CD icon.

You can browse only when creating a mounted volume on the local computer. You must specify the path in the text box if using Disk Management to manage a remote computer.

Unmounting a Volume

Unmounting a volume is equally easy. Open the Disk Management node, right-click the volume you want to unmount, and choose Change Drive Letter and Path. Select the path you want to remove and click Remove. Click Yes to verify the operation or No to cancel it.

Hierarchical Storage Management

Windows Server 2003's version of Hierarchical Storage Management (HSM) is a service named Remote Storage or Remote Storage Services (RSS). If the term is new to you, it means this: HSM is a service that *relocates* data that is *idle* or inactive to a *cheaper* storage location in order to keep *valuable hard disk space* from getting full.

Notice the italics in the preceding definition of HSM. First, the idea of relocation is important. The data is not backed up, nor is HSM a substitute for the disaster recovery procedures discussed in Chapter 21, even though the data is stored on tape. Candidate data is migrated to a storage medium that should always be available to a user, so if the house burns down, the HSM data is lost.

To further qualify the relocation of data, if the user requires access to the data, the data should be made available as if it were in online files, requiring no extra step to access it. The only difference the user might notice is the lag time between the application issuing a file manipulation command (such as Open, Copy, or Delete or execution) to the file system and the recalling of the file from remote storage.

Second, HSM is applied to files that are idle or stale (excluding system files or similarly flagged files). In other words, idle files become candidates for relocation when they have not been accessed for a predetermined period of time. The terms *data* and *file* are often used interchangeably with respect to HSM. In reality, the contents of the file, the data, are what are relocated. The file remains behind, like an empty envelope, which acts as a marker.

Third, *cheaper* is a key term in defining HSM, because the storage medium chosen as the target location should be cheaper than your average hard disk drive. The concept is worthwhile: Why store unused files on expensive hard disks? The problem with this tenet, however, is that hard disks are getting cheaper all the time, and their capacity is almost doubling every few months. They may soon become cheaper than so-called cheaper storage media, such as tapes. We will return to cost after a full discussion of Remote Storage.

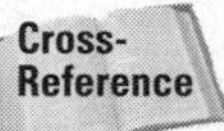

Disk Management and Removable Storage services are discussed in Chapters 19 and 20.

Finally, the most important component in the definition of HSM is *valuable hard disk space.* Without the component that frees up hard disk space, HSM would be, in many respects, worthless. As with disk quotas (see Chapter 19), HSM can be used to effectively maintain and manage hard disks and prevent them from exceeding certain usage levels. This service applies to the need to make hard disk resources available to users for online storage, as well as the maintenance of applications.

To understand the service and its benefits, let's look at an example. Take a busy newsroom at the local newspaper publisher, which represents an extreme case of file turnover. A group of reporters and editors generates a lot of files every day. Stories are written, then edited, and then imported into layout and production systems before being sent to the printers.

Most of the files will be used and then abandoned on the same day they are created; many of them will be accessed over a course of several days, perhaps to earmark the stories for weekend editions or to refer to for follow-up reports and articles. About 80 percent of the files will become idle after the first day following their creation; by the third day after the files are created, about 95 percent of them will be idle; and by the following week, almost all the files created will be idle. Does it then make sense to keep them lying around taking up hard disk space?

Using Remote Storage, you can configure the file system to relocate the files to removable storage. If a file needs to be accessed, it can be recalled from the library at any time. By the time the files are relocated, they will not be needed as urgently as they were on the day they were created, so the few seconds it takes to retrieve a file's data is not a critical factor. The Remote Storage thus makes for a very effective electronic newspaper morgue.

How HSM Works

HSM is made possible by *reparse points* and other components in the Windows Server 2003 NTFS file system, discussed earlier in this chapter. It is provided by a combination of services derived from the file system, fixed storage, and the removable storage technology owned by Veritas Software Corporation. HSM is managed by the MMC snap-in called Remote Storage.

HSM is split between two tiers of storage. The first tier comprises local storage, the volumes supported on the local machine under the control of the local operating system. *Local* is the key term here because, currently, Windows Server 2003's HSM does not extend to storage area network (SAN) volumes, paths to remote volumes, or storage anywhere other than in the local machine. And there is currently nothing "remote" about the service.

The second tier comprises removable storage. Removable storage can consist of any local removable media technology, such as a tape drive library. (The Removable Storage service, which configures removable storage hardware and creates and manages media pools, is discussed in Chapters 19 and 20.) The idle data is transferred to and from the aforementioned tiers.

You configure the Remote Storage service to maintain your hard disk at a certain level of "free space." You also need to identify for how long files should be idle and how often and when relocation should occur. The Remote Storage service handles everything automatically.

Installing and Configuring Remote Storage

As mentioned earlier, HSM is installed and managed on the local machine by way of the Remote Storage snap-in. The service is not installed on your server by default. To install the service and MMC snap-in, open the Control Panel and double-click the Add or Remove Programs icon. Click the Add/Remove Windows Components option in the dialog box that loads. This loads the Windows Components Wizard. Select (check) Remote Storage from the list and then click Next. Then proceed to install the service. Restart the server if prompted.

As soon as Remote Storage is installed, you can run it from the Administrative Tools menu by choosing Start ➪ Administrative Tools ➪ Remote Storage, or by running `RSADMIN.MSC` from the command line or the Run menu. (If you are viewing the classic Start button then you may need to select All Programs first.)

Unless you have the supported removable storage media already configured (see Chapters 19 and 20), you should not run Remote Storage. As soon as the snap-in runs, Remote Storage starts to check supported removable media is available. If you do not have supported media and hardware installed, Remote Storage will report an error. The snap-in will still open, but the Remote Storage options will be disabled.

Managed Volumes

Configuring a volume for HSM using Remote Storage puts it under Managed Volume status. To manage a volume, you need to open the Remote Storage snap-in and perform the following steps:

1. Add a Managed Volume and configure it for Remote Storage.
2. Configure the Managed Volume properties.
3. Configure the Remote Storage service.

Add a Managed Volume and configure it for Remote Storage

Select the Managed Volumes folder in the Remote Storage tree. Right-click it and then select New ⇨ Managed Volume(s). This action launches the Add Volume Management Wizard. Click Next to proceed with the wizard. If the wizard finds volumes that can be managed, it will list them in the next page of the wizard. If no volumes are found, the wizard will not proceed further.

There could be a number or reasons why the wizard would fail to detect a volume suitable for management. First, the volumes may not be formatted with the NTFS file system. Second, the underlying hardware supporting the hard disks might not be compatible with Windows Server 2003. Third, all volumes in the system may already be under Remote Storage management.

We found that a simple volume in a Compaq hard disk array (excluded from any RAID level) had to be reformatted twice before Remote Storage noticed it. This points to a likely hardware compatibility problem.

If one or more volumes are listed, select the volume to manage and click Next. The Volume Settings dialog box, illustrated in Figure 26-21, enables you to set the desired amount of free space and the file relocation parameters according to your application, circumstances, or needs. Make the changes or leave the defaults intact, and click Next. You will be asked to confirm the configuration before committing the changes. Click Finish to commit the configuration.

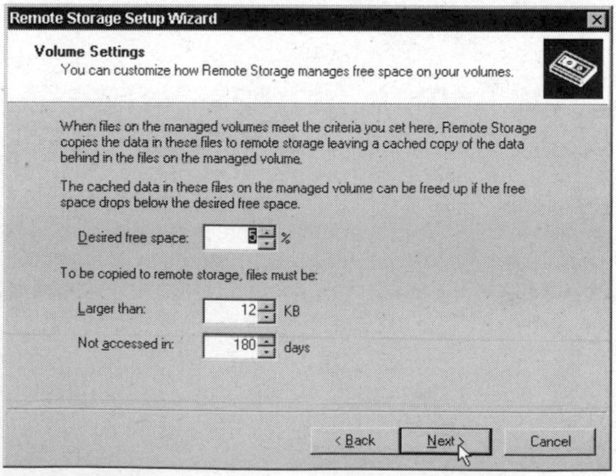

Figure 26-21: The Volume Settings dialog box.

Configure the Managed Volume properties

After you have added the volume, you will notice the managed volume listed in the Remote Storage snap-in, as illustrated in Figure 26-22. You can change the configuration of the volume at any time. Double-click the volume in the list, and the volume's property pages will appear.

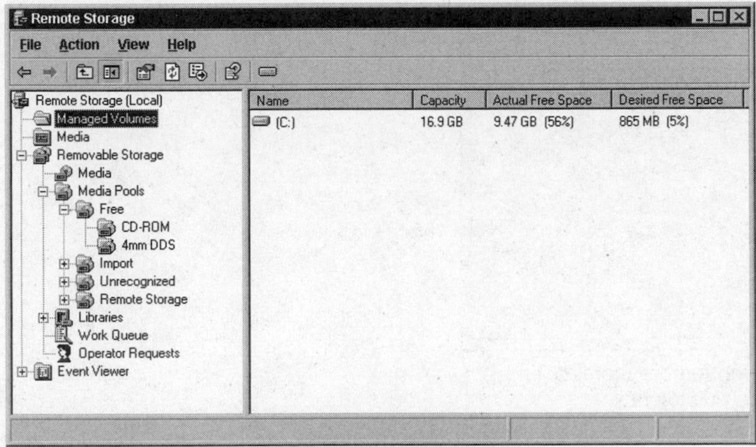

Figure 26-22: The Remote Storage snap-in.

In addition to the remote storage options, a third tab on the property page enables you to exclude or include files in the relocation process. You will notice that all system files are automatically excluded from relocation.

Configure the Remote Storage service

Your final step in configuring HSM is to configure the Remote Storage service. Select Remote Storage at the top of the tree and right-click it. Select Properties from the pop-up menu. The Remote Storage (Local) Properties dialog box appears. This collection of property pages, illustrated in Figure 26-23, lets you configure a schedule for the relocation of data, set a recall limit, and gives you the ability to make copies of the removable media holding the relocated data.

The recall limit, which is set to 60 recalls by default, lets you specify how many times a file can be recalled from storage within a certain Registry defined time frame. When the limit is reached, all additional recall attempts are refused. In other words, the request is not passed to the Remote Storage service. There is a good reason for this property, and we will discuss it shortly.

You can also configure Remote Storage to make duplicate copies of the removable media on which relocated media is stored. To use the copy service, you need two tape drives supporting identical media. The copy service is disabled if a second drive is unavailable.

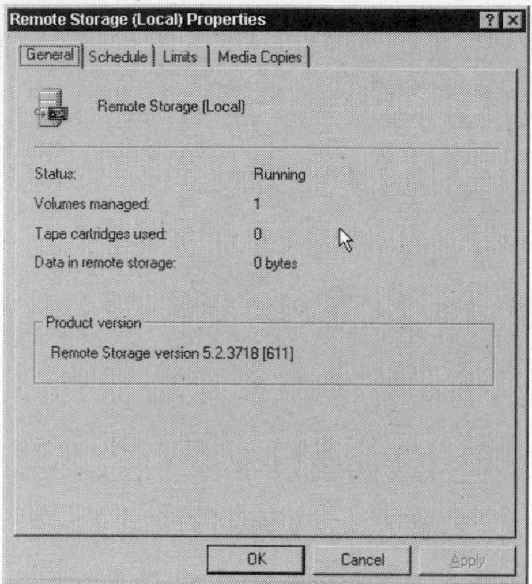

Figure 26-23: The Remote Storage (Local) Properties Settings dialog box.

Limitations of Remote Storage

HSM is not a new concept; it has been available on legacy systems for many years. The ideal server-based HSM system should conform to several wishes before it can be classified as a true HSM system, the dream of every network administrator. The most important of these wishes, according to our vision of the ideal HSM system, are as follows:

- ✦ The HSM system must be a network service, able to coexist with any distributed file system.
- ✦ The HSM system must support a recall override or recall prevention option.
- ✦ The HSM system must coexist with standard backup and restore procedures and technology.
- ✦ The HSM system must support all forms of removable or remote media, on any server on the network (running on Windows 2000 or .NET, of course).

The HSM system made possible by the Remote Storage service has several limitations. First, the Remote Storage service is currently available only to the server on which it is installed. This means that you have to install the service and compliant hardware on every server you wish to place under HSM or Managed Volume status. This is clearly a lot more expensive than disk quota management.

Many companies spend a lot of money investing in a good tape library system for the benefit of all servers. To replicate the investment on each server on which you need HSM would wipe out the cost benefit; sticking in new hard disks would be cheaper. A good tape system starts at about $4,000 and runs to more than $20,000 for a good DLT or DAT library system (see Chapter 20 for details on DLT and DAT systems). However, you can pick up a single 70GB hard disk for under $500. Double this for the media duplication feature discussed earlier. Incidentally, the cheaper tape backup hardware discussed in Chapter 20, like QIC, is not supported by Remote Storage.

Second, the current version of Remote Storage does not support the ability to override recalls. This means that all software that attempts to read a file will inadvertently recall it from the library or tape drive system, unless the software has been built with Remote Storage support (such as the Backup utility that ships with Windows Server 2003).

Granted, software will have to become Remote Storage aware, but this will be a problem for many applications, such as third-party backup software, antivirus software, indexing software, document management systems, and so on. It will take a while before all software is endowed with the ability to work on managed volumes, but it would be nice to set times or other parameters that would cause the recall not to fire. As mentioned earlier, the recall limit is a step in this direction, but it would have been better to program the service to recognize who is reading a file marker before recalling the file. The operating system knows which service or user account is accessing a file.

HSM might save you time and money managing a hard disk, but you could lose that benefit with the added diligence required in the backing up and restoring of data. Once the data has been relocated, Remote Storage leaves a file marker or placeholder on the media. (The marker is represented by the same icon owned by the file, but superimposed with a small clock.) So, what does your backup program back up . . . a placeholder, a token of what was once valuable data? And what do you restore in the event of a hard disk crash . . . the version in the backup or the version on the Remote Storage folder?

Also, Remote Storage brings with it the possibility of losing relocated data. Placeholders and caching data can get deleted and corrupted, possibly even becoming the target of e-terror. The media used to store the data is not impervious to damage or loss. The additional brain strain is not what many Windows server administrators would like. The ideal HSM system should be fully integrated with a backup program.

Some third-party HSM products have catered to many of the above limitations, including Veritas, which contributed much of the backup, remote, and removable storage applications in Windows 2000 and Windows Server 2003.

Despite these reservations, we are referring to the first version of what is clearly a valuable addition to the operating system. As the previous example in the newsroom demonstrated, it can be put to good use, and it works very well. If you wish to investigate the Remote Storage Service further, go to Microsoft's Web site and search there using the keyword RSS.

File Services for Macintosh

File Services for Macintosh is an optional service in Windows Server 2003 that makes it possible for Macintosh users to access folders and files stored on a Windows Server 2003. The Macintosh clients have full read/write capabilities (subject to permissions, of course) in the shared volume. Other clients that have access to the share — such as Windows clients on the network — can read and write to the share, also subject to their permissions. This means that File Services for Macintosh not only lets Macintosh users access folders and files on a Windows Server 2003, but also lets Windows and Macintosh users share files.

File Services for Macintosh (FSM) supports both TCP/IP and AppleTalk networks, but AppleTalk must naturally be installed on the Windows Server to support AppleTalk clients. The client must be running AppleShare client version 3.7 or later. If the client has both TCP/IP and AppleTalk installed, it attempts TCP/IP and failing that, attempts AppleTalk.

Installing FSM on a Windows Server does not automatically give all Macintosh users access to shares on the server. Instead, the administrator must share a volume specifically for Mac access. When you share a folder, you can configure it for Windows clients, Mac clients, or both.

Tip: If Services for NetWare are installed on the server, you can also configure a share for access by NetWare clients.

Windows clients browse to the share and access files in it in the same way they do for other, non-Mac shares. The subfolders and files appear in a hierarchical structure just like any other Windows-hosted folder. Mac users can browse the shares through the Chooser and see the content in a Mac-like folder structure. So, to both types of clients, the share looks and functions like their "native" server shares.

Note: FSM shares can only be hosted on NTFS volumes.

FSM Security

You don't need to manage a separate set of authentication credentials for Mac clients that need to access FSM shares on a Windows Server 2003. FSM uses the native Windows Server 2003 security infrastructure to authenticate clients. This includes user accounts and groups — both local and AD — as well as NTFS access permissions. From an administrative standpoint, Mac users are therefore no different from Windows users in terms of providing access to shared folders. Although you don't need to do so, you can create Mac-specific groups and place all Mac client accounts in those groups to help you keep Mac and Windows clients logically separated.

FSM supports three authentication mechanisms for Mac clients:

- **Guest.** You can configure a share to allow access using the built-in Windows Server 2003 Guest account. Mac clients do not need to provide a password to connect using the Guest account.
- **Cleartext passwords.** Mac clients can provide a local or domain user account and password, and the password is transmitted across the network in cleartext.
- **Encrypted passwords.** FSM supports two authentication methods that support encryption to provide more secure authentication. Apple Standard Encryption supports passwords of up to eight characters. MS-User Authentication Method (UAM) supports passwords up to 14 characters, but requires AppleShare 3.8 or later on the client. If both cleartext and encryption are supported by the server, the Mac client automatically uses encryption.

FSM does not support Kerberos authentication. In addition, for Mac clients to use encrypted authentication, their passwords must be stored using reversible encryption. You can configure this through group policy at the domain level through the policy `\Windows Setting\Security Settings\Account Policies\Password Policy\Store Passwords Using Reversible Encryption`. After the policy takes effect, the users must change their passwords for the new password to be stored using reversible encryption. You can also change the password administratively to make the change take effect.

Mac clients, just like Windows clients, can authenticate using the local domain or a trusted domain. If the user specifies an account in the form *user*, Windows Server 2003 attempts to authenticate the user with a matching local account, if any. It then attempts the server's domain, followed by all trusted domains until it finds a matching account name (which is not necessarily the correct account). The user can also specify the account in the form *domain\user* and Windows Server 2003 authenticates the user using the specified domain.

In all respects except one, Mac client accounts are the same as all other accounts. However, you can specify the primary group for an account through the Member Of tab in the accounts properties. The primary group comes into play when the Mac user creates a folder or file. FSM associates the user's primary group with the newly-created item.

FSM File Permissions

Macintosh permissions apply to a volume or folder, but not to individual files. NTFS permissions, however, can apply to individual files as well as folders and volumes. FSM takes into account the NTFS permissions set at the server and the Mac permissions set by the Mac client on the folder when determining access. If the file permissions are more restricted than the Mac permissions, those file permissions apply.

Mac OS versions prior to 8.5 support the following permissions:

✦ **See Files.** Users can list and read files in the folder.

✦ **See Folders.** Users can see subfolders contained in the folder.

✦ **Make Changes.** Users can create, modify, move, rename, and delete files.

✦ **Cannot Move, Rename, or Delete.** User cannot perform these actions in the folder.

Mac OS versions 8.5 and later support these additional permissions:

✦ **Read-Only.** Users can read but not modify the file.

✦ **Write-Only.** Users can create new files and folders.

✦ **Read and Write.** Users can create, modify, and delete files and folders.

✦ **None.** Users have no access.

FSM translates permissions between Windows and Mac clients. Table 26-6 lists these permissions.

Table 26-6: Services for Macintosh Permission Translation

Windows Server 2003 permissions	*Macintosh permissions*
Read	See Folders, See Files
Write, Delete	Make Changes

In addition to using NTFS and Macintosh permissions to protect folders in an FSM share, you can also apply a volume password. The Mac users must specify this volume password along with their username and password to connect to and use the shared volume. Volume passwords do not apply to Windows clients who access the share. FSM does not assign a volume password when you create the Mac volume, but you can assign it afterwards.

Tip

Volume passwords are case-sensitive.

FSM File Name Considerations

Windows Server 2003, like previous Windows platforms, supports both short and long file names. Short file names are often called 8.3 names because the name is limited to eight characters, with a three-character file extension. Windows Server 2003 is limited to 256 characters for long file names.

Windows imposes some restrictions on file names that the Macintosh operating system does not. The Mac OS supports all Mac characters for file names except a colon, which means it allows characters not allowed by Windows. Services for Macintosh FSM therefore needs to do a little translation of file names to ensure cross-platform functionality. For example, when a Mac client creates a file with a long file name, Windows Server 2003 creates a short 8.3 file name for the file. It also translates extended characters in the file name to equivalent Unicode characters to make them compatible for Windows clients. Likewise, FSM performs the translation for files created by Windows clients, making them compatible for Mac clients.

Installing File Services for Macintosh

Like other optional services, you add File Services for Macintosh with the Add or Remove Programs object in the Control Panel. Click Add/Remove Windows Components, open Other Network File and Print Services, select File Services for Macintosh, and click OK. Then click Next and follow the remaining prompts to install the service.

Adding a Macintosh Volume

In Windows NT, adding and managing Macintosh volumes meant a trip to the venerable File Manager. In Windows Server 2003, however, you use the Computer Management console to manage Macintosh volumes.

To create a Mac volume, open the Computer Management console and open the Shared Folders branch. Right-click the Shares node and choose New Share to start the Share a Folder wizard (see Figure 26-24). Enter the path to the folder in the Folder to Share field or click Browse to browse for the folder (or to create a new folder). Specify in the Share Name field the name by which Windows users will see the shared folder. Add an optional description in the Share Description field, if desired. Select Apple Macintosh to allow Mac clients to see and access the share; then specify the share name for Mac users in the Macintosh Share Name field.

Click Next and set permissions for the share. The wizard provides some predefined sets of permissions, and you can also assign custom permissions.

When you complete the wizard, Windows Server 2003 actually creates two shares, assuming you selected the Microsoft Windows option to share the folder for Windows users. You can use different share names, if desired, for each target client group.

You can set some additional properties for the share. Still in the Shares node of the Shared Folders branch, right-click the Mac share and choose Properties to display the property sheet shown in Figure 26-25. Use the options on the General tab to set the number of allowed concurrent users, assign a volume password (discussed previously), set the volume as read-only, and enable/disable Guest access to the volume. You use the Security tab to set NTFS permissions on the share just as you would for any NTFS folder.

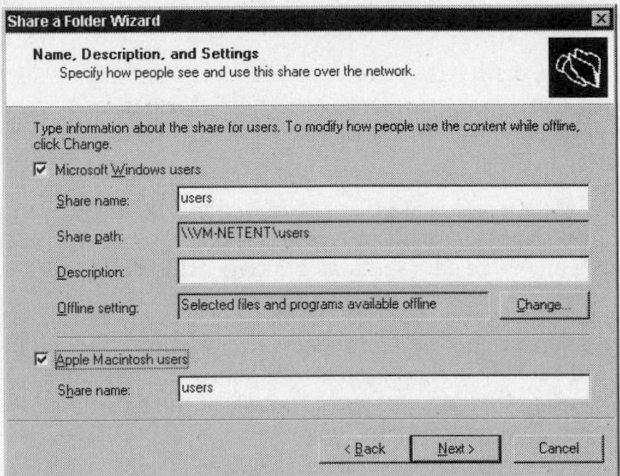

Figure 26-24: Use the Create Shared Folder wizard to set up an FSM volume.

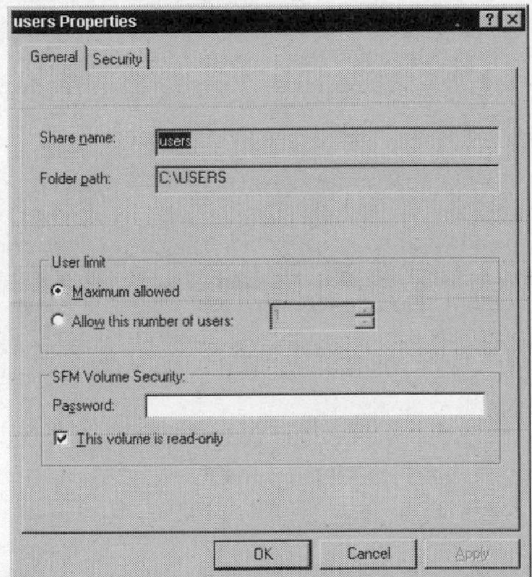

Figure 26-25: Configure volume password and other properties with the General tab of the share's property sheet.

Removing a Macintosh Volume

You can easily remove an FSM volume when your Mac users no longer need access to it. Removing a volume doesn't actually delete the data or folder, but rather removes the share. You can re-establish the share later, if needed. To remove a share, click the Shares node of the Shared Folders branch of the Computer Management console. Right-click the FSM shared volume and click Stop Sharing, then click Yes when prompted to confirm.

Backup and Recovery Considerations

FSM uses NTFS data streams to store file data. Data common to PC and Mac clients is stored in the data fork, and Mac-specific data such as code, font, and other information is stored in the resource fork. Other Mac-specific information is contained in other data streams.

The data fork, where the actual file data is stored, is the only data that PC clients see. The Mac clients, however, use all of the data streams. FSM takes care of handling the streams and giving each client the appropriate data, making it transparent to the user. When you consider backup and recovery, however, these alternate data streams become critically important.

If you back up the Macintosh volumes from your Windows Server 2003, you need to make sure you choose a backup tool that supports backing up these data streams — not all backup solutions support them. The result of backing up and restoring a Mac volume with a backup application that doesn't specifically support FSM volumes is that all of the additional data is lost, potentially rendering the restored data unusable by Mac clients.

Services for Unix

Windows Server 2003, like Windows 2000 Server before it, includes Print Services for Unix, which provides printing integration between Windows and Unix platforms. Windows Server 2003 doesn't provide file services for Unix platforms, but Microsoft offers an add-on product called Services for Unix (SFU) that does provide file and related services for Unix platforms.

SFU includes several components, including:

- **NFS.** SFU includes client, server, and gateway components to support Network File System (NFS) file sharing between Windows and Unix platforms. The Client component enables Windows clients to access files on Unix-based NFS servers. The Server component exports shares hosted on Windows servers as NFS file systems, enabling multi-platform NFS clients to access those files. The Gateway component enables a Windows Server 2003 to act as a gateway for NFS shares on Unix hosts, making the shares appear as if they were shared from the Windows Server, eliminating the need for NFS client software on the client workstations.
- **Server for PCNFS.** This component is provided to support earlier NFS clients that do not support User Name Mapping for obtaining UID and GID information from Unix servers. The NFS Client component in SFU version 2 and later supports User Name Mapping, making Server for PCNFS unnecessary.
- **Server for NIS.** This component enables a Windows Server 2003 domain controller to act as a Network Information Service (NIS) master NIS server for multiple NIS domains. Server for NIS makes it possible to manage Windows and NIS domains from a single administrative point and common set of tools.
- **Password Synchronization.** This component provides password synchronization between Windows and Unix environments. Users or administrators can change their Windows passwords and have their corresponding passwords on all target Unix systems synchronized accordingly. This SFU component can significantly reduce administrative overhead and frustration from users who would otherwise have to juggle multiple accounts and passwords.
- **Telnet Client/Server.** SFU includes a Telnet server for Windows Server 2003, as well as client software. The client supports NTLM authentication, IPv6, and the common features you would expect from a Telnet client. The Server component of SFU enables

Windows Server to function as a Telnet server. The server component is not required for Windows Server 2003 and Windows 2000 Server, which both include a native Telnet server service.

✦ **User Name Mapping.** The User Name Mapping (UNM) service lets you map user and groups between Windows and Unix servers to support NFS, Interix, and Remote Shell Service authentication. UNM supports one-to-one and one-to-many account mapping.

✦ **Cron and Remote Shell Service.** The Cron service enables users to schedule Unix commands, and the Remote Shell Service enables a Windows Server 2003 to accept remote commands, much like the Unix rsh daemon.

✦ **Interix UNIX Environment.** Interix is a multi-user Unix environment that runs under the Windows operating system. By providing a Unix compliant environment, Interix enables you to run Unix commands and applications, port applications between Unix and Windows, and accomplish related tasks.

✦ **ActiveState Perl.** ActiveState ActivePerl is a Windows implementation of the Perl distribution that includes Perl installers, Core Perl, Perl Package Manager, Perl for ISAPI, PerlScript, and PerlEz. ActivePerl enables a Windows Server 2003 to process Perl/CGI scripts.

SFU contains several components and naturally requires some understanding of Unix to implement successfully. Complete coverage of the product would take much more space than we have available, so we'll assume first that you have some Unix background, and second that you're mainly looking for tips on getting the services up and running as quickly as possible. So, think of the following sections as a primer on SFU that will help you put it in place quickly. We'll focus on three main areas: NFS, NIS, and account synchronization/authentication as they relate to file systems and file access/sharing. You can experiment and fine-tune the installation based on your specific needs as you become more familiar with it.

Installing Services for Unix

As mentioned previously, SFU is not included with Windows Server 2003, but rather is available as an add-on produce from Microsoft. If you're not sure yet whether you want to invest in SFU, you can download an evaluation copy from Microsoft's Web site at `www.microsoft.com/windows/sfu/default.asp`.

To install SFU, run Setup from the CD or from the file set extracted from the evaluation download. Installation is much like any other server application and includes a wizard to step you through the process. Setup offers Standard or Custom installation; choose Custom if you want to specify which components are installed, or choose Standard to install all components except the SDKs and related documentation.

SFU must be installed in a folder that does not have spaces in the folder path name. So, choose a folder such as C:\SFU.

You should have no problems with the majority of the Setup wizard. However, you do need to make two decisions during installation that affect security. First, the wizard asks if you want to enable setuid behavior for Interix programs. With setuid enabled, a process that executes a file that has the UID and GID bits set gains the UID and GID of that file. This can pose a security risk because it could allow unauthorized users to execute tasks that should be reserved for administrators. For that reason, Setup does not enable setuid behavior by default. If you know you will have applications that require it, enable the setting. Otherwise, leave it disabled for better security.

The second choice involves case sensitivity. Windows Server 2003 is not case sensitive in terms of file recognition, but it does preserve case for file names. For example, you can create a file named `UPdown.txt` and Windows will maintain the case, but will treat the file the same as `updOWN.txt` for recognition. For example, you couldn't have files with those two names in the same folder.

With case sensitivity enabled for SFU, Server for NFS and the Interix subsystem treat files as case-sensitive. This poses a potential security risk in that a virus or Trojan horse application could be placed in a folder with a valid executable of the same name, but with a different file name case. A user might attempt to execute the valid file but instead, the virus/Trojan horse would execute. If you don't foresee this as being a problem or need case sensitivity recognized, then enable case sensitivity during SFU installation.

Setup also prompts for the User Name Mapping server. You can specify it during installation or leave it blank and add it later through the management console.

Tip SFU needs to be installed on all domain controllers to ensure proper password synchronization.

Configuring User Name Mapping

One of the first tasks you'll need to perform is to configure User Name Mapping, because it is required by services such as Server for NFS. User Name Mapping associates Windows and Unix accounts to support a single client logon.

To configure UNM, start by opening the Services for Unix Administration console and then click the User Name Mapping node in the left pane. The Configuration tab lets you choose between NIS and PCNFS as the type of server that will provide the Unix user and group names. NIS requires no additional server options to define the server. If you choose PCNFS, you must specify the path and file name for the files that contain the password file and group file. These files are copied from the PCNFS server and must reside on the local server.

After you specify the server you need to create user/group maps. You can create simple or advanced maps. Use simple maps when the user or groups names are identical between the Windows and Unix environments, or use advanced maps when the names are not identical or you need to create a one-to-many mapping.

Creating a simple map

In the SFU console, open the User Name Mapping node and click the Maps tab in the right pane. Select the Simple Maps check box, then click Add and in the resulting dialog box (see Figure 26-26), select the Windows domain from the drop-down list. Then, enter the name of the NIS server domain in the NIS Domain Name field, and if the server is located in a different subnet, enter the server name in the NIS Server Name field. Then click OK to create the map.

Tip You can add multiple maps to the list, and SFU processes them in order from top to bottom.

Creating an advanced map

If the account or group names are not identical between Windows and Unix, or you need to create a one-to-many mapping, create an advanced map. In the SFU console, click the Maps tab, and click the Show User Maps link to expand the console (Figure 26-27).

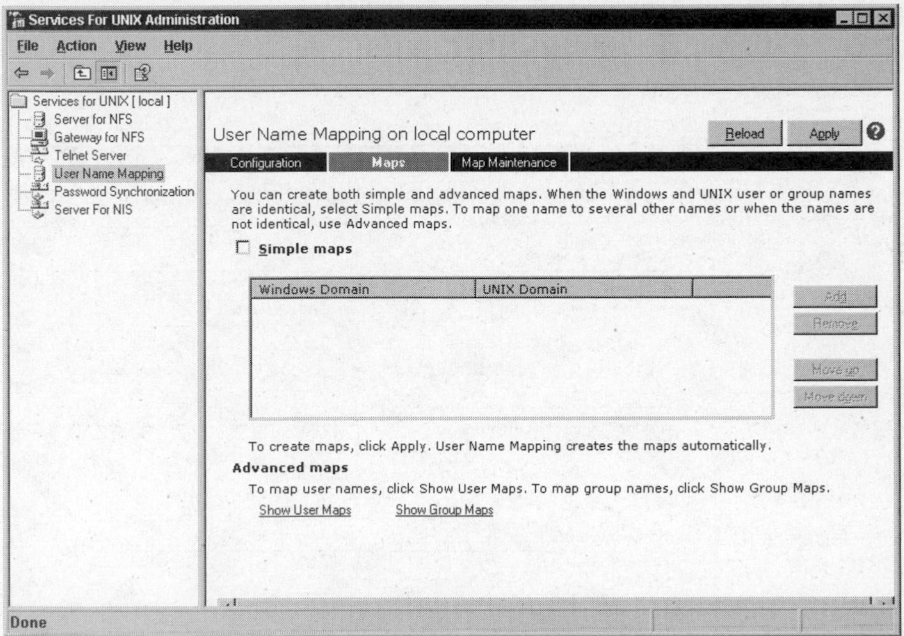

Figure 26-26: Configure simple maps through the SFU console.

Start by listing the Windows domain in which the accounts reside; then click List Windows Users to show the names in the Windows Users list. Click List Unix Users to show the Unix users in the Unix Users list. Now it's a simple matter of selecting a Windows name, a Unix name, and clicking Add to create the map. Repeat the process to create additional one-to-one or one-to-many mappings.

Tip If you map multiple Windows user accounts to a single Unix name, you need to specify one map as the primary. Select the map in the list and click Set Primary.

Mapping groups is essentially identical to mapping accounts/names. Click the Show Group Maps link, then follow the general procedure previously described to create the maps. As with account maps, you need to specify a primary map if you map multiple Windows groups to a single Unix group.

Setting map refresh

The default interval at which User Name Mapping updates the maps is one day. If your accounts, groups, and maps seldom change, you can increase the interval. In a more dynamic environment, you might need to decrease the interval.

To configure the map refresh interval, open the SFU console and open the User Name Mapping node. Click the Configuration tab and set the refresh interval using the options at the bottom of the page. Click Synchronize Now to update the maps immediately.

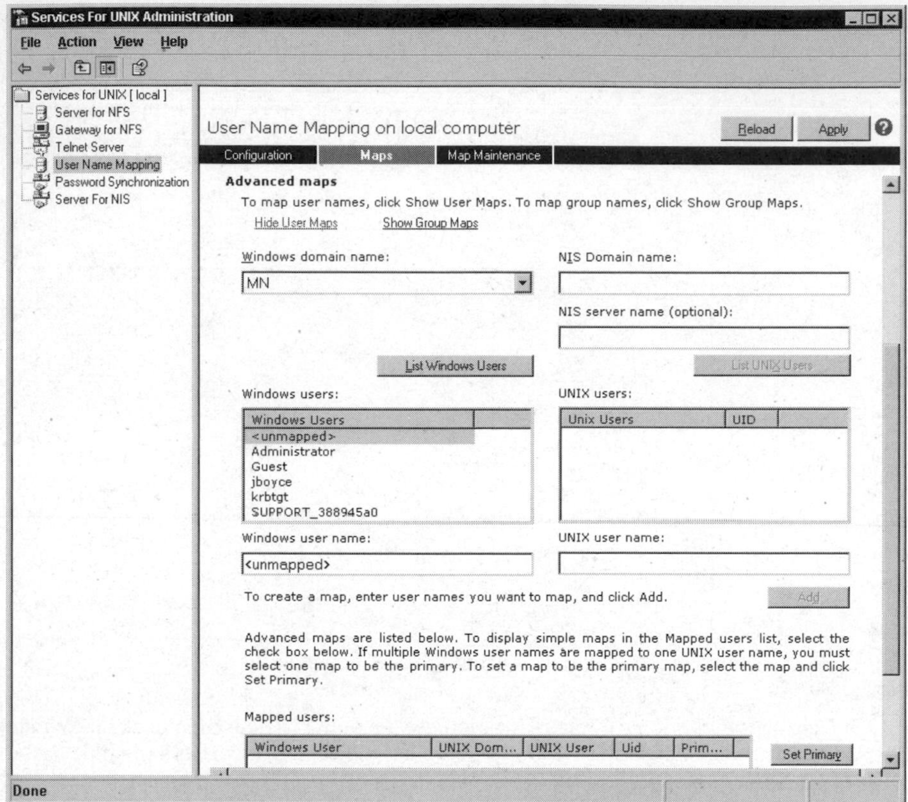

Figure 26-27: Advanced maps allow nonuniform mapping and one-to-many maps.

Backing up and restoring maps

You'll no doubt want to back up your user and group maps, particularly if you spend the time to create several advanced maps. When you back up maps, Server for NFS creates a backup file containing the map data, which you can later use to restore the maps if they are lost.

To backup the maps, open the SFU console and then open the User Name Mapping node. Click Map Maintenance in the right pane, and enter the full path and file name for the backup file in the top text box. Then, click Back Up to create the file. SFU backs up the server type (NIS or PCNFS), domain maps, advanced user and group maps, and password and group files. SFU does not back up the password and group files if you back up a remote server that is configured to use PCNFS source files.

To restore maps, navigate to the User Name Mapping node in the SFU console and click Map Maintenance. Enter the full path and file name of the backup file in the bottom text field, then click Restore. If you restore the maps on a server configured to use PCNFS source files, SFU automatically places the file in the PCNFS folder of the SFU installation and configures the server to use that location.

If you need to restore the maps to a server pool, copy the restored file to the same folder on the other servers in the pool, then configure each of the other servers to use the specified location for the map data. If restoring on a cluster, restore to one server in the cluster, then configure it to use the maps from the specified location. The cluster will automatically replicate the change to other cluster nodes.

Configuring NFS

The Server for NFS component in SFU enables a Windows Server 2003 to function as an NFS server, offering folders and files to NFS clients. This makes it possible for Unix hosts and other platforms running an NFS client to access folders and files on a Windows Server 2003. If you didn't install the Server for NFS component when you installed SFU, you can use the Add or Remove Programs applet in the Control Panel to add it. You also need to add the Server for NFS Authentication component if it isn't installed yet on the server. Adding the Server component automatically adds the Authentication component.

NFS overview

You have two options for authentication with NFS: use Server for NFS Authentication, or allow anonymous access to the shares. Using anonymous access is fine if you have no critical data or have no security concerns in allowing anonymous access to the NFS shares and their contents. However, it's more likely that you will want to control access, so we'll take that approach in this chapter. Authentication is explained in more detail in the next section.

Unix systems have different file name conventions than Windows systems, and because Unix clients will be placing files in the Windows file system, Server for NFS needs some mechanism to remap special characters that are not allowed in the Windows file systems. You accomplish this by creating a character-mapping file that tells Server for NFS how to handle the translation.

You also need to decide how you want Server for NFS to handle case sensitivity. Unix systems are case sensitive, but Windows Server 2003 is case preserving/case insensitive. .NET maintains the case of a file but does not consider case when locating files. In no case can two files with the same name but with different case be stored in the same folder on a Server for NFS share because of the underlying reliance on the Windows Server 2003 file systems.

By default, Server for NFS considers case sensitivity when matching directory and file names, but you can configure Server for NFS to ignore case. We'll cover how to do that shortly.

The type of underlying file system also has some bearing on how Server for NFS handles files. FAT and CDfs don't provide the ability to set individual ACLs, providing very little security. If you share a FAT or CDfs share through Server for NFS, the server returns the owner and group provided during authentication (the requester) as the owner and group for the file or folder in question. Essentially, this translates into, "Everyone owns this file." Clients cannot change ownership of folders or files on FAT and CDfs shares.

The level of access a user has in a FAT or CDfs NFS share depends on the share permissions you apply to the share, just as for Windows clients who access a FAT/CDfs-based share. Users who are granted Read access to the mount point receive read and execute for owner, group, and other (`-r-xr-xr-x`). Users who are granted read/write or root access to the mount point receive read, write, and execute permissions (`-rwxrwxrwx`).

Tip Share a FAT folder or volume as read-only if you want to prevent modifications to the files.

NTFS is a completely different animal in terms of file permissions. NTFS provides extensive access control, and those access permissions need to be mapped to their Unix equivalents. Unix is more restrictive in that it supports only three levels of permissions for owner, group, and other. NTFS allows you to set permissions for individual or groups independent of other permission sets.

The Services for Unix Help documentation includes a more extensive discussion of how Server for NFS translates NTFS permissions to Unix file modes. In a nutshell, understand that SFU translates the NTFS permissions to maintain the level of access defined in NTFS for the Unix clients. You should avoid using `chmod` and similar Unix tools to change permissions on files or folders stored on an NTFS share, because the ACE for Everyone, owner, and primary group will be modified, leading to potentially unforeseen consequences. Instead, use NTFS permissions at the server to change permissions for folders and files when needed.

Configuring authentication

NFS clients can authenticate against domain accounts or accounts on the local Windows Server. If you're going to rely on domain accounts, you must install Server for NFS on each domain controller in the target domain. Server for NFS authenticates through the User Name Mapping server you've specified in SFU's configuration.

See the section titled "Configuring User Name Mapping" earlier in this chapter for a discussion of authentication and account/group mapping.

When an NFS client requests access, Server for NFS accepts the UID and GID from the client and passes them to the UNM server. The UNM server explores its database and returns the account based on the UID and group membership based on the GID. If there is no match, Server for NFS returns an error to the client.

If Server for NFS is configured to allow anonymous access and the client submits an anonymous request, Server for NFS passes the anonymous UID and GID, instead.

Server for NFS passes the account and group information to Server for NFS Authentication, which logs on the user either locally or in the domain, depending on the credentials provided. Server for NFS Authentication responds with the user credentials, which Server for NFS then uses to request file access on the client's behalf. By default, SFU forces re-authentication if the client connection is inactive for ten minutes, but you can disable this behavior or change the interval, if needed, through the SFU console (explained later).

If you have not yet done so, you need to specify the UNM server that SFU will use for authentication. Open the SFU console and click on the Services for Unix branch, then click Settings in the right pane. This page provides only one option — Computer Name — where you specify the name of the UNM server. With that done, configure user and group mappings as described in the previous section.

Configuring logging

Unless you have no security concerns for NFS (unlikely), one of your next steps should be to configure logging for Server for NFS. Enabling and configuring logging provides a trace path for identifying security problems and troubleshooting access problems.

To configure logging, open the SFU console and click the Server for NFS node, then click Logging in the right pane. You can configure NFS to log to the event log, to a text file, or both. If you use a log file — which must be located on the local server — you can set a limit on the file's size.

See section titled "Event Viewer" in Chapter 7 for detailed information on configuring the size of the Windows event logs, as well as the rollover behavior when the log fills up.

After you set the log location, you can choose which events to log. Simply place a check beside the events you want to log.

Configuring file locking

The Locking tab in the Server for NFS page lets you configure file locking for NFS. Server for NFS uses mandatory locks for all file requests, including those that come in through NFS, and Windows Server 2003 enforces those locks. You can configure the period that Server for NFS waits for clients to submit requests to reclaim a lock in the event the connection is disrupted. To do so, open the Server for NFS node of the SFU console, then click the Locking tab. Specify the waiting period in seconds in the field provided. You can also use this tab to view and release existing locks, if needed.

Configuring file name translation

Earlier in this section you read how Server for NFS must translate Unix-allowed file name characters to the Windows file systems. You control how characters are mapped by creating a translation file.

The translation file is a text file with each line in the file specifying a character-to-character mapping in the following form:

0x*nn* 0x*nn* : 0x*nn* 0x*nn* ; [comment]

The column to the left of the colon specifies the Unix character and the column to the right of the colon specifies the character to which it will map on the Windows Server 2003. For example, you might want to change the colon (:) character, which is allowed in Unix file names, to a dash (-) on the Windows Server 2003 because a colon is an invalid file name character under Windows. The following would accomplish the mapping:

0x00 0x3a : 0x00 0x2d ; maps : to -

Everything to the right of the semicolon is treated as a comment and ignored for purposes of mapping the characters.

Setting up the map is a matter of deciding which characters need to be mapped, and to what they will be mapped, then creating an entry in the file for each required translation. Take care not to create multiple mappings for the same client-side character, and don't remap periods, which are required by both Unix and Windows Server 2003.

After you create the translation text file, place it on the server and set permissions on the file or its parent folder to prevent unauthorized changes. Then, open the Server for NFS branch in the SFU console, and click the Server Settings tab in the right pane. The File Name Handling group of controls lets you enable translation and configure the location of the translation file.

To support Unix's convention of treating as hidden files those files whose names begin with a period, enable the option identified for that purpose in the File Name Handling group.

Setting authentication renewal and case sensitivity

The Server Settings tab (see Figure 26-28) also provides controls you can use to control authentication renewal and other behaviors. By default, Server for NFS requires a client to re-authenticate after 10 minutes. You can use the options in the Authentication Options group to change that interval, or if desired, disable authentication renewal. For example, security might not be a major issue for you for the NFS shares, so you could turn off authentication renewal to reduce server overhead and improve client performance.

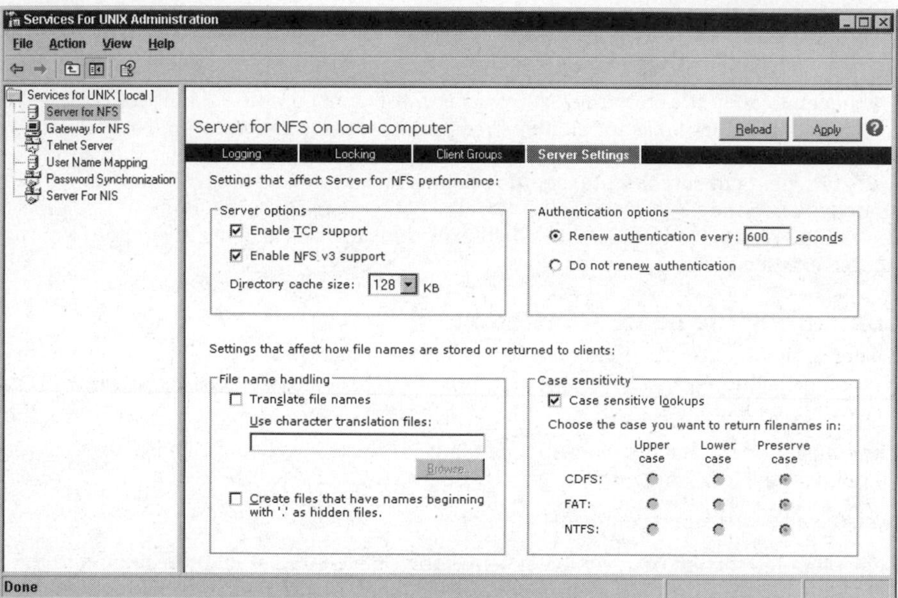

Figure 26-28: Configure authentication renewal and other settings through the Server Settings tab.

While you're working in the Server Settings tab, take a few seconds to configure how Server for NFS handles case sensitivity for each of the three supported file systems: CDfs, NTFS, and FAT. Server for NFS by default preserves case for each of the three file systems, but you can configure it to return file names as either uppercase or lowercase, if desired, rather than preserving the case.

Sharing a folder

After you've configured Server for NFS to behave in the way you need, you're ready to start making folders available through NFS. You configure sharing for NFS in much the same way you configure sharing for Windows. Open in Explorer the parent folder, right-click the folder or volume you want to share, and choose Sharing and Security; then click the NFS Sharing tab (see Figure 26-29), and click the option Share this folder.

As you can for a Windows share, you can set the share name by which NFS will make the resource available. Use the Encoding drop-down list to specify the character encoding type to be used for the folder (the default is ANSI). If you want to allow anonymous access to the resource, select the option Allow anonymous access. You can change the anonymous UID and GID from their defaults of -2, if needed.

Next, you need to configure permissions for the share to define the permissions that NFS clients will have in the share. Click Permissions to open the NFS Share Permissions dialog box (see Figure 26–30). By default, Windows Server 2003 grants all computers read-only access.

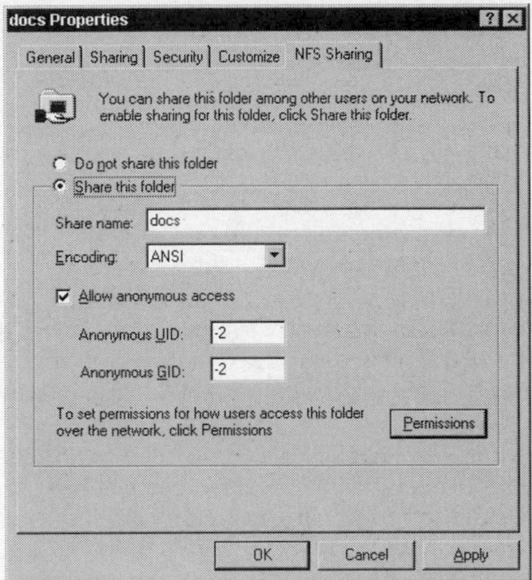

Figure 26-29: Use the NFS Sharing tab to share a folder through NFS.

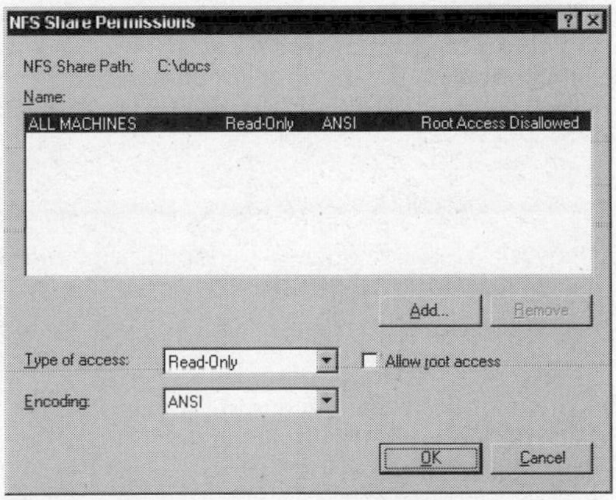

NFS Share Permissions
NFS Share Path: C:\docs
Name:
ALL MACHINES Read-Only ANSI Root Access Disallowed
Add... Remove
Type of access: Read-Only Allow root access
Encoding: ANSI
OK Cancel

Figure 26-30: Configure permissions with the NFS Share Permissions dialog box.

To add a new client or group, click Add to open the Add Clients and Client Groups dialog box. Select and add the name, select the desired access type from the drop-down list, set the encoding type, and if you want to grant root access, select the option Allow root access. Then click OK. You can change these properties from the NFS Share Permissions dialog box, if needed. When you're satisfied with the permission sets, click OK to close the NFS Share Permissions dialog box, then click OK to close the properties for the folder or volume.

Setting Up an NFS Gateway Server

Server for NFS enables Unix and other NFS clients to access files shared on a Windows Server 2003 computer. To provide bi-directional NFS support between your clients, you also need to install and use Gateway for NFS, which is also included with SFU. Gateway for NFS enables Windows clients to access NFS shares on remote NFS servers as if those shares were located on the Windows Server 2003. The Windows Server handles the necessary translation and authentication, and to the client, the folders and files appear as if they were local to the Windows Server. The clients need no NFS client software to access shares.

Windows clients can optionally run Client for NFS to access NFS shares directly, rather than using Gateway for NFS as the bridge to the NFS servers. A direct connection provides better performance, so clients that use NFS shares frequently should run Client for NFS, instead.

Gateway for NFS does not install by default when you install SFU, so you need to add it through the Add or Remove Programs applet in the Control Panel. However, Gateway for NFS and Client for NFS cannot be installed on the same computer. If you already have the client installed, remove it and install the gateway. Installing the gateway requires a server restart.

Configuring Gateway for NFS

There isn't much to configuring Gateway for NFS. After you configure the UNM server that SFU will use for authentication (explained earlier in this chapter), you only need to configure the default permissions that Gateway for NFS will use when creating new files on remote NFS shares. To do so, open the SFU console and click the Gateway for NFS node. In the right pane, use the File Access control group on the File Permissions tab to specify the default permissions for user, group, and others.

Creating a new NFS LAN

After you install Gateway for NFS and then browse the Entire Network object in My Network Places, you'll find a new icon named NFS Network. This icon opens a folder showing the NFS LANs available on your network, making it easy for you to browse for NFS resources. By default, Gateway for NFS adds a LAN configuration to show all of the NFS servers in the network segment in which the Gateway for NFS server resides. You can create additional LANs as needed.

To create a LAN, open My Network Places, open Entire Network, and right-click NFS Network. Click Add/Remove NFS LANs to open the Add/Remove NFS LANs dialog box. Click Add LAN to open the Add Broadcast LAN dialog box (see Figure 26-31).

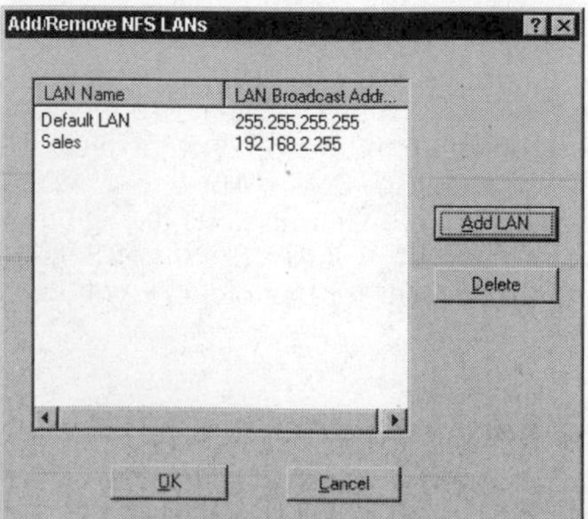

Figure 26-31: Add NFS LANs to the NFS Network folder to simplify browsing for NFS servers.

In the Name field, enter a descriptive name for the NFS LAN. Then, enter the IP address of any host in the LAN. Enter the subnet mask in the Subnet Mask field and press Tab. You'll find that Gateway for NFS automatically creates Broadcast Address for LAN setting based on your entries. Then click OK. Repeat the process to add other LANs as needed.

When you open the NFS Network folder, Windows Server 2003 shows an icon for each of the defined LANs, but it also shows an icon named Favorite LAN. You can manually add hosts to the Favorite LAN folder to quickly access NFS servers. Right-click the Favorite LAN icon and click Add/Remove Hosts. In the resulting Favorite LAN dialog box, click Add Host. Enter the host name and address and click OK.

Next, you need to configure individual shares. Open the Gateway for NFS Configuration tool from the Windows Services for Unix menu in the Start menu, which opens the Gateway for NFS Shares dialog box (see Figure 26-32).

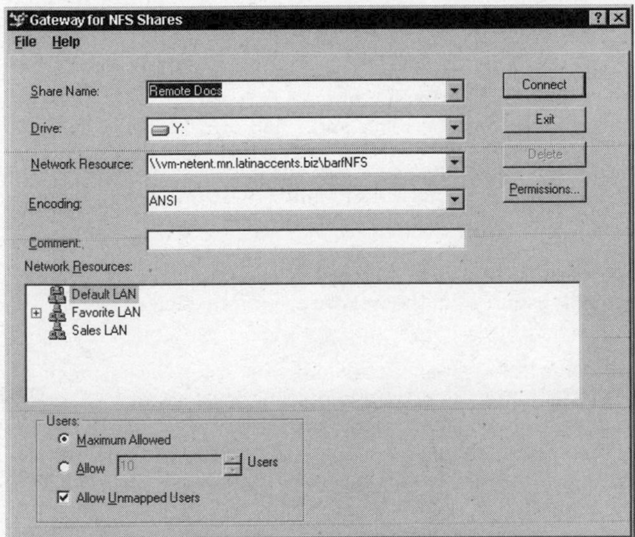

Figure 26-32: Use the Gateway for NFS Shares dialog box to map local drive letters on the server to remove NFS shares.

In the Share Name field, specify the name by which you want clients to access the share. Then select a local drive letter from the Drive drop-down list to associate with the share. Select the encoding type and add an optional comment. In the Users group, specify the maximum number of concurrent client connections to the remote share. Select the option Allow Unmapped Users if you want to allow users with no name mapping to have access to the share. Click Permissions to fine-tune permissions for the share, and then click Connect. Repeat the process to create other shares, then click Exit.

Note If you enable unmapped users, those users receive the permissions of an anonymous Unix user on the remote host.

Integrating NFS Shares in Dfs

Earlier in this chapter we explained how you can use the Distributed File System (Dfs) to create a homogenous file system space from disparate systems. You can integrate NFS shares in the Dfs structure with relative ease. The key is that you must install the Client for NFS on the server(s) where the Dfs root is hosted. After you map to the remote NFS share you can create a link to it in Dfs.

See the section titled "Managing the Distributed File System" earlier in this chapter for a detailed explanation of how to create and manage Dfs roots and links.

NetWare Integration

Windows Server 2003 continues to provide integration with the Novell NetWare network operating system. While Microsoft has practically leapfrogged Novell as the network operation system vendor of choice, there are still so many NetWare networks in place today that even the future Windows Server 2006 and possibly even Windows Server 2010 will still be integrating with this king of the command line from the 1980s and 1990s era.

Why integrate with NetWare? This is a good question that has only two possible answers. The first answer is that you have a large NetWare network in place that you are not about to just switch off, and that you need to keep around for awhile to support critical legacy applications and even huge user universes. But you desire to bring Windows Server 2003 into the picture for some of the fancy stuff it is capable of doing. Such a scenario requires you to integrate the two network operating systems if resources in the NetWare world needed to be accessed by Windows Server and vice versa.

The second reason is that you have a NetWare network and your company has decided to migrate to Windows Server 2003 with the aim of quietly putting the NetWare network to sleep. This also requires integration because you cannot simply close down your NetWare shop, pack up your files and folders, and carry them across the street to the Window's world. No matter whether you are leaving NetWare or just flirting with Windows Server 2003, integrating the two operating systems is required.

One of the most common reasons for integration is to move NetWare file services to Windows Server 2003 or Windows 2000. The following list provides examples of NetWare services and the Windows 2000 or Windows Server 2003 services you would be looking to migrate to:

✦ **File services.** You cannot easily move NetWare data to a Windows Server 2003 file server primarily because you lose all security coverage over your data when you break a file server off from the NetWare bindery or NetWare Directory Services (NDS); thus integration allows you to move your data between the two systems over a period of time, allowing you to move your files from one security boundary to another.

✦ **Print services.** Retaining NetWare print services lets Windows clients print to NetWare print queues before Windows Server 2003 printer services are in place or before applications and users have access to Windows Server 2003 print queues. Strange as it may seem, legacy applications have hard-coded paths to both printers and file shares on a NetWare network.

✦ **ZENWorks.** If you still have clients using the ZENWorks application launcher, you'll need to keep NetWare and NDS around until alternatives, such as using Group Policy to deploy applications or Systems Management Server, can be put in place.

- **Migrating from GroupWise.** Many companies are moving to Microsoft Exchange 2000 Server and the only way to migrate e-mail is through the integration of the two e-mail systems. Of course, you may be going from Exchange to GroupWise; you would still need to integrate the two systems despite the Novell advert that says you simply switch Exchange. This is required before any GroupWise mailbox can be converted to Exchange.

Migrating from GroupWise to Exchange is one of the most complex operations requiring NetWare and Windows Server 2003 integration and several layers besides file system integration. You cannot easily move mailbox data between the two e-mail systems. Converting a mailbox can sometimes takes hours and a lot of processing power. A large network of 1,000 users typically takes from a month to two months to migrate. This means that while you are migrating 10 to 20 users a month to Exchange, the new Outlook users still need a way to communicate with the co-workers stranded in GroupWise until the migration team can get around to them. So complex is the integration and coexistence of GroupWise/Exchange and NetWare/Windows that a complex migration effort can take up to a year to complete.

While this chapter is primarily about file systems, GroupWise-Exchange integration and coexistence requirements are the same.

Migration/Integration Tools

The tools Microsoft has provided for integration with NetWare are so slick that they annoy a lot of NetWare engineers as you will see. The tools include the following:

- **IPX/SPX Protocol.** This protocol, deftly named NWLink, supports the IPX/SPX protocol for talking to NetWare. While later versions of NetWare, such as NetWare 5.0, support TCP/IP, the older versions of NetWare operate on the IPX/SPX stack and thus require that your Windows Server 2003 install the NWLink services.

- **Client Services for NetWare.** This gateway tool allows a Windows Server 2003 to connect to a NetWare server. With it you can access the NetWare files system and printer resources, and integrate Active Directory with NDS for GroupWise/Exchange integration. This gateway also lets you pull the Novell NetWare client from your workstations because they use the gateway as a proxy into the NetWare world.

- **File and Print Services for NetWare.** This tool is referred to by the acronym FPNW and is one of several tools that ships on the CD called Windows Services for NetWare. This tool still does not come free with Windows Server 2003. Yes, you have to buy it from Microsoft and we are not sure why. Perhaps it has something to do with not wanting the ability of a Windows server operating system to spoof a NetWare server to come built into the operating system. (The Services for NetWare CD also includes Directory Synchronization Services and Directory Services Migration tools for moving users, security settings and files from NDS, or a bindery-based NetWare network, discussed in Chapters 12 and 27, respectively.)

Getting Ready to Integrate

Before any level of integration can be achieved, whether for moving data from GroupWise to Exchange or from a NetWare file server to a Windows Server 2003 file server, the first item on the list of things to do is to add the necessary protocol support.

You're likely to have IP in place already, so go directly to adding the IPX/SPX support as demonstrated in Chapter 15. Most NetWare networks, including intraNetWare, will likely be running IPX/SPX as well so consider it as highly likely you will need to add IPX/SPX and the NWLink service.

Client services for NetWare

The most important step in providing integration is to add the gateway services. The gateway is exactly that, a gateway between the NetWare world and the Windows world. In Windows NT, Microsoft called it Gateway Services for Netware (GSNW). Then in Windows 2000, it called in Gateway (and Client) Services for Netware, not being able to make up its mind before the product shipped in December 1999. Now in Windows Server 2003, they have finally settled on Client Service for NetWare (CSNW).

Whatever it is called, it still works the same way it did in the past. The gateway is installed on a Windows Server and using a single user account from Active Directory to access the NDS tree or the bindery, it allows all workstations and servers on the Windows network to access resources on the other side of the gateway where the NetWare network resides.

This service performs a critical and extremely valuable service for Windows clients, one that probably does not sit too well with Novell. You see the gateway accesses NetWare resources as a proxy for Windows clients, and as such you really only need a single NetWare license to let your entire Windows network access a NetWare share.

It is important to note, however, that the gateway is not a long-term solution and is really only suitable for migration and integration. So don't think it solves your steep NetWare licensing needs. First of all, there are limitations with the number and size of the files that the gateway account can access. Second, security over the data on the NetWare file servers is nonexistent. The reason is simple. Your clients are accessing the NetWare files via the proxy services of the gateway account, an account with administrative privileges. This means that all users accessing the file shares through the gateway have access to each others files and data because they are essentially all administrators.

The way to mitigate this is to mount user shares into a standalone Dfs (a domain Dfs will not work) and map your user's drives to their own shares. You can also use the drive mapping command line, `SUBSTR`, to map drives to NetWare files shares through the gateway.

The previous solutions are not long-term features. In addition, the gateway (sorry client) services, which were used by the user account to access the gateway and the resources you use to map to the NetWare file shares are all temporary. They existed long enough for you to move data through the gateway and then close it down when migration has been achieved. Naturally the gateway is not a very reliable or secure service and Microsoft warns you not to prolong its use. This is likely the reason Novell has pretty much ignored the fact that anyone can access its world through a single user gateway account.

To add the gateway, perform the following tasks:

1. Open the Properties tab of your server's local area network interface adapter and click the install button to select a network client service. The dialog box shown in Figure 26-33 loads.

2. Select Client Service for NetWare and click OK. Now if you have integrated with NetWare from Windows NT 4.0 Server or Windows 2000 Server, you'll notice now that the service is no longer called GateWay (and Client) Service for NetWare.

3. Reboot your server and get your NetWare data ready for action. You'll be prompted to connect to the NetWare connection server as soon as the operating system comes back up.

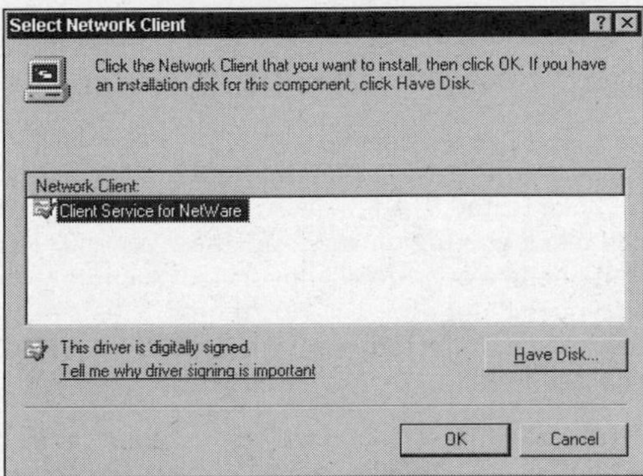

Figure 26-33: Add the NetWare client to the network interface on which the NetWare server resides.

By this time you should know whether you are going to connect to a NetWare bindery, in which case you'll be asked for the name of a preferred server, or you'll have the information you need to connect to a NDS tree. If the latter is the case you'll have the name of a default tree and context ready to go.

When the server reboots before you even get to see the desktop, the dialog box in Figure 26-34 pops up and asks you for the bindery or NDS information. You can also specify a login script to run when the server logs into NetWare.

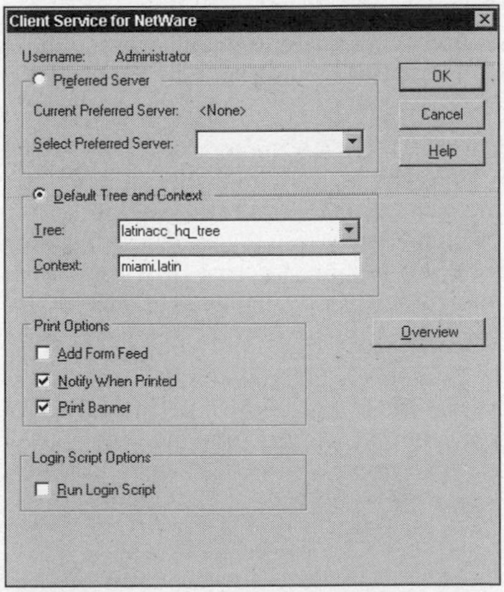

Figure 26-34: Configure NetWare client settings with the Client Service for NetWare dialog box.

Notice from this dialog box the name of the user account the client service is attempting to log on with to the NetWare server. Now, if you've done this before, you know the user account you logged onto the console with is the user account you must create for the gateway to be authenticated to NDS.

Microsoft doesn't tell you this for some reason; and any documentation that suggests otherwise has not actually done integration. We have tested it — for many file server integrations and some very complex GroupWise migrations. If you log onto Windows Server 2003 as Harry and attempt to connect to NetWare account Sheila when the client service prompts you for your NetWare user account and password, you will not connect. No amount of hair pulling and screaming will help you when your user ID gets rejected, even when you know it exists in NDS. Good luck searching for the reason on TechNet.

You will need to create a user account in NDS called Harry and give him administrative privileges in NDS, or log on as Sheila. Only then will you be able to connect. The reason is simple: CSNW, like GSNW before it, connects under the context of the logged on user on the Windows Server 2003 console, because the gateway is not really a service but a background console application running in the context of the logged on user's account.

You will know that you have connected when you can verify client connectivity by browsing to one of the familiar SYS volumes on the NetWare server. Welcome to NetWare.

To access folders and files on the NetWare server, see Chapter 27, Sharing and Securing Files and Folders. Print Services, Chapter 28, also provides some information allowing you to use the file system integration to access the NetWare print servers.

Summary

The topic of file systems in Windows Server 2003 covers a very broad range of technologies and features. Choosing the best file system naturally depends on several factors, but in most cases, the best choice for providing the broadest range of features and the best security is NTFS.

NTFS not only provides enhanced security through NTFS object permissions, but also, the fact that it can be extended through the use of file system filters from Microsoft and third parties enables certain capabilities not offered by FAT16 or FAT32. These additional capabilities include the Distributed File System (Dfs), which enables you to create a single, homogenous file system namespace from shares on multiple computers across the enterprise. This homogenous file system simplifies administration, improves availability and failover capability, and most important, greatly simplifies user access to shared resources.

Another feature made possible by NTFS in Windows Server 2003 is mounted volumes, which bring the same concept to the local file system that Dfs brings to the enterprise. You can use mounted volumes to create a homogenous file system namespace from multiple physical and logical volumes on the local computer, making those volumes appear as an integral part of a single logical volume.

Two mutually exclusive features made possible with NTFS are compression and encryption — you can use one or the other, but not both. NTFS can provide on-the-fly compression and decompression of files to increase storage capacity by as much as 80-90 percent, with the process remaining completely transparent to the user. The Encrypting File System (EFS), which is discussed in the next chapter, functions as an installable file system filter that performs encryption and decryption on-the-fly and transparently to the user. EFS provides a high degree of security for sensitive data that could be susceptible to theft, such as in notebook computers.

We talked about the Windows Server 2003 HSM system known as Remote Storage, a useful tool that adds to the suite of volume management tools that comes with the operating system.

Finally, we covered additional services that enable you to support Macintosh, Unix, and NetWare clients from a Windows Server 2003. File Services for Macintosh (FSM) is included with Windows Server 2003 and allows Macintosh clients to use a Windows Server 2003 as a file server. It also allows PC users to access Macintosh files stored on the server. Services for Unix and Services for NetWare are two add-on products from Microsoft that let you support Unix and NetWare clients for file services on a Windows Server 2003.

✦ ✦ ✦

CHAPTER 27

Sharing and Securing Files and Folders

✦ ✦ ✦ ✦

In This Chapter

Understanding the concept of shares, permissions, and ownership

Developing strategies for effective folder, file, and data security

Configuring a file server role

Using the Encrypting File System

✦ ✦ ✦ ✦

This chapter provides an understanding of access control to network file and folder resources. Chapter 26 provides an in-depth review of the Windows Server 2003 file system, especially NTFS and the DFS. Now, we look at the file system from other viewpoints: users and applications and, of course, administrators. We also examine and configure the Encrypting File System (EFS) in this chapter.

Windows Server 2003 has enhanced the file-server role of the operating system with some cool new features, as the following list describes:

- **Remote Document Sharing:** This feature enables access to files on Web servers through standard file-system calls through the new Web Distributed Authoring and Versioning protocol (WebDAV). This is sure to become very popular for use with document-sharing and document-control systems such as SharePoint, as you discover in Chapter 29.
- **Enhanced Distributed File System:** Although this was the subject of Chapter 26, we talk about mapping to file services on the DFS in the section "Connecting to shares," later in this chapter.
- **GUID Partition Table:** The 64-bit support on Windows Server 2003 Enterprise Edition and Datacenter Edition includes a new disk-partitioning technology that replaces the master boot record (MBR) found on all 32-bit operating systems. Although the new technology is largely hidden from the user and the administrator, it greatly improves reliability and performance over that of the legacy MBR.

Most data is generated and stored on computer systems, using the file and folder metaphors inherited from our three-dimensional world. Since the advent of local and wide area networks, and particularly the Internet, however, your files and folders are accessible to anyone with a computer and a network connection unless you secure them. You need to secure the data within their files and the folders that contain those files while at the same time providing controlled access to authorized users. The NT File System (NTFS) enables you to do that on the following three security access levels:

- ✦ Shares
- ✦ Folder permissions and file permissions (called NTFS permissions)
- ✦ Encryption

NTFS creates a hierarchy of folders in a volume, all starting from a root folder (see also DFS and mounted volumes in Chapter 26 and drive mappings in Chapter 19). The earlier versions of NTFS could store only a single folder hierarchy on a single hard drive or volume, maintained on a single computer. As we state in Chapter 26, the folder hierarchy (or folder namespace) can traverse or span hard-disk volumes on any computer on the network. To keep things simple in this chapter, we discuss folder and files independently of where they may be located on the network.

Sharing and Securing Your Data

Windows Server 2003, as do all modern graphically managed or command-line managed operating systems, enables you to manage your files and folders in the same way as in your hardcopy filing systems: in folders and filing cabinets. Think about the file room in a law firm or a newspaper morgue. It is unlikely you would be permitted to just walk into this room: It is usually locked or guarded, and you would need authority to enter, but you know that it's there. The company does not hide it away from you, because it is a shared resource, and the company usually wants you to know about it because you may need data in it to do your work.

Shares are the clubhouses of the network. A share is where users and groups of users go to share resources. You enable folder-sharing for your users and applications by creating a share, or in the lingo of mainframes, midrange, and legacy systems, a *share-point.* By owning the files and folders on your own machine (and we discuss ownership in the following section), you automatically have full access and control over your folders and their contents. Administrators own all the folders that they create anywhere on the network and can thus share them.

Do not confuse the term *share-point* with the new Microsoft SharePoint Team Services that ships with FrontPage.

Getting back to your brick and mahogany file room: By having access to the file room, you do not necessarily have access to every file or folder that it contains. Depending on your rank in the company, the department that you work for, and the work that you do, you may or may not have permission to open a file cabinet, read a file, check it out, change its contents, or add data to it. Similarly, by being a member of a group of users or by having individual authority, you may gain access to the NTFS share, but some files are not for your eyes. Others are accessible for reading only — you may not be permitted to change, delete, copy, or move them. The levels of access that you have to the folders and files are called *permissions.* Administrators, members of administrative groups (Administrator, Domain Administrators, or groups delegated administrative rights), and the owners of objects can assign permissions and control access to these objects, and they can also encrypt the files.

Over the years, we have found that most calls to the support desk come in if a user or a group cannot connect to shared resources, such as folders, files, and printers. If users cannot connect and get the `Access denied` message, they assume that the world has ended, such is the extent of their panic. Usually, the culprit is a simple case of an incorrect permission. We have seen how permission misadventure causes much consternation and is a waste of time, however, so we stress that every administrator should become an expert in this subject.

Folder and file encryption is the third mechanism that you can now use for protecting your files and folders. It was added to the Windows 2000 file system and is naturally also supported on Windows Server 2003. If you add support for cryptography and distributed security services, such as Kerberos and digital certificates, to the file system, you have what is known as the *Encrypting File System*, or *EFS*. The EFS is fully discussed in the section "Securing Files by Using the Encrypting File System," later in this chapter.

Ownership

Another means of understanding shares or share-points is by understanding *ownership*. Ownership is not a configuration setting or a mere value in the registry or Active Directory; it derives from the security services of the NTFS and the Win32 security system (which are discussed in more detail in Chapter 3).

If you've done some Windows programming, that usually helps you to understand ownership. The Win32 API has a function that creates objects such as folders and files. If the function that you are calling can take a security parameter, you can lock the object (pass a security descriptor) and keep other processes from accessing it. The lock is like a key that you, the owner, get to keep after you create the object. That is the essence of ownership. Of course, the whole process is managed by the OS and requires no user actions.

Whenever a process creates a file or a folder — objects — the file system assigns that process the rights of ownership and passes it a key. The process created it, so that process owns it . . . and it can do whatever it wants with that object. If *you* create a folder on the computer that you are logged onto or within a folder namespace to which you have access, *you* own the folder. Only you and the processes that operate within your security context (activated by the validation of your password) can access that folder.

Now, if other users or processes need access to the folder you just created, do you enable them to take ownership — hand them the key? No, not normally, because if you did, you would be losing your right to the object. By creating a share, you are essentially inviting others to access the folder (with restrictions, of course), but you don't give them the key. If someone else with bad intentions got hold of your keys, they may come back after dark and destroy your network. Remember the old adage: Possession is nine-tenths of the law. And remember what we say about safeguarding the Administrator account in Chapter 13. You can do tremendous damage with 50 lines of code and access to the Administrator account.

The owner of an object can actually enable a specified user or a group to take over the ownership of the object. (We get to that process in the section "Taking Ownership," later in this chapter.) Taking ownership is a one-way action. You can take ownership, but you cannot bestow it or return it. You can enable someone else to take ownership; you assign that person this permission. Ownership can be transferred only if the would-be benefactor is willing to take it. Because it lacks the capability to transfer ownership unilaterally, NTFS prevents users from hiding dirty work. In other words, you cannot lock up a folder and throw away the key and then make it look as though someone else did the damage.

Configuring the File Server Role

Before you can offer file services to your users, you need to configure the server to perform the role of a file server. As you learn in Chapter 6, installing a server from scratch makes this happen because the file server role is one of the most common roles for a server. Optimizing a server for file services would not make any sense, however, if the server is destined to become a database server or some Active Directory role server. Later, you may decommission a database server and use it for file services . . . and then you need to reconfigure it for the role of file server.

The flowchart shown in Figure 27-1 identifies the sequence of file-server chores that you are likely to perform in configuring your file server.

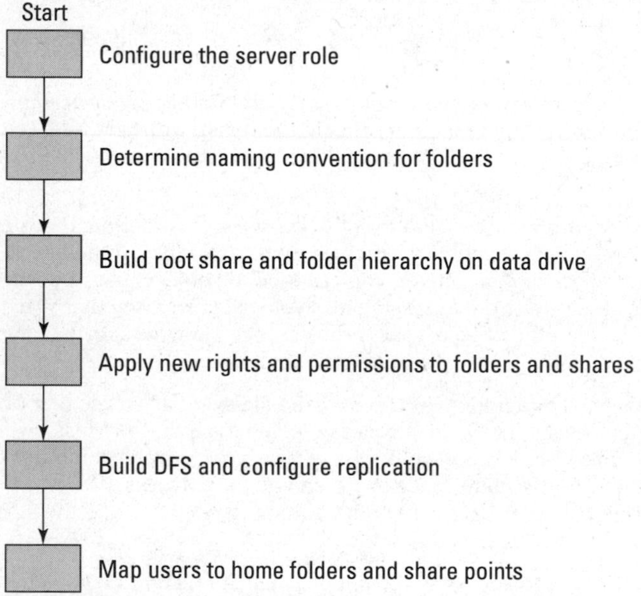
Start
Configure the server role
Determine naming convention for folders
Build root share and folder hierarchy on data drive
Apply new rights and permissions to folders and shares
Build DFS and configure replication
Map users to home folders and share points

Figure 27-1: The steps that you take to create, configure, and manage file servers.

First you need to create the file-server role. After you have a file server up and running, the first step is to determine whether you need to set up additional file servers and configure a Distributed File System (DFS); if you do not need a DFS, you proceed directly to configuring a folder hierarchy and a collection of shares on one or more standalone file servers. After your file server is performing optimally, you need to turn your attention to the EFS.

The premier file-server management tool on Windows Server 2003 is the *File Server Management console*. The console is shown in Figure 27-2 and is a more dedicated management facility for file servers than is the Computer Management console introduced in Windows 2000. Although you can still perform many file-server chores from the Computer Management console, Windows Explorer, and even the command line, the File Server

Management console provides a powerful interface for the most common file-management responsibility, managing shares and sessions.

The easiest way to open the File Server Management console is to execute `filesvr.msc` from the command line. You find this Microsoft Management Console (MMC) tool in the `system32` folder, and from there, you can create a shortcut on the desktop or link it to your menus.

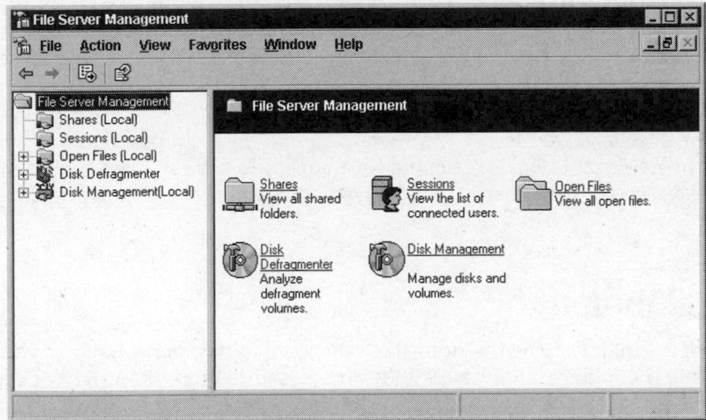

Figure 27-2: The File Server Management console.

You may notice that the console caters to the three areas that dominated the Computer Management console in Windows 2000: the creation and management of file shares, session management, and disk management. Disk management is discussed in Chapters 19 and 26, so we do not cover this topic any further here. Instead, we get directly to the issues of shares in the following sections.

Publishing Shares in Active Directory

The idea of *published shares* is no longer new to the Windows networking environment, but it did begin with Active Directory. Windows Server 2003 users connect to shared resources on the domain by looking them up in Active Directory or mapping them out by using logon scripts.

Although connecting or mapping to share points published in Active Directory is useful, the DFS provides the most utility and value for a company with extensive or widely distributed file serving needs. We explore the use of the DFS in the section "Connecting to Shares," a little later in this chapter.

Creating shares on Windows Server 2003 is really easy, and if you have Windows experience, you need to read the following section only as a refresher and to pick up subtle yet important differences. Establishing shares on remote computers is another story, however, and the process is handled now by the File Server Management console (and the Computer Management console) described in the section "Configuring the File Server Role," later in this chapter. You can also create shares from Windows Explorer, the command line, and the Manage Your Server console as you set up your server in the file-server role. You can also create shares from the Active Directory Users and Computers console.

Creating a Share

As you first create a share, the file system automatically gives *Read* access to the *Everyone* group, unless you have taken steps to prevent that, as we discuss in the section "Share Attributes," later in this chapter. If the contents of the files are sensitive, you need to remove the Everyone group and assign access only to authorized users or groups. Although *Read* access stops unauthorized users from adding files to the folder or deleting files, it does not stop anyone from reading the files. And *Read* access for Everyone means that all users can unnecessarily see the share-point, which is not a good idea, because shares should be shown on a need-to-know basis.

In Chapter 13, we encourage you to use common-sense management practices and avoid assigning rights to individual users. The same advice applies to shares. Share folders with groups, not individuals, and don't share to the Everyone group unless you have a good reason to do so.

Sharing a local folder

If you are the owner of the folder or the folders within the local folder namespace or you have administrative access to the folders, sharing a folder involves little more than right-clicking the new or existing folder and then choosing Sharing and Security from the pop-up menu. Select the Share this Folder option in the folder's Properties dialog box that appears. (It is open to the Sharing tab.) The Share Name field is enabled. This is shown in Figure 27-3. (A Web Sharing tab also appears on this dialog box if you have Internet Information Server installed on the server.)

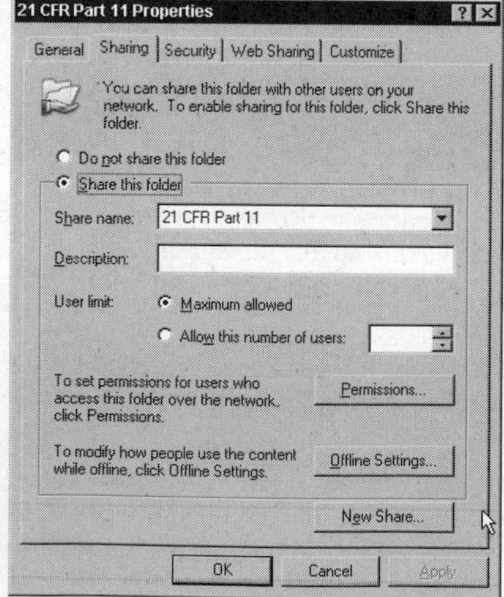

Figure 27-3: The Sharing tab on the `21 CFR Part 11` folder's Properties dialog box.

As soon as the fields on this dialog box are enabled, you can enter the following share data:

✦ **Share Name:** The actual folder name is used as the default share name, but you can change this to reflect any name that better suits the application for the share. A good idea is to use the best share name for the share, possibly one that clearly informs the user of the purpose of the share or that provides a hint of the share's contents. A folder may, for example, be already named `SQLDATA`, and rather than changing that name, which would affect other applications, a better choice would be to make the share name `SQL Server databases`. Share names can be up to 80 characters in length, and they can contain spaces. If your users are attaching to the share from the command line or you have applications that may send share attach commands to the system console, however, you should stick to single names of between eight and 12 characters (and even stick to eight-character names with three-character extensions for those still using software built during the previous millennium). The best command-line-compliant substitute for the aforementioned share name is simply `Data`.

✦ **Description:** The Description field takes more than 100 characters, so you can be creative here. Populating this field wherever possible is a good idea because the data shows up in Explorer and Active Directory whenever users browse for a share. Although we've said that you can be creative, be conservative, too. A hundred-character comment field forces most users to waste time scrolling to the right.

✦ **User Limit:** On server shares, you have no maximum connection limit, but you can restrict connections to shares for application-specific purposes or licensing by selecting the Allow this Number of Users radio button and then incrementing the number in the spin box to the right of the option. The Maximum Allowed radio button then toggles off. Client operating systems such as Windows 2000 Professional and Windows XP Professional prohibit more than ten concurrent connections and make several other exclusions that you eventually discover . . . which is why they do not make good file servers in a busy, yet small office.

✦ **Permissions:** This button opens the Permissions dialog box. As soon as you enter the share name and description, you can click the Permissions button to admit users to the share and set the access types that you want. Permissions are discussed in depth in the section "Share Attributes," later in this chapter.

✦ **Offline Settings:** This button was called Cache Settings in Windows 2000. Clicking it opens another dialog box that enables you to configure offline access to the shared folder. Offline folder and file access is touched on in the section "Offline Access," later in this chapter, and explained in the context of Group Policy and change control in Chapter 14.

After you create a share, you have the option of creating another share. Clicking the New Share button clears the fields in the dialog box but does not replace the old share; you can share a folder as many times as you want, each time with different access clients and permissions. Any time that you need to end a share, just select the share name from the drop-down list and click the Remove Share option, which becomes visible after the creation of a second share. If you need to stop sharing the folder completely, click the Do Not Share this Folder radio button and then click Apply. This option terminates all shares on the folder.

Establishing shares by using the File Server Management console

You can connect to a remote computer and create a share-point on it in two ways. The first and hardest way is by using the `NET SHARE` command at the command prompt. The second, and by far the easiest way, is by opening the File Server Management console. (You can also use the Computer Management console, as mentioned in the section "Configuring the File Server Role," earlier in this chapter. If your Computer Management console shortcut is missing, you can simply create a new one by linking to the `compmgmt.msc` snap-in in the Windows Server 2003 installation folder — usually `Windows` or `Winnt` — and in the `system32` subfolder.)

After the File Server Management console is open, select the first option, Shares (Local) in the folder tree in the left-hand pane. Right-click it and choose Connect to Another Computer from the pop-up menu, as shown in Figure 27-4. You can connect to a computer listed in Active Directory (the best way), or you can connect to a computer listed in the domain. After you have opened the remote computer into the File Server Management snap-in, you can manage the remote computer's shared folders. From here on, the process of creating the share-point is no different from creating shares on the local machine.

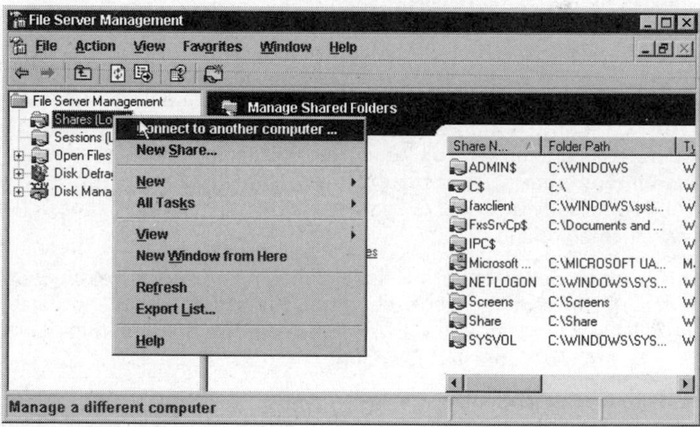

Figure 27-4: Right-clicking Shares (Local) in the File Server Management console to access its pop-up menu.

To connect to another computer, simply enter the name of the file server to connect to in the Another Computer field of the Select Computer dialog box, as shown in Figure 27-5, and click OK.

To create the share on the local or remote computer, run the File Server Manager option (which you launch from the Manage Your Server console or by directly launching the File Server Management console (`filesvr.msc`) in the `Windows\system32` folder).

If you don't want to keep opening the Manage Your Server console to launch the File Server Manager, you can place the `filesvr.msc` shortcut on the Administrative Tools menu and rename it File Server Manager.

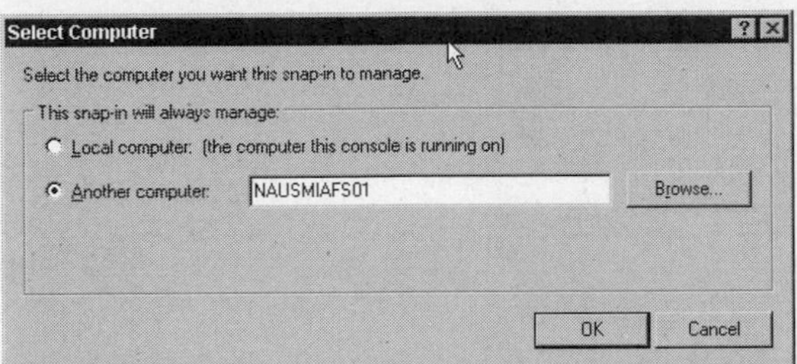

Figure 27-5: The Select Computer dialog box enables you to specify a file server to connect to or the option to browse for the server in Active Directory.

Expand the nodes, select Shares, and right-click it. Then choose New Share from the pop-up menu. The Share a Folder Wizard opens and enables you to provide shared-folder parameters, as shown in Figure 27-6.

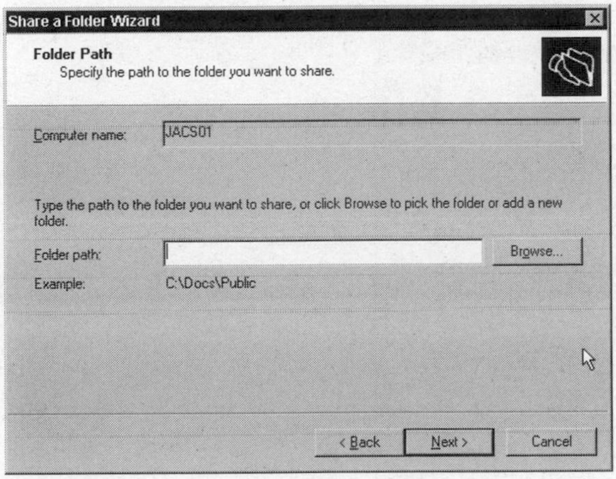

Figure 27-6: The Share a Folder Wizard.

Enter the path to the shared folder in the Folder Path field and then click Next. The Name, Description, and Settings screen of the wizard appears and enables you to target the share to Windows or Macintosh users, as shown in Figure 27-7.

Fill in this screen of the wizard and click Next to set up permissions for your users, as shown in Figure 27-8; then, after setting your permissions, click the Finish button and you are done.

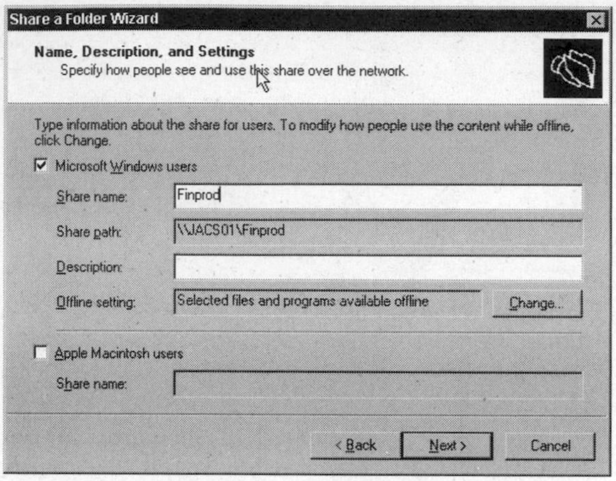

Figure 27-7: The Name, Description, and Settings screen of the Share a Folder Wizard.

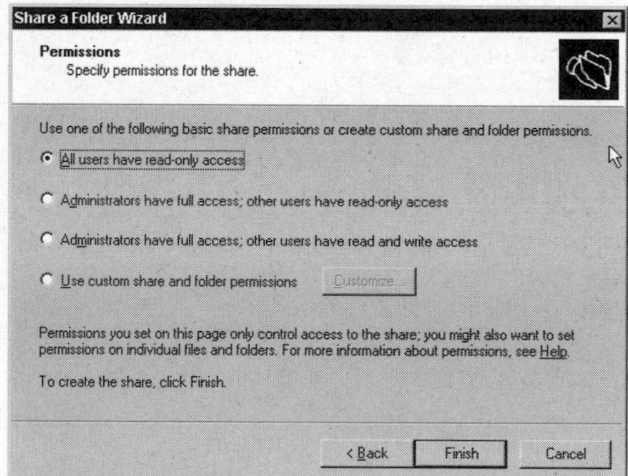

Figure 27-8: The Permissions screen of the Share a Folder Wizard.

Share Attributes

Share access can be given directly to users or processes or implicitly through group membership. Shared folders possess the following attributes:

✦ Folder shares work only on folder objects and not on the files that folders contain. You cannot select a file, `x-file`, and share it as `x-file` on the network. But you can share a folder called `thexfiles` and enable users to access the files in that folder.

- The default access permission on a share is *Full Control*. This permission is assigned to the Everyone group, with *Read* access. So, if you create such a share and have your Guest account enabled and not governed by any domain policy, every computer user has access to it. But you are a common-sense administrator, and you are sure to follow our advice and make sure that your network is locked down . . . or else.
- Shares can be established on most file systems, including FAT. But NTFS permissions, discussed in the section "Securing Files and Folders by using Permissions," later in this chapter, are peculiar to the Windows NT, Windows 2000, and Windows Server 2003 operating systems.
- Shares are visible to you (if they are not hidden), even if you do not have permission to access the folder through share permission or security settings. This frustrates many NetWare file-server administrators, who can hide the share on that type of server from users who don't need to know that it exists.
- Share access also applies to the local user logged onto the computer that is hosting the shared folder. This feature is extremely important because it means that you can prevent users who log on locally from accessing folders. And it's a surefire way of protecting your data on a notebook computer.
- A shared folder on your machine is represented as an icon with a hand holding the folder. But across the network, the icon does not include the hand; the icon is either visible to the user as a folder sitting on the network or it is not seen at all because it is hidden. Hiding shares is a valuable security and administration tool that we discuss in the section "Connecting to Shares," later in this chapter.

Table 27-1 lists the folder permissions that apply to Windows Server 2003 shares. Remember that the access level is at the share only; NTFS permissions provide the "second line of defense" to locked-down resources at the object level. You set share permissions through the Share Permissions dialog box, which you can access by clicking the Permissions button on the Sharing page of the folder's Properties dialog box (refer to Figure 27-3). If you click this button, the dialog box shown in Figure 27-9 opens.

Table 27-1: Shared Folder Permission Types

Permission	*Privilege*
Read	The user can see the entire shared folder tree (root shared folder and subfolders). The user can also see all the files in the folder tree (traversing) and open them for reading. The user can execute applications in the shared-folder hierarchy.
Change	This privilege inherits the Read privileges and also enables the user to change the folders and the data in the files within the shared folder's namespace. The user can also change file attributes and can copy, move, and delete files and folders. The user cannot change the actual share.
Full Control	This privilege enables the user to take ownership of the files and folders, within the shared folder's namespace. It inherits the privileges of the Read and Change permissions. Under NTFS, only Full Control enables a user to change permissions and take ownership of a file or folder.

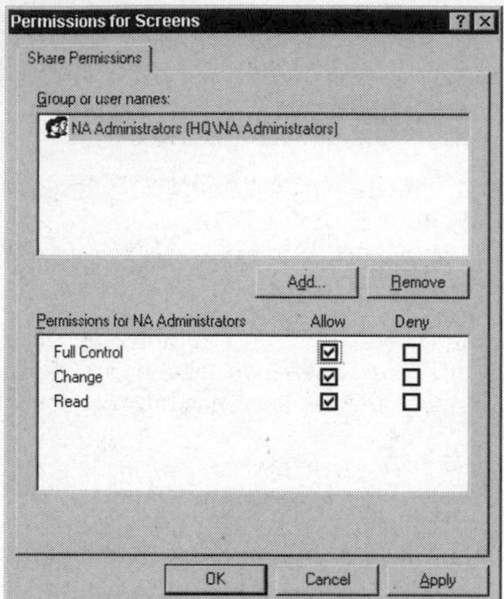

Figure 27-9: Setting share permissions for a folder.

Deny

You can deny access to any of the permissions described in Table 27-1 by clicking the appropriate Deny check box on the Share Permissions tab in a folder's Permissions dialog box. If you deny Full Control, for example, you drop the privilege level down to Change. Deny is useful if you want to single out a user and deny that user permission. Deny is the strongest of permission attributes; in other words, it takes precedence over every permission. If a user in a primary group has full access to a share, but you deny access directly or via a secondary group, for example, the individual user is denied access despite the access given in the primary group. Taking the user out of a group, however, is better than keeping him in the share and specifically denying him access individually.

Accumulation of share permissions

Share permissions accumulate. If a user is a member of one group that is given Read access but is also a member of another group that is given Change access (to the same share), the user's cumulative permissions in the share are Read and Change. The user's effective permission is Change, because it includes Read permission.

Moving or copying folders

If you move a folder, the shares assigned to it are deleted. The folder is not shared at the new location. If you copy a folder, the new copy is not shared, but the source folder remains shared.

Intradomain shares

Shares are not restricted to the users and groups of the domain in which they are created. If a trust relationship exists between two domains, a user or group in one domain can be given access to the share in another domain (see Chapters 3, 9, and 14). The administrator of Domain A can provide access to a user or to a global or universal group from Domain B.

Who can share folders

Members of the predefined Administrators, Server Operators, and Power Users groups can share folders. In a domain on a member server, the members of the Administrators or Server Operators groups can share folders that exist on any computer on the network. On a standalone computer, only the administrator and members of the Power Users and local Administrators groups can share a folder.

Workgroups do not make for such flexible sharing. Only members of the local Administrators group and the Power Users group can share folders. (But remember that, if you own the folder, you can share it. And an administrator can take ownership at any time.)

Hidden shares

The capability to hide shares is a useful feature of the Windows OS. It makes up for the problem of shares being visible to everyone on the network, even to users who do not have access to the shares. Relative hiding of shares is probably a very difficult and cumbersome technology to introduce into the OS, but exposing shares only to users who have access to them makes sense. To the other users, the shares should not be visible . . . but available only on a need-to-know basis. Active Directory goes a long way in making selectively exposing shares to users possible by locating published shares in organizational units.

Hiding shares is possible simply by ending the share name with the dollar sign ($). You can still connect to the share if you have access to it, but it does not appear on the browse list (because nothing ending with the dollar sign appears in the browse list). You connect to the share by using the Run dialog box, as explained in the following section, or at the command line by using `NET SHARE`.

Here is a good example of a hidden share in action: A certain company in Florida transmits millions of dollars of direct-deposit information to the bank every afternoon. The application resides at the data center in Miami, but it logs into a hidden share on the wide area network after an application in Los Angeles writes the direct-deposit information to a file in the same hidden share. Both applications or processes are members of the Banking group, and they have Read and Write access to the file in the share. No one else can see the share on the network, and the cloaking affords the share a measure of concealment. Of course, digging around on computers and looking for hidden shares is possible. But did you know that you can hide *servers* as well? Run the command `NET CONFIG SERVER /HIDDEN:YES`, and the server stops appearing on the Browse list. You can still contact it if you know the IP address. To put the server name back on the Browse list, change the `/HIDDEN:` option to `NO` in the command.

Connecting to Shares

Ensuring that users have access to shares, typically through drive mappings, is one of the most frequently visited tasks that the network administrator has on his plate. You have several ways to connect to shares that are not visible in a browse list. You can connect by using interactive tools, such as Windows Explorer, or at the command line. You can also connect to published shares in Active Directory. DNS directs you to the domain controller hosting Active Directory, so connecting to a share is as simple as browsing for a Web page.

To connect to a share by using the Map Network Drive Wizard (an option that assigns a drive letter), follow these steps:

1. Right-click the My Network Places icon on the desktop and then select Map Network Drive from the pop-up menu. The Map Network Drive dialog box appears. (*Note:* My

Network Places is not on the default desktop in Windows Server 2003, but it is available in Windows Explorer and on the desktop of the alternate Windows 2000 (Classic) Start Menu.)

2. Type the UNC path to the folder in the Folder field if you know it, or click Browse to search for the exact folder.
3. Enter a drive letter of your choice in the Drive field or use the default.
4. Select the Reconnect at Logon check box if you want the connection to remain persistent. Click OK to finish.

   You can also connect to the share under another username. All you need is the user's logon name and password. This option is useful if you need to connect to a resource on a domain for which you are not fully authenticated.

To connect to a share by using the Run dialog box, follow these steps:

1. Choose Start ➪ Run.
2. In the Run dialog box, type the UNC path to the folder if you know it or click Browse to search for the exact folder. Click OK.

To connect to a share from My Network Places, follow these steps:

1. Open My Network Places.
2. Find the computer that contains the share and locate the folder in the browse list.
3. After you find the share, double-click it to establish the connection.

To connect to a share in the Active Directory, follow these steps:

1. Open My Network Places.
2. Expand the Active Directory node until you locate the domain in which you want to locate a published share.
3. After you find the share, double-click it to establish the connection.

Connecting users to published shares

You can connect users to shares published in Active Directory. This enables you to map users to shares according to their membership in Organization Units. Say, for example, that you have an OU called US MIA, which belongs to NA OU; users who work in Miami should map drives to the file shares that they need in this OU. As long as a user is a member of the OU, that user can gain access to the share.

You can automate share connection via login scripts, which we demonstrate later in this section. Providing shares and mapping users drives to them is performed according to the flowchart shown in Figure 27-10.

First you need to create some standards for the company. Table 27-2 lists the mapped drives standard assigned to the various hubs and sites in the Latin Accents company.

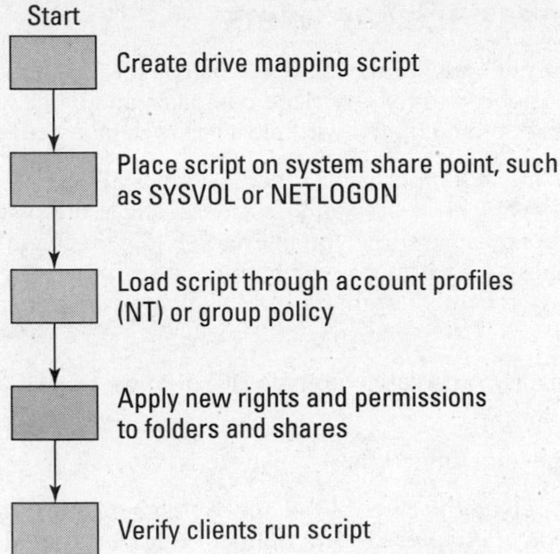
Start
Create drive mapping script
Place script on system share point, such as SYSVOL or NETLOGON
Load script through account profiles (NT) or group policy
Apply new rights and permissions to folders and shares
Verify clients run script

Figure 27-10: The procedures for setting up drive mappings for the members of various organizational units.

Table 27-2: Shared Folder Permission Types

Drive Letter	*File Server Share*
J (user folders)	`\\ServerName\BusinessGroup\Users\UserName`
K (common folders)	`\\ServerName\BusinesGroup\Common`
W (application data)	`\\ServerName\BusinesGroup\Applications`

Now you can create your shares and hide them as shown earlier by using the trailing dollar sign in the share name (for example, `\\ServerName\BusinessGroup\ShareName$`). This takes the share name off any browse lists. Next, you provide a login script for the user, as we demonstrate in the following section.

You have several reasons for mapping to shared resources in this manner. First, doing so enables administrators to control what users have mapped access to. Forcing or simply enabling users to map to shared resources such as folders and printers tends to result in an administrative nightmare as well as a security risk.

Second, by not advertising the shares to browse lists, you add an extensive security layer on the shared resources. Security is further enhanced by locking the shares down so that users can access them only via login scripts or Group Policy, which are further protected with permissions and access control.

Third, script or policy-driven mapping keeps the mapping uniform and standard. In other words, users' home directories are mapped to J, all application data is mapped to W, and the common folders are mapped to K.

Mapping out the DFS namespace for users

As Chapter 26 demonstrates, one of the wonders of Windows Server 2003 is the Distributed File System, or DFS, namespace. A DFS is a good idea for any sized company, and living without one is hard after you apply it to a distributed company with file servers in many cities.

Latin Accents' Miami hub also supports a site in Rio de Janeiro that has a busy file server. So we decided to build a DFS file system that spans both sites and provides a single file-system namespace to our users. After the DFS is built, as we show you in Chapter 26, you can map your user's directory to folders in the namespace without needing to create hundreds of shares on the actual file servers. If you have recently escaped from a NetWare/NDS network, this section should pique your interest.

No matter where your user logs on, as long as you create a domain DFS, that user can map to a home folder and other folders as needed.

To set up the DFS and map users to a home folder in it, follow these steps:

1. Create a DFS root. This is done by opening the Distributed File System console under Administrative Tools, as we show you in Chapter 26, and right-clicking Distributed File System to launch the New Root Wizard. Your DFS root is at the start, or root, of the folder branch containing all your users' home directories. The New Root Wizard takes you to the screen shown in Figure 27-11. Before you create the root name, add a dollar sign (`$`), as shown, to the end of the name to hide it on browse lists. After you have created the DFS root, you are done working on shares. All you need to do is map users to their folders on the namespace.

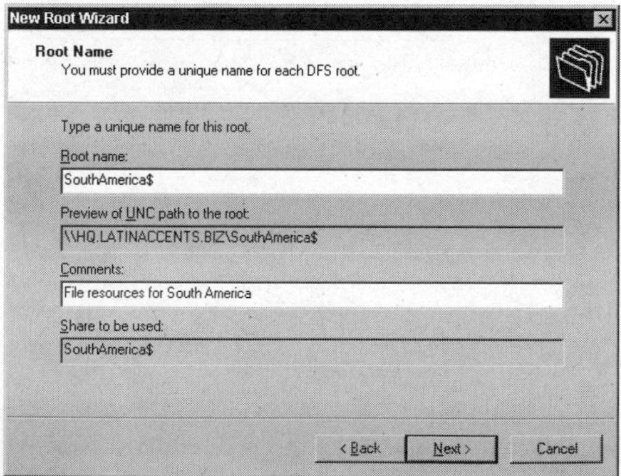

Figure 27-11: The new root name, with a trailing dollar sign ($) for hiding it, in the New Root Wizard.

2. Create a simple batch file to be processed as a logon script. You can go to town with VBScript or JScript stuff, but for logon scripts, a simple batch (`*.bat`) file works. (And you thought that DOS was dead.) Figure 27-12 provides an example of a logon script to map users to home folders. (*Note:* You are not limited to batch language, and on Windows Server 2003, you can script this in more than 20 languages.)

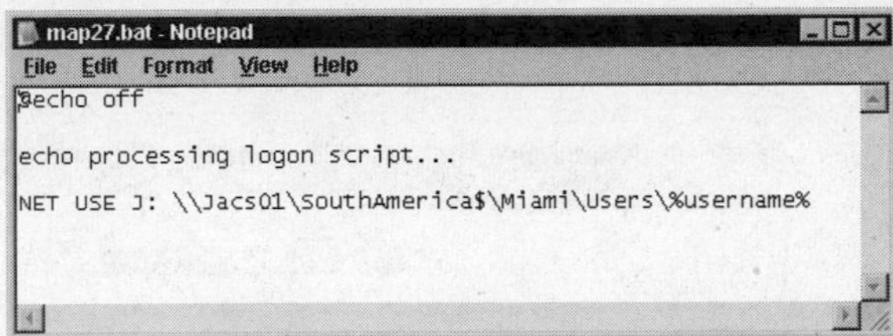

Figure 27-12: Creating a logon script in Notepad to map users to home folders in the DFS.

3. Now you need to place the script, or batch file, in a share that all client computers can access. `SYSVOL` or `NETLOGON` are usually the safest bets. You must make sure that your client computers can see the volumes whenever they authenticate to the domain or the script does not get processed. Run the `NET USE` command at a client workstation, and you soon discover what the client workstations are using on the server. The `Shares` folder in the File Server Management console, however, provides you with the server-side information as shown in Figure 27-13.

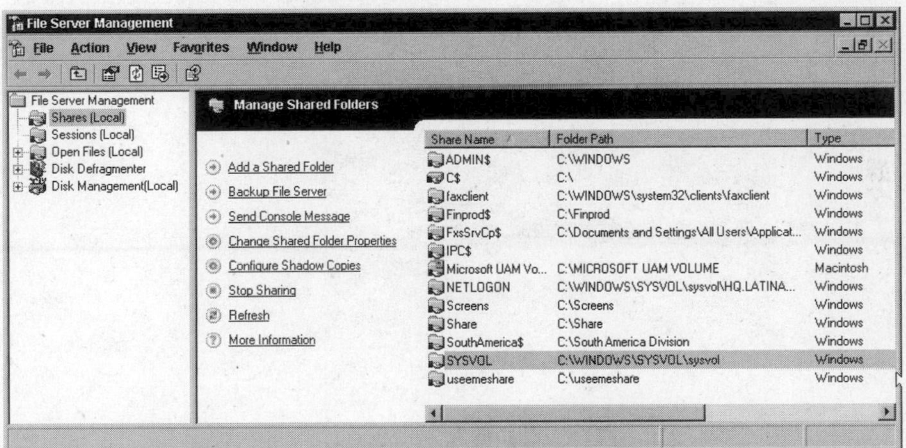

Figure 27-13: Checking out the shares in the File Server Management console.

4. The next job is to enable Group Policy for the users. Create a Group Policy Object to affect the users in the organizational unit to control and then open the Group Policy Object Editor to edit the object, as shown in Figure 27-14. Expand the User Configuration node through Windows Settings and Scripts (Logon/Logoff). (This process is described in detail in Chapter 14.)

5. Double-click Logon in the right-hand pane, as shown in Figure 27-14, and enter the path to the logon script on the server in the dialog box shown in Figure 27-15. Remember to use a UNC path or your clients may think that they need to process a script that's sitting on their own hard-disk drives.

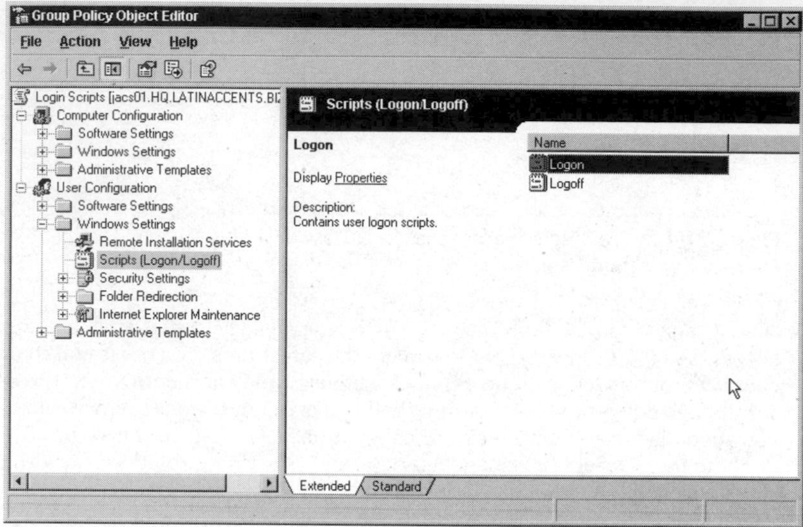

Figure 27-14: Configuring Group Policy to process logon scripts.

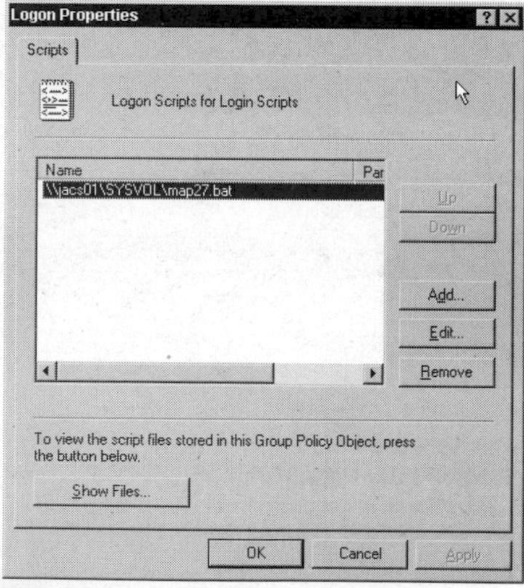

Figure 27-15: Providing the UNC path to the logon script for a Group Policy Object.

6. Save the policy, and the job is done. Now, whenever users in the OU are under the influence of the policy logon, their J drives are automatically mapped as `Jeffrey.Shapiro` on `Jacs01\SouthAmerica$\Miami\Users (J:)`.

Administrative Shares

As you install Windows Server 2003, NTFS automatically creates administrative shares on your local volume. These shares are placed in strategic administrative folders, the most important being the one where you installed the Windows Server 2003 system files. These administrative shares are listed in Table 27-3.

Table 27-3: Administrative Shares

Share	*Purpose*
Roots (`C$`, `D$`, `E$`, and so on)	The root of every volume on a Windows Server 2003 (and even on Windows 2000, NT 4.0, and earlier servers) is shared. So if you can map to the share, you can access the entire volume.
`ADMIN$`	This share is the system root, the Windows Server 2003 system folder hierarchy. To map to this share, simply use `\\SERVERNAME\ADMIN$`.
`PRINT$`	This share is created as you install the first shared printer on the server. This share is established at `\\SERVERNAME\SPOOL\DRIVERS`, and its purpose is to enable clients to remotely pull printer drivers for installation on their machines. The Everyone group has Read access to this share, and administrators can install new drivers to the share as needed by using Full Control.
`Netlogon`	This share is used for the Net Logon service, which is the mechanism to service logon requests to the server. It is also used for locating logon scripts. This share is not automatically created in Windows 2003 Server. See also Chapter 14 for login information.
`IPC$`	This is the share for the Named Pipes protocol, which provides intra- and interprocess communications between applications.

Shutting off these shares is possible, but doing so may result in unpredictable results. You can, for example, shut down the `NETLOGON` share to prevent anyone from trying to obtain authentication at your machine — and you may have legitimate reasons for doing so — but the correct way is to stop the `Net Logon` service.

We have found that you can delete the share if you are an administrator or have ownership of the share. If you try to change permissions on the share, however, Windows Server 2003 denies access with a nasty message saying that built-in shares cannot be modified — absurd in light of the fact that you can delete the administrative shares at any time after you unseat the ownership.

Incidentally, if you delete an administrative share, it returns after you reboot the computer. The administrative shares are controlled by the server service. Anytime that you restart this service, such as at reboot time, the shares are reestablished and reset to the factory default.

You may be concerned that the administrative shares pose a potential danger, and they do. In fact, all shares are dangerous if not managed with common sense. Mapping to the shared roots on each drive is feasible, if you know how to use a server. If you can connect, you get total access to the drive and the entire folder hierarchy within.

You would be right to say that these shares are the equivalent of leaving the hen-house door open for the fox to walk right in. Only administrators, however, have access to these shares. That limitation, however, is still not comforting, and the whole administrative-share quirk is another reason why we lock up the Administrator account. As long as the Administrator account's identity and password are locked away and security policy is in force, you do not experience any hacking of these shares.

Common-Sense Strategies for Sharing Folders

Shares are not an easy facility to manage, and often they conflict with applications, restrict the wrong people, and expose the network to security risks. The following sections include strategies for closing holes in your network with respect to shares.

Restricting shares

Many administrators prefer to keep shares wide open by leaving the Everyone group in the share with full access. Instead, they control access to subfolders via folder and file permissions. We understand this policy, and the reason for it is to relieve some of the administrative burden (one less thing to worry about). But is this common-sense management? Not if it means that you are leaving doors unlocked on your network.

The problem is that the subfolders below the share become accessible to the users who are given access at the share-point. And if the Everyone group has access to the root, it has access to all the subfolders. So by not restricting the share, you are in effect giving yourself more work to do, because you must go to every subfolder and apply NTFS permissions. On a complex folder hierarchy, the task of locking up all the subfolders could prove next to impossible. If you want to keep shares (and your network) secure, your best course is to remove the Everyone group from the share and admit only the groups that require access to the folder namespace. Further security can be applied by using the file and folder permissions.

Limiting use of the Everyone group makes troubleshooting user-related problems easier. The Everyone group forces you to be cognizant of every user account in your domain and every domain with which you share trusts.

Setting up application share-points

If users need to access a remote application, shortcuts are created on their systems (manually or via profiles, logon scripts, and Group Policy). The users run the applications from the network shares, and the applications run in the local memory space on the client computer. Most well-designed Win32 applications can be executed multiple times in this fashion. And you are often asked to install an application on the applications server and then share that folder. The following strategies are suggested for creating application shares:

- ✦ Create an application share-point. On our servers, we call this share the "Apps" share-point.
- ✦ Under the Apps share-point, you can create a share for each application that you are installing and then share each respective install folder. Creating more shares may not be necessary, however, because the subfolders are accessible to those given access to the share-point. If you need to restrict access to a subfolder, simply ensure that only the authorized group has access, through folder permissions, which are discussed throughout the latter part of this chapter.

✦ Provide access to an administrators group (or whatever suits your purpose) for the root (Apps) share and make sure that the group has the Full Control privilege assigned. This enables only application administrators to manage the applications, such as patches and upgrades. You may also add a special *applications admins* group with Change control enabled to permit technicians or consultants to troubleshoot the applications.

✦ Remove the Everyone group from the share and provide access to either the Users group or a specific group that requires the access. Make sure that these groups have only the Read privilege assigned.

Setting up data share-points

Data shares contain files that users or applications need to share. Users mostly share spreadsheet and document files, while applications (clients) need access to databases. Common-sense practice is to keep the data share-points separate from application share-points, because data shares require more that just Read access.

Data backup is another good reason for separate data share-points. Your backups should not be repetitively backing up application files (see Chapter 20), and the share is easy to identify and back up. The following list describes how to create a data share-point:

✦ Create a root data share-point for applications. Name the shares after the groups or projects that require them — for example, `Part 11 compliance docs` or `materials management`. Naming the shares after the application name is confusing, and you may have many shares that contain data generated by the same application. A share named Microsoft Access Files, for example, would be a bad idea. (We manage several hundred servers, and they all contain Microsoft Access files.)

✦ Give your users Change access so that their applications can update files and save the data. Administrative groups should be given Change or Full Control as needed.

Offline Access

On Windows Server 2003, you can also configure shared folders and their contents for offline access. The contents of these shares can therefore be seconded to the target computer. The remote or standalone computer disconnects from the network and maintains a mirror, or shadow copy, of the folder and files. You continue to work with the offline resource as if you are connected to it on the server. The following steps described how to setup folders for offline access:

1. Open Windows Explorer, right-click a shared folder, and choose Sharing and Security or Properties from the pop-up menu. The folder's Properties dialog box appears.

2. On the shared folder's Properties dialog box, select the Sharing tab and click the Offline Settings button. The Offline Settings dialog box appears, as shown in Figure 27-16. All shares are cached for offline use by default, so you can select the Files or Programs From the Share Will Not Be Available Offline radio button if you do not need to cache the contents of the folder.

3. To keep caching for offline access, you can choose one of the options shown in Figure 27-16 and outlined in Table 27-4.

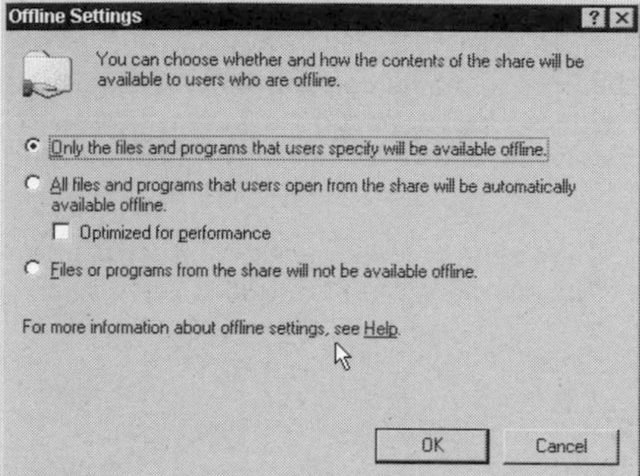

Figure 27-16: The Offline Settings dialog box.

Table 27-4: Caching Settings

Caching Option	*Purpose*
Only the files and programs that users specify are available offline.	This option enables users to select the files to be marked for offline access. This is the default setting for all shares, but only files marked for offline use are activated. Every file marked for offline is cached, regardless of whether the file was opened or not.
All files and programs that users open from the share are automatically available for offline use.	This option enables every file in the folder that is opened to be automatically cached. This option saves on bandwidth because only files actually used are cached. You can further instruct the file server to optimize the Offline setting activity to be optimized for performance. This is especially useful in low-bandwidth connections, like a frame relay WAN, or for added file server scalability.
Files or programs from the share are not available offline.	Selecting this option prevents users from obtaining offline access to files and programs.

Offline attributes

The following are attributes of the offline access features of Windows Server 2003:

- ✦ After a computer first connects to the share on the network, any files marked for caching on the server are copied to the client computer's hard disk.
- ✦ After a computer connects back to the share on the network, any files that have been updated on the client computer are copied to the server.
- ✦ After the user logs off the network, the server and the client synchronize the files automatically.

Synchronizing cached resources

To manage the synchronization between offline files and folders and their sources on the server clients, you need to open Windows Explorer and choose Tools ➪ Synchronize from the menu bar. In the Items to Synchronize dialog box, first select the items in the list to synchronize and then click the Synchronize button.

The synchronization management options, as shown in Figure 27-17, can be used to determine when offline files are synchronized with the versions on the servers. You can do either a quick or a full synchronization. The latter takes longer but ensures that the current versions are saved to the network and copied to the client.

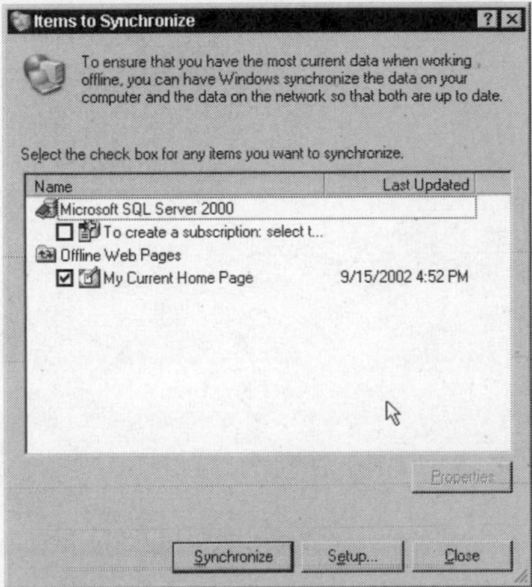

Figure 27-17: The Items to Synchronize dialog box.

Securing Files and Folders by Using Permissions

As you learn in Chapter 3, permissions are the means by which you control access to network objects. After shares, they are the second and third lines of defense in protecting data and network resources. File and folder permissions are controlled by NTFS. This section deals specifically with the permissions that control access to volumes, folders, and files, as opposed to permissions that control access to share-points.

Permissions kick in as soon as you format a volume to NTFS. Volumes are protected with NTFS permissions, just as are folders and files. As soon as you have formatted a volume to NTFS 5.0, right-click the name of the volume in Windows Explorer and choose the Properties command on the ensuing pop-up menu. Click the Security tab of the Properties dialog box that appears. You should now notice a bunch of groups that have default access to the folder. The most suspicious group is Everyone.

These settings are still consistent with the Windows 2000 default, where the default behavior of the OS is to give Everyone access as well — that is, assign it rights to access the files in the folder. This access has now been locked down further in Windows Server 2003. Although the Everyone group is still added to the security settings, by default it gets no rights. We still advise that you change this default behavior, however, and get the Everyone group out of the default groups that are given some sort of access to every new folder that's created. You do so as shown in the flowchart in Figure 27-18.

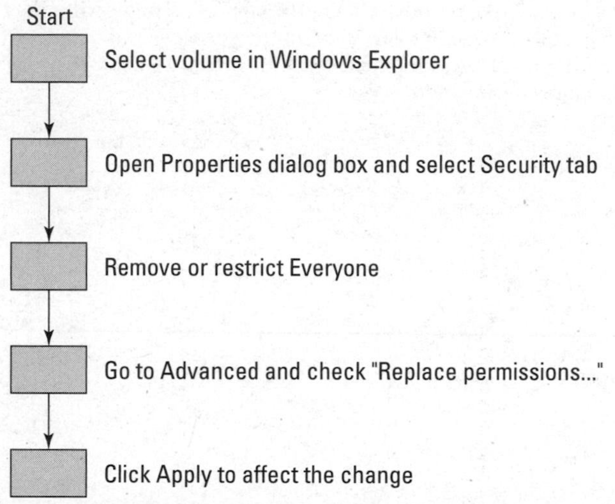
Start
Select volume in Windows Explorer
Open Properties dialog box and select Security tab
Remove or restrict Everyone
Go to Advanced and check "Replace permissions..."
Click Apply to affect the change

Figure 27-18: The steps to removing access to new folders for the Everyone group.

To remove the group, follow these steps (and please proceed with caution):

1. Select the disk volume in Windows Explorer and right-click it to select the Properties option, which loads the volume's Properties dialog box. Then select the Security tab on the dialog box.
2. Click the Advanced button on the Properties dialog box. The Advanced Security Settings dialog box opens. If the Everyone group is included in the list of groups, remove the group or disable (deselect) any rights that it may have. Your best course is to remove the group because not having the group in the list in the first place is more secure than just denying it any rights. Plus selecting Deny shuts down the whole share because it literally locks out *everyone*.
3. Select Replace Permissions on All Child Objects the radio button and click Apply. Do not deselect the Inheritable Permissions radio button. You are warned about the change; click OK in the warning dialog box to continue. The Everyone group is now removed from the list of groups that have access to all objects on the drive.

Now, only your select administrators can create and manage new folders on the volume. The default thus prevents all and sundry from creating a folder on the volume. And each time that you create a folder, you automatically assign your administrators' group to the folder and nothing else. This setup makes for good security practice and keeps the doors locked until the folder is ready for group access.

If you decide not to remove the Everyone group, remember that the group is automatically given carte blanche access to any share that you create (albeit with no rights).

Setting up security as just described can be done on a drive that's in service for only a short time but is safest and most easily done on a new volume.

We strongly recommend that you remove the Everyone group from the root of the volume. If you don't, you're creating a security risk, because giving Everyone permission at the root of the folder hierarchy and then forgetting about it is all too easy. If your volume has been in service for a while, however, removing the Everyone group this way may do some damage if you have been loose in dishing out rights to "Everyone." Many shares and access rights are given access to Everyone, so removing it this way is likely to prevent access to a user or an application that depended on it being there.

The Permission Types

Table 27-5 lists the folder permissions that you can apply. Folder and file permissions are accessible from the Security tab of the folder's Properties dialog box. To access the folder's Properties dialog box (such as folder 21 CFR Part 11 Properties), right-click the folder and choose Properties from the pop-up menu. Then select the Security tab, as shown in Figure 27-19.

Table 27-5: Folder Permissions

Permission	*Purpose*
Full Control	This permission enables the user to take ownership and perform all the actions of the following permissions.
Modify	This permission enables you to authorize users to delete the folder under management and all earlier permissions.
Read & Execute	This permission enables you to authorize the user to traverse the folders from a root folder down. It also enables the user to read the files and execute applications in the folder under management and all subfolders.
Read	This permission is the first that provides access to the folder's contents. Without this permission, the user would get the dreaded `Access Denied` message. This permission enables the user to see ownership, permissions, and file attributes. All Write permissions are grayed out.
Write	This permission enables you to authorize the user to create files and folders in the folder. It also gives the user the capability to change file attributes and view ownership and permissions.
List Folder Contents	This permission enables the user to see files and subfolders in the folder under management.
Special Permissions	This permission's check box is not selectable until special or advanced permissions are enabled. Advanced permissions are accessible only by clicking the Advanced button.

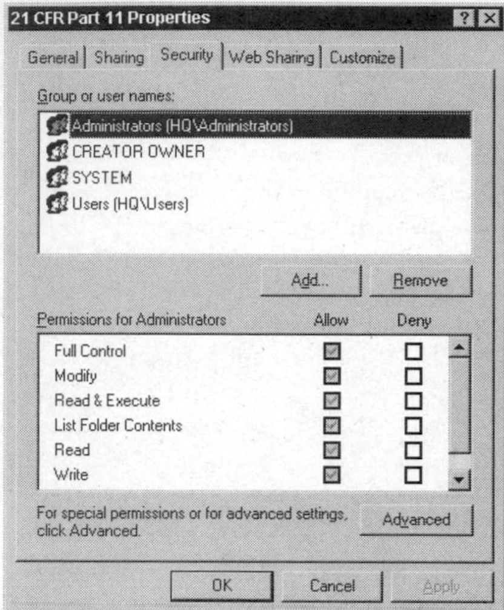

Figure 27-19: The Security tab on the folder's Properties dialog box.

Table 27-6 lists the permissions that are possible to assign on files.

Table 27-6: File Permissions

Permission	***Purpose***
Full Control	This permission enables the user to take ownership and perform all the actions of the following permissions.
Modify	This permission permits the user to delete and perform all the actions permitted by the previous permissions.
Read & Execute	This permission permits the user to run applications and also applies the Read permissions to the file.
Read	This permission permits the user to read the files and view their attributes, ownership, and permissions.
Write	This permission permits the user to change the files' contents and attributes and to view ownership and permissions.
Special Permissions	This permission's check box is not selectable until special or advanced permissions are enabled. Advanced permissions are accessible only by clicking the Advanced button.

NTFS 5.0 also enables you to assign advanced versions of the permissions that we describe in the preceding tables. These permissions are more specific versions of the general permissions. In other words, they enable you through the extended selection lists accessible from the Advanced button to pinpoint the level of access that you want to provide to the user, such as *only* read a file or *only* execute an application . . . as opposed to the Read and Execute options in the basic permissions.

To assign Advanced permissions, click the Advanced button on the Security page of the file or folders Properties dialog box; then click the Edit button on the dialog box that appears. This launches the Advanced Security Settings dialog box, as shown in Figure 27-20.

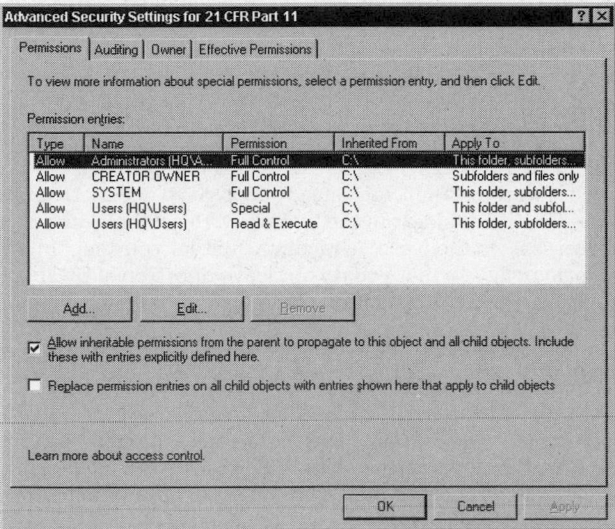

Figure 27-20: The Advanced Security Settings dialog box for a folder.

You can deny permissions at any time by selecting the Deny check box to the right of the permission. If you deny Full Control, you effectively deny all other permissions as well.

The Permission list on the Security tab and in the Advanced Security Settings dialog box is an abstraction of the Access Control List (ACL) that is maintained by the file system. The ACL can be accessed directly — but only programmatically.

Permissions Attributes

You can assign multiple permission types to users, groups, and computer accounts for tighter control of access to folders and files. As with shares, you need to understand the attributes of permissions to more effectively achieve your objectives. Permissions possess the following attributes:

- ✦ Permissions are cumulative. A user's total authority is the sum of all permissions granted to him over the use or access of an object. If, on a given collection of files, a user is granted Read permission by virtue of his or her membership in the Readers Group, for example, and is a member of an Application Access Group that bestows the Execute permission on the same set of files, the user's total access is Read and Execute.
- ✦ The Deny permission option overrides any and all permissions granted to a user for the specific object. If a user has Full Control of an object by virtue of membership in several groups, assigning him the Deny option in only one group locks that user out of the file or folder completely.

✦ File permissions are *not* stronger than folder permissions. Any file permission bestowed to a user does not override or supercede any permission granted at the folder level. In other words, if you give a user access to a file (even Full Control) but deny the user access at the folder level, the user cannot access the file. This mechanism prevents the user from connecting to the file from the command line by specifying a UNC path to the file.

Inheritance

The permissions that you assign to a given folder or file can, by default, propagate down to the child folders and files. In other words, if the Everyone group is given access to a folder and inheritance is turned on for all the subfolders in the hierarchy, the subfolders also enable the Everyone group to have access, as do the files. We recommend that you keep inheritance turned off by default or via domain policy so that you do not leave doors open by acts of omission or by failure to keep an eye on the propagation chain reaction.

Of course, the inheritance option is useful if you need to build a huge folder hierarchy and automatically provide one group with specific permission access to the entire folder and file namespace.

To prevent or enable permission inheritance, simply deselect or select the Allow Inheritable Permissions option on the Advanced Security Settings dialog box (accessed by clicking the Advanced button on the file or folder's Properties dialog box. You are prompted to Copy or Remove the inherited permissions every time that you elect to deselect the check box. By turning inheritance off for a folder, you make the folder the new parent, and if subfolders have inheritance turned on, they become children.

In the section "Common Sense Strategies for Sharing Folders," earlier in this chapter, where we advised you to remove the Everyone group from the volume's Group or User names list, we made special note to ensure that you kept the Reset Permissions on All Child Objects and Enable Propagation of Inheritable Permissions check box selected. The option can be selected from any level in the folder hierarchy. The option brings back not-too-fond memories of the Replace Permissions on Subfolders and Files option on NT 4.0 and earlier versions of NTFS.

By running this option, you are replacing — not merging — the permissions on all child folders and files on the volume. So any permissions applied to subfolders and files are lost. If that is not your desired end, you could end up losing weeks of work restoring permissions so that users and applications can operate. And the situation gets worse: This action cannot be undone. You can only rebuild what you had from backups and documentation. Proceed with care here, as the wrong step could cost you dearly.

Taking Ownership

Administrators, owners, or users with Full Control of an object can set up a user or a group to take ownership of the object. This is done by first admitting the user or group to the *access control list* (*ACL*), via the Group or User names list, and selecting the Take Ownership check box on the Permission Entries list, as described in the section "The Permission Types," earlier in this chapter, or by giving the potential owner Full Control (which is a security risk). See Figure 27-21.

Administrators, as long as they inherit their power from an administrator's group, can take ownership of objects regardless of the permissions in the object's ACL.

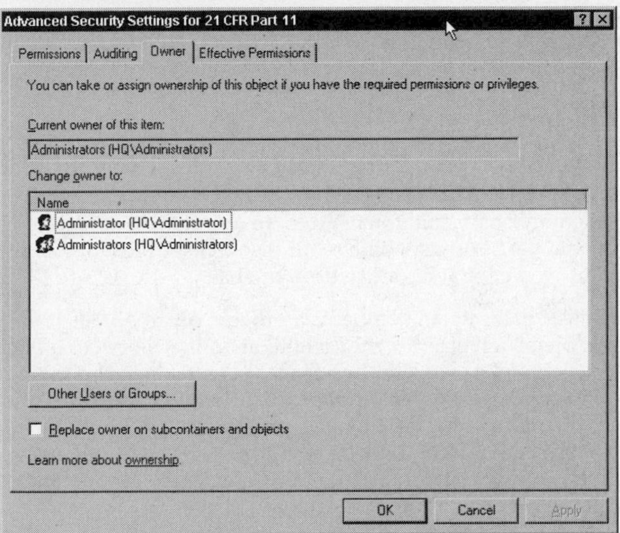

Figure 27-21: The Owner tab on the Advanced Security Settings dialog box.

To take ownership of the object, follow these steps:

1. Open to the Security tab of the Properties dialog box for the object in question. (See the section "The Permission Types," earlier in this chapter.) Click the Advanced button and then select the Owner tab from the Advanced Security Settings dialog box.

2. Select the Replace Owner on Subcontainers and Objects check box to take ownership of all child subfolders and files contained by the parent folder.

3. In the Change Owner To list box, select the User or Group account name that is taking ownership and click Apply.

Copying and Moving

Often, you may need to move or copy folders and their contents to other volumes or containers on the network. You cannot do so, even as an administrator, if you do not have ownership or the permission to move or copy the folders. But you can take ownership and then assign yourself the necessary permissions.

Before you move a folder or a file, you should check and document the ownership and rights before the actual copy or move. After you have successfully completed the process, you can reapply any permissions along the way.

The following security behavior applies to copying, moving, and ownership of files and folders:

- ✦ Whenever you copy or move a file or a folder to a container within the same volume or on another volume, the permissions assigned to the object are dropped, and the object and its contents and children inherit the permissions assigned to the destination container.

- ✦ You cannot copy or move a folder or a file to the destination container if the destination container has not given you Write access, regardless of which volume you are moving or copying to.

- The user account that performs the actual copy or move becomes the owner of the objects after they reach their destination; usually that's the administrator.
- Permissions and ownership do not change at the source objects.

Strategies for Managing Permissions

Assigning permissions is not a complex art, but you need to be orderly and consistent about the process. It looks easy, but on a big network with a lot of resources, thousands of users, and mission-critical applications, you cannot afford to drop the ball.

Here's a good example: Every night at a certain company, a process on an AS/400 connects to a share on a Windows network, opens a file, and writes a million dollars worth of business to the file. As soon as the file is closed and saved, another process connects to the same file and performs special functions on the data. What would happen if, by some mistake on the part of the administrator, the permission on that file was changed, and the file could not be opened? A million dollars worth of business could potentially be lost. In our case, we had alerts on the AS/400 that raised an alarm if the process failed. And the only damage done was that the administrator was beeped at three in the morning to fix the problem.

Consider the following guidelines in working permissions:

- Create groups for access to folders and files and assign them only the permissions required to work on the files. If the group needs only the Read permission on the file, assign only Read permission to that group.
- Have team leaders or department heads formally request all permission levels for their teams or departments, and have them put the requests in writing. Then assign rights only according to the written request. That way, should a user accidentally delete a file, the damage is not on your head. All requests for permissions should be channeled through the help or support desk, where a case can be opened specifically for the purpose.
- Document everything that you do on a permissions case. You always have something to refer back to if problems crop up later. Often, you get a request to restore a folder and permissions back to the way that they were previously because of some problem resulting from the change. Folders and files get deleted, and the backups do not always contain the latest permissions work performed on the object. Make sure that your documentation is clear and concise so that other administrators or support-desk staffers can handle the case.
- Use the Deny option only if implicitly denying access to a user or group is essential or urgent. Opt instead to remove a user from a group or remove the group from access control.
- Assign permissions on a folder-by-folder or file-by-file basis. Make sure that the permission requestor opens a separate support case for each permission required on a folder or a file.
- Avoid propagation where at all possible. In other words, don't simply set permissions for a root or parent folder and then leave all subfolders exposed to the inherited permissions. By the same token, don't just add a group to the parent folder if they specifically need access to only a single subfolder or file. (Prevention is better than a cure in dealing with deleted or damaged files.)

- In today's world of viruses and denial-of-service attacks, assigning only Read and Execute permissions to application folders or files makes sense (see Chapter 3). Doing so prevents any hostile attempt to delete or infect files in a folder or to replace the file with a Trojan horse.
- In working with public data folders, assign the Read and Execute permissions and the Write permission to the group requiring access to existing files. This practice enables the group to read or execute a file and to save changes whenever necessary. Adding the built-in Creator Owner principal to the folder and assigning it Full Control is a good and safe practice. Users who create their own files can thus safely perform all necessary functions on the file and even delete it, if need be.
- Assigning permissions to files at every corner can be tedious. Classifying files according to their level of importance and application and then grouping them in folders only makes sense. Doing so enables you to assign permissions to the folders and not to each file.

For most enterprise work environments, share and folder and file permissions are sufficient security. If someone steals a server or a hard disk, however, and attempts to access its files from another operating system, that person may gain unfettered access to the data. If the data needs to be protected from such an attack, no NTFS permissions can keep the data safe. You need to encrypt your data, and that can be done in Windows Server 2003 by using the Encrypting File System, as was the case with Windows 2000.

Securing Files by Using the Encrypting File System

Windows Server 2003 adds to the *Encrypting File System* (*EFS*), introduced in Windows 2000. The EFS enables users and administrators to encrypt and protect the file system in situations where the system is subject to unauthorized physical access. The additions, however, have more to do with managing file encryption and recovery than with the employment of stronger file encryption.

The EFS is an ideal agent for data protection in any situation, including that of a server in a small office that typically is not locked in a secure computer room or that of a public place that uses a server to support a transient work force, such as a circuit court or polling station. EFS is invaluable on workstations where hard disks are accessible or on notebooks that are easy pickings for the criminally motivated. A *storage area network* (*SAN*) is also an ideal candidate for EFS, as in an intranet that enables many people to access secure corporate data, such as 401K or similar employee-related information that should not fall into unauthorized hands. EFS provides on-the-fly encryption and decryption, working transparently to the user, just as NTFS compression works behind the scenes without any interaction with the user. Although EFS does not protect the data from unauthorized access across the network, it does secure the data from a disgruntled employee who physically removes the storage device from the network.

NTFS provides a means of protecting data while it is safely tucked in a user's computer or on a server and that computer or server is not subject to a direct hacker attack. But little prevents someone from stealing a computer or a removable storage device and gaining access to the device by cracking the password or using one of the tools that are floating around the Internet — or are available commercially — that enables access to NTFS volumes while bypassing NTFS security. The only viable solution, other than using only internal devices and wrapping hefty chains around your computers, is to use encryption.

Encryption on individual files is not always an answer either. Many applications create temporary files as you work with a document, and these temporary files are not encrypted unless you use an encryption system that automatically encrypts everything in the folder where the temporary files are created. EFS addresses this potential problem.

EFS supports encryption of folders and files on NTFS volumes but does not support encryption on FAT volumes. (Because encryption is integrated with the NTFS, it relies on NTFS reparse points and an installable NTFS filter.) You can use encryption on folders and files stored locally as well as on remote servers. Encryption, however, doesn't protect file data as it moves from the remote server to your workstation across the network (or vice-versa), because the network traffic is unencrypted. If you need to ensure security throughout the entire process, use IPSec to encrypt network traffic (see Chapters 3 and 18).

Windows Server 2003 warns you that a file to be moved or copied from one encrypted file system to another is going to be decrypted. You had no such warning in Windows 2000, and as a result, many files were inadvertently left insecure.

How EFS works

EFS employs *public-key encryption* and the *CryptoAPI* architecture to encrypt and protect files. Windows 2003 Server encrypts each file with a unique, randomly generated file-encryption key. These keys are independent of the user's public/private-key pair. By using a different key for each file, Windows 2003 Server provides a very secure encryption method that is difficult to compromise at all, much less on a widespread basis (decrypting an entire volume of encrypted files, for example). The current implementation of EFS uses the *Data Encryption Standard X* (*DESX*), which provides 128-bit encryption, until recently available in Windows 2000 only in North America (see Chapter 3).

As an administrator, you need to do very little, if anything, to enable users to encrypt and decrypt files. EFS automatically creates a public-key pair and a file-encryption certificate for a user the first time the user attempts to encrypt a file. This eliminates the need for you to create a certificate or key pair for each user who needs or wants to use EFS. The users' encryption certificates and keys are stored in their profiles, so they are available each time that a user logs on.

Whenever a user encrypts a file, EFS automatically generates a *bulk symmetric encryption key* and then encrypts the file by using the bulk encryption key. EFS then uses the user's public key to encrypt the bulk encryption key. (The user's key is called a *File Encryption Key,* or *FEK.*) EFS stores the FEK for an encrypted file within an attribute called the *Data Decryption Field* (*DDF*) in the file itself. In addition, EFS also encrypts the bulk encryption key by using the recovery agent's public key. This FEK is stored in the *Data Recovery Field* (*DRF*) of the file. The DRF can contain data for multiple recovery agents. Each time that EFS saves the file, it generates a new DRF by using the current recovery-agent list, which is based on the recovery policy (explained in the following section). Figure 27-22 shows the encryption process.

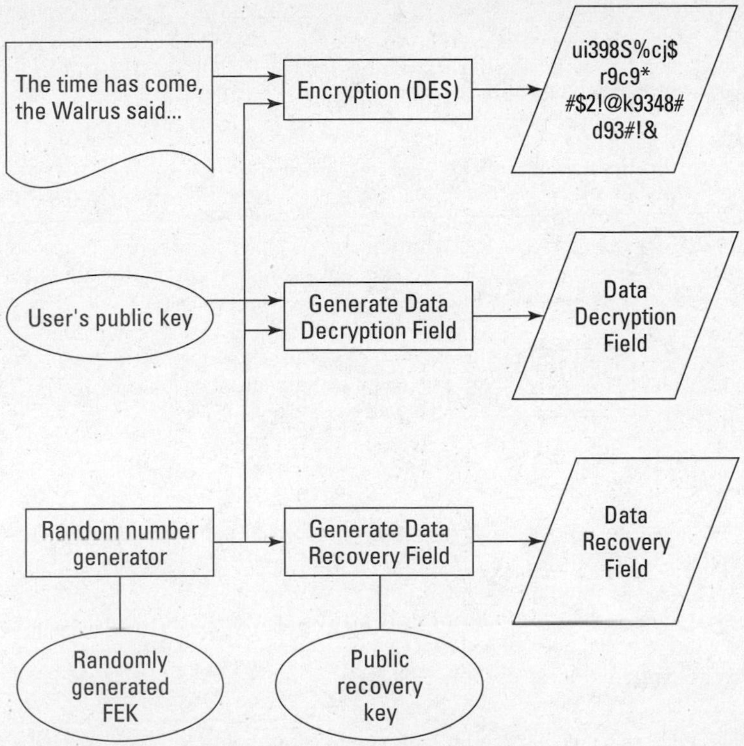

Figure 27-22: The encryption process used by EFS.

Encryption and decryption happens transparently to the user as the file is read from and written to the disk. So, a user can simply open an encrypted document by using the document's parent application without any special procedures. The application doesn't need to be EFS-aware because the encryption/decryption happens at the file-system level, independent of the application. EFS uses the private portion of the user's key pair to decrypt the FEK and enable the user to view the data. If the user doesn't supply the necessary private key required by the file (which happens automatically through the user's certificate store), the user receives an `Access Denied` message. Figure 27-23 shows the decryption process.

Note

EFS does not require an entire file to be decrypted as it is being read. Instead, decryption occurs on a block-by-block basis, so only those portions of the file actually read are decrypted. As a result, EFS is extremely fast, and overhead is not noticeable in accessing encrypted files.

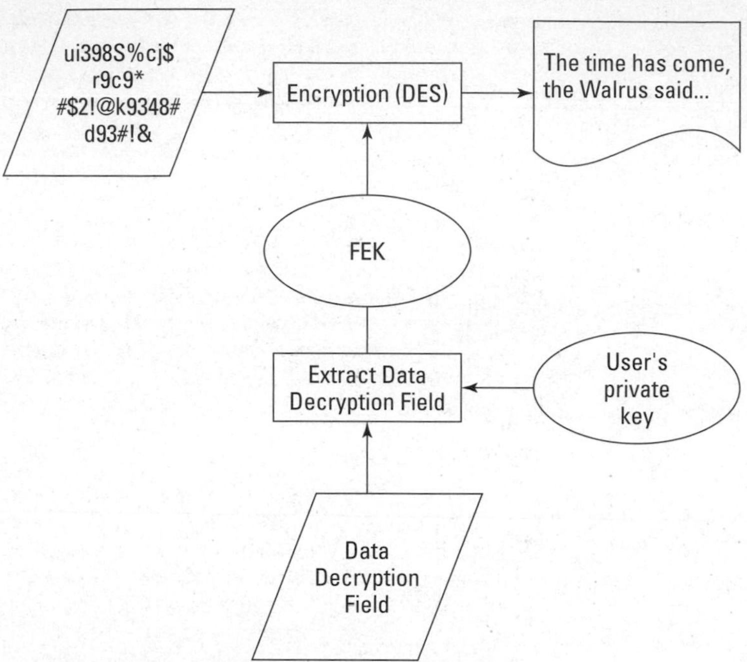

Figure 27-23: The decryption process used by EFS.

EFS under Windows 2000 was not designed to enable encrypted data to be easily shared among users; you could, however, enable multiple users to access and work with encrypted folders and files. The users simply needed to share the same encryption keys. For more information, see the section "Sharing Encrypted Data," later in this chapter. Windows Server 2003 makes encrypted folder and file sharing a lot easier.

Recoverability and the encryption recovery policy

In most situations, you want the capability to recover encrypted data if a user leaves the organization or loses his encryption certificate and keys. EFS ensures recoverability of encrypted files by administrators by requiring that at least one data-recovery key be present on the system. These recovery keys enable a *recovery agent* who has the necessary public key to decrypt a file's FEK and, thereby, decrypt a file. The recovery key doesn't enable the recovery agent to retrieve any other information such as the user's private key, ensuring continued security for the user (if still gainfully employed) while still enabling the agent to recover data.

On Windows 2000/Windows Server 2003 domains, the Domain Administrators account is configured automatically as the recovery agent in a domain. The local Administrator account is defined as the recovery agent on standalone computers and those participating in a workgroup. The recovery process is identical to the decryption process shown in Figure 27-23, except that the EFS uses the recovery agent's private key instead of the user's private key to decrypt the data.

You can define an encryption recovery policy at the domain level and enforce that policy on all computers in the domain through domain/group policies. Administrators can delegate recovery policies to specific security-administration accounts through the delegation features inherent in Active Directory (AD). This capability enables administrators to delegate authority for encrypted data recovery to one or more security administrators. EFS also enables multiple recovery-key configurations, which provides redundancy and greater flexibility in configuring and implementing the encryption policy.

If you have no domain (such as in a standalone, workgroup, or home-office environment), EFS automatically creates recovery keys and saves them as machine keys, enabling the local Administrator account to perform encryption recovery.

The EFS recovery policy is part of the domain security policy for computers participating in a domain and part of the local security policy for computers in a workgroup or for standalone computers. In each case, the security policy is applied through `Security Settings\Public Key Policies\Encrypted Data Recovery Agents`. You can use the Local Security Policy or Domain Security Policy MMC consoles, as appropriate, to add and configure recovery agents and their certificates. This includes importing and exporting certificates. By implementing the recovery policy in the system security policy, Windows 2003 Server provides centralized replication, enforcement, and caching of the policy. Because the user's security credentials are cached, the user can continue to work with encrypted files even if his system is not currently connected to the network.

Note See the section "Configuring and Using a Recovery Policy," later in this chapter, for information on configuring the security policy and performing recovery operations.

Windows Server 2003 no longer requires that the recovery be in effect on the domain to decrypt files. Although the policy is configured for standalone computers as part of local policy, the recovery on a Windows Server 2003 domain is configured as needed at the site, domain, and OU level; it can also be configured at the individual computer level. The policy applies to all Windows 2000, XP, and Windows Server 2003 computers that are within a defined scope of the policy. The recovery certificates are issued by a *Certificate Authority* (*CA*) using the Certificates console.

Using EFS

Because EFS is integrated with NTFS 5.0 and installed automatically, no installation or configuration is required for a user to begin encrypting folders and files. As long as a recovery agent is defined, the user can encrypt files. If no recovery agent is defined, EFS is disabled. Because Windows Server 2003 by default creates the recovery certificate and installs it in the domain or local security policy, as appropriate to the system, users can begin using encryption with Windows Server 2003 right out of the box.

Although you can encrypt individual files, applying encryption on a folder-by-folder basis (or in cases requiring extreme security, on a volume-by-volume basis) is best. The main reason for not applying encryption to individual files is that many programs create temporary files as you work with a document (Microsoft Word being a good example), and EFS does not automatically encrypt these temporary files. To do so, the application would need to be EFS-aware and notify the operating system that the temporary file needs to be encrypted. By encrypting a folder, you effectively encrypt the contents of the folder. As you create new files in the folder (including automatically created temporary files), those new files are encrypted and enjoy the same security as the other files in the folder.

If you encrypt a folder, you aren't actually encrypting the NTFS field that defines the folder but rather are setting the folder's encryption attribute. EFS uses this attribute to determine how to handle file creation and modification operations in the folder.

Recovery policy

The following three types of recovery policy can be defined in the domain by administrators:

✦ **Recovery-agent policy:** This is the default recovery policy. As soon as an administrator adds one or more recovery agents, the recovery-agent policy is in effect. These agents have the responsibility of recovering the encrypted data within the scope of their administration.

✦ **Empty-recovery policy:** This policy comes into effect if an administrator deletes all the recovery agents and their public-key certificates. Such a policy actually means that no policy exists. For Windows 2000 and Windows Server 2003 servers on the domain, this requires EFS to be disabled.

✦ **No-recovery policy:** If an administrator deletes all the private keys associated with recovery policy, a no-recovery policy is in effect. Recovery of data, therefore, is not possible because you have no way to activate a recovery agent. Depending on the environment, this may be a desirable situation.

Encrypting and decrypting through Windows Explorer

Encrypting a folder or file is easy. Just right-click the object and choose Properties from the pop-up menu to display its property page. On the object's General property page, click Advanced to open the object's Advanced Attributes dialog box (see Figure 27-24). Select the Encrypt Contents to Secure Data check box, click OK, and then click OK again to close the object's property sheet.

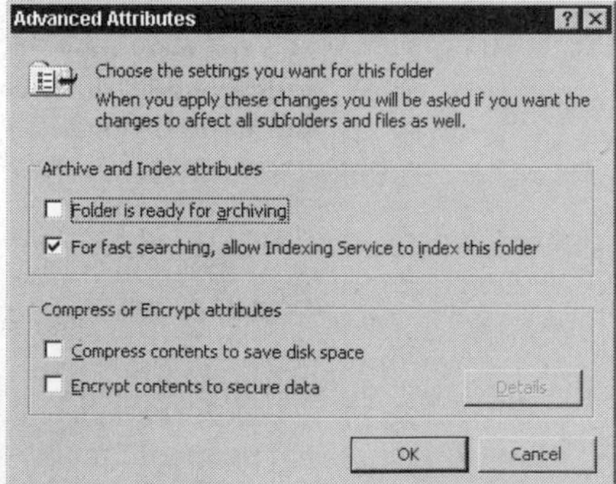

Figure 27-24: The Advanced Attributes dialog box.

NTFS compression and encryption are mutually exclusive, so encryption is not supported for compressed folders or files or vice-versa. If you enable encryption of a compressed folder or file, the file is decompressed. If you compress an encrypted folder or file, it is decrypted. This decryption doesn't happen automatically per se, but if you select the Compress Contents to Save Disk Space check box on the Advanced Attributes dialog box, the Encrypt Contents to Secure Data option is automatically deselected.

If you encrypt a folder, Windows Server 2003 displays the Confirm Attribute Changes dialog box, as shown in Figure 27-25. If you select Apply Changes to this Folder Only, EFS encrypts the folder but not any of its contents, including subfolders or files. Any new objects that you create in the folder, however, are encrypted. If instead you choose Apply Changes to this Folder, Subfolders, and Files, EFS encrypts not only the folder, but also all its child objects.

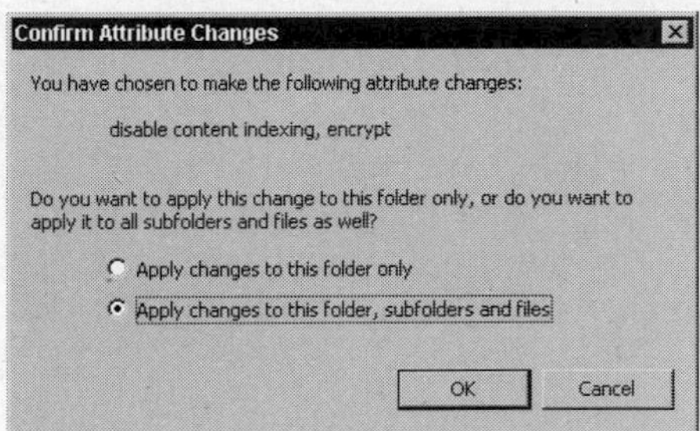

Figure 27-25: The Confirm Attribute Changes dialog box.

Encrypting and decrypting by using the command prompt

If you work substantially in a command console or need to integrate encryption processes in batch files, you can use the `CIPHER` command to encrypt and decrypt folders and files. Following is the syntax for the command:

```
CIPHER [/E | /D] [/S:directory] [/A] [/I] [/F] [/Q] [/H] [pathname [...]]
CIPHER /K
CIPHER /R:filename
CIPHER /U [/N]
CIPHER /W:directory
CIPHER /X[:efsfile] [filename]
```

The following list summarizes the command options for `CIPHER`:

- ✦ `/E`: Encrypts the specified folders. New files added are encrypted.
- ✦ `/D`: Decrypts the specified folders. New files are not encrypted; does not affect existing encrypted child objects.
- ✦ `/S`: Performs the specified operation on folders in the given directory and all subfolders.
- ✦ `/A`: Performs the specified operation for files as well as folders.
- ✦ `/I`: Continues the specified operation even if errors occur. By default, `CIPHER` stops whenever an error is encountered.
- ✦ `/F`: Forces the encryption operation on all specified objects, including those already encrypted. Objects already encrypted are skipped by default.
- ✦ `/Q`: Reports only essential information.
- ✦ `/H`: Displays files with hidden or system attributes; these files are omitted by default.
- ✦ `/K`: Creates a new file-encryption key for the user who is running `CIPHER`. All the other options are ignored if this option is used.

- `/N`: Prevents keys from being updated. It works with the `/U` option
- `/R`: Generates an EFS recovery-agent key and associated certificate and then writes the files to a PFX file (which contains certificates and private key information) and CER files, which contain only certificate information. The administrator then adds the contents of the CER file to the EFS recovery policy to create a recovery agent for users. The PFX file is then imported to recover individual files.
- `/U`: Used to affect all the encrypted files on a volume to update user file-encryption keys and recovery-agent keys if they are changed.
- `/W`: Wipes data off volumes.
- `/X`: Used for backing up EFS certificates.
- `pathname`: Specifies a file, or directory.

If used without parameters, `CIPHER` displays the encryption state of the current directory and any files contained in the folder. You can use multiple directory names and wildcards. Use spaces between multiple parameters.

Copying, moving, or renaming encrypted files

As with compression, a folder's encryption attribute also has an effect on the files that you copy or move between encrypted and nonencrypted folders or files and folders that you rename. The following list summarizes the effect of the encryption attribute in copying, moving, and renaming objects:

- **Copying and moving encrypted folders or files to unencrypted folders (NTFS volumes):** The copies are encrypted regardless of the encryption attribute of the destination folder. If you are copying to another computer, the objects are encrypted only if the destination computer permits encryption. In a domain environment, the destination computer must be trusted for delegation — remote encryption is not enabled by default.
- **Copying and moving unencrypted folders or files to encrypted folders (NTFS volumes):** The folders or files are encrypted if copied or moved through the Explorer interface. This applies to copies on the same computer and to a remote computer that supports encryption. The `COPY` console command causes the destination file to be encrypted, but the `MOVE` command does not because it simply renames the file.
- **Copying and moving encrypted or unencrypted files to FAT volumes:** Windows displays a prompt indicating that the files cannot be encrypted and gives you the option to copy or move the files anyway, losing encryption. An exception to this is if you use the Backup utility to back up the files to a Backup file (BKF) on a FAT volume. In this case, the file remains encrypted in the backup set.

The `COPY` command used in a command console has been modified to support encryption. You can use the `/D` switch to copy an encrypted file to a non-EFS capable volume, but the file loses its encryption. Following is an example:

```
COPY /D sourcefile destinationfile
```

The `XCOPY` command also supports copying to non-EFS capable volumes. `XCOPY`, however, uses the `/G` switch for this functionality. The syntax is similar to that for the `COPY` command.

If you rename a folder or file, the encryption attribute is unaffected. So you can rename an encrypted folder or file in place, and it remains encrypted. In addition, you can rename a folder or file to a different location (essentially a move operation), and the folder or file remains encrypted, even if it's renamed to an NTFS folder that is not encrypted.

Accessing encrypted data remotely

To access encrypted data, you must have the necessary security certificate and key. If you're logging on from the computer where you encrypted the files, you have that certificate and associated private key in your local certificate store, provided you log on using the same account as when you encrypted the files. To access the encrypted data remotely from another computer, you must do one of two things: Use a roaming profile or import the certificate to the computer. If you use a roaming profile, your security certificates follow your logon, making them available regardless of your logon location.

If you're not using a roaming profile, you need to import the certificate that you used when the files were encrypted. You also can share a security certificate to enable multiple users to access the same set of encrypted folders and files. The following section explains how to share a security certificate.

Sharing encrypted data

To use files on a computer other than the one where they were encrypted, you must have the required certificate and its associated private key on the computer at which you're logged on. This is true whether you're accessing data that you or someone else encrypted. So you need to install the certificate and its associated key on your computer. You do so by using the Certificate Manager, which you can load as a snap-in for the MMC. First, you export the certificate and its key on the computer where the files were encrypted, and then you import the key to the other computer(s) where you want to access those files.

Using certificate services to share encrypted data requires you to install a *public key infrastructure* (*PKI*) and establish a Windows 2000 or Windows Server 2003 network as a local or private Certificate Authority (CA). We introduce Windows PKI in Chapter 3.

To export the certificate and key, follow these steps:

1. Log on with the account that was used to encrypt the files and then open the Certificates MMC console snap-in focused on the user account.
2. Open the Personal folder and then open the Certificates folder and locate the certificate issued for EFS. (Select the Intended Purpose column for Encrypting File System.) This is shown in Figure 27-26.

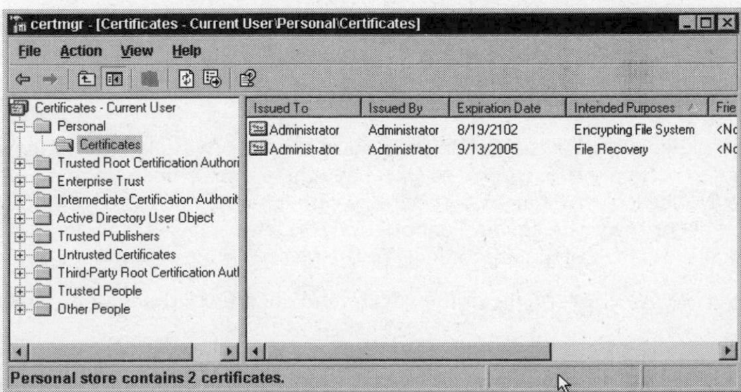

Figure 27-26: The Certificates console.

3. Right-click the certificate in the right-hand panel and choose All Tasks ⇨ Export from the pop-up menu to start the Certificate Export Wizard.
4. In the wizard, choose the Export option to export the private key and click Next.
5. The default PKCS format option should be automatically selected on the next screen of the wizard; if not, select it (see Figure 27-27). Choose options from the wizard based on the following list and then click Next again:
   - **Include All Certificates in the Certification Path if Possible:** Select this option if you need to export multiple certificates from the selected store. In most cases, you do not need to select this option, as you probably have only one EFS certificate in your personal store.
   - **Enable Strong Protection (Requires IE 5.0, NT 4.0 SP4 or Above):** This option enables *iteration count,* which provides stronger security. This option is compatible with Internet Explorer 5.0 and NT 4.0 Service Pack 4 or higher. If you are exporting the key to systems that don't fit those criteria, deselect this option.
   - **Delete the Private Key if the Export Is Successful:** This option, if selected, deletes the private key associated with the certificate. In most cases, you probably do not want to delete the private key so that you can continue to use the certificate on the originating system.

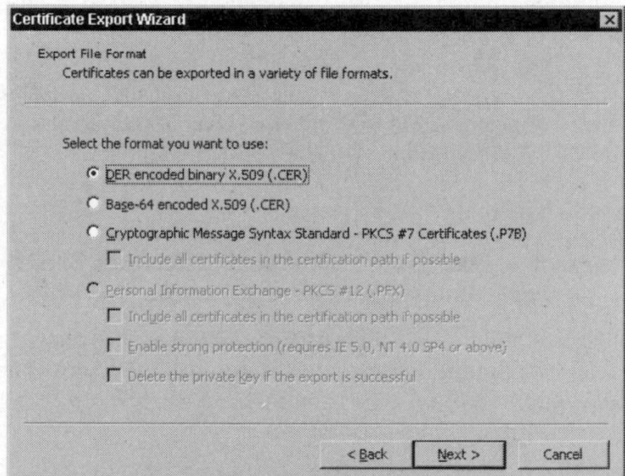

Figure 27-27: Use the Certificate Export Wizard to export the EFS certificate to other computers.

6. Specify and confirm a password in the wizard for the private key being exported. Doing so ensures that only those persons who have the password can Import and use the certificate. Notice that you can export the key with a blank password, but doing so reduces security for the key and enables anyone with access to the export file to import and use the certificate to decrypt the files.
7. Specify a file name for the file in the wizard and click Next; then click Finish to create the file.

After you have exported the certificate file, you need to import the file on the computer(s) and accounts from which you want to access the encrypted files. Follow these steps to import the certificate:

1. Log on at the computer where you want to use the certificate, or in the case of a roaming profile, simply log on at any computer in the domain, using the account through which you want to access the encrypted data.

2. Open the Certificate Manager MMC console; then open the Personal folder.

3. Right-click the Personal folder and choose All Tasks ➪ Import from the pop-up menu to start the Certificate Import Wizard.

4. Within the wizard, locate the file created in the preceding steps and click Next to display the File to Import screen of the wizard, as shown in Figure 27-28.

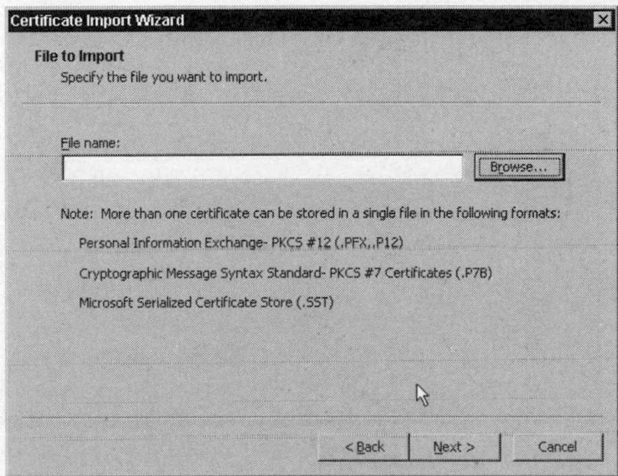

Figure 27-28: The File to Import screen of the Certificate Import Wizard enables you to search for the file to import by clicking Browse.

5. After you're prompted, specify the password for the private key in the certificate; then select options based on the following list:

   - **Enable Strong Private Key Protection:** Select this option if you want Windows Server 2003 to prompt you each time that the private key is used by an application. This helps you track when the key is used.

   - **Mark the Private Key as Exportable:** Select this option if you want the capability to export the key in the future. If you don't select this option, you can't export the key.

6. Specify that you want to place the certificate in the Personal store and follow the prompts to complete the wizard and the import process.

You can provide the exported certificate to other users who need to access the encrypted data. You can distribute the file as you would any other, such as by e-mail attachment or by placing the file in a network share. Because both methods make the file publicly available, you should make sure that you use a password in exporting the certificate and give the password only to those users who need to import and use the certificate.

Encrypting files for multiple users

After files are encrypted, you can share the files by using the new file-sharing feature of Windows Server 2003. First, encrypt the files as described in the preceding section and then click the Details button on the Advanced Attributes dialog box to add users to the encrypted file. The user is added only if he has a valid EFS certificate.

You cannot share a file until it is encrypted, and the Details button is enabled only after you open the Advanced Attributes dialog box again. This is shown in Figure 27-29.

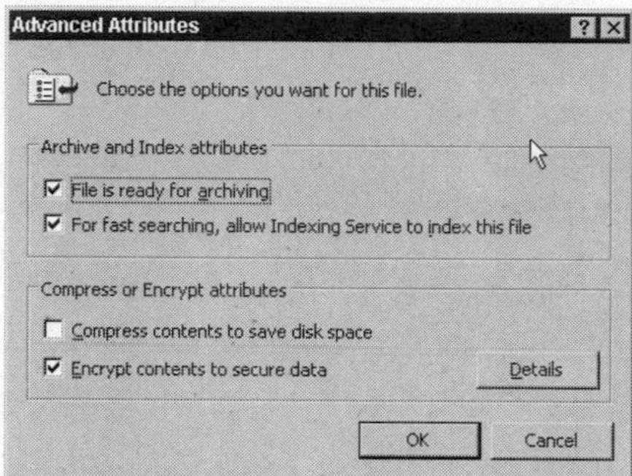

Figure 27-29: The Advanced Attributes dialog box, ready for sharing EFS files.

You are now ready to add users. To do so, follow these steps:

1. Click Details, and the Encryption Details dialog box shown in Figure 27-30 opens. This dialog box shows existing users and the certificates cached in the Other People and Trusted People certificate stores on the local machine. The dialog box enables you to add users found in Active Directory as well.

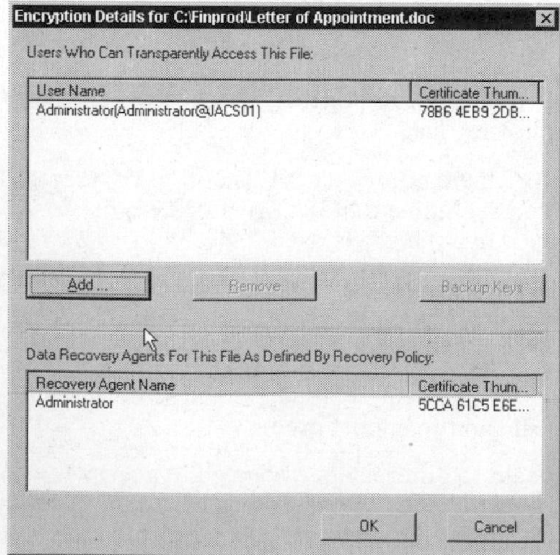

Figure 27-30: The Encryption Details dialog box for adding users.

2. To add new users, click the Add button. The Select User dialog box, as shown in Figure 27-31 opens, displaying the users who can be added from the local machine. To find a user in Active Directory, click the Find User button.

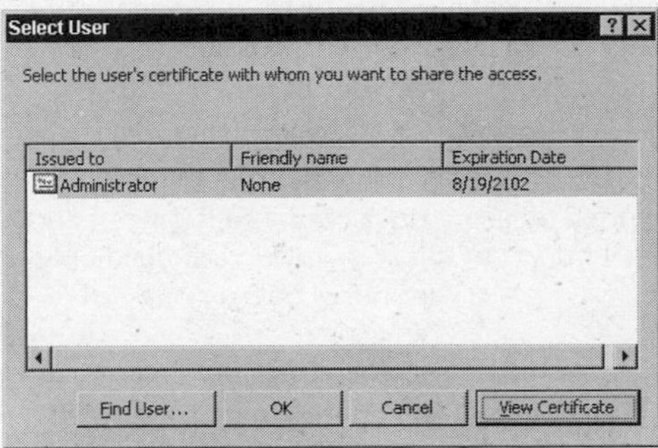

Figure 27-31: The Select User dialog box for adding more users to the encrypted file.

3. From the Select Users dialog box, you can choose to view a certificate. Click the View Certificate button and the certificate appears on-screen, as shown in Figure 27-32. Click the Details tab to view data concerning the key, as shown in the figure.

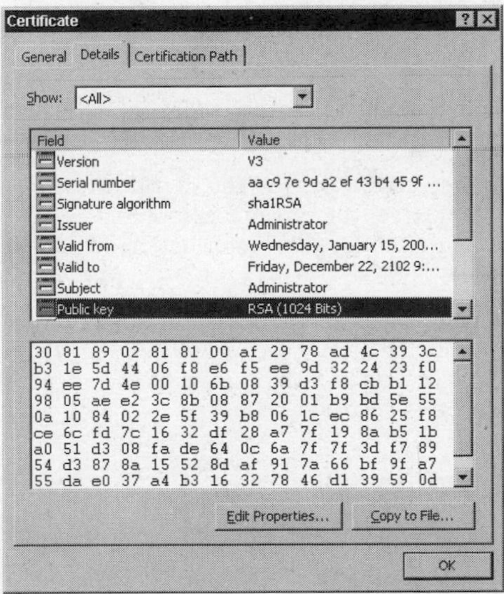

Figure 27-32: Viewing the user's Certificate details.

You cannot add groups of users to encrypted files. And the EFS header for a file has a limit or 256K for metadata. You can, however, add 800 users to the encrypted file.

Backing up and recovering encrypted data

The Windows 2003 Server Backup program can back up and restore files for which the backup operator (or account) doesn't have adequate permissions to actually view the data. The same is true for encrypted data. Backup can back up and restore encrypted data regardless of whether the backup account has the EFS certificate necessary to decrypt the data. The backup and restore operations also have no effect on the encryption state of the files — the files remain encrypted and secure.

You can also back up directly from the command line by using the /X parameter, as described in the section "Encrypting and Decrypting by using the Command Prompt," earlier in this chapter, or by clicking the Backup Keys button in the Encryption Details dialog box (refer to Figure 27-30).

Note

Even if encrypted files are backed up to media that doesn't support encryption (such as FAT volumes or floppies), Backup maintains the encryption on the files. If an unauthorized user gains access to the backup set and restores it—whether to FAT or NTFS volumes—the encrypted data is not restored. Backup creates the target files, but the files are empty.

Situations may arise where you need to recover encrypted data as a recovery agent. A user who has encrypted data on his computer may leave the organization, for example, or lose his certificate. In this situation, any recovery agent who has the appropriate recovery certificate, which Windows Server 2003 creates automatically, can recover the encrypted data.

Follow these steps to restore encrypted files:

1. Back up the encrypted files to a BKF file on a floppy disk or hard disk accessible from the recovery agent's computer.
2. Log on to the recovery agent's computer and restore the files from the backup set to a secure NTFS folder.
3. If you don't already have the required certificate, use the Certificates console to import the recovery key and certificate to the recovery agent's computer. (See the section "Sharing encrypted data," earlier in this chapter, for information on how to open the Certificates console).
4. Open the property sheet for each file and deselect the encryption option to turn off the file's encryption attribute (decrypting the file). You can now send the decrypted files to any user who needs them. If the data needs to be re-encrypted, do so by using a certificate shared by those users who need to access the data.

Configuring and using a recovery policy

EFS requires that a recovery agent be designated before encryption can occur. On a standalone computer or on those in a workgroup, the local Administrator account is designated as a recovery agent by default, and the appropriate recovery key is placed in the Administrator's personal certificate store. In a domain, the Domain Administrator account is designated as the default recovery agent. You can continue to use the default recovery agents, if you want, or modify the recovery policy to accommodate specific security needs, such as redefining the role of recovery agents within the domain or disabling EFS on certain computers. The following sections examine several administrative issues related to configuring and using a recovery policy.

Securing the default recovery key – workgroup/standalone computer

At the initial logon with the Administrator account on a standalone computer or a computer in a workgroup, Windows Server 2003 creates a default recovery policy on the computer that makes the local Administrator account the recovery agent for EFS. Windows Server 2003 does so by creating a recovery certificate for the administrator and placing it in the administrator's personal store.

In some situations, you may want to secure the local recovery key to prevent the local administrator account from being used to recover encrypted data. You may instead want to delegate this capability to a specific user. To secure the recovery key, you need to export the key to a file and then remove the certificate from the local computer. Give the key to the designated recovery agent for import on the agent's computer or place the certificate file in a secure location for import whenever it is needed.

See the section, "Sharing Encrypted Data," earlier in this chapter, if you're not sure how to export the recovery certificate. After you successfully export the certificate, remove the certificate from the local computer to prevent it from being used for EFS recovery.

Securing the default recovery key – domain

You may want to secure the default recovery key in a domain environment as well. You may, for example, want to create a group of administrators specifically for the purpose of EFS recovery rather than enable any domain administrator to perform recovery. To secure the default recovery key in a domain, log on as Administrator on the first domain controller in the domain. Then use the procedure described in the preceding section to export the certificate to a file and delete the certificate from the Domain Administrator account's certificate store.

Obtaining a file-recovery certificate

If you are using the default recovery policy in a domain, requesting recovery certificates isn't necessary because the necessary certificates are already in place in the Domain Administrator's certificate store. If you are instead delegating recovery responsibility to a specific group of users or to individual accounts, you may want to use a Certificate Authority (CA) to generate recovery certificates when requested by recovery agents.

You don't specifically need to use a CA to distribute recovery certificates. You can simply export the default domain-recovery certificate from the Domain Administrator's certificate store and then give the certificate to individual users designated as recovery agents for import on their computers. Using multiple certificates, however, can increase security by not putting all your recovery eggs in one basket. Instead, you can rely on the CA to issue a unique recovery certificate to each recovery agent.

Because this chapter focuses on file systems, it does not cover how to set up a CA. Instead, the following steps explain the general procedure for providing a means for recovery agents to request recovery certificates:

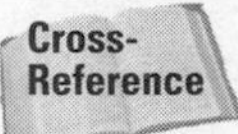

See the *Windows Server 2003 Security Bible* (published by Wiley) for details on how to set up a CA.

1. If no CA is currently installed, log on to a domain controller and run the Add/Remove Programs object in the Control Panel. Install Certificate Services.

2. Create a group called Domain Recovery Agents in the domain and add the appropriate users to the group. Configure policies on the CA to enable the designated users or group to request recovery certificates from the CA. To do so, open the Certificate Authority console, right-click the server, and choose Properties. Click the Security tab, and grant Enroll and Read permission as needed.

3. Have each recovery agent request a recovery certificate from the CA. To start this process, the agents open the Certificates MMC console, right-click their Personal store, and choose All Tasks ➪ Request New Certificate from the pop-up menu to start the Certificate Request Wizard.

4. The wizard automatically locates a CA in the domain, but the agent can choose a specific CA if needed. Through the wizard, the agent specifies that he wants to obtain an EFS Recovery Agent certificate and follows the wizard's prompts to obtain the certificate.

5. If the certificate is not automatically published to the AD, the agent needs to copy the certificate without the private key to a CER file. The domain administrator then uses this file to add the certificate to the domain recovery policy. Use the Certificates console to copy the certificate to the CER file (that is, to export the certificate to the file).

6. The agent exports the certificate to a secure PFX file by using the Certificates console and places the PFX in a secure archive. Then the agent deletes the certificate from the local computer, again through the Certificates console. This ensures that the certificate is applied through the domain policy rather than through the local policy.

Defining a domain-wide recovery policy

After you set up a CA and the designated recovery agents have their certificates exported to CER files, you need to set up the domain-wide recovery policy. You do so by adding the recovery agents and their respective certificates to the default domain policy. The presence of the certificates in the `Security Settings\Public Key Policies\Encrypted Data Recovery Agents` container implicitly defines the domain recovery policy. Follow these steps to define the domain recovery policy:

1. Set up a CA and a Recovery Agents group and have the agents request certificates and export them to CER files.

2. Collect the CER files into a common secure location on your local computer or on the domain controller.

3. Open the Default Domain Security Settings console by choosing Start ➪ Programs ➪ Administrative Tools ➪ Default Domain Security Policy.

4. In the Default Domain Security Settings console, open to Public Key Policies in the left-hand pane.

5. Right-click the Encrypting File System folder in the right-hand pane and choose Add Data Recovery Agent from the pop-up menu to start the Add Recovery Agent Wizard. (This process is shown in Figure 27-33.)

6. Follow the wizard's prompts to complete the installation. Repeat the process to add any additional certificates. (If the certificates are already published in AD, they are listed in the wizard. You can also browse to the folder containing the CER files.)

See Chapter 3 for a discussion of Certificate Authorities and how to set them up in Windows Server 2003.

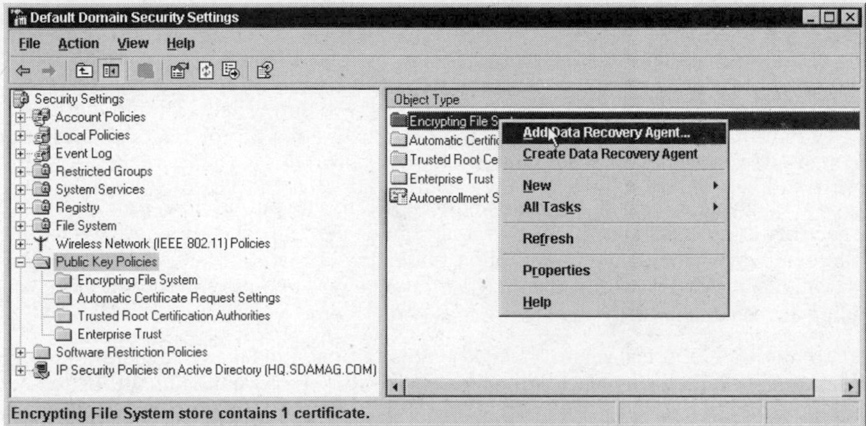

Figure 27-33: The Default Domain Security Settings console.

Defining a recovery policy for an organizational unit

You define a recovery policy for an OU in essentially the same way that you define the domain-wide recovery policy. Rather than working at the domain level, however, you work at the level of the OU. Follow the same steps in the OU as those described in the preceding sections for the domain, adding recovery-agent certificates at the appropriate container in the OU.

Forcing EFS use

In some situations, particularly with notebook computers that contain sensitive data, you may want to force the use of EFS. Because encryption and decryption happens transparently to the user, forcing the use of EFS doesn't affect the user in any way and ensures that, if a notebook is stolen, the files on it are relatively safe from compromise.

To force EFS use, format the drives on the computer by using NTFS. Apply object permissions to folders to prevent the user from storing documents in any folder other than those you configure for encryption. You may restrict the user to only working within the My Documents folder, for example, setting permissions on all other folders to prevent the user from creating documents in them. Then configure My Documents for encryption. Secure the default recovery key if present on the computer by exporting it and then removing the certificate from the computer.

Disabling EFS

In some situations, you may want to disable EFS for specific standalone computers or certain computers in an OU. You can disable EFS by applying an empty recovery policy to the computer — one that contains no recovery certificates and, therefore, disables EFS. If the user tries to create an encrypted folder or file, he receives an `Access Denied` message.

An empty recovery policy is different from no recovery policy in a domain. With no recovery policy in place, the recovery policies defined at higher levels in the AD are inherited by the local computer. If no policy exists at a higher level, the local policy applies.

On a standalone computer or one in a workgroup, simply export the recovery certificate from the local Administrator's personal certificate store and then remove the certificate from the computer (along with any other recovery certificates, if installed). This defines an empty local policy, effectively disabling EFS. In a domain, define the empty policy at the OU level.

Summary

This chapter describes how you share folders to enable users to access shared or network applications and to provide access to shared data. As we note, shares should not be left wide open by admitting the Everyone group to the share with Full Control. Users should be admitted to shares as members of groups and not individually.

Folder and file permissions are the domain of the NTFS. The permissions provide true network security and access control. Permissions can be complex and cumbersome to manage on a large network with many users, groups, and network resources. We stress strong documentation, change-control record keeping, and tracking as common-sense practices in providing access and security to network files and folders.

In situations where physical security of a server is critical, the Encrypting File System (EFS) provides an excellent means of securing files on the server, preventing unauthorized access through file copy to a disk or backup to offline storage. If you intend to implement EFS, keep in mind that encryption and compression are mutually exclusive, so if you're going to use EFS, it must be on an uncompressed volume.

✦ ✦ ✦

Print Services

This chapter covers everything you need to know about the Windows Server 2003 printing service. Despite all of our efforts to create a paperless office, hardcopy and thus printers are not going away. For all intents and purposes, for good or for evil, printers are becoming more sophisticated, cheaper, and easier to use. And Windows Server 2003 isn't helping to conserve trees. In fact, the operating system now includes support for more than 3,000 printers, as well as support for industrial, high-performance, printing supporting devices that would cost a small island.

In addition, technologies such as e-mail and the World Wide Web have not done much to alleviate the need for printers. Instead, they have often succeeded in shifting the burden of hardcopy output from the sender to the receiver. Today, even attorneys e-mail contracts — and then ask you to print them out, sign, and return them.

The network operating system lives and dies by its ability to host access to printers. The print service is the third leg of the "stool" that makes up a network operating system. Without it, a network OS simply falls over. Windows Server has inherited a rich and robust printing service, culled from years of research and development and the experiences of over a hundred million users. It is one of the reasons that Windows 2000 has done so well.

For the most part, installing printers and printing is a no-brainer — that is, until the printer stops printing. So, possessing a good understanding of the elements and components of Windows networking services to troubleshoot is vitally important.

As an administrator, you need to understand the logical environment to troubleshoot printer problems effectively. Therefore, this discussion begins with introducing the components that make printing actually happen and then moves on to installing printers. After the discussion, your properties-and-parameters setup will mean more to you. After you're equipped with the fundamentals, you can explore print-service troubleshooting.

You should understand that the components we discuss now are extremely complex objects and APIs that make up the Windows Server print service. In this book, our purpose is to provide you with enough information to visualize the components, and therefore be able to solve printing problems in Windows Server environments in an effective manner.

✦ ✦ ✦ ✦

In This Chapter

✦ ✦ ✦ ✦

Understanding Windows Server Printer Services

To help you avoid getting hung up on terminology and concepts, look at the printer services from two different points of view—the logical environment, and the physical environment. The logical environment is an abstraction of the physical device that the user sees. It includes the software required to interface to the physical environment. The physical environment represents the devices from which the final printed medium (usually paper) emerges.

Printer Services: The Logical Environment

First of all, printers have no user interface other than a cryptic keypad and a small LCD screen. Their job is to receive data and to convert the data into information that a printer's electronics understands. The printer language or software lays out the page according to specifications in the data and goes about the task of sending this information to the physical parts that print the images onto a hard medium.

So if you're not able to print, and all the logical printer components check out, the only course of action for a faulty printer is to ship it back to the factory or call a service technician (assuming you know little about corona wires, drums, and hoppers). For the most part, you need only know how to turn the printer or plotter on and off, change toner and paper, connect its interface cables, and clean it.

Windows Server, on the other hand, is both printer-aware and user-aware. Its task is to provide a logical printer interface that users can see and managers can manage and troubleshoot, as well as a holistic printer spooling and pooling environment. The logical printer, represented by the `printer` object, its icons, and properties, is representative of the hardware. The printer icon, or the printer share, is all the knowledge workers need to know about printing.

You can install logical printers on your client computers (*local printers*), but most of the time the logical printers are installed on servers dedicated to hosting logical printers (*network printers*).

The following list describes the basic user procedure to connect to and use a printer:

1. Install a logical local or remote printer you have access to (the installation is persistent).

2. After you are connected, you can manage certain properties of the logical printer, such as paper size and layout, bins and trays, resolution and color, number of pages and copies, and so on.

3. You, or at least your users, then print documents and graphics to the logical printer. The action of printing is often called a *job*. The job encapsulates printing instructions for the printer service, telling the logical printer how the job should be printed to the physical printer. When a client application prints a document or image, the application calls the Windows graphic device interface (GDI), which loads the driver for the target printer. (The driver is downloaded from the server if it does not exist on the client machine. On Windows Server clients, the drivers get downloaded with every print job.)

   Using the driver for the target printer, the GDI renders the document in the printer language of the physical printer. After complete, the GDI then calls the local spooler, hands off the job, and closes. At this point, the GDI's work is done, and the client computer sends the job to the print server, via a routing service. The routing service transports the print job over the network using the remote procedure call service, the NetBIOS redirector, or other service (in the case of Unix, OS/2, and so on).

4. After it has received the job from a print router or other interface, the logical printer, also called the printer service or client spooler, loads the necessary driver, which tells it how to interface to the physical printer and how to send it the document. This is done via the services of print providers and processors.

5. The print processor checks the job's data types and alters them or leaves them alone depending on the requirements and the data types received. The print processor ensures the job prints correctly.

6. If the data types call for separator page processing, the jobs are handed off to the separator page processor. The separator page is added to the front of the job.

7. Meanwhile, as the printer administrator, you manage the logical printer's properties (the logical printer is an object), such as where it resides on the network, who has access to it, when they can use it, and so on.

The printer service, illustrated in Figure 28-1, includes several components and concepts, which are described in the following sections.

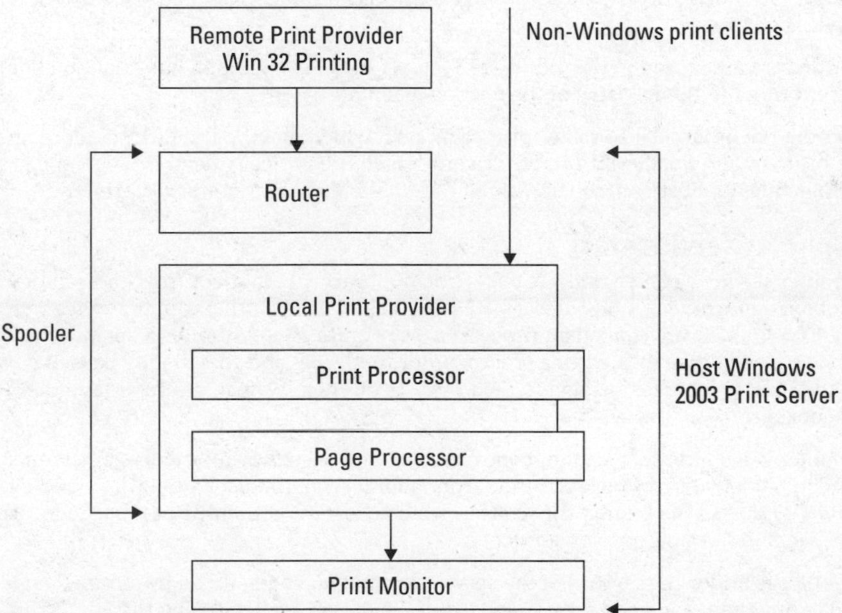

Figure 28-1: The Windows Server Print Service represented as a stack of services.

Print routers

Print routers sit between the client application and the print server (which can also be on the local machine, if printing to the parallel or serial port). The first job of the router is to route print jobs to the correct servers and print services. The second job of the router, once the target server is found, is to make sure the client has the correct driver for the job. The router checks the target server's driver with the client's, and if the client's driver is older or absent, the router updates the driver on the client machine.

Routers are usually Win32 services. In other words, they cater to Windows printing. All other network clients, such as Unix, OS/2, Midrange systems, and the Mac environment, get their jobs to the Windows Server print service via APIs that interface directly with the server service stack.

Printer drivers

Printer drivers are the first variable components you provide when setting up logical printers. They are the software components sent to the user's software to enable it to create print jobs according to the capabilities of the target printers.

Printer drivers are built for specific printers or printer families. For example, you need a printer driver for jobs printed to the Hewlett-Packard LaserJet III printers and different drivers for jobs printed to LaserJet 4 and LaserJet 5 printers, respectively. However, LaserJet 4 and 5 drivers can print standard jobs printed to the LaserJet III printers, but the older LaserJet III printers may not print a complex job generated by the LaserJet 4 or 5 driver.

Printer drivers are installed when you install and configure logical printing devices. You can also select alternative drivers after the logical printer has been installed. This is discussed later in this chapter.

Printer drivers are stored in the `\system32\spool\drivers\` folder. Information about the drivers is stored in the Registry of the hosting machine.

The drivers are grouped into raster printer drivers, which include the PCL standard and dot matrix printers and PostScript printer drivers, which are typically used for high-end graphics and publishing applications, the domain of the Apple/Mac computers and printers.

The spooler service stack

The spooler service is an engine — a collection of libraries — that controls each and every print job on a machine. It's best described as a stack starting with a router service that can receive jobs handed off from client processes (see Figure 28-1). After arriving into the stack, the job is passed down to the print processor for rendering and then finally passed down to the Print Monitor for transmission to the I/O ports on the physical interfaces at either local or remote ports.

The spooler is also the service that controls client and server printer management, installation and administration of logical printers, and more. From the user's point of view, it's the functionality that exists behind the icons to which users send their print jobs. Each Windows Server machine has one spooler service.

The spooler is under the control of the service control manager. It can be stopped and started at any time. You need only shut down the spooler service (using the `net stop spooler` command) to stop all printing services on a machine. The spooler is part of the Win32 subsystem and is never deleted or relocated. It's owned by the local system account, and a number of child processes and services depend on it.

The spooler service is also responsible for client-side printer management. In fact, when you stop the service, the machine can't request or send print jobs to the logical shared printers on a server machine. In other words, the spooler service acts as both a client or server service, as needed.

The spooler service creates the files (spool jobs or files) in the directory where it resides. The service and files are installed by default in the `\winnt\system32\spool\printers` folder. So if your server hosts a large number of print jobs, you should consider redirecting the print jobs to a volume dedicated to servicing printers. Changing the path value in the printer's Registry key does this. The key in question is:

```
HKEY_LOCAL_MACHINE\SYSTEM\CurrentControlSet\Control\Print\Printers
```

And the value is a drive letter and subfolder path, not the UNC path. After the value has changed, stop and restart the print service. You can also set up separate folders for each printer's job, which is discussed next.

The spooler output files

These are the files that are generated by the spooler service (specifically the print provider component) for each job it handles. After the job has been sent to the printer successfully, the spooler files are deleted. The spooler output files consist of two types of files — the spool file and the shadow file. They serve the following purpose:

- ✦ **Spool file:** This file has the `.spl` extension and is the print job — what gets sent to the printer.
- ✦ **Shadow file:** This file has the `.shd` extension. It contains the information needed for the print job, and is useful only to the print service components. It contains information related to the job's position in the queue, the job's owner, the printer's destination, and so on.

To redirect the spool files for each printer to a separate volume or folder, change the target printer's default spool directory key. The key in question is:

```
HKEY_LOCAL_MACHINE\SYSTEM\CurrentControlSet\Control\Print\Printers
```

Drill down to the printer in question and then look for the SpoolDirectory data item. You can then change the value (the default is blank). Remember that the value must be a drive letter and folder, not UNC. This is demonstrated in Figure 28-2. The reason for redirecting these spool files to custom directories is explained next.

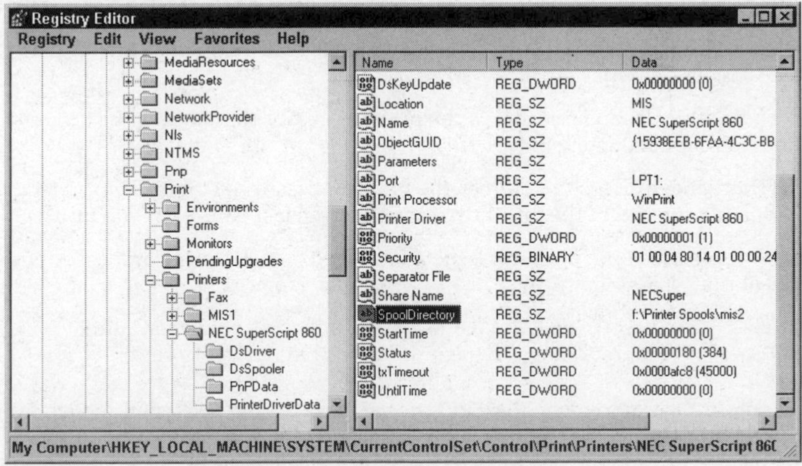

Figure 28-2: Changing the spool directory for a printer.

Print queues

Windows print queues are the previously mentioned print files (the collection of `.spl` files) waiting in the spool folder to be printed. Each spooled job prints in the order it is received. You can use the `net print` command at the command line to manage a job (see Appendix A), or you can work with the document interactively via the respective printer's management interface (accessing the printer management interface for both local and remote computers is discussed later in this chapter).

If you manage a lot of printers, redirecting each printer's spool files to a separate folder can make it easier to manage the printer queue from the command line. If a print job hangs for some reason, you may begin your diagnostics with the print queue. If the queue receives the file from the user, the client spooler service process is not the problem. The next diagnostic step is to determine why the job is sitting in the queue but going nowhere.

The print processor

The print processor is the `winprint.dll` file that resides in the `\system32\spool\prtprocs\w32x86` folder. This library of functions takes the print job data sent by the spooler and renders it into data the printer can understand (if the data is already understandable, it isn't rendered). Most print jobs don't require any intervention by the print processor, unless you have peculiar output requirements.

The default data type spooled to printers by the processor is NT EMF, which can be handled by most printers. EMF stands for Enhanced Metafile Format, and most printers can read it. You don't have to intervene and change the print processor libraries very often because the client applications determine the data type to be sent and because you can't choose or force a job to be handled by any particular print processor. This work is handled automatically.

Windows Server comes with built-in print processors. The one installed by default is known as Winprint, and it handles the standard data types printed by Windows applications. Another important print processor is SFMPSPRT — the Macintosh print processor — which handles jobs sent to PostScript printers. The Macintosh print processor is installed when you install Macintosh services on the host machine. Winprint can handle the following data types:

✦ **NT EMF ver 1.00x:** EMF stands for Enhanced Metafile Format. These files can be printed to most printers.

✦ **RAW:** This data type job indicates to the print processor that nothing further needs to be done to print the document.

✦ **RAW (FF appended):** This type forces the print processor to check if a form feed has been added to the end of the job — to ensure that the last page exits the printer.

✦ **RAW (FF auto):** This type does not issue a form feed, and the print processor adds it to the end of the job automatically.

✦ **TEXT:** This data type is usually issued for printers that do not accept direct text. The print processor renders the text to meet the needs of the target printer.

Note

The Macintosh print processor, SFMPSPRT, renders jobs to non-postscript printers for the benefit of Mac clients. However, the output is limited to the very basic "playout" (to use a Mac-DTP phrase for sending a job to the printer). The default data type is PSCRIPT1, which is a Windows bitmap format that prints to the non-postscript printers. The best you can do for Mac clients is to install PostScript printers (or face the wrath of the Mac maniacs), which provides the high resolution and graphics capabilities DTP publishers require, regardless if the client is Mac or Windows or Linux.

Ports

The term *port* is loosely used to refer to the hardware connections that enable a data stream to flow from one device or media to another. Print servers and printer interface equipment use ports to represent network and cable connections. Ports are assigned network addresses and reside between the printer and the spooler service. We deal with server ports later in the chapter.

Print monitors

Print monitors are important components to understand. They are soft devices that control the transmission process of the print job to the I/O ports on the devices that interface with the physical printer. Windows Server supports several standard print monitors. Print monitors perform the following tasks in the print service:

- ✦ They open up a connection between the print processor and the port. The connection is then used to transfer the data to the I/O ports of the physical printer or remote printer interface. In essence, they touch the actual ports at the interfaces on the remote print servers or printer interface devices.
- ✦ They monitor the print job for error messages, progress, and completion.

The print monitor essentially monitors the entire print job and reports status back to the spooler. If a print job times out, for whatever reason, the monitor notifies the spooler, and the spooler sends a message to the client.

Several print monitors are built into Windows Server. You can see the list when attempting to create a new port for the job data connection. Unfortunately, Windows Server, as with its predecessor, tends to create confusion between the monitor type and the actual I/O port, as illustrated in Figure 28-3.

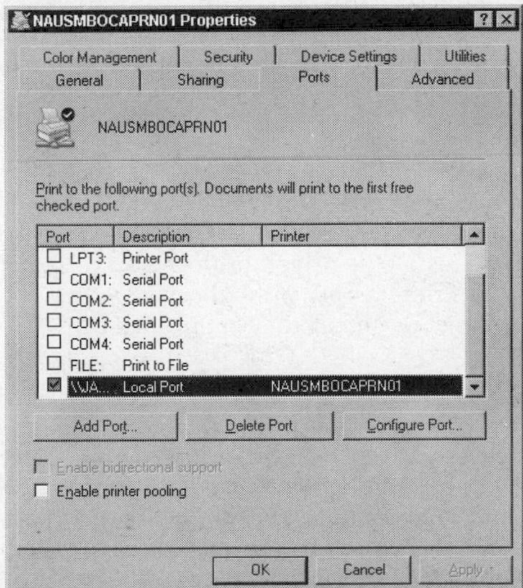

Figure 28-3: The Ports tab in the Properties dialog box.

Why is it so important to understand the role of the monitor? It's usually the first component in the print service stack that alerts you to a print problem, and its most common reason—inability to communicate with the local or remote port. If the print monitor reports that there's a problem connecting to a remote port, you have a network problem (IP, IPX/SPX, or lower on the network stack). Usually, a trip to the printer finds the network cable kicked out of the network drop or the interface unit.

Various monitors come bundled with Windows Server.

Local print monitor

The local print monitor (formerly `localmon.dll` and now built into `localspl.dll`) manages the following ports:

- **Parallel Interface:** This interface caters to print jobs that are sent to the parallel port on the computer initiating the job. Every machine supports parallel port printing. You choose this monitor when you set up a *local* printer connected directly to the host. The local printer can also be shared, which makes it a network printer.
- **Serial Interface:** This interface provides the same service as the parallel interface. The data, however, is transmitted through the serial interface, a communications port (such as COM1 or COM2), instead of the parallel interface. Serial interfacing is not common on printers.
- **USB, Infrared, and Wireless (the likes of 802.1X and Bluetooth):** Windows Server 2003 supports USB printing, infrared and various shades of wireless printing. The local print monitor and its user interface components provides the means to set up these printers in the same location as the legacy parallel and serial interfaces and the remote ports (such as LPR and IP).
- **File:** This interface enables you to spool the job to a file name. The job is identical to jobs that are spooled directly to print interfaces, local or network. The option of wrapping up the data into a file enables you to relocate the file to another system for printing. In other words, the physical printer does not have to be present or locatable on your network to be of service.

  This option is convenient if you do not actually own or have access to the target physical printer. If you need to print to very expensive printers, such as the Linotronic typesetters and heavy-duty PostScript printers run by service bureaus and printing companies, you can print the job to a file and then send the file to the service via the Internet or on a disk. All you need to do is install the driver for the target printer. (By the way, PostScript print files are binary.) Print files are printed using various commands at the command prompts of the target machines they get printed from.

LPR print monitor (TCP/IP printing)

As soon as you put some distance between the physical printers and the computers from which you are requesting the print service, you establish a network-printing environment. The protocol suite of choice for a heterogeneous computing/printing environment is TCP/IP, and you would be well advised to aim for a homogenous TCP/IP printer network. In particular, the Line Printer Remote (LPR) and Line Printer Daemon (LPD) service is used as a standard for TCP/IP printing. It was derived from the Berkeley Unix standards. LPR and LPD printing becomes available on Windows Server 2003 only after Services for Unix are installed on the server.

Windows Server supports LPR/LPD printing with the services of the LPR/LPD environment (`lpd.exe`) and the LPR print monitor (`lpr.exel`). The LPR monitor is installed by default when you install Windows Server. If you install Services for, Unix, additional TCP/IP printing support is added to the printing system to support printers connected to Unix servers.

The LPR port can be used for all TCP/IP printing environments, especially for connecting to remote printer interface devices that do not support a custom TCP/IP daemon or service. You can also use the LPR service to connect to printers hanging off the local ports of Unix computers and big iron, such as VAX, MVS, and AS/400.

The LPR/LPD facilities are provided by the TCP/IP Print Server service, which is installed when you install Windows Server. Typing **LPR** at the command prompt returns several Command Line commands for LPR printing.

Standard TCP/IP print monitor

Windows Server also installs by default a standard TCP/IP print monitor that enables you to create a port to any network interface device or printer that supports IP.

Third-party print monitors

Third-party monitors may need to be loaded when you install printers that require custom or proprietary print monitors. All printer manufacturers create print monitors that can be installed into the printer service at any time, post-installation of Windows Server. These include the following legacy print monitors:

✦ **Digital's print monitor:** Note the apostrophe after Digital. The possessive denotes that the monitor is technology belonging to Digital Equipment Corporation (or DEC, which is now part of Hewlett-Packard Company) and not "digital" as in binary, which is a common presumption.

  The Digital print monitor is not installed as a default monitor and ships with DEC products, such as the DEColorwriter. It requires the DECnet protocol from Digital, which runs atop TCP/IP, typical of the network protocol tomfoolery of the last century.

✦ **Hewlett-Packard's print monitor:** The older Hewlett-Packard monitor talks to HP's printers and plotters and JetDirect devices. This monitor requires the DLC protocol be added to the network services. The old HP monitor is essentially useless because it does not support TCP/IP. In the event you need to install it, possibly to enable the server to cater to printing from the mainframe and mid-range environments, you need to remember that DLC is not a routable protocol. The server and printer need to be on the same network segment.

  The JetDirect print monitor is a new technology that can use several protocols, including TCP/IP and IPX/SPX. The JetDirect print monitor is installed during installation of the JetDirect printer drivers and management software. You can route IP print job packets to a JetDirect card anywhere on the planet.

✦ **Lexmark print monitor:** Another big printer manufacturer is Lexmark. Windows Server supports both Lexmark DLC and TCP/IP print monitors.

✦ **Macintosh print monitor:** This monitor (SFMMON) is installed automatically when you install Services for Macintosh and the AppleTalk protocol. AppleTalk is all you need to print to Apple printers and other PostScript printers. And you get the full features of the PostScript printer environments, including high resolution, color, separations, and more.

Printer Services: The Physical Environment

To use Windows Server printer services, you need a computer that can act as a host for the services. If you support a large network, it's a good idea to dedicate a server to the role of printer server.

All of the Windows Server operating systems support printer server services. The only difference is the degree of availability. The servers (Standard, Enterprise, and the 64-Bit Edition (Data Center)) are designed to host a large number of connections, while Windows 2000 Professional/XP is restricted to no more than ten concurrent connections (as was its predecessor, Windows NT Workstation 4). Windows 2000 Advanced Server, Server 2003 Enterprise and the above mentioned enables you to cluster the printer service for maximum availability.

Experience has shown us over the years that the size of the company or group has little to do with how much hardware you need to throw at print services. For instance, we manage small insurance companies that print five times the number of documents that our larger clients do. Here are some "street" rules for determining the hardware resources needed for a print server:

- ✦ If you can determine that RAM holds 10MB of print data at any given time, provide at least 30MB for expansion.
- ✦ Provide three to five times more hard disk space for print spools and queues or enable the volumes to be easily extended (see Chapter 19). This might be hard for you to determine when first setting up the print service on a server, but you can easily predict your needs. If all your users are printing concurrently — or at least within a few minutes of each other — total up the size of all their documents in the spool folders. These documents sit in the spooler on the hard disk until the service sends them to the printer, so provide at least three times more hard disk space than the total of all document sizes sent to the printer. You never know when someone will decide to send the entire tax rulebook of the Internal Revenue Service to the printer, over the weekend.
- ✦ Printing is also a demanding service. At one of our clients, we have as many as 40 printers on one server alone, so it makes sense to make sure the print server machine has a processor to be proud of.
- ✦ Color printing or printing complicated graphics requires a lot of processor bandwidth. A dedicated server should service these needs, especially in terminal environments.

Print servers

Several hardware components combine to complete the printing system. Unfortunately, the names of the components do not always mean the same thing to everyone. The print server, in our book, is a computer that "serves" printer interfaces to users on the network, as previously discussed. Printer interfaces (logical printers) are established on the server and act as representatives or portals to the printers either on the network or attached directly to the parallel ports of the computer.

Print devices

A *print device* is what Microsoft calls the physical printer hardware. If you ask your user where his or her print device is, he or she will probably draw a blank, but the term seems to have become a Microsoft standard. To stay on the same page as your customers, you should stick with *printer* and forget trying to overcomplicate things with redundant phrases.

Local printers are connected directly to the parallel, serial, USB and wireless ports of computers, while network printers can interface directly to the network with the help of network interface components. The components can be network interface devices or network interface cards (NICs) built directly into the printer.

Network interface devices

The makers of these interface boxes say they have a claim to the term *print server,* and some even stamp "print server" on their product. But refer to them by their brand names, such as Lantronix box or JetDirect card — it results in less explaining.

These guys are very useful and exist for the following reasons:

- ✦ They obviate the need to hook up a computer parallel port to every printer in the office. Instead, the printer cable is attached to a parallel port on the box, which attaches to the network via a network interface port.
- ✦ In large companies, the print servers (computers) are locked away in cooled server rooms, and the printers are either located near their users or in printing rooms. The interface device enables the printer and the print server computer to co-exist some distance away from each other. At one of our clients, we support label printers in many distribution centers that are installed at loading docks and bays where food is packed and shipped. We would not want to locate an expensive Pentium or AS/400 at every dock just to print labels.
- ✦ They provide a network interface to the printer, enabling you to place a printer at any convenient location where you have a network drop.
- ✦ They support a variety of networks, such as Token Ring and Ethernet, and also support all the most popular protocols, especially TCP/IP.
- ✦ They come packed with smart electronics and embedded software that enables you to manage their network protocols, such as assigning network addresses, printing capability, and communications with the printer. They come equipped with terminal access and daemons for remote management. You can telnet into them or even access their internals from a Web browser.
- ✦ They enable you to connect more than one printer to the network at a single network drop and address (many printers on one IP or IPX address). The interface directs the inbound job to an IP port assigned to the printer. (Remember that standard TCP/IP supports up to 65,536 ports.)
- ✦ They come with built-in memory to further queue documents sent by the server.

These interfaces are very useful, inexpensive, and compact. Keep them hidden out of harm's way, such as under the printer, in a printer cabinet, or behind the printer stand. We have a collection of dead Lantronix boxes — each no bigger than a pack of West Virginia's filtered finest — which have been tortured with cigarette butts, coffee spills, shoe prints, and electric shock. They also have a habit of going into indefinite seclusion, never to be seen or heard again.

Print Services Strategy

Providing print services to the enterprise should be a well-planned exercise. Although it appears easy enough to install printers, it makes sense to create blueprints or policy governing printer installation, usage, access, naming, administration, and more.

Often, you arrive at a company only to find that your predecessor knew his or her printing environment like a palm tree knows where its coconuts fall. Troubleshooting such an environment is almost impossible, and it's best to scrap what you inherited and start all over again. Your best course of action would be to create a new logical printer environment and then move users to the new environment in phases.

As a starting point, the guidelines for setting up a strategic print service plan are discussed below.

Printer Taxonomy

Printers that users print to are not the actual printer devices, but logical printers set up in Windows Server, and these printers can thus go by several aliases. As discussed later, one physical print device can be used by several groups that "map" to the printer as different shares, targeting different aliases. You must establish a consistent and practical naming scheme or convention to cater to a varied user environment.

Although it may not seem important if you already have hundreds of printers set up in many different places or if the printer administrator's job recently became your responsibility, it is important to create a naming scheme for your printers if you do not have any. A large company could have as many as 1,000 physical printers plugged in everywhere, and their logical printer namespace may contain as many as 1,500 names.

The naming scheme should be simple. Put *HP* in all Hewlett-Packard printer names, *Xe* in all Xerox printer names, *Ne* in NEC printer names, and so on. For example: HP5LSI_MIS1 is the share name for the main MIS Hewlett-Packard 5LSI printer. And the name HP5LSI_MIS2 may be the same printer shared for after-hour use.

On the other hand, you can also name printers by their location in the world. This is particularly useful if you have printers located all over. A naming convention could be two letters for region or continent, such as NA for North America; two letters for country, such as US; two or more letters for city, such as BOCA, and then the number of the printer or device, such as PRN01. The name of a printer could end up as NAUSBOCAPRN01.

If you are naming by location and type of device, populate the description and comment fields for each printer, as is discussed later in this chapter.

Keep the names simple and try not to leave blank spaces, such as HP MIS1b. Blank spaces make it difficult for advanced users or administrators to map to printers from the command line using the `net use` command, or from within scripts. Names with spaces need to be enclosed between quotes and that wastes time. Rather, use underscores to represent spaces in the name.

Also try to keep the name as short as possible. The name does not need to explain life itself. You can be as descriptive as is necessary in the description fields and in the Active Directory, as you'll soon discover. We have encountered printer names you need a cipher to read. If the admin can't shout the name across the room or over the telephone — "you need to map to HP_MIS1b" — then the name is too complex. Consider this e-mail recently received from an associate in a sister company: "You can send the reports to $_IKY14_T_MAT_MGT5." This "fifth" printer allegedly belonged to the materials management group on the 14th floor of the "Tier" building somewhere in Kentucky.

Easy share names also work well for users. In our accounting department, we named all our printers HP_ACT1 to HP_ACT12. The ACT is short for accounting, but it did not take long before our users associated the printers with Shakespeare.

Creating Print Groups

Here we go again reminding you not to give share access or permissions to individuals (in permissions and access control), but rather to work with groups. Even if the printer belongs to a group of one person, you never know when someone else may need to print to the same printer. A good example is an executive who has a personal printer in his or her office. So, you create the logical printer in Windows Server and add only the name of the executive to the `printer` object's access control list. But what happens when the assistant needs to print to that printer? If a group has access, then the assistant can be added to the group.

Using groups in access control and permissions makes for effective printer management. Under our corporate policy of controlled access, groups are only given access to certain printers at certain times and for certain jobs. We believe it's best to limit group access to all network printers. Otherwise, a disaster awaits. We've seen stuff such as a user sending ten copies of a 1,500-page report to a small printer that could not handle the job, and thus causing urgent smaller documents to wait indefinitely for a chance to get to the printer. If you plan well, you won't have to spend half your life deleting and purging failed jobs from print queues.

Not too long ago, we received a call from the CEO's assistant saying he sent a highly secret document to the wrong printer, which he couldn't find — anxiety was mounting. We found the document before it printed by tracing the queues and looking for his call sign (ownership). Now the CEO can only print to a printer that does not specifically deny him access.

Controlling access to printers is discussed later in this chapter.

Creating a Print Network

Creating a print network, used exclusively for printers, is a worthwhile exercise. It helps keep other devices and machines from invading the printer's address space and makes it easier to manage the printer requirement. Here are some points to consider:

✦ **TCP/IP:** The protocol of choice for most printer networks is TCP/IP. If possible, you should stick to one network protocol. Managing a network of more than one protocol adds dollars to your total cost of ownership. Most models and makes support TCP/IP. Even modern PostScript printers can be assigned an IP address, even though AppleTalk drives them. Older printers and environments (such as VMS, MVS, NetWare, and so on) prefer to talk LAT, IPX, Pathworks, and so on, but for a Windows Server print network, you may as well introduce Klingon into the school syllabus.

✦ **Subnet:** For organizations with a large number of printers, it's best to create one or more subnets exclusively for printers. One Class C subnet caters to 254 printers or more on printer interface devices, which would probably be more than enough addresses for a company of 3,000 paper monkeys. If you manage a number of interconnected offices or sites on a WAN, reserving a block of addresses out of the Class C (say 10 or 20) on the site should suffice. You don't need to add a second subnet to the site just for a bushel of printers; it only adds stress to the routing and replication bandwidth on which DNS and Active Directory depend.

✦ **DHCP:** Ensure the printer IP address range does not get used by DHCP. This is easily handled by reserving the block of addresses in the DHCP service (see Chapter 16).

Keeping Drivers Current

The print routers in Windows 95, 98 (with the latest service packs), NT, 2000, Me and XP clients can receive the printer driver from the server every time they make a connection. Make sure that you keep current and available the printer drivers for every make and model of printer you deploy. Windows Server 2003 ships with more than 3,000 drivers, as opposed to the 2,500 (give or take a few) that shipped with Windows 2000, so the library on the disk is more than sufficient (although there weren't drivers for our Zebra printers, as discussed later in this chapter).

The following provides two good reasons for this important task:

✦ **Staying current:** By regularly updating the drivers, you ensure that users always have access to the latest feature the drivers publish and that you have maintenance releases that fix earlier release defects. Printer drivers become out-of-date very quickly. You can keep drivers current by downloading them from the Internet using the Windows Update service, explained in the first chapter.

✦ **Availability:** Making sure servers hold and keep current printer drivers for every printer you deploy ensures that whenever a client connects to a printer (an old or new logical printer) the latest driver is available. This keeps printing delays to a minimum and the volume of support calls down.

Installing and Setting Up Printers

When you install printers on a server, they usually install as local printers printing to remote TCP/IP ports. Local printers, by definition, are printers that coexist with a server, which acts as its proxy. Local printers are shared as files and folders so that user groups may map to them and use their services.

Just because the physical printer is established out on the network somewhere does not mean it's a network printer; it must still be installed as a local printer (remember, you are installing a logical printer). Installing the network printer option does not make your server a proxy for the printer. It only gives you the ability to connect to and print from the remote network printer. Installing a network printer only makes you another client, and that is not your objective.

Before you begin installing a new local printer, there are a number of parameters and data you need handy, as follows:

✦ If you have a TCP/IP printer network, as most organizations now have, assign the new IP address for the remote port, be it on a printer interface device or on the printer itself. Ensure that the DHCP server reserves the IP address and mark the IP address as assigned on an IP address allocation list or database you keep.

✦ If you are setting up a port on a remote printer interface device, make up a network name for the device. The name can be derived from the name of the device given by the manufacturer, a serial number, and even a MAC (hardware) address.

✦ Have all printer drivers handy. If you do not maintain an install directory on the server, as explained in Chapter 6, you may need your Windows Server 2003 install CDs within arm's reach.

Installing the Local Printer

Follow these steps to install a local printer:

1. Log on to the Print Server computer as an administrator group member. You can do this from the console or log on over a terminal session.
2. Select ➪ Start ➪ Settings ➪ Printers and Faxes. The Printers and Faxes folder loads, as illustrated in Figure 28-4. (This is classic path to the Printers and Faxes folder. You can also get to by opening Control Panel which contains the Printers and Faxes link or icon (depending on the view).

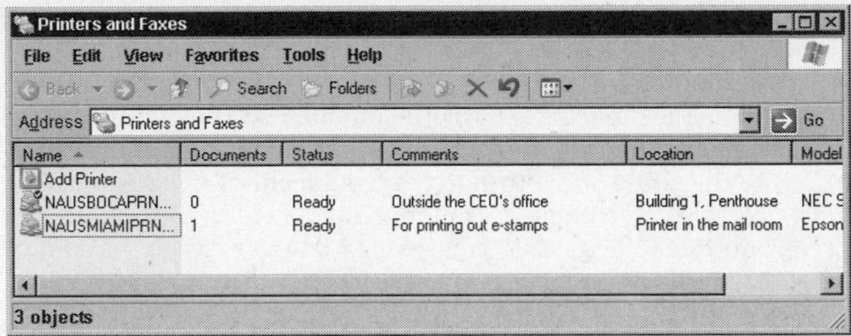

Figure 28-4: The Printers folder.

3. Double-click the Add Printer icon. This launches the Add Printer Wizard. Click Next to arrive at your first totally confusing screen. The wizard asks you to install a local or network printer, but describes the "Local printer" as being directly connected to the computer. Forget that useless advice. The printer server can be connected directly to your server, or your server can be in Little Rock, Arkansas, USA, and the printer can be in Zululand, Natal, South Africa. As mentioned earlier in this chapter, choose Network Printer only if the printer you are installing is not going to be serviced by the local computer as its printer server, host, or proxy.

4. Choose the plug and play option if you are setting up a PnP printer for the first time. Choosing this option for a printer that is already installed wastes time because PnP discovery takes longer than sharing your knowledge of which driver is on the system or on the CD in your hand.

5. The next page is the Port Selection page. If the printer is indeed installed in Zululand, you need an IP address for the port on the printer or on the print device interface box to which your Zulu printer is connected. Note that you can also choose a parallel port (the LPT port) or a COM port if the printer actually is connected to the server computer with a data cable.

   For demo purposes, let's assume the printer is a Zebra printer located 9,000 miles away in Zululand. In this case, you must create an LPR port and assign it the IP address you have handy. (If you do not have the IP address handy, stop everything, and go and get it.)

6. On the "Select a Printer Port" screen of the Add Printer wizard check the "Create a new port" option and then choose the LPR port option from the "Type of port" dropdown combobox. Click Next, and the Add LPR-compatible printer dialog box loads. You are prompted to provide a name or IP address for the port. If at all possible, provide the IP address, because name resolution just slows things down (the IP address should be permanently assigned to this port in any event).

   Also provide the name, as we also requested you do earlier. The far-away Zebra printer is hanging off a Lantronix computer, so the typical name we use identifies the port as being on a Lantronix printer "server." This is illustrated in Figure 28-5.

Add LPR compatible printer

Name or address of server providing lpd: 100.50.2.2

Name of printer or print queue on that server: ZULU1_Zebra5 (MPS)

OK

Cancel

Help

Figure 28-5: Adding an LPR port.

7. Because we discussed the function of the print monitor earlier, note here that the LPR print monitor immediately tries to touch the remote IP address. The LPR Port Configuration Warning shown in Figure 28-6 pops up if the IP address or remote server does not respond to a test packet sent by the monitor. At this point, you can choose to abandon the installation in order to test the IP address or the remote device, or you can carry on with the setup and return to the troubleshooting later. Either option brings you back to the same point. It's not much of a deal to return later to change the IP address or other settings, as demonstrated later.

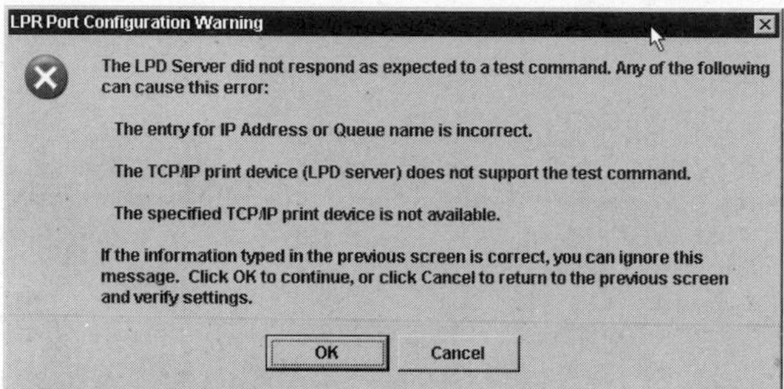

Figure 28-6: An LPR port error.

This message may occur for several reasons.

- The IP address could be bad or unreachable. Troubleshoot the address, using `ping`, `tracert`, and other TCP/IP tools described in Chapter 15.
- If the address is valid, the interface device may not be working properly. Diagnose that problem with the tools that ship with the device.
- The device may not be connected to the network, or it may be connected but not have power. Whatever the reason, someone at the remote site must troubleshoot the device. Many interface devices enable you to connect to the printer and dump, or print setup and diagnostics information to the printer. Printing out the configuration and setting in the device tells you if the device has the correct IP address installed and if the device is working properly. Many modern printers also have the ability to print configuration and address information. If the device is set up with the wrong IP address, as is usually the case, then a simple change gets your device installed and working.

8. Click Next to load the printer driver for the printer from the manufacturer list, illustrated in Figure 28-7. If the printer you are installing is not in the list (Figure 28-7 indicates the absence of Zebra printers), you need to get the driver from the Internet or from a CD that ships with the printer. Click Next after you have selected the driver. If the driver is already installed on the system, Windows prompts you accordingly to replace or use the existing driver.

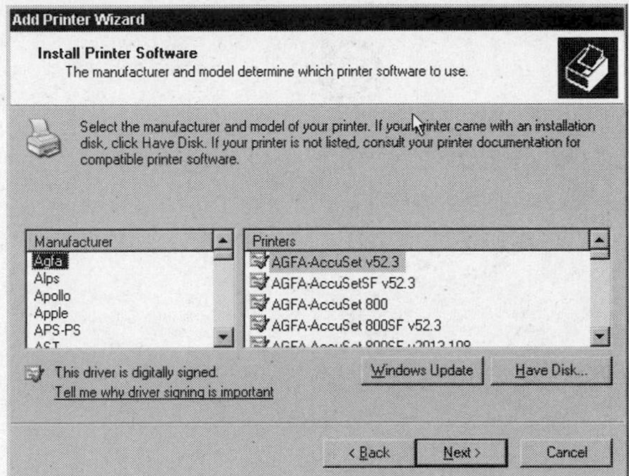

Figure 28-7: The manufacturer's list of printers.

9. Click Next to name the printer, as illustrated in Figure 28-8. Keep in mind the naming consistency convention. In the illustration, the name denotes a Zebra printer for the "shipping" group.

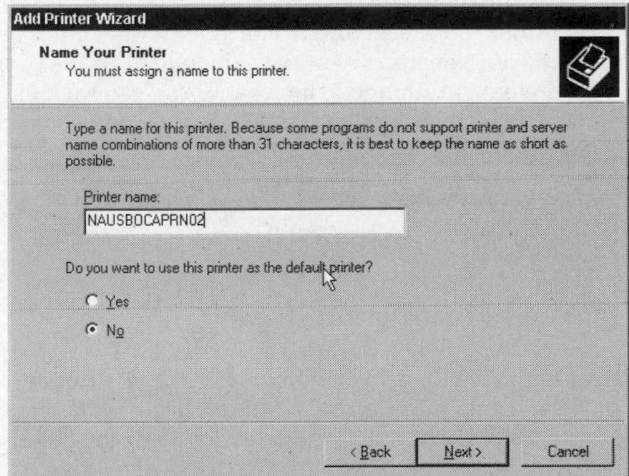

Figure 28-8: Naming the logical printer.

10. Click Next to share the printer; then click Next to provide information about the location and use of the printer. This is demonstrated in Figure 28-9.

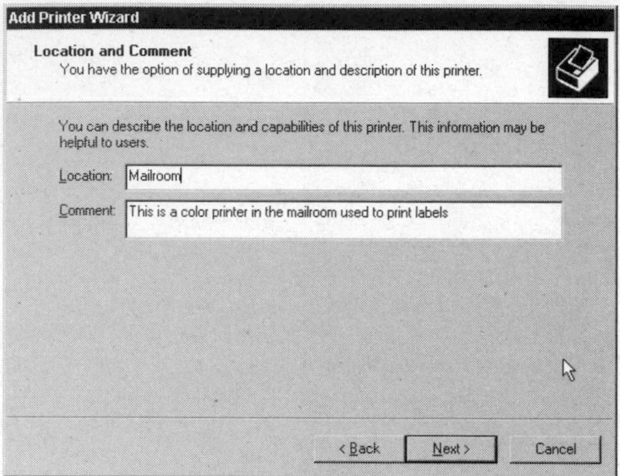

Figure 28-9: Location and comment information.

11. Finally, you can choose to print a test page. Do it. Click the test page but do not use the troubleshooter. In other words, respond YES to the prompt asking if the test page printed correctly, even if you have no idea what came out, halfway across the planet. It's not that we don't trust the troubleshooter. If we agreed that the test page did not print, we would not be wasting time hyper-linking our way around the help system. After you've troubleshot several printer problems, the troubleshooter becomes a waste of time. The test page is more useful as a means of sending a document to the printer without having to leave the printer configuration to send a page. You can then check the queue of the printer. If the test page has not printed after a few minutes, you need to troubleshoot. Meanwhile, your new printer service is installed.

A local printer has now been installed. Before you have access to it, you must still do some fine-tuning.

Publishing Printers

Printers are a resource, but you can either make them available to users or you can hide them. When printers are made available — when they can be found on the network — users try to connect to them and print, oblivious to any permissions or policy you may have set. If you don't want certain printers used by various groups, you have to lock them down, even hide them away.

Conversely, if you are going to make a printer share available, you should make it easily locatable, not only to ease your work load, but also so that the user or the administrator installing the printer as a network printer can find it. This is what we call *publishing printers*.

Locating Printers

Printers can easily be located by browsing the printer servers, as is the case with legacy Windows NT printer servers. The printer can then be installed on a client machine for printing — using the Add Printer Wizard or via the `net use` command.

Locating the printer in Active Directory

You can also publish printers in Active Directory. You can search an enterprise for a printer that serves your purpose. Let's say you are looking for a printer that is able to print on both sides of the page and that has stapling ability.

If the printer has been published in Active Directory, you can find it by asking the directory to search for printers matching your specifications, as illustrated in Figure 28-10. You can then look up the printer's manager or contact person and request access to the printer. This is great for large or widely dispersed organizations, where machine count can run into the hundreds and thousands.

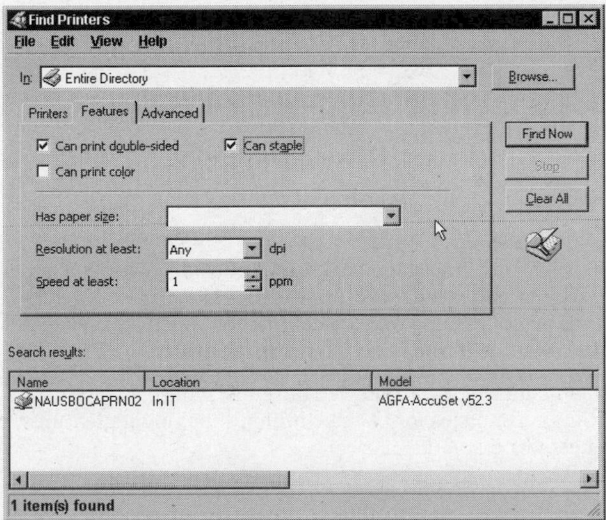

Figure 28-10: Searching for a printer in the directory.

So how do you publish or list the printer in Active Directory? You don't have to do anything other than ensure that the server is an active member of a domain. When a server is authenticated as a domain jrs member, Windows Server 2003 enables the server to publish its shares in the directory. You can also expressly refuse to publish the shares by unchecking the List in the Directory check box found on the Shares tab or the printer properties.

However, the print server need not be a domain member to make its print shares available. You can map to the printer share of a standalone machine in the directory as follows:

1. Select the OU in AD in which to publish the share. Right-click the OU, select New, and then choose Printer.
2. Enter a UNC name to the share name, as illustrated in Figure 28-11. Although the dialog box makes reference to pre-Windows Server 2003 print shares, this is how you list standalone Windows Server 2003 print server shares in the directory. You can also map to the IP address used by the server with `\\192.168.10.57\HP1`.

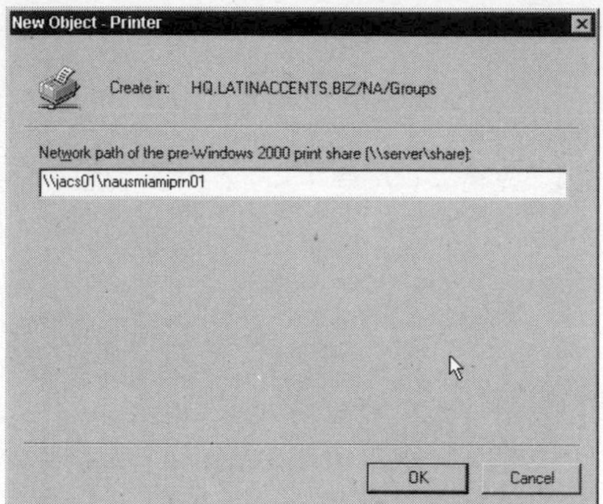

Figure 28-11: Manually listing a printer in Active Directory.

Locating printers over the Web

With the Internet Information Server fully integrated into the Windows Server 2003 operating systems, clients can connect to the print server's printers via the HTTP protocol if IIS services are installed and started. Upon connecting to a logical printer share on the server, the server automatically updates the client with the necessary printer driver.

This is a wonderful service for large intranets and service bureaus, where a print manager with a flare for HTML can customize the pages for each printer, publishing its features, connection parameters, usage requests, and so on.

Clients connect to the printer using their Web browsers as follows:

- **HTTP//*servername*/printers:** This Web page lists all the logical printers hosted by the server identified in the URL. The information entered when the printer was first installed is listed on the page, as well as status information, and so on.
- **HTTP//*servername/logicalprinter_share:*** This URL connects you directly to the logical printer.

Hiding Printers

You can hide print shares the same way you hide folders (see Chapter 27) by appending the dollar sign ($) onto the end of the share name such as `HP_MIS8$`. You can still map to the share from the command line, using the `NET USE` command, but then you must know the exact printer share name.

If you want to hide the share, remember not to list it in the directory when you first install it as a local printer.

Printer Pools

Pooling is another means of publishing printers. Several printers can be grouped together to form a contiguous print resource. Note the check box on the Port tab that is checked, as illustrated in Figure 28-12.

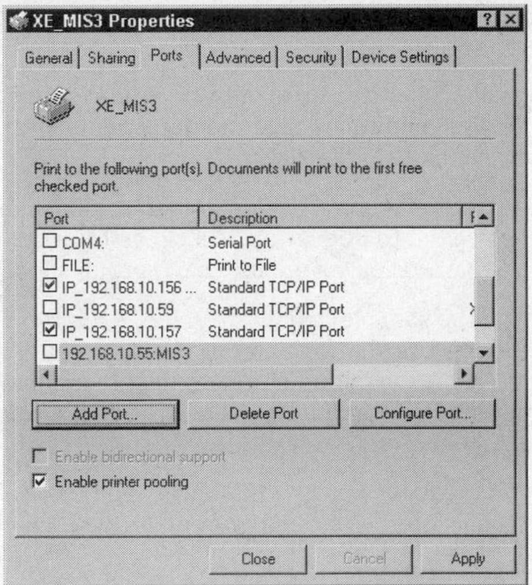

Figure 28-12: Pooling logical printers.

Printer pooling is ideal for a shop that is printing a high volume of documents. Print jobs do not have to wait for a job on one printer to finish. If another printer is free, the jobs automatically route to the first free printer.

To create a pool of printers, do the following:

1. Install your group of identical printers as local printers. Create as many ports as printers to be added to the pool.
2. Check the Enable Printer Pooling check box.
3. Check all the ports on which a member of the pool is installed (illustrated in Figure 28-12). It's important to ensure that each port has an identical printer connected to it.

Loading Printer Ports

Windows Server 2003 enables you to create multiple logical printers and assign them to the same port. We coined the term "loading the ports" to describe this technique. Another way to look at this is as a many-to-one printer setup: many logical printers to one physical printer or port. Each logical printer is a separate instance of the `printer` object. In other words, you can create several logical printers, all printing to the same physical device and the same physical port.

The following list describes the benefits of loading printer ports:

- ✦ **Printer configuration:** Each logical printer can be configured differently for various reasons. Availability, sharing, permissions, and device settings can be different for each logical printer. On one printer, you might provide access to group A to print certain jobs, while on another logical printer you might provide access to a totally different group running other jobs. One printer might be available at night, while another is only available during the day (when the office is busier).
- ✦ **Job Prioritizing:** Certain logical printers can be given priority over print jobs. Setting the `priority` property of the logical printer achieves this. One printer can be set up

under a high priority to only enable access to users who can justify high-priority printing privileges.

- **Delegating Admin functions:** Each logical printer has its own print manager and queue. Document administrators can be assigned to manage the documents in the queues belonging to the logical printers installed in their OUs.
- **Sharing physical printers:** Several organizational units, or departments, can share a single printer. Instead of lumping all the users into one group, it makes better sense to create a logical printer for each group. Separator pages identify each group's job.

Prioritizing jobs can't be done automatically on the same logical printer. If one job requires priority over another job, you can pause the lesser priority job and enable the urgent job to "jump the queue." This becomes tricky and tiresome when lots of documents are queued. It is better to create another logical printer on the same port and then set a higher print priority for the latter logical printer. How can this be done?

The logical printer has a `priority` property that can be set from the lowest value of one to the highest value of 99. Jobs that are sent to the printer with the higher priority setting print before the lower priority jobs.

This is achieved as follows:

1. Create a second logical printer on the same port (loading) as the regular printer.
2. Select the printer in the Printer manager and right-click its icon. Select properties and zero in on the Advanced tab. In the priority setting box, select the priority (you can make it the highest if this printer is the most important) and then click OK. (See Figure 28-13, which illustrates the Advanced tab.)

Now when users need to print urgent jobs, they can print to the second printer. You should create a special group for the latter printer, which can be used for people who have priority over others. Whenever someone needs to print a job urgently, you can temporarily admit him or her to the group.

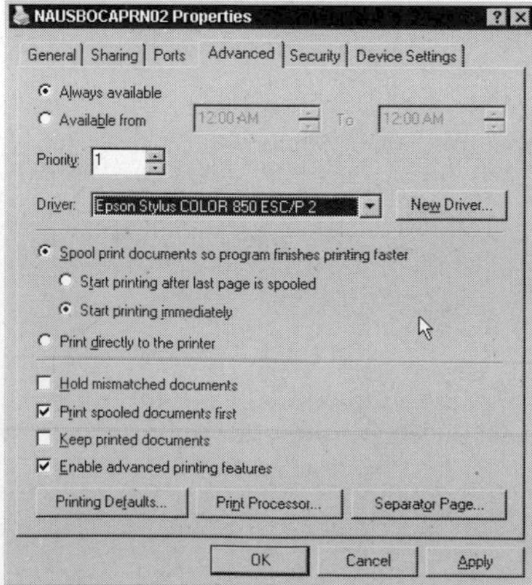

Figure 28-13: The Advanced tab in the Properties dialog box.

Printer Administration

Long gone are the days when the only printers we set up in the average office were simple laser printers and dot matrix printers. Today, it would be ridiculous to expect the OS to cater to all the features of the myriad of printer brands and models. Instead, Microsoft publishes APIs that enables the printer manufacturer to hook into system management facilities to manage and configure the printer. Still, a number of common features are accessible from the printer configuration dialog boxes.

There are three tiers of Windows Server 2003 administration of printers. First, we can control how and what printers print, and when they can print it. This is printer-centric management. Second, we can control which jobs print; we can delete them, pause them, redirect them, and cancel them. This is job-centric management. Finally, we can publish printer shares and control who has access to the printer, when they have that access, and what they can print. This is printer access control. Let's first deal with printer management functions.

Printer Management

The job of the printer manager requires strong organizational skills. Using the techniques provided in this chapter, you can create logical printers, install network interface devices, install physical printers onto the network interface devices, provide access to the printers, delegate administration, and more. In essence, as a printer manager, you have to do everything this chapter covers, including the following chores.

Setting separator pages

Setting separator pages, or banners if you prefer NetWare terminology, can be tedious work, but in very busy printing environments producing substantial documents, they are essential.

Separator pages separate jobs. They also can be used to provide information about jobs and can print at the beginning of each print job, in front of the first page. They do not affect the printing order of the jobs, nor the pagination. Consider the following key reasons for using separator pages:

- **Tracking down job owners:** We have several high-end printers to which many people print every day. At the end of each day, there were hundreds of documents that were forgotten by their owners. At the end of the week, a huge pile of uncollected documents was getting thrown out (Web pages, white papers, press releases, e-mail, and so on). The situation got worse by the day, and it did not take long to recognize the waste of time and materials. The situation called for separator pages, to enable a printer administrator to collect the jobs, identify the owners, and threaten them with disciplinary action if they did not collect their output. Habitual offenders were told they needed to clean up their acts or they would lose their printing privileges.
- **Separating the print jobs in long runs:** If your printer is receiving large volumes of print runs, or continuous reports, the only way to pull complete jobs from the run or sort them easily is with separator pages. We have several printers that typically print reports on a round-the-clock basis, and all the jobs are separated by separator pages.
- **Organizing chaos at high-traffic printers:** After printing, many job owners dash off to the printer and wait for the paper to slide out of the hopper. If the printer is busy printing, eager-job-beavers grab every freshly printed page, collecting pages and even whole jobs before other users can get to them. Meanwhile, uncollected jobs get stored in the pickup tray as mentioned above, and if separator pages don't exist, it does not take long to create job mayhem.

✦ **Job information:** Separator pages can be used with sophisticated printers to print job information, such as the owner, language used (if the printer supports language changing on the fly), and so on.

Windows Server 2003 provides four types of separator page files. They are stored in the `systemroot\System32` folder. Table 28-1 describes these pages.

Table 28-1: Separator Pages

Separator File	*Purpose*
PCL.SEP	Switches a dual-language HP Printer to PCL mode printing
PSCRIPT.SEP	Switches a dual-language HP Printer to PostScript mode printing
SYSPRINT.SEP	Used for PostScript printers
SYSPRTJ.SEP	Same as SYSPRINT.SEP but uses Japanese characters

The pages described in the Table 28-1 are not actually printed. They are script files that contain codes to instruct the print provider to print a separator page, and what to print on it. You can open and edit these files and customize them for your purpose. By default, the separator file instructs the printer to print the job owner's name, date, and job number.

To create your own separator file, copy the existing one (so you have an original to go back to) and modify the copy as needed. You can rename the file whatever you like, but give it the `.sep` extension. The contents of the Windows Server 2003 PCL file are as follows:

```
\
\H1B\L%-12345X@PJL ENTER LANGUAGE=PCL
\H1B\L&l1T\0
\M\B\S\N\U
\U\LJob : \I
\U\LDate: \D
\U\LTime: \T
\E
```

Note that the first character in each line of code is the backslash (\). This is the character that denotes or signifies that the character following a \ *is* the escape code. You could use a character such as the @ sign as the escape code signifier (such as @E). The Windows Server 2003 Escape codes are as follows:

✦ `\B\M` Text is printed in double-width blocks until \U.

✦ `\B\S` Text is printed in single-width blocks until \U.

✦ `\E` Page eject.

✦ `\H`*n* Initiates a control sequence where *n* is a hex code for the target printer (see printer manual).

✦ `\F`*path* Prints the contents of a file at *path*.

✦ `\I` Job number.

✦ `\L`*xxx* Prints the characters in *x* following the escape code.

✦ `\n` Skips *n* lines (zero moves to the next line).

✦ `\N` Switches a dual-language HP Printer to PCL mode printing.

- ✦ `\T` Time the job was printed.
- ✦ `\U` Turns off block character printing.
- ✦ `\Wnn` Width of the separator page in characters.

Separator pages are set up on the print server computer as follows:

1. Select the printer from the Print manager dialog box. Right-click and select Properties. Then go to the Advanced tab, as illustrated in Figure 28-13.
2. Click Separator Page. You can type the name and path of the separator page, or you can browse for it. OK your way out of the Properties dialog box. The print provider now prints the separator page.

Some last advice about separator pages: They work well in high-print or high-job volume situations but are annoying on the small stuff. For every single sheet you print, out pops a separator page you have to throw away. To save the forests and your sanity, keep separator pages off the small jobs. The best way of switching separators off small jobs is to have the small-stuff printers print to an alternative logical printer, as described in the previous section, "Publishing Printers."

Mixing and matching forms and trays

Most printers today come with multiple trays for labels, envelopes, paper and form sizes, and more. And single-tray printers can be manually fed a form or enable the physical printer to automatically feed the form. You can configure your printer to enable application users to select the paper or form size they need right from their applications.

To assign a form to a particular tray or form feeder, do the following:

1. Select the printer from the Print manager dialog box. Right-click, select Properties, and go to the Device Settings tab.
2. Click the tray you want to assign paper sizes to. A drop-down menu appears enabling you to select from the list of standards-based paper sizes. Select a size and then click OK. The tab is illustrated in Figure 28-14.

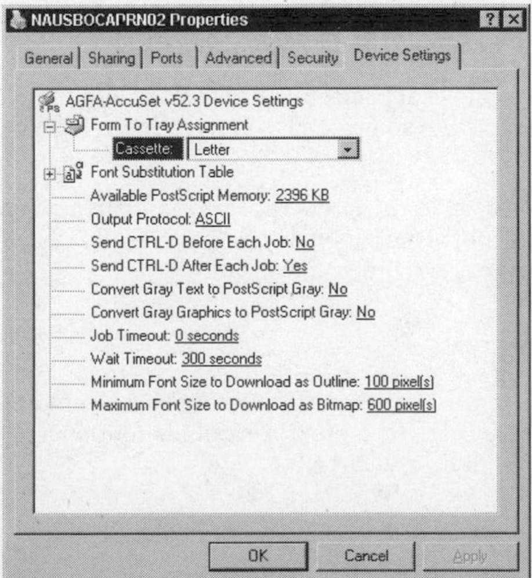

Figure 28-14: Device settings.

Job Management

Server 2003 and printer administrators frequently get called to manage print jobs or documents. Windows Server 2003 enables you to delegate the job management function on an OU-to-OU basis. The following task list describes the job management functions that can be assigned to job management administrators. The job management options are accessible from the context menu (right-clicking), the Printer menu, and the Document menu in the respective print queues dialog box, as illustrated in Figure 28-15.

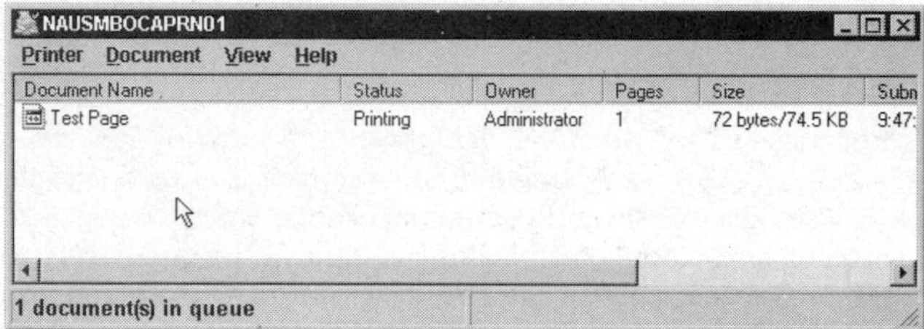

Figure 28-15: The Print queue dialog box for printer NAUSMBOCAPRN01.

✦ **To pause a job:** Double-click the printer to open the queue or print job manager. Then select a printing document and right-click or click the Document menu. Select the pause option. A check mark appears next to the document to indicate that it's paused.

✦ **To pause all jobs:** Right-click the printer queue and then select the option Use Printer Offline. All jobs are suspended.

✦ **To resume a job:** There are two ways to resume a job. You can pull down the Document menu again and select the Resume option, or you can right-click the job again and re-click the pause option to clear the check mark.

✦ **To cancel all jobs:** Right-click the queue window on any job and select the option to Cancel all Documents.

✦ **To delete a single job:** Select the document and hit the Delete key.

You can redirect stalled jobs to another physical printer rather than delete them and have to resubmit them. The logical printer remains the same — all you have to do is change the port and physical printer.

Open the properties of the logical printer, go to the Ports tab, and select a new port. As long as you know that the printer on the new port is working, is the same as the one you are redirecting from, and uses the same driver, your documents will print.

Advanced Spool Options

The default options on the Advanced tab work for the majority of printing environments. But the tab has a number of options available that are useful for troubleshooting and managing printers. The Advanced tab is illustrated in Figure 28-14.

Available time

A logical printer is usually always available. However, it may be necessary to shut it down for any number of reasons, during the day. Some printers are so large and complex that refilling their trays can take up a lot of time, hoppers and bins may need to be cleaned, toner may need to be refilled, and so on.

In addition, you may shut down a logical printer to prevent certain groups from using it during specific daytime hours. For example, you might have a group that needs exclusive access to the printer at a certain time, and they can't afford to have other users printing at the same time (check printing is a good example).

To shut down the logical share at a certain time, toggle to the Time available option to enable the option and set the time range.

Remember that setting an available time for a logical printer does not shut down the physical printer at the time range you set. If other logical printers point to the same physical printer and availability is set to Always, the other users can print. If you need to shut down the printer completely at a certain time, make sure all logical printers have the same available time range set.

To spool or not to spool

As mentioned earlier, you can opt to send print jobs directly to the printer. Simply toggle the options to use the spooler or to print directly to the printer. If you choose the latter, the print job bypasses the spooler and prints directly to the printer.

Choose the latter option only in rare situations, such as a broken spooler, because you otherwise lose the benefits of spooler-managed printing. For starters, print jobs complete much faster at the application level if they are sent to the spooler. A large document can tie up your application for hours as it prints directly to the printer and you must wait for each printed page to emerge from the printer before the next page is sent.

Still, you might have a special reason to print directly to the printer, and you should explore the use of a sophisticated printer interface device that has sufficient memory to act as a buffer.

Most of the time, however, all logical printers make use of the spooler. But you can toggle between printing immediately when the spooler receives a page or waiting until it has received the entire document before it starts sending the job.

Choosing the latter delays printing, but it ensures that the entire job spools correctly before the printing process starts. You would do this if you had a large job to print and the application that produced the job was no longer available. Such a situation is encountered at print service bureaus where customers bring in print files for processing.

Holding mismatched documents

Check this option for most of your logical printers, especially if they represent sophisticated devices with multiple feeders and hoppers. This option instructs the spooler to examine the codes in the print document and checks them against the setup of the physical printer. For example, let's say you print to a bulk cassette or special-size form feeder from the application, but that option has been disabled in the printer's device settings or it's offline for some reason. Instead of throwing an error, the printer holds the job until the problem has been corrected. This is illustrated in Figure 28-16.

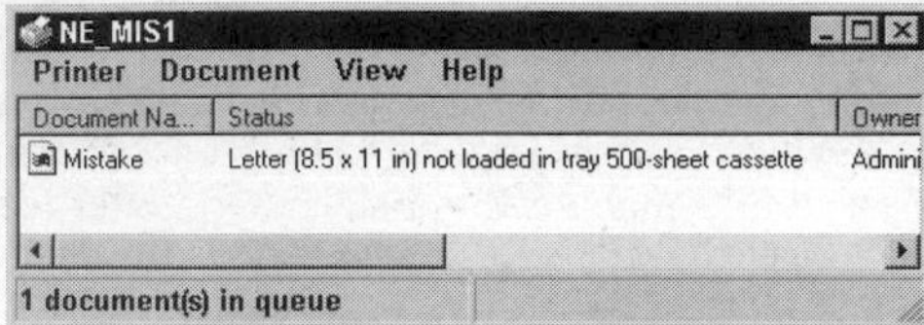

Figure 28-16: Mismatched documents are held.

The spooler does not hold up valid jobs from printing. While your job is on hold, you can correct the problem at the actual printer or delete the job (Cancel) and reprint with new parameters.

Printing spooled documents first

When you tell the spooler to give jobs that have completed spooling priority over jobs that are still spooling, it overrides any priority a job has. In other words, if you are spooling a job consisting of 1,000 pages, why should all the one-page jobs have to wait in line?

If you turn this feature off in situations where all the jobs are roughly the same size, the spooler then prints the jobs in the order it receives them.

Keeping printed documents

This is another feature that at first seems to make no sense—until you get a job to print that takes hours to set up. A good example of such a job is a sheet of labels for ZIP disks, or address labels, or CD labels, or high-resolution color jobs that don't change graphically but need to be reprinted from time to time.

If you have such a need, you can create a logical printer that keeps the documents after they have printed. When you need to reprint the job, right-click the job you need and select Restart from the Context menu. Figure 28-17 illustrates the result.

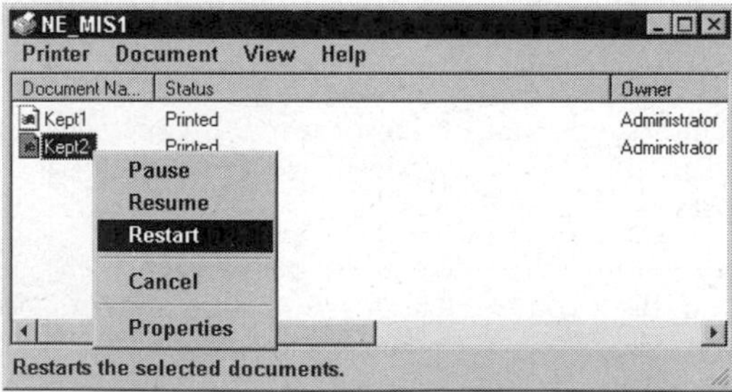

Figure 28-17: Keeping jobs that have printed.

Creating a special printer that keeps the jobs makes more sense than toggling this property every time you want to keep the document and run the risk of every user's job having to be manually deleted from the hard disk. Use the techniques described earlier for creating a logical printer that redirects its jobs to a folder you created instead of the default queue folder, so that jobs that should be deleted do not get co-mingled with your persistent jobs.

Another means of keeping the job is to print to a file and then print it from the command line whenever you need it. This might be a better option for you if the environment in which you are working is not sufficiently secure and you run the risk that the queue gets "flushed" and your job gets lost. The `Copy` command prints documents from the command line.

Access Control

Providing access to printers is similar to providing access to files and folders. To give users access to the printers on the print server, you first have to share the printer. Sharing also enables the users to browse the network to find the printers. Providing access to printers is almost identical to providing access to share-points. There is only one difference: You can't decide who has access to the print share. Microsoft has hard-coded the share to be open to everyone. Sounds horrible? Fear not.

You can restrict access to printers via security permissions (access control). As with file shares, you may be tempted to just leave the Everyone group in the printer access control list. This may be a good idea if you have a huge printer or a collection of pooled printers set up as a free-for-all, only printing to blank white paper (and you are really certain that no one can walk up to the printer and stick letterhead in the tray). In other situations, especially when it comes to smaller printers, or highly specialized printers (such as check and label printers) and plotters, it becomes essential to restrict the printers to only the groups specifically using the printers.

Consider creating groups along application needs and then admitting the application users to these groups. For example, we have a group of users who work with PeopleSoft applications all day long, and we installed a special Xerox system that prints payroll checks. To prevent people from printing to the checks in the tray, only members of the PeopleSoft-Check Printers group have access to this printer.

You can also provide access to — and information about — all printers in the organization by publishing the printers in the Active Directory (which is done automatically when you install printers on any server that is a domain member). And you can delegate the administration task to printer administrators in any group established on an OU-per-OU basis. We discuss this later in the chapter.

Assigning permissions according to role

Windows Server 2003 separates access to printers into three roles or classes of users: people who print, people who manage the documents or jobs, and people who manage the printers. Incidentally, users can be assigned all the permissions. Table 28-2 summarizes the printer permissions.

Table 28-2: Printer Permission Types

Access	*Print*	*Manage Documents*	*Manage Printers*
Print	Yes	Yes	Yes
Manage own job	Yes	Yes	Yes
Manage other's job	No	Yes	Yes
Connect	Yes	Yes	Yes
Control Print Jobs	No	Yes	Yes
Delete all Jobs	No	No	Yes
Share Printers	No	No	Yes
Configure Printers	No	No	Yes
Delete Printers	No	No	Yes
Change Permissions	No	No	Yes

The Manage own job permission enables the user to pause jobs, resume jobs, restart jobs, and cancel any job he or she owns. Users have no access to documents in the queue over which they have no ownership. Administrators, however, have the ability to take ownership of documents.

The `printer` object is similar to the `file` object. You can assign the above permissions, and you can also specifically deny any of them. Be careful though — denying some permission may affect other weaker permissions. For example, if you deny Connect, it's as good as removing the group from the access control list. Deny is stronger than the "allow" permissions of any other group and overrides other permissions granted.

Permissions have been fully outlined in Chapter 27. Refer to this chapter for techniques and suggestions.

Delegating printer and document administration

Delegating responsibility for the management of print jobs and printers is important, especially in large organizations. Instead of sending all the problems that users get from printers to one person, you should set up two printer groups per OU and assign people from the OU to deal with the OU's printer problems and needs, assuming you have the staff. The following list is a suggestion for the two groups.

- ✦ **Print Job Admins:** The members of this group manage print jobs. They can pause, restart, redirect, and cancel jobs. This group cannot delete jobs, nor can they change printer properties.
- ✦ **Printer Admins:** The members of this group can perform print job management, install printers, configure printers, and delete printers. They can also change permissions, take ownership, and publish printers in the directory.

Creating groups and delegating administrative control is discussed in Chapters 11, 12, and 13.

Taking ownership

You can take ownership of a logical printer in the same way you take ownership of a file or folder. Ownership rules for printers are no different than the ownership rules for files and folders. For example: The person who created the logical printer owns it; the user owns the created print job. Ownership is discussed in Chapter 3 and Chapter 27.

To take ownership of a printer, perform the following:

1. Open the logical printer's properties and then select the Security tab. Click the Advanced button.
2. The Advanced Security Settings dialog box appears. Click the Owner tab. Your user account (your logon) and the Administrators group appear in the list of owners. Select the account and click Apply or OK. Click OK again to close the Properties dialog box.

It's important to remember that you can't take ownership if you are not a member of an administrator's group that has been assigned the Manage Printers permission.

Troubleshooting

Now that you understand the Windows Server 2003 printing services, you're better equipped to troubleshoot printer problems when they occur, and they will occur. Out of all the services the mighty Windows Server 2003 networking environment has to offer, the printer services generate the most support calls, behind resource access issues. The following troubleshooting suggestions and tips are a place to start to resolve printing problems as quickly as possible.

Server-side Print Problems

We like to refer to jobs that do not print as being *blocked.* Blocked jobs arrive at the queues and just sit there, or they time-out with an error. Most calls to a support or help desk are complaints that jobs have spooled to the logical printer but are not emerging from the physical printer.

If a job is sitting in the queue and not indicating an error, it's possible that a mismatched document has been trapped by the printing service. Mismatch problems are easily corrected, as previously mentioned.

Jobs that throw an error indicate they were unable to print to the physical printer. If the job can't print and an error is reported, the following steps should be taken to alleviate the situation and correct the problem:

1. **Check the port assigned to the logical printer:** If the port is an IP address, ping it. If you get a reply from the port, you have connectivity to the network components involved in the printing process. In other words, jobs can get to the server and the server can see the port, or at least the print monitor can. (If you are some distance away from the print server, open a terminal session to the server and ping the port from the session.) If the IP address is correct and you get a reply from the port, you can check the IP port off your list. If the port is a parallel or serial cable connected directly to the server, you need to perform specific diagnostics there as well.

Network addressing is seldom the problem, especially if you maintain your IP printing network as suggested earlier (and if your printer has been printing before and no IP address conflicts appear in the event logs).

2. **Check the hard disk space, memory, and event logs:** Resource starvation is one of the biggest causes of printer spooler service shutdown. (With Windows Server 2003, you can set and enforce disk quotas — as described in Chapter 16 — to help prevent your print server from running out of hard disk space.) Freeing up space or shutting down memory hogs may be all it takes to get printing again. The event logs can tell you when the first jobs failed. These events may tie in with other errors that could point to a reason for the sterile jobs.

   You can also check the driver. Although this is an unlikely point of failure with a printer that has been printing with no problems to date, the driver may have been changed or deleted by another administrator.

   If you can't get the print service printing to the physical printer within, say, five minutes of getting a call for help, go to step 3.

3. **Attempt to redirect the jobs:** Redirect the jobs to another port and physical printing device as described earlier in this chapter under the "Publishing Printers" section. This is a quick fix that does not impact users and alleviates the pressure stemming from impatient users. They still print to the same logical printer.

   If the new target physical printer is located somewhere else in your offices, notify users where they can collect their jobs. Please don't redirect the jobs to another city in another state as one CNE once did. And make sure you are redirecting the jobs to another printer of the same type and using the same driver.

   If you can't redirect the jobs and the other port is printing — and the blocked jobs are not — you most likely have a problem with the spooler and spooler files. This could have been caused by the lack of resources. You need to act fast and proceed to step 4.

4. **Stop and restart the spooler service on the print server computer:** If resources starvation is the problem or the spooler is down for some reason, the spool files can become corrupted. In fact, consider giving the spooler a sharp crack on the head when everything else seems to check out. Restart the spooler and then stop and restart it again. If the spooler starts up normally and responds quickly to the restart command, but the jobs are still not printing, it's likely that they are corrupt. Delete the jobs — kill the spool files and the shadow files. (You may have to take ownership to delete the files. If new jobs are still not printing, it's a drastic situation.) The files to delete are the SPL file and SHD files, previously discussed in this chapter.

5. **Take the logical printer offline:** The best way to do this is to prevent access to the logical printer completely. Selecting the option to "Use the printer offline" does nothing but cause the queues to fill up with more sterile print jobs. Your users print and then rush to the printers to stare at empty hoppers like deer in headlights. It's better to tell them they have been denied access, and they will know why. We prefer to remove access from the printer completely. Go to the Security tab on the Properties dialog box and uncheck the permissions assigned to the groups using the printer. You may have to perform this exercise with several logical printers all using the port on which there is an error.

6. **Notify users that there is a problem, and notify your help or service desk:** When users discover they can't access a printer, they call for help. It's better to preempt the calls.

7. **If you can see the port, attempt to log in:** Some ports enable you to telnet into the interface box. If you can log in to the port, you can get diagnostics from the port. Many manufacturers now ship software that can query the printer for errors and diagnostics. If the printer reports errors, you may have to call in a service technician. If the printer is checking out, you may have a problem with the printer interface device — such as the JetDirect card or the Lantronix device. Often, we have found these to be problem children that were fixed when we downloaded new versions of their firmware.

8. **Check for problems on the client:** If clients are printing and you are not seeing the jobs in the queues, then check the client. Odds are it's not a server-related problem. The spooler service on the client may be stopped.

Client-side Print Problems

Client-side printing problems are different from server-side problems, although they are certainly interrelated and may stem from the server. The following list represents the most "popular" client-side print problems you may encounter:

1. **Pages print incorrectly or are garbled:** The cause of this problem is usually that the client has received the wrong printer driver. Check the server configuration and make sure the client is getting the correct driver. Remember, you may need drivers for all versions and types of operating systems running on your clients, possibly one for every version of Windows too.

   The clients may also generate error messages saying that they need to install a printer driver when connecting to a specific printer on a Windows Server 2003 printer server. This means that the correct drivers are installed on the Windows Server 2003 server, but they are not automatically sent to the legacy client every time the client prints.

   Finally, another cause of garbled text could be related to the physical printer. It may have special font requirements, it may be set to print only PostScript when the job you're sending is PCL (which could happen when you print to a file or restart a job from some time back), or the printer may be low on memory or faulty.

2. **Only some clients print:** This means the client has been misconfigured. Chances are the client has printed — but to the wrong printer. You can minimize this problem by providing adequate information about the location of printers.

Enabling Bi-directional Printing

Enabling bi-directional printing enables smart printers equipped with the ability to transmit data to the printing service to talk to the server in real-time. It also makes it easier to find out why a printer is not printing when all else checks out. This means that the physical printer has the ability to report to the server that it requires paper, servicing, toner, or reports its overall status, and more.

The default operation is bi-directional printing disabled. The option is found on the Ports tab of the printer properties. It's grayed out if the port selected does not support bi-directional printing. This does not mean you won't get sufficient status information from the printer because Windows polls the printer for information. But Windows only polls for standard information (out of paper, and so on), and the messages are not as detailed.

Auditing Printer Usage and Management

Windows Server 2003 enables you to track print job success and failure on a logical printer. Check out Chapter 23 on auditing Windows objects, if you have not already done so, and how to prepare the system for auditing.

You can audit access and usage to a logical printer as follows:

1. Select the printer you wish to audit for printing and management. Right-click, and select Properties; then select the Security tab.
2. On the Security tab, click the Advanced button, which launches the Access Control Setting dialog box for the logical printer. Click the Auditing tab.
3. On the Auditing tab, click Add and select the group or groups you want to access. Choose the Success or Failure audits you want to trap and then click Apply.

That's all there is to auditing printer usage. To check the audits, refer to the System log in Event Viewer.

Summary

This chapter was designed to get you up to speed on the elements of the Windows Server 2003 print services. We believe it's important to understand the service — from the manager or administrator perspective — in order to correctly troubleshoot printing problems.

Print services are a vital function of the network; they represent an important part of a network operating system. It's also important to build a blueprint or comprehensive plan of your printing environment or service, and to set down policy and procedures for using printers. If you establish a printing network and manage it correctly (such as reserving a specific range of network addresses and establishing printer user groups), you should not have many problems and be able to boast high availability of printing services.

✦ ✦ ✦

Web, FTP, and Intranet Services

In This Chapter

This chapter covers configuring and managing an Internet or intranet server for HTTP, FTP, SMTP, and NNTP services and security. You learn how to set up a Windows Server 2003-based Web server to host Web and FTP sites, act as an e-mail server, and host newsgroups.

What's New in IIS 6.0

Although Internet Information Services (IIS) 6.0 at first blush might resemble IIS 5.0, there are some significant changes under the covers. While these changes are mainly architectural, they make IIS 6.0 more fault tolerant and secure, and a better performer.

New server role

Windows Server 2003 incorporates the .NET framework, and other services, providing additional capabilities and redirecting the focus of Windows Server 2003 to run as an application server rather than just a Web server. To that end, Microsoft has added a new server role called *application server* that you can enable through the Manage Your Server console.

If you browse through the Add/Remove Windows Components in the Add or Remove Programs applet in the Control Panel, you find that Internet Information Services is no longer a primary installation option. Browse through the Application Server option, however, and you find Internet Information Services hiding underneath. The installation options for IIS are the same, but simply buried one level deeper. So, you can install IIS as a suboption, or you can install it as part of the Application Server role, which also adds ASP .NET, COM+, DTC, message queuing, and the Application Server console. The approach you take depends on whether you need these additional components.

Processing changes

One of the most significant changes in IIS 6.0 is an architectural change that provides much better request processing. In IIS 5.0, `inetinfo.exe` was the primary process that handled all requests, passing out requests to `dllhost.exe`. In contrast, IIS 6.0 comprises the following two components:

✦ **Http.sys:** This kernel-mode driver listens for HTTP requests and queues the requests for processing, one queue per application pool. As a kernel-mode driver, `http.sys` is not susceptible to user-mode code that could otherwise crash the service.

✦ **WWW Service Administration and Monitoring Component:** This service-level component provides IIS configuration, monitoring, and process management functions. As with `http.sys`, it does not enable third-party code to run, thus making the server less susceptible to errant applications.

In IIS 6.0, *worker processes* are the mechanisms that provide application and process execution. An *application pool* comprises a request queue within `http.sys` and one or more worker processes. The new WWW service DLL is loaded into and runs within the context of the worker process. The application pool can service one or more Web applications, with applications assigned to application pools based on the application's URL. Multiple application pools handle multiple applications and sites. Worker process isolation ensures that an application or site cannot crash another. In addition, worker processes isolate core IIS functions such as configuration, management, and request queuing from application code, preventing errant application code from crashing these core IIS services and functions.

These architectural changes make IIS more robust and more fault tolerant. In addition to essentially eliminating crashes caused by applications, these changes also mean you don't need to reboot the server to clean up site or application crashes, or make changes to individual sites. The combination of these IIS architectural changes and other general changes to Windows Server 2003 enable it to run more concurrent processes, which also means better scalability for IIS under Windows Server 2003.

To provide full compatibility for custom applications developed for IIS 5.0, IIS 6.0 includes a mode called *IIS 5.0 isolation mode*. IIS 5.0 isolation mode functions in much the same ways as native IIS 5.0, with everything in user mode running nearly as it does with IIS 5.0. In isolation mode, all requests pass through `Inetinfo.exe`, with IIS 6.0 handling the queuing.

The WWW service in IIS 6.0 is the only component service that makes use of the new architectural changes. The FTP, NNTP, and SMTP services continue to function as they did in IIS 5.0 with requests being processed by `Inetinfo.exe`.

See the section, "Managing Application Pool Settings," later in this chapter to learn how to configure and manage application pool settings and performance.

Security changes

In keeping with its reported focus on security, Microsoft has implemented several changes in IIS 6.0 to make it more secure. For example, Setup does not install IIS by default when you install Windows Server 2003. But when you do install IIS, by default it only serves static content. When you upgrade previous Windows versions to Windows Server 2003, Setup disables IIS, if it exists on the server prior to installation. IIS can also be disabled through group policy in Windows Server 2003, giving administrators the ability to gain control over IIS across the enterprise.

Several security-related changes affect the way IIS 6.0 functions, as well. IIS worker processes and all ASP built-in functions run in a low-privileged user context, which can significantly reduce the ability of a hacker or worm to execute attacks against the server. In addition,

IIS accepts requests only to files with known extensions, prevents command-line tools from executing via the Web server, exits a worker process if a buffer overflow occurs, and verifies that content exists before passing the request to a request handler. Several settings — including timeouts and upload limits — have been tweaked so their default settings provide better security.

Passport and other security changes

IIS 6.0 adds support for Microsoft Passport for authentication. Administrators can map Passport to Active Directory accounts so that after a user authenticates with his Passport, access to site resources can be controlled by that AD account. This eliminates the need for users to remember a server- or site-specific set of credentials.

IIS 6.0 also takes advantage of new authentication features in Windows Server 2003 to enable administrators to allocate access on a URL or task basis for situations in which controlling access by NTFS ACLs isn't feasible. Thus, you can control access to sites and resources within the site with greater flexibility.

In addition, IIS takes advantage of Windows Server 2003's *constrained delegation*, which enables administrators to delegate authentication for individual computers or services. For example, a Web application could constrain delegation to enable it to request back-end services on behalf of a user within that user's security context.

Management and administration changes

IIS 6.0 implements several changes that affect manageability and administration. The metabase has been moved from a proprietary binary file (`Metabase.bin`) to plain-text, XML-formatted files. Moving to XML offers several advantages, including the ability to view and directly edit metabase data with a standard text editor. The move to XML also makes for easier backup and restore, as well as import/export of metabase data between servers. A clear view into the metabase enables administrators and developers to identify problems in the metabase and extend the schema.

IIS also provides automatic metabase version history for information and restore operations, which can greatly simplify restore and rollback. The metabase can be modified while the server is running simply by modifying the `Metabase.xml` file. Metabase backups are encrypted with a user-supplied password rather than the machine key, enabling server-independent backup and restore.

To further improve manageability, IIS 6.0 includes several VB-based scripts that administrators can use to control sites and services, perform backup and restore operations, configure server extensions, and perform several other tasks. These scripts reside in `%systemroot%\System32`. IIS 6.0 also incorporates an expanded Web-based administration toolset for remote site and server management.

Several other new or improved features in IIS 6.0 either increase performance, scalability, or management. These features are covered where applicable throughout the remainder of this chapter.

Overview of Web and FTP Server Administration

Windows 2000 provided an extensive range of services for configuring and managing an Internet or intranet server based on Windows 2000. Windows Server 2003 expands those services, making Windows Server 2003 an even better platform for distributing Web-based content. This chapter explains each of the services and also examines global issues such as building a management team to manage your servers and the services they provide.

Because designing and implementing an Internet or intranet server is a complex task that requires its own book, this chapter can't cover every facet of IIS. Instead, you can examine the most common issues and learn the procedures to follow to accomplish various tasks. In some cases, we'll refer you to other sources for more details, if you need them.

Web-related services

Windows Server 2003 incorporates several services geared toward Internet and intranet clients, collectively known as Internet Information Services (IIS):

- **Background Intelligent Transfer Service (BITS) Server Extensions:** These extensions support bandwidth throttling and restartable file transfers.
- **Internet Information Services Manager:** This management console enables you to manage IIS and its components services.
- **World Wide Web Server:** This service enables you to configure Windows Server 2003 to function as an HTTP server for the World Wide Web (WWW). Through this service, a Windows Server 2003 computer can host multiple Web sites. The World Wide Web Server is also required by certain other services primarily to provide remote administrative access to the server and those dependent services.
- **File Transfer Protocol (FTP) Server:** The FTP protocol provides for file transfer between computers. Although many sites now provide their file distribution efforts with the HTTP server, FTP is still the most widely used mechanism for serving files for upload and download via the Internet or an intranet. Through the FTP service, a Windows Server 2003 computer can host multiple FTP sites.
- **Simple Mail Transport Protocol (SMTP) Service:** The SMTP protocol and service enables you to configure a Windows Server 2003 as an SMTP e-mail server.
- **Network News Transfer Protocol (NNTP) Service:** The NNTP protocol and service enables you to configure a Windows Server 2003 to act as a news server. You can host public, private, read-only, moderated, and authenticated newsgroups, and take news feeds from other NNTP servers on the Internet to create a public news server.
- **FrontPage 2002 Server Extensions:** FrontPage Server Extensions enable the HTTP service in Windows Server 2003 to support FrontPage Webs, which are Web sites developed with Microsoft FrontPage. In general, the FrontPage Server Extensions enable remote authoring and management of FrontPage sites.
- **Internet Printing:** Select this option to have Setup create the Printers virtual folder and put in place the support files necessary to enable HTTP-based printer discovery, installation, and printing.

In addition to these services, Windows Server 2003 includes additional components that install as part of the Application Server role. When you install the Application Server role, Setup by default adds some, but not all, of the components listed under the Application Server item in the Add/Remove Windows Components applet. Except where noted, Setup adds the following components:

- **Application Server Console:** This administrative tool brings together three consoles to help you manage the server. Use the .NET Configuration console to manage .NET configuration (applications, assemblies, security policies, etc.), the Internet Information Services Manager to manage IIS sites and services, and the Component Services console to manage COM+ and Distributed Transaction Coordinator DTC.
- **ASP .NET:** This item installs the components needed to run .NET ASP applications on the server.
- **Enable Network COM+ Access:** This component enables the server to host distributed COM+ applications.
- **Enable Network DTC Access:** This option is not installed by default, but if enabled the server participates in network DTC transactions.
- **Internet Information Services:** The Application Server option installs Common Files, Internet Information Services Manager, and the World Wide Web Service. In this latter service, only the WWW service is installed by default. Additional components including Background Intelligent Transfer Service Server Extensions (BITS), FTP, FrontPage Extensions, Internet Printing, NNTP, and SMTP are not installed.
- **Message Queuing:** This service, which is not installed by default for an Application Server role, adds support for reliable, transactional message queuing.

If you are building a public Web server to provide extensive client support, e-commerce, and other Internet services (if you're an ISP, for example), you probably want to look at solutions other than just the services built into Windows Server 2003. For example, Microsoft Commercial Internet Server brings together all the services mentioned so far plus additional ones (SQL Server, Site Server) to enable you to create a full-service Web server. Microsoft Content Management Server (CMS) provides the framework by which you can distribute site development, enabling nonadministrators to easily add content to a dynamic site. CMS also provides content activation/expiration and other mechanisms to control site content.

If you're enthralled by the capabilities that Microsoft's Content Management Server can bring to your sites, but can't afford the stellar pricing, check out Web Update Builder from `www.xemico.com`, which offers a limited set of similar features at a considerably lower cost. Also check out Macromedia Contribute, which you will find at `www.macromedia.com/software/contribute`. Contribute provides an excellent set of tools that offer the capability for non-developers to contribute to Web site content.

The core services included with Windows Server 2003 offer a solid platform for developing an intranet server or a public Internet server geared toward hosting your own company or organization site. We focus on these core services in this chapter, but mention other solutions where applicable.

Web services checklist

Before beginning the process of installing and configuring IIS and related services, plan the server implementation and ensure the server is ready for IIS. The following serves as a checklist for planning and preparing IIS installation and configuration:

- **Define the server mission:** By knowing what you expect the server to provide to clients, you can determine which IIS services and related services are required for installation. The role the server plays has a bearing on the server's hardware and connection requirements, as well as how you configure security. Know ahead of time exactly which functions you want the server to perform and whether those functions are to be made available to anonymous users or restricted to specific groups or individuals. If you're setting up a Web server to host several sites for your company or for your clients, for example, you probably want to invest in a high-performance server with RAID, high-capacity backup hardware, and at a minimum, a T1 Internet connection.
- **Establish the Internet connection for a public server and acquire IP addresses:** If your server is connected to the Internet, contact your ISP to establish the connection (if one isn't already in place) and acquire the necessary IP addresses for the server to support its mission.
- **Implement network protection:** If your server will be or is connected to the Internet, implement a firewall (or at the very least a proxy server) to secure the server and its content against malicious attacks.
- **Prepare the hardware, OS, and file system:** Based on the server's mission, determine the type of hardware required to adequately support the mission. Install Windows Server 2003 and test the server. Then, determine where to store IIS services and content and convert those volumes to NTFS (not required but highly recommended for security).
- **Install and configure TCP/IP:** IIS services require TCP/IP whether you are installing an Internet or intranet server. Install TCP/IP and configure the server's settings according to the server's mission. If the server hosts multiple sites, bind multiple IP addresses (as many as required) to the TCP/IP protocol.

See Chapter 12 for detailed information on installing and configuring TCP/IP.

- **Secure the server's non-IIS services and files:** Review the server's other services and files and secure them with object permissions and account restrictions to prevent unauthorized access to these services and files.
- **Install and configure DNS to support your domain(s):** If you are providing your own Domain Name Service (DNS) namespace resolution, set up and configure the DNS service, either on the IIS server or on a different server. Create the initial zones to be hosted by the IIS server and create resource records, as needed. If an ISP or other organization is providing DNS services, ensure that those services are in place and the necessary zones and records are ready.
- **Install IIS services:** Install the IIS services necessary to support the server's mission.
- **Secure directories and develop user access permissions and policies:** After setting up the IIS services, review the object permissions for content folders and for user accounts and groups to ensure adequate security for the server and its content.

✦ **Create and test sites:** Create sites that support the server's mission and test those sites for functionality. Configure the sites to accommodate specific resource needs, such as throttling bandwidth or limiting connections.

It may take several weeks of careful study, planning, and implementation to accomplish the process described in the preceding checklist. Each step is critical to successful implementation of an IIS server. Many of these topics are covered elsewhere in this book. Part IV, for example, covers TCP/IP configuration, DNS, DHCP, remote access, and related topics. See Chapter 3 for a discussion of local and network security issues relevant to IIS. See Chapter 22 for information on how to use object permissions to restrict access to files and folders, which helps control IIS content access.

Installing IIS 6.0

It's a relatively simple process to install IIS through the Add/Remove Programs wizard in the Control Panel. However, you can take one of two approaches depending on the role your server will play. If you are setting up an application server rather than a more traditional Web server, add the Application Server item from the Add/Remove Windows Components applet in the Control Panel:

1. Install, configure, and test any required non-IIS services, according to the server function (DHCP, DNS, TCP/IP, Index Server, and so on).
2. Open the Control Panel and double-click the Add or Remove Programs icon.
3. In the wizard, click Add/Remove Windows Components.
4. After Windows Server 2003 scans the server for installed components, it displays a component list (Figure 29-1). Select the Application Server item and then click Next.
5. Follow the remaining prompts to complete the installation process. Windows Server 2003 should require no additional input other than providing the Windows Server 2003 CD for Setup to copy the required files to the system.

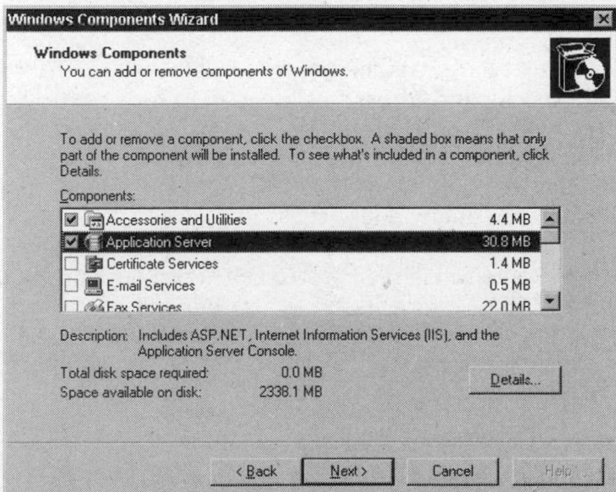

Figure 29-1: Use Add/Remove Programs to add IIS service components to the server.

If you are setting up a traditional Web server rather than a .NET application server, or you want to install additional IIS services not installed with the Application Server item, you can install IIS selectively. The following tells you how:

1. Open the Add or Remove Applications applet in the Control Panel, and click the Add/Remove Windows Components button.
2. Double-click Application Server to open the Application Server component list, then double-click Internet Information Services.
3. In the Internet Information Services list, select the individual IIS components you want to install.
4. Click OK; then click Next, and follow the wizard's prompts to complete the installation.

Configuring and Managing HTTP Services

The World Wide Web Server component of IIS enables a Windows 2000 Server computer to function as a Web server for HTTP content. The Web service offers several features that provide considerable control over content, security, and bandwidth, making IIS a good option for Windows 2000 Server-based Web servers. This section of the chapter focuses specifically on IIS in a traditional Web server capacity, rather than application server. Following chapter sections explain the Web service's features and how to configure and manage Web sites under IIS. The section, "Managing an Application Server," later in this chapter, focuses on the implementation of IIS in Windows Server 2003.

In this section of the chapter we assume you've installed all components and services listed under the Internet Information Services item in the Add/Remove Windows Components applet.

Default sites created by Setup

When you install the Web service, IIS creates three sites by default, which appear in the Internet Information Services MMC console. The sites serve the following functions:

✦ **Default Web Site:** The Default Web Site is the site that IIS serves to HTTP requests that are not associated with a specific IP address/host header. IIS creates the Terminal Services virtual directory (Tsweb) and Internet printing virtual directory (Printers) under this site. The Printers folder enables the server to support Internet Print Protocol (IPP) printing from Web-based clients. The Default Web Site is configured for port 80 with no host header, and anonymous access is allowed.

Setup no longer installs the remote administration Web site, which enables you to manage the server remotely through HTTP. However, you can use the Add or Remove Programs applet in the Control Panel to add this site. Click Add/Remove Windows Components and in the Windows Components Wizard, open the Application Server\Internet Information Services\World Wide Web Service group and add the Remote Administration (HTML) component.

✦ **Microsoft SharePoint Administration:** This site enables management of SharePoint services on the server. The site is configured to use a randomly-assigned port with anonymous and Integrated Windows Authentication enabled.

See Chapter 28 for a detailed discussion of IPP and how to configure Windows Server 2003 to support IPP printing from Internet and intranet clients.

The default site is bound to all unassigned IP addresses. Thus, the site responds to all IP addresses bound to the server, which are not assigned to other sites. The default site has other implications, particularly on a server hosting multiple sites. For example, if you assume that all sites on the server use the same IP address, employ host headers to direct incoming client requests to a specific site. If a particular site is not available (because it is stopped, for example), IIS serves the default site to the client. So, take the time to develop a default Web site that accommodates situations in which a client is “accidentally” directed to the site. Think of the default as your “error handler” for incoming Web requests. Design the default site to redirect the clients back to the correct site.

Configuring Web sites

Setting up a Web site under IIS is not a difficult task, but it takes several steps to accomplish it. This section explains how to set up new sites and configure existing sites.

Preparing the server

To set up a site, prepare the site’s folders. Often, the simplest approach is to place all of a site’s files within a single physical folder structure with all content residing in that folder and its physical subfolders. However, IIS doesn’t impose a single folder structure. You can create a virtual structure using a folder on the local server, a share on another server, and virtual folders. All of these appear as a single, logical folder structure to the client and function accordingly within the site content. At this stage, determine how you will store the site files, whether they’ll be on a single server or multiple servers, and what NTFS permissions you need to apply to the folders to control access if not using anonymous access or using a combination of anonymous and authenticated access. Create the folders on the target computer(s) and configure permissions, as required.

If you are creating a Web farm comprising multiple servers for one or more sites, consider using DFS because it enables you to replicate site content between servers. Use Active Directory-enabled DFS to provide replication across the domain, if desired. Also check out Microsoft Application Center 2000, which provides Web farm configuration, clustering, and deployment tools. You will find more information at `www.microsoft.com/applicationcenter`.

Next, verify that you have the necessary IP address bound to the server. If the server only hosts one site, you only need one IP address. You must bind multiple IP addresses to the server, use multiple TCP ports, or use host headers to host multiple sites (explained in the following section). Use the TCP/IP protocol properties in the network connection’s settings to view and add IP addresses.

Finally, verify that the necessary DNS zone is created for the domain on the site’s designated name server(s) and that the zone is populated with the appropriate resource records. For example, if you’re setting up a Web and FTP server for the `latinaccents.biz` domain, create a DNS zone on your DNS server for `latinaccents.biz` with the appropriate Start of Authority (SOA) and Name Server (NS) records for the zone. Then, create host (A) records for WWW and FTP that point to the appropriate IP addresses for those services on your IIS server. Lastly, make sure that the domain is registered with the root servers and that the root servers’ records point to your DNS server for name resolution.

See Chapter 17 for detailed information on configuring DNS zones and records.

Creating and configuring the site in IIS

Several steps are required to create and configure a Web site in IIS, although the process of simply putting up a site is relatively simple. Applying advanced properties can take a little longer if you have special needs for the site or want to provide additional customization of properties or behavior. Start with running the Web Site Creation Wizard.

Running the Site Wizard

To add a site, open the Internet Information Services Manager console from the Administrative Tools folder. Expand the server where you want to add the site, right-click the Web Sites container, and choose New ⇨ Web Site to start the Web Site Creation Wizard. The wizard prompts for the following information:

✦ **Description:** This is the description that appears in the IIS console to identify the site.

✦ **IP Address:** Select the IP address for the site from the drop-down list. Each site needs a unique IP address unless you use host headers or a different port, as described in the following.

✦ **TCP port:** The default HTTP port is 80, but you can specify any valid port that doesn't conflict with other services on the server. Specifying a nondefault port adds a bit of security because the clients must know the port number to connect and specify it in the URL, as in `http://www.latinaccents.biz:8080`, using port 8080 as an example. See `http://www.iana.org/assignments/port-numbers` for an up-to-date list of registered well-known TCP port numbers.

✦ **Host Header:** The host header is the domain name requested by the client's URL, such as `support.latinaccents.biz` in the URL `http://support.latinaccents.biz/contacts`. The host name is passed by the client's browser to the server, and IIS can use that host name to determine which site to serve up on a multi-site server. See the section "Configuring Multiple Sites with a Single IP" later in this chapter for more information.

✦ **SSL port:** If you are using Secure Socket Layer (SSL) to create a secure Web site, specify the SSL port number. The default port number is 443.

✦ **Path to the home directory:** Type or browse to the path that serves as the site's primary folder. You can specify a local folder, network share, or UNC path name.

✦ **Allow anonymous access:** Select this option to enable anonymous connections to the site. Deselect this option to use Windows accounts (local or domain) to authenticate within the site.

✦ **Access permissions:** Configure the type of access permissions you want clients to have to the site. Available options include the following:

- **Read:** Enable clients to read the site's content.
- **Run Scripts:** Enable clients to run scripts such as ASP, JSP, and so on.
- **Execute:** Enable clients to execute applications such as ISAPI, CGI, and so on.
- **Write:** Enable clients to post content to the site.
- **Browse:** Enable clients to browse the directory structure for the site.

After you create the site through the wizard, set some additional properties to define the site's content, permissions, and so on. The following sections explain these steps.

Configuring default documents

Most sites incorporate at least one *default document*. This is the HTML or ASP document presented to the client, if no document is submitted in the URL. For example, browsing to `http://www.latinaccents.biz` displays whatever default document is configured for the `www.latinaccents.biz` site (such as `default.htm`, or `default.asp`). However, the client could also request a specific document, such as `http://www.latinaccents.biz/contacts.htm`. In this case, IIS would serve up the document `Contacts.htm`, assuming it existed within the site's root folder.

You can configure multiple default documents. If one specified in the list is not available, IIS serves the next document in the list. You configure the document priority when you assign the default documents. To do so, open the IIS console, right-click the Web site you want to modify, and choose Properties. On the Documents property page, select Enable Default Content Page, then either verify that you're using one of the default document names (`Default.htm`, `Default.asp`, or `index.htm`) for the primary document in the target folder, or click Add to add the document name you want to use. After adding all appropriate names, use the Move Up and Move Down arrows to change document order.

Configuring the Home Directory

When you add the site through the wizard, you specify the local folder, network share, or UNC path to serve as the home directory for the site. Another step in configuring the site is to fine-tune the home directory properties. To do so, right-click the site in the IIS console, choose Properties, and click the Home Directory tab to display the Home Directory page shown in Figure 29-2. The tabs displayed in the property sheet for the site vary according to the options you have installed for the server.

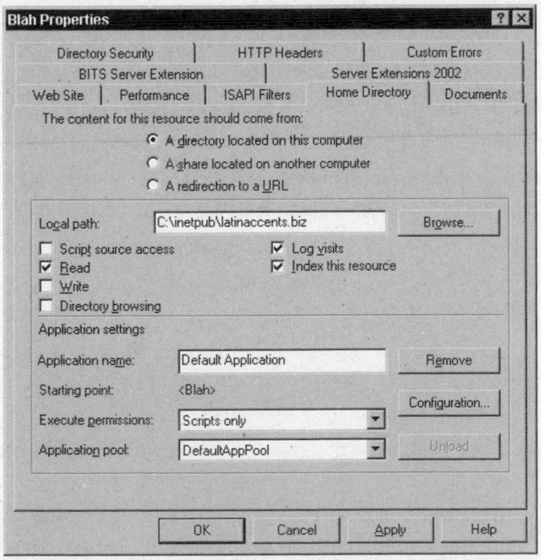

Figure 29-2: Use the Home Directory page to fine-tune permissions or redirect the site to a different home directory.

As Figure 29-2 illustrates, you can change the home directory location, if needed. Use the check boxes on the dialog box to define access permissions and enable logging and indexing. You also can apply a fine degree of control over application execution and debugging through the Application Settings group of controls. Fine-tune the settings based on the site's function, intended clients, and your security needs.

Configuring security

A site's Directory Security property page enables you to configure access and security for the site. Through the Directory Security page, you can enable or disable anonymous access and specify authentication options (clear text, digest authentication, integrated Windows authentication, or Passport). You also can specify a range of IP addresses that are either granted or denied access, giving you a means of restricting access to a specific subnet. This is particularly useful for enabling access only to intranet users in a specific physical location, such as a department or throughout the entire organization (to prevent outside connections to the site).

You also can use the Directory Security page to configure certificates and enable SSL. See the section "Enabling Secure Sockets Layer" later in this chapter for more information.

Configuring other site settings

You can get most sites up and running through the tasks and options discussed to this point; however, each site provides several other property pages you can use to configure a wide variety of site properties to control performance, configure additional security options, and so on. While this chapter can't cover them all in detail, the following list summarizes the types of tasks you can accomplish through other property pages:

✦ **Performance:** The Performance page provides a means for controlling site performance. You can enable and configure bandwidth, which limits the load on the server imposed by the site. You can also limit the number of concurrent connections, if desired.

✦ **ISAPI Filters:** ISAPI filters respond to events during processing of HTTP requests and can provide background processing for site traffic. Use the ISAPI Filters page to install and enable or disable ISAPI filters.

✦ **HTTP Headers:** This property page controls several features related to HTTP headers for the site, including the following:

- **Content expiration:** Use this feature to specify when content expires to enable clients and scripts that test for content expiration and automatically refresh content from the site.
- **Custom HTTP headers:** Add custom HTTP headers to the site to enable custom processing within scripts/browsers.
- **Content rating:** Enable and configure the site's content rating to enable rating filters to identify and potentially block the content from the client based on its rating values.
- **MIME mapping for the site:** Configure new file type associations for content on the site.

✦ **Custom Errors:** Defines the error messages received by clients, such as the page that appears when the client requests a page that doesn't exist (the Not Found error). The error pages by default are stored in `*systemroot*\help\iisHelp\common`. You can edit the files with any HTML or text editor to customize the pages.

✦ **Server Extensions 2002:** The Server Extensions page enables you to configure Server Extensions (also referred to as FrontPage Server Extensions), which control options for Web authoring through FrontPage and related applications. See the section "Configuring FrontPage Server Extensions" later in this chapter for additional information.

✦ **BITS Server Extensions:** Use this tab to configure file transfer for the site. See the section, "Configuring BITS," later in this chapter for more information.

Configuring multiple sites with a single IP address

Although you can configure multiple Web sites on a single server using unique IP addresses for each one, this can pose a problem in instances in which only a limited number of addresses are available (if your ISP only provides a small subnet, for example). The IP address is just one of three properties that define the site. The other two are the TCP port and *host header*. The TCP port is the port through which the site communicates, and the host header is (usually) the site's domain name. Our example the `latinaccents.biz` main site uses an internal address of 192.168.0.3, the default TCP port 80, and the host header `www.latinaccents.biz`. The support site could use 192.168.0.3, port 80, and a host header of `support.latinaccents.biz`. Sites on the same server can share any two of these properties, but one must be different. In this case, the host header for each site is unique.

Host headers enable you to share an IP address with multiple sites because most browsers (Internet Explorer 3.0 and Netscape 2.0, and later) support the use of host headers. These browsers pass the host header information to the server, and the server directs traffic to the appropriate site based on that header. Figure 29-3 illustrates how host headers direct traffic to the correct site.

Note Browsers that support HTTP 1.1 support host headers. Certain older browsers also support host headers even though they don't support HTTP 1.1. In addition, sites configured for SSL cannot use host headers, since the header information is encrypted. SSL sites must use a unique IP address.

To configure the host header for a site, right-click the site in the IIS console and choose Properties. Click Advanced on the Web Site property page. In the Advanced Multiple Web Site Configuration dialog box, select the site identity you want to modify and click Edit. Specify the domain portion of the site's URL (`www.latinaccents.biz` or `support.latinaccents.biz`, for example) as the host header, then close the site's property sheet. Finally, make sure you modify the DNS records for each domain to point the host (`www`, `support`) to the appropriate IP address.

Note Although you can direct traffic to a specific site with a non-unique IP address by specifying a different port number for each site, that typically requires that the client know the port number ahead of time. You can develop a primary site using port 80, which serves as a jumping-off point to these other nondefault port sites, but you would need to incorporate the appropriate port value in all hyperlinks within each site. The better, cleaner solution is to use host headers.

You have two options for supporting client browsers that do not support host headers: cookies or URL-munging (embedding the host name in the URL). Because these topics apply in a limited number of situations (most browsers in use support host headers), they are not covered in this chapter. Point your browser to `http://www.microsoft.com/windows2000/en/advanced/iis/default.asp?url=/windows2000/en/advanced/iis/htm/core/iisuphh.htm` to learn how to enable support for browsers that don't support host headers.

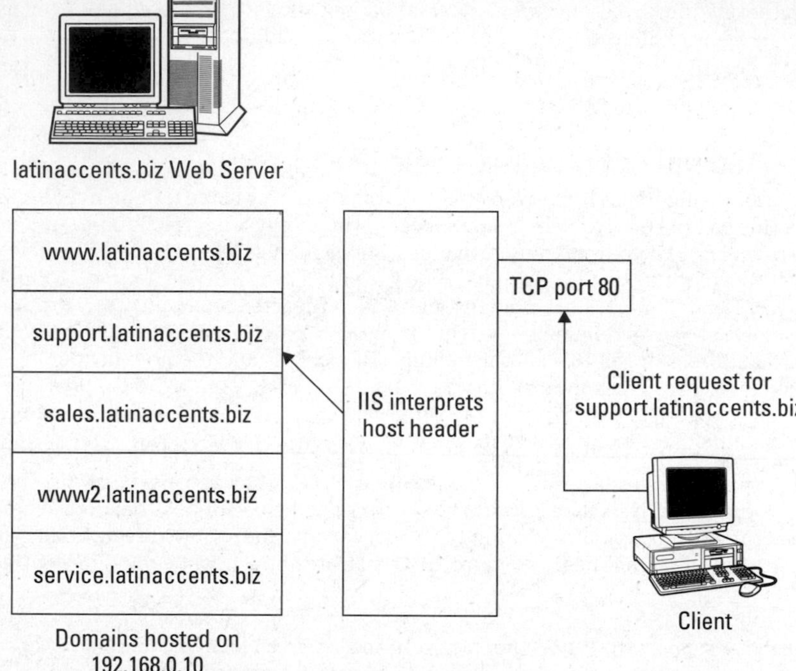

Figure 29-3: Host headers direct traffic to the appropriate site when a single IP is used for multiple sites.

Configuring FrontPage server extensions

Microsoft FrontPage is an HTTP development application that enables you to create, modify, and publish Web sites to a server that supports FrontPage Server Extensions. While few Web development companies consider FrontPage a viable tool for professional Web development, many companies or organizations use it to enable end-users to create and update their own site areas or departmental sites. This section covers the FrontPage Server Extensions in the event you need to install them on a Web server to enable users to manage sites on the server.

FrontPage Server Extensions and Microsoft SharePoint Team Services are integrated in Windows Server 2003. This section of the chapter explains how to configure basic FrontPage Server Extensions settings on a virtual server.

Installing FrontPage Server Extensions is really a two-step process. You must install the extensions on the server and install the extensions to each Web site that requires them. To install FrontPage Server Extensions on the server, open the Control Panel and run the Add/Remove Programs object. Click Add/Remove Windows Components, open Application Server, double-click Internet Information Services, and select FrontPage 2002 Server Extensions. Click OK and follow the prompts to complete the installation to the server.

Next, install Server Extensions on each site for which FrontPage is used. You do so through the IIS console. Open the IIS console, right-click the site, and choose All Tasks ⇨ Configure Server Extensions 2002. IIS opens a Web-based interface you can use to configure the Server Extensions Configuration Wizard. Verify in the Server to Extend field that you are extending the correct site, enter an account with administrative privileges for the site, and click Submit.

After you configure server extensions on a site, you can manage extension settings through the site's property sheet. Right-click the site, choose Properties, and then click Server Extensions to display the Server Extensions tab. Click Settings to open the Web page shown in Figure 29-4.

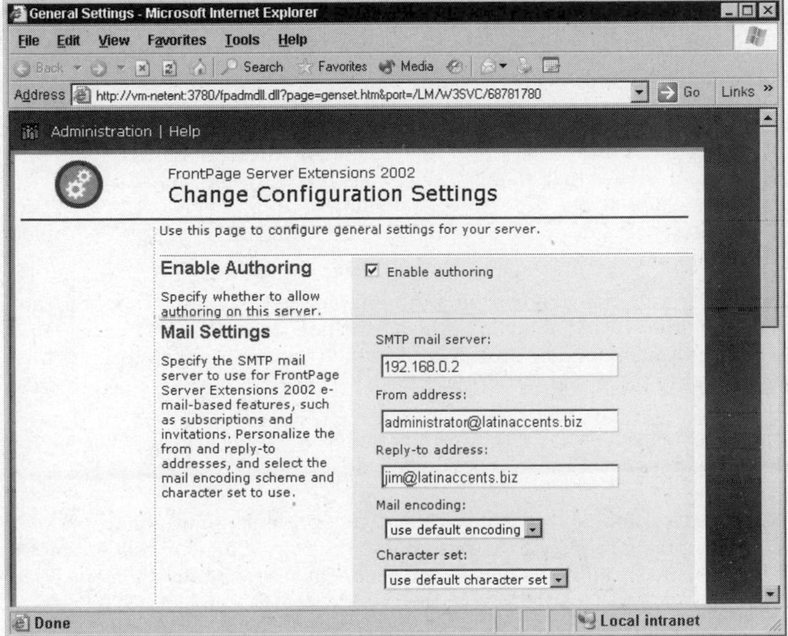

Figure 29-4: FrontPage extension options on the Server Extensions page.

The Enable Authoring option determines whether authors can use FrontPage to access and modify the content of the root web for the selected site. The Mail Settings group enables you to specify the settings FrontPage Extensions uses for the site to send mail, such as when the site submits a form by e-mail. The settings include the following:

- ✦ **SMTP mail server:** Specify the IP address or FQDN of the SMTP server that you want IIS to use to send outgoing messages. If the SMTP virtual server is running on the local computer and you have it configured to respond on all unassigned IP addresses, you can enter **localhost** in this field. Otherwise, you must specify the local IP address explicitly or the FQDN of the server.
- ✦ **From address:** Enter in this field the e-mail address you want outgoing messages to use as the sender's address.

- **Reply-to address:** Specify here the address to which replies to outgoing messages will be directed. This value need not be the same as the From address value.
- **Mail encoding:** Select the format for outgoing messages.
- **Character set:** Specify the character set to use for outgoing messages.

Use the Performance Tuning options to configure cache and other values that affect site performance. Selecting an option from the Tune for drop-down list fills in the fields with appropriate values. You can then fine-tune the individual settings, if desired.

The Client Scripting group includes one option that specifies the types of scripts, if any, can run on the site. Select Use Default from the drop-down list if you want to use the scripting language defined at the server level. Select no scripting to disable scripting altogether, or select either VBScript or JavaScript to restrict scripting to a specific language.

The options in the Security Settings group control authoring. The options include the following:

- **Log authoring actions:** Select this option to have authoring actions logged to the `Author.log` file in the site's `_vti_log` folder. The log file is an ASCII file with several possible types of entries that identify the actions taken by authors and the source IP address for each action. See the Microsoft document at `http://support.microsoft.com/default.aspx?scid=kb;en-us;Q278432` for information on log file format and logged methods.
- **Require SSL for authoring and administration:** Enable this option to require authors to use SSL to author in and administer the site, which provides a higher degree of security. You must also configure the site for SSL, which you accomplish through the Directory Security tab of the site's properties.

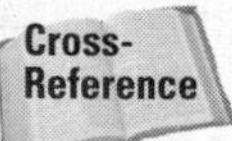

See the section in this chapter, "Enabling secure socket layer," which follows to learn how to configure a site to support SSL.

- **Allow authors to upload executables:** Select this option if you want authors to be able to publish executable files (such as .EXE files) to the site. Enabling this option exposes the site and clients to additional security risks because executables may be infected by viruses and/or contain Trojan horse or worm code, or other malicious code.

When you're satisfied with the settings for the server, click Submit to submit the changes.

Enabling secure socket layer

IIS fully supports Secure Socket Layer (SSL) connections to provide secured transactions between the client browser and the server. SSL is typically used to provide secure credit card transactions and other e-commerce functions, but SSL can be used in any situation in which you want the traffic flowing between the client and server to be encrypted and secure from outside tampering or hijackers. For example, you might want to use SSL for site authoring.

Enabling SSL requires following several steps:

1. Obtain a certificate from a Certificate Authority (CA) for the server. If you have Certificate Services installed on a Windows 2000 Server or Windows Server 2003 in your enterprise, you can obtain a certificate from that CA. Otherwise, you need to obtain a certificate from another CA, such as Thawte or VeriSign. See Chapter 3 for additional information on certificates and CAs. The following steps assume you're using a Windows 2000/Windows Server 2003 running Certificate Services either on a local computer or a computer in your enterprise to generate certificates for you.

If you choose to issue your own certificate, understand that users will receive a security prompt when they view the site if your certificate is not added to the list of trusted authorities. In general you should obtain a certificate from a public CA for public sites, but can certainly use your own certificates for internal sites where it is easy to add the certificate to a users' list of trusted authorities.

2. Open the IIS console and then the properties for the site for which you want to obtain a certificate to enable SSL. Open the Directory Security page.

3. Click Server Certificate to start the Web Server Certificate Wizard. Within the wizard, select the option to create a new certificate. (You have the option of assigning an existing certificate and importing a certificate from a Key Manager backup file, but this procedure assumes you're requesting a new certificate.)

4. Complete the wizard to create the request. You can submit the request immediately if an Enterprise CA is available on the network. IIS cannot recognize a standalone CA server on the same computer or detect one on the network. In this situation, create the request using the wizard, which creates an encrypted text file. You then run the wizard again to submit the encrypted request to the CA. The remaining steps assume you're creating the file and submitting later. Use the following list as a guide to respond to the wizard's prompts:

Note

The first page of the wizard offers several options for creating a new certificate, assigning an existing certificate, or importing from another system. The following options assume you select the Create a New Certificate option. The other methods are discussed a bit later in this chapter. The following steps assume the CA is running Windows 2000 Server. If you are using a Windows Server 2003 CA, some of the prompts will be slightly different, but overall the process is the same.

- **Prepare the request now, but send it later:** Use this option if you have no enterprise CA in your enterprise, or want to submit to a standalone CA.
- **Send the request immediately to an online certification authority:** Use this option to submit the request immediately to an enterprise CA (dimmed if IIS doesn't detect an available CA).
- **Name:** Friendly name for the certificate.
- **Bit length:** A longer bit length increases security but can decrease performance.
- **Select cryptographic service provider (CSP) for this certificate:** Select this option if you want to select between DH or RSA providers for the certificate.
- **Organization:** Specify the name of your organization (typically, the business name).
- **Organizational Unit:** Specify a department or other OU to further define the certificate.
- **Common name:** Specify the domain name (such as `www.latinaccents.biz`) for a site hosted on the Internet. You can specify a DNS name or NetBIOS name for a site hosted on your intranet.
- **Regional information:** Specify country, state, city, or other regional information for your organization.
- **File name:** Specify a file name under which the certificate request will be saved.

5. With a Web browser, connect to the CA using `http://ServerCA/CertSrv`, where *ServerCA* is the DNS name or IP address of the certification server. Choose Request a certificate and then click Next.
6. Select Advanced Request and click Next.
7. Choose Submit a certificate request by using a base-64-encoded CMC or PKCS #10 file, or submit a renewal request by using a base-64-encoded PKCS #7 file; then click Next.
8. Click Browse and browse for the file created in step 4; then click Read to read the file into the form. Or, open Notepad and then open the certificate request created in step 4. Copy the text from the file and paste the text into the Saved Request text box on the form. Make sure to select Web Server from the Certificate Template drop-down list; then click Submit.
9. Follow the prompts provided by the CA to complete the request. Depending on how the certificate server is configured, you're granted the certificate immediately or you have to return to the page after an Administrator has issued the certificate. In either case, you have the option of downloading the certificate in DER or Base 64 encoded formats. Either format is acceptable.
10. Open the IIS console and open the property sheet for the site and then open the Directory Security page. Click Server Certificate to run the wizard again, which recognizes that a certificate request is pending for the site. Through the wizard, specify the location of the certificate file provided by the CA in step 9 and then complete the wizard to install the certificate.
11. On the Directory Security page, click Edit to display the Secure Communications page (Figure 29-5). Configure options based on the following list, then close the property sheet and stop/start the site in preparation for testing the site:
    - **Require Secure Channel (SSL):** Select this option to require the client to use SSL to connect to the site. Deselect the option to enable unencrypted access to the site.
    - **Require 128-bit encryption:** Select this option to require the client to use 128-bit encryption.
    - **Client certificates:** Specify how client certificates are treated. For a public Web site, choose Ignore client certificates. Select Accept client certificates to enable clients to optionally use client-side certificates to authenticate on the site. Select Require client certificates to force clients to use a certificate.
    - **Enable client certificate mapping:** Use this option to enable clients to use their client-side certificates to authenticate against user accounts on the server. This enables you to integrate client logon with your Windows user accounts and groups.
    - **Enable certificate trust list:** Select this option and use the associated controls to define a list of CAs that are trusted for the site.

After configuring the site, test it to ensure it functions properly. Open a browser on another system and connect to `https://site name`, where *site name* is the Web site's DNS name or the NetBIOS server name (intranet). If you receive an error that the site can't be displayed, open the Directory Security properties for the site and view the certificate. Make sure the Issued To field for the certificate matches the name of the site (`www.latinaccents.biz`, for example) or the NetBIOS name of the server (for an intranet site). If it doesn't, remove the certificate and request a new certificate with the correct name.

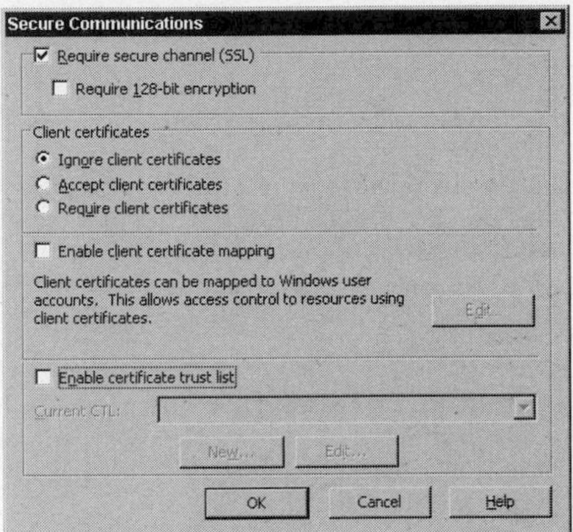

Figure 29-5: The Secure Communications page.

If the certificate's Issued To field shows a username or Administrator, you probably neglected to select Web Server from the Certificate Template drop-down list when you requested the certificate. Resubmit the request with the correct template.

Configuring BITS

BITS stands for Background Intelligent Transfer Service, and BITS provides smart, bi-directional file transfer capability for IIS, enabling it to control bandwidth and offer restartable file transfers. BITS continues a file transfer even after a user closes the application in which the transfer was started, as long as the user remains logged on. If the user logs off or the network connection is interrupted, the session is placed on hold and then reinitiated when the user logs on again or the connection is re-established.

One reason to use BITS is that it adjusts the bandwidth used for file transfers according to the load on the client computer. As the load increases on the system, BITS reduces the bandwidth used for the file transfer to allow more bandwidth for other operations.

BITS does not initiate a connection on its own — the user must perform an interactive logon to enable the connection to be re-established. The user can log on through the Welcome screen, log on to a terminal service client, or log on through fast user switching (Windows XP). Terminal service logon is supported for Windows XP but not for Windows 2000.

You can also use BITS programmatically with services to perform file transfers, provided the service uses the LocalSystem, LocalService, or NetworkService system accounts. These accounts are always logged on, so file transfer works as long as the computer is on and a network connection is established.

BITS enables and supports authentication using challenge-response and basic authentication. For basic authentication, the client must specify the credentials in the connecting URL, such as `http://jboyce:mypassword@www.latinaccents.biz/downloads/contract.doc`. The downside to using basic authentication is that the credentials are sent in plain text and are therefore susceptible to sniffing and interception. For challenge-response authentication, BITS uses the client's credentials. You can use SSL to provide additional security when you need to use basic authentication.

BITS version 1.5 and later support authentication through a proxy server, but BITS 1.0 does not.

The configuration of the security properties for the file transfer directory has an impact on BITS. If you configure the directory for both anonymous and authenticated access and use ACLs to control access to files, BITS transfers may fail because IIS will not attempt to authenticate the client but instead uses anonymous access. If the ACLs on the target files or folders don't enable anonymous access, the client won't be able to access them. So, if you intend to use authenticated access for uploads or downloads, segregate those files or folders in a separate location from anonymous content and configure the virtual directory properties accordingly.

If you want to use BITS to control file transfer, configure the BITS server extensions for the virtual directories. Open the IIS console, expand the site, right-click the directory, and choose Properties. Then click the BITS Server Extensions tab (Figure 29-6).

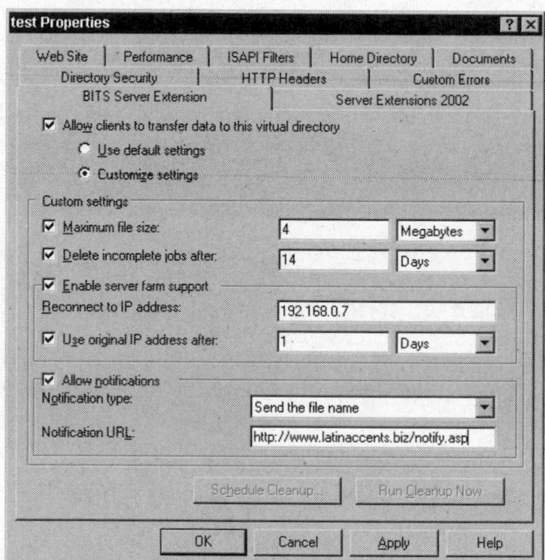

Figure 29-6: Configure file transfer with the BITS Server Extensions tab.

The BITS Server Extensions tab contains the following settings:

- ✦ **Allow clients to transfer data to this virtual directory:** Select this option to enable clients to use BITS to upload files to the virtual directory. BITS uploads and script/executable permissions are mutually exclusive. If you enable BITS, IIS disables script and executable permissions on the virtual directory for security reasons. Re-enabling the permissions causes all BITS transfer requests to be denied. This setting corresponds to the `BITSUploadEnabled` metadata value.
- ✦ **Use default settings:** Use this option to configure BITS with its default values.
- ✦ **Customize settings:** Select this option if you want to impose file size limits or make other modifications to the default BITS settings.

- **Maximum file size:** Use this option to limit the file size that a client can upload to the virtual directory. This setting corresponds to the `BITSMaximumUploadSize` metadata value.
- **Delete incomplete jobs after:** Use this option to specify the length of time that BITS should maintain a connection. If the session times out, BITS closes the connection and cleans up the data associated with it. This setting corresponds to the `BITSSessionTimeout` metadata value.
- **Enable server farm support:** Select this option to enable clients to reconnect to a server farm that does not use shared storage. If a session is interrupted, the client reconnects to the host specified by the Reconnect to IP address value (which should be the local server). If you don't enable this option, disconnected sessions can be reconnected to another server in the farm, making transfer restarts impractical. BITS cleans up the failed transfer on the original host after the timeout period is reached.
- **Reconnect to IP address:** Specify the IP address of the server to which the client should reconnect if the connection fails. This should be an IP address that maps to the local server (local address or a NAT-mapped IP address) to ensure that the transfer reconnects to the same server. If you specify a different server, the transfer restarts from scratch and BITS cleans up the failed connection's data on the local server after the timeout period is reached. This value corresponds to the `BITSHostID` metadata value.
- **Use original IP address after:** Specify the period of time after a disconnect that the client should attempt to reconnect to the original host address before reverting to the hostname specified in the file transfer job. This setting corresponds to the `BITSHostIdFallbackTimeout` metadata value.
- **Allow notifications:** Enable this option to specify how the client passes the file name to the server application (see the following options). Disabling this option is equivalent to setting the `BITSServerNotificationType` metadata value to 0.
- **Notification type:** Select Send the file name from the drop-down list to have the client pass the location of the upload file in a header to the applications server. Select Send the data to have the client pass the contents of the file in the body of the request to the application server. The former option corresponds to setting `BITSServerNotificationType` to 1, and the latter corresponds to a `BITSServerNotificationType` value of 2.
- **Notification URL:** This setting specifies the URL for the application server and works in conjunction with the Notification type setting. Do not include a query string in the URL. If the remote name passed by the client includes a query string, BITS appends it to the specified URL. For example, if the client requests `http://snoopy/files/dogfood.txt?user=joeblow` and you specify a URL of `http://bart/morefiles/file.asp`, BITS uses `http://bart/morefiles/file.asp?user=joeblow`. Or, if the client specifies `http://snoopy/files/dogfood.txt` and the notification URL is set to simply `files.asp`, BITS uses `http://snoopy/files/files.asp` as the URL. This setting corresponds to the `BITSNotificationURL` metadata value.
- **Schedule Cleanup:** Click to configure the scheduled times that BITS cleans up incomplete sessions.
- **Run Cleanup Now:** Click to force an immediate cleanup.

After reading this section, you may have realized that using BITS isn't a simple point-and-click solution, but rather requires server-side coding to implement. You can find extensive BITS development documentation in MSDN, with the document currently at `http://msdn.microsoft.com/library/default.asp?url=/library/en-us/bits/bits/about_bits.asp`.

Backing up and restoring Configuration data

As mentioned at the beginning of this chapter, IIS 6.0 stores configuration data in plain text, XML-formatted files. You can export a site or virtual directory's configuration to an XML file for archival/backup purposes and easily restore the configuration from the file.

To back up the configuration for a site or virtual directory, right-click the virtual server or directory and choose All Tasks ➪ Save Configuration to a File. Specify the file name and path in the resulting dialog box, and optionally specify that you want to encrypt the file. IIS creates an XML file in the specified location.

You can add a virtual server or virtual directory from a configuration file, which is useful when you need to restore a failed server or want to migrate a virtual server from one physical server to another. To add a virtual server from a configuration file, open the IIS console, right-click the Web sites container, and choose New ➪ Web Site (from file). Enter the XML file and path in the resulting dialog box, click Read File, select the location to restore, and click OK. If the file is encrypted, IIS prompts you for the password.

You can also back up and restore all of the virtual HTTP servers on a physical server, which is extremely useful for quickly restoring a server after a failure or migrating servers. To back up all sites, right-click the Web sites container and choose All Tasks ➪ Save Configuration to a File. Specify the file name and path and optional encryption settings to create the file. To restore all virtual servers, repeat the process described above to read the XML file and restore the configuration, repeating the process as needed to restore each virtual server.

Optionally, you can backup and restore at the server level rather than the Web sites container. IIS automatically backs up configuration data, but you can explicitly create a backup and/or restore the configuration of all FTP and Web sites on the server. To create an explicit backup, open the IIS console and right-click the server, then choose All Tasks ➪ Backup/Restore Configuration. Click Create Backup, specify a name for the backup, optionally enable encryption, and click OK. IIS creates a pair of files prefixed with the specified name in the `%systemroot%\System32\inetsrv\MetaBack` folder, and stores the configuration in those files. You can later right-click the server, choose All Tasks ➪ Backup/Restore Configuration, and select and restore a specific configuration by name. You can also migrate the backup files to another server and restore the configuration there.

Managing the Web server

The Internet Information Services Manager MMC console provides the primary means through which you manage IIS Web sites. You can use the console to set site properties; stop, pause, and start a site; set properties on documents within a site; configure FrontPage Server Extensions; define custom headers and error pages; and all other management tasks.

Use the IIS console to manage IIS services and sites locally or to connect to other servers on your network. To connect to another server, right-click on Internet Information Services in the console tree and choose Connect from the context menu. Or, choose Action ➪ Connect from the console menu. Specify the name of the computer to manage and click OK. You also can connect to systems on a remote network if you first establish a VPN connection to the network. After establishing the VPN connection, connect with the IIS console to the remote server as you would for a local server.

IIS also provides a means of managing Web sites through a browser. The Administration Web site, which you can add as an optional component, enables you to use a browser to perform administration tasks on all of the Web sites hosted on the server. Connect to `http://<server>:<port>`, where `<server>` is the IP address or host name of the server, and `<port>` is the port assigned to the Administration Web site, to manage it remotely.

Use port 8098 if you want to use SSL for greater security.

By default, the Administration site enables access from all IPs, a change from IIS 5.0 in which the Administration Web site was restricted only to localhost access by default. You may configure the virtual server to restrict access based on IP address, doing so adds greater security to your Web server. Open the properties for the Administration Web site and click the Directory Security tab. Click Edit in the IP address and domain name restrictions group, then specify the individual computers, group of computers, or domain from which the server can be managed. If you prefer, you can grant all computers access to the server, but this isn't recommended for security reasons.

The Administration Web site in Windows Server 2003 offers much more flexibility over server management than its Windows 2000 counterpart. You can manage all Web sites, as well as general HTTP and FTP server and log settings, but you can't manage individual FTP sites. However, you can manage many general server settings, including the following:

✦ **Server Identification:** Change the server name and domain membership.

✦ **Network Interfaces:** Configure all network interfaces on the server.

✦ **Administration Web site:** Set the ports and allowed addresses for the Administration Web site.

✦ **Global Settings:** Configure DNS resolution, modify the Hosts file, and modify the `Lmhosts` file for the server. These settings affect all network interfaces on the server.

✦ **Administrator Account:** Change the password for the administrator account.

✦ **Telnet:** Enable Telnet access to the server.

✦ **Users and Groups:** Create user accounts and groups.

✦ **Date/Time:** Set the server's data and time.

✦ **Logs:** View and configure the application, security, system, and Web administration event logs.

✦ **Alert E-mail:** Enable and configure settings for e-mail alerts generated by the server.

✦ **Shutdown:** Schedule the server for shut down or restart, or immediately shut down or restart the server.

✦ **Remote Desktop:** Connect to the server using Remote Desktop (requires either Windows XP on the client computer or the Remote Desktop client software installed for other client platforms).

✦ **Language:** Change the language used by the server.

Oddly enough, even with Microsoft's new focus on security, the Administration Web site is not very secure. True, it does require authentication and a nonstandard port connection, but this isn't a substitute for restricting the site to localhost access initially. For that reason, you should configure the properties on the Administration Web site to lock it down as soon as you add IIS to the server.

Unfortunately, you can't manage SMTP or NNTP services through a browser. If you need to administer these remotely, connect to the network with a VPN and use the IIS console instead.

You can stop and start the WWW service remotely by connecting to the server through a Telnet session and issuing the commands `NET STOP W3SVC` or `NET START W3SVC`, respectively. This requires that the Telnet service be running and configured to enable you to log on through Telnet.

Disabling Web server extensions

The IIS console enables you to view Web server extensions and their allowed/prohibited state, as well as configure those services. Click the Web Service Extensions container in the left pane and note the service settings in the right pane. Double-click a service, click the Required Files tab, select a file, and click Prohibit to prevent access to that extension.

Managing Application Pool Settings

The first section of this chapter briefly explained IIS's new architecture and its use of application pools and worker processes to handle Web server requests more efficiently and with greater robustness. The IIS console provides the means by which you configure application pools to tune performance. As with sites, you can set general default properties. You can also set properties uniquely for each application pool. Right-click the Application Pools container and choose Properties to set general properties, or expand the container, right-click an application pool, and choose Properties to configure that pool.

The Recycling tab, shown in Figure 29-7, controls how IIS recycles worker processes. Recycling worker processes helps guard against failed processes and draining of system resources. You can configure the server or application pool to recycle worker process at a predetermined interval, after a specified number of requests, or a defined schedule. You can also configure the server or pool to recycle when a process uses a set amount of virtual or physical memory.

The Performance tab (Figure 29-8) controls additional settings that affect worker process timeout, the HTTP request queue, and other performance-related items. Use the Idle timeout setting to control how long a worker process can be idle before it is shut down. Use the Request queue limit values to enable and set a limit on the number of requests the kernel request queue will accommodate.

Use the Enable CPU monitoring option group to have IIS monitor CPU utilization and take action when utilization becomes too high. If you choose the No action option, IIS writes an error to the event log. If you choose the Shutdown option, IIS initiates a shutdown of all processes in the pool when the specified maximum usage is reached.

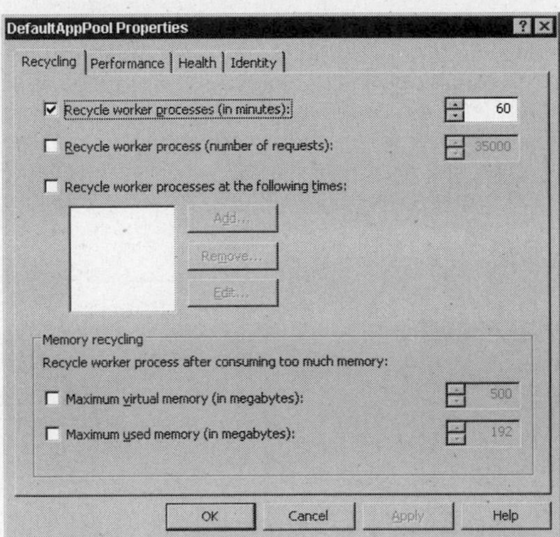

Figure 29-7: Use the Recycling tab to configure worker process recycling.

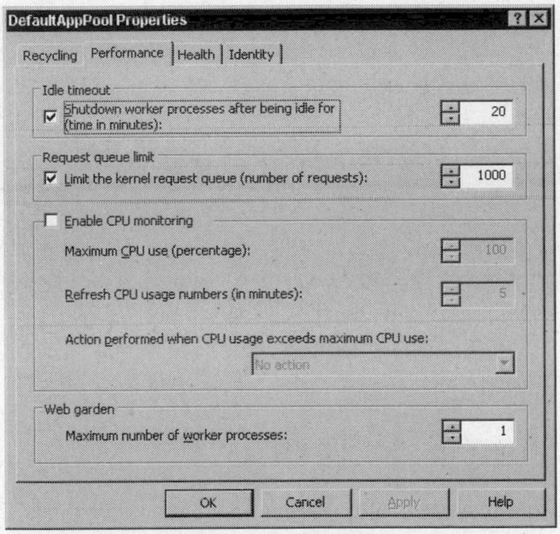

Figure 29-8: The Performance tab.

The Web garden option specifies the maximum number of worker processes in an application pool. By default, only one process is allowed (and therefore, no garden), but you can configure the pool to allow multiple worker processes. This enables the application pool to distribute processing tasks to multiple processes, potentially improving performance and reliability.

Use the Health tab (Figure 29-9) to configure worker process health monitoring. The Enable pinging group lets you configure IIS to ping worker processes periodically to determine if they are still alive. Use the Enable rapid-fail Protection options to have the server respond with 503 Service Unavailable messages if a specified number of worker process failures occur within a given time period. Using this feature helps detect and isolate application pools in which worker processes are failing frequently and improves overall server performance. The Startup time limit and Shutdown time limit options specify the allowed startup and shutdown time for worker processes in the application pool. IIS treats as unavailable those processes that don't start or stop in the specified time.

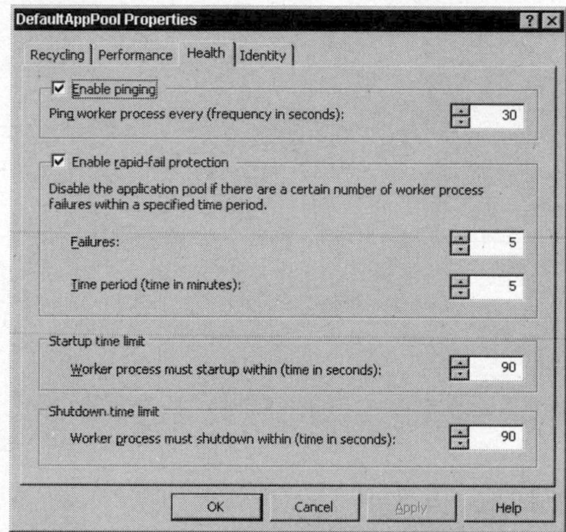

Figure 29-9: The Health tab.

Finally, the Identity tab enables you to configure the service under which the application pool functions. You can select from Network Service, Local Service, or Local System accounts, or you can choose a custom account. The account must be a member of the IIS_WPG group if you choose a custom account.

Configuring and Managing FTP Services

File Transfer Protocol (FTP) enables users to upload and download files to and from the server. While HTTP is becoming more common as a means for file transfer, FTP still serves an important role in providing file transfer services. While HTTP restricts clients to a browser for uploading and downloading files, FTP enables clients to use a browser, FTP command line, or third-party FTP utility to transfer files. IIS provides the capability to restart failed FTP transfers, enabling a client to reconnect to the server and restart the transfer from the point of failure rather than transferring the entire file again.

Setting up an FTP site is much like setting up a Web site. The following section explains the process.

Creating and configuring FTP sites

As with HTTP, IIS creates a default FTP site that responds to FTP requests on all unassigned IP addresses. You can configure this site to use as your only FTP site, or you might prefer to create other FTP sites, particularly if you are hosting multiple domains on a particular server.

Either before or after setting up the FTP site on the server, make sure you create the necessary DNS zone and records to accommodate the site. If you don't already have a DNS zone set up to accommodate the FTP site, create the zone on your DNS server with the appropriate SOA and NS records. Then, create a host (A) record that defines the host portion of the site name. For example, in the zone `latinaccents.biz`, you might create an A record for FTP that points to the IP address assigned in IIS for the FTP site, enabling clients to connect to the site using the URL `ftp://ftp.latinaccents.biz`. After you've configured the appropriate DNS records, you're ready to begin creating the site.

Creating an FTP site

To create a new site, open the IIS console, right-click FTP Sites in the tree, and choose New ⇨ FTP Site to start the FTP Site Creation Wizard. The wizard prompts you for the following information:

- **Description:** This is the friendly name for the site that appears in the IIS console.
- **IP address:** Specify the IP address for the FTP server or choose All Unassigned to have the FTP server respond to all requests for which an IP is not specified or not available (such as when a virtual server is stopped).
- **TCP port:** Specify the TCP port to be used by the FTP site. The default is 21. You can use a different port to increase security, but clients will have to know beforehand what port to use to connect to the server.
- **FTP User Isolation**: Use the options on this page to optionally restrict users to their specific FTP folders. Choose Isolate Users to require the user to have a folder, either physical or virtual, within the root of the FTP site that matches his account name. Choose Isolate Users Using Active Directory to require the user to be assigned an FTP home directory through his account properties in the AD.
- **Path:** Specify the path to the folder that will serve as the FTP site's root folder.
- **Read/Write:** Choose Read to enable download and Write to enable upload (subject to NTFS permissions you apply to the site's folders, if applicable).

Configuring site properties

After you create a site, you can configure its properties to fine-tune its function. Right-click the site in the IIS console and choose Properties to display its property sheet (Figure 29-10). You'll find that the properties for an FTP site are similar to those for a Web site, although there are fewer properties.

The FTP Site Connections group on the FTP Site page lets you configure the number of concurrent connections allowed to the site and the connection timeout period. You might wish to limit the number of connections for sites with high traffic or low bandwidth to improve performance for connected users. Increase the connection timeout value if clients are experiencing difficulty maintaining a connection during large transfers or times when there is significant traffic on the site.

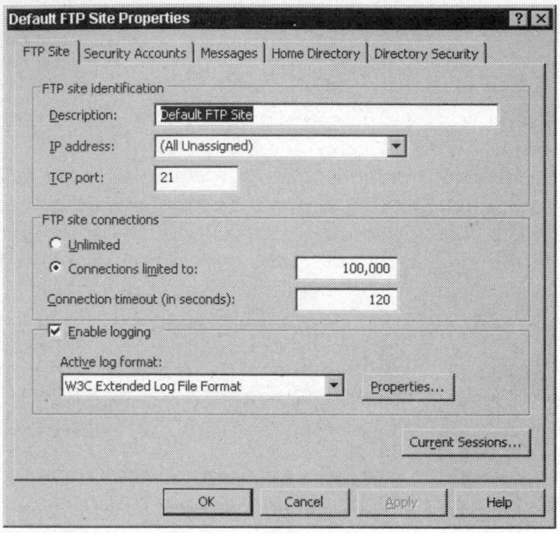

Figure 29-10: The property sheet for an FTP site.

The Enable logging option enables you to turn on connection logging and specify the log file format. Use the Current Sessions button to view a list of currently connected users and, if desired, disconnect one or more of them.

Setting security

The Security Accounts page of the FTP site's properties enables you to configure how IIS grants access to the FTP site. The Allow anonymous connections option, when selected, enables users to connect to the site with the username *anonymous.* If you deselect this option, users must specify a valid user account and password on the server or within the domain in order to authenticate and log on to the FTP site. When anonymous connections are enabled, IIS uses the user account and password specified in the Username and Password fields of the Security Accounts page. By default, the account is IUSR_*server,* where *server* is the name of the computer. In general, you shouldn't change this account, but you can if you prefer to make it more difficult for hackers to guess the default anonymous account. If you specify a different account, make sure you configure the account's rights and permissions on folders accordingly to enable the account to be used successfully for anonymous logon.

To log on for FTP, an account must have the right to log on locally. The IUSR account by default has this right. To enable other user accounts to log on for FTP, however, you need to grant those accounts the right to log on locally. Although you can do this on an account-by-account basis, it's best to create an FTP group, grant the group the right to log on locally, and then place in the group any users who need authenticated (non-anonymous) FTP access.

Tip

If a virtual folder with the same name as a user exists within the FTP site, IIS automatically connects the user to that virtual folder when he or she logs on, making the virtual folder the user's home folder. For example, assume the site contains a virtual folder `jboyce`. When jboyce logs on to the FTP site, he or she is automatically placed in the folder pointed to by the `jboyce` virtual folder. An added benefit is that other users don't see the virtual folders, regardless of their logon accounts. They can, however, change to them manually if they know the virtual folder name. Their access to the folder is subject to its NTFS permissions. See the section "Configuring the site's directory structure" later in this chapter for additional information.

You can use either local or domain accounts for FTP authentication. Users who need to authenticate with an account in a trusted domain can specify the domain and account in the form *domain\account*.

The FTP Site Operators control group on the Security Accounts page defines the accounts or groups that are designated as site operators. A site operator has limited administrative privileges within the site and can configure properties that affect the site. Site operators do not have the ability to modify global IIS properties or properties for other sites unless their accounts are designated within that site as a site operator account or group.

Configuring logon and logoff messages

In most cases, you probably will want to define messages that appear when the user logs on or off the FTP site or when the maximum number of connections is reached for the site. You configure these messages through the Messages property page for the site. In particular, consider posting a welcome message that adequately addresses your company's legal rights should the site be misused by unauthorized personnel (typically applies to a private FTP site rather than a public site). The following is a sample of such a message, although you should consult with the company's legal counsel to be certain the message addresses your needs:

> WARNING: Access to this system by authorized personnel only. All users will be monitored for security purposes and potential law enforcement. Unauthorized use will be subject to criminal and civil prosecution and penalties.

Configuring the site's directory structure

An FTP site's home directory is defined when you create the site, but you can modify the directory through the Home Directory page of the site's properties in the IIS console. The site's home directory can be a folder on the local computer or a share on the network. Subfolders of the home directory appear within the site's folder structure just as they do on the local computer or network share.

You can configure a site's home directory for Read, Write, and Log Visits. Read enables users to download from the site, and Write enables them to upload to the site, subject to any NTFS permissions you might apply to the folder and its contents. The Log Visits option turns on access logging to the selected folder if logging is enabled for the site in the FTP Site property page.

In addition to defining the home directory, you also can configure *virtual folders* for the FTP site. A virtual folder functions as part of the site's directory structure but is effectively hidden from users — it doesn't show up when users browse the site or issue a DIR command from an FTP prompt. However, users can connect to the folder in one of two ways: specify the folder explicitly in the browser or FTP prompt, or connect with a user account that matches the virtual folder's alias name.

To create a new virtual folder, open the IIS console, right-click the FTP site where you want to create the folder, and choose New ⇨ Virtual Directory. A wizard prompts you for the folder's alias name, path, and Read/Write properties. After you create the folder, right-click the folder in the IIS console and choose Properties to set its properties, which are similar to those for a home directory but more limited.

As with a home directory and its child objects, a virtual folder's NTFS permissions control access to the folder and its contents in conjunction with the Read and Write properties you set for the folder when you create it in IIS.

Configuring directory security

By default, all FTP users are granted access to all folders in a site. You can, however, restrict access to individual computers and groups of computers, just as you can with a Web site's folders. You configure access through the Directory Security page of the site's or folder's property sheet, configuring them differently if needed.

Managing the FTP server

The primary tool used to manage the FTP service is the IIS console. As with Web sites, you can connect with a VPN to the network where the server is located and use the IIS console remotely to administer FTP sites on the server. However, you can't use the HTML version of the Internet Services Manager to manage FTP sites or services because it restricts you to managing only the default Web site.

You can stop and start the FTP service from a command prompt (including through a Telnet session to a server) using the `NET STOP MSFTPSVC` and `NET START MSFTPSVC` commands.

FTP client access

Clients connect to an FTP site using a Web browser, FTP command-line utility (included with all Windows platforms, Unix, and other platforms), or third-party FTP utility. When connecting from Internet Explorer 5.0 or later, clients specify the user account for the connection within the URL if using an account other than anonymous to access the site. Enter the URL in the form `ftp://`*`user`*`@`*`site`*, where *`user`* is the account name and *`site`* is the FTP site name. Logging on as user jboyce to the site `ftp.latinaccents.biz`, for example, requires a URL of `ftp://jboyce@ftp.latinaccents.biz`. Internet Explorer prompts for the password. To log on using the anonymous account, specify anonymous in the URL.

For information on using the FTP command, open a console prompt and enter `ftp`, then enter the **?** command to view a description of the FTP command's options. The advantage to using a command prompt is its support for scripting and several other features not offered by Internet Explorer.

Configuring and Managing SMTP Services

Simple Mail Transport Protocol (SMTP) is the primary protocol for transferring e-mail on the Internet. The SMTP Service included with IIS doesn't turn a server running IIS into a full-blown e-mail server, but instead it provides a means for you to create *virtual e-mail servers* that forward mail to designated full-featured e-mail servers that provide client support (POP3, for example). In effect, the SMTP service is primarily a message-forwarding service. Its advantage is that capacity to create multiple e-mail identities and servers to go along with each domain hosted on the server. The SMTP service can handle incoming mail from clients on the Internet or mail generated within a Web site.

The SMTP Service included with Windows Server 2003 offers the following key features:

- **Integrated Management:** The SMTP service uses the same IIS console for management as Web, FTP, and NNTP services, providing a single point for management of all services. You also can use SNMP, the Windows Server 2003 event logs (and Event Viewer), and SMTP transaction logs to monitor the service.
- **Directed mail drop and delivery:** The SMTP service can be configured to drop all incoming mail into a drop directory on the server, enabling other applications on the server to use the SMTP service as a mail receiver. Applications also use a pickup directory to send messages — properly formatted messages placed in the pickup directory are delivered automatically by the SMTP service. Applications also send messages via the SMTP server's TCP port(s).
- **Ability to restrict messages:** You can configure each SMTP server for a variety of restrictions that limit message size, number of recipients, and so on. You also can restrict message relay to prevent a server from being used as a relay for spamming.
- **Routing options:** The SMTP Service provides several options to control message routing and delivery. You can route messages directly, use a smart host as an interim relay agent, and configure other settings to fine-tune message routing.
- **Secure transmission:** The SMTP Service supports anonymous as well as authenticated access to each virtual server, and it also supports Transport Layer Security (TLS) for encryption of incoming messages.
- **Transaction logging:** You can perform extensive logging of SMTP transactions for troubleshooting and tracking server usage.

Overview of the SMTP service

The SMTP service included with IIS enables a Windows Server 2003 computer to function as an SMTP mail server (e-mail delivery agent). The SMTP service does not provide for mailboxes on the server or client support for POP3, so it isn't really designed to function as a full-featured mail server such as Microsoft Exchange or other e-mail server applications. However, you can use the SMTP service to process messages coming from clients on the Internet, from the local LAN, or from applications on the server itself.

The SMTP service works essentially as a file transfer agent. When you create a virtual SMTP server, you define the server's home directory. IIS creates the specified folder and creates the following four subfolders by default:

- **Badmail:** This folder stores undeliverable messages that can't be returned to the sender.
- **Drop:** This folder stores all incoming messages for the domains handled by the virtual server.
- **Pickup:** This folder stores all outgoing messages. The SMTP service monitors the `Pickup` folder, and as soon as a properly formatted message is placed in the folder, the service collects the message and attempts delivery.
- **Queue:** This folder holds messages waiting delivery. When a message can't be delivered because of a communications failure or other problem, it leaves the message in the `Queue` folder for later delivery attempts based on the settings configured for the server (discussed later in this chapter).
- **MailBox**, **Route**, and **SortTemp**. The SMTP service uses these folders as working directories to sort and process messages.

Messages come to the server from the Internet, the LAN, or from an application on the server itself. These messages arrive at the server through the virtual server's designated TCP port (25 by default), or in the case of LAN or local messages, are also placed directly in the `Pickup` folder. The SMTP service processes the message into the `Queue` folder and initiates delivery. The SMTP service places the message in the `Drop` folder if the message is for a local recipient, or the service relays the message to the appropriate server if the message is for a remote recipient. Figure 29-11 illustrates the process.

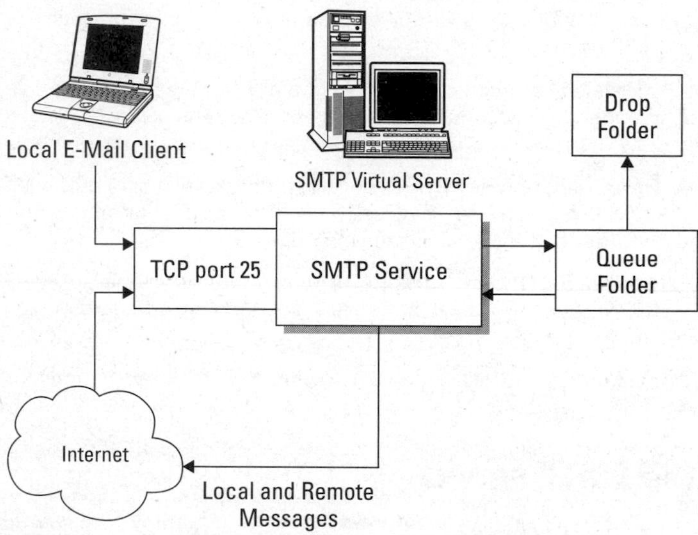

Figure 29-11: SMTP processing incoming messages.

For local recipients, delivery ends when the message is placed in the `Drop` folder. The process for remote delivery is different. SMTP attempts to connect to the receiving mail server, and if the server can't be reached or a communications error occurs, SMTP places the message in the queue for later delivery at intervals you designate for the server in its Delivery property page (discussed later in this chapter). Once the receiving server acknowledges the message receipt, SMTP removes the message from the Queue folder, indicating a completed delivery.

Tip SMTP supports Transport Layer Security (TLS) for remote delivery, providing enhanced security by encrypting all outgoing messages. You can enable or disable TLS for individual remote domains, giving you control over the remote domains for which SMTP uses TLS.

If you prefer, route outgoing messages from a virtual server to a *smart host,* which essentially serves as an intermediary and takes care of transmitting the messages to their destinations. The primary use of a smart host is to direct messages through a connection that might be faster or less costly than the one the server otherwise uses for a direct delivery. A smart host is specified in one of two ways: for the entire virtual server or for each remote domain hosted on the server. The domain setting overrides the server setting, enabling you to route all outgoing messages through a single smart host except for specific domains, which can be directed to other smart hosts. Figure 29-12 illustrates the use of smart hosts for routing message delivery.

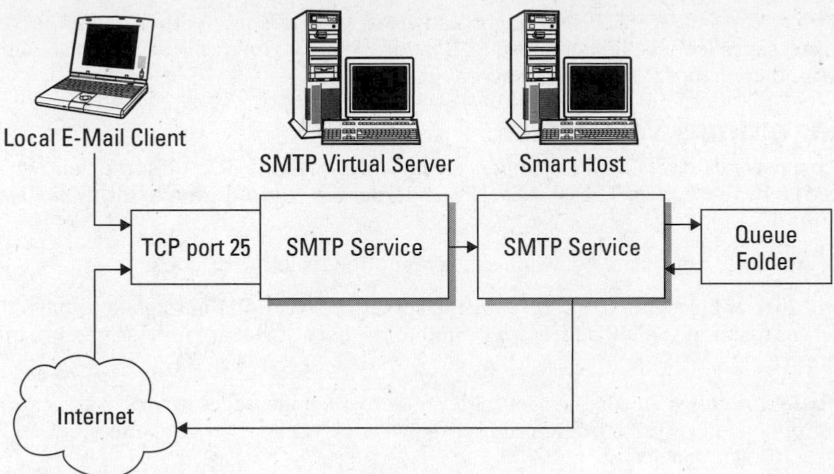

Figure 29-12: Smart hosts act as routing intermediaries.

SMTP offers support for several options for controlling security and connections for both incoming and outgoing messages. For example, you can limit the number of connections for both incoming and outgoing connections, specify timeout for connections, and limit the number of connections per domain (outgoing). To secure both incoming and outgoing access, SMTP supports anonymous authentication, basic (clear text) authentication against Windows 2000 and .NET domain accounts, TLS encrypted authentication, and Windows Security Package (WSP)—the authentication mechanism built into Windows 2000 and .NET. This last option enables clients to use the same single sign-on for mail server authentication as for other enterprise resources, but it requires the use of an e-mail client that supports WSP authentication. The version of Outlook Express included with Windows 2000 and later supports WSP.

Installing SMTP

Windows Server 2003 does not install the SMTP service by default, but you can use the `Add or Remove Programs` object in the Control Panel to add the service. To do so, follow these steps:

1. Open the Control Panel, open Add or Remove Programs, and click Add/Remove Windows Components.
2. Double-click Application Server, double-click Internet Information Services, select SMTP Service, and click OK.
3. Click Next to run the wizard and add the service.

Configuring SMTP

As with the Web and FTP services, IIS automatically creates an SMTP server that, by default, responds to all unassigned IP addresses. Configure the default SMTP server to process messages as a backup for any other SMTP virtual server that happens to be offline.

In addition to the default SMTP server, you can create any number of other virtual servers to process messages for specific domains and IP addresses. The following sections explain how to create and configure SMTP virtual servers under IIS.

Creating a virtual SMTP server

To create a new virtual SMTP server, open the IIS console, right-click the server, and choose New ➪ SMTP Virtual Server. The New SMTP Virtual Server Wizard prompts for the following information:

- **Name**: This is the name by which the server appears in the IIS console.
- **IP address:** Select the IP address for the server or select All Unassigned to have the server respond to all IP addresses bound to the server that are not assigned to other sites.
- **Home directory:** This is the root folder under which messages in process are stored. For enhanced security, this should be an NTFS folder. SMTP creates the required folder structure automatically.
- **Domain:** Each virtual server has one default domain that is used to stamp messages from addresses that don't have a domain. The DNS name is specified in the server's TCP/IP properties or any unique DNS name. You can create additional domains after the virtual server is created. See the following section for more information on domain settings.

After you create the virtual server, it appears in the IIS console with two child objects: Domains and Current Sessions. The `Domains` object contains the domains assigned to the server. You can use this object to create and delete domains and configure their properties. Use the `Current Sessions` object to view current connections to the virtual server and, if needed, disconnect sessions.

Managing SMTP domains

SMTP supports two types of domains: *local* and *remote*. Local domains are hosted on the virtual server, and remote domains are hosted elsewhere. As mentioned previously, each virtual SMTP server has one default local domain that is used to stamp messages from addresses that don't specify a domain. Logically, only one domain can be the default domain, but you can create multiple alias domains that use the same settings as the default domain. Messages that arrive for an alias domain are stamped with the default domain name and placed in the default domain's `Drop` directory.

When you create an SMTP virtual server, IIS creates a default domain for that server based on your response in the New SMTP Virtual Server Wizard. Use the IIS console to configure the properties for the default domain, create local alias domains and remote domains, and change the default domain.

Creating domains

To create a new domain, follow these steps:

1. Open the IIS console and open the virtual server where you want to create the domain.
2. Right-click on the Domains node and choose New ➪ Domain to start the New SMTP Domain Wizard. Because the default domain already exists, you can only create remote and alias domains.

3. Select the desired type and specify the name for the domain. You can use the computer host name specified on the DNS tab of the server's TCP/IP properties for an alias domain, or you can specify a unique name for the domain that can optionally be supported by valid DNS entries in the domain's DNS server. However, the name specified for the domain in the SMTP service has no bearing on name resolution for incoming messages.

If the default domain uses the DNS name specified in the server's TCP/IP properties and you change the server's host name in its TCP/IP properties, you don't have to change the domain name in the SMTP service. IIS automatically uses the new name at startup.

Note The options in the wizard are identical regardless of the type of domain you create.

Setting default domain properties

Open the IIS console, open the Domain node for the desired server, right-click the default domain in the list, and choose Properties. Configure the following two options for the local default domain:

- **Drop directory:** Use this property to specify the location of the `Drop` directory for the domain. You can specify any local directory other than the `Pickup` directory.
- **Enable drop directory quota:** Select this option to enable quotas to be enforced on the `Drop` directory. If this option is enabled, SMTP limits the capacity of the `Drop` folder to ten times the value specified by the Limit Message Size To setting on the Messages page of the properties for the virtual server. If the capacity is exceeded, an error is generated and logged to the SMTP log.

Note Properties can't be changed for an alias domain. An alias is simply the default local domain.

Changing the default domain

You can't delete the default domain, but you can designate a different local domain as the default, leaving the previous default domain as an alias or deleting it after setting up a new default domain. To change the default domain, first create an alias domain using the properties you want for the new default domain. Then, in the IIS console, right-click the newly created local alias domain and choose Set as default. SMTP designates the domain as the default and sets the old domain as an alias.

Configuring remote domain properties

The properties for a remote domain are different from those of the default local domain. To configure the properties for a remote domain, follow these steps:

1. Open the IIS console and locate the remote domain in the appropriate SMTP virtual server.
2. Open the Domains node, right-click the remote domain to modify, and choose Properties. IIS displays a property sheet for the domain similar to the one shown in Figure 29-13.

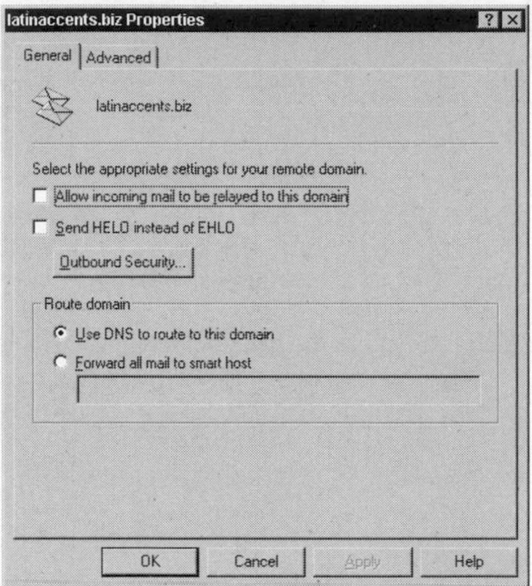

Figure 29-13: Properties for a remote domain.

3. Use the General tab to configure the following options:

   - **Allow incoming mail to be relayed to this domain:** SMTP by default prevents messages from being relayed to the remote domain unless otherwise specified in the Access property page for the virtual server (covered in the following section of this chapter). Select this option to override the settings on the Access page and allow message relay to the remote host.
   - **Send HELO instead of EHLO:** Servers that support ESTMP (Extended SMTP) supply a list of supported extensions when a connection is made using the EHLO command rather than the standard HELO command. Servers that do not support ESMTP generate an error if a connection attempt is made using EHLO instead of HELO. Select this option to have SMTP use standard HELO commands, instead of EHLO when connecting to the remote domain.
   - **Outbound security:** Click this button to configure security options for the outbound connection to the remote domain. Configure the type of authentication (anonymous, basic, WSP, or TLS) and user account or password required by the remote server, if any.
   - **Use DNS to route to this domain:** Select this option to have SMTP attempt to deliver messages directly to the remote host using DNS lookup rather than forwarding to a smart host for delivery.
   - **Forward all mail to smart host:** Select this option to forward all messages for the remote domain to the specified smart host. You can enter a Fully Qualified Domain Name (FQDN) or IP address for the smart host. If entering an IP address, enclose the address in brackets to identify the entry to SMTP as an IP address, bypassing DNS lookup and speeding up the connection process. Specifying a smart host in this field overrides the smart host setting, if any, specified in the general properties for the virtual server for the selected remote domain only.

Use the Advanced tab to configure which remote hosts use remote triggered delivery (ATRN, or Authenticated TURN) to pull messages bound for them from the virtual server. Remote triggered delivery enables the remote host to pull messages from the virtual server at its own designated times to reduce network bandwidth utilization at peak times or to accommodate other administrative or performance requirements on the remote host or network. Rather than attempt to deliver messages waiting in the queue to these remote hosts, SMTP simply places the messages in the queue and waits for the remote host to connect and issue an ATRN command to retrieve the messages. The options on the Advanced page are self-explanatory.

Setting general properties

SMTP provides several property pages you can use to configure global options for each virtual server that determine how the virtual server functions. Open the IIS console, right-click the SMTP virtual server you want to manage, and click Properties. The following sections explain the options you can set.

General

The General tab enables you to configure several global properties for the site, which are explained in the following list:

- **IP Address:** Select a single IP address or select All unassigned.
- **Advanced:** Click to add multiple IP addresses for the server or to change address/port assignments for the server.
- **Limit Number of Connections To**: Select this option to limit the number of concurrent connections to the server, and enter a number for the maximum connections in the associated text field.
- **Connection Time-Out (Minutes)**: Set the timeout for incoming and outgoing connections.
- **Enable logging:** Select this option to turn on SMTP service logging; then select a log format from the associated drop-down list. Click Properties to configure log properties such as how often a new log is created, the log size limit, log file directory, and the types of events that are logged.

Access

Use the Access tab to configure properties that control remote server and client access to the virtual server and their ability to relay through the server. The Access control group enables you to configure the types of authentication accepted by the server and includes anonymous access, basic authentication against a specified Windows 2000 or .NET domain, TLS encryption, and WSP. Selecting the anonymous access option and deselecting all others effectively turns off authentication for the virtual server and enables all clients to access the server.

The Secure Communication group on the Access page enables you to request and install a certificate for securing access to the server through TLS encryption. Click Certificate to run the Web Server Certificate Wizard, which enables you to request, install, and configure a certificate for enabling TLS on the virtual server. The process is essentially identical to that for installing a certificate to enable SSL on a Web site. You can request a certificate from a CA in your enterprise or from an outside CA. See the section "Enabling secure socket layer" earlier in this chapter for a discussion on requesting and installing a certificate.

Use the Communication button to enable and configure TLS. Select the Require secure channel option on the resulting Security dialog box to require TLS encryption for remote clients to connect to the virtual server. You also can configure the server to require stronger 128-bit encryption, if needed.

The Connection Control group on the Access page enables you to specify which computers can access the SMTP virtual server, giving you the means to restrict access as needed. As with Web and FTP sites, you can restrict access by enabling or denying access to a specified group. You can add computers to the group to be allowed or denied access by single IP, subnet (group), or domain name.

The last group on the Access tab — Relay restrictions — lets you configure the list of computers that is either allowed or denied the privilege of relaying messages through the server (Figure 29-14). As with connection control, you can specify a single IP, subnet, or domain to allow or deny the privilege. The Allow all computers option at the bottom of the dialog box allows all clients that successfully authenticate to relay messages through the server even if they would otherwise be denied access based on their IP address or domain.

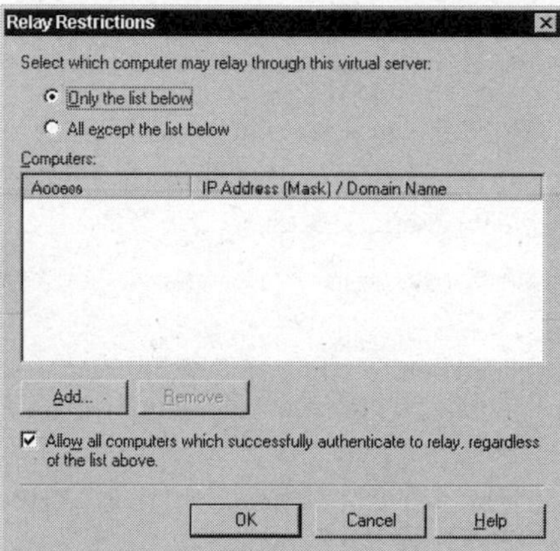

Figure 29-14: The Relay Restrictions dialog box.

Messages

The Messages tab for an SMTP virtual server enables you to apply limits on message size, session size, number of messages per connection, and number of recipients per message. These options can help reduce spamming and can serve to reduce the load on the server.

The option "Send copy of Non-Delivery Report to" enables you to specify an e-mail address to which a copy of non-delivery reports (NDRs) are sent. NDRs are generated when SMTP is unable to deliver a message, such as when a bad mailbox or domain is specified in the address. The message is returned to the sender with an NDR, but you may also forward a copy to an administrative account for monitoring. Numerous NDRs for messages bound for the same domain can indicate a connectivity, name resolution, or similar problem with a remote host, and receiving the NDRs can be a heads-up alert that a potential problem exists.

The last option on the Messages page enables you to change the location of the `Badmail` folder for the virtual server. By default, bad messages are stored in the `Badmail` folder under the SMTP mail root folder that is specified when the server is created. Using this setting, you can redirect the folder, if needed.

Delivery

SMTP tries to send messages as soon as they are ready, except in the case of a remote domain that uses remote triggered delivery to trigger the virtual server to transmit messages to it. The Outbound group of controls on the Delivery property page enables you to specify the frequency of retransmission attempts, when the server sends a delay notification to the sender, indicating the message's delay and expiration time period before it's returned with an NDR. This group also controls the delay notification and expiration times for local messages.

Outbound connection security options are configured through the Delivery page. As with incoming connections, you can configure the virtual server to use anonymous access, basic authentication against the remote server's security database, WSP, and enable TLS. Refer to the section "Access" earlier in this chapter, if you need more information on configuring these properties.

Clicking the Advanced button on the Delivery page displays the Advanced Delivery dialog box shown in Figure 29-15, which enables you to configure advanced routing options for the virtual server. The following list explains the options:

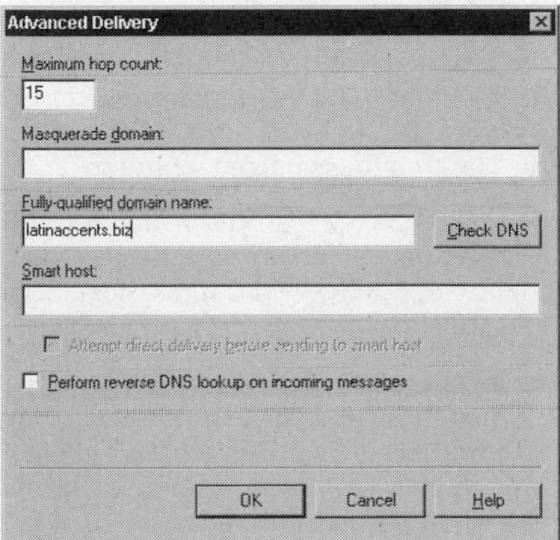

Figure 29-15: The Advanced Delivery dialog box.

✦ **Maximum hop count:** Each server that a message passes through on its way to delivery is called a *hop.* The total number of hops is called the *hop count.* The SMTP server counts the number of hops listed in each message's header and compares it with the hop count specified by this setting. SMTP returns the message to the sender with an NDR if the number of hops exceeds this setting. The default value is 15. Decreasing the value can help reduce spamming because spammed messages often route through multiple servers to reach their final destinations. Increase the value if you're having trouble getting messages delivered because the hop count is exceeding that set for the server.

✦ **Masquerade domain:** This property enables you to insert a masquerade domain name in the Mail From lines in each message's protocol for readability or to match an existing domain naming policy. For example, you might replace `mail2.latinaccents.biz` with simply `latinaccents.biz`.

- **Fully-qualified domain name:** The SMTP service automatically uses the FQDN derived from the host and domain name properties on the host server's DNS property page (TCP/IP properties) for connectivity. If the host or domain name changes, SMTP adjusts automatically and uses the new name. However, you might choose to specify an explicit FQDN for each virtual server, especially when hosting multiple virtual domains on a single server. So, the server's native FQDN might be `server1.latinaccents.biz`, but you're hosting the domain `support.latinaccents.biz` and want to differentiate it with its own FQDN. In this case, create MX and A resource records in the appropriate DNS server for `mail.support.latinaccents.biz`, and use that as the FQDN for the virtual server that supports that domain.

- **Check DNS:** Click this button to perform a name server lookup on the FQDN specified in the fully-qualified domain name field to verify that it is a valid name. SMTP checks the name servers listed in the host server's DNS properties for a corresponding zone and host record.

- **Smart host:** Use this option to direct all outgoing mail to an intermediate host that handles delivery of the messages. This property applies to all messages coming through the virtual server, regardless of the destination domain. You can configure individual domains within the virtual server to use another smart host, if desired. The smart host setting defined in each remote domain's properties overrides the host setting defined here. Specify the FQDN or IP address of the host that handles message delivery. If specifying an IP address, enclose the address in brackets, such as `[192.168.0.24]`, to indicate to SMTP that the entry is an IP address and to bypass name resolution.

- **Attempt direct delivery before sending to smart host:** Select this option if you want the virtual server to attempt to deliver messages before forwarding them to the smart host. By default, the SMTP service does not attempt delivery if a smart host is specified, but selecting this option causes it to do so.

- **Perform reverse DNS lookup on incoming messages:** By default, SMTP does not attempt to verify that the client's IP address matches the DNS name submitted by the client when establishing the connection with the server. It's possible for a client to spoof its DNS name to enable it to relay through your server or otherwise hide its true origin. The only way for the SMTP service to verify the identity of the client is to perform a reverse lookup. If the reverse lookup fails, SMTP inserts "unverified" after the IP address in the message header. No change occurs if the reverse lookup succeeds. For the reverse lookup to succeed, the originating domain's DNS zone must contain a host record for the originating host. With this option enabled, SMTP performs a reverse lookup for every message received by the virtual server, which can negatively impact server performance if the server receives a large number of messages on a regular basis.

LDAP routing

The SMTP service can use Lightweight Directory Access Protocol (LDAP) to resolve sender and recipient addresses. The directory service stores information about clients, including e-mail addresses and other data. By configuring the SMTP service to use LDAP, you enable it to perform such tasks as resolving a distribution list into individual addresses stored on a directory server. The SMTP service can use the Active Directory, Site Server Membership Directory (MCIS 2.0 or later), or Exchange (Site Server 3.0 or later) LDAP service. Select the option Enable LDAP Routing to configure the virtual server to use LDAP. You specify the LDAP server, schema, authentication settings, and base container in the directory at which to begin the search.

Security

Use the Security tab to grant users Operator status for the SMTP virtual server, giving them the ability to perform limited administrative functions on the virtual server.

Configuring and Managing NNTP Services

Network News Transport Protocol, or NNTP, serves as the protocol by which news messages are distributed across the Internet. This chapter assumes you have some familiarity with NNTP and understand its purpose and function. We focus on how to install and configure NNTP under IIS in Windows Server 2003 to create a local news server to host your organization's newsgroups.

Installing NNTP

As with the other IIS services, you add NNTP through the `Add or Remove Programs` object in the Windows .NET Control Panel. After you start the `Add or Remove Programs` object, click Add/Remove Windows Components, double-click Application Server, double-click Internet Information Services, and select NNTP Service. Click OK, click Next, and follow the prompts provided to complete the software installation.

Configuring NNTP

As with the other IIS services, IIS sets up a default NNTP virtual server when you install the NNTP service. The default NNTP virtual server is bound to all unassigned IP addresses by default, which causes it to respond to all IP addresses bound on the server that are not assigned to another NNTP virtual server. If another virtual server defined on the server isn't available, the default server responds to client and server NNTP requests. You can modify the configuration of the default NNTP virtual server and use it as the only one on the server, or you can create multiple virtual servers to accommodate multiple domains or other organization units.

Creating NNTP virtual servers

Creating an NNTP virtual server is relatively simple thanks to the New NNTP Virtual Server Wizard provided by IIS. To run the wizard, open the IIS console, right-click the server where you want to add the virtual server, and choose New ➪ NNTP Virtual Server. You also can right-click an existing NNTP virtual server and choose New ➪ Virtual Server. Specify the following information in the wizard:

- ✦ **Name:** This is the friendly name for the virtual server as it appears in the IIS console.
- ✦ **IP Address:** Select a single IP from the drop-down list or select All Unassigned to have the server respond to all NNTP requests not serviced by another virtual server on a specific IP.
- ✦ **TCP Port:** Specify the TCP port the virtual server should monitor for NNTP traffic. The default port is 119. For communication using SSL, the default port is 563.
- ✦ **Path:** Specify the path to the folder the NNTP virtual server should use for its general, noncontent files. These include temporary files, drop folder for incoming messages, pickup folder for outgoing messages, and so on.

✦ **File System** or **Remote Share:** Specify whether the NNTP virtual server uses a local folder or remote share to store news content.

✦ **Path to Content Folder:** Choose the folder where the NNTP virtual server stores newsgroup folders, messages, and related data. For enhanced security, this should be on an NTFS volume so you can apply additional restrictions, if needed, through NTFS object permissions.

When you create an NNTP virtual server, IIS creates three newsgroups by default: `control.cancel`, `control.newgroup`, and `control.rmgroup`. These three special newsgroups are used to enable clients to cancel messages, create newsgroups, and remove newsgroups, respectively. If a client posts a message to a newsgroup but then decides to cancel the message and remove it from the group, he or she can click the message and choose Message ⇨ Cancel Message (using Outlook Express as the example NNTP client). Outlook Express posts a cancel message to the control.cancel newsgroup, and the NNTP virtual server processes the request, removing the selected message if it was posted by the client requesting the cancellation, and if the user has access to the control.cancel newsgroup (explained shortly).

The control.newgroup newsgroup processes newsgroup messages typically generated by a server to create new newsgroups. The `control.rmgroup` newsgroup processes messages from servers to remove newsgroups. Generally, NNTP client programs such as Outlook Express don't support the ability to generate `newgroup` (create a new newsgroup) or `rmgroup` (remove an existing newsgroup) messages. This feature is generally provided for other servers to be able to create and remove newsgroups from the virtual server.

Applying security through physical and virtual directories

When you create a virtual server, the NNTP service creates a folder structure to contain the newsgroups. For example, create a newsgroup called `support.technical`, and NNTP creates a folder under the NNTP root folder called `Support\Technical`. Messages for that newsgroup are stored in that folder. However, you can build a distributed file structure for a news server by using virtual directories and/or DFS.

As with Web and FTP sites, an NNTP virtual directory can be located on the server's file system or on a remote share. A virtual directory serves as the root of a portion of the newsgroup hierarchy. Take the `latinaccents.biz` news server as an example. It contains several newsgroup areas of interest including sales, support, help, and general. The general and sales portions of the newsgroup hierarchy are stored on the server under the NNTP root folder. The support and help portions, however, are stored on a remote share managed by the technical support department. Figure 29-16 illustrates the virtual server structure.

Virtual directories offer multiple advantages. They enable you to distribute the newsgroup hierarchy onto multiple volumes to accommodate space requirements and improve performance. On a system with several SCSI physical volumes, each volume can be reading or writing concurrently with others. This improves performance in situations where the newsgroups stored on the individual volumes see a lot of traffic. While the system is posting messages to one volume, it can be retrieving messages from others. If all the newsgroups were stored on a single volume, access would have to be sequential rather than concurrent. Distributing the newsgroup hierarchy to network shares also offers the same advantage but naturally generates additional network traffic. A final advantage to virtual folders is that you can grant administrative access to certain portions of the newsgroup structure. The technical support staff can manage the folders stored on their server, for example.

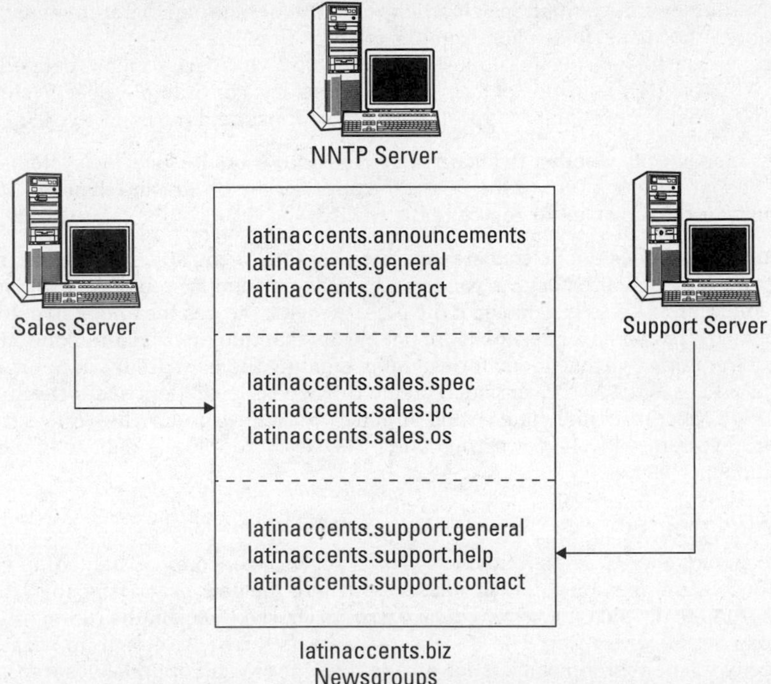

Figure 29-16: A virtual server can use virtual directories to distribute the newsgroup hierarchy on multiple systems.

Whether you're using physical or virtual folders, you can configure security on individual folders, which applies security for the newsgroups stored in those folders. For example, you can protect a private newsgroup by simply applying permissions so that only those persons who should have access to the newsgroup do so. Assigning permissions in this way requires that the folders be located on NTFS volumes. To restrict access to a newsgroup, simply configure the NTFS object permissions for the newsgroup's folder to enable read and write access for only the individual accounts or groups that should have access. Allow read and deny write permissions for specific users or groups to enable those clients to view messages but not post.

Creating virtual folders

As the following indicates, creating virtual folders is an easy task:

1. Create the physical folder to be assigned as the virtual folder.
2. Open the IIS console and open the NNTP virtual server under which the virtual folder will be created.
3. Right-click the Virtual Directories node and choose New ⇨ Virtual Directory to start the New NNTP Virtual Directory Wizard.

4. Specify in the Newsgroup Subtree field, the root of the newsgroup hierarchy to be stored under the virtual folder. For example, to store all of the `support.* newsgroups` under the virtual folder, specify support as the subtree. Or, specify a more defined structure to host only a portion of a newsgroup category. For example, specify support.help to host support.help, support.help.self, support.help.pub, and so on.

5. You must also specify whether to locate the virtual folder on the local file system or on a network share through the wizard. Select the appropriate option and then specify the local folder or remote share to complete the wizard.

Creating a virtual folder does not in itself create any newsgroups. You still must create those to be hosted in each virtual directory. As you learn in the next section, you don't explicitly define where a newsgroup is stored. Instead, the NNTP service creates the folder structure for the newsgroup based on its name and, if applicable, its matching virtual directory. After creating a support subtree virtual folder, for example, creating the newsgroups support.help and support.pubs causes the NNTP service to create the necessary folders under the support virtual directory. If there is no matching virtual directory for a newsgroup, the NNTP service creates the folder structure for the newsgroup under the NNTP root folder defined in the virtual folder's global properties.

Creating newsgroups

You can create any number of newsgroups on a virtual server to accommodate your needs. Open the IIS console and then open the virtual server where the newsgroup is hosted. Right-click the Newsgroup node and choose New ⇨ Newsgroup. Or, right-click in the Newsgroup pane and choose New ⇨ Newsgroup. The NNTP service starts the New Newsgroup Wizard in which you specify the newsgroup name (such as `support.help`) and optional description and pretty name. Clients can download newsgroup descriptions along with newsgroup names and search by description as well as by name. The client can retrieve the pretty name if the client software is capable of issuing the list `prettynames` command, and the pretty name serves as an alias for the newsgroup.

By default, NNTP creates nonmoderated newsgroups with read and write access. Any client can post messages in a nonmoderated newsgroup subject to his or her access to the newsgroup, as defined by its NTFS object permissions. In a moderated newsgroup, however, messages are sent to a moderator who accepts and posts the message or rejects it.

You can configure a newsgroup's properties to make it read-only, define it as a moderated newsgroup, and change its description or pretty name. To do so, right-click the newsgroup in the IIS console and choose Properties. Except for the Moderated option, the options are self-explanatory. The section "Moderating newsgroups" later in this chapter offers more information on configuring and managing moderated newsgroups.

Defining expiration policies

If you allow all messages to remain indefinitely on a server with a large number of newsgroups or messages, performance rapidly deteriorates, users have difficulty finding messages, and you eventually run out of storage space. To overcome these potential problems, define *expiration policies* that determine how long a message resides on the server before it expires and is removed. Create a single policy to control all newsgroups or create multiple policies to expire only specific newsgroups.

To create an expiration policy, open the IIS console and then open the NNTP virtual server to which you want to apply the policies. Right-click the Expiration Policies node and choose New ⇨ Expiration Policy to start the New NNTP Expiration Policy Wizard. Within the wizard, specify the following information:

✦ **Expiration Policy Name:** This is the friendly name for the policy as it appears in the IIS console.

✦ **Affected Newsgroups:** You can apply the policy to all newsgroups on the virtual server or only to selected newsgroups on the server. If you choose to apply the policy selectively, the wizard displays a dialog box to add newsgroups to the policy. Add the applicable newsgroup names one at a time. Use a wildcard to specify all newsgroups within a specific category, such as `support.*` or `alt.*`.

✦ **Expiration period:** Specify the number of hours that messages can remain in a newsgroup covered by this policy. The default is 168 hours (7 days).

Moderating newsgroups

As mentioned earlier in this chapter, you can allow anyone to post messages to a newsgroup (subject to their access restrictions) or create a moderated group. In a moderated group, a moderator receives all posted messages and either accepts or rejects them. Accepted messages are posted to the newsgroup, and rejected messages are not (and optionally returned to the sender). Messages can be sent to the moderator through the SMTP service or placed directly in an SMTP virtual server's Pickup folder. The messages are then forwarded to the specified moderator(s).

Any NNTP client can post to a moderated newsgroup because the client-side process is the same as for a nonmoderated newsgroup; however, the moderator needs to use an NNTP client that supports moderator features.

Setting up a moderated newsgroup is a multi-step process, as follows:

1. Open the IIS console, and right-click the NNTP virtual server you want to configure; then choose Properties.

2. Click the Settings tab, and in the field "SMTP server for moderated newsgroups," specify the DNS name or IP address of the SMTP server to which moderated messages are sent, or specify the local Pickup folder for the SMTP virtual folder. The directory for the default SMTP server is `\Inetpub\Mailroot\Pickup`. You specify either option in the SMTP Server for Moderated Groups field.

3. In the Default moderator domain field, specify the qualified domain name for the domain that handles all moderated newsgroups for which there is no specified moderator. These messages are sent to *`newsgroup@default_moderator_domain`*, where *`newsgroup`* is the newsgroup name and *`default_moderator_domain`* is the domain specified by this setting. The name you specify must be a valid DNS name.

4. In the Administrator Email Account field, specify the e-mail address to which nondelivery notices should be sent for newsgroup articles that can't be delivered to the designated moderator. To enable sending NDRs, create the `DWORD` value MailFromHeader in the registry. Use `Regedit` or `Regedt32` to add the `DWORD` value `HKEY_LOCAL_MACHINE\SYSTEM\CurrentControlSet\Services\NntpSvc\Parameters\MailFromHeader` and set the value to 1.

5. The account under which the NNTP service runs needs to be defined as an account on the SMTP server if you use the SMTP service to deliver moderated messages. By default, this is the System account. Verify that this is the case by first verifying the NNTP service's account in the Services console (or Services node of the Computer Management console). Then, verify that the designated account exists on the SMTP server or in the domain.

6. In the IIS console, open the NNTP virtual server, right-click the newsgroup you want to moderate, and choose Properties. On the newsgroup's property sheet, select the Moderated option, and in the `Moderator` field, specify the e-mail address of the moderator. Or, click Set Default to set the moderator to *newsgroup@default_moderator_domain*, where *newsgroup* is replaced with the name of the newsgroup and *default_moderator_domain* is the domain defined as the default in the virtual server's global properties. Note that only the newsgroup portion of the address appears in the box, and that periods are replaced by dashes (support.help becomes support-help, for example). The domain is appended automatically, which enables the NNTP service to route the messages correctly even if the domain membership of the server changes.
7. Close the newsgroup property sheet, and post some test messages to verify that everything works properly.

Indexing the news server

The Indexing Service can index news messages stored in virtual directories. To configure indexing, verify that Index Server is running on the server; then open the IIS console, and open the NNTP virtual server in question. Open the Virtual Directories node, right-click the virtual directory to index, and choose Properties. On the virtual directory's property sheet, select the Index news content option and click OK.

Using SSL

You can configure an NNTP virtual server to require SSL connections for enhanced security. As with securing a Web server for SSL, you first need to obtain a certificate to install on the server. Follow these steps to enable SSL:

1. Open the IIS console, right-click the NNTP virtual server, and choose Properties.
2. On the Access tab, click Certificate to start the wizard. Prepare a certificate request using the wizard. Be certain to specify the FQDN of the NNTP virtual server as the common name for the certificate if users are connecting to the server through DNS lookups, or specify the IP address as the common name if users are using the IP address. If connecting on an intranet, specify the NetBIOS name as the common name. See the section "Enabling secure sockets layer" earlier in this chapter, if you need additional help creating the certificate request.
3. Open a browser and submit the request to a CA to obtain the certificate. See "Enabling secure sockets layer" earlier in this chapter, if you need more detailed information.
4. Open the Access tab for the NNTP virtual server and click Certificate again to process the pending request and install the certificate.
5. Open the Virtual Directories node, right-click the newsgroup subtree for which you want to require SSL, and choose Properties. Apply SSL to the Default subtree to require SSL for all newsgroups.
6. Click Secure on the newsgroup's General property page. Select the option Require secure channel to enable SSL. You can optionally enable 128-bit encryption. Click OK and then close the property sheet for the newsgroup.
7. Configure an NNTP client to access the news server using SSL and test operation of the server.

Controlling access to the server

The Access tab for an NNTP virtual server enables you to determine which clients have access to the server and the type of authentication methods employed. To configure access, open the IIS console, right-click the NNTP virtual server, and choose Properties. Click the Access tab; then click Authentication to display the Authentication Methods dialog box shown in Figure 29-17.

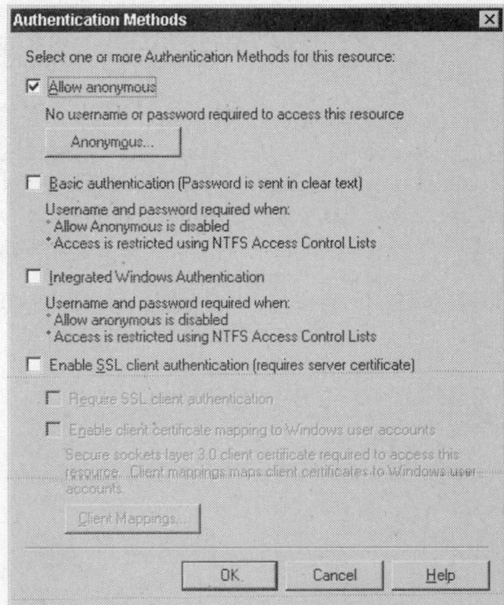

Figure 29-17: The Authentication Methods dialog box.

You can configure the server to enable anonymous access, eliminating the need for a client to have or provide a valid user account for authentication. As with the HTTP and FTP services, IIS uses a predefined anonymous account to authenticate the users. Select the option Allow anonymous to enable anonymous access. Click Anonymous if you need to change the user account and password the NNTP server uses to authenticate anonymous access.

You also can disable anonymous access and require clients to log on to the server, restricting who can access the server because only those users with valid accounts can access it. You can use basic clear-text authentication, WSP, or SSL. If you use SSL, you can optionally require the clients to have SSL certificates and enable client certificates to be mapped to user accounts on the server or in the server's domain.

In addition to defining the authentication options, you also can restrict access to the server to individual computers, subnets, or domains. On the server's Access property page, click Connection to display the Connection dialog box. As with other services, you can allow all except those listed or deny all except those listed. Add computers to the list by their individual IP addresses, specify a group via a subnet entry, or specify a domain name. You can use the DNS Lookup button to look up the IP address of a computer if you know its DNS name.

Summary

Windows .NET offers a good set of tools in IIS to enable you to build a full-featured Web server for HTTP, FTP, SMTP, and NNTP protocols. You can host multiple Web sites and provide secure access and authentication through SSL and other mechanisms. The FTP server provides a means for serving files throughout your enterprise or to clients on the Internet. The SMTP service makes it possible to create multiple virtual SMTP e-mail servers that can serve as main transfer agents for your company or domains you host for others. The NNTP server enables you to set up public and private news servers that support both anonymous or authenticated access, as well as secure access through SSL.

If you're an ISP or company that needs to do e-commerce, however, IIS by itself isn't the solution. Instead, you need to look to Microsoft's MCIS, Site Server, SQL Server, and other Web server applications to provide the types of services you no doubt need to offer your customers. But if you're looking to build an Internet presence for your company, need to do a moderate amount of site hosting, or are looking to build an intranet for your company, IIS is a good choice.

✦ ✦ ✦

Terminal Services

◆ ◆ ◆ ◆

In This Chapter

Exploring the Terminal Services architecture

Planning Terminal Services

Installing and deploying Terminal Services

This chapter explores thin-client/server computing and discusses the pros and cons of deploying *Terminal Services* to support a thin-client/server infrastructure. Thin-client/server technology has been proven to drastically lower total cost of ownership (TCO) and virtually eliminate workstation obsolescence for a vast majority of computer applications. It is also provides cost-effective, rapid, and simple means of deploying Windows XP/Server 2003-based desktops in a legacy Windows environment.

Thin-Client/Server Computing

Terminal Services represents a major paradigm shift in computing in general and in client/server (C/S) computing in particular. Its revolutionary approach met initially with mixed reactions but quickly gained overwhelming acceptance and popularity.

The term *terminal services* is a bit of misnomer because the technology exceeded by far the capabilities of old-fashioned terminal emulation. Originally, in fact, thin-client software was intended to function as nothing more than a dumb terminal. It was supposed to be limited to receiving the display and sending user key strokes and mouse clicks, while all processing, execution, and storage access took place on the server. The transferred data was so miniscule that it did not need significant bandwidth (only 10 to 28 Kbps). This provided satisfactory user access to a company's computing resources, even through dial-up connections.

This initial, modest design has been significantly changed to enhance users' convenience and productivity. New features enable the redirection of resources between local system and remote server. Users can access their local drives directly from the session, experience streaming audio that's delivered to the server playing through their local speakers, copy text from a document viewed in a remote session and paste it to another one, opened locally, or print that document to their local printer. Before we cover all these features in more detail, we review the history behind them.

Throughout this chapter, we refer to the technology as *terminal services,* while its Microsoft implementation is referred to as *Terminal Services* (capitalized).

Refresher: client/server computing model

Popularity of the client/server computing model is probably best exemplified by the phenomenon of the Internet. Clients connect to it and request information and services, typically in the form of news, e-mail, or files. Web servers handle almost all the data processing; the clients handle the rendering of the images and the user interface. By placing the majority of the workload on a server, the client does not require any significant amount of processing power, services, memory, or storage. In fact, the browser can be installed into a very "thin" client device, such as small mobile phones.

Notice, however, that although servers have been getting bigger, faster, and fancier, so, too, have the clients. The average workstation on the market probably carries a more powerful processor and a faster motherboard than the servers that have been faithfully plugging away 24 hours a day, seven days a week for the past five or more years. Is anything wrong with that? Yes, in an enterprise-computing environment, something is wrong there.

Although computer prices are coming down all the time, the cost of administration has been going up. Any business that employs more than a handful of computer users and deploys fancy workstations for its people has another cost. This cost is called *TCO*, which stands for *Total Cost of Ownership*. And it is not merely a buzzword. The number of times it is used throughout this book is not coincidental.

The total cost of a computer is more than the total cost of the CPU, monitor, and input devices. It also includes the cost of maintaining that equipment so that the users get the best possible service from it and that the company derives the maximum benefit from its investment. Each workstation also requires software, and a cost is involved in distributing that software to each workstation and in keeping the software current, configured, and in service. You need to lock down your workstations so that users cannot change settings, fiddle with hardware, save rubbish to the hard disk, or do anything that would put the computer out of commission and pile on your workload. The larger the enterprise and the more remote offices that it has, the harder it is providing any manner of attention to each workstation. In addition, shortly after new workstations are rolled out at considerable cost, they become obsolete.

This is what we call the *true cost of ownership* (TCO); the cost of the technology and your effort to get the most mileage for your investment.

Windows Server 2003 and Windows XP Professional were designed with the goal in mind of reducing total cost of ownership. They provide very tightly integrated, homogenous C/S environment, in which clients and servers cooperate in a well-defined partnership. But for a lot of companies with huge investments in legacy and homogenous networking environments, upgrading all clients to Windows XP Professional may be impractical and very expensive.

What is the solution? What can be done to reduce the cost of technology and of ownership? To find the answer, we had to look in our past . . . to the mainframe computing model.

Total recall: The mainframe computing model

Before the advent of the PC and graphical user interface systems, knowledge workers, primarily in large organizations, worked at dumb terminals connected to a mainframe. The only devices at the desktop were the keyboard and a monitor. This model is still in wide use.

The mainframe model is ideal from a client-TCO point of view. Aside from the fact that the mainframe costs a lot of money, you need to administer or install virtually nothing at the desktop. The users cannot compromise the system by inserting anything in a floppy disk drive, and you have no local software or hardware to install. The only thing that can fail on the desktop is the terminal or the keyboard, and they rarely do.

If new equipment is needed for a user, it can be shipped to that user, who unpacks it and plugs it in . . . no complex installation. All the user must do is plug the terminal into the power socket and into the network jack. Everyone's computing environment is centrally administered. Before PCs and servers, most large companies employed only a handful of operators on their mainframes.

But these early terminal systems were arcane to use and dumb, and to a large extent, nothing has changed in recent years. Everyone must learn cryptic terminal shortcuts and stare at green or amber characters. The GUI changed everything; it made interacting with the computer simpler and more productive. As the PC and its operating system matured, every small business could afford computing power formerly available only to the multinational or Fortune 500 companies.

So what if we can take the C/S model, its graphical user interface, and affordable, powerful, and widely used applications and morph them into the mainframe-computing model? One company decided that it was worth betting the farm to create such a computing environment.

Enter Citrix Systems

Citrix Systems, Inc., came up with the idea of "thin" clients: nothing more than a monitor, a keyboard, and a mouse connecting the user to a server where the overwhelming majority of the user environment and all the user's desktop applications are running. In other words, the user's application processing space (CPU, storage, memory) is on the server. In this aspect, the thin-client computing model is practically identical to the mainframe model. Citrix made this possible through the introduction of the Multi-Win technology and *Independent Computing Architecture* (referred to as *ICA* throughout the rest of this chapter) protocol. Multi-Win enables the running of multiple simultaneous desktop sessions on a single Windows server, while the ICA protocol carries communication between these sessions and client devices. ICA is very bandwidth-efficient as well as network-protocol- and client-operating system-independent. Citrix's first product, WinFrame, was developed for Windows NT 3.51 Server, in close partnership with Microsoft.

Microsoft quickly realized that the Citrix invention had incredible potentials. It licensed Multi-Win technology from Citrix and entered the market with its own version of thin-client technology, the Windows NT 4.0 Terminal Server Edition. The Terminal Server communicated with clients by using Microsoft's *Remote Desktop Protocol* (*RDP*), similar in some aspects to ICA, but TCP/IP-specific and available initially only to Windows clients. Starting with Windows 2000, a multi-user kernel (enabling multiple users to interactively use the same computer) became integrated into the operating system.

The Microsoft and Citrix partnership splits the client market into two realms. Citrix gets a majority of the market for non-Windows clients. Although currently rather limited, it is an important segment of the market, which is showing all the signs of fast growth. Citrix also makes its money from enhanced administration and application publishing — technologies needed in large terminal-server farm deployments (a collection of multiple servers managed as a single unit). Microsoft's share consists of all Windows systems, including the ones running MetaFrame, because one of the prerequisites of Citrix MetaFrame is installation of the Microsoft Terminal Services.

Because Citrix MetaFrame runs as an add-on to Windows Terminal Services, it needs to be purchased separately. Make sure that you consider carefully whether its benefits justify the added (substantial) product and licensing costs. Citrix targets large Web farms by providing support for centralized administration, dynamic load balancing, automated application deployment, and simplified printer management. It also supports a wider range of client operating systems and devices than does Windows Terminal Services alone. At the time of the writing of this book, Microsoft's Terminal Services client software was available for all Windows platforms and Macintosh-based systems (Mac OS X), while Citrix included virtually all others (such as MS-DOS, Unix, Linux, and network computers such as Sun Java Station or IBM Network station).

If support for a variety of client platforms is your primary concern (and the extra management features of MetaFrame are of lesser importance to you), however, you can use much less expensive third-party add-ons. These add-ons provide connectivity to Windows Terminal Server from non-Window platforms by using Remote Desktop Protocol. Among most popular choices are the Unix-based RDP client available for download from `www.rdesktop.org` and HOBLink JWT from HOB, Inc., which supports a much wider range of platforms (Apple Mac OS, Unix, Linux, OS/2). If you are interested in extending the support of Terminal Services to applications running on platforms other than Windows, you may want to take a look at Tarantella from Tarantella Inc. (at `www.tarantella.com`), which has its own unique approach to terminal-services architecture.

Citrix products and Windows Terminal Services have brought us the best of both computing models: a mainframe computing model requiring no computer or administration at the desktop, with access to the Windows graphical interface and Win32- or even Win64-bit applications running on the server. This model is called *thin-client computing* because the client needs only a minimal set of resources to load the remote desktop software and connect to the server.

The thin-client/server computing model

Citrix's slogan for thin-client/server computing is availability for "any client over any network connection." The model's simple dictate is this: Any client can connect to the server, which enables 100-percent server-based processing, management, deployment, and support for mission-critical, productivity, Web-based, or desktop applications. In short, just about anything that you can do on the workstation can be done at the server.

Thin clients come in many forms. With simpler ones, the electronics fit into a keyboard, and you have no need for a hard disk and more than a couple megabytes of RAM. More elaborate types run embedded versions of Windows NT or CE. The hardware makers, such as Wyse, Inc., offer specialized, inexpensive, and compact Windows-based terminal devices running ICA or RDP software.

Setting up the client is easy. Most of the time, it just involves plug and play. As with the mainframe terminal, you simply connect a client terminal to a network, turn it on, and you're at the Windows logon screen. All client and session administration is done at the server. Maintenance is typically limited to occasional firmware updates.

The Thin-Client/Server Revolution

Before we start analyzing architecture, functionality, deployment, and management of Terminal Services (TS), we first want to look briefly at their benefits and discuss circumstances in which they may not be suitable. You need to know what criteria to apply in deciding whether a particular system constitutes a good candidate for thin-client technology. (Not all of them do.)

Start by splitting the workstation role into two categories: *data I/O applications* and *processor- and graphics-intensive applications.* You can probably be more specific, but for the majority of companies, these two categories work just fine.

Good candidates: Data I/O applications

Data I/O, in this case, does not refer only to the input or output of data from and to a database, but also includes word processing, working with spreadsheets, e-mail exchanges, browsing the Web, and so on. Data I/O applications are ideal candidates for deployment in the thin-client/server model.

Consider this scenario: If all the workers do all day is key information into the applications; create reports, documents, and letters; print; and so on, they are ideal candidates for Terminal Services. After the users have logged on and loaded their applications, they do not run any processes that suddenly consume a lot of memory or processing bandwidth, so why would they need the overhead of a fancy workstation?

And what about high-end data I/O applications — the ones that use up memory and processor cycles generating reports, calculating spreadsheets, and re-indexing thousand-page documents? Choosing where to do the processing is relative to the IS environment, the user experience, the number of sessions (users) on the servers, the size or quantity of CPUs on the server, and so on. For a more in-depth analysis, refer to Chapter 7, where we discuss configuring an application server.

Poor candidates: Processor- and graphics-intensive applications

Processor- and graphics-intensive applications use a lot of memory and always need dedicated processor time. Such applications may not be suitable for deployment in a thin-client/server arrangement. They include graphics design, desktop publishing, computer-aided design or engineering (CAD/CAM) applications, and software development tools — essentially, any resource-hungry application.

Many modern word-processing suites double as desktop publishing (DTP) environments and can command more resources from the server than the average letter writer. Vast repagination, indexing, search and replace, hyphenation and justification, printing, and layout processing may be better served on a dedicated workstation. Many companies, however, still opt to keep processor-intensive applications such as DTP on the terminal server and simply add more CPU power and RAM to meet the demand. This becomes even easier with the Windows Server 2003 platform, which pushes memory and processing limits well beyond what used to be available.

Applications with special hardware requirements are also not good candidates for Terminal Services deployment. A typical example would be a video-editing application that depends on powerful, specialized electronics or peripheral devices.

Poor candidates: Bad software

As you probably suspect, requirements for software running in a multi-user environment are much more stringent than they are for regular desktop application. Such applications should have the Certified for Windows 2000 and Windows Server 2003 logo, assigned by Veritest (at `www.veritest.com`) after passing rigorous compatibility tests. If you are forced to install an application that has not been certified, verify through testing that it can handle multi-user access. Older programs, not designed for a terminal server, can still be modified to run correctly through the use of application compatibility scripts (discussed in the section "Application Compatibility Scripts," later in this chapter). The chances that you can get hold of existing ones, either from software manufacturers or via the thin-client user community (such as the one at `www.thethin.net`) are reasonably good. Avoid installing 16-bit applications, however, replacing them with 32-bit versions whenever possible.

The benefits of thin-client/server computing

To evaluate applicability of thin-client/server computing in your environment, you need to be familiar with its benefits. The following sections describe them in detail.

Non-Win32 workstations

If you have a number of computers that are running 16-bit versions of Windows or a non-Windows operating system and you need to extend Windows to these desktops, Terminal Services is ideal. You may, however, need to invest in additional software, such as Citrix MetaFrame. This applies to workstations running Unix, Linux, or DOS and a number of thin-client devices with an embedded ICA client or those operating in non-TCP/IP environment.

No applications on the workstation

If you can boot clients to Windows NT, 9*x*, 2000, or XP but do not want to have particular applications running on the workstations for whatever reason, Terminal Server is your answer. Consider loading the terminal client to give the users access to these applications on the server in full interactive Win32 sessions.

You can, for example, put all your 9*x* clients into a workgroup and not connect them to any domain. They can load without requiring authentication, obtain an IP address from a DHCP server, and then load the Terminal Server client in full-screen mode. The user does not even see the old Windows 9*x* desktop, and the first logon screen is the Windows Server 2003 Terminal Server session at the server.

No workstation hardware

If you need to extend the Windows XP desktop to a user at a location that currently has no PCs (and no budget for any) consider Terminal Server. Thin-client devices are cheaper than PCs. Their RAM requirements are much lower than a typical workstation running Windows XP locally, and a number of Terminal Server clients need no hard disks and only a few megabytes of RAM to run. The required components are so small that they fit inside the average keyboard.

A thin-client device is also the way to go if the environment is not conducive to workstation deployment. Such an environment can be the loading dock at a factory, the customer-service desk at a depot of sorts (such as customs receiving), or retail stores. The Terminal Server client can be installed on Windows CE or other embedded operating systems. If you're connected to a mobile or wireless communications network, you can use your handheld to connect to the server while sunning yourself on the beach.

Obsolescence resistance

The Terminal Server client device is obsolescence-resistant. Unlike a PC, a thin-client device can serve its role for years with merely a few firmware upgrades. All the Terminal Server client needs is enough electronics to provide network interface and keyboard/display I/O and no more than a few MB of RAM to run the communication protocol and terminal client software.

Centralized support environment

User sessions are centrally managed from the server. You can even log on to the server under the user's logon ID to see the exact desktop that the user sees without ever needing to make a trip to the client's location. Sessions can be managed, users can be sent messages, and you can also shadow the session and view directly the actions of the client.

No workstation administration

You no longer need to concern yourself about administration or control of the workspace environment at the user's location. Granted, group policies in Windows Server 2003 are highly advanced, but you may save a lot of time and money by limiting desktop or workspace management only to portable or notebook computers or in situations in which the user needs to continue working, regardless of the state of the network connection.

Reduced risk of virus infection

By relocating the workspace to the server, you reduce or even completely eliminate the introduction of viruses to the network or servers from the user's machine. Managing anti-virus (AV) software on remote computers is time-consuming and complex. In traditional client/server computing environments, anti-virus software on workstations tends to become disabled or seriously out of date if not adequately maintained. In a Terminal Server environment, you load the AV engine on the server, and protection is automatically extended to all users for the duration of their sessions.

Eliminate the risk of clients introducing illegal software

Clients can be locked down to prevent the user from introducing illegal copies of software into the enterprise. Although you can control this to a fine degree with policies on workstations, this task is much easier accomplished on the server.

Remote access

If you have users working from home or a small remote office, they can connect to Remote Access Server (RAS) and then open a Terminal Server session to the server. And to cut the cost of the RAS option further, you can have clients connect to your intranet portal via Virtual Private Network (VPN) across the Internet and then establish the Terminal Server session.

The cons of thin-clients

You also, naturally, face some drawbacks in using the Terminal Services solution. Apart from the initial learning curve and deployment, you should also keep in mind the situations described in the following sections.

The cost of 5-9 uptime

Introduction of Terminal Services results in increased reliance on server availability. Intermittent network failures or temporary problems with a server become painfully apparent to your clients if all applications and resources that they use are server-based.

Ensuring that your server and network are very stable and, preferably, redundant is critical before you start implementing a Terminal Services solution on a larger scale. Ideally, your terminal servers should be configured as a load-balanced cluster with a Session Directory Server. Your goal should be the 5-9 mark, designating 99.999 percent uptime (which translates into roughly only five minutes of service interruptions a year). For more information on clustering technologies available on the Windows Server 2003 platform (including Network Load Balancing of Terminal Services with Session Directory Server), refer to Chapter 25.

Entry cost of software

Using thin-client on the desktop enables you to enjoy savings in hardware and desktop operating-system software. Unfortunately, this gain may prove difficult to realize because of the initial cost of terminal-server farm software, hardware, and licensing costs. You need to factor this into your budget and plan for the long-term benefits to sell your management on the viability of the Terminal Server solution.

The falling prices of PCs

The processing power of computers at the same price level doubles roughly every 18 months. The market has consistently proven this axiom correct. This fact may actually be used as a strong argument against implementing thin-client solutions. After all, if hardware is getting cheaper, why not run applications locally instead of burdening the server with all the processing tasks. Such a course reduces your dependency on the server and network conditions. It also enables you to fully utilize (otherwise idle) resources distributed among all your workstations.

This reasoning, however, does not take into consideration all the issues mentioned in the section "Benefits of thin-client/server computing," earlier in this chapter, that contribute to Total Cost of Ownership. Distributed environments tend to be much more difficult and costly to maintain, secure, and troubleshoot.

Terminal Services Architecture

Windows Server 2003's Terminal Services consists of a number of components, which evolved from the original Citrix's MultiWin technology, as described in the following list:

- ✦ **Multi-User Kernel:** Multi-user concurrent processing is handled by multi-user extensions to the kernel. In Windows Server 2003 and Windows 2000, these extensions are an integral part of the operating system.

✦ **The Remote Desktop Protocol (RDP):** The Windows Server 2003 platform includes Microsoft's proprietary (but based on ITU T.120 standard) Remote Desktop Protocol. (Citrix's ICA protocol is available only after the installation of Citrix MetaFrame on top of Windows Terminal Services.) The RDP runs on top of TCP/IP. (It cannot be used with any other network protocols.)

The new RDP Version 5.2 introduced in Windows Server 2003 offers improvements in the areas of functionality and performance. System administrators should appreciate most the automatic redirection of the client's local and network mapped drives. Among other new features are the redirection of audio, Windows Clipboard, time zones (where clients automatically operate in their local time zones, regardless of location of the server), and locally attached printers. You can launch remote sessions in a full-screen, true-color, 24-bit mode and take advantage of standard Windows shortcuts. From a remote desktop session (but not from the console), you can control other remote desktop and console sessions, even across terminal servers. RDP also supports dynamic bandwidth allocation, an important component of the Microsoft Quality of Service technology.

As far as security is concerned, four levels of encryption are available. The default High 128-bit level is intended for communication between XP and Windows Server 2003 systems. The FIPS (Federal Information Processing Standard) encryption level follows U.S. government requirements. The Client Compatible option uses the maximum level of encryption supported by the client. The Low-level option secures the client communication with 56-bit encryption.

✦ **The Remote Desktop Connection (formerly known as Terminal Services Client):** This lightweight program running on the thin-client device is responsible for displaying the server session on the client's desktop. Its primary responsibility is establishing and maintaining a connection to the server via Remote Desktop Protocol.

✦ **The Remote Desktop Web Connection (a new version of the Terminal Services Advanced Client introduced in Windows 2000 SP1):** This Web-based version of the client enables a user to connect to a Terminal Services server via Internet Explorer.

✦ **The Remote Assistance:** This is a software component that takes advantage of the Remote Desktop functionality by enabling a remote operator (known in Microsoft terminology as an *expert*) to attach to a console session of a "novice" and view or control the session. Although Remote Desktop Connections are used for accessing remote systems to run applications and perform administrative tasks, Remote Assistance, as the name clearly indicates, is used primarily for troubleshooting and end-user training purposes.

✦ **The Terminal Services Licensing Service:** This service is needed if you are running a full Terminal Server component (discussed in the section "Full Terminal Server," later in this chapter). The service provides licenses for clients connecting to the server.

✦ **Terminal Services Administration Tools:** These utilities, implemented as Microsoft Management Console snap-ins, are used for configuration and for session and license management.

Terminal Services on Windows Server 2003 can operate in two modes: Remote Desktop for Administration (the equivalent of Windows 2000 Terminal Server in Remote Administration mode) and Full Terminal Server (previously known as the Application Server mode).

Remote Desktop for Administration

If you're using the Remote Desktop for Administration mode, each server can be accessed and managed as if you were sitting in front of its console. Anyone who has suffered working at a server in a cold and cramped server room is sure to appreciate this service. It is intended strictly for server administration and, therefore, is restricted both in terms of the number of simultaneous connections and the permissions to use them. More specifically, it can support up to two remote-desktop and one console (remote or local) connections. The console access is exclusive, which means that only one can be active at any time (similar to how Remote Desktop Connection functions on a Windows XP Professional system). The right to use connections is, by default, granted exclusively to members of the local Administrators group (although this right can be extended to other accounts — more about this in the section "Enabling Terminal Services," a little later in this chapter). On the other hand, no extra licenses are required to accommodate remote connections. Remote Desktop for Administration is really a subset of the complete multi-user environment, minus the overhead of the services that support concurrent application access and that require licensing. The service is native to each edition of Windows Server 2003, so you no longer have any need for third-party remote-control software, such as VNC, pcANYWHERE, or Carbon Copy, on any of your servers. Restriction to one connection per server, prevalent among these programs, also no longer applies.

Full Terminal Server

In Full Terminal Server component mode, any number of remote users (restricted not by any limit set within the operating-system code but only by licensing, network, or hardware-capability constraints) can connect simultaneously to the server. Because this mode is intended primarily for application sharing, additional software components, which are responsible for handling multi-user application access, are activated. This, in turn, introduces performance overhead (which is more significant than in Remote Desktop for Administration mode). Full Terminal Server component mode has also separate licensing requirements, discussed in the section "Terminal Services Licensing," later in this chapter.

Enabling Terminal Services

Enabling Terminal Services for use on the server requires you to make a few choices. First, you need to decide on the mode that Terminal Server is to run in: *Remote Desktop for Administration* or Full *Terminal Server* component. This decision should be fairly easy, because as noted in the preceding sections, each mode has its own purpose. Performance, simultaneous connection limit, and licensing implications make using one as a substitute for the other entirely impractical. Keep in mind that the Remote Assistance feature, which also utilized Terminal Server functionality, remains available regardless of which mode you choose.

Remote Desktop for Administration mode does not need to be installed because it is built into all the Windows Server 2003 platforms. For security reasons, however, it is disabled by default. To enable it, you need to launch the System applet located in the Control Panel; on the Remote tab of the System dialog box that appears, select the Allow Users to Connect Remotely to this Computer check box. You also need to specify which accounts can use Remote Desktop. This is done by populating the built-in Remote Desktop Users group. You can add new users or groups to this group by using either typical administrative tools (Active Directory Users and Computers in a domain environment or Local Users and Groups on a nondomain controller) or by clicking the Select Remote Users button on the Remote tab in the System Control Panel applet. Although the local Administrators group is not included in Remote Desktop Users, all its members are granted the right to run a Remote Desktop session implicitly.

This becomes a bit more involved if you are trying to enable Remote Desktop access to domain controllers. Incidentally, this was also an issue in the previous version of Windows, although for a different reason. In Windows 2000, the Log on Locally user right was required for a terminal server session logon. This worked fine on member servers, where this right is granted to the local Users group (containing Domain Users). On domain controllers, however, only a few groups (Administrators and Server, Backup, and Account Operators) are permitted to log on interactively, which prevents everyone else from connecting via Terminal Server sessions. The problem surfaced more frequently in running Windows 2000 Terminal Services in application mode (because these are intended for regular users), but it could also confuse operators managing servers via Terminal Server in administration mode (in case they did not happen to belong to one of the privileged groups).

Remembering that the Log on Locally right is no longer required to access a Windows Server 2003 server via a Remote Desktop session (in either mode) is important. In spite of this, if you're using default settings, the same issue persists on Windows Server 2003 domain controllers. To resolve the problem, you need to modify the Default Domain Controllers Group Policy Object by enabling the Allow Logon through Terminal Services option (located under Computer Configuration\Windows Settings\Security Settings\Local Policies\User Rights Assignments) and adding to it all accounts that you want to grant rights to run Remote Sessions on domain controllers. If you want to explicitly deny access to Terminal Services for a specific user or group, you can use the Deny Logon through Terminal Services option.

Keep in mind, however, that Microsoft added the extra step of modifying the Default Domain Controllers Group Policy Object for a reason. Granting direct logon access to domain controllers for nonprivileged accounts is bad practice from a security perspective. Using domain controllers as terminal servers is much worse (because doing so affects both security and performance). If you work for a smaller company and are forced to implement such solution, however, make sure that you secure all affected servers. Otherwise, you greatly increase the risk of compromising Active Directory or incurring damage to the registry and file system.

You also cannot connect to a Terminal Services session by using an account that has a blank password (which you should not even have in the first place).

Full Terminal Server component mode can be installed either as part of an unattended installation of the base operating system or post-installation by using the Windows Components Wizard (see Chapter 7). It is available in Standard, Enterprise, and Datacenter versions but not in the Windows Server 2003 Web server version (which is limited to Remote Desktop for Administration only). Figure 30-1 shows the option screen presented to you by the Windows Components Wizard.

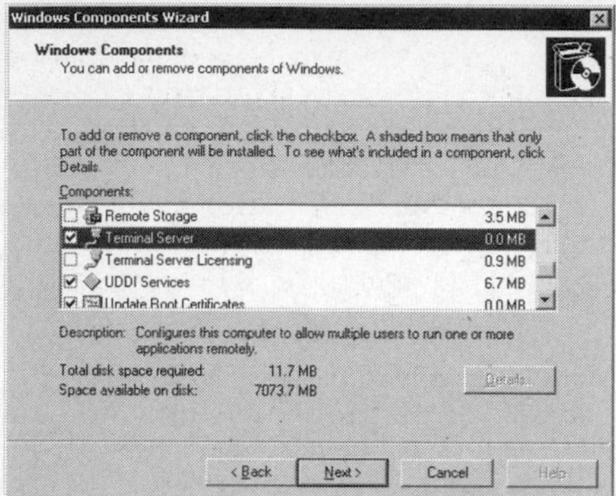

Figure 30-1: The Full Terminal Server component installation screen.

As part of the Windows Component Wizard process, you are also prompted to choose between full and relaxed security. You need to base your decision on security requirements and the types of applications that are to be shared on the Terminal Server. Full security is more restrictive in providing access to file-system and registry locations. This selection, however, may prevent older programs, not designed specifically for the Windows Server 2003 platform, from functioning correctly. If you are planning on running such software, you should select the Relaxed Security option. You also should realize that any previously installed applications may not work correctly and require full reinstallation. This results from the fact that the standalone-application installation process is different from the shared application, running on a Terminal Server.

Another side effect of installing a Full Terminal Server component is the addition of all members of the local Users group to the built-in Remote Desktop Users group. This happens only at the time of installation, so any subsequent changes to one of these groups do not affect in any way the other. Switching to Full Terminal Server mode changes also the appearance of the Remote tab on the System Properties dialog box (accessible from the System applet in the Control Panel). Without the Full Terminal Server component installed, the System Properties dialog box's Remote tab contains a Select Remote Users button, used for populating the Remote Desktop Users group. This tab is gone after you switch to Full Terminal Server mode. You can use this as an indication as to whether the Full Terminal Server component has been installed. Alternatively, you can launch the Terminal Services Configuration utility from the menu bar by choosing Administrative Tools ⇨ Terminal Services Configuration Utility (refer to Figure 30-3, later in this chapter). After the Terminal Services Configuration window appears, select the Server Settings option. The mode is shown in the data panel at the right of the tree, listed under the Licensing entry. Without the Terminal Server component, this is set to Remote Desktop for Administration; after its installation, it can be set to either Per Device or Per Session. Alternatively, you can type the following at the command prompt:

```
query termserver
```

After pressing the Enter key, you see a list of all the domain servers with the Terminal Server component installed.

Connections to Full Terminal Server are separately licensed and require the presence of a Licensing server. Microsoft, however, grants a rather generous 120-day grace period for setting up the Licensing server, which means that your server is fully operational as soon as the Terminal Server component is installed.

The third type of Remote Desktop connection — Remote Assistance — was first implemented in Windows XP. It is intended for administrative and desktop-support personnel (called *experts* in the context of Remote Assistance session) to connect to existing console sessions for the purpose of troubleshooting or assisting their primary users (*novices*). The Remote Assistance session can be initiated by either a novice (sending an invitation via Windows Messenger, e-mail, or as a file) or an expert (sending an offer via the same means). In either case, the novice makes the final decision whether the session is established or not.

Remote Assistance is, by default, disabled on each type of Windows Server 2003 server. On an individual system, you can enable it by selecting the Turn on Remote Assistance and Allow Invitations to be Sent from this Computer check box on the Remote tab of the System Control Panel applet. This and other settings can be configured by using Local Group Policy. In a domain environment, you should use Group Policy Objects on a domain, organizational unit, or site level. Group Policies enable you to control every aspect of Remote Assistance configuration.

Administering Terminal Services

Two standard administrative tools are used to manage or administer Terminal Services: *Terminal Services Manager* and the *Terminal Services Configuration*. The *Terminal Server Licensing* program is used specifically to control licensing settings. In addition, numerous aspects of Terminal Server management can be also handled by using Terminal Services Group Policies, Active Directory Users and Computers, the Terminal Server Extensions to Local Users and Groups MMC Snap-In, several command-line utilities, and the Terminal Services WMI Provider. The following sections describe these tools.

The Terminal Services Manager

The *Terminal Services Manager*, as shown in Figure 30-2, can be used to manage multiple Windows Server 2003 servers running Terminal Services. It is an MMC snap-in with the tree pane on the left containing a list of servers, arranged in three nodes (This Computer, Favorite Servers, and All Listed Servers). The details pane on the right displays the properties of the server that's selected in the left pane. These properties are arranged in three tabs — Users, Sessions, and Processes. The Processes tab lists all processes on the server, each with its associated user. You can use it to terminate individual processes if you suspect that they have a negative effect on the stability of the server or user sessions. The Users and Session tabs provide you with the same set of right-click menu options (except for the Log Off option), which apply to users and sessions, respectively. These options are described in the following list:

- ✦ **Connect:** Connects to and, effectively, takes over and disconnects another remote session. If the session belongs to another user, you need Full Control or User Access permissions on the connection level (granted through the Terminal Services Configuration utility) and are prompted for a password. By using this option, you can take over a runaway session, close safely all the applications saving the data, and log off. This is one of a few operations that are not *console-capable*, which means that you can neither run it directly from the console nor connect to a console session.
- ✦ **Disconnect:** Administratively terminates the connection but does not end the session.
- ✦ **Send Message:** Used mostly to notify users about some planned action on the server (such as a shutdown).

- **Remote Control:** Enables you to take over another session without disconnecting its current user. The user, by default, is prompted for permission. (This is configurable on the connection and user levels.) Because both of you are sharing the session, you can see each other's actions. You terminate the remote-control session by pressing one of the available special key combinations (by default, Ctrl +*, where * is the one located on the numeric keypad — so make sure that your keyboard has one). This is another example of operation that is not console-capable. Remember that, to remotely control another session, your screen resolution must be the same as or higher than that of the other session.
- **Reset:** Forcefully terminates the session, killing all its processes. Use it only as the last resort. You cannot reset a console session.
- **Status:** Displays statistics for the user or session (depending on the tab).
- **Log Off:** Logs off a user. (It is available only on the Users tab.) This is less drastic than Reset but still can result in data loss. You cannot log off a console session from a remote session.

The Users tab provides a listing of all users who are currently running sessions on the server. This feature may prove useful if the number of connections to the server is limited (for example, if you're operating in Remote Desktop for Administration mode). If you want to run a session to the server that has reached its connection limit, you can contact directly to one of the connected users and request that user to log off (via the Send Message option or via more traditional methods such as a phone call or yelling down the hall). You can even use the Log Off option if you suspect that the session is not being actively used. You can often determine this by looking at the list of processes for this session (as listed on the Processes tab). Keep in mind that forcing a user to log off from a session by using active processes may result in a data loss.

Regardless of the number of sessions on the server, you always see one in the Listen state with a very high ID number (65536 or higher), as shown in Figure 30-2. This session is not actively used by any particular user. Its purpose is to prepare the resources that are necessary for Terminal Server to accept the next connection request, which speeds up connection time.

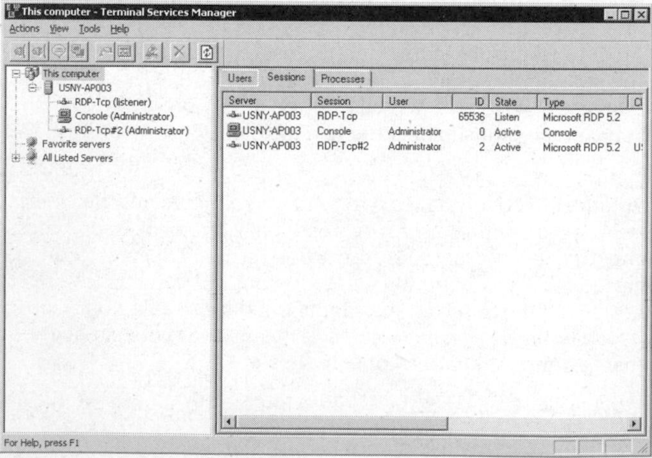

Figure 30-2: The Terminal Services Manager.

Terminal Services Configuration

The *Terminal Services Configuration* utility, as shown in Figure 30-3, enables you to manage connection protocols and settings on a local server. This MMC-based snap-in is located in the Administrative Tools menu. The console-tree pane contains two folders: Connections and Server Settings.

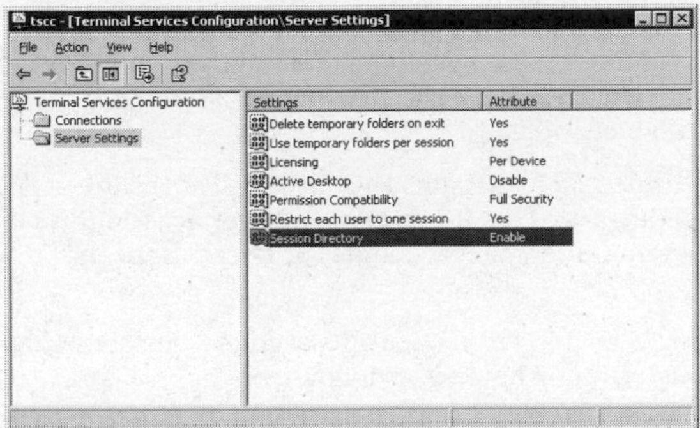

Figure 30-3: The Terminal Services Configuration utility.

By default, the only entry listed in the Connections container is RDP-Tcp. (Although you can create additional RDP-Tcp connections on a server with multiple network adapters, the one created by default is likely the only one that you need.) Installation of Citrix MetaFrame would create one or more entries for an ICA connection (depending on the number of installed protocols and network adapters that they are bound to). Double-clicking the connection entry displays its properties in the Properties dialog box. On this dialog box, you have access to a number of connection parameters on the following set of tabs:

- ✦ **General:** Contains the connection's Encryption Level setting (High or Client Compatible, FIPS Compliant, and Low).
- ✦ **Logon Settings:** Used to provide authentication information for the connection. Typically, you would use the client's provided logon information (default), but you can also set it to the same account for every session by selecting the Always Use the Following Logon Information option and providing login information.
- ✦ **Sessions:** Controls time limits on disconnected, active, and idle sessions and determines whether reconnections are permitted from any client or only previous clients. After the configurable time limit runs out, an active or idle session can be either disconnected or terminated. Similarly, a disconnected session can be automatically terminated after an arbitrarily chosen time interval. By default, all these settings are inherited from the user account duration (set on the Remote Control tab of the user account's Properties dialog box). For details, refer to the section "Active Directory Users and Computers and Terminal Server Extensions to Local Users and Groups," later in this chapter.
- ✦ **Environment:** Specifies the program that is launched for every session via this connection. After the program is exited, the connection terminates. This tab overrides session- and user-level settings.

- **Remote Control:** Determines remote-control permission settings (enabling viewing only or interacting with the session).
- **Client Settings:** Controls resource redirection and color depth of the screen.
- **Network Adapter:** Used to select the network adapter used for the connection and to limit the number of concurrent connections. By binding RDP traffic to only a specific network card, you can prevent terminal-server access from unsecure networks.
- **Permissions:** Sets the permission level for the connection. This tab is typically unnecessary (because users can be granted access by adding them to the Remote Desktop Users group), unless you want to delegate some of the administrative rights (such as the right to remotely control other sessions) to other users.

All the connection level settings are turned off by default. This, in turn, causes the user-level settings to take precedence. These settings are configured by using user account properties in Active Directory Users and Computers (for domain accounts) or Local Users and Groups (for local server accounts).

The Server Settings folder in the console tree (refer to Figure 30-3) gives you access to server-specific settings (also available through Group Policies), as follows:

- **Delete Temporary Folders on Exit:** Saves the disk space used by temporary files on the server.
- **Use Temporary Folders per Session:** Secures user-specific temporary files.
- **Licensing:** Displays the Terminal Server licensing type. Available choices depend on the Terminal Services mode. In Remote Desktop for Administration mode, no additional licensing is needed. In Terminal Server mode, you can choose between Per Device and Per Session licensing. For details, refer to the section "Terminal Services Licensing," later in this chapter.
- **Active Desktop:** Enables or disables Active Desktop for remote sessions. In Remote Desktop for Administration mode, this setting is enabled. Installing the Terminal Server component changes the default to disabled.
- **Permissions Compatibility:** Displays a Full (more secure) or Relaxed (less secure, which may be require to run older applications) Security entry. Full Security is the only option in Remote Desktop for Administration mode. With Terminal Server installed, you can switch between the two.
- **Restrict Each User to One Session:** If this setting is enabled, it ensures that your users can reconnect to disconnected sessions. This, however, does not apply to situations where a single user configures multiple RDP connections, each with a different program to start after the connection is established. In this case, a single user still can create multiple sessions, one per each separately configured connection. The setting is, by default, disabled in Remote Desktop for Administration mode and enabled after Terminal Server is installed.
- **Session Directory:** This setting, available only after Terminal Server is installed, enables the use of Session Directory for setting up Terminal Server clusters. If you decide to enable it, you need to provide the name of the cluster, the Session Directory server, and the network adapter that Session Directory server should redirect client requests to. To find out more about Session Directory and Terminal Server clusters, refer to Chapter 25.

Server settings configured by using the Terminal Server Configuration tool take precedence over those set by a client (in establishing a Remote Desktop connection) and those configured by using the Local Users and Groups utility. On the other hand, they are overwritten, in case of a conflict, by local or Active Directory-based Group Policies. Using Group Policies (instead of Server Settings) is the recommended way to administer multiple servers.

Note

Automatic client-drive redirection is a new feature of Terminal Services available only for connections involving XP and Windows Server 2003 systems. The client local and network mapped drives appear during the Remote Desktop session in the format `DriveLetter on ClientComputer` (for example, `C on USNY-WKS001`). This feature is also available through Citrix ICA-based products. If you need to access a client's local drives via Terminal Server sessions in earlier versions of Windows, you must create drive mappings manually (or through a batch file). In such a case, they look the same as any other network mapped drive (which may be confusing to clients).

Terminal Services Group Policies

Windows Server 2003 has a number of Group Policy settings located under the Terminal Services folder (which you access from the Windows Components subfolder of the Administrative Templates folder for both Computer and User Configuration nodes). For more information on this subject, refer to Chapter 14.

The Terminal Services environment, serving multiple users, is obviously more vulnerable than a traditional, single-user desktop. Enhancements in Windows Server 2003 Group Policies (such as Software Restriction policies) enable you to control this environment even better than you could in Windows 2000. You may want to consider creating a separate organizational unit containing exclusively Terminal Services servers. This enables you to set policies that differ from those applied to workstations or other servers. You can, for example, prevent the activation of a user-based Software Installation policy for Remote Desktop logons by using Group Policy loopback processing in Replace mode, as explained in Chapter 14.

Terminal Services Group Policies apply only to Windows Server 2003 servers.

Active Directory Users and Computers and Terminal Server extensions to Local Users and Groups

Remote Desktop connections can be managed on a per-user basis. For domain users, this is done by using Active Directory Users and Computers, while Local Users and Groups is used for local accounts. The Terminal Server-related settings are located on four tabs of a user account's Properties dialog box, as the following list describes:

- The *Environment tab* can be used to set a program that automatically starts at logon. (The same option can be set on a per-connection level by using the Terminal Services Configuration tool.) It also contains three check boxes controlling client drives, printer mappings, and inheriting the client's default printer option.
- The *Sessions tab* controls timeouts for disconnected, active, and idle sessions and reconnection behavior (which are identical to Session settings that can be configured on a per-connection level).

✦ The *Remote Control tab* contains the Enable Remote Control check box. After remote control is enabled, you can also specify whether a user's permissions are required and what level of control is permitted (interacting with the session or viewing it only). This tab, again, has equivalent connection-level settings, configurable by using the Terminal Services Configuration tool.

✦ The *Terminal Services Profile tab* enables you to set a profile and the home directory paths used for logons via Remote Desktop connection, which are separate from those used for non-Terminal Services logons. The Allow Logon to Terminal Server check box on this tab is useful if you want to prevent a particular user from using Terminal Services altogether. This tab has no equivalent connection-level settings.

All these settings can be also configured by using Group Policies (which is the recommended approach).

In dealing with nondomain accounts, you can use the Terminal Services extension to the Local Users and Groups snap-in. This extension is added automatically on Windows Server 2003 servers. The Terminal Server settings are identical to the ones available for domain accounts if you're using Active Directory Users and Computers.

Command-line utilities

You can perform a number of Terminal Server administrative tasks by using command-line utilities. This approach may prove useful if you manage your server through a Telnet session or if you want to automate management via custom batch files. The following list describes a few examples of the command-line utilities that you can use:

✦ `Change logon /disable`: Temporarily disables all Remote Desktop logons. This does not affect existing sessions.

✦ `Change logon /enable`: Restores Terminal Server availability.

✦ `Change user /install`: Used prior to installing applications on a Windows Server 2003 server running Full Terminal Server. This utility changes the way that configuration files and registry entries are handled during the installation, which is critical for enabling shared access to the application.

✦ `Change user /execute`: Switches to the default execute mode. Run this command after installation of an application is completed.

✦ `Logoff` *`14`*: Forces logoff of a user running session number 14. Be aware that forcing a logoff may result in the loss of data.

✦ `Msg` *`12`* `/server:`*`USNY-AP003 Please logoff in 10 minutes`*: Sends a message to a user running session ID 12 on the server `USNY-AP003`. You can also send messages to multiple sessions (by separating session numbers by commas). Instead of session IDs, you can also use session or usernames (or the name of a file containing their listings).

✦ `Query process /server:`*`USNY-AP003`*: Displays a list of all the processes launched by all users on the server `USNY-AP003`.

✦ `Query user /server:`*`USNY-AP003`*: Displays a list of all the users connected via Remote Desktop to the server `USNY-AP003`.

✦ `Reset session` *`13`* `/server:`*`USNY-AP003`*: Terminates session number 13 on the server `USNY-AP003`. Remember that terminating a session may result in a loss of data.

✦ `Shadow` *`15`* `/server:`*`USNY-AP003`*: Starts the remote control of session number 15 on the server `USNY-AP003`.

✦ `Tscon` *`11`* `/password:`*`Pa$$w0rd`*: Enables you to connect from a Remote Desktop connection to session number 11 on the same Terminal Server (where *`Pa$$w0rd`* is the password of the user of that session).

✦ `Tsdiscon` *`10`* `/server:`*`USNY-AP003`*: Disconnects session 10 on the server `USNY-AP003`. With default settings in place, all processes launched during that session continue to run.

✦ `Tskill` *`569`* `/server:`*`USNY-AP003`*: Terminates a process with process ID 569 on the server `USNY-AP003`. You can use the `query process` command (shown in the third paragraph of this list) to obtain the process ID.

✦ `Tsshutdn` *`90`* `/server:`*`USNY-AP003`* `/delay:`*`60`*: Initiates a shutdown of the server `USNY-AP003`. The shutdown is orderly and consists of several stages. First, connected users are notified about the impending lost of connectivity and are granted 90 seconds (the first parameter) before a forced logoff. After all sessions are logged off, the system waits 60 seconds (the parameter used with the `/delay` switch) to terminate all processes. This is followed by the shutdown. `/Powerdown` and `/Reboot` switches are also available. This command should be used to shut down a Terminal Server rather than the traditional method (via the Start ⇨ Shutdown command or from the Windows Security dialog box).

For a complete listing of all command-line utilities used for managing Terminal Server refer to the online Help files included with Windows Server 2003.

Terminal Services WMI Provider

Windows Server 2003 servers include the Terminal Services WMI Provider, which enables the checking and modifying of Terminal Services. The provider offers a scripting interface, which can be used for automating standard administrative tasks. For full documentation about Terminal Services WMI classes, properties, and methods, refer to the Microsoft Platform Software Development Kit available from the Microsoft Web site.

Terminal Services Licensing

Licensing requirements for the Remote Desktop connections to Windows Server 2003 servers are dependent on three factors: the mode in which Terminal Services are running (Remote Desktop for Administration or Full Terminal Server), the operating system on the client device that's running Remote Desktop session, and the number of Terminal Servers configured with per-device and per-session licensing. (Per-device licensing requires temporary or full license for each connecting device; per-session counts only concurrent connections to the server.) In Remote Desktop for Administration mode, no additional licenses are needed, regardless of the type of clients. This changes after you install the Terminal Server component. To comply with licensing requirements, you need to set up the Terminal Server Licensing Server (which involves the installation of a licensing component and its activation) and, depending on your client population and the licensing mode that you set on terminal servers, purchase a number of client licenses.

In general, with the Full Terminal Server component installed, you use one or more of the following types of client licenses:

✦ **Temporary Terminal Server Client Access Licenses:** These licenses are sufficient to provide unlimited connectivity to clients who are running Windows 2000, XP Pro, or Windows Server 2003 operating systems and, for a limited amount of time (up to 120 days), to all the other clients (including non-Windows operating systems). These temporary licenses, stored typically on a client in the form of a digital certificate, are valid for 120 days after they are issued by the activated Licensing Server. Even if all your clients are running Windows 2000, XP, or Windows Server 2003 operating systems, you still need an activated Licensing Server in your environment, although you don't need to purchase any license packs for them. Keep in mind that the temporary licenses can be used only for clients connecting to Terminal Server configured in the per-device licensing mode.

✦ **Full Terminal Server Client Access Licenses:** These are granted to all clients not covered by temporary Terminal Services Client Access Licenses (CALs). This may happen as soon as such clients request a license (if Terminal Services Licensing Server has available CALs) or at the time that their temporary licenses expire (if CALs have been installed after the initial client connection). Prior to Windows Server 2003, Microsoft offered only per-device licenses, which meant that you needed to ensure that you had a license for every device that connected to any of your Terminal Servers. Although this worked fairly well in intranet scenarios, it was impractical for providing Terminal Services to Internet users. Partial relief was provided by the Internet Connector License, which enables up to 200 concurrent connections (using per-session and not per-device licensing). The Internet Connector License, however, had significant limitations. It could be used only for anonymous connections and was restricted to non-employees. In Windows Server 2003, Microsoft switched to per-device and per-session licensing. The following paragraphs describe the differences between these two types of licensing:

- *Per-device licensing* works the same way as it did in Windows 2000 Service Pack 3. Just as is the temporary Terminal Services Client Access License, the full per-device license is stored on a client machine in the form of a digital certificate. Also just like temporary Terminal Services CAL, the full per-device license expires within a random time interval shorter than 120 days. Although the idea of a "temporary" full license may sound like an oxymoron, Microsoft has a very good reason for it. Because a full Terminal Services CAL is stored locally on a client device, it would be permanently lost in the case of hard-drive failure. By using a temporary full license, this problem is avoided in the following way. After the client OS is rebuilt, it requests a new license. Even if no full Terminal Services CALs are available (because the one that formerly belonged to the client is lost), the client can operate for the first 120 days by using temporary Terminal Services CALs. Before the 120-day period passes, the full license is returned to the license pool (as soon as it expires) and assigned to the original owner. Full Terminal Services CALs are renewed whenever a client negotiates new connection. Terminal Server checks the expiration date of the license and renews it automatically if the expiration date is near.

- *Per-session licensing* is a replacement for Windows 2000 Terminal Server Internet Connection licensing. Instead of being assigned on per-device basis, it works on a per-connection basis. An important point to remember is that per-session licensing applies to every connection to the server, including these initiated from Windows 2000, XP, and Windows Server 2003 systems.

Each Terminal Server must operate on either a per-device or a per-session licensing basis. The type of licensing is set in the Terminal Server Configuration MMC snap-in (by using the Licensing entry in the Server Setting folder). Each server configured by using per-session licensing contacts the Terminal Server Licensing Server and uses the next available per-session license from the pool of available ones.

Keep in mind that the licenses described in the preceding list do not include the Windows Server 2003 product license and Windows Server 2003 Client Access Licenses, which are required regardless of the use of Terminal Server.

In publishing applications via Terminal Services — in addition to operating-system and Terminal Server licensing — you also need to comply with multi-user application licensing rules. The use of third-party products enhancing Terminal Services functionality, such as Citrix MetaFrame, further increases your licensing and product costs.

Whenever Windows Server 2003 running the Full Terminal Server component receives a connection request, it first tries to retrieve a license from the client. Clients typically cache previously obtained licenses locally in the registry. (This does not apply to non-Windows operating systems, however, for which the per-device Client Access License is stored on the Licensing Server.) If such a license exists and is valid, the connection is established. Otherwise, the Terminal Server tries to contact a Terminal Server Licensing Server containing a licensing database.

Specifics of the mechanism used to obtain the license depend on the client device's operating system, Terminal and Licensing Server configuration, and the length of time that the Terminal Server and Licensing Server have been operational.

Terminal Server can ignore the absence of a Licensing Server for the first 120 days after you install the Full Terminal Server component (but contacts it as soon as the Licensing Server becomes available). After this grace period passes, all further connection requests are rejected. So within the 120 days after the installation date of your first Terminal Server, you also need to have a fully functional Licensing Server.

To accomplish this task, follow these steps:

1. Install the Terminal Server Licensing component (via the Add or Remove Programs applet in the Control Panel) on a Windows Server 2003 or Windows 2000 server.

   A Licensing Server can be configured to serve an entire enterprise or only a single domain or workgroup. Enterprise Licensing Server responds to requests for licenses from any server from the same site (as long as it belongs to the same forest). Domain Licensing Server provides licenses only to servers from the same domain. For installation of Enterprise Licensing Server you must be logged on by using an account with the Enterprise Admin privileges, because the process results in the creation of an entry in Active Directory at the location `CN=TS-Enterprise-License-Server,CN=site-name,CN=Sites,CN=Configuration,DC=domain,DC=com`. Terminal Servers search for Licensing Servers by querying all domain controllers in their domain for the reference to a server that's running the Terminal Server licensing service. If several of them are available, the server chooses one at random and requests a license from a license-key pack matching the client type. If none is available in the same domain, the server searches Active Directory for the Enterprise Licensing server at the location listed earlier in this step.

You can configure Terminal Services to request the License Key Pack from a specific License Server by specifying the NetBIOS name of this server in the `DefaultLicenseServer` registry entry of type `REG_SZ` at the following location:

```
HKEY_LOCAL_MACHINE\SYSTEM\CurrentControlSet\Services\
TermService\Parameters
```

If you decide to use this configuration, remember that, if the specified server is not available, the Terminal Server does not try to contact another one.

2. After the Licensing Server component is installed, you need to activate it.

   The activation process is a one-time event that involves obtaining a Licensing Server ID (based on your Licensing Server product ID) from Microsoft Clearinghouse (which you can contact via a direct (from the Licensing Server) or indirect (from any other computer) Internet connection to the Microsoft Clearinghouse Web site or by phone). You perform it by choosing Action ➪ Activate Server from the Terminal Server Licensing administrative tool's menu bar. You are asked to provide your contact and company information.

3. If you have clients running operating systems other than Windows 2000 and XP Professional, you need to purchase client licenses.

   You need to take care of this within 120 days after Licensing Server activation. During this time, your clients can use temporary licenses. After this second grace period expires (the first one, also lasting 120 days, follows the installation of the Terminal Server), full client licenses are required. You need to decide what type of licensing agreement you are going to use. Several options are available (for example, retail license packs, Microsoft Open License, Enterprise agreement, and so on), so review them carefully before you decide which one works best for you. Another critical decision that you need to make concerns the type of licenses you're going to use (per-device, per-session, or a mix of both). Your choice depends mostly on whether your clients are internal or external and what types of operating system they run.

   After both decisions are made, you can purchase licenses directly from Microsoft or a reseller (typically in the form of license packs, although this depends on the type of licensing agreement you go with) and install them on the Licensing Server by running the Terminal Server Client Access License Installation Wizard (which you launch by choosing Action ➪ Install Licenses from the Terminal Server Licensing utility's menu bar). If you have a direct link to the Internet from the Licensing Server, the wizard connects to the Microsoft Clearinghouse and leads you through the CAL installation process. Otherwise, you need to connect to the Microsoft Web site via a browser on another computer or contact the Clearinghouse via phone. You are asked to provide the Client Access License's 25-character code and 35-character Licensing Server ID. Both of them are used to generate a unique, 35-character client license key pack ID, which activates the licenses.

Because that list of available licenses is stored in a database on a Licensing Server, you should back it up regularly. Your backup, at the very least, should include System State data and the folder in which the Licensing Server component is installed (the `%SystemRoot%\System32\LServer` folder, by default). As a last resort, in case your restore fails, you need to contact the Microsoft Customer Support Center.

Remote Desktop for Administration features

In Remote Desktop for Administration mode, the server uses minimal resources to support sessions. This mode provides the most suitable Terminal Services configuration for servers running mission-critical applications such as SQL Server or Microsoft Exchange, where application access would interfere with critical services.

Two remote desktop connections available in this mode (in addition to remote or direct console access) should be sufficient in almost any environment.

If you decide to use a Remote Desktop for Administration session for installation or upgrades (such as the installation of service packs, the promotion and demotion of domain controllers, and so on), you should use the console connection. Although standard sessions work fine in the majority of the cases, having a view of the console session enables you to see all pop-up messages, alerting you of some issues that may crop up relating to the installation. Depending on installation procedure, some of these messages may be visible from the console only. To establish a console connection, you can launch the Remote Desktop client (`MSTSC.EXE`) by using the `/console` switch from the command line. Take, for example the following line:

```
Mstsc /v:USNY-TS001 /console /w:800 /h:600
```

This command would initiate the Remote Desktop connection to the server `USNY-TS001` (in the 800 x 600 window), directly to its console. Keep in mind that, if someone were logged on to the console locally at the target server, this would automatically lock that session (just as a remote connection to a computer running Windows XP would do). This happens because two users cannot independently use the same session.

Note Unfortunately, you cannot set the Console option through the GUI by using the Remote Desktop Connection applet (which is available from the Start menu by choosing Start ➪ All Programs ➪ Accessories ➪ Communications). You can, however, save all the other connection settings in a file—say, `MyConnection.RDP`—and then launch the `MSTSC` utility from the command prompt by using the syntax `Mstsc MyConnection.RDP /console`.

You can also disconnect from the computer instead of logging off (by using the Disconnect option available from the Shut Down Windows dialog box) and leave your sessions running for later access. This can be done in a scenario where a complex install takes a lot of time. You can begin the installation or upgrade and then leave the session running while you disconnect. (The session's disconnect parameters must be appropriately set; refer to the section "Administering Terminal Services," earlier in this chapter, for details.) Later on, you can reconnect to the existing session (from the same or another computer).

Note A user running a session has two ways to end a remote connection: *Disconnect* and *Logoff*. Disconnect leaves the session running for a configurable period of time. Logoff terminates the session, closes any applications that are open, and cleans up resources the session had open or used.

The Remote Desktop for Administration supports all the RDP features. These include automatic drive, printer, and port mapping; local and remote Clipboard sharing; session remote control; full-screen mode with support for Windows keyboard shortcuts; two encryption levels, up to 24-bit color; and automatic session reconnection. The end result is an extremely powerful solution for remote management of Windows Server 2003 servers. You do, however, need to keep several important considerations in mind, as the following list describes:

- **Do not use remote administration for application serving.** Although you can certainly run administration tools and applications by using remote administration, you should not install general multi-user applications for access to the server as a quasi-application server (to circumvent licensing). The remote administration services do not use all the multi-user components necessary for application sharing (plus you are limited to only three connections).
- **Make sure that the Terminal Services session is set to Disconnect on Broken.** The Disconnect or Broken option, configurable on the per-user and per-server levels, ensures that, if you suddenly lose a connection to the server, which can easily happen over an unreliable connection, the session is placed into Disconnect state (rather than being terminated). In Disconnect state, the processes that you launched while connected remain running. So if you were performing a delicate operation at the time—such as defragmenting a disk—the session termination does not kill the processes. If you reset the session on disconnect, you can do some serious damage, because Reset forces the termination of each user process.
- **Use Remote Desktop wisely.** You have a limit of two simultaneous remote desktop connections per server and one console connection. What can you do if two existing connections are already initiated by two administrators logged on with their accounts? You have several options. One is to enforce a policy of only enabling a special domain account (for example, RDADMIN) to connect to the server. By default, Terminal Services restrict each user to one session only (although this can be changed by using the Terminal Services Configuration utility—described in the section "Terminal Services Configuration," earlier in this chapter). This way, multiple administrators can connect (although not at the same time) to a single session in progress. Although this method forcibly disconnects a currently connected user, all processes running within the connection are unaffected. You must ensure that your RDADMIN administrator account and the server are configured not to reset after session disconnect. You also need to make sure that any administrative work is performed by using this shared account. The main problem with this approach is accountability. Information Security groups do not like shared accounts, because they make auditing, tracking, and attributing changes to individual administrators difficult, if not impossible. Other options involve session sharing through Remote Assistance or using administrative tools to determine who is connected to the server. After you have this information, you can either ask that person to log off or, in extreme cases, terminate the session yourself (as described in the section "Administering Terminal Services," earlier in this chapter).
- **Coordinate remote administration.** For the reason described previously, coordinate remote administration wisely. Grant access to a server's remote desktop sessions only to a small group of administrators. Make sure that you and the other administrators communicate concerning the work on the server (such as installing software or configuring storage). Whenever you log in to a server through Terminal Services, check to see whether anyone else is logged in by launching the Terminal Services Manager or running the `query user` command from the command prompt in the session.

Full Terminal Server Features

Full Terminal Server mode is used mainly to provide access to the Windows desktop and applications via Remote Desktop sessions. With default settings in place, users can launch a session and view the Windows Server 2003 desktop instead of their own. At that point, they can launch applications the same way that they would locally. You can also restrict a user's access to one particular application. The first of these two options is referred to as *desktop deployment* and the second as *application publishing.*

Desktop deployment

Desktop deployment is straightforward. Users simply connect to the server and interact with the desktop as if it were local. In the desktop-deployment scenario, configure your Windows client to take one of the following two routes in providing a session to the client:

- ✦ Configure a Remote Desktop connection that enables the user to work in the remote (TS) environment and leave the user the option to work locally. This option should be provided only to experienced users — and possibly only to technical personnel — because it can be disconcerting and counterproductive for the users to be toggling between two desktops. Over a fast intranet, the sessions are so responsive that discerning between the remote and local desktop is almost impossible. In such a case, you can use the capability to display the connection bar (which you find at the top of the window) of Windows Server 2003 Remote Desktop sessions that are running in full mode. This configurable feature can help you determine whether you are viewing a local or remote desktop.
- ✦ Configure a connection that is activated at logon time. You need a script or batch file to automate this process and place the user at the Terminal Services logon prompt in the full screen mode. You can accomplish this by using a precreated custom Remote Desktop Connection saved as a Remote Desktop file (with an `RDP` extension) and using it as a parameter for `MSTSC.EXE`. This way, local desktop is completely hidden from the user's view. Your script can also shut down the local workstation after the user logs off or disconnects from the Terminal Server.

You can switch between the full-screen and windowed mode by pressing the Ctrl+Alt+Break key combination.

Application-publishing deployment

In this scenario, your user authenticates to the domain and works on the local machine normally, either on the intranet or via remote access. Access to an application on the Terminal Server is provided through a specially configured Remote Desktop connection that launches it as soon as the session is established and the user logs on. (This is done by using entries on the Programs tab of the Remote Desktop Connection dialog box.) If you want to eliminate the need for a user to log on (to make access to applications quick and transparent), you need to also type a username, password, and domain for the connection in the appropriate fields on the General tab. You can even change the icon of the connection to reflect the icon of the program that you intend to publish.

To simplify access to an icon that's representing the connection, place it on the user's desktop. After the user double-clicks the icon, the application launches as if it were installed locally.

Installing applications

Installing applications in Remote Desktop for Administration mode requires no special installation procedures. This changes, however, in running Windows Server 2003 with the Full Terminal Server component. As you can imagine, having multiple instances of the same software running at the same time affects application installation, configuration, and management procedures.

The Terminal Server can operate in one of two modes: *install* and *execute*. If you need to install applications on the server, place the server in the install mode. (If you forget to do so, Windows Server 2003 displays a friendly reminder.) This can be done either by running the Add or Remove Programs Control Panel applet or by using the command `Change User /Install`. If you use the Add or Remove Programs applet, you automatically exit install mode after the Installation Wizard completes. Otherwise, you need to remember to run `Change User /Execute` at the end. You can verify the mode that you are in by running `Change User /Query`.

To run interactive installation by using the Add or Remove Programs Control Panel applet, follow these steps:

1. Open the Control Panel and click the Add or Remove icon.
2. In the Add or Remove Programs dialog box that appears, click the Add New Programs option and then click CD or Floppy. This action loads the Installation Wizard.
3. Ensure that media with source files are available and click Next to locate the install program. In the Run Installation Program page that appears, click Next. The Installation program launches, with the operating system monitoring the process. The Wizard also displays a dialog box with a reminder to click Finish only after the installation is complete.
4. After the installation is complete, you may get a message telling you to reboot. Make sure that you *do not*. Select the Restart the Machine Later option. Click the Finish button. After the install Wizard closes, you can restart the server.

Deploying Windows Installer-based applications (those depending on technology used by Microsoft to deploy its applications) to Terminal Servers involves some special considerations. Installations, in this case, should be modified through *transforms* (`MST` files that can be executed during the installation to change its outcome), which cause all required application features to be installed locally. Features set to be installed on demand would fail if used within a Terminal Server session because users would not have sufficient permissions to install them. The same restriction applies to applications deployed via Software Deployment Group Policies (which require applications to be packaged in Windows Installer format). You should prevent assigning or publishing applications to users during their logon to Terminal Servers. One way to accomplish this is to place Terminal Servers in a separate organizational unit, create a new Group Policy Object, ensure that no Software Installation entries are in its User Configuration container, and apply this Group Policy in the loopback Replace mode.

Application Compatibility Scripts

The majority of older applications do not have built-in provisions to operate in a multi-user environment, so most of the time, they need to be appropriately tweaked if installed on a Terminal Server. This is typically accomplished through the use of Application Compatibility Scripts. The scripts are batch files, commonly available from an application vendor, Microsoft (some are included with the operating system), or Internet-based support groups. Their role is to emulate a standalone application environment on a multi-user system. They may need to be run during installation, user logon, and uninstallation. Depending on their role, they are located in `Install`, `Logon`, and `Uninstall` subfolders of the `%SystemRoot%\Application Compatibility Scripts` folder. Those required on every logon are invoked through a sequence of batch files initiated by the Terminal Server logon script `USRLOGON.CMD` (residing in the `%SystemRoot%\System32` folder), which runs whenever any user logs on to Terminal Server (regardless of the user's logon script). The logon scripts are automatically added to this sequence by the Application Compatibility installation script.

Fortunately, Application Compatibility Scripts are becoming things of the past. A growing number of newer applications do not require them.

Installing Microsoft Office 2000 on a Terminal Server

An MS Office 2000 installation uses Windows Installer technology. Any generic Windows Installer-based installations uses an `MSI` file, while additional modifications are performed by using so-called *transforms* (files with the MST extension). Microsoft Installer Transformation File for Terminal Server (`TERMSRVR.MST`) was developed specifically for Terminal Server-based installations. The transform is included with the MS Office 2000 Resource Kit and is downloadable from the Microsoft Web site. Its main purpose is to ensure that all the installation features are run from the local computer (because, for example, the Installed on First Use option is not suitable for the Terminal Server environment), but it also includes other Terminal Server-specific changes. You can further modify it by using the Custom Installation Wizard (which is also part of the MS Office Resource Kit). In running the wizard, you need access to the `DATA1.MSI` file from the MS Office 2000 installation CD, which is used as the base for modifications.

After you have the final transform file (this may be the original `TERMSRVR.MST` or your own customized version), you can launch setup from either the Add or Remove Programs Control Panel applet or from the command prompt after running `change user /install`. In the first case, select the Add New Programs option and click the CD or Floppy button. This displays the Open dialog box. Next, double click the MS Office 2000 `SETUP.EXE` installation file. In the same Open dialog box, type the additional parameter specifying the location of the transform file. Assuming, for example, that your transform is located in the `C:\Temp` folder, you would type the following line:

```
SETUP.EXE TRANSFORMS=C:\Temp\TERMSRVR.MST
```

In the second case, type the same line at the command prompt. The rest of the process is straightforward. You can also run the process remotely by using the Remote Desktop console session.

After installation completes, you can customize each of the Office applications by launching them and making changes by using their menu options. Then you can capture these settings by using the Profile Wizard (also provided with the Resource Kit) and save them, along with the Profile Wizard executable (`PROFLWIZ.EXE`), to an `OPS` file locally on the Terminal Server in a read-only folder that's accessible to all members of Remote Desktop Users group. To replicate your settings to all users who are accessing the server, create an entry referencing your `OPS` file in the following registry key:

```
HKEY_LOCAL_MACHINE\SOFTWARE\Microsoft\Windows NT\CurrentVersion\Terminal
Server\Install\Software\Microsoft\Windows\CurrentVersion\RunOnce
```

The entry needs to be of REG_SZ type, but its name is not relevant. Assuming that you saved both files in the C:\Program Files\ORK location, the entry would have the following value (where CUSTOM.OPS is the file containing your custom settings):

```
C:\Program Files\ORK\PROFLWIZ.EXE /r CUSTOM.OPS /q
```

Optionally, you can also take advantage of other Resource Kit utilities, such as the following:

- *MS Office 2000 Group Policy Templates* that enable you to control many MS Office 2000 settings. Their installation automatically places the required ADM files in the %SystemRoot%\INF folder.
- *OUTLFEAT.XLS* containing the listing of many Microsoft Office features (such as Office Assistant), for which installation can be controlled via modifications to the TERMSRVR.MST file.
- *The Motionless Office Assistant* (implemented as STILLOGO.ASC) that is a replacement for the animated Office Assistants included with the original installation of MS Office 2000. Eliminating animation decreases bandwidth utilization and avoids unnecessarily burden on the processor. For additional information, refer to the documentation provided with the MS Office 2000 Resource Kit.

Installing Microsoft Office XP on a Terminal Server

The installation of MS Office XP is much more straightforward. The Setup program is capable of detecting that it is running on the Terminal Server and it does not require special transforms to make adjustments appropriate to a multi-user, low-bandwidth environment. All features, for example, are set to one of two states: *Run from My Computer* or *Not Available*. All menu animation features are automatically turned off, and splash screens are switched to the text-based format. If you intend to make changes to the default settings, you need to use the Office XP Custom Installation Wizard included in the Office XP Resource Kit. In addition, just as in Office 2000, you can further customize options within each of the Office applications by capturing them in an OPS file by using the Office XP Profile Wizard. Changes can even be applied after the installation is completed (which is not possible in MS Office 2000) by using the Office XP Custom Maintenance Wizard.

Printer management

Printer management has most likely been the primary cause of administrative headaches in earlier versions of Terminal Server. Fortunately, Microsoft introduced some clever improvements in this area in Windows Server 2003. In dealing with printing from Terminal Server sessions, two main issues basically need to be considered: the redirection of printers that are attached locally to client devices and the creation of mappings to network printers that are located in the client's vicinity.

If a printer is attached to an LPT, COM, or USB port on a client device, Terminal Server has the capability to automatically create this printer within a Remote Desktop session. That way, whenever a client prints, the print job is redirected to the local printer (as is usually desired). The only caveat that causes a fair amount of confusion is the fact that the appropriate printer driver must be installed on the Terminal Server. This printer driver must match the one attached to the client device. Unfortunately, the detection mechanism may not always be accurate, especially if the client is running an older version of Windows or using an OEM driver. (You can track a failed printer mapping by checking the Event log.) Although Microsoft significantly increased the number of natively supported printers in Windows Server 2003, you still face a good chance that your clients may require the installation of third-party drivers. Make sure that you test them before installing such drivers on a production system, because poorly written print drivers are notorious for affecting Terminal Server's stability. If the printer is not matched automatically, you can also map it manually. To do so, first redirect the port (LPT or COM) to which the printer is attached. Then, by using the Add Printer Wizard, map a new printer (using the appropriate driver) and configure it to use the redirected port. This port appears under a list of ports on the Terminal Server in the format `computername:port`, where `computername` is the name or IP address of the client device and `port` is local port designation (such as LPT 1). Very conveniently, information about manually mapped printer is stored on the client device, so such a printer is recreated automatically at the beginning of every subsequent session.

Terminal Server is not capable of automatically mapping a client's network printers. You can try to resolve this issue by assigning roaming profiles for your users (because that is where network printer mappings are stored) or by creating mappings through a logon script invoked whenever a user logs on to the Remote Desktop session. Remember, however, that, in this case, you also need to make sure that matching printer drivers are installed on the Terminal Server.

If the functionality built into Windows Server 2003 does not meet your expectations, you can explore some third-party products. triCerat's ScrewDriver, Charon System's UniPrint, EleSoft's ElePrint, and, obviously, Citrix MetaFrame are a few examples of interesting solutions dealing with Terminal Server printing issues.

Remote Assistance Features

Remote Assistance is intended for troubleshooting and end-user-training purposes. It is available only between computers running either Windows XP Professional or Windows Server 2003 servers.

Remote Assistance resembles a remote control feature of Terminal Server, because it provides access to an existing session. The session in this case, however, is a standard desktop session, not a remote one. Just as a remote-control mechanism does, remote assistance offers a number of security features. By default, this functionality is disabled on each type of Windows Server 2003 server. Access to it can be controlled on a per-user, per-group, per-machine, or AD-container level (through Group Policies). On a single desktop, it can be turned on or off by accessing the System applet in the Control Panel, selecting the Remote tab, and selecting the Turn on Remote Assistance and Allow Invitations to Be Sent from this Computer check box. A Remote Assistance session does not jeopardize security or confidentiality, because its establishment requires explicit end-user consent. A user not only creates a password-protected invitation to an expert, but also must acknowledge warning prompts displayed before the session starts. Although the invitation can be reused for a specific, user-defined amount of time, the user who created the invitation can revoke it by forcing its expiration. The invitation can be sent through Windows Messenger, e-mail, or as a file. An expert can also offer assistance to a remote user. The offer triggers a message on the user's screen asking for permission to initiate a session. After a user accepts the offer, a new session launches.

Terminal Services Clients

In this section, we take a look at Terminal Services from the client's perspective, covering different client types with their deployment strategies and configuration options. We present the steps necessary to install the Remote Desktop Connection, the Remote Desktop MMC snap-in, and the Remote Desktop Web Connection, as well as the ways of connecting to servers and optimizing performance and bandwidth utilization of the connections.

Deploying Terminal Services to clients

In general, three types of Terminal Services clients are designed for the Windows Server 2003 server platform. The first type, known simply as *Remote Desktop Connection*, takes the form of the executable file `MSTSC.EXE`. This utility is included, by default, in Windows XP Professional (Version 5.1) and Windows Server 2003 servers (Version 5.2). The version included in Windows Server 2003 has the capability to automatically reconnect a disconnected session (in addition to all the features of Version 5.1). You can install Remote Desktop Connection on other Windows 32-bit platforms by using one of the procedures described in the following sections. The second type, called *Remote Desktops* is implemented as an MMC snap-in. The third type is browser-based *Remote Desktop Web Connection*, which provides access to Terminal Services from Internet Explorer.

Although you can still use earlier versions of the Terminal Services client software to access Windows Server 2003 servers remotely, you cannot take advantage of any new features introduced in the Windows Server 2003 Remote Desktop.

Option 1: Installing Remote Desktop Connection

To install the Remote Desktop Connection software (`MSTSC.EXE`) use any of the following options:

- ✦ Run the `SETUP.EXE` file from the root of a Windows Server 2003 server installation CD. On the initial flash screen, select Perform Additional Tasks. Clicking the first option on the next screen, Set up Remote Desktop Connection, launches the installation.
- ✦ Run the `MSRDPCLI.EXE` file from the `SUPPORT\TOOLS` folder of a Windows Server 2003 server-installation CD. This launches the installation directly.
- ✦ Share the `%SystemRoot%\System32\Clients\Tsclient` folder on a Terminal Server as Terminal ServicesClient. Set the permissions to Read. Your Win32 clients need to connect to the `\\`*`Server`*`\TSClient\Win32` folder and run `SETUP.EXE`. (You need to replace the *Server* entry with the name or IP address of the Terminal Server).
- ✦ Use the Group Policy Software Deployment feature (or any other software deployment tool) to distribute `MSRDPCLI.MSI` from the `%SystemRoot%\System32\Clients\Tsclient` folder to target computers. This is a standard Windows Installer-based package, which can be installed silently.

The installation steps are very straightforward. After the initial informational screen, you simply need to accept the licensing agreement, provide customer information, and decide whether software is available only for the currently logged-on user or for all users.

Unlike with Windows 2000 Terminal Services client software, no floppy-based installation is available in Windows Server 2003.

Option 2: Installing the Remote Desktops MMC snap-in

The Remote Desktops MMC snap-in is included in full set of Windows Server 2003 Administrative Tools, which, at the time of writing, can be installed on Windows XP Professional by running the `ADMINPAK.EXE` file (included with the Windows Server 2003 OS and downloadable from the Microsoft Web site). The snap-in enables you to store and run multiple connections as part of a single MSC file. It also has a Connect to Console option, missing from the standard Remote Desktop Connection. On the other hand, it does not enable you to set Full Screen mode (for obvious reasons) or customize the use of graphical features available on the Experience tab of the Remote Desktop Connection Properties dialog box.

Option 3: Installing the Remote Desktop Web Connection

The Remote Desktop Web Connection is a Web application that can be launched from Internet Explorer. It consists of an ActiveX control and a set of customizable Web pages residing on a Windows Server 2003-based Web Server.

Remote Desktop Web Connection involves three computers: a client, a Windows Server 2003 Web Server with Internet Information Services running World Wide Web Service, and a Terminal Server to which the client wants to connect.

A Windows Server 2003 Web Server needs to have the Remote Desktop Web Connection software installed. This is done by using the Windows Component Wizard (accessed from the Add or Remove Programs applet in the Control Panel). The Remote Desktop Web Connection is listed under subcomponents of the World Wide Web Service (which, in turn, are subcomponents of Internet Information Services). Installation creates a folder, `%SystemRoot%\Web\TSWeb`, shared as a virtual Web folder, and populates it with all necessary files.

The client must be running Internet Explorer Version 4.0 or later. A target system must be either a legacy server running Terminal Services or Windows Server 2003 with Remote Desktop access enabled.

Connecting to the server

The way that you connect to a target server depends on the type of connection that you are using.

If you're using Remote Desktop Connection, you launch it from the Start menu by choosing Start ➪ All Programs ➪ Accessories ➪ Communications ➪ Remote Desktop Connection. In the Computer text box of the Remote Desktop Connection dialog box that appears, you can enter either the name of the target server (NetBIOS or DNS) or its IP address. If you connect consistently to the same server, using the same settings, you can store your connection information in a Remote Desktop file (with the extension `RDP`) and place a shortcut to it on a desktop.

A number of Remote Desktop Connection settings can be modified. They are accessible after clicking the Options button in the Remote Desktop Connection dialog box. (You can also modify them by using Group Policies.) The General tab contains the target computer's name and the user credentials. From here, you can also save the connection settings (including the user password) to an `RDP` file. From the Display tab, you set the remote desktop size (with full-screen mode as the default) and specify color depth (true color is available). The Local Resources tab controls the redirection of sound, Windows key combination shortcuts, and local devices (disk drives, printers, and serial ports). On the Programs tab, you can specify a program to be launched on the server as soon as you log in. Finally, the Experience tab determines which GUI features (such as wallpaper, menu animation, and so on) are available. Enabling each of the GUI features affects the bandwidth, so your default choices depend on the connection speed. This feature is available to Windows 9*x*, Me, CE, 2000, XP, and Windows Server 2003 clients.

You can also launch the Remote Desktop Connection from the command line by specifying the name of the executable (`MSTSC.EXE`) with appropriate parameters, as in the following example:

```
Mstsc /v:USNY-AP003 /w:800 /h:600
```

This command initiates a Remote Desktop connection with server `USNY-AP003`. The width and height (in pixels) of the session window is determined by the `/w:` and `/h:` parameters.

With the Remote Desktops MMC snap-in, the process is slightly different. Each new connection becomes a separate icon in the tree pane underneath the Remote Desktops node. For each one, you first specify the target server, the credentials used to connect to it, and whether you want to connect to the console. After the entry appears in the tree pane, you can further modify it by setting the desktop size, a program to be launched at startup, and local drive redirection.

Whenever using a Remote Desktop Web Connection, a client starts by typing `http://`*`WebServerAddress`*`/TSWeb/` in the Internet Explorer Address box (where *`WebServerAddress`* is the IP address or name of a Web server with the Remote Desktop Web Connection component installed). This causes the browser to display the Remote Desktop Web Connection page (`default.htm`). From there, the client would type the name of a target Terminal Server in the Computer text box, select the window size, and specify whether to log on using the current account. At the same time, the browser would attempt a download and installation of the ActiveX component `MSRDP.OCX`. (Depending on the browser settings, the client may get prompted to permit these actions to take place.) After the installation is complete, the browser window displays the Remote Desktop Connection session. Unfortunately, to enable clients to modify options other than screen size or automatic passing of logon information, you would need to manually modify the Remote Desktop Web pages. The security settings of the Internet Explorer may also affect some of the connection parameters. This applies especially to clients operating in Internet and Restricted Sites zones. In such cases, starting connection in a full-screen mode or automatically launching a program after the connection is established is not possible.

The Remote Desktop Web Connection uses port 80 during initial HTTP communication with a Web server. As soon as the ActiveX component is downloaded, the client initiates an RDP session directly with the Terminal Server over port 3389. Web servers and Terminal Servers never communicate with each other.

Optimizing remote desktop connections

Remote desktop sessions should be capable of gracefully handling changing bandwidth conditions. One day, the user may connect to the server over a 100-Mbit backbone; the next day, a connection may be initiated from a hotel room via RAS over a 28.8-Kbit dial-up line. Responsiveness has been improved by the implementation of bitmap caching and compression enhancements, which optimizes packet utilization and frame size. You can further optimize bandwidth use and server performance by following these suggestions:

- **Keep the use of graphics low.** Eliminate blinking cursors, the clock in the notification area, and animated features, such as the Microsoft Office Assistant. Disable Active Desktop, wallpaper, and application splash screens.
- **For Remote Desktop Connection, use the speed selections on the Experience tab.** Each selection enables a different set of features dealing with the graphical interface, such as bitmap caching, showing the content of a window while dragging it, the animation of menus and windows, and displaying themes or wallpaper. The Modem (28 Kbps), option, for example, activates only bitmap caching, while the Modem (56 Kbps) option adds to it a display of themes. If you are not satisfied with any of the preconfigured options, you can customize them on your own.
- **Do not run legacy applications on the server.** These include DOS and 16-bit Windows apps.
- **Set time limits on idle and disconnected sessions.** This helps promote the efficient use of Terminal Server resources.

If your Terminal Servers provide critical services to the business, you can configure Windows Server 2003 servers into load-balanced clusters that offer maximum performance and reliability. You can find out more about clustering Terminal Servers in Chapter 25.

Session encryption levels

Clients connect to Terminal Server by using one of two permitted encryption levels. In both cases, the standard RSA RC4 method is used. The Client Compatible level checks the maximum encryption level supported by a client. This setting is then matched by the server. Typically, you would use it in environments with legacy clients. A high level forces 128-bit encryption. If a client does not support it, the session is not established. The decision as to which one to choose depends on clients' operating systems, the desired degree of security, and server utilization. A high encryption level substantially increases your CPU overhead.

You can switch between the two levels on the General tab of the RDP-Tcp Properties dialog box in the Terminal Services Configuration utility, as shown in Figure 30-4.

Remote administration and Telnet

So far, this chapter has discussed the implementation of thin-client technology on the Windows Server 2003 platform based on the Remote Desktop component. Remote Desktop provides convenient access to a familiar Windows desktop, physically running on a remote server.

A graphical interface, however, despite its obvious benefits, can be painfully slow across low-speed connections (especially if you're using more graphically intensive administrative tools). In addition, running a Windows desktop session may not be possible in trying to connect to Windows Server 2003 servers from non-Windows clients (without third-party add-ons). Fortunately, you can easily deal with these limitations by using Telnet. This character-based terminal-emulation protocol has been favored by Unix administrators for years. Its practical value in the Windows environment was limited because the majority of administrative tools in previous versions of Windows were GUI-based. This changed in Windows Server 2003. Because practically every administrative task can be now performed via command-line utilities, Telnet has a much better chance of becoming an important component of every Windows administrator's toolkit.

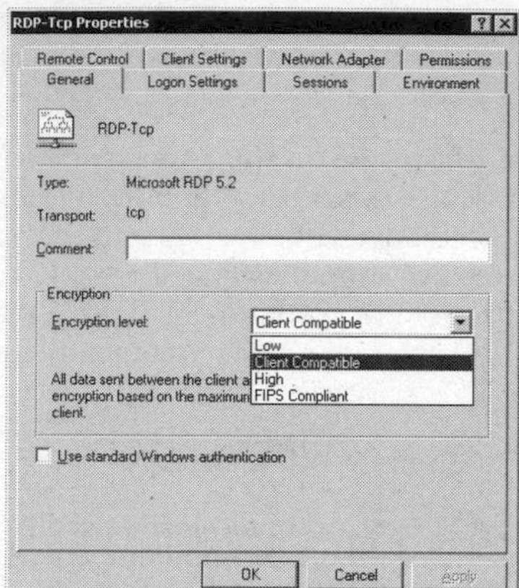

Figure 30-4: Changing the encryption level.

Telnet is a part of the TCP/IP suite of protocols. It consists of a client and a server component. The client component is included in every standard TCP/IP implementation, regardless of the operating system. The server component in a Windows Server 2003 server is implemented as a service, managed via the Services MMC snap-in. It enables up to two concurrent incoming connections (although the version of Telnet included in the Microsoft Windows Services for Unix does not have this limitation). The service, by default, is disabled. For the server component to start accepting connections, you need to first change its startup parameters to manual or automatic and then start it.

Telnet access is granted only to the local Administrators group. If you want to enable non-privileged accounts to log on via Telnet session, you need to create a TelnetClients local group and add these accounts to it.

To initiate a Telnet session from a client, type **Telnet** at the command prompt or choose Start ➪ Run and type it in the text box of the Run dialog box (and click OK). Either action launches a command-prompt window running the Microsoft Telnet Client. Typing **help** or a single question mark (**?**) lists the available commands. Among the most common ones are the following:

✦ `o` *`hostname port`*: Opens a Telnet connection to a hostname on the specified port. (If you do not specify the port, default 23 is used.) The logon triggers the default Telnet login script stored in `%SytemRoot%\system32\Login.cmd`. You can modify this file if you intend to customize the logon process for all the Telnet users.

✦ `c`: Closes the current connection.

✦ `q`: Exits Telnet.

✦ `set ntlm`: Sets NTLM authentication for any new connections (providing that the remote system is either Windows 2000 or Windows Server 2003). This option uses your current credentials for Telnet connection. Otherwise, you are prompted for a logon name and password. Using NTLM is recommended because of its security benefits. Without it, the username and password are sent to the remote server as plain text and can be easily captured with a network monitor. In addition, NTLM simplifies connecting to network resources from within a Telnet session.

✦ `unset ntlm`: Switches back to non-NTLM authentication.

✦ `display`: Displays the current settings.

Summary

Windows Server 2003 Terminal Services and the thin-client/server computer model represent a major paradigm shift in computing. In this chapter, our objective is to introduce you to this technology. We also talk about how it can contribute to lowering your total cost of ownership (TCO).

We introduce you to the two operation modes of the server: Remote Desktop for Administration and Full Terminal Server. Remote Desktop for Administration mode provides a straightforward mechanism for managing servers from a remote location in an environment identical to that of the direct console access. Terminal Services, intended for user access, offers a new, cost-effective way of accessing computing resources, presented in a familiar, friendly GUI-based manner.

✦ ✦ ✦

Index

SYMBOLS AND NUMERICS

A

Continued

Continued

C

Continued

Continued

Continued

Continued

Continued

E

Continued

F

Continued

G

Continued

J

K

L

Continued

M

Continued

N

Continued

O

P

Continued

Q

R

Continued

Continued

Continued

T

Continued

U

V

Continued